THE CAMBRIDGE HISTORY OF IRAN

IN EIGHT VOLUMES

Volume 5

THE CAMBRIDGE HISTORY OF IRAN

Volume 5

THE SALJUQ AND MONGOL PERIODS

edited by
J.A.BOYLE
Professor of Persian Studies, University of Manchester

CAMBRIDGE
AT THE UNIVERSITY PRESS
1968

Published by the Syndics of the Cambridge University Press
Bentley House, 200 Euston Road, London, N.W.1
American Branch: 32 East 57th Street, New York, N.Y. 10022

Library of Congress Catalogue Card Number: 67–12845

Standard Book Number: 521 06936 X

Printed in Great Britain
at the University Printing House, Cambridge
(Brooke Crutchley, University Printer)

CONTENTS

PLATES

BETWEEN PAGES 640 AND 641

15 Rustam slays Isfandiyār (Courtesy of the Fogg Art Museum, Harvard University. Gift of Mr Edward W. Forbes).

16 Illustration of a planetary model from a copy of Quṭb al-Dīn al-S̲h̲īrāzī's *al-Tuḥfa al-s̲h̲āhiya* (folio 62v of Aya Sofya MS 2584, reproduced by permission of the Director, Süleymanie Library, Istanbul).

ACKNOWLEDGMENTS

The editors and publishers are grateful to those who have given permission to reproduce plates in this volume.

PREFACE

It is remarkable how little attention has been given in the West to a period of great significance in the evolution of Persian, European and indeed world history. Of the Saljuq Turks the only up-to-date account is Claude Cahen's chapter in the Pennsylvania *History of the Crusades*. Of the Īl-Khānid dynasty there has been no detailed study in the English language since Part III of Howorth's *History of the Mongols* (*The Mongols of Persia*) published as long ago as 1888 and now completely antiquated. In the present volume an attempt is made to cover not only the political but the religious, cultural, administrative and socio-economic history of Saljuq and Mongol Iran. In choosing my collaborators in this task the principle I adopted was to approach scholars who might, I thought, be disposed to expand, abridge or revise what they had already written elsewhere on their specialized subject, sometimes in a language other than English. Few unpublished works have been more frequently consulted than Professor A. K. S. Lambton's dissertation *Contributions to the Study of Seljūq Institutions* (London, 1939). It is highly gratifying that she should have consented to expound her present-day views on this subject in chapter 2 ("Internal Structure of the Saljuq Empire"). As the author of *Persia religiosa* (Milan, 1959) Professor Alessandro Bausani was the obvious choice for chapters 3 ("Religion in the Saljuq Period") and 7 ("Religion under the Mongols"). To Professor M. G. S. Hodgson, who has written the standard work on the Persian Ismā'īlīs, *The Order of Assassins* (The Hague, 1955), we are indebted for chapter 5 ("The Ismā'īlī State"). Professor I. P. Petrushevsky's monumental *Zemledelie i agrarnïe otnosheniya v Irane XIII–XIV vekov* ("Agriculture and Agrarian Conditions in 13th- and 14th-century Iran") (Moscow–Leningrad, 1960) is still not translated into English or indeed into any West European language; but we now have an English summary in chapter 6 ("The Socio-Economic Condition of Iran under the Mongols"). I was particularly fortunate in persuading Professor Jan Rypka, the doyen of European Iranists, to contribute chapter 8 ("Poets and Prose Writers of the Late Saljuq and Mongol Periods"). Professor Rypka's *magnum opus*, published first in Czech (Prague, 1956) and then in German (Berlin, 1959) is now available in an English translation under the title *History of Iranian Literature* (Dordrecht, Holland, 1968). Chapter 9 ("The Visual Arts 1050–1350") is by a leading expert on

Middle Eastern art, Professor Oleg Grabar of the University of Ann Arbor, and chapter 10 ("The Exact Sciences in Iran under the Saljuqs and Mongols") by Professor E. S. Kennedy of the American University, Beirut, our greatest authority on Islamic science. The opening chapter on the political and dynastic history of the Saljuqs and their successors down to the Mongol invasion I entrusted to Dr (now Professor) C. E. Bosworth, whose doctoral thesis (afterwards expanded into *The Ghaznavids*) I had recently examined. Chapters 1 and 4 ("Political and Dynastic History of the Īl-Khāns") provide the chronological setting for the remainder of the volume.

On chapter 4 it is necessary to add a few details. The sources, particularly for the period of the Mongol invasion, are extremely discordant: it is not unusual to find two or even three mutually contradictory descriptions of the same occurrence. Even for the later Īl-Khānid period, our two main authorities, Rashīd al-Dīn and Vaṣṣāf, though viewing events from the same coign of vantage, are by no means always in agreement. It has often been necessary to draw attention to such discrepancies and even occasionally to reproduce side by side the two or more conflicting versions of a campaign or battle. In quoting the sources I have, whenever practicable, referred the reader to European translations. The relevant parts of Rashīd al-Dīn's encyclopaedic work have now been translated into Russian, a language no longer, as in Professor Browne's day, even less read in Western Europe than Persian. For permission to reproduce passages from a paper entitled "The Mongol Invasion of Eastern Persia 1220–23" read at the Middle East Centre, Cambridge, in November 1962, and afterwards published in *History Today* for September 1963, I am indebted to the courtesy of Professor Arberry and the editors of the journal.

The system of transliteration requires a word or two of explanation. In the case of Persian and Arabic words it is, broadly speaking, that recommended by the Royal Asiatic Society, modified here and there to conform with the practice in vol. 1. Thus the Persian province of Azerbaijan appears as Āzarbāijān (and not Ādharbāijān or Āẕarbāijān); *-iyya* alternates with *-īyeh* in name-endings; and place-names in the neighbouring Arab countries appear sometimes in their conventional English forms whilst in other cases they are rigorously transliterated like the Persian names. It is to be hoped that the specialist will make allowances for such inconsistencies, which will not disturb the general reader. In the case of Turkish and Mongol words it has been thought proper to reproduce the actual pronunciation of the more elaborate vowel system rather than simply to transliterate the Arabic script, e.g. Boz-Aba (Turkish "Grey Bear") and not Būzāba, Öljeitü (Mongol "Blessed, Fortunate") and not Ūljāitū. As a guide to the pronunciation for the general reader it is sufficient to say that *c͟h* is pronounced as the *ch* in *church*, *ḍ* and *d͟h* (by the Persians) as *ẓ*, *k͟h* as the *ch* in *loch*, *g͟h* as the French *r grasseyée*, *s͟h* as the *sh* in *ship*, *t͟h* (by the Persians) as *s* and *z͟h* as the French *j* or the *s* in *leisure*; that no distinction is made by the Persians between the dotted and undotted forms of *h*, *s*, *t* and *ẓ*; and that the vowels in Persian and Arabic words have their Italian values, while Turkish and Mongol *ö* and *ü* are pronounced as the corresponding German vowels (French *eu* and *u*) and *ï* as the Russian *ы* (Polish *y*).

In conclusion I should like to record my thanks to my friends Charles F. Beckingham, Professor of Islamic Studies in the University of London, and Frank R. C. Bagley, Lecturer in Persian in the University of Durham, for reading the galley proofs of chapters 4 and 8 respectively and making a number of valuable suggestions.

J. A. B.

Manchester, February 1968

CHAPTER I

THE POLITICAL AND DYNASTIC HISTORY OF THE IRANIAN WORLD (A.D. 1000–1217)

I. THE EASTERN IRANIAN WORLD ON THE EVE OF THE TURKISH INVASIONS

For nearly a thousand years—indeed, until our own century—Iran has generally been ruled by non-Persian dynasties, usually Turkish but sometimes Mongol or Kurdish. This domination at the highest level has had less effect on Iranian national psychology and literary consciousness than might be expected, for all of the alien ruling dynasties have come from races of low cultural development, and thus they have lacked the administrative expertise necessary for ruling a land of ancient settlement and civilization. Whether consciously or unconsciously, they have adopted Iranian culture at their courts, and they have been compelled to employ Iranian officials to administer the country and collect the taxes.

The first such alien rulers were the Saljuq Turks, who appeared in the Iranian world in the first half of the 5th/11th century. For them as well as for their successors, the process of assimilation to the indigenous culture and practices of Persia was not uncongenial, because they were able to draw on the country's ancient traditions of exalted monarchic power and submissiveness by the people. Moreover, in these traditions kingly authority was identified with divine authority, which helped the dynasties to rise above their tribal origins. The Saljuqs had originated as chieftains of nomadic bands in the Central Asian steppes. Their powers and ambitions often hedged about by a complex of traditional tribal rights and customs, the steppe leaders were little more than *primi inter pares* amongst the heads of all the prominent tribal families. With their entry into the Iranian world, the Saljuqs and their successors found the instruments at hand with which to make themselves, if they so desired, despots of the traditional Persian stamp: these instruments were a settled administration, a steady revenue from taxation, and usually a personal guard and standing army.

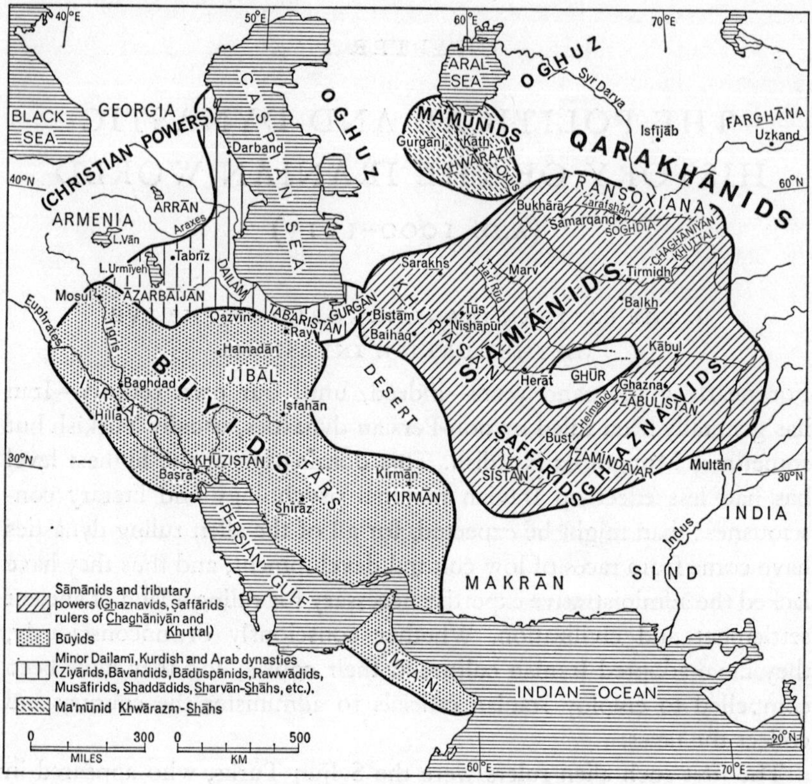

Map 1. The Iranian world, *c.* 388/998.

Yet the process of self-magnification had a reverse side. What was to be done with the ladder by which these leaders had risen? For their supporters had included fellow tribesmen, e.g. the Saljuqs' Türkmen; military retainers, such as the Turkish and Mongol soldiers of the Mongol Qa'ans, and fellow sectaries and religious devotees, such as the Ṣafavids' Qïzïl-Bāsh. In the Saljuq period the Oghuz and other Türkmen were a pressing problem for the sultans. How could the Türkmen be reconciled to the new concept of royal power—especially when they saw the old tribal custom, which defined and guaranteed each man's personal position and duties, quietly set aside and replaced by the Islamic *sharī'a* and by the Iranian governmental ethos, in both of which political quietism and virtually unconditional obedience to the monarch were enjoined? This question, in varying terms, runs through much of Iran's history in the last nine centuries, underlying many of its revolutions and crises of power. It is particularly important in the age of the Saljuqs, when the sultans were never able satisfactorily to resolve this tension in their empire.

Whilst it is true that the coming of the Saljuqs inaugurated the age of alien, especially Turkish, rule, the change was not absolutely abrupt. We shall first of all be concerned with the eastern Iranian world, comprising Khurāsān, the adjoining regions of modern Afghanistan, and the lands of the Oxus and Syr Darya basins. At the opening of the 5th/11th century, the Iranian world still extended far beyond the Oxus, embracing the regions of Khwārazm, Transoxiana (called by the Arabs *Mā warā' al-nahr*, "the lands beyond the river"), and Farghāna. In pre-Christian and early Christian times the Massagetae, the Sakae, the Scyths, the Sarmatians, and the Alans—all Indo-European peoples—had roamed the Eurasian steppes from the Ukraine to the Altai. The pressure of Altaic and Ugrian peoples from the heartland of Central Asia and Siberia gradually pushed the limits of Indo-European occupation southwards, but until the end of the 4th/10th century the lands along the Oxus and south of the Aral Sea, together with the middle and upper reaches of the Syr Darya as far as its sources in the slopes of the T'ien Shan, were still generally ruled by royal dynasties or local princes who were apparently Iranian. The picture presented by the holders of power is thus relatively straightforward, except that the Iranian names and titles of petty rulers and local landowners (*dihqāns*) in such frontier regions as Isfījāb, Īlāq, and Farghāna do not make it absolutely certain that they were racially Iranians. However, a demographic analysis of the whole population in this Iranian-ruled area involves certain difficulties. From the earliest times Transoxiana has been a corridor through which peoples from the steppes have passed into the settled lands to the south and west; thus history and geography have worked against an ethnic homogeneity for the region. Whether the invading waves have receded or been swallowed up in the existing population, a human debris has inevitably been left behind. This was undoubtedly the origin of the Turkish elements in eastern Afghanistan, for these Oghuz and Khalaj were nomads on the plateau between Kābul and Bust when Muslim arms first penetrated there in the early centuries of Islam, and they survived as an ethnic unity throughout the periods of the Ghaznavids, Ghūrids, and Khwārazm-Shāhs. It has been plausibly argued by J. Marquart that these Turks were remnants of peoples brought from north of the Oxus by the confederation of the Ephthalites or White Huns, whose leaders seem to have been of the same race as the Iranians.[1]

In Transoxiana and Khwārazm, the infiltration of Turkish elements must also have begun early. Topography—i.e. the mountain chains running east and west, the land-locked river basins and oases—made Transoxiana and especially Soghdia (the basin of the Zarafshān river) a politically fragmented region. In the 1st/7th and 2nd/8th centuries the region was a battleground where Iranian rulers fought the invading Arabs from the south as well as the Western Türk or T'u-chüeh from the north, with the Chinese keeping an eye on what was nominally a distant province of their empire. Turkish warriors were frequently invited from outside by the local rulers in an effort to repel the Arabs, but it is also possible that some of these troops were recruited from the Turks already settled within the borders of Transoxiana.[2] For not all Turks were pastoral nomads or forest hunters. In such comparatively favoured spots of Central Asia as the Orkhon and Selenga valleys in Mongolia, and the Chu valley and shores of the Ïsïq-Köl in Semirechye ("land of the seven rivers", or the northern part of the modern Soviet Kirghiz republic and the parts of the Kazakh republic adjoining its northern borders)—in all these areas Turkish agriculturalists had been able to make a living in peaceful periods.[3] Similarly, the rural peasantry and even the town populations of Transoxiana and Khwārazm may well have contained Turkish elements from an early date. Firdausī's *Shāh-Nāma* speaks of Iran and Tūrān, i.e. the Iranians and the Turks, as two naturally antipathetic groups: "two elements, fire and water, which rage against each other in the depths of the heart",[4] but the economic facts, well brought out by the Arabic geographers, belie this. They say that the economy of the pastoralist Turks from the steppe was complementary to and interdependent with the economy of the agricultural

[1] J. Marquart, "Ērānšahr nach der Geographie des Ps. Moses Khorenac'i", *Abh. der Königl. Gesell. der Wiss. zu Göttingen*, p. 253; *idem* and J. J. M. de Groot, "Das Reich Zābul und der Gott Žūn", *Festschrift Eduard Sachau* (Berlin, 1915), pp. 257–8. The Iranian ethnic nature of the Ephthalites has recently been affirmed by R. Ghirshman, *Les Chionites-Hephtalites* (Cairo, 1946). For a contrary opinion see E. G. Pulleyblank, "The Consonantal System of Old Chinese: Part II", *Asia Major*, N.S., vol. IX (1963), pp. 207–65 (258–60).

[2] Cf. R. N. Frye and A. M. Sayïlï, "Turks in the Middle East before the Saljuqs", *J[ournal of the] A[merican] O[riental] S[ociety]*, pp. 196 ff.; see also a forthcoming chapter by C. E. Bosworth on the Turks in the early Islamic world, in C. Cahen (ed.), *Philologiae Turcicae Fundamenta*, vol. III (Wiesbaden).

[3] Cf. O. Lattimore, "The Geographical Factor in Mongol History", *Geographical Journal* vol. XCI (January 1938), pp. 1–20.

[4] Cf. T. Kowalski, "Les Turcs dans le Šāh-nāme", *Rocznik Orientalistyczny*, vol. XV (1939–49) pp. 87 ff.

oases and towns of the Iranian Tājīks. The settled regions supplied the nomads with cereals, manufactured goods, and arms, and the nomads reared stock animals and brought dairy products, hides, and furs to the farmers. In Transoxiana and Khwārazm, wrote al-Iṣṭakhrī (*c.* 340/951), the Oghuz and Qarluq from beyond the Syr Darya and from the Qara Qum steppes supplied horses, sheep, camels, mules, and asses.[1] It is likely, too, that some of the pastoralists remained in the market centres of the settled region and gradually settled down within its borders.

The rule of native Iranian dynasties in Khwārazm, Transoxiana, and Khurāsān foundered by the opening decades of the 5th/11th century. The Sāmānids of Bukhārā had ruled in the latter two provinces, first as local administrators for the 'Abbāsid governors of Khurāsān, and then as virtually independent sovereigns.[2] In the last decade of the 10th century their rule sustained almost simultaneous attacks from two Turkish powers, the Qarakhānids and the Ghaznavids. The Qarakhānids originated from a confederation of Turkish tribes who had long occupied the steppes that stretched from the middle Syr Darya to the T'ien Shan. Their nucleus seems to have been the Qarluq tribe and its component peoples of the Yaghma, Tukhsï, and Chigil. The Qarluq were an old people in the steppes, known from the 1st/7th century as a constituent group within the Türkü empire. Already the characteristic title for their chiefs, *Ilig*, appears in the Turfan texts of that period; and in later times Muslim sources often refer to the Qarakhānid dynasty as that of the Ilig-Khāns. Within the various confederations that took shape in the steppes after the collapse of the Türkü empire in 125/741, the head of the Qarluq assumed the title first of *Yabghu* and then of *Qaghan* (Arabic form, *Khāqān*), or "supreme monarch". The adoption of this latter title was to become characteristic of the Qarakhānids, whereas the Saljuqs never felt entitled to adopt it. In the course of the 4th/10th century the Qarluq became Muslim; the first ruler to become converted is traditionally held to be Satūq Bughra Khān (d. ? 344/955), who assumed the Islamic name of 'Abd al-Karīm and reigned from Kāshghar and Talas over the western wing of his people.

[1] al-Iṣṭakhrī, *Kitāb masālik al-mamālik*, p. 274; cf. Bosworth, *The Ghaznavids: their Empire in Afghanistan and Eastern Iran 994–1040*, pp. 154–5.

[2] There exists no special monograph devoted to the Sāmānids; the best account of this very important but still obscure dynasty remains that by W. Barthold in his *Turkestan down to the Mongol Invasion*, G[ibb] M[emorial] S[eries], vol. v, pp. 209 ff. See also Frye's brief survey, "The Samanids: a Little-Known Dynasty", *Muslim World*, pp. 40–5; and *idem*, *The History of Bukhara* (a translation of Narshakhī's *Ta'rīkh-i Bukhārā*), the notes to which contain much valuable information on the Sāmānids.

Those who worked in the pagan outer darkness of the steppes were mainly the dervishes or Ṣūfīs, i.e. religious enthusiasts whose orthodoxy was suspect, and who were often *persona non grata* to the orthodox Sāmānid government and religious institution. Nevertheless the Qarakhānids became firm Sunnīs once they entered the Islamic world.[1]

The Qarakhānid Bughra Khān Hārūn or Ḥasan, a grandson of Satuq Bughra Khān, temporarily occupied the Sāmānid capital of Bukhārā in 382/992. As he passed through Transoxiana he met with little opposition: indeed, he was encouraged in his action by the rebellious Sāmānid general Abū 'Alī Sīmjūrī and also by discontented dihqāns. Faced with the Qarakhānid invasion from the north and the revolt of the generals Abū 'Alī Sīmjūrī and Fā'iq Khāṣṣa in Khurāsān, the Sāmānid amīr Nūḥ b. Manṣūr (366–87/976–7 to 997) was compelled to call in from Ghazna another of his Turkish slave commanders, Sebük-Tegin.[2]

Abū Manṣūr Sebük-Tegin (d. 387/997) was the founder of the Ghaznavid dynasty and father of the famous Maḥmūd of Ghazna (388–421/998–1030).[3] Sebük-Tegin came originally from Barskhan, a settlement on the shores of the Ïsïq-Köl, whose ruler, according to the anonymous author of the Persian geographical treatise *Ḥudūd al-'ālam* ("Limits of the World"), was one of the Qarluq. It seems therefore probable that the Ghaznavids were of Qarluq origin. In a tribal war Sebük-Tegin was captured by the neighbouring Tukhsï and sold in a Sāmānid slave market at Chāch. Because of his hardiness and his skill with weapons, he rose rapidly from the ranks of the Sāmānids' slave guards, coming under the patronage of Chief Ḥājib or Commander-in-Chief Alp-Tegin. In 351/962 he accompanied his master to Ghazna, where Alp-Tegin henceforth established himself as ruler, and in 366/977 Sebük-Tegin succeeded to power there, continuing, like his predecessors, to regard himself as governor there on behalf of the Sāmānids.[4] In 384/994 the amīr Nūḥ b. Manṣūr summoned Sebük-Tegin to Khurāsān to fight the rebellious generals but this led to the establishment of the Ghaznavids in Khurāsān and all the Sāmānid

[1] The Qarakhānids and the Qarluq, from whom the dynasty very probably sprang, have been studied by O. Pritsak. Amongst his many articles on them, see especially "Karahanlïlar" in *İslâm Ansiklopedisi*; and on the origins of the dynasty, "Von den Karluk zu den Karachaniden", *Zeitschrift der Deutschen Morgenländischen Gesellschaft*, pp. 270–300.

[2] Cf. Barthold, *Turkestan*, pp. 254–61.

[3] On the Ghaznavid dynasty, see B. Spuler, "Ghaznavids", *Encyc. of Islam* (2nd ed.); M. Nāẓim, *The Life and Times of Sulṭān Maḥmūd of Ghazna*; and Bosworth, *The Ghaznavids*.

[4] On Sebük-Tegin's early life and his rule as governor in Ghazna, see Nāẓim, *op. cit.* pp. 28–33, and Bosworth, *The Ghaznavids*, pp. 35–44.

provinces south of the Oxus. These territories were definitely annexed in 388/998 by Abu'l-Qāsim Maḥmūd b. Sebük-Tegin. Meanwhile it had proved impossible to dislodge the Qarakhānids from the Syr Darya basin, and in 389/999 the Sāmānid dynasty was definitely overthrown in Transoxiana by the Ilig Naṣr b. 'Alī (d. 403/1012–13), nephew of Bughra Khān Hārūn. The heroism of the last of the Sāmānids, Ismā'īl al-Muntaṣir, could achieve nothing in the face of the division of the Sāmānid empire between the Ilig and Maḥmūd. In 391/1001 these two came to a formal agreement whereby the Oxus was to be the boundary between the two kingdoms, and in 395/1005 Ismā'īl was killed through the treachery of an Arab nomad chief in the Qara Qum desert.[1]

In the adjacent province of Khwārazm, the classical Chorasmia, the days of rule by native Iranian monarchs were also numbered. For several thousand years the region of the lower Oxus had held a complex of rich agricultural oases linked by irrigation canals, the full extent of which has only recently come to light through the researches of Soviet archaeologists. (The Iranian scholar al-Bīrūnī says that the Khwārazmian era began when the region was first settled and cultivated, this date being placed in the early 13th-century B.C.) That the ancient dynasty of Afrīghid Khwārazm-Shāhs survived for nearly three centuries after the coming of Islam to their land is unique in the Islamic world: al-Bīrūnī lists twenty-two rulers of this line running from A.D. 305 to 385/995.[2] However, the vandalism of Qutaiba b. Muslim's invading Arabs in 93/712 had an enfeebling effect on the culture of ancient Khwārazm, and this seems to have been aggravated by economic decline, whose symptoms, according to S. P. Tolstov, included the neglect of irrigation works and the decline of urban life. The system of large fortified estates, which is characteristic of Khwārazmian agrarian society at this time, was a response to increasing external pressure from Turkish steppe peoples, who were attracted not only by prospects of plunder but also by the winter pasture available along the shores of the Oxus. The Turkicizing of the population of Khwārazm probably began during this period.[3] In the 4th/10th century there were

[1] Barthold, *Turkestan*, pp. 261–721; and *idem*, "A Short History of Turkestan", in *Four Studies on the History of Central Asia*, vol. 1, pp. 21–4.

[2] al-Bīrūnī, *al-Āthār al-bāqiya 'an al-qurūn al-khāliya* (tr. E. Sachau, *The Chronology of Ancient Nations*), pp. 40–2.

[3] Sachau, "Zur Geschichte und Chronologie von Khwârizm", *S*[*itzungs-*] *B*[*erichte der*] *W*[*iener*] *A*[*kad. der*] *W*[*iss.*], Phil.-Hist. C., vol. LXXXIII, 1873; vol. LXXIV, 1873, pp. 471 ff.

villages with Turkish names on the right bank of the Oxus. The Ghaznavid historian Abu'l-Faḍl Baihaqī speaks of Qïpchaq, Küjet, and Chaghraq Turks harrying the fringes of Khwārazm in 422/1030,[1] and a few years after this the Saljuqs and their followers spent some time on Khwārazmian pastures before moving southwards into Khurāsān. The higher culture of Iranian Khwārazm offered resistance to the process of Turkicization, but the trend nevertheless continued over the next centuries (see pp. 141–2 below).

In spite of this, the downfall of the native Afrīghid dynasty of Khwārazm-Shāhs in 385/995 came about through internal disturbances. Gurganj, a town on the left bank of the Oxus, had grown in importance as the terminus of caravan trade across the Oghuz steppes to the Volga and southern Russia, thereby eclipsing the ancient capital on the right bank of Kāth. A local Gurganj family, the Ma'mūnids, succeeded in deposing the last Afrīghid, Abū 'Abdallāh Muḥammad, and assumed the traditional title of Khwārazm-Shāh. But their tenure of power was brief. The Sāmānids had been nominal suzerains of Khwārazm, though in practice they had rarely interfered there; now the shadow of their supplanter, Maḥmūd of Ghazna, grew menacing for the Ma'mūnids. In 406/1015–16 Abu'l-'Abbās Ma'mūn b. Ma'mūn married one of the Ghaznavid sultan's sisters, Ḥurra-yi Kaljī; nevertheless, Ghaznavid pressure was relentless. The 'Abbāsid caliph in Baghdad sent directly to the Khwārazm-Shāh a patent of investiture for Khwārazm, a standard, and the honorific titles '*Ain al-Daula wa Zain al-Milla* ("Eye of the State and Ornament of the Religious Community"); but the shah did not dare to receive these publicly in his capital Gurganj for fear of provoking Maḥmūd's wrath. In the sultan's imperial strategy, possession of Khwārazm was necessary to turn the flank of the Qarakhānids, amongst whom the ruler of Samarqand and Bukhārā—'Alī b. Ḥasan Bughra Khān, known as 'Alī-Tegin (d. 425/1034)—was showing himself an implacable enemy of the Ghaznavids. After an ultimatum to the Khwārazmians, which contained humiliating demands and required the renunciation of national sovereignty, Maḥmūd's troops invaded and annexed Khwārazm in 408/1017. The sultan then installed as Khwārazm-Shāh Altun-Tash, one of his most trusted slave generals and a former *ghulām* or military retainer of his father Sebük-Tegin; for the next seventeen years Khwā-

506; A. Z. V. Togan, "The Khorezmians and their Civilisation", Preface to Zamakhsharī's *Muqaddimāt al-Adab*, pp. 9–43; S. P. Tolstov, *Auf den Spuren der Altchoresmischen Kultur*, pp. 9 f.

[1] Baihaqī, *Ta'rīkh-i Mas'ūdī*, p. 86; cf. Bosworth, *The Ghaznavids*, p. 109.

razm remained a salient of Ghaznavid power that reached into the steppes.[1]

Some Western orientalists have viewed the downfall of these north-eastern Iranian dynasties through a certain romantic haze. They have idealized the Sāmānids, at whose court the renaissance of New Persian culture and literature began—a court adorned by such figures as Balʿamī, Rūdakī, and Daqīqī; or, mourning the passing of the Khwārazm-Shāhs, whose kingdom nurtured the polymath al-Bīrūnī, they have called it the end of an epoch, after which Iran lost political control of its destiny for many centuries.[2] On the other hand, as V. Minorsky has justly pointed out, there have been few laments for the passing of those Iranian dynasties farther west, that also went down in the course of the 5th/11th century under Turkish pressure; yet the Būyids' court at Ray and Shīrāz, the Kākūyids' at Iṣfahān, and the Ziyārids' court at Gurgān and Ṭabaristān gave shelter to such diverse geniuses as al-Mutanabbī, Avicenna, and al-Bīrūnī. To some extent these Western attitudes reflect those of the contemporary Sunnī Muslim sources which are distinctly favourable to dynasties like the Ṭāhirids and Sāmānids, sprung from the landed classes, while they are hostile to those of plebeian origin, e.g. the Ṣaffārids or to those tinged with Shīʿism or unorthodoxy, such as the Būyids and Kākūyids.[3]

The collapse of the native Iranian dynasties of the north-east was followed within a few decades by a major migration of Turkish peoples, the Oghuz, from the outer steppes. Similar population movements have been recurrent features of the history of this region from early times, for the Oxus and Syr Darya basins are a transitional zone between Central Asia and the lands of ancient civilization in the Near East. The mountain chains of the Alburz [Elburz], Pamirs, and Hindu Kush are high and, being geologically young, are sharp and jagged, yet they have never seriously hindered the passage of armies and other peoples; nor have invaders from the steppes ever found that the transition to the Iranian plateau necessitated much change in their way of life. In order for a pastoralist economy to survive, each summer the flocks and

[1] Sachau, *S.B.W.A.W.* vol. LXXIV (1873), pp. 290–301; Barthold, *Turkestan*, pp. 233–4, 275–9; *idem*, "Short History of Turkestan", pp. 18–19; Tolstov, *Auf den Spuren*, pp. 253–63, 286–91.

[2] See, for example, T. Nöldeke, *Das Iranische Nationalepos*, pp. 40–1; and G. E. von Grunebaum, "Firdausī's Concept of History", in *Islam, Essays in the Nature and Growth of a Cultural Tradition* (London, 1955), pp. 168–84.

[3] See V. Minorsky, Review of Spuler's *Iran in frühislamischer Zeit* in *Göttingische Gelehrte Anzeigen*, vol. CCVII (1953), pp. 192–7.

herds should be driven out of their winter grounds to pastures, or *yailaqs*, in the hills. Thus the terrain of Iran was quite well suited to the traditional way of life of Central Asian invaders. For instance, the oases of Khurāsān could provide rich pasture for herds, and certain *chamans* (pasture grounds), e.g. the Ūlang-i Rādkān between Mashhad [Meshed] and Khabūshān, and the Marg-i Ṣā'igh near Nasā, have played significant parts in Iranian history as the camping and grazing grounds of armies. As the Türkmen moved westwards, they found the valleys of Āzarbāījān and Armenia and the plains of Anatolia highly suitable for their flocks. In this way the Saljuq and Mongol invasions inevitably had an effect on landholding and land utilization in the Iranian world.

Yet these considerations do not explain why the Türkmen succeeded in bringing about permanent changes in the ethnography and economy of the Iranian world, whereas most of the earlier invaders had eventually been absorbed into the existing way of life. It was certainly not through sheer weight of human numbers, for there were not many Türkmen bands in Khurāsān during the reign of Mas'ūd b. Maḥmūd of Ghazna (421–32/1030–41), although the damaging effects of their sheep and goats as they nibbled across the country's agricultural oases were indeed serious.[1] It seems that in the first half of the 5th/11th century, the Iranian bastion of the north-east, whose age-old function had been to hold closed this corridor for peoples, lost its resilience and no longer possessed the absorptive power it had once had. In the previous century the Afrīghid Khwārazm-Shāhs had every autumn led an expedition into the steppes against the Türkmen; and the Sāmānid amīrs launched punitive expeditions and slave raids across the Syr Darya, such as the famous campaign of Ismā'īl b. Aḥmad (279–95/892–907) against the Qarluq at Talas in 280/893.[2] It is true that the groundwork for this collapse had been in some measure prepared, with Turks taking part in the internal wars of Transoxiana and also settling peacefully within its borders. Furthermore, from the early 3rd/9th century onwards Muslim rulers in all parts of the eastern caliphate had been growing more dependent on Turkish slave troops, which increased the flow of Turks through Transoxiana and Khurāsān. This traffic in human beings became an important source of revenue for the Sāmānids, who issued licences and collected transit dues; at the same time the amīrs became

[1] Cf. Bosworth, *The Ghaznavids*, pp. 128, 224, 226, 241, 259–61.

[2] Barthold, *Turkestan*, p. 224; *idem*, "Short History of Turkestan", pp. 19–20; Tolstov, *Auf den Spuren*, pp. 262–3; Bosworth, *op. cit.* pp. 31–3.

dependent on Turkish ghulāms for their own bodyguard, seeking to use them as a counterbalance to the indigenous military class of the dihqāns.[1]

To sum up: the disappearance of the native Khwārazm-Shāhs and Sāmānids meant the end of two firmly constituted states in the eastern Iranian world, and the result was a power vacuum. The authority of the Qarakhānids in Transoxiana and that of the Ghaznavids in Khurāsān and Khwārazm had no organic roots; in the first region it was diffused and less effective than Sāmānid rule had been, and in the other two regions it was despotic, capricious, and operating from a very distant capital, Ghazna. These points will be examined at greater length in the next section.

II. KHURĀSĀN: THE DECLINE OF GHAZNAVID POWER AND THE ESTABLISHMENT OF THE SALJUQS

All through their period of domination the Qarakhānids in Transoxiana remained a tribal confederation and never formed a unitary state. Their territories straddled the T'ien Shan, where their yailaqs lay, and on the facts of geography alone it is hard to see how such an empire could have been governed by one power. Originally the dynasty did have a certain unity, although there was from the start the old Turkish double system of a Great Khan and a Co-Khan. But as early as the first decades of the 5th/11th century the sources mention internecine strife in the family; and two distinct branches—which may be called after their characteristic Islamic names, the 'Alids and Ḥasanids—begin to emerge. After 433/1041–2 there were lines of eastern and western Qarakhānids, established at first in Balāsāghūn and Uzkand respectively, and then in Kāshghar and Samarqand. Within the family there existed the complicated system of a double khanate and subordinate under-khans, so that several princes might hold power simultaneously in various regions; and the family's titulature and onomasticon, combining both Turkish tribal and totemistic titles with Islamic names and honorifics, was confused and constantly changing. The task of sorting out the genealogy of the dynasty has thus been very difficult; only the researches of the numismatist R. Vasmer and the Turcologist O. Pritsak have thrown light on it.[2]

[1] Bosworth, pp. 208–9.

[2] Cf. Pritsak, "Karahanlılar", *İslâm Ansiklopedisi*; *idem* "Karachanidische Streitfrage", *Oriens*, pp. 209–28; and "Titulaturen und Stammesnamen der altäischen Volker", *Ural-Altäische Jahrbücher*, vol. XXIV (1952), pp. 49–104.

In the early part of the 5th/11th century the administration of Transoxiana reverted to a pattern resembling that which had prevailed on the eve of the Muslim conquests: small city-states were scattered along the Zarafshān, and the middle Syr Darya was under the general supervision of Qarakhānid princes. With this trend towards regionalism, the landed aristocracy enjoyed a resurgence of power. The dihqān of Īlāq, on the north bank of the Syr Darya, began for the first time to mint his own coins.[1] The general weight and expense of administration decreased. A continuator of Narshakhī, the historian of Bukhārā, records that the land tax of Bukhārā and its environs was everywhere lightened after the fall of the Sāmānids, in part because irrigation works were neglected and land became water-logged and unproductive.[2] Hence after the disappearance of the Sāmānid amīrs, with their centralizing administrative policy and their standing army, Transoxiana was ill-prepared to meet fresh waves of invaders from the steppes.

We have seen that Khurāsān passed into the Ghaznavids' hands. Towards the end of his life the restless dynamism of Sulṭān Maḥmūd made him press westwards across Iran against his rivals the Dailamī Būyids, various branches of whom ruled in western and central Iran and in Iraq (see below, section III, pp. 25 ff.). The Shīʿism of the Būyids and their tutelage of the ʿAbbāsid caliphs in Baghdad gave the early Ghaznavids plausible pretexts for intervention in the west. They had grandiloquent plans for liberating the caliphs, opening up the pilgrimage route to Mecca and Medina, and then pushing on to attack the Shīʿī Fāṭimids in Syria and Egypt; but the Türkmen's pressure in the east ensured that these designs remained only dreams.[3] It was not until 420/1029, the last year of his life, that Maḥmūd came to Ray in northern Iran and deposed its Būyid ruler Majd al-Daula Rustam b. ʿAlī (387–420/997–1029). At the same time that the province of Ray and Jibāl was being annexed, another Dailamī ruler, the Kākūyid ʿAlāʾ al-Daula Muḥammad b. Dushmanziyār of Iṣfahān (398–433/1008 to 1041–2), was made a tributary, and various petty Kurdish and Dailamī rulers of north-western Persia, such as the Musāfirids of Ṭārum, were also forced to recognize the sultan. The Ziyārid Manūchihr b. Qābūs (403–20 or 421/1012–13 to 1029 or 1030) was already

[1] Barthold, "Short History of Turkestan", in *Four Studies*, vol. I, pp. 23–4.

[2] Narshakhī, *Taʾrīkh-i Bukhārā*, ed. Mudarris Riḍavī, pp. 39–40 (Frye tr., p. 33).

[3] Cf. Bosworth, "The Imperial Policy of the Early Ghaznawids", *Islamic Studies*, pp. 67–74; *idem*, *The Ghaznavids*, pp. 52–4.

paying tribute to Maḥmūd; now he had to allow Ghaznavid armies transit through his territories and was forced on at least one occasion to contribute troops to them. (For a detailed survey of these minor Dailamī dynasties, see below, section III.) In the province of Kirmān in south-eastern Iran, which was under the control of the Būyids of Fārs and Khūzistān, Maḥmūd had in 407/1016–17 attempted to set his own nominee on the throne, but without lasting success; thereafter he left Kirmān alone. One of Mas'ūd b. Maḥmūd's armies did temporarily occupy the province in 424/1033, but was shortly afterwards driven out by the returning Būyids.[1]

When Maḥmūd died in 421/1030, the territory of the Ghaznavid empire was at its largest. It had become a successor state to the Sāmānids in their former lands south of the Oxus, but its original centre was Ghazna and the region of Zābulistān on the eastern rim of the Afghan plateau. As soon as he came to power in Ghazna in 366/977, Sebük-Tegin began a series of raids against the Hindūshāhī rajahs of Vaihand, and Maḥmūd gained his lasting reputation in the Islamic world as the great *ghāzī* (warrior for the faith), leading campaigns each winter against the infidels of the plains of northern India. Maḥmūd's thirst for plunder and territory, and also his need to employ a standing army of some 50,000 men, combined to give Ghaznavid policy a markedly imperialist and aggressive bent;[2] whilst from the religious aspect, the Ghaznavids' strict Sunnī orthodoxy enabled the sultan to pose as the faithful agent of the caliph and to purge his own dominions of religious dissidents such as the extremist Shī'ī Ismā'īlīs and the Mu'tazilīs.

The spoils of India were insufficient to finance this vast empire; the steady taxation revenue from the heartland of the empire, Afghanistan and Khurāsān, had to supplement them. Khurāsān suffered most severely from the exactions of Ghaznavid tax collectors, who were driven on by the sultan's threats of torture and death for those who failed him. For some ten years, until his dismissal and death in 404/1013–14, the Vizier Abu'l-'Abbās al-Faḍl Isfarā'inī mulcted the merchants, artisans, and peasants of Khurāsān, causing misery and depopulation. In the words of the Ghaznavid historian 'Utbī, "Affairs were characterized there by nothing but tax levies, sucking which sucked dry, and attempts to extract fresh sources of revenue, without any construc-

[1] Cf. Nāẓim, *The Life and Times of Sulṭān Maḥmūd of Ghazna*, pp. 77–9, 80–5, 192–3; Bosworth, *Islamic Studies*, pp. 69–72.

[2] On the Ghaznavid military machine, see Bosworth, "Ghaznevid Military Organisation", *Der Islam*, pp. 37–77.

tive measures". Hence after a few years there was nothing more to be got in Khurāsān, "since after water had been thrown on her udder, not a trickle of milk could be got nor any trace of fat".[1]

Mas'ūd continued to act irresponsibly in Iran. When Ray had first been conquered there had been some sympathy for the Ghaznavids, for they delivered the people from the Shī'ī Būyids and their turbulent soldiery. But the exactions of the Ghaznavid officials soon alienated all support: "Tash Farrāsh [the Ghaznavid military governor] had filled the land with injustice and tyranny, until the people prayed for deliverance from them [the Ghaznavids] and their rule. The land became ruined and the population dispersed."[2] This policy of *Raubwirtschaft* prevented the growth of any bond of sympathy or feelings of interdependence between the sultan and his Iranian subjects. Loyalty and patriotism as we know them had no meaning in the Islamic world at this time, as can be seen in Maḥmūd's words to the people of Balkh after the Qarakhānid invasion of 397–8/1006–8: he reproached them for putting up a spirited defence against the besiegers, because some of the sultan's personal property had been destroyed in the fighting. On their side, the attitude of the merchants and landowners of Khurāsān was purely pragmatic; they tolerated Ghaznavid rule as long as it could secure the external defence of the province. In Mas'ūd's reign it became clear that the Ghaznavids could not provide this protection, so there was no reason for the Khurāsānian cities to retain any further loyalty to them. Even as early as 397/1006, a considerable number of the dihqāns and notables had inclined towards the Qarakhānid invaders.[3]

The Ghaznavids failed, therefore, to identify themselves with the historic interests of Khurāsān, that is, with the securing of internal prosperity, an atmosphere in which commerce and agriculture could flourish, and with the preservation of the north-eastern frontier against external invaders from Central Asia. In both spheres their achievements fell short of those of earlier, Iranian rulers of the province, such as the Sāmānids. The racially Turkish Ghaznavids adopted the government's traditional institutions and practices, encouraged Iranian culture, and held court with the magnificence of Iranian monarchs;[4] but their

[1] 'Utbī, *al-Ta'rīkh al-Yamīnī*, vol. II, pp. 158–9; cf. Bosworth, *Ghaznavids*, pp. 65 ff., 86–9.

[2] Ibn al-Athīr, *al-Kāmil fi'l-Ta'rīkh*, vol. IX, p. 292; cf. Bosworth, *Ghaznavids*, pp. 85–6.

[3] Baihaqī, *Ta'rīkh-i Mas'ūdī*, p. 551; 'Utbī, II, p. 77; cf. Barthold, *Turkestan*, p. 291, and Bosworth, *Ghaznavids*, pp. 253, 259–66.

[4] Cf. Bosworth, *Ghaznavids*, pp. 129–39.

identification was not deep enough, or perhaps it did not have time to develop: the sultans ruled in Khurāsān for only forty years, and in Ray and Jibāl for only seven or eight years. In basic outlook the sultans remained in large measure Turkish *condottieri*, thus the lure of India and their dreams of expansion towards Iraq and beyond distracted them from proper attention to the defence of the Oxus line. Until it was too late, the Ghaznavid sultans regarded the Türkmen as minor irritants, just one more wave of raiders from the steppes who would either sweep through Iran to regions beyond or else become absorbed into the existing economy and social structure of Persia.

When the Saljuqs first appeared in Transoxiana and Khurāsān in the 5th/11th century, they came as marauders and plunderers. It has been suggested that the Turkish peoples' conversion to Islam and their consequent zeal for *jihād* (holy war) helped them to overrun so much of the Middle East.[1] It is true that in the course of the 5th/11th century the Türkmen carried on warfare against the Byzantines and the Christian kingdoms of Armenia and the Caucasus, and that the Saljuqs achieved some prestige in the eyes of the orthodox by overthrowing Shīʿī Būyid rule in western Iran. Sunnī writers even came to give an ideological justification for the Turks' political and military domination of the Middle East. The Iranian historian Rāvandī dedicated his history of the Saljuqs, the *Rāḥat al-ṣudūr wa āyat al-surūr* ("Solace of Hearts and Signal for Gladness", begun in 599/1202), to one of the Saljuq sultans of Rūm or Asia Minor, Ghiyāth al-Dīn Kai-Khusrau b. Qïlïj-Arslan. Rāvandī tells of a hidden, supernatural voice from the Kaʿba at Mecca, which spoke to the Imām Abū Ḥanīfa and promised him that as long as the sword remained in the hands of the Turks, his faith (that of the Ḥanafī law school, which was followed *par excellence* by the Turks) would not perish. Rāvandī himself adds a pious doxology: "Praise be to God, He is exalted, that the defenders of Islam are mighty and that the followers of the Ḥanafī rite are happy and joyful! In the lands of the Arabs, Persians, Byzantines, and Russians, the sword is in the hands of the Turks, and fear of their sword is firmly implanted in all hearts!"[2]

Yet these considerations, valid though they may be for the second half of the 5th/11th century and after, have no relevance for the

[1] This view is put especially clearly by August Müller in his *Der Islam im Morgen- und Abendland* (Berlin, 1884–7), vol. II, pp. 53–4.

[2] Rāvandī, *Rāḥat al-ṣudūr*, pp. 17–18; cf. O. Turan, "The Idea of World Domination among the Mediaeval Turks", *Studia Islamica*, vol. IV (1955), pp. 84–5.

preceding decades of the Saljuq invasions of Khurāsān. Barthold has pointed out that the Ṣūfī shaikhs who worked in the steppes were usually evangelical hell-fire preachers, who dangled their audiences over the pit rather than painting for them the delights of a warriors' paradise.[1] Moreover, it is hard to see that the orthodox Muslim *faqīhs* and theologians, who came mainly from the property-owning classes, could positively have welcomed the Qarakhānids or Saljuqs. It is safest to treat this passing of Transoxiana and Khurāsān into Turkish hands as acts of resignation by the landowning and religious interests, which feared the centralizing policy of the Sāmānid amīrs more than they did the incoming Qarakhānids; moreover the merchants and landowners had despaired of getting further help against the Türkmen from the distant government in Ghazna.

The Saljuqs belonged to the Oghuz Turks, who appear in history as a grouping of nine tribes, the Toquz Oghuz. These tribes formed part of the eastern Türkü and are mentioned in the royal annals of the confederation, the Orkhon inscriptions of Outer Mongolia, written in the first half of the 2nd/8th century. When that empire collapsed in 125/741 and a fresh confederation was formed, the Oghuz chief eventually came to hold the military office of Yabghu of the "right wing of the horde", although he never acquired the supreme title of Qaghan. Towards the end of the 2nd/8th century the Oghuz moved westwards through the Siberian steppes to the Aral Sea and to the Volga and southern Russia. With their attacks on Ushrūsana in the reign of the Caliph al-Ma'mūn (198–218/813–33), they come within the purview of Islamic writers.[2]

Some Oghuz also moved into the Dihistān steppes north of the Atrak river, and others took over the existing settlements at the mouth of the Syr Darya, where the Islamic sources of the 4th/10th century mention three Turkish towns: Jand, Khuvār, and the "new town" of Yengi-Kent. Most of the Turks were Oghuz, and they included both nomads and sedentaries. They acquired a certain amount of culture, for this region had economic connexions with Khwārazm and Transoxiana, but the cultural and material level of those Oghuz who were nomads between the Dihistān steppes and the Urals remained perceptibly lower. The Arab traveller Ibn Faḍlān was passing through their territories in 309–10/921–2 on an embassy from the caliphate to the Bulghars of the middle Volga, and he met a band of Oghuz who were

[1] *Histoire des Turcs d'Asie Centrale*, pp. 57–9.
[2] Cf. Bosworth, *Ghaznavids*, pp. 210–11.

living in extreme wretchedness and wandering "like straying wild asses". Ibn Faḍlān met amongst them certain leaders whose titles recur in later Saljuq history; their chief had the title of Yabghu, whilst the military leader was called *Ṣāḥib al-jaish* (*Sü-Bashï* or *Sü-Begi* in Turkish), or "army leader"; and there was a subordinate commander called the Lesser *Yinal*. It is in the 4th/10th century too that the term "Türkmen" first appears in Islamic sources; about 370/980 the geographer Maqdisī, speaking of two strongholds in the province of Isfījāb, calls them "frontier posts against the Türkmen". It is not clear whether the term has a political or an ethnic denotation, but in the 5th/11th century and after it was undoubtedly applied to the south-western Turks, the Oghuz and Qïpchaq, whereas the term "Turk" is used for the more easterly Turks of the Qarluq group. Ghaznavid sources frequently call the incoming Oghuz "Türkmen", and in his "Mirror for Princes" (the *Siyāsat-Nāma*) the Saljuq vizier Niẓām al-Mulk uses the term for the tribal followers of the Great Saljuqs who had remained nomads within Iran and the lands to the west.[1]

According to Maḥmūd Kāshgharī, author of the pioneer Turkish–Arabic dictionary, the *Dīwān lughāt al-Turk* (completed 466/1074), the leading tribe of the Oghuz, from whom their princes sprang, was the Qïnïq. The Saljuq family (it does not seem originally to have been any bigger social unit than this) belonged to the Qïnïq.[2] At the end of the 4th/10th century the ruler of the Oghuz was the Yabghu, who had a winter capital at Yengi-Kent in the Syr Darya delta, and whose authority ranged over the steppes from there to the Volga. The lower Syr Darya was at this time in the zone where Islam and paganism met, and where Muslim *ghāzīs* (fighters for the faith) were active; at one stage in their rise to power the Saljuqs themselves operated here as typical ghāzīs. According to the *Malik-Nāma*, an account of Saljuq origins which Cahen believes to have been written for Sulṭān Alp-Arslan, the progenitor of the Saljuq family was one Duqaq, called *Temür-Yalïgh* ("iron-bow"). He and his son Saljuq served the "king of the Turks", i.e. the Yabghu, with Saljuq holding the important military office of Sü-Bashï. Certain sources state that Duqaq and Saljuq served the king

[1] Cf. Togan, "Ibn Faḍlāns Reisebericht", *Abhandlung für die Kunde des Morgenlandes*, vol. XXIV (1939), pp. 15–17 (tr., pp. 28–31); Tolstov, *Auf den Spuren*, pp. 263 ff.; İ. Kafesoğlu, "A Propos du nom Türkmen", *Oriens*, vol. XI (1958), pp. 146–50; Bosworth, *Ghaznavids*, pp. 211–18.

[2] Kāshgharī, *Dīwan lughāt al-Turk*, vol. I, pp. 55–9; cf. Cahen, "Les Tribus Turques d'Asie Occidentale pendant la Période Seljukide", *W*[*iener*] *Z*[*eitschrift für die*] *K*[*unde des*] *M*[*orgenlandes*], pp. 179–80.

of the Khazars, whose kingdom embraced the lower Volga and southern Russia, but this seems to be merely a memory of earlier Oghuz-Khazar connexions. Eventually the Yabghu became jealous of Saljuq's power, and the latter was forced to flee with his retainers and their flocks to Jand; it was in the region of Jand, apparently in the last decade of the 10th century, that the Saljuq family became Muslim and then turned to *ghazw*, or raiding, against those Turks who remained pagan, including the Yabghu of Yengi-Kent. The fierce hostility between these two branches of the Qïnïq was not resolved until 433/1042, when the Saljuqs took over Khwārazm and drove out the Yabghu's son and successor, Shāh Malik b. 'Alī (see below, section IV, p. 52).[1]

Over the next decades the Saljuqs (now led by the three sons of Saljuq who had reached manhood, Mūsā, Mīkā'īl, and Arslan Isrā'īl, as well as by Mīkā'īl's two sons Toghrïl Beg Muḥammad and Chaghrï Beg Dā'ūd) hired out their services to the warring factions of Transoxiana and Khwārazm, fighting for anyone who would assure them pasture for their herds. Indeed, some sources specifically say that it was pressure of population and the need for pasture which compelled them to move southwards. They can have had no thoughts of a more ambitious role in the Iranian world, even though the *Malik-Nāma* (preserved in al-Ḥusainī's historical account of the dynasty, *Akhbār al-daula al-Saljūqiyya*) describes a dream in which Saljuq saw himself urinating fire, whose sparks spread all over the world: a shaman (priest-doctor) interpreted this to mean that a son of his would rule over all the world. The Yabghu of Yengi-Kent became a Muslim in 393/1003 and aided the last of the Sāmānids, Ismā'īl al-Muntaṣir (see p. 7 above). His Saljuq rivals, who on the fall of the Sāmānids had moved to pastures near Bukhārā, therefore gave their services to the Sāmānids' enemies, the Qarakhānids. Toghrïl and Chaghrï fought for a Qarakhānid called Bughra Khān (possibly the ruler of Talas and Isfījāb, Yïghan-Tegin b. Qadïr Khān Yūsuf) and then joined forces with their uncle Arslan Isrā'īl in the service of a rival Qarakhānid, 'Alī-Tegin of Bukhārā and Samarqand. Their followers were now living on winter pastures at Nūr Bukhārā or Nakhshab, near 'Alī-Tegin's capital, moving eastwards into Soghdia for the summer.[2]

When in 417/1026 'Alī-Tegin was temporarily defeated by the united

[1] Cahen, "Le Malik-Nameh et l'Histoire des Origines Seljukides", *Oriens*, pp. 41–4; Bosworth, *Ghaznavids*, pp. 219–23.

[2] Cahen, *Oriens*, pp. 44–52; Bosworth, *op. cit.* pp. 223–4.

forces of Maḥmūd of Ghazna and Qadïr Khān Yūsuf of Kāshghar and Khotan, the Saljuq bands split up once more. Arslan Isrā'īl's followers, comprising 4,000 tents, complained of the oppression of their own chiefs and requested permission from Maḥmūd to settle on the northern fringes of Khurāsān near Sarakhs, Abīvard, and Farāva; they promised to act as auxiliaries for the Ghaznavids and to refrain from encroaching on the settled land. Either at this point or shortly afterwards, Arslan Isrā'īl himself fell into Maḥmūd's hands and later died in prison. Toghrïl and Chaghrï remained in the neighbourhood of Bukhārā with 'Alī-Tegin; after 420/1029 they quarrelled with the Qarakhānid, yet in 423/1032 the Saljuqs were to be found fighting on 'Ali-Tegin's side against the Ghaznavid general Altun-Tash at the battle of Dabūsiyya. When in 425/1034 'Alī-Tegin died, they moved into Khwārazm at the invitation of Altun-Tash's son Hārūn, who was then in virtual rebellion against Maḥmūd. At this point the old enmity between the Saljuqs and the line of the Oghuz Yabghus of Yengi-Kent flared up: the Saljuqs were overwhelmingly defeated by Shāh Malik of Jand, who aimed at annexing Khwārazm for himself.[1]

The Saljuqs' only recourse now was to follow the example of Arslan Isrā'īl's band and head southwards for Khurāsān. A group of 7,000 or 10,000 Türkmen were led by Toghrïl, Chaghrï, Mūsā Yabghu (the Saljuqs had themselves assumed this title in rivalry to the Yabghus of Yengi-Kent and Jand), and by Ibrāhīm Ïnal, who is described as a son of Toghrïl's mother and the leader of the Ināliyān, a section of the Türkmen mentioned separately in the sources. Their defeat in Khwārazm had left the Ināliyān in a state of utter wretchedness, and in 426/1035, in a very humble letter to Mas'ūd of Ghazna's vizier, the leaders described themselves as "the slaves Yabghu, Toghrïl, and Chaghrï, Clients of the Commander of the Faithful" and asked that the towns of Nasā and Farāva be granted to them. The existing depredations caused by the wave of Türkmen who had entered Khurāsān in 416/1025, the so-called "'Irāqī" Türkmen, were now aggravated by the Saljuqs' spoliations. They sent cavalry columns into Afghanistan as far as Gūzgān, Tukhāristān, and Sīstān, where they carried off livestock, pastured their sheep on agricultural land, and interrupted the caravan trade, generally terrorizing the towns of Khurāsān and causing starvation in both countryside and town. For the seven years 422–9/1031–8, until the town capitulated to Toghrïl, no sowing was possible outside

[1] Cahen, pp. 52–5; Bosworth, pp. 224–5.

the walls of Baihaq (modern Sabzavār), and during all this time mutton was unobtainable there.[1]

The Ghaznavid sultans alternated between attempts at conciliation and punitive expeditions. They tried to enrol the Saljuq leaders as frontier guards against further Türkmen inroads, giving them each in 426/1035 the title *Dihqān* and the insignia and dress of a governor, and they even offered marriage alliances to Toghrïl, Chaghrï, and Mūsā Yabghu. But it was soon obvious that the Saljuqs, being nomads, were unfamiliar with the concepts of defined frontiers and the sanctity of landed property. During the period 426–31/1035–40 large Ghaznavid armies were almost continually in the field against the Türkmen. The sultan blamed his Turkish ghulām commanders for pusillanimity and incompetence, even accusing them of collusion with the Saljuqs. The Ghaznavid armies were better led, better armed, and probably numerically superior to the poorly armed, half-starved nomad bands, and at first glance the advantages were all on one side. Yet though the sultan's forces scored some successes in pitched battles, they were never able to follow them up. The nomads had a clear advantage in mobility. They were unhampered by the elephants, siege machinery, and camp-following without which no Ghaznavid army could move; they were more hardened to the extremes of climate, the lack of water, and the famine conditions then prevailing in Khurāsān; and they did not have to operate, as did the Ghaznavid armies, from fixed bases.[2]

Meanwhile, the position of the Khurāsānian towns became perilous. There was little danger that the Saljuqs would storm them directly, for the nomads were unequipped for siege warfare and fought shy of it. The great cities surrendered voluntarily to them: Marv in 428/1037 and Herāt and Nīshāpūr in 429/1038 (this last was recovered by the sultan's forces and not lost again till 431/1039). In each case the notables and landowners took the initiative in making peace, having despaired of receiving adequate protection from the sultan in Ghazna, who only latterly came to Khurāsān to lead his armies. Economic and commercial life was at a standstill. The 8th/15th-century historian Mīrkhwānd describes the distressed state of the Nīshāpūr area thus: "That region became ruinous, like the dishevelled tresses of the fair ones or the eyes of the loved ones, and it became devastated by the pasturing of [the Türkmen's] flocks."[3] Of the Saljuq chiefs, only Toghrïl seems at this

[1] Cahen, pp. 55 ff.; Bosworth, pp. 225–6. [2] Cahen, pp. 57 ff.; Bosworth, pp. 241–9.
[3] Mīrkhwānd, *Rauḍat al-ṣafā*, vol. IV, p. 102.

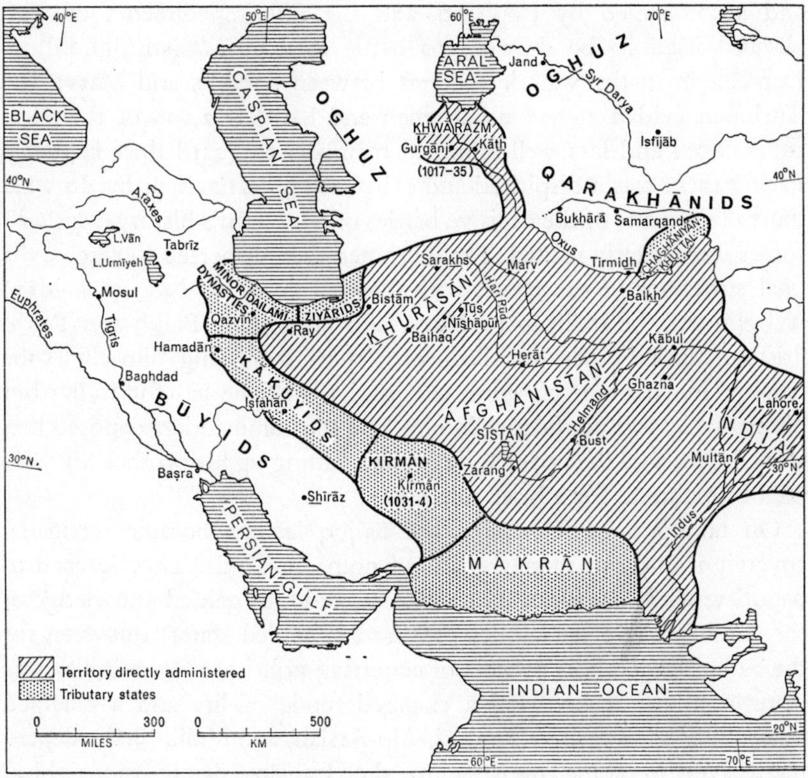

Map 2. The Ghaznavid empire at its greatest extent, *c.* 421/1030.

point to have had an eye to the future and to have adopted a statesmanslike attitude. He had difficulty in restraining his own brother from looting Nīshāpūr, and the task was *a fortiori* more difficult where the ignorant and rapacious masses of the Türkmen were concerned. On occupying Marv, however, Chaghrī did give orders that tillage should be restored and refugees summoned back.[1]

Ghaznavid authority was declining even in the more easterly regions of Bādghīs and Tukhāristān, where the mountainous terrain was less suitable for the nomads to operate in. Law and order broke down, *ʿayyārs* or brigands flourished, and the officials and leading citizens in cities such as Herāt began to negotiate with the Saljuqs for the surrender of their cities.[2] The final, decisive blow to Ghaznavid authority in the west came in 431/1040. A large army, led personally by Sulṭān Masʿūd

[1] Bosworth, *Ghaznavids*, pp. 252–65.

[2] *Ibid.* pp. 265–6.

and accompanied by elephants and the full impedimenta of war, allowed itself to be drawn into battle at the *ribāṭ* (stronghold) of Dandānqān in the waterless desert between Sarakhs and Marv. The Türkmen fielded 16,000 cavalrymen and had left 2,000 of their less experienced and less well-mounted members to guard their baggage. Facing them was a dispirited and exhausted Ghaznavid army. In what must rank as one of the decisive battles of Khurāsān's history, Mas'ūd's forces were utterly routed. The Türkmen then dispersed to receive the final surrender of the cities, with Toghrïl going to Nīshāpūr, Mūsā Yabghu and the Ināliyān to Marv, and Chaghrï to Balkh and Tukhāristān. Mas'ūd's nerves failed completely. Resigning himself to the Saljuqs' inevitable occupation of Ghazna itself, he left for India; but his army had lost confidence in him, and the commanders deposed him when he reached the upper Indus valley, setting up his brother Muḥammad b. Maḥmūd for a brief sultanate.[1]

On taking over Khurāsān, the Saljuq leaders became territorial sovereigns and not merely chiefs of nomadic bands. They learned to negotiate with the rulers of other states, and they gained knowledge of the administrative techniques practised in settled states. But even for the Saljuq leaders this process of acquiring political responsibility was disturbing, for it involved a changed mode of life and a changed outlook. Sultans such as Toghrïl, Alp-Arslan, and Malik-Shāh adapted themselves in some measure to the Iranian–Islamic monarchical tradition, leaning more and more heavily on their Iranian officials. Yet in his *Siyāsat-Nāma* the great vizier Niẓām al-Mulk lamented that the sultans were neglecting the wise administrative practices followed by the Ghaznavids and other former rulers; thus the Iranian officials were never able to mould their masters into the exact shape they would have liked. As soon as Khurāsān and western Iran had been overrun, various members of the Saljuq family were allotted regions to govern (see p. 49 below). Nevertheless their frequent rebellions—those of Ibrāhīm Ïnal, of Qutlumush b. Arslan Isrā'īl, and even of the senior member of the family, Mūsā Yabghu—show that these provincial rulers never understood their subordinate position in the hierarchy of power that was roughly taking shape under the sultan. As for the masses of the Türkmen, now nominally Muslim, they remained at a cultural level little higher than that which they had enjoyed in the

[1] Baihaqī, *Ta'rīkh-i Mas'ūdī*, pp. 616–34, 653–4; Gardīzī, *Zain al-akhbār*, pp. 107–12; Ibn al-Athīr, *al-Kāmil*, vol. IX, pp. 329–33; Spuler, *Iran in frühislamischer Zeit*, pp. 123–4.

steppes, and their irreconcilable attitude towards any settled government was kept alive by the arrival of fresh tribal elements from Central Asia, who were attracted westwards by prospects of plunder.

Toghrïl's first occupation of Nīshāpur, the administrative capital of Khurāsān, elated him. He behaved as independent ruler of the province, installing himself in the sultan's palace in the suburb of Shādyākh and sitting upon Mas'ūd's throne (this last profanation so roused Mas'ūd that he subsequently had the throne broken up). According to the historian of the Saljuqs, 'Imād al-Dīn, who wrote in 579/1183, Toghrïl "forbade, gave orders, made grants, levied taxes, administered efficiently, abolished things, ordered affairs correctly, entrusted matters and presided every Sunday and Wednesday over the investigations of complaints".[1] The *khuṭba* (Friday sermon) was read in his name, and he assumed the royal title *al-Sulṭān al-Mu'aẓẓam* ("Exalted Ruler").[2] Despite all this, it is possible that the pro-Saljuq sources which depend on the *Malik-Nāma* exaggerate the degree of Toghrïl's political sophistication at this time. As late as 430/1039 the Saljuqs still had a great fear of Sulṭān Mas'ūd's power, and they doubted whether they would be able to hold on in Khurāsān; it seems that they still placed Mas'ūd's name in the khuṭba alongside their own. But at the same time Toghrïl was in touch with the caliph, employing a *faqīh* as his secretary and envoy from Nīshāpūr. After the Dandānqān victory, this man was dispatched to Baghdad with the Saljuqs' *fatḥ-nāma* (formal announcement of victory), a document written on the battlefield with materials salvaged from the abandoned Ghaznavid chancery.[3]

III. WESTERN AND CENTRAL IRAN IN THE FIRST HALF OF THE 5TH/11TH CENTURY

With the east secured by the success at Dandānqān, the lands farther west now lay open to Saljuq attack. In 431/1040 western and central Iran were in the last phase of what V. Minorsky has called the "Dailamī

[1] Investigation into complaints of tyranny (*maẓālim*) was one of the traditional duties of Islamic rulers; cf. H. F. Amedroz, "The Mazalim Jurisdiction in the Akham Sultaniyya of Mawardi", *J*[*ournal of the*] R[*oyal*] *A*[*siatic*] *S*[*ociety*] (1911), pp. 635–74.

[2] Baihaqī, p. 553; Bundārī, *Zubdat al-nuṣra wa nukhbat al-'uṣra*, in *Recueil de Textes relatifs à l'Histoire des Seljoucides*, vol. II, p. 7; Ẓahīr al-Dīn Nīshāpūrī, *Saljūq-Nāma*, p. 15; Rāvandī, p. 97; Ibn al-Athīr, vol. IX, p. 328; Mīrkhwānd, vol. IV, p. 102; Bosworth, *Ghaznavids*, pp. 256–7, 267.

[3] Baihaqī, pp. 570, 628; Bundārī, p. 8; Nīshāpūrī, p. 18; Rāvandī, p. 104; Ibn al-Athīr, vol. IX, p. 312; Bosworth, *Ghaznavids*, pp. 243–4, 268.

interlude" of Iranian history.[1] Headed by the various branches of the Būyids, dynasties of Dailamī origin flourished not merely in their *Urheimat*, the mountains of northern and north-western Iran, but also as far south as lower Iraq and the shores of the Persian Gulf. Intermingled with these dynasties were some Kurdish rulers, notably the ʿAnnāzids of the Shāhanjān tribe (*c.* 381–511/*c.* 991–1117), successors in Ḥulwān and Kirmānshāh to the Ḥasanūyids. Other semi-nomadic Kurds were the effective holders of power in the mountainous regions of Kurdistān and Luristān; in the eastern part of Fārs, around Dārābjird, the Shabānkāra'ī Kurds were especially influential. The Marwānids of Diyārbakr, Akhlāṭ, and Malāzgird (372–489/983–1096) were also of Kurdish origin, but they rose to power as vassals of the Fāṭimids. During the long reign of Naṣr al-Daula Aḥmad b. Marwān (401–53/1011–61), his cities of Āmid, Mayyāfāriqīn, and Ḥiṣn Kaifā in Diyārbakr enjoyed considerable material prosperity and a vigorous cultural life; an invasion of the Oghuz in 443/1041–2 was beaten off, and the annalist Ibn al-Athīr records that the sense of security and the prevailing justice in Ibn Marwān's dominions were such that people actually dared openly to display their wealth.[2] A local historian of Mayyāfāriqīn, Ibn al-Azraq (d. after 572/1176–7), describes enthusiastically how Naṣr al-Daula lightened taxes and, as part of his charitable works, supplied the town with piped water. However, the Marwānid territories came under Saljuq suzerainty soon after Naṣr al-Daula's death. They were divided between his two sons, and in 478/1085–6 Saljuq armies under Fakhr al-Daula Ibn Jahīr and his son ʿAmīd al-Daula Ibn Jahīr conquered Diyārbakr (see p. 98 below).[3]

On the western edges of the Iranian plateau, where it merges into the plains of Iraq, al-Jazireh, and northern Syria, there were various Arab amirates including the Mazyadids of Ḥilla, the ʿUqailids of Mosul, and the Mirdāsids of Aleppo. Militarily they depended on the Bedouins of the region; strategically they were important, first because they commanded the approaches into eastern Anatolia, Armenia, and western Iran, and second, because they were in the buffer zone between the rival dynasties of the Būyids and Fāṭimids and later between the

[1] On the region of Dailam and its role in Iranian history at this time, see below, pp. 30 ff.; see also the references in n. 2, p. 30 below.

[2] Ibn al-Athīr, *al-Kāmil*, vol. x, p. 11.

[3] Cf. Amedroz, "The Marwānid Dynasty at Mayyāfāriqīn in the Tenth and Eleventh centuries A.D.", *J.R.A.S.* pp. 123–54; and Zetterstéen, "Marwānids", *Encyc. of Islam* (1st ed.).

Saljuqs and Fāṭimids. Their religion, like that of almost all the Arabs of the Syrian desert and its fringes, was Shī'ī. In the fourth and fifth decades of the eleventh century these amirates were threatened by the Oghuz marauders who preceded the arrival of Toghrïl and the Saljuqs, and their grazing grounds were encroached upon by the Türkmen's flocks. In general they adopted a hostile attitude towards Toghrïl when he appeared in Iraq; the Mazyadid Dubais gave much support to Arslan Basāsīrī, who was his own brother-in-law (see pp. 46–7).

The Dailamī dynasty of the Ziyārids (*c.* 316–483/928–1090) reigned in the Caspian provinces of Gurgān and Ṭabaristān, and also at times in the province of Qūmis to the south of the Alburz mountains.[1] They arose from one of the fiercest and most ambitious Dailamī *condottieri* of the early 4th/10th century, Mardāvīj b. Ziyār (d. 323/935). Later in the century the Ziyārids' strategic position, commanding the routes which connected western Iran and Iraq with Khurāsān and Central Asia, allowed them to play a prominent role in the struggles between the Sāmānids and Būyids in northern Iran. The most famous of the dynasty, Shams al-Ma'ālī Qābūs b. Vushmagīr (366–403/977 to 1012–13), united something of his grandfather's ferocity with an enlightened love of letters and culture; some of his Arabic and Persian verses are known, and al-Bīrūnī and Avicenna both spent some time at his court. Though Mardāvīj himself had been violently anti-Muslim, his successors were Sunnīs (this was unusual amongst the generally Shī'ī Dailamīs), and almost at the end of the dynasty Kai-Kā'ūs still called himself *Maulā Amīr al-Mu'minīn*, the "Client of the Commander of the Faithful".[2] Qābūs felt the pressure of the Ghaznavids and was compelled to recognize the suzerainty of Maḥmūd, although 'Utbī's grandiose claim, that "Jurjān and Ṭabaristān as far as the shores of the Caspian and the region of Dailam, by dint of the combining of circumstances, became just like one of the Sultan's own dominions", is certainly exaggerated. Falak al-Ma'ālī Manūchihr b. Qābūs, the original patron of the Ghaznavid poet Manūchihrī Dāmghānī, became Maḥmūd of Ghazna's son-in-law; he ruled somewhat uneasily in the sultan's shadow, but did succeed in retaining some freedom of action.[3]

[1] For general surveys of this dynasty, see C. Huart, "Les Ziyârides", *Mémoirs de l'Acad. des Inscriptions et Belles-Lettres*, vol. XLII (1922), pp. 357–436; *idem*, *Encyc. of Islam* (1st ed.); and H. L. Rabino di Borgomale, "L'Histoire du Mâzandarân", *J*[*ournal*] *A*[*siatique*], vol. CCXXXIV (1943–5), pp. 229–33.

[2] Kai-Kā'ūs b. Iskandar, *Qābūs-Nāma*, p. 5 (tr. R. Levy, *A Mirror for Princes*, p. 1).

[3] 'Utbī, *al-Ta'rīkh al-Yamīnī*, vol. II, p. 15; cf. Nāẓim, *Life and Times of Sulṭān Maḥmūd of Ghazna*, pp. 77–9.

With Manūchihr's death in 420/1029 or 421/1030 (the date of 424/1033, given by the local but non-contemporary historians Ibn Isfandiyār and Ẓahīr al-Dīn Mar'ashī, is too late), the Ziyārid dynasty ceased to count for anything outside the specific boundaries of Gurgān and Ṭabaristān. At this point the family's chronology and order of succession become confused and uncertain.[1] Of all the existing accounts—in Ibn Isfandiyār, Ẓahīr al-Dīn Mar'ashī (whose material here derives from the former source), Ibn al-Athīr, and Baihaqī—only the last is contemporary. It seems that Manūchihr's son Anushīrvān succeeded, but since he was a minor, effective power was held by his maternal uncle and chief minister, Abū Kālījār b. Vaihān al-Qūhī. This man was Mas'ūd of Ghazna's father-in-law, but in 425/1034, while the sultan was away in India, he seized the opportunity to ally with the Kākūyid 'Alā' al-Daula of Iṣfahān, and together they cut off tribute and rebelled. The violent behaviour of a Ghaznavid punitive expedition, which was sent in the next year and which penetrated as far westwards in Ṭabaristān as Nātil, alienated all sympathy for Mas'ūd in the Caspian provinces.[2] Despite this disharmony, Abū Kālījār and the sultan had a common interest in warding off the Türkmen, for the line of the Atrak river and the Dihistān region had been from early Islamic times a *thaghr* (frontier region) against the Türkmen of the Qara-Qum and beyond.

Abū Kālījār maintained contact with Mas'ūd till 431/1040; thereafter he had to make his own terms with the Saljuqs, but in fact all mention of him now disappears from the sources. In 433/1041–2 Toghrïl arrived in Gurgān accompanied by one Mardāvīj b. Bishūī; this man and Anushīrvān b. Manūchihr divided power between themselves, placing Toghrïl's name in the khuṭba and paying an annual tribute to him.[3] Shortly afterwards a collateral branch of the Ziyārids took over, continuing as Saljuq vassals. From 441/1049–50 until a date after 475/1082–3 the was ruler 'Unṣur al-Ma'ālī Kai-Kā'ūs b. Iskandar, author of another famous "Mirror for Princes", the *Qābūs-Nāma*. Before coming to the throne, he had spent some years in Ghazna as a boon-companion of Sulṭān Maudūd b. Mas'ūd, but he also had connexions with the north-western corner of the Iranian world: he

[1] An attempted elucidation is made by C. E. Bosworth in his article, "On the Chronology of the Ziyārids in Gurgān and Ṭabaristān", *Der Islam*, pp. 25–34.

[2] Baihaqī, *Ta'rīkh-i Mas'ūdī*, pp. 340, 376, 394, 451–63; Ibn Isfandiyār, *Ta'rīkh-i Ṭabaristān*, p. 235; and Ibn al-Athīr, *al-Kāmil*, vol. IX, p. 301.

[3] *al-Kāmil*, vol. IX, p. 340.

had fought in Armenia and Georgia with the Shaddādid amīr Abu'l-Asvār Shāvur b. Faḍl (d. 459/1067), lord of Dvin and Ganja (see below, pp. 34–5), and he spent some time amongst the Shaddādids.[1] It is probable that Kai-Kā'ūs ruled only in the mountainous interior of Gurgān and Ṭabaristān while nominees of the Saljuqs held the coast. His son Gīlān Shāh was the last of the line; the chief of the Assassins of Alamūt, Ḥasan-i Ṣabbāḥ, conquered the mountain regions of Ṭabaristān, and after *c.* 483/1090 the Ziyārids disappear from history.[2]

Ibn Isfandiyār records that Ṭabaristān suffered much during the reign of the Saljuq sultan Alp-Arslan, because his troops moved frequently through the region. (This was in the seventh decade of the century: see pp. 64 ff., below.) However, the Ziyārids' western neighbour, the Bāvandid Ispahbadh Qārin b. Surkhāb, was able to consolidate his power in the mountains. Thus it was the coastal plain which suffered, whilst the mountains either remained in the hands of local chieftains or else fell under Assassin control. In the 5th/11th and 6th/12th centuries the Caspian provinces often served as a corridor for the passage of nomads from Central Asia, but the coastal lands were unsuitable for their permanent settlement: the damp and malarial climate of the region and its dense vegetation and forest are singled out for mention by many of the Islamic geographers, and one writer calls Gurgān "the graveyard of the people of Khurāsān".[3] Down to the nineteenth century the raids and transits of the Türkmen must have retarded agriculture, though the fertility of the area gave it considerable natural resilience.

The Bāvandid Ispahbadhs (45–750/665–1349) had their roots in the pre-Islamic Iranian past, for they sprang from the Sassanian Kā'ūs b. Qubādh, brother of Anushīrvān the Just. Their Kā'ūsiyya branch reigned till 397/1006–7, followed by the Ispahbadhiyya from 465/1073 till 606/1210; and then, under Mongol suzerainty, the Kīnkhwāriyya held sway from 635/1237 onwards. They ruled in Ṭabaristān (or Māzandarān, as it became known in the course of the 6th/12th century),[4] often relinquishing control of the plains to rulers such as the 'Alid

[1] *Qābūs-Nāma*, pp. 24–5, 135–6 (Levy tr., pp. 35–7, 230, 234).

[2] Ibn Isfandiyār, *Ṭabaristān*, p. 236; Ẓahīr al-Dīn Mar'ashī, *Ta'rīkh-i Ṭabaristān u Rūyān u Māzandarān*, pp. 143–4. However, Rabino di Borgomale (*J.A.* p. 233) mentions a later possible scion of the Ziyārids.

[3] Tha'ālibī, *Laṭā'if al-Ma'ārif*, p. 113.

[4] See Nöldeke, *Das Iranische Nationalepos*, p. 61, for a discussion of this change in nomenclature.

Dā'īs, the Būyids, and the Ziyārids; but they retained authority in the mountains. The Kā'ūsiyya reigned from Firīm or Shahriyār-Kūh in the mountains to the south-west of Sārī, and they were Shī'īs, as the formula on their coins—"'Alī is the Friend of God"—shows.[1] The last Ispahbadhs of this line were connected by marriage to the Būyids and Ziyārids; one of them was Rustam b. Marzbān (d. ?407/1016–17), author of a well-known collection of fables, the *Marzbān-Nāma*, and a vassal of the Būyid Majd al-Daula of Ray. The line ended in 397/1006–7, with the death of Shahriyār b. Dārā at the hands of Qābūs b. Vushmagīr.

Other members of the Bāvandid dynasty survived, and as the Ziyārids gradually lost control of the Caspian littoral to the Türkmen invaders, the Ispahbadhiyya entrenched themselves in the mountains. In the early Saljuq period they extended down to the coast; in the third quarter of the 11th century Rustam b. Shahriyār founded a *madrasa*, or college, at Sārī, which became the capital of their principality. These Ispahbadhs were generally vassals of the Saljuqs; in the reign of Sulṭān Muḥammad b. Malik-Shāh, for example, there was a son of the Ispahbadh Ḥusām al-Daula Shahriyār b. Qārin at the court of Iṣfahān, and another son married one of the sultan's sisters. On the other hand, they were not invariably servile towards their suzerains. When the same Saljuq sultan sent an expedition against the Ismā'īlīs of Alamūt, Shahriyār was offended by the sultan's peremptoriness, refused all help, and routed a Saljuq punitive force sent against him. This expedition was probably in 501/1107–8 or 503/1109–10 under the sultan's vizier and Amīr Chavlī; see section VIII, pp. 118–19, below.[2]

During the 6th/12th century the Caspian provinces frequently fulfilled one of their historic roles, that of a refuge area, with the Bāvandids giving shelter to various Saljuq contenders for the sultanate, as well as to a Ghaznavid prince, to the sons of the Khwārazm-Shāh Quṭb al-Dīn Muḥammad b. Anūsh-Tegin, and even to the son of the Mazyadid Ṣadaqa b. Manṣūr. With the decline of Saljuq power, the Ispahbadh Shāh Ghāzī Rustam b. 'Alī (534–58/1140–1 to 1163) became a major figure in the politics of northern Iran, pursuing an independent policy aimed at the expansion of his principality. He campaigned each

[1] P. Casanova, "Les Ispehbeds de Firîm", *Essays to E. G. Browne* (Cambridge, 1922), pp. 117–26.

[2] Ibn Isfandiyār, *Ṭabaristan*, pp. 240–2; cf. M. G. Hodgson, *The Order of Assassins, the Struggle of the Early Nizârī Ismâ'ilîs against the Islamic World*, pp. 97, 100.

year against the Ismā'īlīs of Alamūt and led one unsuccessful expedition against the Oghuz of the Dihistān steppe. Ẓahīr al-Dīn Mar'ashī calls him the richest and greatest of the rulers of Ṭabaristān: he conquered Gurgān and Qūmis, and his power in the west extended as far as Mūghān. He helped the Saljuq Sulaimān-Shāh to gain the sultanate (see below, pp. 169 and 176), and in reward he was given Ray and Sāveh. Shāh Ghāzī's grandson Ḥusām al-Daula Ardashīr b. Ḥasan (576–602/1171–2 to 1205–6) aided Sulṭān Toghrïl b. Arslan and the atabeg Pahlavān Muḥammad b. Eldigüz (see p. 179 below), and he also had friendly relations with the Khwārazm-Shāh Tekish b. Il Arslan, the Ayyūbid Saladin, and the Caliph al-Nāṣir. But pressure from the aggressive Khwārazm-Shāhs became hard to resist, despite the Ispahbadhs' attempts to conciliate them by marriage alliances. In the reign of Nāṣir al-Daula Rustam b. Ardashīr, the Ismā'īlīs overran most of the Bāvandid territories in Ṭabaristān, and when in 606/1210 he was assassinated, the Khwārazm-Shāh 'Alā' al-Dīn Muḥammad seized the Caspian provinces and the Ispahbadhiyya line of the dynasty came to an end.[1]

The Bādūspānids were western neighbours of the Bāvandids in Ṭabaristān, ruling for nearly a thousand years (*c.* 45–1006/665 to 1597–8) in the mountains of Rustamdār, Rūyān, Nūr, and Kujūr, and bearing the princely titles of *Ispahbadhs* and *Ustūndārs*. The dynasty, which traced its origins to a Sassanian governor of the Caspian provinces, vanished only when the Ṣafavid Shāh 'Abbās exterminated its last members. At times the Bādūspānids recognized Ṣaffārid and Būyid suzerainty, and later they were generally subordinate to the Bāvandids. Shahrnūsh b. Hazārasp (510–23/1116–17 to 1129) married a sister of Shāh Ghāzī Rustam, and his brother Kai-Kā'ūs b. Hazārasp (523–60/1129–65) was also an ally of the Bāvandids and a resolute foe of his neighbours the Ismā'īlīs; but unlike the Ziyārids and Bāvandids, the Bādūspānids obtruded little on Iranian affairs outside their own corner of the Caspian region. Ibn Isfandiyār says that it was Kai-Kā'ūs b. Hazārasp and his descendants who became followers of the Sayyid Abu'l-Ḥusain al-Mu'ayyad Billāh, yet according to Ẓahīr al-Dīn Mar'ashī it was not until a Bādūspānid of the 9th/15th century imposed

[1] Ibn Isfandiyār, pp. 256–7; Ibn al-Athīr, *al-Kāmil*, vol. XII, pp. 166–7; Juvainī, *Ta'rīkh-i Jahān-Gushā* (tr. J. A. Boyle, *The History of the World-Conqueror*), vol. I, pp. 340–1; Rabino di Borgomale, "Les Dynasties du Mâzandarân", *J.A.* (1936), pp. 409–37; *idem*, *J.A.* (1943–5), pp. 218–21; Kafesoğlu, *Harezmşahlar devleti tarihi (485–617/1092–1229)*, pp. 180–2; Frye, "Bāwand", *Encyc. of Islam* (2nd ed.).

Shī'ism on Rūyān and Rustamdār that most of the population there adopted that faith.[1]

Between Ṭabaristān in the east and Āzarbāījān and Mūghān in the west lay Gīlān and Dailam. Strictly speaking, Gīlān was the coastal plain and Dailam the mountainous interior through which ran the Safīd Rūd and Shāh Rūd, but up to the 5th/11th century the Muslims applied the term Dailam to the whole region. Islam was late in coming here; the Dailamī mountaineers were notorious for their depredations in the settled lands to the south of the Alburz, and Qazvīn was long regarded as a thaghr against these infidels. In the early part of the 3rd/9th century Dailam was a centre for 'Alid propaganda, and the local people were gradually won over to Shī'ism. Here then is why the majority of Dailamī dynasties in the 4th/10th and 5th/11th centuries were Shī'ī.[2]

The 4th/10th century was the period of the Dailamīs' greatest expansion; in the next century they tended to give way in Iran to Turkish dynasties such as the Ghaznavids and Saljuqs. The oldest of the Dailamī dynasties was that of the Justānids, who ruled at Rūdbār. Some seven or eight members of the family are known, the first of whom was mentioned in 189/805 when the Caliph Hārūn al-Rashīd received at Ray the submission of "the lord of Dailam". But the dynasty declined as their rivals of the Kangarid or Musāfirid family grew more powerful in Dailam. The last Justānid ruler definitely known was defeated by the Dailamī general Asfār b. Shīrūya (d. ?319/931). However, the dynasty may have survived much longer than this, for in 434/1042–3 Toghrïl Beg received at Qazvīn the submission of the "King of Dailam", and Kasravī has surmised that this was a surviving member of the Justānids. Less certain is a mention by the Persian traveller Nāṣir-i Khusrau, who passed through the region in 437/1046; he spoke of "the Amīr of Amīrs, who is from the Kings of Dailam", but this may refer to one of the Musāfirids.[3]

The Musāfirids or Sallārids were originally and more correctly called Kangarids.[4] They arose in Dailam in the early years of the 4th/10th

[1] Rabino di Borgomale, *J.A.* (1936), pp. 443–74; *idem*, *J.A.* (1943–5), pp. 221–2; B. Nikitine, "Bādūsbānids", *Encyc. of Islam* (2nd ed.).

[2] On Dailam and the Dailamīs, see Aḥmad Kasravī, *Shahriyārān-i gum-nām*, vol. I, pp. 2–20; Minorsky, *La Domination des Daïlamites*, pp. 1–5; *idem*, "Daylam", *Encyc. of Islam* (2nd ed.).

[3] Ibn al-Athīr, *al-Kāmil*, vol. IX, p. 348; Nāṣir-i Khusrau, *Safar-Nāma*, p. 5. On the dynasty in general, see Kasravī, *Shahriyārān*, vol. I, pp. 22–34; Rabino di Borgomale, "Les Dynasties Locales du Gîlân et du Daylam", *J.A.* pp. 308–9.

[4] Cf. Kasravī, *op. cit.* pp. 36–7, on the name of this dynasty.

century through the efforts of Muḥammad b. Musāfir, who was allied by marriage to the older dynasty of the Justānids, and whose power grew at the latter's expense. A contemporary Būyid source says that it was this marriage connexion plus the acquisition of the fortress of Samīrān in the region of Ṭārum which established the Musāfirids' fortunes.[1] Samīrān was then one of the key fortresses of Dailam, just as Alamūt was to be in Saljuq times, and several Islamic travellers and geographers described its wonders. After the deposition of Muḥammad b. Musāfir in 330/941, there were two lines of Musāfirids. One remained in the ancestral centre of Ṭārum; the other expanded northwards and westwards into Āzarbāījān, Arrān, and eastern Transcaucasia. This branch pushed as far as Darband on the Caspian coast, but its power was eventually destroyed by the Rawwādids. The Ṭārum branch lost Samīrān to the Būyid Fakhr al-Daula in 379/989, but they recovered it on that ruler's death, and in the period of his son Majd al-Daula's minority, the Musāfirids pressed southwards to Zanjān, Abhar, Suhravard, and Sarchahān.[2] The ensuing decades of Musāfirid history are very dark, but the dynasty was directly threatened when in 420/1029 Maḥmūd of Ghazna seized Ray (see p. 12 above). Against the Musāfirid Ibrāhīm b. Marzbān the sultan sent a "descendant of the Kings of Dailam", probably a Justānid, and then Mas'ūd b. Maḥmūd came in person and captured Ibrāhīm. Although a Ghaznavid garrison was left in Ṭārum, by 427/1036 it was again in Musāfirid hands.[3] The early Saljuqs did not try to establish direct rule in Dailam, but were content to exact tribute; then in 434/1042–3 Toghrïl came westwards, retrieved Ray from the hands of his half-brother Ibrāhīm Ïnal, and gained submission from "the Sālār of Ṭārum" on the basis of 200,000 dīnārs' tribute. Nāṣir-i Khusrau speaks with admiration of Samīrān and of the security and justice prevailing in the lands of the "Marzbān al-Dailam, Jīl-ī Jīlān, Abū Ṣāliḥ [Justān b. Ibrāhīm], Maulā Amīr al-Mu'minīn". In 454/1062, shortly before his death, Toghrïl went to Samīrān and again took tribute from the local ruler Musāfir. After this the sources are quite silent about the dynasty, and it is likely that the line was extinguished when, as the geographer

[1] Letter of Abū 'Ali al-Ḥasan b. Aḥmad to the Ṣāḥib Ibn 'Abbād, in Yāqūt, *Mu'jam al-Buldān*, vol. III, pp. 256–7, *s.v* "Samīrān".

[2] Yāqūt, *loc. cit.*; Ibn al-Athīr, vol. IX, pp. 262–3; Münejjim Bashī, in Minorsky, *Studies in Caucasian History*, p. 165.

[3] Baihaqī, *Ta'rīkh-ī Mas'ūdī*, pp. 16, 18, 49, 218; Ibn al-Athīr, *al-Kāmil*, vol. IX, pp. 262–3, 304; Minorsky, *Caucasian History*, pp. 165–6.

Yāqūt relates, the Ismā'īlīs of Alamūt destroyed the fortress of Samīrān.[1]

The Rawwādids (latterly the form "Rawād" is commoner in the sources) were another product of the upsurge of the mountain peoples of northern Iran; their domain was Āzarbāījān, and particularly Tabrīz. Strictly speaking, the Rawwādid family was of Azdī Arab origin, but by the 4th/10th century they were accounted Kurdish. At the opening of the 'Abbāsid period Rawwād b. Muthannā had held a fief which included Tabrīz. Over the course of the next two centuries his descendants became thoroughly Kurdicized, and the "Rawwādī Kurds" emerged with Iranian names, although the local poet Qaṭrān (d. *c.* 465/1072) still praised them for their Arab ancestry. Early in the 4th/10th century the Sājid line of Arab governors in Āzarbāījān collapsed, and the region became politically and socially disturbed. A branch of the Musāfirids of Ṭārum first emerged there, but despite Būyid help the Musāfirid Ibrāhīm b. Marzbān was deposed in *c.* 370/980–1, probably by the Rawwādid Abu'l-Haijā' Ḥusain b. Muḥammad (344–78/955–88); certainly it was the Rawwādids who succeeded to all of the Musāfirid heritage in Āzarbāījān.[2]

The most prominent member of the dynasty in the 5th/11th century was Vahsūdān b. Mamlān b. Abi'l-Haijā' (*c.* 410–46/*c.* 1019–54). It was in his reign that the Oghuz invaded Āzarbāījān. These were some of the first Türkmen to come westwards, being the so-called "'Irāqīs", or followers of Arslan Isrā'īl, expelled from Khurāsān by Maḥmūd of Ghazna (see pp. 38 and 40–1). Vahsūdān received them favourably in 419/1028, hoping to use them as auxiliaries against his many enemies, such as the Christian Armenians and Georgians and the rival Muslim dynasty of Shaddādids. He even married the daughter of an Oghuz chief, but it still proved impossible to use the anarchic nomads as a reliable military force. In 429/1037 they plundered Marāgheh and

[1] Nāṣir-i Khusrau, p. 5; Ibn al-Athīr, vol. IX, p. 348, vol. X, p. 15; Minorsky, *Caucasian History*, p. 166; and Cahen, "L'Iran du Nord-Ouest face à l'expansion Seldjukide, d'après une source inédite", *Mélanges d'Orientalisme Offerts à Henri Massé* (Tehran, 1963), pp. 65–71. On the dynasty in general, see Huart, "Les Mosâfirides de l'Adherbaïdjân", *Essays to E. G. Browne*, pp. 228–56; E. D. Ross, "On Three Muhammadan Dynasties in Northern Persia in the Tenth and Eleventh Centuries", *Asia Major*, pp. 213–15; Kasravī, *Shahriyārān*, vol. I, pp. 36–49; Minorsky, "Musāfirids", *Encyc. of Islam* (1st ed.); and *idem*, *Caucasian History*, pp. 158–66 (= the section from the Ottoman historian Münejjim Bashī's *Jāmi' al-duwal* on this dynasty).

[2] Kasravī, *op. cit.* vol. II, pp. 163–4, 176; Minorsky, *Caucasian History*, pp. 162–4. On the dynasty in general, see Kasravī, vol. II, pp. 160–225; Minorsky, "Tabrīz" and "Marāgha", *Encyc. of Islam* (1st ed.).

massacred large numbers of Hadhbānī Kurds.[1] Vahsūdān allied with his nephew, the chief of the Hadhbānīs, Abu'l-Haijā' b. Rahīb al-Daula, against the Türkmen; many of them now migrated southwards towards Iraq, and in 432/1040–1 Vahsūdān devised a stratagem by which several of the remaining leaders were killed. The rest of the Oghuz in Āzarbāījān then fled to the territory of the Hakkārī Kurds south-west of Lake Vān. Vahsūdān's capital, Tabrīz, was destroyed by an earthquake in 434/1042, and fearing that the Saljuqs would take advantage of his resulting weakness, he moved to one of his fortresses; but the city was soon rebuilt, and Nāṣir-i Khusrau found it populous and flourishing.[2]

Despite Vahsūdān's apprehension, a considerable time elapsed before the Saljuqs themselves moved against Āzarbāījān. Meanwhile the main threats came from independent Türkmen bands who passed continuously through the province towards Armenia and the Caucasus; it was in 437/1045 that Qubādh b. Yazīd, ruler of Shīrvān in the eastern Caucasus, was forced to build a defensive wall round his capital Yazīdiyya.[3] In 446/1054 Toghrïl at last resolved to bring Āzarbāījān and Arrān under his sway. Vahsūdān, making no attempts at opposition, handed over his son as a hostage. The sultan then passed to the Shaddādid capital of Ganja and also received the homage of other minor rulers of eastern Transcaucasia before pressing westwards into Anatolia as far as Malāzgird and Erzerum.[4]

In 450/1058 the eldest of Vahsūdān's sons, Mamlān, was confirmed by Toghrïl in his father's territories, but the last days of the dynasty are obscure, as indeed is most of the history of Āzarbāījān at this time. The Ottoman historian Münejjim Bashī (d. 1113/1702), whose vast historical compilation incorporates some ancient and otherwise lost sources for the history of north-western Iran and the Caucasus region, says that the Rawwādids came to an end in 463/1070–1 when Alp-Arslan returned from his Anatolian campaign (see pp. 63–4 below) and deposed Mamlān. However, one later member of the family is known: Aḥmadīl b. Ibrāhīm b. Vahsūdān held Marāgheh and took part in the Crusading warfare in Syria, and the name Aḥmadīl was perpetuated by the line of his own Turkish ghulāms, who began to

[1] According to the 7th/13th-century biographer Ibn Khallikān, the Ayyūbid Sulṭān Saladin came from this tribe of Kurds; cf. Minorsky, *Caucasian History*, pp. 124–5, 128–9.

[2] Nāṣir-i Khusrau, *Safar-Nāma*, p. 6; Ibn al-Athīr, *al-Kāmil*, vol. IX, pp. 269–72, 351; Kasravī, *Shahriyārān*, vol. II, pp. 174–209.

[3] On the dynasty of the Shīrvān-Shāhs, see p. 35 below.

[4] Ibn al-Athīr, vol. IX, pp. 410–11; Kasravī, *op. cit.* pp. 211–14; Minorsky, *A History of Sharvān and Darband in the 10th–11th Centuries*, pp. 33, 65–6.

rule at Marāgheh after his death in 510/1116. (For these Aḥmadīlīs see below, pp. 170–1.)[1]

The Shaddādids of Arrān and Dvin (*c.* 340–468/951–1075) were almost certainly Kurds, as Münejjim Bashï suggests. They arose from a Kurdish adventurer called Muḥammad b. Shaddād, who established himself in Dvin in the middle of the 4th/10th century, the town being held at that time by the Musāfirids. The ethnic origins of the family are complicated because its members frequently adopted Dailamī names, such as Lashkarī and Marzbān, and even the Armenian one of Ashot; but their basic Kurdishness seems very likely, and the variety of their onomasticon is doubtless a reflexion of the confused ethnic and political condition of the region.[2] Muḥammad b. Shaddād could not hold on to Dvin, but in 360/971 his sons Lashkarī and Faḍl displaced the Musāfirids by agreement with the notables of Ganja. Faḍl eventually secured power in Arrān and reigned there for close to half a century (375–422/986–1031). Armenian sources stress his violence and military vigour: he recovered Dvin, fought the Georgian Bagratids and the Armenian rulers of Anī, Ałvank' (Albania), and Tashīr, and he subdued the Hungarian Sevordik' in the upper Kur valley. His construction of a fine bridge over the Araxes in 421/1030 points towards ambitions against the Rawwādids in Āzarbāījān. Faḍl's son and grandson had to cope with attacks from the Georgians, from other Caucasian mountaineers such as the Alans or Ossetes, from the Russians, and the Rawwādid Vahsūdān b. Mamlān. In about the year 440/1048–9 there was a Byzantine invasion under the eunuch Nicephorus, aimed principally at the Shaddādid branch in Dvin. Ominous, too, was the appearance of the Oghuz, from whom the Rawwādids south of the Araxes suffered severely. The historians al-'Aẓīmī and Ibn Duqmāq record an attack by Qutlumush b. Arslan Isrā'īl on Ganja in 438/1046–7, and there may have been other incursions which have not been noted in the chronicles.[3]

The Shaddādids reached their zenith under Abu'l-Asvār Shāvur b. Faḍl, who ruled in Dvin from 413/1022 to 441/1049 and then in Ganja till 459/1067. The Byzantines' devastation of the Dvin area probably

[1] Ibn al-Athīr, *al-Kāmil*, vol. IX, p. 448, vol. X, p. 361; Kasravī, *Shahriyārān*, vol. II, pp. 214–16; Minorsky, *Caucasian History*, pp. 167–9.

[2] Minorsky, *ibid.* pp. 5, 33–5. On the dynasty in general, see Ross, "Banū Shaddād", *Encyc. of Islam* (1st ed.); *idem*, *Asia Major* (1925), pp. 213–19; Kasravī, *Shahriyārān*, vol. III, pp. 264–313; Minorsky, *Caucasian History*, pp. 1–77.

[3] Kasravī, *op. cit.* vol. II, pp. 203–4, vol. III, pp. 274–8; Minorsky, *op. cit.* pp. 16–17, 40–9, 54–64; and Cahen, "Qutlumush et ses Fils avant l'Asie Mineure", *Der Islam*, p. 20.

influenced his decision to leave Dvin, where he had faced Armenian princes on his west and south. In 434/1042–3 or 435/1043–4, at the instigation of the Byzantine emperor, Abu'l-Asvār invaded the principality of Ani and thereby acquired a great contemporary reputation as a "warrior for the faith", praised for his courage and sagacity by the Ziyārid Kai-Kā'ūs b. Iskandar, who fought with him as a ghāzī against the Christians. Abu'l-Asvār submitted to Toghrïl in 446/1054–5, and towards the end of his life he was associated with Türkmen expansion into Armenia and Anatolia; in 457/1065 he became governor of Ani, which had been captured from the Christians in the previous year.[1] Before that he had been involved with his neighbours the Shīrvān-Shāhs. In the latter half of the 2nd/8th century the Arab family of the Yazīdids had governed Arrān for the 'Abbāsids.[2] During the ensuing decades they were pushed northwards by Dailamī pressure, becoming completely Iranian in their way of life, and though they acquired close marriage connexions with the Shaddādids, these did not prevent Abu'l-Asvār from invading the territories of his nephew the Shīrvān-Shāh Farīburz b. Sallār (455–after 487/1063–after 1094) on four separate occasions during these years.[3]

In the end, the extension of Saljuq power into this north-western region, under the leadership of Alp-Arslan and his ghulām commander 'Imād al-Dīn Sav-Tegin (? Shād-Tegin), proved fatal to the Shaddādids. Abu'l-Asvār's son Faḍl II was captured by the Georgians, and the Shīrvān-Shāh invaded Arrān. An army under Sav-Tegin passed through Arrān in 460/1068, and seeing internal dissensions within the Shaddādid family, the sultan allotted fiefs in Darband and Arrān to his general. Sav-Tegin once more appeared with an army, this time in 468/1075, and Faḍl III b. Faḍl II was obliged to yield his ancestral territories. This ended the main line of the Shaddādids, though the members of a junior branch, descended from Abu'l-Asvār's son Manūchihr, became governors on behalf of the Saljuqs in Anī, and the family can be traced there till the Georgians recaptured the town in 556/1161.[4]

[1] *Qābūs-Nāma*, pp. 24–5 (Levy tr., pp. 35–7); Ibn al-Athīr, *al-Kāmil*, vol. IX, p. 411; Kasravī, *Shahriyārān*, vol. III, pp. 292–304; Minorsky, *Caucasian History*, pp. 19–22, 50–6.

[2] The Yazīdids originated with one Yazīd b. Mazyad, but the designation "Mazyadid" for this dynasty is best avoided, since it is likely to cause confusion with the Mazyadids of Ḥilla.

[3] *Ibid.* pp. 20–1, 74–5; *idem*, *A History of Sharvān and Darband* (= an anonymous *Ta'rīkh Bāb al-Abwāb* preserved in Münejjim Bashī), pp. 34–5, 56–65.

[4] Kasravī, *op. cit.* vol. III, pp. 304–12; Minorsky, *Caucasian History*, pp. 23–5. On the Shaddādids of Anī, see Kasravī, vol. III, pp. 316–27, and Minorsky, *op. cit.* pp. 79–106.

We have noted that on the eve of the Saljuq invasions, the western and central parts of the country were in the last phase of the Dailamī ascendancy in Iran: indeed the principal Dailamī dynasty, that of the Būyids, was already in a state of confusion and decay when Toghrïl moved westwards from Khurāsān. The Būyids had brought with them from their Caspian homeland a patrimonial conception of power in which each member of the dynasty acquired a share of territory and power; from the very start there had been three Būyid principalities in Iran. Moreover, since the Būyids came to rule over such scattered provinces as the Iranian ones of Jibāl, Fārs, Khūzistān, and Kirmān, and the Arab ones of Iraq and even Oman, the lack of geographical cohesion in their empire undoubtedly favoured the dispersal of political power among several members of the family. In the middle decades of the 4th/10th century the Būyids were held together by family solidarity, which was furthered by the energy and capability of such amīrs as the original three sons of ʿAlī b. Būya and those of the next generation, including ʿAḍud al-Daula Fanā-Khusrau (d. 372/983) and Fakhr al-Daula ʿAlī (d. 387/997). But ʿAḍud al-Daula made plans to perpetuate after his own death the unified rule which he had achieved in his lifetime, and the family henceforth became fragmented and divided against itself. Militarily the Būyids at first depended for infantrymen on their fellow Dailamīs, supplemented by Turkish cavalrymen; but in the 5th/11th century the recruitment of Dailamī soldiers seems to have dwindled (the reasons for this are unclear) and the amirs became almost wholly dependent on Turkish mercenaries, over whom they frequently lost control.[1]

On the religious plane the Būyids' tenure of power was definitely favourable to the consolidation of ʿAlid and Twelver Shīʿī organization and doctrine, but with the rise of the Turkish dynasties in eastern Iran, intellectual as well as political trends were no longer so clearly helpful for the Būyids. Political Shīʿism was clearly failing to gain power in the eastern Islamic world, and even the successes of the Nizārī Ismāʿīlīs were to be fairly limited geographically. In addition, the caliphate of al-Qāʾim (422–67/1031–75) witnessed a certain revival of ʿAbbāsid power, at least in Iraq; here in 437/1045–6, after a century in which the caliphs had been politically impotent under Būyid control,

[1] Cf. Bosworth, "Military organisation under the Būyids of Persia and Iraq", *Oriens*, vol. XVIII (1968). There exists no special monograph on the Būyids, but a valuable provisional survey is given by C. Cahen in his "Buwayhids", *Encyc. of Islam* (2nd ed.).

al-Qā'im appointed a forceful, strongly Sunnī vizier, the Ra'īs al-Ru'asā' Abu'l-Qāsim Ibn al-Muslima.[1] Intellectually the Sunnī revival had already been visible in several phenomena, such as the madrasa-building movement, the gradual rise to respectability of the As͟h'arī *kalām* or theological system (although it was a long time before this process was completed), and the vitality of the conservative and traditionalist law school of Ḥanbalism. The incoming Saljuq rulers enthusiastically aided the progress of this revival.[2]

The territories held by the Būyids in 421/1030 were still extensive. The most serious inroads on their possessions had been made in northern and central Iran. Ray and Jibāl had not been under strong rule since Fak͟hr al-Daula's death, when power there had been divided between his two young sons, Majd al-Daula at Ray and S͟hams al- Daula at Hamadān and Kirmāns͟hāh. Majd al-Daula was an ineffectual ruler, and in practice his territories were governed by his mother Sayyida. After her death in 419/1028, he was unable to keep order or control his troops, and he foolishly appealed to Maḥmūd of G͟hazna for help. This request was the pretext for Maḥmūd's Jibāl campaign. In 420/1029 he sacked Ray, deposed Majd al-Daula, and carried him and his son off as prisoners to K͟hurāsān, installing a G͟haznavid governor in Ray. From here, operations were carried out against the Musāfirids of Ṭārum. The area to the south and west of Ray, including Iṣfahān, Hamadān, and Kirmāns͟hāh, had passed out of Būyid control before this time, but into the comparatively friendly hands of the Kākūyids, another dynasty of Dailamī origin which was closely connected to the Būyids.

The Kākūyids exercised considerable, if transient, authority in central Iran. The founder of the line, Rustam b. Marzbān Dus͟hmanziyār, attracted the favour of the Būyids of Ray by helping them against the Ziyārids. His son 'Alā' al-Daula Muḥammad[3] was first appointed by the Būyids to govern Iṣfahān, and he later adopted this as the capital of his principality.[4] After 398/1007–8 he was virtually independent of Būyid control, extending his power over the towns of Hamadān, Dīnāvār, and S͟hābūr-K͟hwāst. From Ṭabaristān to K͟hūzistān, Ibn Kākūya was continually involved in warfare, and, with the resources

[1] Ibn al-Jauzī, *al-Muntaẓam fī ta'rīk͟h al-mulūk wa'l-umam*, vol. VIII, pp. 127, 200–1; Ibn al-At͟hīr, *al-Kāmil*, vol. IX, p. 362.

[2] For more on the Sunnī revival, see section VI, pp. 70 ff.

[3] In the sources he is generally called Ibn Kākūya, for *kākū* in the Dailamī dialect is said to mean "maternal aunt", and 'Alā' al-Daula was the son of Majd al-Daula's maternal aunt.

[4] An alternative etymology, from a place-name, is suggested by Rabino di Borgomale in *J.A.* (1949), pp. 313–14.

of the rich cities of central Iran at his disposal, he hired mercenaries. Thus in 428/1037, in preparation for an attack on the Ghaznavid-held city of Ray, he was using his wealth to recruit not only local Kurdish and Dailamī troops but also the "'Irāqī" Türkmen, these last comprising some who had come directly from the Balkhān-Kūh area to the east of the Caspian together with others who had just fled westwards from Nīshāpūr. Indeed, Ibn Kākūya's dynamism was a major factor in the brevity of Ghaznavid rule in western Iran. Although he was twice driven from Iṣfahān, by Mas'ūd of Ghazna in 421/1030 and by another Ghaznavid army in 425–7/1034–6, his resilience was such that on each occasion he re-established himself, and the sultan had to recognize him as his vassal.

It was the growing power of the "'Irāqī" Türkmen in northern and central Iran which curbed Ibn Kākūya's ambitions. Deflected from Āzarbāījān by the Rawwādid Vahsūdān b. Mamlān and the Kurdish chieftain Abu'l-Haijā' b. Rahīb al-Daula, two groups of these Oghuz turned to attack Ray (428/1037 or 429/1038) and Hamadān (430/1038–9). Shortly afterwards, the Kākūyids became Saljuq vassals. On the battlefield of Dandānqān in 431/1040, Toghrïl awarded Ray and Iṣfahān to Ibn Kākūya's son Abū Manṣūr Farāmurz; on Ibn Kākūya's death in 433/1041–2 Farāmurz succeeded him in Iṣfahān, and Farāmurz's brother Abū Kālījār Garshāsp was given Hamadān. Farāmurz attempted to keep on equal terms with both the Saljuqs and the Būyid al-Malik al-Raḥīm, yet he only managed to exasperate Toghrïl. In 442/1050–1 the sultan besieged and captured Iṣfahān and moved his capital thither from Ray; in exchange, Farāmurz received Yazd and Abarqūh, while Garshāsp lost Hamadān and Kangāvar to Ibrāhīm Ïnal and died in exile amongst the Būyids in Khūzistān.[1] Later descendants of Farāmurz adapted themselves more smoothly to Saljuq masters. His son Mu'ayyid al-Daula 'Alī, ruler of Yazd, married one of Chaghrï Beg's daughters, and in 488/1095 he died fighting for Tutush b. Alp-Arslan against Berk-Yaruq (see below, p. 107). 'Alī's son 'Aḍud al-Dīn Abū Kālījār Garshāsp also held Yazd, and, being high in Muḥammad's favour, he married a sister of Sultans Muḥammad b. Malik-Shāh and Sanjar; but Sulṭān Maḥmūd b. Muḥammad dispossessed him of Yazd, and henceforth he became a fierce partisan of Sanjar, urging him in 513/1119 to join battle with Maḥmūd at Sāveh (see below, pp. 135–6).[2]

[1] Baihaqī, *Ta'rīkh-i Mas'ūdī*, p. 628; Ibn al-Athīr, vol. IX, pp. 339, 384–5.

[2] Muḥammad b. Ibrāhīm, *Ta'rīkh-i Saljūqiyān-i Kirmān* in *Recueil de Textes*, vol. I, p. 26. Cf. M. T. Houtsma, "Zur Geschichte der Selǵuqen von Kermân", *Z.D.M.G.* pp. 374–5;

The Būyid territories in Iraq and southern Iran were broadly divided between Jalāl al-Daula Abū Ṭāhir Shīrzīl and his nephew 'Imād al-Dīn Abū Kālījār Marzbān in 421/1030. The former was *Amir al-Umarā'* or "Supreme Commander"—as the Būyid rulers in Iraq called themselves—in Baghdad and the rest of Iraq excepting Basra, but though he ruled from 416/1025 to his death in 435/1044, his authority was never very firm. It is true that in Baghdad the caliph did not yet feel strong enough to exert much political pressure. In 429/1037–8 al-Qā'im was powerless to prevent Jalāl al-Daula from assuming the ancient Sassanian title of *Shāhanshāh* ("King of Kings"), although five years later his opposition to the amīr's appropriation of poll-tax revenues collected in Baghdad from the People of the Book (i.e. Christians and Jews) did deter the Būyid from trying to take them again the next year.[1] The real holders of power in the city were the violent and undisciplined Turkish and Dailamī soldiery, the opposing Ḥanbalī and Shī'ī mobs, and the ubiquitous 'ayyārs.[2] Furthermore, a good proportion of the Turkish troops supported the claims of Abū Kālījār, who ruled in Baṣra, Khūzistān, Fārs, Kirmān, and Oman. In the years after 423/1032, Jalāl al-Daula was thrice expelled from his own capital by pro-Abū Kālījār forces; on one Friday in the year 428/1037, the khuṭba in Baghdad was made for four different persons, the caliph, Jalāl al-Daula, Abū Kālījār, and the 'Uqailid Qirwāsh b. al-Muqallad. After this, however, the two Būyid rulers made peace, and 'Irāq was comparatively peaceful until Jalāl al-Daula's death in 435/1044.[3]

The vigorous Abū Kālījār was master in his Iranian territories to an extent that Jalāl al-Daula never enjoyed in Iraq. As well as his father's heritage of Khūzistān and Fārs, he fell heir to the adjoining province of Kirmān when in 419/1028 his uncle Qiwām al-Daula Abu'l-Fawāris died, and this province he successfully defended against an incoming Ghaznavid army. Jalāl al-Daula had intended that his son Abū Manṣūr

Bundārī, *Zubdat al-nuṣra*, p. 133; Ibn al-Athīr, *al-Kamil*, vol. x, pp. 315, 387. On the dynasty in general, there is an indifferent article by Huart in *Encyc. of Islam* (1st ed.), *s.v.*; much more informative is that by G. C. Miles, "The Coinage of the Kākwayhid Dynasty", *Iraq*, pp. 89–104.

[1] Ibn al-Jauzī, *al-Muntaẓam*, vol. VIII, pp. 97–8, 113–14; Ibn al-Athīr, vol. IX, pp. 312–13, 350. Cf. Amedroz, "The Assumption of the Title Shâhanshâh by Buwayhid Rulers", *Numismatic Chronicle*, pp. 393–9.

[2] On the *'ayyārs* and other groups who flourished in times of stress and weak government, see Cahen, *Mouvements Populaires et Autonomisme Urbain dans l'Asie Musulmane du Moyen Âge*, *passim*.

[3] H. Bowen, "The Last Buwayhids", *J.R.A.S.* pp. 228–9.

Khusrau Fīrūz, called al-Malik al-'Azīz (d. 441/1049), should succeed him, but al-'Azīz's ineffectual character was no match for his cousin Abū Kālījār's military and financial resources. It was Abū Kālījār alone who was able to pay the *ḥaqq al-bai'a*, or the subsidies demanded by the Būyid troops on the accession of a new ruler, and for the last four years of his life, until his death in 440/1048, he was ruler of the whole of the Būyid possessions in Iraq and southern Iran.[1]

Towards the end of his reign, Abū Kālījār realized that the Türkmen were becoming a major threat to his dynasty, and indeed, within fifteen years of his death, the Turks were to extinguish the independent rule of the Dailamīs. We have already touched upon the raids of the Oghuz into western Iran and beyond. Several Christian sources—such as Matthew of Edessa, Samuel of Ani, Vardan, and the continuator of Thomas of Ardzrun, as well as a Muslim source that depends on the *Malik-Nāma*—all of these place the first penetration of Armenia at a date between 407/1016–17 and 412/1021, when Türkmen under the leadership of Chaghrī Beg ravaged the district of Vāspūrakān between Lakes Vān and Reẓā'īyeh. But this is almost certainly too early.[2] The stimulus for these movements by the Oghuz was Maḥmūd of Ghazna's seizure of Arslan Isrā'īl (*c.* 418/1027), after which his Türkmen followers spread out in various directions plundering aimlessly. Since many of these came to western Iran, which is often called in early Muslim sources 'Irāq-i 'Ajam "Persian Iraq", they became known as the 'Irāqī Türkmen. Although the names of several of their leaders are known, it does not seem that they had any one outstanding leader; thus they were a more anarchic group than those Türkmen headed by the Saljuq leaders.

Over the next few years the various Oghuz bands were a turbulent factor in the politics of central and western Iran, where Ghaznavids, Būyids, Kākūyids, and local Kurdish chiefs endeavoured to use them against their rivals. The insecurity of this period prompted the construction of town walls in various places: in 429/1038 'Alā' al-Daula Ibn Kākūya fortified Iṣfahān, and between 436/1044–5 and 440/1048–9 the Būyid 'Imād al-Dīn Abū Kālījār put a wall round Shīrāz for the

[1] Baihaqī, *Ta'rīkh-i Mas'ūdī*, pp. 423, 426, 429–32; Ibn al-Athīr, *al-Kāmil*, vol. IX, pp. 282 *bis*, 353; Bowen, *op. cit.* pp. 231–3.

[2] The historicity of this expedition is maintained by Kafesoğlu in "Doğu Anadoluya ilk Selçuklu akīnī (1015–21) ve tarihî ehemmiyeti", *Köprülü Armağanī*, pp. 259–74; but that an expedition was possible at such an early date is denied by Cahen, "A Propos de Quelques Articles dans le Köprülü Armağanī", *J.A.* vol. CCXLII (1954), pp. 271–81.

first time in its history;[1] rich cities such as Ray and Hamadān were other natural targets for the predatory Og͟huz. By themselves the Türkmen were militarily and psychologically unfitted for siege warfare (p. 20 above), yet they could benefit from temporary alliances with one or another side in local disputes. It was because of a triple alliance against him, consisting of the Og͟huz, the Būyid Fanā-K͟husrau, who was a son of the dispossessed Majd al-Daula, and finally the Dailamī ruler of Sāveh, Kām-Ravā, that Ibn Kākūya was forced to evacuate Ray after taking it over from the G͟haznavids in 428/1037. A fearful slaughter followed, and this was repeated in 420/1038–9 when the Og͟huz and Fanā-K͟husrau's Dailamīs captured Hamadān, expelling Ibn Kākūya's son Gars͟hāsp. Prudently, the inhabitants of Qazvīn bought off the Og͟huz for 7,000 dīnārs.[2]

Armenia, Diyārbakr, al-Jazīreh, and Iraq likewise suffered from the Og͟huz, who spread out from Āzarbāijān after Vahsūdān treacherously massacred several of their leaders in 432/1040–1. The establishment of Ibrāhīm Ïnal at Ray in 433/1041–2, and then at Hamadān the next year, drove more numbers of the 'Irāqī Türkmen out of Jibāl into Iraq and al-Jazīreh. It seems that Tog͟hrïl and the Saljuq leaders were already endeavouring to exercise some control over the whole body of Türkmen in the Iranian world, and this was being resisted by the anarchistic 'Irāqīs. When Tog͟hrïl came westwards he notified Gök-Tas͟h, Bug͟hra, and other leaders, then he encamped at Zanjān, hoping to win them over. But they were too suspicious, and told him: "We realize full well that your intention is to seize us if only you can get hold of us. It is fear of you which has made us stay apart and encamp here, and if you persist in trying to get your hands on us, we will make for K͟hurāsān or Rūm, and will never under any circumstances join up with you." Tog͟hrïl nevertheless regarded himself as overlord of all the Og͟huz, and in 435/1044, after Gök-Tas͟h's followers had savagely sacked Mosul, he wrote to Jalāl al-Daula, the ruler of 'Irāq, excusing the Türkmen's conduct; they were, said Tog͟hrïl, mere dependents of the Saljuqs, rebellious slaves who deserved severe punishment.[3]

---

[1] Ibn al-Balk͟hī, *Fārs-Nāma*, p. 133; Yāqūt, *Mu'jam al-buldān*, vol. III, p. 351, *s.v.* "S͟hīrāz"; but according to Ḥamd Allāh Mustaufī (*Nuzhat al-qulūb*, p. 113) it was Ṣamṣām al-Daula b. 'Aḍud al-Daula who first put a wall round S͟hīrāz.

[2] Ibn al-At͟hīr, *al-Kāmil*, vol. IX, pp. 269–71.

[3] *Ibid.* pp. 272, 275, 348.

IV. TOGHRÏL'S STRUGGLE WITH THE BŪYIDS AND THE CONSOLIDATION OF THE EASTERN CONQUESTS

After settling affairs in Khwārazm and the Caspian provinces, Toghrïl came westwards to Jibāl in 434/1042/3 and took over from Ibrāhīm Ïnal the city of Ray, which was to serve briefly as his capital.[1] Ibrāhīm Ïnal now moved into Kurdistān to conduct operations against the Kākūyids and the Kurdish 'Annāzids, but he was already showing signs of the rebelliousness that was to lead to his downfall. In 441/1049–50 he was arrested by Toghrïl, then later released and restored to favour; on this occasion Toghrïl gave him the choice of staying with him or of being allocated a territory which he could carve out as his own principality.[2]

The Oghuz successes in Iran and the consequent crumbling of Ghaznavid and Būyid defences inevitably attracted more Türkmen from Central Asia; indeed, the westward deflexion of unruly elements was now becoming one of Toghrïl's instruments of policy. We are badly informed about the tribal affiliations of the Türkmen in Iran at this time. After their appearance in the accounts of Saljuq origins, the Qïnïq disappear wholly from mention. The 7th/13th-century Armenian historian Vardan calls Toghrïl "leader of the Döger", another Oghuz tribe, who, unlike the Qïnïq, did play a significant role in northern Iran; and Cahen has suggested that in his capacity as chief of a coalition of tribes, Toghrïl might be considered the head of the Döger. Only in the 6th/12th century do we have some information about the activities of individual Oghuz tribes,[3] though we do know that in the middle decades of the 5th/11th century there had been a considerable influx of Central Asian elements into northern Iran and thence to the borders of Armenia and Byzantium.

From this same period dates the especial importance of Āzarbāījān as a base for Türkmen expansion. This area lay at one end of the route through Ray and northern Iran along which Türkmen passed from Khurāsān and beyond, and its fertile valleys—Āzarbāījān is one of the few regions of Iran where dry farming can be practised to any considerable extent—provided pasture for the nomads' herds. Political authority in the region was fragmented, which gave numerous oppor-

[1] See also p. 33 above.

[2] Ibn al-Athīr, *al-Kāmil*, vol. IX, pp. 380–1.

[3] Cf. Cahen, "Les Tribus Turques d'Asie Occidentale pendant la Periode Seljukide", *W.Z.K.M.* pp. 178–87.

tunities for employment in the service of local rulers. Moreover, as a frontier province sharing a border with Christian powers, Āzarbāījān had long-established traditions of ghāzī warfare, in which families like the Shaddādids were prominent, as we have seen. All these factors combined to make Āzarbāījān a concentration-point for the Türkmen, and at this period it began to acquire the Turkish ethnic and linguistic colouring which it still has today.[1] Over the next century or so, ghāzī elements from this area put pressure on the Christian kingdoms of Armenia and Georgia, while at the same time they infiltrated into Anatolia, founded ghāzī states such as those of the Dānishmanids and Mangüjekids, and laid the foundation for a Saljuq sultanate at Rūm which would endure for many decades after the Great Saljuqs had disappeared from Iran and Iraq.

It is unlikely that the Saljuq Sultans Toghrïl and Alp-Arslan conceived of their mission in the west as an all-out offensive against Christian Armenia, Georgia, and Byzantium.[2] Their main interests were, first, to occupy and bring under direct control the rich lands of ancient Iranian civilization: Khurāsān, Jibāl, and Fārs; and second, they wanted to hold Iraq as a bastion against the Fāṭimids and their satellites in Syria and al-Jazīreh. Warfare in Armenia and Anatolia was therefore left primarily to the Türkmen and ghāzīs, troublesome and undisciplined marauders whose presence in the settled lands of Īrān and Iraq would have been an embarrassment to the sultans. Ibrāhīm Ïnal does not represent the more mature outlook of the sultans, but on one occasion he expressed what must have been their desires. In 440/1048 he sent a large body of Oghuz ghāzīs from Transoxiana to raid Byzantium. He told them previously, "My territory [the region of Hamadān and Ḥulwān] is not extensive enough to support you or provide for your needs. The most sensible policy for you is to go and attack Rūm, fight in the way of God, and gain booty. I will follow after you and assist you in this." He and Qutlumush b. Arslan Isrā'īl then led them personally as far as Malāzgird, Erzerum, and Trebizond, eventually capturing the Georgian prince Liparit (called in the Islamic sources "[Li]fāriṭ").[3]

[1] Cf. *idem*, "La Premiere Pénétration Turque en Asie-Mineure", *Byzantion*, pp. 5–15.

[2] Cahen, "La Campagne de Mantzikert d'après les sources Musulmanes", *Byzantion*, pp. 621 ff.

[3] Ibn al-Athīr, *al-Kāmil*, vol. IX, pp. 372–3; Barhebraeus, *Chronography*, p. 206; E. Honigmann, *Die Ostgrenze des Byzantinischen Reiches von 363 bis 1071 nach griechischen, arabischen, syrischen und armenischen Quellen* (= A. A. Vasiliev, *Byzance et les Arabes* vol. III], pp. 179–81;

Yet this policy was not of infinite applicability. Many tribal leaders viewed with suspicion the moves by Toghrïl and Chaghrï to appropriate the rich land of Iran for themselves, as well as their claims to a general control over all the Oghuz. Ibrāhīm Ïnal's own jealousies and ambitions could not be stilled, and it is clear that he represented a substantial body of conservative Türkmen feeling. Toghrïl's magnanimity was now stretched to breaking point. In 451/1059 Ibrāhīm Ïnal and the two sons of his brother Er-Tash rebelled, at a time when affairs in Baghdad and Iraq were critical for Toghrïl, and the latter had to appeal for help from Chaghrï's son Alp-Arslan in Sīstān, who came with his brothers Qavurt and Yāqūtī. When the revolt was suppressed, Ibrāhīm Ïnal was found strangled with a bowstring; Ibn al-Jauzī adds that Toghrïl had now destroyed all trust and loyalty on the part of the Türkmen.[1]

Sporadic Türkmen revolts, such as those of Ibrāhīm Ïnal, of Qutlumush and his brother Rasūl-Tegin, together with events in 'Irāq and Īrān, prevented Toghrïl himself from taking much part in the raids against Rūm. In 446/1054 he went to Āzarbāījān to receive the homage of the Rawwādids and Shaddādids, at Tabrīz and Ganja respectively. He then led his forces into the region of Vān and against Trebizond and Kars, but without decisive result, and with the onset of winter the siege of Malāzgird had to be lifted.[2] In the following years Qutlumush and Yāqūtī were raiding Armenia and eastern Anatolia, and in 450/1058 Kars and Malatya fell. Just before his death Toghrïl appeared briefly in Āzarbāījān (454/1062), but in general he was content to leave the conduct of warfare in the hands of Yāqūtī.[3]

Toghrïl's other great concern was his position *vis-à-vis* the Būyids and the caliph. Toghrïl and 'Imād al-Dīn Abū Kālījār, leader of Khūzistān and Fārs, had come to an understanding: the Saljuq had restrained Ibrāhīm Ïnal from raiding Būyid territory in Luristān and Fārs and had married one of Abū Kālījār's daughters, whilst the Būyid's son Fūlād-Sutūn had married one of Chaghrï's daughters

M. H. Yinanç, *Anadolu'nun fethi*, pp. 46–8; Cahen, *Byzantion* (1948), pp. 15–16; Minorsky, *Studies in Caucasian History*, p. 57; Cahen, "Qutlumush et ses Fils avant l'Asie Mineure", *Der Islam*, p. 20.

[1] Bundārī, *Zubdat al-Nuṣra*, pp. 15–16; Ibn al-Jauzī, *al-Muntaẓam*, vol. VIII, p. 202; Ḥusainī, Ṣadr al-Dīn 'Alī, *Akhbār al-daula al-Saljuqiyya*, pp. 19–20; Ibn al-Athīr, vol. IX, p. 444; Barhebraeus, p. 213; Mīrkhwānd, *Rauḍat al-ṣafā'*, vol. IV, p. 106.

[2] Ibn al-Athīr, IX, 410–11; Barhebraeus, p. 207; for much more detailed information in the Christian sources, cf. Honigmann, *Die Ostgrenze des Byzantinischen Reiches*, pp. 181–2; Yinanç, *Anadolu'nun fethi*, pp. 49–50; and Cahen, *Byzantion* (1948), pp. 16–17.

[3] Yinanç, *op. cit.* pp. 50–7.

(439/1047–8).[1] Abū Kālījār died the next year, before he could recover his province of Kirmān from the Saljuq Qavurt b. Chaghrï Beg, and he was succeeded by his eldest son Khusrau Fīrūz, who took the title *al-Malik al-Raḥīm* ("the merciful king"). It was fortunate for Toghrïl's ambitions that al-Malik al-Raḥīm's succession was disputed by his brother Fūlād-Sutūn, for a period of internal strife within the Būyid family now ensued, in which several of Abū Kālījār's sons (at least nine of them are known) took part. Al-Malik al-Raḥīm was never able to rule outside Iraq, and Fārs and Khūzistān were generally in the hands of Fūlād-Sutūn and several other brothers. It was inevitable that one of the contending parties should call in the Saljuqs. In 444/1052–3, Oghuz raiders had penetrated as far as Shīrāz. In the next year Fūlād-Sutūn inserted Toghrïl's name in the khuṭba in his capital of Shīrāz for the first time, and in 446/1054–5 Toghrïl sent a group of Türkmen to take over Khūzistān.[2]

We have seen that when in 426/1035 the three Saljuq leaders crossed the Oxus, they styled themselves "Clients of the Commander of the Faithful", and that when he captured Nīshāpūr and assumed the title of "Exalted Sultan", Toghrïl opened up diplomatic relations with the caliphate (pp. 19 and 23 above). The Saljuqs soon saw the weakness of Būyid rule in Iraq. In 441/1049–50 Saljuq pressure compelled Naṣr al-Daula Ibn Marwān to put Toghrïl's name in the khuṭba in Diyārbakr,[3] and northern Iraq, already much ravaged by Oghuz raids, was open to attack by the Saljuqs. Toghrïl's march to Baghdad has often been viewed as a Sunnī crusade to rescue the caliph from his Shī'ī oppressors, and it is true that it was the Shī'ī proclivities of a Turkish commander in Baghdad, Arslan Basāsīrī, which prompted al-Qā'im's appeal to Toghrïl. We can only guess at Toghrïl's inner motives, but it is surely relevant to note that his Iranian advisers included many officials from Khurāsān, the most strongly Sunnī part of Iran. The sources give varying lists of the viziers who are said to have served Toghrïl, but the backgrounds of these men are predominantly Khurāsānian, and most of them started their careers with the Ghaznavids. Thus the Ṣāḥib Ḥusain Mīkālī, whom Ibn al-Athīr includes in his list, entered the Saljuqs' service some time after being captured from the Ghaznavids; he came from a prominent Nīshāpūr family which had

[1] Ibn al-Athīr, *al-Kāmil*, vol. IX, pp. 365–6.
[2] *Ibid.* pp. 401–2, 414; Bowen, "The Last Buwayhids", *J.R.A.S.* pp. 233–7.
[3] Ibn al-Athīr, vol. IX, p. 380; Barhebraeus, *Chronography*, pp. 205–6.

produced a long line of Ḥanafī scholars and traditionists as well as administrators.[1] The most famous of Toghrïl's viziers was the 'Amīd al-Mulk Abū Naṣr Kundurī, who had been recommended to Toghrïl shortly after the latter's occupation of Nīshāpūr. Kundurī was a fierce Ḥanafī, and when Toghrïl gave permission for the khuṭba in Khurāsān to include the cursing of the Shī'a, Kundurī added the cursing of the Ash'arīs, who tended to be of the Shāfi'ī law school; this caused prominent scholars such as al-Qushairī and Abu'l-Ma'ālī al-Juvainī to flee to the Ḥijāz.[2] Hence there is much justification for regarding the early years of the Great Saljuq sultanate as strongly Sunnī and Ḥanafī in ethos and outlook.

Al-Malik al-Raḥīm's seven-year reign in Baghdad (440–7/1048–55) was racked by continual violence and rioting, with hostility polarized around the figures of the caliph's Vizier Ibn al-Muslima on one side, and the Turkish general Abu'l-Ḥārith Arslan Basāsīrī on the other. The vizier accused Basāsīrī of being in touch with the Fāṭimid caliph of Egypt, al-Mustanṣir (427–87/1036–94), the 'Abbāsids' great rival, and it is true that a Fāṭimid *dā'ī* (agent), al-Mu'ayyad fi'l-Dīn Shīrāzī, became very active in Iraq shortly after this time.[3] In 447/1055 Toghrïl was assembling forces at Hamadān, Dīnāvār, Kirmānshāh, and Ḥulwān, and he now announced his intention of making the pilgrimage to Mecca and then of mounting a crusade against the Fāṭimids. Al-Malik al-Raḥīm and the caliph accepted Toghrïl's appearance at Baghdad in Ramaḍān 447/December 1055, but the Būyid prince was unable to preserve his power: he was arrested and deposed by Toghrïl that same month, and spent the remaining four years of his life in Saljuq captivity.[4] In this fashion, the rule of the Dailamīs in 'Irāq was extinguished after over a century's tenure of power, although Būyid rule continued for a few years more in Fārs.

At this time Fūlād-Sutūn was ruling in Fārs with the support of the Vizier Abū Manṣūr al-Fasawī, called Muhadhdhib al-Daula, but chaos increased there with the rise of a chieftain of the Shabānkāra'ī Kurds,

[1] Ibn al-Athīr, vol. IX, p. 359; on the Mīkālīs, see the notes to Sa'īd Nafīsī's edition of Baihaqī's *Ta'rīkh-i Mas'ūdī*, vol. III, pp. 969–1009; see also Bowen, "Notes on some Early Seljuqid Viziers", *B[ulletin of the] S[chool of] O[riental and] A[frican Studies]*, vol. XX (1957), pp. 107–8.

[2] Ibn al-Athīr, *al-Kāmil*, vol. X, p. 21; but according to Bundārī, p. 30, Kundurī later moderated his Ḥanafī views and sought to reconcile the Ḥanafīs and Shāfi'īs.

[3] Cf. M. Canard, "al-Basāsīrī", *Encyc. of Islam* (2nd ed.).

[4] Bundārī, *Zubdat al-nuṣra*, pp. 10–11; Ibn al-Athīr, *al-Kāmil*, vol. IX, pp. 418–22; Barhebraeus, *Chronography*, pp. 207–9; Mīrkhwānd, *Rauḍat al-ṣafā'*, vol. IV, pp. 105–6; Bowen, *J.R.A.S.* (1929), pp. 237–8.

Abu'l-'Abbās Faḍlūya, who in 454/1062 overthrew and killed Fūlād-Sutūn, setting up one of the latter's brothers as a Būyid puppet ruler. However, Faḍlūya was defeated in this same year by a Saljuq army from Kirmān under Qavurt; the khuṭba in Shīrāz was then made in Toghrïl's name and the rule of the Būyids finally ended there.[1] Another of Abū Kālījār's sons, Abū 'Alī Fanā-Khusrau, prospered under later sultans, residing on his fief at Naubandajān in Fārs, enjoying the privileges of a standard and a salute of drums, and dying full of days and honour in 487/1094. The sources also mention one of Jalāl al-Daula's sons, Abū Manṣūr 'Alī, who held the fiefs of al-Madā'in and Dair al-'Āqūl in Iraq until 490/1097.[2]

In 'Irāq, Basāsīrī had allied with his brother-in-law the Mazyadid Dubais in an open campaign under the Fāṭimid white colours, having received an investiture patent from al-Mustanṣir in Cairo. Toghrïl remained in Baghdad for thirteen months without personally meeting al-Qā'im, all communication being handled by their respective viziers. After campaigning in al-Jazīreh, Toghrïl entered Baghdad once more, and at the end of 449/beginning of 1058 he was at last received by the caliph. 'Imād al-Dīn describes at length the splendour of the occasion, during which al-Qā'im bestowed on Toghrïl the honorifics *Rukn al-Daula* ("Pillar of the State") and *Malik al-Mashriq wa'l-Maghrib* ("King of the East and West"), together with seven robes of honour in the 'Abbāsid colour of black and two crowns signifying rule over the Arabs and 'Ajamīs.[3] Later the distraction caused by Ibrāhīm Ïnal's rebellion allowed Basāsīrī and the 'Uqailid Quraish b. Badrān to re-enter Baghdad in 450/end of 1058, when they attracted strong popular support, both Sunnī and Shī'ī; now the Fāṭimid khuṭba was made, the caliph expelled, and the old enemy Ibn al-Muslima savagely executed.[4] A year passed before Toghrïl was able to return. Basāsīrī had been abandoned by the Fāṭimids and, in the final battle, by Dubais too, and in 451/1060 he was killed. Thus Fāṭimid ambitions in Iraq were finally thwarted and a decisive check placed first on the Shī'ī element in Baghdad (where the Saljuqs now carried out an intensive purge) and second on the Shī'ī-tinged Arab amīrs of Iraq.[5]

[1] Ibn al-Balkhī, *Fārs-Nāma*, p. 166.

[2] Bowen, *op. cit.* pp. 241–5.

[3] Bundārī, pp. 13–14; Ḥusainī, *Akhbār al-daula*, pp. 18–19; Barhebraeus, pp. 209–12; Mīrkhwānd, vol. IV, p. 106.

[4] Bundārī, *Zubdat al-nuṣra*, pp. 15–16; Ibn al-Tiqtaqā, *Kitāb al-Fakhrī*, pp. 263–4 (tr. C. E. J. Whitting, pp. 285–6); Maqrīzī, *Itti'āẓ al-Hunafā'* (Cairo, 1367/1949), pp. 62–3; Canard, *Encyc. of Islam* (2nd ed.).

[5] Ḥusainī, *Akhbār al-daula*, pp. 20–1; Ibn al-Athīr, *al-Kāmil*, vol. IX, p. 448; Barhebraeus, *Chronography*, pp. 213–15; Ibn Khallikān, *Wafayāt al-a'yān*, vol. I, pp. 172–3.

Toghrïl's campaigns in Iraq not only relieved the caliph of his enemies, but also crystallized the new division of power and influence in the central lands of the *Dār al-Islām*. This duality—between the caliph-imāms as spiritual heads and the Saljuq sultans as secular rulers—had eventually to be recognized in Islamic constitutional theory, although it had not occurred in time to be considered in the famous treatise of al-Māwardī (d. 450/1058), *al-Aḥkām al-sulṭāniyya* ("The Principles of Government"). Toghrïl seems to have exulted in his role as deliverer of the caliph: a document of 454/1062, issued by Toghrïl's chancery and quoted by the Baghdad historian and theologian Ibn al-Jauzī, is headed, "From the exalted Emperor of Emperors, King of the East and West, Reviver of Islam, Lieutenant of the Imām, and Right Hand of the Caliph of God, the Commander of the Faithful".[1] He now sought to draw the two houses more closely together. In 448/1056 al-Qā'im had married one of Chaghrï's daughters, Arslan Khātūn Khadīja; Toghrïl himself aspired to marry one of the caliph's daughters. That an 'Abbāsid bride should be given to a rough Türkmen was, however, a different matter, and al-Qā'im replied that such alliances were not customary amongst the caliphs. To the importunings of Kundurī, which were supported by the caliph's own daughter Arslan Khātūn, al-Qā'im proudly replied, "We are the children of al-'Abbās, the best of mankind; both the Imamate and temporal leadership shall remain in us until the Day of Resurrection. He who supports us will be guided aright, but he who opposes us will fall into error".

Yet to the caliph's moral authority Toghrïl could oppose a judicious measure of *force majeure*. The caliphate at this time was relying financially on gifts from outside powers and their envoys, on the sale of honours, and on revenues granted to them by the secular rulers of Iraq. On Toghrïl's orders, Kundurī threatened to sequestrate the caliph's *iqṭā's* (estates), leaving him only with those which his father al-Qādir had possessed.[2] al-Qā'im had no alternative but to comply, and in 454/1062 the marriage contract was made at Tabrīz by Toghrïl's representative, the Ra'īs al-'Irāqain Abū Aḥmad al-Nihāwandī, and by that of the caliph, Abu'l-Ghanā'im b. al-Muhallabān. The sultan himself was absent in Armenia, and did not meet his wife in

[1] Ibn al-Jauzī, *al-Muntaẓam*, vol. VIII, p. 223.

[2] Bundārī, *Zubda tal-nuṣra*, pp. 11–12, 19–20; Ḥusainī, *Akhbār al-daula*, pp. 17–18; Ibn al-Athīr, *al-Kāmil*, vol. IX, p. 424; Barhebraeus, *Chronography*, p. 209.

Baghdad until the following year, 455/1063, shortly before his death at Ray.[1]

The conventional eulogies on his death stress Toghrïl's piety and clemency on the one hand, and his vigour, even harshness, on the other. We need only note that it was surely a remarkable man who, in a life span of seventy years, could rise from a hand-to-mouth existence as a nomadic chief to a position of sovereignty over lands extending from Kirmān to Diyārbakr. At the time of his death the regions of Anatolia, northern Syria, and the Caucasus still provided ample scope for the energies of ghāzīs and tribesmen, although the Türkmen revolts which Toghrïl had to quell were a reminder that the Saljuq leaders' progress from steppe chieftains to monarchs in the Iranian style would not be untroubled.

Whilst Toghrïl was occupied with the west, Khurāsān and the east remained under the control of Chaghrï Beg, according to the division of authority made by the Saljuqs after the Dandānqān victory. Chaghrï was allotted Khurāsān and all the lands north of the Oxus that he might conquer, while Marv became his capital; down to the end of Sanjar's reign, Marv was to remain the centre of Saljuq administration for the east. If he could wrest them from the sultans, Mūsā Yabghu was to have the frontier territories which accompanied the Ghaznavid empire: i.e. Herāt, Pūshang, Isfizār (Aspuzār), Ghūr, Sīstān, and Bust; but his main efforts were in fact to be directed in the direction of Sīstān (see below, pp. 50–1). Qavurt, Chaghrï's eldest son, was to expand southwards and occupy Kirmān, Kūhistān, and Ṭabas, the latter being an important fortress and trading-post on the route that skirted the great salt desert and connected Khurāsān with Kirmān. Ibrāhīm Ïnal, Qutlumush b. Arslan, and Chaghrï's other two sons, Yāqūtī and Alp-Arslan, accompanied Toghrïl westwards.[2]

Chaghrï thus remained ruler in the east until his death in 452/1060, though in the final years his son and successor Alp-Arslan took an increasing share in the business of ruling. Noting the paucity of information in the sources on Chaghrï's personality and his system of government, Cahen has concluded that he was a somewhat colourless person.[3] He does seem to have been content with the very extensive

[1] Bundārī, pp. 22, 25–6; Ḥusainī, p. 21; Barhebraeus, p. 215; Ibn Khallikān, *Wafayāt al-aʿyān*, vol. III, p. 232.

[2] Ẓahīr al-Dīn Nīshāpūrī, *Saljūq-Nāma*, p. 18; Rāvandī, *Rāḥat al-Ṣudūr*, p. 104. A slightly different account of their spheres of influence occurs in Bundārī, *Zubdat al-nuṣra*, pp. 8–9, and Ḥusainī, *Akhbār al-daula*, p. 17.

[3] "Čaghrī", *Encyc. of Islam* (2nd ed.).

power which he wielded in the east, and was never tempted into the acts of rebelliousness which characterized the careers of so many lesser Saljuq amīrs. Toghrïl, suzerain of the whole of the Saljuq dominions, was without male heir, and thus it was almost certain that one of Chaghrï's own sons would succeed to the unified sovereignty of east and west, which in fact happened under Alp-Arslan. The two brothers always remained on friendly terms. Chaghrï accepted Toghrïl's intervention in Sīstān on behalf of Mūsā Yabghu and his son, and when Ibrāhīm Ïnal rebelled, Toghrïl received valuable help from Chaghrï's sons.

Chaghrï had wide responsibilities in the east. Beyond the Atrak and the Oxus, Dihistān and Khwārazm had to be defended against Qïpchaq pressure and a possible revival of Qarakhānid activity. But relations with the Ghaznavids were his foremost concern. Only gradually over the next few decades did the Ghaznavid sultans become reconciled to the permanent loss of their Khurāsānian provinces. Ibrāhīm b. Mas'ūd is said to have mourned his inability to recover the lost territories: "He used to say, 'If only I had been in my father Mas'ūd's place after the death of my grandfather Maḥmūd, the bastions of our kingdom would not have collapsed. But now, I am too weak to regain what they have taken, and neighbouring kings with extensive territories and powerful armies have conquered it.'"[1]

Sīstān had been ruled in the 4th/10th century by amīrs descended from collaterals of the Ṣaffārid brothers Ya'qūb and 'Amr b. Laith. But in 393/1002 Maḥmūd of Ghazna deposed the Amīr Khalaf b. Aḥmad (d. 399/1008–9) and annexed Sīstān to his empire. The unknown but very patriotic author of the *Ta'rīkh-i Sīstān*, a local history of the province, regards the coming of the Turks, i.e. the Ghaznavids, as a major disaster for his country.[2] Because of feelings like this, Sīstān under Ghaznavid rule was usually racked by the activities of patriotic 'ayyārs. Mas'ūd ruled Sīstān through a scion of the Ṣaffārid dynasty, Amīr Abu'l-Faḍl Naṣr. Türkmen raids on Sīstān are recorded from *c.* 427/1036 onwards, and soon afterwards the Saljuqs were definitely called in by some Sagzī rebels against the Ghaznavids. Er-Tash (d. 440/1048–9), who is described as a brother of Ibrāhīm Ïnal, came and compelled Abu'l-Faḍl to make the khuṭba in the name of Mūsā Yabghu, who was then in Herāt; after Dandānqān, Mūsā came in person to Sīstān. Abu'l-Faḍl remained faithful to his new Saljuq masters: his

[1] Ibn al-Athīr, *al-Kāmil*, vol. x, p. 111. [2] *Ta'rīkh-i Sīstān*, p. 354.

brother Abū Naṣr Manṣūr married a Turkish princess, and when in 432/1041 Sulṭān Maudūd b. Mas'ūd of Ghazna (432–41/1041–50) sent an army into Sīstān, Abu'l-Faḍl and Er-Tash eventually repulsed it decisively. Abu'l-Faḍl also purged the land of Ghaznavid sympathizers, who seem to have been especially well represented amongst the religious classes.[1]

The frontier between this south-easternmost outpost of Saljuq influence and the Ghaznavid empire was finally stabilized in the lower Helmand valley between Sīstān and Bust. In 434/1042 Maudūd repulsed an attack on Bust by Abu'l-Faḍl and Er-Tash, but it was Sulṭān 'Abd al-Rashīd b. Maḥmūd who took the offensive in this region. In 443/1051–2 his slave general Toghrïl invaded Sīstān and drove out Abu'l-Faḍl and Mūsā Yabghu, who were forced temporarily to flee to Herāt.[2] Saljuq suzerainty was re-established in Sīstān, but it seems that Chaghrï Beg now asserted his own superior rights over Sīstān, first sending his son Yāqūtī and then in 448/1056–7 coming personally to Zarang, the capital of Sīstān, where he minted his own coins. Relying on his position as ruler of Khurāsān and the east, Chaghrï clearly hoped to reduce Mūsā Yabghu to a subordinate status in which Sīstān should be held as an apanage of Khurāsān. But later in that year, Mūsā appealed to Toghrïl as supreme head of the Saljuq family. Toghrïl, who was in 'Irāq, thereupon sent Mūsā a patent of investiture for Sīstān and ordered that the khuṭba and the *sikka* (right of coinage) should both be in Mūsā's name, as before. Mūsā's son Qara-Arslan Böri resumed these rights on his father's behalf, and the local administration of the province remained in the hands of the Ṣaffārid Abu'l-Faḍl until his death in 465/1073, when his son Bahā' al-Daula wa'l-Dīn Ṭāhir took over.[3]

Towards the middle of Mas'ūd of Ghazna's reign, Khwārazm had fallen under the control of rebellious governors, who had taken advantage of the province's geographical isolation and its remoteness from Ghazna. It came briefly into the hands of Hārūn b. Altun-Tash Khwārazm-Shāh, and then, after his murder in 426/1035, into those of his brother Ismā'īl Khandān. Both of them lent their support to the Saljuqs—e.g. Hārūn supplied them with arms and beasts of burden—for they were enemies of the Ghaznavids.[4] Shāh Malik, the Oghuz ruler of Jand, therefore allied with Mas'ūd, and in 429/1038

[1] *Ibid.* pp. 354, 364–8; Ibn al-Athīr, vol. IX, pp. 330–1, 346.

[2] *Tar'īkh-i Sīstān*, pp. 368, 371–2; Ibn al-Athīr, vol. IX, pp. 354, 399; Jūzjānī, *Ṭabaqāt-i Nāṣirī* (tr. H. G. Raverty), vol. I, p. 99.

[3] *Ta'rīkh-i Sīstān*, pp. 375–82.

[4] Baihaqī, *Ta'rīkh-i Mas'ūdi* (ed. Ghanī and Fayyāḍ), p. 684.

the sultan sent him a patent of investiture for Khwārazm, with the implicit invitation to overthrow Ismā'īl. In the winter of 432/1040–1 Shāh Malik marched across the desert into Khwārazm to assert his claim, and after a long and singularly bloody battle, he went to the capital and proclaimed the khuṭba for Sulṭān Mas'ūd, although by this time Mas'ūd was in fact dead.[1]

The Saljuqs had meanwhile taken over Khurāsān, and were now able to turn their attention to Khwārazm and settle scores with their ancient enemy. Toghrïl and Chaghrï combined for this campaign, and in 433/1042 they drove Shāh Malik from Khwārazm. He fled with his forces across the Dihistān steppe to Kirmān and Makrān, and Pritsak has surmised that he was unable to return to his former territories in the Syr Darya delta because these had now passed into the hands of the Qïpchaq. Eventually Shāh Malik was captured in Makrān by Er-Tash, who had been securing Sīstān; he was then handed over to Chaghrï, who killed him. Khwārazm was placed under a Saljuq governor, and the only other information recorded about this region during the rest of Chaghrï's lifetime is a revolt by the governor of Khwārazm, which was suppressed personally by Chaghrï at the end of the fifth decade of the eleventh century. In the course of this campaign, Chaghrï also received the submission of the "Amīr of Qïpchaq", who became a Muslim and married into Chaghrï's family.[2]

As well as securing the defence of his south-western frontier in the Sīstān and Bust area, Maudūd of Ghazna managed to halt the Saljuqs in north-western Afghanistan and even to push them back temporarily. He drove them from Balkh, Herāt returned to Ghaznavid allegiance, and Tirmidh, the important bridgehead on the Oxus, remained in his hands for some years more. An army which he had fitted out for the reconquest of Khurāsān was in 435/1043–4 defeated by Alp-Arslan, but Maudūd's prestige was so great that the "King of the Turks in Transoxiana" (probably the Qarakhānid Böri-Tegin, the later Tamghach-Khān Ibrāhīm b. Naṣr of Samarqand) submitted to him, and eventually Maudūd married one of Chaghrï's daughters.[3] Towards the

[1] *Ibid.* pp. 689–90; Ibn al-Athīr, *al-Kāmil*, vol. IX, pp. 345–6; Sachau, "Zur Geschichte und Chronologie von Khwârizm", *S.B.W.A.W.* pp. 309–12; Barthold, *Turkestan*, p. 302.

[2] Ibn Funduq, *Ta'rīkh-i Baihaq*, p. 51; Ḥusainī, *Akhbār al-daula*, pp. 27–8; Ibn al-Athīr, vol. IX, p. 346, vol. X, p. 4; Mīrkhwānd, *Rauḍat al-ṣafa'*, vol. IV, p. 105; Sachau, *op. cit.* pp. 303–12; Pritsak, "Der Untergang des Reiches des Oğuzischen Yabğu", *Köprülü Armağanï*, pp. 405–10.

[3] Ibn al-Athīr, vol. IX, pp. 334–54; Barthold, *Turkestan*, pp. 303–4.

end of his reign he planned another *revanche* against the Saljuqs in Khurāsān, by means of subsidies and promises of territory which stirred up several of their enemies. The Kākūyid former ruler of Hamadān, Abū Kālījār Garshāsp, sent a contingent of troops, while the "Khāqān, King of the Turks" (doubtless Böri-Tegin again), with his commander Qashgha, attacked Tirmidh and Khwārazm respectively. Unfortunately for Maudūd, these strategies came to naught with his own death. At some time before his death, Tirmidh had been finally lost to the Ghaznavids; the Saljuqs were now in possession of the upper Oxus valley as far as Qubādhiyān and Vakhsh, and these regions were now entrusted to one of Alp-Arslan's officials, Abū 'Alī b. Shādhān.[1]

The decade 1050–60 was a troubled one for the Ghaznavids. Of the four short reigns in it, the most important were those of 'Abd al-Rashīd b. Maḥmūd (441–4/1050–3) and Farrukh-Zād b. Mas'ūd (444–51/1053–9), and these two were separated by the short but violent usurpation of the throne by the Turkish slave commander Toghrïl.[2] The fact that the Saljuqs derived no great advantage from these disturbances shows that they had reached the natural geographical limits of their expansion in the east. Indeed, at one point 'Abd al-Rashīd successfully launched a counter-attack, defeating Chaghrï and forcing the Oghuz to withdraw for a while from Sīstān and Kirmān (see above, p. 51). Farrukh-Zād repelled Chaghrï's forces from Ghazna and captured several important Saljuq commanders before he in turn was defeated by Alp-Arslan. Thus the warfare was in general indecisive, and the two sides were fairly evenly balanced. Farrukh-Zād's brother and successor, Ibrāhīm b. Mas'ūd, accordingly made a formal peace treaty with Chaghrï.[3] Ibrāhīm's long reign marked a period of prosperity and consolidation for the Ghaznavid empire, and the frontier with the Saljuqs remained essentially stable during his lifetime.[4] The Ghaznavid empire was henceforth based upon the two centres of Ghazna in Afghanistan and Lahore in northern India; from the time of the reign of Maudūd these are the only two mints recorded for the Ghaznavids, in contrast to the multiplicity of mints used in the previous reigns.[5]

[1] Ḥusainī, pp. 27–8; Ibn al-Athīr, vol. IX, pp. 381–2; Barthold, *loc. cit.*

[2] For an attempt to sort out the confused chronology of this decade, see Bosworth, "The Titulature of the Early Ghaznavids", *Oriens*, pp. 230–2.

[3] Ḥusainī, *Akhbār al-daula*, pp. 28–9; Ibn al-Athīr, *al-Kāmil*, vol. IX, pp. 398–401, vol. X, pp. 3–4; and Jūzjānī (Raverty tr.), vol. I, pp. 98–9, 103–4, 133.

[4] For the relations between Ibrāhīm and Malik-Shāh, see section VII, pp. 93–4 below.

[5] Cf. D. Sourdel, *Inventaire des monnaies musulmanes anciennes du Musée de Caboul*, pp. XV–XVI.

V. THE REIGN OF ALP-ARSLAN

Before he died, Toghrïl seems to have designated as his successor Chaghrï's younger son Sulaimān, a virtual nonentity who is hardly mentioned in the sources before this. Yet the union of both eastern and western lands under one Saljuq sultan surely demanded the strongest possible man at the top. Direct, unified rule by one man had never before been achieved, and there were powerful centrifugal forces at work in the Saljuq dominions, including the ambitions of other members of the Saljuq family and the naturally anarchical tendencies of the Türkmen. These latter considerations were probably in the minds of several Saljuq slave commanders, whose own interests lay in a strong central authority and the maintenance of a powerful professional army. Two such men, Yaghï-Basan and Erdem, proclaimed at Qazvīn the succession of Sulaimān's brother, Abū Shujā' Alp-Arslan Muḥammad. Sulaimān himself was the candidate of Toghrïl's vizier and adviser, the 'Amīd al-Mulk Kundurī, who doubtless hoped to perpetuate his own influence in the state; it was patent that if Alp-Arslan came to the throne, it would be the star of his own vizier and protégé, Niẓām al-Mulk, which would rise, whereas that of Kundurī would fall. The percipient Niẓām al-Mulk therefore threw his weight into the struggle on his master's side, and since Alp-Arslan already had possession of Khurāsān and was obviously superior in military experience, Kundurī and Sulaimān had to yield. Speedy recognition of Alp-Arslan's claim was imperative at this point, for Qutlumush and a large Türkmen following were lurking in the Alburz mountains to the south of the Caspian, awaiting the chance to descend on the key cities of Ray and Qazvīn and thus seize power.[1]

Alp-Arslan's succession was duly effected, and Kundurī's fall was now inevitable. Shortly after the new sultan's accession in 455/1063, Kundurī was arrested and later executed on the prompting of Niẓām al-Mulk. Kundurī is said to have reflected philosophically that his old master Toghrïl had given him secular power, and now his nephew was going to give him a martyr's crown for the next world; but he warned Niẓām al-Mulk with the words, "You have introduced a reprehensible innovation and an ugly practice into the world by executing a [dismissed] minister and by your treachery and deceit, and you have not fully considered what the end of it all will be. I fear that

[1] Bundārī, *Zubdat al-nuṣra*, p. 28; Ibn al-Athīr, *al-Kāmil*, vol. x, pp. 18–19.

this evil and blameworthy practice will rebound on the heads of your own children and descendants." The 'Abbāsid caliph's assent was now secured for Alp-Arslan's assumption of the sultanate. In his embassy Alp-Arslan tactfully allowed Toghrïl's widow, the daughter of al-Qā'im, to return home; he never attempted to emulate his uncle and contract a liaison with the 'Abbāsids, nor does it seem that he ever even visited Baghdad. The caliph agreed to designate the new sultan "Trusted Son", and he bestowed on him the honorifics *'Aḍud al-Daula* ("Strong Arm of the State") and *Ḍiyā' al-Dīn* ("Light of Religion") in 456/1064.[1]

Alp-Arslan's reign of ten years (455–65/1063–73) and the succeeding twenty years' rule of his son Malik-Shāh form the apogee of the Great Saljuq sultanate. During these decades the Saljuq dominions were united under the rule of one man, and the energetic and unceasing journeys and campaigns of the sultans meant that this unity was far from theoretical. Īrān was now enjoying an intellectual and cultural florescence as well as a considerable commercial and agricultural prosperity. The chaos caused by the Türkmen and their flocks was alleviated both by the policy of diverting them westwards as far as possible, and also by the Saljuq governors' control over the provinces. After the great famine and pandemic of 448–9/1056–7 (its effects were felt in regions as far apart as Egypt, the Yemen, and Transoxiana), Iran was relatively free of the plagues and other misery which had earlier come in the wake of warfare and other devastation.[2] There are indications that in the cities of Khurāsān, firmer rule and internal pacification checked the endemic violence of the 'ayyārs and the sectarian factions (*'aṣabiyyāt*). According to the historian of Baihaq, Ibn Funduq, Malik-Shāh's death was followed by a period of bloody sectarian strife and the dominance of 'ayyārs in the towns.[3] For Iran as a whole, however, trade with Central Asia and the Qïpchaq steppe, together with trade through Kirmān and the Persian Gulf, was facilitated. Although there may have been a decline in the commerce of the Persian Gulf during the 5th/11th century—Lewis has surmised that the diversion of trade from India to South Arabia, the Red Sea,

[1] Bundārī, pp. 29–30; Ẓahīr al-Dīn Nīshāpūrī, *Saljūq-Nāma*, pp. 23–4; Rāvandī, *Rāḥat al-ṣudūr*, p. 118; Ḥusainī, *Akhbār al-daula al-Saljūqiyya*, pp. 23–6; Ibn al-Athīr, vol. x, pp. 20–3, 37; Ibn Khallikān, *Wafayāt al-a'yān*, vol. III, pp. 300–1.

[2] Ibn al-Jauzī, *al-Muntaẓam*, vol. VIII, pp. 170–1, 179–81; Ibn al-Athīr, vol. IX, pp. 434–5, 438–9.

[3] *Ta'rīkh-i Baihaq*, pp. 274–5.

and Egypt was a deliberate, anti-'Abbāsid policy on the part of the Fāṭimids of Cairo—Kirmān nonetheless prospered under the descendants of Qavurt. In the last decades of the 5th/11th century and the early ones of the next, the towns of Kirmān or Bardasīr and Jīruft enjoyed great mercantile activity, and their commercial quarters contained colonies of foreign traders from as far afield as Byzantium and India.[1]

This combined period of thirty years may also be characterized as the age of the great Vizier Niẓām al-Mulk, or *al-Daula al-Niẓāmiyya* as Ibn al-Athīr specifically calls it, and it is worth pausing to consider this outstanding figure of Iranian history. Not only was he mentor to the Saljuq sultans, encouraging them to act as sovereign monarchs in the Iranian tradition, but in his *Siyāsat-Nāma* or "Book of Government" he provided a precious source of information on the political ethos of the age and on the administrative and court procedures then prevalent in eastern Islam. He typifies the class of Iranian secretaries and officials upon whom the sultans relied, and his book is not merely a theoretical "Mirror for Princes" but also a blueprint according to which Niẓām al-Mulk hoped to fashion the sultan and his empire.

Abū 'Alī Ḥasan b. 'Alī Ṭūsī (408 or 410–85/1017 or 1019–92) was given the honorific *Niẓām al-Mulk* ("Order of the Realm") at some point early in his career, perhaps by Alp-Arslan in Khurāsān. Like so many of the Saljuqs' Khurāsānian servants, he had begun as an official of the Ghaznavids. He never ceased to have as his ideal the centralized despotism of the Ghaznavids, and in the *Siyāsat-Nāma* it is not surprising to find forceful monarchs such as Maḥmūd of Ghazna and the Būyid 'Aḍud al-Daula continually held up as models for the Saljuqs to emulate. Niẓām al-Mulk's family background and early life are well-documented by Ibn Funduq, for the family had marriage connexions with the Sayyids of Baihaq.[2] His studies with the Imām Muwaffaq, one of the outstanding Shāfi'ī *'ulamā* of Nīshāpūr, helped to form his enthusiasm for both the Shāfi'ī law school and the Ash'arī kalām, while his zeal for education, and for these two fields of knowledge in particular, were later put into practice by his extension of the madrasa system (see pp. 72–4 below).

[1] Muḥammad b. Ibrāhīm, *Ta'rīkh-i Saljūqiyān-i Kirmān*, pp. 2, 25–6, 49. Cf. Houtsma, "Zur Geschichte der Selǵuqen von Kermân", *Z.D.M.G.* pp. 372, 380; B. Lewis, "The Fatimids and the Route to India", *Revue de la Faculté des Sciences Economiques de l'Université d'Istanbul*, vol. XI (1953), pp. 50–4.

[2] Cf. *Ta'rīkh-i Baihaq*, pp. 73–83.

After the expulsion of the Ghaznavids from Khurāsān, the young Niẓām al-Mulk spent three or four years in Ghazna and then entered the service of Chaghrï and Alp-Arslan in his native Khurāsān. It may be that he saw himself as a representative of the Persian dihqān and official classes, with a duty and mission to perpetuate the traditions of those classes by civilizing their Turkish masters and thereby preserving Īrān from Türkmen anarchy. On the death of Alp-Arslan's vizier, Abū 'Alī b. Shādhān, Niẓām al-Mulk took over the post, and thus with Chaghrï's death he became the administrator of all Khurāsān. We have seen that his fame aroused the jealousy of Toghrïl's vizier, Kundurī, who attempted to push the candidature of Sulaimān and so prevent Alp-Arslan and Niẓām al-Mulk from gaining supreme power in the Saljuq dominions. During Alp-Arslan's reign Niẓām al-Mulk had a free hand in directing the administration of the empire; in addition, he spent much time on military duties, accompanying his master and also undertaking expeditions of his own, such as those of 459/1067 and 464/1071–2 in Fārs, whose success greatly increased his prestige.

Bowen has tabulated five main points of policy in Alp-Arslan's reign, although, he says, whether they were formulated by the sultan himself or by his minister is uncertain.[1] First, the Türkmen were employed for raiding the Christian kingdoms of Asia Minor and the Caucasus, as well as the lands of the Shī'ī Fāṭimids in Syria; hence at the outset of his reign, when his position as sultan was far from secure, Alp-Arslan thought it wise to lead a campaign into Georgia and Armenia (see below, p. 62). Second, the irresistibility of the sultan's forces was demonstrated—coupled, however, with clemency towards and the reinstatement of rebels who submitted. Next, local rulers, both Sunnīs and Shī'īs, were maintained in such regions as Iraq, Fārs, Āzarbāījān, and the Caspian provinces, while members of the Saljuq family were used as provincial governors. Fourth, to prevent the kind of crisis that had occurred on Toghrïl's death, there was the early appointment of Malik-Shāh as *valī 'ahd* (heir) even though he was not the eldest son. And finally, good relations were established with the 'Abbāsid caliphs. Bearing these policies in mind, we shall now consider the events of the reign, so far as they relate to the history of the Iranian world, under the three headings of dynastic affairs in the heartlands of the empire; the campaigns in the west; and the securing of the east.

[1] "Niẓām al-Mulk", *Encyc. of Islam* (1st ed.); see also Cahen, "Alp Arslan", *Encyc. of Islam* (2nd ed.).

When Alp-Arslan obtained the throne, the most immediate problem was to secure it against his uncle Qutlumush b. Arslan Isrā'īl. In his claim Qutlumush had voiced the old Turkish idea of seniorate, or the right of the eldest competent male member of the family to have supreme control: "By right, the sultanate should come to me, because my father was the senior and leading member of the tribe."[1] There is no doubt that this argument appealed to many of the Türkmen. Qutlumush raised the standard of revolt at Sāveh in 456/1054, accompanied by his brother and by large numbers of Türkmen. Against him, Niẓām al-Mulk fitted out for the sultan an army whose chief commanders were, as their names show, slave soldiers; prominent among them was the eunuch Sav-Tegin, who became one of Alp-Arslan's most trusted generals. In this way the two opposing sides exemplified the dual aspect of the Saljuq military and ruling institution: on one side there were the free-ranging, independent, tribally organized Türkmen; and on the other was the new, professional army of the sultan, predominantly slave soldiers whose only loyalty was to the sultan, on whom they depended for their salaries or for grants of land. With typical Türkmen disregard for the agricultural economy of the region, Qutlumush devastated the neighbourhood of Ray, but was defeated in battle and was afterwards found dead in mysterious circumstances.[2]

Difficulties also arose in Alp-Arslan's reign when another important member of the Saljuq family, the sultan's own elder brother Qara-Arslan Qavurt, ceased to be content with a subordinate position. Kirmān had formed part of the Būyid territories in southern Iran held by 'Imād al-Dīn Abū Kālījār (see above, p. 39). The origins of Saljuq rule in the province are not very clear, for the accounts in Ibn al-Athīr and in Muḥammad b. Ibrāhīm's special history of the Saljuqs of Kirmān do not coincide in all points, and the opening pages of the latter work are in any case lost. But the Ghaznavid defeat of Dandānqān certainly allowed Saljuq raiders to penetrate southwards through Kūhistān and the towns of Ṭabas and Qā'in in order to attack the oases of Kirmān province. Whether it was Ibrāhīm Ïnal or Qavurt who was attacking Bardasīr, the chief town of Kirmān, in

[1] Ẓahīr al-Dīn Nīshāpūrī, *Saljūq-Nāma*, p. 22.

[2] Bundārī, *Zubdat al-nuṣra*, pp. 28–9; Ẓahīr al-Dīn Nīshāpūrī, *loc. cit.*; Ḥusainī, *Akhbār al-daula*, pp. 30–2; Ibn al-Athīr, *al-Kāmil*, vol. x, pp. 23–4; Ibn Khallikān, *Wafayāt al-a'yān*, vol. III, p. 236; Cahen, "Qutlumush et ses Fils avant l'Asie Mineure", *Der Islam*, pp. 23–4.

434/1042–3 is unclear, but the Būyid vizier Muhadhdhib al-Daula was sent out from Fārs to defend it, and it seems to have remained in Būyid hands for a few years more. However, shortly before Abū Kālījār's death in 440/1048–9, the Dailamī commander of Bardasīr, Bahrām b. Lashkarsitān, delivered the capital into Qavurt's hands.[1] In this way the rule of Qavurt and of his descendants became established in the province for the next 140 years, and until the irruption of the Ghuzz in the latter half of the 6th/12th century, Kirmān enjoyed a period of comparative stability and prosperity—especially since it lay on the overland trade-route from Khurāsān to the Gulf and to the lands farther east. Muḥammad b. Ibrāhīm stresses Qavurt's just rule: the Türkmen were allotted fiefs in Kirmān, but the amīr himself was careful to pasture his own extensive flocks well out in the steppe, where agricultural land would not be damaged. He also sent an expedition against the Kūfīchīs or Qufṣ, the Balūchī mountaineers whose banditry had long made the southern and eastern parts of the province insecure; the Saljuq invasion of Kirmān seems to have given a general stimulus to the eastward migration of the Balūchīs into Makrān and the modern Balūchistān.[2] Qavurt was even strong enough to mount an expedition across the Persian Gulf and seize the former Būyid dependency of Oman from the local Khawārij; it was to remain under Saljuq suzerainty until *c.* 536/1140.[3]

When his father Chaghrï died, Qavurt recognized the succession of Alp-Arslan in the east, and after Toghrïl died and Alp-Arslan came to Kirmān in 456/1064, Qavurt recognized him as supreme Saljuq sultan and gave him his allegiance. This he withdrew three years later, removing his brother's name from the khuṭba.[4] Alp-Arslan then came with an army and restored the status quo, granting Qavurt full forgiveness; yet the latter was never fully reconciled to the exaltation of another man over the whole of the Saljuq family, and when Malik-Shāh took over his father's throne, Qavurt rebelled against the new sultan (see below, pp. 88–9). After the siege of Jīruft in Kirmān in 459/1067, Alp-Arslan's army marched into Fārs, which five years previously had been conquered by Qavurt from the Shabānkāra'ī

[1] Muḥammad b. Ibrāhīm, *Kirmān*, pp. 2–3, cf. Houtsma, *Z.D.M.G.* (1885), pp. 367–8; Ibn al-Athīr, vol. IX, pp. 349–50.

[2] Muḥammad b. Ibrāhīm, pp. 4, 7–8 (cf. Houtsma, *op. cit.* pp. 368–9); R. N. Frye, "Remarks on Baluchi History", *Central Asiatic Journal*, p. 47.

[3] Muḥammad b. Ibrāhīm, pp. 8–10, cf. Houtsma, *op. cit.* pp. 369–70.

[4] Ibn al-Athīr, vol. x, pp. 28, 36–7.

chieftain Faḍlūya, though it had afterwards slipped from Saljuq control. In the course of this campaign in Fārs several fortresses were taken: indeed, the conquest of Iṣṭakhr is said to have given a great fillip to Niẓām al-Mulk's fame. A further campaign against Faḍlūya was required in 461/1069, but this particular menace was now removed by the capture and killing of Faḍlūya and of his brother Ḥasan or Ḥasanūya.[1]

It has been noted that Alp-Arslan never visited Baghdad personally.[2] He was nevertheless concerned to maintain his rights in Iraq, and above all to watch over the Arab amīrs there and ensure that they did nothing more to encourage the Fāṭimids' ambitions in Iraq. The sultan's military representative in the Iraq was *shaḥna*, a position normally given to one of his ghulām commanders. As far as possible, the sultan always appointed a man who was *persona grata* to the 'Abbāsid caliph. Al-Qā'im objected to Ai-Tegin, appointed in 464/1071, because his son had killed one of the caliph's ghulāms; so Alp-Arslan and Niẓām al-Mulk agreed to remove him and substitute Gauhar-Ā'īn, a former ghulām of the Būyid Abū Kālījār.[3] As was customary, administrative and diplomatic contact between the sultanate and caliphate was channelled through the respective viziers. When in 450/1058 Ibn al-Muslima was killed, his successor as vizier to al-Qā'im was the capable and energetic Fakhr al-Daula Muḥammad b. Jahīr, who had formerly served the 'Uqailids, Mirdāsids, and most recently the Marwānid Naṣr al-Daula.[4] Over the next fifteen years Ibn Jahīr strove to maintain the influence of the caliphate in Iraq. By a skilful cultivation of the Arab amīrs, most of whom were Shī'īs, he won their allegiance to the 'Abbāsids. Niẓām al-Mulk was on friendly terms with his opposite number, and in 462/1069–70 his daughter Ṣafiyya was married to Ibn Jahīr's son 'Amīd al-Daula. At the same time he received from the caliph the honorifics *Qiwām al-Dīn* ("Support of Religion") and *Raḍī Amīr al-Mu'minīn* ("Favoured One of the Commander of the Faithful"). Indeed, in 460/1068 al-Qā'im had temporarily dismissed Ibn Jahīr for his subservience to the Saljuqs, "because", in the words of Ibn al-Jauzī, "you have put on robes of honour from 'Aḍud al-Daula

[1] Ibn al-Balkhī, *Fārs-Nāma*, p. 166; Bundārī, *Zubdat al-nuṣra*, pp. 30–1; Ibn al-Athīr, *al-Kāmil*, vol. x, pp. 36–7, 48–9; Bowen, "The Last Buwayhids", *J.R.A.S.* p. 244.

[2] Ibn Khallikān, *Wafayāt al-a'yān*, vol. III, p. 235.

[3] Bundārī, p. 44; Ibn al-Jauzī, IX, pp. 115–16; Ibn al-Athīr, x, pp. 47–8, 200–1.

[4] Bundārī, pp. 24–5; Ibn al-Athīr, vol. x, pp. 14–15; Cahen, "Djahīr (Banū)", *Encyc. of Islam* (2nd ed.).

[i.e. from Alp-Arslan]".[1] The sultan used caliphal support in 458/1066 to make his son Malik-Shāh valī 'ahd; at a ceremony near Marv, the assembled amīrs took an oath of allegiance to Malik-Shāh and his name was placed in the khuṭba. At the same time, Alp-Arslan publicly allotted the governorships of Khwārazm, Khurāsān, the upper Oxus lands, and the Caspian provinces, to several of his brothers, sons, and other relatives. The seal was set on cordial relations with the caliph when in 464/1071–2 Alp-Arslan's daughter was married to al-Qā'im's son and heir, who was later to become Caliph al-Muqtadī.[2]

Saljuq policy in Iraq and the Syrian desert fringes was to maintain the existing power of the Arab amīrs while keeping them under close surveillance. Thus it was from the sultan in the first place that the 'Uqailid Sharaf al-Daula Muslim b. Quraish of Mosul (d. 478/1085) sought the grant of Anbār, Hīt, and other places in central 'Irāq, and only afterwards did he get caliphal confirmation. In Baṣra, the sultan in 459/1067 restored to the governorship and to the tax-farm there the Kurd Tāj al-Mulūk Hazārasp b. Bankīr, and he linked his fortunes to those of the Saljuqs by giving Hazārasp one of his own sisters in marriage. After Hazārasp's death three years later, this same sister was again given in a political marriage, this time to the 'Uqailid Sharaf al-Daula Muslim.[3] Thanks to this policy, Iraq enjoyed a period of tranquillity after the violence of Toghrïl's reign. The Fāṭimids did not dare to interfere there, and their influence also diminished in some parts of the Arabian peninsula. In 462/1070 the sharīf of Mecca, Muḥammad b. Abī Hāshim, came to Alp-Arslan with the news that the khuṭba in Mecca was now being made for the 'Abbāsid caliph and the Saljuq sultan, and no longer for the Fāṭimid al-Mustanṣir; and further, the Shī'ī *adhān* (call to prayer) had been abolished. The sultan attempted to make this *volte-face* permanent by allotting the sharīf a generous pension.[4]

It was his activities in the west, and above all his victory at Malāzgird (Mantzikert), which established Alp-Arslan in the eyes of posterity as a Muslim hero. In some respects this victory was a fortuitous one, for a crusade against the Christians does not appear to have been one of the mainsprings of the sultan's policy. Wittek and Cahen have shown that in dealing with the overrunning of Anatolia at this time,

[1] Bundārī, pp. 34–6; Ibn al-Jauzī, *al-Muntaẓam*, vol. VIII, p. 249; Ibn al-Athīr, vol. X, pp. 39, 41. [2] *Ibid.* pp. 34, 48.

[3] Bundārī, *Zubdat al-nuṣra*, pp. 31, 36–7; Ibn al-Athīr, vol. X, pp. 35, 37, 41.

[4] *Ibid.* p. 41.

we must distinguish clearly between the official policy of the Saljuq sultans and the uncontrolled activities of Türkmen raiders. The moderate, even magnanimous, attitude adopted by Alp-Arslan towards the defeated Byzantine Emperor Romanus Diogenes shows that his most basic policy at this time was essentially one of co-existence between the two great empires, Christian and Islamic. Just as the Og͟huz bands when they first entered K͟hurāsān had been unable to conceive that the formidable G͟haznavid empire might crack under their puny attacks, so the Byzantine empire, which had withstood many Muslim attacks in the past, was regarded by the Saljuqs as ageless and invincible. The Türkmen, on the other hand, sought plunder and pasture for their herds wherever they could find them. They too had no thoughts of overthrowing Byzantine rule in Anatolia, for they were militarily incapable of besieging and taking the Byzantine strongholds there; but their spreading out through the Anatolian countryside inevitably led to the surrender of the Greek cities, which were now encircled and cut off from their rural hinterland. In effect, the Türkmen on the Byzantine and Armenian frontiers in eastern Anatolia swelled the ranks of older Muslim g͟hāzī elements, Arab, Kurdish, and Dailamī—warriors who had long faced their Byzantine counterparts, the *akritai*. With this increase of Turks on the frontiers, the Turkish terms *aqïnjï* (raider) and *uj* (properly extremity, border > fighter on the border) come into use side by side with that of g͟hāzī.[1]

Shortly after his accession, Alp-Arslan, accompanied by his son Malik-S͟hāh and by Niẓām al-Mulk, campaigned in Armenia, capturing Ani from its Byzantine garrison. Gagik-Abas of Kars submitted and the sultan penetrated into Georgia, where he consolidated his influence by marrying a niece of the Georgian King Bagrat IV, but in 460/1068 a further campaign against Georgia was necessary.[2] In 459/1067 Alp-Arslan was in Arrān, where he received the tribute of the S͟haddādid Faḍl II b. S͟hāvur and also of the S͟hīrvān-S͟hāh Fak͟hr al-Dīn Farīburz b. Sallār; in the ensuing years Turkish g͟hulām governors were appointed for the western shores of the Caspian as far north as Darband.[3]

[1] Cf. P. Wittek, "Deux Chapîtres de l'Histoire des Turcs de Roum", *Byzantion*, pp. 285–302; *idem*, *The Rise of the Ottoman Empire* (London, 1938), pp. 16 ff.; Cahen, "La Première Pénétration Turque en Asie-Mineure", *Byzantion*, pp. 5 ff.

[2] Bundārī, *Zubdat al-nuṣra*, p. 31; Ḥusainī, *Ak͟hbār al-daula*, pp. 35–8, 43–6; Ibn al-At͟hīr, *al-Kāmil*, vol. x, pp. 25–8; W. E. D. Allen, *A History of the Gorgian People*, pp. 90–2; Honigmann, *Die Ostgrenze des Byzantinischen Reiches*, pp. 185 ff.; R. Grousset, *Histoire de l'Arménie des Origines à 1071*, pp. 610–16; Minorsky, *Studies in Caucasian History*, pp. 64–7.

[3] Minorsky, *A History of Sharvān and Darband*, pp. 37–8, 41, 66.

Meanwhile, virtually independent Türkmen bands were already raiding far into Anatolia: in 459/1067 Caesarea (Kayseri) in Cappadocia was sacked; in the next year Armorium in Phrygia, and in the next year Iconium (Konya). Despite all this, the Byzantines still occasionally followed their traditional practice of employing predatory bands such as these Türkmen as auxiliaries (*foederati*) against other Türkmen.

The attacks on central Anatolia menaced the Byzantine lines of communication that stretched through the Taurus and Cilicia to their cities of Antioch, Edessa, and Malatya in northern Syria and Diyārbakr. The Emperor Romanus accordingly sent an army to northern Syria, which secured the defence of these cities and then took the offensive against the Muslims: Artāḥ, between Antioch and Aleppo, and Manbij on the Euphrates were both captured, and Aleppo itself was menaced. It is likely that a truce was made in 462/1070 between Alp-Arslan and Romanus, since the sultan now felt free to turn his attention to what had long been a favoured project of his: the expulsion of the Fāṭimids from Syria and even perhaps a march on Egypt. According to two writers, the historian of Aleppo, Ibn al-'Adīm, and the Egyptian Ibn Muyassar, an appeal was made to Alp-Arslan at this time by a certain rebel against the Fāṭimids in Egypt. Yet whatever type of truce may have been made, no real cessation of hostilities in Anatolia was possible, for the sultan had very little control over the activity of the Türkmen there.[1]

In the spring of 463/1071 Alp-Arslan was in northern Syria when he heard the news that Romanus had assembled a vast army at Erzerum and had marched eastwards into Armenia. The sultan was taken by surprise and treated this as a breach of the truce. With wild exaggeration, Muslim and Christian sources variously number the emperor's army at between 200,000 and one million; more reliable sources say that it included Frankish, Russian, Khazar, Pecheneg, Oghuz, and Qïpchaq mercenaries, as well as Greeks and Armenians. The pitched battle which took place at Malāzgird was the first major one that the Turks had ever ventured against a Byzantine army. It ended in disaster for the Greeks, the supreme indignity being the capture of the Basileus by the Muslims. But even in his hour of victory Alp-Arslan did not endeavour to destroy the Byzantine empire. Romanus was allowed to ransom himself, promising tribute and a

[1] Cf. Cahen, "La Campagne de Mantzikert d'après les sources Musulmanes", *Byzantion*, pp. 621–5; *idem*, *Byzantion* (1948), pp. 29–30; Honigmann, *Die Ostgrenze*, pp. 117–22.

marriage alliance, and it is possible that he promised to cede such cities as Malāzgird, Edessa, Antioch, and Manbij; as it was, the deposition and death of Romanus rendered all these provisions void.[1]

The defeat at Malāzgird was a symptom rather than a cause of the Greeks' downfall in eastern Anatolia. In the years just before this, the will to resist among the Byzantine akritai had been weakening, especially as many of these warriors were Armenians, resentful of Byzantine political and ecclesiastical policy in their country; moreover the poor quality of Romanus's army, huge though it may have been in numbers, was reflected in what was at least a trickle of desertions to the enemy. From 464/1072 onwards, eastern and central Anatolia lay open to the Türkmen, who speedily overran all the region except for the strongholds in the Taurus. Alp-Arslan's victory at Malāzgird also meant that, apart from the districts of Tashīr and eastern Siunik', Armenia passed definitely into Muslim hands; and within the next decade or so, the Byzantines, resolutely anti-Armenian to the end, exterminated several survivors of the native Bagratid and Ardzrunid dynasties.[2] Thus in succeeding centuries only the tiny kingdom of Georgia survived as an independent Christian power in the Caucasus.

Alp-Arslan took steps early in his reign to secure his eastern frontiers, where there were old rivals such as the Qarakhānids and Ghaznavids whose attitude might flare up into hostility should a favourable opportunity present itself. The western Qarakhānid khanate of Soghdia and Farghāna was at this time under the rule of Tamghach-Khān Ibrāhīm b. Naṣr (*c.* 444–60/*c.* 1052–68). The historical sources and the "Mirrors for Princes" both portray this khan as a man of outstanding justice and piety: he cultivated the 'ulamā, was careful not to introduce uncanonical taxation, and protected the common people against banditry and exploitation by commercial interests.[3] Already in Toghrïl's lifetime Alp-Arslan had demonstrated by a show of force against the Qarakhānids that his father's old influence along the Oxus valley was to be upheld; now that Alp-Arslan was supreme sultan, he invaded the territories of Tamghach-Khān Ibrāhīm, causing the latter to protest to the caliph about this unprovoked aggression. Over the following years, however, Alp-Arslan adopted a more pacific policy here and

[1] Bundārī, pp. 38–44; Ibn al-Jauzī, vol. VIII, pp. 260–5; Ḥusainī, pp. 46–53; Ibn al-Athīr, vol. x, pp. 44–6; cf. Cahen, *Byzantion* (1934), pp. 627 ff.; Honigmann, *op. cit.* pp. 189–90; Grousset, *op. cit.* pp. 626–9.

[2] Grousset, pp. 616–17, 629–35.

[3] Cf. Barthold, *Turkestan down to the Mongol Invasion*, pp. 311–13.

endeavoured to secure harmony with the Qarakhānids through a series of marriage alliances. He himself married the widowed daughter of Qadïr Khān Yūsuf, formerly ruler of Kāshghar and Khotan; his daughter 'Ā'isha was given to Ibrāhīm's son and successor, Shams al-Mulk Naṣr; and his son Malik-Shāh married another Qarakhānid princess, who eventually gave birth to the future Saljuq Sulṭān Maḥmūd (see below, p. 103).[1]

The links between the two Turkish houses were therefore ostensibly close, though they did not prevent tension from arising at the end of Alp-Arslan's reign between the sultan and Shams al-Mulk Naṣr (460–72/1068–80). In 465/1072 Alp-Arslan crossed the Oxus on a bridge of boats with an army alleged to number 200,000, but this campaign was cut short by his death: he was stabbed by a local castellan whom he had condemned to death. Shams al-Mulk thereupon took the offensive and carried the war over to the Saljuq side of the Oxus. He captured Tirmidh and ejected Ayaz b. Alp-Arslan from Balkh before the new sultan Malik-Shāh could intervene and cause the Qarakhānid forces to retreat.[2] Throughout this period relations with the Ghaznavids were harmonious, and the frontier agreed upon by Chaghrï Beg and Sulṭān Ibrāhīm b. Mas'ūd remained respected.[3]

Apart from dealings with these two great powers, Alp-Arslan had had to contend with a certain amount of unrest and rebelliousness on the eastern fringes of the empire, where some local rulers and governors tried to take advantage of the troubled circumstances surrounding the sultan's accession. In 456/1064 he had to subdue and finally kill the rebellious amīr of Khuttal and the governor of Chaghāniyān (whether these were the descendants of former local rulers or merely nominees of the Saljuqs is unknown), while a revolt of his uncle Fakhr al-Mulk Mūsā Yabghu in Herāt also had to be suppressed.[4] In the following year the sultan undertook an expedition from Marv to Khwārazm and then into the Üst Urt and Qïpchaq steppes, the ancestral home of the Oghuz; and at this time he did in fact take the opportunity of visiting Jand, where Saljuq b. Duqaq was buried. These events are

[1] Ibn al-Athīr, vol. IX, p. 212, vol. X, p. 28; cf. Sachau, *S.B.W.A.W.* (1873); Barthold, *op. cit.* p. 314.

[2] Bundārī, *Zubdat al-nuṣra*, pp. 45–7; Ẓahīr al-Dīn Nīshāpūrī, *Saljūq-Nāma*, pp. 28–9; Ḥusainī, *Akhbār al-daula*, pp. 53–4; Ibn al-Athīr, *al-Kāmil*, vol. X, pp. 49–50; Ibn Khallikān, *Wafayāt al-a'yān*, vol. III, p. 235; Barthold, *op. cit.* pp. 314–15.

[3] Ibn al-Athīr, vol. X, p. 28; Jūzjānī, *Ṭabaqāt-i Nāṣirī*, ed. 'Abd al-Ḥayy Ḥabībī, vol. I, p. 239 (Raverty tr., vol. I, pp. 103–4).

[4] Ibn al-Athīr, vol. X, p. 22.

treated in some detail by Mīrkhwānd, but both the events and the personages involved remain somewhat shadowy and mysterious. It appears that Alp-Arslan was formally recognized in Khwārazm as sultan and that he then left as governor there his son or brother Arslan-Arghun;[1] from Khwārazm he led a punitive campaign against the Qïpchaq, penetrating as far as the Manqïshlaq peninsula on the eastern Caspian shore.[2]

We have seen that when Malik-Shāh was made heir to the throne in 458/1066, Alp-Arslan chose the occasion to redistribute governorships in the east among members of the Saljuq family. According to Ibn al-Athīr, Ṭabaristān was given to Ïnanch Yabghu (? Bïghu), Balkh went to the sultan's brother Sulaimān, Khwārazm to his brother Arslan-Arghun, and Chaghāniyān and Tukhāristān to his brother Ilyās; Marv was given to his youngest son Arslan-Shāh, the district of Bāghshūr (near Marv ar-Rūd) to Mas'ūd b. Er-Tash, and Isfizār to Maudūd b. Er-Tash.[3] That he continued to grant the eastern fringes as appanages for lesser members of the family, despite the opportunities this gave for rebelliousness, seems to show that the sultan was still mindful of traditional obligations to family members; it further seems to imply that he now considered western Iran and Iraq to be the Saljuq empire's centre of gravity and the regions most demanding of his personal presence.

VI. NIẒĀM AL-MULK AND THE ZENITH OF THE GREAT SALJUQ EMPIRE

Jalāl al-Daula Mu'izz al-Dīn Abu'l-Fatḥ Malik-Shāh (465–85/1072–92) continued and in some ways surpassed the triumphs of his father. The lands of the Great Saljuqs were never more extensive than during Malik-Shāh's reign. In the east there was something like a state of equilibrium with the Ghaznavid Sulṭān Ibrāhīm, although the pretensions of the Qarakhānids in Tukhāristān and in the other lands to the south of the Oxus—pretensions which had already caused anxiety to Alp-Arslan—made the north-eastern frontier a certain source of worry in the early part of Malik-Shāh's reign. When internal dissension

[1] On the confusion surrounding this personage, see Cahen, "Arslan-Arghūn", *Encyc. of Islam* (2nd ed.).

[2] Ḥusainī, p. 40; Ibn al-Athīr, vol. x, p. 33; Mīrkhwānd, *Rauḍat al-ṣafā'*, vol. IV, pp. 111–12; Sachau, *S.B.W.A.W.* pp. 313–14.

[3] Ibn al-Athīr, vol. x, p. 34; cf. Ḥusainī, p. 41.

within the Qarakhānid dominions afforded a chance for intervention, the sultan undertook an important campaign into Transoxiana and beyond, carrying Saljuq arms into places where they had never been seen before, such as Talas and Kāshghar. In the north-west, Saljuq troops operated amongst the Muslim amīrs of Mūghān, Arrān, and Shīrvān, and also amongst the Christian peoples of the southern Caucasus. In Anatolia, following Malāzgird and the Muslim conquest of Armenia, Qutlumush's two sons Sulaimān and Manṣūr took advantage of the collapse of the Byzantine *limes* (frontier defence line) to raid as far as the shores of the Aegean. The generally hostile attitude of these two Saljuq princes towards Malik-Shāh, the son of their father's rival and vanquisher, makes it questionable whether the Türkmen conquests in Anatolia were in any measure attachable to or dependent upon the Great Saljuq empire. In the Arab lands south of Anatolia, however, the sultan's direct influence was extended by several means: through the agency of such slave commanders as Aq-Sonqur, Bursuq, and Khumar-Tegin; by Türkmen *begs*, e.g. Artuq and Atsïz b. Uvak; by members of the Saljuq royal family, such as Tutush b. Alp-Arslan; and also by the two Ibn Jahīrs, father and son, who were Arab soldier-officials. These latter extinguished the independence of the Marwānids, whose attitude in the Saljuq-Fāṭimid conflict had been at times ambiguous; in addition they reduced the power of other Arab amīrates such as the 'Uqailids, they mopped up survivals of Greco-Armenian resistance in northern Syria, expelled the lieutenants of the Fāṭimids from the whole of Syria and the greater part of Palestine, and they even undertook successful expeditions into the Arabian peninsula as far as the Yemen in the southwest and al-Aḥsā' in the east.

Such an achievement is an impressive one for a comparatively young man—Malik-Shāh was only thirty-seven when he died—and it contrasts with the disunity and the squabbling amongst the sultan's children after his death in 485/1092. Thereafter, Saljuq power in Iraq and western Īrān was to become increasingly enfeebled. Khurāsān and the east were under the rule of Sanjar, the most capable of Malik-Shāh's sons and the one favoured by a long life, and this region enjoyed the greatest degree of stability and continuity of rule in the first half of the 6th/12th century; yet even here, Sanjar's dominion was to end in tragedy and confusion at the hands of intransigent Türkmen tribesmen.

Malik-Shāh's achievement was by no means a wholly personal one; indeed, the contribution of Vizier Niẓām al-Mulk was even greater than that of his master. Whereas in the years before 465/1072 Niẓām al-Mulk had served men of maturity and experience, such as Chaghrï Beg and Alp-Arslan, now his sultan was a young man of eighteen whom he hoped to control and adapt to his own ideal of a despotic monarch in the Iranian-Islamic tradition. His entire period as vizier to the Saljuq sultans extended over thirty years, not counting his service to the prince Alp-Arslan when Toghrïl was still sultan.[1] His famous boast to Malik-Shāh, made just before his assassination in 485/1092 and when his enemies at court were concerting their plans against him, was tactless but substantially true:

Tell the Sultan, "If you have not already realized that I am your co-equal in the work of ruling, then know that you have only attained to this power through my statesmanship and judgement." Does he not remember when his father was killed, and I assumed responsibility for the conduct of affairs and crushed the rebels who reared their heads, from his own family and from elsewhere, such as so-and-so and so-and-so (and he named a whole group of those who had risen up in revolt)? . . . Tell him that the stability of that regal cap is bound up with this vizierial inkstand, and that the harmony of these two interests is the means of securing all objects sought after and the ultimate cause of all objects gained. If ever I close up this inkstand, that royal power will topple.[2]

Niẓām al-Mulk acted in effect as the *atabeg*, or tutor, of Malik-Shāh. This Turkish title, meaning literally "Father-commander", was not in wide use till after Malik-Shāh's death, when there were several young Saljuq princes who were provided with atabegs (see below, pp. 111–12); but Niẓām al-Mulk himself received the title amongst the epithets bestowed on him at the beginning of Malik-Shāh's reign, and he was usually addressed by the sultan as "Father".[3]

Niẓām al-Mulk directed policy primarily through the Great Dīvān or administrative office (*Dīvān-i Vaẓīr, Dīvān-i Sulṭān*), the executive centre of the state, over which he presided. He had considerable influence within the sultan's standing army and an important voice in the nomination of amīrs for specific campaigns. On occasion he

[1] Ibn al-Athīr, *al-Kāmil,* vol. x, pp. 137–8.

[2] *Ibid.* pp. 138–9; abridged in Bundārī, *Zubdat al-nuṣra,* p. 63, Ẓahīr al-Dīn Nīshāpūrī, *Saljūq-Nāma*, p. 33, Rāvandī, *Rāḥat al-ṣudūr*, p. 134, Ḥusainī, *Akhbār al-daula al-Saljūqiyya*, p. 69, and Ibn al-Jauzī, *al-Muntaẓam*, vol. IX, p. 67.

[3] Cahen has pointed out that according to Ḥusainī (*op. cit.* p. 29), the young Alp-Arslan apparently had an atabeg ("Atabak", *Encyc. of Islam*, 2nd ed.).

would still undertake expeditions himself, but increasing age and the feeling of power which he already derived from being at the centre of things in his dīvān, led him during Malik-Shāh's reign to prefer the role of organizer and diplomat to that of field commander. Either this dīvān, which was normally located in the sultan's capital of Iṣfahān, or else while he was accompanying the monarch on his campaigns and missions, Niẓām al-Mulk supervised the operation of the subordinate departments: those of the *Mustaufī* (Chief Accountant), of the *Munshī'* or *Ṭughrā'ī* (Chief Secretary), of the *'Āriḍ al-Jaish* (Chief of Military Affairs and Organization), and of the *Mushrif* (Chief of Intelligence and Investigation Services). This central bureaucracy, whose five-part division obviously follows that of the Ghaznavids, he succeeded in moulding largely to his own liking. He filled it with officials who were either from his own family or were his protégés and supporters; in many cases the two categories became coterminous through the marriages which he arranged. In the early part of Malik-Shāh's reign two men are specially mentioned in the sources as having aided Niẓām al-Mulk in making the bureaucracy a pliant instrument for the execution of his policy: the *Ṣāḥib Dīwān al-Inshā' wa'l-Ṭughrā* ("Head of the Department of Correspondence and the Seal"), one Kamāl al-Daula Abū Riḍā Faḍlallāh; and the *Ṣāḥib al-Zimām wa'l-Istīfā* ("Head of the Department of Financial Control and Accounting"), a man named Sharaf al-Mulk Abū Sa'd Muḥammad.[1]

Niẓām al-Mulk's own children were a numerous and ambitious clan; Rāvandī numbers his sons at twelve, all of whom, so he says, held some office or other.[2] Certainly we find several of them entrenched in lucrative posts throughout the empire, not only in the central bureaucracy but also in the strategically important provincial governorships, where the vizier required trusty supporters to put his decrees into practice. Shams al-Mulk 'Uthmān was governor of Marv. Jamāl al-Mulk Manṣūr was governor of Balkh till his murder in 475/1082; in Alp-Arslan's times his pride had made him reject his father's request that he should act as vizier to the prince Malik-Shāh. "It is not fitting", he said, "for someone like me to act as vizier to a mere boy."[3] Mu'ayyid al-Mulk 'Ubaidallāh's power and influence were almost as great as

[1] Bundārī, pp. 59 ff.

[2] *Rāḥat al-ṣudūr*, p. 133. According to a report in Mīrkhwānd (*Rauḍat al-ṣafā'*, vol. IV, p. 115), these twelve sons received as much honour in the people's eyes as did the twelve Imāms of the Shī'a.

[3] Bundārī, *Zubdat al-nuṣra*, pp. 73–4; Ibn al-Jauzī, *al-Muntaẓam*, vol. IX, p. 67.

those of his father. At one point Niẓām al-Mulk hoped to impose him on the ʿAbbāsid caliph as his vizier, but al-Muqtadī strenuously objected; eventually Mu'ayyid al-Mulk replaced Kamāl al-Daula as Ṭughrā'ī in the Saljuq administration. In 475/1082–3 Mu'ayyid al-Mulk entered Baghdad from Iṣfahān and assumed the privilege, normally bestowed only by express royal command on the greatest men in the state, of having a salute of drums and military music (*nauba*) playing outside his house at three of the daily prayer times; a handsome payment persuaded him to desist from this. Likewise, when Niẓām al-Mulk's daughter died in 470/1077–8, her father secured for her body the privilege of burial in the grounds of the caliphal palace at Baghdad.[1] It was not surprising that the vizier's opponents accused him and his family of arrogance and of the abuse of political and social power.

In addition to his own family, Niẓām al-Mulk had a numerous following of secretaries and officials who were seeking his patronage, together with a personal household of ghulāms who were said to number several thousand.[2] According to Anushīrvān b. Khālid, parents hastened to send their children to the great vizier's household for their education.[3] For his part, Niẓām al-Mulk was always careful to attract useful, capable men into his service and into the administration, and the power of this retinue is shown by their activities after Niẓām al-Mulk's death. Within a short time his ghulāms had wreaked vengeance on his old rival Tāj al-Mulk Abu'l-Ghanā'im, who was widely suspected of having instigated Niẓām al-Mulk's murder. More important, his descendants played a prominent part in public affairs for at least half a century after his death, many of them acting as viziers and officials for the Saljuq sultans and for the caliphs, despite the fact that only one or two of these officials seem to have had outstanding ability.

Niẓām al-Mulk also tried to buttress the structure of the Saljuq empire, and to counter the splendour and prestige of the Fāṭimid caliphate in Cairo, by encouraging the progress of the Sunnī revival in Iraq and Iran. The sources attribute to him a decisive role as the protagonist of Sunnī orthodoxy, saying that he restored political and social order in Iran by repairing the damage to state and religion wrought by the heretical and tyrannical Būyids. Later in Malik-Shāh's

[1] Bundārī, pp. 52, 60, 73; Ibn al-Athīr, *al-Kāmil*, vol. x, pp. 82–3, 85.

[2] Ibn al-Athīr, vol. x, p. 84; according to Ḥusainī, *Akhbār al-daula*, p. 67, he had over 20,000 ghulāms.

[3] Bundārī, p. 57.

reign, the Ismāʿīlīs or Assassins appeared in several areas of Iran, disturbing in some measure the course of this return to orthodoxy; since several of the Assassin strongholds were in the Alburz mountains, the region in which the province of Dailam lay, it is not unreasonable to see this outbreak of political and religious heterodoxy as a recrudescence of earlier Iranian opposition to the orthodox institutions of the Baghdad caliphate and of Sunnī Islam. However, the Ismāʿīlī movement in Iran never constituted a major threat to the established institutions, and it is likely that Ismāʿīlism's conspiratorial methods, in particular its weapon of political assassination, caused contemporaries to exaggerate its importance. [For a detailed treatment of Ismāʿīlism in Iran, see below, pp. 422–82.]

It seems that Niẓām al-Mulk desired to speed up the provision of educational institutions within the eastern Sunnī world and to make them comparable with those still flourishing in Umayyad Spain and Fāṭimid Egypt. There is some controversy about his exact motives in founding these *madrasas*, or colleges of higher learning, which were named *Niẓāmiyyas* in his honour. Did he seek to create a network of these institutions personally dependent on himself, meaning to further his own political plans; or was his aim the more general one of raising intellectual standards throughout eastern, non-Fāṭimid Islam, with the madrasas fitting into a pattern of state-supported education?[1] The latter view is probably the more likely one in the context of contemporary events. The Sunnī madrasa-building movement had begun in the second half of the 4th/10th century and was in full swing well before Niẓām al-Mulk's time. It was a response first to the challenge of Muʿtazilī thought, and subsequently to the Fāṭimid institutions for training Shīʿī *dāʿīs* or propagandists: i.e. the Azhar mosque of the Fāṭimid general Jauhar and the Caliph al-Muʿizz (founded in 359/970), the *Dār al-Ḥikma* ("House of Learning") of the Caliph al-Ḥākim (founded in 395/1005), and the various local *dār al-daʿwas*, or rallying-places and centres for propaganda. To implement Niẓām al-Mulk's administrative policies throughout the Saljuq empire required the training of reliable personnel as secretaries and officials, and herein probably lies the key

[1] For these two views, see the articles of G. Makdisi, "Muslim Institutions of Learning in Eleventh-century Baghdad", *B.S.O.A.S.* pp. 1–56, and A. L. Tibawi, "Origin and Character of *al-Madrasah*", *B.S.O.A.S.* pp. 225–38. Tibawi's standpoint is nearer to that of the earlier, classic writers on the subject: see Goldziher, "Education—Muslim", *Encyc. of Religion and Ethics;* and Pedersen, "Masdjid", *Encyc. of Islam* (1st ed.). On the madrasa under the Saljuqs see also below, pp. 214–17 and 289–90.

to his motives. Moreover, not only was madrasa education free, as of course it was in other educational institutions, but generous living allowances were allotted to students at the Niẓāmiyyas.[1]

Tāj al-Dīn al-Subkī, the 8th/14th century compiler of a biographical dictionary of Shāfiʿī scholars, attributes to Niẓām al-Mulk the foundation of a madrasa in every important city of Iraq and Iran, and he specifically mentions nine of them: the ones at Baghdad and Nīshāpūr (the two most famous Niẓāmiyyas), and those at Balkh, Herāt, Marv, Āmul in Gurgān, Iṣfahān, Baṣra, and Mosul.[2] This prominence of Khurāsānian cities may not be fortuitous. During the 5th/11th century Sunnī scholarship in Khurāsān was at its most brilliant. It had behind it a long tradition of political and cultural orthodoxy, stretching back through the Ghaznavids and Sāmānids to the Ṭāhirids, whereas central and western Iran were for a long time in the Saljuq period still politically and religiously suspect because of their association with heterodox Dailamī dynasties. Niẓām al-Mulk regarded the appointment of suitable scholars to teach at his Niẓāmiyyas as a personal responsibility. When the Baghdad Niẓāmiyya opened in 459/1067, he took considerable pains to secure for it the scholar Abū Isḥāq al-Shīrāzī, and later, in 484/1091, he brought the theologian and philosopher Abū Ḥāmid al-Ghazālī to lecture there when the latter was only thirty-three and little known outside his native Khurāsān. On Malik-Shāh's first visit to Baghdad in 479–80/1081, after the conclusion of the campaign in northern Syria, Niẓām al-Mulk personally lectured on *ḥadīth* or tradition at his madrasa and dictated to the students there.[3]

The use of scholars from Khurāsān is bound up with another controversial aspect of Niẓām al-Mulk's educational policy: the degree to which he specifically hoped to further his own Shāfiʿī law school and the Ashʿarī kalām. Many of the sources may have overemphasized the Shāfiʿī and Ashʿarī nature of the teaching at the Niẓāmiyyas. Before the great vizier achieved such power in the Saljuq state, these doctrines were very suspect to men such as Toghrïl and

[1] Subkī, *Ṭabaqāt al-shāfiʿiyya al-kubrā*, vol. III, p. 137, rightly refutes the assertion made in many sources, that the great vizier was the first person to build madrasas; but, says Subkī, he may have been the first to assign allowances to the students. However, even this is dubious.

[2] See his article on Niẓām al-Mulk, *op. cit.* vol. III, pp. 135–45.

[3] Ibn al-Jauzī, *al-Muntaẓam*, vol. IX, pp. 36, 55; Ibn al-Athīr, *al-Kāmil*, vol. X, p. 104; Subkī, vol. IV, pp. 103–4; cf. W. Montgomery Watt, *Muslim Intellectual, a Study of al-Ghazali* (Edinburgh, 1963), pp. 22–3.

his minister Kundurī;[1] and Niẓām al-Mulk's support for the doctrines did not guarantee their acceptance and recognition, especially outside Khurāsān. In Baghdad and the western provinces they were anathema to conservative religious circles, Ḥanafī as well as Ḥanbalī, who regarded them as alien, Khurāsānian imports. If the Niẓāmiyyas were institutions for the propagation of Shāfi'ism and Ash'arism, they failed in Iraq and western Iran. Although the 'Abbāsid caliphs were Shāfi'īs, the Saljuq sultans themselves remained staunch Ḥanafīs, and the fervent Ḥanafī Rāvandī, who wrote his history of the Saljuqs in the opening years of the 13th century, still couples together for denunciation the Rāfiḍīs (i.e. the extremist Shī'īs and Ismā'īlīs) and the Ash'arīs. 'Imād al-Dīn stresses the violent Ḥanafī partisanship shown by several of Sulṭān Mas'ūd b. Muḥammad's ghulām amīrs. Between the years 536/1141–2 and 542/1147–8 he speaks of the persecution and expulsion of Shāfi'ī scholars by Saljuq governors and commanders in Baghdad, Ray, and Iṣfahān, where some Shāfi'īs found it politic to change to Ḥanafism.[2] In Baghdad the Niẓāmiyya declined in the 6th/12th century, and it was the Ḥanbalī colleges which were intellectually the most vital in Baghdad at this time. But perhaps the most significant piece of evidence which we have against any undue partisanship by Niẓām al-Mulk is his soothing pronouncement, as reported by the fiercely Ḥanbalī Ibn al-Jauzī, when the Ḥanbalīs of Baghdad were protesting against the public teaching of Ash'arism:

> The Sultan's policy and the dictates of justice require us not to incline to any one rite [*madhhab*] to the exclusion of others; we aim at strengthening orthodox belief and practice [*al-sunan*] rather than at fanning sectarian strife. We have built this madrasa [i.e. the Niẓāmiyya] only for the protection of scholars and in the public interest, and not to cause controversy and dissension.[3]

Niẓām al-Mulk was not by any means the sole person to busy himself with founding madrasas. Makdisi has drawn up an impressive list of the Ḥanafī, Shāfi'ī, and Ḥanbalī colleges which were flourishing in Baghdad at this time, and he has pointed out that the madrasa built around the shrine of the Imām Abū Ḥanīfa (this was built in 457–9/1065–7 under the authority of Alp-Arslan's mustaufī, Sharaf al-Mulk Abū Sa'd Muḥammad) was doubtless of equal importance to the

[1] Kundurī's hatred for and persecution of the Ash'arīs are stressed in several of the sources, e.g. in Ibn Khallikān, *Wafayāt al-a'yān*, vol. III, pp. 297–8.

[2] Bundārī, *Zubdat al-nuṣra*, pp. 193–4, 220–1; Rāvandī, *Rāḥat al-ṣudūr*, pp. 30–2.

[3] Ibn al-Jauzī, vol. VIII, p. 312.

Niẓāmiyya, though less publicized in the sources.[1] Niẓām al-Mulk's example stimulated other leading figures to found educational institutions; in 480–2/1087–9 his own great enemy, the mustaufī Tāj al-Mulk Abu'l-Ghanā'im, founded a Shāfi'ī madrasa in Baghdad, the *Tājiyya*, where Abū Bakr al-Shāshī and Abū Ḥāmid's brother Abu'l-Futūḥ al-Ghazālī both taught.[2]

Despite his commanding position in the Saljuq state, Niẓām al-Mulk's authority did not go unchallenged. His arrogant trust in his own powers and indispensability did not endear him to other courtiers or even to the sultan himself, once he had outgrown his initial dependence on the vizier. Nor was Niẓām al-Mulk without enemies within the Saljuq administration itself, in large measure because of his partisanship and his way of pushing his own relatives and protégés. The officials of the bureaucracy had entered their profession in the expectation of a reasonable rotation of offices in which persons of merit would have a fair chance of obtaining the most coveted and lucrative posts, such as the directorship of the central Dīvāns and of the provincial administrative organs. Niẓām al-Mulk's long tenure of office, together with his control of so much of the stream of patronage, upset these expectations; at the best of times not everyone could be satisfied, but Niẓām al-Mulk now stood as a tangible target for frustrated and ambitious rivals. On the whole, his firm policy and his emphasis on military preparedness made him popular in the army, but it was natural that those commanders close to the sultan or personally attached to him should come to share Malik-Shāh's restiveness.

For the first seven years of the sultan's reign, the authority of Niẓām al-Mulk had gone unchallenged; then in 472/1079–80 two of Malik-Shāh's slave generals precipitated a major crisis by their act of defiance of the vizier's power. The shaḥna of Baghdad, Sa'd al-Daula Gauhar-Ā'īn, and the governor of Fārs and Khūzistān, Najm al-Daula Khumar-Tegin al-Sharābī, were Niẓām al-Mulk's deadly enemies, and together killed one of his protégés, Ibn 'Allān, the Jewish tax-farmer of Baṣra, and despoiled him of his wealth. The sultan sought the vizier's pardon but no retribution was exacted, which showed that the latter's partisans were not personally above the law.[3] In the next year Malik-Shāh insisted, against Niẓām al-Mulk's advice, on dismissing from the army

[1] *B.S.O.A.S.* (1961), pp. 17–44; Ibn al-Athīr, vol. x, p. 23.
[2] *al-Kāmil*, vol. x, pp. 120, 147; Ibn al-Jauzī, ix, pp. 38, 46.
[3] *al-Muntaẓam*, vol. viii, p. 323; Ibn al-Athīr, vol. x, p. 75.

7,000 Armenian mercenaries (see below, p. 81). In an effort to counter the vizier's influence, he began to encourage the latter's opponents in the administration, and two rival parties now emerged.

The central figure in the opposition was Tāj al-Mulk Abu'l-Ghanā'im Marzbān b. Khusrau Fīrūz, who came from a vizierial family in Fārs. Through the patronage of the slave general Sav-Tegin he had risen in royal favour, becoming successively vizier to the sultan's male children (known as *maliks*), then treasurer, overseer of the palace buildings, and finally head of the *Dīwān al-Inshā' wa'l-Ṭughrā*. At his side were other high officials: first the son of Kamāl al-Daula Abū Riḍā, the Sayyid al-Ru'asā' Abu'l-Maḥāsin Muḥammad, hostile to Niẓām al-Mulk even though he was the vizier's son-in-law;[1] next, 'Amīd al-Daula Ibn Bahmanyār, vizier to the governor of Fārs, Khumar-Tegin; and finally the 'Āriḍ Sadīd al-Mulk Abu'l-Ma'ālī al-Mufaḍḍal, one of Tāj al-Mulk's protégés. Ibn Bahmanyār tried in 473/1080–1 to procure the poisoning of Niẓām al-Mulk, but he failed and was blinded by the vizier.[2] Another manifestation of the feeling against Niẓām al-Mulk was the circulation at court of satirical poetry and slanderous stories aimed at him and his sons. One of Malik-Shāh's court jesters, Ja'farak, had been active in this work, and in retaliation Jamāl al-Mulk al-Manṣūr b. Niẓām al-Mulk, governor of Balkh, came in a rage to Iṣfahān in 475/1082–3 and tore out the jester's tongue, killing him in the process. Malik-Shāh made no open protest, but he had the civil governor of Khurāsān, Abū 'Alī, secretly poison Jamāl al-Mulk at Nīshāpūr; he then hypocritically commiserated with Niẓām al-Mulk.[3]

Where Ibn Bahmanyār had failed to secure the vizier's downfall, the Sayyid al-Ru'asā' Abu'l-Maḥāsin, one of the sultan's intimates, now tried, accusing Niẓām al-Mulk of amassing wealth and offices for his family. The vizier did not deny this, but retorted that these were the just rewards for his service to three generations of Saljuq rulers; that the thousands of Turkish ghulāms in his service added to the sultan's military potential; and that much of his wealth was expended on pious and charitable works which redounded equally to the sultan's glory. Malik-Shāh did not feel able to withstand the power of Niẓām al-Mulk's ghulāms and the general support for him within the Saljuq army.[4] He let Abu'l-Maḥāsin be blinded and imprisoned, while the

[1] See above, p. 69.
[2] Bundārī, *Zubdat al-nuṣra*, pp. 59–62; Ibn al-Jauzī, vol. VIII, p. 330.
[3] Bundārī, pp. 73–4; Ibn al-Jauzī, vol. IX, p. 5; Ibn al-Athīr, vol. X, pp. 79–80.
[4] Cf. Ḥusainī, *Akhbār al-daula*, p. 67.

latter's father Kamāl al-Daula lost to Niẓām al-Mulk's son Mu'ayyid al-Mulk his office of Ṭughrā'ī (478/1083–4).[1]

In this way Niẓām al-Mulk surmounted a prolonged period of crisis: but opposition would again build up towards the end of his life, this time centred round Tāj al-Mulk and the sultan's first wife, the Qarakhānid princess Jalāliyya Khatun or Terken Khatun (usually spelt "Turkān" in the sources), whom he had married in 456/1064.[2] For although Niẓām al-Mulk achieved a dominant position in the administration, he never enjoyed equal influence at the court (*dargāh*). It is for this reason that in his *Siyāsat-Nāma* much is said about how the sovereign should comport himself and how the court institutions and officials should be organized to serve the ideal of a despotic state, but there is little about the procedures of the dīvāns, which the vizier had already largely moulded to his own satisfaction. Further, the vizier did not consider that the Saljuq court was organized with requisite strictness and care for protocol, especially in comparison with the Ghaznavid court; nor was the sultan distant and awe-inspiring enough. Niẓām al-Mulk expatiates on such topics as the arrangement of royal drinking sessions, the need to keep an open table and thus maintain traditions of hospitality, and the creation of a proper circle of *nadīms*, or boon companions, around the ruler. Offices vital for the maintenance of order and discipline at court and within the empire at large have been allowed to lapse, he alleges.[3] The fearsome *Amīr-i Ḥaras* (Captain of the Guard), who maintained discipline through his force of lictors or club-bearers, has lost importance; the *Vakīl-i Khāṣṣ* (intendant of the court and of the sultan's private domains) has declined in status. The court ghulāms, who perform many personal services for the sultan—one is the armour-bearer, another the keeper of the wardrobe, another the cup-bearer, etc.—are no longer adequately trained. Worst of all, Alp-Arslan has allowed the *Barīd* (intelligence network), which Niẓām al-Mulk considers one of the pillars of the despotic state, to decay, on the grounds that it engendered an atmosphere of mistrust and suspicion amongst friend and foe alike.[4]

Niẓām al-Mulk is further apprehensive about the relationship between

[1] Bundārī, pp. 60–1; Ibn al-Jauzī, vol. IX, pp. 6–7; Ibn al-Athīr, vol. X, p. 85.

[2] See above, section v, p. 65.

[3] *Siyāsat-Nāma*, chs. xvii, xxix, xxxv (tr. H. Darke, *The Book of Government or Rules for Kings*, pp. 92–4, 122–3, 127–30).

[4] *Siyāsat-Nāma*, chs. x, xiii, xvi, xxvii, xxxix (Darke tr., pp. 74–5, 78 ff., 92, 105 ff., 135); Bundārī, *Zubdat al-nuṣra*, p. 67; cf. Barthold, *Turkestan down to the Mongol Invasion*, p. 306.

the dargāh and the dīvāns, and concerned lest the court should interfere in the mechanism of administration. Thus he says the sultan's nadīms should never be allowed to hold official posts; letters sent directly from the court to the dīvāns should be as few as possible; only in emergencies should ghulāms be used as court messengers, and especial care should be taken with verbal commands from the sovereign, their transmission supervised and their subject matter checked before they are executed.[1]

Niẓām al-Mulk's position *vis-à-vis* the sultan was thus to some extent unsatisfactory, and his influence at the subordinate households of the sultan's wives and those of the princes (*maliks*) was still weaker. Terken Khatun's household became the focus of opposition, for Tāj al-Mulk was also her personal intendant (*vakīl*). The vizier doubtless had Terken Khatun in mind when in the *Siyāsat-Nāma* he denounced the malevolent influence of women at court, citing their misleading advice to the ruler and their susceptibility to promptings from their attendants and eunuchs.[2] Terken Khatun's son Dā'ūd had been his father's favourite, but he died in 474/1082. Six years later Malik-Shāh had caliphal approval when he proclaimed as heir another of her sons, Abū Shujā' Aḥmad, and gave him a resplendent string of honorifics: *Malik al-Mulūk* ("King of Kings"), *'Aḍud al-Daula* ("Strong Arm of the State"), *Tāj al-Milla* ("Crown of the Religious Community"), and *'Uddat Amīr al-Mu'minīm* ("Protecting Force of the Commander of the Faithful"); but in the following year he too died. After these disappointments it was not surprising that Terken Khatun wanted to promote the succession of her third son Maḥmūd (b. 480/1087), despite the fact that he was the youngest of all the possible candidates. Berk-Yaruq, Malik-Shāh's son by the Saljuq princess Zubaida Khatun (she was the daughter of Yāqūtī b. Chaghrī Beg), had been born in 474/1081, and there were also two younger sons, Muḥammad and Sanjar, born of a slave wife in 474/1082 and 477/1084 respectively.[3] Niẓām al-Mulk and much of the army supported Berk-Yaruq because he was the eldest and, so far as could be seen, the most capable claimant. There were, however, further collateral members of the Saljuq family who thought that they had a claim to the succession, and on Malik-Shāh's death there was to be a period of civil war and confusion before Berk-Yaruq established his right to the throne.

[1] *Siyāsat-Nāma*, chs. xi, xii, xv, xvii (Darke tr., pp. 75–7, 91–4); cf. Barthold, *op. cit.* pp. 308–9.

[2] Ch. xlii (Darke tr., p. 185).

[3] Cf. İ. Kafesoğlu, *Sultan Melikşah devrinde Büyük Selçuklu imparatorluğu*, pp. 200–1.

Despite the ideals of men like Niẓām al-Mulk, the constitution of the Saljuq empire remained at this time far from monolithic. Malik-Shāh called himself *Sulṭān-i A'ẓam*, "Supreme Ruler", but the title of sultan was gradually adopted by other members of the family, in particular by Sulaimān b. Qutlumush in Rūm, who was, as we have seen, on cool terms with Malik-Shāh and who acted as a virtually independent sovereign. Normally the Saljuq princes below the supreme sultan were known by the titles of *malik* (ruler) or simply *amīr* (prince, commander).[1] We have to conceive of the Saljuq empire as a series of political groupings rather than as a unitary state. The most extensive and powerful grouping was that surrounding Malik-Shāh himself, with his power centred on Iṣfahān and exercised immediately over central and western Iran, Iraq, and Khurāsān. But beyond this his direct influence diminished. On the fringes of Iraq and Syria several Arab amirates were his tributaries and their functions were to repel Fāṭimid influence in the Syrian desert and to supply troops for the sultan's army. In the mountainous interiors of Fārs and Kurdistān, Kurdish tribes such as the Shabānkāra enjoyed a large degree of autonomy, and their dislike of outside control made them a frequent source of trouble to the sultans.

In the frontier areas of Āzarbāījān, the Caucasus, Armenia, Anatolia, Khwārazm, and the eastern fringes of Khurāsān, Saljuq influence was upheld by the Saljuq princes and governors and also by Türkmen begs.[2] To the Türkmen tribesmen the sultan in Iṣfahān was a very remote figure, and it was natural that their first allegiance should be given to their own tribal chiefs who were there with them. The begs themselves regarded the sultan more as a supreme tribal khan than as an autocratic sovereign. For the three generations down to Berk-Yaruq the sultanate had descended from father to son, but in the eyes of Türkmen leaders and even of many members of the Saljuq family, this fact did not establish a precedent. At times of stress and crisis, tribal beliefs about succession—e.g. the idea of a division of the family patrimony, and the traditional supremacy of the eldest capable male in the princely family—came to the surface. On Malik-Shāh's death, Berk-Yaruq had to contend not only with the claims of his half-brother Maḥmūd, but also with the pretensions of his maternal uncle Ismā'īl b. Yāqūtī and of his paternal uncles Tutush and Arslan-Arghun.

[1] Cf. M. F. Sanaullah, *The Decline of the Saljūqid Empire*, pp. 1–2; Kafesoğlu, *op. cit.* p. 143.
[2] Cf. Kafesoğlu, pp. 159–63.

Many old Turkish traditions and practices were still of significance during Malik-Shāh's reign, although this is frequently obscured by the exclusively Arabic and Iranian nature of the historical sources. For example, on his death-bed Alp-Arslan had recommended that his brother Qavurt should marry his widow, according to the Turkish levirate; the purpose of this custom was to keep wealth within the family (and perhaps, in this case, to prevent undue fragmentation of the empire which Alp-Arslan had assembled).[1] Again, the early sultans, from Toghrïl to Malik-Shāh, kept up the practice of giving regular feasts (*shölen*), just like those which tribal leaders held for their retainers. Malik-Shāh gave one in his palace each Friday, where, amongst others, scholars and theologians came and held disputations. On the other hand, he neglected to give the customary banquets for the Chigil tribesmen of the Qarakhānid forces at Samarqand and Uzkand whilst on his Transoxianan campaign of 482/1089, and his consequent loss of prestige is chided by the *Siyāsat-Nāma*.[2]

Much attention had therefore still to be given to the claims of the Türkmen of the empire, who were established in those regions of Īrān suitable for pastoral nomadism, i.e. northern Khurāsān, Gurgān and Dihistān; Āzarbāījān, Arrān, and parts of Kurdistān and Luristān. One would not expect that Niẓām al-Mulk, the supreme exponent of the Iranian tradition of order and hierarchy in the state, would have much sympathy with the turbulent and non-assimilable Türkmen. Yet in the *Siyāsat-Nāma* he recognizes that they have legitimate claims upon the dynasty: in the early days of the Saljuq sultanate, he says, they were its military support, and they are of the same racial stock as the sultans.[3] It is likely that as early as Malik-Shāh's reign the fiscal agents of the central administration were trying to extend their operations into the outlying tribal areas. Furthermore, the sultan was now established at Iṣfahān, not at Nīshāpūr, Marv, or Ray, and therefore he was much occupied with events in 'Irāq and northern Syria. Because he was less accessible to the Türkmen, their just complaints of encroachments on their rights had little chance of being heard at court. This was to be demonstrably true in Sanjar's reign (511–52/1118–57).

[1] Ibn al-Athīr, *al-Kāmil*, vol. x, p. 52; Barhebraeus, *Chronography*, p. 224; cf. Kafesoğlu, *op. cit.* p. 17 n. 30.

[2] Ch. xxxv (Darke tr., pp. 127–8); cf. I. H. Uzunçarşīlī, *Osmanlī devleti teşkilâtīna medhal* (Istanbul, 1941), pp. 33–4; Kafesoğlu, *op. cit.* pp. 137–8.

[3] Ch. xxvi (Darke tr., p. 105).

Militarily the sultan no longer depended primarily on the Türkmen bands. Continuity in military and political affairs required a permanent, professional force. The empires of Alp-Arslan and Malik-Shāh could not have held together on the deaths of those sovereigns without a loyal core of permanent troops and slaves, directed on the first occasion by Niẓām al-Mulk and on the second by his sons and retainers. The constitution of the army now approximated more to the Ghaznavid pattern.[1] There was in the standing army a nucleus of either ghulāms or slave troops, and the rest were mercenaries. Both groups were drawn from various nationalities, including Turks, Armenians, Greeks, Arabs, and Slavs; Niẓām al-Mulk especially commended the employment of Dailamīs, Khurāsānīs, Georgians, and Shabānkāra'ī Kurds. This army was normally stationed in the capital, and its commanders were directly under the sultan's orders; according to Rāvandī, the number of cavalrymen was not allowed to fall below 46,000.[2]

The ghulām commanders were extensively used by the sultan for personal service in the palace and for such administrative posts as provincial governorships; and the course of events during Malik-Shāh's reign amply demonstrates that, in contrast to the rebelliousness of certain members of the Saljuq family, the faithfulness of the ghulāms towards their master rarely faltered. The sources are not very explicit, but it is probable that the Saljuq maliks in their appanages, as well as the slave generals who were detailed for provincial governorships, also had households of ghulāms and permanent forces of their own. The *Siyāsat-Nāma* advises the great men of state to expend their wealth on military equipment and the purchase of ghulāms rather than on luxury articles for consumption; and we have seen that the vizier himself justified his extensive following of personal ghulāms by the plea that the sultan's general striking power was thereby increased (see p. 75 above).[3]

The maintenance of a standing army was naturally expensive. Reliance on a professional army instead of on tribesmen or local levies has in the course of human history generally meant a rise in state expenditure, resulting in fresh taxation and an increase in the central power of the state. Though Malik-Shāh must have welcomed such an accession of power, he was seized at times with desires for economy,

[1] For this last, see Bosworth, "Ghaznevid Military Organisation", *Der Islam*, pp. 37–77.

[2] *Siyāsat-Nāma*, ch. xxiv (Darke tr., pp. 103–4); Rāvandī, p. 131.

[3] *Siyāsat-Nāma*, ch. xxxi (Darke tr., p. 124); cf. Kafesoğlu, *op. cit.* pp. 155–9.

feeling perhaps that the burden was excessive, and that troops could safely be dismissed in the peaceful intervals between campaigns. Against this, Niẓām al-Mulk advocated a permanently high level of expenditure on the army, believing this to be the prime buttress of royal power, and he regarded projects for economies as pernicious. At the beginning of Malik-Shāh's reign the vizier had increased the soldiers' allowances by 700,000 dīnārs in order to secure their loyalty against possible rivals for the succession. In 473/1080–1, however, the sultan reviewed the army at Ray and, in the teeth of the vizier's opposition, discharged from it thousands of Armenian mercenaries. Niẓām al-Mulk expostulated:

There are no secretaries, merchants, tailors, or craftsmen of any kind amongst these persons—the only profession they have is soldiering. If they are discharged, we can never be sure that they will not set up some person from amongst their own number and make him Sultan. We shall have to deal with them, and until we overcome them, we shall expend several times more than we normally allot for their salaries.

The sultan would not listen, and the unemployed troops went off to Pūshang and joined his brother Tekish, who used them in a rebellion against Malik-Shāh.[1] Again, towards the end of the reign someone at court, probably from the circle of Tāj al-Mulk and Terken Khatun, suggested to Malik-Shāh that because of the general peace then prevailing, the greater part of the standing army could be dismissed and its numbers thereby cut from 400,000 to 70,000. The vizier denounced this project by saying that it would create 330,000 enemies for the sultan, stop the empire's momentum of expansion, and reduce the kingdom to a state of defencelessness.[2]

The standing army was supported partly by payments in cash or kind, and partly by revenues from lands or fiefs (*iqṭa*'*s*) assigned to the soldiers. The chapter of the *Siyāsat-Nāma*, in which Niẓām al-Mulk asserts the necessity of having reserves of cash to pay those soldiers and ghulāms who do not have iqṭā's; he also points to the fact that both systems exist side by side.[3] Thus it is inaccurate to say that pay-

[1] Ibn al-Athīr, vol. x, pp. 52, 76.

[2] *Siyāsat-Nāma*, ch. xli (Darke tr., pp. 170–1). There is a disparity between the vizier's figure for the army and that given by Rāvandī, but the higher figure may perhaps be a grand total that includes provincial levies, Türkmen, and other troops outside the core of the standing army.

[3] Ch. xxiii (Darke tr., pp. 102–3). On the complex question of iqṭā's under the Būyids and Saljuqs, see Barthold, *Turkestan*, pp. 307–8; Cahen, "L'Évolution del'Iqta' du IXe au XIIIe Siècle", *Annales: Économies, Sociétés, Civilisations*, pp. 32 ff.; A. K. S. Lambton, *Landlord and Peasant in Persia*, pp. 49–76.

ment through fiefs was universal in the Saljuq empire at this time. The central treasury, which held large reserves of cash and treasure, was always sought by claimants to the throne whenever a sultan died; Tāj al-Mulk and Terken Khatun secured it in 485/1092 and used it to buy military support for Maḥmūd's candidature (see below, p. 103).[1] The system of iqṭā's was certainly not invented by Niẓām al-Mulk, despite the assertions of such authorities as 'Imād al-Dīn and al-Ḥusainī. The only novelty in the vizier's use of the system appears to be that mentioned by Rāvandī, namely, that he allotted to each soldier "grants of taxation" in various provinces of the empire so that wherever a soldier was campaigning, he would have at hand some means of support.[2]

It has been stressed that the so-called Empire of the Great Saljuqs, far from being a homogeneous, centralized political entity, was really an assemblage of provinces that differed in their geography, their social systems, and historical backgrounds. In the case of the iqṭā' system, the distinction between the old Būyid lands in the west and the old Ghaznavid ones in the east is significant. Amongst the Būyids and amongst the Ḥamdānids in al-Jazīreh and northern Syria, the main prop of the military regime had been a system of grants of taxation issued to each soldier—theoretically for life only—and collected from the peasants by the fiscal agents of the non-resident grantees (this is the type of fief which the jurist al-Māwardī calls *iqṭā'āt al-istighlāl*, or assignments of revenue for living-allowances). This system of iqṭā's was taken over unchanged by the Saljuqs in the western Iranian lands, and it is this one which Niẓām al-Mulk discusses in the *Siyāsat-Nāma*. His chief concern here is to guard against abuses by the fief-holders (*muqṭa's*) and to prevent the land thus granted from slipping out of the state's control. Consequently, he asserts the sultan's ultimate ownership of all land, perhaps in accordance with the Sassanian idea of the ruler's absolute ownership of his kingdom, or perhaps with the aim of extending the ruler's authority over the peasants and thus protecting them from any arbitrariness by the fief-holders. Other safeguards suggested by the vizier are that the peasants should have free access to the court; that the muqṭa' should collect no more than the sum specified, and only at the appropriate time in the agricultural year; and

[1] Ibn al-Athīr, *al-Kāmil*, vol. x, pp. 142, 145.

[2] Bundārī, *Zubdat al-nuṣra*, p. 58; Ḥusainī, *Akhbār al-daula*, p. 68; Rāvandī, *Rāḥat al-sudūr*, p. 131.

that fiefs should be changed round every three years to avoid the perpetuation of abuses.[1]

In this system the fief-holders tended to acquire direct rights to exploit the estates granted to them; however, there also existed pure grants of taxed revenue, which carried no rights over the tax-paying land. In 457/1065, in exchange for the fiefs of Qum and Kāshān, Alp-Arslan granted to the Būyid Abū 'Alī Fanā-Khusrau b. Abī Kālījār 50,000 dīnārs from the taxes of Baṣra, together with the right of residing there but with no further privileges. Al-Ḥusainī says that when Niẓām al-Mulk paid the soldiers' allowances of 1,000 dīnārs each, half of this was charged to the revenues of Samarqand (from whose Qarakhānid ruler the Saljuqs drew tribute) and half to the revenues of Anatolia, which again was not under the direct control of the sultan. This report may well be exaggerated, probably to emphasize the extent of the Saljuq empire and the careful control which the vizier kept over it; but it does show that money payments could be assigned where there was no question of tenurial rights involved.[2] [For more on the iqṭa's, see chapter 2, pp. 230 ff.]

The position was different in Khurāsān and in the marches along the Atrak, Murghāb, and upper Oxus. As Niẓām al-Mulk notes, "former kings", i.e. the Sāmānids and Ghaznavids, did not generally give land-grants to their soldiers: such factors as the economic richness of Khurāsān and the proximity of India as an inexhaustible source of plunder enabled them to pay their troops at stipulated points of the year in cash as well as kind.[3] It is true that the concepts of the fief and of commendation by the weak to the strong (*taljī'a*) were known in the east, for the explanation of their technical terminology is given in al-Khuwārizmī's encyclopaedia of the sciences, the *Mafātīḥ al-'ulūm* (written *c.* 367/977).[4] But their occurrence was exceptional. Under the Saljuqs Khurāsān remained what it had always been, a border land; now, however, it looked out upon the Saljuqs' rivals, the Qarakhānids and Ghaznavids, and it formed a corridor through which Türkmen from Central Asia passed to the west. Like Āzarbāījān in the north-west—also a frontier march, to which similar considerations applied—

[1] *Siyāsat-Nāma*, chs. v, xxxvii (Darke tr., pp. 33 ff., 152) cf. Lambton, *op. cit.* pp. 66–7.

[2] Sibṭ b. al-Jauzī, *Mir'āt al-Zamān*, quoted by Bowen, *J.R.A.S.* (1929), pp. 243–4; Husainī, p. 68. The well-known story that Niẓām al-Mulk made financial drafts on Antioch in order to pay the boatmen who ferried Malik-Shāh's army across the Oxus, clearly has a similar aim of vaunting the extent of the empire.

[3] *Siyāsat-Nāma*, ch. xxiii (Darke tr., p. 103); cf. Bosworth, *Der Islam* (1960), pp. 71 ff.

[4] Ed. G. van Vloten, pp. 60, 62.

Khurāsān was peopled extensively with Türkmen pastoralists. They could not be fitted into the Būyids' static framework of fiefs, and their interspersion among the sedentary Tājīk agricultural population created many problems for the central financial system. Instead of fiefs, the nomads had been granted collective grazing rights since Ghaznavid times, and in the Saljuq period these rights provided the livelihood and maintenance of the Türkmen. Furthermore the Saljuq military organization, despite increasing emphasis on professionalism, still gave these Türkmen a significant role to play. Kafesoğlu has shown that outside Iran and Iraq, the majority of new territories added to the Saljuqs' empire or sphere of influence were conquered by Türkmen: men such as Atsïz b. Uvak in Syria, Artuq on the fringes of Arabia, and Sulaimān b. Qutlumush in Anatolia; and the number of Türkmen who could be called upon to swell the Saljuq army was probably 300,000 or more.[1]

Because of their strategic importance, Khurāsān and the upper Oxus lands were usually granted at this time to members of the Saljuq family. At the beginning of each reign there was a general allocation of these eastern governorships,[2] and since administrative continuity and a permanent state of defence were necessary, changes were as far as possible avoided; thus conditions favoured the growth of hereditary lines. In the sources, most of which are non-contemporary, these appanages are often called iqṭa'ṡ; but this is probably an anachronism, for in the latter half of the 5th/11th century the land system of the east was clearly different from that of the west. The Saljuq principality of Kirmān under Qavurt and his descendants was typical of these eastern appanages. Hereditary succession continued here for over a century, not only because the province was somewhat isolated from the rest of Iran, but because it adjoined Sīstān and southern Afghanistan where the Ṣaffārids and Ghaznavids had to be watched. Likewise in the west the positions of Tutush in Syria and Sulaimān in Rūm were analogous to those of the Saljuq maliks in the east, and once again a frontier situation helps to explain the existence of their existence.

The sources all praise Malik-Shāh and his vizier as the architects of an empire where prosperity reigned and security was established. There is much in this view, for the age of Alp-Arslan and Malik-Shāh

[1] Kafesoğlu, *Sultan Melikşah devrinde Büyük Selçuklu imparatorluğu*, pp. 162–3.

[2] Cf. Ibn al-Athīr, vol. x, pp. 34, 51-2; Kafesoğlu, *Sultan Melikşah*, pp. 152–3.

was one in which the Great Saljuqs were at last in strong control: rebellious members of the family were firmly handled, a powerful fighting machine enabled the momentum of expansion to be kept up, and the leading talents of the Iranian administrative tradition were taken into the service of the regime. The sources contrast this period, if only implicitly, with the dissension among Malik-Shāh's sons and the eventual splitting of the fabric of the empire. Of greater value than the stylized eulogies of Muslim authors is the high praise given to both Alp-Arslan and Malik-Shāh by Armenian and Syriac Christian writers.

According to the 8th/14th-century historian and geographer Ḥamd Allāh Mustaufī, who is quoting a certain *Risālat-i Malikshāhī*, the annual revenue of Iran during Malik-Shāh's reign amounted to 215 million dīnārs.[1] Despite heavy expenditure on the administration and army, which was only partly alleviated by the practice of granting iqṭā's, a good proportion of the sultan's income was used to erect tangible memorials to his power—roads, walls, charitable and educational institutions, mosques, and palaces. The capital Iṣfahān benefited especially. There he laid out several palaces and gardens, together with a madrasa, the citadel of the town, and a fortress at nearby Dizkūh, where his armoury and treasury were housed; it was in fact this stronghold which fell into the hands of the Ismā'īlīs during Berk-Yaruq's reign.[2] In the frontier regions and in those provinces where there was a large proportion of Türkmen pastoralists, the provision of town walls was of prime importance. In the exposed province of Khurāsān, for example, Malik-Shāh built a wall round Marv that measured 12,300 paces, and he laid out the town of Panj-Dih in the district of Marv ar-Rūd; in 464/1071–2 Niẓām al-Mulk raised the height of the walls around Baihaq, which were previously only as high as two men.[3] Internal security and the safe movement of travellers and merchants were facilitated by the building of *ribāṭs* and caravanserais. In stressing the sultan's piety, the sources describe his zeal in keeping the pilgrimage route from Iraq to the Ḥijāz in good order; e.g. he provided beacons, wells, and cisterns, and he compensated the amīr of the *Ḥaramain* (or "two holy places") with a subsidy, in order that a

[1] *Nuzhat al-Qulūb*, pp. 33–4.

[2] Rāvandī, pp. 132, 156; Ibn al-Athīr, vol. x, p. 215; cf. Kafesoğlu, *Sultan Melikhşah*, p. 167.

[3] Ibn Funduq, *Ta'rīkh-i Baihaq*, p. 53; Ḥamd Allāh Mustaufī, *op. cit.* pp. 154–5.

tax levied on pilgrims might be abolished: hence from 479/1086 till the sultan's death, the pilgrimage was performed each year without mishap.[1] The Saljuq amīrs and great men of state were similarly encouraged by the sultan and by Niẓām al-Mulk to expend their wealth on good works. As for Malik-Shāh's reputation as a just and equitable ruler, Ḥusain b. Muḥammad al-Ḥusainī relates how the sultan sent heralds all round the empire, had boards put up in the towns, and had the *khaṭībs* (official preachers) proclaiming from the pulpits—all to announce that he would personally hear and investigate every complaint of injustice.[2]

We have little direct information on the economic condition of Iran at this time, although the sources frequently mention that by the middle of the reign, in 476/1083–4, there was unparalleled security on the roads and prices were low throughout the empire.[3] The measures to improve internal security and communications must have helped economic growth, as must the lightening or abolition of many transit dues and market tolls. Khurāsān continued to flourish, once the Türkmen nomads had been assigned a definite place in the agrarian structure of the province, and in the second half of the 5th/11th century it was still the centre of the most lively intellectual currents in Iranian life. Kirmān, according to Muḥammad b. Ibrāhīm, flourished under the firm rule of the local Saljuq line. There Qavurt suppressed the Balūchī brigands and put watchtowers, cisterns, and caravanserais along the caravan route through the desert to Sīstān; foreign merchants were encouraged to trade with India and the east via Kirmān, so that colonies of foreigners grew up in the capital there, and Qavurt was careful to maintain a high standard of coinage.[4]

Conditions in the adjacent province of Fārs were less encouraging. Whereas Qavurt was largely successful in stopping the depredations of the Balūchīs, Fārs continued to be racked by brigands and by internecine warfare amongst the local Kurdish tribes of the Shabānkāra. Ibn al-Balkhī, writing in the first decade or so of the 12th century, records that the Saljuq governors in Fārs—first Najm al-Daula Khumar-Tegin and then, after *c.* 493/1099, Fakhr al-Dīn Chavlī—sent many

[1] Bundārī, pp. 69–70; Ḥusainī, pp. 73–4; Ibn al-Athīr, vol. x, p. 144.

[2] Ḥusain b. Muḥammad al-Ḥusainī, *Tarjama-yi Maḥāsin-Iṣfahān*, pp. 140–1. (al-Ḥusainī's Persian translation of al-Māfarrūkhī's local history of Iṣfahān.)

[3] E.g. *ibid.* p. 85.

[4] Muḥammad b. Ibrāhīm, *Ta'rīkh-i Saljūqiyān-i Kirmān*, pp. 4 ff. Cf. Houtsma, "Zur Geschichte der Selǵuqen von Kermân", *Z.D.M.G.* pp. 369 ff.

expeditions against the bandits but failed to pacify the province. Shīrāz, once the flourishing capital of the Būyids, was sacked on several occasions by both Türkmen and Shabānkāra'īs, and she did not recover till the end of the 6th/12th century. The trade from the orient to the port of Sīrāf on the coast of Fārs was permanently ruined and the town itself depopulated by the piracy of the amīrs of the island of Qais, whom frequent Saljuq expeditions failed to subdue.[1]

VII. EVENTS DURING MALIK-SHĀH'S REIGN

The military and political events of Malik-Shāh's reign can conveniently be reviewed under three headings: first, the crushing of opposition from ambitious members of the Saljuq family; second, the humbling of external foes on the eastern and north-western frontiers of Iran; and third, relations with the caliphate and the extension of Saljuq power into Syria and the Arabian peninsula.

It was fortunate that Alp-Arslan lingered on for four days after he had been fatally wounded on the Oxus banks in Rabī' I 465/November 1072 (see above, p. 65); for within these four days he was able to set out his final wishes. He had a numerous family, including his sons Malik-Shāh, Ayaz, Tekish, Tutush, Böri-Bars, Toghan-Shāh, and Arslan-Arghun, but since 458/1066 Malik-Shāh had been recognized as heir. Niẓām al-Mulk now secured recognition for him by sending to Baghdad asking that the khuṭba be made in his name. Malik-Shāh himself dropped back to Nīshāpūr, the key city of Khurāsān, and with the treasure from its citadel Niẓām al-Mulk increased the salaries of the troops by a total of 700,000 dīnārs, "and thereby won over the hearts of the regular army ['*askar*] and the auxiliary troops [*ḥashar*]". Not only was it necessary at this point to secure the loyalty of the army against possible rivals, but the Saljuqs were in the midst of a campaign against the Qarakhānids, and the vizier did not want the pressure on them relaxed. Alp-Arslan was mindful of the claims of his other relatives when he enjoined Malik-Shāh to look after their due rights. His brother Qavurt, he said, was to continue in Kirmān and the parts of Fārs which he then held, and he was to receive a stipulated sum of money; his son Ayaz should rule the upper Oxus provinces from Balkh, for which he would have his grandfather Chaghrī's annual

[1] Ibn al-Balkhī, *Fārs-Nāma*, pp. 136–7; J. Aubin, "La Ruine de Sîrâf et les routes du Golfe Persique aux XIe et XIIe Siècles", *Cahiers de Civilisation Médiévale*, pp. 295–301.

allowance of 500,000 dīnārs, but Malik-Shāh was to keep a garrison in the citadel of Balkh.[1]

Obviously Qavurt was Malik-Shāh's most serious potential rival, for he was Alp-Arslan's brother and a commander of great experience. Moreover he had ruled in Kirmān for over thirty years. His Türkmen followers had settled on estates in the province (Muḥammad b. Ibrāhīm calls them *iqṭā'*s), but Qavurt's success in taking over Kirmān early in Toghrïl's reign had attracted thither larger numbers of Türkmen than that relatively poor region could stand. Qavurt's policy had therefore been to divert them into those outlying parts that were infested with Balūchī brigands, and he also sent a force under his son Amīrān-Shāh against Sīstān. As a further outlet for expansion he mounted an expedition against Oman, and after crossing the Persian Gulf in ships chartered from the local ruler of Hurmuz, he deposed the Būyid governor and brought Oman under Saljuq suzerainty. Qavurt, in fact, behaved almost as an independent ruler, adopting the royal insignia of a parasol (*chatr*), stamping on documents a *tughra* or official emblem—this was the Saljuq bow and arrow symbol—and assuming regal titles.[2]

On hearing the news of Malik-Shāh's accession, Qavurt hurried back to Kirmān from Oman, losing several ships and many men in the crossing. He set before Malik-Shāh a claim based on the principle of seniority: "I am the eldest brother, and you are a youthful son; I have the greater right to my brother Alp-Arslan's inheritance." Against this, Malik-Shāh asserted the concept of father–son succession: "A brother does not inherit when there is a son." Qavurt then occupied Iṣfahān, and in 465/1073 a three-day battle took place outside Hamadān. Fighting with his seven sons at his side, Qavurt expected the support, and even the defection to him, of much of his opponent's army. The Turks and Türkmen in Malik-Shāh's forces did show this expected sympathy, although the sultan's ghulām commanders, such as Sav-Tegin and Gauhar-Ā'īn, stood firmly by their master. There was sharp tension in Malik-Shāh's army between the Turkish elements and the contingents of Arabs and Kurds led by the 'Uqailid Sharaf al-Daula Muslim b. Quraish and the Mazyadid Bahā' al-Daula Manṣūr b. Dubais. The latter groups played a decisive part in crumpling up

[1] Bundārī, *Zubdat al-nuṣra*, p. 48; Ḥusainī, *Akhbār al-daula al-Saljūqiyya*, pp. 55–6; Ibn al-Athīr, *al-Kāmil*, vol. x, pp. 51–2.

[2] Muḥammad b. Ibrāhīm, *Ta'rīkh-i Saljūqiyān-i Kirmān*, pp. 1–12. Cf. Houtsma, "Zur Geschichte der Selǵuqen von Kermân", *Z.D.M.G.* pp. 367–71.

Qavurt's right wing, and this blow against their fellow Turks so incensed Malik-Shāh's own Turkish troops that some of them turned aside to plunder the baggage of the Arabs and Kurds as well as that of the caliph's envoy. This episode brings out the differing outlooks of the two constituents of the Saljuq army, the Turkish tribesmen and the multi-national professional and slave soldiery; the unreliability of the former must now have been quite clear to the sultan.

With Qavurt defeated and captured, Malik-Shāh was disposed to be merciful to his uncle, who at one point offered to retire to Oman; but Niẓām al-Mulk was adamant, insisting that clemency would only be taken as a sign of weakness. According to Ẓahīr al-Dīn Nīshāpūrī, the sultan's army was still restive and threatening to support Qavurt if their pay and shares in the booty were not increased. Qavurt was strangled with a bowstring, presumably to prevent the spilling of royal blood, and two of his sons were at least partially blinded. Malik-Shāh then appointed as amīrs Rukn al-Daula Qutlugh-Tegin over Fārs and Sav-Tegin over Kirmān. To mark the prominent role taken by the Arabs and Kurds, they were granted extensive fiefs and extra shares in the plunder.[1]

Malik-Shāh eventually restored Kirmān to Qavurt's sons; Rukn al-Daula Sulṭān-Shāh ruled from 467/1074 to 477/1085, followed by 'Imād al-Daula Tūrān-Shāh from 477/1085 to 490/1097. At one point Sulṭān-Shāh's loyalty to the Saljuqs became ambiguous, and in 473/1080–1 Malik-Shāh marched to the capital of Bardasīr, receiving there Sulṭān-Shāh's homage and contenting himself with the destruction of one of the towers in the citadel. Tūrān-Shāh, the last survivor from amongst Qavurt's sons, was praised for his justice and piety, and his tomb became a place of pilgrimage. His vizier was the capable al-Mukarram b. al-'Alā', who won the gratitude of the common people of Bardasīr by removing the turbulent Turkish soldiery from quarters within the town to a new suburb (*rabaḍ*) outside it, where he also built himself a palace and erected several public buildings.[2] It seems that the Saljuqs of Kirmān kept control of Fārs, for Ibn al-Athīr records that in 487/1094, presumably just before her death, Terken Khatun deputed

[1] (Anon.), *Mujmal al-tawārīkh wa'l-qiṣaṣ*, p. 408; Bundārī, pp. 48–9; Muḥammad b. Ibrāhīm, pp. 12–13 (cf. Houtsma, *op. cit.* p. 370); Ẓahīr al-Dīn Nīshāpūrī, *Saljūq-Nāma*, p. 30; Rāvandī, *Rāḥat al-ṣudūr*, pp. 126–8; Ḥusainī, *Akhbār al-daula*, pp. 56–8; Ibn al-Athīr, vol. x, p. 53; Ibn Khallikān, *Wafayāt al-a'yān*, vol. II, p. 587.

[2] Bundārī, pp. 71–2; Muḥammad b. Ibrāhīm, pp. 17–21 (cf. Houtsma, *op. cit.* pp. 371–3); Ibn al-Athīr, vol. x, pp. 74–5 *bis*.

the Amīr Öner to wrest Fārs from Tūrān-Shāh. The attempt failed, in part because the sympathies of the local people were with Tūrān-Shāh, who is reported to have been mortally wounded in the fighting.[1] Bahā' al-Daula Īrān-Shāh succeeded his father for a reign of five years (490–5/1097–1101), and during this time Fārs continued to be a subject of dispute with the Great Saljuq sultans. Öner was again sent into Fārs, this time by Berk-Yaruq to subdue Īrān-Shāh's allies the Shabānkāra'ī Kurds, but he had to retire in defeat to Iṣfahān.[2] In the eyes of the chroniclers, the most noteworthy feature of Īrān-Shāh's reign was his alleged acceptance of Ismā'īlī propaganda, which is reputed to have been disseminated in Kirmān shortly after 486/1093. According to Ibn al-Athīr it was brought by a secretary from Khūzistān, one Ibn Zur'a, but Muḥammad b. Ibrāhīm says that it originated with the amīr's companion, Kākā Balīmān; it is possible that these two are one person. Īrān-Shāh was opposed by his own atabeg, Nāṣir al-Daula (this is the first tutor mentioned in the history of the Kirmān Saljuqs), by the orthodox ulema, and also by his own commanders. The representatives of the religious institution finally issued a *fatwā* (legal decision) authorizing the heretic ruler's deposition; Īrān-Shāh fled, but was finally trapped and killed.[3]

Shortly after Qavurt's revolt and death, Malik-Shāh received with much relief the news of his own brother Ayāz's death. Balkh and Tukhāristān were now granted to another of his brothers, Shihāb al-Dīn Tekish, who installed himself in these territories after 466/1073–4, the year in which Malik-Shāh defeated the Qarakhānid Shams al-Mulk and ejected his troops from the south bank of the Oxus. A further brother, Böri-Bars, was given the governorship of Herāt, Gharchistān, and Ghūr, while the sultan's uncle 'Uthmān b. Chaghrī Beg received Valvālij in eastern Tukhāristān.[4] For some years Tekish governed his province without recorded incident, until in 473/1080–1 the arrival of the 7,000 mercenaries whom Malik-Shāh had discharged, and who now sought to enter Tekish's service, tempted him to rebel. But the sultan beat him in the race to secure Nīshāpūr, the capital of Khurāsān, and after being besieged in Tirmidh, Tekish was compelled

[1] *al-Kāmil*, vol. x, p. 163. This conflicts with Muḥammad b. Ibrāhīm, who places his death in 490/1097.

[2] Ibn al-Athīr, vol. x, p. 192.

[3] *Ibid.* pp. 213, 219–20; Muḥammad b. Ibrāhīm, pp. 21–5 (cf. Houtsma, *op. cit.* pp. 373–4); Hodgson, *The Order of Assassins*, p. 87.

[4] Bundārī, *Zubdat al-nuṣra*, p. 49; Ḥusainī, *Akhbār al-daula*, pp. 58–61; Ibn al-Athīr, vol. x, p. 64.

to yield. His brother pardoned him. Four years later, however, whilst Malik-Shāh was at the opposite end of the empire in Mosul, where Fakhr al-Daula Ibn Jahīr and Artuq Beg had been conducting operations against the 'Uqailids, Tekish again rebelled in Khurāsān. His forces were held up at the fortress of Sarakhs, and the sultan managed to gain time for the march across Iran. Tekish was captured and now paid the penalty for his disloyalty: he was blinded and imprisoned, and his territories given to his son Aḥmad.[1] The firmness of Malik-Shāh and Niẓām al-Mulk in dealing with rebels from the Saljuq family forms a contrast to Alp-Arslan's comparatively lenient treatment of such claimants; but it seems to have had an exemplary effect, for there was no more trouble from the rest of the family for the remaining years of Malik-Shāh's reign.

It has been noted that towards the end of Alp-Arslan's reign, when warfare had broken out between the Saljuqs and the Qarakhānid Shams al-Mulk Naṣr b. Ibrāhīm, the sultan's assassination gave the khan the opportunity to invade Tukhāristān (see p. 65 above). Malik-Shāh's brother Ayāz was unable to withstand the invaders, but once the new sultan was firmly on the throne, he came eastwards in 466/1073–4, drove Shams al-Mulk's brother from Tirmidh, and pushed on to Samarqand; the khan was now forced to seek the intercession of Niẓām al-Mulk and sue for peace. Malik-Shāh entrusted the key of Tirmidh to Sav-Tegin, with instructions for its refortification with stone walls and a ditch, and it was then that he gave the governorship of Balkh and Tukhāristān to Tekish.[2] At some point in his reign Shams al-Mulk became involved in a war with the eastern branch of the Qarakhānids, who were ruled by the two sons of Qadïr-Khān Yūsuf of Kāshghar and Khotan. Forced to abandon to them Farghāna and the province of Īlāq north of the Syr Darya, he must have become eager to preserve peaceful relations with the Saljuqs.[3]

Like his father, Shams al-Mulk was famed for his equity and piety, particularly in the sphere of public buildings and charitable works. He built celebrated ribāṭs at Khardhang near Karmīniyya and also at Āq-Kutāl on the Samarqand–Khujand road; the splendid palace of Shamsābād near Bukhārā, and a Friday mosque in that city. Nevertheless he fell foul of the religious classes, and in 461/1069 was driven to

[1] Bundārī, p. 71; Ḥusainī, *op. cit.* p. 64; Ibn al-Athīr, vol. x, pp. 88–9.

[2] Ḥusainī, *op. cit.* pp. 59–61, 63; Ibn al-Athīr, vol. x, pp. 63–4; cf. Barthold, *Turkestan down to the Mongol Invasion*, pp. 314–15; Kafesoğlu, *Sultan Melikşah*, pp. 19–20, 28–9.

[3] Ibn al-Athīr, vol. IX, p. 212.

execute the Imām Abū Ibrāhīm Ṣaffārī. In the brief reign of Shams al-Mulk's brother Khiḍr Khān (472–3/1080–1) the western kingdom of the Qarakhānids is said to have reached its zenith of prosperity and splendour.[1]

Nothing is recorded of Saljuq-Qarakhānid relations for several years until the accession in Transoxiana of Aḥmad Khān b. Khiḍr (473–82/1081–9), the nephew of Malik-Shāh's wife Terken Khatun. Saljuq influence beyond the Oxus continued to be strong, and it is in this period that the double honorifics *al-Dunyā wa'l-Dīn* (" . . . of the Secular World and of Religion") first appear amongst the Qarakhānids (coin of 474/1081–2).[2] However, Aḥmad Khān stirred up the opposition of the orthodox religious institution to such a pitch that in 482/1089 a Shāfi'ī faqīh, one Abū Ṭāhir b. 'Aliyyak, came to Malik-Shāh's court seeking aid.[3] The sultan was at this time at the peak of his prestige. He had successfully settled affairs in Syria and al-Jazīreh, humbling the pretensions of his brother Tutush and installing several of his reliable ghulām commanders as governors (see below, p. 98); he had also brought off a diplomatic *coup* by marrying his daughter to Caliph al-Muqtafī. He was accordingly well disposed to listen to the Transoxianan faqīh's appeal for intervention against the impious khan. The sultan occupied Bukhārā without difficulty; Samarqand was obstinately defended by its inhabitants, but Malik-Shāh broke into it, captured Aḥmad Khān, and deported him to his capital Iṣfahān. Leaving the civil governor of Khwārazm to hold Samarqand, the sultan now pushed on to Talas and into Semirechye with the aim of bringing the eastern Qarakhānids equally under his suzerainty. At Uzkand he received the personal submission of the Khān of Kāshghar, Hārūn b. Sulaimān b. Qadïr-Khān Yūsuf (d. 496/1103); the khan promised to place Malik-Shāh in the khuṭba and offered one of his daughters in marriage to one of the sultan's sons.

Meanwhile, the kingdom had become temporarily endangered by revolts among the people of Samarqand and among the Chigil or Qarluq tribesmen who had passed from Qarakhānid into Saljuq service; Niẓām al-Mulk explains that Malik-Shāh's failure to give the customary feasts for them had displeased them. A three-cornered struggle began with the appearance of Ya'qūb-Tegin, brother of the

[1] Barthold, *op. cit.* pp. 315–16, who is quoting Niẓāmī 'Arūḍī Samarqandī.
[2] Pritsak, "Karahanlïlar", *İslâm Ansiklopedisi*.
[3] 'Aliyyak's obituary is in Ibn al-Jauzī, *al-Muntaẓam*, vol. IX, pp. 58–9.

Khān of Kāshghar, and Malik-Shāh had to undertake the recovery of Samarqand and a further trip to Uzkand. Saljuq fortunes were helped by the eternally present family conflicts of the Qarakhānid dynasty. A new aggressor appeared, Toghrïl b. Ïnal, who drove the khan out of Kāshghar.[1] The sultan's representatives Tāj al-Mulk now brought the khan and his brother Ya'qūb-Tegin together, and left them to regain their territories as best they could; the sultan himself returned to Khurāsān, and at some unknown time later restored Aḥmad Khān to Samarqand.[2] Soon afterwards, in 488/1095, Aḥmad Khān was overthrown and executed by the agents of the religious leaders in Samarqand, on the grounds that he had embraced Ismā'īlī doctrines (see below, p. 106).[3]

Although there had been peace between the Ghaznavids and Saljuqs during Alp-Arslan's reign, the troubled events surrounding Malik-Shāh's accession tempted Ibrāhīm of Ghazna to try and regain former Ghaznavid territory in Badakhshān and Tukhāristān. He attacked Malik-Shāh's uncle, the Amīr al-Umarā' 'Uthmān b. Chaghrï Beg, at a place named Sakalkand, then he sacked it and carried 'Uthmān ignominiously off to Ghazna. (Since the latter was soon afterwards made Governor of Valvālīj, he must have been speedily ransomed or released from captivity.) Malik-Shāh sent an army under Gümüsh-Tegin Bilge Beg and his slave Anūsh-Tegin Gharcha'ī, and the *status quo* was presumably restored (465/1073). Little more is recorded of relations between the two sultans, though one other expedition by Malik-Shāh against the Ghaznavids is mentioned. This got as far as Isfizār in western Afghanistan, where it was halted by a clever piece of psychological warfare on Ibrāhīm's part which made the Saljuq sultan believe that his own army was disaffected.[4]

The Ghaznavid empire in eastern Afghanistan and northern India flourished during Ibrāhīm's forty-year reign, and the sultan acquired a great reputation as a patron of learning and religion, building many mosques, madrasas, and public buildings. He made several fresh

[1] Perhaps originally the ruler of Barskhan, Toghrïl b. Ïnal was probably also Qadïr Khān Jibrā'īl b. 'Umar who was to invade Transoxiana in 495/1102: see below, sec. x, p. 109.

[2] *Siyāsat-Nāma*, ch. xxxv (Darke tr., p. 128); *Mujmal al-tawārikh*, p. 408; Bundārī, *Zubdat al-nuṣra*, pp. 55, 71; Narshakhī, *Ta'rīkh-i Bukhārā*, p. 34 (Frye tr., p. 29); Ẓahīr al-Dīn Nīshāpūrī, *Saljuq-Nāma*, p. 31; Rāvandī, *Rāḥat al-ṣudūr*, pp. 128–30; Ḥusainī, *Akhbār al Daula*, pp. 65–6; Barthold, "History of the Semirechyé", in *Four Studies*, vol. 1, pp. 97–8; *idem*, *Turkestan*, pp. 316–18; Kafesoğlu, *Sultan Melikşah*, pp. 119–23.

[3] Ibn al-Athīr, *al-Kāmil*, vol. x, pp. 165–6.

[4] Ḥusainī, p. 16; Ibn al-Athīr, vol. x, pp. 53, 110; I. M. Shafi, "Fresh Light on the Ghaznavids", *Islamic Culture*, pp. 206–11; Kafesoğlu, *op. cit.* p. 30 n. 49.

conquests of fortresses in the Punjab, and after 469/1076–7 he assigned the governorship of India to his son Saif al-Daula Maḥmūd, patron of the famous poet Mas'ūd-i Sa'd-ī Salmān. Ibrāhīm and Malik-Shāh negotiated as equals, and marriage links between the two houses were kept up. Ibrāhīm's son, the later 'Alā' al-Daula Mas'ūd III (492–508/1099–1115), had married a daughter of Alp-Arslan, and later he was to marry one of Malik-Shāh's daughters, Jauhar Khatun, known in Ghazna as *Mahd-i 'Irāq*, "the wife from Iraq [i.e. western Persia]".[1] The extent of Saljuq influence in Ghazna at this time can be seen in the Ghaznavid sultans' formal assumption of a typically Saljuq title—*al-Sulṭān al-Mu'aẓẓam*—in addition to their own normal ones of *Amīr* and *Malik*; the title first appears on the coinage of Farrukh-Zād.[2]

Sīstān had come under Saljuq suzerainty soon after the Ghaznavids' expulsion from Khurāsān. Though it remained under the general supervision of the Saljuqs of Kirmān, it was left in practice to its own ancient rulers of the Ṣaffārid line (see above, pp. 50–1). In 465/1073, the year of Malik-Shāh's accession, it passed to Amīr Bahā' al-Daula wa'l-Dīn Ṭāhir, but his authority was soon disputed by other powerful nobles of Sīstān, in particular by one Badr al-Dīn Abu'l-'Abbās. The mediation of Malik-Shāh's governor in Khurāsān was sought, yet internal strife ended only when Ṭāhir was strangled by his opponent in 480/1088. Abu'l-'Abbās now moved against Kūhistān, but he too died shortly afterwards. Malik-Shāh himself was at this time occupied in Transoxiana; in 485/1092, however, the Saljuq amīr Qïzïl-Sarïgh linked up with one of the local amīrs of Sīstān, and until the sultan's death joint operations were conducted against the Ismā'īlīs of Kūhistān. In Sīstān itself, Ṭāhir's son Tāj al-Dīn Abu'l-Faḍl Naṣr came to power in 483/1090–1 as a Saljuq vassal, and after a long reign largely coterminous with that of Sanjar, he died a centenarian in 559/1164.[3]

Malik-Shāh's concern with the north-western frontiers of Iran was twofold: first, to secure Arrān and thus protect Āzarbāījān, and second, to hold the route that led up the Araxes into Armenia against any Georgian attack. During his reign, Āzarbāījān conserved its importance both as a region of Türkmen concentration and as the base from which Türkmen amīrs fighting in Anatolia drew replenish-

[1] Ḥusainī, *loc. cit.*; Ibn al-Athīr, vol. x, p. 111; Jūzjānī, *Ṭabaqāt-i Nāṣirī* (Raverty tr., vol. 1, pp. 103–4, 107); Mīrzā Muḥammad Qazwīnī, "Mas'ud-i Sa'd-i Salman", *J.R.A.S* pp. 711–15; Kafesoğlu, *Sultan Melikşah*, pp. 29–30.

[2] Sourdel, *Inventaire des Monnaies Musulmanes Anciennes du Musée de Caboul*, pp. xiii–xiv.

[3] (Anon.), *Ta'rīkh-i Sīstān*, p. 383; Kafesoğlu, *op. cit.* pp. 117–19.

ments for their forces; this importance was recognized by the sultan's eventually placing the whole of the Arrān–Āzarbāījān area under his cousin Quṭb al-Dīn Ismāʿīl b. Yāqūtī, who was given the title Malik.

When Malik-Shāh came to the throne, he considered that he needed to strengthen the somewhat nominal dependence of Faḍl (Faḍlūn) III b. Faḍl II, the Shaddādid ruler of Ganja and Dvin who had succeeded his father in 466/1073. Accordingly, the sultan sent an expedition to Arrān; Ganja was occupied and Faḍl deposed, receiving in exchange Astarābād in Gurgān. Sav-Tegin, already familiar with the area from his campaigns there in Alp-Arslan's time, was installed in Ganja as governor (?468/1075–6; the chronology of these events is uncertain). But aggressive activity by the king of Georgia, Bagrat IV's son Giorgi II (1072–89), led to the temporary recapture of Kars by the Christians. The sultan came personally to Georgia in 471/1078–9, and shortly afterwards he entrusted operations there to the Türkmen amīr Aḥmad, who regained Kars in 473/1080 and, after returning to his base in Arrān, sent two more Türkmen begs, Yaʿqūb and ʿĪsā Böri, against Georgia. They penetrated as far as Lazistān and the Chorukh valley on the Black Sea coast and they also threatened Trebizond; according to Anna Comnena, this city was in fact taken, but was recaptured soon afterwards by a Byzantine general.[1]

A revolt by the restored Shaddādid Faḍl III, probably after the death of Sav-Tegin in 478/1085, necessitated Malik-Shāh's appearance in the Caucasus in 478/1086. After receiving the homage and tribute of the Shīrvān-Shāh Farīburz b. Sallār, the sultan reached the Black Sea coast, where the slave commander Bozan was detailed to take Ganja. Faḍl was finally deposed and the Shaddādid line in Ganja extinguished, although the collateral line in Ani, under Amīr Abu'l-Faḍl Manūchihr, one of Malik-Shāh's faithful vassals (?464–*c.* 512/?1072–*c.* 1118), continued to flourish in the 6th/12th century. The Shīrvān-Shāh seems to have exercised some influence over Arrān, but much of the Araxes basin was doubtless parcelled out into military fiefs and absorbed into the existing pattern of Türkmen occupation in Āzarbāījān; the region as a whole was under the control of Quṭb al-Dīn Ismāʿīl.[2]

[1] Allen, *A History of the Georgian People*, pp. 93–4; Yinanç, *Anadolu'nun fethi*, pp. 110–13; Cahen, "La Première Pénétration Turque en Asie-Mineure", *Byzantion*, p. 49; Minorsky, *Studies in Caucasian History*, pp. 67–8.

[2] *Caucasian History*, pp. 68, 81–2; *idem*, *A History of Sharvān and Darband*, pp. 68–9; *idem*, and Cahen, "Le Recueil Transcaucasien de Masʿûd b. Nâmdâr (début du VIe/XIIe siècle)", *J.A.* pp. 119–21.

The sons of Qutlumush had arrived in Anatolia at the beginning of Malik-Shāh's reign and had put themselves at the head of certain of the Türkmen bands which were gradually isolating and compelling the surrender of the remaining Byzantine strongholds in Anatolia. The later historiography of the Rūm Saljuqs posits that Malik-Shāh officially invested these sons with the governorships of Anatolia, intending the region to be an appanage of the Saljuq empire as Khurāsān, Kirmān, and Damascus had been under Tutush. In fact, relations here were never very cordial. Assumption of the title Sulṭān by Qutlumush's sons (this occurred after *c.* 473/1080–1) seems to have been a unilateral act and cannot have pleased Malik-Shāh, whose own title of Supreme Sulṭān implied an overlordship of the Saljuq family. Indeed, in 467/1075 two of Qutlumush's sons—Alp-Ilig and Daulab, in the view of Cahen—were fighting in Palestine for the Fāṭimids against Malik-Shāh's lieutenant Atsïz b. Uvak.[1]

In Anatolia itself, the other sons Sulaimān and Manṣūr were taking advantage of the succession disputes which racked Byzantium until the last and most successful claimant, Alexis Comenus (1081–1118), emerged triumphant. The various contenders—Michael Dukas, Nicephorus Botaniates, Nicephorus Melissenos, and Alexis himself—all sought help from the Turks, with the result that by 474/1081 Sulaimān's forces had reached the shores of the Sea of Marmara and had taken Nicea (Iznik). Malik-Shāh regarded his cousins in Anatolia as semi-rebels, and he cannot have viewed their successes with enthusiasm; his attitude towards Byzantium was no doubt the same as his fathers: that the two empires of the Greeks and the Saljuqs should exist side by side (see p. 62 above). Barhebraeus speaks of a punitive expedition under Amīr Bursuq, sent by Malik-Shāh *c.* 470/1077–8; though it succeeded in bringing about Manṣūr's death, Sulaimān had to be left with most of the western and southern parts of Anatolia.[2] In Cappadocia, Pontus, and the east there were several other Türkmen begs, some related to the Saljuqs, others independent of them. Certain of the legends and traditions which surround the beginnings of the Türkmen Dānishmand Beg ascribe to him a part in the victory of Malāzgird, and they ascribe a similar role to Artuq, Mengüjek, and Saltuq, other Türkmen amīrs who later became famous.[3] In reality,

[1] Cf. Cahen, *Byzantion* (1948), pp. 35–6. [2] Barhebraeus, *Chronography*, p. 227.

[3] This tradition is found in the works of the 8th/14th-century historian of the Rūm Saljuqs, Aqsarāyī, and it is also mentioned by the later Ottoman historians.

Dānishmand Beg does not become a historically authenticated figure till the time of the First Crusade, in Berk-Yaruq's reign, but it is quite possible that the foundations of the important Dānishmanid principality were being laid in the regions of Sīvās, Kayseri, Amasya, and Tokat during the latter part of Malik-Shāh's reign.[1]

However, events in the Anatolian interior were of less immediate importance to the Great Saljuqs than were those taking place on the south-eastern fringes of Anatolia, in al-Jazīreh and in Syria. South of the Taurus and the Anatolian plateau we are outside the Irano-Turkish world on which the Saljuqs' political power and culture were based, and only a brief outline of the extension of Saljuq influence as against that of the Fāṭimids in Syria and Arabia need be given here. The tasks of Saljuq arms and diplomacy in the shifting and complex politics of this region to the south of Anatolia were, first, to ensure that cities like Antioch, Aleppo, and Edessa were in friendly Sunnī Muslim hands; and second, to bring into the Sunnī–Saljuq sphere of influence the local Arab amirates (e.g. those of the Mirdāsids, the Banū Munqidh of Shaizar, and the Banū 'Ammār of Tripoli) as well as the tribal groups, such as those of Kilāb and Numair, many of which were Shī'ī and possibly pro-Fāṭimid in sentiment. Roving Türkmen bands injected a fresh element of unrest into the region; and in the years after Malāzgird an ephemeral but significant Greco-Armenian principality grew up along the Taurus under the leadership of Philaretos, a former general of Romanus Diogenes, who extended his power from Ḥiṣn Manṣūr, Abulustān, and Mar'ash, over the cities of Malatya, Samosata, Edessa, and Antioch.[2]

Malik-Shāh's reign saw the destruction of the Marwānids, the long-established Kurdish dynasty in Diyārbakr, although there are no indications that this action came from deliberate Saljuq policy; it was some decades since Fāṭimid influence had been a danger in this area. After the death of Naṣr al-Daula Ibn Marwān in 453/1061, the power and splendour of the dynasty waned perceptibly under his sons, and its end came when the private ambitions of the Banū Jahīr finally worked upon Malik-Shāh and Niẓām al-Mulk.[3] Accompanied by a Saljuq army

[1] Cahen, *Byzantion* (1948), pp. 35 ff.; I. Mélikoff, *La geste de Melik Dāniṣmend, étude critique du Dāniṣmendnāme* (Paris, 1960), vol. 1, pp. 71 ff.; *idem*, "Dānishmendids", *Encyc. of Islam* (2nd ed.).

[2] J. Laurent, "Des Grecs aux Croisés; Etude sur l'Histoire d'Edesse entre 1071 et 1098", *Byzantion*, pp. 387 ff.; Honigmann, *Die Ostgrenze des Byzantinischen Reiches*, pp. 142–6; Cahen, *Byzantion* (1948), pp. 39–41.

[3] See p. 24 above.

and by the ghulām generals Qasīm al-Daula Aq-Sonqur and Gauhar-Ā'īn, and later helped by Artuq Beg, Fakhr al-Daula Ibn Jahīr conducted a long and strenuous campaign in 477–8/1084 against the Marwānids in Āmid, Mayyāfāriqīn, and Jazīrat ibn 'Umar, afterwards annexing Diyārbakr to the Saljuq empire and appropriating for his personal use the Marwānids' treasury.[1]

The disappearance of the Marwānids was a palpable threat to another local power, the 'Uqailids. By 477/1084 the dominions of the very capable Sharaf al-Daula Muslim b. Quraish stretched from Mosul through Diyār Rabī'a and Diyār Muḍar to Manbij and Aleppo, and he had reached an entente with the Armenian general Philaretos. At the beginning of his reign Malik-Shāh had sent his brother Tutush to hold Syria as an appanage, and from his base of Damascus, Tutush and later Artuq Beg conquered all the territories in southern Syria and Palestine formerly held by Atsïz b. Uvak. The prize of Aleppo brought Tutush into rivalry with its ruler, Sharaf al-Daula Muslim, and in 477/1084 a complex pattern of warfare broke out in the region of Aleppo and Antioch, involving Tutush, Sharaf al-Daula Muslim, Philaretos, Sulaimān b. Qutlumush, and an army from Iṣfahān under the personal command of Malik-Shāh and his generals Bozan and Bursuq. In the fighting the 'Uqailid was killed (478/1085), while Sulaimān either died in battle or else committed suicide (479/1086). The sultan's Syrian campaign was crowned with triumph as one after another Mosul, Ḥarrān, Aleppo, and Antioch submitted, and he was at last able to let his horse stand on the shores of the Mediterranean. When Tutush and Artuq had withdrawn to Damascus and Jerusalem respectively, Malik-Shāh installed ghulām governors in Antioch (Yaghï-Basan), Aleppo (Aq-Sonqur), and Edessa (Bozan).[2]

Saljuq influence during his reign was even carried into the Arabian peninsula. In 469/1076–7 Artuq marched through al-Aḥsā' in eastern Arabia as far as Qaṭīf and Baḥrain Island, attacking the local Qarmatian sectaries *en route*. After the sultan's second visit to Baghdad, in 484/1091, he conceived the idea of making it the centre of his empire (see below, p. 101), and it was probably in connexion with this that he deputed

[1] Bundārī, *Zubdat al-nuṣra*, pp. 75–6; Ibn al-Athīr, *al-Kāmil*, vol. x, pp. 86–8, 93–4; Amedroz, "The Marwānid Dynasty at Mayyāfāriqīn in the Tenth and Eleventh Centuries A.D.", *J.R.A.S.* pp. 146 ff.; Kafesoğlu, *Sultan Melikşah*, pp. 46–56; Cahen, "Djahīr (Banū)", *Encyc. of Islam*.

[2] Ibn al-Athīr, vol. x, pp. 75–72 *bis*, 74, 82, 89–91, 96–8, 107; Barhebraeus, pp. 230–1; Kafesoğlu, *op. cit.* pp. 40–5, 86–94.

Gauhar-Ā'īn and Chabaq to bring the Ḥijāz and the Yemen under his power. Through his diplomacy the khuṭba at Mecca was returned to the 'Abbāsids in 468/1075–6, which meant in effect that he had outbid the Fāṭimids for the support of the venal Sharīf of Mecca—although according to Ibn al-Jauzī, there was also a project for the sharīf to marry one of the sultan's sisters. In the last year of Malik-Shāh's life, Gauhar-Ā'īn sent a force of Türkmen under Tirsek and Chabaq, and the Yemen and Aden were temporarily occupied.[1]

The exclusion of the 'Abbāsid caliphs from secular affairs in Iraq was maintained during Malik-Shāh's reign, and on his first visit to Baghdad, in 479–80/1086–7, he had received the formal grant of this secular authority from al-Muqtadī. Within Baghdad the sultan's *shaḥna*, or military commander, was Gauhar-Ā'īn, who had been appointed in his father's reign. Not only did he have the task of keeping public order in the city and of mediating among the hostile factions of Shī'īs, Ḥanbalīs, 'ayyārs, and so on, but Gauhar-Ā'īn also had a general responsibility for the security of Iraq; thus when in 483/1090 a force of 'Āmirī Bedouins from the Qarmatians of al-Aḥsā' sacked Baṣra, he had to come from Baghdad and restore order.[2] Financial and civil affairs in the capital and in Iraq in general—including supervision of those iqṭā's allotted to the caliph, together with the transmission to him of their revenues—were the responsibility of a civilian *'amīd* or governor. In the latter part of Malik-Shāh's reign, when relations between sultan and caliph became very strained, the 'amīd clearly had the power of making life unpleasant in many ways for the caliph. One 'amīd, Abu'l-Fath b. Abī Laith, even interfered with the caliph's own court and retinue, until in 475/1082–3 al-Muqtadī complained to the sultan and Niẓām al-Mulk.[3]

For most of Malik-Shāh's reign Niẓām al-Mulk was left to mould Saljuq policy towards the caliphate, and this meant that he was thrown into close contact with the caliph's viziers; down to 507/1113–14, with only a few breaks, the vizierate for the 'Abbāsids continued to be held by the Banū Jahīr, namely Fakhr al-Daula and his sons 'Amīd al-Daula and Za'īm al-Ru'asā'. Saljuq pressure on the caliphate increased during this period, as the firm hand of Gauhar-Ā'īn in Baghdad showed. At the opening of the reign Niẓām al-Mulk had reversed his previously conciliatory attitude, and the climax of this new harshness came in

[1] Bundārī, pp. 70–1; Ibn al-Jauzī, vol. VIII, p. 298; Ibn al-Athīr, vol. x, p. 137.
[2] *al-Kāmil*, vol. x, pp. 103–4, 121–3. [3] *Ibid.* p. 81.

471/1079, when he secured Fakhr al-Daula's dismissal on the pretext that he was behind Ḥanbalī attacks on the Niẓāmiyya madrasa. He even tried, without success, to impose on the caliph his own son Mu'ayyid al-Mulk as vizier. The family's fortunes were restored through the tact of 'Amīd al-Daula Ibn Jahīr, who came personally to Niẓām al-Mulk's camp to intercede for his father's restoration, and who in the following years grew so close to Niẓām al-Mulk that he was given successively two of the vizier's daughters in marriage.[1] Over the next few years the Banū Jahīr oscillated between support for the interests of the sultan and for those of the caliph. In 474/1081–2 Fakhr al-Daula and Niẓām al-Mulk arranged the betrothal of one of Malik-Shāh's daughters to the caliph, but the condition was imposed on al-Muqtadī that he should take no concubine and no other wife but this Saljuq princess. Hence by 476/1083–4 al-Muqtadī had lost all patience, and he installed as vizier a firm supporter of his own interests, Abū Shujā' al-Rūdhrāwarī; Niẓām al-Mulk was furious that his ally 'Amīd al-Daula should be dismissed, and according to Sibṭ b. al-Jauzī he even contemplated abolition of the caliphate.[2]

Harmony was restored for a time when Malik-Shāh, victorious after his Syrian campaign, visited Baghdad for the first time. Niẓām al-Mulk took the opportunity of impressing the caliph with the military might of the sultanate by parading before him the Saljuq amīrs—they numbered over forty—while he detailed their iqṭā's and the number of their retainers. The sultan's euphoria at this time was such that he increased the caliph's own iqṭā's, and at the same time abolished throughout Iraq illegal taxes, transport dues on goods, and the transit payment levied on pilgrims.[3] The marriage alliance with the caliphate was celebrated in 480/1087 with enormous pomp, in the presence of Niẓām al-Mulk, Abū Sa'd the Mustaufī, Terken Khatun, and the caliph's vizier Abū Shujā'. Very soon a son was born, the short-lived Abu'l-Faḍl Ja'far.[4] Niẓām al-Mulk's reception at Baghdad turned him into a warm partisan of the caliphate, but the marriage did not bring the expected harmony between sultan and caliph. As early as 481/1088 the Turks who had accompanied the Saljuq princess were expelled

[1] *Ibid.* pp. 74–5; Ibn al-Jauzī, vol. VIII, pp. 317–19.

[2] Bundārī, pp. 72–3, 77–8; Ibn al-Jauzī, vol. IX, pp. 2–3, 5–6; Ibn al-Athīr, vol. X, pp. 77, 83; Bowen, "Niẓām al-Mulk", *Encyc. of Islam* (1st ed.).

[3] Bundārī, pp. 80–1; Ibn al-Jauzī, vol. IX, pp. 28, 30, 35–6; Ibn al-Athīr, vol. X, pp. 103–5, 111.

[4] *al-Kāmil*, vol. X, pp. 106–7; Ibn al-Jauzī, vol. IX, pp. 30, 36.

from the caliph's harem because of their rowdiness. By the next year the princess was complaining to her father of al-Muqtadī's neglect of her, so Malik-Shāh demanded the return of his daughter and his grandson Ja'far; she died shortly after reaching Iṣfahān, but her son, the so-called "Little Commander of the Faithful", became the sultan's favourite.[1]

During Malik-Shāh's second visit to Baghdad relations with al-Muqtadī were at their nadir, and the sultan ignored him. He resolved, however, to make Baghdad his winter capital, and in the winter of 484–5/1091–2 extensive building operations were begun in the city, comprising a great mosque, markets, and caravanserais, while the important ministers such as Niẓām al-Mulk and Tāj al-Mulk were ordered to build houses there for themselves. The sultan came to Baghdad again at the end of 485/1092. Niẓām al-Mulk had just been assassinated and the sultan, freed from all restraint, decided to expel the caliph from his ancient capital, delivering this ultimatum to him. "You must relinquish Baghdad to me, and depart to any land you choose." It seems that the sultan had the idea of setting up his grandson Ja'far as caliph, even though his tender age of five years made him ineligible according to Islamic law. As events turned out, al-Muqtadī was saved when Malik-Shāh died from a fever, fifty-three days after the passing of Niẓām al-Mulk.[2]

During the last two or three years of Malik-Shāh's reign, certain disquieting events occurred which showed that his impressive empire was not unassailable. In 483/1090, for example, Baṣra was savagely sacked by Qarmatians.[3] More serious was the emergence of several centres of Ismā'īlī activities within the empire, notably in Syria, al-Jazīreh, and Persia. Propagandists having connexions with the Nizārī faction in Fāṭimid Egypt began work in such parts of Iran as Kirmān, Tukhāristān, Kūhistān, Qūmis, the Caspian provinces, and Fārs (see above, p. 90). Those regions where there were already pockets of Shī'ism or of older Iranian beliefs seem to have been particularly susceptible. The Ismā'īlīs were even active in the capital city of Iṣfahān, under the dā'ī 'Abd al-Malik b. 'Attāsh and his son Aḥmad, who in Berk-Yaruq's reign was to seize the nearby fortress of Shāhdīz. Another dā'ī, Ḥasan-i Ṣabbāḥ, worked in Ray during Malik-Shāh's time, and in

[1] *al-Muntaẓam*, vol. IX, pp. 44, 46–7; Ibn al-Athīr, vol. X, pp. 109, 116.

[2] Bundārī, p. 70; Ẓahīr al-Dīn Nīshāpūrī, p. 35; Rāvandī, p. 140; Ibn al-Jauzī, vol. IX, pp. 60–2; Ibn al-Athīr, vol. X, pp. 133–5; Barhebraeus, pp. 231–2.

[3] Ibn al-Athīr, vol. X, pp. 121–3.

483/1090 he seized the fortress of Alamūt in the Alburz mountains near Qazvīn. In the last year of his life Malik-Shāh, conscious of this threat to the line of communications through northern Persia, sent the amīrs Arslan-Tash and Qïzïl-Sarïgh against the Ismā'īlīs of Alamūt and Kūhistān, respectively, but operations were broken off at his death.[1]

At Ṣiḥna, a place in Fārs on the Iṣfahān–Baghdad road, Niẓām al-Mulk had met death at the hands of a Dailamī youth, ostensibly a *fidā'ī* (assassin) of the Ismā'īlīs.[2] Several sources state that shortly before this killing, the sultan had dismissed him and several of his protégés in the administration, putting in their places Tāj al-Mulk and his friends; it is also possible that Niẓām al-Mulk, now at an advanced age, laid down office of his own accord. Yet one of the earliest sources, Anushīrvān b. Khālid, says nothing of Niẓām al-Mulk's departure from office. Contemporaries generally attributed his death to the machinations of Malik-Shāh and Tāj al-Mulk, and the view is expressed by the later historian Rashīd al-Dīn (d. 718/1318) that the vizier's enemies at court concocted the murder in association with the Assassins; in view of Rashīd al-Dīn's access to the Ismā'īlī records at Alamūt, the story is worthy of consideration. The last weeks of Malik-Shāh's own life were spent in drawing up his extravagant plans for the deposition of al-Muqtadī. After 485/1092 the caliphs would never again have to fear so powerful a member of the Great Saljuq dynasty.[3]

VIII. THE FIRST SIGNS OF DECLINE: BERK-YARUQ AND MUḤAMMAD B. MALIK-SHĀH

The twelve years that followed Malik-Shāh's death were ones of internal confusion and warfare, ended only by Berk-Yaruq's death in 498/beginning of 1105. Despite this, the external frontiers of the empire held firm thanks to Malik-Shāh and his vizier, whose policy had been to buttress the north-western frontiers through the concentration of

[1] Cf. *ibid.* pp. 215–17; Juvainī, *Ta'rīkh-i Jahān-Gushā*, vol. II, pp. 666 ff.; Kafesoğlu, *op. cit.* pp. 128–35; Hodgson, *The Order of Assassins*, pp. 47–51, 72–8, 85–7.

[2] Bundārī, pp. 62–3; Rāvandī, p. 135; Ibn al-Jauzī, vol. IX, pp. 66–7; Ḥusainī, *Akhbār al-daula*, pp. 66–7; Ibn al-Athīr, vol. X, pp. 137–9; Ibn Khallikān, *Wafayāt al-a'yān*, vol. I, pp. 414–15; Subkī, *Ṭabaqāt al-Shāfi'iyya al-kubrā*, vol. III, pp. 142–4; Kafesoğlu, *op. cit.* pp. 203–7.

[3] Cf. Houtsma, "The Death of the Niẓām al-Mulk and its Consequences", *Journal of Indian History*, pp. 147–60; Bowen, *Encyc. of Islam* (1st ed.); and K. Rippe, "Über den Sturz Niẓām-ul-Mulks", *Köprülü Armağanï*, pp. 423–35.

Türkmen in Āzarbāïjān and Arrān, and to hold the Qaraḵẖānids firmly in check on the north-eastern borders. Sanjar's governorship in eastern Ḵẖurāsān and Tuḵẖāristān from 490/1097 onwards discouraged possible moves by the Ghaznavids at this time, though they might well have seen in this period of Saljuq confusion a heaven-sent chance to recover their *terra irredenta*. Only in the extreme west was there potential disquiet with the appearance in 1097 of the First Crusade: within three years the Franks had entrenched themselves on the Levant coast, had advanced as far as western Diyārbakr, and had taken such key cities as Jerusalem, Antioch, and Edessa. Yet the Islamic world had seen aggressive infidels on its borders before. Moreover the Saljuq sultans were never directly threatened by the Crusaders, and they regarded the troubles of Tutush and his family in Syria as his own affair. When the news of the First Crusaders' successes in Syria first reached Baghdad, Berk-Yaruq wrote letters to the various amīrs urging them to go and fight the unbelievers (Rabīʿ II 491/March 1098), but this exhortation seems to have exhausted his concern.[1] There are few indications that thoughts of the Frankish threat seriously worried at any time the contestants who fought over the heartland of the empire, Iran and Iraq.

When Malik-Shāh died, Tāj al-Mulk and Terken Ḵẖatun acted vigorously. Their policy in building up a party amongst Niẓām al-Mulk's enemies in the army and bureaucracy, together with the fact that they happened to be in Baghdad at the crucial time, enabled them to place the four-year-old prince Maḥmūd on the throne as sultan, the caliph being reluctantly forced to grant him the honorific *Nāṣir al-Dunyā waʾl-Dīn* ("Helper in Secular and Religious Affairs"). Occupation of Iṣfahān was now the next aim, for despite large accession subsidies the army was again restive for pay. Maḥmūd was placed on the throne in Iṣfahān and the royal treasuries thrown open. Meanwhile the rival party of the Niẓāmiyya, which contained the great vizier's relatives and partisans, led by the ghulām Er-Ghush, had managed to seize the armaments stored up by the vizier at Iṣfahān and had taken with them to Ray the twelve-year-old Abuʾl-Muẓaffar Berk-Yaruq (Turkish for "strong brightness"). At Ray the *raʾīs*, or chief notable, crowned him sultan. Anushīrvān b. Ḵẖālid states that only obscure people and opportunists supported Berk-Yaruq and that the majority favoured Maḥmūd; but this merely reflects Ḵẖālid's partisanship for Berk-Yaruq's

[1] Ibn al-Jauzī, *al-Muntaẓam*, vol. IX, p. 105.

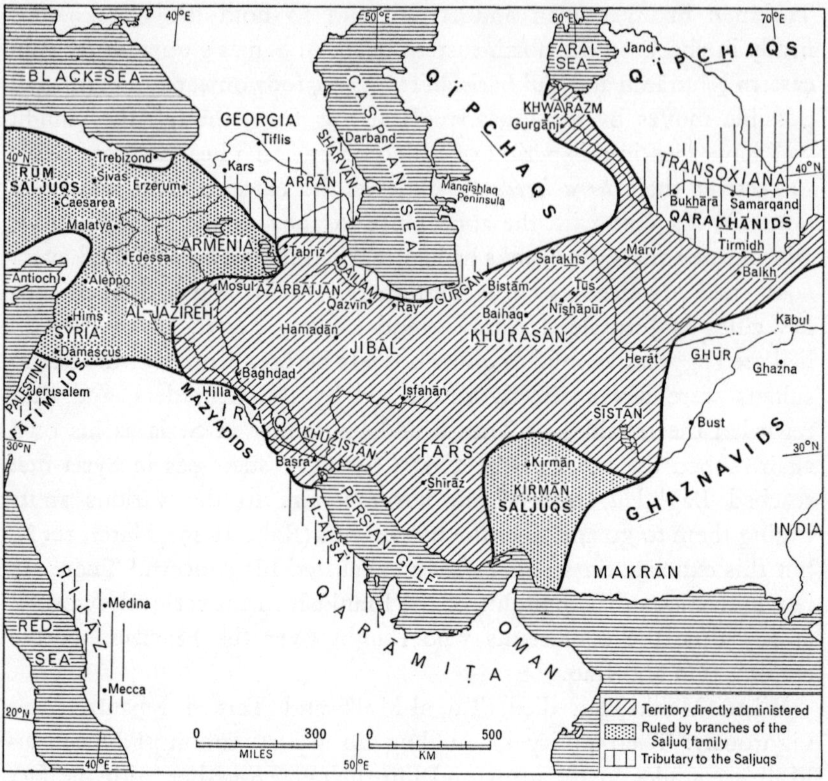

Map 3. The Saljuq Empire at the death of Malik Shāh (485/1092).

rival Muḥammad, under whom he later became Mustaufī and ʿĀriḍ al-Jaish.[1]

As a youth approaching manhood, Berk-Yaruq was clearly more fitted to hold together his father's heritage, and in the struggle against Tutush and Muḥammad he generally had the support of the Niẓāmiyya. This does not necessarily imply that the Niẓāmiyya had a collective policy, for none of the sons of Niẓām al-Mulk was his father's equal in ability, and opportunism and personal factors seem often to have swayed them. At the outset they desired vengeance on Tāj al-Mulk, who was captured on the defeat of Terken Khatun in 485/beginning

[1] Bundārī, *Zubdat al-nuṣra*, pp. 82–3; Ḥusainī, *Akhbār al-daula al-Saljūqiyya*, pp. 74–5; Ẓahīr al-Dīn Nīshāpūrī, *Saljūq-Nāma*, pp. 35–6; Rāvandī, *Rāḥat al-ṣudūr*, pp. 140–2; Ibn al-Athīr, *al-Kāmil*, vol. x, pp. 145–6; Barhebraeus, *Chronography*, p. 232. For general surveys of Berk-Yaruq's reign, see M. F. Sanaullah, *The Decline of the Saljūqid Empire*, pp. 83–113 and Cahen, "Barkyāruk", *Encyc. of Islam* (2nd ed.).

of 1093. Mindful of his capabilities, however, Berk-Yaruq wished to make him vizier, and Tāj al-Mulk mollified a good proportion of the Niẓāmiyya by judicious payments; but an irreconcilable element of them finally secured his death.[1] In the next few years personal animosities among Niẓām al-Mulk's sons placed them on opposite sides in the conflict. Berk-Yaruq's first vizier was the drunkard 'Izz al-Mulk Ḥusain, and then in 487/1094 the capable Mu'ayyid al-Mulk 'Ubaidallāh. Unfortunately, the hostility of the sultan's mother Zubaida Khatun led to his dismissal, and a further son, Fakhr al-Mulk Abu'l Muẓaffar, was appointed in his place. The latter and Mu'ayyid al-Mulk were strong enemies, for they had quarrelled over some jewels left by their father, and henceforth Mu'ayyid al-Mulk became the guiding spirit behind Muḥammad's bid for the sultanate.[2]

Terken Khatun's final act was to invite another member of the Saljuq family, Ismā'īl b. Yāqūtī, to march against Berk-Yaruq. Although Ismā'īl collected an army from the Türkmen of Āzarbāījān and Arrān, he was defeated and Berk-Yaruq's former atabeg Gümüsh-Tegin put him to death. From Iṣfahān Terken Khatun tried to make contact with Tutush, but she died suddenly in 487/1094, to be followed a month later by her son Maḥmūd.[3]

Early in this year Berk-Yaruq disposed of two other possible rivals, his uncle Tekish, who had been blinded by Malik-Shāh and imprisoned at Takrīt, and Tekish's son; Tekish, in an attempt to overthrow the youthful sultan, had allegedly been in touch with former supporters in his old appanage of Tukhāristān.[4] Despite the firmness of Alp-Arslan and Malik-Shāh, the traditional idea of a paternal inheritance divided amongst members of the family, coupled with the absence of any clear succession law, came to the surface in these uncertain times. In addition to his struggle with Terken Khatun, Berk-Yaruq was faced with a *coup d'état* in the east by one uncle, Arslan-Arghun, and in the west by a bid for the sultanate from another uncle, Tāj al-Daula Tutush.

Arslan-Arghun's rebellion was the less dangerous, for he seems to have had only the limited aim of making Khurāsān an autonomous province for himself. On hearing of Malik-Shāh's death he left his iqṭā' in Jibāl, seized several of the cities of Khurāsān, and demanded

[1] (Anon.), *Mujmal al-tawārīkh*, pp. 408–9; Ibn al-Athīr, vol. x, pp. 146–7.

[2] Bundārī, pp. 83–6; Ibn al-Athīr, vol. x, pp. 192–5.

[3] *Mujmal al-tawārīkh*, p. 409; Ẓahīr al-Dīn Nīshāpūrī, p. 36; Rāvandī, p. 141; Ibn al-Jauzī, vol. IX, p. 84; Ibn al-Athīr, vol. x, pp. 152, 159, 163; Barhebraeus, pp. 232–3.

[4] Ibn al-Athīr, vol. x, p. 162.

recognition as tributary ruler of the whole province except for Nīshāpūr. Against him Berk-Yaruq sent his uncle Böri-Bars b. Alp-Arslan, who had some initial successes but was captured in 488/1095 and strangled. Arslan-Arghun now began a reign of terror in Khurāsān, purging it of disaffected amīrs and demolishing the walls and fortifications of potentially rebellious places. It was his excesses which caused one of his own ghulāms to murder him in 490/1097. Berk-Yaruq had meanwhile appointed his half-brother Sanjar as governor in Khurāsān, providing him with an atabeg and vizier. A feeble attempt to set up Arslan-Arghun's young son in Balkh collapsed, and Berk-Yaruq and his army spent seven months at Balkh suppressing a further revolt by a Saljuq claimant, Muḥammad b. Sulaimān b. Toghrïl, who had received aid from the Ghaznavids (for more on this see p. 136 below). Beyond the Oxus, the situation in the Qarakhānid lands was somewhat troubled after the deposition and death of Aḥmad Khān in 488/1095 (see p. 93 above), which was followed shortly afterwards by the death of his successor Mas'ūd; Berk-Yaruq now confirmed the succession in Samarqand on Sulaimān and then on Maḥmūd Khān.[1]

The threat from Tutush was far more serious, for it threatened the whole basis of Berk-Yaruq's sultanate. Soon after his brother's death, Tutush had left Damascus accompanied by the ghulām commanders whom Malik-Shāh had installed in Syria, Aq-Sonqur, Yaghï-Basan, and Bozan; and in 486/1093 in the city of Baghdad he proclaimed himself sultan. He routed the Arabs of the 'Uqailid Ibrāhīm b. Quraish of Mosul, and in Baghdad itself Malik-Shāh's former shaḥna, Gauhar-Ā'īn, showed himself favourable to the new ruler. Soon afterwards his plans were disrupted by the desertion of Aq-Sonqur and Bozan, but in the next year Tutush killed these two undependable commanders and resumed the attack. Berk-Yaruq was recognized in Baghdad by the new caliph, al-Mustaẓhir (487–512/1094–1118), who granted him the honorific *Rukn al-Dīn* ("Pillar of Religion"), but Tutush was soon in occupation of all the western lands of the empire, and Berk-Yaruq had the misfortune to fall into the hands of Maḥmūd's partisans at Iṣfahān, who planned to blind him and so render him unfit for the sultanate. Before doing this, however, they decided to wait and see whether the child Maḥmūd should recover from his

[1] Bundārī, *Zubdat al-nuṣra*, pp. 85, 255–9; Ibn Funduq, *Ta'rīkh-i Baihaq*, pp. 53, 269; Ẓahīr al-Dīn Nīshāpūrī, *Saljuq-Nāma*, p. 37; Rāvandī, *Rāḥat al-ṣudūr*, pp. 143–4; Ḥusainī, *Akhbār al-daula*, pp. 78, 84–7; Ibn al-Athīr, *al-Kāmil*, vol. x, pp. 178–81; Barthold, *Turkestan down to the Mongol Invasion*, p. 318.

smallpox. As we have seen, he did not recover: thus Berk-Yaruq's sight was saved, and those many amīrs who feared Tutush now rallied to the sultan. Even so, his position still seemed desperate, for he himself was suddenly stricken with smallpox; but now he had the help of Mu'ayyid al-Mulk as vizier, and he was even given a breathing space when Tutush withdrew temporarily to Ray, probably because the provisioning of his large army in mid-winter was proving difficult. Berk-Yaruq soon collected 30,000 troops and defeated Tutush near Ray; during the battle one of Aq-Sonqur's ghulāms avenged his master and slew Tutush (488/1095). The remnants of his army fled to Syria, and Berk-Yaruq seemed secure on the throne.[1]

The seat of Berk-Yaruq's personal power was essentially Iraq and western Iran. Khurāsān, of course, always remained important to the Saljuqs because it had been the cradle of their power, and in the brief period of peace before the rise of his rival Muḥammad, the sultan devoted to it as much attention as he was able. He went personally to suppress Arslan-Arghun's revolt, but shortly after his return to Iraq in the latter part of 490/1097, he had to send the *Amīr-i Dād* ("Chief Justiciar") Ḥabashī b. Altun-Taq to deal with Qodun, the governor of Marv, and with another amīr, Yaruq-Tash. These two had killed the Saljuq governor of Khwārazm, Ekinchi b. Qochqar, and had tried to annex the province for themselves, but Ḥabashī suppressed the outbreak and appointed as Khwārazm-Shāh a man named Quṭb al-Dīn Muḥammad b. Anūsh-Tegin Gharcha'ī, founder of the line of shāhs who were to play such a big role in Persian history in the decades before the Mongol invasions (see below, pp. 185 ff.). After this, distractions in the west forced Berk-Yaruq to leave Khurāsān to Sanjar.[2]

Likewise, he granted Ganja to Sanjar's uterine brother, Muḥammad, with Qutlugh-Tegin as his atabeg; very soon Muḥammad threw off the latter's control, killing him and taking over the whole of Arrān. Syria was always of peripheral importance to Great Saljuqs, and Berk-Yaruq never went there in person, despite al-Mustaẓhir's message to

[1] *Mujmal al-tawārīkh*, p. 409; Bundārī, pp. 84–5; Ẓahīr al-Dīn Nīshāpūrī, p. 36; Rāvandī, pp. 142–3; Ibn al-Jauzī, *al-Muntaẓam*, vol. IX, pp. 76–7, 80, 84–5, 87–8; Ḥusainī, pp. 75–6; Ibn al-Athīr, vol. x, pp. 149–51, 155–9, 166–7; Ibn Khallikān, *Wafayāt al-a'yān*, vol. I, pp. 273–5.

[2] Ibn al-Athīr, vol. x, pp. 181–3; Juvainī, *Ta'rīkh-i Jahān-Gushā*, vol. I, 277–8; Sachau, "Zur Geschichte und Chronologie von Khwârazm", *S.B.W.A.W.* pp. 314–16; Barthold, *Turkestan*, pp. 333–4; İ. Kafesoğlu, *Harezmşahlar devleti tarihi*, pp. 37–8.

him in 491/1098 expressing alarm at the successes of the Crusaders. Tutush's two sons Riḍwān and Duqaq were left in Aleppo and Damascus respectively, where they were duly provided with atabegs. The formerly 'Uqailid amīrate of Mosul then passed to a succession of Turkish and Türkmen commanders. In central Iraq, Saif al-Daula Ṣadaqa (479–501/1086–1108) made the Mazyadids a considerable power in this period. He intervened frequently in the confused affairs of Baghdad—this city alternated between allegiance to Berk-Yaruq and to his rivals Tutush and then Muḥammad—and in 496/1103 he added the formerly 'Uqailid town of Hīt to his possessions.[1] Farther south, in the marshlands of the Baṭīḥa, there was the local dynasty of the Banū Abi'l-Jabr under Muhadhdhib al-Daula Abu'l-'Abbās. Baṣra and Wāsiṭ were nominally under Berk-Yaruq's control, but the Turkish muqṭa's of this region were in practice little troubled.[2] In Khūzistān and its chief town Shustar, Toghrïl's former amīr Bursuq and his four sons established themselves as hereditary muqṭa's. These sons remained generally attached to Berk-Yaruq's cause, and the sultan on more than one occasion dropped back from central Iran into Khūzistān to rest and to assemble fresh armies.[3]

The remaining years of Berk-Yaruq's reign, from 490/1097 to 498/1105, were taken up with the struggle against his half-brother Abū Shujā' Muḥammad Tapar (*Tapar* = Turkish for "he who obtains, finds"),[4] who, in accordance with his claim to the sultanate, secured from the caliph in 492/1099 the honorific *Ghiyāth al-Dunyā wa'l-Dīn* ("Support in Secular and Religious Affairs").[5] These years were full of warfare and of shifting alliances amongst the Turkish amīrs. Muḥammad received much help from Sanjar; he also had at his disposal the administrative skill of Mu'ayyid al-Mulk, and the bulk of the Niẓāmiyya now fought on his side. For his part, Berk-Yaruq had only his own military skill and the loyalty of a nucleus of amīrs, including Ayāz and the governor of Hamadān, Il Ghāzī. Even for the support of the sons of Bursuq he had to pay a price: in 492/1099 Zangī and Aq-Böri insisted that he sacrifice his vizier Majd al-Mulk Abu'l-Faḍl

[1] Ibn al-Athīr, *al-Kāmil*, vol. x, pp. 247–8. Several of the sources state that it was Ṣadaqa who built for the dynasty a splendid new capital at Ḥilla, but this is not accurate: see G. Makdisi, "Notes on Ḥilla and the Mazyadids in Mediaeval Islam", *J.A.O.S.* pp. 249–62.

[2] Cf. Ibn al-Athīr, vol. x, pp. 232–4.

[3] Cf. Cahen, "Bursuk", *Encyc. of Islam* (2nd ed.).

[4] Cf. P. Pelliot, *Notes sur l'histoire de la Horde d'Or* (Paris 1950), pp. 182–3.

[5] Ibn al-Athīr, vol. x, pp. 195–6.

al-Balāsānī, who had S̲h̲ī'ī sympathies and was allegedly privy to the Ismā'īlīs' assassination of Bursuq.[1] The accusation that he had Ismā'īlī sympathies was frequently hurled at Berk-Yaruq by his opponents. On the occasions when his fortunes were low he certainly seems to have accepted Ismā'īlī troops in his army;[2] and it is said that when besieging Terken K̲h̲atun and Maḥmūd in Iṣfahān, he feigned sympathy in order to get the support of local Ismā'īlīs. But there are no signs of an active sympathy with these schismatics, which would have brought down on his head fierce condemnation from the Sunnī religious institution and from the 'Abbasid caliph.

A former governor of Fārs whose reputation there had been damaged by his failure to quell the S̲h̲abānkāra, the Amīr Öner, was persuaded by Mu'ayyid al-Mulk to rebel against Berk-Yaruq. In 492/1099 Öner took 10,000 troops to Ray, but his rising collapsed when he was murdered by a Turkish g̲h̲ulām; as so often happened when an army became leaderless, the troops mutinied, plundered the dead commander's treasury, and then scattered. Mu'ayyid al-Mulk now fled to Ganja, becoming vizier to Muḥammad, who at this point formally proclaimed himself sultan. The killing of his own vizier al-Balāsānī created a crisis of confidence for Berk-Yaruq. He still had a fair-sized army under Inal b. Anūs̲h̲-Tegin, as well as the help of one of Niẓām al-Mulk's sons, 'Izz al-Dīn Manṣūr; yet Iṣfahān refused to admit him, and then his mother Zubaida K̲h̲atun was captured at Ray and strangled by Mu'ayyid al-Mulk. Support for Muḥammad was growing among the Turkish amīrs of Iraq and al-Jazīreh, men such as Kür-Bug̲h̲a in Mosul and C̲h̲ökermis̲h̲ in Jazīrat ibn 'Umar; in Kurdistān the 'Annāzid Surk̲h̲āb b. Badr joined him, and in Baghdad Gauhar-Ā'īn secured the k̲h̲uṭba for him.[3]

Still further changes of allegiance took place. When in 493/1100 Berk-Yaruq faced his brother in battle, he had at his side Gauhar-Ā'īn, Kür-Bug̲h̲a, Surk̲h̲āb, and the Mazyadid 'Izz al-Daula Muḥammad b. Ṣadaqa. This clash, the first of five between the rival sultans, nevertheless ended disastrously for Berk-Yaruq. He fled from Hamadān to Nīs̲h̲āpūr, seeking for help from the governor Ḥabashī, and it is on this march through northern Iran that he is said to have joined forces with

[1] Bundārī, pp. 87–8; Ẓahīr al-Dīn Nīs̲h̲āpūrī, pp. 37–8; Rāvandī, pp. 145–6; Ibn al-Ath̲īr, vol. x, pp. 196–7.

[2] Cf. Hodgson, *The Order of Assassins*, pp. 86–8.

[3] Bundārī, pp. 84–91; Ẓahīr al-Dīn Nīs̲h̲āpūrī, p. 37; Rāvandī, pp. 144–5; Ibn al-Jauzī, vol. ix, pp. 109–10; Ḥusainī, pp. 76–7; Ibn al-Ath̲īr, vol. x, pp. 192–7.

5,000 Ismāʿīlī troops, presumably from Dailam or Kūhistān. He then marched across Iran to K͟hūzistān, where Bursuq's sons Zangī and Il-Begi gave him their support, and in the second battle with Muḥammad, in 494/1101, the latter was defeated and Muʾayyid al-Mulk captured. In revenge for his mother, and because the vizier had imputed to him Ismāʿīlī sympathies, Berk-Yaruq killed him personally.[1]

Muḥammad now called in Sanjar from Balk͟h, and the union of their two armies caused support to melt from Berk-Yaruq. Part of his forces had to be detached and sent with Kür-Bug͟ha to Āzarbāijān, where Maudūd b. Ismāʿīl b. Yāqūtī was in revolt against Berk-Yaruq and was vowing vengeance for his father. Problems of logistics and an inability to pay his troops troubled the sultan. He appeared in Baghdad with 5,000 unruly cavalrymen who plundered the Sawād and made his cause very unpopular, and when he tried to get a subsidy from the caliph by asking for the arrears of tribute from the Mazyadid ruler Ṣadaqa, he only caused the latter to declare for Muḥammad.[2] Now he had to retreat southwards into K͟hūzistān, destroy the bridges behind him to prevent pursuit. Muḥammad's followers had jeeringly called his troops *Bāṭiniyya*, and at some point during his withdrawal from Baghdad, Berk-Yaruq carried out a purge of the Ismāʿīlīs in his army. The organizer of Ismāʿīlī propaganda in the army is said to have been one of the last scions of the Kākūyids, Muḥammad b. Dus͟hmanziyār of Yazd; whether this fact is an instance of Dailamī heterodoxy, or just a fiction hiding other reasons for his killing, is unknown.[3]

The third battle, at Rūd͟hrāvar in 495/1102, consisted of indecisive personal combats, after which negotiations were opened up and a settlement reached. Muḥammad was to bear the title of Malik and have Arrān, Āzarbāijān, Diyārbakr, al-Jazīreh, and Mosul; whilst Berk-Yaruq was to have all the rest and the title of Sulṭān. But Muḥammad repudiated this in less than two months and arrogated for himself the sultan's privilege of five *naubas* (salutes of military music). He was routed in a fourth battle and shut himself in Iṣfahān, after hurriedly restoring the walls around ʿAlāʾ al-Daula Ibn Kākūya's palace. Berk-Yaruq now

---

[1] *Mujmal al-tawārīk͟h*, pp. 409–10; Bundārī, pp. 88–9, 260; Ẓahīr al-Dīn Nīs͟hāpūrī, pp. 38–9; Rāvandī, pp. 148–9; Ibn al-Jauzī, vol. IX, pp. 112–13, 123, 129; Ibn al-At͟hīr, vol. X, pp. 198–202, 205–7.

[2] For more on Ṣadaqa, see below, p. 115.

[3] Bundārī, p. 261; Ibn al-Jauzī, vol. IX, pp. 120, 122–4; Ḥusainī, pp. 77–8; Ibn al-At͟hīr, vol. X, pp. 207–10, 220–1. According to the *Mujmal al-tawārīk͟h*, p. 409, another Kākūyid, ʿAlī b. Farāmurz b. ʿAlāʾ al-Daula, fought for Tutus͟h and was killed with him at the battle of Dās͟hīlū (see above, p. 107).

began a nine-month siege of the city during which the occupants suffered terrible deprivations, though Muḥammad managed to escape. Simultaneously the struggle for power in Baghdad and Iraq was being carried on by Berk-Yaruq's shaḥna, Gümüsh-Tegin al-Qaiṣarī, and Muḥammad's shaḥna Il Ghāzī b. Artuq. Then in 496/1103 Berk-Yaruq marched into Āzarbāijān against Muḥammad and Maudūd b. Ismā'īl b. Yāqūtī, and a fifth and last battle, again a defeat for Muḥammad, took place at Khuy between Lakes Urmīyeh and Vān.[1]

Berk-Yaruq's illnesses and the exhaustion of his resources inclined him to make peace in 497/1104, even though he held at this time most of western and central Iran, along with Iraq and Diyārbakr. There was to be a full *divisio imperii*, each ruler becoming sultan in his own lands. Muḥammad was to have north-western Iran, Diyārbakr, al-Jazīreh, Mosul, and Syria; Berk-Yaruq was to have the core of the empire, Jibāl, Ṭabaristān, Fārs, Khūzistān, Baghdad, and the Ḥaramain, i.e. Mecca and Medina; whilst Sanjar was to remain in Khurāsān, making the khuṭba for Muḥammad. Whether this precarious arrangement would have lasted can only be surmised. A year later Berk-Yaruq died, leaving an infant son Malik-Shāh as his successor and Ayāz as his atabeg. Ayāz and Il-Ghāzī proclaimed him in Baghdad, but Muḥammad marched there *via* Mosul and Ayaz, and Vizier al-Ṣafī Sa'd al-Mulk Abu'l-Maḥāsin decided that resistance was hopeless. Muḥammad thus became sultan over the whole of the Saljuq territories.[2]

The verdict of posterity has been that Berk-Yaruq was not a man of his father's calibre. Yet it is not surprising that he burnt himself out by the age of twenty-five, for he campaigned ceaselessly, was often ill, and was several times wounded by assassins. He was never able to dislodge Muḥammad from Āzarbāijān, and he had continuously to defend the core of his territories, Fārs and Jibāl, while also attempting to maintain his influence in Iraq.

The divisions of power between Berk-Yaruq and Muḥammad demonstrated cogently how vital was the principle of a patrimonial share-out. The role of the ghulām commanders and the Türkmen begs becomes very prominent in this period, and local Türkmen dynasties

[1] Bundārī, p. 261; Ibn al-Jauzī, vol. IX, pp. 131, 133–4; Ḥusainī, pp. 77–8; Ibn al-Athīr, vol. x, pp. 224–36.

[2] *Mujmal al-Tawārīkh*, p. 410; Bundārī, pp. 89–90; Ibn al-Jauzī, vol. IX, pp. 138, 141–3; Ibn al-Athīr, vol. x, pp. 253–5, 260–8; Sibṭ b. al-Jauzī, *Mir'āt al-zamān fī ta'rīkh al-a'yān*, vol. I, pp. 8, 12–13; Barhebraeus, pp. 238–9.

begin to form: the sons of Bursuq in Khūzistān; the Artuqids in Diyārbakr; at Khilāṭ the Shāh-Armanids, descendants of Ismā'īl b. Yāqūtī's ghulām Sukmān al-Quṭbī; and shortly afterwards the Zangids, descendants of Aq-Sonqur, in Mosul. Other local dynasties, e.g. the 'Annāzids and Mazyadids, persisted and even strengthened their position. After Malik-Shāh's death there were many young Saljuq princes in provincial appanages, each normally provided with a Turkish ghulām as his atabeg. These tutors not only exercised power on their charges' behalf, but often succeeded in arrogating effective power for themselves, especially after the death of Sulṭān Muḥammad in 511/1118; towards the middle of the century, for example, the family of Eldigüz, atabeg of Arslan b. Toghrïl b. Muḥammad, founded a powerful, autonomous dynasty in the north-west.[1] A further notable feature of the 6th/12th century was a rise in the prestige and actual power of the 'Abbāsid caliphate, due in large part to the need of rival claimants for caliphal support and confirmation of titles.

Many of the troops of Berk-Yaruq and Muḥammad were furnished by the Turkish amīrs, whose frequent changes of side show that their interest lay in opposing the reconstitution of an effective central power; yet their attitude did ensure that, however crushingly any contestant was defeated, he could generally reassemble forces fairly quickly. The worst sufferers were, of course, the populations of Iran and the Sawād of Iraq, across which armies were constantly marching. The rival sultans were rarely able to collect regular territorial taxation, and irregular levies were therefore resorted to, above all when cities changed hands: e.g. Muḥammad's generals Inal b. Anūsh-Tegin and his brother 'Ali collected 200,000 dīnārs from Iṣfahān in 496/1102.[2] To satisfy the soldiery, estates were often confiscated and parcelled out as iqṭā's amongst them; it was said against Berk-Yaruq's vizier, al-'Amīd al-A'azz Abu'l-Maḥāsin al-Dihistānī, that he even seized private properties and turned them into iqṭā's.[3] Practices like these inevitably contributed to economic and social regression after the period of internal peace under Malik-Shāh.

Scorched-earth tactics were another recognized military measure. When in 498/1105 Chökermish was threatened at Mosul by Muḥammad, he gathered everyone inside the walls of the city and then devastated the surrounding countryside. The ravages of Sanjar's army in 494/1101

[1] Cf. Cahen, "Atabak", *Encyc. of Islam* (2nd ed.).

[2] Ibn al-Athīr, vol. x, p. 243.

[3] Bundārī, p. 89.

as he marched through Qūmis to join Muḥammad at Ray were particularly severe, causing famine and reducing people to cannibalism.[1] This general decline in security also encouraged sectarian and factional disturbance. In the cities of Khurāsān, for instance, the old *'aṣabiyyāt* (factions), involving unpopular groups such as the Shī'a and Karāmiyya, flared up; in Kurdistān there was fighting between the 'Annāzid Surkhāb and the Türkmen of the Salghur tribe, who had been dispossessing the indigenous Kurds of their pastures.[2]

Above all, the sources state that disturbed conditions favoured the spread of Ismā'īlism, especially in Kūhistān and Fārs. In northern Syria Riḍwān b. Tutush earned himself eternal obloquy from Sunnī historians by his use of local Ismā'īlīs in warfare against his brother. Berk-Yaruq massacred Ismā'īlīs in western Iran and Baghdad, and other amīrs carried out operations in Dailam, Fārs, and Khūzistān, without, however, permanently dislodging the sectaries from their strongholds.[3] Some of the greatest successes of the Bāṭiniyya in this period were in Kūhistān, where large stretches of territory were under their regular control. Mentioned amongst their allies is a certain al-Munawwar, a descendant of the Sīmjūrid family who in the 4th/10th century had held Kūhistān from the Sāmānids. Sanjar sent both regular troops and ghāzīs into the province, but the most he could achieve was an agreement with the Ismā'īlīs that they should voluntarily limit their activities.[4]

Muḥammad reigned for thirteen years as undisputed sultan (498–511/1105–18), while his brother Sanjar remained at Balkh as his viceroy in the east, receiving the title of Malik. Whilst the sources are lukewarm about Berk-Yaruq, they eulogize Muḥammad as "the perfect man of the Saljuqs and their mighty stallion", praising his zeal for the Sunna and his hatred of the Bāṭiniyya.[5] They do not, on the other hand, reveal him to be a more capable ruler or soldier than Berk-Yaruq. Several facts explain Muḥammad's popularity in pious circles. First, it was his fortune to secure sole power after the kingdom had been

[1] Ibn al-Athīr, vol. x, pp. 207, 262; cf. Sanaullah, *Decline of the Saljūqid Empire*, pp. 70 ff. In 494/1101 Sanjar is said to have taxed even baths and caravanserais at Nīshāpūr (Ibn al-Jauzī, vol. IX, p. 123), and the violence and oppression of his ghulāms and agents at Baihaq is mentioned by Ibn Funduq, p. 269.

[2] Ibn al-Athīr, vol. x, p. 238–9.

[3] *Ibid.* pp. 217–18, 220–1; cf. Sanaullah, *op. cit.* pp. 66–8, and Hodgson, *The Order of Assassins*, pp. 88 ff.

[4] Ibn al-Athīr, vol. x, pp. 217, 221–2, 260; cf. Hodgson, *op. cit.* pp. 74–5, 88.

[5] Bundārī, p. 118.

gripped by civil war for years, and at a time when it was economically exhausted and ready to accept anyone who could give peace. This period of peace enabled the sultan to give moral encouragment and a certain amount of indirect military help to the Syrian amīrs, who were struggling to contain the Crusaders; even more important, he was able to take action against the Ismā'īlīs in Persia, who, profiting by the previous disorders, had consolidated their position in Dailam, Fārs, and Kūhistān. Finally, Muḥammad was the last Great Saljuq to have firm and undisputed control of western Iran and Iraq, the heartland of the sultanate since Toghrïl's time. After his death his sons ruled successively as subordinates of Sanjar, and the centre of gravity of the sultanate tended to shift eastwards to its birthplace, Khurāsān. Since the sources are usually partial to Niẓām al-Mulk and his descendants, their picture of Muḥammad is influenced by the fact that he received support from the majority of the Niẓāmiyya, which began when Mu'ayyid al-Mulk first espoused his cause in 492/1099. Muḥammad also employed Naṣīr al-Mulk b. Mu'ayyid al-Mulk, first as his chief secretary and then as vizier to his sons; and in 500/1107 Niẓām al-Mulk, Ḍiyā' al-Mulk Aḥmad b. Niẓām al-Mulk, became his own vizier for four years, the sultan insisting on having one of the family because of their innate capability and auspiciousness (*baraka*).[1]

The ambiguous attitudes and shifting allegiances of the Turkish, Kurdish, and Arab amīrs of Jibāl, Iraq, al-Jazīreh, and Diyārbakr had added much to the confusion of Berk-Yaruq's reign. Muḥammad now endeavoured to curb these amīrs by reducing over-mighty subjects and diverting energies into the holy wars in Syria. But like all preceding sultans, he had to deal first of all with rival claims from members of his own dynasty. In 499/1105–6 Mengü-Bars b. Böri-Bars rebelled at Nihāvand. He tried to draw the sons of Bursuq to his side, but the sultan captured and jailed him together with other potential claimants, the sons of Tekish. In the following year Qïlïch-Arslan b. Sulaimān, who had been fighting the Franks at Edessa, came to Mosul at the invitation of Zangī b. Chökermish, established himself there, and claimed the sultanate for himself; eventually defeated by Muḥammad's general Chavlï, and knowing himself to be a rebel who could expect only short shrift from the sultan, Sulaimān drowned himself to avoid capture.[2]

[1] *Ibid.* pp. 89, 93, 96 ff.; Ibn al-Jauzī, vol. IX, p. 150; Ibn al-Athīr, vol. X, p. 304.

[2] Ibn al-Jauzī, vol. IX, p. 146; Ibn al-Athīr, vol. X, pp. 274, 286–7, 293–8; Sibṭ b. al-Jauzī, vol. I, p. 22.

It was a measure of Muḥammad's sense of strength that in 501/1108 he decided to overthrow the Mazyadid Saif al-Daula Ṣadaqa. During the fighting between Berk-Yaruq and Muḥammad, the so-called "King of the Arabs" had usually lent his support to the latter, but neither side had had a preponderance in central Iraq and the rivalry of the two Saljuqs had probably been helpful to Mazyadid interests. At first Ṣadaqa continued in high favour. Deputed to recover Baṣra, he and Muhadhdhib al-Daula of the Banū Abi'l-Jabr expelled from there a Turkish amīr who had installed himself during the previous disturbances, and the city was now restored to Saljuq control. Then in 498/1105 he received the grant of Wāsiṭ.[1] But slanders about Ṣadaqa seem to have been spread at the Saljuq court by the 'Amīd Abū Ja'far al-Balkhī: he was even accused of Ismā'īlī inclinations, possibly because of his strongly Shī'ī beliefs.

Yet the sources unite in stressing how Ṣadaqa embodied the traditional Arab virtues of liberality and hospitality. His house in Baghdad was "the inviolate refuge of all those in fear" (Ibn al-Jauzī), and "in his reign, Ḥilla was the halting-place of the traveller, the refuge of the hopeful ones, the asylum of the outcast, and the sanctuary of the terrified fugitive" (Ibn al-Ṭiqṭaqā). Indeed, it was his sheltering of the refugee Dailamī governor of Āveh and Sāveh which gave the sultan a pretext to move against him; before this Ṣadaqa had behaved very circumspectly, refusing in 500/1107 to go to the aid of Zangī b. Chökermish in Mosul lest the sultan be offended. In a battle in the marshlands of al-Za'farāniyya, Ṣadaqa's Arabs and Kurds were defeated by Muḥammad's forces, amongst whom were the sons of Bursuq and the Kākūyid Abū Kālījār Garshāsp; the sultan's palace ghulāms and Turkish archers played a prominent part in decimating Ṣadaqa's front-line troops, and Ṣadaqa himself was killed. It was not Muḥammad's aim to occupy the Mazyadid capital of Ḥilla; he contented himself with carrying off Ṣadaqa's son Dubais and even appointed Ṣadaqa's old commander-in-chief as governor of the city.[2]

For several years al-Jazīreh and Mosul had been disputed among various local amīrs. The region was strategically important as a frontier march against the Türkmen elements in Diyārbakr and

[1] Ibn al-Athīr, vol. x, pp. 276–9, 283–4, 302–3.

[2] Bundārī, *Zubdat al-nuṣra*, p. 102; Ẓahīr al-Dīn Nīshāpūrī, *Saljūq-Nāma*, p. 39; Rāvandī, *Rāḥat al-ṣudūr*, p. 154; Ibn al-Jauzī, *al-Muntaẓam*, vol. ix, pp. 156–7, 159; Ḥusainī, *Akhbār al-daula*, pp. 80–1; Ibn al-Athīr, *al-Kāmil*, vol. x, pp. 306–14; Sibṭ b. al-Jauzī, *Mir'āt al-zamān*, vol. i, pp. 25–7; Ibn al-Ṭiqṭaqā, *al-Fakhrī*, pp. 269–70 (Whitting tr., pp. 291–2).

Armenia, many of whom were grouped around the Artuqid ruler of Nisībīn, Il-Ghāzī, and around Sukmān al-Quṭbī of Akhlāṭ; it was also a frontier against the Crusaders, who were pressing eastwards from Edessa. Furthermore, in these years Riḍwān of Aleppo was trying to bring Mosul into his own sphere of influence and thereby utilize its resources for his wars against the Franks. Muḥammad tried to stabilize the position by the direct appointment of successive ghulām governors in Mosul: Chavlï Saqao, Maudūd b. Altun-Tegin, Aq-Sonqur al-Bursuqī, and Ai-Aba Juyūsh (?Chavush) Beg, the last two being made atabegs to his son Mas'ūd. He hoped, too, to use these amīrs and their troops against the Franks in Syria. His relations with the spiritual head of Sunnī Islam, the 'Abbasid caliph, were cordial, and in 502/1108–9 a marriage was arranged between al-Mustaẓhir and Muḥammad's sister, the daughter of Malik-Shāh.[1] Appeals for help against the Franks came from the hard-pressed people of Aleppo and even from the Byzantine Emperor Alexis Comnenus. From 501/1107–8 onwards, Fakhr al-Mulk Ibn 'Ammār, the dispossessed ruler of Tripoli, haunted the Saljuq court, until Muḥammad was moved to send troops and money to his cousin Duqaq of Damascus for the relief of Tripoli.[2] Chavlï, Maudūd, Aq-Sonqur, and Bursuq b. Bursuq all campaigned in Syria with little success, mainly because of the coolness of Il-Ghāzī and of Tugh-Tegin of Damascus, who in 509/1115 allied with the Franks. The crushing victory of the Crusaders at Dānīth in that year, coupled with the death of the Saljuq rulers in Syria, put an end to Muḥammad's hopes of intervening in Syria.

Little is mentioned of internal conditions in western and central Iran during Muḥammad's reign, apart from the continuing activities of the Ismā'īlīs. On the north-western frontier an attack on Ganja by the Georgians was repelled (503/1109–10).[3] After the suppression of Mengü-Bars' revolt in Jibāl, the sultan took the opportunity of exchanging the iqṭā's held by Bursuq's sons in Khūzistān for others in the region of Dīnāvār, presumably to reduce the concentration of their power in the south-west.[4] Fārs was governed by Fakhr al-Daula Chavlï Saqao from 498/1104 to 500/1106, and then again from 502/1109 till his death eight years later. According to Ibn al-Athīr's account, Chavlï ruled oppressively, using Muḥammad's infant son Chaghrï, for whom he

[1] Ḥusainī, pp. 81–2; Ibn al-Athīr, vol. x, pp. 330, 339; Sibṭ b. al-Jauzī, vol. 1, p. 27.

[2] Ibn al-Athīr, vol. x, pp. 315–17, 339; cf. Sibṭ b. al-Jauzī, vol. 1, pp. 31, 35–7, 46.

[3] Ibn al-Qalānisī, *Dhail ta'rīkh Dimashq*, p. 167; Ḥusainī, p. 81.

[4] Ibn al-Athīr, vol. x, p. 274.

was atabeg, as a cloak for his tyrannies and expropriations. On the other hand Ibn al-Balkhī, Chavlï's contemporary and the local historian of Fārs, mentions several measures taken by the atabeg to restore order and prosperity. The chief obstacle to order in Fārs remained the Shabānkāra'īs, and Chavlï began systematically to reduce their castles, capturing over seventy of them and dismantling the fortifications of most of them. Campaigns were also launched against the tribal chiefs of the Kurds, such as Ḥasan b. al-Mubāriz of Fasā and Abū Saʿd b. Muḥammad b. Masā of the Karzuvī tribe. The chief of Dārābjird, Ibrāhīm, was expelled and forced to flee to Kirmān, where his kinsman by marriage, the Saljuq ruler of Kirmān, sheltered him. Chavlï accordingly marched against Kirmān in 508/1114–15 to demand the extradition of the Shabānkāra'īs who had fled there, but he was unable to get beyond a point on the frontier between Fārs and Kirmān.[1] However, Chavlï had many positive achievements in Fārs to his credit: the rebuilding of towns, the restoration of agriculture, and in particular the repair of irrigation works and dams, such as the Band-i Qaṣṣār in the district of Lower Kurbāl and the dam in the district of Rāmjird, which was named "Fakhristān" in his honour. On the whole, Muḥammad's reign witnessed a distinct improvement in the pacification of Fārs; the sultan himself conciliated the tribal chieftains and kept a group of Shabānkāra'ī leaders permanently in his service at court.[2]

Kirmān was ruled from 495/1101 to 537/1142 by Muḥiyy al-Islām Arslan-Shāh b. Kirmān Shāh. Although he ruled longer than any other Saljuqs of Kirmān, Muḥammad b. Ibrāhīm has very little to say about his reign, presumably because it was in general peaceful and uneventful. He does mention Arslan-Shāh's encouragement of the ulema and scholars, and states that in his reign Kirmān reached new heights of commercial prosperity; chaos and piracy in the Persian Gulf meant that much trade was coming overland, and the trading suburb of the capital expanded greatly. The continued existence of this compact Saljuq amirate in eastern central Iran, with its permanent force of Türkmen soldiery, made it a haven for political refugees and for those seeking military help; it was during this period that Kirmān sheltered the Ghaznavid Bahrām-Shāh b. Masʿūd III. Arslan-Shāh also intervened at Yazd on behalf of the last members of the Kākūyid family,

[1] Muḥammad b. Ibrāhīm, Taʾrīkh-i Saljūqiyān-i Kirmān, p. 26 (cf. Houtsma, "Zur Geschichte der Selǧuqen von Kermân", Z.D.M.G. p. 374); Ibn al-Athīr, vol. x, pp. 361–5.
[2] Ibn al-Balkhī, Fārs-Nāma, pp. 128, 130, 151–2, 157–8 (tr., pp. 29, 32, 39, 65–6, 74); Bundārī, p. 122.

who held their fiefs there, and afterwards he received this town from one of the Kākūyid disputants. Keeping up links with the Great Saljuqs, Arslan-Shāh married one of Sulṭān Muḥammad's daughters, and was careful not to infringe on the rights of Sanjar in Khurāsān. Thus whilst welcoming Bahrām-Shāh, he refused to give him military help, referring him to Sanjar as the senior representative of the Saljuqs in eastern Iran; it was in fact with Sanjar's help that Bahrām-Shāh was placed on the throne at Ghazna in 510/1117 (see below, pp. 158–9).[1]

The freedom from external pressure left Muḥammad free to tackle the question of the Ismā'īlīs with some success, although he never permanently quelled them. The political assassinations carried out by the Bāṭinī fidā'īs created an unpleasant atmosphere of suspicion and fear within the sultanate, while the denunciation of "heretics" is a common feature of Muḥammad's reign. In 500/1107 Vizier Sa'd al-Mulk Abu'l-Maḥāsin was denounced by one of his enemies and executed, together with many of the Dīvān officials;[2] fifteen years later, under Maḥmūd b. Muḥammad, the celebrated poet and stylist al-Ṭughrā'ī was executed on a trumped-up charge of heresy (see pp. 158–9 below). Under the influence of the ra'īs of Iṣfahān, 'Abdallāh al-Khaṭībī, Muḥammad purged the administration of many allegedly Ismā'īlī sympathizers, and started a policy of favouring Khurāsānīs at the expense of "'Irāqīs" (i.e. those from western Iran or 'Irāq 'Ajamī), on the plea that the Khurāsānīs were stronger supporters of orthodoxy.[3]

Amongst the military operations against the Bāṭiniyya, the capture of Shāhdīz near Iṣfahān and that of Khānlanjān in 500/1107 brought the sultan much prestige; despite the fact that some of the defenders escaped to Kūhistān and to other fortresses in Fārs, Aḥmad b. 'Abd al-Malik b. 'Aṭṭāsh and his son were both killed.[4] Alamūt, the seat of Ḥasan-i Ṣabbāh, was besieged either in 501/1107–8 or two years later by Vizier Ḍiyā' al-Mulk and Amīr Chavlī; it was the vizier's failure here which led to his downfall. In 505/1111–12 the sultan sent the governor of Āveh and Sāveh, Anūsh-Tegin Shīrgīr (?b. Shīrgīr), who captured various castles in the region of Qazvīn and Dailam. Towards

[1] Muḥammad b. Ibrāhīm, pp. 25–7 (cf. Houtsma, *Z.D.M.G.* pp. 374–5).
[2] Bundārī, p. 92; Ibn al-Athīr, vol. x, p. 304.
[3] Bundārī, pp. 95–6.
[4] *Ibid.* p. 91; Ibn al-Qalānisī, pp. 151–6 (text of *fatḥ-nāma*); Ẓahīr al-Dīn Nīshāpūrī, pp. 40 ff.; Rāvandī, pp. 155 ff.; Ibn al-Jauzī, vol. ix, pp. 150–1; Ibn al-Athīr, vol. x, pp. 299–302; Sibṭ b. al-Jauzī, vol. i, pp. 19–20; cf. Hodgson, *The Order of Assassins*, pp. 95–6.

the end of the reign Anūs̲h̲-Tegin again besieged Alamūt and was near to capturing it when the news of the sultan's death arrived and the army thereupon dispersed, allowing all its stores and baggage to fall into the Assassins' hands.[1]

IX. THE SALJUQ SULTANATE IN THE WEST UNDER THE SONS OF MUḤAMMAD B. MALIK-S̲H̲ĀH

Muḥammad died in 511/1118 and in his last illness he appointed his son Maḥmūd as successor. Maḥmūd reigned for fourteen years (511–25/1118–31) with the honorific *Mug̲h̲īt̲h̲ al-Dunyā wa'l-Dīn* ("Bringer of Help in Secular and Religious Affairs"). But there were four other sons, Masʿūd, Tog̲h̲rïl, Sulaimān S̲h̲āh, and Saljuq S̲h̲āh, who at various times and in various parts of the empire also held power. Indeed, Muḥammad's sons held the sultanate in the west for the next three or four decades, and all but Saljuq S̲h̲āh reigned in turn.[2]

The centrifugal tendencies of the previous two reigns, held in check for a time by Muḥammad, now had free play. The succession in western Iran and Iraq was permanently in dispute, often with as many as three or four claimants at one time, each backed by his atabeg or guardian. The sultans had to find support amongst the powerful Turkish amīrs, and this usually meant the alienation of territory and of fiscal rights in the form of iqtaʿs, as well as the interference of amīrs even within the sultans' own bureaucracy. Anus̲h̲īrvān b. K̲h̲ālid, who was Maḥmūd's vizier in 521/1127 and 522/1128 and thus had first-hand experience of affairs, laments the decline of the Saljuq state after Muḥammad's death: "In Muḥammad's reign", he says, "the kingdom was united and secure from all attacks; but when it passed to his son Maḥmūd, they split up that unity and destroyed its cohesion. They claimed a share with him in the power, and left him only a bare subsistence."[3]

In the east Maḥmūd's uncle, Sanjar, remained the senior member of the dynasty. Although it had become the practice for the supreme sultanate to devolve on the ruler of western Iran and Iraq, Sanjar's

---

[1] Bundārī, p. 117; Ibn al-Qalānisī, p. 162 (year 501); Ḥusainī, pp. 81–2; Ibn al-At̲h̲īr vol. x, pp. 335 (year 503), 369–70; Juvainī, *Taʾrīk̲h̲-i Jahān-Gus̲h̲ā*, vol. ii, pp. 680–1; cf. Hodgson, *op. cit.* pp. 97–8.

[2] Bundārī, *Zubdat al-nuṣra*, p. 118; Ibn al-At̲h̲īr, *al-Kāmil*, vol. x, pp. 367–9; Sibṭ b. al-Jauzī, *Mirʾāt al-zamān*, vol. i, pp. 69–70.

[3] Bundārī, p. 134. For a detailed account of Maḥmūd's sultanate, see M. A. Köymen, *Büyük Selçuklu Imparatorluğu tarihi*, vol. ii, *İkinci Imparatorluk Devri*, pp. 5–148, 164–73.

seniority gave him a special standing under Turkish customary law. This seems to be reflected in his decision to assume his father Malik-Shāh's old title *Mu'izz al-Dunyā wa'l-Dīn* ("Strengthener in Secular and Religious Affairs") as soon as Muḥammad had died; and on coins minted by Maḥmūd in the west, Sanjar's name is accorded primacy over his own. Whenever there was doubt over the succession in the west, it was to Sanjar that the problem was taken; on Maḥmūd's death in 525/1131, the Caliph al-Mustarshid refused to interfere personally, but referred the claimants Mas'ūd b. Muḥammad and Dā'ūd b. Maḥmūd to Sanjar, who in fact decided in favour of Toghrïl.[1] The later years of Sanjar's rule in the east were clouded by external threats and internal unrest among the Ghuzz tribesmen, but in the earlier period his territories enjoyed relative peace, and this contrasted notably with the instability and confusion of the west, where the atabegs and other amīrs had secured much of the substance of power.

At the outset of his reign, in 513/1119, Maḥmūd had to face an invasion of his lands by Sanjar, who alleged that the Chief Ḥājib 'Alī Bār had secured an objectionable ascendancy over the young ruler, and that Maḥmūd was encouraging the Qarakhānids to attack him from behind. He came with a powerful army, whose commanders were said to include five kings: Sanjar, the rulers of Ghazna and Sīstān, the Khwārazm-Shāh Quṭb al-Dīn Muḥammad, and the Kākūyid 'Alā' al-Daula Garshāsp, Ismā'īlīs and pagan Turks were among its troops, and there were forty elephants.[2] Sanjar defeated Maḥmūd at Sāveh, and pushed on through Jibāl as far as Baghdad. When peace and amity were finally restored, Maḥmūd was given one of Sanjar's daughters in marriage and was made his uncle's heir, but he in turn had to relinquish important territories in the north of Iran. Sanjar remained in occupation of Ṭabaristān, Qūmis, Damāvand, and, most important of all, Ray, which was to serve as a kind of watchtower over western Iran.

Nor did Maḥmūd have much direct control over the north-western provinces. His brother Toghrïl had received from Sultan Muḥammad the iqṭā's of Sāveh, Āveh, and Zanjān, with Amīr Shīrgīr designated as his atabeg. At the instigation of a new atabeg, Kün-Toghdï, Toghrïl had rebelled against Maḥmūd, and although the rebels were forced to withdraw to Ganja, they strengthened their position through Sanjar's

[1] Ibn al-Athīr, vol. x, pp. 385, 474 ff.; Köymen, *op. cit.* p. 21. For a further discussion of Sanjar's constitutional position, see below, section x, pp. 135–7.

[2] Ibn al-Jauzī, *al-Muntaẓam*, vol. IX, p. 205; Sibṭ b. al-Jauzī, vol. I, p. 77.

Diktat to Maḥmūd. They further obtained Gīlān and Dailam, in addition to Qazvīn and several towns of the north-west, and from this base Toghrïl successfully defied Maḥmūd for the whole of the latter's reign.[1]

Mas'ūd b. Muḥammad was malik of Mosul, al-Jazīreh, and Āzarbāījān, and Ai-Aba Juyūsh Beg was his atabeg. Ample support for Mas'ūd's ambitions came from the troops of local Türkmen and Kurdish chiefs—especially from 'Imād al-Dīn Zangī, the son of Malik-Shāh's ghulām commander Qasīm al-Daula Aq-Sonqur. Moreover, the Mazyadid Dubais b. Ṣadaqa was eager to see Maḥmūd and Mas'ūd embroiled in warfare. According to Ibn al-Jauzī, "Saif al-Daula [Dubais] rejoiced at the conflict between the two sultans and believed that he and his power would be preserved as long as they were involved together, just as his father Ṣadaqa's position had been favoured by the hostility of the two sultans [Berk-Yaruq and Muḥammad]".[2] Mas'ūd and Juyūsh Beg rebelled openly in 514/1120, but Maḥmūd's general Aq-Sonqur Bursuqī defeated them at Asadābād. Only Mas'ūd's vizier Ḥasan b. 'Alī al-Ṭughrā'ī lost his life; Mas'ūd himself was pardoned and Juyūsh Beg conciliated. Two years later Juyūsh Beg was deputed to suppress a revolt in Āzarbāījān led by Toghrïl and his new atabeg Aq-Sonqur Aḥmadīlī, muqṭa' of Marāgheh. Dubais, however, was forced to flee to his wife's relatives, the Artuqids of Mārdīn, and then to the safety of the inaccessible marshes in the Baṭīḥa of southern Iraq. Mosul was granted to Aq-Sonqur Bursuqi, and in Diyārbakr the death of Il-Ghāzī b. Artuq caused a split in the Artuqid family and a division of their territories which for the moment neutralized this quarter for the sultan.[3]

Dissension within the Saljuq family allowed the 'Abbāsid caliphs to increase their secular power in the course of the 6th/12th century. This process is discernible under the capable caliphs al-Mustarshid (512–29/1118–35) and al-Muqtafī (530–55/1136–60), and it becomes particularly marked in the long and successful reign of al-Nāṣir (575–622/1180–1225).[4] During Maḥmūd's reign the hostility of the Shī'ī Mazyadids

[1] Bundārī, pp. 125–35, 264–5; Ẓahīr al-Dīn Nīshāpūrī, *Saljūq-Nāma*, p. 53; Rāvandī, *Rāḥat al-ṣudūr*, p. 205; Ḥusainī, *Akhbār al-daula al-Saljūqiyya*, pp. 88–90; Ibn al-Athīr, vol. x, pp. 383–9; Sibṭ b. al-Jauzī, vol. I, pp. 77–8.

[2] Ibn al-Jauzī, vol. IX, p. 218; Ibn al-Athīr, vol. x, pp. 378–81.

[3] Ibn al-Qalānisī, *Dhail ta'rīkh Dimashq*, pp. 202–3; Ẓahīr al-Dīn Nīshāpūrī, p. 54; Ibn al-Jauzī, vol. IX, pp. 217–18; Ḥusainī, pp. 96–7; Ibn al-Athīr, vol. x, pp. 378–81, 395–7, 414–15, 421–2, 426; Sibṭ b. al-Jauzī, vol. II, pp. 89–91; Ibn Khallikān, *Wafayāt al-a'yan*, vol. I, 463; Köymen, *op. cit.* pp. 27–41.

[4] For more on al-Nāṣir, see section XII, pp. 168–9 below.

prevented al-Mustarshid from ever alienating the Saljuqs too much. Indeed, Ibn al-Athīr says that the sultans left Dubais in power merely as a check on the caliph; when al-Mustarshid died and Dubais's role here was finished, Mas'ūd executed him.[1] On one occasion the caliph had to implore Maḥmūd to remain in the capital as a safeguard against Dubais, who had sworn to raze Baghdad to the ground. In 516/1122 al-Mustarshid was obliged to accept as his vizier the brother of Maḥmūd's own vizier, Shams al-Mulk 'Uthmān b. Niẓām al-Mulk, and when the latter was executed in 518/1124 al-Mustarshid had to remove the brother from office correspondingly. However, in company with Aq-Sonqur Bursuqī the caliph defended Baghdad against Dubais and in 517/1123 took the field personally against him; this act, together with his seizure and destruction of wine in the sultan's market at Baghdad in 514/1120, signified his growing self-confidence. The sultan's shaḥna in Baghdad, Sa'd al-Daula Yürün-Qush, was perturbed enough in 510/1126 to warn Maḥmūd of the caliph's rising confidence and military expertise, and he foresaw an attack on the sultan's rights in Iraq if the latter did not come personally to enforce them. Maḥmūd did come to Baghdad and besiege al-Mustarshid in the eastern part of the city, forcing him to make peace and hand over the stipulated tribute.[2]

Dubais joined with Toghrïl in 519/1125 to harass the sultan and caliph in Iraq; but they were unable to remain there, and Maḥmūd pursued them through Jibāl into Khurāsān, where they took refuge with Sanjar. They then aroused Sanjar with stories of Maḥmūd's disaffection and his closeness to the caliph, causing Sanjar to come westwards to Ray in 522/1128. But the two sultans were reconciled there, and Dubais was forced to flee to Ḥilla, Baṣra, and finally Syria, where he fell into the hands of Zangī and narrowly escaped death. Two years later Mas'ūd came to Sāveh from Khurāsān, where he had been staying with Sanjar; it was feared that the latter was instigating him to rebel, but the two brothers made peace at Kirmānshāh, and Maḥmūd granted to Mas'ūd the iqṭā' of Ganja.[3]

Being so pre-occupied with internal difficulties, Maḥmūd could give

[1] Ibn al-Jauzī, vol. x, pp. 52–3; Ḥusainī, p. 108; Ibn al-Athīr, vol. x, pp. 349–50.

[2] Ibn al-Qalānisī, pp. 215–16, 217–18; Ibn al-Jauzī, vol. IX, pp. 218, 232–4, 245–6; Ibn al-Athīr, vol. x, pp. 425, 428–30, 433–4, 447–50; Sibṭ b. al-Jauzī, vol. I, pp. 100–1; Köymen, *op. cit.* pp. 43 ff.

[3] Ibn al-Qalānisī, pp. 230–1; Ibn al-Jauzī, vol. IX, pp. 252–4, vol. x, pp. 8–9, 20; Ibn al-Athīr, vol. x, pp. 459, 469–71; Köymen, *op. cit.* pp. 75–91, 117–29.

only intermittent attention to the external frontiers of his part of the empire. During his reign the main danger zone was in the north-west, Arrān and the Caucasus, where the Georgians became very active under "The Restorer", David IV (1089–1125). He not only brought into Georgia large bands of slave troops and Qïpchaq mercenaries, but he ceased the payment of tribute to the Saljuqs and interfered with the seasonal migrations of the Türkmen into Georgia. Maḥmūd sent an expedition against him in 515/1121 in which the Artuqid Il-Ghāzī, Toghrïl, Dubais, and Kün-Toghdï took part, but the Muslim army was destroyed and the triumphant Georgians entered Tiflis, dislodging the local Muslim family of the Banū Ja'far. It was probably in 517/1123, shortly after the fall of Tiflis, that David scored a further success by entering Ani without striking a blow. There he deposed the Shaddādid amīr Abu'l-Asvār II b. Manūchihr (? 503–17/? 1110–23), restored the Armenian cathedral to its Christian usage, and installed in Ani an Armenian governor. This governor was later threatened by a Saljuq army under Sanjar, probably in 520/1126, and returned the city to Faḍl III b. Abu'l-Asvār II (reigned *c.* 520–4/*c.* 1126–30). Georgian expansion eastwards to Shamākhī and Darband also affected the Muslim principality of Shīrvān, and in 517/1123 Maḥmūd came to this province. He seized the Shīrvān Shāh (possibly Manūchihr II b. Farīdūn) and behaved so repressively that Shīrvān's annual tribute to the Saljuq treasury now dried up; in the end, a threatened attack by David the Restorer compelled the sultan to withdraw.[1] Ibn al-Athīr alleges that in the course of an expedition in 524/1130, just before his death, Maḥmūd captured the Ismā'ilī stronghold of Alamūt; but the verdict of another source, that the sultan achieved no successes here, is probably nearer the truth.[2]

In judging Maḥmūd as a ruler, the sources praise his justice and clemency and also his excellence as an Arabic scholar, saying that he attained a level of literacy not common among the Saljuqs.[3] Conversely, Anūshirvān b. Khālid assesses his conduct of administration severely. He lists ten great faults of his reign, including the alienation of Sanjar

[1] Ibn al-Qalānisī, pp. 204–5; al-Fāriqī, *Ta'rīkh Mayyāfāriqīn*, in Ibn al-Qalānisī, *Dhail ta'rīkh Dimashq*, pp. 205–6 n.; Bundārī, pp. 139–41; Ibn al-Athīr, vol. x, pp. 398–9, 434; Sibṭ b. al-Jauzī, vol. I, pp. 101–2; Minorsky, "Tiflis", and Barthold, "Shirwānshāh", in *Encyc. of Islam* (1st ed.); Allen, *A History of the Georgian People*, pp. 96–100; Minorsky, *Studies in Caucasian History*, pp. 83–5.

[2] Ibn al-Athīr, vol. x, p. 469; cf. Hodgson, *The Order of Assassins*, p. 102.

[3] Bundārī, p. 156; Ẓahīr al-Dīn Nīshāpūrī, p. 53; Rāvandī, p. 203; Ḥusainī, p. 99; Ibn al-Athīr, vol. x, p. 471.

and Dubais, the dispersal of royal ghulāms, a moral deterioration at court, and the squandering of the treasure amassed by his father. Much obloquy is heaped on his viziers, such as the tyrannical Shams al-Mulk ʿUthmān, but above all on Qiwām al-Dīn Abu'l-Qāsim al-Darguzīnī, or al-Ansabādhī, who acted as ʿĀriḍ al-Jaish and then as vizier for Maḥmūd; on his dismissal he acted as vizier for Toghrïl in Āzarbāījān, again achieving a reputation for tyranny, till in 527/1133 Toghrïl executed him. Anushīrvān sneers at his peasant origin; he also accuses him of friendliness towards the Bāṭiniyya, of using his official position to get rid of enemies, and of financial rapacity.[1] Yet it must be remembered that the sultan's financial position was usually parlous. His direct rule extended only to Jibāl, northern Fārs, and the Baghdad area, with a summer capital in Hamadān and a winter one in Baghdad, and from these regions he had to find iqṭāʿs for the soldiers directly in his employ. Because of financial problems, the sphere of operations of his dīvāns was drastically reduced, and the vizier was compelled to get money by seizures and confiscations. One vizier, Kamāl al-Mulk ʿAlī al-Simirumī, earned great unpopularity in 514/1120 by reimposing the local tolls and market taxes (*mukūs*) which had been abolished thirteen years previously by Sulṭān Muḥammad.[2] Accordingly, it is not surprising that Maḥmūd got through the greater part of the treasure chest—it contained eighteen million dīnārs in cash alone—which his father had assembled.[3]

A further period of crisis and chaos occurred in 525/1131 when Maḥmūd died. At Hamadān his young son Dā'ūd was proclaimed sultan by al-Darguzīnī, with Aq-Sonqur Aḥmadīlī assuming the office of atabeg. Dā'ūd was recognized in Jibāl and Āzarbāījān, but in Iraq Masʿūd proclaimed himself sultan, and in Fārs and Khūzistān another brother, Saljuq-Shāh, supported by the Atabeg Qaracha, also claimed the throne. The caliph referred the disputants to Sanjar, as senior member of the dynasty, but Sanjar's intervention only brought into the arena his own protégé, Toghrïl, whose claim he now pushed. Sanjar came to Jibāl in person and set Toghrïl on the throne, giving him al-Darguzīnī as his vizier; he also invited Dubais b. Ṣadaqa and Zangī to invade Iraq and embarrass Masʿūd's ally the caliph. Complex military operations followed, but Sanjar's withdrawal to Transoxiana,

[1] Bundārī, pp. 120–4, 138, 144 ff., 163, 166–9; Ibn al-Athīr, vol. x, pp. 482–3.

[2] Ibn al-Jauzī, vol. ix, pp. 218, 239; Ibn al-Athīr, vol. x, p. 425; Sibṭ b. al-Jauzī, vol. i, p. 91; cf. pp. 107–9.

[3] Bundārī, pp. 155–6; Ḥusainī, pp. 98–9; cf. Ibn Khallikān, vol. iii, p. 346.

where a Qarakhānid revolt had broken out, left Toghrïl in a very shaky position (see below, p. 139). He could find no popular support in Jibāl, where the people of Iṣfahān refused to admit him to their city, and after being twice defeated by Mas'ūd, he fled to Ray and then to Ṭabaristān, where the Bāvandid Ispahbadh 'Alā' al-Daula 'Alī b. Shahriyār (511–34/1117–40) sheltered him during the winter of 527/1132–3. Mas'ūd's involvement with Dā'ūd, who was holding out in Āzarbāījān, permitted Toghrïl to gather together an army and make a successful *revanche*. Mas'ūd was driven from Hamadān and fled to Baghdad in a wretched state. When at last Toghrïl seemed secure on the throne, he fell ill at Hamadān; and at the beginning of 529/1134, after a troubled reign of only two years, he died.[1]

A race for the throne occurred when the news spread of Toghrïl's end. Mas'ūd was in Baghdad, but he managed to clear a way through the mountain snows, using camels to trample a road; he was received in Hamadān by the amīrs and proclaimed sultan with the honorific *Ghiyāth al-Dunyā wa'l-Dīn*. In this fashion he began a reign of nearly twenty years (529–47/1134–52), the longest of any sultan in the west since Malik-Shāh's time. He employed as his vizier Anushīrvān b. Khālid and entrusted to his tutelage his brother Dā'ūd b. Muḥammad.[2]

As in Maḥmūd's time, the sultan's authority was in practice confined to Jibāl and central Iraq. When Mas'ūd obtained the throne, the rival claimant Dā'ūd b. Maḥmūd, who had been cheated of the succession on his father's death two years before, remained in Āzarbāījān, and over the following years he made several attempts from this base to seize the sultanate. Eventually conciliated by Mas'ūd's recognition of him as the valī 'ahd, he now married one of the sultan's daughters and settled down at Tabrīz, but in 538/1143–4 he was assassinated by the Ismā'īlīs, allegedly at the instigation of Zangī, who feared that Mas'ūd was about to send Dā'ūd to take control of his own region of northern Syria.[3] In the later years of Mas'ūd's reign the north-west passed into the hands of a series of powerful Turkish amīrs who behaved as virtually independent rulers. After the death of Qara-Sonqur in 535/

[1] Bundārī, pp. 156–72; Ẓahīr al-Dīn Nīshāpūrī, pp. 54–5; Rāvandī, pp. 208–9; Ibn al-Jauzī, vol. x, pp. 20–1, 25, 35–6, 41; Ḥusainī, pp. 99–105; Ibn al-Athīr, vol. x, pp. 471, 474–80, 482–3, vol. xi, pp. 6, 10–11; Sibṭ b. al-Jauzī, vol. i, pp. 136, 145; Köymen, *Büyük Selçuklu Imparatorluğu tarihi*, vol. ii, pp. 174–218, 237–50.

[2] Bundārī, pp. 174–5; Ẓahīr al-Dīn Nīshāpūrī, pp. 55–6; Rāvandī, pp. 226–7; Ibn al-Athīr, vol. x, p. 345; Köymen, *op. cit.* pp. 250–4.

[3] Bundārī, p. 195; Ḥusainī, p. 114.

1140–1, Chavlī Jāndār took over in Āzarbāījān, Arrān, and Armenia, finally becoming the atabeg to Mas'ūd's son Malik-Shāh.[1] Chavlī's own death occurred in 541/1146, after which 'Abd al-Raḥmān Toghan-Yürek succeeded him as atabeg to the young prince and added the governorship of Arrān and Āzarbāījān to his existing iqṭā' of Khalkhāl; but in 541/1147, alarmed at Toghan-Yürek's power, the sultan procured his murder (see p. 132 below).[2] Nevertheless, the end of Mas'ūd's sultanate saw power in Āzarbāījān being monopolized by two Turkish amīrs, Shams al-Dīn Eldigüz, the atabeg of Arslan b. Toghrïl, and Aq-Sonqur (or Arslan) b. Aq-Sonqur Aḥmadīlī of Marāgheh.

Fārs was for many years ruled by the Amīr Boz-Aba, the irreconcilable enemy of Sultan Mas'ūd ever since 531/1136–7, when the sultan had killed Boz-Aba's companion, the atabeg Mengü-Bars. Boz-Aba maintained himself in Fārs till Mas'ūd captured him in battle and executed him (542/1147–8).[3] In the years before this violent end, the amīr had successfully fought off attempts by other amīrs to oust him from possession of Fārs, in favour of the princes for whom they were atabegs. Thus in 533/1138–9 the atabeg Qara-Sonqur, together with Dā'ūd and Saljuq-Shāh, the sons of Sultan Muḥammad, had invaded Fārs and placed Saljuq-Shāh on the throne at Shīrāz as local malik; but once Qara-Sonqur had departed, Boz-Aba came back, seized Saljuq-Shāh, and jailed him. At the end of his life Boz-Aba espoused the cause of two of Mahmūd's sons, Muḥammad and Malik-Shāh, and for a brief moment before his final downfall placed them on the throne in Jibāl (see below, p. 131).[4]

With regard to Saljuq influence in Iraq and al-Jazīreh, the most significant event in Mas'ūd's reign was the meteoric rise of 'Imād al-Dīn Zangī b. Aq-Sonqur, a Turkish amīr of slave origin. Zangī's sphere of expansion was essentially that of the Arab lands in al-Jazīreh, Diyārbakr, and northern Syria, but the possession of Mosul gave him an important base for penetration northwards and eastwards into Kurdistān, and on several occasions he allied with the discontented Turkish amīrs in Iran against the sultan and caliph. Indeed, Mas'ūd, came to regard him as the arch-instigator of the rebellious coalitions which encompassed him. As governor of Wāsiṭ and Baṣra in Sulṭān Maḥmūd's time, Zangī had successfully administered the difficult and confused delta region of Iraq, and in 521/1127, with the death of the

[1] Bundārī, pp. 195, 203–4.
[2] Ibn al-Athīr, vol. xi, pp. 76–7.
[3] Bundārī, pp. 184, 219–20; Ibn al-Athīr, vol. xi, 78–9.
[4] Bundārī, pp. 219–20.

governor of Mosul, 'Izz al-Dīn Mas'ūd al-Bursuqī, Maḥmūd appointed Zangī in his stead; he also gave him the custody of his sons Alp-Arslan and Farrukh-Shāh, so that Zangī now became an atabeg.[1]

From Mosul, Zangī began a policy of conquest against the Arab and Türkmen rulers of Diyārbakr and northern Syria, as well as against the Franks and Byzantines. First he captured Aleppo, Ḥimṣ, and Ḥamā, and then in 539/1144 he achieved the success which made him the idol of Sunnī historians, the capture of Edessa from Count Jocelyn II. His death came in 541/1146 at the hands of his own ghulāms whilst he was besieging the 'Uqailid Sālim b. Mālik in Qalāt Ja'bar.[2] Although his exploits had made him a Sunnī hero, Zangī was always hostile to the 'Abbasids. In Mas'ūd's reign he allied with the Shī'ī Mazyadids and with the deposed Caliph al-Rāshid against the Caliph al-Muqtafī of Baghdad; and in 528/1134, during Toghrïl's reign, his extensive operations in the Hakkārī region of Kurdistān and Armenia were provoked by the Kurdish chiefs' help to al-Mustarshid, given in the previous year when the caliph had besieged Zangī in Mosul and expelled him from it.[3]

At the close of the year in which Mas'ūd was acknowledged sultan (529/1135), Caliph al-Mustarshid was assassinated by a Bāṭinī, thus ending a reign full of military and political activity. His son al-Rāshid reigned only for one year (529–30/1135–6), and his deposition at Mas'ūd's instigation marks the high tide of Saljuq influence in Baghdad at this time. The new caliph, al-Muqtafī b. al-Mustaẓhir (530–55/1136–60), proved to be a capable and energetic warrior as well as a religious figurehead. Receiving at the outset of his reign the revenues which his father had held, he began to build up a personal army of Armenian and Greek ghulāms, excluding Turks because he found them unreliable.[4] He strengthened the wall which al-Mustarshid and his vizier Abū Naṣr Aḥmad b. Niẓām al-Mulk had built round Baghdad in 517/1123, and he also dug a trench around the city.[5] He was therefore able on several occasions to defy the sultans, and when Mas'ūd died and a period of even greater disunity within the Saljuq dynasty ensued, he extended caliphal authority over the whole of lower and

[1] Ibn al-Athīr, vol. x, pp. 453–7.

[2] Ibn al-Qalānisī, pp. 284–7; Bundārī, pp. 208–9; Ibn al-Athīr, vol. xi, pp. 71–4.

[3] *al-Kāmil*, vol. xi, pp. 2–3, 7–9; cf. K. Zettersteen, "Zengī, 'Imād al-Dīn", *Encyc. of Islam* (1st ed.).

[4] Bundārī, p. 235; Ibn al-Athīr, vol. xi, p. 28.

[5] Bundārī, *loc. cit.*; Ibn al-Jauzī, vol. ix, pp. 233–4; Ibn al-Ṭiqṭaqā, p. 273 (Whitting tr., pp. 295–6).

central Iraq to a degree unknown since the early 4th/10th century. As Ibn al-Ṭiqṭaqā says: "In his reign there occurred much civil strife and warfare between him and the Sultan of Persia, in which the victory lay with him; his reign was also characterized by much activity on the part of ʿayyārs and evil-doers [the sources stress the sharp rise of *ʿiyāra*, i.e. brigandage and mob violence, in the capital at this time], for the suppression of which he took firm steps."[1]

In the early months of Masʿūd's sultanate, relations with al-Mustarshid deteriorated rapidly. The caliph prepared for war, helped by some Turkish amīrs who had deserted Masʿūd, and also by Bursuq b. Bursuq of Khūzistān, who linked up with him in Jibāl; whilst Dā'ūd in Āzarbāījān arranged to join forces with the caliph at Dīnāvār. Nevertheless, Masʿūd coped easily with this coalition. In a battle at Dāi-Marg near Hamadān, which was really little more than a skirmish, the caliph's Turkish troops deserted to the Saljuq army. The caliph himself was taken prisoner, and shortly afterwards was murdered by Ismāʿīlīs in the sultan's camp at Marāgheh, whither Masʿūd had gone in pursuit of Dā'ūd. Masʿūd confiscated al-Mustarshid's estates and property in Baghdad and is said to have looted ten million dīnārs worth of goods, the chests of coin alone requiring one hundred and seventy mules to carry them away. From Khurāsān, Sanjar had written enjoining Masʿūd to treat the caliph with respect, although according to ʿImād al-Dīn, contemporaries whispered that Sanjar himself was really behind al-Mustarshid's assassination.[2]

The new caliph al-Rāshid was quickly involved in hostilities with Masʿūd over the non-payment of a tribute customarily due to the sultan. Barring Masʿūd's representative Yürün-Qush from Baghdad, he formed a grand coalition against the sultan, embracing Dā'ūd from Āzarbāījān, Zangī from Mosul, Ṣadaqa b. Dubais, and his "atabeg" ʿAntara b. Abi'l-ʿAskar (the appearance of this typically Turkish office amongst a purely Arab dynasty is interesting), together with Bursuq b. Bursuq, the son of Aq-Sonqur Aḥmadīlī, and the Turkish governors of Qazvīn and Iṣfahān. In the extreme south Masʿūd's brother Saljuq-Shāh came from Khūzistān and seized Wāsiṭ. But Masʿūd remained master of events. He captured Baghdad, and the caliph fled with

[1] Bundārī, pp. 235–6; Ibn al-Ṭiqṭaqā, p. 276 (Whitting tr., pp. 298–9).

[2] Bundārī, pp. 176–8. See also Niẓāmī ʿArūḍī, *Chahār Maqāla*, pp. 36–7 (E. G. Browne tr., pp. 23–4); Ẓahīr al-Dīn Nīshāpūrī, p. 56; Rāvandī, pp. 227–8; Ibn al-Jauzī, vol. x, pp. 43–9; Ḥusainī, pp. 106–8; Ibn al-Athīr, vol. xi, pp. 14–17; Sibṭ b. al-Jauzī, vol. i, pp. 156–8; Juvainī, *Ta'rīkh-i Jahān-Gushā*, vol. ii, pp. 683–5; Ibn Khallikān, vol. iii, p. 364.

Zangī to Mosul. Mas'ūd now assembled the religious dignitaries of the capital and pointed out how al-Rāshid had broken his vow of allegiance and his promise never to take up arms against the sultan. Al-Rāshid's financial requisitions for his soldiers had made him unpopular; a fatwā, or judicial opinion, was secured for his deposition, and his uncle set up as al-Muqtafī (530/1136).[1] This triumph was the peak of Mas'ūd's career. His general Qara-Sonqur followed it up by routing Dā'ūd at Marāgheh; Saljuq-Shāh's position in Khūzistān became unsafe and he actually had to appeal to Mas'ūd for assistance. The sultan obtained the loyalty of Ṣadaqa by marrying the latter's daughter, and he also appointed Ṣadaqa's brother Muḥammad to govern Ḥilla, while the new caliph married Mas'ūd's sister Fāṭima.[2]

There still remained the threat from Malik Dā'ūd and the ex-caliph al-Rāshid, who gathered round themselves in Āzarbāījān a group of amīrs fearful of a rise in the sultan's power. Al-Rāshid had already appealed to Sanjar for help against Mas'ūd, but Sanjar's preoccupations with Transoxianan affairs compelled him to refuse.[3] Mas'ūd defeated and killed the chief of these rebellious amīrs, Mengü-Bars, governor of Fārs, but he was in turn defeated by Amīr Toghan-Yürek, who captured and killed the Mazyadid Ṣadaqa and the sons of Qara-Sonqur, the atabeg of Āzarbāījān. From the south Saljuq-Shāh made an attempt on Baghdad. Al-Rāshid, Dā'ūd, and Boz-Aba established themselves in the Saljuq capital Hamadān; but al-Rāshid was unable to make any further headway, and a group of his Khurāsānian soldiers, possibly having Ismā'īlī sympathies, murdered him at Iṣfahān in 532/1137–8.[4]

Dā'ūd seems now to have despaired of achieving the sultanate for himself, and to have settled for a limited sphere of authority in Āzarbāījān, where for the remaining six years of his life he was governor under the Atabeg Ayaz. To Saljuq-Shāh, Mas'ūd allotted the governorship of Akhlāṭ, Malāzgird, and Arzan in eastern Anatolia, all the former territories of the Shāh-Armanid Nāṣir al-Dīn Sukmān II; and the amīr of Tabrīz, Qïz-Oghlu (?Ghuzz-Oghlu), led an expedition thither to take up possession.[5] In the next year, 533/1138–9, seeking

[1] Ẓahīr al-Dīn Nīshāpūrī, p. 56; Rāvandī, p. 229; Ibn al-Jauzī, vol. x, pp. 54–62; Ḥusainī, pp. 108–9; Ibn al-Athīr, vol. xi, pp. 22–4, 26–9; Sibṭ b. al-Jauzī, vol. i, p. 158.

[2] Ibn al-Jauzī, vol. x, pp. 67, 72; Ibn al-Athīr, vol. xi, pp. 29–30; Sibṭ b. al-Jauzī, vol. i, p. 161.

[3] Ḥusainī, p. 109.

[4] Ibn al-Jauzī, vol. x, pp. 67–8, 72, 76; Ḥusainī, pp. 109–10; Ibn al-Athīr, vol. xi, pp. 39–41; Sibṭ b. al-Jauzī, vol. i, pp. 164, 167–8; Juvainī, vol. ii, pp. 685–6.

[5] Bundārī, p. 185; Ḥusainī, p. 111.

revenge on Boz-Aba for the killing of his son, Qara-Sonqur took with him both Dā'ūd and Saljuq-Shāh (the latter having been recalled from Akhlāṭ) on an expedition to Fārs. Saljuq-Shāh was placed on the throne as malik of Fārs, but in the following year he was deposed by Boz-Aba, thenceforth disappearing from history and probably dying in captivity. Thus Fārs and Khūzistān remained in the hands of Boz-Aba.[1] In 535/1140–1 Mas'ūd sent two generals against him, Ismā'īl Chahārdāngī and Alp-Qush Khūn-Kar, but they were unable to collect sufficient funds in Iraq for the expedition, and after some futile operations in the Baṭīḥa it was abandoned.[2]

Shortly before this expedition, Qara-Sonqur had had to deal with a descent of the Georgians on Ganja. During Maḥmūd's reign Ganja had been recaptured for a while by one of its ancestral Shaddādid rulers, Faḍl III b. Abi'l-Asvār II, but soon afterwards it fell under the power of a Turkish amīr, Toghan-Arslan al-Aḥdab ("the hump-backed"), ruler of Bitlis and Arzan, whose son Qurtī was probably responsible for Faḍl's death in 524/1130. The Georgian attack was led by a noble of the Orbeliani family, Ivane b. Abī Laith; it came on top of a serious earthquake at Ganja and caused great loss of life and property, but was repulsed by Qara-Sonqur when he arrived in Arrān.[3]

In the middle years of his reign, Mas'ūd fell more and more under the influence of the Turkish amīrs. Their ability to dictate to the sultan, even in matters concerning the central bureaucracy, was clearly shown in 533/1139 when they secured the dismissal and death of Mas'ūd's vizier. Mas'ūd had found his first vizier, Anushīrvān b. Khālid, too mild and lenient; his second one, al-Darguzīnī, a relative of the vizier to Maḥmūd and Toghrïl, was useless and incompetent, so in 533/1139 Mas'ud appointed to the vizierate his treasurer, Kamāl al-Dīn Muḥammad. Distinguished for his equity and probity Kamāl al-Dīn abolished vexatious taxes and investigated complaints of tyranny. He was zealous in asserting the sultan's financial rights, and uncovered thefts and embezzlements. Not surprisingly he made many enemies, so that Qara-Sonqur threatened a refusal to march against Fārs and a withdrawal of allegiance in favour of one of the Saljuq claimants if the over-zealous vizier were not removed; Mas'ūd was obliged to agree to this and to appoint Qara-Sonqur's personal vizier as his own chief minister.

[1] Bundārī, pp. 188–9; Ẓahīr al-Dīn Nīshāpūrī, p. 57; Rāvandī, p. 231; Ḥusainī, pp. 111–13; Ibn al-Athīr, vol. XI, p. 49.
[2] *al-Kāmil*, vol. XI, pp. 51–2.
[3] Bundārī, p. 190; Ibn al-Athīr, vol. XI, p. 52; cf. Minorsky, *Caucasian History*, pp. 85–6.

After this, says Ibn al-Athīr, "Things became difficult for Sulṭān Mas'ūd. He was impotent to prevent the amīrs from parcelling out the whole land as iqṭā's for themselves, so that in the end he had no territory left at all for himself, but merely the name of Sulṭān."[1]

Qara-Sonqur died at Ardabīl in 535/1140–1, much mourned by the people of Āzarbāījān. When he was dying, he named the Amīr Chavlī Jāndār as his successor in Āzarbāījān and Arrān, and Mas'ūd had to agree to this. In Ray, the Amīr 'Abbās—he was a slave of Jauhar, Sanjar's former governor there—consolidated his power. He collected round himself a large slave guard and soon acquired a reputation as a hammer of the Ismā'īlīs in the Alburz area, who had killed his master Jauhar; and on one occasion he led an expedition against Alamūt.[2] At the sultan's court, the loyalty of the Chief Ḥājib 'Abd al-Raḥmān Toghan-Yürek was a dubious quantity, in part because of jealousy of Mas'ūd's favourite, Khāṣṣ Beg Arslan b. Palang-Eri. In his struggle against the disaffected amīrs centred round 'Abbās of Ray, Toghan-Yürek, and Boz-Aba of Fārs, Mas'ūd could generally count upon the support of the two leading figures in Āzarbāījān, Chavlī (until his death in 541/1146), and Eldigüz, who was atabeg to Arslan b. Toghrīl and for a time had been Mas'ūd's shaḥna in Baghdad.

The sultan resolved to bring 'Abbās to heel and came to Ray with an army, but he was bought off by rich presents from the amīr. A series of conspiratorial negotiations between 'Abbās and Boz-Aba now began, culminating in 540/1145–6 in a definite rebellion. Boz-Aba brought to Iṣfahān and Hamadān the two princes Muḥammad and Malik-Shāh, sons of Sulṭān Maḥmūd, while the sultan left Baghdad for Kirmānshāh, and was joined by Eldigüz and other amīrs of Āzarbāījān whose assistance he had invoked. 'Abbās marched from Ray with yet another Saljuq prince, Mas'ūd's brother Sulaimān-Shāh. Meanwhile, the sultan had pushed on to Marāgheh, where he was joined by Chavlī. A battle near Kāshān was imminent, but Sulaimān-Shāh and 'Abbās withdrew towards Ray and then to Ardahān, pursued by Mas'ūd. Boz-Aba was compelled by these desertions to fall back on Iṣfahān with the two Saljuq maliks; from there, with Chavlī in pursuit, he escaped to Fārs. Despite this apparent success, Mas'ūd's position was far from strong; the loyalty of his Chief Ḥājib, Toghan-Yürek, was

[1] Bundārī, pp. 185–6; Ẓahīr al-Dīn Nīshāpūrī, p. 57; Rāvandī, pp. 230–1; Ibn al-Jauzī, vol. x, pp. 78–9; Ḥusainī, pp. 111–12; Ibn al-Athīr, vol. xi, pp. 42, 46.

[2] Bundārī, pp. 190–2; Ẓahīr al-Dīn Nīshāpūrī, p. 58; Rāvandī, p. 232; Ḥusainī, p. 113; Ibn al-Athīr, vol. xi, pp. 76–7.

uncertain, for it was believed that his sympathies inclined towards the rebels. The sultan made peace with ʿAbbās and received the custody of Sulaimān-Shāh, who was now consigned to imprisonment. When Chavlī died, Toghan-Yürek received what he had long coveted, the governorship of Arrān and Āzarbāijān, and at the same time he was made atabeg to Masʿūd's son Malik-Shāh. Moreover the sultan was compelled to accept as his own vizier the personal vizier of Boz-Aba, Tāj al-Dīn Ibn Dārust, and Toghan-Yürek directed all his efforts towards bringing Boz-Aba back into favour at court.[1]

In the west the spectacular successes of Zangī were continuing, and from his Mosul base he was gradually mopping up the remaining independent amīrs of al-Jazīreh and Diyārbakr, while also making war on the Kurdish chiefs of the Hakkārī region. Zangī had in his care a Saljuq prince, Sulṭān Maḥmūd's son Alp-Arslan, and was waiting to place this candidate on the throne as soon as Masʿūd should die. In 538/1143–4 Masʿūd prepared a punitive expedition against Zangī, regarding him as a source of persistent rebelliousness, but again he was bought off by the promise of a payment; even then, the sultan did not exact the whole of the sum due, hoping that he could still conciliate Zangī.[2] In central Iraq Baghdad was racked by ʿiyāra and the Mazyadid ʿAli b. Dubais roused the local Arab population of the Ḥilla district and wrested the capital from his brother Muḥammad. He defeated an army sent by the shaḥna of Baghdad, and, despite a brief occupation by Masʿūd's troops in 542/1147–8, retook Ḥilla and remained in possession of it.[3]

The death of Zangī in 541/1146 relieved the sultan of this source of worry, and in the same year he also succeeded in breaking out of the iron grip of the Turkish amīrs. He procured the assassination of Toghan-Yürek at Ganja, and that of ʿAbbās, who was then deputy-chief ḥājib, at the court in Baghdad.[4] In place of Toghan-Yürek, Khāṣṣ Beg Arslan b. Palang-Eri was appointed atabeg to Malik Muḥammad, while the obnoxious vizier Ibn Dārust was sent back to Boz-Aba in Fārs. Boz-Aba, his position obviously weakened by the elimination of his two great allies, now marched to Iṣfahān and Hamadān, accompanied by the princes Muḥammad and Malik-Shāh,

[1] Bundārī, pp. 214–15; Ẓahīr al-Dīn Nīshāpūrī, pp. 58–62; Rāvandī, pp. 232–7; Ibn al-Jauzī, vol. x, pp. 116, 119; Ḥusainī, pp. 114–18; Ibn al-Athīr, vol. xi, pp. 69–9.

[2] *al-Kāmil*, vol. xi, pp. 61–2, 66–7.

[3] Ibn al-Jauzī, vol. x, pp. 116, 125.

[4] Ẓahīr al-Dīn Nīshāpūrī, pp. 62–3; Rāvandī, pp. 237–9; Ibn al-Jauzī, vol. x, pp. 119, 123; Ḥusainī, pp. 118–19; Ibn al-Athīr, vol. xi, pp. 76–7; Sibṭ b. al-Jauzī, vol. i, p. 193.

whom he set up in the <u>kh</u>uṭba of those two cities. Mas'ūd hurried from Baghdad, summoning aid from <u>Kh</u>āṣṣ Beg, Eldigüz, and <u>Sh</u>īrgīr in the north-west, and their forces united at Hamadān before Boz-Aba was able to give battle to Mas'ūd alone. There followed a fierce engagement at Marg-i Qara-Tegin, in which the army of Fārs was routed and Boz-Aba and the son of 'Abbās were killed. At the conclusion of this campaign, Mas'ūd married his nephew Muḥammad to his own daughter Jauhar, the widow of Dā'ūd b. Maḥmūd, granted him <u>Kh</u>ūzistān, and proclaimed him the official heir to the throne.[1]

The sultan's excessive favour to <u>Kh</u>āṣṣ Beg, together with fears among the remaining amīrs that their fate would be similar to that of Boz-Aba and his allies, contributed to the formation of a fresh coalition of rebellious amīrs in 543/1148, this time including many of Mas'ūd's former supporters. Forces were sent from Arrān and Āzarbāījān by Eldigüz and Qaiṣar; from Jibāl by Alp-Qu<u>sh</u> and Tatar; from Wāsiṭ by Turuntai; from Ḥilla by 'Alī b. Dubais. Other amīrs provided further troops, and they were all joined outside Baghdad by Malik Muḥammad. Mas'ūd entrusted the defence of the city to the caliph, who deepened the protective trench round Baghdad and issued to the citizens a general summons to arms; the sultan himself then withdrew to the fortress of Takrīt. After heavy fighting, the allies dispersed. Alp-Qu<u>sh</u> then attempted to place Malik-<u>Sh</u>āh b. Maḥmūd on the throne at Baghdad, but his attack on the city was repelled by al-Muqtafī. Sanjar came to Ray in the winter of 544/1149–50, a reconciliation with Mas'ūd took place, and he promised to end <u>Kh</u>āṣṣ Beg's ascendancy.[2]

During Mas'ūd's absence at Ray, several of the previous rebels, including Yūrün-Qu<u>sh</u>, Turuntai, and 'Alī b. Dubais, again massed their troops in Iraq, this time in company with Malik-<u>Sh</u>āh. They sought the caliph's assurance that he would make the <u>kh</u>uṭba for their nominee, but on Mas'ūd's return to Baghdad the coalition fell apart. During the last year or so of the sultan's life Malik-<u>Sh</u>āh's pretensions remained an active threat to security until finally, when he raided Iṣfahān and drove off cattle from there, Mas'ūd sent troops against him. Mas'ūd's death came in the next year, 547/1152, at Hamadān. "With him", says Ibn al-A<u>th</u>īr, "the fortunes of the Saljuq family

---

[1] Bundārī, pp. 219–20, 222; Ẓahīr al-Dīn Nī<u>sh</u>āpūrī, pp. 63–4; Rāvandī, pp. 241–3; Ibn al-Jauzī, vol. x, p. 124; Ḥusainī, pp. 119–20; Ibn al-A<u>th</u>īr, vol. xi, pp. 77, 78–9.

[2] Bundārī, p. 224; Ẓahīr al-Dīn Nī<u>sh</u>āpūrī, pp. 46, 64; Rāvandī, pp. 174–5; Ibn al-Jauzī, vol. x, pp. 131–3, 137–8; Ḥusainī, pp. 120–1; Ibn al-A<u>th</u>īr, vol. xi, pp. 87–8, 94.

died; after him, there was no banner for them to depend on or rally round—'Qais's death was not the death of a single man, but rather the collapse of a whole tribe's foundations.'"[1]

All this time the local Saljuq line in Kirmān obtruded little on the wider scene of events in Iran. The long and peaceful reign of Arslan-S͟hāh had ended in a burst of violence in 537/1142, when, during a quarrel over the future succession, the most aggressive and capable of Arslan-S͟hāh's sons, Muḥammad, seized his father, killed him, and then imprisoned and blinded some twenty of his own brothers and nephews.[2] The claims of another brother, Saljuq-S͟hāh, were dashed in a battle outside Jīruft, and he fled across the Persian Gulf to al-Aḥsā' and Oman. There he assembled a force with the intention of invading Kirmān, but Muḥammad's agents obtained his imprisonment in Oman. Thereafter, Muḥammad was undisturbed on his throne; only at the end of his reign did Saljuq-S͟hāh manage to escape and return to Kirmān, where he met defeat and death at the hands of the new amīr, Toghrïl-S͟hāh b. Muḥammad.

Muḥammad b. Arslan-S͟hāh assumed the honorific *Mug͟hīt͟h al-Dunyā wa'l-Dīn* and reigned for fourteen years (537–51/1142–56). His prestige was such that neighbouring potentates sought his protection and help. The governor of Ṭabas in southern K͟hurāsān, menaced by the G͟huzz tribesmen who got out of control towards the end of Sanjar's reign in the east, yielded up his town to Muḥammad, in whose hands it remained until the rise of Sanjar's former g͟hulām, Mu'ayyid al-Dīn Ai-Aba, in K͟hurāsān (see below, pp. 154–5).[3] More important was the temporary acquisition of Iṣfahān, transferred to Muḥammad by the commander who had governed it on behalf of the Saljuqs of the west. Although Muḥammad was clearly a bloodthirsty tyrant, he contrived by his ostentatious piety to make a good impression on the chroniclers. Muḥammad b. Ibrāhīm, the local historian, praises the amīr for his pensions to the ulema and his bursaries to poor students. He encouraged astronomy and the compilation of astronomical tables (*taqvīms*); he built mosques and libraries in the chief towns of Kirmān, e.g. Bardasīr, Jīruft, and Bam; and he never killed anyone without first obtaining for this a fatwā from the religious authorities.[4]

[1] Bundārī, pp. 226–7; Ẓahīr al-Dīn Nīs͟hāpūrī, p. 65; Rāvandī, p. 245; Ibn al-Jauzī, vol. x, pp. 147, 151; Ibn al-At͟hīr, vol. xi, pp. 94, 105.

[2] On Arslan-S͟hāh, see above, pp. 117–18.

[3] *al-Kāmil*, vol. xi, p. 121.

[4] Muḥammad b. Ibrāhīm, *Ta'rīk͟h-i Saljūqiyān-i Kirmān*, pp. 28–34. Cf. Houtsma, "Zur Geschichte der Selǵuqen von Kermân", *Z.M.D.G.* pp. 375–7.

X. SANJAR'S SULTANATE IN THE EAST, AND THE RISE OF THE KHWĀRAZM-SHĀHS AND QARA-KHITAI

The fortunes of the eastern provinces of the Saljuq empire were directed for over fifty years by Abu'l-Ḥārith Aḥmad Sanjar (*Sanjar* = Turkish for "he who thrusts, pierces") b. Malik-Shāh.[1] After the death of Arslan-Arghun in 490/1097, Berk-Yaruq had appointed his half-brother Sanjar, then a lad of ten or twelve years, to the governorship of Khurāsān (see above, p. 107). Sanjar remained ruler of the east until shortly after his escape from captivity amongst the Ghuzz; the hardships which he had suffered there seem to have hastened his death in 552/1157.

In the civil strife of Berk-Yaruq's reign, Sanjar took the side of his full brother Muḥammad Tapar, but from the constitutional point of view he regarded himself during this period as subordinate to the sultan in Iraq and western Iran; thus on a coin of his from Marv, probably minted in 499/1105–6, he calls himself simply *Malik al-Mashriq* ("King of the East") and gives the title *al-Sulṭān al-Mu'aẓẓam* ("Exalted Sultan") to Muḥammad.[2] However, when the latter died in 511/1118, Sanjar was not disposed to accept a similar status in regard to his nephew Maḥmūd b. Muḥammad. In the past, as we have said, the supreme sultanate had gone to the Saljuq who held Iraq and western Iran, and at the beginning of his reign Maḥmūd's alliance with the Qarakhānids against his uncle might have been a sign of his determination to assert himself as head of the family and thus reduce Sanjar's pretensions.[3] But the older Turkish principle of the seniorate now came to the fore, and Sanjar became generally regarded as supreme head of the family. Indeed, Maḥmūd had to acknowledge his own subordination at an early date: coins struck by him at Iṣfahān and dated 511/1118 and 512/1118–19 give Sanjar the title *al-Sulṭān al-Mu'aẓẓam*, whereas Maḥmūd is given simply his name and patronymic.[4]

Sanjar's campaign in western Iran and his defeat of Maḥmūd at Sāveh in 513/1119 gave him the opportunity clearly to demonstrate his superior status (see pp. 119–20 above). At Ray he treated Maḥmūd as his close vassal. Out of deference to Sanjar, Maḥmūd had to abandon

[1] Cf. Pelliot, *Notes sur l'Histoire de la Horde d'Or*, pp. 176–80.

[2] Köymen, *Büyük Selçuklu Imparatorluğu tarihi*, vol. II, p. 25. On the general topic of Sanjar's constitutional relations with the other Saljuqs, see Köymen, pp. 5–27, 250–4.

[3] Ḥusainī, *Akhbār al-daula al-Saljūqiyya*, p. 88; cf. Bundārī, *Zubdat al-nuṣra*, pp. 120–1.

[4] Köymen, *op. cit.* p. 25.

his personal privileges as sultan, such as the five-fold *nauba* (salute of military music). He had to hold Sanjar's bridle when he mounted; to prostrate himself before Sanjar; to walk on foot by his side from the audience chamber to Sanjar's personal tent, and to reside in the quarters of Sanjar's children and wives. Maḥmūd's chief officials received investiture patents directly from Sanjar, and Sanjar kept in his hands the city of Ray, perhaps not merely because of its strategic importance but also because during Toghrïl Beg's time it had been the capital of the Saljuqs in Iran. In Iraq Sanjar ordered the reappointment there of the s̲h̲aḥna whom Maḥmūd had dismissed. In return, Sanjar made Maḥmūd his heir, and the two names henceforth appear together on Sanjar's coins. Whilst it is true that after 519/1125 Maḥmūd minted coins on which he himself was styled *al-Sulṭān al-Muʿẓẓam* and Sanjar was not mentioned, he remained essentially subordinate to his uncle.[1]

The relationship of Sanjar to his nephews stayed the same during the succeeding reigns of Toghrïl and Masʿūd, particularly since Toghrïl was directly beholden to him for his authority. However, at the outset of his reign Masʿūd rejected a command from Sanjar to execute certain amīrs in his entourage, and thereby announced that he would not be a blind puppet of his uncle.[2] Sanjar, increasingly preoccupied with such problems as the rise of the K̲h̲wārazm-S̲h̲āhs and of the Qara-K̲h̲itai, allowed Masʿūd more freedom of action than might otherwise have been the case; yet with the passage of time the unparalleled length of Sanjar's rule in the east only strengthened his moral position as supreme sovereign.

After Berk-Yaruq nominated him to the governorship of the east, Sanjar and his amīrs had been faced with a certain amount of opposition from rival Saljuq princes. In 490/1097 Muḥammad b. Sulaimān b. C̲h̲ag̲h̲rï Beg Dā'ūd, whom the sources call *Amīr-i Amīrān* ("Supreme Commander"), obtained a force from the G̲h̲aznavids and attempted to seize power in K̲h̲urāsān; he was defeated by Sanjar's army and blinded. In the following year a Saljuq named Daulat-S̲h̲āh, apparently a descendant of Er-Tas̲h̲ b. Ibrāhīm Ïnal, collected in Tuk̲h̲āristān a force of Türkmen malcontents, but was likewise defeated and blinded by Sanjar.[3]

---

[1] Bundārī, pp. 128-9; Ḥusainī, pp. 88-9; Ibn al-At̲h̲īr, *al-Kāmil*, vol. x, p. 394; Köymen, *op. cit.* pp. 8 ff.

[2] Ibn al-Jauzī, *al-Muntaẓam*, vol. x, pp. 43-4; cf. Köymen, *op. cit.* pp. 250-4.

[3] Ibn al-At̲h̲īr, vol. x, pp. 181, 191.

In the early years of Berk-Yaruq's reign, the central and western parts of Khurāsān (i.e. Nīshāpūr, Ṭūs, Isfarā'in, Nasā, etc.), together with Qūmis and Gurgān, were governed from Dāmghān by the *Amīr-i Dād* Ḥabashī b. Altun-Taq. Sanjar's base was at this time farther east, at Balkh, and it was a prime task for him and his amīrs, Kündigüz, Er-Ghush, and Rustam, to dislodge Ḥabashī from Khurāsān. In the ensuing warfare Ḥabashī secured the help of 5,000 Ismā'īlī troops from Ṭabas—then in the hands of a Bāṭinī governor, Ismā'īl Kalkālī—and he was also joined by Sulṭān Berk-Yaruq, who had been compelled to flee eastwards after his defeat in 493/1100 at the hands of Muḥammad (see above, p. 109). Ḥabashī and Berk-Yaruq were nevertheless defeated by Sanjar and his amīrs at a place called Naushajān, Ḥabashī being captured and then killed, and Berk-Yaruq retiring to Gurgān and later Iṣfahān.[1] From this time onwards the whole of Khurāsān up to and including Qūmis was firmly in Sanjar's hands, and he subsequently moved his capital to the more central city of Marv. Now he could take direct action against the troublesome Ismā'īlīs of Kūhistān; two expeditions against Ṭabas by the Amīr Boz-Qush are recorded, in both of which regular troops and volunteers took part (494/1101 and 497/1104).[2]

Thus in these years, when he was still just one of the Saljuq maliks and subordinate to the sultans in the west, Sanjar was primarily concerned to consolidate his power within Khurāsān and to provide financial help or refuge to his brother Muḥammad in his struggle against Berk-Yaruq.[3] But this period was also one of turmoil and instability in the neighbouring kingdom of the Qarakhānids, vassals of the Saljuqs from Malik-Shāh's time, and Sanjar was soon drawn into the affairs of Transoxiana. As pointed out on pp. 5–6 above, the rule of the Qarakhānids in Transoxiana, Semirechye, and Kashgharia was essentially that of a loose tribal confederation, and internal dynastic conflicts were frequent. Sanjar was able to follow his Saljuq predecessors' examples and utilize these disputes for his own purposes.

An important religious and political phenomenon is discernible in the Qarakhānid cities of Samarqand and Bukhārā from the middle years of the 5th/11th century onwards. This is the tension between the

[1] *Ibid.* x, pp. 201–2 (the fullest and most convincing account); Bundārī, pp. 259–60; and Ḥusainī, p. 87 (a divergent account); cf. Hodgson, *The Order of Assassins*, pp. 86–7.

[2] Ibn al-Athīr, vol. x, pp. 221–2, 260. Cf. Hodgson, *op. cit.* p. 88; and see above, section VIII, pp. 118–19.

[3] Cf. Bundārī, pp. 260–1.

khans and the orthodox religious institution, despite the ostentatious Sunnī piety and zeal for charitable works shown by many of the khans. It is difficult in any period of Islamic history to discern the true feelings of the urban masses; at certain critical points, for example, they seem to have supported the khans, and it was a revolt of the artisans of Bukhārā which in 636/1238–9 ended the domination of the Burhānī *ṣudūr*. On the other hand the military leaders, always jealous of any increase in the central power, gave direct assistance to the religious classes on several occasions. The just and devout Tamghach Khan Ibrāhīm was driven to execute Shaikh Abu'l-Qāsim Samarqandī; then in the reign of Aḥmad b. Khiḍr the faqīhs called in the Saljuq Malik-Shāh and in the end had the khan deposed and executed for alleged Ismā'īlī sympathies (pp. 92–3 above). The power of this clerical caste can be seen in the appearance of lines of hereditary religious leaders, especially in Bukhārā, who often bear the honorary titles of *Ṣudūr* or "prominent men" (sing. *Ṣadr*). Similarly in the 5th/11th century there had been the *imāms* (religious leaders) of the Ṣaffārī family; but Sanjar, in the course of his Transoxianan expedition of 495/1102, deposed the reigning ra'īs and imām of Bukhārā, Abū Isḥāq Ibrāhīm Ṣaffārī, and replaced him by the well-known scholar 'Abd al-'Azīz b. 'Umar of the Burhān family. He invested him personally with the *ṣadāra* (religious leadership) and gave him a sister in marriage, so that 'Abd al-'Aziz and his successors of the Āl-i Burhān became immediate vassals of the Saljuqs. Some decades later these ṣudūr dealt directly with the Qara-Khitai invaders of Transoxiana and collected the taxes of the Bukhārā region for them. The authority of the Burhānīs accordingly had a political and fiscal aspect as well as a religious one. The family retained its power under the Khwārazm-Shāhs and early Mongols, in spite of a dark period when the Shāh 'Alā' al-Dīn Muḥammad deposed Ṣadr Burhān al-Dīn Muḥammad b. Aḥmad, and subsequently permitted his mother Terken Khatun to execute the imām.[1] The line ended only with the popular rising of 636/1238–9 in Bukhārā, after which a fresh series of ṣudūr, that of the Maḥbūbīs, begins.[2]

The western Qarakhānid throne in Transoxiana had been given by Berk-Yaruq to Sulaimān b. Dā'ūd b. Tamghach Khān Ibrāhīm in

[1] Nasawī, *Histoire du Sultan Djelal ed-Din Mankobirti*, p. 23 (tr. pp. 41–2); cf. Barthold, *Turkestan*, pp. 379, 430.

[2] Cf. Barthold, pp. 313, 316–17, 320–2; O. Pritsak, "Āl-i Burhān", *Der Islam*, pp. 81–96; Qazvīnī's n. xi in Niẓāmī 'Arūḍī, *Chahār Maqāla* (E. G. Browne revised tr., pp. 110–12).

490/1097; the throne then passed quickly to a Maḥmūd-Tegin and to Hārūn b. Sulaimān b. Qadïr Khān Yūsuf, who died in 495/1102. In this year Transoxiana was invaded by Qadïr Khān Jibrā'īl b. 'Umar of Talas and Balāsāghūn, who led an army which included both Muslim and pagan Turks. Berk-Yaruq and Muḥammad were at this time involved in warfare, whilst Sanjar was in Baghdad, and the Qarakhānid Muḥammad b. Sulaimān b. Dā'ūd fled to Sanjar's capital at Marv; but Qadïr Khān Jibrā'īl pressed through Transoxiana, across the Oxus, and into Khurāsān, aided by the defection of one of Sanjar's own amīrs, Kün-Toghdï. In the end the invader was halted and then defeated and killed near Tirmidh by Sanjar, who had hurried eastwards, whilst Kün-Toghdï fled to the court of the Ghaznavid Mas'ūd III b. Ibrāhīm. Sanjar then sent troops into Transoxiana and placed Muḥammad on the throne in Samarqand; the latter took the Turkish ruling title of Arslan-Khān and remained ruler there till 524/1130. Sanjar also concerned himself with the religious leadership in Transoxiana, and it was at this point that he gave the leadership of the Ḥanafīs there to Ṣadr 'Abd al-'Azīz b. 'Umar of the Āl-i Burhān. Like his father, Arslan-Khān Muḥammad was linked to the Saljuqs by a marriage alliance with one of Sanjar's daughters, and on two occasions in the next few years (496/1103 and 503/1109) Sanjar gave him military help against another Qarakhānid claimant, Saghun Beg.[1] This rival has been identified by Pritsak as the Ḥasan b. 'Alī whom Sanjar was to place on the throne of Samarqand in 524/1030. The poet and literary stylist Rashīd al-Dīn Vaṭvāṭ gives Ḥasan Khān the title of Kök-Saghun, and it is probable that he came from the line of 'Alī b. Bughra Khān Hārūn, known as 'Ali-Tegin, who had ruled in Soghdia a century before and whose descendants had remained in Farghāna.[2]

This rivalry excepted, Arslan-Khān Muḥammad enjoyed a reign which was peaceful almost to the end of this life. He became noted as a great builder, rebuilding the citadel and walls of Bukhārā and constructing there a fine Friday mosque and two palaces. He undertook regular campaigns into the surrounding steppes, presumably against pagan Qïpchaq, bringing back slaves and gaining the title Ghāzī.[3] Despite these laudable activities, the tension between the dynasty and the religious classes was not stilled. It may well have been

[1] Bundārī, p. 262; Ḥusainī, p. 90; Ibn al-Athīr, vol. x, pp. 239–41, 252; Barthold, *Turkestan*, pp. 318–19; *idem*, "History of the Semirechyé", in *Four Studies on the History of Central Asia*, vol. 1, p. 98.

[2] Cf. Pritsak, "Karahanlïlar", *İslâm Ansiklopedisi*.

[3] Bundārī, p. 264.

religious elements who in 507/1113–14 complained to Sanjar about the khan's tyranny, a trait which does not accord with the rest of our knowledge of him. In any case the khan was obliged to seek the intercession of the Khwārazm-Shāh Quṭb al-Dīn Muḥammad and of Sanjar's Amīr Qaimaz, and to go personally and meet the sultan.[1] At the end of his reign Arslan-Khān Muḥammad became embroiled with the Saljuqs. By now a sick man, he ruled in association with his son Naṣr. But an 'Alid faqīh and the ra'īs of Samarqand, leaders of a group representing religious interests, conspired together and killed Naṣr, whereupon the khan appealed to Sanjar for help and appointed another son, Aḥmad, in Naṣr's place. Aḥmad assumed the title of Qadïr-Khān and took draconian measures against the leaders of the plot, but Sanjar was now on his way with an army. Friction occurred between the khan's followers and the Saljuq army, and Sanjar captured Samarqand, plundering part of the city (524/1130). The sick Arslan-Khān surrendered to Sanjar, and, because he was the father of Sanjar's Qarakhānid wife Terken Khatun, was allowed to stay in the sultan's harem. He died soon afterwards, and in his place Sanjar appointed Ḥasan b. 'Alī; on his death in 526/1132, Sanjar chose Arslan-Khān's brother Ibrāhīm, and he was followed by a third son of Arslan-Khān, Maḥmūd, later to be ruler of Khurāsān during Sanjar's captivity amongst the Ghuzz (see below, pp. 153–7).[2] It was this Maḥmūd who was reigning in Transoxiana when the Qara-Khitai appeared there a few years later.

The province of Khwārazm had passed into Saljuq hands on the defeat of Shāh Malik, the son of the Oghuz Yabghu of Jand and Yengi-Kent (see p. 18 above). It had then come under governors representing the Saljuqs, and for the next few decades Khwārazm made little impact upon eastern Islamic history. Alp-Arslan came thither in 457/1065 to suppress a revolt, visiting Jand and pushing westwards across the Üst Urt plateau towards the Manqïshlaq peninsula (see p. 65 above).[3] He then appointed Arslan-Arghun as governor, and this man remained in office during the early part of Malik-Shāh's

[1] Ibn al-Athīr, vol. x, pp. 348–9.

[2] Bundārī, *loc. cit.*; Ẓahīr al-Dīn Nīshāpūrī, p. 44; Rāvandī, p. 169; Ḥusainī, p. 92; Ibn al-Athīr, vol. x, pp. 465–6; Juvainī, *Ta'rīkh-i Jahān-Gushā*, vol. 1, pp. 278–9; Barthold, *Turkestan*, pp. 320–2; Köymen, *Büyük Selçuklu Imparatorluğu tarihi*, pp. 158–63.

[3] The Soviet authority on this region, S. P. Tolstov, has surmised from the name of one of these rebels in Khwārazm, given by Mīrkhwānd as Faghfūr, that this man might possibly have been a survivor from the old Afrīghid line of Khwārazm-Shāhs. See *Auf den Spuren der altchoresmischen Kultur*, p. 292.

reign: an exception to the general rule of the time, for Khwārazm was usually granted to ghulām commanders rather than to members of the Saljuq dynasty itself, who, by the province's isolation, might rebel. It seems that the revenues of Khwārazm were used in Malik-Shāh's reign to defray the expenses of a particular office in the royal household, that of the keeper of the wash-bowls (*tasht-dār*), for the ghulām Anūsh-Tegin Gharcha'ī held this office and also bore the title "*shaḥna* of Khwārazm".[1]

The presence of Turkish governors in Khwārazm after the overthrow of the Ma'mūnid Shāhs in 408/1017—at first they had ruled on behalf of the Ghaznavids, and then on behalf of the Saljuqs—must have favoured the process whereby Khwārazm was gradually transformed from an ethnically and culturally Iranian land into a Turkish one. For many centuries the distinctive local language of Khwārazm had been an Iranian tongue with affinities to Soghdian and, to a lesser extent, to Ossetian. It was still in full use during the Saljuqs' hegemony, not merely for speech but also for writing, with special diacritical marks added to the Arabic alphabet to express the sounds peculiar to Khwārazmian; these are found in some manuscripts of the Khwārazmian al-Bīrūnī's works. Khwārazmian speech probably lasted in upper Khwārazm till the end of the 8th/14th century, but in lower Khwārazm and Gurgānj, the region nearest to the Aral Sea, the process of Turkicization was complete in the 7th/13th century, according to information deducible from the travel narrative of the Franciscan John of Plano Carpini. Today the Khwārazmian language has to be reconstructed from such materials as odd words and phrases in al-Bīrūnī's works, from the glosses on an Islamic legal text, and from a single literary work, a Khwārazmian version of an introduction to Arabic grammar and language by the famous exegete and grammarian, al-Zamakhsharī (d. 538/1141).

Geographically Khwārazm was a peninsula of advanced cultural and economic life jutting out into the Turkish steppes, and thus its Iranian character was made vulnerable to external ethnic and political as well as linguistic pressure. In the second half of the 5th/11th century these steppes were controlled by Turks of the Qïpchaq, Qanghlï, Qun, and Pecheneg groups, not all of whom had yet become Muslim; the middle stretches of the Syr Darya were still *Dar al-kufr* ("lands of unbelief") in the 6th/12th century. The Saljuq governors recruited auxiliary troops

[1] Juvainī, trans. Boyle, pp. 277–8; *Turkestan*, pp. 323–4.

from these nomads, and in the latter half of the 6th/12th century the Khwārazm-Shāh Atsïz and his successors relied heavily on the Qïpchaq, Qanghlï, Yimek, and associated tribes for their armies. Hence they were brought within the boundaries of sedentary Khwārazm, and by settlement and intermarriage the older Iranian population was eventually diluted; already in the 5th/11th century the physical approximation of the Khwārazmian people to the Turkish type was noted.[1]

This linguistic and ethnic change was not, however, accompanied by any material or cultural impoverishment. Under the dynasty of Atsïz, Khwārazm became for the first and last time in its history the centre of a great military empire which embraced large parts of Central Asia and Iran. The Khwārazmians were always great travellers, and their merchants continued to journey across the Eurasian steppes as far as southern Russia and even the Danube basin, where certain place-names attest their presence. Intellectually, Khwārazm was never so brilliant as in the 6th/12th and 7th/13th centuries, when it produced great theologians and literary men, and in particular remained a centre of Arabic learning. The much-travelled geographer Yāqūt (d. 626/1229), writing on the eve of the Mongol invasion, said that he had never seen such urban and agricultural prosperity as in Khwārazm; and the walled cities and fortified villages, canals and irrigation works disclosed by Soviet archaeologists confirm the view that the area of cultivated land expanded in the course of the 6th/12th century.[2]

In the latter part of Malik-Shāh's reign the governor of Khwārazm was, at least titularly, the ghulām Anūsh-Tegin Gharcha'ī. (The *nisba* probably refers to the region of Gharchistān in northern Afghanistan, where Anūsh-Tegin had been originally bought by a Saljuq amīr; Kafesoğlu has conjectured that he was of Khalaj Turkish origin.)[3] Ekinchi b. Qochqar, a ghulām of Qun origin, was appointed as Khwārazm-Shāh, probably on the occasion of Berk-Yaruq's expedition to Khurāsān in 490/1097 against Arslan-Arghun. As Minorsky has

[1] Cf. A. Z. V. Togan and W. Henning, "Über die Sprache und Kultur der alten Chwarezmier", *Z.D.M.G.* vol. xc; Togan, *The Khorezmians and their Civilisation*, pp. 20 ff.; Henning, "The Khwarezmian Language", *Zeki Velidi Togan'a Armağanï* (Istanbul, 1955), pp 420–36; *idem*, in *Handbuch der Orientalistik*, vol. iv, *Iranistik*, no. 1, *Linguistik* (Leiden, Cologne, 1958), pp. 56–8, 81–4, 109–20.

[2] Togan, *loc. cit.*; Barthold, *Histoire des Turcs d'Asie Centrale*, pp. 109–15; Tolstov, *Auf den Spuren*, pp. 295–310.

[3] See his long discussion of Anūsh-Tegin's origin in his *Harezmşahlar devleti tarihi*, pp. 38–43.

pointed out, Ekinchi must have had considerable renown, as well as a great knowledge of events in the region of Khwārazm and the steppes, to be nominated to this important post.[1] At the end of the same year, however, Ekinchi was killed by rebellious Saljuq amīrs, so that Berk-Yaruq's representative in Khurāsān, the Amīr-i Dād Ḥabashī, appointed in his stead Anūsh-Tegin's son Quṭb al-Dīn Muḥammad. As Khwārazm Shāh from 490/1097 till his death in 521/1127 or 522/1128, Quṭb al-Dīn had the reputation of being a just ruler who was always obedient to his master Sanjar.[2] At various points during the Saljuq succession-disputes in western Iran, he fought for Sulṭān Muḥammad b. Malik-Shāh and for Sanjar, and in 507/1113–14 he mediated between Arslan-Khān Muḥammad of Samarqand and Sanjar (see above, p. 140).

'Alā' al-Dīn Atsïz succeeded his father and reigned as nominal vassal of the Saljuqs till his death in 551/1156. He came to the governorship of Khwārazm with a reputation, like that of Quṭb al-Dīn Muḥammad, for loyalty and submissiveness towards Sanjar. Despite this, the course of events was to show that Atsïz had his own ambitions to make Khwārazm as autonomous as possible, and although he had many reverses he pursued this goal with determination, feeling his way between the two neighbouring powers of the Saljuqs and the Qara-Khitai, and laying the foundation for the fully independent policy of his successors. Juvainī and 'Aufī also praise Atsïz for his culture and learning, ascribing to him the composition of verses in Persian.

In his early years as Khwārazm-Shāh, Atsïz aimed primarily at securing the long and vulnerable frontiers of his principality against the nomads; since many of these were still pagans, his efforts earned him amongst the orthodox the title of Ghāzī. Of particular strategic importance here were the steppes between the Aral and Caspian seas, together with the adjacent Manqïshlaq peninsula where many nomads had summer pastures, and the lower Syr Darya region from Uṭrār down to Jand. Both these areas had long been spring-boards for attacks on Khwārazm, and it was to Manqïshlaq and Jand that the followers of Ekinchi b. Qochqar's son Toghrïl-Tegin had fled in 490/1097 after the latter's bid to regain Khwārazm had been frustrated by Quṭb al-Dīn Muḥammad.[3] Atsïz attended Sanjar regularly, being

[1] Minorsky, *Sharaf al-Zamān Ṭāhir Marvazī on China, the Turks and India* (London, 1942), pp. 101–2.

[2] Ibn al-Athīr, vol. x, pp. 181–3; Juvainī, vol. 1, pp. 277–8, quoting Ibn Funduq's *Mashārib al-tajārib* (probably also the source for Ibn al-Athīr).

[3] Ibn al-Athīr, vol. x, p. 183.

with him, for example, in the Transoxianan campaign of 524/1030, but he did not neglect the frontiers of Khwārazm. According to Ibn al-Athīr, he had already secured Maqïshlaq during his father's lifetime, and in 527/1133 he led a campaign from Jand into the Qïpchaq steppes; Yāqūt quotes a line of verse in praise of the Manqïshlaq victory. After 536/1141 he secured the lower Syr Darya against the Qara-Khitai by paying them an annual tribute in cash and kind.[1]

It was not long before Atsïz's relation with his suzerain Sanjar became strained. The sultan allegedly began to grow cold towards the Khwārazm-Shāh during the campaign of 529/1135 against the Ghaznavid Bahrām-Shāh (p. 159 below), and in a proclamation of victory issued after his triumph at Hazārasp, Sanjar accused Atsïz of killing Muslim ghāzīs and *murābiṭūn* (frontier fighters) at Manqïshlaq and Jand. In 533/1138 Atsïz rebelled openly, flooding much of the land along the Oxus to impede the advance of Sanjar's army. Yet this did not prevent the sultan from defeating the Khwārazmian army, which included some pagan Turks, at the fortress of Hazārasp; he then executed Atsïz's son Atlïgh. He occupied Khwārazm and granted it to his nephew Sulaimān-Shāh b. Muḥammad, providing him with a vizier, an atabeg, and other administrative officials, but the advent of direct Saljuq rule proved irksome to the Khwārazmians. As soon as Sanjar had left for Marv, Atsïz returned from his refuge in Gurgān, and the people rose and expelled Sulaimān-Shāh. Then in 534/1139–40 the Khwārazm-Shāh took the offensive, capturing Bukhārā from its Saljuq governor and destroying the citadel there. The extent to which Atsïz clearly commanded the sympathies of the Khwārazmians is an indication of the province's continued individuality and its need for a local ruler who could look after its special political and commercial interests. For all this, Sanjar's power and prestige were still formidable, and in 535/1141 Atsïz found it expedient to submit to him.[2]

Four months later, Sanjar's unexpected and crushing defeat by the Qara-Khitai in the Qaṭvān steppe was obviously opportune for Atsïz, so much so that several sources accuse him of having incited the

[1] *Ibid.*; Yāqūt, "Manqashlāgh", *Mu'jam al-buldān*, vol. v, p. 215; Juvainī, vol. i, pp. 278–9, 356; Barthold, *Turkestan down to the Mongol Invasion*, p. 324; *idem*, "A History of the Turkman People", in *Four Studies*, vol. iii, pp. 126–7; and Kafesoğlu, *Harezmşahlar devleti tarihi*, p. 45.

[2] Continuator of Narshakhī, *Ta'rīkh-i Bukhārā*, p. 30 (R. N. Frye tr., pp. 24–5); Ibn al-Athīr, vol. xi, pp. 44–5; Juvainī, vol. i, pp. 279–82; Barthold, *Turkestan down to the Mongol Invasion*, pp. 324–6; Köymen, *Büyük Selçuklu Imparatorluğu tarihi*, vol. ii, pp. 312–23; Kafesoğlu, *op. cit.* pp. 46–9.

Qara-Khitai to rise against the sultan as an act of revenge for the killing of his son Atlïgh;[1] but according to Juvainī, the invaders also passed from Transoxiana into Khwārazm, devastating the province and compelling Atsïz to pay tribute. When Sanjar fell back before the Qara-Khitai to Tirmidh and Balkh, Atsïz made two incursions into Khurāsān in the course of 536/1141–2. In the first expedition he took Sarakhs and Marv, either killing or carrying off several of the local ulema, and appropriating the state treasury at Marv; he then returned the next spring to occupy Nīshāpūr (where the khuṭba was made for him over the next three months), Baihaq, and other parts of Khurāsān. Through his court poet Rashīd al-Dīn Vaṭvāṭ, the Khwārazm-Shāh boasted that the power of the Saljuqs was at an end and his own dynasty was in the ascendant, but early in 537/1142 Saljuq rule was re-established in Khurāsān. In retaliation, the sultan in 538/1143–4 invaded Khwārazm, besieged Gurgānj, and compelled Atsïz to submit and to return the treasuries taken from Marv; but once more the country proved too hostile for the Saljuqs to remain there.[2]

To Sanjar's troubles with the Qara-Khitai were now added the first rumbles of discontent from the Ghuzz in Khurāsān. Atsïz again showed himself rebellious, plotting the sultan's assassination by means of hired Ismā'īlīs and executing an envoy sent from the court at Marv. In 542/1147 Sanjar marched into Khwārazm for the third time, capturing Hazārasp and Gurgānj, but in 543/1148 he allowed the Khwārazm-Shāh to make a grudging submission. Atsïz's adventures in Khurāsān and his attempts to throw off Saljuq suzerainty accordingly came to nought, so he turned once more to his original sphere of activity, the steppes surrounding Khwārazm. One of the consequences of his preoccupation with events in Khurāsān and the south had been the loss of Jand, which had passed to one Kamāl al-Dīn b. Arslan-Khān Maḥmūd, apparently a Qarakhānid and son of the khan who ruled in Samarqand from 526/1132 to 536/1141. An expedition left Khwārazm in the summer of 547/1152 and occupied Jand without striking a blow. Although Juvainī states that Kamāl al-Dīn had been a friend of Atsïz and of Vaṭvāṭ, he was seized and jailed for the rest of his life. Jand was now placed under the governorship of Atsïz's son and

[1] E.g. Ibn al-Athīr, vol. xi, p. 53.

[2] Ibn Funduq, *Ta'rīkh-i Baihaq*, p. 272; Bundārī, pp 280–1; Ẓahīr al-Dīn Nīshāpūrī, p. 46; Rāvandī, p. 174; Ḥusainī, pp. 95–6; Ibn al-Athīr, vol. xi, pp. 53, 58–9, 63; Juvainī, vol. i, 280–4; Barthold, *op. cit.* p. 327; Köymen, *Büyük Selçuklu Imparatorluğu tarihi*, pp. 336–45; Kafesoğlu, *Harezmşahlar devleti tarihi*, pp. 54–7.

successor Il-Arslan—an illustration of the importance attached to the town.[1]

During Sanjar's captivity amongst the Ghuzz, Atsïz remained essentially loyal to the Saljuq connexion. He did try to get Sanjar to grant him Āmul-i Shaṭṭ, the strategically important crossing on the river Oxus, but its castellan refused to yield up his charge. At one point the Khwārazm-Shāh's brother Ïnal-Tegin marched into Khurāsān, where he devastated the Baihaq oasis in 548–9/1154; Ibn Funduq says that the resultant destruction and depopulation were still visible fourteen years later.[2] The Qarakhānid Maḥmūd Khān, who had been chosen as ruler of Khurāsān by that part of Sanjar's army which had not joined the Ghuzz, now began negotiating with Atsïz for the dispatch of a Khwārazmian army into Khurāsān to quell the Ghuzz. Atsïz and his son Il-Arslan set out for Khurāsān, leaving a further son Khitai-Khān as regent of Khwārazm (551/1156), and whilst at Shahristān they received news of Sanjar's escape from the Ghuzz. Maḥmūd Khān and the other Saljuq amīrs now regretted having invited the ambitious Atsïz into Khurāsān, but in fact the latter behaved with restraint and did nothing provocative. He met Maḥmūd Khān and summoned for aid the Ṣaffārid Abu'l-Faḍl, the Bāvandid Ispahbadh Shāh Ghāzī Rustam, and the Ghūrid 'Alā' al-Dīn Ḥusain; he sent Sanjar a florid letter of congratulation; and he warned Ṭūṭī Beg, most prominent of the Ghuzz leaders, of the consequences of further rebelliousness. Whatever Atsïz's real intentions, all was now ended, for he died at this point, nine months before Sanjar's own death. Thus he died as a vassal of the Saljuqs, yet the conquests he had made in the steppes and the assembling of a powerful mercenary army enabled his successors to make Khwārazm the nucleus of a powerful empire in the decades before the Mongol invasion: an empire whose part in attracting the Mongols westwards was to have incalculable consequences for the greater part of the Islamic world.[3]

Until the eighth century A.D., there had been a certain amount of direct contact between the Iranian and the Chinese world. The T'ang dynasty (618–906) never believed that Transoxiana and the formerly Buddhist lands on the upper Oxus were totally lost to the Chinese

[1] Juvainī, vol. I, pp. 284–5; Barthold, *op. cit.* pp. 327–9; Köymen, *op. cit.* pp. 345–53; Kafesoğlu, *op. cit.* pp. 58–61.

[2] Juvainī, vol. I, pp. 285–6; Ibn Funduq, p. 271.

[3] Ibn al-Athīr, vol. XI, p. 138; Juvainī, vol. I, pp. 286–7; Barthold, *op. cit.* pp. 330–1; Köymen, *op. cit.* pp. 452–63; Kafesoğlu, *op. cit.* pp. 65–72.

empire, although the immense distances involved made any direct control almost impossible. Nevertheless, after the disintegration of the Western Türk's steppe empire in the first half of the eighth century, the Chinese tried to assert their authority in Transoxiana. In 133/751 the Arab general Ziyād b. Ṣāliḥ defeated near Talas a Chinese army that had appeared in the Syr Darya valley, and the possibility of Chinese political control in this region vanished forever.[1] But commercial and religious movements across Central Asia continued for many centuries to bring some Chinese cultural influences and some luxury imports into the Iranian world. Chinese prisoners taken by Ziyād b. Ṣāliḥ are said to have taught the Muslims of Samarqand the art of paper-making, and fine porcelain brought from China became highly prized in the Islamic world.[2]

In the early part of the 6th/12th century there was an intrusion of the Chinese world into eastern Iran, in the shape of the Qara-Khitai invaders from northern China, although the Mongol invasions of the 7th/13th century were to prove more important in spreading Far Eastern cultural and artistic ideas in the Persian world. The domination of the Qara-Khitai affected only Transoxiana and, for a brief while, a strip to the south of the Oxus around Balkh; they did not exterminate existing ruling houses, as the Mongols were to do, but were content to receive tribute and to exercise a supreme overlordship. Perhaps the most significant feature of their dominion in Transoxiana and Semirechye was the temporary check it gave to the spread of Islam in the steppes. The Qara-Khitai possessed the traditional tolerance of the steppe peoples, who have always been at the receiving end of the great religions of Asia.[3] They accorded the indigenous Muslims of Transoxiana no special preference among the adherents of other faiths; but neither did they persecute them. Ibn al-Athīr says that the first Gür-Khān ("Supreme, Universal Khan") was a Manichaean;[4] indeed, when the Christians of Europe first heard dimly of the defeats suffered by the Muslim Saljuqs and Khwārazm-Shāhs, they thought that a great Christian power had arisen in Central Asia, and in this way legends about "Prester John" began to circulate in the West. What is

[1] Cf. Barthold, *op. cit.* pp. 195–6; H. A. R. Gibb, *The Arab Conquests in Central Asia* (London, 1923), pp. 95–8; R. Grousset, *L'Empire des steppes*, pp. 165–72.

[2] Cf. Thaʿālibī, *Laṭā'if al-maʿārif*, p. 126; P. Kahle, "Chinese Porcelain in the Lands of Islam", in *Opera Minora* (Leiden, 1956), pp. 326–61.

[3] Cf. D. Sinor's chapter, "Central Eurasia", in *Orientalism and History* (Cambridge, 1954), pp. 82–103.

[4] *al-Kāmil*, vol. xi, p. 55.

certain is that Qara-Khitai impartiality allowed the repressed adherents of non-Islamic faiths to flourish more openly, and this can be seen in the missionary enterprise and expansion begun in this period by the Nestorian Christians of eastern Iran and Central Asia.[1] Grousset's verdict, that "the foundation of the Qara-Khitai empire may be viewed as a reaction against the work of Islamization accomplished by the Qarakhānids", may in this wise be true.[2]

Ethnically the Qara-Khitai were most probably Mongols.[3] In Chinese sources they are first called the "K'i-tan" and then, after 947, the "Liao"; over the next two centuries they became deeply Sinicized and in the Chinese annals are accounted a native dynasty. In the tenth century they founded a vast empire stretching from the Altai to the Pacific, with its centre in northern China. The name of their empire, in the form Khatā or Khitā, was first applied by the Muslims to northern China, passing from them to the Europeans, whence the older English Cathay. Between 1116 and 1123, however, the K'i-tan were overthrown in China by a fresh wave of barbarian invaders, the Jürchet, a Tungusic people from the Amur valley and northern Manchuria. A section of the K'i-tan migrated westwards into Central Asia, where Islamic historians knew them as the Qara-Khitai, i.e. Black (or perhaps "Powerful, mighty") Khitai.

This section came in two groups. One went into eastern Turkestan and came up against the branch of the Qarakhānids ruling there. Arslan-Khān Aḥmad defeated them before they could reach Kāshghar and captured their leader (whom Ibn al-Athīr calls al-Aʿwar, "the One-eyed"); in a letter from Sanjar to the caliph in 527/1133 this victory is mentioned as a recent event. The other group, numbering some 40,000 tents, took a more northerly route through the Altai and came into the territories of the Qarakhānid ruler of Balāsāghūn, who tried to use the invaders against his own Qarluq and Qanghlï enemies but instead found himself deposed. The Qara-Khitai leader, whose name appears in Chinese sources as Yeh-lü Ta-shih (d. 537/1143), now made the Chu valley the centre of his empire and assumed the title of Gür-Khān. His followers campaigned against the Qanghlï in the steppes stretching

[1] Cf. Barthold, *Zur Geschichte des Christentums in Mittel-Asien* (Tübingen, Leipzig, 1901), pp. 55 ff.; *idem*, *Histoire des Turcs d'Asie Centrale*, pp. 99–101.

[2] *L'Empire des steppes*, p. 221.

[3] Cf. Sir Gerard Clauson, "Turk, Mongol, Tungus" *Asia Major*, N.S. vol. VIII (1960), pp. 120–1; but in a postscript on p. 123 he admits the possibility that the K'i-tan spoke a language of their own, unrelated to the Altaic tongues.

towards the Aral Sea, against the Kirghiz in the steppes to the north of the Chu, and against the Qarakhānids in Kāshghar and Khotan. In 531/1137 they made contact with the Transoxianan Qarakhānids and defeated Maḥmūd Khān b. Arslan Muḥammad of Samarqand in the Syr Darya valley at Khujand.

The Qara-Khitai halted here for four years, but in 536/1141 internal disputes in Samarqand opened the whole of Transoxiana to them. Several years earlier, Maḥmūd Khān had invoked the aid of his suzerain Sanjar against the unruly Qarluq. According to 'Imād al-Dīn, their families and flocks had increased in number in the Samarqand region and had been damaging property and tillage; yet 'Imād al-Dīn also stresses the initial peaceableness of the Qarluq, who were harried by the sultan's agents, had their pastures reduced and their women and children enslaved, but still offered to pay Sanjar an extensive tribute in beasts. Only after this did they appeal to the Qara-Khitai to intercede for them with the sultan. Sanjar brusquely rejected this approach, and seems deliberately to have made it a *casus belli* against the Qara-Khitai. The latter now invaded Transoxiana in force, and in 536/1141 a bloody battle was fought in the Qaṭvān steppe in Ushrūsana, to the east of Samarqand. The Muslim losses were huge, and Amīr Qumach, the amīr of Sīstān, and Sanjar's Qarakhānid wife were all captured. Sanjar and Maḥmūd Khān abandoned Transoxiana and fled to Tirmidh; the Gūr-Khān occupied Bukhārā, killing the Burhānī *ṣadr* Ḥusām al-Dīn 'Umar, and he sent an army under his commander Erbüz to ravage Atsïz's dominions in Khwārazm.[1]

Sanjar's defeat meant the permanent loss of Saljuq sovereignty beyond the Oxus, while the Muslims there fell under "infidel" control. In practice the Qara-Khitai were not fanatics, and Islamic sources speak of the equitable government of the first Gūr-Khāns, whereas there had been frequent complaints about the oppression of Sanjar's amīrs. According to the later historian Muṣliḥ al-Dīn Lārī, the people of Herāt rejoiced in 542/1147 when their city passed from the tyranny of the Saljuqs to the just rule of 'Alā' al-Dīn Ḥusain Ghūrī; and the

[1] Niẓāmī 'Arūḍī, *Chahār Maqāla*, pp. 37–8 (tr., pp. 24–5); Bundārī, *Zubdat al-nuṣra*, pp. 276–8; Ẓahīr al-Dīn Nīshāpūrī, *Saljūq-Nāma*, pp. 45–6; Rāvandī, *Rāḥat al-ṣudūr*, pp. 172–4; Ḥusainī, *Akhbār al-daula*, pp. 93–5; Ibn al-Athīr, *al-Kāmil*, vol. XI, pp. 54–7; Juvainī, *Ta'rīkh-i Jahān-Gushā*, I, pp. 354–6; Barthold, *Turkestan down to the Mongol Invasion*, pp. 326–7; *idem*, "History of the Semirechyé", pp. 100–4; *idem*, "A Short History of Turkestan", pp. 26–30; *idem*, *Histoire des Turcs d'Asie Centrale*, pp. 94 ff.; Grousset, *L'Empire des steppes*, pp. 219–22; Köymen, *Büyük Selçuklu Impartorluğu tarihi*, pp. 323 ff.

boundless justice of the first Gür-Khān forms the subject of one of Niẓāmī 'Arūḍī's anecdotes in the *Chahār Maqāla*.[1] Within their newly acquired territories the Qara-Khitai allowed a wide degree of local autonomy: often, for example, existing political and tribal institutions were retained and their members required to collect and forward taxation to the Gür-Khāns' *ordu* (military camp) in the Chu valley; this was the arrangement eventually made with the ṣudūr of Bukhārā.

What did suffer irreparably was Sanjar's own prestige, and he spent the rest of his reign striving to preserve his remaining possessions. Beyond Khurāsān were young and expanding powers such as the Khwārazm-Shāhs and Ghūrids; within there was mounting insubordination among the Saljuq amīrs and increasing lack of control over the Türkmen. Atsïz seized his chance to invade northern Khurāsān in 536/1141–2, and in a proclamation to the people of Nīshāpūr he said that Sanjar's defeat was a divine retribution for ingratitude towards his loyal servant the Khwarazm-Shāh.[2] News of the Qara-Khitai victory reached the Christian West, causing an access of hope that the tide might now be turning against Islam. In letting Sanjar be defeated, writes Sibṭ b. al-Jauzī, "God took vengeance for [the murdered caliph] al-Mustarshid and let loose on him ruin and destruction". From this we may conclude that caliphal circles in Iraq at this time enjoyed a certain amount of *Schadenfreude*, even though Sanjar had in the preceding year attempted to improve relations with Baghdad by returning to al-Muqtafī the Prophet's cloak (*burda*) and the sceptre (*qaḍīb*), which had been taken from al-Mustarshid.[3]

The historians describe Khurāsān as being in a flourishing state during Sanjar's time, and this may well be true of at least the first decades of his reign. He preserved an unusually long continuity of administration, during which the seat of government, Marv, became a vital centre for culture and intellectual life.[4] A comparatively rich documentation, in the form of collections of official correspondence, shows that the sultan was aware of his responsibility for provincial administration, even though this was usually delegated to ghulām military commanders or occasionally to Saljuq maliks. However, it is not so clear from these documents how much check and control from the centre there really was. In an investiture patent for the governor-

[1] Niẓāmī 'Arūḍī, *loc. cit.*
[2] Barthold, *Turkestan down to the Mongol Invasion*, p. 327.
[3] Sibṭ b. al-Jauzī, *Mir'āt al-zamān*, vol. 1, p. 180; Ibn al-Athīr vol. xi, p. 52.
[4] Cf. Juvainī, vol. 1, p. 153.

ship of Gurgān, given to his nephew Mas'ūd b. Muḥammad (later sultan in the west), Sanjar points out the importance of such duties as the defence of the region against the pagan Turks of Dihistān and Manqïshlaq, a strict adherence to the tax rates laid down by the central dīvān in Marv, and the adoption of a generally kind attitude towards the people.[1] Nevertheless, social unrest in the countryside and the violence of 'ayyārs and religious factions in the towns were certainly not stilled in Sanjar's reign. There was, for instance, an *émeute* in 510/1116–17 at Ṭūs when the tomb of the Shī'ī Imām 'Alī al-Riḍā was attacked, presumably by Sunnī partisans; the local governor then built a high wall round the shrine.[2] The Ismā'īlīs continued to be active, especially in Kūhistān. In 520/1126 troops under Sanjar's Vizier Mu'īn al-Mulk Abū Naṣr Aḥmad marched against Turaithīth, or Turshīz, in Kūhistān, and also against Ṭarz in the Baihaq district, and Ibn Funduq mentions operations in others years against the Ismā'īlīs of Ṭarz. In 530/1136 the Saljuq governor at Turshīz was forced to call in Ghuzz tribesmen against the Ismā'īlīs, but on this occasion the cure proved worse than the disease. Sanjar's captivity amongst the Ghuzz and the breakdown of all central government in Khurāsān inevitably favoured the activities of the Bāṭiniyya. In 549/1154 a force of 7,000 Kūhistān Ismā'īlīs banded together to attack Khurāsān whilst the Saljuq forces were being distracted by the Ghuzz. They marched against Khwāf in northern Kūhistān, but were decisively repelled by the amīrs Muḥammad b. Öner and Farrukh-Shāh al-Kāsāni. However, in 551/1156 they sacked Ṭabas, causing great bloodshed and capturing several of Sanjar's officials and retainers.[3]

One of Sanjar's most pressing problems was that of controlling the pastoralist nomads, who, since the Saljuq invasions of the previous century, had become a permanent element in the demography and economy of Khurāsān. These Türkmen increased in numbers in the latter part of Sanjar's reign, perhaps because of pressure both from ethnic movements in the Qïpchaq steppe and from the rising power of the Qara-Khitai in Transoxiana. It was of course always difficult for the Saljuq administration to maintain a firm external frontier along

[1] Muntajab al-Dīn Juvainī, *'Atabat al-kataba*, pp. 19–20, quoted in Lambton, "The Administration of Sanjar's Empire as illustrated in the *'Atabat al-Kataba*", *B.S.O.A.S.* pp. 376–7.

[2] Ibn al-Athīr, vol. x, p. 366.

[3] Ibn Funduq, pp. 271, 276; Ibn al-Athīr, vol. x, p. 445, vol. xi, pp. 131–2, 143; Yāqūt, *Mu'jam al-buldān*, vol. iv, p. 33; le Strange, *The Lands of the Eastern Caliphate*, pp. 354–5; Hodgson, *The Order of Assassins*, pp. 100–2.

the Atrak and Oxus, but by exacting taxation either on flocks or individual tents, it did try to control those nomads who were within the boundaries of the empire. Although the Türkmen were an unruly and intractable class, a permanent drag on the machinery of settled government, the Saljuqs always felt that they had obligations to them because they had been the original support of their dynasty, and Niẓām al-Mulk's opinion concerning the Türkmen's rights continued to have validity (see p. 79 above). Since they were a clearly defined class of the population, special administrative arrangements were often made for the areas where they were most numerous. One such region was that of Gurgān and Dihistān, and there is extant the text of a diploma from Sanjar's chancery to Ïnanch Bilge Ulugh Jāndār Beg appointing him military administrator of the Türkmen there. In this document Ïnanch Bilge is enjoined to treat the Türkmen well, to share out water and pasture fairly, to refrain from imposing fresh taxes, and generally to act as the channel between the nomads and the sultan.[1]

The military campaigns which increasingly occupied Sanjar after 529/1135 imposed fresh financial burdens on his subjects; the sultan is said to have expended three million dīnārs on his campaign of 536/1141 against the Qara-Khitai, not counting the cost of the presents and robes of honour which had to be offered during the course of this expedition into Transoxiana.[2] Both sedentaries and Türkmen began to feel increased pressure from the sultan's financial agents, and it was a group of Oghuz or Ghuzz who occupied pastures in Khuttal and Tukhāristān, on the upper Oxus banks, who finally rebelled against these demands.

Ibn al-Athīr quotes "certain historians of Khurāsān" (presumably including Ibn Funduq, author of the *Mashārib al-tajārib*), and asserts that these particular Ghuzz had been driven from Transoxiana by the Qarluq, and had then been invited into Tukhāristān by the local amīr Zangī b. Khalīfa al-Shaibānī. Whilst in their previous home they had been allowed by Atsïz to spend the winter pasturing on the borders of Khwārazm. They were divided into two tribal groups, the *Bozuq* under Qorqut b. 'Abd al-Ḥamīd, and the *Üch-Oq* led by Ṭūṭī Beg b. Isḥāq b. Khiḍr; other amīrs are named as Dīnār, Bakhtiyār, Arslan,

[1] Muntajab al-Dīn Juvainī, pp. 81 ff., quoted in Lambton, *B.S.O.A.S.* (1957), p. 382; see also Lambton's *Landlord and Peasant in Persia*, pp. 56–8.

[2] Ḥusainī, p. 95.

Chaghrī, and Maḥmūd.[1] Sanjar's representatives at Balkh was the ghulām amīr 'Imād al-Dīn Qumach, formerly the sultan's atabeg, who is described as both governor of the province of Tukhāristān, where he held extensive iqṭā's, and shaḥna of the Türkmen there. The capture of Sanjar in 548/1153 was only the climax of a period of discord—a discord aggravated by Qumach's harshness; before this, Ṭūṭī Beg and Qorqut had been faithful attendants at Sanjar's court.[2]

When Qumach defeated his enemy Zangī b. Khalīfa, he at first confirmed the Ghuzz in their Tukhāristān pastures. He also recruited them as auxiliary troops when the Ghūrid 'Alā' al-Dīn Ḥusain attacked Balkh in 547/1152, but the Ghuzz soon defected to the Ghūrids, enabling 'Alā' al-Dīn temporarily to capture Balkh.[3] Henceforth, Qumach's hostility towards the Ghuzz was sharpened. They were accustomed to paying an annual tribute of 24,000 sheep for the sultan's kitchens, but this was being extracted with increasing brutality, and when at last the Ghuzz killed a tyrannical tax collector (*muḥaṣṣil*), Qumach had a pretext for attacking and expelling them. He assembled against them an army of 10,000 cavalry. To placate him, the Ghuzz offered a payment of 200 dirhams per tent. Qumach refused this, and in the ensuing battle he and his son 'Alā' al-Dīn Abu Bakr were both slain. Fearing the sultan's wrath, the Ghuzz offered a large propitiatory payment in cash, beasts, and slaves, together with an annual tribute; under the influence of his amīrs, Sanjar rejected this peace-offering and in 548/1153 set out from Marv with an army. Twice defeated by the Ghuzz, he fell back to Marv but was forced to evacuate the capital, and on leaving it he and several of his amīrs were captured by the Ghuzz.

Marv, meanwhile, was plundered and claimed by the Ghuzz leader Bakhtiyār as his personal iqṭā', and the Ghuzz swept on through the other towns of Khurāsān. In 549/1154 Nīshāpūr was attacked and, after a struggle, its citadel taken; Ibn al-Athīr's source says that corpses were piled up in the streets and that the Ghuzz dragged out those sheltering in the Manī'ī mosque and burnt its famous library. Only the

[1] Ibn al-Athīr, vol. XI, p. 116; Barthold, *A History of the Turkman People*, pp. 119–20. The whole episode of the Ghuzz rebellion has been examined in detail by Köymen in two articles: "Büyük Selçuklular Imparatorluğunda Oğuz Isyanī", and "Büyük Selçuklu Imparatorluğu Tarihinde Oğuz istilâsi", in *Ankara Üniv. Dil ve Tarih-Coğrafya Fakültesi Dergisi*, pp. 159–73, 563–620 (German tr., 175–86, 621–60); see also his *Büyük Selçuklu Imparatorluğu tarihi*, vol. II, pp. 399–466.

[2] Bundārī, p. 281.

[3] Ibn al-Athīr, vol. XI, pp. 107–8, 116–18.

Mashhad 'Alī al-Riḍā at Ṭūs, and those towns such as Herāt and Dihistān which had strong walls, escaped them. Initially the Türkmen seem to have been actuated by a special animosity against the Saljuq court and administration; all the amīrs captured with Sanjar were executed, and many members of the religious institution, which was closely linked with the established order, were put to death. Even so, the sources may well exaggerate the numbers of those killed. Köymen has added up all those scholars whom the sources say were murdered by the Ghuzz, and his figure of fifty-five is hardly a colossal one.[1] The limited numbers of dead given by contemporary biographers such as Sam'ānī and Ibn Funduq are clearly more reliable than the vast figures given by later historians. It is also certain that indigenous anti-social elements in Khurāsān seized the opportunity offered by the Ghuzz rebellion to pursue their own paths of violence and rapine; it is recorded, for example, that in Nīshāpūr at this time the local 'ayyārs behaved worse than the Ghuzz.[2]

On first being captured, Sanjar did not realize the serious position he had fallen into—for were not the Ghuzz from the same stock as himself? They placed him on the throne each day and, initially at least, kept up the pretence that he was the master and they his obedient slaves. But he was closely guarded, and Juvainī says that after an attempted escape Sanjar was kept in an iron cage; it is likely that towards the end he suffered contemptuous treatment, hunger, and other deprivations, for according to Sibṭ b. al-Jauzī, Sanjar's name became proverbial amongst the people of Baghdad for wretchedness and humiliation.[3] The Saljuq army was left headless, and ambitious amīrs were now able to indulge their desires for power. Many of the less-disciplined rank-and-file either joined the Ghuzz or else ravaged the province independently; in 522/1157 a section of the army of Khurāsān attacked the caravan of the Pilgrimage of Khurāsān at Bisṭām, killing, plundering, and leaving the pilgrims in such a defenceless state that they were an easy prey for the local Ismā'īlīs.[4]

The most important of Sanjar's amīrs, together with his vizier Nāṣir al-Dīn Ṭāhir b. Fakhr al-Mulk b. Niẓām al-Mulk, came to

[1] Cf. Köymen, *Büyük Selçuklu*, pp. 430–45.

[2] Bundārī, pp. 281–4; Ẓahīr al-Dīn Nīshāpūrī, pp. 48–51; Rāvandī, pp. 177–82; Ibn al-Jauzī, vol. x, p. 161; Ibn al-Athīr, vol. xi, pp. 116–21; cf. Lambton, *Landlord and Peasant in Persia*, pp. 58–9.

[3] Ḥusainī, p. 125; Ibn al-Athīr, vol. xi, p. 133; Juvainī, vol. i, p. 285; Sibṭ b. al-Jauzī, vol. i, p. 227.

[4] Ibn al-Athīr, vol. xi, pp. 148–9.

Nīshāpūr after the sultan's capture and decided to set up the Saljuq Sulaimān-Shāh b. Muḥammad as their sultan; Sulaimān-Shāh had long lived at the court, and as Sanjar's valī 'ahd had been mentioned in the khuṭba of Khurāsān. He and a detachment of the Saljuq army left Marv to engage the Ghuzz and recapture Sanjar, but they fled at the first encounter with them. Indeed, Sulaimān-Shāh proved a feeble and ineffective ruler at a time when strong leadership in the face of two centrifugal forces, the ambitious Saljuq amīrs and the destructive Ghuzz, was necessary. After the Vizier Ṭāhir died, to be succeeded by his son Niẓām al-Mulk Ḥasan, Sulaimān-Shāh decided to abandon the struggle to enforce his rights as sultan. In 549/1154 he finally left Khurāsān for Atsïz's court, where for a time he was well received and married one of the shah's nieces. But he fell out of favour and had to leave Khwārazm; so he decided to try his luck in western Iran and Iraq, where the succession after his brother Maḥmūd's death had not been satisfactorily settled; finally he arrived in Baghdad (see p. 176 below).

The army of Khurāsān now offered the throne to the Qarakhānid Maḥmūd Khān. After the Qara-Khitai victory of 536/1141 Maḥmūd had fled with Sanjar, while the Qara-Khitai had set up Maḥmūd's brother Tamghach-Khān Ibrāhīm III as their ruler in Samarqand; he retained the throne as their tributary until he was killed in 551/1156 by his own Qarluq troops (see p. 187 below). Maḥmūd was the son of Sanjar's sister, who had married Arslan-Khān Muḥammad, and this Saljuq connexion, together with his princely blood from the house of Afrāsiyāb, made him a suitable candidate for the throne. The Saljuq sultan in the west, Muḥammad b. Maḥmūd, agreed to the choice and sent from Hamadān an investiture diploma.[1] Yet the fact that the Saljuq amīrs were quite prepared to abandon the direct line of the Saljuqs illustrates clearly the decline in Sanjar's prestige and that of the dynasty in general.

The real power in Khurāsān was falling into the hands of the Saljuq amīrs, and in the next few years the province became parcelled out amongst these commanders. The most powerful and successful of these was Sanjar's former ghulām Mu'ayyid al-Dīn Ai-Aba (d. 569/1174), who for almost twenty years was to be one of the most prominent figures in Khurāsānian affairs. Ibn Funduq calls him the "Khusrau [Emperor] of Khurāsān, King of the East".[2] Ai-Aba began by driving the Ghuzz out of Nīshāpūr, Ṭūs, Nasā, Abīvard, Shahristān, and

[1] Bundārī, p. 284; Ẓahīr al-Dīn Nīshāpūrī, p. 52.

[2] Ibn Funduq, p. 284.

Dāmghān, henceforth establishing himself at Nīshāpūr as the local ruler. There he became known for his justice and good rule—e.g. he lowered taxation and conciliated the landowning classes—so that his effective power began to spread all over the province. Similarly another one of Sanjar's ghulāms, Ikhtiyār al-Dīn Ai-Taq, left Khurāsān when the Ghuzz rebellion broke out and assumed power at Ray, where, his power legitimized by the western sultan Muḥammad b. Maḥmūd and by Sulaimān-Shāh in Marv, he built up a large army and made himself a considerable power in northern Iran. When Maḥmūd Khān was made sultan of Khurāsān, Ai-Aba at first refused to hand over power to him; only after long negotiations did he agree to become Maḥmūd's tributary, whilst nevertheless keeping effective control over the parts of Khurāsān which he held.[1] Maḥmūd felt unable to subdue the Ghuzz single-handed and invited in the Khwārazm-Shāh Atsïz, who died, however, before any practical steps against them could be taken (see above, p. 146).

As for the Ghuzz themselves, their disunity and low level of political and social sophistication prevented them from establishing a territorial administration in Khurāsān, despite their military successes. Hence they did not emulate the Saljuq invaders of a century or so before; on this situation Rāvandī comments that the Ghuzz had the military power but lacked the essential qualities of justice and righteousness without which no state can be founded.[2] They do, however, seem to have had some slight diplomatic contact with those powers outside Khurāsān who had seized on Sanjar's embarrassments as a chance to advance their own claims. 'Alā' al-Dīn Ḥusain corresponded with them over the extradition of the poet Anvarī, who had satirized the Ghūrid ruler. And we have seen that under Shāh Ghāzī Rustam, the Bāvandids of Ṭabaristān expanded beyond their mountain principality into Qūmis and Dailam, where in 552/1157 Shāh Ghāzī devastated Alamūt and enslaved a large number of Ismā'īlīs (pp. 28–9 above). It seems that early in Shāh Ghāzī's reign the Ismā'īlīs had murdered his son, and this would account for his unrelenting enmity towards them. The Ghuzz leaders Ṭūṭī Beg and Qorqut, who exercised some degree of authority among them, sent envoys to Shāh Ghāzi, encouraging his ambitions for the conquest of western Iran and promising him a share of Khurāsān in return for his alliance.[3]

[1] Ibn al-Athīr, vol. XI, pp. 121–2.
[2] Rāvandī, p. 186.
[3] Köymen, *Büyük Selçuklu*, pp. 424–8; Hodgson, *Order of Assassins*, p. 145.

Towards the end of Sanjar's three-year captivity, the disunity and fragmentation of the Ghuzz became more pronounced. Then in 551/1156 a group of the Ghuzz were suborned, and Sanjar succeeded in escaping to Tirmidh and Marv. A year later, at the age of seventy-one, Sanjar died, and with him the authority of the Saljuqs in eastern Iran virtually ceased; Sanjar himself while on his deathbed appointed the Qarakhānid Maḥmūd Khān as his successor. The death of a monarch who had reigned for over sixty years as malik and then as sultan seemed to contemporaries the end of an epoch, and they expressed wonder at the might of a man whose name was in the khuṭba from Mecca to Kāshghar.[1]

XI. THE EASTERN FRINGES OF THE IRANIAN WORLD: THE END OF THE GHAZNAVIDS AND THE UPSURGE OF THE GHŪRIDS

Under Ibrāhīm of Ghazna's son 'Alā' al-Daula Mas'ūd III (492–508/1099–1115) the Ghaznavid empire extended over the regions of Ghazna, Kabul, Bust, Quṣdār, Makrān, and northern India. It continued to be oriented primarily towards the Indian subcontinent, and the dynasty continued to be respected as the spearhead of the faith in the Islamic world. Mas'ūd had close marriage ties with the Saljuqs—his wife Mahd-i 'Irāq was Sanjar's sister—and all through his reign peaceful relations were maintained with the Saljuqs.

Between the Ghaznavid territories and Saljuq Khurāsān lay the buffer province of Ghūr, in central Afghanistan, a mountainous and inaccessible region which was at times subordinate to Ghazna, or to the Saljuqs, but on the whole little disturbed by either. At one point Ibrāhīm of Ghazna had marched into Ghūr at the invitation of some of the chiefs there and had deposed Amīr 'Abbās b. Shīth of the local Shansabānī line. He then set up 'Abbās's son Muḥammad as amīr of Ghūr, and Muḥammad remained till his death a faithful vassal of the Ghaznavids. In his grandson 'Izz al-Dīn Ḥusain, however, who came to power in 493/1100 and began a long reign in Ghūr as tributary to Sanjar and the Saljuqs, we see an indication of the relative decline of the Ghaznavids. It seems that in 501/1107–8 Sanjar led a raid into Ghūr; the stimulus for this is not known, but it is likely that the Ghūrī tribesmen, always notorious for their banditry, had been harassing the fringes of Saljuq territory in Bādghīs and Kūhistān. Sanjar captured

[1] Cf. Ẓahīr al-Dīn Nīshāpūrī, p. 45; Rāvandī, p. 171; Ibn al-Jauzī, vol. x, p. 178.

Ḥusain, and Ghūr must now have passed into the Saljuq sphere of influence. According to the Ghūrid historian Jūzjānī, Ḥusain sent annually to Sanjar the specialities of his region, arms and armour and dogs of the fierce local breed.[1]

Therefore the energies of Mas'ūd III of Ghazna were in large part deflected towards India, where his son 'Aḍud al-Daula Shīr-Zād was viceroy at Lahore. During this time the general Toghan-Tegin is said to have penetrated farther across the Ganges than anyone had ever done since the great Maḥmūd's time.[2] Mas'ūd died in 508/1115, and after the brief reign of Shīr-Zad another son, Arslan-Shāh, became sultan for three years (509–12/1115–18).

A succession struggle between Arslan-Shāh and another brother of his, Bahrām-Shāh, brought about the intervention of Sanjar and a Saljuq declaration of suzerainty over the Ghaznavid empire. Arslan-Shāh imprisoned all his numerous brothers, and only Bahrām-Shāh managed to escape to Khurāsān, where he sought Saljuq assistance. Arslan-Shāh also treated with indignity his father's widow, Sanjar's sister, even though she was probably his own mother.[3] Hence Sanjar had a double pretext for intervention. To Sulṭān Muḥammad in western Iran, the supreme head of the dynasty Arslan-Shāh complained about Sanjar's threatening attitude, but this did not avert a Saljuq invasion from Khurāsān. Accompanied by a contingent under the tributary Ṣaffārid amīr of Sistān, Tāj al-Dīn Abu'l Faḍl, the Saljuq army appeared at Bust and defeated Arslan-Shāh. Sanjar now came personally, refusing all peace offers. In a battle outside Ghazna Arslan-Shāh had 30,000 troops and 120 elephants, each with four armed men on its back. But Sanjar gained the victory, and he entered Ghazna to acquire an immense booty of treasure and jewels, and to place Bahrām-Shāh on the throne (510/1117). The latter agreed to pay an annual tribute of 250,000 dīnārs and to make the khuṭba for Muḥammad and Sanjar—the first time that the Saljuq khuṭba had ever been heard in Ghazna. Not even Malik-Shāh had achieved this, for when he had desired to introduce it Niẓām al-Mulk had deterred him, out of respect for the old-established Ghaznavid dynasty. On Sanjar's departure Arslan-Shāh came back

[1] Jūzjānī, *Ṭabaqāt-i Nāṣirī*, vol. 1, pp. 258–9, 332–5 (Raverty tr., vol. 1, pp. 149, 332–7).

[2] *Ibid.* vol. 1, p. 240 (tr., pp. 106–7). Cf. Mīrzā Muḥammad Qazwīnī, "Mas'ud-i Sa'd-i Salman", *J.R.A.S.* pp. 733 ff.

[3] This filiation is put forward by Gulam Mustafa Khan in "A History of Bahram Shah of Ghaznin", *Islamic Culture*, pp. 64–6.

from Lahore and reoccupied Ghazna briefly, but Bahrām-Shāh, again securing Saljuq help, captured and executed his brother.[1]

Bahrām-Shāh now began a reign of thirty-five years (512–47/1118–52) as a vassal of the Saljuqs; this we know because all his coins, except those of Indian type minted at Lahore, have Sanjar's name before his own. His reign was one of particular cultural splendour, and it forms a late flowering of the civilization of the Ghaznavids. Led by Sayyid Ḥasan and Sanā'ī, there was a numerous circle of court poets; it was to the sultan that the latter dedicated his *magnum opus*, the *Ḥadīqat al-ḥaqīqa*, and likewise to him that Abu'l-Ma'ālī Naṣrallāh dedicated his Persian translation of *Kalīla wa Dimna*. However Bahrām-Shāh had to quell revolts by the governor of India, Muḥammad Bahlīm; and then in 529/1135 the sultan himself became restive under Saljuq domination. Despite wintry conditions, Sanjar, accompanied by the Khwārazm-Shāh Atsïz, marched through northern Afghanistan and occupied Ghazna. Bahrām-Shāh, who had meanwhile fled, returned shortly afterwards and submitted to Sanjar, who restored him to his throne and then returned to Balkh.[2]

But Bahrām-Shāh's reign was not to end peacefully. The long dominion of the house of Sebük-Tegin was drawing to its close, and the instrument of its overthrow was not to be Sanjar, occupied as he was in Khurāsān and Transoxiana, but the Shansabānī rulers of Ghūr. That this line of petty chiefs should burst forth and compete on equal terms with such dynasties as the Saljuqs, the Ghaznavids, and the Khwārazm-Shāhs, is one of the most remarkable phenomena of the period. Yet the forces underlying this dynamism are very imperfectly understood. The medieval topography and history of Ghūr are known only fragmentarily for its isolation made the Islamic geographers and historians neglect it almost totally; and our knowledge of the Shansabānī dynasty would be meagre indeed were it not for the *Tabaqāt-i Nāṣirī* of the 7th/13th-century author Jūzjānī, in effect a special history of the Ghūrids.[3]

Until the 5th/11th century, Ghūr remained a pagan enclave ringed

[1] Bundārī, *Zubdat al-nuṣra*, pp. 262–3; Ẓahīr al-Dīn Nīshāpūrī, *Saljuq-Nāma*, p. 44; Rāvandī, *Rāḥat al-ṣudūr*, pp. 168–9; Ḥusainī, *Akhbār al-daula al-Saljūqiyya*, p. 91; Ibn al-Athīr, *al-Kāmil*, vol. x, pp. 353–6; Jūzjānī, vol. 1, p. 241 (tr., vol. 1, pp. 107–9).

[2] Bundārī, p. 264; Ḥusainī, p. 92; Ibn al-Athīr, vol. xi, pp. 17–18; Jūzjānī, vol. 1, pp. 241–2 (tr., vol. 1, p. 110); Juvainī, *Ta'rīkh-i Jahān-Gushā*, vol. 1, p. 279; A. J. Arberry, *Classical Persian Literature*, pp. 88–97.

[3] Cf. Arberry, pp. 152–5, and C. E. Bosworth, "Early Sources for the History of the First Four Ghaznavid Sultans (977–1041)", *Islamic Quarterly*, pp. 16–17.

with Muslim ribāṭs and known chiefly as a source for slaves. Islam first came with the early Ghaznavids. After his expedition of 401/1010–11 Maḥmūd left teachers to instruct the Ghūrīs in the precepts of Islam, and he appointed as ruler there a pliant member of the Shansabānīs, a family from Āhangarān on the upper Harī Rūd. This chieftain is praised by Jūzjānī as the man who firmly implanted Islam in Ghūr, but it is likely that paganism persisted there at least till the end of the century. Originally the Shansabānīs were merely one family of petty chiefs among many in Ghūr, but by their ruthlessness and ambition they gradually made themselves supreme there. The main branch of the family became established in the 6th/12th century at Fīrūzkūh, and *pari passu* with the decline of the Ghaznavids the fortunes of the Ghūrids rose.[1]

With 'Alā' al-Dīn Ḥusain b. 'Izz al-Dīn Ḥusain (544–56/1149–61) the Ghūrids broke out of the confines of their own province and succeeded to the heritage of the Ghaznavids, eventually becoming the greatest single power on the eastern fringes of the Islamic world. As early as 542/1147 the Ghūrids were tempted to intervene at Herāt, when its governor rebelled against Sanjar. Bahrām-Shāh feared the nascent strength of the Ghūrids, and although 'Alā' al-Dīn's brother Quṭb al-Dīn Muḥammad was related by marriage to the Ghaznavids, the sultan nevertheless had him poisoned; Jūzjānī traces the enmity between the two dynasties to this event.[2] Bahrām-Shāh killed a further brother, Saif al-Dīn Sūrī, and it was left to 'Alā' al-Dīn Ḥusain to take vengeance. He led an army from Fīrūzkūh into Zamīndāvar, where, despite the formidable array of elephants fielded by Bahrām-Shāh, he defeated the sultan three times and pursued him into Ghazna. The capital was now given over to a frightful seven days' orgy of plundering and destruction, which earned for 'Alā' al-Dīn the title *Jahān-Sūz* ("World-Incendiary"); as a final gesture of spite, the corpses of all but three of the Ghaznavid sultans were exhumed and burnt (545/1150–1).[3]

[1] On the topography and early history of Ghūr, see *Ḥudūd al-'Ālam* (ed. Minorsky), pp. 342–4, and Bosworth, "The Early Islamic History of Ghūr", *Central Asiatic Journal*, pp. 116–33. For general surveys of the Ghūrid dynasty, see Bosworth, "Ghūrids", *Encyc. of Islam* (2nd ed.); and Wiet's historical chapter in A. Maricq and G. Wiet, *Le Minaret de Djam, la Découverte de la Capitale des Sultans Ghorides* (*XIIe–XIIIe siècles*), *Méms. de la Délég. Archéol. Française en Afghanistan*, pp. 31–54.

[2] Ẓahīr al-Dīn Nīshāpūrī, p. 47; Rāvandī, p. 176; Ibn al-Athīr, vol. xi, pp. 107–8; Jūzjānī, vol. i, p. 336 (tr., vol. i, p. 340).

[3] Niẓāmī 'Arūḍī, *Chahār Maqāla*, p. 46 (tr., pp. 30–1); Ibn al-Athīr, vol. xi, pp. 89–90, 107–9; Jūzjānī, vol. i, pp. 242, 338, 341–6 (tr., vol. i, pp. 110–11, 342, 347–57).

Bahrām-Shāh fled to his Indian possessions. Only when the Ghūrid army had left did he return to Ghazna, and there he died shortly afterwards (547/1152). His son Khusrau-Shāh succeeded, but Ghūrid pressure compelled him to retire to Lahore, where he died in 555/1160.[1] The final Ghaznavid sultan, Khusrau-Malik, was, like his father, ruler in the Punjab only. The fifteen years' occupation of Ghazna by a group of Ghuzz from Khurāsān, who had seized the city after 'Alā' al-Dīn Ḥusain's death, temporarily held up the Ghūrid advance into the Indian plain; but 'Alā' al-Dīn's nephew, Ghiyāth al-Dīn Muḥammad b. Sām, attacked and expelled the Ghuzz from Ghazna, and by 579/1183–4 he was besieging Lahore. In 582/1186–7 Ghiyāth al-Dīn Muḥammad finally annexed the Punjab, deposing Khusrau-Malik and carrying him off to imprisonment in Ghūr, thus extinguishing the Ghaznavid line.[2]

To the west of Ghūr the main obstacle to the Shansabānīs' expansion was at first the Saljuqs. 'Alā' al-Dīn, elated by his capture of Ghazna, was little disposed to continue as Sanjar's tributary. He stopped the payment of tribute and in 547/1152 advanced down the Harī Rūd, but after being decisively defeated by Sanjar at Nāb near Herāt, he was captured and held prisoner until a large ransom was paid over. Before his death 'Alā' al-Dīn abandoned the title of Malik, with which his dynasty had so far been content, and in imitation of the Saljuqs and Ghaznavids called himself *al-Sulṭān al-Mu'aẓẓam*.[3] From this time onwards the Ghūrid dynasty split into two and ultimately three lines. The main one established itself in Ghūr proper, where Quṭb al-Dīn Muḥammad (540–1/1145–6) founded the fortress of Fīrūzkūh in a strategic position on the headwaters of the Harī Rūd, and this became the sultans' summer capital.[4] The second branch reigned from Bāmiyān over Tukhāristān and Badakhshān (and also, according to Jūzjāni, over the Transoxianan territories of Chaghāniyān and Vakhsh); these regions had been conquered by 'Alā' al-Dīn after his Ghazna victory and given to his brother Fakhr al-Dīn Mas'ūd, who bore the title Malik. And third, after expelling the Ghuzz from Ghazna in 569/1173, Ghiyāth al-Dīn Muḥammad set up his brother Shihāb al-Dīn or Mu'izz al-Dīn Muḥammad, as sultan in Ghazna, while he himself retained the

[1] Ibn al-Athīr, vol. xi, pp. 124, 173; Jūzjānī, vol. i, pp. 242–3 (tr., vol. i, pp. 111–13).

[2] Ibn al-Athīr, vol. xi, pp. 110–12; Jūzjānī, vol. i, pp. 243–4, 357, 396, 398 (tr., vol i, pp. 114–15, 376–7, 448–9, 455–9, 455–7).

[3] Niẓāmī 'Arūḍī, pp. 104, 132 (tr., pp. 74, 96); Ibn al-Athīr, vol. xi, pp. 107–9; Jūzjānī, vol. i, pp. 346–8 (tr., vol. i, pp. 357–61).

[4] *Ibid.* vol. i, pp. 335–6 (tr., vol. i, pp. 339–40). Cf. Maricq in *Le Minaret de Djam*, pp. 55–64.

ancestral territory of Ghūr and ruled from Fīrūzkūh as supreme head of the dynasty.[1]

The empire reached its apogee in the generation or so spanned by the reigns of Ghiyāth al-Dīn Muḥammad (sultan in Ghūr, 558–99/1163–1203) and of his younger brother Mu'izz al-Dīn Muḥammad (sultan in Ghazna, 569–602/1173–1206). The partnership and amity between the two was a rare phenomenon for the age, but the dual aspect of the empire—i.e. its expansionist policy in Khurāsān and the west, and its succession to the Ghaznavid ghāzī-tradition in India and the east—favoured such a division of power. In India Mu'izz al-Dīn campaigned in the Punjab and the Ganges valley, capturing Delhi in 589/1193; he wrested Multan from the local Ismā'īlīs in 571/1175–6, and he penetrated to the coasts of Sind and Gujerat.[2] Although latterly he became preoccupied with the defence of the Khurāsānian conquests, his Turkish ghulām commanders, such as Quṭb al-Dīn Aibeg, Ikhtiyār al-Dīn Muḥammad Khaljī, and Nāṣir al-Dīn Qabacha, continued to carry on raids in India; and such was the quality of Mu'izz al-Dīn's leadership and the loyalty which he inspired that these slave amīrs in India continued proudly to call themselves "Mu'izzī", and to place the dead sultan's name on their coins for some decades after the Ghūrid dynasty proper had disappeared.[3]

The "World-Incendiary" 'Alā' al-Dīn Ḥusain was briefly succeeded by his son Saif al-Dīn Muḥammad (556–8/1161–3), who reversed his father's policy of toleration towards the Ismā'īlīs in Ghūr and drove them out to Kūhistān.[4] Indeed, the Ghūrids now become conspicuous for their Sunnī piety, earning laudatory mention in the sources. Abandoning their support of the literalist Karāmiyya sect, which was strong amongst the people of Ghūr, they adhered to the Shāfi'ī law school, with its greater social prestige and intellectual reputation.[5] Ghiyāth al-Dīn kept up cordial relations with the 'Abbāsid caliphs in Baghdad. Ambassadors were frequently exchanged, and the sultan sought membership in one of the chivalric orders, known collectively

[1] Jūzjānī, vol. I, pp. 384–6 (tr., vol. I, pp. 421–4).

[2] See the list of his conquests *ibid.* vol. I, p. 407 (tr., vol. I, p. 491).

[3] Cf. Jūzjānī's *ṭabaqa* or section on the Mu'izziyya sultans of Hind, *ibid.* vol. I, pp. 415–38 (tr., vol. I, pp. 508–95).

[4] *Ibid.* vol. I, pp. 349, 350–1 (tr., vol. I, pp. 363, 365); cf. Bosworth, *Central Asiatic Journal* (1961), pp. 132–3.

[5] Ibn al-Athīr, vol. XII, pp. 99–100, 101–2; Jūzjānī, vol. I, pp. 362–4 (tr., vol. I, pp. 384–5); Bosworth, "The Rise of the Karāmiyyah in Khurasan", *Muslim World*, vol. L (1960), 5–14; and *idem*, in *Central Asiatic Journal* (1961), pp. 128–33.

as the *futuwwa*, by means of which al-Nāṣir was seeking to restore the secular and moral power of the caliphate (see p. 168 below).[1] The caliph also encouraged Ghūrid ambitions in Khurāsān as a counter-weight to the Khwārazm-Shāhs, whose advance into western Iran was causing deep concern in Baghdad.

When Saif al-Dīn Muḥammad was killed in battle with the Ghuzz near Marv, his cousin Ghiyāth al-Dīn was raised to the throne at Fīrūzkūh by the army.[2] Ghiyāth al-Dīn had first of all to deal with a coalition of his enemies raised up by his uncle Fakhr al-Dīn Mas'ūd of Bāmiyān, who claimed that the throne should have passed to him by right of seniority. In a battle at Rāgh-i Zar, between Herāt and Fīrūzkūh, he defeated Fakhr al-Dīn and killed the Turkish governors of Balkh and Herāt, Qumach and Yïldïz, both former ghulāms of Sanjar. Fakhr al-Dīn was restored to Bāmiyān in 559/1163, and Ghiyāth al-Dīn began to extend his authority over outlying parts of Afghanistan. Gharchistān, Gūzgān, Bādghīs, and Zamīndāvar were all secured, and the Ghuzz were ejected from Ghazna. Khurāsān, where the collapse of Saljuq power had left a vacuum, now claimed his attention. In 571/1175–6 Sanjar's old ghulām Bahā' al-Dīn Toghrïl had to abandon Herāt to the sultan. Shortly afterwards the amīr of Sīstān, Tāj al-Dīn Ḥarb b. Muḥammad, acknowledged Ghiyāth al-Dīn as his suzerain and on several occasions sent troop contingents to the Ghūrid armies; even the amīrs of the Ghuzz in Kirmān, who had succeeded there to the local Saljuq dynasty, sent envoys to Fīrūzkūh.[3]

Jūzjānī alleges that there was originally an *entente* between Ghiyāth al-Dīn and the Khwārazm-Shāh Tekish, yet this seems unlikely, for a clash between these two great powers of the east was not long delayed.[4] For some time Ghiyāth al-Dīn sheltered Tekish's fugitive brother Sulṭān-Shāh, although he refused to give him military aid. Sulṭān-Shāh eventually got help from the Qara-Khitai and assembled at Marv an army with which to attack the Ghūrid province of Bādghīs. In response Ghiyāth al-Dīn summoned troops from Bāmiyān and Sīstān, as well as from his brother Mu'izz al-Dīn in Ghazna, and in 586/1190 he defeated Sulṭān-Shāh near Marv, taking over some of his Khurāsānian territories.[5]

1 Cf. Jūzjānī, vol. I, pp. 301–2, 361 (tr., vol. I, pp. 243, 382–3).
2 Ibn al-Athīr, vol. XI, p. 193; Jūzjānī, vol. I, pp. 351–4 (tr., vol. I, pp. 366–70).
3 *Ibid.* vol. I, pp. 354–8, 385–6 (tr., vol. I, pp. 371–8, 424–5).
4 *Ibid.* vol. I, p. 360 (tr., vol. I, p. 382).
5 Ibn al-Athīr, vol. XII, p. 38; Jūzjānī, vol. I, pp. 301–2, 358–9 (tr., vol. I, pp. 245–9, 378–9).

In addition to their territories north of the Oxus, the Qara-Khitai had a foothold in Tukhāristān, south of the river. Dislodging the infidels from here became the goal of the Bāmiyān Ghūrids, who, as supporters of orthodoxy, welcomed this opportunity for jihād. In 594/1198 Bahā' al-Dīn Sām occupied Balkh after the death of its Turkish governor, who had paid tribute to the Qara-Khitai.[1] In the same year a general war broke out in Khurāsān between the Ghūrids on one side and the Khwārazm-Shāhs and their Qara-Khitai suzerains on the other. Fighting had begun in 590/1194, when the death of the last Saljuq sultan in the west, Toghrïl b. Arslan, had brought the Khwārazm-Shāh to the borders of Iraq (see p. 182 below). Although the caliph al-Nāṣir had wittingly set this train of events in motion, he now sent envoys to Fīrūzkūh imploring Ghūrid help. Ghiyāth al-Dīn accordingly threatened to attack Tekish's Khurāsānian possessions unless the latter abandoned his threatening attitude towards the caliph. For his part, Tekish sought the help of the Qara-Khitai, and together they sent an army into Gūzgān, threatening Fīrūzkūh and demanding of the Bāmiyān Ghūrids that they pay tribute for Balkh. Tekish himself marched against Herāt, but in a battle on the Oxus banks the Qara-Khitai were routed by the amīrs of the Ghūrids. Ghiyāth al-Dīn and Mu'izz al-Dīn then took over Marv, Sarakhs, Nasā, Abīvard, Ṭūs, and Nīshāpūr, and they installed in Marv Tekish's fugitive grandson Hindū Khān. Finally Mu'izz al-Dīn conducted some operations in Kūhistān against the Ismā'īlīs, after which Khurāsān was entrusted to a Ghūrid prince, Ḍiyā' al-Dīn or 'Alā' al-Dīn Muḥammad (597/1200).[2]

The Ghūrids were unpopular among the people of Khurāsān, and they found it hard to maintain their authority there. According to Juvainī, Mu'izz al-Dīn imposed financial levies and confiscated properties in Ṭūs, and carried off for his army grain which had been committed to the protection of the Imām 'Alī al-Riḍā's shrine. He was compelled to spend much of his time attending to the defence of these western conquests, especially as Ghiyāth al-Dīn was becoming incapacitated by gout or rheumatism and eventually died in 599/1202.[3]

On his brother's death, Mu'izz al-Dīn allotted various parts of the Ghūrid empire to his relatives, with Ghūr itself going to Ḍiyā' al-Dīn

[1] Ibn al-Athīr, vol. XII, p. 88; Jūzjānī, vol. I, p. 358 (tr., vol. I, p. 378).

[2] Ibn al-Athīr, vol. XII, pp. 108–13; Jūzjānī, vol. I, pp. 301, 359–60 (tr., vol. I, pp. 242–3 379–81); Juvainī, vol. I, pp. 315 ff.; Kafesoğlu, *Harezmşahlar devleti tarihi*, pp. 148–51.

[3] Ibn al-Athīr, vol. XII, pp. 117–19; Jūzjānī, vol. I, p. 361 (tr., vol. I, p. 383); Juvainī, vol. I, p. 319.

Muḥammad.[1] The Khwārazm-Shah 'Alā' al-Dīn Muḥammad came to besiege Herāt; Mu'izz al-Dīn pursued him back into Khwārazm, but the flooding of the Khwārazmian countryside made progress impossible for the Ghūrid troops. The shah also called in the Qara-Khitai once more, and a large army, whose commanders included Tayangu of Ṭarāz and the Qarakhānid ruler of Samarqand, 'Uthmān b. Ibrāhīm, joined Muḥammad and drove the Ghūrids out of Khwārazm; then, in a great battle at Andkhūi on the Oxus, the Qara-Khitai routed Mu'izz al-Dīn (601/1204). Only the mediation of 'Uthmān Khān, who did not want to see the Ghūrid sultan captured by pagans, permitted Mu'izz al-Dīn's withdrawal to his own land. Of his former lands in Khurāsān, only Herāt remained to him, and he found it expedient to make peace with the Khwārazm-Shāh even though the caliph continued to incite him against Muḥammad, urging an alliance with the Qara-Khitai if this would further their design.[2] The suppression of a revolt in the Punjab occupied Mu'izz al-Dīn's closing months, for on the way back to Ghazna he was assassinated, allegedly by emissaries of the Ismā'īlīs whom he had often persecuted during his lifetime (602/1206).[3]

Within a decade of his death the Ghūrid empire fell apart, passing briefly into the hands of the Khwārazm-Shāhs. The Ghūrid forces comprised not only local Ghūrī, Afghan, and Sagzī troops, but also the Turkish ghulāms who were found in almost all eastern Islamic armies at this time. Mu'izz al-Dīn's skill had kept all these elements together, but now the Turkish commanders in Ghazna and India began to act as an independent body. The dead sultan had no son of his own; for his successor the Turkish troops inclined to his nephew Ghiyāth al-Dīn Maḥmūd b. Ghiyāth al-Dīn Muḥammad, whereas the Ghūrī commanders favoured Bahā' al-Dīn Sām of Bāmiyān and then, after the latter's death, his two sons. In the end Ghiyāth al-Dīn Maḥmūd prevailed, driving out the governor of Ghūr, Ḍiyā' al-Dīn Muḥammad, who was the candidate of the local Karāmiyya adherents, and ascending the throne at Fīrūzkūh.[4]

[1] Jūzjānī, vol. I, p. 401 (tr., vol. I, pp. 472–3); Kafesoğlu, *Harezmşahlar devleti*, p. 155.

[2] Nasawī, *Histoire du Sultan Djelal ed-Din Mankobirti*, p. 22 (tr., pp. 38–9); Ibn al-Athīr, vol. XII, pp. 117–19, 121–4; Jūzjānī, vol. I, pp. 401–3 (tr., vol. I, pp. 473–81); Juvainī, vol. I, pp. 321–5; Kafesoğlu, *op. cit.* pp. 156–61.

[3] Ibn al-Athīr, vol. XII, pp. 139–41, 142–5; Jūzjānī, vol. I, pp. 403–4 (tr., vol. I, pp. 481–5); Juvainī, vol. I, p. 326.

[4] Ibn al-Athīr, vol. XII, pp. 146–9; Jūzjānī, vol. I, pp. 370–1, 372–4 (tr., vol. I, pp. 394, 396–9).

However, the new sultan was inferior to his predecessors, and never managed to establish his direct authority over the eastern fringes of the Ghūrid empire. The Turkish commander Tāj al-Dīn Yïldïz squashed the Bāmiyān Ghūrids' pretensions to rule in Ghazna, but only reluctantly and tardily did he recognize Ghiyāth al-Dīn Maḥmūd.[1] The latter dared not leave Ghūr unprotected and march to Ghazna; the full measure of his clumsiness was seen when he called in the Khwārazm-Shāh and Ḥusain b. Kharmīl, governor of Herāt, to expel Yïldïz from Ghazna and enforce his rights there (603/1206–7). The end of the Fīrūzkūh Ghūrids was now near. Balkh and Tirmidh had both fallen to the Khwārazm-Shāh, the latter being handed over to the Qara-Khitai. The shah was defeated and temporarily held captive by the Qara-Khitai, but he returned to the attack and after a thirteen months' siege took Herāt, the key to the Harī Rūd valley. His forces then invaded Ghūr and captured Ghiyāth al-Dīn Maḥmūd (605/1208–9). The latter remained sultan, but only as the Khwārazm-Shāh's puppet. He was assassinated either two or four years later, and his son Bahā' al-Dīn Sām was carried off to Khwārazm shortly afterwards. Ghazna was taken in 612/1215–16, Yïldïz was driven into India, and the shah's son Jalāl al-Dīn was installed as governor of Ghazna. In the same year the Bāmiyān line of the Ghūrids was extinguished, and Ghūr now relapsed into an obscurity almost as deep as before.[2]

The "Ghūrid interlude" in eastern Iranian history thus lasted for only a few decades, yet it constituted a remarkable achievement for the chieftains of such a remote corner of Afghanistan. The Ghūrid sultans had drawn upon the manpower resources of their native Afghanistan as well as upon professional mercenaries from outside, and they had skilfully utilized Sunnī religious sentiments in their struggles with the 'Abbasids' enemies, the Khwārazm-Shāhs, and with the pagan Qara-Khitai. Unfortunately for the Ghūrids' ambitions, the resources which they could command, human and moral, did not prove quite enough for the double role in Khurāsān and northern India which the sultans aspired to play.

[1] Ibn al-Athīr, vol. XII, pp. 141–6, 153–6, 163–6; Jūzjānī, vol. I, pp. 409 ff. (tr., vol. I, pp. 494 ff.).

[2] Nasawī, pp. 140–1 (tr., pp. 233–4); Ibn al-Athīr, vol. XII, pp. 149–53, 163–6, 172–6, 202–3; Jūzjānī, vol. I, pp. 309, 374 ff. (tr., vol. I, pp. 267, 400 ff., 505–6); Juvainī, vol. I, 327–36, 352–4; Kafesoğlu, *op. cit.* pp. 161–5, 178, 193–6.

XII. THE LAST DECADES OF SALJUQ RULE IN THE WEST

The last forty years of Saljuq rule in Iraq and western Iran were characterized by three main trends, each of which was the accentuation of an earlier trend. First, the political and military influence of the ʿAbbāsid caliphate continued to rise. Second, the Turkish amīrs and atabegs in the various provinces of the western Saljuq empire consolidated their power, in some cases forming hereditary lines. And finally, the real power of the Saljuq sultans themselves, their dynasty now deeply disunited within itself and dependent on the military support of the Turkish amīrs, continued to decline, and not even the despairing revival of activity on the part of Togh̲rïl b. Arslan, last of the sultans, could arrest this process and stave off total ruin. Hence the last decade of the 6th/12th century sees western Iran, the territory up to the edge of the Iraqi plain, incorporated into the vast empire which the K̲h̲wārazm-S̲h̲āhs assembled on the eve of the Mongol invasions.

As we have seen, Caliph al-Muqtafī began vigorously to assert the secular rights of his office (pp. 128–9 above). Two centuries of Būyid and Saljuq control in Baghdad had fostered the idea that the caliph's power was purely spiritual, and that temporal affairs should be left to the amīr or sultan who held the military and political supremacy at the time. This idea was now challenged. Ibn al-At̲h̲īr sums up this novel trend in his obituary notice on al-Muqtafī:

> He was the first Caliph to get sole power over Iraq, to the exclusion of any Sultan, since the time when the Dailamīs [the Būyids] first appeared. He was also the first Caliph to have firm control over the Caliphate and over his troops and retainers since the time when the slave troops secured an ascendancy over the Caliphs in al-Munstaṣir's time [i.e. in the latter part of the 3rd/9th century] to the present day, with the possible exception of al-Muʿtaḍid's reign.[1]

Al-Muqtafī recruited troops extensively and was said to have a network of spies and intelligence agents in all lands, while in the field of diplomacy he supported Turkish amīrs in the provinces, e.g. the Eldigüzids in Āzarbāījān, as a check on the Saljuq sultans. After the death of Masʿūd b. Muḥammad the sultans were excluded from Baghdad; Masʿūd's s̲h̲aḥna there, Masʿūd Bilālī, was expelled when his master died, the caliph took over the sultan's palace and properties and henceforth no s̲h̲aḥnas were tolerated in Baghdad.[2] For much of

[1] Ibn al-At̲h̲īr, *al-Kāmil*, vol. XI, p. 169.
[2] *Ibid.* pp. 105–6.

al-Muqtafī's reign and throughout the following one of al-Mustanjid (555–66/1160–70), the rights of the caliphate were strongly upheld by the viziers 'Aun al-Dīn Yaḥyā Ibn Hubaira (d. 560/1165) and his son 'Izz al-Dīn (d. 561/1166 or 562/1167). 'Aun al-Dīn was a staunch Ḥanbalī, and his fiscal policy of making lands once again directly taxable alienated those Shī'īs whose shrines were in central Iraq.[1] He was also a capable general, and in 549/1154, after he defeated the Turkish amīrs and their protégé Arslan b. Toghrïl, he was rewarded by the unusual honorifics of *Sulṭān al-'Irāq* ("Sultan of Iraq") and *Malik al-Juyūsh* ("Monarch of the Military Forces").[2]

With the accession of al-Nāṣir (575–622/1180–1225), the caliph became a central figure in eastern Islamic diplomacy and politics. He gave little attention to the west, leaving the struggle with the Crusaders to Saladin and the Ayyūbids, but he was intensely concerned with such events in the East as the expansion of the Khwārazm-Shāhs, whom he endeavoured to check first through the Ghūrids and then through the Mongols. On the moral and ethical plain he made use of the futuwwa, or chivalric orders, becoming himself a member of the Rahhāṣiyya order in 578/1182–3. He reorganized these futuwwa bands and sought to enroll in them the rulers of the Islamic world, with himself as the head, thus linking together both Sunnī and moderate Shī'ī elements. Rulers such as the Ayyūbids, the Rūm Saljuqs, and the Ghūrids became affiliated with the Rahhāṣiyya order, and under al-Nāṣir's grandson al-Mustanṣir even the Khwārazm-Shāh Jalāl al-Dīn, son of al-Nāṣir's old enemy 'Alā' al-Dīn Muḥammad, was admitted.[3]

An event which caused a great sensation in the Islamic world was al-Nāṣir's success in securing the return of the Persian and Syrian Ismā'īlīs to the fold of orthodoxy. In 608/1211–12 the Grand Master of Alamūt, Jalāl al-Dīn Ḥasan III b. Muḥammad, restored the practices of orthodox Islam in the regions under his control, building mosques, burning heretical books, and receiving from the caliph titles of honour such as no previous Grand Master had ever enjoyed. On the Talisman Gate which he built at Baghdad the victorious caliph was depicted tearing apart the jaws of two dragons; the great epigraphist Max van

[1] *Ibid.* pp. 211–12; Ibn al-Ṭiqṭaqā, *al-Fakhrī*, p. 281 (Whitting tr., p. 304); cf. Ibn al-Jauzī, *al-Muntaẓam*, vol. x, pp. 214–17; Sibṭ b. al-Jauzī, *Mir'āt al-Zamān*, vol. 1, pp. 255–61, 267.

[2] Ibn al-Athīr, vol. xi, p. 130.

[3] *Ibid.* vol. xii, pp. 286–7; cf. F. Taeschner, "Das Futuwwa-Rittertum des islamischen Mittelalters", *Beiträge zur Arabistik, Semitistik und Islamwissenschaft*, pp. 353–7.

Berchem interpreted these dragons to represent the two great enemies of the caliphate, the Ismāʿīlī Grand Master and the Khwārazm-Shāh ʿAlāʾ al-Dīn Muḥammad.[1]

The death of Sulṭān Masʿūd without direct heir nevertheless left several Saljuq princes with claims to the sultanate, including his brother Sulaimān-Shāh and the sons of his brothers Maḥmūd and Toghrïl. With the exception of Muḥammad b. Maḥmūd, whom ʿImād al-Dīn praises as the most majestic, most learned, and most just of the Saljuqs,[2] these contenders were of mediocre capability. They were almost wholly dependent on the Turkish amīrs for support, since in this period several of the provincial amīrs kept Saljuq princes at their courts, using them as shields for their own ambitions. Eldigüz, atabeg of Arrān and of part of Āzarbāïjān, at first pushed the claims of Malik-Shāh b. Maḥmūd; but he also had with him Arslan b. Toghrïl, who was moreover the atabeg's own stepson—for Eldigüz had married Toghrïl's widow, and it was the children of this union, Pahlavān and Qïzïl-Arslan, who continued the line of the Eldigüzids.[3] Ibn Aq-Sonqur, the Aḥmadīlī Atabeg of Marāgheh and Tabrīz, likewise had with him a Saljuq prince, apparently a son of Muḥammad b. Maḥmūd. Sulaimān-Shāh b. Muḥammad b. Malik-Shāh was held prisoner for some time by the Zangid ruler of Mosul, Quṭb al-Dīn Maudūd, until he was released to reign for a brief period in Hamadān as sultan (555–6/1160–1). On the death of Malik-Shāh b. Maḥmūd, his son Maḥmūd was taken by his supporters to Fārs, where the Salghurid atabeg Muẓaffar al-Dīn Zangī seized him and held him at Iṣṭakhr as a possible claimant.[4]

The north-western provinces of Iran remained quite outside the sultans' sphere of direct influence. Power here was divided between the Eldigüzids and the Aḥmadīlīs. Shams al-Dīn Eldigüz (d. 570/1174–5 or possibly 571/1175–6) was originally a slave of Sulṭān Maḥmūd's vizier, al-Kamāl al-Simirumī; then he passed into the possession of

---

[1] Ibn al-Athīr, vol. xii, p. 195; Juvainī, Taʾrīkh-i Jahān-Gushā, vol. ii, pp. 364, 391, 699 ff. Cf. M. van Berchem, "Das Baghdad Talismantor", in Archaeologische Reise im Euphrat-und Tigris-Gebiet, ed. F. Sarre and E. Herzfeld (Berlin, 1911), vol. i; van Berchem, "Epigraphie des Assassins de Syrie", J.A. ser. 9, vol. ix (1897), pp. 474–7; Taeschner, "al-Nāṣir", Encyc. of Islam (1st ed.); idem, "Das Futuwwa-Rittertum", pp. 377–8. See also, The Order of Assassins, pp. 215–25, where Hodgson combats van Berchem's interpretation of the Talisman Gate decoration (pp. 222–3 n. 31).

[2] Bundārī, Zubdat al-nuṣra, p. 288.

[3] Ibid. p. 297; Ẓahīr al-Dīn Nīshāpūrī, Saljūq-Nāma, p. 75; Ḥusainī, Akhbār al-daula al-Saljūqiyya, pp. 133, 197; Ibn al-Athīr, vol. xi, pp. 168, 176.

[4] Ẓahīr al-Dīn Nīshāpūrī, pp. 75–6; Ḥusainī, pp. 142–3; Ibn al-Athīr, vol. xi, pp. 135–7, 177, 208; Jūzjānī, Ṭabaqāt-i Nāṣiri, vol. i, p. 270 (tr., vol. i, pp. 174–5).

Sulṭān Mas'ūd, who appointed him governor of Arrān.[1] For some time he kept aloof from the quarrels over the sultanate, until the fortunate marriage which he had made with Toghrïl's widow Mu'mina Khatun enabled him to champion the succession of Arslan b. Toghrïl; the latter he duly set up at Hamadān on the murder of Sulaimān-Shāh in 556/1161.[2] His son Nuṣrat al-Dīn Pahlavān Muḥammad was Sulṭān Arslan's half-brother, and Pahlavān succeeded not only to the paternal territories in Arrān and much of Āzarbāījān, but also to Jibāl, Iṣfahān, and Ray, with his brother Qïzïl-Arslan 'Uthmān ruling in Tabrīz as his subordinate. Pahlavān held Arslan and his young son and successor Toghrïl under close tutelage until his death *c.* 581/1186. Only with Qïzïl-Arslan's rule did Toghrïl manage to burst out of this constriction, and after the Eldigüzid's murder in 587/1191 he briefly turned the tables on Qïzïl-Arslan's successor, Qutlugh Inanj b. Pahlavān. The Eldigüzid line did not, however, survive beyond the first quarter of the 7th/13th century. For much of Iran, the irruption of the Khwārazm-Shāhs marked the end of an epoch, and in 622/1225 Sulṭān Jalāl al-Dīn finally deposed Öz-Beg b. Pahlavān.[3] Thus the historical significance of the Eldigüzids lies, first, in their virtually undisputed rule over much of north-western Iran for several decades (just before his death Qïzïl-Arslan was even bold enough to claim the sultanate for himself);[4] and second, in their role as champions of Muslim arms on the north-eastern frontier, where they faced the resurgent power of the Georgian kings (see pp. 178–9 below).

The Aḥmadīlīs of Marāgheh took their name from the Rawwādid Aḥmadīl b. Ibrāhīm of Tabrīz, who was murdered in 510/1116.[5] In accordance with the prevalent practice, his Turkish slave Aq-Sonqur took the surname of his master's family, Aḥmadīlī, and founded a line which endured in Marāgheh for over a century, until, like the Eldigüzids, it was extinguished by the Khwārazm-Shāhs. Aq-Sonqur became atabeg to Dā'ūd b. Maḥmūd and supported his brief tenure as sultan in Āzarbāījān and Jibāl in 525–6/1131–2. The name of his son and successor is somewhat uncertain, but in the sources he is often

[1] Minorsky has pointed out (*B.S.O.A.S.* [1949–50], p. 877) that the date 568/1172–3—which Ibn al-Athīr gives as the year of Eldigüz's death—is wrong; the correct date is either that of Ḥusainī (570) or of Fāriqī and Rāvandī (571), and probably the latter.

[2] Ẓahīr al-Dīn Nīshāpūrī, p. 75; Ibn al-Athīr, vol. XI, pp. 175–7, 255–6.

[3] See Houtsma, "Ildegiz" and "Ṭughril II b. Arslān", and Zetterstéen, "Pehlewān, Muḥammad b. Ildegiz" and "Kïzil Arslan", in *Encyc. of Islam* (1st ed.).

[4] Bundārī, p. 302; Ibn al-Athīr, vol. XII, p. 49.

[5] On the Rawwādids, see above, pp. 32 ff.

called Aq-Sonqur; he now became the Eldigüzids' rival for power in the north-west. Whereas Eldigüz pressed the claims of Arslan b. Toghrïl, Aq-Sonqur II was in 554/1159 entrusted with the infant son of Muḥammad b. Mas'ūd; he refused to recognize the succession of Arslan in 556/1160, and the Caliph's vizier 'Aun al-Dīn Ibn Hubaira incited him to set up as a rival the Saljuq child whom he had in his keeping.[1] Falak al-Dīn b. Aq-Sonqur II lost Tabrīz in 570/1174–5 to Pahlavān b. Eldigüz, and conflict between the two families persisted into the next century. The Aḥmadīlī 'Alā' al-Dīn Qara-Sonqur or Körp-Arslan, patron of the poet Niẓāmī, attempted in 602/1205–6 to despose the drunk and incompetent Eldigüzid Nuṣrat al-Dīn Abū Bakr b. Pahlavān, but the latter reacted with unwonted vigour and captured Marāgheh from 'Alā' al-Dīn, allotting him in exchange Urmīyeh and Ishnū. When in 605/1208–9 'Alā' al-Dīn's infant son and successor died, almost all the Aḥmadīlī lands fell to Abū Bakr, although scions of the family are still heard of after the engulfing waves of the Khwārazm-Shāhs and Mongols had passed over Āzarbāījān.[2]

In Armenia the Shāh-Armanids, descendants of the ghulām Sukmān al-Quṭbī, were frequently involved in the politics and warfare of Āzarbāījān, tending to take the side of Aq-Sonqur II against the Eldigüzids. But when Naṣr al-Dīn Sukmān died without heir in 581/1185, a bloodless struggle for power took place between Pahlavān b. Eldigüz, who had married a daughter to the aged Shāh-Arman in order to acquire a succession claim, and the Ayyūbid Saladin. In the end, Pahlavān took over Akhlāṭ, whilst Saladin annexed Mayyāfāriqīn in Diyārbakr, a possession of the Artuqids of Mārdīn which had been latterly under the protectorship of the Shāh-Arman.[3] Mosul and the Jazīreh remained under Zangid rule, although the relentless advance of Saladin into the Jazīreh posed a serious threat to the Zangids, driving the last Shāh-Arman and the atabeg 'Izz al-Dīn Mas'ūd b. Quṭb al-Dīn Maudūd into alliance against Ayyūbid aggression.[4] After the death of Saladin in 589/1193, the Zangids recaptured most of the towns and fortresses of the Jazīreh.

From *c.* 550/1155 till his death in 570/1174–5, a Türkmen of the Avshar tribe of the Oghuz, named Ai-Toghdï or Shumla, maintained

[1] Ẓahīr al-Dīn Nīshāpūrī, p. 76; Ibn al-Athīr, vol. XI, p. 177.

[2] *al-Kāmil*, vol. XI, p. 280, vol. XII, pp. 157, 182; cf. Minorsky, "Marāgha", *Encyc. of Islam* (1st ed.), and *idem*, "Aḥmadīlī", *Encyc. of Islam* (2nd ed.).

[3] Ibn al-Athīr, vol. XI, pp. 339–41; Barhebraeus, *Chronography*, pp. 318–19.

[4] Ibn al-Athīr, vol. XI, pp. 317–23.

control in Khūzistān.[1] Between 553/1158 and 556/1161, Malik-Shāh b. Muḥammad took from him part of Khūzistān, but thereafter it reverted entirely to Shumla, who held it till his death in battle against Eldigüzid forces. On two occasions, in 526/1167 and 569/1173–4, Shumla had tried to encroach on caliphal territory in Iraq, but was repulsed by forces from Baghdad; in 564/1169 he temporarily occupied Fārs at the invitation of the army of the Salghurid ruler of Fārs, Muẓaffar al-Dīn Zangī, who had become unpopular for his tyranny.[2] Like other provincial amīrs, Shumla sheltered a Saljuq prince, the son of Malik-Shāh b. Maḥmūd, and after Shumla's death this prince continued to harry the borders of Iraq. One of Shumla's sons reigned in Khūzistān for a further twenty years till his death in 591/1195, when al-Nāṣir's vizier Mu'ayyid al-Dīn Ibn Qaṣṣāb invaded the province, annexing it and carrying off Shumla's grandsons to Baghdad. The caliph then appointed ghulām commanders to rule Khūzistān, but in 603/1206–7 he was faced with a rebellion there of one of his former ghulāms, who had built up a coalition of local Kurdish chiefs, the Salghurid ruler of Fārs, 'Izz al-Dīn Sa'd, and the former Eldigüzid ghulām Ai-Toghmïsh, now ruler of Ray, Iṣfahān, and Hamadān. The threat was surmounted, but the caliph had to suppress a further revolt in Khūzistān in 607/1210–11.[3]

In Fārs the Salghurid family of Atabegs ruled for some 120 years as tributaries first of the Saljuqs, then of the Khwārazm-Shahs, and then of the Mongols. They were of Türkmen origin, and the Salghur (or Salur) tribe seems to have played an important role in the establishment of the Saljuq sultanate of Rūm. The line of atabegs is usually said to start in 543/1148 with Muẓaffar al-Dīn Sonqur, who took advantage of the troubles of Sulṭān Mas'ūd b. Muḥammad by extending his power over Fārs; the sources state that Sonqur was a nephew of the previous ruler in Fārs, Boz-Aba, though this affiliation is uncertain. Sonqur's son Zangī (d. 570/1174–5) was confirmed in Fārs by Sulṭān Arslan b. Toghrïl, and the province seems to have enjoyed a moderate prosperity under his rule; but the real florescence of this minor dynasty came in

[1] *Ibid.* p. 133; Bundārī, pp. 286–7; Ibn al-Jauzī, vol. x, pp. 161, 255. Cf. Cahen, "Les Tribus Turques d'Asie Occidentale pendant la période Seljukide", *W.Z.K.M.* p. 181; M. F. Köprülü, "Afshār", *Encyc. of Islam* (2nd ed.).

[2] Ibn al-Jauzī, vol. x, p. 221; Ibn al-Athīr, vol. xi, pp. 156–7, 173–4, 216–17, 229, 270, 280; Sibṭ b. al-Jauzī, vol. i, p. 268.

[3] Ibn al-Athīr, vol. xi, pp. 291–2, vol. xii, pp. 70–1, 170, 190–1; Sibṭ b. al-Jauzī, vol. i, pp. 330, 445; Ibn al-Ṭiqṭaqā, p. 289 (tr., p. 312).

the reign of 'Izz al-Dīn Sa'd (590–628/1194–1231). It was from this ruler that the poet Sa'dī derived his *takhalluṣ* (*nom de plume*), his father having been in the atabeg's service. After an eight-year struggle with his cousin Toghrïl, Sa'd had to restore internal prosperity to his devastated province; he subdued the Shabānkāra'ī Kurds and attacked Kirmān, but finally had to submit to the Khwārazm-Shāh 'Alā' al-Dīn Muḥammad and to cede part of his territory to him (see p. 184 below).[1]

Just as the rebellion of the Ghuzz in Khurāsān led directly to the decline and disappearance of Saljuq power in that province, so the irruption of these nomads into Kirmān brought about the end of the local Saljuq dynasty there. In 582/1186 the last Saljuq of Kirmān, Muḥammad Shāh b. Bahrām-Shāh, fled before the Ghuzz leader Malik Dīnār; yet for some years before that the Saljuq family in Kirmān had been seriously weakened by internecine conflict, for Toghrïl-Shāh b. Muḥammad[2] left four sons, Bahrām-Shāh, Arslan-Shāh, Tūrān-Shāh, and Terken-Shāh, all of whom except the last subsequently achieved the throne.[3]

Bahrām-Shāh ruled in Jīruft from 565/1169–70 to 570/1174–5, proclaimed ruler there by the eunuch atabeg Mu'ayyid al-Dīn Raiḥān, in whose hands lay much of the real power. But the other important town of Bardasīr, was held by Quṭb al-Dīn Muḥammad (son of an earlier and now displaced atabeg, Boz-Qush), who eventually espoused the cause of Arslan-Shāh when he made a bid for the throne. On his behalf Tūrān-Shāh also appeared from Fārs with forces supplied by the Salghurid Zangī. Bahrām-Shāh got aid from Mu'ayyid al-Dīn Ai-Aba in Nīshāpūr, but Arslan-Shāh returned to the attack, this time with forces lent by Sulṭān Arslan b. Toghrïl and the atabeg Eldigüz. In the end, Arslan-Shāh and Bahrām-Shāh agreed to partition Kirmān between them, the former to have two thirds and the latter to have the eastern third of the province.[4]

Both were in fact dead by 572/1176–7, and the third brother Tūrān-

[1] Ḥamd Allāh Mustaufī, *Ta'rīkh-i Guzīda*, pp. 505–7 (tr., pp. 120–2); Mīrzā Ḥasan Shīrāzī Fasā'ī, *Fārs-Nāma-yi Nāṣirī*, cited in Lambton, *Landlord and Peasant in Persia*, p. 76 n. 1; T. W. Haig, "Salghurids", and Köprülüzāde Fu'ād, "Salur", in *Encyc. of Islam* (1st ed.); and Cahen, *W.Z.K.M.* (1948–52), pp. 180–1.

[2] On Toghrïl-Shāh b. Muḥammad, see p. 134 above.

[3] Muḥammad b. Ibrāhīm, *Ta'rīkh-i Saljūqiyān-i Kirmān*, pp. 36–8; cf. Houtsma, "Zur Geschichte der Selǵuqen von Kermân", *Z.D.M.G.* p. 378.

[4] Muḥammad b. Ibrāhīm, pp. 38–56; cf. Houtsma, *op. cit.* pp. 378–86; Ḥusainī, pp. 164–6; Ibn al-Athīr, vol. XI, pp. 235–6.

Shāh came to the throne for a seven years' reign (572/1176–7 to 579/1183–4). His reign, too, was stormy; at the outset the Salghurid Zangī allied with the atabeg Muḥammad b. Boz-Qush to force Tūrān-Shāh off the throne, and shortly afterwards a force of Ghuzz invaded Kirmān penetrating as far as Makrān and Fārs. Expelled from the Sarakhs area of Khurāsān by the Khwārazm-Shāh's brother Sulṭān-Shāh, these Ghuzz comprised 5,000 mounted men plus their dependants. Their arrival threw Kirmān into chaos, and their own depredations together with the nibbling of their flocks brought economic dislocation and then famine. The trading suburb or *rabaḍ* of Bardasīr, once an international resort for merchants and caravans, was destroyed, and never in this period did it revive. Kirmān now became the base for Ghuzz raids as far as Iṣfahān, Fārs, and Sīstān.[1] Tūrān-Shāh's nephew and successor Muḥammad-Shāh (579–82/1183–6) found the old centre of Bardasīr too stricken by ruin and famine to serve as his capital, so he transferred to Bam. Nevertheless he was unable to withstand the pressure of the Ghuzz, and in the end he abandoned Kirmān, seeking help first in Fārs and Iraq and then from Tekish in Khurāsān. Despairing of recovering Kirmān, Muḥammad-Shāh finished his days in the service of the Ghūrids.[2]

Kirmān was now fully in the hands of the Ghuzz leader Malik Dīnār, who had come there in 582/1186 from Nīshāpūr after the death of Toghan-Shāh b. Ai-Aba (p. 190 below).[3] As ruler of Kirmān, Malik Dīnār showed statesmanship and foresight; he took measures for the restoration of agricultural and economic prosperity, conciliated the ulema, and tried to legitimize his rule by marrying a Saljuq princess, the daughter of Toghrïl-Shāh. He led expeditions against the local rulers of Hormuz and the island of Qais and made them his tributaries. When Malik Dīnār died in 591/1195, his incompetent son Farrukh-Shāh was unable to control the Ghuzz, and as a ruling force the horde now disintegrated. Farrukh-Shāh had been ready to recognize the suzerainty of the Khwārazm-Shāhs, by then the greatest single power in Iran, and after his death in 592/1196 Tekish's authority was established in Kirmān through the agency of the atabeg Nuṣrat al-Dīn b. Muḥammad Öner. Faced by a powerful Khwārazmian army, the Ghuzz of Kirmān gave up the attempt to retain their power there and

[1] Muḥammad b. Ibrāhīm, pp. 101–2, 106–20; cf. Houtsma, *op. cit.* pp. 386–90.

[2] Muḥammad b. Ibrāhīm, pp. 124–36; cf. Houtsma, *op. cit.* pp. 390–1, and Kafesoğlu, *Harezmşahlar devleti tarihi*, p. 107 n. 111.

[3] Ibn al-Athīr, vol. xi, pp. 248–9; Juvainī, vol. i, p. 294.

abandoned the province, entering the ranks of the Khwārazmian army after a twenty-year domination of Kirmān.[1]

Thus in the second half of the 6th/12th century, the Saljuqs of Iraq and western Iran ruled no more than the province of Jibāl; Hamadān and Iṣfahān were the centres of their power, though they did have occasional control over Ray. When the fugitive Sulaimān-Shāh came in 550/1155 to Baghdad, Caliph al-Muqtafī recognized him as sultan but required in return that Sulaimān-Shāh should never make any hostile move against Iraq; and after the failure of Sulṭān Muḥammad's siege of Baghdad in 551–2/1157, the sultans never again seriously tried to assert their former authority there.[2]

On the death in 547/1152 of Sulṭān Mas'ūd, the Amīr Khāṣṣ Beg Arslan, in accordance with the dead monarch's wishes, proclaimed Malik-Shāh b. Maḥmūd as his successor. Al-Muqtafī seized the opportunity for a great onslaught on Saljuq authority in Iraq. Mas'ūd's old shaḥna in Baghdad, Mas'ūd Bilālī, was driven out, the sultan's properties expropriated, and even poets attached to the Saljuq court circle, including the famous Ḥaiṣ-Baiṣ, were arrested, whilst caliphal forces took over the outlying towns of Ḥilla, Kūfa, and Wāsiṭ.[3]

Malik-Shāh was allowed to reign only for a few months, and in 548/1153 he was replaced by his brother Muḥammad, who was brought from Khūzistān. During his six years as sultan, Muḥammad tried energetically to restore the slipping authority of his dynasty in Iraq. The caliph was at this time clearing Iraq of the remaining Turkish elements, who had rallied round Mas'ūd Bilālī in Takrīt. These amīrs brought out from captivity in Takrīt the young Saljuq prince Arslan, and set him up as sultan; according to 'Imād al-Dīn, the commanders had said to Mas'ūd Bilālī, "Fetch Malik Arslan b. Toghrïl, the Sultan's nephew, so that the troops and the Türkmen contingents may take heart from his presence". At first forced back on Baghdad, the caliph assembled an army of Arabs and Kurds, and with his vizier, 'Aun al-Dīn Ibn Hubaira, he led them in 549/1154 to victory at Bazimzā near Baghdad against Mas'ūd Bilālī, Al-Qush, and their protégé Arslan.

[1] Muḥammad b. Ibrāhīm, pp. 138–201; cf. Houtsma, *op. cit* pp. 392 ff.; Nasawī, *Histoire du Sultan Djelal ed-Din Mankobirti*, pp. 27–8 (tr., pp. 46–9); cf. Kafesoğlu, *op. cit.* pp. 144, 196–8.

[2] Ibn al-Jauzī, *al-Muntaẓam*, vol. x, pp. 161, 164; Ibn al-Athīr, *al-Kāmil*, vol. xi, p. 139.

[3] Bundārī, *Zubdat al-nuṣra*, pp. 227–9; Ẓahīr al-Dīn Nīshāpūrī, *Saljūq-Nāma*, pp. 66–7; Rāvandī, *Rāḥat al-Ṣudūr*, pp. 249–56; Ibn al-Jauzī, vol. x, pp. 147–8, 153–4; Ḥusainī, *Akhbār al-daula*, pp. 129–30; Ibn al-Athīr, vol. xi, pp. 105–7; Sibṭ b. al-Jauzī, *Mir'āt al-zamān*, vol. i, pp. 212–13.

The latter fled into Kurdistān and eventually found shelter with his stepfather Eldigüz.[1]

The Saljuq prince Sulaimān-Shāh b. Muḥammad Tapar had been his uncle Sanjar's heir in Khurāsān, but the ascendancy of the Ghuzz drove him westwards, and in 550/1155 he appeared at Baghdad with a small force. Al-Muqtafī saw in him a useful weapon against Sulṭān Muḥammad, and he recognized Sulaimān-Shāh as a rival sultan, placing his name in the khuṭba. He also provided him with an army, but his bid for power in Jibāl was easily defeated by Muḥammad. The latter was naturally incensed at the caliph's aid to his rival, and he summoned all his forces for a siege of Baghdad in 551–2/1157. As well as the Saljuq army from Hamadān, Zangid forces under Zain al-Dīn 'Alī Küchük came from Mosul, and contingents came from the Mazyadids in Ḥilla and from southern Iraq. Heavy fighting, both on land and on the rivers, followed. Ibn Hubaira had laid in good stocks of food for the army, but the interruptions to commerce made the spirits of Baghdad's merchant classes flag. The vizier distributed money and presents amongst the besiegers, together with skilful propaganda about the impiety of attacking the caliph; he also wrote to Eldigüz inciting him to make a countermove in Jibāl and to set up there a Saljuq prince as rival to Muḥammad. This diplomacy had its effect. The army of Mosul grew lukewarm, and when Muḥammad received the news that Eldigüz had come with the princes Arslan and Malik-Shāh and had occupied the capital Hamadān, he lifted the siege. He drove Eldigüz back into Āzarbāījān and cleared his partisans from Ray and Iṣfahān, but by now he was a sick man. He was unable to consummate his marriage with the daughter of Muḥammad b. Arslan-Shāh of Kirmān, and remained in Hamadān till his death in 554/1159 at the age of thirty-two.[2]

There was dissension among the amīrs regarding a successor. Muḥammad's own infant son was committed to the Aḥmadīlī Aq-Sonqur II at Marāgheh. Some amīrs favoured Malik-Shāh b. Maḥmūd, to whom Muḥammad had latterly allocated the province of Fārs; and though he managed to conquer part of this from Shumla, he died at

[1] Bundārī, pp. 236–40; Ẓahīr al-Dīn Nīshāpūrī, pp. 67–8, 75; Rāvandī, pp. 258 ff.; Ibn al-Jauzī, vol. x, pp. 156–8; Ḥusainī, pp. 131–3; Ibn al-Athīr, vol. xi, pp. 106–7, 125, 128–30; Barhebraeus, *Chronography*, pp. 282–3.

[2] Bundārī, pp. 240–2, 251–3, 285–8; Ẓahīr al-Dīn Nīshāpūrī, pp. 68–72, 75; Rāvandī, pp. 262–70; Ibn al-Jauzī, vol. x, pp. 161, 164–5, 168–75; Ḥusainī, pp. 131–3, 143; Ibn al-Athīr, vol. xi, 135–7, 140–2, 166; Barhebraeus, p. 285.

Iṣfahān in 555/1160, reputedly poisoned by the Vizier Ibn Hubaira, for Malik-Shāh had been threatening to march against the caliph in Baghdad.[1] Others supported Arslan b. Toghrïl, but a majority, including Ïnanch Sonqur, the powerful governor of Ray, favoured Sulaimān-Shāh on grounds of seniority and acceptability to al-Muqtafī. Saulaimān-Shāh was accordingly released from captivity at Mosul, and with difficulty established himself at Hamadān. He reigned for a few months only in the year 555/1160, during which time he leant heavily on the support of such amīrs as Ïnanch Sonqur and Sharaf al-Dīn Gird-Bāzū, while from fear of Eldigüz he was compelled to invest Arslan with the governorship of Arrān and make him his heir. Sulaimān-Shāh dreamed of re-establishing Saljuq influence in Baghdad by the appointment there of a shaḥna, but the negotiations with al-Mustanjid were inconclusive. Sulaimān-Shāh's drunkenness and general ineffectiveness soon lost him the amīrs' support. They invited Eldigüz to set up Arslan as sultan; Gird-Bāzū arrested Sulaimān-Shāh, who was first imprisoned and then in 556/1161 strangled with a bowstring.[2]

In this fashion Arslan was installed at Hamadān in 556/1161 as nominal sultan. He remained under the tutelage of Eldigüz, who took the title of *Atabeg al-A'ẓam* ("Supreme Atabeg") and his vizier was Shihāb al-Dīn Muḥammad Nīshāpūrī, formerly minister to Ïnanch-Sonqur of Ray. Arslan now married Muḥammad's widow, the Khatun-i Kirmānī.[3] This succession was nevertheless disputed. Ïnanch of Ray was temporarily mollified by the marriage of his daughter to Pahlavān b. Eldigüz, but the caliph refused to recognize Arslan as sultan, fearing the constitution of a powerful Saljuq–Eldigüzid state in western Iran. His vizier stirred up Aq-Sonqor II Aḥmadīlī, who had with him the son of Muḥammad b. Maḥmūd, and Aq-Sonqur in alliance with the Shāh-Arman of Akhlāṭ routed the army of Pahlavān on the banks of the Safīd Rūd. Ibn Hubaira further encouraged the Salghurid Zangī in Shīrāz to press the succession claims of Maḥmūd b. Malik-Shāh b. Maḥmūd.[4]

A coalition of discontented amīrs, including Ïnanch-Sonqur, 'Izz al-Dīn Satmaz, and Alp-Arghun of Qazvīn, marched on Hamadān,

[1] Bundārī, pp. 286–7, 295; Ibn al-Athīr, vol. XI, pp. 173–4.

[2] Bundārī, pp. 288–9, 293–6; Ẓahīr al-Dīn Nīshāpūrī, pp. 72–4, 76; Rāvandī, pp. 274–9; Ibn al-Jauzī, vol. X, pp. 192, 196; Ḥusainī, pp. 143–4; Ibn al-Athīr, vol. XI, 166, 168, 175–7.

[3] Bundārī, pp. 296–7; Ẓahīr al-Dīn Nīshāpūrī, p. 76; Rāvandī, p. 286.

[4] Ibn al-Athīr, vol. XI, pp. 177–8.

but in a battle at Marg-i Qara-Tegin they were defeated by Sulṭān Arslan, Eldigüz, and Gird-Bāzū. Īnanch fled first to the Bāvandid Caspian territories and then to the Khwārazm-Shāh Il-Arslan. Despite the support of a Khwārazmian army, his invasion of the Qazvīn–Zanjān area proved a failure, and the excesses of his troops alienated the local people (562/1166–7). Īnanch then took refuge in Gurgān, returning later with Bāvandid support, and this time recapturing Ray. But Eldigüz came in 564/1169 with an army to besiege Īnanch in the citadel of Ṭabarak, after which he suborned some of Īnanch's ghulāms to kill him. Ray was then granted to Pahlavān, with the Vizier Sa'd al-Dīn al-Ashall left there to administer it.[1]

Eldigüz's diplomatic and military activity reached well beyond the borders of his territories of Āzarbāījān and Jibāl. Mu'ayyid al-Dīn Ai-Aba of Khurāsān had long been one of Eldigüz's friends, and in 558/1163 he placed Sulṭān Arslan in the khuṭba of the towns in his possession. Therefore in 562/1167, when Khwārazmian pressure seemed to be uncomfortably close, it was natural that Ai-Aba should write to Eldigüz, warning him of Il-Arslan's ambitions not merely in Khurāsān but in the whole of Iran; Eldigüz wrote to the shāh warning him that Khurāsān was part of Sulṭān Arslan's territories, and he came himself to Bisṭām to check a Khwārazmian move against Khurāsān.[2] In 563/1168 Pahlavān led an army against the Aḥmadīlīs and forced them to make peace; Eldigüz sent to Mosul and had Quṭb al-Dīn Maudūd read the khuṭba for Arslan, and in 564/1169 he sent an army to Kirmān to aid the claimant Arslan-Shāh.[3]

The defence of the north-west was one of Eldigüz's particular concerns, for the period of the Eldigüzids in Āzarbāījān coincided with a phase of renewed activity by the Bagratid kings of Christian Georgia. Under Dmitri (1125–54 or 1156), the Georgian monarchy was largely occupied with internal struggles against the Orbeliani family of nobles, but in 549/1154, apparently at the invitation of the local Shaddādid ruler Fakhr al-Dīn Shaddād, the Georgians descended on Ani and defeated and captured 'Izz al-Dīn Saltuq of Erzerum.[4] The reign of

[1] Bundārī, pp. 298–300; Ẓahīr al-Dīn Nīshāpūri, pp. 76–81; Rāvandī, pp. 290 ff.; Ḥusainī, pp. 145–53; Ibn al-Athīr, vol. XI, pp. 177–9, 229–30.

[2] *al-Kāmil*, vol. XI, pp. 192–3; Ḥusainī, pp. 162–4.

[3] Muḥammad b. Ibrāhīm, p. 52; cf. Houtsma, *Z.D.M.G.* (1885), pp. 380–1; Ḥusainī, pp. 162–6; Ibn al-Athīr, vol. XI, p. 208.

[4] Fāriqī, in Ibn al-Qalānisī, *Dhail ta'rīkh Dimashq*, p. 328 n.; Ibn al-Athīr, vol. XI, pp. 125–6, 133; Minorsky, "Caucasica II. 1. The Georgian Maliks of Ahar", *B.S.O.A.S.* vol. XIII/4 (1951), pp. 874–7; *idem, Studies in Caucasian History*, pp. 86–7.

Dmitri's son Giorgi III (1156–84) was one of internal prosperity and warfare against the Muslims. In 556/1161 Ani passed from Faḍl IV b. Maḥmūd to the Christians, and in the next year a Georgian army took Dvin. These successes provoked a grand Muslim coalition of Sulṭān Arslan, Eldigüz, Aq-Sonqur Aḥmadīlī, and the Shāh-Arman Sukmān b. Ibrāhīm, which in 557/1162 invaded Georgia and defeated King Giorgi.[1] Eldigüz's efforts gradually slowed down Georgian expansion, though we still find the Christians raiding as far as Ganja in 561/1166 and even intervening at Darband to assist the Shīrvān-Shāh Akhsitan, who was related by marriage to the Bagratids.[2]

Under Queen Tamara (1184–1212) the dynamism of the Georgians reached its peak. Guided by her *Amīr-Spasalari* (Commander-in-Chief) Zakharia Mkhargrdzeli and his brother the "atabeg" Ioanne, she deliberately diverted attention from internal questions by directing Georgian energies outwards. The later Eldigüzids were not of the calibre of Eldigüz and Pahlavān. In the succession struggles amongst the latter's sons, Amīr Amīrān 'Umar fled at one point to Queen Tamara, and from her and her vassal the Shīrvān-Shāh he received help against his brother Abū Bakr. Later realizing that he could not stand up to Georgian arms, Abū Bakr contracted a marriage with a Georgian princess in order to safeguard his position.[3] In the succeeding years the Georgians took Dvin, Kars and Ardābīl; they operated in the west without hindrance as far as Malāzgird, Akhlāṭ, Arjīsh, and Erzerum, eventually coming up against the Saljuqs of Rūm; and after 600/1204 Tamara gave aid to the fugitive Comneni in Trebizond. Most of these conquests were not held for very long, and though Giorgi IV (1212–23) continued to draw tribute from Erzerum, Ganja, Nakhchivān, and Akhlāṭ, the Mongols appeared in the Caucasus in 617/1220 and a period of disaster began for the Georgians.[4]

When Eldigüz died at Nakhchivān in 570/1174–5 or 571/1175, his son Pahlavān Muḥammad succeeded to his position as atabeg. Sulṭān Arslan had long resented his subordination to Eldigüz, and it seems that at this juncture he endeavoured to break away from Eldigüzid

[1] Fāriqī, in Ibn al-Qalānisī, pp. 360–4; Ẓahīr al-Dīn Nīshāpūrī, p. 77; Rāvandī, pp. 287–8; Ḥusainī, pp. 156–62; Ibn al-Athīr, vol. XI, pp. 184, 188–9; Minorsky, *Caucasian History*, pp. 89 ff.; M. Canard, "Dwīn", *Encyc. of Islam* (2nd ed.).

[2] Ḥusainī, pp. 185 ff.

[3] *Ibid.* pp. 185–6; Ibn al-Athīr, vol. XII, pp. 120, 160.

[4] Ḥusainī, pp. 188–9; Ibn al-Athīr, XII, pp. 133–4, 159, 169, 184. Cf. Allen, *A History of the Georgian People*, pp. 100–10; Minorsky, "Tiflis", *Encyc. of Islam* (1st ed.).

control. Some discontented amīrs having provided him with money and troops, he moved to Zanjān intending to conquer Āzarbāījān; but in 571/1176, at the age of forty-three, he fell ill and died. 'Imād al-Dīn asserts—and it is not improbable—that Pahlavān had conveniently poisoned the sultan. Pahlavān now set up Arslan's young son Toghrïl as sultan, and successfully fought off an attempt to seize the throne, made by Arslan's elder brother Muḥammad, who had been living in Khūzistān.[1]

Pahlavān died in 582/1186, and in accordance with the Turkish practice of seniorate his position as atabeg fell to his childless brother Qïzïl-Arslan 'Uthmān. But Pahlavān also divided his personal territories among his four sons, who were to be under Qïzïl-Arslan's general supervision, and this partition was to prove a source of dissension and weakness. Pahlavān's wife Ïnanch Khatun, daughter of Ïnanch-Sonqur of Ray, supported the claims of her two sons against the other two children, sons of Pahlavān by slave mothers; one of these latter, Abū Bakr, was particularly favoured by Qïzïl-Arslan and seemed likely to succeed, as in fact he did, to the whole of the Eldigüzid inheritance.[2]

The new Sulṭān Toghrïl, last of the Saljuqs in Iran, is praised in the sources for his manifold qualities, scholarly as well as soldierly. He soon became restive under Qïzïl-Arslan's tutelage, for whereas he had been on good terms with Pahlavān, the new atabeg treated him harshly.[3] Toghrïl allied with the forces supporting Ïnanch Khatun's son Qutlugh Ïnanch Muḥammad in opposition to Qïzïl-Arslan and Abū Bakr. In 583/1187 he was in Māzandarān seeking help from the Bāvandid Ḥusām al-Daula Ardashīr. Also in this year he sent an envoy to Baghdad asking that the old palace of the Saljuq sultans be repaired in order that he might occupy it. Al-Nāṣir's answer was to raze the palace to the ground and to send an army of 15,000 troops, under his vizier Jalāl al-Dīn 'Ubaidallāh b. Yūnus, to support Qïzïl-Arslan, who agreed to become the caliph's direct vassal. Toghrïl defeated the caliphal forces at Dāi-Marg near Hamadān in 584/1188, but he lost support by his arbitrary behaviour and his execution of opponents in Hamadān. Qïzïl-Arslan now set up Sanjar b. Sulaimān-Shāh as a rival sultan and drove Toghrïl into the Lake Urmīyeh

[1] Bundārī, p. 301; Ẓahīr al-Dīn Nīshāpūrī, p. 82; Rāvandī, p. 351; Ibn al-Jauzī, vol. x, p. 264; Ḥusainī, pp. 168–71; Ibn al-Athīr, vol. xi, pp. 255–6, 257. Cf. Houtsma, "Some Remarks on the History of the Saljuks", *Acta Orientalia*, pp. 140–2.

[2] Ḥusainī, pp. 172–5; Ibn al-Athīr, vol. xi, pp. 346–7.

[3] Abū Ḥāmid Muḥammad b. Ibrāhīm, *Dhail-i Saljuq-Nāma*, p. 86.

region; and though he tried despairingly to obtain help from the Ayyūbid Saladin and to conciliate the caliph, even sending one of his infant sons to Baghdad as a hostage, Toghrïl was obliged in 586/1190 to surrender to Qïzïl-Arslan, who imprisoned him and his son Malik-Shāh in a castle near Tabrīz.[1]

Qïzïl-Arslan now claimed the sultanate for himself, assuming the appropriate style and privileges; but in the next year he was mysteriously murdered, possibly by one of his own amīrs, possibly by Ïnanch Khatun, whom Qïzïl-Arslan had married on his brother's death. Toghrïl's subsequent execution of Ïnanch Khatun may point to the second alternative.[2] After two years' incarceration, Toghrïl was released by one of the amīrs of Āzarbāījān. Near Qazvīn he speedily defeated Ïnanch Khatun's two sons, Qutlugh-Ïnanch and the Amīr-Amīrān 'Umar, and drove them into Āzarbāījān (588/1192). There they were again defeated, this time by their half-brother Abū Bakr who was then at Nakhchivān, but they later returned with help from Georgia and Arrān and defeated Abū Bakr. Toghrïl was now master of Jibāl, Hamadān, and Iṣfahān, and he had also secured the treasuries left by Pahlavān. But an enemy more dangerous than the Eldigüzids had meanwhile appeared.[3]

Qutlugh-Ïnanch had summoned help from the Khwārazm-Shāh Tekish, who in 588/1192 came to Māzandarān and then Ray, and demanded that the khuṭba of western Iran recognize his name immediately after that of the caliph. After this was granted, however, he was obliged to return to Khurāsān on receiving news of a projected attack on Khwārazm by his brother Sulṭān-Shāh. Tekish therefore made peace with Toghrïl, but the sultan felt that a Khwārazmian army in Ray, with its commanding position of the roads into Jibāl and Āzarbāījān, was a threat which could not be endured; and no doubt he felt too that his prestige was involved. Tekish had distractions in Khurāsān, and does not seem at this point to have been implacably hostile towards Toghrïl, despite urgings from Caliph al-Nāṣir.

In 589/1193 Toghrïl marched eastwards and cleared the Khwārazm-

[1] Bundārī, pp. 301–2; Abū Ḥāmid, pp. 86–9; Rāvandī, pp. 339–62; Ibn Isfandiyār, *Ta'rīkh-i Ṭabaristān*, p. 252; Ḥusainī, pp. 176–80; Ibn al-Athīr, vol. xi, pp. 347, 371, vol. xii, pp. 15–16; Ibn al-Ṭiqṭaqā, p. 288 (tr., p. 311); Houtsma, *Acta Orientalia* (1924), pp. 145–50.

[2] Bundārī, p. 302; Abū Ḥāmid, p. 89; Rāvandī, pp. 363, 367; Ibn Isfandiyār, p. 254; Ḥusainī, pp. 181, 184; Ibn al-Athīr, vol. xii, pp. 49–50; Sibṭ b. al-Jauzī, vol. i, p. 406; Houtsma, *op. cit.* pp. 142–4.

[3] Abū Ḥāmid, pp. 89–90; Ravandī, pp. 365–9; Ḥusainī, pp. 182–7; Ibn al-Athīr, vol. xii, p. 61.

ian garrison out of Ray; and in the following year he defeated Qutlugh-Ïnanch there, despite the 7,000 Khwārazmian reinforcements which the Eldigüzid had obtained from Dāmghān. Tekish returned to Ray in 590/1194. Against the advice of his amīrs, Toghrïl refused to withdraw and negotiate a peace, or even to wait for additional troops to come up from Iṣfahān and Zanjān. In a battle outside Ray the Saljuq army was defeated and Toghrïl killed at the age of twenty-five, his head being sent by Tekish to Baghdad. In this fashion, the sources note, the Saljuq dynasty ended as it began, with a Toghrïl; though in fact two of the dead sultan's sons remained in the custody of the Khwārazm-Shāhs till their execution at the time of the Mongol invasion of Khwārazm in 616/1219–20, and a daughter of Toghrïl survived to marry first the Eldigüzid Öz-Beg b. Pahlavān and then the Khwārazm-Shāh Jalāl al-Dīn himself.[1]

Tekish occupied Hamadān and the whole of Jibāl, making Qutlugh-Ïnanch governor over it, but much of the land was divided into iqṭā'ś for his amīrs, and he left his sons Yūnus Khān and Muḥammad Khān in control.[2] It was readily predictable that the caliph would find the proximity of Tekish uncomfortable, and deep mutual suspicion arose. Al-Nāṣir's vizier, Mu'ayyid al-Dīn Ibn al-Qaṣṣāb, had taken over Khūzistān on the death of Shumla's son, and in 591/1195 was joined there by Qutlugh-Ïnanch, who had quarrelled with the Khwārazmian Commander-in-Chief Shams al-Dīn Mayanchuq. The two of them invaded Jibāl and drove the Khwārazm-Shāh's son from Hamadān and then Ray into Qūmis and Gurgān. Returning to Hamadān in 592/1196, Tekish disinterred and mutilated the body of Ibn al-Qaṣṣāb; but disorder in his territories on the lower Syr Darya compelled his withdrawal once more (see p. 191 below).[3]

The caliph judged it wise to bow in some degree to the military superiority of the shah, and in 595/1199 he sent to Tekish an investiture patent for the sultanate of Iraq, Khurāsān, and Turkestan. Reports about Mayanchuq's misconduct brought Tekish westwards once again

[1] Bundārī, pp. 302–3; Abū Ḥamid, pp. 90–1; Rāvandī, pp. 370–4; Ḥusainī, pp. 189–93; Nasawī, pp. 21, 39, 118–19, 153–4 (tr., pp. 37, 66, 96–8, 254–7); Ibn al-Athīr, vol. XII, pp. 69–70; Jūzjānī, vol. I, p. 267 (tr., vol. I, pp. 166–7); Juvainī, *Ta'rīkh-i Jahān-Gushā*, vol. I, pp. 299–303; Barhebraeus, pp. 344–5; Barthold, *Turkestan down to the Mongol Invasion*, pp. 366–7; Houtsma, *op. cit.* pp. 150–2; Kafesoğlu, *Harezmşahlar devleti tarihi*, pp. 116–19, 123–6.

[2] Abū Ḥāmid, p. 92; Rāvandī, p. 385; Ibn al-Athīr, vol. XII, pp. 69–70; Jūzjānī, vol. I, p. 304 (tr., vol. I, pp. 249–50); Barhebraeus, p. 345; Kafesoğlu, *op. cit.* pp. 126–7.

[3] Rāvandī, p. 389; Ibn al-Athīr, vol. XII, pp. 72–3; Juvainī, vol. I, pp. 303–4; Kafesoğlu, *op. cit.* pp. 131–7.

in this same year, and after the rebellious governor had been pursued into Dailam and defeated, the shāh turned to attack the Ismā'īlīs there, capturing the fortress of Arslan-Gushāi near Qazvīn.[1] In all these campaigns the Khwārazmian army included a large proportion of Türkmen troops from the Qïpchaq steppes, many of whom were still pagan; the army became hated in western Iran for its violence and rapine, which Rāvandī says were worse than the excesses of the Christian Georgians and Franks and even of the pagan Qara-Khitai. When in 596/1200 Tekish died, the people of Jibāl rose and massacred all the Khwārazmians they could find.[2]

Al-Nāṣir now agreed to partition western Iran between himself and Nūr al-Dīn Gökche, a former Eldigüzid ghulām who had taken over Ray, Sāveh, Qum, and Kāshān; the caliph was to have Iṣfahān, Hamadān, Qazvīn, and Zanjān.[3] Thus the nominal authority of the Eldigüzids survived in northern Jibāl and Dailam, and when in 600/1203–4 Gökche was killed in battle with another of Pahlavān's old ghulāms, Shams al-Dīn Ai-Toghmïsh, the latter set up Öz-Beg b. Pahlavān as titular ruler of Gökche's territories. In Āzarbāījān, Abū Bakr b. Pahlavān held on and secured a reputation with posterity for his patronage of scholars and his foundation of mosques and madrasas. With Ai-Toghmïsh's aid in 602/1205–6 he fought off an attack by the Aḥmadīlī ruler of Marāgheh, 'Alā' al-Dīn Qara-Sonqur, and three years later he took over almost all the Aḥmadīlī possessions (see above, pp. 170–1).[4] The Eldigüzid ghulāms remained a potent force in Jibāl and in 608/1211–12 a further upheaval took place in which Ai-Toghmïsh was replaced by Mengli. Mengli's power soon excited the fears of neighbouring powers, however, and in 612/1215–16 the caliph organized a grand coalition against him, including Öz-Beg, the amīrs of al-Jazīreh and Kurdistān, and the Ismā'īlī Grand Master Ḥasan III, newly returned to the fold of orthodoxy (see p. 168 above). Mengli was defeated in battle and eventually executed by Öz-Beg, who now appointed the ghulām Saif al-Dīn Ïghlamïsh as governor of Jibāl.[5]

Tekish was followed as Khwārazm-Shāh by his son 'Alā' al-Dīn Muḥammad. At the end of his life Tekish had demanded of al-Nāṣir

[1] Ibn al-Athīr, vol. XII, pp. 100–1; Juvainī, vol. I, pp. 310–12; Kafesoğlu, pp. 141–5.

[2] Rāvandī, pp. 393 ff.; Barthold, *Turkestan down to the Mongol Invasion*, pp. 347–8.

[3] Rāvandī, p. 400; Ibn al-Athīr, vol. XII, pp. 76–7.

[4] *al-Kāmil*, vol. XII, pp. 156–7, 168, 182; Jūzjānī, vol. I, p. 270 (tr., I, p. 173); Kafesoğlu, *op. cit.* pp. 180–1.

[5] Ibn al-Athīr, vol. XII, pp. 200–1; Kafesoğlu, *op. cit.* pp. 199–201; Hodgson, *Order of Assassins*, pp. 220–2.

that his son's name be put in the khuṭba at Baghdad, but for many years his successor was too occupied with his opponents the Ghūrids, the Qara-Khitai, and the Qïpchaq to contemplate expansion in the west. However, in 614/1217, on the very eve of the Mongol invasion, 'Alā' al-Dīn Muḥammad demanded recognition by the caliph and came westwards. Ïghlamïsh in Jibāl recognized him, but was shortly afterwards murdered by an Ismā'īlī assassin. The Salghurid atabeg Sa'd b. Zangī, seeing a chance to add Jibāl to his existing province of Fārs, marched on Ray only to meet defeat and capture at the hands of the Khwārazmian army. He was forced to pay a tribute of a third of his annual revenues for the rest of his life, and to allot certain of his territories as fiefs for Khwārazmian commanders. In return, Sa'd was given a Khwārazmian bride together with help to recover his province, for in his absence his son Abū Bakr Qutlugh Khān had taken over Fārs; later one of Sa'd's daughters was to marry Sulṭān Jalāl al-Dīn.[1]

'Alā' al-Dīn Muḥammad knew from captured diplomatic correspondence that the caliph had in the past incited the Ghūrids against him and was now using Ismā'īlī assassins to remove his opponents.[2] Because of his anti-caliphal attitude he was unable to count on Sunnī opinion, and so the shāh adopted a pro-Shī'ī policy. He secured a fatwā from the religious authorities of his empire saying that al-Nāṣir was unfit to rule and that the 'Abbāsids had usurped the caliphate from the house of 'Alī, and he proclaimed the Sayyid 'Alā' al-Mulk Tirmidhī as Anti-Caliph. He began a march on Baghdad, but in the winter of 614/1217–18 snowstorms of unparalleled ferocity, together with harrying by hostile Türkmen and Hakkārī Kurds, halted him on the borders of Iraq and Iran. Hearing of the Mongols' appearance in the east, the shāh returned to Khurāsān, leaving his son Rukn al-Dīn Ghūr-Sanjï with the care of eastern Iran.[3]

[1] Nasawī, *Histoire*, pp. 3, 13–14, 19–20, 167 (tr., 6, 24–6, 33–5, 278); Ibn al-Athīr, vol. XII, pp. 206–7; Jūzjānī, vol. I, pp. 271–2 (tr., vol. I, pp. 176–8); Juvainī, vol. II, pp. 365–6; Ḥamd Allāh Mustaufī, *Ta'rīkh-i Guzīda*, pp. 496, 506–7 (tr., pp. 114–15, 120–1); Kafesoğlu, *Harezmşahlar devleti tarihi*, p. 204.

[2] Juvainī, vol. II, pp. 390–1; cf. Jūzjānī, vol. I, pp. 301–2 (tr., vol. I, p. 243).

[3] Nasawī, pp. 11–21 (tr., pp. 20–36); Ibn al-Athīr, *al-Kāmil*, vol. XII, pp. 206–7; Juvainī, vol. II, pp. 364–7, 392, 474; Sibṭ b. al-Jauzī, vol. II, pp. 582–3; Ḥamd Allāh Mustaufī, *op. cit.* p. 496 (tr., pp. 114–15); Barthold, *Turkestan*, pp. 373–5; Kafesoğlu, *op. cit.* pp. 202–5, 214–20. [Ed.: Ibn al-Athīr's mention of the Mongols is anachronistic; he probably meant the Qïpchaq Turks on Muḥammad's northern frontier. See Barthold, *Turkestan*, p. 369.]

XIII. KHURĀSĀN IN THE SECOND HALF OF THE 6TH/12TH CENTURY, AND THE EXPANSION OF THE KHWĀRAZM-SHĀHS

After Sanjar's death in 552/1157, Khurāsān remained politically fragmented. For despite the authority which should have come to him when Sanjar nominated him as heir, the Qarakhānid Maḥmūd Khān was never able to enjoy more than a limited authority. Amongst the former ghulāms of Sanjar's army the most powerful single figure was Mu'ayyid al-Dīn Ai-Aba of Nīshāpūr. Maḥmūd Khān, unable single-handed to make much headway against him, allied with Ai-Aba, confirmed him in the governorship of Nīshāpūr and Ṭūs, and fell more and more under his influence.[1] The end of the eastern branch of the Saljuqs left a power vacuum in Khurāsān, and this inevitably invited the intervention of external powers such as the ambitious Bāvandid Shāh Ghāzī Rustam (534–58/1140–63) and the Khwārazm-Shāh Tāj al-Dunyā wa'l-Dīn Il-Arslan (551–68/1156–72). The internal politics of Khurāsān were for twenty years dominated by the disputes of the Turkish amīrs and the Ghuzz tribesmen, with the Khwārazm-Shāhs stepping in only so far as their dependence on the Qara-Khitai allowed. But after the capture of Herāt by the Ghūrids in 571/1175–6, a new major power appeared in the province, and down to the last decade of the century there was a three-cornered struggle for hegemony in Khurāsān involving the Ghūrids, the Khwārazm-Shāh Tekish, and his estranged brother Sulṭān-Shāh. Squeezed among these combatants, the Ghuzz tribesmen were either compelled to migrate to adjacent regions such as Kirmān, or else they were absorbed into the Khwārazmian and Ghūrid armies.

In the rivalry after Sanjar's death between Ai-Aba and Ikhtiyār al-Dīn Ai-Taq, the latter received help from Shāh Ghāzī Rustam (p. 156 above). Ai-Taq collected an army in Māzandarān, but was defeated by Ai-Aba and Maḥmūd Khān. A peace between the two sides in 553/1158 freed Ai-Aba to deal with Sonqur 'Azīzī, another of Sanjar's former ghulāms, who had rebelled in Herāt during Ai-Aba's preoccupation with Ai-Taq. Ai-Aba and Maḥmūd Khān then attempted to subdue the independent Türkmen bands who were established in several parts of Khurāsān, but found this an uphill task; they were defeated by the Ghuzz, who followed up this victory by occupying Marv and then raiding Ai-Aba's towns of Sarakhs and Ṭūs. The Ghuzz now

[1] Ibn al-Athīr, *al-Kāmil*, vol. xi, pp. 121, 171–2.

offered their allegiance to Maḥmūd, and the khan, although personally distrustful of the Türkmen, saw a chance to reduce his dependence on Ai-Aba. From his refuge in Gurgān he sent his son Jalāl al-Dīn Muḥammad to the Ghuzz, who had meanwhile taken Nīshāpūr and temporarily expelled Ai-Aba (554/1159).[1]

However, Ai-Aba returned in the same year and firmly resumed power in Nīshāpūr, taking stern measures to repress the *fitna*, or internal strife, which had been raging there.[2] It seems that the collapse of Saljuq authority in Khurāsān had given free rein to local faction and violence. Agriculture was interrupted by the trampling of opposing armies as well as by the nomads' flocks, and famine resulted. Religious and social sectarianism, the curse of the Khurāsānian cities, flared up on several occasions: in Astarābād Shāh Ghāzī Rustam had to mediate between Shī'īs and Shāfi'īs, and in Nīshāpūr in 556/1161 Ai-Aba jailed the *naqīb* (head) of the 'Alids, holding him responsible for clashes which had ruined much of the city and had caused the destruction of such a famous library as that of the 'Uqailī mosque.[3] Maḥmūd Khān soon tired of his *entente* with the Ghuzz, and in 556/1161 decided to make his peace with Ai-Aba; but the latter seized, blinded, and imprisoned the khan and his son Jalāl al-Dīn Muḥammad, and made the khuṭba in Nīshāpūr for himself alone.[4]

Ai-Aba was now systematically extending his power. He disputed the possession of Pūshang and Herāt with the Ghūrids; he conquered Qūmis and installed as governor of Bisṭām one of his ghulāms, although this last was in 559/1164 driven out by the Bāvandids. In the previous year the sultan in the west, Arslan b. Toghrïl, had given him presents and an investiture patent, and he accordingly placed Arslan in the khuṭba of those parts of Khurāsān held by him (i.e. Nīshāpūr, Ṭūs, Qūmis, and the region between Nasā and Ṭabas).[5] The Amīr Ai-Taq had been defeated by a group of Ghuzz under the Yazïr chief Yaghmur Khān, but had obtained help first from the Bāvandids and then from the Khwārazm-Shāh; he finally planted himself in Gurgān and Dihistān, and there made the khuṭba for Il-Arslan. Other towns of Khurāsān, such as Balkh, Marv, Sarakhs, Herāt, and Ṭāliqān, along with the region

[1] *Ibid.* pp. 146–7, 149–50, 152–5.
[2] *Ibid.* pp. 171–2.
[3] *Ibid.* pp. 154–5, 165, 171–2, 179.
[4] *Ibid.* pp. 179–80; Ẓahīr al-Dīn Nīshāpūrī, *Saljūq-nāma*, p. 52; Juvainī, *Ta'rīkh-i Jahān-Gushā*, vol. 1, p. 289.
[5] Ibn al-Athīr, vol. XI, pp. 185–6, 192–3, 206; Jūzjānī, *Ṭabaqāt-i Nāṣirī*, vol. 1, p. 273 (tr., vol. 1, pp. 180–1); Kafesoğlu, *Harezmşahlar devleti tarihi*, p. 77.

of Gharchistān, were in the hands of Ghuzz amīrs or former ghulām commanders of Sanjar's army, who made the khuṭba first for the dead Sanjar and then for themselves.[1] The amīr of Herāt, Ai-Tegin, died in 559/1164, and rather than face an occupation by the Ghuzz, the local people handed the city over to Ai-Aba. The latter also sent expeditions against the Ghuzz in Marv and Sarakhs, but his attempt to occupy Nasā was forestalled by the appearance of a Khwārazmian army. Il-Arslan's troops threatened Nīshāpūr for a while, but then turned westwards and drove the shāh's erstwhile protégé Ai-Taq from Dihistān (560/1165). Ibn Funduq mentions the presence of Khwārazmian troops at Baihaq and Nīshāpūr in 561–2/1166–7, but the time for the shāhs' full-scale intervention in Khurāsān was not yet come, for they still had many problems to face north of the Oxus.[2]

Both the Khwārazm-Shāhs and the Qarakhānids remained vassals of the Qara-Khitai, though the latter were little disposed to interfere in the internal administration of Khwārazm or of Bukhārā and Samarqand, provided that order was kept and the required taxation forwarded to the Gür-Khān's *ordu* (military camp) in Semirechye. Unfortunately for the Qarakhānids, many elements within their territories made for disorder, and the ensuing troubles brought about interference in Transoxiana from both the Khwārazm-Shāhs and the Qara-Khitai. The endeavours of the khans to consolidate their authority had often in the past caused clashes with the military classes, whose interests lay in a weak central power. Disputes with the Qarluq tribal divisions culminated in the murder of Tamghach-Khān Ibrāhīm III of Samarqand in 551/1156. His successor Chaghrï Khān, or Kök-Saghïr 'Alī Khān, sought revenge by slaying the leader of the Qarluq and driving out others of their chiefs to Khwārazm. According to the account in Ibn al-Athīr, Chaghrï Khān tried to carry out the orders of his suzerain the Gür-Khān by disarming the Qarluq and planting them in Kashgharia as agriculturists—and this, not surprisingly, provoked a Qarluq revolt.

Whatever the exact sequence of events, the result was an invasion of Transoxiana by Il-Arslan on behalf of the Qarluq (553/1158). Chaghrï Khān appealed to the Qïpchaq of the lower Syr Darya and to the Qara-Khitai, but the Qara-Khitai army was reluctant to face a battle with the

[1] Ibn al-Athīr, vol. XI, pp. 192–3, 205–6; Barthold, "A History of the Turkman People", pp. 122–3; Kafesoğlu, *Harezmşahlar devleti tarihi*, pp. 76–7.

[2] Ibn Funduq, *Ta'rīkh-i Baihaq*, p. 2841; Ibn al-Athīr, vol. XI, p. 208; Kafesoğlu, *op. cit.* pp. 77–8.

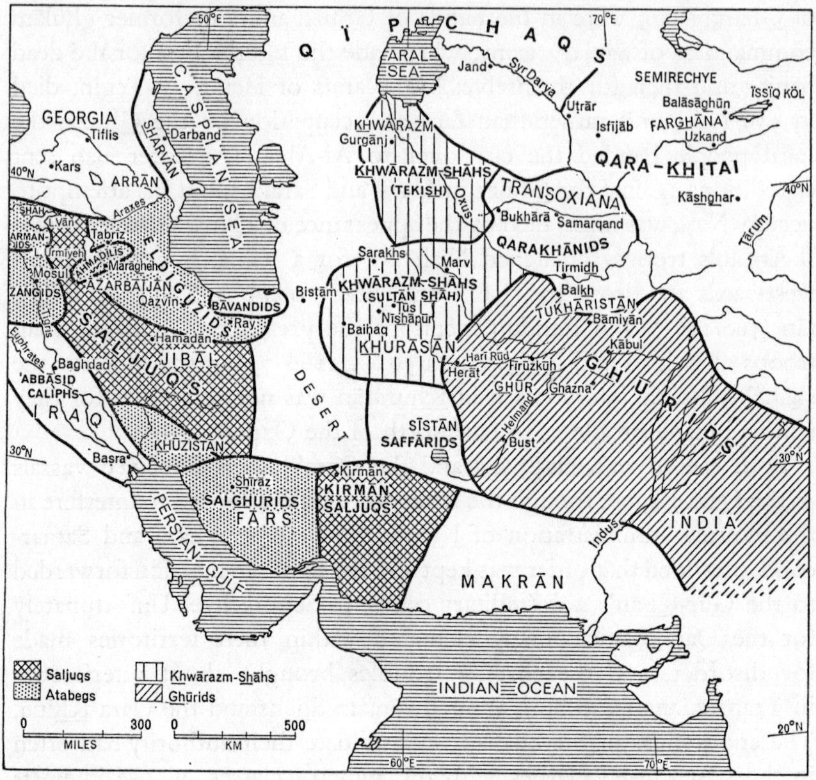

Map 4. The Iranian world, *c.* 575/1180.

Khwārazmian troops, and a peace was arranged whereby Chaghrï Khān had to take back the Qarluq chiefs with full honours.[1] There was a further revolt of the Qarluq in the reign of Chaghrï Khān's brother and successor Qïlïch Tamghach-Khān Mas'ūd II (556–74/1160–78), but this was suppressed, and the khan was then free to send an expedition across the Oxus and carry on warfare against the Ghuzz of Khurāsān.[2]

The Khwārazm-Shāh Il-Arslan died in 567/1172, after fighting off an invasion of the Qara-Khitai provoked by tardy payment of tribute to the Gür-Khān.[3] He was eventually succeeded by his eldest son 'Alā'

[1] Ibn al-Athīr, vol. XI, p. 205; Juvainī, *Ta'rīkh-i Jahān-Gushā*, vol. I, pp. 288–9; Barthold, *Turkestan down to the Mongol Invasion*, pp. 333–4; Pritsak, "Karahanïlar", *İslam Ansiklopedisi*; Kafesoğlu, *op. cit.* pp. 80–2.

[2] Muḥammad b. 'Alī al-Ẓahīrī al-Kātib al-Samarqandī, *A'rāḍ al-riyāsa fī aghrāḍ al-siyāsa*, quoted in Barthold, *Turkestan*, p. 336; Pritsak, *op. cit.*

[3] Ibn al-Athīr, vol. XI, p. 246; Juvainī, vol. I, p. 289; Barthold, *op. cit.* pp. 336–7; Kafesoğlu, *op. cit.* pp. 82–3.

al-Dīn Tekish, in whose long and important reign (567–96/1172–1200) Ghūrid ambitions in Khurāsān were combatted and Khwārazmian arms carried into western Iran against the last Saljuq sultan. At the moment of Il-Arslan's death Tekish was governor of Jand, a strategic outpost against the Qïpchaq, but distant from the centre of power in Khwārazm. Hence the Queen-Mother Terken Khatun placed Tekish's younger brother Sulṭān-Shāh on the throne. Tekish appealed to the Qara-Khitai, and an army under the first Gür-Khān's son-in-law Fuma (chinese *fu-ma* = son-in-law of the emperor) placed him on the throne before the end of 567/1172 without bloodshed. Sulṭān-Shāh in his turn sought help from Ai-Aba of Nīshāpūr; Ai-Aba led an expedition into Khwārazm, but it ended in disaster for him, as he was captured by Tekish and killed. Sulṭān-Shāh fled successively to Dihistān, to Nīshāpūr, and finally to Ghiyāth al-Dīn's court at Fīrūzkūh in Ghūr.[1]

Tekish owed his throne to the Qara-Khitai, yet he looked for an early opportunity to throw off their authority. The sources stress that whereas the first Qara-Khitai in Transoxiana had behaved with exemplary impartiality and equity, their tax collectors became increasingly arrogant and oppressive. Moreover the central power of the Qara-Khitai dynasty, never very cohesive, was weakened by the long periods of regency exercised by women, and this may well have caused a relaxation of control over subordinate officials.[2] It was of course convenient for the shahs to raise the banner of jihād against the infidels, and towards the end of Tekish's reign and in that of his son 'Alā' al-Dīn Muḥammad, this crusading attitude had some value as a counterbalance to the shāhs' unpopularity in orthodox circles, which was due to their anti-caliphal policy (see above, p. 184).

Tekish's pretext for revolt came from the alleged extortions of the Qara-Khitai tribute collector. Sulṭān-Shāh, who was to be a thorn in his brother's flesh for a number of years, judged it a suitable moment to get Qara-Khitai help in regaining the throne which he had briefly occupied in Khwārazm. The Qara-Khitai army under Fuma was halted in Khwārazm by the traditional manoeuvre of opening the dykes, but Sulṭān-Shāh, aided by a detachment of Qara-Khitai troops, was more successful in Khurāsān. He drove the Ghuzz Malik Dīnār out of Sarakhs and defeated Ai-Aba's son and successor Toghan-Shāh, so

[1] Ibn al-Athīr, vol. XI, pp. 247 ff.; Juvainī, vol. I, pp. 289–91; Barthold, *op. cit.* pp. 337–8; Kafesoğlu, *op. cit.* pp. 84–6.

[2] Cf. Juvainī, vol. I, pp. 75, 292, 342, 358; Barthold, "History of the Semirechyé", pp. 104–5.

that Nīshāpūr and Ṭūs both fell into his hands (576/1181).[1] It seems also that Sulṭān-Shāh harried the fringes of Ghūrid territory in Bādghīs, and during the following years he held several towns in Khurāsān, acting as a third force between Tekish and Ghiyāth al-Dīn Muḥammad. He occasionally lent his support to the Ghūrids, but in general he pursued an independent policy.[2]

Tekish's immediate interests lay in preserving a balance of power in central Khurāsān between Sulṭān-Shāh and Toghan-Shāh, and in turning his brother against the Ghūrids in Marv and other cities. The unwarlike Toghan-Shāh found his position in Nīshāpūr increasingly untenable; he failed to get adequate help from Tekish or from the Ghūrids, despite his marriage with one of Ghiyāth al-Dīn's daughters, and many of his amīrs drifted to the side of Sulṭān-Shāh.[3] In 581/1185 or the next year he died, leaving a son, Sanjar-Shāh, as his successor, but real power was now held by Sanjar-Shāh's atabeg, Mengli Beg or Mengli-Tegin. On hearing about the disorders in Khurāsān, Tekish came southwards in 582/1186, avoided Sulṭān-Shāh, now ruling in Marv, and besieged Sanjar-Shāh and Mengli Beg in Shādyākh, the suburb of Nīshāpūr to which the city had been moved after the Ghuzz devastations.[4] After a second siege in 583/1187, Tekish captured Shādyākh and executed Mengli Beg. Sanjar-Shāh was carried off to Khwārazm and later blinded for continuing to intrigue with the people of Nīshāpūr. This city was now placed under Tekish's son Malik-Shāh, the former governor of Jand; and though Sulṭān-Shāh still coveted Nīshāpūr, he was forced to make peace with his brother in 585/1189 when Tekish came once more to Khurāsān. Sulṭān-Shāh was, moreover, hard-pressed by the Ghūrids; in that same year Ghiyāth al-Dīn came from Fīrūzkūh and by 586/1190 had defeated him and stripped him of many of his possessions. But from his centre of Sarakhs, Sulṭān-Shāh once again came to blows with his brother, for while Tekish was absent in western Iran during 588/1192 he prepared to attack Khwārazm (see p. 181 above). Tekish had to hurry back, but

[1] Malik Dīnār later passed into Kirmān and extinguished the local Saljuq line there: see above, section XII, pp. 174–5.

[2] Ibn al-Athīr, vol. XI, pp. 247 ff.; Jūzjānī, vol. I, pp. 302–3 (tr., vol. I, pp. 245–8); Juvainī, vol. I, pp. 292–3; Barthold, *Turkestan*, p. 339; Kafesoğlu, *Harezmşahlar devleti tarihi*, pp. 88–91. 98–101.

[3] Jūzjānī, vol. I, p. 274 (tr., vol. I, p. 182).

[4] Cf. Ibn al-Athīr, vol. XI, pp. 180–1; and for the general history of Shādyākh, see the copious materials collected by Sa'īd Nafīsī in the notes to his edition of Baihaqī's *Ta'rīkh-i Mas'ūdī*, vol. II, pp. 897–914.

the death of Sulṭān-Shāh in the following year relieved him of danger from this quarter.[1]

Tekish was also concerned with the northern frontiers of his empire. Along the frontiers of Khwārazm and the lower Syr Darya, where Jand was held by the shāhs, there lived a number of Türkmen, and even though many of them were still pagan, the Khwārazm-Shāhs had to achieve some sort of *modus vivendi* with them. As part of this policy marriage links were cultivated, and the famous Terken Khatun, wife of Tekish and mother of 'Alā' al-Dīn Muḥammad, is variously described in the sources as being from the Qanghlï or the Baya'ut tribe of the Yemek, being the daughter of the Qïpchaq Khān.[2] Tekish admitted large numbers of the Qïpchaq and their associated peoples into his armies, and it was in large measure these barbarians who gave the Khwārazmian troops in Iran a reputation for excessive violence and cruelty. According to Sulṭān Jalāl al-Dīn's biographer Muḥammad Nasawī, the majority of 'Alā' al-Dīn Muḥammad's top commanders were from Terken Khatun's tribe (which he names as the Yemek), and the need to attach them to his side was one reason why the shah leant so heavily on his mother for advice.[3]

But diplomacy did not always work, and punitive expeditions into the steppes were also necessary. In the winter of 591/1194–5 Tekish led an expedition to Sïghnaq and Jand against the Qïpchaq chief Qayïr Buqu Khān; and though he was defeated after some of the Qïpchaq troops in the Khwārazmian army defected to the enemy, Tekish was nevertheless able to utilize a dispute between the khan and his nephew Alp-Direk, first to capture the khan and then to release him against the refractory nephew.[4]

With regard to Khwārazmian policy in Transoxiana, there is a mention in some of the shāhs' official correspondence of an expedition to Bukhārā in 578/1182, when the local *ṣudūr* surrendered to Tekish.[5] Alone of the historians, Ibn al-Athīr records a further expedition in

[1] Ibn al-Athīr, vol. XI, p. 249, vol. XII, pp. 38, 67; Jūzjānī, vol. I, pp. 274, 303–4 (tr., vol. I, pp. 181–2, 248–9); Juvainī, vol. I, pp. 293–301; Barthold, *op. cit.* pp. 340, 342, 346; Kafesoğlu, *op. cit.* pp. 103–6, 113–22.

[2] Nasawī, *Sīrat Jalāl al-Dīn*, pp. 25, 42 (tr., pp. 44, 72); Jūzjānī, vol. I, pp. 300, 306 (tr., vol. I, pp. 240, 254); Juvainī, vol. II, 465; cf. Kafesoğlu, *op. cit.* pp. 130–1.

[3] Nasawī, pp. 28, 42, cf. pp. 56–7, 162–3 (tr., pp. 50, 72, cf. pp. 96, 286–8).

[4] Juvainī, vol. I, pp. 304–5, 309–11; Barthold, *op. cit.* pp. 340, 342–4; Kafesoğlu, *op. cit.* pp. 128–30.

[5] Bahā' al-Dīn Muḥammad al-Baghdādī, *al-Tawassul ila'l-Tarassul*, in Barthold, *Turkestan*, pp. 341–2; Kafesoğlu, *op. cit.* pp. 95–8.

594/1198. In his struggle with the Ghūrids, it is said, Tekish had sought help from the Qara-Khitai, and the latter had crossed into Tukhāristān hoping to recover from the Ghūrids of Bāmiyān the town of Balkh, formerly tributary to the Gür-Khān. The Qara-Khitai were soundly beaten, and they now blamed Tekish for involving them with the Ghūrids (see pp. 164–5 above). After rapidly making peace with the Ghūrid Sulṭān Ghiyāth al-Dīn, Tekish turned on the Qara-Khitai. He repelled an invasion of Khwārazm and pursued the enemy to Bukhārā, whose population rallied to the Qara-Khitai and held out against the shāh until the city was at last stormed. From the silence of Juvainī and the other sources, Barthold has doubted the historicity of this last campaign in Transoxiana.[1]

Tekish died in 596/1200 and was succeeded by his second son Quṭb al-Dīn Muḥammad, who now assumed the honorific *'Alā' al-Dīn* ("Eminence of Religion"). Muḥammad's nephew Hindū-Khān b. Malik-Shāh had pretensions to the throne, and his cause was espoused by the Ghūrids, who seized several towns of Khurāsān from the new Khwārazm-Shāh and set up Hindū-Khān at Marv.[2] Ghūrid rule in Khurāsān was unpopular, and Muḥammad soon restored the position there. On his return from India in 601/1204, Mu'izz al-Dīn Ghūrī took the offensive and invaded Khurāsān, but he was defeated by the Khwārazm-Shāh and his Qara-Khitai allies (pp. 165 above). After Mu'izzal-Dīn's death in 602/1206, the threat from the Ghūrids' imperial policy receded. Herāt was finally taken in 605/1208–9, and in the same year a rebellion led by Közli (governor of Nīshāpūr) and his son was suppressed.[3] In the Caspian provinces there was a succession struggle after the death of the Bāvandid Ḥusām al-Daula Ardashīr in 602/1205–6, which permitted Muḥammad's brother 'Alī Shāh to step in and make the new Bāvandid ruler a Khwārazmian vassal.[4] As for western Iran, it was neutralized by the rivalries of the caliph, the last Eldigüzids, and other Turkish amīrs (see pp. 182–3 above). Yet despite this secure position, Muḥammad was not yet prepared definitely to defy his Qara-Khitai suzerains. In 602/1206 he restored to them the recaptured town of

[1] Ibn al-Athīr, vol. XII, pp. 88–90; Barhebraeus, p. 347; Barthold, *op. cit.* pp. 344–6; Kafesoğlu, *op. cit.* p. 97 n. 84.

[2] Ibn al-Athīr, vol. XII, pp. 103–4; Jūzjānī, vol. I, pp. 304–5 (tr., vol. I, pp. 251–2); Kafesoğlu, *op. cit.* pp. 148 ff.

[3] Ibn al-Athīr, vol. XII, pp. 172–5; Jūzjānī, vol. I, pp. 307–8 (tr., vol. I, pp. 257–60); Juvainī, vol. I, pp. 333–40; Kafesoğlu, *op. cit.* pp. 167–72.

[4] Ibn Isfandiyār, *Ta'rīkh-i Ṭabaristān*, pp. 256–7; Ibn al-Athīr, vol. XII, pp. 166–7; Kafesoğlu, *op. cit.* pp. 166–7.

Tirmidh, and indeed Jūzjānī alleges that before Tekish died he enjoined his son never to quarrel with the Qara-Khitai.[1]

In Muḥammad's subsequent struggle with the Qara-Khitai, the last Qarakhānid ruler of Samarqand, the "Sultan of Sultans" 'Uthmān Khān b. Ibrāhīm (600–8/1203–4 to 1212), played a prominent role; but the details and chronology are unclear, for our main authority, Juvainī, gives two parallel but widely differing accounts of events. Barthold thought that on the whole the second one accorded best with what is known from other sources, and it is this version which is essentially followed below.[2] Like his father, Muḥammad had to safeguard his northern frontier, and he led a successful campaign against the Qïpchaq (probably to be placed in the summer of 605–6/1209). Elated with this victory, and no longer requiring the Qara-Khitai for his struggle with the Ghūrids, Muḥammad began preparing the ground in Transoxiana. He came to Bukhārā and negotiated with 'Uthmān Khān and with other local magnates who were discontented with the exactions of the Qara-Khitai financial agents.[3] It is dubious, however, whether the Muslim cause in Transoxiana would have made much headway against the still-formidable Qara-Khitai power had it not been for the general revolt of the Gür-Khān's Muslim vassals in eastern Turkestan.[4] On the crest of these disorders the Naiman Mongol chief Küchlüg rose to power in the eastern part of the Qara-Khitai empire after his flight westwards from his rival Chingiz-Khān.[5] In Samarqand, 'Uthmān Khān had been offended by the Gür-Khān's refusal to give him a daughter in marriage and had proclaimed his allegiance to the Khwārazm-Shāh, but this assertion of independence ended in failure for the Qarakhānid, whose capital was occupied by a Qara-Khitai army (probably in 606/1209–10).[6]

However, Küchlüg's successes in Semirechye compelled the Gür-Khān to leave Samarqand. The Khwārazm-Shāh Muḥammad, in alliance once more with 'Uthmān Khān, followed the retreating Qara-

[1] Ibn al-Athīr, vol. XII, pp. 152–3; Jūzjānī, vol. I, p. 302 (tr., vol. I, p. 244); Barthold, *Turkestan*, p. 352; Kafesoğlu, *op. cit.* pp. 164–5.

[2] Juvainī, vol. I, pp. 341–52 (first version), pp. 354–61 (second version); cf. Barthold, *op. cit.* pp. 335 ff., and Kafesoğlu, *op. cit.* pp. 172 ff., for full critiques and discussions. The account in Ibn al-Athīr, vol. XII, pp. 171–9, accords best with the second version.

[3] Ibn al-Athīr, vol. XII, pp. 171–2; Juvainī, vol. I, pp. 342–3; Kafesoğlu, *Harezmşahlar devleti tarihi*, pp. 183–4.

[4] Juvainī, vol. I, p. 359.

[5] Cf. Barthold, "A Short History of Turkestan", pp. 33–5; *idem*, "History of the Semirechyé", pp. 106–9; Grousset, *L'Empire des Steppes*, pp. 269–71, 294–6; Kafesoğlu, *op. cit.* pp. 189–93.

[6] Juvainī, vol. I, pp. 359–60; Kafesoğlu, *op. cit.* pp. 176–7, 182–3.

K̲h̲itai and won a victory near Talas, capturing the Qara-K̲h̲itai general Tayangu. Although the Gür-K̲h̲ān defeated Kü̲c̲h̲lüg, his army mutinied and Kü̲c̲h̲lüg successfully put himself at the head of the rebels. A Mongol detachment under Qubilai Noyan, one of C̲h̲ingiz-K̲h̲ān's generals, had appeared in northern Semirechye, and the Gür-K̲h̲ān was obliged to surrender to Kü̲c̲h̲lüg and abdicate all real power; he died shortly afterwards.[1] The substitution of Muslim K̲h̲wārazmian rule for that of the pagan Qara-K̲h̲itai in Transoxiana proved unwelcome both to the local rulers there and to the population at large. The Qarak̲h̲ānid ruler of Uṭrār, Tāj al-Dīn Bilge-K̲h̲ān, rebelled against the K̲h̲wārazm-S̲h̲āh, and 'Ut̲h̲mān K̲h̲ān decided, despite his marriage to Muḥammad's daughter, to renew his connexion with the Qara-K̲h̲itai.[2] After a general massacre in Samarqand of the hated K̲h̲wārazmians, the s̲h̲āh came and took a terrible vengeance: the city was ruthlessly sacked, and 'Ut̲h̲mān K̲h̲ān and other members of his dynasty executed (608/1212). In the general slaughter of the Qarak̲h̲ānids, only Tāj al-Dīn Bilge-K̲h̲ān of Uṭrār seems to have survived for some years more.[3]

Extinguishing the remnants of the western Qarak̲h̲ānids was not difficult for Muḥammad, but he was much less successful against Kü̲c̲h̲lüg, who had taken over the former Qara-K̲h̲itai territories. Even after his Talas victory the K̲h̲wārazm-S̲h̲āh was unable to bring relief to the Muslim inhabitants of Balāsāg̲h̲ūn, a town that had then been sacked by the Gür-K̲h̲ān's army;[4] and he was equally impotent to protect the Muslim population of Kas̲h̲g̲h̲aria against Kü̲c̲h̲lüg's fiercely anti-Muslim policy there. Nor could he even guard the people of northern Transoxiana: according to Muslim sources, he had to evacuate the inhabitants of Farg̲h̲āna, C̲h̲āc̲h̲, and Isfījāb and devastate these provinces, thereby rendering them useless to Kü̲c̲h̲lüg; on the other hand, a Chinese traveller who passed through the Syr Darya valley a few years later does not mention any signs of ruin there.[5]

---

[1] Nasawī, pp. 7–8 (tr., pp. 12–14); Ibn al-At̲h̲īr, vol. XII, pp. 176–7; Jūzjānī, vol. I, pp. 309–10 (tr., vol. I, pp. 261–2); Juvainī, vol. I, pp. 360–1; Barthold, *Turkestan*, pp. 358–9, 363–4; Kafesoğlu, *op. cit.* pp. 183–5, 192–3.

[2] Nasawī, p. 22 (tr., pp. 38–9—with *ibn 'amm*, "cousin", mistranslated as "nephew"), says that Tāj al-Dīn Bilge-K̲h̲an was 'Ut̲h̲mān K̲h̲ān's cousin.

[3] *Ibid.* pp. 22–3 (tr., pp. 38–41); Ibn al-At̲h̲īr, vol. XII, pp. 177–8; Juvainī, vol. I, pp. 347–9; Barthold, *op. cit.* pp. 364–6; Pritsak, "Karahanlílar", *Islâm Ansiklopedisi*; Kafesoğlu, *op. cit.* pp. 187–9.

[4] Juvainī, vol. I, p. 360; Barthold, *op. cit.* pp. 358–9; Kafesoğlu, *op. cit.* pp. 185–6.

[5] Ibn al-At̲h̲īr, vol. XII, p. 179; E. Bretschneider, *Mediaeval Researches from Eastern Asiatic Sources* (London, 1910), vol. I, pp. 75 ff.; cf. Barthold, "A Short History of Turkestan", p. 35.

Although Küchlüg's transient empire would eventually crumble before the advance of Chingiz-Khān, the removal of Küchlüg only postponed the day of reckoning for the Khwārazm-Shāh.

XIV. THE PERIOD IN RETROSPECT

Between A.D. 1000 and 1200 the Islamic cult and faith became completely accepted in the Iranian world: herein lies the social and religious significance of these two centuries. The process of conversion actually went on till the early 5th/11th century, by which time the only substantial remaining pockets of paganism were on the far eastern fringes, in what is now Afghanistan; the remote region of Ghūr was probably the last to accept the new faith (see p. 157 above). On the whole, the Iranian peoples accepted Islam speedily and peacefully; this was especially true of the landowning classes, anxious to preserve their social and tenurial privileges under the new Arab régime. Nevertheless, the period up to the 4th/10th century was punctuated by several socio-religious protest movements, in some of which elements of the older faiths of Iran, such as Mazdakism and Zoroastrianism, rose to the surface; and on one occasion the political and military leader Dailamī Mardāvīj b. Ziyār (d. 323/935) ostentatiously paraded his hostility to Islam. After the year 1000 such anti-Islamic currents die away. It was not that feelings of social protest and resentment against the ruling and official classes disappeared altogether, but rather that they were channelled into such activities as *'iyāra* (brigandage and mob violence) and into such movements as Ismā'īlīsm and radical Shī'ism. Only in the Ṣafavid period did Shī'ism become the dominant faith in Persia proper (the Iranian parts of Central Asia and Afghanistan were only marginally affected by this process); but in the pre-Mongol period we hear of lively Shī'ī activity in several towns of Persia, and it is probable that the bases of later dominance were quietly being consolidated amongst the 'Alid communities of these places.

Of significance to the whole of the Middle East, and not merely to the Iranian world, were the ethnic, political, and military changes caused by the incoming movements of Turkish peoples from beyond the Oxus and Syr Darya. Turks had long been familiar enough in the Iranian world as peaceful settlers on the north-eastern frontiers, as nomadic predators on the agricultural lands there, and as mercenary soldiers in the armies of the Baghdad caliphs and their provincial epigoni, but it was only in the Saljuq period that this trickle of individuals became a flood. However, the Turks' westward movement was not confined to the period of the Saljuq invasions in the middle 5th/11th century—the number of incomers at this time was not unduly large; rather, it continued steadily up to and after the Mongol invasions. Some tribes of southern Iran, such as the Bahārlū, the Aināllū, and the Qashghai traditionally date their migration thither to post-Mongol times. In the Saljuq period there were always many outlets for Türkmen energies in the frontier warfare with the Byzantines and the Christian powers of the Caucasus, as well as in the complex warfare between Arab amīrates and the Crusaders in Syria and Palestine, and many Türkmen passed through Iran to these western battlefields. Others, however, found suitable pasture grounds for their flocks within Iran, especially in such favourable regions as Āzarbāījān, the Caspian coastlands of Mūghān, Gurgān and Dihistān, and in the oases of Khurāsān. Hence there begins the process of settlement that has made Āzarbāījān, parts of Kurdistān, including the Hamadān region, and a large section of Fārs, Turkish-speaking.[1]

The migrating peoples were originally the rank and file of Turkish tribal and military aristocracies, and in our period these leaders imposed their political authority over the Iranian world at large. This trend towards Turkish political domination began when the Iranian Samanids and the Afrīghid and Ma'mūnid Khwārazm-Shāhs were replaced by the Ghaznavids and Qarakhānids. The Ghaznavids were of servile origin, but their steppe beginnings were speedily overlaid by the Iranian culture and the Iranian administrative techniques which they adopted. The Qarakhānids initially represented a still lower level of assimilation into the Iranian–Islamic culture. In 5th/11th- and 6th/12th-century Transoxiana the trend towards this assimilation was always offset by the fresh arrivals of Turkish peoples from the outer steppes. The Saljuqs and the Oghuz approximated at first to the social and cultural level of the earliest Qarakhānids—if, indeed, they were not at a lower one. Yet, like the Ghaznavids, the Saljuq leaders soon discovered practical advantages in the Iranian–Islamic tradition of statecraft and government: its exaltation of the sovereign above his people; its ideal of state centralization, and of a professional, standing army to buttress the ruler's power; and its concepts of passivity and obedience with which the subject masses were inculcated. Aided by Iranian advisers such as Kundurī and Niẓām al-Mulk, the Saljuqs Toghrïl, Alp-Arslan, and

[1] Cf. Lambton, *Landlord and Peasant in Persia*, p. 77 n. 1.

Malik-Shāh passed from the position of mere tribal chiefs, with only circumscribed authority, to that of "Most Exalted Sultans" (*Salāṭīn-i A'ẓam*) with the full panoply of a hierarchical court, an Iranian-staffed bureaucracy, and a multi-national, partly slave army to execute their plans.

It is not surprising that tension arose between the sultans in their newly acquired splendour and aloofness, and the Türkmen rank and file. In the early stages of the Saljuq invasions these Türkmen had been the Saljuq family's ladder to power, but in the later years of the 5th/11th century the new professional and slave army was making them militarily less vital. Concentrated as they tended to be in the remoter parts of Āzarbāījān or Khurāsān, Gurgān or Fārs, the Türkmen—who in any case were never a very articulate group—could be heard only with difficulty in the sophisticated, Iranian atmosphere of the sultans' court in Iṣfahān, Hamadān, or Baghdad. It soon became apparent to the Türkmen that there had grown up a gulf between themselves and the sultans, and that the latter were quite prepared to use Arab or Kurdish or any other troops against their fellow Turks. Hence they tended to rally round those members of the Saljuq family who were discontented or who had been passed over for the succession despite their valid claims of seniority within the family; such aspirants as Ibrāhīm Īnal, Qutlumush b. Arslan Isrā'īl, and Qavurt were accordingly able to use Türkmen resentment against the sultans to support their own pretensions. A clear-sighted statesman like Niẓām al-Mulk recognized the Türkmen's legitimate claims to gratitude and advocated attention to their needs; but after his death such counsels were heard less often. It was the blundering and officious handling of the Türkmen by Sanjar's officials and commanders that led to the outburst of Ghuzz violence in Khurāsān at the end of his reign, resulting in the capture and detention of the sultan himself, the nomads' overrunning the main towns of Khurāsān, the end of direct Saljuq power in north-eastern Iran, and the eventual destruction of the Saljuq principality of Kirmān (see above, pp. 152 ff.).

During the second half of the 6th/12th century the trend towards a uniform Turkish domination of the Iranian world was temporarily halted in the east by the Ghūrid dynasty in Afghanistan, whose rulers, originally mountain chieftains in Ghūr, had become sovereigns of an empire that stretched from Bisṭām in the west to the Ganges valley in the east. This achievement was only transient, for it was destroyed by the dynamism of the Khwārazm-Shāh 'Alā' al-Dīn Muḥammad. Yet the shāh's victory was largely Pyrrhic: he overstrained his military resources in fighting the Ghūrids and in mounting a campaign in western Iran against the 'Abbāsid caliph (a campaign that brought him much obloquy in orthodox Sunnī circles), and he himself went down before the rising power of the Mongols. In Afghanistan today the Ghūrids have been assigned an important place in the country's history—they are described as the first native Islamic dynasty to make Afghanistan the centre of an empire—and attempts have been made to show that the Ghūrids were Pashto-speaking, and that the earliest Pashto literature sprang from their court circle.[1]

Already by the latter part of Toghrïl's reign the Saljuq sultan depended to a considerable extent on a professional, standing army, which comprised a nucleus of slave commanders and their retainers (ghulāms) drawn from a multiplicity of nationalities: Turks, Armenians, Greeks, Kurds, Caucasians, and even negroes. This nucleus was supplemented by contingents from tributary Arab, Kurdish, and Persian rulers in Iraq, Kurdistān, the Caspian provinces, Sīstān, and so on. The Türkmen tribesmen continued to be of military significance in the 5th/11th century, but the sultans gradually adopted a policy of diverting the Türkmen begs and their followers to the frontiers of the empire, to Anatolia, the Caucasus, Syria, etc., where there were plentiful opportunities for jihād against the Christians or against heterodox Muslim groups such as the Syrian Ismā'īlīs and the Fāṭimids.

Maintaining a standing army was expensive; and since an increase was required in the state's revenue, the degree of centralization and administrative complexity inevitably grew also. Niẓām al-Mulk built up a nexus of relatives and clients within the central government and in the key posts of the provincial administrations, and in this way surveillance over the empire was far-reaching in Malik-Shāh's reign. The basic solution for paying the army was an extended and regularized system of iqṭā's, land grants, whose revenues were used to support the soldiers. Here the Saljuqs were not innovators, for the system had its roots in the Arab caliphate, and had been widely used in the 4th/10th century by such dynasties as the Būyids and Ḥamdānids; but with the political decline of the Būyids and their inability to control their troops,

[1] See examples of allegedly Ghūrid Pashto poetry in M. M. Kaleem's section on Pashto literature in *The Cultural Heritage of Pakistan*, ed. S. M. Ikram and Sir Percival Spear (Karachi, 1955), pp. 145–6, 149; but cf. G. Morgenstierne, "Afghān; iii. Pashto literature", *Encyc. of Islam* (2nd ed.). The earliest authenticated written Pashto literature comes, in fact, from the early 17th century.

their iqṭāʿ system in western Iran became disordered and riddled with abuses. In the 5th/11th century the Saljuq central government regularized the position of the iqṭāʿ-holders (muqṭaʿs). In his *Siyāsat-Nāma* Niẓām al-Mulk regards the system as firmly established in his time, and he is mainly concerned to prevent the muqṭaʿ from becoming over-powerful, i.e. oppressing the peasantry and denying the sultan his ultimate rights over the land. Nevertheless, the power of the muqṭaʿs over the estates grew steadily, especially in the 6th/12th century when control from the centre weakened. Many estates originally granted as iqṭāʿs (and therefore revocable, at least in theory) must at this time have passed into legally private ownership (*milk*).

What was in effect a large-scale application of the iqṭāʿ system was the Saljuq sultans' practice of granting provinces or regions as appanages for other members of the family. This arose originally from Turkish tribal practice, where a tribal chief's patrimony was often divided amongst his male relatives while the most senior relative remained overlord. Given the size of the Saljuq empire in the second half of the 5th/11th century, such a measure of administrative devolution was sensible enough; it was only in the next century, when the empire was losing its cohesion, that the Saljuq maliks in the provinces successfully used their appanages to defy the central power and further their own ambitions.[1]

The degree of unity achieved in the Saljuq empire under Alp-Arslan and Malik-Shāh could not be maintained by their successors. Yet the power of the dynasty, at least in the first half of the following century, was far from ineffective. Undoubtedly as capable an administrator and as vigorous a campaigner as his father Malik-Shāh had been, Sanjar ruled directly over Khurāsān and the east, and after his brother Muḥammad's death in 511/1118 he exercised ultimate sovereignty over his relatives the Saljuq sultans in western Iran and Iraq. Some western sultans, e.g. Maḥmūd and Masʿūd b. Muḥammad, Muḥammad b. Maḥmūd, and the last of the line, Toghrïl b. Arslan, were vigorous and capable rulers, but their freedom of action decreased and their resources became more exiguous as the century progressed.

There are three main reasons why the Saljuqs found their effective power reduced during the 6th/12th century.[2]

[1] Cf. Lambton, *op. cit.* pp. 53 ff.

[2] Cf. H. A. R. Gibb, "An Interpretation of Islamic History", *Cahiers d'Histoire Mondiale*, vol. I (1953), pp. 54 ff. [= *Muslim World*, vol. XLV (1955), pp. 124 ff.].

First, the institution of the atabegate developed and flourished in this century, especially after the death of Muḥammad b. Malik-Shāh. Beginning as genuine tutors attached to the households of young Saljuq princes, Turkish slave commanders often secured an ascendancy over their charges and then set them aside, ruling themselves as provincial governors or in the end as independent potentates. By the second half of the century, Turkish provincial governors were founding dynasties and calling themselves atabegs even when they had never had a Saljuq prince in their charge (e.g. the Salghurids of Fārs: see above, p. 172).

In the succession disputes which now racked the Saljuq empire in the west, the atabegs espoused various Saljuq candidates and gave them military support, hoping thereby to place a weak and pliant ruler on the throne. For their part, the sultans could not easily control these centrifugal tendencies. The rise of such atabeg dynasties as the Zangids in Mosul, the Eldigüzids and Aḥmadīlīs in Āzarbāijān and Arrān, the Salghurids in Fārs, and so on, meant that the territory in the west directly administered by the sultans was shrinking. Yet they still had to maintain armies against rivals to the succession, against overbearing atabegs, and against the increasingly activist policy of the ʿAbbasid caliphs. The territory which they controlled was inadequate for granting iqṭāʿs to their troops, and the troubled social and political conditions of the period cannot have favoured the regular collection of taxation from the population. The sultans were forced willy-nilly into alliances and coalitions with the atabegs and other Turkish military commanders in order to draw upon their troops. Thus the sultans had little space in which to manoeuvre, and by the time of Arslan b. Toghrïl, the creature of the Eldigüzids, it had shrunk to narrow proportions.

Second, the century sees a rise in the material power and prestige of the ʿAbbasid caliph of Baghdad. The end of the "Dailamī interlude" in Iranian history meant the failure of the Shīʿī bid for supreme authority in Iran. The Fāṭimids were repulsed from Iraq and northern Syria by the incoming Saljuqs, and after the death in 487/1094 of al-Mustanṣir, they were no longer a vigorous and expansionist power. Although Ismāʿīlism increased in strength after the Nizārī split from the main Fāṭimid line of al-Mustaʿlī, it was notable more for its terrorism than for its political and territorial achievements; only in Kūhistān, parts of Dailam, and in parts of Fārs did the Ismāʿīlīs control substantial stretches of territory.

The 'Abbāsids, having survived a period of degradation in the 4th/10th century, now had the secular support of the strongly Sunnī Saljuqs. The early Saljuqs allowed the caliphs little more practical political power than had the Būyids. However, they had to defer to the caliphs, who were the moral and spiritual leaders of the Sunnī world, for it was by no means obvious even in Malik-Shāh's time that the Fāṭimids' ability to harm the Saljuqs had passed its peak. Only at the very close of his reign, when the steadying influence of Niẓām al-Mulk had just been removed, did Malik-Shāh seem to harbour thoughts of displacing the 'Abbāsids from Baghdad (see p. 101 above); but the sultan's own death ended this project. After the nonentities and weaklings of the early Būyid period, the 'Abbāsid family was now yielding some capable and effective caliphs: e.g. al-Mustaẓhir, al-Mustarshid, al-Muqtafī, and al-Nāṣir. They in turn were aided by such outstanding vizierial families as the Banū Jahīr in the 5th/11th century and the Banū Hubaira in the next one. When disputes arose over the succession to the sultanate, the caliphs seized the opportunity first to consolidate their hold over Baghdad and central Iraq (after 547/1152 no Saljuq shaḥna was allowed in the capital), and then to intervene directly in the warfare in Iraq and western Persia; such caliphs as al-Mustarshid, al-Rāshid, and al-Muqtafī personally took the field at the head of their forces. The rise in the caliphate's power and prestige reached its peak under al-Nāṣir, who, by his patronage of the Futuwwa, together with a diplomacy that embraced such distant dynasties as the Ghūrids, the Ayyūbids, and the Rūm Saljuqs, made the caliphate for the first time in centuries an international power in the Islamic world.

Thirdly, a final blow to Saljuq power came from the Khwārazm-Shāhs, a new and aggressive power that arose in the north-east of the Iranian world during the 6th/12th century. Their origin was not dissimilar to that of several other provincial lines which sprang from atabegs or local slave governors, but the peripheral position of Khwārazm and its old traditions of independence favoured a long and uninterrupted tenure of power by Anūgh-Tegin Gharcha'i and his descendants. The shāhs became virtually independent after Sanjar's death, subject only to the suzerainty of the Qara-Khitai. Their imperialist ambitions, blocked in the east by the Qara-Khitai, accordingly turned southwards and westwards into Iran. A struggle with the Ghūrids for power in Khurāsān long prevented the shāhs from taking advantage of the fragmented condition of western and central Iran, and it was only in the last years of the 6th/12th century that Tekish vanquished the last Saljuq Sulṭān Toghrïl b. Arslan and moved Khwārazmian troops to the borders of Iraq (see above, pp. 182–3). Al-Nāṣir deployed all his diplomatic weapons against the Khwārazm-Shāh, encouraging the Ghūrids and Qara-Khitai against him and organizing in Iran coalitions of atabegs and local governors threatened by the Khwārazmian advance. (It does not seem, however, that the caliph encouraged the Mongols to attack the Khwārazmians from the rear.)[1] Also, the caliph threw his moral and spiritual weight against the shāhs for their impiety in threatening the caliphate and their pro-Shī'ī activities. Certainly the Khwārazmians made themselves intensely unpopular in Iran, but whether the caliph's could have stayed the Khwārazmian march on Iraq is an unsolved question of history. The distant pressure of the Mongols was already being felt on the borders of Transoxiana and Khwārazm, and within the next fifty years both the caliphs of Baghdad and their opponents the Khwārazm-Shāhs were to go down for ever before the hordes of Chingiz-Khān and Hülegü.

[1] This accusation appears only in late sources; see Barthold, *Turkestan down to the Mongol Invasion*, pp. 399–400.

CHAPTER 2

THE INTERNAL STRUCTURE OF THE SALJUQ EMPIRE

The period of the Great Saljuqs can largely be regarded as representing or corresponding to the early Middle Ages. To make this division is not to underestimate the fundamental fact of the unbroken thread of Persian history in Islamic times. Stretching back behind the Saljuq period is a long continuity of administrative practice, but under the Saljuqs the old institutions gained a new meaning; developments that had begun in the preceding period crystallized, and new elements of worth were added to the Persian heritage. The Saljuqs did not formulate the details of the new system: this was mainly the work of the officials of the bureaucracy and of the religious institution, who were for the most part Persians and not Turks. But the Saljuqs were in some measure responsible for the spirit in which the new system worked.

Many Saljuq institutions lasted in their outward forms (though the terminology was in some cases changed) until the twentieth century; and without a knowledge of these, and an attempt to trace them back to earlier times, we cannot fully comprehend the questions that began to agitate Iran in the nineteenth century and the solutions sought to them. Politically and religiously Iran has travelled far from the theory of a theocracy in which the caliph exercised constituent authority and legitimized the sultan's assumption of power; and economically from the *iqṭāʿ* in its various forms and the guilds and corporations of Saljuq society. But it was not until the twentieth century that the Constitutional Revolution separated modern Iran from medieval Persia.

In many ways the Saljuq period did not differ from the preceding or succeeding periods. It was a time of chronic wars; and hardship, famine, pestilence, violence, ignorance, and superstition were all common. But, on the other hand, it was a time during which Iranian civilization reached heights of religious and secular achievements that have not been easily surpassed. Men such as Ghazālī, Shahristānī, Nasafī, Niẓām al-Mulk, ʿUmar Khayyām, Abū Saʿīd b. Abiʾl Khair, Anvarī, and Muʿizzī all lived in these years. Important technical innovations were made in pottery and metal-work. A high degree of technical skill was achieved by weavers; and new elements of scale and spatial composition were introduced into architecture. The Saljuq state was the organizing force that brought about conditions in which the arts flourished, and the talents of these men and many others burgeoned and thrived. It must not be supposed, however, that uniformity was established throughout the empire at any one time or throughout the period in any one place. There was a great diversity of climatic and physical conditions within the empire; and in spite of the unifying factor of Islam and the general levelling tendency of Turkish military government, there was much local particularism and variety in the social ethics of different groups and communities. There was, for example, a standing opposition between the settled and the semi-settled population; between Turk and non-Turk; and between the military and the rest of the population. There was also a dichotomy between the men of the cities, with their highly developed crafts and industries and traditions of civilization, and the population living on the land, whose main function was to provision the cities and above all to provide for the needs of the army.

The sources, unfortunately, do not tell us much about the daily life of the people, or how this was affected by the influx of large numbers of Türkmen nomads. Presumably the produce from the nomads' flocks made an important contribution to the supplies of the towns; and there was a constant infiltration of nomads into the towns and villages. The sources are also silent on the details of the sultan's administration. It is also difficult to interpret such information as they give, owing to a frequent lack of precision in the use of technical terms. Nor is it possible to obtain a clear picture of the characters of the sultans and their officials. The achievements of the period have been attributed by many writers to the viziers, in particular to Niẓām al-Mulk (d. 485/1192), the vizier first of Alp-Arslan and then of Malik-Shāh. A close examination of the sources would suggest that this view is too general. There can be little doubt of the competence of Toghrïl Beg and Alp-Arslan as leaders of men; Malik-Shāh was not a mere figure-head; and Muḥammad b. Malik-Shāh seems also to have had a more than ordinary degree of competence. The sources attribute justice and good government to Malik-Shāh and Sanjar, as they do to Niẓām al-Mulk; while many of the later sultans are charged with dissipation and negligence in state affairs. In general the sultans were men of action and men of affairs. Their lives were largely spent travelling about their empire on expeditions of one sort or another. Their main recreation was probably the chase; the breeding of horses and falcons was widely maintained. Their personal attainments in the arts may not have been high, but under their rule and patronage great development took place. The relatively stable and effective administration established under their leadership enabled the various classes to carry on their lives and occupations in comparative security. Men of learning and of religion, including the Ṣūfīs, were held in high respect; and the local people were left to practice their local customs. This is not to say that injustice and oppression did not occur, but on the whole it did not reach lengths which the population felt to be intolerable. There was unusually little internal rebellion (as distinct from struggles for power among rival amīrs), though the spread of the Ismā'īlī movement suggests that a strong undercurrent of social discontent existed.

In spite of the fragmentation of the *dār al-Islām*, the function of the state was still to defend the Muslim community and Muslim lands; and its purpose was to create conditions in which the Muslim could live the good life. The traditional view that stability was assured by the maintenance of right religion and justice was broadly accepted. Ibn al-Balkhī, who wrote during the reign of Muḥammad b. Malik-Shāh, is expressing this view when he states, "Those possessed of learning have said, 'When a king is adorned by religion and his rule is stable because of justice, kingship will not disappear from his house unless, God forbid, some disorder appears in religion or he commits tyranny'."[1] There was no separation between church and state; men were not conscious of belonging to two communities. Rather, *dīn* (religion) and *daulat* (state) were two sides of one coin. Non-conformity and political opposition were thus inseparable. Patriotism was an unknown virtue. All the sultan expected of his subjects was that they should pay their taxes and pray for his welfare, while they expected from him security and justice. The state did not demand, or receive, the loyalty of the common man. Loyalty, so far as it transcended the bounds of the tribe, guild, quarter, or city, was accorded not to the state but to Islam or the *sharī'a*. So long as the sultan represented the sharī'a he commanded, in some measure, the loyalty of the people, but as soon as he ceased to represent the sharī'a they too ceased to feel any loyalty towards him.

By the time of the rise of the Saljuqs, the classical theory of the

[1] *Fārs-Nāma*, ed. G. Le Strange and R. A. Nicholson (Gibb Memorial Series, London, 1921), new series, vol. 1, p. 34.

caliphate no longer corresponded—if it ever had—with practice. The caliphate had become merely a symbolic office maintaining links with the past; and the conception of the sultanate as a simple delegation of authority by the caliph to the temporal ruler could hardly be maintained in the political circumstances which prevailed. For some governors had seized their provinces by force, while others, though they were not rebels, were not subject to the appointment of the caliph: an irregular situation, which threatened the life of the community. The latter was supposed to exist in order to carry out the precepts of the shari'a; and unless the shari'a was its basis, there was no reason for its existence. It was thus imperative that the situation should be regularized; and Māwardī (d. 450/1058), writing during the Būyid domination, made an attempt to legalize what was in effect a usurpation of power. He asserted that even if the caliph was placed under restraint ("control over him having been seized by one of his auxiliaries, who arrogates to himself the executive authority"), he could still hold the office of caliph, and such an anomalous situation could stand provided the usurper conformed to the ordinances of the faith and the requirements of justice.[1] Having in mind perhaps such independent rulers as Maḥmūd of Ghazna, Māwardī also put forward the view that "certain concessions might be made to the governors of outlying regions, without prejudice to the rights of the caliph as effective ruler of the central provinces", provided, first, that the governor agreed to preserve the dignity of the caliphate and show such respect for it as would preclude any idea of insubordination; and secondly, that he undertook to govern according to the shari'a. The caliph for his part should validate all religious appointments and decisions hitherto made by the governor, and the two parties would make a pact of friendship and mutual assistance.[2]

By thus keeping those who had usurped power within the framework of the community Māwardī enabled it to survive and prepared the way for the new relationship between the caliphate and sultanate which was to be worked out under the Saljuqs. The early Saljuq sultans insisted on receiving diplomas from the caliphs, partly to place themselves on a level with the Ghaznavids and to legalize their rule, and partly to acquire prestige by adopting the role of the defenders of orthodox Islam. The sultans after Malik-Shāh also endeavoured to obtain the

[1] See H. A. R. Gibb, "al-Māwardī's Theory of the Caliphate", in *Studies on the Civilisation of Islam*, ed. Stanford J. Shaw and William R. Polk (London, 1962), pp. 159–60.
[2] *Ibid.* p. 163.

caliph's recognition, largely in order to strengthen themselves against rivals. The early period saw not merely the reimposition of Sunnism after a time of Shīʿī supremacy, but a reaffirmation of the caliph's position as head of the Islamic community, together with the incorporation of the sultanate as a necessary element into the ideal of Islamic government. From this stemmed a new system of administration composed of a series of interconnected jurisdictions whose stability depended, not on a separation of the civil arm from the military, but on orthodoxy or "right religion" and the personal loyalty of sultan to caliph and of subordinate officials to the sultan. The man who formulated this new relationship between the caliphate and the sultanate was Ghazālī (d. 505/1111). He envisaged a new association between the caliph and the sultan and assumed co-operation between them. On the one hand the caliph was to be designated by the sultan, who, through his exercise of constituent authority, recognized the institutional authority of the caliph; and on the other hand the validity of the sultan's government was established by his oath of allegiance to that caliph who authorized his rule. In this way the sultan recognized that the sharīʿa was the organizing principle of the Sunnī community, while the caliph acknowledged that the sultanate, by establishing order and maintaining discipline, provided conditions in which Islamic institutions could continue and the Muslim fulfil his true destiny.[1]

Because the power of the Saljuqs rested upon the sharīʿa, it differed from the power of the Būyids, which had been usurped.[2] This was of more than theoretical importance. The Saljuqs made possible the preservation of the religious life of the community, and religion for the Muslim embraced virtually all aspects of the life of the community. This is not to say that Ghazālī regarded the Saljuqs' government as a truly Islamic government. His works contain several allusions to the injustice of the Turks. In an undated letter to Abu'l Fatḥ ʿAlī b. Ḥusain Mujīr al-Dīn (Sanjar's first vizier, who was succeeded in 488/1095 by Fakhr al-Mulk b. Niẓām al-Mulk), Ghazālī stated that he had left Ṭūs so that he need not witness the actions of merciless tyrants.[3]

[1] For a discussion of Ghazālī's theory see L. Binder, "Al-Ghazali's Theory of Islamic Government", in *The Muslim World* (1955), pp. 229–41.

[2] The new relationship between the caliph and the sultan is reflected in the *laqabs* given to the Saljuq sultans, which contained the word *dīn* (religion) in contradistinction to those of the Būyids, which contained the word *daula* (state). Toghrïl Beg was given the *laqab* Rukn al-Dīn and Jalāl al-Daula. Alp-Arslan was an exception to the general rule: his *laqab* was ʿAḍud al-Daula.

[3] *Faḍā'il al-anām*, ed. ʿAbbās Iqbāl (Tehran, 1333/1964), p. 54.

In Dhu'l Qa'da in 488/1095 he abandoned all the occupations in which he had been engaged, including the office of *mudarris* (head) of the Niẓāmiyya in Baghdad, and a year later he vowed never to take money from a sultan, to attend the audience of a sultan, or to engage in legal disputations (*munāẓara*) in public.[1] In 499/1106, however, he resumed teaching in the Niẓāmiyya in Nīshāpūr on the orders of Sanjar.

In the *Naṣīḥat al-mulūk*, addressed to Sanjar, Ghazālī puts forward his conception of the sultanate as distinct from the caliphate. Describing the sultan as the Shadow of God upon Earth, he maintains that the divine light has been given to him. This, at first sight, seems incompatible with his theory of the caliphate. In the *Naṣīḥat al-mulūk*, however, Ghazālī was not concerned with the relationship between the caliphate and the sultanate. What he had in mind here was not the preservation of the religious life of the community, which he had discussed elsewhere, but the maintenance of the power of the sultanate, which, if that life was to be preserved, was necessary for the establishment of order. Nor was he concerned to argue the shar'ī basis of the sultanate (this he had already established elsewhere), but rather to ensure that the power of the sultanate should be used with justice. "Know", he writes, "that God has singled out two groups of men and given them preference over others: first prophets, upon them be peace, and secondly kings. Prophets He sent to His servants to lead them to Him and kings to restrain them from [aggression against] each other; and in His wisdom He handed over to them (kings) the well-being of the lives of His servants and He gave them (kings) a high status."[2] Obedience to and love for kings was therefore incumbent upon men, and, conversely, opposition and enmity towards them were unseemly; but only he who acted with justice was the true sultan.[3]

The advice which Ghazālī gives to Sanjar in the *Naṣīḥat al-mulūk* is concerned mainly with ordinary political moral duties based on grounds of political expediency. Ghazālī's exposition of government here is permeated by the Islamic ethic, but it also contains a theory of government that derives from, or is strongly influenced by, the old Persian theory of state. In that theory there was a strong connexion between the Zoroastrian religion and the Sassanian state. This state in turn was

[1] *Ibid.* p. 45.

[2] Ed. Jalāl Humā'ī (Tehran, A.H. 1315–17), p. 39.

[3] See further my articles, "Justice in the Medieval Persian Theory of Kingship", *Studia Islamica* (fasc. XVIII), pp. 91–119; and "The Theory of Kingship in the *Naṣiḥat al-Mulūk* of Ghazālī", *The Islamic Quarterly* (1954), pp. 47–55.

identified with the social order; and the king, whose power was absolute, ruled by divine right and was the centre of the universe.[1] Ghazālī's theory of the caliphate was in due course to be forgotten, but the theory of government put forward in the *Naṣīḥat al-mulūk* was to have considerable influence on later thinkers.

A similar theory is clearly seen in the documents for the investiture of governors, and in other writings of the Saljuq period.[2] In this theory the sultan was regarded as the Shadow of God, by whom he was directly appointed and endowed with justice and wisdom. The historic imamate was completely ignored, and no authorization or validity was sought for the sultan's government. Thus a diploma (*taqlīd*), issued by Sanjar's dīvān for a certain 'Imād al-Dīn Muḥammad b. Aḥmad for the office of *qāḍī* of Nīshāpūr, begins: "Since God...has placed the reins of kingship in our grasp and caused the shadow of His great favour and compassion to be spread over our affairs and raised us to the rank and status of [having] the name of 'The Shadow of God upon Earth'..."[3] Similarly, a diploma (*manshūr*) for the *nā'ib* of Ray opens, "Since God, glory and exaltation be to Him, by His perfect action has bestowed upon us the lordship of the world and placed in our control the affairs of the kingdoms of the world (*ḥall va 'aqd-i maṣālik-i mamālik-i jahān*) and the ordering of the affairs of the people of the world, and has caused the standards of our rule to be signs of His power and might, may He be honoured and glorified..."[4]

The basic importance of justice is recognized. A taqlīd for the office of *vālī* of Gurgān, also issued by Sanjar's dīvān, states: "The foundation of kingship and the basis of rulership (*jahāndārī*) consist in making [the world] prosperous; and the world becomes prosperous only through

[1] See further R. C. Zaehner, *The Dawn and Twilight of Zoroastrianism* (London, 1961). Sassanian traditions had already begun to influence Islamic thought in Umayyad and early 'Abbāsid times. See further H. A. R. Gibb, "The Evolution of Government in Early Islam", in *Studies on the Civilisation of Islam*, pp. 34–45.

[2] A number of documents belonging to the Saljuq period have been preserved in various collections: notably the *'Atabat al-kataba* of Muntajab al-Dīn Badī' Atabeg Juvainī, who was head of Sanjar's *dīvān-i inshā'*. This collection contains a number of diplomas of appointment of various officials. The *Munsha'āt-i 'ahd-i Saljūqī va Khwārazmshāhī va avā'il-i 'ahd-i Mughul* which to some extent duplicates the *'Atabat al-kataba*, and the *Munsha'āt* of Evoghlī Ḥaidar, a later collection, also contain some Saljuq documents. These are supplemented by various collections of model diplomas and letters, mainly of the second half of the sixth/twelfth century, notably *al-Tawassul ila'l-tarassul* of Bahā al-Dīn Baghdādī and the *Dastūr-i Dabīrī* of Muḥammad b. 'Abdi'l-Khāliq al-Maihanī. For a brief discussion of these and other collections see H. Horst, *Die Staatsverwaltung der Grosselǧūqen und Ḫōrazmšahs (1038–1231)* (Wiesbaden, 1964).

[3] *'Atabat al-kataba*, ed. 'Abbās Iqbāl (Tehran, 1329/1950), p. 9.

[4] *Ibid.* pp. 69–70.

justice and equity; and the justice and equity of a ruler (*jahāndār*) are attainable only through efficient governors of good conduct and officials of praiseworthy beliefs and laudable ways of life, and only so does prosperity reach the people of the world."[1] The first duty of the sultan was to rule, and the justification both of his authority and of the political and social order was that they enabled the classes to fulfil their different functions. Thus a manshūr for the offices of vālī and shaḥna of Balkh opens:

The stability of the empire (*daulat*) and the ordering of the affairs of the kingdom (*mamlakat*) are among the fruits of the spreading of justice and the dispensation of compassion (*iḥsān*), to which we are commanded by the creator, may He be exalted and sanctified... Justice consists in...keeping every one of the people of the world—the subjects (*ra'āyā*), servants (*mustakhdamīn*), officials (*mutaqallidān-i a'māl*), and those charged with religious or secular affairs (*mubāshirān-i umūr-i dīnī va dunyavī*)—in their proper ranks and due stations.[2]

The interdependence of kingship and religion is emphasized. Kings were needed for the preservation of Islam, and temporal stability was guaranteed by the protection of religion. An authorization (*tafvīḍ*) to teach in a number of *madrasas* in Balkh states. "The foundation of kingship (*daulat*) and the basis of dominion consist in the observation of the laws of God, glory and exaltation be to Him, and in giving precedence to the raising of the banners of religion and the revivication of the signs and practices of the sharī'a, and in respecting and honouring the *sayyids* and '*ulamā* who are the heirs of the prophet..."[3] In return for the favour conferred upon him by God, the sultan was not to neglect in any way the ordering of the affairs of the world and the interests and protection of the people, who were a trust from God. The righteous were to be rewarded and the unrighteous punished.

A similar theory to that contained in these documents and in the *Naṣīḥat al-mulūk* is expressed more explicitly in terms of political expediency by Niẓām al-Mulk in the *Siyāsat-Nāma*. "God most high", he states, "chooses someone from among the people in every age and adorns him with kingly virtues and relegates to him the affairs of the world and the peace of his servants."[4] The sultan was to order the world so that the people might be secure in their various pursuits, and he was to strive to make the world prosperous by such means as the improve-

[1] *Ibid.* p. 30.
[2] *Ibid.* p. 74.
[3] *Ibid.* p. 33.
[4] Ed. Schefer, Persian text (Paris, 1891–3), p. 5.

ment of irrigation and communications and the building of cities. The object of temporal rule was to fill the earth with justice; this was to be achieved by the maintenance of each man in his rightful place, which, in turn, would assure stability.

Niẓām al-Mulk's view of religion was largely utilitarian. His apparent horror of and opposition to Shī'ism in all forms was based on political rather than religious grounds. He saw a close connexion between stability and right religion.

What a king needs most is right religion, because kingship and religion are two brothers [he writes]. Whenever any disturbance appears in the kingdom, disorder also occurs in religion; and people of bad religion and malefactors appear. Whenever there is disorder in the affairs of religion the kingdom is disturbed, and the power of malefactors increases; and they cause the kings to lose their dignity and make them troubled at heart; innovations appear and rebels become powerful.[1]

Justice, however, rather than right religion was the ultimate basis of Niẓām al-Mulk's theory. "Kingship", he states, "remains with the unbeliever but not with injustice."[2] But there were no sanctions except moral sanctions, and Niẓām al-Mulk clearly believed that rights were acquired and maintained by force. The power of the ruler was absolute, it required no authorization, and the administration was centralized in his person. Against his arbitrary power the population had no rights and no freedom. It was this theory of kingship which was ultimately to prevail in Persia. Under the Saljuqs, however, the rule of the sultans still had a shar'ī basis. This did not stop the arbitrary use of power by the government and its officials, but on the whole it prevented it from reaching lengths which were intolerable to the people.

During the Saljuq period the ruling and orthodox institutions were drawn more closely together, although the functional division between them was more sharply defined than heretofore.[3] All affairs, religious and temporal, became the concern of the sultan. This was inevitable when "right religion" was regarded as the basis of the stability of the state. The caliph remained the supreme authority in matters relating to the legal administration; but once he had authorized the sultan's assumption of power, his main function concerned the performance of prayers and religious leadership. When Toghrïl Beg brought the caliph back to Baghdad in 451/1059–60 after Basāsīrī had fled, his minister

[1] *Siyāsat-Nāma*, p. 55.

[2] *Ibid.* p. 8.

[3] See Gibb, "An Interpretation of Islamic History", in *Studies on the Civilisation of Islam*, p. 24.

'Amīd al-Mulk Kundurī took charge of the administration of Baghdad, and as compensation for this he gave an allowance to the caliph. From this time onwards the caliph was no longer liable to arbitrary deposition, as he had been in Būyid times. He was allowed to enjoy his allowance and the income of his personal estates without fear of any demand being made on him or of his estates being confiscated. The dignity and good name of his office were in some measure restored. But the respect the Saljuqs showed him, although considerable, was limited; and whereas his residence in Būyid times had been the refuge for all who feared the Būyids, a like situation was not tolerated by the Saljuqs. Further, they sought to control the caliph through marriage alliances and occasionally through appointments to his vizierate.

In Muḥarram 448/1056 Arslan-Khatun, Chaghrï Beg Dā'ūd's daughter, was betrothed to the Caliph al-Qā'im. Bundārī states that al-Qā'im intended by this marriage to strengthen the sultan's prestige and cement his friendship with him.[1] In 453/1061 Toghrïl Beg sent the qāḍī of Ray to Baghdad to ask for the hand of the caliph's daughter in marriage. Ibn al-Jauzī states that Toghrïl Beg's former wife, who had died in 452/1060–1, had recommended him to take this step.[2] The demand caused the caliph great vexation: even the Būyids had never forced him to such an action. He tried to get it withdrawn and commanded his envoy to demand 300,000 dīnārs from Toghrïl Beg if he insisted on the marriage. Kundurī told the caliph's envoy bluntly that a refusal was out of the question. Eventually, after a series of threats and counter-threats, the marriage contract was ratified outside Tabrīz in Sha'bān 454/1062. In the following year Toghrïl Beg came to Baghdad and demanded the caliph's daughter. It was pointed out to him that the object of the marriage had been honour and not union, and that if the caliph's daughter was to be seen by him it should be in Baghdad. Eventually she was taken to the sultan's residence in the city and he paid her elaborate homage. When Toghrïl Beg left Baghdad in the following year, the caliph unwillingly gave permission for his daughter to accompany him.

In 464/1071–2 al-Qā'im asked the hand of Alp-Arslan's daughter on behalf of his *valī 'ahd* (heir apparent), who was to become caliph as al-Muqtadī. The latter also demanded the hand of Malik-Shāh's

[1] *Daulat al-Saljūq* (Cairo, A.H. 1318), p. 11.
[2] *Al-Muntaẓam* (Haidarabad, A.H. 1357–59), vol. VIII, p. 218.

daughter by his favourite wife Terken Khatun. This alliance caused the relations between the caliph and the sultan to become strained, because after being taken to the caliph's residence in 480/1087, Malik-Shāh's daughter complained of the caliph's neglect of her, and returned to her father in 482/1089. As a result of his daughter's unhappy marriage to the caliph, Malik-Shāh appears to have conceived a hatred of him. In 484/1091, when he came to Baghdad, he ignored the caliph's presence and insisted that the caliph should revoke the nomination of his eldest son (who subsequently became caliph as al-Mustaẓhir) in favour of Abu'l Faḍl Ja'far, the caliph's son by Malik-Shāh's daughter and retire to Baṣra (or, according to some accounts, to Damascus or the Ḥijāz). The caliph was loth to agree and asked for a delay to make plans for his departure. Meanwhile Malik-Shāh left Baghdad in Rabī' I 485/1092 for Iṣfahān, taking Abu'l Faḍl Ja'far with him. Shortly afterwards Malik-Shāh was assassinated and al-Muqtadī was relieved of the demand. There are several subsequent instances of marriages between the houses of the sultan and the caliph.

In Baghdad, from the time when Toghrïl Beg took over the administration until the caliphate of al-Mustarshid (512–29/1118–35), administrative authority in Iraq was under the sultan and his officials. The chief of these, the *shaḥna*, was the sultan's ambassador to the caliph, and his duty was to watch over the power of the caliph and his officials; he was normally a Turkish amīr and had certain military functions also. In the city of Baghdad there was to some extent a conflict of jurisdiction. The population tended to refer to the caliph, who was always accessible to them, even though he could do little but refer back to the sultan or his representatives. Responsibility for local order and security seems to have been shared somewhat between the shaḥna and the caliph's officials. The caliph's vizier also exercised some kind of judicial authority in Baghdad, and from time to time he held a *maẓālim* court. Certain taxes, including *jizya*, were levied by the caliph's officials. There are also instances of the caliph's making levies on the population for the repair of the city walls.

During the reign of Malik-Shāh various attempts were made by Niẓām al-Mulk to establish his nominee in the caliph's vizierate. This strained the relationship between Niẓām al-Mulk and the Caliph al-Muqtadī, but the vizier's hostility to the caliph was subsequently transformed by al-Muqtadī's gracious reception of him on the occasion of his first visit to Baghdad for the wedding of Malik-Shāh's daughter. In the enmity which later developed between the caliph and Malik-Shāh, Niẓām al-Mulk championed the caliphate.

After the death of Muḥammad b. Malik-Shāh in 511/1117, the caliph, reaping the benefit of the first three sultans' policy to strengthen the caliphate, began to play an important part in the struggle for temporal power; and ultimately a state was established in Iraq over which he exercised full control, temporal as well as religious. But as he began to take part in the struggle for temporal power, the religious sanctity of his office declined and he became subject, like any other temporal ruler, to attack and capture. The first caliph to assemble an army and lead it in person in Saljuq times was al-Mustarshid. Finally after the death of Mas'ūd b. Muḥammad in 547/1152, al-Muqtafī turned the shaḥna and the sultan's other officials out of Iraq and took possession of their *iqṭā*'s (assignments) and allowances, appointing his own officials over the districts of Iraq, and sending spies and *ṣāḥibān-i khabar* (official informants) to all the cities of Iraq.[1]

In addition to the reaffirmation of the caliph's position as head of the Islamic community, an important step towards strengthening and regimenting the religious institution was the development of the madrasas. The initiator of this movement was Niẓām al-Mulk, whose purposes were presumably to provide government officials trained in the tenets of orthodoxy who would replace the former secretarial class and implement his political policies; and secondly, by using the 'ulamā educated in the madrasas, he hoped to control the masses and combat the spread of the Ismā'īlī sect, which had begun to threaten the existence of the state.[2] One of the results of the development of the madrasas was to bring about the integration of the members of the bureaucracy with the religious classes. Under the early 'Abbāsids there had been a separation between the 'ulamā on the one hand and the secretarial class and literary men on the other. Converts to Islam from the secretarial class, such as Ibn al-Muqaffa', had played an immensely important part in the intellectual life of the community. On the whole, however, they had failed to resolve fully the tension between Islamic

[1] Bundārī, p. 215.

[2] Cf. Asad Talas, *La Madrasa Niẓamiyya et son histoire* (Paris, 1939), p. 1; and G. Makdisi, "Muslim institutions of learning in eleventh-century Baghdad", in *B.S.O.A.S.* pp. 51 ff. In the device of forming an administrative class belonging to the religious institution, Sir Hamilton Gibb also sees an attempt "to preserve the spiritual independence of the orthodox institution against the increasing power and absolutism of the temporal princes, and at the same time to maintain (or to re-create) the unity of the Community", "An Interpretation of Islamic History", in *Studies on the Civilisation of Islam*, p. 24.

teaching and the traditions and ideals inherited from the old Persian theory of state. Even Niẓām al-Mulk for all his orthodoxy failed to create an acceptable synthesis of the two. With the growth of the madrasas the secretarial class and the literary men on the one hand, and the ʿulamā on the other, moved closer together because they shared a common training in the madrasas, which became in effect Sunnī strongholds. The former became more fully Islamicized, and the latter perhaps more Persianized. The dichotomy between the two traditions, the old Persian and the Islamic, remained, but under the Saljuqs more integration was achieved than ever before.[1]

The madrasas were not, as is sometimes alleged, founded by Niẓām al-Mulk, nor were they the only centres of higher learning in the Saljuq period.[2] But he was responsible for the new era of brilliance which began under the Saljuqs and which caused his schools to eclipse all other contemporary institutions of learning. He was also responsible for turning them into seminaries of Sunnī orthodoxy, in the same way the *dār al-ḥikma* in Egypt, founded in 395/1005, had been a centre of S͟hīʿī propaganda. Already in the fourth/tenth century there had been madrasas in Nīs͟hāpūr, which, in size of population and development of culture and industry, was able to compete with the Fāṭimid capital and with Baghdad. The madrasas in K͟hurāsān were possibly influenced by the convents or hospices belonging to the Karrāmiyya—an Islamic sect founded by Abū ʿAbdullāh Muḥammad b. Karrām al-Sagzī (d. 255/869), which flourished in K͟hurāsān in the early fifth/eleventh century[3]—and perhaps they were also influenced by the Buddhist *vihāra*. They were a powerful means of propagating Islam independently of the Islamic government.[4] Their transformation into Sunnī strongholds under the Saljuqs was due to the necessity for combating both S͟hīʿī propaganda, whether Ismāʿīlī or It͟hna ʿAs͟harī, and the dissident Sunnīs of the Karrāmiyya convents.[5]

Numerous madrasas were built by the Saljuq rulers, by their ministers and others. Nāṣir-i K͟husrau relates that a madrasa was being built in S͟hawwāl 437/1046 by order of Tog͟hrïl Beg in Nīs͟hāpūr; C͟hag͟hrï Beg

[1] Cf. also Gibb, *loc. cit.* pp. 24–5.

[2] See G. Makdisi, "Muslim Institutions", *op. cit.* pp. 4 ff.

[3] See Ribera y Tarragó, "Origen del Colegio Nidami de Baghdad", in *Disertaciones y opúsculos*, I (1928), pp. 361–83.

[4] See V. V. Bartold, *Zwölf Vorlesungen über die Geschichte der Türken Mittelasiens*, tr. into German by Theodor Menzel (Berlin, 1935), p. 60.

[5] L. Massignon, "Les Medresehs de Baghdad", in *Bulletin de l'Institut français d'archéologie orientale* (1909), pp. 77–8.

Dā'ūd founded a madrasa in Marv; Alp-Arslan in Baghdad, Muḥammad b. Malik-Shāh in Iṣfahān, and Toghrïl b. Muḥammad in Hamadān. The most famous madrasas, however, were those founded by Niẓām al-Mulk, and they were known as Niẓāmiyya. The best known was in Baghdad, which was opened in Dhu'l Qa'da 459/1067.[1] There were also Niẓāmiyya in Nīshāpūr, in Āmul, Mosul, Herāt, Damascus, Jazīrat Ibn 'Umar, Balkh, Ghazna, Marv, and Baṣra. These were probably not all founded by Niẓām al-Mulk as a private individual, but were at least partly paid for and endowed by the royal revenue of which he had control (see below, pp. 249ff.). Others emulated him in the building of such schools. For example, Sharaf al-Mulk, Malik-Shāh's *mustaufī*, built a madrasa in Baghdad in 459/1066–7. Its construction began after work on the Niẓāmiyya had started, though it appears to have been inaugurated before the Niẓāmiyya.[2] Sharaf al-Mulk also built a madrasa in Marv. Tāj al-Mulk Abu'l Ghanā'im (d. Muḥarram 486/1066), Niẓām al-Mulk's rival who succeeded him in the vizierate, founded the Tājiyya madrasa in Baghdad. The building began in 480/1087–8 and the inauguration took place two years later. Many of the amīrs also built madrasas. Thus Khumar-Tegin, who was in the service of Tutush b. Alp-Arslan, built a madrasa in Baghdad and called it after his master. Muḥammad b. Yaghï-Sïyan (d. 501/1107–8) built a number of madrasas in his iqṭā' in Āzarbāījān. Several existed in Fārs, including the one built by 'Alā al-Daula in Yazd in 513/1119–20. Jamāl al-Dīn Iqbāl, the *jāndār*, founded one in Hamadān. There were also madrasas founded by women. For example, Zāhida Khatun, wife of the amīr Boz-Aba, built and endowed one in Shīrāz.

Many of the madrasas were founded for the followers of a particular rite; sometimes for a particular scholar. Niẓām al-Mulk, who was himself a Shāfi'ī, laid down that the *mudarris*, *vā'iẓ*, and librarian of the Niẓāmiyya in Baghdad should be Shāfi'īs. The teaching programme of the Baghdad Niẓāmiyya comprised the Qur'ān, *ḥadīth* (traditions), *uṣūl al-fiqh* (jurisprudence) according to the Shāfi'ī rite, *kalām* (scholastic theology) according to Ash'arī doctrine, *'arabiyya* (Arabic language and literature), *adab* (belles lettres), *riyāḍiyya* (mathematics), and *farā'iḍ* (laws of inheritance). It is possible that Niẓām al-Mulk first made general the

[1] The building was begun in Dhu'l Ḥijja 457/1065. Ṭuṭurshī in the *Sirāj al-mulūk* relates the story of its construction and the embezzlement of part of the funds allocated for this (Alexandria, A.H. 1289), pp. 216–18. See also Hindū-Shāh b. Sanjar, *Tajārib al-Salaf*, ed. 'Abbās Iqbāl (Tehran, A.H. 1313), pp. 270 ff.

[2] G. Makdisi, "Muslim Institutions", pp. 19–20.

practice of establishing allowances for the students (*ṭullāb*) of the madrasas, and stipends for those teaching there.[1] Endowments were administered by a *mutavallī* (an administrator or trustee), appointed usually by the founder, and after his death, if no other arrangements had been laid down, he was succeeded by the qāḍī.

The head of the madrasa, the *mudarris*, was in charge of its affairs and responsible for the general conduct of the students, some of whom, like some of the teachers, appear to have been organized in guilds. Both students and teachers lived in the madrasas. Frequently, the mudarris held some other office also, such as that of qāḍī or *khaṭīb* (preacher). His tenure of office varied; it was normally for life except in the Niẓāmiyyas. The office of mudarris in the large madrasas was one of importance, and if the holder had a reputation as a scholar, students would come from great distances to study under him. Exceptionally there were women students and teachers.[2]

The Niẓāmiyya madrasas, the one founded by Sharaf al-Mulk, the mustaufī, and various others had libraries attached to them. There were also a number of independent libraries, some dating from before the Saljuq period, and also libraries in some of the Ṣūfī *ribāṭs* (hospices). A few madrasas had hospitals attached to them. Presumably the hospital founded by Niẓām al-Mulk in Nīshāpūr was connected with his madrasa there.

The power of the sultan was in theory limited by the sharī'a, to which he, like all Muslims, was subject. But the sanction of the sharī'a in this case was simply moral because no means was devised to enforce his subjection to it. Under the Saljuqs there was, besides the Islamic and old Persian elements, a third element in the theory of the sultanate which, though not formally expressed in any written exposition, had some influence on practice. This was tribal custom. The Saljuqs had come to power with the support of the Ghuzz tribes, and their claim to the leadership of these tribes rested in the first instance on military prowess. Originally they were the hereditary leaders of a small group; gradually, as success attended their activities, the majority of the Ghuzz became associated with them. Their leadership, once established, was maintained by military might coupled with conciliation and consultation, though they never succeeded in establishing full control and unity

[1] Tāj al-Dīn al-Subkī, *Ṭabaqāt al-Shāfi'iyya*, vol. III, p. 137, quoted by De Slane in his introduction to Ibn Khallikān, *Wafayāt al-a'yān* (Paris, London, 1842–71), p. xxviii. See also Makdisi, *op. cit.* pp. 50 ff.

[2] Cf. Ibn Khallikān, vol. I, pp. 625, 551.

over the Ghuzz. The outlying groups, although nominally acknowledging the overlordship of the sultan, acted independently or semi-independently. Politically the Saljuq empire was a loose confederation of semi-independent kingdoms over which the sultan exercised nominal authority. Saljuq princes were known as *maliks* in contradistinction to the paramount ruler, the sultan.[1] Only for a brief period towards the end of Malik-Shāh's reign was any degree of unity achieved.

Originally the Saljuqs seem to have held that their leadership was vested in the family as a whole; and that the various sections of their loose confederation were each led by a member of the family. They were thus in the beginning the leaders of their people but not territorial sovereigns, and they probably thought that their rule extended wherever their people roamed in search of pasture, and not, in any case at first, that it was tied to a given area. During the early period of expansion the khuṭba was read in some cities in Khurāsān in the name of Toghrïl Beg, and in others in the name of Chaghrï Beg Dā'ūd, although Chaghrï Beg never disputed the primacy of his brother.

This conception of the Saljuq family as the guardian of a tribal confederation had already been considerably modified before the death of Toghrïl Beg in 455/1063, and under Alp-Arslan the Persian ideal of an autocratic sovereign was to some extent adopted. It was almost inevitable that once the Saljuqs were no longer merely the leaders of a tribal migration but were the rulers of a territorial empire, they would be forced to seek some more stable basis of power than the Ghuzz, or the "Türkmen", as the Islamicized Ghuzz within the Saljuq empire were called. This change of basis began to take place under Alp-Arslan, perhaps even under Toghrïl Beg, and it was finally completed under Malik-Shāh. From then the ultimate guarantee of the sultan's rule was the standing army composed of slaves and freedmen. This change was gradual: any sudden rupture with the past would have alienated the Türkmen tribes, who continued to be an important element in the Saljuq forces. Niẓām al-Mulk recognized this danger. In his *Siyāsat-Nāma* he stated that the Saljuq dynasty was under an obligation to the Türkmen, owing to blood ties and to the part they played in the foundation of the empire. For this reason the disorders they created could not be suppressed by severe measures. He recommended therefore that a thousand young Türkmen should be enrolled in the service of the sultan and trained as *ghulāms* (slaves) of the court, the number to

[1] After the Saljuq period the title *malik* was debased and applied to prominent amīrs.

be increased if necessary to five or even ten thousand. Many Türkmen were enrolled in the sultan's service in this way.

As the sultan's basis of power changed, so the custom of the steppe and of government by consultation and conciliation were replaced by the absolutism and arbitrary power of the old Persian ruling tradition, and also by a distrust of all to whom power was delegated. In spite of this, the original conceptions—of the leadership of the group being inherent in the Saljuq family, and of the empire as a loose confederation whose different parts were led by members of the family—never entirely disappeared; and they are discernible in the atabegate as well as the iqṭā' (see p. 231 below).[1]

It was perhaps natural that the conception of the sultan as arbitrary ruler should first be challenged by members of the Saljuq family itself; and the fact that there was no stable system of succession encouraged them to dispute when a weak prince or a child succeeded to the throne. The normal practice was for the sultan to nominate his valī 'ahd. No regulations governing his choice were laid down, and sometimes the wives of the sultan exerted influence in the matter. If a prince's mother was free-born and a Saljuq, for example, this was probably favourable for his chance of succession. Berk-Yaruq's mother was free-born and a Saljuq, and this was allegedly one of the reasons that led to his becoming sultan.

The fact that the sultan proclaimed one of his sons as his valī 'ahd did not always ensure his succession, however. Toghrïl Beg, who had no children himself, married one of Chaghrï Beg Dā'ūd's wives after Chaghrï Beg's death, and proclaimed her son Sulaimān as his valī 'ahd. On the death of Toghrïl Beg, his vizier, 'Amīd al-Mulk Kundurī put Sulaimān on the throne; but seeing that the amīrs opposed that accession he proclaimed Alp-Arslan, an older son of Chaghrï Beg by another wife, as sultan in Qazvīn, and he had the khuṭba read in Ray in the names of both. Yabghu b. Mīkā'īl, governor of Herāt, and Qutlumush each rebelled in 456/1063–4. Alp-Arslan defeated them and was later reconciled to both. Qara-Arslan in Kirmān also rebelled some three years later (459/1066–7). He too was reinstated after being defeated. It may well be that the opposition which Alp-Arslan encountered from Yabghu and Qutlumish marked a turning-point in the relations between the sultan and his family. As the conception of autocratic ruler replaced that of ruling khan, the moral basis of Saljuq

[1] Various tribal influences are also to be seen in the royal insignia of the Saljuqs.

authority was weakened. Alp-Arslan may well have realized that some substitute had to be found for the former tribal loyalties to which the Saljuqs owed their position, and that if he was to keep even a limited control over the members of the family, then a standing army loyal to himself was necessary.

In 458/1065–7 Alp-Arslan determined to appoint Malik-Shāh as his valī ʿahd, and he had his name included in the khuṭba after his own. This was probably normal practice. At the same time as this nomination, Alp-Arslan divided part of the kingdom among his relatives in order to abate any quarrel with the succession of Malik-Shāh (see p. 235 below). In spite of this, various members of the family disputed his accession on the death of Alp-Arslan. Qavurd, the ruler of Kirmān, wrote to Malik-Shāh stating that it was more fitting for him to succeed, on the grounds that he was Alp-Arslan's eldest brother while Malik-Shāh was only a young son.[1] Malik-Shāh, who was then aged about eighteen, replied that a brother did not inherit if there was a son. This, however, was Islamic and not tribal law. Qavurd made a determined effort to seize the throne, but he was defeated and killed. Tekish, to whom Balkh and Tukhāristān had been assigned, rebelled twice, in 473/1080–1 and 477/1084–5; on the second occasion he was captured and blinded. Toghrïl b. Ïnāl also made an abortive attempt in 482/1089–90 to establish his independence in the neighbourhood of Nasaf. In Syria, which Malik-Shāh had assigned to Tutush in 470/1077–8, the sultan's nominal authority seems to have been recognized, though he twice had to intervene in person.[2] Tutush came himself to pay his respects to Malik-Shāh in Baghdad in 484/1091.

Malik-Shāh nominated Aḥmad, the eldest son of Zubaida Khatun, as his valī ʿahd, but he died in 481/1088–9. A new heir was not nominated, and when Malik-Shāh died four years later, civil war ensued. Terken Khatun, his last wife, a Qarakhānid princess, succeeded in persuading the caliph to have the khuṭba read in Baghdad in the name of her son Maḥmūd, in return for which she handed over Abu'l Faḍl Jaʿfar, the son of Arslan Khatun and al-Muqtadī, who had been with Malik-Shāh since his mother had returned from the caliph's court. (Jaʿfar died the following year; and Terken Khatun herself died in 487/1094.) Meanwhile the Niẓāmiyya *mamlūks* (slaves) carried off Berk-

[1] *Akhbār al-daulat al-Saljūqiyya*, ed. Muhammad Iqbal (Lahore, 1933), p. 56. Sanjar later opposed the accession of Maḥmūd b. Muḥammad on the grounds of his youth.

[2] See H. A. R. Gibb, *The Damascus Chronicle of the Crusades* (London, 1932), pp. 20–1.

Yaruq, who had been imprisoned in Iṣfahān on Terken Khatun's orders, and proclaimed him sultan. He was at this time a boy of thirteen and in no position to assert himself as the leader of his people.

Ismā'īl b. Yāqūtī, his maternal uncle, who was in Āzarbāījān, was persuaded by Terken Khatun to side against Berk-Yaruq. He was eventually killed by the Niẓāmiyya mamlūks, as was Tāj al-Mulk Abu'l Ghanā'im, who had collaborated with Terken Khatun. Tutush and Arslan Arghūn, both brothers of Malik-Shāh, also rebelled in Syria and Khurāsān respectively. The former was defeated in 487/1096, and the latter three years later. Berk-Yaruq's half-brother Muḥammad rebelled in 492/1098–9. After many vicissitudes, Berk-Yaruq established a slight supremacy in 497/1103–4 at the cost of much disorder throughout the country and a decline in the prestige of the sultanate. By the terms of the peace concluded between them, Muḥammad's status was virtually that of an independent ruler. On his deathbed in 498/1105, Berk-Yaruq nominated his son Malik-Shāh as his valī 'ahd, but although the khuṭba was read in his name in Baghdad, Muḥammad soon succeeded in establishing himself as sultan. During the reign of Muḥammad, his full brother Sanjar (whom Berk-Yaruq had sent with his atabeg Qumach to Khurāsān in 490/1097) was nominally the ruler of Khurāsān on behalf of Muḥammad, but he was virtually independent. On the death of Muḥammad, Sanjar defeated Maḥmūd b. Muḥammad, whom Muḥammad had nominated as his valī 'ahd at Sāveh in 513/1119, and he then made himself sultan. He did not, however, move to a more central position but reinstated Maḥmūd in those districts which he had held in western and southern Persia and Iraq, while he himself returned to Khurāsān. Maḥmūd and his successors are referred to in the sources as sultans, but although they enjoyed a certain measure of independence, their status, until the death of Sanjar, was only that of maliks. It is not clear why Sanjar remained in Khurāsān: he may not have had any personal following outside that province, or he may have considered it unwise to absent himself permanently from the eastern frontiers since the tribes of Central Asia were again in a state of unrest and pressing in upon the Saljuq empire; or it may be that he was influenced by the wishes of his mother, who was Muḥmūd's grandmother and who is alleged to have persuaded him to make peace with Maḥmūd. Whatever the causes, the arrangement was unsatisfactory. Sanjar was forced to intervene in the western provinces on various occasions, and was unable either to restrain the increasing ambitions of the amīrs and atabegs or, ultimately, to prevent the disintegration of the empire.

Geographically the Saljuq empire was divided into provinces which corresponded broadly with the provinces that had formed the Sassanian empire. An elaborate system of roads, which also went back to the pre-Islamic period, radiated from Baghdad to serve not only the movement of armies but also that of merchants. The most famous of these was the great Khurāsān trunk road going east from Baghdad via Kirmānshāh, Hamadān, Ray, Nīshāpūr, and Marv to the frontier towns on the Jaxartes. Cross-roads branched off from Kirmānshāh to Tabrīz and Ardabīl; from Hamadān to Iṣfahān; from Ray to Zanjān and Tabrīz; and from Nīshāpūr roads went to Ṭabas, Qā'in, Herāt, and Sīstān. Another route led south-east from Baghdad to Baṣra, from whence there lay a road to Ahvāz and Shīrāz, where roads from Iṣfahān and Ray, from Yazd and Nīshāpūr, and from Sīrjān, Kirmān, and Sīstān all converged.[1] The administrative divisions of the empire did not correspond precisely with the provincial divisions, although when the empire began to fragment it tended to break up into geopolitical units centred on the major provinces of Khurāsān, Āzarbāījān, Iraq, Kirmān, and Fārs. Administratively the empire fell into two broad divisions: an area directly administered by the sultan's dīvān, and an indirectly administered area. In general, the former tended to increase up to the end of the reign of Malik-Shāh and subsequently to decrease. The indirectly administered area was alienated from the direct control of the sultan's dīvān and assigned to the amīrs and others as iqṭā's (see p. 235 below). These did not correspond to a fixed area, and they varied greatly in size. They tended to be smaller than the geographical provinces and to be centred on the most important town of a district.

The main centres of the empire under Toghrïl Beg at the beginning of his rule were Nīshāpūr and Ray, the latter being his capital for a time. In his final years he spent much time in Iṣfahān, his chief residence for some twelve years, where he expended on public buildings and improvements a sum exceeding 500,000 dīnārs.[2] Nāṣir-i Khusrau, who passed through Iṣfahān in 444/1052, stated that it was the most populous and flourishing city that he had seen in Persian-speaking lands.[3] Royal

[1] See further, G. Le Strange, *The Lands of the Eastern Caliphate* (Cambridge, 1905).

[2] E. G. Browne, "Account of a rare manuscript history of Isfahan", *J.R.A.S.* (1901), pp. 667 ff.

[3] *Safar-Nāma*, ed. C. Schefer, Persian text (Paris, 1881), p. 92.

patronage continued under Alp-Arslan, who was greatly pleased with Iṣfahān and treated its people with marked favour. Malik-S͟hāh chose it as his capital and did much building in the city and the neighbourhood. Marv, too, enjoyed a special position, as the capital of C͟hag͟hrī Beg Dā'ūd and later of Sanjar; and Malik-S͟hāh also built a suburb there called Panj Dih. Tog͟hrïl Beg built a new quarter at Baghdad on the Tigris, which included a Friday mosque and bazaars, and was surrounded by a wall. There Malik-S͟hāh built his mosque known as Jāmi' al-Sulṭān, the foundations of which were laid in 485/1092.

The sultans spent much of their time on military campaigns and travelling about their empire. The *dargāh*, or court, did not remain in the capital but was to be found wherever the sultan was. Government officials such as the vizier, accompanied him, and presumably the "private" treasury often went with him as well. To what extent a distinction was made between the sultan's private treasury and the state treasury is not clear, nor do we know what monies were paid into the former. The vizier was in charge of the state treasury, but there appears to have been a special treasurer directly under the sultan in charge of the private treasury. Malik-S͟hāh is said to have built a fortress outside Iṣfahān, known as S͟hāhdīz (this the Bāṭinīs subsequently captured), in which his treasury, armoury, and young slaves in training were kept when he was absent on campaigns.[1]

Alp-Arslan and Malik-S͟hāh also had stores of money in strongholds in different parts of the kingdom, chiefly to facilitate their military expeditions. Alp-Arslan is said to have had a store in the fortress of Gīv near Farahān so that if he was travelling between K͟hurāsān and Iraq he could obtain from there anything he needed. On one occasion when he reached Farahān on his way to Anatolia, he is reported to have taken from it one million dīnārs for the expenses of the expedition.[2] Malik-S͟hāh had similar strongholds: one such was the fortress of Quhandiz near Nīs͟hāpūr.[3] Sanjar's treasury was apparently kept in Marv, his capital. When he was absent fighting the Qara-K͟hitai in 532/1137–8, the K͟hwārazm-S͟hāh, Atsïz, captured Marv and took Sanjar's jewels. Subsequently Sanjar invaded K͟hwārazm and recaptured them.[4]

The sultan's wives and womenfolk also frequently accompanied him

[1] Rāvandī, *Rāḥāt al-ṣudūr*, ed. Muhammad Iqbāl (Gibb Memorial Series, new series, vol. II, London, 1921), p. 156.

[2] *Naṣā'iḥ-Nāma*, attributed to Niẓām al-Mulk; MS. in my possession, fol. 30, cols. *a–b*.

[3] Cf. *Ak͟hbār al-daulat al-Saljūqiyya*, p. 56.

[4] Bundārī, p. 257.

on expeditions. In 536/1141, when Sanjar was defeated on the Qaṭvān steppe by the Qara-Khitai, his wife Terken Khatun was captured, but she was subsequently released. Some of the sultan's wives wielded unusual influence. Toghrïl Beg's wife, who died in Zanjān in 452/1060–1 and was buried in Ray, was, according to Ibn al-Jauzī, a wise woman to whom Toghrïl Beg entrusted his affairs.[1] Terken Khatun played an active part in the struggle for the succession after her husband Malik-Shāh's death. Some of the wives had their own dīvāns and viziers, and were women of substance; Sanjar's mother, for instance, had her own mamlūks.[2] It appears to have been usual for the sultans' wives to have personal estates. Simīrūm was part of the pension of Guhar Khatun, Muḥammad b. Malik-Shāh's wife. There are also many instances of a sultan's granting iqṭā's to Saljuq women and to women who married into the Saljuq house. For example, when Toghrïl Beg married the caliph's daughter in 454/1062, he assigned to her Ba'qūbā and all that his late wife had held in Iraq. After putting down the rebellion of Qara-Arslan in Kirmān and reinstating him in the province, Alp-Arslan allocated to Qara-Arslan's daughters, in response to their father's request, 100,000 dīnārs, iqṭā's, garments, and money for the expenses of marriage celebrations.

Marriage alliances played an important part in Saljuq policy. In addition to the marriage alliances made with caliphs, there were numerous marriages between Saljuqs and members of former local ruling houses such as the 'Uqailids, the Būyids, Kākūyids, Mazyadids, and others.

Members of the bureaucracy, the religious classes, and learned men frequented the court, but except for the sultan's private household, it was essentially a military court, composed, from the reign of Alp-Arslan onwards, mainly of amīrs and members of the standing army (*'askar*). Those amīrs who held "administrative" iqṭā's (see p. 233 below) often found it necessary to have their agents at court to keep them informed of current developments and to watch over their interests. In addition, there were numbers of hostages taken from various tribal groups—Türkmen, Kurds, Shabānkāra, and others—and from former ruling families, and they remained at court as sureties against the rebellion of their relatives.

The amīrs were mainly *mamlūks* (slaves) or freedmen. Their status was

[1] *Al-Muntaẓam*, vol. VIII, p. 218.

[2] Al-Muqarrab Jauhar had originally been her *mamlūk* and was transferred to Sanjar on her death in 517/1123 (Bundārī, p. 250).

not originally equal to that of the free-born, but they could and did attain to the highest positions in the state, and then they themselves aquired mamlūks. In some cases both slaves and freedmen married into the royal house. The atabegate is further proof that no social stigma attached to the slave or freedman from the time of Malik-Shāh on. Whether this was the case in the early days of Saljuq expansion, however, is not clear. Isrā'īl b. Saljuq, when he sent a message to his family urging them to fight for the kingdom of Maḥmūd b. Sebük-Tegin, is alleged to have spoken of him with contempt as the son of a freed slave (*maulā*).[1] By Islamic law the possessions of a mamlūk escheated to his master; in practice, however, on the death of a royal mamlūk the sultan often granted his possessions to one of the mamlūk's descendants. Freedom was bought by the mamlūk, given by the sultan, or else usurped; and if a mamlūk attained to a position of power he became virtually free. Many of the later sultans, who came to the throne in extreme youth, were dominated by the amīrs. Even Sanjar, if Bundārī is to be believed, fell under the influence of successive mamlūks, whom he singled out for special favour. At least two of them are alleged to have been murdered on his orders after they fell from favour.

The amīrs were divided broadly into three groups: those at the sultan's court; "landed" amīrs, i.e. those holding "administrative" iqṭā's; and "wandering" amīrs, who owed no permanent allegiance to anyone, but moved about the empire serving different leaders and taking possession of districts as opportunity arose. The grouping of the amīrs was not constant, however. Those at court frequently changed, and the distinction between a "landed" and a "wandering" amīr was not fixed; thus a wandering amīr who usurped possession of a district and was then confirmed in his possession of it by the sultan became a landed amīr. As a class the amīrs had no community of interest. Apart from rare instances their jealousies prevented close co-operation among them except for a limited time. Just as the sultan used marriage alliances to strengthen his position, so the amīrs by intermarriage among themselves and with the ruling house sought to strengthen their own position. Their power, relative to that of the sultan on the one hand and the bureaucracy on the other, increased noticeably after the reign of Malik-Shāh. They were quick to resent any attempt to reimpose control over them, and their disobedience after the accession of Maḥmūd b. Muḥammad was a marked feature of the times.

[1] Rāvandī, p. 91.

The chief official of the court until towards the end of the reign of Muḥammad b. Malik-Shāh was the *vakīl-i dar*, who appears to have been a kind of intermediary between the sultan and the vizier. According to Bundārī his position was more privileged than that of the *ḥājibs* (chamberlains). He had to be "eloquent and able to triumph in difficult situations in matters of speech, independent in establishing proof if necessary; [his words] free from banality and distinguished by grace, and able to understand the different moods and characteristics of the sultan".[1] His precise relation to the vizier, the head of the dīvān, is not entirely clear. Ibn Balkhī states that in his time the vakīl-i dar was the vizier's deputy.[2] Towards the end of Muḥammad b. Malik-Shāh's reign the vakīl-i dar was replaced by the *amīr ḥājib*, who was a member of the military classes and not of the bureaucracy. Although this change was apparently provoked by the incompetence of a certain Zakī, who had been appointed vakīl-i dar by Sa'd al-Mulk Abu'l Maḥāsin Āvajī, the vizier of Muḥammad b. Malik-Shāh, it may signify a decline in the position of the vizier, as well as the increased militarization of the state.

Niẓām al-Mulk describes the functions of the ḥājib in terms of those of a court official. But since the court was a military court, the amīr ḥājib was normally a Turkish amīr and the men under him military slaves. He was therefore concerned with the maintenance of military discipline as well as with court ceremonial. He became the most important official at court, while the *amīr ḥaras* (chief of the guard) and the *jāndār* (chief executioner) ranked after him. Bundārī states that the amīr ḥājib (or *amīr-i bār*) regulated the audiences of the sultan and transmitted the sultan's commands to the vizier.[3] 'Alī b. 'Umar, the amīr ḥājib of Muḥmūd b. Muḥammad, eventually became *'āriḍ al-jaish* (muster-master) of the army. Many of those who held the office of amīr ḥājib were among the most powerful amīrs of the day.

There were a series of other officials at the court, such as the *ākhur-sālār* (master of the horse), who looked after the royal stables. Sanjar appears to have had extensive herds of horses, as probably did many of the other sultans; and there was also a *khwān-sālār*, who was in charge of the royal kitchens. The latter was no small charge, for tribal custom demanded that the ruler should keep an open table, and this involved the daily provision of food for large numbers. Alp-Arslan was stated to have fifty head of sheep slaughtered daily, which, together with other

[1] Bundārī, p. 86. [2] *Fārs-Nāma*, p. 91. [3] P. 107.

food, were eaten by the amīrs and the poor. Under Sanjar the G͟huzz paid an annual tribute of 24,000 sheep to the royal kitchen.

Among the sultan's most important functions—and in this the traditions of the steppe and of Islamic government coincided—was to judge. Both traditions required that he should be accessible to his people. His chief medium as a judge was the *maẓālim* court, which, according to Islamic theory, it was his prerogative to hold. This court was also the main channel of contact between the sultan and his subjects, though its effectiveness as such was limited. The procedure of the court and its rules of evidence differed from those of the s͟har'ī courts: i.e. it was necessary that the man who presided over the maẓālim court should possess the power to exercise his functions and to apply the rules of justice, which was not the case with the qāḍī, who presided over the s͟har'ī courts. The first reference to a maẓālim court held by a Saljuq sultan is to the one held by Tog͟hrïl in Nīs͟hāpūr in 429/1038. Malik-S͟hāh is also alleged to have given justice personally. Niẓām al-Mulk maintained that it was indispensable for the ruler to hold a maẓālim court twice a week to exact redress from the unjust, to dispense justice, and to listen to the words of his subjects without an intermediary.[1] This recommendation, however, was based on expediency rather than on a love of justice. "Always", states Niẓām al-Mulk, "there will be many persons at the court demanding redress for injustice, and if they do not receive an answer they will go away, and foreigners and envoys who come to the court and see this complaining and disturbance will think that great tyranny takes place at this court."[2]

The majority of the Saljuq sultans, however, in all probability delegated their function of presiding over the maẓālim court to the vizier or the qāḍī and in the provinces to the great amīrs and Saljuq maliks who held large areas as "administrative" iqṭa's and often in turn delegated their functions to their representatives. Thus under the Saljuqs as under earlier rulers the maẓālim court became, not an exceptional appeal to the sultan in person, but an everyday application to his representative to be dealt with according to a settled practice.[3] The general tendency was for the maẓālim jurisdiction relative to the s͟har'ī courts to extend. Many of the cases coming before the maẓālim court were probably concerned with the collection of taxes and general

---

[1] *Siyāsat-Nāma*, p. 10. [2] *Ibid.* p. 207.
[3] Cf. H. F. Amedroz, "The *Maẓālim* Jurisdiction in the Ahkam Sultaniyya of Mawardi", in *J.R.A.S.* (1911), p. 655.

litigation. It also dealt with cases against government officials. Its decisions were carried out by the shaḥna and his officials, or by the military.

Another of the sultan's important functions was to defend his country and his people in war. In this, too, the tradition of the steppe and of Islamic government coincided. The first three sultans led the army in person. After the death of Malik-Shāh, with the accession of young boys to the throne, this was not always the case. As a result the ties between the sultan and the army were weakened, and the soldiers tended more and more to give their loyalty to their immediate commanders rather than to the sultan. Desertions in the later period became relatively frequent. Moreover the jealousies and quarrels of the amīrs detracted from the efficiency of the army as a fighting force. The core of the standing army was formed by mamlūks and freedmen. On campaigns they were joined by contingents furnished by the amīrs and by tribal auxiliaries. The armies of the amīrs were also in many cases composed round a nucleus of slave troops. The mamlūks and freedmen of the amīrs and others, if they did not pass on the death of their masters to their heirs, were sometimes incorporated into the royal ʿaskar, forming a division known by the name of their late master. Throughout the Saljuq empire there were also bodies of unemployed soldiery, who were ready to join the standard of any leader in the hope of plunder. Their existence facilitated the assembling of an army at short notice, but it also made easy the rebellion of discontented maliks and amīrs.

For the most part the mamlūks of the standing army were Turks who had been captured or bought on the eastern frontiers of the Islamic world. A number of Georgians, Greeks, and Armenians, who had been captured on the western frontiers—or, like some of the Turks, were the children of such captives—were also enrolled in the standing army. Many of the mamlūks were carefully trained to fulfil their various functions, which were administrative as well as military.[1] The most important group in the army after the Turks, however, were the Dailamites, who were chiefly infantry, whereas the Turks were cavalry. Niẓām al-Mulk advocated that the army should be "mixed", half Turkish and half Dailamite. In practice, although the army was composed of different elements, the Turkish greatly predominated.

[1] Niẓām al-Mulk states that the system of training that had prevailed under the Sāmānids had fallen into disuse by his day (*Siyāsat-Nāma*, p. 94).

Tribal auxiliaries were provided mainly by Türkmen. There were also Kurds, Arabs, and Shabānkāra. Quite apart from the family ties between Saljuqs and Türkmen, it was a matter of moment for the sultan to treat them well, because, in addition to their being a useful reinforcement to his army, they were a potential source of strength for the enemy. They were extremely mobile and could assemble in a short space of time. Their guiding motive was plunder. Tribal auxiliaries were in some cases employed by the amīrs, and by local rulers such as the Mazyadids.

The chief weapon of the army was the bow and arrow. This the cavalry used from the saddle, shooting without dismounting or halting. Spears, of which the *khaṭṭī* spear was the most renowned, swords, clubs, shields, and a kind of horse armour, were in use. The Khurāsān army under Sanjar had elephants. Greek fire was used and a siege engine known as the *manjanīq*. This latter was not particularly effective, and if the provisions of the besieged town held out the defenders were usually able to withstand the besiegers. A more deadly siege weapon was the mine, which was used by the Saljuq armies in Syria. The army was in some cases accompanied by a field hospital. The one attached to Maḥmūd b. Muḥammad's army was equipped with instruments, medicines, and tents, and staffed by doctors and orderlies (*ghulāms*); for its transport it had two hundred Bactrian camels.[1]

The cavalry manoeuvred with speed and flexibility: one of their favourite manoeuvres was the feigned retreat. Warfare was necessarily seasonal. Most of the forces assembled by the amīrs tended to disperse at harvest time; and they were generally reluctant to be absent from their iqṭā's for long periods, lest a rival should attack their possessions during their absence or the sultan should assign them to some other amīr.

It is difficult to arrive at accurate figures for the size of the standing army. The numbers given by the sources, which are probably only broad approximations, often include the armies of the amīrs and tribal auxiliaries which joined the sultan when he went on a campaign. Toghrïl Beg's standing army was probably fairly small. Alp-Arslan at the time of his assassination was accompanied by 2,000 slaves. Malik-Shāh, when he was valī 'ahd, had 15,000 soldiers attached to him; as sultan, he is said to have had 40,000 horses always in his service. In 473/1080–1 he is alleged to have dismissed 7,000 Armenians, who then

[1] Bundārī, p. 124. Ibn al-Khallikān, however (vol. II, p. 82), gives the figure of camels needed to transport it as forty.

joined Tekish in his rebellion. Niẓām al-Mulk complains of an attempt made by one of Malik-S̲h̲āh's entourage, probably towards the end of his reign, to induce him to economize on military expenditure and cut down the size of his army. He points out that the strength of the empire lay in proportion to the strength of the sultan's army, and that if men were dismissed they would be a potential centre of disorder and rebellion.[1] Generally speaking, it would seem that in the later period the standing army decreased and numbered only 10–15,000. Against this the number of troops mustered by the amīrs tended to increase.

The army was accompanied by a military bazaar and a host of camp followers. Berk-Yaruq, when he came to Iṣfahān in Jumādā I 495/1102, was reported to have been accompanied by 15,000 horses and 100,000 camp followers. The army did not always move with its followers, however. When Alp-Arslan marched against the Byzantines and defeated them at Mantzikert in 463/1071, for example, he sent his baggage and women to Tabrīz.

The provisioning of the army as it moved through the country was a matter of no small difficulty. Niẓām al-Mulk recommended that fodder and stores should be kept at different places in the country through which the ruler was likely to pass with his army. Land was to be acquired in the neighbourhood, and its produce, when not required by the army, was to be sold and the proceeds remitted to the treasury. Under Malik-S̲h̲āh this plan was followed to some extent; later it probably fell into disuse. Whereas Malik-S̲h̲āh does not appear to have suffered any major obstacle to the provisioning of his army, the later sultans encountered difficulties.

The pay of the standing army and of the amīrs who provided contingents for the royal army was controlled by the Military Inspection Office, the *dīvān-i ʿarḍ* (also called the *dīwān al-jais̲h̲*), which was a department of the central dīvān (see below). They were paid partly by cash and partly by drafts on the revenue[2] and by iqṭāʿs. Niẓām al-Mulk urged that the wages of the soldiers who did not have iqṭāʿs should be held liquid, that they should be paid at the right time, and if possible by the sultan in person. In practice their pay was often in arrears, though

[1] *Siyāsāt-Nāma*, p. 144.

[2] Bundārī states that Niẓām al-Mulk would allot to a soldier (*jundī*) 1,000 dīnārs annually, half of which would be on a town in Asia Minor (Rūm) and half on a place in the most distant part of K̲h̲urāsān; and that the total would be paid immediately without any charge (p. 55). Cf. also *Ak̲h̲bār al-daulat al-Saljūqiyya*, p. 68. Houtsma thinks, probably rightly, that 1,000 dīnārs is a scribe's error for 100 dīnārs.

a part of it was commonly given to them at the outset of a campaign. After the death of Malik-Shāh difficulties in financing the army became more frequent; and insubordination in the army was especially noticeable from this time onwards. This stringency was due partly to the fact that there was a decrease in the directly administered area, and hence a decrease in the revenue coming into the treasury; and partly to the fact that civil war had brought about a general decline in prosperity. In addition to their regular pay the soldiers received *ad hoc* payments such as accession gratuities and presents on special occasions, as well as a share of the booty taken in battle.

Bundārī's well-known statement that Niẓām al-Mulk introduced the practice of granting iqṭā's to the soldiery is manifestly untrue. Such grants were already common practice under the Būyids. What Niẓām al-Mulk probably did was to regularize the practice and in some measure to unify the "military" and the "administrative" iqṭā'. Both existed under the Būyids, but the "administrative" iqṭā' was the exception then, whereas under the Saljuqs it became the dominant type of iqṭā' and the most important institution of their empire. In order to appreciate its nature and the way it developed, the earlier history of the iqṭā' must be briefly considered.

The iqṭā' emerged in the fourth/tenth century against a background of change in the economic and social environment (though not in the purpose of government) of the 'Abbāsid caliphate. As it evolved, in response to the state's dominant need to finance its operations and to pay its civil and military officers, the iqṭā' seized upon and transformed two institutions: the amīrate or provincial government on the one hand; and, on the other, the tax farm, whether the ḍamān or the *qabāla* which was an undertaking to pay the tax quota of a community, assessed at a fixed sum and paid according to the lunar year. The provincial government had its vicissitudes. Eventually the difficulty of finding money to pay the officials of the bureaucracy and the army led to a breakdown of the administrative system and a wholesale extension of the farming of the taxes. Already by the death of the Caliph al-Ma'mūn in 218/833 the balance between the civil and military arms of the administration had been upset, and the money received from the farming of taxes soon ceased to be sufficient to pay the army leaders and their troops. As the revenue came in with increasing irregularity, the practice grew of assigning the taxes, not to the tax-farmers, but to the military themselves.

Once a military leader was assigned the right to collect the taxes of a large area, it became relatively easy for him to establish his semi-independence. Moreover, when the taxes still failed to come in regularly, rights over the land itself were then assigned to him: in other words, the tax-farm swallowed up the land-revenue system and in turn became assimilated to the provincial government. These grants to the military were known as iqṭāʿ. The militarization of the state was marked not only in Iraq and the neighbourhood under the Būyids, but also in the east under the Sāmānids and more especially under the Ghaznavids. The growing tendency of the military to be occupied, not only with the arts of war, but also with administration, obscured to some extent the true nature of the iqṭāʿ system, the origins of which were bureaucratic and not feudal.

In still earlier times hereditary grants of *ʿushr* land were called iqṭāʿ, whereas non-hereditary grants made from land other than *kharāj* land were called *tuʿma*.[1] Land that paid a fixed sum to the treasury and was immune from the entry of the tax-collector was called *īghār*; and an annual but renewable tax-free grant was called *tasvīj*. Both were made on kharāj land. The iqṭāʿs granted to the military under the Būyids were probably made mainly on kharāj land and not ʿushr land, though by that time the distinction between these two types had become somewhat blurred. They were thus an extension of the īghār and tasvīj rather than the original iqṭāʿ. In fact, jurists such as Māwardī distinguish between the new and the old iqṭāʿ (which were properly grants of ʿushr land), calling the latter *iqṭāʿ al-tamlīk* and the former *iqṭāʿ al-istighlāl*. The difference between them was that the iqṭāʿ al-tamlīk was a grant of ownership, its purpose the extension of cultivation, whereas the iqṭāʿ al-istighlāl was a grant of the usufruct, and its purpose was remuneration for services.

Under the Būyids the men to whom the new type of iqṭāʿ, the military iqṭāʿ, was granted did not normally live in the area granted to them, but merely sent their agents to collect their revenues. In theory these iqṭāʿs were not hereditary but were subject to periodic redistribution. The holder had to perform military service and was theoretically subject to detailed regulations and inspection. The amīrs who held these iqṭāʿs had no responsibility for the payment of the soldiery, who

[1] ʿUshr land was land which paid land tax at the rate of one-tenth of the produce; *kharāj* land paid at a higher rate. The classification of lands on the basis of these two rates was an intricate problem; see F. Løkkegaard, *Islamic Taxation in the Classic Period* (Copenhagen, 1950), pp. 72 ff.

received iqṭāʿs or pay from the state. A provincial governor distributed the area under his jurisdiction as iqṭāʿs, but he did this as an official of the state and not because the area formed part of his private domain. Legally the possession of an iqṭāʿ did not give the *muqṭaʿ* (the holder or grantee) any juridical rights over the inhabitants, but in practice there were widespread usurpations by the military under the Būyids. Moreover, the tendency for the functions of the provincial governor, the provincial military commander, the tax-collector, the tax-farmer, and the muqṭaʿ to be combined in one person led to the emergence of large properties virtually independent of the central government. The tendency for the *de facto* powers of the muqṭaʿ to increase was also strengthened by the fact that governors frequently received some areas in their provinces by way of iqṭāʿs; in such cases they combined in these districts their economic power as muqṭaʿ with their functions as governor, and tended to exercise the powers of both throughout the province.[1] There were also cases under the Būyids where a muqṭaʿ was given, in addition to his functions as muqṭaʿ, the administrative duties and obligations of a provincial governor; but this type of iqṭaʿ was the exception in Būyid times, and did not become widespread until the Saljuq period.[2]

The "military" iqṭāʿ under the Būyids was controlled by the military divan, the *dīwān al-jaish*, at whose head was the *ʿāriḍ* or muster-master. Thus the military dīvān was concerned not only, or even primarily, with military administration, but rather with the fiscal value (*ʿibra*) and characteristics of each iqṭāʿ, and with the re-allocation of iqṭāʿs as they fell vacant.[3] This intimate connexion between the assessment of taxes and the levy of troops continued in the Saljuq period; but as the "military" iqṭāʿ became assimilated to the "administrative" iqṭāʿ, the careful estimate of the exact fiscal value of each tended to be replaced by an approximate value; eventually the iqṭāʿ came to be defined not by fiscal value but by service; and then, through usurpation, it became an hereditary domain over which the muqṭaʿ had governmental prerogatives.[4]

Throughout the Saljuq empire there was considerable variety of practice as well as of terminology, and the term *iqṭāʿ* is used in the

[1] Cf. C. Cahen, "L'Evolution de l'iqtaʿ du ixe au xiiie siècle", in *Annales E.S.C.* (1953), pp. 35–6.

[2] See further my article, "Reflexions on the *iqṭāʿ*" in *Arabic and Islamic studies in honor of Hamilton A. R. Gibb*, ed. George Makdisi (Leiden, 1965), pp. 358–76.

[3] Cf. C. Cahen, pp. 36–7.

[4] Cf. C. Cahen, p. 43.

sources to cover a number of different types of grants. Thus it was used to mean (1) a grant on the revenue, or a grant of land for (*a*) military service and (*b*) in lieu of salary; (2) the grant of a district, and jurisdiction over it, to Saljuq maliks, amīrs, and others, which was virtually a grant of provincial government; (3) a tax farm (though this is more often referred to as *ḍamān*); and (4) the grant of (*a*) a personal estate and (*b*) an allowance or pension. Iqṭā‘s to the sultan's wives and other Saljuq women, to the caliph, and to members of the religious classes fall into the last category. It must not be assumed, however, that all iqṭā‘s fall neatly into one or other of these categories, or that all iqṭā‘s belonging to the same category necessarily conformed to the same pattern. There was no doubt a general tendency to follow accepted precedent, which resulted in a general similarity of usage, but this does not exclude the possibility of a variety of special provisions according to circumstances.

Niẓām al-Mulk, discussing the relations of the muqṭa‘s to the population, states:

> Let those who hold *iqṭā‘s*, know that they have no authority over the peasants beyond this, that they should take the due amount which has been assigned to them from the peasants in a good way, and that when they have done so the peasants shall be secure in their persons, and their money, wives, children, goods, and farms shall be secure and the *muqṭa‘s* have no claim over them... Let the *muqṭa‘s* know that the country and the subjects (*ra‘iyyat*) all belong to the sultan. The *muqṭa‘s*, who are set over them, and the governors (*vālīān*) are like *s͟haḥnas* in relation to the subjects, as the king is to others [i.e. those subjects not on assigned lands].[1]

Though it would seem from the above that Niẓām al-Mulk has primarily in mind the "military" iqṭā‘, his coupling of the muqṭa‘ with the vālī suggests that he was discussing something rather different from the "military" iqṭā‘ of the Būyid period. In another passage he states that if attention were ever drawn to the ruin and dispersal of the inhabitants of any district, the matter should at once be investigated and the condition of the muqṭa‘ and *‘āmil* inquired into, in order to prevent the land becoming waste, the peasants dispersing, and money being levied unjustly.[2] This suggests that the idea of increasing cultivation had to some extent been carried over from the old iqṭā‘ al-tamlīk to the new type of iqṭā‘ which was developing under the Saljuqs; and, further, that the "military" and the "administrative" iqṭā‘ were becoming assimilated to each other. This is borne out by Bundārī's statement

[1] *Siyāsat-Nāma*, p. 28. [2] *Ibid.* p. 119.

that Niẓām al-Mulk, seeing the disorder of the country and the irregularity of the payment of taxes, assigned the country to the soldiers (*ajnād*), handing over to them its produce so that they had an interest in its prosperity.[1] It is thus difficult in Saljuq times to make a clear distinction between the "military" and the "administrative" iqṭāʿ. All grants were entirely a matter of grace, and revocable at will by the sultan.

Grants of "administrative" iqṭāʿs to Saljuq maliks do not differ materially from similar grants to the great amīrs, though in the former it is possible to see the influence of the custom of the steppe, according to which the ruling khan did not exercise power, to the exclusion of the other members of his family but rather as the head of a council of elders. The Saljuq malik normally resided in the area assigned to him. These grants were not intended to be permanent, but a tendency arose for different branches of the family to regard certain districts as their own iqṭāʿ. In the case of the Saljuqs of Kirmān, Rūm, and Syria, this led to the establishment of three independent kingdoms.

When he appointed Malik-Shāh as his valī ʿahd in 458/1066, Alp-Arslan gave iqṭāʿs to various members of his family: Inanch Yabghu received Māzandarān; Sulaimān b. Dā'ūd received Balkh, his sons Arslan-Arghu and Arslan-Shāh were given Khwārazm and Marv respectively; Alp-Arslan's brother Ilyās received Chaghāniyān and Tukhāristān; Masʿūd b. Er-Tash had Baghshūr, and Maudūd b. Er-Tash had Isfizār. On his deathbed Alp-Arslan made further assignments. He bestowed upon his son Ayāz what had formerly belonged to Dā'ūd in Balkh, and he also earmarked for him 500,000 dīnārs; but the fortresses in those districts he assigned to Malik-Shāh, and he gave Fārs and Kirmān to Qavurt b. Dā'ūd, allocating to him also a sum of money.

These and similar grants made by later sultans are referred to in the sources as iqṭāʿs. They were in all cases simply delegations of authority and did not contain any implication of vassalage or permanent rights, though these were sometimes usurped. The duties delegated were the normal duties of a Muslim ruler, including the patronage of religion and of the religious classes, preservation of public order, holding or supervising the maẓālim court, collecting taxes, and paying salaries and allowances. In some cases the duty of consultation was also enjoined upon the malik. This derived from two sources: the custom of the steppe and the Quranic principle of "Consult them in affairs". The

[1] P. 55.

terms of the grant varied. In most cases complete financial control was given to the malik, in the sense that all revenue was collected by him. He was usually instructed not to increase taxation, and was in any case limited in this by local custom and Islamic theory. The degree to which he could sub-assign the area under him varied. Sanjar, reinstating Maḥmūd b. Muḥammad after his rebellion in 513/1119, appears to have acted exceptionally when he retained Ray as a precaution in case Maḥmūd should rebel again.[1] During the reign of Mas'ūd b. Muḥammad, Ray was also excluded from the area he ruled, and was assigned by Sanjar to al-Muqarrab Jauhar. It was subsequently held by the latter's mamlūk 'Abbās, whom Mas'ūd killed in 541/1146–7.

Similarly, the assignments made to the great amīrs, which were also delegations of some or all the ruler's normal duties within the area assigned, are usually referred to in the sources as iqṭā's when they are in the western provinces, and their holders are called muqṭa's. Occasionally the term *vālī* is used, apparently as a synonym for muqṭa'. In Khurāsān, Gurgān, and in the neighbouring districts, these grants during Sanjar's reign were known by the traditional terms for a provincial government, *vilāya*, *'amal*, *riyāsa*, and *niyāba*, and the term iqṭā' appears to have been used in a more specific sense, corresponding rather to the "military" iqṭā'. Each iqṭā' was supposed to bring in a definite sum of money, in return for which the holder furnished the ruler with a specified number of troops; and a register of the iqṭā's and of the number of troops the muqṭa's were supposed to furnish was kept in the dīvān. Thus the diploma issued by Sanjar's dīvān to Aḍud al-Dīn for the office of governor of Gurgān required him to look carefully into the iqṭā's according to their original descriptions, and to recover for the dīvān anything that had been fraudulently incorporated into someone's iqṭā' without his or the sultan's permission. Any grant that had fallen into disuse was not to be conferred on a new holder without the sultan's order.[2]

In the early period of Saljuq expansion much of the country was administered by the former local ruling families who acted first as Saljuq tributaries, and finally, so far as they retained part or the whole of their possessions, as Saljuq governors or muqṭa's. These governor-

[1] Ibn al-Athīr, *al-Kāmil fi'l-ta'rīkh*, ed. C. J. Tornberg (Leiden, 1851–76), vol. x, pp. 388–9. Ḥamd Allāh Mustaufī in the *Tārīkh-i Guzīda* states that Sanjar kept something in the possession of his dīvān in every district (ed. E. G. Browne, Gibb Memorial Series, London, 1910), vol. xiv, p. 458).

[2] *'Atabat al-kataba*, p. 31.

ships, like the grants to the amīrs, are also called in the sources iqṭā'ṣ, and the conditions under which they were granted were virtually the same as for the amīrs.[1] From the death of Malik-Shāh, an increasing amount of the country was alienated from the central government as "administrative" iqṭā'ṣ granted to the amīrs, until finally the area directly administered by the sultan became almost negligible. These grants also derived from the absolute sovereignty of the sultan and were entirely arbitrary, subject to re-grant at irregular intervals and to revocation without cause. The holder owed the obligation of obedience and service to the sultan. He was required to furnish the sultan with troops, and also with money when called upon to do so. In the event of his making fresh conquests, he was probably expected to remit something in cash or kind to the sultan. There was no obligation of protection or maintenance on the part of the sultan, nor was there a contract involving mutual fealty.

The extent to which the muqṭa' exercised financial control varied. Niẓām al-Mulk's exposition in the *Siyāsat-Nāma* gives the impression that it was limited; and Bundārī's statement, concerning Niẓām al-Mulk's alleged practice of assigning the pay of the military on different districts (p. 55) suggests that either considerable areas of the empire were at that time directly administered, or that the central government retained control over all or some of the provincial taxes. Usually, however, despite the statement of Niẓām al-Mulk, the muqṭa' probably exercised complete financial control over an "administrative" iqṭā'. Moreover, within his iqṭā' he was able to make sub-assignments to his own followers; and their relation to him was similar to that existing between him and the sultan. Amīrs who attained to a status of semi-independence as local rulers freely assigned the area under their control. There were also muqṭa'ṣ who farmed out the taxes of some of the territory assigned to them. They usually had freedom of choice in the appointment of administrative officials in their assignments. If the muqṭa' held an extensive area, of necessity he appointed deputies and subordinate officials to act for him; and the fact that the muqṭa' was often absent from his iqṭā' on military campaigns with the sultan, or on the sultan's behalf, also sometimes made it necessary for him to appoint a deputy to act for him.

No means were devised by the central government to maintain

[1] The iqṭā'ṣ granted as personal estates to members of former local ruling families fall into a different category.

control over the "administrative" iqṭā' or to prevent a muqṭa''s injustice or rebellion except the threat of superior forces. In theory the oppressed could seek redress from the sultan, but in practice the latter was accessible only if he happened to be passing through the area or its neighbourhood. Ibn al-Athīr relates a case of two men from Lower Iraq demanding redress from Malik-Shāh in 485/1092 against their muqṭa' Khumar-Tegin, the shaḥna of Baghdad, who, they alleged, had extorted 1,600 dīnārs from them. Malik-Shāh dismissed Khumar-Tegin from his iqṭā', returned the money to the plaintiffs, and gave them both an additional 100 dīnārs.[1] Niẓām al-Mulk states that the muqṭa' should be forbidden from preventing his subjects coming to court to demand redress, and he should be punished and his iqṭā' cancelled if he does so.[2]

Acts of usurpation were common; and as the power of the amīrs increased, the grant of an "administrative" iqṭā' tended to become merely the recognition of an amīr's possession of a district. Further, the sultan would sometimes play off one amīr against another by assigning the same district to them simultaneously; and frequently an amīr had to take possession of his iqṭā' by force. In theory the grant of an "administrative" iqṭā' was not hereditary; but as their power grew, a hereditary tendency appeared, and several amīrs transferred their iqṭā's to their sons or dependants by inheritance or by disposing of them by testament.

Certain court offices had particular districts attached to them as iqṭā's to provide for their upkeep, or else the iqṭa's were a special charge on the revenue of a particular district. Thus the *tash-khāna* (the royal pantry) in the time of Malik-Shāh was a charge on the kharāj of Khwārazm, and the *jāma-khāna* (Royal Wardrobe) on the revenue of Khūzistān. Atsïz, who was the *tash-dār* of Malik-Shāh, eventually established virtual independence in Khwārazm and founded an independent dynasty. Various officials were also paid by grants of land or grants on the revenue, both also known as iqṭā's. A number of the shaḥnas of Baghdad, for instance, held Takrīt as an iqṭā'. Wāsiṭ and Ḥulwān at different times were also held as an iqṭā' by the shaḥnas of Baghdad. The vizier was paid in part by iqṭā's (see below, p. 261). Ibn Balkhī states that in his time (i.e. during the reign of Muḥammad b. Malik-Shāh), Jahrūm, in Fārs, was part of the allowances (*mavājib*) of the valī 'ahd;[3] but this may have resembled the kind of iqṭā' granted as

[1] Vol. x, p. 144. [2] *Siyāsat-Nāma*, p. 28. [3] *Fārs-Nāma*, p. 131.

a pension or allowance rather than the iqṭā‘ attached to a particular office.

The iqṭā‘ system did not in itself involve decentralization or even a relaxation of the authority of the central government. Under a strong ruler it contributed to the strength and cohesion of the state, but under a weak ruler it led to political disintegration. When, after the death of Malik-Shāh, the muqṭa‘s began to establish their semi-independence by usurpation, the link between the sultan and his subjects became increasingly tenuous. Thus by abuse the system contributed to the political disintegration of the empire, but not necessarily to its economic decay, since the individual muqṭa‘ was restrained, by self-interest if nothing else, from reducing his iqṭā‘ to a state of ruin; indeed, he often succeeded in transforming it into a virtually hereditary domain. Also by abuse the system contributed to the growth of "private" armies, and to the virtual subjection of the peasantry; but against this the muqṭa‘ protected them from both the depredations of neighbours and the extortions of government officials.

After the death of Malik-Shāh it became increasingly common for iqṭā‘s to be granted to maliks who were still boys, in which case the land was administered by the malik's atabeg. The atabegate was an institution belonging especially to the Saljuq period, though its origins are possibly to be sought in the social organization and customs of the Türkmen. The first well-attested grant of the title *atabeg* is the one to Niẓām al-Mulk by Malik-Shāh when he succeeded to the throne.[1] According to the *Akhbār al-daulat al-Saljūqiyya*, Alp-Arslan also had an atabeg during the lifetime of his father, in the person of Quṭb al-Dīn Kül-Sarïgh (?Qïzïl-Sarïgh);[2] and Ibn Khallikān states that when Chaghrï Beg Dā'ūd appointed Niẓām al-Mulk to look after Alp-Arslan, he said to the boy, "consider him as a parent and do not disobey his counsels".[3] If this was so, it would seem that the atabegate in its original form was primarily a social institution, and that the later and more familiar form was an aberration due to the militarization of the state. All or most of the later atabegs, with the exception of ‘Alī b. Abī ‘Alī al-Qummī, who was one of Berk-Yaruq's atabegs, were amīrs. Normally, too, the atabeg was married to the mother of the malik who was entrusted to his care.

The atabegate as it developed under the Saljuqs had two aspects,

[1] Ibn al-Athīr, vol. x, p. 54. See also Cahen's article "Atabak", in *Encycl. of Islam*, new ed.

[2] Pp. 28–9.

[3] Vol. I, p. 413.

a social and a political. The atabeg was in charge of the prince's education. This presumably was the object of the appointment of 'Alī b. Abī 'Alī al-Qummī as atabeg to Berk-Yaruq—who was not, contrary to the usual custom, given an iqṭā' during the reign of Malik-Shāh. If a young malik was assigned a province or district the atabeg attached to him was responsible for its administration and therefore it was natural that those appointed to the office were almost without exception Turkish amīrs.

In its political aspect, one of the objects of the atabegate was to control the malik and prevent his rebellion in the province assigned to him. This was probably Berk-Yaruq's dominant motive in appointing atabegs to his brothers Muḥammad and Sanjar. Muḥammad, however, when he felt strong enough to be independent, killed his atabeg, Qutlugh-Tegin, and took possession of Arrān. Maḥmūd b. Muḥammad, in appointing Kün-Toghdï as atabeg to his brother Toghrïl in 513/1119–20, had apparently a similar end in view; but Kün-Toghdï, although he had instructions to bring Toghrïl to Maḥmūd, instead induced him to rebel.

As the power of the amīrs increased relative to that of the sultans, the atabegate came to be used, not so much to prevent the rebellion of a Saljuq prince, as to retain the nominal allegiance of a powerful or rebellious amīr; and such conquests as the latter made were nominally under the sultan's ultimate sovereignty. This was the general tendency from the reign of Muḥammad b. Malik-Shāh onwards. As it became more marked, the atabeg was often made the nominal as well as the actual governor of the province, and the malik was sent with him only as a matter of form. Thus in 502/1108–9 Fārs was assigned to Chavlï Saqao and not to his two-year-old ward Chaghrï b. Muḥammad.

The career of Chavlï Saqao is typical of that of the great amīrs of the time, and illustrates the prevailing instability, the mutual jealousies of the amīrs, and the growing weakness of the sultan *vis-à-vis* the amīrs. Chavlï Saqao was a native of the district lying between Rām Hurmuz and Arrajān, and in due course he established himself on the borders of Fārs and Khūzistān. Muḥammad b. Malik-Shāh after his accession sent Maudūd b. Altun-Tegin to besiege him, and after seven months Chavlï submitted and came to Muḥammad in Iṣfahān. In 500/1106 he was assigned Mosul and other districts, which were then in the possession of Chökermish. Chavlï set out for Mosul and captured Chökermish near Irbīl. The people of Mosul thereupon made Zangī b. Chökermish governor in his father's stead, and wrote for help to Ṣadaqa, the Mazyadid, Qïlïch-Arslan, and to Bursuqī, who was then shaḥna of Baghdad.

Chavlï laid siege to Mosul, but retired to Sinjār on the approach of Qïlïch-Arslan. There he was joined by Il-Ghāzī b. Artuq and by a number of Chökermish's followers; later he joined Riḍwān and took Raḥba. He then defeated Qïlïch-Arslan on the Khābūr River and returned to Mosul, the gates of which were opened to him. Having established himself there he withdrew his allegiance from Muḥammad b. Malik-Shāh; and when Muḥammad made preparations to march against Ṣadaqa in 501/1107–8, Chavlï, together with Il-Ghāzī b. Artuq, sent an offer of support to Ṣadaqa. Meanwhile the spoliation of Chavlï's domains was proposed by Muḥammad to the Banī Bursuq, Maudūd b. Altun-Tegin, and to a number of other amīrs. Chavlï, accordingly having prepared Mosul for siege, left his wife to defend the city and himself went to collect reinforcements. At Niṣībīn he was joined, somewhat unwillingly, by Il-Ghāzī b. Artuq, and also by Abū Najm and Abū Kāmil Manṣūr, the sons of Ṣadaqa. He agreed to go with them to Ḥilla and they decided to make Bektash b. Tutush b. Alp-Arslan their spokesman. But the Ispahbud Sabāvū, who had subsequently joined them, advised Chavlï to go again to Syria because the sultan was in or near Iraq. Chavlï accepted his advice. Allying himself to Baldwin of Edessa and Jocelin, he went to Syria but was defeated by Tancred in 502/1108. Muḥammad b. Malik-Shāh meanwhile sent Ḥusain b. Qutlugh-Tegin to Chavlï to win back his allegiance. Chavlï agreed to submit if the siege of Mosul was raised, and he offered to send his son to the sultan's court as a hostage. However, Maudūd, who was besieging Mosul, refused to raise the siege, and Mosul fell shortly afterwards. Realizing that he could not hope for success in Syria or the Jazīreh, Chavlï then determined to go to Muḥammad b. Malik-Shāh in the hope that Ḥusain b. Qutlugh-Tegin would intercede for him. He reached Iṣfahān, surrendered Bektash b. Tutush to Muḥammad, and made his peace with him. Muḥammad then sent Chavlï to Fārs as atabeg to his son Chaghrï. Fārs at the time was in a state of disorder and not under the effective control of the sultan; hence the sultan in sending Chavlï to Fārs was not running any immediate risk of renewed rebellion, since Chavlï would first have to restore obedience in the province. In fact, Chavlï was largely successful in subduing the Shabānkāra, who had reduced the Shāpūr district of Fārs to a state of ruin and disorder, and in bringing back a considerable measure of prosperity to the province. He died in Fārs in 510/1116–17.

As the political aspect of the atabegate began increasingly to dominate its social aspect, a malik was sometimes entrusted to a succession of different atabegs, as happened, for example, with Mas'ūd b. Muḥammad. Or an amīr was put in charge of a succession of maliks. Qasīm al-Daula Aq-Sonqur Bursuqī is a case in point. He was originally a mamlūk of Bursuq, who was made shaḥna of Baghdad by Toghrïl Beg in 452/1060–1 and subsequently served Alp-Arslan, Malik-Shāh, and Berk-Yaruq. Aq-Sonqur Bursuqī was made shaḥna of Baghdad by Muḥammad b. Malik-Shāh in 498/1105. After the death of Maudūd b. Altun-Taq, the muqṭa' of Mosul, he was assigned Mosul and the Jazīreh in 508/1114–15, appointed atabeg to Mas'ūd b. Muḥammad, and ordered to organize a *jihād* (holy war) against the Franks in Syria. In 509/1115–16 Muḥammad b. Malik-Shāh assigned Mosul to Cha'ush Beg, who also became atabeg to Mas'ūd. Bursuqī retired to Raḥba, which he held as an iqṭā'. Muḥammad b. Malik-Shāh died in 511/1117. In the following year Bursuqī was appointed shaḥna of Baghdad by Maḥmūd b. Muḥammad, but Mengü-Bars was appointed to the same office almost immediately afterwards. Mas'ūd then assigned Marāgheh to Bursuqī as an iqṭā' in addition to Raḥba. Dubais b. Ṣadaqa the Mazyadid meanwhile urged Cha'ush Beg to rebel against Maḥmūd, to seek the kingdom in the name of Mas'ūd, and also to seize Bursuqī. The latter, learning of this plan, joined Maḥmūd. For a brief period the khuṭba was read in Āzarbāījān, the Jazīreh, and Mosul in the name of Mas'ūd. Battle was joined between him and Maḥmūd in 514/1120 and Mas'ūd was defeated, after which Maḥmūd sent Bursuqī to Mas'ūd with a pardon. In 515/1121 Bursuqī was assigned Mosul by Maḥmūd and was ordered to undertake a jihād against the Franks. The following year Bursuqī was given Wāsiṭ as an additional iqṭā', together with the office of shaḥna of Baghdad; he was also reappointed atabeg to Mas'ūd and married to Mas'ūd's mother, who had been seized by Mengü-Bars on the death of Muḥammad b. Malik-Shāh in 511/1117 before the expiry of her *'idda* (the legal period of retirement assigned to a widow before she may marry again).[1] Seven years later, Bursuqī was dismissed from the office of shaḥna of Baghdad at the caliph's request. Maḥmūd then made him atabeg to one of his sons, sent him back to Mosul, and ordered him once again to undertake a jihād against the Franks. After taking Aleppo he returned to Mosul, where he was assassinated by a Bāṭinī in 520/1126.

[1] Ibn al-Athīr, vol. x, pp. 380, 391; Bundārī, p. 159; Ibn al-Athīr, *al-Daulat al-Atabakiyya Mulūki 'l Mawṣil*, in *Receuil des historiens des croisades, Sources Arabes*, vol. II, pt. 2, p. 46.

While the sultan thus hoped to retain the nominal allegiance of the great amīrs through the atabegate, they, on the other hand, saw in it a means to establish their virtual independence. In view of the fact that sovereignty was considered inherent in the Saljuq family, it was important for an amīr to secure the person of a Saljuq malik in whose name he could act. The atabegate provided him with a ready means of doing so. Further, in view of the jealousies among the amīrs, it was easier for them to establish virtually independent kingdoms under the guise of atabegates in the outlying provinces than to dominate the sultanate itself, and there are cases of amīrs demanding or taking forcible possession of some malik, with the nominal acquiescence of the sultan, in order to increase their prestige. Thus Mengü-Bars,[1] having made himself master of Fārs in succession to Qaracha al-Sāqī (Saljuq-Shāh b. Muḥammad's atabeg, whom Sanjar had killed in 526/1132) wrote to Toghrïl b. Muḥammad and demanded that he send his son Alp-Arslan to him; if his demand was met, he offered to recognize Toghrïl as sultan. In due course Toghrïl sent Alp-Arslan to Mengü-Bars.

'Imad al-Dīn Zangī, who had originally been in the service of Bursuqī, was another case in point. He made himself master of Mosul in 521/1127 on the death of Bursuqī's son 'Izz al-Din. Two Saljuq maliks were under his care. One he had captured from Dubais b. Ṣadaqa the Mazyadid, to whom the malik had been entrusted.[2] The other was Alp-Arslan b. Maḥmūd, who was known as al-Khafajī. According to Ibn al-Athīr, Zangī pretended to hold the country on behalf of the malik Alp-Arslan, in whose name he sent envoys and answered letters, awaiting the death of Mas'ūd b. Muḥammad, at which time he, Zangī, would assemble an army and seek the sultanate in the name of al-Khafajī.[3] As it happened Zangī died before he could put his plan into action. The fact, however, that an amīr of his power and virtual independence should be found pursuing such a policy, is striking evidence of the added prestige which the possession of a Saljuq malik gave to an amīr. Once an atabeg had firmly established his power, however, the dependent malik was allowed to fall into obscurity, and the atabeg, acting as a virtually independent ruler,

[1] Not to be confused with Mengü-Bars the shaḥna of Baghdad, mentioned above, who was killed in 513/1119–20.

[2] There is some confusion in the sources over the names of these two maliks and the events connected with them: cf. Bundārī, p. 187, Ibn Khallikān, vol. I, p. 330, and Ibn al-Athīr, *al-Daulat*, pp. 126–7. The prince captured from Dubais was probably one of Maḥmūd b. Muḥammad's sons, whom Dubais had seized in 523/1129 (Ibn al-Athīr, vol. x, p. 461).

[3] *Al-Daulat*, pp. 126–7.

transmitted his province to his descendants. The political atabegate thus became a potent factor in the disintegration of the great Saljuq empire. From the reign of Mas'ūd b. Muḥammad on, Āzarbāījān and Fārs were the scene of various attempts by atabegs to establish their independence, and eventually in both provinces independent dynasties were set up.

Although after the death of Malik-Shāh, if not before, most of the empire was alienated in the form of iqṭā's from the control of the central government, there were other areas, towns and districts, where a rather different arrangement prevailed, for they were under an official known as the shaḥna. He was in effect a military governor appointed by the sultan or his governor. One of his main functions was to carry out the decisions of the qāḍī's court, when coercive force was necessary for this; and similarly to support other officials, such as the *'āmil* (tax-collector), in the execution of their duties. A muqṭa' had full control of an "administrative" iqṭā', and he exercised by delegation virtually all the functions of the ruler. But the shaḥna usually had no power to appoint district officials (apart from those in his own dīvān), and he was concerned merely with the maintenance of order, so that the collection of taxes and the general administration could be carried on.[1] The position of the shaḥna of Iṣfahān, for example, was clearly that of a military governor only. On her deathbed in 487/1094, Terken Khatun ordered the shaḥna of Iṣfahān to hold the kingdom for her son Maḥmūd. Various shaḥnas of Ray are mentioned in the sources, including 'Abbās the mamlūk of al-Muqarrab Jauhar.[2] Ray, like Iṣfahān, was at one time the Saljuq capital, and, as stated above, was retained by Sanjar in the possession of his dīvān. This is not to say, however, that the shaḥna was to be found only in directly administered areas.[3] Exercising the functions delegated to him by the ruler, the holder of an "administrative" iqṭa' sometimes appointed shaḥnas; but generally speaking, although there are numerous references to

[1] Cf. Diploma for a *shaḥna*, Muḥammad b. 'Abd al-Khāliq al-Maihanī, *Dastūr-i Dabīrī*, ed. Adnan Erzi (Ankara, 1962), pp. 113–14.

[2] See my article, "The Administration of Sanjar's Empire as illustrated in the '*Atabat al-kataba*", in *B.S.O.A.S.* (1957), pp. 380 ff.

[3] Cf. also H. Horst, *Die Staatsverwaltung der Grosselǧūqen und Ḫōrazmšāhs*, p. 94, n. 2. Preserved in the '*Ataba al-kataba* is a document issued by Sanjar's dīvān for one Saif al-Dīn Yaran-Qush, for the office of shaḥna of Juvain; this document contains a somewhat puzzling statement, to the effect that the office of shaḥna in Juvain belonged to the dīvān of Sanjar's sister Nūr(?) Bilge, and was conferred upon Saif al-Dīn by her dīvān (by virtue of the document issued by Sanjar).

shaḥnas in the north-eastern provinces in the time of Sanjar, references to them in the western provinces are less common. The shaḥna appears to have been paid by local dues levied in accordance with custom.

There are occasional references in the sources to revenue farms (*ḍamān*). These verged on the "administrative" iqṭā', but whereas the muqṭa' usually had complete control over the general administration of the district and maintained armed forces which he used, if called upon, in the service of the sultan, the revenue farmer was concerned only with the collection of taxes. Further, the farmer's contract was for a stipulated period, probably one or three years. The number and size of these farms were relatively small. Most of the references are to the early period of Saljuq rule, and to the area in and around Iraq. Toghrïl Beg farmed Baṣra and Ahvāz to Hazārasp b. Bānkīr in 448/1056–7 for 300,000 dīnārs and 60,000 dīnārs respectively.[1] In 451/1059 the farmer was changed, but in 456/1064 Baṣra was again in the hands of Hazārasp, and in 459/1066–7 Alp-Arslan farmed it to him together with Wāsiṭ for 300,000 dīnārs. In 451/1059 Wāsiṭ was farmed by Toghrïl Beg to a certain Abū 'Alī b. Faḍlān for 200,000 dīnārs; and in 455/1063 to another revenue farmer for the same sum. In 452/1060–1 and 455/1063 Toghrïl Beg farmed Baghdad for three years, on the first occasion for 400,000 dīnārs and on the second (to a different revenue farmer) for 150,000 dīnārs. Malik-Shāh farmed Baṣra first to a Jew named Ibn 'Allān, and then in 472/1079–80 to Khumar-Tegin, who gave him 100,000 dīnārs a year and 100 horses. With Gauhar Ā'īn, the shaḥna of Baghdad, Khumar-Tegin had apparently plotted the fall of Ibn 'Allān. The latter took refuge with Niẓām al-Mulk. But Khumar-Tegin and Gauhar Ā'īn, since they were personal enemies of Nizām al-Mulk, slandered Ibn 'Allān before the sultan and persuaded him to have the man drowned.[2] Alp-Arslan also farmed Fārs to Faḍlūya, the Shabānkāra leader.

For the most part the tribal groups in the Saljuq empire were not directly administered by the central government. The Kurds and Arabs, for instance, were left mainly under the local rulers or else came under a muqṭa'. The question of direct administration did not therefore arise. The same is largely true of parts of Ṭabaristān. The Shabānkāra in

[1] Ibn al-Athīr, vol. IX, p. 422; *Fārs-Nāma*, p. 121. Ibn al-Jauzī states that Kundurī farmed these districts to Hazārasp for 300,000 *sulṭānī* dīnārs (vol. VIII, pp. 168–9).

[2] Ibn al-Athīr, vol. X, p. 75 *bis*; Ibn al-Jauzī, vol. VIII, p. 323. Prior to this, Ibn 'Allān had farmed some of the private domains of the caliph and had defaulted on his contract (Ibn al-Athīr, vol. IX, p. 454).

Fārs were also under their own leaders for much of the period until they were temporarily subdued by Chaulī Saqao.

The most important tribal group as regards both numbers and influence was the Türkmen. But because of their numbers and the Saljuqs' early relation with them, their control presented a special problem. Throughout the period they tended to continue moving in a westerly direction. Alp-Arslan's policy was to employ them in raids outside the *dār al-Islām*, and many of them pushed on into Syria and Asia Minor. Others, however, remained in the provinces over which the sultan maintained control. Some were incorporated into the service of the sultan (see p. 218 above), but the majority continued to follow a nomadic or semi-nomadic existence, moving from winter to summer pastures and migrating in search of new pastures. The main concentrations of Türkmen were to be found in Iraq, the Jazīreh, Āzarbāījān, Gurgān, and the neighbourhood of Marv. These concentrations were not necessarily constant throughout the Great Saljuq period. The power of the sultan held the Türkmen more or less in check until the death of Malik-Shāh. The weakening of the empire after his death and the dissolution of the kingdom created by Tutush in Syria restored their freedom, and within two or three years several of them had formed independent principalities.[1] The fact that some of them had been officers of the sultan—Il-Ghāzī b. Artuq, for example, was a shaḥna of Baghdad on behalf of Muḥammad b. Malik-Shāh in 495/1101–2—helped them to transform themselves quickly into small territorial princes when the sultan's authority declined.

The Türkmen who remained in Gurgān and the neighbourhood of Marv during the reign of Sanjar came under his central dīvān. The official charged with their administration was also known as a shaḥna. His functions were primarily to maintain order and prevent the tribes encroaching on their neighbours, and to collect from them pasture dues and other taxes due to the government. In a diploma issued by Sanjar's dīvān, appointing Ïnanch Bilge Ulugh Jāndār Beg to the office of shaḥna of the Türkmen in Gurgān, it is recognized that they formed a special class. The jāndār beg was, among his other duties, to allot pastures and water to each leader according to the number of his households and followers.[2]

The Ghuzz in the neighbourhood of Marv and on the borders of the

[1] See Gibb, *Damascus Chronicle*, p. 25.
[2] See "The Administration of Sanjar's Empire", p. 382.

empire apparently regarded themselves as the special subjects of the sultan. They were difficult to control, and relations between them and Sanjar's dīvān were marked by a standing opposition between the settled and semi-settled population. Extortion was practised in the collection of the annual tribute of sheep, which they paid to the sultan's kitchen, and eventually they were driven to rebellion. Sanjar was then induced by his amīrs to march against them, and was defeated and captured by the Ghuzz in 548/1153–4; he remained a prisoner in their hands for three years. Although on this occasion the sultan's officials appear to have been at fault, the problem was by no means a simple one, because the Ghuzz were increasing in numbers and encroaching on the settled areas; and after the death of Sanjar in 552/1157, they overran parts of Khurāsān and Kirmān.

In exercising his functions as judge and guardian of public order, and in delegating these functions in the provinces to the muqṭa'ˁs, the sultan acted through the dargāh. A whole range of other functions, including in particular the collection of taxes, was exercised by the sultan through the central dīvān, the main department of the bureaucracy. In the dargāh, which was militarized and composed largely of Turkish amīrs, the sultan was accessible to his subjects for the redress of grievances; in the dīvān, which was mainly staffed by men who were not Turks and who had inherited the administrative traditions of the preceding dynasties, he came into contact with his subjects in a different way: namely, over the collection of taxes. He delegated his functions in the dīvān to the vizier, who at the height of his power supervised all aspects of the administration, secular and religious, and was more than just the head of the financial administration. Niẓām al-Mulk envisaged him as the keystone of the empire. "When the vizier is of good conduct and judgement", he states, "the kingdom flourishes and the army and subjects are contented, quiet and wealthy, and the ruler happy at heart; but when the vizier is of evil conduct, indescribable confusion appears in the kingdom, and the ruler is always distressed and afflicted in mind and the kingdom disturbed."[1]

The relationship between the dargāh and the central dīvān was not clearly formulated. The connecting link between them until the decline of the vizierate was the vizier himself. ʻAmīd al-Mulk Kundurī, Toghrïl Beg's vizier, and Niẓām al-Mulk both had direct access to the sultan; but under the later sultans, as stated above, the amīr ḥājib

[1] *Siyāsat-Nāma*, pp. 18–19.

appears to have been to some extent interposed between them. So far as the vizier conducted the sultan's relations with foreign rulers and with the caliphate, he acted in some measure as an official of the dargāh. When the caliph gave an audience to Malik-Shāh and his amīrs in 479/1086–7, Niẓām al-Mulk presented the amīrs to the caliph. On the accession of a new caliph it was often, though not invariably, the vizier who gave the oath of allegiance to him on behalf of the sultan. Negotiations for marriage alliances with the caliph were also usually carried out by the sultan's vizier. 'Amīd al-Mulk Kundurī acted on behalf of Toghrïl Beg when he demanded the hand of the caliph's daughter; and the negotiations for the marriage of Malik-Shāh's daughter to the caliph in 474/1081–2 were carried out by Niẓām al-Mulk. Similarly, Kamāl al-Dīn Abu'l Barakāt al-Darguzīnī, Mas'ūd b. Muḥammad's vizier, was his *vakīl* in the marriage of his sister Fāṭima to the caliph in 531/1137; and Ḍiyā' al-Mulk Aḥmad b. Niẓām al-Mulk, who was vizier to Muḥammad b. Malik-Shāh from 500/1107 to 504/1110–11, was *mutavallī* on behalf of the sultan's sister when she was married to the Caliph al-Mustaẓhir in 502/1109.

When the vizier deputized for the sultan in the maẓālim court, he was exercising functions that belonged to the dargāh rather than to the dīvān. Similarly, his supervision of the religious institution was delegated to him in his capacity as the sultan's deputy, and not specifically because he was the head of the bureaucracy, except perhaps so far as the administration of *auqāf* (religious endowments) was concerned. He had no power to appoint qāḍīs, *muḥtasibs*, khaṭībs or other officials of the religious institutions, though he may have advised the sultan on the matter. The main object of his supervising the religious institutions was probably to prevent any tendency towards heresy, because this was believed to threaten political stability. The early sultans, Toghrïl Beg, Alp-Arslan, Malik-Shāh, and Muḥammad b. Malik-Shāh, were strictly orthodox and Ḥanafīs by rite. The vizier in the early period was usually a Ḥanafī or a Shāfi'ī. Kundurī was a fanatical Ḥanafī, and instituted the commination of Shī'īs (*rāfiḍīs*) and Ash'arīs from the *minbars* of the mosques. Niẓām al-Mulk, who was a Shāfi'ī, abolished this practice. Under the later sultans strict orthodoxy was not insisted upon. Anushīrvān b. Khālid, who became vizier to Maḥmūd b. Muḥammad in 521/1127 and to Mas'ūd b. Muḥammad in 529/1134–5, was a Shī'ī; and Berk-Yaruq's mustaufī Majd al-Mulk Abu'l Faḍl Barāvistānī Qummī was, according to Ibn al-Athīr, a secret Shī'ī.

The main function of the vizier as head of the dīvān was a financial one. It was his duty to regulate the sources of revenue and to increase the revenue without causing injury to agricultural prosperity. He was expected to keep the finances of the state in a healthy condition and to hold sufficient revenue in reserve to meet emergencies.

The revenue of the empire derived from ordinary and extraordinary taxes, and from various other sources. Ordinary taxes comprised (*a*) canonical taxes: namely, *kharāj* (land tax), pasture taxes (*marā'ī*), and *jizya* (poll-tax on members of the protected communities, the *dhimmīs*); and (*b*) uncanonical taxes (*mukūs*), such as those on merchandise, tolls and customs, and a variety of dues (*rusūm*), including those levied for the payment of officials. Extraordinary taxes consisted of levies made for specific purposes. These were of two kinds: cesses imposed on existing taxes (e.g. for defaulters, arrears, and chipped and broken coins), which in the course of time tended to become assimilated to the original tax; and *ad hoc* levies, which were often extremely burdensome. Because Niẓām al-Mulk thought it necessary to state in the *Siyāsat-Nāma* that the taxes should not be demanded before harvest time, it may be inferred that they were, in fact, not infrequently demanded in advance—a practice that caused much hardship. Diplomas issued to officials concerned in tax collection, i.e. to provincial governors and others, frequently included instructions that the taxes should be levied only at the fixed rates and at the proper time. Since, however, the assessment was sometimes made in one kind of dīnār and paid in currency dīnārs, by manipulating the conversion rate of one dīnār to another it was possible to raise the amount of the tax without actually raising the nominal rate at which it was levied.

The land tax was assessed in one of three ways, by measurement (*misāḥa*), as a proportionate share of the crop (*muqāsama*), or at a fixed sum (*muqāṭa'a*). It was paid in cash and kind. Alp-Arslan is said to have levied kharāj in two annual instalments. The *Akhbār al-daulat al-Saljūqiyya* records that he was satisfied with the original kharāj (*al-kharāj al-aṣlī*), i.e. the ordinary or original assessment to which additional taxes had not been added, or which had not been raised by a manipulation of the conversion rates. Pasture taxes were levied on the nomadic or semi-nomadic population in one of two ways: either (1) they were based on the tent or family or on the number of head of stock owned, or (2) the community was assessed at a lump sum. Poll-taxes did not form an important item of revenue in Saljuq times. After Alp-

Arslan took Ani, the Byzantines are alleged to have agreed to pay jizya; and Alp-Arslan appointed the 'amīd of Khurāsān to collect this. Malik-Shāh is also stated to have received jizya from the Byzantine emperor; but both these payments, in so far as they were made, were in the nature of tribute rather than actual jizya.

The nature, method of assessment, and collection of uncanonical taxes varied widely throughout the empire. The matter of their levy moreover, involved a conflict between religious scruples and financial practice; attempts were made from time to time to revoke them, but never with lasting success. Malik-Shāh remitted additional levies (*qismat va taqsīṭ*) from the people of Iṣfahān;[1] and in 479/1086–7 he ordered the abolition of the mukūs levied on traders who handled all kinds of merchandise in Iraq and Khurāsān.[2] He also abolished all tolls and escort dues (*khafarāt*) paid by travellers throughout his dominions. Muḥammad b. Malik-Shāh, on his arrival in Baghdad in Sha'bān 501/1108, abolished the mukūs, *ḍarā'ib* (? imposts), market taxes, transit dues, and other similar dues which had been levied in Iraq and all his provinces, and tablets to this effect were hung up in the markets. When he went back to Iṣfahān, the mukūs were again levied on the merchants in Baghdad according to custom; on his return to Baghdad he re-affirmed their repeal. Toghrïl Beg, on the other hand, reimposed the mukūs and the practice of confiscating inheritances. Maḥmūd b. Muḥammad, on the advice of his vizier Kamāl al-Mulk Simīrumī, also decided to reimpose the mukūs in Iraq in 515/1121–2, but after the assassination of Kamāl al-Mulk in the following year, he revoked the mukūs and abolished the taxes that the vizier had imposed on merchants and dealers. Their abolition was brief, however, because Mas'ūd b. Muḥammad is recorded as having revoked the mukūs in 533/1138–9, and tablets to that effect were put up in the Friday mosques and markets.

Remissions of taxes were occasionally granted on special occasions or because of some natural calamity. Toghrïl Beg, for example, remitted the taxes of Iṣfahān for three years when he took the city in 443/1051. Individuals, such as members of the religious classes, were also sometimes given immunity from taxes as a special favour.

A fairly important source of revenue was provided by confiscations

[1] Ḥusain b. Muḥammad b. Ābī, *Tarjuma-i Maḥāsin-i Iṣfahān*, ed. 'Abbās Iqbāl (Tehran, 1328/1949), p. 140.

[2] Ibn al-Jauzī makes no mention of this under the year 479, but states that the *ḍarā'ib* and *mukūs* were abolished in Baghdad according to the decree of the Caliph al-Muqtadī in 480 (vol. IX, p. 39).

and fines. Toghrïl Beg confiscated 100,000 dīnārs and 20,000 dīnārs from an 'Alid and a Jew respectively in Baṣra in 449/1057–8. Under Alp-Arslan there were said to have been no confiscations, but after the death of Malik-Shāh, the mulcting of officials on their dismissal was common. This was a measure partly of the growing financial stringency, and partly of the increase in dishonesty and corruption among the official classes. Intrigue and insecurity were the normal concomitants of official life. Men of influence and power accumulated wealth to defend their personal interests against any future intrigues by their rivals, or against a loss of the sultan's favours, and those who were ambitious for office accumulated wealth in order to buy it. Through these corrupt practices many officials amassed, temporarily at least, considerable riches. Abu'l Qāsim Anasābādī Darguzīnī, who eventually became vizier to Toghrïl b. Muḥammad, founded his fortune when vizier to Muḥammad b. Malik-Shāh's amīr ḥājib, 'Alī b. 'Umar. The latter alleged that on his deathbed the sultan had ordered 200,000 dīnārs to be distributed among his enemies and those who had complaints against him; but when this sum was obtained from the treasury most of it was misappropriated by Darguzīnī. He appears to have been one of the most corrupt of the Saljuq officials, making large sums of money from confiscations and fines. Bundārī states that he fined Qutlugh Rashīdī, the chamberlain (*ustād al-dār*) of Maḥmūd b. Muḥammad, 110,000 dīnārs, also that he extracted from a merchant of Hamadān 30,000 dīnārs, and 20,000 and 70,000 dīnārs respectively from the ra'īs of Hamadān and the ra'īs of Tabrīz, together with 150,000 dīnārs from Tāj al-Dīn Daulatshāh b. 'Alā' al-Daula and his mother and vizier. Bundārī's own family also suffered at the hands of Darguzīnī. He relates that his uncle 'Azīz al-Dīn, who was employed in the *dīvān-i istīfā* of Maḥmūd b. Muḥammad, was imprisoned by Maḥmūd in return for 300,000 dīnārs from Darguzīnī, who also imprisoned Bundārī's father and another uncle, Ḍiyā' al-Dīn, and seized their estates.

Corruption became widespread under Muḥammad b. Malik-Shāh, and relatively large sums were involved. Bundārī relates that a number of prominent persons wanted to make their nominee ra'īs of Hamadān in place of the existing ra'īs, Abū Hāshim. Accordingly they imposed a fine of 700,000 dīnārs upon him, besides what was confiscated from his numerous retainers. Muḥammad b. Malik-Shāh sent Anushīrvān b. Khālid, who was then his treasurer, to collect the money. After

Anushirvān had paid the money into the sultan's treasury he told the sultan of the plot against Abū Hāshim. Muḥammad thereupon reinstated him as ra'īs and sent him magnificent presents and robes of honour.[1] Rāvandī gives a slightly different version of this incident. He alleges that Ḍiyā' al-Mulk Aḥmad b. Niẓām al-Mulk, Muḥammad's vizier, determined to attack the ra'īs and gave the sultan 500,000 dīnārs to hand him over, but that Abū Hāshim, hearing of this, came to Iṣfahān and bought himself off for 800,000 dīnārs in return for which Muḥammad handed Ḍiyā' al-Mulk over to him.[2]

Zain al-Mulk Abū Sa'īd b. Hindū, who became mustaufī in 498/1104–5 during the vizierate of Sa'd al-Mulk Abu'l Maḥāsin Āvajī, was alleged to have been extremely corrupt, and when Sa'd al-Mulk was killed in 500/1107, Muḥammad b. Malik-Shāh seized and imprisoned him for two years. He was subsequently reinstated and became Muḥammad's vizier. But in 506/1112–13 a number of amīrs conspired against him and offered to give 200,000 dīnārs of his wealth to the sultan's treasury if they were allowed to seize him. The sultan agreed; he was handed over to one of the amīrs, put to death, and his goods plundered. When Sanjar seized Muḥammad b. Fakhr al-Mulk b. Niẓām al-Mulk, who was his vizier from 500/1106 to 511/1118, the sum of 1,000,000 dīnārs in cash, together with jewels and other possessions, was found belonging to him.[3]

Further sources of revenue were the money received from the buying of offices (though offices were not put up to auction as they had been in Būyid times), and also presents from those who wished to secure or regain the sultan's favours; it is probable that revenue from these sources, as well as from confiscations and fines, went for the most part into the sultan's treasury and not the public treasury. Fakhr al-Mulk b. Niẓām al-Mulk gave Berk-Yaruq many presents, including tents, weapons, jewelled implements, Arab horses, hunting birds, and an armourer's shop (*zarrād-khāna*) when he joined him in 488/1095 and became vizier. Similarly in 494/1101, after defeating Muḥammad b. Malik-Shāh, and capturing his vizier Mu'ayyid al-Mulk b. Niẓām al-

[1] Pp. 89–90.

[2] *Rāḥat al-ṣudūr*, pp. 162–5. Ibn al-Athīr states that Abū Hāshim, whose maternal grandfather was Ibn 'Abbād, the famous Būyid vizier, was extremely wealthy, and that Muḥammad b. Malik-Shāh on one occasion mulcted him of 700,000 dīnārs. He died, according to Ibn al-Athīr, in 502/1109 (vol. x, pp. 332–3).

[3] Muḥammad b. Fakhr al-Mulk had apparently accepted a bribe from Arslan Shāh to induce Sanjar to abandon his march on Ghazna. Sanjar seized him on his return from Ghazna (Ibn al-Athīr, vol. x, p. 385; Bundārī, p. 244).

Mulk, Berk-Yaruq agreed to accept the latter as his own vizier in return for 100,000 gold dīnārs; but the new sultan later regretted his decision and killed the vizier before the transaction was completed.[1] Shams al-Mulk 'Uthmān b. Niẓām al-Mulk is alleged to have given his brother Ḍiyā' al-Mulk Aḥmad, vizier to Muḥammad b. Malik-Shāh 2,000 dīnārs to make him *'āriḍ al-jaish* in place of Anushīrvān b. Khālid. The sultan and his ministers probably exacted sums of money and presents in return for the grant of robes of honour and similar favours.

Tribute was paid to the Saljuqs by various local rulers, but this was not a regular source of revenue. In the early period of expansion, in the time of Toghrïl Beg, the local rulers made sundry payments to the Ghuzz; these were not tribute as they are sometimes represented in the sources, but rather payments to mercenaries which naturally ceased when the Ghuzz left the district. Later as the power of the Saljuqs increased and they began to reduce the local rulers to submission, the terms imposed often included the payment of a sum of money. But in due course most of the local rulers, if they continued to possess some or all of their former territories, were absorbed into the iqṭā' system. Occasionally in the later period tribute was imposed on a neighbouring ruler. Malik-Shāh, for example, imposed an annual tribute of 40,000 dīnārs on the ruler of Shīrvān, but this was not regularly paid;[2] and Sanjar, when he took Ghazna in 510/1116–17, settled an annual tribute of 250,000 dīnārs on Bahrām Shāh.

Lastly there was the revenue from the private estates that the sultan owned in various parts of the empire, including landed estates, *qanāts*, and real property (*mustaghallāt*) in towns. There is no indication of their total extent or income. In Kūfa the private domains of the sultan were farmed in 452/1060 for 40,000 dīnārs a year. It is not clear whether the

[1] Rāvandī's account of this incident is as follows: Mu'ayyid al-Mulk raised the money in a week, and it was agreed that the day after he paid it he should become vizier. However, disputes arose between him and the officials of the treasury over the value of what he had produced in cash and kind; and he haggled over this and annoyed them. On the next day when the sultan was having a siesta in his tent, the *tasht-dār*, thinking the sultan was asleep, said to a group of people, "How lacking in zeal these Saljuqs are! Now he (Berk-Yaruq) is going to make vizier again and trust a man who has given him so much trouble, who once induced a slave of his father [i.e. the amīr Unar] to seek the kingdom, and prepared for himself an insignia of royalty, and on another occasion went to Ganja and brought out his (the sultan's) brother [to seek the kingdom]...". The sultan heard this, came out of his tent, sent for Mu'ayyid al-Mulk, cut off his head, and turned to the *tasht-dār* and said, "See the zeal of the Saljuqs". Whereupon the *tasht-dār* fled and did not dare look upon the sultan again (*Raḥāt al-ṣudūr*, p. 147).

[2] Bundārī, p. 128. According to the *Akhbār al-daulat al-Saljūqiyya*, the sum fixed was 70,000 dīnārs (p. 73).

income from the sultan's private estates was paid into his treasury or the public treasury. So far as the revenue was collected and the estates administered by the tax collectors (*'ummāl*) of the *dīvān-i istīfā-yi mamālik*, it would seem likely that it was paid into the public treasury.

The most important charge upon the revenue was the payment of the standing army and expenditure on military expeditions. Secondly, there was the upkeep of the court, which was only partly met by special levies such as the provision of sheep by the Ghuzz for Sanjar's kitchen. There were probably various other special levies of a minor kind. Cloth for robes of honour and for the various needs of the court and the army may have been partially secured by levies in kind on craftsmen, or by requiring them to carry out work for the dargāh or dīvān as part or all of the tax demand upon them. In some cases, however, this appears to have been done against a payment of money. Ibn Balkhī states in the *Fārs-Nāma* that the weavers of Kāzarūn used to receive from the dīvān an advance on their woven cloth, the delivery of which would be made by some trusted man, the price being fixed by brokers.[1]

Except when they were paid by iqṭā', officials were largely remunerated by special dues (*rusūm*, *marsūmāt*), which were presumably paid directly to them, and in some cases collected by them personally and were not remitted to the dīvān although they were included in the revenue assessments.

Among incidental but regular expenses there were the pensions and allowances paid to the *sayyids* and others of the religious classes, as well as alms given by the sultan in Ramaḍān. For example, Alp-Arslan gave annually 1,000 dīnārs in Balkh, Marv, Herāt, and Nīshāpūr, and 10,000 dīnārs at his court. Malik-Shāh and Sanjar were both liberal in their gifts and alms. The latter on one occasion is alleged to have distributed the greater part of the contents of his treasury, giving away over 700,000 gold dīnārs during five consecutive days, while the value of the horses and garments he bestowed was even greater.

The government revenue tended to increase up to the reign of Malik-Shāh, when the empire achieved its greatest size, stability, and prosperity. Subsequently the revenue declined, partly because an increasing area was alienated from the control of the central government, and partly because of the growing instability. The balance between order and disorder was at all times precarious, and rapid fluctuations in local prosperity took place. Thus parts of Fārs, which were reduced to a state

[1] Pp. 145–6.

of decay and disorder by the depredations of the Shabānkāra, returned to relative prosperity under Chaulī Saqao. Ḥamd Allāh Mustaufī, who was for many years a mustaufī in the service of the Īl-Khāns and has left a valuable account of Persia in the latter days of the Īl-Khāns, states that the revenue of Fārs in Saljuq times amounted to 2,335,000 currency dīnārs, whereas in his own time it had been 2,871,200 currency dīnārs.[1] According to Mustaufī, the revenue of 'Irāq-i 'Ajam had been 25,200,000 odd currency dīnārs in Saljuq times,[2] while in his day it fell to 350,000 currency dīnārs.[3] He states on the authority of the lost *Risālat-i Malik-shāhī* that the total revenue of Malik-Shāh was 215,000,000 gold dīnārs, which amounted to some 500,000,000 currency dīnārs.[4] In spite of the depreciation in the value of the coinage, this figure appears somewhat improbable, for the entire revenue of the Islamic empire under the early 'Abbasids was only some 25 million dīnārs.[5]

Whatever reserves Malik-Shāh may have accumulated during his reign were rapidly dissipated by his successors. Terken Khatun, when she went to Iṣfahān after her son Maḥmūd was proclaimed sultan distributed all the stores that had accumulated; and when Berk-Yaruq besieged Iṣfahān she emptied the treasury and gave gold without stint to the amīrs and the standing army. Berk-Yaruq was frequently in difficulty for money. When Abu'l Maḥāsin Dihistānī was appointed vizier in 493/1099–1100 there was no money in the treasury, and when Berk-Yaruq reached Baghdad in 494/1101 he had no funds and sent to the caliph for help; after negotiations the caliph sent him 50,000 dīnārs.

The financial situation improved slightly under Muḥammad b. Malik-Shāh. Bundārī states that he found a balance sheet (*tafṣīl*) in the handwriting of his uncle, which stated that Muḥammad's treasury contained 18,000,000 dīnārs apart from gold ornaments, jewels, and garments embroidered with gold and silver thread. The improvement, however, was short lived; at the beginning of the reign of Maḥmūd b. Muḥammad the treasury he inherited from his father was emptied by his followers. Bundārī relates that on one occasion Maḥmūd and his officials lacked funds even to provide the daily allowance of beer for themselves. They accordingly sent to the brewer a number of empty boxes from the treasury so that with the proceeds of their sale he might

[1] *Nuzhat al-qulūb*, ed. G. Le Strange (Gibb Memorial Series, Persian text; London, 1915), p. 113.

[2] Variant reading 2,568,000. [3] *Nuzhat*, p. 48. [4] *Nuzhat*, p. 27.

[5] See Alfred Von Kremer, "Ueber das Budget des Harun", in *VII International Congress of Orientalists* (Vienna, 1888).

obtain what he needed. On another occasion Maḥmūd b. Muḥammad is alleged to have asked his treasurer, who had also served his father, for some perfume. The treasurer asked for a few days' delay to procure it. He then brought thirty *mithqāls* (1 *mithqāl* = 4·3 grammes). Maḥmūd said to him, "Tell the company how much perfume there used to be in my father's treasury". He answered, "In the fortress of Iṣfahān there was nearly 180 *riṭls* (1 *riṭl* = 140 *mithqāls*) in golden, silver, crystal, and china vessels, and we had in the 'field' treasury 30 *riṭls*".[1]

Mas'ūd b. Maḥmūd's treasury was also usually empty. Such revenue as arrived from the outlying districts he used to distribute among his audience at once. His vizier Kamāl al-Dīn Muḥammad al-Ḥusain, attempting to reform abuses in the financial administration, organized the collection and payment of taxes and revived practices which had been neglected. In doing this he exposed the fraudulent practices of officials and others; he also tried to break the power of the amīrs and prevent their corrupt practices. He achieved some measure of success and succeeded in collecting the taxes with greater regularity, but eventually his opposition to the amīrs cost him his life. It appears that he had attempted to bribe 'Izz al-Mulk Ṭāhir b. Muḥammad Burūjirdī, then vizier to Qara-Sonqur, to hand over his master for 500,000 dīnārs.[2] 'Izz al-Mulk refused; Kamāl al-Dīn then made Mas'ūd frightened of Qara-Sonqur, and together they summoned the amīr Boz-Aba from Fārs, hoping to use him to overthrow Qara-Sonqur. The latter, however, reacted strongly; he summoned Saljuq-Shāh b. Muḥammad and prepared to set out for Fārs to take it from Boz-Aba and give it to Saljuq-Shāh. Dā'ūd and his atabeg Ayāz, who was one of Qara-Sonqur's followers, also joined them. Setting out with the two Saljuq maliks from Āzarbāījān with an army of 10,000 men, Qara-Sonqur reached Hamadān, whence he sent 'Izz al-Mulk Burūjirdī to Mas'ūd with an ultimatum that Kamāl al-Dīn be killed or handed over to them; Mas'ūd was obliged to give way and Kamāl al-Dīn was executed by them in 533/1139. Establishing 'Izz al-Mulk Burūjirdī as Mas'ūd's vizier, Qara-Sonqur then went to Fārs. Having taken possession of the province, he handed it over to Saljuq-Shāh and returned to Āzarbāījān. Boz-Aba, however, recaptured Fārs shortly afterwards.

[1] Bundārī, pp. 141–2.

[2] Qara-Sonqur had been appointed atabeg to Toghrïl b. Muḥammad and Mas'ūd b. Muḥammad in 521/1127. He fled from Mas'ūd in 527/1132–3 and remained in Āzarbāījān after defeating Dā'ūd b. Maḥmūd in 530/1135–6.

Of the later sultans Sanjar was the only one who had a relatively well-filled treasury, containing rare and valuable objects, including necklaces, pearls, priceless pendants, and other jewels; purses full of money, and garments. His jewels were kept in sealed drums.

The dīvān over which the vizier presided, the *dīvān-i aʿlā* as it was called, had four main departments: (1) the *dīwān al-in<u>sh</u>ā' wa'l ṭu<u>gh</u>rā*, sometimes called the *dīvān-i rasā'il* or the *dīvān-i in<u>sh</u>ā'*; (2) the *dīwān al-zamām wa'l istīfā* (also called the *dīvān-i istīfā-yi mamālik*); (3) the *dīvān-i i<u>sh</u>rāf-i mamālik*; and (4) the *dīvān-i ʿarḍ*.

The dīvān-i in<u>sh</u>ā' was primarily concerned with the supervision of incoming and outgoing correspondence, and all diplomas of appointment to the various offices of state, including "administrative" iqṭāʿs, were prepared in and issued from this office. Its head was called the *ṭu<u>gh</u>rā'ī*. According to Bundārī, the chief requisite for his office was an ability to execute "curved" handwriting (*al-<u>kh</u>aṭṭ al-qausī*).[1] In fact, however, since considerable importance was attached to literary form, the ṭu<u>gh</u>rā'ī was probably often a master of literary style, as indeed was Mu'ayyid al-Daula Muntajab al-Dīn Badīʿ Atabeg Juvainī, the head of Sanjar's dīvān-i in<u>sh</u>ā'. Further, since the office was a stepping-stone to the vizierate, and its holder acted as deputy-vizier in the absence of that official, the attainments expected of the ṭu<u>gh</u>rā'ī were clearly more than those of a calligrapher.

The dīvān-i istīfā-yi mamālik was concerned with the revenue accounts, tax assessments, collection, and expenditure; its head was the *mustaufī al-mamālik*. There exists no detailed information of the exact procedure followed in this department in Saljuq times,[2] or of its relations to the dīvān-i i<u>sh</u>rāf-i mamālik. It was presumably divided into a number of sub-departments, also called dīvāns: e.g. the *dīvān-i muʿāmila va qismat* appears to have been concerned among other things with tax contracts of the muqāṭaʿa type. The empire, so far as it was not alienated from the direct control of the central dīvān in the form of "administrative" iqṭāʿs, was divided into tax districts, each presided over by a mustaufī or ʿāmil. The tax statement was prepared in the dīvān-i istifa-yi mamālik and sent to the district mustaufī, who allocated the amount demanded within the district, and was responsible

[1] P. 77. The *ṭu<u>gh</u>rā* was originally a calligraphic emblem put on rescripts and farmans. Each ruler had his own *ṭu<u>gh</u>rā*.

[2] See, however, H. Horst, *Die Staatsverwaltung*, pp. 71 ff.

for the local expenditure of revenue on allowances, pensions, and salaries. Collection was carried out by the local tax-collectors (*'ummāl*) and by their subordinates, the *muḥaṣṣils* and *mutaṣarrifs*. Oppression in the collection of taxes was not uncommon; and a proportion of the total sum levied must have frequently failed to reach the treasury.[1] Tax collection in "administrative" iqṭā's and provincial governments was in general the responsibility of the muqṭa' or provincial governor, who had his own dīvān. In theory the muqṭa's and provincial governors had no power to alter taxation, but in practice they exercised a wide discretion in such matters and were not subject to effective control by the dīvān-i istīfa-yi mamālik.

After the reign of Malik-S͟hāh an increasing proportion of the empire was alienated from the direct control of the central dīvān. When Sanjar reinstated Maḥmūd b. Muḥammad as the ruler of the western provinces of Persia in 513/1119–20, no land remained under his dīvān because Sanjar had made various assignments to Tog͟hrïl b. Muḥammad and Saljuq-S͟hāh b. Muḥammad, and various amīrs had taken possession of other districts; the only source of revenue remaining to Maḥmūd's dīvān, according to Bundārī, was confiscations.

The dīvān-i is͟hrāf-i mamālik was concerned with the auditing of financial transactions. Its head was the *mus͟hrif-i mamālik*. Niẓām al-Mulk seems to have envisaged the dīvān-i is͟hrāf as ideally exercising supervision and inspection over the administration in general, and not only its financial matters. In practice, however, the mus͟hrif seems to have been concerned with finances only. There were district or provincial mus͟hrifs in the same way that there were district or provincial mustaufīs. The function of the provincial mus͟hrif was:

To account for (*zīr-i qalam-i k͟hwīs͟h dārad*) everything which went on in the (provincial) dīvān concerning different kinds of financial transactions (*mu'āmilāt*), the conclusion of agreements (*'uqūd-i qabālāt*), adjustment of accounts (*taujīh*), pasture taxes (*marā'ī*), alms taxes (*ṣadaqāt*), the allocation of allowances (*iṭlāq-i jāmagiyyāt va jarāyāt*), particulars of accounts (*tafṣīl-i muḥāsibāt*), the conduct of monetary affairs (*ḥall va 'aqd va k͟hafḍ va raf'*), and the collection and disbursement of revenue; and to certify (*ma'lūm dārad*) all the landed estates (*amlāk*) and real property (*mustag͟hallāt*) of the sultan, the revenue from *k͟harāj* and *'us͟hr* (*māl-i k͟harāj va k͟hazānat va g͟hallāt-i 'us͟hr va irtifā'āt*), and salaries (*marsūmāt*), and to take cognizance of whatever sums, great or small, relating to the collection and disbursement of revenue were new, and not omit to record them so that the smallest item of revenue in

[1] Cf. *Faḍā'il al-anām*, p. 59.

cash or kind should not be levied or expended without his knowledge and authorization. He was to take cognizance of everything that went on in the office of the *ra'īs* in the way of meetings, the allocation and assessment of tax quotas (*qism va taqsīṭāt*), and alterations [in these], and to conceal nothing; to keep himself informed of what went on in the mint and concerning seals (*muhr*), coins (*sikka*), and the standards used in every forge. No overseers of markets (*muqaddimān-i asvāq*) or headmen of districts (*zu'amā-yi navāḥī*) were to be appointed without his knowledge, and he was to appoint vigilant and efficient deputies so that he would know what went on and how those in charge of affairs conducted their business and the state of agriculture and the development [or otherwise] of the district. He was to look into the matter of seed, draught animals, means of cultivation, estimates of the value of crops, and measures, and should consider whether they were too high or too low; he should always have available an amended and up-to-date register and a clear and accurate statement of the extent of the tax districts and their conditions, so that if asked about these he could give an answer. He was to investigate the affairs of the taxpayers and peasants (*dahāqīn va ra'āyā*) so that the tax collectors (*'ummāl va mutaṣarrifān*), scribes, and officials should not make improper demands or impose any extra burden upon them.[1]

From this document it is clear that the mushrif was concerned with overseeing the collection and disbursement of taxes, and with whatever affected this. Since the prosperity of the empire depended ultimately on the well-being of agriculture, and since, too, over-taxation would lead to the ruin of the countryside and in the last resort to the flight of the peasantry, he was given a general authority over agricultural matters. To what extent and in what way action was taken when a mushrif reported adversely on the action of officials or others in the area under his jurisdiction, is not clear; and there is little reason to suppose that his presence was effective in curtailing corruption and extortion. The dīvān-i ishrāf and the district mushrifs also exercised general supervision over the administration of *auqāf*, although these were normally under the immediate charge of the qāḍī; this supervision followed from the fact that the *dīvān-i auqāf* handled the collection and expenditure of funds.

The fourth department of the dīvān-i a'lā was the dīvān-i 'arḍ, headed by the 'āriḍ al-jaish (also called the *ṣāḥib-i dīvān-i 'arḍ*), or the muster master. The military registers and records of the "military" iqṭā's were kept in this department, and everything relating to the pay of the standing army and of the amīrs went through it. It was also concerned with recruitment and with assembling and reviewing troops

[1] Muḥammad b. 'Abd al-Khāliq al-Maihanī, *Dastūr-i Dabīrī*, pp. 111–12. See also Horst, *Die Staatsverwaltung*, pp. 133–4.

before military expeditions. Up to the end of the reign of Malik-Shāh the 'āriḍ al-jaish was a member of the bureaucracy. Later the office was held from time to time by a Turkish amīr.

Through the dīvān-i 'arḍ the vizier exercised, in theory at least, supervision over the fiscal value of "military" iqṭā's; but he did not in practice control their allocation. It seems unlikely that the "administrative" iqṭā's went through this department except exceptionally; and unlikely that the vizier, through the 'āriḍ al-jaish, controlled their allocation, though at the height of his power Niẓām al-Mulk no doubt exercised considerable influence over these grants. Occasionally other viziers exercised similar control. For example, 'Izz al-Mulk Ṭāhir b. Muḥammad al-Burūjirdī, vizier to Mas'ūd b. Muḥammad, was alleged to have assigned the provinces independently of Mas'ūd; and Kamāl al-Dīn Muḥammad b. al-Ḥusain, who made an abortive attempt to reform the financial administration (see p. 256 above), gave iqṭā's and allowances to the amīrs in strict accordance with the numbers of their armies. Niẓām al-Mulk recommended that the muqṭa's and also the tax collectors (*'ummāl*) should be changed every two or three years so that they would not establish themselves in a strong local position. The dīvān, however, was seldom strong enough to act upon this advice.

Often the heads of the various departments of the dīvān had deputies, who acted on their behalf in their absence on campaigns or missions for the sultan. Abu'l Qāsim Anasābādī Darguzīnī, whom Sanjar appointed vizier to Toghrïl b. Muḥammad in 526/1132, was at the same time made Sanjar's vizier; he remained in Iraq with Toghrïl and appointed a deputy to act for him at Sanjar's court. This was an exceptional case. Plurality of office, however, against which Niẓām al-Mulk inveighs in the *Siyāsat-Nāma*, was not uncommon. There was also a series of subordinate officials and scribes (*kuttāb*) in the different departments of the dīvān. The choice of departmental heads of the dīvān and of subordinate officials was in practice often in the hands of the vizier, whose fall would frequently entail the dismissal of his supporters and clients also.

After the death of Niẓām al-Mulk the prestige and influence of the vizierate declined, and the sultan tended to deal directly with the heads of the different departments. Berk-Yaruq's mustaufī, Majd al-Mulk Abu'l Faḍl Barāvistānī, dominated the Vizier Fakhr al-Mulk b. Niẓām al-Mulk, and became the most powerful official in the bureaucracy (see below, p. 267).

Although the vizier was the head of the bureaucracy and his functions mainly administrative, he was nevertheless expected to accompany the sultan on military expeditions. Thus Niẓām al-Mulk was present with Alp-Arslan on most of his campaigns; and in 464/1071–2 Alp-Arslan sent him at the head of a large force to Fārs, where he defeated Faḍlūya, the Shabānkāra leader. When vizier to Muḥammad b. Malik-Shāh, Khaṭīr al-Mulk Abū Manṣūr Maibudī was entrusted with the defence of one of the gates of Iṣfahān during its siege by Berk-Yaruq in 495/1102; but he deserted his post and went to Maibud. On some occasions it appears to have been the vizier and not the sultan who dispatched military expeditions. For example, Niẓām al-Mulk sent an army to besiege Alamūt in 485/1092 after hearing that Ḥasan-i Sabbāḥ had taken it; and Sanjar's vizier, Mukhtaṣṣ al-Mulk Abū Naṣr Aḥmad Kāshī, sent an army against the Ismā'īlīs of Turshīz and Baihaq in 520/1126.

The vizier was probably paid mainly by iqṭā's. Ibn al-Khallikān alleges that one-tenth of the produce of the soil was usually granted as an iqṭā' to the viziers in the Great Saljuq period.[1] If so, this type of iqṭā' was clearly something rather different from the "administrative" or the "military" iqṭā'. When Niẓām al-Mulk was accused by Abu'l Maḥāsin b. Kamāl al-Daula, deputy-head of the dīvān-i rasa'il, and by others before Malik-Shāh of misappropriating the revenue, he admitted to taking one-tenth of Malik-Shāh's wealth, which he alleged to have spent on the standing army, on alms, gifts, and auqāf. This story may be the foundation for Ibn Khallikān's statement. If, in fact, such an allocation was made to the vizier, it was probably not so much in lieu of salary as to enable him to meet the expenses of his office, such as the giving of alms and presents and the provision of allowances for the religious classes and others. It must also be remembered that the area under the direct administration of the central government was probably never the majority of the empire, and therefore the sum involved was not as large as might appear at first sight.

Most viziers also held assignments of land, but whether this was granted to them as personal estates or in lieu of salary is not always clear. In either case such assignments differed from the "military" and "administrative" assignments, for the holder was not under obligation to furnish the sultan with troops; and, further, he did not live on his iqṭā'. Nevertheless, since the maintenance of private armies by influential people was the general rule, the produce of these assignments was probably largely spent on the upkeep of troops.

[1] Vol. III, p. 297.

Another source of wealth for the vizier was confiscation and fines. Further, since he was one of the most influential men in the empire, those who desired office, whether at the centre or in the provinces, and those who feared they had incurred the sultan's displeasure endeavoured to buy the vizier's support. 'Amīd al-Mulk Kundurī, after his abortive attempt to place Sulaimān b. Chaghrī on the throne, and knowing that Niẓām al-Mulk's jealousy had been aroused and that he had schemed for his arrest, sought to make his peace with Niẓām al-Mulk. In Muḥarram 456/December 1063–January 1064, Kundurī went to Niẓām al-Mulk and left with him 500 dīnārs tied up in a handkerchief. This availed him nothing and he was killed shortly afterwards. When Malik-Shāh seized and blinded Abu'l Maḥāsin b. Kamāl al-Daula in 476/1083–4 after his failure to encompass the fall of Niẓām al-Mulk, Kamāl al-Daula gave Niẓām al-Mulk 200,000 dīnārs.[1] This suggests that there had been a significant increase in the amount of money changing hands in this way. When the Banī Jahīr, who had been in the caliph's vizierate, were disgraced in 493/1099–1100, their possessions were sold and the proceeds went to Mu'ayyid al-Mulk b. Niẓām al-Mulk, Muḥammad b. Malik-Shāh's vizier. When the latter was killed by Berk-Yaruq, his possessions were taken by Berk-Yaruq's vizier, al-'Izz Abu'l Maḥāsin Dihistānī. When the latter was murdered in 495/1101–2 his wealth was shared between his successor in the vizierate, Khaṭīr al-Mulk Abū Manṣūr Maibudī, and the sultan. One of the most active viziers in respect to confiscation was Kamāl al-Dīn Abu'l Barakāt Darguzīnī. Shams Mulk b. Niẓām al-Mulk, who was vizier to Maḥmūd b. Malik-Shāh in 516/1122–3, is also alleged to have oppressed and fined the people, and consequently to have been hated by them.

The vizier was himself obliged to spend large sums of money to retain the favour of the sultan, and, if possible, to forestall the intrigues of rivals. On one occasion Niẓām al-Mulk sent a certain Ashtar to accompany Alp-Arslan's envoy on a return mission to Shams al-Mulk, the ruler of Transoxiana, and to report what had transpired. It so happened that Shams al-Mulk's envoy mentioned that Niẓām al-Mulk was a *rāfiḍī* (i.e. a Shī'ī). Ashtar at once informed Niẓām al-Mulk. The vizier was much perturbed at this and spent, according to his own account, 30,000 gold dīnārs to prevent the report—false though it was—reaching the sultan's ears.[2]

[1] Ibn al-Athīr, vol. x, p. 85. According to Bundārī, Kamāl al-Daula gave 300,000 dīnārs to the sultan's treasury (p. 57).

[2] *Siyāsat-Nāma*, pp. 88–90.

The expenses of a vizier's establishment were considerable. His court was the refuge of innumerable persons who sought redress, office, or some other favour. When Niẓām al-Mulk came to Baghdad with Malik-Shāh in 480/1087–8 many beggars and others came to his court; and none (to quote Hindū-Shāh, author of the *Tajārib al-salaf*) went away disappointed. When he left Baghdad he ordered the gifts he had made to be counted: they amounted to 140,000 dīnārs. The second time he came to Baghdad he did not at first give any presents, but after a member of the religious classes remonstrated with him, he resumed his former practice. Tāj al-Mulk Abu'l Ghanā'im—Terken Khatun's vizier, who, with Majd al-Mulk Barāvistānī, the mustaufī, and with Abu'l Ma'ālī Sadīd al-Mulk, the 'āriḍ al-jaish, plotted for the downfall of Niẓām al-Mulk—accused him of spending 300,000 dīnārs annually on the *fuqahā* (jurists) and Ṣūfīs. According to al-Ṭuṭurshī, Niẓām al-Mulk spent double that sum annually on madrasas, *ribāṭs* (hospices), and pensions for the pious and the poor. Indeed the vizier, like the sultan, was expected to keep an open table and to show generosity to the poor and the religious classes, and since these obligations arose in part from his official position, it is not unlikely that the money spent on pensions and madrasas was derived, partly at least, from the state revenue.

The vizier in some cases had his own "private" army; and that of Niẓām al-Mulk was of considerable size. His mamlūks were known as the Niẓāmiyya mamlūks, and after his death they played an important part in securing the accession of Berk-Yaruq; then, in revenge for the death of their former master, they killed Tāj al-Mulk Abu'l Ghanā'im, who had been designated to succeed him as vizier to Malik-Shāh but had not formally assumed office before Malik-Shāh died.

It was usual for the vizier to rise to his office through the subordinate ranks of the dīvān. Many held the office of mustaufī, 'āriḍ al-jaish, or ṭughrā'ī before becoming vizier. Some entered the dīvān-i a'lā after being employed in the provinces or in the dīvān of an amīr or a Saljuq princess. Transfer from the dīvān of one Saljuq malik to another was also not uncommon. Thus viziers and departmental heads of the dīvān enjoyed a common background and training. There was, however, occasionally recruitment to the bureaucracy from other classes; and an able man, if he was prepared to accept patronage and adopt the various devices which led to success in official life, could rise to the top. Abu'l Qāsim Anasābādī Darguzīnī was the son of a peasant of Anasābād near Hamadān. He came to Iṣfahān as a child and subsequently entered the services of Kamāl al-Mulk Simīrūmī, acting as vizier to Guhar Khatun, Muḥammad b. Malik-Shāh's wife. He then became vizier to the amīr ḥājib, 'Alī b. 'Umar, at which time he laid the foundations of his fortune (see p. 251 above). He ultimately became vizier to Sanjar and Toghrïl b. Muḥammad, and was executed by the latter in 527/1133. Kamāl al-Mulk Simīrumī himself was the son of a man who farmed Simīrum, which belonged to Guhar Khatun's dīvān. He entered the service of Guhar Khatun's dīvān and in due course her vizier, when he went to Baghdad, made Kamāl al-Mulk his deputy. Kamāl al-Mulk rehabilitated Guhar Khatun's dīvān and succeeded in ingratiating himself with her; and on the death of the vizier he became the head of her dīvān. She recommended him to the sultan, who made him mushrif al-mamālik, and then mustaufī. Finally he became vizier to Maḥmūd b. Muḥammad in 512/1118–19. Muḥammad b. Sulaimān Kāshgharī, who became Sanjar's vizier, was previously a merchant. He was not a popular or successful vizier. Trade, it seems, was not a suitable training for the bureaucracy. Zakī, whose incompetence, as stated above, had contributed to the replacement of the vakīl-i dar by the amīr ḥājib, was a rich Qazvīnī merchant.

The most famous of all the Saljuq viziers was Niẓām al-Mulk. Five of his sons, two of his grandsons, and one great-grandson held the office of vizier to one or other of the sultans or maliks after him, though none of them achieved his eminence. He was the son of a man who had been made the tax-collector and revenue farmer (*bundār*) of Ṭūs, by the Ghaznavid 'amīd of Khurāsān. At the beginning of the Saljuq expansion the country was in a state of disorder and the taxes were not being collected. The 'amīd of Khurāsān demanded from Abu'l Ḥasan, Niẓām al-Mulk's father, the arrears of Ṭūs, which he was unable to pay in full. In the prevailing confusion the administration began to disintegrate and many of the Ghaznavid officials dispersed. Abu'l Ḥasan eventually found his way to Ghazna, with his son Niẓām al-Mulk, who was still a child. In due course the latter entered Ghaznavid service, but after Balkh fell to the Saljuqs in 432/1040–1 he attached himself to the 'amīd of Balkh, Ibn Shādān. His experiences with Ibn Shādān were not altogether happy. It is related—perhaps apocryphally—that whenever the 'amīd thought Niẓām al-Mulk had accumulated any wealth, he would say, "O Ḥasan, you have grown fat" and mulct him. When this had happened several times Niẓām al-Mulk fled to Marv.[1] There, by

[1] Muḥammad Mufīd, *Jāmi'-i Mufīdī*, ed. Iraj Afshār (Tehran, 1342/1963), vol. I, p. 54.

some means or other, he joined the service of Alp-Arslan. Kundurī, who had been Toghrïl Beg's vizier, was dismissed by Alp-Arslan shortly after his accession, and Niẓām al-Mulk became vizier, which office he also held under Malik-Shāh. Ghazālī, who was Niẓām al-Mulk's contemporary, compared him to the Barmakids; and he appears to have enjoyed a great reputation among all classes of the population, including the army. Such was his prestige that the caliph allowed him to be seated in his presence. On the occasion of the betrothal of Malik-Shāh's daughter to the caliph in 474/1081–2, when the sultan's retinue went to the caliph's court, Niẓām al-Mulk, at the caliph's command, rode while everyone else walked; and when they reached the caliph's audience Niẓām al-Mulk was seated on a throne (*masnad*) and given a robe of honour with a border (*ṭarāz*) on it, inscribed: "In the name of the just and perfect vizier, Niẓām al-Mulk, *raḍī amīri'l mu'minīn*."[1]

To what extent Niẓām al-Mulk's reputation for justice was merited is difficult to judge. His lavish expenditure on pensions, allowances to the religious classes, and the building of madrasas contributed to his fame and popularity. In a letter to Fakhr al-Mulk b. Niẓām al-Mulk, Ghazālī tells him of his father's ambition not to be surpassed by anyone in good works.[2] He appears on the whole to have counselled moderation and tolerance, though in his early career, at least, he was not above ridding himself of rivals by intrigue, as he did in the case of 'Amīd al-Mulk Kundurī. He was undoubtedly an able and competent administrator, and not without skill in military affairs—a fact which no doubt was of great help to him in his relations with the amīrs, and which enabled him to maintain the prestige of the bureaucracy *vis-à-vis* the military. He appears to have been a good judge of character, an essential attribute of a vizier when power was personal rather than institutional. Bundārī states that he selected each man for the work for which he was best suited and appointed him to office accordingly. The fact that many of his relatives held office under him increased his power though it also aroused the sultan's jealousy.

The office of vizier was potentially, and under Niẓām al-Mulk actually, one of great power, but it also involved its holder in great risks. He had no security of tenure and could be dismissed at will and without cause by the sultan. The power he exercised was delegated to him entirely as a matter of grace: he was the servant, not of the state, but of the sultan, and consequently it was essential for him to retain the

[1] Ibn al-Khallikān, vol. I, p. 413.

[2] See *Faḍā'il al-anām*, p. 30.

satisfaction of the sultan, who, because of the arbitrary nature of power in the medieval Persian state, was inevitably jealous of any influence the vizier obtained. The latter often faced a conflict between his duty towards the people, whether seen in terms of Islam or common justice, and political practice. Ghazālī indeed took the view that the vizier because of his office inevitably became involved in corruption and disobedience to the laws of God.[1] Another story, also perhaps apocryphal, illustrates this point. Niẓām al-Mulk complained to the Imām al-Ḥaramain of Alp-Arslan's secret ill-feeling towards him in spite of his almost superhuman efforts in the interests of the state. The Imām al-Ḥaramain replied that since the wealth and property of the sultan were in the hands of Niẓām al-Mulk, inevitably the sultan suspected him of corruption. He also pointed out that some of the demands sultans made upon their viziers were impossible to fulfil.

The vizier was also likely to incur the dissatisfaction of other members of the sultan's family, who, if their desires were opposed or they were prevented from interfering in affairs, were likely to attribute this to the vizier's opposition; and the vizier's rivals, desirous of self-advancement, would encourage them in this. No vizier who made any serious effort to establish an effective administration was immune from the jealousy and intrigues of his fellows. Niẓām al-Mulk, the strongest and most influential of all the Saljuq viziers, was no exception, and many of his contemporaries attributed his murder—generally thought to have been committed by an emissary of Ḥasan-i Sabbāḥ—to Malik-Shāh and Tāj al-Mulk Abu'l Ghanā'im, Terken Khatun's vizier, who had supported her in her efforts to persuade the sultan to declare her son Maḥmūd as valī 'ahd.

The bureaucracy had no traditions of integrity and independence: the vizier could not expect loyalty from his colleagues, and consequently self-preservation demanded that he should fill key places as far as possible with his relatives and clients, the former because he could in some measure control them and the latter because their hope of advancement would be at least temporarily bound up with his. But by the nature of the case he fought a losing battle. He had to share with his supporters the benefits and spoils of office; and as they rose from poverty to riches, from weakness to power, and insignificance to fame, they were likely to scheme with others to encompass his destruction.

The prevention of corruption in subordinate officials was an ex-

[1] Cf. *Faḍā'il al-anām*, p. 61.

tremely difficult problem for the vizier, and one which, however dealt with, made many enemies for him. There was no adequate system of control or supervision. The *barīd*, which in earlier times had been used for the transmission of messages between government agents in the provinces and the capital, and whose officers kept watch over and reported on events taking place in various parts of the empire, had been abolished. Alp-Arslan's alleged reasons for objecting to it were sound: namely, that those who were loyal would pay no attention to the *ṣāḥib khabar* (the postmaster) and see no need to bribe him, while his enemies would make friends with the ṣāḥib khabar and give him money, with the result that he would report favourably on them and unfavourably on those who were loyal.[1] But in the absence of any effective checks and controls in the administrative system, there could be, as Niẓām al-Mulk recognized, no security for the ruler against rebellion, injustice, or extortion by his officials. Hence Niẓām al-Mulk advocated an efficient system of espionage backed by an armed force strong enough to overpower all opposition. In his view, the sultan should have informers and spies throughout the empire and among all classes of the people, including the qāḍīs. He probably had his own agents in the country, but in spite of his advice, the barīd was not re-established.

Perhaps the most delicate problem of all for the vizier was his relationship with the amīrs. His official business constantly brought him into contact with them. Friendship with them individually attracted the enmity of those excluded from the friendship and aroused the suspicion of the sultan. Up to the death of Niẓām al-Mulk the vizier's influence was greater than that of the amīrs, but after his death they gradually deprived the bureaucracy of all effective power. None after Niẓām al-Mulk really succeeded in reimposing control over the amīrs, and those who tried came to an untimely end. The first and most striking case is that of the mustaufī Majd al-Mulk Barāvistānī, who, having succeeded in getting Fakhr al-Mulk b. Niẓām al-Mulk appointed to Berk-Yaruq's vizierate in 488/1095, made his own influence dominant in the dīvān. He appears to have attempted to keep a tight hold on the amīrs, but in 492/1098–9 Öner rebelled and offered Berk-Yaruq his renewed obedience on condition that Majd al-Mulk was surrendered to him. But before any action could occur, Öner was assassinated. The opposition to Majd al-Mulk was not thereby ended, and later in the same year a number of prominent amīrs demanded that the sultan

[1] *Siyāsat-Nāma*, p. 65.

should hand Majd al-Mulk over to them. Berk-Yaruq refused to surrender him. The rebellious amīrs thereupon entered the sultan's tent, dragged out the mustaufī, and killed him.[1] This incident is significant of the changing relationships between the vizierate and the amīrs; and by the time of Mas'ūd b. Muḥammad, the amīrs began to appoint their own nominees to the office. As stated above, Qara-Sonqur made his own vizier, 'Izz al-Mulk Ṭāhir b. Muḥammad Burūjirdī, the vizier to Mas'ūd b. Muḥammad in 533/1139. After the death of Qara-Sonqur, a group of amīrs led by 'Abd al-Raḥmān b. Ṭughrāyarak persuaded Mas'ūd to seize 'Izz al-Mulk in 539/1144–5 and in the following year (or in 541/1146–7) Boz-Aba, who had become one of the most powerful amīrs in the empire, succeeded in appointing his own vizier, Tāj al-Dīn Abu'l Fath b. Dārast, to the sultan's vizierate. He held office for only a few months, however, before returning to Boz-Aba's service in Fārs. Ibn al-Athīr states that he preferred Boz-Aba's service to the sultan's, whereas Bundārī states that Mas'ūd allowed him to return to Boz-Aba in the hope that he would restrain Boz-Aba from rebellion. Whichever account is nearer to the truth, it is clear that there had been a sharp decline in the power of the sultan's vizierate, as well as a major change in the relations between vizier and amīrs.

The position of the vizier and of government officials in general was extremely insecure. After the death of Niẓām al-Mulk, viziers succeeded one another with great rapidity. This was perhaps partly due to the prevailing financial stringency; the dismissal of a vizier and the confiscation of his wealth by the sultan was a means of temporarily relieving this stringency. After the death of Malik-Shāh the number of viziers who escaped being murdered, imprisoned, or having their wealth confiscated is small. The readiness with which the later sultans listened to intrigues against their viziers contrasts strongly with the conduct of Alp-Arslan, who, on one occasion when he received a letter accusing Niẓām al-Mulk of malpractices, is alleged to have given it to him and said, "If they are right in what they have written, repair your nature and mend your ways; and if they lied then forgive them their slip".[2] But it is also true that since there were no effective controls or checks against corruption within the bureaucratic system itself, then

[1] Rāvandī, pp. 145–7. Ibn al-Athīr's account differs slightly, in that he states that Berk-Yaruq finally agreed to surrender Majd al-Mulk but made the amīrs promise to spare his life. When he was handed over by the sultan, some soldiers killed him before he reached the amīrs (vol. x, pp. 196–7).

[2] Ibn al-Athīr, vol. x, p. 51.

once there was a relaxation in the power of the sultan, intrigue and corruption grew and fed upon each other.

The sultan exercised "administrative" justice in the maẓālim court, personally or through his agents. He delegated his function as judge according to the ideal system of the sharī'a to the qāḍī. In the maẓālim court the administration of justice was exercised on the basis of custom, equity, and governmental regulations; whereas the qāḍī in his court applied the sharī'a according to certain formal rules of evidence and procedure.[1] This court sat in the mosque, in the qāḍī's residence, or some other duly appointed place. It was concerned primarily with the settlement of litigation, the execution of testaments and matters of inheritance, escheat, transfers of property, administration of the affairs of orphans, widows, and of those legally incapacitated, and the appointment of *umanā* (trustees) for this purpose. The qāḍī normally applied the sharī'a according to the rite to which most people in the area under his jurisdiction belonged. Among the qualifications demanded of the qāḍī was that he should be a Muslim, free, and versed in the principles of the law (*uṣūl al-fiqh*).

In spite of the fact that by Saljuq times the jurisdiction of the maẓālim court tended to overlap with and to supersede that of the qāḍī's court, the qāḍī still played an extremely important role in the life of the Saljuq empire. He acted as a link both between the political and the religious institution, and between the sultan and his people; and he maintained and transmitted the traditions of Islamic civilization. From the new relationship between the caliph and the sultan, and from the renewed association of the political and the religious institution, there followed a reappraisal of the position of the religious classes in general and of the qāḍī in particular. Niẓām al-Mulk states the qāḍīs were the deputies (*nā'ibān*) of the ruler, upon whom their support was incumbent. Full respect and dignity were to be accorded to them because they were the deputies of the caliph (*nā'ibān-i khalīfa*), upon whom his mantle (*shi'ār*) had devolved. At the same time, they were also appointed by the secular ruler and did his work.[2] Similarly in contemporary documents the 'ulamā are sometimes referred to as the "heirs of the Prophet" and the qāḍīs as the officers of the sharī'a and "the *umanā* of God in the execution of decrees, the termination of disputes, and in obtaining the rights of the weak".[3] The position of the

[1] See further J. Schacht, *An Introduction to Islamic Law* (Oxford, 1964), pp. 49 ff.

[2] *Siyāsat-Namā*, pp. 40–1.

[3] Cf. *Quis Custodiet*, *Studia Islamica*, fasc. v, p. 132.

qāḍīs *vis-à-vis* the sultan was to some extent analogous with that of the caliph *vis-à-vis* the sultan: the immediate source of their power was the sultan, who exercised constituent authority, but their functional authority was derived from the sh̲arīʿa and the Prophet—hence the reference to them as the "heirs of the Prophet". But whereas the caliph under the new arrangement exercised only spiritual authority, the qāḍīs were incorporated into the political institution.

Once a qāḍī was appointed, it was theoretically incumbent upon government officials to execute his decrees, which were not subject to review, though in cases of injustice an appeal could in theory be made to the maẓālim court. The freedom of action of the qāḍī was limited in practice, first because he had to rely on the officials of the dargāh (or, in the provinces, on the muqṭaʿ) to exccute his decrees; and secondly because he was subject to dismissal by the sultan, or by those to whom the sultan had delegated authority in the provinces.

With their incorporation into the administrative hierarchy, the qāḍī and other officials of the religious institution, such as the k̲h̲aṭīb and muḥtasib, received salaries and allowances as other officials did. Niẓām al-Mulk, writing on the position of the qāḍīs states:

He (the sultan) must know the condition of each one of the qāḍīs of the kingdom individually. Whoever of them is more learned, more abstemious, more honest (*kūtāh-dasttar*), he shall keep in office, but whoever is not he shall be dismissed and replaced by someone more worthy. He shall allocate to each one of them a salary (*mus̲h̲āhira*) sufficient for his livelihood so that he will have no need to commit embezzlement. This is an important and delicate affair because the qāḍīs are empowered over the lives and possessions of the Muslims. If they issue a decree in ignorance, greed, or with deliberate intent, or give a written judgement, it will be incumbent upon other judges (*ḥākimān*) to execute that evil decree while making it known to the sultan so that he may dismiss and punish that person. The officials must support the qāḍī and preserve his prestige. If anyone behaves proudly and does not appear at the [qāḍī's] summons, he shall be made to appear by force and compulsion even though he is a man of standing (*muḥtas̲h̲am*).[1]

The documents of the day also recognize that the office of qāḍī was intimately connected with the well-being and interests of the population. He was in fact often their spokesman, and in times of disorder it was not unknown for him to organize the administration and defence of a city. Usually, moreover, he was a local man, and there was a strong hereditary tendency in the office. The chief qāḍī of a town or

[1] *Siyāsat-Nāma*, p. 38.

district, who was called the *qāḍī al-quḍāt*, was appointed by the sultan, unless he lived in an area alienated from the ruler's direct control, in which case he was probably appointed by the provincial governor or the muqṭa'. He usually had power to appoint deputies in the area under him. In his deed of appointment he was designated as the qāḍī of such and such a place. This was also the case with diplomas issued for mustaufīs, mushrifs, 'āmils, and other officials, who were appointed over specified areas; but whereas they were simply the representatives of the dīvān-i a'lā in the area, the qāḍīs, although appointed by the sultan, exercised their authority both as the "heirs of the Prophet", and as the qāḍīs of a particular area, which gave them a certain independence *vis-à-vis* the central government.

The main duty of the qāḍī under the Saljuqs was probably to watch over the religious institution on behalf of the sultan, especially with a view to preventing unorthodox opinions. Usually, though not invariably, the qāḍī was also entrusted with the supervision of mosques and of the officials of the religious institution, notably the muḥtasib, in the area to which he was appointed. His oversight of the mosques sometimes included power to nominate the imāms, who led the prayers, and the khaṭīb, who read the khuṭba in the Friday mosque. In the chief cities of the empire, however, the latter was frequently nominated by the sultan; and in Marv the office was held by a Shāfi'ī.[1] It was not uncommon for the office of khaṭīb to be held by a qāḍī.

With regard to the administration and supervision of auqāf there was considerable variety of practice. If no *mutavallī* (administrator) had been appointed by the founder, the qāḍī administered the *vaqf* directly; if, however, there was a mutavallī, then the qāḍī merely exercised general supervision over its administration. The qāḍī frequently taught in the local madrasa, and in some cases held the office of mudarris. Often, too, he was a *muftī* and issued *fatwās* (decrees) on theological and juridical matters. Sometimes he also presided over the maẓālim court, as stated above. Lastly the qāḍīs were often used by the sultan as envoys. This was perhaps partly because of the respect in which they were held by the local population; and partly because it was the policy of the Saljuqs to incorporate the religious hierarchy into the administrative hierarchy.

Alp-Arslan appears to have had a chief qāḍī of the empire: *qāḍī-yi jumla-yi mamālik*. According to the document for his appointment, dated Muḥarram 457/December 1064–January 1065, this official was

[1] *'Atabat al-Kataba*, p. 87.

entrusted with the care of mosques and auqāf, and was instructed to hear shar'ī cases and to take good care of the documents (wills, contracts, etc.) deposited with him. The great men of the kingdom, the tax collectors, *ru'asā*, and all the subjects were enjoined to consider him the foremost qāḍī of the empire (*aqḍā'l-quḍāt dar kull-i vilāyāt*).[1] With the increased centralization of the administration in the hands of the vizier during the reign of Malik-Shāh, it is not unlikely that the office of chief qāḍī of the empire fell into disuse. The vizier as head of the financial administration exercised general supervision over auqāf, as stated above; but his precise relationship to the chief qāḍī, and to the provincial qāḍīs—in respect to the supervision of auqāf, as well as to the extent and nature of control held by the *dīvān-i auqāf-i mamālik* over provincial auqāf—is not clear. In some cases the auqāf of a particular district were expressly placed outside the control of this dīvān.[2] It is possible that under Sanjar the *qāḍī-yi lashkar* may have, to some extent, taken the place of the chief qāḍī of the empire. In a diploma for the qāḍī-yi lashkar issued by Sanjar's dīvān for the *qāḍī al-quḍāt*, Majd al-Dīn, he was entrusted with the supervision of auqāf; and the amīrs, army leaders, and the sultan's entourage, Turk and non-Turk, were all instructed to refer their shar'ī cases to him. He was also enjoined to administer the Ḥanafī rite.[3]

While the renewed association between the religious and the political institution did in some ways strengthen the position of the qāḍīs, it also to some extent jeopardized their independence. Niẓām al-Mulk, in fact, proposed that the sultan should appoint a god-fearing man in every town to watch over and give information about the condition of the 'āmil, the qāḍī, the muḥtasib, and the subjects in general.[4]

The muḥtasib, who was under the general supervision of the qāḍī was, like him, normally a member of the religious classes; and through him the sultan came into contact with his subjects in yet another way: by exercising control over the moral welfare of the townspeople. In general the people in the towns were grouped according to their religious, ethnical, and above all professional affinities, because only by grouping themselves into corporations were they able to protect their lives and goods, and to buy intercessions and favours to relieve their lot. The corporate organization of society, which was a marked feature of Islamic society in Persia until modern times, was characteristic also of

[1] See Horst, *op. cit.* pp. 147–8.
[2] *'Atabat al-Kataba*, p. 33.
[3] *Ibid.* p. 59.
[4] *Siyāsat-Nāma*, p. 43.

the Saljuq period. There is evidence of a spirit of corporate feeling among the inhabitants of various cities, which sometimes manifested itself in rivalry between different towns and also in the ability of a town to make a settlement with individual leaders without reference to the central government or its officials. Thus when disorders were committed by the *'ayyār* in Baihaq after the death of Malik-Shāh in 485/1092, a sayyid from a neighbouring village patrolled the city at night with mounted men and footmen so that "no disorderly person or wrongdoer should encroach upon the possessions of the Muslims or their women".[1]

Bodies of 'ayyār were to be found in various cities, notably Baghdad and Nīshāpūr. These groups may have originated as an offshoot of the *futuwwa* organizations. In the *Qābūs-Nāma*, where he discusses the fifth/eleventh-century Persian conception of *javānmardī* or *futuwwa* (chivalry), Kai Kā'ūs ranks soldiers (*sipāhiyān*), *'ayyārān*, and the people of the bazaar as the fourth and last group of those possessing this quality. The other three were first Ṣūfīs, secondly wise men, prophets, and saints, and lastly "spiritual" men and apostles.[2] From his description it seems possible that the futuwwa organizations were dividing along two lines, those who fulfilled their self-imposed duties in an active sphere, and those who interpreted jihād as applying to the inward and spiritual struggle against the temptations of the world. Kai Kā'ūs states: "The most perfect soldier is like the most perfect *'ayyār*, but generosity, hospitality, liberality, gratitude, and probity should be greater in a soldier, and he should be more heavily armed; and while [to prefer] his own loss and the benefit of a friend, obedience, and humility are a virtue in a soldier, they are a fault in an *'ayyār*."[3]

Ibn al-Jauzī (d. 597/1200–1), writing rather later, also identifies the 'ayyār with those who belong to the futuwwa organization. He states:

Amongst those persons who have been made captive by the misrepresentations of Satan are the *'ayyār*; and this body, who are called *fityān*, take the people's goods, and say "a *fatā*, is one who does not commit fornication nor lie, and strives to preserve the honour and reputation of women, and does not violate their privacy. In spite of this, they do not restrain themselves from seizing people's property, not remembering that by their action they oppress the people. They call their organisation (*ṭarīqa*) '*futuwwa*'." It often happens that one of them takes an oath, binding himself to the obligations

[1] Ibn Funduq, *Ta'rīkh-i Baihaq*, ed. Aḥmad Bahmanyār (Tehran, n.d.), pp. 274–5.
[2] Ed. R. Levy, Gibb Memorial Series, p. 141.
[3] *Qābūs-Nāma*, p. 143, taking the variant *ziyān-i khud va sūd-i dūst.*

of *futuwwa*, and abstains from food and drink. Their garments are trousers (*sarāwīl*) with which they invest everyone who enters their organisation, in the same way as the Ṣūfīs clothe the *murīd* in a patched garment (*muraqqa'a*).[1]

The general tendency was for the 'ayyār to degenerate into bands of robbers. Already before Saljuq times they had been a frequent source of trouble to the Sāmānid administration in Khurāsān; and Ya'qūb b. Laith, the founder of the Ṣaffārid dynasty, was himself an 'ayyār. By Saljuq times the 'ayyār were mostly undisciplined mobs who took up arms, robbed and murdered the population, and spread terror among them when opportunity offered.[2]

The city was usually enclosed by a fortified wall, within which there was frequently a citadel: the last refuge of the city's defenders in case of siege, and of government officials in case of revolt. The city was divided into quarters, and in the large cities each quarter was self-contained and sometimes enclosed within its own walls, having its own mosque, bazaar for primary necessities, and public bath. Nāṣir-i Khusrau mentions that all the streets and quarters of Iṣfahān had strong bars and gates in 444/1052.[3] Sometimes the quarters were separated from one another by an occupational grouping. Factional and sectarian strife and rivalry among different quarters was not uncommon, especially in Baghdad. Nīshāpūr was also notorious for factional strife. In 489/1096 riots took place there between the Karāmiyya and other sections of the people; many were killed, and the Shāfi'īs and Ḥanafīs prevailed in the end;[4] and after the Ghuzz captured Sanjar in 548/1153, it is alleged that there were riots in Nīshāpūr every night in one quarter or another, because of religious differences and ancient hatreds.[5] Ṭūs appears to have been another town where lack of unity prevailed. Ghazālī, too, complains of intrigues and envy among its inhabitants.[6]

The *dhimmīs* or members of the "protected" communities, i.e. Christians, Jews, Sabeans, and Zoroastrians (only the first two were found in any number), were segregated in their own quarters. They each had their own organizations and took little part in the life of the Muslim community. They enjoyed freedom of religion and appointed

[1] *Naqd al-'ilm wa'l-'ulamā yā talbīsi Iblīs* (Cairo, A.H. 1340), p. 421. This has been translated by D. S. Margoliouth, under the title "The Devil's Delusion", in *Islamic Culture* (1938).

[2] See further C. Cahen, *Mouvements Populaires et Autonomisme Urbain dans l'Asie Musulmane du Moyen Age* (Leiden, 1959), pp. 30 ff.

[3] *Safar-Nāma*, p. 92.

[4] Ibn al-Athīr, vol. x, pp. 169, 171; Ibn Funduq, pp. 268–9.

[5] Rāvandī, p. 182.

[6] *Faḍā'il al-anām*, p. 53.

their own religious officials, subject probably to the confirmation of the sultan or his officials. They were subject to the payment of *jizya* (poll-tax) and to certain other limitations such as the wearing of distinguishing marks on their clothing; and they were debarred from bearing arms. The Jews were probably largely occupied in trade and commerce. There were Jewish and Christian communities in many of the large cities of the empire, notably Baghdad and Nīshāpūr. Benjamin of Tudela, who travelled some years after the death of Sanjar, mentions Jewish communities in, among other places, Hamadān, Iṣfahān, Nihāvand, and Shīrāz.

On the whole there appears to have been little discrimination against the dhimmīs, though from time to time there were outbreaks of feeling against them. Ibn al-Athīr relates an incident concerning a Jew called Abū Sa'd b. Samḥā, who lived in Baghdad in 484/1091 and was an agent (*vakīl*) for Malik-Shāh and Niẓām al-Mulk. After being struck by a huckster in the street, he went with the shaḥna, Gauhar Ā'īn, to the sultan's camp, which was then in the neighbourhood, to complain of the caliph's vizier, Abū Shujā'—presumably because he was considered responsible for public order so far as it concerned the dhimmīs in Baghdad. Meanwhile, a decree was issued by the caliph forcing the dhimmīs to wear distinguishing marks on their clothing, and they began to flee from Baghdad. But when Abū Sa'd and Gauhar Ā'īn reached the sultan's camp their demand for Abū Shujā''s dismissal from the caliph's vizierate was accepted, and the caliph was forced to comply.[1] It is clear from the fact that new orders for the dhimmīs to wear special clothing were from time to time issued that these orders were not permanently enforced. A new order making it obligatory on the dhimmīs in Baghdad to wear distinguishing marks on their clothes was issued by Maḥmud b. Muḥammad in 515/1121–2.

The most influential and respected section of the local population was that composed of the religious classes, many of whom had a large following among the people. It was perhaps for this reason that they were frequently employed as envoys. Al-Muqtadī sent Abū Isḥāq Shīrāzī on an embassy to Malik-Shāh in 475/1083. In every town through which he passed the people came out with their women and children to welcome him, and sought to touch his stirrups and collect the dust from his mule as a blessing; and in Sāveh various guilds, such as the bakers', fruiterers', confectioners', and others came out to present

[1] Vol. x, pp. 123–4.

offerings of their respective trades and crafts. A *vā'iẓ* (preacher) named 'Abbādī, whom Sanjar sent to the caliph in 541/1166–7, found great acceptance in Baghdad. Mas'ūd b. Muḥammad and others came to hear him preach, and "as for the common people, they abandoned their occupations to be present at his assembly".[1]

The religious classes were organized into corporations; in the large towns the Shāfi'īs and Ḥanafīs (and any other rites that existed) each had their own *ra'īs* or head, who sometimes received a diploma of appointment from the sultan. Abū Sa'd 'Abd al-Karīm b. Muḥammad b. Manṣūr al-Sam'ānī, who received a diploma from Sanjar's dīvān for the office of ra'īs of the Shāfi'īs of Marv and its environs, was also appointed khaṭīb of the Friday mosque and mutavallī of its auqāf, and he was authorized to teach in thc madrasas, including the Niẓāmiyya madrasa, shrines (*mashāhid-i khair*), and Friday mosque. The khaṭībs of the neighbourhood and the mutavallīs of the auqāf were instructed to refer their affairs to him.[2] The 'Alids also formed an important corporation under their own *naqīb*, who in some cases received a diploma of appointment from the sultan; and they were in some measure removed from the authority of other officials. In a diploma issued by Sanjar's dīvān for Murtaḍā Jamāl al-Dīn Abu'l Ḥasan 'Alavī, for the office of naqīb of the sayyids of Gurgān, Dihistān, Astarābād, and the neighbourhood, which office he held by hereditary right, he was enjoined to treat the sayyids with respect according to the degree of their learning (*'ilm*) and piety (*'afāf*), and to transmit to them their livelihood from the customary sources. He was to strengthen the righteous and punish the wicked, to investigate carefully their genealogies, and to expel anyone who falsely claimed to be a sayyid. All the sayyids of Gurgān and Dihistān were to recognize him as their naqīb, to obey him, and refer their affairs to him. The dīvān officials and local officials were to respect him and to entrust to him the affairs of the sayyids without interfering therein.[3]

It was not only the 'ulamā of the religious institution who were held in respect. The Ṣūfīs also enjoyed honour among all classes of the people and were organized in recognized orders and corporations. Some, like Abū Sa'īd b. Abī'l Khair, who was visited on several occasions by various members of the Saljuq family, passed lives of religious devotion; others used the garb of a Ṣūfī to make a livelihood. Among such were

[1] Ibn al-Athīr, vol. xi, p. 78.
[2] *'Atabat al-kataba*, pp. 85–8.
[3] *Ibid.* pp. 63–4.

the guilds of story-tellers against whom Ibn al-Jauzī warned in *The Devil's Delusion*:

In our time the story-tellers act in a way which has no connection with delusion, since it is an evident way of making the stories a source of livelihood and of getting gifts from tyrannical princes and obtaining the like from the gatherers of unlawful imposts and earning money by [their stories] in the provinces. Some of them go to the cemeteries where they dilate upon affection and parting with friends drawing tears from the women, but not exhorting them to take warning.[1]

The more prominent merchants ranked among the "notables" of the city, while the smaller merchants ranked with the craft guilds in the bazaars. The merchant community with the *ṣarrāfs* (brokers) played an important part in financing the operations of the state. Travelling, exporting, and wholesale merchants usually conducted their business in caravanserais, which were situated on the outskirts of the town or in the bazaar itself. According to Nāṣir-i Khusrau, there were fifty good caravanserais in Iṣfahān in his day where the merchants congregated and had rooms.[2] Monetary dealings were handled largely through the ṣarrāfs. Nāṣir-i Khusrau reports that there were 200 ṣarrāfs in one of the bazaars of Iṣfahān in 444/1052, which indicates the commercial importance of Iṣfahān at that time.

The bazaar was usually divided into a number of *sūqs*, belonging to the different craft guilds, most of which had their own separate quarters. However, the craftsmen did not live in the bazaars; these were locked and barred at night, as were the premises of the craftsmen within them. Some guilds, such as the brickmakers' and plasterers', were usually to be found on the outskirts of the city. Trade was carried on daily except on Fridays and religious holidays. Ghazālī has a curious passage in the *Kīmiyā al-sa'āda*[3] on forbidden things (*munkirāt*) in a bazaar, which gives a glimpse of the life of the people. Among the items which should not be sold he mentions effigies of animals for children at the holiday (*'īd*), swords and wooden shields for the Nau-Rūz (the festival of the vernal equinox), and clay pipes for Sada (the festival of the autumnal equinox). These things were not in themselves forbidden but they were a manifestation of Zoroastrian customs, which were contrary to the sharī'a and for this reason unseemly. Further, excessive decoration of the bazaars, making much confectionery and extravagance on the occasion of the Nau-Rūz were not fitting: Nau-Rūz and Sada should be forgotten.

[1] P. 133. The translation is Margoliouth's, in *Islamic Culture* (1938), p. 36.
[2] *Safar-Nāma*, p. 92.
[3] Tehrān, 1333/1964, p. 407.

The guilds had their own leaders. They were probably responsible, not only for the maintenance of professional standards, but also for allocating among the members and then collecting the taxes and levies that were assessed on the guild in a lump sum. The sources tell us little of the actual membership of the guilds and their methods of work. Ghazālī mentions three types of association which were customary but in his view wrong. The first was the association of porters (*ḥammālān*) and artisans (*pīshavarān*), who made the pooling of their individual earnings a condition of their association. The other two did not specifically concern the guilds but were, rather, trading associations. The first consisted of persons who pooled their capital and shared the subsequent loss or gain; and the second was a partnership between two parties, one of whom had standing, while the other put up the money and traded in his partner's name, the profits being shared between them.[1] As in later times, the bazaar was sometimes closed by way of protest against injustice. Thus in 512/1118–19, when one of the soldiers of Mengü-Bars, the shaḥna of Baghdad, broke into the house of a newly married couple, wounded the bridegroom, and raped his wife, the bazaars all closed in protest.

Public morals and the due performance by Muslims of their religious duties were under the general care of the muḥtasib. He had to prevent, for example, prayer that was contrary to the legal rites, the breaking of the fast of Ramaḍān, wine-drinking in public, the playing of illegal musical instruments, and unseemly behaviour in public. He was also charged with overseeing what might be called public amenities. Thus it was his duty to see that no house was raised above another belonging to a Muslim so as to overlook the women's quarters; that no house had projecting rain-spouts or open drainpipes to drench or befoul wayfarers in the street; and that free passage in the streets was not impeded. He was not to allow slaves to be ill-treated, or animals overburdened. He was also to see that the dhimmīs complied with the regulations imposed upon them to distinguish them from Muslims. The muḥtasib's main task, however, was to oversee the markets and to prevent dishonest dealing by merchants and artisans, as well as to supervise the guilds and corporations. He was empowered to inflict summary punishment on offenders.[2] Niẓām al-Mulk states that a muḥtasib should be appointed in every city

[1] *Kīmiyā al-saʿāda*, p. 272.

[2] For a general discussion of the *muḥtasib*'s duties, see R. Levy, *The Social Structure of Islam* (Cambridge, 1957), pp. 334 ff.

to oversee weights and prices, to watch over commercial transactions, prevent fraud and the adulteration of goods, and "to enjoin what is good and forbid what is evil". If the sultan and his officials did not support the muḥtasib, "the poor would be in trouble and the people of the bazaar would buy and sell as they liked, middle-men (*faḍla-khur*) would become dominant, corruption would become open and the *sharī'a* without prestige".[1]

In a diploma issued from Sanjar's dīvān for the muḥtasib of Māzandarān, Auḥad al-Dīn, he is commanded to enjoin what is good and forbid what is evil; to exert himself in the equalization and control of weights and measures (*tasviyat va ta'dīl-i mavāzīn va makā'īl*) so that no fraud would be committed in buying and selling and the Muslims would not be cheated or suffer loss; to ensure that the requirements of the sharī'a would be duly carried out in mosques and places of worship, and that the *mu'adhdhins* and other officials would perform their duties in the proper way and at the stated times; to strive to suppress corrupt persons and to prevent notorious conduct by them in public, the open commission of vice, and any dealing in intoxicating drink in the neighbourhood of mosques, burial places, and tombs. Further, the muḥtasib must see that the dhimmīs wear distinguishing clothing to mark their inferiority among the Muslims; and he must prevent women mixing in assemblies of the *'ulamā* (*majlis-i 'ilm*) and listening to homilies (*mavā'iẓ*).[2]

Saljuq documents not infrequently compare the sultan to a shepherd and state that the subjects were placed in his care as a trust from God. In some measure his function as "the shepherd of his people" was delegated to the qāḍī. In part, however, it was delegated to a local official known as the ra'īs. This term, like various others, is used in a variety of senses and not always with precision. In some instances, as stated above, it is broadly synonymous with a provincial governor; it is also used to designate the head of a religious corporation. But in its most common use the term *ra'īs* designated a local official representing the local people *vis-à-vis* the government in general and the tax administration in particular. In the larger towns he was appointed by the sultan or the muqṭa'. But he was not an official of the central or the provincial government, as were the 'āmil, mustaufī, and mushrif, even though they, too, were sometimes local men; normally he was one of the leaders of local society, for only a man of local influence and standing could carry out his duties. Not only did he stand up for the interests of

[1] *Siyāsat-Nāma*, p. 41.

[2] *'Atabat al-kataba*, pp. 82–3.

the local population against the officials of the bureaucracy and the military classes—those living in the area and passing through it—but he also ensured that the local population paid their taxes in full to the government. There are instances of a ra'īs being sent from one city to another, though this was probably exceptional. Ibn Funduq states that Ḥamza b. Muḥammad, in whose family the office of ra'īs of Baihaq was hereditary, became ra'īs of Baihaq for a time, and then was sent as ra'īs to Tabrīz and Marāgheh.[1] As with the qāḍī, there was probably a hereditary tendency in this office.

Rāvandī relates an incident that shows the importance of the ra'īs as the representative of the local people: when the Niẓāmiyya mamlūks took Berk-Yaruq from Iṣfahān to Ray and seated him on the throne, the ra'īs of Ray, Abū Muslim, the son-in-law of Niẓām al-Mulk, suspended a jewelled crown above his head.[2] In some instances the ra'īs of a town was a man of considerable substance, as was Abū Hāshim, the ra'īs of Hamadān (see above, p. 251).

Since the relations between the government and people were principally in the field of taxation, it follows that the functions of the ra'īs were mainly connected with financial affairs. It was his special duty to safeguard the well-being of the people and to see that their burdens were lightened, and at the same time to ensure the due collection of dīvān taxes, to prevent both tyranny and oppression by the tax-collectors and evasion by the tax-payers. Through him the sultan exercised control over the officials of the dīvān. It was his duty to prevent anything being levied without due authorization from the dīvān, or without some overriding emergency; and when a levy was made on the order of the dīvān, he had to see that it was equitably distributed among all classes of tax-payers. He also supervised all transactions concerned with the revenue; and the 'āmil, shaḥna, and other officials were to keep him fully informed of their activities and not to act without his agreement and approval. In a diploma issued by Sanjar's dīvān for the ra'īs of Sarakhs, he is instructed *inter alia* not to allow demands to be made upon the people on behalf of leading members of the sultan's retinue or by others passing through the district, by the military (*mutajannida*), or by those having drafts for the collection of dues (*'avāriḍ*) or fodder (*'alaf*).[3] Clearly in the absence of coercive force provided by the government, only a man of local standing could hope to carry out such instructions.

[1] P. 94. [2] Pp. 140–1. [3] *'Atabat al-kataba*, p. 41.

The ra'īs had a dīvān or office, and in some cases had the power to appoint deputies to act for him. He was paid by dues (*rusūm*) levied locally. He seems to have had some responsibility for the general conduct of affairs inside the city, and appears on occasion to have had powers of arrest and imprisonment. After Ghazālī had been appointed mudarris of the Niẓāmiyya in Nīshāpūr a group of persons were alleged to have intrigued against him, imputing to him unorthodox views; and one man changed some words in the text of a copy of the *Mishkāt al-anwār* and the *Munqidh min al ḍalāl* with the intention of incriminating Ghazālī. Before signing the copy as correct, however, the author discovered the falsification. When the ra'īs of Khurāsān (= ? Nīshāpūr) learned of this he arrested the man and debarred him from residence in Nīshāpūr. He accordingly left that town and went to the royal camp where he continued his intrigues until finally Sanjar summoned Ghazālī to speak for himself. Ghazālī duly came to court about the year 503/1109–10 and put his opponents to shame.[1]

In this brief examination of the internal structure of the Saljuq empire I have attempted to show that nothing, religious or temporal, lay outside the care and concern of the sultan. Ghazālī's new definition of the relationship between the sultanate and the caliphate was an attempt to authorize the sultan's government (see above, pp. 207 ff.). This went far towards assuring the acceptance of his government as the effective organ through which Islamic government was expressed, or at least as the means for securing conditions in which the Islamic community could carry on its lawful purposes. And the attempt was to this extent successful, that after the caliphate was overthrown by the Mongols, although there was a temporary break with tradition, yet when the Mongol Īl-Khāns were converted to Islam their government was accepted—except by the more legalistically minded—as the government of Islam. On the other hand, the fundamental disharmony in the organization of the state was perpetuated by Niẓām al-Mulk's restatement of "the old Persian tradition of monarchy, with its independent ethical standards based on force and opportunism".[2]

The Saljuqs, who had started out as the leaders of a tribal migration, were gradually transformed, partly under the influence of Ghazālī and

[1] *Faḍā'il al-anām*, pp. 11–12.

[2] Cf. H. A. R. Gibb, "An Interpretation of Islamic History", in *Studies on the Civilisation of Islam*, p. 24.

Niẓām al-Mulk, into the rulers of a centralized state. The formulation of its institutions was largely the achievement of Niẓām al-Mulk, who modified and developed existing forms. The main features of the new organization of state—notably the structure of the dīvān, the iqṭāʿ system, and the close connexion between the assessment of taxes and the levy of troops—are also to be found (with changes in terminology) in the Ṣafavid and Qājār periods. The main institutions of the Saljuq state were essentially bureaucratic, though the fact that many offices of the state were held by the military tends to obscure this fact. The measures taken to solve the two crucial problems of the state, namely the payment of its civil and military officials and the provision of armed forces for the preservation of order and the maintenance of defence, were bureaucratic devices; and though their abuse led to decentralization and ultimately to the disintegration of the state, they did not of themselves involve decentralization.

Through the officials of the dīvān, the muqṭaʿs and provincial governors, the officials of the religious institution, and local officials, the sultan came into contact with all aspects of the life of his people. But in the absence of any effective system of control over them, the officials of the central government showed a recurrent tendency to act unjustly, while local officials became petty despots, and the people in general tended to encroach upon one another's rights. Thus the population felt no real identification with the sultan or his government, which is perhaps why ethics and not politics provided the social ideal, and why the emphasis in the political literature of the time is on justice seen, not in terms of legal justice or anything expressed in specific and practical terms, but as the harmonious relationship between society in a divinely appointed system, the component parts of which were in a perfect equilibrium.

CHAPTER 3

RELIGION IN THE SALJUQ PERIOD

In the religious history of Iran the Saljuq period is particularly interesting, for it is the period of the Ismā'īlīs. As the Ismā'īlī movement is treated in another part of the book, this chapter will be chiefly devoted to the three main aspects of religious life in Iran during this period: the development of Sunnism, the ferment of Shī'ī ideas, and Ṣūfism. Chronologically the Saljuq epoch in Iran extends roughly from the tenth to the twelfth centuries; obviously in this chapter we cannot always keep exactly within these limits.

If we realize that in the years from the death of Ash'arī (935) to that of Ghazālī (1111) the entire theological system of Islam found its final systematization; that it was also the period of Niẓām al-Mulk's *Siyāsat-Nāma* and of extremely interesting Shī'ī–Sunnī polemics; and finally that in the twelfth century the oldest Ṣūfī *ṭarīqat*s (fraternities) were organized, some of the first great Muslim theological universities were founded, and the poet Niẓāmī lived (1141–1209/13): realizing these facts, we can easily see the importance of the Saljuq era. Though not one of the most original, it is certainly one of the most formative epochs in the cultural history of Iran.

(I) SUNNISM

The stronghold of Sunnism was mostly eastern Iran, whereas Shī'ī centres were typical of Persian 'Irāq and Ṭabaristān (especially Qum, Ray and Āveh). Iranian Sunnism was chiefly Ḥanafī and Shāfi'ī, and these two schools were not often on good terms. In the *Kitāb al-naqḍ*, a Shī'ī polemic work of the first half of the twelfth century by Naṣīr al-Dīn Abu'l-Rashīd al-Qazvīnī, an attempt is made at a sort of sectarian geography of Iran. The author observes that Khurāsān and Transoxiana and part of 'Irāq were Ḥanafī and Mu'tazila in theology; Āzarbāījān up to the borders of Anatolia, and Hamadān, Iṣfahān, Sāveh, and Qazvīn were Shāfi'ī, while their theology represented various schools (Ash'arī, Ḥanbalī, etc.); the areas of Luristān, Khūzistān, Karaj, Gulpāigān, Burūjird, Nihāvand were full of "anthropomorphists" (*Mushabbiha*, *Mujassima*); and in Māzandarān, Qum, Kāshān and Āveh there were Shī'īs.

A later work, also by a Shīʿī author, the *Tabṣirat al-ʿawāmm* (beginning of the thirteenth century), shows us the religious pattern of Saljuq Iran in more detail. The author distinguishes seven Sunnī "sects", distributed more or less as follows:

1. *Dā'ūdī*, "now no more in existence".

2. *Ḥanafī*, theologically divided into *Muʿtazila*, *Najjāriyya*, *Karāmiyya*, *Murjiʿa*, and *Jabriyya*. The people of Khwārazm are Ḥanafī–Muʿtazilī, the people of Bukhārā and the "peasants" (*rustā'ī*) of Kāshān are Ḥanafī–Najjārī; in Ghūr and Sind there are Karāmīs, whereas the Ḥanafīs of Kūfa and Baghdad are Murjiʿa, and the Ḥanafīs of Khurāsān, Transoxiana, and Farghāna are Jabrī, as are the Turks.

3. *Mālikī*, theologically divided into *Khārijī* (*sic*), *Muʿtazila*, *Mushabbiha*, *Sālimiyya* (the Mālikīs of Baṣra), *Ashʿarī*.

4. *Shāfiʿī*, theologically divided into six groups: *Mushabbiha* or "anthropomorphists" (Hamadān, Qara, Burūjird, Iṣfahān, Yazd, Herāt, Salmās, Shīrāz, etc.); *Salafī*, i.e. more moderate Mushabbiha; *Khārijī* led by Ḥusain Karābīsī (according to this author all the Khārijīs of Baṣra, Oman, and Isfarā'in are Shāfiʿī–Karābīsī); *Muʿtazila*, having as their imām Māwardī and Rāghib Iṣfahānī (the inhabitants of Mufradāt, a town in Khūzistān between Baṣra and ʿAskar-i-Mukarram, are Shāfiʿī–Muʿtazila, who "in older times" were numerous in Fasā, and even "now" in Shīrāz there is a half-ruined caravanserai, an old *vaqf* of the Shāfiʿī-Muʿtazila of Fasā); *Ashʿarī*; and *Yazīdī*, who are spread from Zūr to Syria (of Mushabbiha and Khārijite [*sic*] tendencies, they consider Abū Bakr, ʿUmar, ʿUthmān, Muʿāwiya and Yazīd to be "God-guided caliphs", but they often use *taqiyya* and include ʿAlī also in the list of God-guided caliphs).

5. *Ḥanbalī*. 6. *Thaurī* (?). 7. *Isḥāq-Rāhawī*: all three with Mushabbiha tendencies.

This rather confused list is interesting for its information on the geographical distribution of religious centres in Saljuq Persia. Of particular interest is the continuation of centres with Khārijite tendencies. Yāqūt too (1179–1229) informs us that in this period there were many Khārijites in Sīstān: they were not afraid of declaring openly their Khārijism, and they wore a special garb.

As always happens in formative ages, religious debates and quarrels, often ending in massacres, were frequent. Even in moments of grave dangers religious antagonism was strong and active; according to

Rāvandī's *Rāḥat al-ṣudūr*, in Nīshāpūr after the terrible onslaught of the Ghuzz (1154) every night one sect would assault a quarter of the town inhabited by members of an enemy sect, and there they would kill and burn. Similar things happened in Shīrāz between Ḥanafīs and Shāfi'īs, in Ray between both of them and the Shī'īs, and between all of them and the Ismā'īlīs. To isolate a single racial or national element in Shī'ī–Sunnī disputes of this age is totally impossible. A verse like the following, composed in Arabic by an unknown poet of Ray and mentioned in the Shī'ī work *Kitāb al-naqḍ*, is typical:

Truly man is distinguished only by religion, and piety (*taqwā*) cannot be abandoned on account of racial reasons (*'alā'l-nasab*). Islam exalted the Persian Salmān, polytheism humiliated the noble Abū Lahab!

The same important text speaks of persecutions of Mushabbiha in Iṣfahān at the time of the Saljuq princes Maḥmūd and Mas'ūd, while in Ray Ḥanafīs of Mu'tazilī tendencies were compelled by force to declare that the Qur'ān was increate. The Saljuq Mas'ūd b. Muḥammad, influenced by Mu'tazilī suggestions, persecuted followers of Mushabbiha, Jabrīyya, and Ash'arī tendencies in Qazvīn, Ray, Iṣfahān, Baghdad and other places.

The *Kitāb al-naqḍ*, particularly significant as it is a Shī'ī work, shows clearly that the great majority of Iranians were at that time Sunnī with Ash'arī and even Mushabbiha tendencies; and the city of Iṣfahān is mentioned as a "capital city of Sunnism". As often happens in fiery polemics, all parties abundantly used an insulting and abusing language, misrepresented facts, and so on. Poets also took part in the disputes: e.g. the famous Ẓahīr-i Faryābī (d. 1201) jeered at Mu'tazilas, and Khāqānī (d. 1199) attacked *falāsifa* (philosophers), Mu'aṭṭila, and Mu'tazila. Shī'īs were fond of accusing all Sunnīs of anthropomorphism and even of Ismā'īlism, "because they apply *ta'līm* and *taqlīd* as the Ismā'īlīs!"[1] An ex-Shī'ī convert to Sunnism wrote, soon before 1161, an anti-Shī'ī book with the significant title "Some of the ignominies of the Shī'īs" (*Ba'ḍu faḍā'iḥ al-rawāfiḍ*), which contained a list of sixty-seven of these "ignominies". Qazvīnī's *Kitābu 'l-naqḍ*, written as an answer to that book, bears the complete title: "Some vices of the Sunnīs: a destruction of the ignominies of the Shī'īs" (*Ba'ḍu mathālib al-nawāṣib fī naqḍ ba'ḍ faḍā'iḥ al-rawāfiḍ*). His book emphasizes especially the Mushabbiha aspects of Sunnism, and accuses the Sunnīs of being blind

[1] *Kitāb al-naqḍ*, p. 489.

followers of the tradition, believers in predestination and enemies of the family of the Prophet. The Sunnīs, for their part, tended to assimilate all forms of Shī'ism to Ismā'īlism (at that time the supreme public danger). The book *Faḍā'iḥ al rawāfiḍ* says: "Shī'ism is the corridor leading to heresy" (*rāfiḍī dihlīz-i mulḥidīst*). And when the same book says that the Shī'is are Zoroastrians under Muslim garb, it is repeating an older accusation (its initiator may have been Ibn Ḥazm, d. 1064), which is at the root of some unfounded modern assertions of a special similarity between Shī'ism and Zoroastrianism. An interesting anti-Shī'ī accusation in this book is the statement that the Shī'is propagandize especially in the lower classes and amongst ignorant artisans and that they are *dahriyya* (materialists).

It is practically impossible to delineate here a history of the development of Sunnī ideas solely within Iran, regarded as a racial or national unit. The fact that Ghazālī was Iranian is not of great importance, as he wrote in Arabic and his works were studied even as far away as Spain; whereas in Iran Sunnīs, and also Shī'is, studied the religious works of their fellow believers spread throughout that vast unit which was the Islamic world. A chapter on Ghazālī and his significance in the history of Muslim philosophy and theology can be found in any work on the history of Islam and has no place here. We will simply remark that he is one of the best representatives of that solid, clear, Khurāsānian Sunnism that has been for centuries the religious milieu in which the greatest Iranian geniuses, literary and otherwise, have been bred. Of this Sunnism Ghazālī is, in a way, the résumé and the practical end: after him Sunnism did not produce much that is significant in the theological field. On the other hand, Ghazālī's radical mistrust of human reason and his consequent condemnation of philosophy; his intellectual aristocratism (he discouraged the common people from studying theology, saying they must only believe); his so often unjustly praised introduction of a moderate mysticism into orthodoxy, which killed all the most enthusiastic and progressive aspects of mysticism; his wish to make jurisprudence mystical and mysticism juridical—all of these achievements represent an end rather than a beginning, and their enormous influence has been quite detrimental for later Muslim culture.

But the Saljuq period in Iran is not only the period of Ghazālī. It is, as we said before, a *formative* age in which, side by side with the great synthesis of Ghazālī, there existed other tendencies that are still alive and influential. It is the period in which the Mu'tazila school was being finally vanquished by the Ash'arites, except for some nuclei of resistance in 'Irāq, Khwārazm, and Transoxiana. Four of the most famous figures here were:

Juvainī (d. 1085), the master of Ghazālī, known as *Imām al-Ḥaramain*; in his epoch the greatest Shāfi'ī–Ash'arī theologian of Khurāsān, and author of the important treatises *Irshād*, *Khāmil*, *Ghiyāthu 'l-Umam*, *Muḥaqqiq 'l-Ḥaqq*. He had many pupils besides Ghazālī. One of them was 'Imād al-Dīn Kiyā Harāsī (d. 1110) of Ṭabaristān.

Another Shāfi'ī–Ash'arī scholar of Saljuq Iran was al-Shahrastānī (d. 1153), who served Sulṭān Sanjar and is chiefly famous as the author of the great heresiographical manual, *al-Milal wa'l-niḥal*. He lived in Khurāsān (Shahristān is a town there, near Nasā) and in Khwārazm. Amongst other works he wrote a commentary on the Qur'ān. His *Muṣāri'a* is a polemical work against Avicenna, who is a favourite target of Ash'arī attacks.

Ibn al-Jauzī (d. 1201) the author of the celebrated *Talbīs Iblīs*, "The Tricks of Satan", another heretical treatise; he lived in Baghdad and was so much venerated by all religious parties that sometimes disputes between Shī'is and Sunnīs were brought to him to be arbitrated.

Fakhr al-Dīn Rāzī (d. 1210), the author of the famous *Tafsīr* of the Qur'ān, a real encyclopaedia, of which somebody has said, *Fihi kullu shai' illā'l-tafsīr* ("In it there is everything save a commentary on the Qur'ān!"). He also wrote the *Muḥassil afkār al-mutaqaddimīn* (a rich historical summary of the ideas of Muslim theologians); one *risāla* (treatise) on the Prophet's Ascension, and other similar tracts. The famous *al-Kashshāf*, a Mu'tazila commentary on the Qur'ān by al-Zamakhsharī (d. 1144), is also a fruit of the Persian religious genius of the Saljuq epoch.

The growing influence of the orthodox Ash'arite school brought with it, of course, a decline in the speculative sciences. Ghazālī's *Tahāfut al-Falāsifa* ("Destructio philosophorum") is only the most authoritative example of many similar attacks on philosophy, i.e. on purely speculative, Aristotelian and Neo-Platonic philosophy. A typical specimen of the orthodox Ash'arite attitude of this time towards science is this sentence in the theological treatise *Majmū'a al-rasā'il al-kubrā*: "Only the science transmitted to posterity through the Holy Prophet is worthy of the name of science (*'ilm*). Other sciences are either sciences but not useful (*nāfi'*), or they are not sciences and not useful, or they are not sciences, but only called such, and not useful. If they are sciences and useful they are certainly contained in the Prophet's heritage."[1] According to Ghazālī the three chief errors of the "philosophers" are the following: "They admit in God only the science of the Universals and not of particular things; they do not believe in the resurrection of the body and in the reality of eschatological facts; they regard the world as being uncreated."

Although an uninterrupted chain of masters and pupils connected him with the great Master Avicenna, the philosopher—Farīd Ghīlānī of Balkh (twelfth century) nevertheless wrote a treatise (*Risāla ḥudūth al-ʿālam*) in confutation of Avicenna, and especially of his theory of the uncreatedness of the world. As Avicenna had long been regarded as the philosopher *par excellence*, many of these attacks simply took the form of attacks on him personally. He was criticized from two sides: from the left, by such rationalist philosophers as Averroes (d. 1199), who thought his Aristotelian tendencies were impure; and from the right by such theologians as Shahrastānī, Farīd Ghīlānī, and Fakhr al-Dīn Rāzī, and even by poets influenced by the general Ashʿarite atmosphere (e.g. Sanāʾī, d. 1141, and Khāqānī, d. 1199).

Amongst the most important religious philosophers of the Saljuq epoch we may mention several in particular.

Abu'l-ʿAbbās Faḍl b. Muḥammad al-Lūkarī of Marv, a pupil of Avicenna's pupil Bahmanyār, was the author of the *Bayān al-ḥaqq bi-ḍiman as-ṣidaq* and other works. The *Bayān al-ḥaqq*, still unpublished, utilizes parts of previous works by Fārābī, Avicenna, and others, and is divided into five parts: logic, natural history, theology, metaphysics, ethics. Lūkarī exercised a great influence on the Persian philosophers of this age for he had numerous pupils, though not all of them remained faithful to Avicennism, as we saw. Amongst his pupils were Abū Ṭāhir Tabasī of Marv (d. 1145) with his pupil Abū Saʿīd Funduwarjī, and also the qāḍī ʿAbd al-Razzāq Turkī, al-Īlāqī, the aforementioned Farīd Ghīlānī, the physician Ḥasan Qaṭṭān of Marv, and Asʿad al-Maihanī (d. 1133).

Lūkarī was a contemporary of the great astronomer and poet ʿUmar Khayyām, who, though not strictly a philosopher or a theologian, must be mentioned here if only because he symbolizes a different direction of Persian thought in this age. The orthodox opinion on him is well expressed in the mystical work *Mirṣād al-ʿibād* by Dāya (1223), in which Khayyām, though praised as "famous for his talents, his wisdom,

[1] Cairo, 1324, p. 238.

intelligence and doctrine", is associated with "those unfortunate philosophers and materialists, who, detached from divine blessings, wander in stupefaction and error". In one of his quatrains (129 of Furūghī's edition) Khayyām himself refuses the title of *falsafī* ("philosopher"), in the sense of an Aristotelian one, saying he desires simply "to know who I am". An anecdote reported in the *Tatimma ṣiwān al-ḥikma* connects the name of 'Umar Khayyām with that of another philosopher and physician of this age, Abu'l-Barakāt Hibat Allāh al-Baladī or al-Baghdādī (d. 1152), a Jew who served under the 'Abbāsid Caliph al-Mustarshid Bi'llāh, and, taken prisoner by the Saljuq prince Mas'ūd, accepted Islam. Abu'l-Barakāt is the author of famous books such as *al-Mu'tabar*, *Kitāb an-nafs*, and a commentary on Aristotle's psychology. He strongly criticized Avicenna, and according to the anecdote mentioned above, 'Umar Khayyām, requested by the Kākūyid prince 'Alā' al-Daula of Yazd to express his opinion on the dissension between the two philosophers, is said to have remarked: "Abu'l-Barakāt does not even understand the sense of the words of Avicenna, how can he oppose what he does not know?"

The names of other philosophers of this age—such as Abū Sa'īd al-Ghānimī, author of *Qurāḍat at-ṭabī'īyāt*; Zain al-Dīn al-Sāwī, a contemporary of Sulṭān Sanjar, a pupil of Īlāqī and author of treatises on logic, and so on—would mean little to the non-specialist reader.

The importance of the Saljuq period lies especially in the fact that religious learning was organized in great teaching institutions, which might be considered to be amongst the first universities of the civilized world. For in this way the bases were laid for almost all the organized institutions of Muslim religious culture. In this work the great vizier Niẓām al-Mulk was most active; the institutions he founded took the name of *Niẓāmiyya*, and they were like colleges, with scholarships, good salaries for the professors, and a traditional and well-organized course of studies. Especially famous were the Niẓāmiyyas of Baghdad (founded in 1065–7) and Nīshāpūr, though others were present in all the chief towns of the Saljuq sultanate. The professors in Baghdad and Nīshāpūr were appointed by Niẓām al-Mulk and, after his death, by his heirs. All the other colleges were imitations of the Niẓāmiyya: one of the most important of this period is the *Mustanṣiriyya* of Baghdad, founded in the years 1228–34 by the 'Abbāsid Caliph al-Mustanṣir Bi'llāh. The teaching in all these universities (*madrasas*) was done by the *mudarrises* (professors) and their *mu'īds* (assistants). The professor used to teach seated on a *kursī* (a sort of chair), and he wore a special gown called a *ṭarḥa* and a turban; two mu'īds were seated at his side, repeating his words to the students and explaining difficult points. The *curriculum studiorum* consisted of *fiqh* (Muslim law) *ḥadīth* (traditions of the Prophet), *tafsīr* (exegesis of the Qur'ān), literary theory, mathematics, and medicine. Every student had his own *ḥujra* (a small room) and a monthly stipend. In these madrasas, and also elsewhere, there were rich libraries. To take only an example given by Yāqūt in his *Mu'jam*: in Marv there were ten vaqf libraries, some of them containing 12,000 volumes. Books could be borrowed without any restrictions (Yāqūt himself had two hundred in his house at one time!).

(2) SHĪ'ISM

Before the sixteenth century, when it succeeded in becoming the official religion of an organized political unit, Ṣafavid Iran, Shī'ism consisted chiefly of widespread "centres of resistance", a sort of fermentation of ideas to which it is very difficult to assign a well-defined geographical area. Such centres were by no means limited to Iran, which in Saljuq times was perhaps a more Sunnī country than was Anatolia or Syria; but since Persia was to become—and not always by peaceful means—a Shī'ī country four centuries later, it is of special interest to study the position of Shī'ism in the Saljuq era, in order to try to discover some elements of historical continuity. The chief sources for our study are the two controversial works mentioned above, the *Kitāb al-naqḍ* of Qazvīnī, and the *Faḍā'iḥ ar-rawāfiḍ*, together with the "History of Religions", *Tabṣiratu 'l-'awāmm*, by Sayyid Murtaḍā Rāzī.

Of the numerous Shī'ī sects only four retain importance in this period in Iran: (1) the *Naṣīrī*, a name given in the twelfth and thirteenth centuries to those extremists who attributed to 'Alī divine or quasi-divine powers (all other Shī'īs, including Ismā'īlīs, considered these heretical and *kāfir* (unbeliever)); (2) the *Zaidīs*; (3) the *Ismā'īlīs*; and (4) the *Imāmīs* (Twelvers).

The Zaidīs in the Saljuq period were subdivided into four communities: the *Jārūdiyya/Sarḥūbiyya* were followers of Abu'l-Jārūd, a contemporary of the imām al-Bāqir, who, as a reproach for his "hypocrisy" (*nifāq*), had called him Sarḥūb, one of the names of Satan; then there were the *Jarīriyya/Sulaimāniyya*; the *Batriyya*, followers of Kuthaiyyir an-Nawwā' al-Abtar; and the *Ya'qūbiyya*.

The Jārūdiyya considered the leaders of the Islamic community before ʿAlī to be usurpers and *kāfir* (unbelievers). Some of them believed that their *Mahdī* was the lord of Ṭāliqān (in Badakhshān), Muḥammad b. ʿAlī b. ʿUmar b. ʿAlī b. Ḥusain b. ʿAlī, imprisoned by the Caliph al-Muʾtaṣim (833–42). Others proclaimed as Mahdī the prince of Kūfa, Yaḥyā b. ʿUmar b. Yaḥyā b. Ḥusain b. Zaid b. ʿAlī, eventually killed during the caliphate of al-Mustāʿīn (862–6).

The Jarīriyya/Sulaimāniyya held different views from the Jārūdiyya, especially with respect to the transmission of the imamate. For the Jārūdiyya, as for the Twelvers, it was transmitted by *naṣṣ* (explicit designation by the former imām), whereas the Jarīriyya/Sulaimāniyya adopted the Sunnī idea of the transmission of the imamate by *shūrā* (consultation). For them Abū Bakr and ʿUmar were sinners but not kāfir. Not so ʿUthmān, who, having introduced (according to them) anti-Islamic *bidʿas* (innovations, heresies) was truly a kāfir.

The Batriyya were even more moderate than the Jarīriyya, holding the idea that, though ʿAlī was after the Prophet the noblest of creatures, the caliphates of Abū Bakr and ʿUmar were still legitimate, because ʿAlī himself had abandoned his pretensions to the imāmate; similar ideas were defended also by the Yaʿqūbiyya.

Theologically the Zaidīs were Muʿtazila, and in jurisprudence they were practically identical with the Sunnīs inasmuch as they considered *qiyās*, *raʾy*, *ijtihād*, and *istiḥsān* to be good *sharʿī* sources of law. They regarded as invalid all imāms after ʿAlī son of Ḥusain, and as kāfir all those who did not accept, after him, the imāmate of Zaid and the holy war.

In the Saljuq period Zaidīs were still comparatively strong in those regions that had been their stronghold in the ninth and tenth centuries, i.e. Dailam, Gīlān, Ṭabaristān, and Gurgān. In some of these areas during the lifetime of the author of the *Kitāb al-naqḍ*, the Zaidīs still read the *khuṭba* in the name of their imāms, and struck coins in their name.

Apart from the Ismāʿīlīs (treated in another chapter of this volume) the strongest Shīʿī sect of the Saljuq epoch were the *Imāmiyya*, or Twelvers, as Western orientalists call them. The Saljuqs affirmed their power in Iran just at the moment when Shīʿī elements—comparatively strong in Dailam, Ṭabaristān, Persian and Arab ʿIrāq, Khūzistān, and Kirmān—together with the powerful Ismāʿīlī movement were preparing the way for the destruction of the ʿAbbāsid caliphate. Based on the strong Sunnī centres of eastern Iran, and finding its best and most honest representative in the great personality of Niẓām al-Mulk, the vizier of Malik-Shāh, the inflexible Sunnism of the Saljuqs gave new life to the moribund Sunnī caliphate of Baghdad. This passage from the famous *Siyāsat-Nāma* of Niẓām al-Mulk is illuminating:

In the days of Mahmud, Mas'ud, Tughril, and Alp-Arslan (may Allah have mercy on them) no Zoroastrian or Jew or Rafidi would have had the audacity to appear in a public place or to present himself before a great man. Those who administered the affairs of the Turks were all professional civil servants and secretaries from Khurasan, who belonged to the orthodox Hanafi or Shafi'i sects. The heretics of Iraq were never admitted as secretaries and tax collectors; in fact the Turks never used to employ them at all; they said, "These men are of the same religion as the Dailamites and their supporters; if they get a firm footing they will injure the interests of the Turks and cause distress to the Muslims. It is better that enemies should not be in our midst." Consequently they lived free from disaster.[1]

This passage shows how one of the racially purest Iranian zones, Khurāsān, was strongly Sunnī, whereas Shī'ism seemed identified with 'Irāqī, western Iranian, and even Arabic tendencies: further proof, if necessary, that the present Shī'ism of Iran has nothing to do with race.

The *Siyāsat-Nāma* is full of episodes and anecdotes showing the strong anti-Shī'ī tendencies of the influential author, who, for propagandist reasons, often lumped all Shī'īs together with the much-feared Ismā'īlīs; indeed Shī'ī resentment was one of the causes of Niẓām al-Mulk's eventual dismissal, after which Shī'ī influence began to grow. Nevertheless, in spite of the Saljuqs' anti-Shī'ī policy, Shī'ī centres were flourishing in Iran, as elsewhere, during this period. Shī'īs had their own madrasas, mosques, and libraries, and, as the protests expressed in the above passage show, they even succeeded in penetrating into court life: thus Hibat Allāh Muḥammad b. 'Alī (known as Ibn al-Muṭṭalib) was a minister of the Caliph al-Mustaẓhir; Sa'd al-Mulk Āvajī was vizier to Sulṭān Muḥammad b. Malik-Shāh, and Sharaf al-Dīn Anushīrvān b. Khālid Kāshānī was vizier to both the Caliph al-Mustarshid and Sulṭān Maḥmūd b. Malik-Shāh. That orthodox Sunnīs were preoccupied with the slow penetration of Shī'ī elements into official posts is also clear from the *Faḍā'iḥ al-rawāfiḍ*, which expresses the fear of an alliance between "Turks" (i.e. the Saljuq ruling class) and Shī'ism: "Now [*c.* 1165] there is no *sarāi* of Turks that has not at least ten or fifteen *ravāfiḍ*, and many of them are employed as *dabīrs* in the *dīvān*s."[2] The Shī'ī author of the *Kitāb al-naqḍ* even has words in praise of the "Turks" who sometimes used to protect the Shī'īs in the period following

[1] Darke tr., pp. 164–5

[2] Pp. 53–4.

the death of Niẓām al-Mulk and Malik-Shāh. Shīʿī influences were particularly strong in Khwārazm, perhaps because this region was a traditional stronghold of Muʿtazilism: it is known that at the beginning of the thirteenth century the Khwārazm-Shāh Muḥammad went so far as to propose the ʿAlid ʿAlāʾ al-Mulk as caliph, and to invite the ʿulamā of his country to declare the ʿAbbāsids unworthy of the caliphate, which should have belonged to the Ḥusainīs.[1]

Amongst the propaganda techniques used by the Shīʿīs to spread their beliefs and influence was that of the *manāqibīs* or *manāqib-khwān*s. *Manāqib* means "virtues" and *manāqib-khwān* is a singer who extols the virtues of ʿAlī and his descendants in streets and bazaars. The manāqibīs had existed in Iraq since the Būyid period, and their activity had continued more or less secretly into the period of the early Saljuqs in ʿIrāq and Ṭabaristān; in order to avoid persecutions they often migrated from place to place. The *Kitāb al-naqḍ*, speaking of the situation after the death of Malik-Shāh, says that the manāqib-khwāns used to sing *qaṣīdas* in praise of the Shīʿī imām because he had attacked the Sunnī "usurpers". These qaṣīdas also contained doctrinal and theological elements, such as the concept of *tanzīh* (the absolute transcendence of God, as opposed to anthropomorphism); that of *ʿadl* (the justice of God, as opposed to the Ashʿarī idea of His arbitrary power); that of the imāms' *ʿiṣma* (infallibility and impeccability), of their miracles, and so on. Moreover in their fantastic tales of the military exploits of ʿAlī and his paladins, the poems were like "religious epical songs". Unfortunately these older poems are almost completely lost, but we have good specimens of this kind of folk-religious Shīʿī epic in the Ṣafavid period. The *Kitāb al-naqḍ* gives us also the names of some Shīʿī poets (to be distinguished from the *manāqibīs*, who were mere singers), of whom the most famous in the twelfth century was Qivāmī of Ray.

To counterbalance the manāqib-khwāns' influence the Sunnīs employed *faḍāʾil-khwāns* (also meaning "singers of virtues"), who exalted the superior virtues of Abū Bakr and ʿUmar and insulted the Shīʿīs. The *Kitāb al-naqḍ*, in a very interesting passage, tells us that their poems were imitations of those of the Shīʿīs (and this is probably correct), that in them they taught the dogmas of *jabr* (predestination) and *tashbīh* (anthropomorphism), and instead of singing of the "true" holy wars of ʿAlī and his companions, "they invented false wars and unfounded stories concerning Rustam, Suhrāb, Isfandiyār, Kāʾūs, Zāl, etc., and

[1] Juvainī, *Taʾrīkh-i Jahān-Gushā*, vol. II, pp. 96–7.

sent their singers to spread these idle tales (*turrahāt*) in all the bazaars of the country, as a confutation (*radd*) of the bravery and virtue of the Prince of the Believers (ʿAlī). This heretical practice (*bidʿat*) is still observed now, and it is truly a heresy and an aberration to sing the praises of Zoroastrians (*gabrakān*) in the holy Nation of Muḥammad (blessings on him!)".[1] Imāmite Shīʿism appears here, in its true light, as an essentially *Islamic* movement, which, in Iran, not only had nothing to do with pre-Islamic ideas, but condemned them more strongly than it did the traditional Iranian Sunnism.

According to some texts it is also in this epoch that the *taʿziya*s (of not in the modern sense theatrical plays) experience a sort of revival. These mourning ceremonies in commemoration of the martyrdom of Ḥusain at Karbalā seem to have been started or developed first under the Būyids, and under the Saljuqs they were sometimes practised by the Sunnīs too (Ḥanafī and Shāfiʿī), and "even in strong Sunnī towns, like Hamadān".

Where in Iran were the Shīʿīs most numerous at this period? The list of such places has become almost a τόπος in various religious books of this epoch, leading one to suspect that it is a formula inherited from older heretical treatises rather than a result of actual observations of facts. The places most commonly mentioned in connexion with the Shīʿīs are Qum, Ray, and Āveh (this last being Āveh of Sāveh, mentioned also by Yāqūt as a fervent Shīʿī centre). Summing up the information given in the *Tabṣiratu ʾl-ʿawāmm*, the *Kitāb al-naqḍ*, and the *Rāḥat al-ṣudūr*, we see that, besides Baghdad and its famous Shīʿī quarter of Karkh, the "Shīʿī centres" in Saljuq Iran were chiefly considered to be Kāshān, Tafrish, Āveh, Qum, Ray, Qazvīn, Sārī, Iram, and zones in Māzandarān; in Khurāsān there were some Shīʿīs in Nīshāpūr and Sabzavār. But rather than denoting organized Shīʿī communities, some of these names hint at the presence of generically Shīʿī ferment, sometimes in the sense of Ismāʿīlī or *Bāṭinī* ferment. I wonder whether verses like those of Shams al-Dīn Lāgharī, quoted in the *Rāḥat al-ṣudūr*, may be taken as real proofs of the presence of organized Twelver Shīʿī communities in the localities mentioned:

> Sire, the place of Bāṭinīs are Qum, Kāshān, Āba, and Tabrish;
> Vindicate, therefore, the honour of the Four Companinns [the "orthodox" caliphs of the Sunnīs], and throw fire into these four places,
> Then burn Farāhan and Muṣliḥgāh, so that the recompense of thy meritorious works may be multiplied!

[1] Pp. 34–5.

More reliable information is that given by the *Kitāb al-naqḍ*, which mentions the following Shī'ī madrasas of this epoch (second half of the twelfth century): in Ray, a traditional centre of Shī'ism, the madrasa founded by Sayyid Tāj al-Dīn Muḥammad Gīlakī, a contemporary of Toghrïl Beg, and the madrasas of Shams al-Islām Ḥaskā Bābūya and many others, some containing from 200 to 400 pupils; in Qum the madrasa of Athīr al-Mulk, of Sayyid 'Izz al-Dīn Murtaḍā, and so on (altogether eight are mentioned for Qum); and in Kāshān the madrasas called Ṣafawiyya, the Najdiyya, the Sharafiyya, etc., with learned masters like Imām Żiyā' al-Dīn Abu'l-Riḍā Faḍl Allāh b. 'Alī al-Ḥusainī. In Āveh the madrasas 'Izz al-Mulkī, 'Arabshāhī, and others are mentioned; in Varāmīn the Riḍawiyya and Fatḥiyya, and in Sabzavār there were "good *madrasas* and teachers, which from generation to generation taught the Law of Islam".[1]

Shī'ī culture in this epoch produced remarkable religious works. More or less at the beginning of the period the important Qur'ānic commentary of the Shī'ī doctor Abū Ja'far Ṭūsī (d. 1068) was composed, and a summary of it by Ibn Idrīs al-Ḥillī belongs to the twelfth century (Ḥillī died in 1182). In the first half of this century the Shī'īs produced a Qur'ānic commentary in Persian, that of Jamāl al-Dīn Rāzī; and another venerated Shī'ī scholar, Shaikh Ṭabarsī (d. 1153), composed three Qur'ānic commentaries, the most important of which is the *Majma' al-bayān* in Arabic (translated into Persian in the nineteenth century). The majority of Shī'ī theologians of this period were polemicists, but they laid the bases of that methodical Shī'ī theology which flourished especially in the next century in the personality of Naṣīr al-Dīn Ṭūsī—sometimes considered the greatest of all Shī'ī theologians. Amongst the Shī'ī polemical works we may mention Shaikh Ṭūsī's *Ithbāt al-wājib* and *Talkhīṣ ash-shāfī*; a summary of a work by Sayyid Murtaḍa (d. 1045); written against *al-Mughnī fī 'l-imāma* by the Qāḍī 'Abd al-Jabbār Mu'tazilī of Hamadān (d. 1023), and concerned with such problems as the legitimacy of the imāmate. Another polemical writer was Abu'l-Qāsim Ḥusain b. Muḥammad of Iṣfahān, known as Rāghib (d. 1108), who wrote *al-Dharī'a ilā makārim al-sharī'a*. Qazvīnī's *Kitāb al-naqḍ*, composed around 1165, has already been mentioned. This epoch produced a remarkable number of those compositions, partly heresiographic and polemical, partly theological and historical, which could be defined as forerunners of our modern

[1] Qazvīnī, p. 174.

handbooks of comparative religion. The oldest one in Persian was written in 1092 by a Shī'ī, Abu'l-Ma'ālī Muḥammad 'Ubaid Allāh, and bore the title *Bayān al-adyān* ("An Explanation of Religions"). To the later Saljuq period belongs the *Tabṣirat al-'awāmm* of Sayyid Murtaḍā Dā'ī Ḥasanī of Ray, also a sort of encyclopaedia of religions containing useful data.

(3) ṢŪFISM

The second half of the eleventh century, all of the twelfth, and the beginnings of the thirteenth may be considered one of the most important periods in the history of Ṣūfism, not only in Iran but everywhere. In the second half of the eleventh century in Transoxiana, Khurāsān, and Iraq, great Ṣūfī saints lived, each one in small convents (*khānqāh*), praying, meditating, and teaching new pupils. As we said in relation to Ghazālī, it is in the Saljuq period that Ṣūfism, after years of distrust and even persecution by members of the orthodoxy, found its way in a modified form into Sunnī orthodoxy itself. Qushairī and then Ghazālī, both Ash'arī (at first sight a rather anti-mystical position!), gave to Ṣūfism full rights of citizenship in Sunnism; whereas Shī'ism (seemingly a more favourable ground for mystical ideas) generally, at least in older periods, opposed Ṣūfism, sometimes in a very violent manner.

It is in the twelfth century that the oldest organized *ṭarīqats* of Ṣūfism were founded, and some important parts of the ṭarīqat ritual were introduced. Massignon and Kahle are of the opinion that the initiation ritual of the Ṣūfī brotherhoods was first created in this century, imitating the Qarmaṭī (Ismā'īlī) ritual.

Further, the document of initiation (*ijāza*) with its *silsila*, a sort of spiritual chain of the names of all the Masters of the brotherhood, seems to have been used for the first time towards the end of the Saljuq period, in 1227.[1] It is also in this century that the coenobitic life of *ikhwān* (brothers) in a cloister (*khānqāh*) found its first developments, though we may find traces of a communal life of mystics in earlier texts.[2] The first organized Ṣūfī brotherhood in Iran were the Kāzarūniyya (Shīrāz, 1034), in its beginnings a mystical school rather than a real "order"; but most important were the three branches of an originally common school (Junaidīya): i.e. the Khwājagān (founded by Yūsuf Hamadānī, d. 1140), which spread, especially in Turkestān, through its branch

[1] See Massignon's article "Ṭarīḳa", in *Encyclopaedia of Islam*.

[2] Another word for *ikhwān*, mostly in Anatolia, was *akhī*.

the Yasaviyya; secondly, the Kubrāwiyya (founded in K͟hurāsān by Najma 'l-Dīn Kubrā, d. 1221); and thirdly, the famous Qādiriyya, organized in Baghdad some decades after the death of its spiritual originator, the famous saint ʿAbd al-Qādir Gīlānī, d. 1166). To these first ṭarīqats we may add the Rifāʿiyya, with its centre in Baṣra (founded by al-Rifāʿī, d. 1183), the Suhravardiyya of Baghdad, founded by ʿAbd al-Qāhir Suhravardī (d. 1167) and ʿUmar Suhravardī (d. 1234), and later the C͟his͟htiyya, which spread through the eastern zones of Iran, Afghanistan, and India in the thirteenth century; its centre was Ajmīr, India, where the tomb of its founder Muʿīn al-Dīn C͟his͟htī (d. 1236) is situated.

At the beginning of the Saljuq era some of the great Ṣūfīs of the older pre-ṭarīqat period of Ṣūfism were still living in Iran. Abū Saʿīd b. Abī'l-K͟hair, the first mystical poet of Iran (d. 1048–9), and the equally famous Ṣūfī theoretician Qus͟hairī (d. 1073) were both active in K͟hurāsān, where they left many disciples. Soon after them come such men as Hujvīrī, K͟hwāja Aḥmad Sarak͟hsī, and Abū ʿAbdallāh Bākū; the C͟his͟htīs, spiritual offspring of K͟hwāja Aḥmad C͟his͟htī, d. 966 (C͟his͟ht is a town in K͟hurāsān), included Muḥammad b. Abī Aḥmad, Yūsuf b. Muḥammad b. Samʿān (d. 1067), and Quṭb al-Dīn b. Maudūd C͟his͟htī (d. 1133), all very well known at the time of the Greater Saljuqs. It was in the same region, K͟hurāsān, that the fame of K͟hwāja ʿAbdallāh Anṣārī (d. 1089), the great writer and saint buried in Herāt, began to spread in this period. Some time earlier, K͟hwāja Yaḥyā b. ʿAmmār al-S͟haibānī, disciple of the S͟hīrāzī saint Ibn K͟hafīf, had gone to Herāt and was active there in spreading Ṣūfī teachings. One of the greatest Ṣūfīs of K͟hurāsān was the S͟haik͟h al-S͟huyūk͟h Abū ʿAlī Fārmadī, who lived in the second half of the eleventh century. He was a spiritual disciple of Abu al-Ḥasan K͟harraqānī, Abū Saʿīd b. Abī'l-K͟hair, Abu'l-Qāsim Gurgānī, and of Qus͟hairī, and in his turn became master of the Sunnī theologian al-G͟hazālī, whose brother Aḥmad G͟hazālī, author of the mystical work *Sawāniḥ*, is also a very famous Ṣūfī of this epoch (d. 1123). Fārmadī was also the master of S͟haik͟h Abū Bakr b. ʿAbdallāh Nassāj of Ṭūs, who in his turn had numerous pupils at the end of the twelfth century. Pupils of Aḥmad G͟hazālī included the famous author of the *Maqāmāt*, Badī ʿal-Zamān Hamadānī (killed as a heretic in 1131), S͟haik͟h Abu'l-Faḍl Bag͟hdādī (1155)—the first link in the spiritual chain of Niʿmatallāh Walī (d. 1430), a later founder of the mystic order of the Niʿmatallāhī—and Ḍiyāʾ al-Dīn Suhravardī.

In Transoxiana the above-mentioned Khwāja Abū Ya'qūb Yūsuf Hamadānī, of the school of Fārmadī and founder of the Yasaviyya/Khwājagān brotherhood, had many pupils, among whom 'Abd al-Khāliq Ghijduwānī, 'Abdallāh Barqī, Ḥasan Andaqī, and Aḥmad Basavī are particularly famous.

In Khwārazm the greatest Ṣūfī of this epoch was Abu'l-Janāb Najm al-Dīn al-Khīwaqī, known as Kubrā, who was killed in 1221 during the invasion of his native country by the Mongols. He is also known as *Shaikh-i Valī-Tarāsh* ("the Creator of Saints"), because of the great number of Ṣūfī disciples who followed his teachings, and he founded the Ṣūfī brotherhood of the Kubrāwiyya. He was, like all the great Ṣūfīs of Iran in this time, a Sunnī (Shāfi'ī): "We think", he wrote, "that the best creatures are Muḥammad, the Prophet of God, then Abū Bakr, then 'Umar, then 'Uthmān, then 'Alī; and we love the people of His house, the Good, the Pure ones, from whom God took away any trace of impurity and whom He made pure and near to Him." That he showed a particular veneration for 'Alī and his descendants (in Mongol times this respect was to become accentuated in some of his disciples) is a common quality of Ṣūfism and not peculiar to him. Amongst his first disciples were Abū Sa'īd Majd al-Dīn Sharaf b. Mu'ayyad Baghdādī (d. 1211 or 1219, a native of Baghdādak in Khwārazm, not to be confounded with Baghdad), and Sa'd al-Dīn Muḥammad b. Mu'ayyad Ḥamūya (d. 1252), author of difficult and still not sufficiently studied esoteric and cabbalistic works such as the *Kitāb sajanjal al-arwāḥ*, in which, according to some, he expressed Shī'ī tendencies: e.g. after Muḥammad, he said, there was a chain of twelve *auliyā*, saints, not imāms. Saif al-Dīn Bākharzī (d. 1260) was another disciple, active in Bukhārā and author of famous quatrains; other Ṣūfīs were Jamāl al-Dīn Jīlī, Bābā Kamāl Jundī, Najm al-Dīn Rāzī, called Dāy, author of the famous mystical work *Mirṣād al-'ibād* (1223); and Bahā' Valad (d. 1230), father of the greatest Ṣūfī of Iran, Jalāl al-Dīn Rūmī.

As is clear from all these data, the development of Ṣūfism in this epoch took place especially in the eastern, more strictly Sunnī, zones of the Iranian cultural world. In the western part of this world, with its spiritual centre in Baghdad, Ṣūfism was spread above all by the Suhravardiyya brotherhood, founded, as we saw, by Abū Ḥafṣ 'Umar Suhravardī, the real founder of the ṭarīqat of this name, though its silsila goes back to his uncle 'Abd al-Qāhir, a pupil of Aḥmad Ghazālī. Abū Ḥafṣ 'Umar is the author of many books (*Kitāb al-'awārif*, *Kashf an-naṣā'iḥ*, *I'lām al-taqī*, *I'lām al-hudā*, etc.) and had very famous students, including the great poet Sa'dī, the poet Auḥad al-Dīn Kirmānī, and Aḥmad Basavī.

As we said before, most Shī'īs in this epoch were much more anti-Ṣūfī than the Sunnīs were; the pro-Ṣūfī attitude of many Shī'ī communities of later ages, and especially of modern Iran, is an interesting phenomenon in the religious history of the country, which cannot, however, justify the anachronistic attitude of those modern Iranian scholars who try to attribute Shī'ī tendencies to Ṣūfīs of earlier epochs. The Shī'ī attitude towards Ṣūfism in the Saljuq period is clearly exemplified by the Shī'ī "History of Religions", the *Tabṣirat al-'awāmm* by Sayyid Murtaḍā Rāzī, who distinguishes the Ṣūfīs of his epoch into six sects: (1) The pantheists, followers of the ideas of al-Ḥallāj (d. 922), who affirm the *ittiḥād* (the complete unification, or fusion, of the soul of the mystic with God); (2) the *'Ushshāq* (lovers), who preach detachment and love of God as propaedeutic to the acquisition of occult doctrines; (3) the *Nūriyya* (from *nūr* = "light"), who affirm the existence of two kinds of veils between man and God, a veil of light and a veil of fire (*nūr* and *nār*); (4) the *Vāṣiliyya*, who say that the practices of the *sharī'a* are a useful preparation for approaching God, but are no longer needed by those who have reached (*vāṣil*) God. (And, our Shī'ī author adds deprecatingly, all the Ṣūfīs of the period are *vāṣil*!); (5) those who deny the utility of science and logic, saying that arguments based on them are vain, since the only true science lies in humble obedience to the Master; they say also that faith is not a created thing or attitude, but a divine act, and all divine acts are uncreated; and finally (6) those immoral and despicable Ṣūfīs who assume the garb of wandering beggars.

The same author affirms that "all the Ṣūfīs are Sunnīs", which is for him a very strong argument for their condemnation; indeed the greatest figures in the history of Ṣūfism (Ḥallāj, Bāyazīd Bisṭāmī, Shiblī, and so on) are stamped with the worst maledictions and treated as pantheists, sorcerers, *zindīqs* (dualists), and, generally speaking, as antinomians.

In spite of the Ṣūfīs' deep penetration into orthodox Sunnī circles—accomplished, as we saw, precisely in this epoch—an anti-Ṣūfī attitude is of course still present in some orthodox Sunnī writers. *Talbīs Iblīs*, by the Ash'arī theologian Ibn al-Jauzī, contains strong attacks on the Ṣūfīs, though the author makes a clear distinction between an older, purer Ṣūfism, and the "modern" one, for which he shows distrust. Ibn al-Jauzī gives us in his book precious information on the Ṣūfī life of his age. He says that the Ṣūfīs of the twelfth century owned many *ribāṭs* in which they led a merry life, whereas for the older mystics the ribāṭs were places of asceticism. Some of the convents had been erected by unjust princes with stolen money, which they wanted to "purify" through these holy foundations (*vaqf*), and those who frequented them were quite different from the Bishrs and Junaids of the past. Imitating the old companions of the Prophet, early Ṣūfīs used as their garment the austere *khirqa* (a robe made of shreds and patches of various colours), but some wore a woollen vest under it. They used to eat but little, and before the ceremony of initiation they fasted for two months. Some Ṣūfīs organized for their *sāliks* (disciples) periods of forty days of half-fasting called *arba'īniyya* (*arba'in* = "forty" in Arabic) during which they ate only fruit; and some of them grew so accustomed to fasting that they had temptations and visions and sometimes fell into immoral habits. Now, however (he adds), there are Ṣūfīs who exaggerate in the opposite direction and eat abundantly. The habits Ibn al-Jauzī most energetically disapproves of in Ṣūfīs are laziness and mendicity, both forbidden by the canonical law of Islam. Nor does *samā'* (singing and dancing) meet with his sympathy, though it was prudently accepted by Ghazālī, who devoted an interesting book of his *Iḥyā'* to the problem of the canonical legality of samā'. Both Ghazālī and Ibn al-Jauzī mention the habit, current amongst Ṣūfīs in their time, of tearing away garments in the paroxysm of ecstatical dances, and of distributing their pieces (considered to be full of *baraka*, or mystical force) to those present. Ghazālī gives a canonical reinterpretation of this, accepting it as a sort of surrogate alms, when the pieces torn away are sufficient to patch garments of poor people.[1] Ibn al-Jauzī also speaks critically of the dangerous practice of the intercourse of Ṣūfīs with the *shāhids* (beautiful youths, symbols of the beauty of the Creator). Ṣūfīs of his time, however, had a strong predilection for celibacy and loved to travel without any provisions, relying only on God (*tavakkul*). Their contempt for the sciences, their calling the canonical law of Islam *'ilm-i ẓāhir* (purely exoteric science) and their own doctrines *'ilm-i bāṭin* (esoteric science), their disdain for logic and law once they had realised their "truths"—none of this met with the approval of the author.

In spite of all such opposition, Ṣūfīs in this epoch were fairly free to teach their doctrines and carry out their practices. They easily found protectors in princes and powerful personalities. One of the greatest of

[1] *Iḥyā'*, vol. II, pp. 209, 22 ff.

their protectors in the Saljuq era was the great vizier Niẓām al-Mulk himself. According to Muḥammad b. Munawwar in his *Asrār al-tauḥīd*, composed in the second half of the twelfth century, he had been in his youth a pupil of the famous Abū Sa'īd b. Abi 'l Khair, and had witnessed miracles performed by that saint. He is said to have remarked: "All that I have, I owe to Shaikh Abū Sa'īd." He founded many khānqāhs, and gave much money to the embryonic Ṣūfī organisms of his age. Not one of the least of the Ṣūfīs' contributions to Iranian culture lay in their ample use of poetry to teach their doctrines: the first great mystic poet, Sanā'ī of Ghazna lived in this epoch.

Though not strictly speaking a Ṣūfī, and active outside as well as inside Iran, Shihāb al-Dīn Suhravardī "Maqtūl" (1153–91)—not to be confounded with the other Suhravardīs mentioned above—is one of the most original thinkers of the eastern Islamic world in this epoch. This "Master of the doctrine of *ishrāq*" (*Shaikh al-ishrāq*) was born in Suhravard, in north-western Iran, and his early education was also in Iranian territory, at Marāgheh and Iṣfahān. He was chiefly active in Syria, where he was killed—allegedly for religious motives, but probably also for political reasons—by order of the great Ayyūbid Sulṭān Ṣalāḥ al-Dīn, the "Saladin" of Western histories and legends. He can be classified neither as a Ṣūfī nor as a philosopher, neither as Sunnī nor as Shī'ī, and in this isolated originality lies his greatness. He could be called perhaps a theosophist, apart from the modern implications of this word, or a gnostic; but many of his ideas (the development of a sort of mystical Neo-Platonism with clear Ismā'īlī influences) and also a great part of his terminology are original and do not follow the accepted patterns. This, and his openly expressed contempt both for the traditional Aristotelian philosophy of the schools and for the orthodox legalism of the theologians, even accentuated his "heterodoxy". Moreover in his works he consciously attempted to revive the older Hermetic/Pythagorian/Iranian tradition. For instance, in his *Talwīḥāt* he says: "...Know thou that the Exalted Wise Men (*al-ḥukamā al-kibār*) of old, since the times in which Wisdom was orally transmitted, such as the Father of the Wise, the Father of Fathers, Hermes, and before him Agathodaimon and Pythagoras and Empedocles and the Prince of the Wise, Plato, were of much greater dignity and of much higher spiritual stature than all those subtle *loici* we know amongst the Muslims...".[1] And in his *Mashāri' wa muṭāraḥāt* he again sets up a sort

[1] Corbin ed., vol. I, p. 111.

of spiritual *silsila* in which old Iranian names occur alongside those of Greeks, Egyptians, and Muslims:

> The last one amongst the Greeks who had an exact notice of that Annihilating Light that leads to the Lesser Death was Plato, the sublime Wise one. And amongst the Great ones, the one who consolidated his knowledge, and whose name remains eternal in the histories, was Hermes. Amongst the "Pahlavis" ["old Iranian traditions", *fahlaviyyīn*] it was the first man [*mālik al-ṭīn*, "the possessor of the clay"] called Gayūmart, and in his school (*shī'a*) Farīdūn and Kai-Khusrau. For what concerns the lights of the mystical path [*sulūk*] in these times nearer to us the leaven of the Pythagorians fell into Akhī Akhmīm [the famous Egyptian Muslim mystic Dhū 'l-Nūn, d. 860] and from him it descended into the Contemplative Wanderer (*sayyār*) of Tustar [Abū Sahl al-Tustarī of the ninth century] and into his school; whereas the leaven of the Khusravānids, in the Mystical Path, descended into the Contemplative Wanderer of Bisṭām [Bāyazīd Bisṭāmī, d. 874] and after him into the Divine Knight (*fatā*) of Baidā [Manṣūr al-Ḥallāj, the mystical martyr, killed in 922] and afterwards into the Divine Wanderer of Āmul and Kharraqān [Abu'l-Ḥasan al-Kharraqānī]...[1]

These doctrines were therefore, for him, the common patrimony from an ancient tradition of which Iran was a part, a tradition that originated in the Hellenistic syncretism of the first centuries of the Christian era. This allegedly "old" doctrine, actually perfected and developed by Suhravardī's undeniable theosophical genius, cannot be outlined here. It is sufficient to say that Suhravardī did not remain an isolated thinker; after he died his ishrāqī ideas, more or less openly professed, found their way first into Iranian Ṣūfism and Shī'ism, and later, sometimes through dim and secret historical channels, even into modern Iranian culture, after their interesting revival in the seventeenth century in the School of Iṣfahān. It is another important seed of thought that first developed in the Saljuq epoch.

To conclude, the importance of the Saljuq period in the religious history of Iran lies in its formative richness, expressed in various directions of thought: first, Ash'arī Sunnism reached its final systematization in the great synthesis of Ghazālī. Secondly, Ṣūfism was first organized into great brotherhoods, and important schools were created. Thirdly, the philosophy of Suhravardī Maqtūl opened up new paths to Iranian theosophical speculation. And fourthly, Shī'ī ferment pullulated in Iran in the double aspect of Ismā'īlism, with its highly interesting esoteric theology, and Twelver Imāmism, which, though now comparatively weak, created a wide network of propaganda centres, during the Saljuq period.

[1] Corbin ed., vol. 1, pp. 502 ff.

CHAPTER 4

DYNASTIC AND POLITICAL HISTORY OF THE IL-KHĀNS

THE MONGOL INVASION

The chronology of Sulṭān Muḥammad's first contacts with the Mongols is extremely confusing, and it is difficult and sometimes impossible to reconcile the accounts of the various authorities. According to Jūzjānī[1] relations had been established as early as 1215. Himself attracted by the riches of China and therefore disturbed by reports of Chingiz-Khān's operations in that region Muḥammad decided to send an embassy to this new rival with instructions to ascertain his military strength and the extent of his successes. The embassy was headed by one Bahā' al-Dīn Rāzī, and Jūzjānī professes to give his somewhat lurid account of the mission in the envoy's actual words. As the party journeyed through the North China plain they descried in the far distance a great white mound, which they took to be a snow-covered mountain but which, as they were informed by their guides, was in fact a huge pyramid of human bones. As they proceeded farther the very ground beneath their feet became dark and greasy from the fat of rotting corpses; and for three full stages they had to make their way through this grisly morass. When they finally arrived before Peking they perceived, beneath a bastion of the citadel, the bones of 60,000 young women who, when the city was captured, had flung themselves from the walls rather than fall into the hands of the Mongols. During the envoys' first interview with Chingiz-Khān the Chin Emperor's son and prime minister were brought in bound in chains, no doubt with an eye to the effect of this spectacle upon the ambassadors. The latter were, however, favourably received, and in a second interview Chingiz-Khān charged them to inform the sultan that he regarded him as the ruler of the West, as he himself was ruler of the East. There should be a treaty of peace and friendship between them, and merchants should be free to travel to and fro between their territories. Among the gifts which he sent with them for presentation to their master was a nugget of gold from the mountains of China

[1] Transl. Raverty, vol. II, pp. 963 ff.

so large that it had to be transported in a waggon. He dispatched with them also a group of his own merchants with a caravan of five hundred camels laden with gold, silver, silks and furs. And here Jūzjānī casts some doubt upon the story by stating, still apparently in the words of Bahā' al-Dīn, that these were the same merchants whose detention and execution at Uṭrār gave rise to the outbreak of hostilities between Chingiz-Khān and the sultan.

The mission to Peking is mentioned by none of the other sources. However, Nasawī's[1] account of an embassy in the opposite direction may well be the description of the same event, viz. the first diplomatic encounter between the Mongols and the Khwārazm-Shāh, wherever and whenever this may have actually taken place. The embassy described by Nasawī reached the sultan somewhere in Transoxiana (probably Bukhārā) early in 1218 bearing presents similar to those enumerated by Jūzjānī, including a precious silk fabric called *torqu*. The message they brought was likewise similar to that recorded by Jūzjānī. Chingiz-Khān had heard of the sultan's victories and wished to conclude a treaty of peace and friendship with him; he wished also for the free and unhampered movement of merchants between their territories. In expressing these wishes, however, he referred to Muḥammad as being "on a level with the dearest of my sons", a phrase which gave deep offence to the sultan. Sending for one of the envoys, a Khwārazmī called Maḥmūd, probably the same Maḥmūd Yalavach who afterwards held high office in the Mongol empire, he questioned him in private about Chingiz-Khān, asking whether it was true that he had conquered the Chinese and captured their capital. Maḥmūd replied that it was indeed so. Even such conquests, the sultan went on, did not give an infidel the right to address him, the ruler of a great empire, as his son, i.e. as a vassal. Perceiving the sultan's anger Maḥmūd added that the Mongols' army could bear no comparison with the Khwārazm-Shāh's forces, and Muḥammad was mollified and agreed to the conclusion of a treaty.

Whatever the truth about the initial embassy to or from Chingiz-Khān, the sources are all in broad agreement about the massacre at Uṭrār. In that town, on Muḥammad's eastern frontier, there arrived at some time in 1218 a caravan of merchants, four hundred and fifty in number according to Juvainī,[2] a figure which tallies with the five hundred camels which, in Jūzjānī's account, were required for the transport of

[1] Transl. Houdas, pp. 57–9.

[2] Transl. Boyle, vol. 1, p. 79.

their wares. The sight of all these riches excited the cupidity of the governor, a relation of the sultan called Ïnalchuq, who had been accorded the title of Qayïr-Khān. He placed the whole party under arrest and dispatched a messenger to Muḥammad, who according to Juvainī was still in Western Persia, to seek his instructions, alleging that the merchants were really spies in the service of the Mongols. Whether the sultan believed this allegation or whether, like Ïnalchuq, he was activated solely by motives of greed, he authorized or at any rate connived at the execution of several hundred fellow-Muslims, many of whom must have been his own subjects. News of this bloodbath was brought to Chingiz-Khān by a member of the party who had contrived to make his escape. Controlling his anger the Mongol conqueror made a last attempt to obtain satisfaction by diplomatic means. A Muslim, formerly in the service of Sulṭān Tekish, was dispatched with two Mongols as companions to protest against Ïnalchuq's action and demand the surrender of his person. Far from acceding to this request the sultan ordered all three envoys to be put to death, a wanton breach of international law which rendered the Mongols' invasion of his territories inevitable.

However, before Chingiz-Khān could attack the sultan it was necessary to deal with two enemies nearer home. Of these the more formidable was the Naiman Küchlüg, who as the sultan's ally had seized the lion's share of the Qara-Khitai empire. An army under the command of the famous Jebe chased him from Kāshghar over the Pamirs into Badakhshān, where, with the co-operation of the local population, he was captured and put to death. In the meantime the remnants of the Merkit had been defeated and annihilated by an army jointly commanded by the great general Sübedei and by Chingiz-Khān's eldest son Jochi. Defeated with Küchlüg on the Irtish in 1206 the Merkit had at first made common cause with the Naiman prince but had then quarrelled with him and withdrawn into the region of the Upper Yenisei. Pursued from thence by the Mongols, they had fled to the territory of the Qïpchaq to the north-east of the Aral Sea; and here, in what is today the Kustanai region of Northern Kazakhstan, they were now overtaken and destroyed.

Sulṭān Muḥammad was in Samarqand when he learnt of the Merkit's approach to the Qïpchaq country. He at once set out to attack them, but upon reaching Jand received the news that the Mongols were close at their heels. Returning to Samarqand for reinforcements he advanced northwards for the second time, hoping, in the words of Juvainī,[1] "to kill two birds with one stone". Between two rivers, apparently the Irgiz and the Turgai, he came upon the scene of the battle. From a wounded man, discovered amongst the piles of dead, it was learnt that it had been fought that very day. Hurrying after the retiring Mongols the sultan caught up with them the next morning. They sought to avoid a conflict insisting that their quarrel was only with the Merkit and that they had no authority to attack the sultan. The latter, however, forced them into a stubborn but indecisive engagement, which continued till nightfall. The Mongols then withdrew under cover of darkness after first kindling fires to conceal their intention; and the sultan entered their camp the next morning only to find it deserted. He returned to Samarqand in a state of panic, the effect of this first encounter with the Mongols being such that he never again ventured to meet them in the open field.

It was probably at Samarqand that Muḥammad first learnt of the approach of Chingiz-Khān's main army. He held the first of several councils of war, in which his son Jalāl al-Dīn,[2] according to Juvainī, or Shihāb al-Dīn Khīvaqī, according to Ibn al-Athīr,[3] advocated the more courageous, if less practical, course of advancing with united forces to meet the enemy at the frontier. The majority were in favour of abandoning Transoxiana to its fate, some advising the sultan to withdraw into Khurāsān and defend the crossings of the Oxus, while others suggested that he should make a stand in the Ghazna region of Afghanistan and, if necessary, fall back on India. He decided to follow this latter advice and having placed considerable garrisons in the various towns of Transoxiana made his way to Balkh en route for Ghazna. At Balkh, however, he was met by an emissary of his son Rukn al-Dīn, the governor of 'Irāq-i 'Ajam, who persuaded him to change his plans and proceed instead to Central Persia. Upon leaving Balkh he sent a patrol to Panjāb or Mēla, the well-known crossing of the Oxus near the mouth of the Vakhsh, to ascertain the course of events. At Tirmidh the patrol came up with the news that Bukhārā had already fallen, soon followed by a report of the capture of Samarqand. Continuing his westward flight the sultan passed by the great natural fortress known later as Kalāt-i Nādirī, and it was suggested to him that he should concentrate troops and supplies in this well-nigh impregnable stronghold. He was

[1] Transl. Boyle, vol. II, p. 370.
[2] *Ibid.* pp. 376–7.
[3] Vol. XII, p. 237.

unable to reach a decision and pressed onwards towards Nīshāpūr, where he arrived on 18 April 1220. Still in a state of panic he urged the inhabitants to disperse throughout the countryside rather than attempt to withstand the irresistible Mongols. Finding them unwilling to quit their homes he bade them repair the fortifications for whose destruction he had himself been responsible. Then gradually recovering his peace of mind and thinking that the Oxus might prove at least a temporary barrier to the Mongols' advance, he gave himself up to pleasure and for a time refused to listen to any serious business. His fears were now so much allayed that he decided to send Jalāl al-Dīn back to Balkh. He had travelled only a single stage of the journey when he learnt that Sübedei and Jebe had already crossed the Oxus and were close at hand. He returned to Nīshāpūr with the news, and the sultan left the town on 15 May just in time to escape the vanguard of the Mongol army, which arrived before the gates on the very next day and at once continued in his pursuit.

The conquest of Transoxiana had been accomplished with incredible speed. After passing the summer of 1219 on the banks of the Irtish Chingiz-Khān had advanced westwards in the autumn through what is now the Soviet Socialist Republic of Kazakhstan. At Qayalïq in the present-day Taldy Kurgan region he was joined by the local Qarluq tribesmen as also by the Qarluq of Almalïq and a contingent of Uighur led by their ruler, the *ïdhuq-qut*. The Mongol army, which in Barthold's[1] estimation numbered between 150,000 and 200,000 men, arrived at some time in the late autumn before the frontier town of Uṭrār. Here Chingiz-Khān divided his forces, advancing himself on Bukhārā with the main body, whilst sending his eldest son Jochi on an expedition down the Syr Darya and leaving his younger sons Chaghatai and Ögedei to lay siege to Uṭrār. Having crossed the Syr Darya the Mongols approached the small fortified town of Zurnūq, which was persuaded to surrender without a fight. Instead, however, of following the normal route towards Samarqand the Mongols were led by Türkmen guides across the Qizil Qum desert to Nūr (now Nurata); and from Nūr, which likewise offered no resistance, Chingiz-Khān arrived before Bukhārā early in February 1220. The garrison, after a siege of only three days, decided to abandon the town and endeavoured to cut their way through the besiegers; but only a few of their number made good their escape. The townspeople were left with no choice but capitu-

[1] *Turkestan*, p. 404.

lation, and the next day they opened their gates to the Mongols. The citadel, however, was still held by a small body of the sultan's troops who continued to offer resistance. This act of defiance was countered by the Mongols' destroying the town by fire and then launching an assault on the fortifications driving the inhabitants in front of them as a kind of cannon fodder. After some twelve days' fighting the citadel was stormed and its defenders massacred to a man. The walls of the town were then razed to the ground, and the Mongols, accompanied by a levy of the able-bodied men of Bukhārā forced into their service to fight in the front ranks against their fellow Muslims, set out for Samarqand. The fortifications of Samarqand had been greatly strengthened and very considerable forces concentrated there, circumstances of which Chingiz-Khān had been informed at Uṭrār and which account for his having first attacked the more westerly Bukhārā. Arriving before the town he passed the first two days in inspecting the walls and outworks, his forces now augmented by the troops of Chaghatai and Ögedei, the victors of Uṭrār. It was at this juncture that, having learnt of Muḥammad's flight, he dispatched Sübedei and Jebe in his pursuit. On the third and fourth days of the siege the defenders made sorties from the town but with such disastrous effect that on the fifth day they decided to surrender. Having first demolished the walls the Mongols drove the inhabitants out into the open country the better to subject the town to pillage. Here too, as in Bukhārā, the citadel garrison fought on after the surrender, but they were soon overpowered and destroyed. As for the civil population they were now divided up, the craftsmen for ultimate transportation to Mongolia as slaves of the Mongol princes and the young men for service in the levy; and the conquest of Transoxiana virtually completed, Chingiz-Khān withdrew into the mountains to the south of the town to remain inactive, resting his men and animals, until the autumn.

In the meanwhile Jebe and Sübedei were sweeping across Persia in pursuit of the sultan. So well, however, had he concealed his tracks that only on one occasion did the Mongols come to close quarters with him and even then he was quickly able to shake them off. It will be convenient, therefore, to consider Muḥammad's movements separately from those of his pursuers. Upon leaving Nīshāpūr he had made off in a north-westerly direction to Isfarā'in and then followed the great trunk road to Ray. At Ray a patrol came up with the news that the enemy was close at hand and he hurried south-westwards to the castle of Farrazīn[1] near the modern Arāk (Sulṭānābād) on the Hamadān–Iṣfahān road, where his son Rukn al-Dīn was encamped with an army of 30,000 men. Upon the very day of his arrival he sent his mother along with his son Ghiyāth al-Dīn to the castle of Qārūn, apparently a mountain stronghold in the neighbourhood of Hamadān, and at the same time dispatched a messenger to summon the atabeg of Great Lur, Nuṣrat al-Dīn Hazār-Asp. In the meantime the sultan consulted the amīrs of 'Irāq-i 'Ajam as to the best means of repelling the invaders. They advised that a stand should be made in the bastion provided by the Kūh-i Ushturān, a lofty mountain chain in the High Zagros. He went to inspect these mountains at close range and then damped his troops' spirits by rejecting out of hand the possibility of their defending themselves in such a terrain. No sooner had he descended from the mountains than the atabeg Nuṣrat al-Dīn appeared in answer to his summons. He too offered a natural stronghold as a base of operations: a mountain valley on the border of Luristān and Fārs, probably the Shi'b-i Bavvān, famed as one of the four Earthly Paradises. Here, the atabeg said, 100,000 foot could be gathered together from Luristān and Fārs to repel the enemy upon his arrival. But the sultan opposed himself to this plan also, suspecting or affecting to suspect that Nuṣrat al-Dīn wished to involve him in his own quarrel with the atabeg of Fārs. He decided to remain in Farrazīn but had no sooner reached this decision than he received news of the Mongols' attack upon Ray; and at the heels of the patrol which brought this news came the Mongols themselves.

They overtook the sultan *en route* to Qārūn and discharged arrows at him without realizing his identity. Escaping on his wounded horse he made his way to the castle, where he remained for only one day before taking guides and stealing off in the direction of Baghdad. The Mongols arrived immediately and launched an assault on the castle thinking the sultan to be still inside it; then realizing their mistake they set off in his pursuit. He shook them off by turning back from the Baghdad road and striking northwards towards the strong castle of Sarchahān in the mountains between Ṣā'in-Qal'a and Sulṭānīyeh. He remained here for seven days before crossing the Alburz into Gīlān; he then turned eastwards along the coast of the Caspian, the Mongols being now once again in close pursuit. Arriving at Dabū in the Āmul area he was advised by the local amīrs to seek refuge in one of the offshore islands, apparently the present-day Āshūrādeh at the entrance to Astarābād bay.

[1] Not Qazvīn as in Barthold, *op. cit.* p. 422. See Juvainī transl. Boyle, vol. II, p. 382 n. 63.

It was here that he died in December 1220, or January 1221, either, as Juvainī[1] would have us believe, from grief at the fate of his womenfolk, who had been captured by the Mongols in a castle on the neighbouring mainland, or, according to Nasawī's[2] more prosaic account, from an acute inflammation of the lungs. Such was the wretched end of a monarch who for a brief interval had ruled over the whole eastern half of the Saljuq empire but whose very conquests had facilitated the Mongol invasion, just as his conduct at Uṭrār had provoked it.

As for the sultan's pursuers, they had followed the normal practice of Mongol advance parties, avoiding combat as much as possible and attacking only when provoked. Thus at Balkh, where the notables of the town had sent a deputation to them with offerings of food (*tuzghu*), they had contented themselves with setting a *shaḥna* or resident over the people and had done them no harm. Even at Zāveh (the modern Turbat-i-Ḥaidarī), where the townspeople had closed their gates and refused their demand for provisions, it was at first their intention to ride on; but angered by jeers shouted at them from the walls they had turned back to storm the town and massacre the population. At Nīshāpūr itself the authorities saw fit to go through the forms of submission and to supply the Mongols' needs. A deputation was received by Jebe, who urged them to destroy their walls and to give provisions to any bodies of troops that passed by. The two generals then parted company, evidently quite uncertain as to the direction of the sultan's flight. Sübedei turned back south-eastwards to Jām and then circled round to the north-west through Ṭūs, Rādkān and Qūchān to Isfarā'in. Here he may have picked up the sultan's trail, for he followed in his tracks along the great Khurāsān trunk road as far as Ray. Meanwhile Jebe, who had made for the district of Juvain to the north-west of Nīshāpūr, had proceeded from thence into Māzandarān, where he carried out great massacres, especially in the Āmul region, before crossing the mountains to link up with Jebe at Ray. What happened at Ray is by no means clear. According to Juvainī,[3] the *qāḍī* and other dignitaries tendered submission to the Mongols, but Ibn al-Athīr speaks of their sacking the town, perhaps as the consequence of a later rebellion.[4] At Ray the Mongols learnt of the sultan's recent departure in the direction of Hamadān, and Jebe set out in his pursuit. Entering Hamadān he received the submission of the governor and set a shaḥna over the town,

[1] Transl. Boyle, vol. II, pp. 385–6.
[2] Transl. Houdas, p. 79.
[3] Transl. Boyle, vol. I, p. 147.
[4] Vol. XII, p. 244.

to which he returned again after the clash with the sultan at Qārūn. From Hamadān he made his way to Sujās to defeat and destroy a large concentration of the sultan's troops under two of his generals. The greater part of 'Irāq-i 'Ajam was then subjected to slaughter and rapine until, with the approach of winter, the Mongols withdrew northwards to the Mūghān Steppe. That troops were sent from these winter quarters in search of the sultan is possible but unlikely; the forces which chased him along the Caspian littoral and which captured the castles in which his harem had sought refuge were probably those left behind by Jebe in the previous summer. In any case, the generals' main attention must have been attracted in another direction, for it was from this base that they launched their first attack on the Georgians, on whom they inflicted a crushing defeat in February 1221. In the spring they returned to Hamadān to put down a revolt and then left 'Irāq for Āzarbāījān, where they pillaged and slaughtered until the atabeg made his submission. It was about this time, according to Rashīd al-Dīn,[1] that they dispatched a message to Chingiz-Khān to the effect that the sultan being now dead they would, in accordance with the khan's *yarlīgh*, continue their conquests for a year or two before returning to Mongolia by way of the Caucasus. It would seem, indeed, that the pursuit of the sultan had been only the first part of their mission. From Āzarbāījān the generals now invaded Georgia for the second time, then passing into Shīrvān forced their way through Darband to descend into the plains of what is now southern Russia. Here they dispersed a coalition of Caucasians and Qïpchaq before advancing westwards into the Crimea to sack the Genoese *empôt* of Soldaia and defeat a Russian army on the Kalka. Then they turned back, crossing the Volga near the present-day Volgograd and finally joining their master somewhere along the route of his homeward journey after carrying out a reconnaissance raid without parallel in history, "an expedition", in the words of Gibbon,[2] "which had never been attempted and has never been repeated".

In the summer of 1220, whilst Jebe and Sübedei were chasing Sulṭān Muḥammad to and fro across Persia, Chingiz-Khān was resting his men and animals in the mountains to the south of Samarqand. It was not until the autumn that he moved southwards against Tirmidh on the northern bank of the Oxus, where today it forms the frontier between Uzbekistan and Afghanistan. The people of Tirmidh, emboldened by the strength of their fortifications, rejected his call to surrender, and

[1] Transl. Smirnova, p. 226.

[2] VII, 10.

paid for their defiance the terrible price that was soon to be exacted from the great cities of Khurāsān. When after eleven days' fighting the town was taken by storm, the whole population, men and women, were driven out on to the plain, and divided amongst the soldiers, by whom they were then put to death, each soldier being responsible for the execution of a fixed number of persons. The story is told that when the Mongols had finished this butchery they caught a woman who had escaped their attention. In exchange for her life she offered them a large pearl but, when they asked to see it, said that she had swallowed it. They at once disembowelled her and found several pearls in her stomach, whereupon Chingiz-Khān ordered all the bodies to be eviscerated. From Tirmidh he now withdrew into the upper reaches of the Vakhsh, i.e. the region of the present-day Tajikistan, where he passed the winter of 1220–1 in operations against the local population. Then, with the approach of spring, he prepared to cross the Oxus and attack Balkh.

On what happened at Balkh the authorities disagree. Ibn al-Athīr[1] says that the town surrendered voluntarily and that in consequence the lives of the inhabitants were spared. On the other hand, according to Juvainī,[2] the population, despite their professions of submission, was subjected to the same wholesale slaughter as the people of Tirmidh. It is probable that, as appears to have been the case at Ray and as we know to have been the case at Herāt, the massacre followed, not upon the original surrender of the town, but upon a subsequent revolt. Whatever the details, the capitulation of Balkh was speedily achieved, and Chingiz-Khān turned westwards to lay siege to Ṭāliqān, a town in the mountains of Jūzjān, probably to be identified with the present-day Chachaktu. The town with its castle (which is given various names, all meaning something like "Hill of Victory") occupied a strategic position in the path of bodies of Mongol troops on their way to Khurāsān, Ghūr and southern Afghanistan; and whenever such parties passed beneath the castle the garrison would make a sortie and attack them, carrying off their prisoners and cattle. So seriously did this harassment affect the Mongols' movements that, some months before Chingiz-Khān's arrival a large force from the main army had been beleaguering the town. Their failure to capture Ṭāliqān accounts for Chingiz-Khān's decision to intervene in person. The subjugation of Khurāsān he deputed to his youngest son Tolui, who carried out the task with a thoroughness from which that region has never recovered.

[1] Vol. XII, p. 255.

[2] Transl. Boyle, vol. I, pp. 130–1.

From Balkh, Tolui proceeded in a westerly direction as far as Marūchaq in what is now the north-western corner of Afghanistan. Then crossing the Murghāb and its left-bank affluent the Kūshk he turned northwards along the river bank, following what, six centuries later, were to be the tracks of the Transcaspian Railway. Marv, at the time of his approach, was in a state of great confusion, the governor being at loggerheads with a great host of Türkmen who had sought refuge in that neighbourhood and whom he had only recently succeeded in dislodging from the town, which they still continued to attack. Having spied out the position of the Türkmen's encampment on the river bank, the Mongols launched a night attack. Surprised in the darkness the Türkmen, despite their numbers, were utterly routed, and such as were not drowned in the river fled in panic. The way now lay open and on the next day, 25 February 1221, the Mongols arrived before the gates of Marv. Tolui in person, with an escort of five hundred horsemen, rode the whole distance around the walls, and for six days the Mongols continued to inspect the defences, reaching the conclusion that they were in good repair and would withstand a lengthy siege. On the seventh day the Mongols launched a general assault. The townspeople made two sallies from different gates, being in both cases at once driven back by the Mongol forces. They seem then to have lost all will to resist. The next day the governor surrendered the town, having been reassured by promises that were not in fact to be kept. The whole population was now driven out into the open country, and for four days and nights the people continued to pour out of the town. Four hundred artisans and a number of children were selected to be carried off as slaves, and it was commanded that the whole of the remaining population, men, women, children, should be put to the sword. They were distributed, for this purpose, amongst the troops, and to each individual soldier was allotted the execution of three to four hundred persons. These troops included levies from the captured towns, and Juvainī records that the people of Sarakhs, who had a feud with the people of Marv, exceeded the ferocity of the heathen Mongols in the slaughter of their fellow-Muslims.

Even now the ordeal of Marv was not yet over. When the Mongols withdrew those who had escaped death by concealing themselves in holes and cavities emerged from their hiding places. They amounted in all to some five thousand people. A detachment of Mongols, part of the rearguard, now arrived before the town. Wishing to have their share of the slaughter they called upon these unfortunate wretches to come out into the open country, each carrying a skirtful of grain. And having them thus at their mercy they massacred these last feeble remnants of one of the greatest cities of Islam.

The sober and careful Ibn al-Athīr,[1] a contemporary of these events, puts the number of the slain at the enormous figure of 700,000. Juvainī[2] gives an even higher figure. He tells how the *sayyid* 'Izz al-Dīn Nassāba "together with some other persons passed thirteen days and nights in counting the people slain within the town. Taking into account only those that were plain to see and leaving aside those that had been killed in holes and cavities and in the villages and deserts, they arrived at a figure of more than one million, three hundred thousand."

From this great shambles Tolui now proceeded south-westwards to Nīshāpūr. After their desertion by Sulṭān Muḥammad the people of Nīshāpūr had at first adopted a conciliatory attitude towards the Mongols, but with the passage of time and the rumours of victories gained by the sultan in Central Persia they had become openly hostile to the invaders. In November 1220 an army of 10,000 men under one Toghachar, a son-in-law of Chingiz-Khān, had appeared before the town. The fierce resistance of the townsfolk caused the Mongols to withdraw but not before Toghachar had been killed in battle. The people of Nīshāpūr were elated with the news of his death, which was, however, soon to prove their own death-warrant. Tolui now approached the town with such vast forces and such abundance of siege instruments that the people at once lost heart and sought to negotiate terms of surrender. Their overtures were rejected, and the assault began on Wednesday, 7 April 1221: the walls were breached on the Friday, and on the Saturday the town was taken by storm. As in Marv, the people were driven out into the open country, and in order to avenge the death of Toghachar it was ordered "that the town should be laid waste that the site could be ploughed upon; and that in the exaction of vengeance not even cats and dogs should be left alive".[3] Toghachar's widow, the daughter of Chingiz-Khān, rode into the town with her escort and took her share in the killing of the survivors. Four hundred craftsmen were spared for transportation to Mongolia; otherwise the

[1] Vol. XII, p. 256.
[2] Transl. Boyle, vol. I, pp. 163–4. On these figures see below p. 484, n. 4.
[3] Transl. Boyle, vol. I, p. 177.

whole population was put to death. The heads of the slain were severed from their bodies and piled in heaps, those of the men being separate from those of the women and children.

"The last of all to suffer", says Juvainī,[1] "was Herāt, and when he [i.e. Tolui] had joined her to her sisters, he returned to wait upon his father." The Persian historian has unfortunately left no detailed account of the capture of the town. Barthold,[2] on the authority of d'Ohsson, whose authority in turn was a fifteenth-century local history of Herāt, says that none of the inhabitants were killed, with the exception of the sultan's troops and that Herāt, in consequence, "suffered least of all". On the other hand, Jūzjānī, a contemporary of the event who had himself taken part in the defence of a mountain fortress at no great distance from Herāt, speaks of its capture after siege of eight months' duration and the subsequent massacre of the entire population. There were in fact two sieges of Herāt, both of which are recorded in detail in a work which was re-discovered only during the present century and was published, on the basis of a unique manuscript, as recently as 1944. This is the *Ta'rīkh-Nāma-yi-Harāt* or "History of Herāt" of Saif b. Muḥammad b. Ya'qūb known as Ṣaifī. A native of Herāt, Ṣaifī was born in that city in 1282 and wrote his history at some time between 1318 and 1322. It contains a great deal of information, not recorded elsewhere, about conditions not only in Herāt itself but in the whole of Khurāsān in the period during and immediately following the Mongol invasion.

According to Ṣaifī's[3] account Tolui, upon his arrival before Herāt, encamped in the meadows near the town and sent an envoy to invite the people to surrender. The envoy was at once put to death on the orders of the malik or governor representing Sulṭān Jalāl al-Dīn. Tolui, in anger, ordered a general assault, which continued for eight days, at the end of which the malik was killed in the fighting. Tolui now intervened in person, riding up to the edge of the moat and making a proclamation, in which he promised to spare the lives of the inhabitants if they surrendered immediately. To this the townspeople agreed and the Mongols kept their word except with regard to the troops of Sultan Jalāl al-Dīn numbering 12,000 men. Tolui set a malik over the town, a Muslim called Abū Bakr of Marūchaq, and also a Mongol shaḥna, a man called Mengetei, a member of Tolui's immediate entourage. Eight days later Tolui left the region to join his father.

[1] *Ibid.* p. 152. [2] *Turkestan,* p. 447. [3] *Op. cit.* pp. 66 ff.

But this was by no means the end of the story. For a time all went well, the people living peaceably under the protection of the Muslim malik and the Mongol shaḥna. And then, all of a sudden, they rose in rebellion and killed both of these officials. Ṣaifī gives two versions of this rising. It was either a spontaneous movement on the part of the Herātīs or else it was engineered by the people of the mountain stronghold of Kālyūn to the north-east of Herāt, who were still holding out against the Mongols, and hoped in this way to enlist the Herātīs as their allies. According to this latter version, the assassinations were carried out by men from Kālyūn who entered the town disguised as merchants with weapons concealed about their persons. Whatever the truth of the matter, the damage was now done. When the news reached Chingiz-Khān he was filled with anger and dispatched the general Eljigidei at the head of 80,000 men to mete out retribution. Ṣaifī[1] records his instructions: "The dead have come to life again. This time you must cut the people's heads off: you must execute the whole population of Herāt."

Eljigidei set out in November 1221. In due course he arrived on the Harī Rūd, and busied himself for the next month with warlike preparations: from the surrounding regions he gathered reinforcements to the strength of 50,000 men. With this great army Eljigidei now laid siege to Herāt. This time the resistance was long and heroic. It was not until June of the following year that the Mongols finally captured the town. Eljigidei carried out his instructions to the letter: the entire population was put to death, "and no head was left on a body, nor body with a head".[2] Ṣaifī assesses the number of those thus massacred at a figure of 1,600,000. (The contemporary Jūzjānī[3] records that in a single quarter there were counted 600,000 dead and on this basis estimates the total number in the whole town at 2,400,000!) For seven days the Mongols were busy with this slaughter and with demolishing the houses, filling in the moats and destroying the fortifications. On the eighth day they set off in the direction of Kālyūn. When they had reached Auba (Obeh) on the Harī Rūd, Eljigidei sent back 2,000 horsemen with instructions to kill any persons they might find who had escaped the massacre by going into hiding. They stayed two days in the town, where they discovered nearly their own number of such wretches; they put them all to death and then returned to the main body.

[1] *Op. cit.* p. 76.

[2] *Op. cit.* p. 80.

[3] Transl. Raverty, vol. II, p. 1038.

The siege of Ṭāliqān, to which we now return, lasted, according to Ibn al-Athīr,[1] ten months (six months before, and four months after the personal intervention of Chingiz-Khān), according to Rashīd al-Dīn,[2] seven months; the town was taken only after the arrival of Tolui's forces fresh from the conquest of Khurāsān, i.e. at some time in the early summer of 1221. On Chingiz-Khān's movements following on the capture of Ṭāliqān the sources are vague and contradictory. He probably remained in the mountains of Jūzjān in the immediate vicinity of Ṭāliqān until he received the news of Sulṭān Jalāl al-Dīn's victory at Parvān.

Jalāl al-Dīn had accompanied his father in his flight across Persia and had been present at his deathbed on the island in the Caspian. Together with his brothers Uzlaq-Sulṭān, the heir-presumptive of Sulṭān Muḥammad (though, according to Nasawī, the sultan, shortly before his death, had altered his will in favour of Jalāl al-Dīn) and Aq-Sulṭān he then left the island and landing on the Manqïshlaq Peninsula made for Gurgānj, his father's capital, which he reached some little time before its investment by the Mongols. The discovery of a plot against his life (in which his brother Uzlaq-Sulṭān seems to have been involved) prompted him to quit the capital almost immediately and make for the territories formerly allotted to him by his father and corresponding more or less to the modern Afghanistan. Crossing the Qara Qum desert accompanied by only three hundred horse he broke through the cordon established by the Mongols along the northern frontiers of Khurāsān and succeeded in reaching Nīshāpūr. His brothers, Uzlaq-Sulṭān and Aq-Sulṭān, who followed the same route shortly afterwards, were less fortunate. They were killed in battle or captured in flight and their severed heads were paraded on the end of lances to strike terror into the population—an indignity afterwards inflicted upon Duke Henry of Silesia.[3] As for Jalāl al-Dīn, he remained in Nīshāpūr only for a day or two before departing, on 10 February 1221, *en route* for Ghazna. His departure nearly coincided with the arrival of the Mongols in his pursuit. They at once took up the chase, but he shook them off and travelling, according to Juvainī,[4] 150 miles in a single day arrived before the walls of Zūzan in Kūhistān. Refused asylum by the people of Zūzan he found shelter in a neighbouring town, which he left at

[1] Vol. XII, p. 255.
[2] Transl. Smirnova, p. 219.
[3] See Carpini, *The Tartar Relation*, transl. George D. Painter, pp. 80 and 82 n. 4.
[4] Transl. Boyle, p. 404.

midnight, only a few hours before the arrival of the Mongols: he had reached the region of Herāt before they finally abandoned their pursuit. The sultan continued on his way to Ghazna, which, at the time of his arrival, was in the hands either of his cousin Amīn Malik, a Qanqlï Turk, who had been malik of Herāt, or of the Ghūrī A'ẓam Malik, the son of 'Imād al-Dīn of Balkh, more probably the latter. Amīn Malik, if not already present, hastened to join the sultan and with his Qanqlï forces, the Ghūrī troops of A'ẓam Malik and a great host of Khalaj and Türkmen tribesmen which had gathered together at Peshawar under Saif al-Dīn Ïghraq, Jalāl al-Dīn now found himself at the head of a well-equipped, if ill-assorted, army of some 60,000 men.

The sultan passed the remainder of the winter in Ghazna and in the first days of spring led his forces northwards to Parvān, a town at the confluence of the Ghōrband and the Panjshīr in a position where many roads met and where he hoped to obtain some information about the course of events. Learning that a Mongol army under the two generals Tekechük and Molghor was laying siege to a castle in the Wāliān Kōtal (to the north-west of Chārīkār) he led an attack against them and had killed a thousand men of the Mongol vanguard before they withdrew across the river (apparently the Ghōrband) and destroyed the bridge. The two armies then discharged arrows at each other across the water until nightfall, when the Mongols retreated and the sultan returned to his base at Parvān. News of this encounter being brought to Chingiz-Khān, presumably by the defeated commanders, he at once dispatched one of his most distinguished commanders, the Tatar Shigi-Qutuqu, at the head of an army of 30,000 men. The Mongols reached Parvān, according to Juvainī,[1] only a week after the sultan's own arrival. Jalāl al-Dīn at once rode out to meet the enemy. Three miles from the town he drew up his forces in battle order, assigning the right wing to Amīn Malik and the left to Ïghraq, while he himself commanded in the centre. He then instructed the whole army to dismount and fight on foot holding on to the reins of their horses. The Mongols concentrated their attack on the right wing under Amīn Malik, which they drove back until repeated reinforcements from the centre and the right turned the tide and they were forced back in turn.

The battle raged to and fro until nightfall when both sides withdrew to their bases. Under cover of darkness the Mongols had recourse to a ruse which, according to Carpini,[2] was part of their normal tactics. They

[1] Transl. Boyle, p. 406.

[2] Transl. Becquet and Hambis, p. 80.

set up dummy warriors on their spare horses, and the next morning the sultan's army were dismayed to descry what appeared to be a line of reinforcements drawn up at the rear of the enemy lines. In their alarm they considered the possibility of flight but, rallied by the sultan, joined battle with the Mongols for the second time. Again they fought on foot and this time the enemy launched their attack on the left wing under Ïghraq. Ïghraq's men stood firm and the Mongols turned and began to make for their base, whereupon, at the sultan's command, the whole army mounted horse and moved forward at the charge. The Mongols fled before them, then turned in a final desperate attack before, with the sultan's personal intervention, they were utterly routed, Shigi-Qutuqu escaping with the remnants of his army to carry the news to Chingiz-Khān.

Few victories have been more short-lived than this, the only serious defeat to be inflicted upon the Mongols during the whole campaign. Jalāl al-Dīn's forces were dispersed upon the very battle-field. In a quarrel over the booty Amīn Malik struck Ïghraq over the head with a whip. Jalāl al-Dīn, fearing the reaction of Amīn Malik's undisciplined followers, saw fit to ignore the incident, and Ïghraq, waiting only till nightfall, withdrew in dudgeon with all his forces as also those of A'ẓam Malik, who had taken his side in the dispute with the Qanqlï. Disheartened by their defection, Jalāl al-Dīn returned to Ghazna, there to make preparations for seeking safety beyond the Indus: the victor of Parvān was soon to become a fugitive before the main army of Chingiz-Khān.

At Ṭāliqān Chingiz-Khān had been joined not only by Tolui but also by his elder sons Chaghatai and Ögedei, who together with his eldest son Jochi had captured the Khwārazmī capital Gurgānj after a siege of seven months. It was thus at the head of vastly augmented forces that he now advanced against Jalāl al-Dīn, apparently setting out from the Ṭāliqān area immediately upon receiving the news of the defeat inflicted upon Tekechük and Molghor. His route lay through the present-day district of Durzāb and Gurziwān, where the resistance of a stronghold (probably the castle of Rang mentioned by Jūzjānī)[1] delayed the army, according to Juvainī,[2] for a full month. The advance was held up at Bāmiyān also, where one of Chaghatai's sons, the favourite grandchild of Chingiz-Khān, was killed and where, in vengeance for his death, it was ordered "that every living creature, from mankind down to the

[1] Transl. Raverty, p. 1003.

[2] Transl. Boyle, vol. 1, p. 132.

brute beasts, should be killed; that no prisoner should be taken; that not even the child in its mother's womb should be spared; and that henceforth no living creature should live therein".[1] The report of Shigi-Qutuqu's defeat at Parvān seems to have reached Chingiz-Khān after this butchery had been completed, for we are told by Juvainī that upon receiving the news he hurried forward by day and night without intermission so that no time was left for the cooking of food. At Parvān he halted long enough to inspect the battlefield and to criticize both his own commanders and the sultan for their choice of positions. In Ghazna, which he entered without opposition, he learnt that Jalāl al-Dīn had left for the Indus only a fortnight before and at once continued in his pursuit. He overtook the sultan on the very banks of the river, probably at Dinkot, near the modern Kālābāgh, whilst the boats were still being assembled for the crossing. Despite his desperate position, hemmed in by the oncoming Mongols in front and with the waters of the Indus in his rear, Jalāl al-Dīn drew up his forces and offered battle. The Mongols first attacked the right wing commanded by Amīn Malik; it was driven back and destroyed, Amīn Malik himself being killed whilst fleeing in the direction of Peshawar. The left wing was likewise driven back: only the centre, where the sultan in person commanded a body of 700 men, continued to stand firm. In charge after charge he attacked different sectors of the semi-circle of troops in front of him, but as more and more detachments arrived he was left with less and less space to manoeuvre until by mid-day it was clear that the situation was hopeless. He mounted a fresh horse, made a final charge to force back the men closing in on him, then turning in the space thus gained he threw off his cuirass and drove his horse over the bank into the water, thirty feet below. His pursuers were about to plunge in after him but were prevented by Chingiz-Khān, who had ridden down to the water's edge to watch the sultan's progress towardst he opposite bank. As he climbed ashore safe and sound, still grasping his sword, lance and shield, the Conqueror pointed him out to his sons with expressions of amazement and admiration. Jalāl al-Dīn's men were less fortunate than their leader: of those that followed him into the Indus the vast majority were killed by Mongol arrows, and Juvainī[2] tells us, on the authority of eyewitnesses, that the whole river, within the range of the bowmen, was red with the blood of the slain.

The Battle of the Indus marks the virtual end of the Campaign in the

[1] Transl. Boyle, vol. I, p. 133.

[2] *Ibid.* vol. II, p. 411.

West. It took place, according to Juvainī,[1] in Rajab of the year 618, i.e. at some time between 21 August and 19 September 1221. Nasawī[2] gives a later and more precise date, viz. the 8th Shawwāl (25 November), which is, however, difficult to reconcile with Juvainī's more detailed account of events leading up to the battle. After gaining this victory Chingiz-Khān followed the Indus some distance upstream, apparently seeking a crossing-place and then turned off into the valley of the Upper Kurram. Here he learnt that Jalāl al-Dīn had recrossed the river to bury his dead. He dispatched Chaghatai in his pursuit whilst proceeding himself with the main army to winter-quarters in a region probably to be identified with the Swat valley. He now conceived the idea of returning to Mongolia by way of Bengal and Assam, but the difficulties of the route were such that he was forced to turn back after travelling only two or three stages and slowly retraced his steps through Afghanistan. The summer of 1222 he spent in pasture lands high in the Hindu Kush, apparently in the region of Parvān. Here he received the first visit of the Taoist monk Ch'ang-ch'un, whom he had summoned from China hoping to receive from him the "medicine of immortality". A second interview was postponed till the autumn because of news of an insurrection by the "native mountain bandits"[3] with which Chingiz-Khān wished to deal in person. This is perhaps a reference to the continued resistance of Herāt or, conceivably, to the situation at Balkh, where, as Juvainī[4] tells us, the Mongols on their return journey killed the survivors of the earlier massacre and demolished any walls that were still left standing. Ch'ang-ch'un passed close to Balkh on his way to the second interview with Chingiz-Khān, and we are told in the account of his travels that the population "had recently rebelled against the Khan and had been removed; but we could still hear dogs barking in the streets".[5] Chingiz-Khān received this visit somewhere to the east of Balkh, perhaps in the Baghlān area; he broke camp on 3 October and crossed the Oxus on a bridge of boats on the 6th. Chaghatai had by now returned from his fruitless search for Sulṭān Jalāl al-Dīn, and a general called Dorbei Doqshin was sent back on the same errand. He was equally unsuccessful although he penetrated as far as Multan and Lahore before the summer heat forced him to withdraw northwards to join his master. Meanwhile Chingiz-Khān had reached the Samarqand area

[1] *Ibid.* vol. I, p. 135.
[2] Transl. Houdas, p. 139.
[3] *The Travels of an Alchemist*, p. 102.
[4] Transl. Boyle, vol. I, p. 131.
[5] *Op. cit.* p. 111.

early in November and encamped some six or seven miles to the east of the town. Juvainī is wrong in stating that he passed the whole winter here, for Ch'ang-ch'un, who left Samarqand on 29 December, caught up with the Mongols a month later on the eastern banks of the Syr Darya. The spring and summer of 1223 were spent in the region of Qulan-Bashï, the pass between the Arïs and Talas basins on the way from Chimkent to Jambul. Here Ch'ang-ch'un took his leave of Chingiz-Khān and we have no precise details regarding the rest of his itinerary: he was on the Black Irtish in the summer of 1224, and it was not till the spring of 1225 that he finally reached his headquarters in Mongolia. In the autumn of the following year he was at war with the Tangut, whose rebellion is said to have been one of the reasons for his return from the West. He died, while the campaign was still in progress, on 25 August 1227.[1]

SULṬĀN JALĀL AL-DĪN

Sulṭān Jalāl al-Dīn remained in India for nearly three years. He was joined, on the very banks of the Indus, by a number of stragglers from his defeated army and after several successful encounters with bodies of Indian troops in the Salt Range found himself at the head of some three to four thousand men. News of the approach of a Mongol army now caused him to withdraw in the direction of Delhi. Somewhere in the Rawalpindi area the Mongols gave up the chase and the sultan, having arrived within two or three days' journey from Delhi, dispatched an envoy to Sulṭān Shams al-Dīn El-Tutmïsh to seek an alliance and ask for temporary asylum. Alarmed at the possibility of involvement in the sultan's fortunes El-Tutmïsh replied with a polite refusal, and Jalāl al-Dīn turned back to the Lahore region, where more fugitives gathered around him and his forces were increased to a total of 10,000 men. Another expedition against the tribes of the Salt Range led to an alliance with the Khokars against Nāṣir al-Dīn Qubacha, the ruler of Sind, who was driven out of Uch and forced to flee upstream to Multān. The summer (apparently of 1222) Jalāl al-Dīn passed in the Salt Range or in the mountains near Lahore and then, with news of the Mongols again in his pursuit, he made his way into Lower Sind, clashing briefly with Qubacha as he passed by Multān, setting fire to Uch, which had risen in revolt, and capturing Sādūsān (the modern Sehwan) before arriving at the seaport of Debul at the mouth of the

[1] For the best account of his career see Grousset, *Le Conquérant du monde.*

Indus. At Debul he received the news that his brother Ghiyāth al-Dīn had made himself master of 'Irāq, where, however, the greater part of the military favoured Jalāl al-Dīn and were demanding his presence there. This news and reports of the Mongols' continuing approach decided the sultan to re-enter Persia by way of Balūchistān and Makrān.

The sultan emerged from these waterless wastes with greatly depleted forces: his army, according to Nasawī,[1] had been reduced to 4,000 men mounted on donkeys and oxen. He was welcomed on the borders of Kirmān by a former official of his father. This was Baraq Ḥājib, a Qara-Khitayan by origin, who had risen to the rank of *ḥājib* or chamberlain in the service of Sulṭān Muḥammad and had then attached himself to Ghiyāth al-Dīn. Appointed governor of Iṣfahān he had quarrelled with Ghiyāth al-Dīn's vizier and was on his way to India to join Jalāl al-Dīn when his party was attacked by the governor of the castle of Guvāshīr (as the town, as distinct from the province, of Kirmān was then known). Baraq turned the tables on his attacker, whom he captured and put to death: the governor's son, driven from the castle, entrenched himself in the inner town, to which Baraq was laying siege when he received the news of the sultan's approach. In addition to other tokens of his loyalty he offered Jalāl al-Dīn the hand of his daughter in marriage. The sultan, as we shall see, was much addicted to such political and, for the most part, temporary alliances: in Ghazna he had married a daughter of the ill-fated Amīn Malik and in India a Khokar princess. The marriage with Baraq's daughter having been duly solemnized the sultan appeared before the gates of Guvāshīr, which at once surrendered to him and in which he now installed himself with his bride and his father-in-law. Some days later he set out on a hunting expedition, from which Baraq excused himself on the grounds of some bodily infirmity. Suspecting his motives Jalāl al-Dīn sent back an officer to summon him to his presence, making out that he was leaving immediately for 'Irāq and wished to consult Baraq on conditions in that province. Baraq's reply, though expressed in courtly language, made it quite plain that he intended to keep Kirmān for himself, an intention made even plainer by his ejecting such of the sultan's followers as still remained in Guvāshīr. Jalāl al-Dīn had no alternative but to swallow his discomfiture and continue on his way, leaving Baraq to consolidate his position and found the local dynasty of the Qutlugh-Khāns (1224–1303). In Fārs the sultan fared better. Pleased with the advent of a rival

[1] Transl. Houdas, p. 157.

to Ghiyāth al-Dīn, who had twice invaded his territory, the Atabeg Sa'd showered presents upon Jalāl al-Dīn, gave him his daughter in marriage and even agreed to the sultan's request for the release from imprisonment of his rebellious son Abū Bakr, afterwards his successor and the patron of the poet Sa'dī. Jalāl al-Dīn remained in Shīrāz only for a month or two after the marriage (perhaps the most permanent of these alliances, for we know that the Salghurid princess accompanied Jalāl al-Dīn in the final flight before the Mongols that culminated in his death at the hands of a Kurdish assassin), and then made his way to Iṣfahān. Here he learnt of Ghiyāth al-Dīn's presence at Ray, whither he proceeded at such speed as to catch his brother and his followers completely unawares. Most of the officers and officials at once declared themselves for Jalāl al-Dīn, and those who, with Ghiyāth al-Dīn at their head, had fled in panic, were soon persuaded to return and tender their submission. Thus, after three years of wandering, the sultan found himself in undisputed possession of part at least of his father's empire.

With the military resources now at his command Jalāl al-Dīn, in the winter of 1224–5, moved southwards into Khūzistān with the object, apparently, of resuming his father's feud with the caliph. Nasawī[1] and Juvainī[2] are, as one would expect, somewhat reticent on this delicate subject and it is only Ibn al-Athīr[3] who gives a detailed account of the campaign. In Muḥarram 622/January–February 1225 the sultan invested Shustar, which was defended with considerable vigour by the caliphal governor of Khūzistān, Muẓaffar al-Dīn Wajh al-Sabu'. As the siege dragged on detachments of the sultan's army infiltrated westwards plundering the country as they went; they reached the districts of Bādurāyā and Bākusāyā on the eastern borders of Arab 'Irāq, and one party turned southwards to clash with the governor (*shaḥna*) of Baṣra. Meanwhile the siege of Shustar, which had continued for two months, was suddenly abandoned, and the sultan set out in the direction of Baghdad. His advance was opposed by an army of 20,000 men under the command of the *mamlūk* Jamāl al-Dīn Qush-Temür. Defeated by a ruse, despite their superior numbers, the caliph's troops were driven back to the outskirts of Baghdad, which, however, the sultan did not closely approach, perhaps because of the formidable preparations that had been made for his reception, making instead for the small town of

[1] Transl. Houdas, pp. 180–1.
[2] Transl. Boyle, vol. II, pp. 421 ff.
[3] Vol. XII, pp. 276–8.

Ba'qūbā some twenty-seven miles to the north of Baghdad. From here the Khwārazmīs proceeded to Daqūqā (the modern Tauk), still pillaging the countryside as they passed by and in particular seizing all the horses and mules on which they could lay their hands; for they had arrived in Khūzistān, according to Ibn al-Athīr, with a great shortage of mounts, such animals as they had being so weak as to be practically useless. Daqūqā was taken by storm and the sultan, angered by the inhabitants' resistance, ordered or countenanced a general massacre. Alarmed by the fate of Daqūqā the people of Baqāzīj on the Lower Zāb asked the sultan for a shaḥna to protect them from his soldiers; he sent them, so it was said, a son of Chingiz-Khān whom he had captured in one of his battles with the Mongols. The sultan himself remained in Daqūqā till the end of Rabī' I (the beginning of May 1225), exchanging messages with Muẓaffar al-Dīn Kök-Böri, the last (1190–1232) of the Begtiginids of Irbīl, with whom he finally concluded a treaty of peace. According to Juvainī,[1] these negotiations followed upon the capture of Muẓaffar al-Dīn in battle as he passed by Daqūqā at the head of reinforcements for the caliph's army. Satisfied with this diplomatic victory or perhaps realizing that his resources were still inadequate for a full-scale assault on Baghdad, the sultan now decided to turn his arms against a far less formidable opponent, Muẓaffar al-Dīn Öz-Beg, the atabeg of Āzarbāījān.

At Marāgheh, which he found still in ruins as the result of the Mongol invasion, Jalāl al-Dīn received the news that Yaghan Taisī, the maternal uncle and atabeg of his brother Ghiyāth al-Dīn, had set out from Āzarbāījān with the intention of seizing the town and region of Hamadān. After his nephew's discomfiture at Ray, Yaghan Taisī had entered Öz-Beg's territory either as his ally against the sultan, as Nasawī[2] would have us believe, or more probably, as Ibn al-Athīr's[3] more detailed account implies, as a freebooter pure and simple. After ravaging a great area of Āzarbāījān he passed the winter of 1224–5 on the seacoast of Arrān, presumably in the Mūghān Steppe, so favoured in later times by the Īl-Khāns. Recrossing Āzarbāījān *en route* for Hamadān he had pillaged the unhappy country for a second time. His advance on Hamadān was due to the instigation of the caliph, who had offered him the town and region as an *iqṭā'*, presumably as an act of reprisal for the sultan's invasion of his own territory. Travelling light and with the

[1] Transl. Boyle, vol. II, pp 423–4.
[2] Transl. Houdas p. 178
[3] Vol. XII, pp. 280–1.

speed that was to become proverbial Jalāl al-Dīn came upon Yag͟han Taisï by night, his encampment surrounded with the horses, mules, donkeys, oxen and sheep which he had carried off from Arrān and Āzarbāijān. The plunderer awoke in the morning to find his forces encircled by an army whose commander he recognized, by the parasol held over his head, as Sulṭān Jalāl al-Dīn. Completely taken aback by the sudden appearance of the sultan, whom he had believed to be still in Daqūqā, he sent his wife, who was Jalāl al-Dīn's sister, to intercede on his behalf. She obtained his pardon, and the sultan, his forces swollen by Yag͟han Taisï's army to some 50,000 horse, returned to Marāg͟heh to prepare for the attack on Tabrīz.

With the approach of the sultan the atabeg had at once deserted his capital for Ganja (the present-day Kirovabad) in Arrān; and, perhaps because of his enemy's departure, Jalāl al-Dīn's first moves were peaceful and conciliatory enough. He sought and obtained permission for his troops to visit the town and purchase provisions; then when complaints were made about their behaviour, he sent in a shaḥna to keep order and protect the populace; only when complaints were lodged against the shaḥna did he finally lay siege to the town. After five days of violent fighting the two sides came to terms, and Tabrīz was surrendered to the sultan on the understanding that Öz-Beg's wife, who had remained in the town, should be granted safe-conduct to her possessions in Ḵhūy and Nak͟hchivān. This lady, a daughter of Tog͟hrïl II, the last of the Saljuqs of 'Irāq, had, according to Juvainī,[1] been in secret correspondence with Jalāl al-Dīn. Estranged from her cowardly and pleasure-loving husband, she had promised to secure the capitulation of the town if the sultan would agree to marry her. Such a marriage was possible because of an oath which Öz-Beg had taken that he would divorce her if he executed a slave, whom he now had in fact executed. Jalāl al-Dīn accepted her proposal; she for her part persuaded the notables of Tabrīz to negotiate the terms of surrender, and the sultan made his triumphal entry on 17 Rajab 622/ 25 July 1225. Ibn al-Ath͟īr[2] has recorded two episodes of his short stay in the town. When Friday came around he attended the service at the mosque, but when the preacher began to pray for the caliph he stood up and remained standing until the prayer was over. Öz-Beg had built at vast expense a beautiful pavilion looking down upon gardens. Having entered and inspected it the sultan declared that it was a place fit only

---

[1] Transl. Boyle, vol. II, p. 424.   [2] Vol. XII, p. 282.

for the slothful and of no use to him. Sloth was certainly not one of Jalāl al-Dīn's failings. Within days, it would seem, of his occupation of Tabrīz he had already embarked upon his first campaign against the Georgians.

For some years previous to the sultan's arrival the Georgians had been engaged in aggressive warfare against the Muslim states on the southern fringes of the Caucasus; and Āzarbāījān, whose ruler had neither the power nor the will to oppose them, had borne the brunt of their attack. Jalāl al-Dīn was accordingly seen in the light of a heaven-sent deliverer, a role which he was only too willing to assume. With such forces as he had at hand he at once advanced into enemy territory, encountering a Georgian army of some 70,000 men on the river Garni in Armenia. The battle, which took place at some time in Sha'bān, 622/August–September 1225, resulted in a crushing defeat for the Georgians; and advancing from the battlefield the sultan captured the old Armenian capital of Dvin, then in Georgian hands. From Dvin he returned to Tabrīz, where the leading men were reported—falsely, according to Nasawī[1]—to be plotting against him, leaving his brother Ghiyāth al-Dīn to carry the war into the borderlands of Eastern Georgia. The conspirators, if such they were, having been duly punished, the sultan left Tabrīz for Khūy, where he fulfilled his promise of marrying Öz-Beg's wife. According to Nasawī[2] and Juvainī,[3] the news was brought to her husband in the castle of Alinja near Julfā, at no great distance from Khūy, and his feelings of shame and mortification were so violent as to bring about his death. It is probable, however, and more in keeping with what is recorded of Öz-Beg's character, that he survived this blow to his personal honour. At any rate we are told by Ibn Al-Athīr[4] that he was still in Ganja some time after the ceremony when the town was occupied by Jalāl al-Dīn's troops. He withdrew into the castle, from which he sent a message to the sultan protesting against, not the violation of his marriage, but the marauding activities of Jalāl al-Dīn's soldiers; and the sultan dispatched a body of troops to protect him from further annoyance.

The war against the Georgians was resumed, according to Nasawī,[5] immediately after the *'īd al-fiṭr*, i.e. at the beginning of October 1225, but it is difficult to believe that all that had happened since the capture

[1] Transl. Houdas, pp. 192 ff.
[2] *Op. cit.* pp. 197–8.
[3] Transl. Boyle, vol. II, pp. 425–6.
[4] Vol. XII, pp. 284–5.
[5] Transl. Houdas, p. 202.

of Tabrīz (at the end of July) could have been crowded into so brief a space of time; and it was probably well into winter (Dhu'l-Ḥijja, 622 = 4 December 1225–1 January 1226, according to Ibn al-Athīr)[1] before the sultan re-entered Georgian territory, his objective being now the capital, Tiflis. Advancing directly northwards from Dvin he crossed the Pambak mountains to encounter the enemy in the Lori steppe in what is now northern Soviet Armenia. The Georgian army, according to Ibn al-Athīr, had been augmented with contingents of Alans (Ossetes), Lezghians and Qïpchaq Turks; but this is probably an anachronistic reference to the confederacy that was formed against the sultan in 1228. Whatever their composition, these forces were defeated, and the sultan advanced into Georgia proper. His progress was slow, whether because of Georgian resistance or because of the rigours of a Caucasian winter, and it was not until the beginning of March 1226 that he finally arrived before Tiflis. Having inspected the fortifications and convinced himself that an open assault would be fruitless Jalāl al-Dīn had recourse to a stratagem. Concealing the greater part of his forces in ambush he approached the town at the head of some 3,000 horse; and the defenders, deceived by appearances, were tempted to make a sortie. The sultan turned in simulated flight and led the Georgians on until they fell into the trap he had set, and the whole Khwārazmī army sprang up from their hiding places, drove the enemy back through the gates and, with the collaboration of the Muslim inhabitants, possessed themselves of the town. The citadel, which lay on the far side of the Kur, seemed secure from attack; but a single day sufficed for the sultan to transport his troops across the river and blockade it from every side. The garrison negotiated favourable terms of surrender and were allowed to withdraw unmolested into western Georgia. It was otherwise with the townspeople. The Christian population, except such as saved their lives by apostasy, were subjected to a general massacre; and all of their churches were razed to the ground.

Jalāl al-Dīn's prestige was now perhaps at its zenith. Tiflis had been in Georgian hands for more than a century and in recovering the city for Islam the sultan had succeeded with apparent ease where the Saljuqs, while still at the height of their power, had repeatedly failed. It was this success no doubt which induced his admirer Mu'aẓẓam, the Ayyūbid ruler of Damascus, to suggest to Jalāl al-Dīn an attack on the Armenian town of Akhlāṭ as a diversionary movement in a campaign against his

[1] Vol. XII, p. 293.

brother Ashraf, the ruler of Ḥarrān and Mayyāfāriqīn, who held the town as the most easterly of his various fiefs. Jalāl al-Dīn was already *en route* for Akhlāṭ when news reached him of suspicious behaviour on the part of Baraq Ḥājib, and he abandoned this new adventure in order to deal with his rebellious vassal. Accompanied by less than 300 horse he rode from the Tiflis region to the borders of Kirmān in the amazingly short space of seventeen days. As on a previous occasion Baraq adopted an attitude of courteous defiance; and, realizing the strength of his position, the sultan had no option but to turn back. He halted at Iṣfahān to rest his horses; and the Iṣfahānī poet Kamāl al-Dīn Ismā'īl composed a fine *qaṣīda*[1] upon his spectacular dash from the Caucasus mountains to the Dasht-i-Lūṭ. Here he received a report from his vizier Sharaf al-Mulk, who during his absence had led a raid into the Erzerum region to replenish the garrison's dwindling provisions; whilst returning through the territories of Akhlāṭ he had been attacked by Ashraf's representative, the *ḥājib* Ḥusām al-Dīn 'Alī of Mosul, who was able to recover the whole of the booty. Despite this provocation Jalāl al-Dīn did not, upon his return to Tiflis in the early autumn, immediately resume his attack upon Akhlāṭ. Instead he laid siege to the Armenian towns of Ani and Kars, both held by the Georgians, which he continued to invest until the beginning of October, when he returned to Tiflis and from Tiflis made a ten-day foray into western Georgia. All of these movements were designed to mask his real intentions and to lull Ḥusām al-Dīn into false security. In this he was not entirely successful, for when he appeared before Akhlāṭ on 7 November the ḥājib had had two days' notice of his approach. In their second assault the sultan's men forced their way into the town, where, however, they committed such atrocities that the population, filled with the courage of despair, were not only able to eject them but also to beat off a further attack launched a few days later. Meanwhile, there had been a heavy snowfall in Armenia and reports had reached the sultan that the Ive Türkmen, thinking he was stuck fast before Akhlāṭ, had occupied Ushnuyeh and Urmīyeh and extended their marauding activities to the very walls of Tabrīz. On 15 December he raised the siege of Akhlāṭ and hastened back to Āzarbāījān.

The Türkmen were soon dealt with, but other preoccupations prevented Jalāl al-Dīn from resuming the assault on Akhlāṭ. In February or March 1227 the Georgians attacked and burnt Tiflis and

[1] See Juvainī transl. Boyle, vol. II, pp. 434–5.

had dispersed before the sultan could overtake them. Then Orkhan, one of his oldest and most trusted commanders, was murdered in Ganja by Ismā'īlī assassins, and to avenge his death the sultan carried fire and sword into all the Ismā'īlī territories from Alamūt to Gird-Kūh. Next came news of a Mongol army advancing westwards and already at Dāmghān on the borders of his territory. The sultan attacked these invaders, put them to flight and followed them in close pursuit for a number of days; he then halted near Ray in case they might rally and return to the attack and receiving a report that large forces were in fact approaching he decided to stay and await their arrival.

Such, according to Ibn al-Athīr,[1] was the sequence of events in 1227. Neither Nasawī nor Juvainī mentions the campaign against the Ismā'īlīs or, what is stranger still, the defeat of the Mongols in the Dāmghān region. All authorities are at any rate agreed that the major encounter with the Mongols occurred in the following year. In 1228, so Ibn al-Athīr[2] tells us, Jalāl al-Dīn fought many battles with the Mongols: his informants differed as to the actual number, but most of them went against him, only in the last was he victorious. This was the Battle of Iṣfahān, fought according to Nasawī,[3] on 22 Ramaḍān 625/25 August 1228, which seems in point of fact to have been a Pyrrhic victory for the Mongols. Nasawī's[4] account of the battle is in broad agreement with Juvainī's[5] less-detailed version. Proceeding direct from Tabrīz to Iṣfahān (and not withdrawing in that direction from Ray as in Ibn al-Athīr's[6] account) the sultan gathered together his forces and calmly awaited the enemy's approach. When the Mongols encamped a day's journey to the east of the town, he did not immediately give battle having been advised by his astrologers not to engage the enemy until the fourth day. The Mongols interpreted his inaction as unwillingness to fight and thinking it might be necessary to lay siege to the town, dispatched a foraging party of 2,000 horse into the Luristān mountains to procure provisions. Jalāl al-Dīn caused them to be followed by a detachment of 3,000 men who, having seized the passes and cut off their retreat, returned to Iṣfahān with 400 prisoners. Of these wretches some were handed over to the qāḍī and ra'īs to be massacred in the streets of the town for the delectation and encouragement of the populace; the rest he decapitated personally in the court-

[1] Vol. XII, pp. 306–7

[2] *Op. cit.* p. 310.

[3] Transl. Houdas, p. 231.

[4] *Op. cit.* pp. 223–32.

[5] Transl. Boyle, vol. II, 436–8.

[6] *Loc. cit.*

yard of his palace, the bodies being dragged out into the open country to be devoured by dogs and vultures. On the day approved by the astrologers the sultan was drawing up his army in battle-order when Ghiyāth al-Dīn, who had been nursing a grudge against his brother, suddenly withdrew along with all the forces under his command. Undisturbed by this defection the sultan, perceiving the enemy's numbers to be inferior to his own, ordered the local infantry to return to the town, as a gesture at once of self-confidence and of contempt for his opponents. Towards evening the right wing of his army charged the Mongols' left, broke through and pursued the fleeing enemy as far as Kāshān. Satisfied with this success Jalāl al-Dīn was resting on the side of a ravine when he was approached by one of his chief officers, who urged him not to let the enemy escape under cover of darkness but to avail himself of the opportunity to destroy them utterly. The sultan at once mounted horse but had hardly reached the end of the ravine before a Mongol force, which had been lying in ambush, charged down upon the left wing driving them back against the centre. The sultan's commanders in the left wing were killed almost to a man, and the centre, where he himself was stationed, was in utter confusion, surrounded on every side by the enemy. His very standard-bearer turned in flight, and Jalāl al-Dīn struck him down with his own hand before cutting his way through the Mongol ranks and making good his escape. What was left of the centre and left wing fled in various directions: some to Fārs, some to Kirmān and some to Āzarbāījān, while those who had lost their horses made their way back to Iṣfahān. Two days later the right wing returned from Kāshān expecting to find the rest of the army equally victorious; learning of their defeat and dispersal they too disbanded, leaving Iṣfahān at the mercy of the invaders. The Mongols, however, who had suffered even greater losses than their opponents, were content to show themselves before the walls of the town; they then retreated northward with such speed that they reached Ray in three days; they continued eastwards to Nīshāpūr and were soon beyond the Oxus. As for the sultan a whole week passed without news of his whereabouts; he was believed dead and there was talk of appointing Yaghan Taisī as his successor. The qāḍī persuaded the citizens to postpone any decision until the ʿīd al-fiṭr; and Jalāl al-Dīn, who had been hiding in the Luristān mountains, appeared just in time to preside over the celebrations. Entering the town amidst universal rejoicings he honoured and promoted those of his commanders and soldiers who had distinguished themselves in the battle whilst punishing others for their absence or inactivity. He remained only a day or two in Iṣfahān before proceeding northwards in the wake of the retreating Mongols; from Ray he dispatched bodies of horsemen even into the desolate wastes of Khurāsān.

Upon returning to Tabrīz the sultan received disturbing news about his brother Ghiyāth al-Dīn. After his defection at the Battle of Iṣfahān Ghiyāth al-Dīn had taken refuge in Khūzistān, where he stood under the direct protection of the caliph; he was now said to be heading northwards towards Iṣfahān. When this report reached the sultan he was playing polo in the great square. With typical impetuosity he flung down his mallet and at once took to the road only to learn *en route* that his brother had sought and obtained asylum with 'Alā' al-Dīn of Alamūt. The Ismā'īlī ruler refused to hand over the fugitive but guaranteed his good behaviour, and, apparently satisfied with his undertaking, the sultan returned to Āzarbāījān. As for Ghiyāth al-Dīn, his confinement in Alamūt soon became irksome and he was lured by Baraq Ḥājib to Kirmān, where both he and his mother (whom Baraq had compelled to marry him) were treacherously put to death.

Late in 1228 Jalāl al-Dīn approached Akhlāṭ for the second time. He now had another score to settle with the ḥājib Ḥusām al-Dīn. The Saljuq princess, Öz-Beg's former wife, was soon completely disenchanted with her new husband and, angered by the discourteous behaviour of his lieutenant the vizier Sharaf al-Dīn during the sultan's absence in Central Persia, had not only invited the ḥājib to invade Āzarbāījān but had accompanied him back to Akhlāṭ. The sultan's troops do not appear on this occasion to have closely invested the town. Instead they pillaged and massacred through the length and breadth of Armenia penetrating to the Plain of Mūsh on the border of Jazīreh or Upper Mesopotamia, and the people of Ḥarrān and Sarūj, thinking the Khwārazmīs intended to winter in that more temperate region, began a general exodus into Syria. Their fears, however, were groundless, for the sultan, when an unprecedented snowfall rendered further operations impossible, withdrew his forces into Āzarbāījān.

A renewal of the campaign in the spring of 1229, was prevented by a threat to the sultan's northern flank. The Georgians, now fully recovered from their earlier defeat, had formed a confederation of the various Caucasian peoples and were advancing southwards with a multinational army that included a contingent of 20,000 Qïpchaq Turks. The two sides came into view of each other at a place with the Georgian name of Mindor near the town of Lori, and it was at once evident that the enemy's forces vastly outnumbered the sultan's. Disdaining his vizier's advice to entrench himself and await reinforcements, the sultan drew up his men in preparation for battle. He then ascended a hill in order to observe the enemy more closely and, descrying the banners of the Qïpchaq on the right wing, dispatched a messenger to remind them of the favours he had rendered them during his father's lifetime. The appeal was successful and the Qïpchaq withdrew from the battlefield. Next, turning to the Georgians drawn up in front of him the sultan proposed a one-day truce, during which the young men of either side might engage in single combat. The proposal was readily accepted, and five champions rode forward in succession from the Georgian ranks, each to be felled by the sultan in person. Then, wearying of the sport and forgetful of the truce, he gave a sign with his whip, and his troops advanced at the charge to drive the enemy before them in headlong flight.

Fresh from this and other victories in the Caucasus area the sultan, at the end of August 1229, sat down before the walls of Akhlāṭ. This time he did not raise the siege with the advent of winter, although the bitter cold and heavy snowfalls obliged the besiegers for a while to forsake their posts and seek shelter in neighbouring villages. Meanwhile food supplies inside the town dwindled and deteriorated, and the besieged, who had begun by eating their sheep and oxen, were reduced to a diet of cats and dogs, and even rats and mice. Akhlāṭ was finally taken on 14 April 1230, and was subjected, apparently against the sultan's better judgment, to three days of looting. Ḥusām al-Dīn, his old adversary, was now dead, having been executed by the mamlūk who had succeeded him as governor, and the sources are silent about the Saljuq princess whom he had abducted. Jalāl al-Dīn indemnified himself for her loss and avenged the slight to his honour by laying hands on a Georgian lady, the wife of Malik al-Ashraf, who had been left behind in the town. It was probably this act which decided Ashraf to join with Kai-Qubād, the Saljuq sultan of Rūm, in taking up arms against Sulṭān Jalāl al-Dīn.

Kai-Qubād had been greatly alarmed, not to say panic-stricken, by the capture of Akhlāṭ, which he saw as an immediate threat to the eastern flank of his territories; and he had dispatched envoy after envoy to the Ayyūbids with frantic appeals for an alliance against the sultan. With the approval of the senior Ayyūbid, Malik al-Kāmil of Egypt, Ashraf mustered his forces—5,000 seasoned troops—at Ḥarrān and moved northwards to link up, at Kai-Qubād's headquarters in Sīvās, with an army of 20,000 Rūmīs. The allies then proceeded eastwards along the highway to Persia and halted in Arzinjān in the valley of the western Euphrates. The sultan, meanwhile, was following the same route in a westerly direction. He had left Akhlāṭ to attack the town of Malāzgird, when the ruler of Erzerum, a cousin of Kai-Qubād, who had supplied him with provisions and forage during the siege, came to inform him of the alliance concluded between his cousin and the Ayyūbids; he advised the sultan to advance to the attack before their forces could combine. Jalāl al-Dīn accepted his advice and had pushed forward as far as Khartabirt, where he fell ill; by the time he had recovered sufficiently to continue the march the allies had already linked up. The first clash with the enemy occurred in the village of Yasī-Chaman, somewhat to the east of Arzinjān, on 7 August, when a detachment of Rūmī troops were surrounded and cut to pieces. Two days later the main armies were in contact and there was some skirmishing; but they did not join battle in earnest until the 10th. The Khwārazmīs were decisively defeated, whether because they lost their bearings in the mist, or because of a sand storm that blew in their faces, or simply because of the weight of the enemy's numbers; and Jalāl al-Dīn fled to Khūy, pausing *en route* at Akhlāṭ only long enough to collect such stores and valuables as could be readily transported.[1]

From Akhlāṭ, which he now reoccupied, Ashraf entered into negotiations with the sultan; and peace was concluded on condition that Jalāl al-Dīn should henceforth respect the territories of both the Ayyūbids and the Saljuqs. With respect to Kai-Qubād the sultan gave this undertaking with great unwillingness and only upon receiving reports that large forces of Mongols had arrived in Central Persia. This was the army, 30,000 strong, under the command of the *noyan* Chormaghun, dispatched by Ögedei, the son and first successor (1229–41) of Chingiz-Khān, to complete the conquest of Persia and make an end of the sultan. It seemed at first as though the Mongols might winter in 'Irāq-i 'Ajam, thus affording Jalāl al-Dīn time to reassemble his forces; but then came news of an army at Sarāb, only sixty miles east of Tabrīz. The sultan set out at great speed for Ahar, where he passed the night; the roof of the palace in which he lodged caved in and he took this for

[1] For a detailed account of this campaign see Gottschalk, *Al-Malik al-Kāmil*, pp. 188 ff.

an evil omen. He made his way to the Mūghān Steppe, where the Mongols all but caught up with him; he shook them off by abandoning his encampment under cover of darkness and hiding in the mountains of Kapan, in what is today the extreme south-east of Soviet Armenia. The winter of 1230–1 he passed in Urmīyeh and Ushnūyeh; later we find him in Arrān sentencing his vizier Sharaf al-Mulk, justly or unjustly, to death and suppressing a revolt in Ganja; then involved in fruitless negotiations with the Ayyūbid governor of Akhlāṭ; and finally *en route* for Diyārbakr, apparently to join the ruler of Āmid in an attack upon the sultan of Rūm. In the middle of August 1231 he encamped in the immediate vicinity of Āmid; he drank heavily that night and was sunk in intoxicated sleep when, at day break, the Mongols launched their attack. Roused by one of his generals he effected his escape whilst the enemy was pursuing the bulk of his army, which, led by the same general, made its way to Irbīl and finally to Iṣfahān. The sultan, meanwhile, with only a small following, rode up to the walls of Āmid and, being refused admission, turned back in the direction of Mayyāfāriqīn and encamped outside a nearby village. Again overtaken by the Mongols he killed two of his pursuers and made off into the mountains. Here, he was captured by the Kurds, who murdered him for his clothes and horse, according to some authorities, or for motives of revenge, according to others. In due course the ruler of Āmid recovered his body and gave it burial; but many refused to believe that he was dead and years later, when the whole of his domains were subject to Mongol rule, pretenders would arise claiming to be Sulṭān Jalāl al-Dīn.

Such was the end of the last of the Khwārazm-Shāhs. Nasawī[1] describes him as a short, dark man, Turkish in appearance and in speech, though he spoke Persian also. Grave and taciturn by nature he smiled rather than laughed and never lost his temper or used abusive language. His qualities, in d'Ohsson's judgment, were those of a Türkmen warrior rather than of a general or a sovereign. This is to do him less than justice. For all his faults, he alone of his contemporaries, as was recognized by friend and foe alike, was a match for the invaders. Jalāl al-Dīn and his army formed a wall between Islam and the Tartars. That wall had now been breached and neither Ayyūbid nor Saljuq was capable of stemming the flood.

[1] Transl. Houdas, pp. 411–12.

THE MONGOL VICEROYS

After the death of Sulṭān Jalāl al-Dīn the military operations of Chormaghun were conducted in the Caucasus, Upper Mesopotamia and Asia Minor, and henceforth he was to exercise only an indirect influence on the course of events in Persia. One consequence of his passage through Iran had been the Mongol re-occupation of Khurāsān and the gradual establishment of a civil administration in that unhappy region now slowly recovering from the state of utter desolation in which it had lain since the invasion. At the time of the conquest of Gurgānj, a certain Chïn-Temür, a Qara-Khitayan by origin, had been appointed *basqaq* of that area. He now received orders to lead his forces westwards in support of Chormaghun and, arriving in Khurāsān, proceeded systematically to reduce the province to subjection, setting basqaqs over such places as had submitted. In this work he was hampered by the activities of two former generals of Sulṭān Jalāl al-Dīn, Qaracha and Yaghan-Sonqur, who were conducting guerrilla warfare against the Mongols in the Nīshāpūr region. News of these operations having reached the Great Khan, he was greatly enraged and instructed the noyan Dayir to set out from his base at Bādghīs and, having first dealt with Qaracha, to put the whole population of Khurāsān to the sword. Dayir's troops were already on the move when he received the news that Qaracha had been driven out of Khurāsān by Kül-Bolat, a lieutenant of Chïn-Temür, and had entrenched himself in Zarang in Sīstān. Dayir proceeded to lay siege to Zarang, which held out for nearly two years, and upon its surrender dispatched messengers to Chïn-Temür asserting his claim to the governorship of Khurāsān. In this he was supported by Chormaghun, who called upon Chïn-Temür to join him in the West, whilst leaving the administration of Khurāsān and Māzandarān in the hands of Dayir. Chïn-Temür decided to appeal to the Great Khan, to whom accordingly he dispatched a mission headed by Kül-Bolat and including several local rulers who had made their submission to the Mongols. Ögedei was pleased with the mission, remarking that Chormaghun, despite the vastly greater territory under his control, had never sent tributary princes to wait upon him; and he issued a yarlïgh or rescript giving official status to Chïn-Temür as the governor of Khurāsān and Māzandarān. A second mission, led by an Uighur Turk called Körgüz accompanied by Bahā' al-Dīn Juvainī, the father of the historian, whom Chïn-Temür had made his *ṣāḥib-dīvān* or minister of finance, was equally successful but brought no benefit to Chīn-Temür, who had died before the mission returned (633/1235–6).

He was succeeded in his office by Nosal, an aged Mongol said to have been more than 100 years old, who died in 637/1239–40, already in effect superseded by the Uighur Körgüz, a clever and ambitious man, who, as the result of a second visit to Mongolia, had been given special powers by the Great Khan. Körgüz proceeded upon his return to hold a census and to reassess the taxes, but was soon obliged to return to Mongolia to answer charges laid against him by the family and dependants of Chīn-Temür. Not only did he triumph over these adversaries, but he was granted letters-patent conferring upon him the civil administration of all the territories held by Chormaghun in Western Asia. Returning to Khurāsān at the end of 1239 he at once sent agents to 'Irāq-i 'Ajam, Arrān and Āzarbāījān to take over from the military commanders, whilst he established his own headquarters in Ṭūs. The town was still in ruins, only some fifty houses remaining standing, but with Körgüz's encouragement and example was now speedily re-built. Public order was restored, and Juvainī tells us,[1] with the usual hyperbole, that an amīr who had previously cut off heads with impunity would not now venture to decapitate a chicken, whilst the morale of the peasantry was so high "that if a great army of Mongols encamped in a field they might not even ask a peasant to hold a horse's head, let alone demanding provisions..." Körgüz's career was, however, nearly at its end. A dispute with his vizier, one Sharaf al-Dīn, a man of the people from Khwārazm, whose character can hardly have been as black as it is painted by Juvainī,[2] caused him to set out upon a fourth journey to Mongolia. This was presumably in the winter of 1241–2, for he was met *en route* with the news of the Great Khan's death, which occurred on 11 December 1241. When passing through the territories of Chaghatai, then only recently dead, he had in the course of an altercation with an official made a remark which had given offence to Chaghatai's widow. Fearful of the consequences of his words in the new and unpredictable situation he hurried back to Khurāsān. His fears were not groundless, for no sooner had he returned to Ṭūs than the emissaries of Chaghatai's family—one of them his successor, Arghun Aqa—arrived in the town. He was arrested and taken first to Ulugh-Ef, the *ordu* of Chaghatai near the present-day Kulja and then to the court of Töregene, the widow of Ögedei and Regent of the Empire (1242–6)

[1] Transl. Boyle, vol. II, pp. 501–2.

[2] *Op. cit.* vol. II, pp. 524–46.

in Qara-Qorum. Here it was ruled that the crime should be tried where it had been committed, in Chaghatai's territory. Körgüz was in consequence brought back to Ulugh-Ef, where, by the orders of Qara-Hülegü, the grandson and first successor (1242–6) of Chaghatai, he was put to a cruel death. Originally a Buddhist despite his name (the Turkish for George) Körgüz had towards the end of his life become a convert to Islam, an indication perhaps of some feeling of solidarity with his Muslim subjects.

Arghun Aqa had already been appointed to succeed Körgüz as the viceroy of the conquered territories in the West, i.e. of a region embracing Iran, the southern Caucasus area and part of Upper Mesopotamia and Asia Minor. He arrived in Khurāsān in 641/1243–4 and left almost immediately on a tour of inspection of 'Iraq-i 'Ajam and Āzarbāījān. From Tabrīz, where he received embassies from the sultan of Rūm and the Ayyūbid rulers of Damascus and Aleppo, he was summoned to attend the *quriltai* or assembly of the Mongol princes at which Güyük, the son of Ögedei, was elected his successor as Great Khan (1246). Confirmed in his office and loaded with honours by the new khan, Arghun returned to Khurāsān in the spring of 1247. He spent some time in Marv before passing on to Ṭūs, where he ordered the rebuilding of the Saljuq palace called the Manṣūriyya. He then relaxed for a while in the meadows of Rādkān, a region of copious springs and lush grass, which seems to have made a special appeal to the Mongols, and in the late autumn of 1247 set out for Tabrīz by way of Māzandarān. At Āmul he was magnificently entertained by Juvainī's father, the ṣāḥib-dīvān, and was about to resume his journey when he received news of intrigues against him in the Mongol capital; and he determined to return thither without delay. On this journey he was accompanied not only by the ṣāḥib-dīvān but also by the latter's son, the future historian. The party had reached Talas, the present-day Jambul in Kazakhstan, when they were met with the tidings of Güyük's death (which had occurred in April 1248); at the same time there came news of the approach of the noyan Eljigidei at the head of a large army. The purpose of this expedition is not clear: it was perhaps intended that Eljigidei, as the khan's personal representative, was to supersede Baiju (who had succeeded Chormaghun in 1242) as commander of the Mongol forces in Western Asia. Arghun hurried forward to meet him and at his insistence returned to Khurāsān to supervise the equipment and provisioning of his army. It was not until the late summer of 1249 that he was able to resume his interrupted journey to Mongolia. His case was duly investigated in the ordu of Oghul-Qaimish, Güyük's widow, then Regent of the Empire; and a decision was reached in his favour. On the homeward journey the party (of which the historian Juvainī was one) halted for a month or two at the ordu of Yesü-Möngke, who now ruled over the apanage of Chaghatai. The party had arrived in Almalïgh in the late summer or early autumn of 1250; they left in the winter, when the roads were blocked with snow, but nevertheless made rapid progress and had soon reached Marv in Khurāsān. Arghun did not remain long in Iran. In August or September 1251 he again set out for the East in order to attend the quriltai which had been summoned to enthrone the new khan, Möngke (1251–9), the eldest son of Tolui. The enthronement had in fact already taken place (on 1 July 1251), though the news did not reach Arghun until his arrival at Talas. It was now mid-winter and the deep snow made travelling almost impossible. Nevertheless the party struggled on and finally came to Besh-Balïq, the old Uighur capital, a little to the north-west of Guchen in Sinkiang. From here Arghun sent a message to inform the new khan of his approach, but the party did not reach the Mongol Court till 2 May 1252, nearly a year after Möngke's enthronement. Arghun reported on the chaotic condition of finances in the territories under his control, and it was decided that a more equitable form of taxation known as *qubchur*, already in force in Transoxiana, should be introduced in the Western countries also. The deliberations over these and other matters lasted so long that it was not until August or September 1253 that Arghun finally took his leave. It was during this lengthy stay in Mongolia that Juvainī, who had again accompanied Arghun, was persuaded to embark upon his history of the Mongol conquests.

Upon his return to Khurāsān Arghun dispatched officials to the various parts of Persia to carry out the fiscal reforms. He himself set out for the Court of Batu, the son of Jochi and founder of the Golden Horde, to deal with certain unspecified business, apparently on the instructions of the Great Khan. Returning by way of Darband he conducted a census and imposed the new qubchur tax in Georgia, Arrān and Āzarbāījān before proceeding to 'Irāq-i 'Ajam. In the meanwhile, availing themselves of his absence, certain of his enemies at the Mongol Court had secured a yarlïgh for the dispatch of an inspector to Khurāsān to examine his accounts. Reports of this official's arrival and activities must have reached Arghun more or less simultaneously with news that the Great Khan's younger brother, Prince Hülegü, was advancing westward at the head of a great army. In November 1255 he waited on Hülegü at Kish, the present-day Shahr-i Sabz in Uzbekistan and accompanied him as far as Shuburqān before continuing on his way to Mongolia once again to triumph over his accusers.

Arghun was to spend the remainder of his life in the service of the Īl-Khans. He returned to the West, according to Juvainī, in September 1258, although Rashīd al-Dīn represents him as being present, in Hülegü's suite, at the siege of Baghdad (January–February 1258). In 1259 and 1260 he was in Georgia introducing the qubchur and conducting military operations against the rebel princes. He held, under both Hülegü and Abaqa, the office of Tax-Farmer General (*muqāṭi'-i mamālik*). As deputy to the viceroy of Khurāsān, Abaqa's younger brother Tübshin, he took part in the war with Baraq, the ruler of Transoxiana, in 1270. He died in the meadows of Rādkān in May or June 1275.

HÜLEGÜ

At the quriltai of 1251 the Great Khan Möngke had decided to complete and consolidate the Mongol conquests by dispatching his brothers Qubilai and Hülegü to China and Western Asia respectively. The victories of Qubilai (Kubla Khan), the successor of Möngke as Great Khan (1260–94) and founder of the Yüan dynasty, fall outside the scope of this volume.[1] As for Hülegü, his instructions were in the first place to destroy the Ismā'īlīs and demolish their castles and then, this task completed, to put down the Kurds and Lurs: the caliph was to be attacked only if he refused to tender his allegiance. Elaborate preparations were made for the passage of Hülegü's army through Central Asia. The road was cleared of boulders and thorny shrubs; bridges were built over small, and ferries provided for the crossing of larger rivers; and all pasturage on either side of the route, from the Khangai mountains to the Oxus, was reserved for the exclusive use of Hülegü's army. That army, probably larger than the forces which Chingiz-Khān led westward in 1219, included contingents from all the Mongol princes, the sons, brothers and nephews of the Great Khan; and special mention should be made, in view of later developments, of the contingent sent by Batu and led by two of Jochi's grandsons, Balaghai and Quli, and one great grandson, Tutar, as also of the contingent from

[1] See Grousset, *L'Empire des steppes*, pp. 349 ff.

Chaghatai's *ulus* led by one of his grandsons, Tegüder. The army likewise included a corps of Chinese mangonel-men and naphtha-throwers for employment in siege operations.

Hülegü advanced westward at a leisurely pace necessitated perhaps by the size and unwieldiness of his forces. Setting out from his own ordu in October 1253 he halted for a time at Ulugh-Ef, where he was entertained by Princess Orqïna, the widow of Chaghatai and now (1252–61) the ruler of his ulus. The summer of 1254 Hülegü passed in mountain pastures somewhere on the eastern borders of Transoxiana. In late September 1255 he encamped in the famous meadows of Kān-i Gil to the east of Samarqand. Here he was visited by Shams al-Dīn Muḥammad, the founder (1245–78) of the Kart dynasty of Herāt, who had demonstrated his loyalty to the Mongols by taking part in their invasion of India in 1246. Early in November Hülegü pressed on to Kish, where, as we have seen, he was joined by the viceroy Arghun Aqa. From Kish he dispatched express couriers to the various Persian rulers informing them of his intention to extirpate the Ismā'īlīs and calling upon them to render assistance or suffer the consequences of their refusal or inactivity. Many of these rulers, including Sa'd, the heir and successor (1226–60) of the Atabeg Muẓaffar al-Dīn of Fārs, came to do homage in person, as did also the rival sultans of Rūm, 'Izz al-Dīn and Rukn al-Dīn. After a month's stay in Kish the army continued on its way to the Oxus, which it crossed on bridges of boats commandeered from the ferrymen. On the left bank of the river Hülegü amused himself with a tiger hunt, in which the hunters rode on Bactrian camels in place of their terrified horses. The next halting-place was in the meadows of Shuburqān (the present-day Shibarkhān in north-western Afghanistan), where only a short stay had been intended; but heavy snowfalls and bitter cold obliged Hülegü to pass the remainder of the winter in this area. In the early spring of 1256 Arghun Aqa took leave of the Mongol prince having first entertained him in "a large tent of fine linen embroidered with delicate embroideries, with gold and silver plate in keeping with it";[1] and Hülegü entered Kūhistān to come for the first time in contact with the Ismā'īlīs.

As the army was passing through the districts of Zāveh and Khwāf, there occurred a number of "incidents", a vague term used by both Juvainī[2] and Rashīd al-Dīn[3] presumably with reference to surprise

[1] Juvainī, transl. Boyle, vol. II, p. 164. [2] *Op. cit.* p. 615.
[3] Transl. Arends, p. 26.

attacks by Ismāʿīlī *fidāʾīs*; and Hülegü dispatched the generals Köke-Ilge and Ket-Buqa to attack the Ismāʿīlī stronghold of Tūn. Ket-Buqa, a Nestorian Christian, famous afterwards as the Mongol commander at ʿAin Jālūt, had had considerable experience in fighting this enemy. At the head of Hülegü's advanced guard, a body of 12,000 men, he had crossed the Oxus in March 1253, captured several places in Kūhistān and then laid unsuccessful siege to the celebrated fortress of Gird-Kūh in May of the same year. In August he had attacked the castle of Shāhdīz near Ray and sent a raiding party still farther west into the Alamūt region. Returning to Kūhistān he had harried the country a second time and captured several strongholds, including Tūn. The town, says Juvainī,[1] "had apparently not yet been humbled and still persisted in its former benightedness..." Köke-Ilge and Ket-Buqa arrived before the gates on 4 April 1256; they took the town on the 16th and slaughtered all the inhabitants, except the younger women, according to Juvainī,[2] or the artisans, according to Rashīd al-Dīn.[3] Their mission accomplished the two generals rejoined the main army, then on its way to Ṭūs.

At Ṭūs as at Shuburqān Hülegü was lodged in a beautiful tent which Arghun Aqa had had especially constructed for his accommodation on the instructions of the Great Khan. After a few days of feasting and revelry he moved on to the gardens of Manṣūriyya, the Saljuq palace restored by Arghun Aqa, where he was entertained with a banquet by Arghun's wives. Leaving Ṭūs the army encamped for a day or two in the meadows of Rādkān before proceeding to Khabūshān (the modern Qūchān), "a town" to quote Juvainī,[4] "which had been derelict and in ruins from the first incursion of the Mongol army until that year, its buildings desolate and the *qanāts* without water and no walls still standing save those of the Friday mosque". The historian, whose motives were not altogether disinterested, for he had purchased a quarter of the town for himself, approached Hülegü on the subject of Khabūshān and obtained his authority for the complete restoration of the town at the expense of the treasury.

Hülegü remained in this region for a month and then resumed the advance westward. On 24 July he was rejoined by the ambassadors he had sent to the Ismāʿīlī Grand Master, Rukn al-Dīn Khur-Shāh, to convey the terms of surrender. From Khurqān near Bisṭām, where he

[1] Transl. Boyle, vol. II, p. 615.
[2] *Op. cit.* p. 616.
[3] Transl. Arends, p 26.
[4] Transl. Boyle, vol. II, p. 617.

had arrived on 2 September, he dispatched a second embassy to Rukn al-Dīn. The Grand Master, acting on the advice of the famous philosopher Naṣīr al-Dīn Ṭūsī and other learned men detained against their will amongst the Ismā'īlīs, decided to send his brother Shahanshāh to make professions of submission. Hülegü received Shahanshāh with every honour and dispatched a third embassy with the message that Rukn al-Dīn should now demonstrate his submission by demolishing his castles. Dissatisfied with the Grand Master's response Hülegü prepared for battle. In the middle of September he advanced from Khurqān at the head of 10,000 men, whilst the various armies converged on Rukn al-Dīn's residence, the well-nigh impregnable castle of Maimūn-Diz,[1] Buqa-Temür and Köke-Ilge approaching by way of Māzandarān, Tegüder and Ket-Buqa by way of Simnān and Khuvār and Tutar and Balaghai from the direction of Alamūt. And again he sent ambassadors, to notify Rukn al-Dīn of his intention and to promise an amnesty if he presented himself in person. As Hülegü passed by Fīrūzkūh the ambassadors returned accompanied by Rukn al-Dīn's vizier, who undertook to destroy the castles but asked that Rukn al-Dīn might be allowed a year's respite before vacating Maimūn-Diz and that the castles of Alamūt and Lanbasar might be spared from destruction. Meanwhile Hülegü continued to advance through Lār and Damāvand, and the castle of Shāhdīz, to which Ket-Buqa had laid siege two years previously, was captured within two days. Yet once again he sent ambassadors to Rukn al-Dīn calling upon him to present himself before him. The Grand Master now agreed to send his son and to demolish all of the castles; and Hülegü halted at 'Abbāsābād near Ray to await the son's arrival. On 8 October Rukn al-Dīn sent a child of seven or eight, his own or his father's by some irregular union. Hülegü sent the boy back on the ground that he was too young and asked instead for one of Rukn al-Dīn's brothers to relieve Shahanshāh. On 27 October the Grand Master sent his brother Shīran-Shāh, who was received by Hülegü near Ray; and he, or more probably Shahanshāh, returned on the 31st bearing a yarlīgh to the effect that provided Rukn al-Dīn dismantled his castles he had nothing to fear.

This message was apparently intended to lull Rukn al-Dīn into false security, just as the latter's embassies had been designed to delay the Mongol's assault until the winter snows rendered it impracticable. The

[1] The site has only recently been identified and investigated. See Willey, *The Castles of the Assassins*, pp. 158 ff.

weather, however, remained unseasonably mild and, his victim being now completely encircled, Hülegü ordered the various armies to close in whilst he himself advanced from the direction of Pishkil-Dara through Ṭāliqān. On 8 November he was encamped on a hilltop facing Maimūn-Diz from the north and the next day surveyed the castle from every side in search of some vulnerable point. The great strength of the fortifications, the approach of winter and the consequent difficulty of procuring supplies were advanced as reasons for postponing siege operations until the spring; but a minority of the princes and generals favoured immediate investment of the castle and Hülegü supported their view. In the event the siege was to last less than a fortnight. Great pine trees, planted in former times by the Ismā'īlīs themselves, were felled by the Mongols to serve as poles for their mangonels; and in addition to these normal siege instruments a Chinese ballista, with a range of 2,500 paces, discharged its missiles against the garrison. In the face of this bombardment the Ismā'īlīs ceased fighting and asked for a truce, which was granted. Then Rukn al-Dīn asked for a yarlīgh granting him safe-conduct if he descended from the castle. This too was granted, the yarlīgh being drawn up by the historian Juvainī who functioned as Hülegü's secretary. Still the Grand Master failed to appear, and the bombardment was resumed on a much larger scale. Now at last Rukn al-Dīn decided to surrender and sent down his brother Shīran-Shāh and one of his sons with a group of notables including Naṣīr al-Dīn Ṭūsī; on the following day, 29 Shawwāl/19 November, according to Juvainī,[1] or on the day after, according to Rashīd al-Dīn,[2] who quotes a chronogram by Naṣīr al-Dīn, he came down himself.

The next day Rukn al-Dīn brought all of his family and following down out of the castle; and the Mongols climbed up to begin the work of demolition. They were attacked by some of the more fanatical fidā'īs, whose desperate resistance was broken only after four days of fighting. Meanwhile, Rukn al-Dīn had been kindly received by Hülegü, though kept as a prisoner at large under the surveillance of a Mongol commander. At Hülegü's behest he dispatched bodies of men to destroy the Ismā'īlī castles in the whole of the region. Forty such castles were demolished, only Alamūt and Lanbasar refusing to admit these emissaries. Alamūt was invested by Balaghai until surrender terms were negotiated through the good offices of Rukn al-Dīn. The work of demolition then began, but the historian Juvainī, with Hülegü's

[1] Transl. Boyle, vol. II, p. 634.

[2] Transl. Arends, p. 29.

permission, was able to salvage part of the celebrated library, as also a quantity of astronomical instruments. Lanbasar was approached by Hülegü in person. Finding the garrison disinclined to surrender he left Dayir-Buqa to lay siege to the castle (which, in the event, was to hold out for a full year) and, on 4 January 1257, set out for his chief ordu, then situated some twenty miles from Qazvīn, where he celebrated the Mongol New Year festival with a week of revelry. Rukn al-Dīn seems to have accompanied Hülegü to his ordu, though his family and possessions had been transferred to Qazvīn. Because he was still of use to him Hülegü continued to treat him with honour and consideration, bestowing upon him a Mongol girl of whom he became enamoured and even humouring him in his curious pastime of watching camel-fights. With the Grand Master's co-operation it had been possible for Hülegü to secure the speedy surrender of scores of Ismā'īlī castles, many of which (as was in fact the case with Gird-Kūh) could have withstood a siege of many years. Once his usefulness was exhausted, however, his presence was a source of embarrassment to Hülegü, who acceded with alacrity to his request that he might be sent to the Great Khan. Rukn al-Dīn did not return from this journey. According to Juvainī,[1] he actually reached the Mongol Court, was reproached by Möngke with the continued resistance of Lanbasar and Gird-Kūh and was murdered by his escort in the Khangai mountains on the way back. Rashīd al-Dīn,[2] on the other hand, tells us that he was put to death on the outward journey, at the express orders of the Great Khan, who protested at the wasting of relay animals upon such a visitor. His departure was the signal for a general massacre of his followers, and all the Ismā'īlīs in Mongol custody, including Rukn al-Dīn's own family at Qazvīn, were put to the sword, not even infants in the cradle being spared. Their wholesale slaughter was carried out, according to Juvainī,[3] not only by order of the Great Khan Möngke but in fulfilment of a *yasa* of Chingiz-Khān himself.

By the virtual extinction of the Ismā'īlī sect Hülegü had rendered a great, if unintentional, service to orthodox Islam. His next blow was to be directed against the founthead of orthodoxy, the 'Abbāsid Caliphate. The Īl-Khān,[4] as we may now call him, proceeded with the same

[1] Transl. Boyle, vol. II, pp. 724–5.
[2] Transl. Arends, p. 30.
[3] *Loc. cit.*
[4] The term means "subject khan" and was applied to the Mongol rulers of Persia (and sometimes to the rulers of the Golden Horde) as subordinates to the Great Khan in Mongolia and afterwards China.

deliberation as in his advance through Central Asia. In March or April 1257 he left the Qazvīn area *en route* for Hamadān and was joined, apparently before reaching his destination, by Baiju, the successor of Chormaghun in the West, whom he presumably instructed on the role of his army in the forthcoming campaign. Hülegü himself, with the Jochid princes Quli, Balaghai and Tutar, encamped on the Hamadān plain, from whence, after a brief stay, he set off in the direction of Baghdad, arriving in Dīnavar on 26 April; he then, for some unknown reason, returned to Hamadān; on 26 July he was in Tabrīz and on 21 September back in Hamadān. Here began what Grousset[1] has called the "dialogue epistolaire" between Hülegü and the caliph, "un des plus grandioses de l'histoire". The gist of Hülegü's first message, shorn of Rashīd al-Dīn's rhetoric, was that the caliph should either present himself in person or send his three principal officers, the vizier, the commander-in-chief and the lesser *davāt-dār* or vice-chancellor; the caliph's reply was to the effect that this raw and inexperienced young man should return whence he had come. There followed a second exchange in similar tone, after which, wishing to secure his passage through the Zagros mountains, Hülegü established contact with the caliph's governor of Dartang and persuaded him to hand over the castles in his area: though the governor afterwards repented of his treason, the castles were retained through the intervention of Ket-Buqa at the head of 30,000 horse. The way being thus cleared, the Īl-Khān consulted his leading men as to the advisability of an attack on Baghdad. The astronomer Ḥusām al-Dīn, who, despite his Muslim name, had been attached to Hülegü by the order of the Great Khan, spoke openly against such a move. Every ruler who had attacked Baghdad and the 'Abbāsids had forfeited his kingdom and his life; and he foretold six natural disasters that would occur if Hülegü made the attempt. Hülegü then turned to Naṣīr al-Dīn Ṭūsī, who had now joined his suite, and asked his opinion. With equal discretion and common sense the philosopher replied that none of these disasters would occur. "What then will happen?" asked the Īl-Khān. "Hülegü will reign in place of Musta'ṣim", he replied; and in a disputation with Ḥusām al-Dīn he had no difficulty in citing a number of cases in which the caliphs had come to a violent end without any consequent calamity.

The decision being now taken, the Mongol armies converged on Baghdad. Baiju, coming from the direction of Irbīl, crossed the Tigris

[1] *L'Empire des steppes*, p. 428.

at Mosul and encamped to the west of Baghdad to await the arrival of the forces from the East. Of these the right wing, commanded by Balaghai, Tutar and Quli, was advancing through Shahrazūr and Daqūqā, the centre under Hülegü himself by way of Kirmānshāh and Ḥulwān, and the left wing under Ket-Buqa by way of Luristān and Khūzistān. Hülegü set out from the Hamadān area in November 1257. From Asadābād he again summoned the caliph to his presence, and at Dīnavar he received the caliph's ambassador again advising him to turn back. He replied that having travelled so far he could not return without having met the caliph face to face. On 6 December he reached Kirmānshāh, which must have offered some resistance, for the town was sacked and the inhabitants massacred. From here he summoned Baiju and his officers to a council of war. They joined him at Ṭāq-i Girrā, the so-called "Zagrian Gates", and, their consultations completed, set off to recross the Tigris and take up their position to the west of Baghdad. Hülegü sent yet another warning to the caliph and, passing through the defile, encamped on the banks of the Ḥulwān river, where he remained from 18 to 31 December. In the meantime, Ket-Buqa had conquered the greater part of Luristān; and Baiju, by 16 January 1258, having crossed the Tigris, had reached the banks of the Nahr 'Īsā. Here Suqunchaq, the future governor of 'Irāq-i 'Arab and Fārs, obtained his permission to lead the advanced forces and pushed forward as far as Ḥarbiyya. The davāt-dār, who commanded the caliph's army, was encamped between Ba'qūbā and Bājisrā. Hearing of a Mongol army approaching from the west he crossed the Tigris and joined battle with Suqunchaq near Anbār. The Mongols retreated to a place which Rashīd al-Dīn[1] calls Bashīriyya, apparently on a branch of the Dujail called Nahr Bashīr. Here they were rallied by Baiju, who came up with the main army. The Mongols then opened a dyke and flooded the whole area behind their opponents, and, attacking at dawn on 17 January, inflicted a heavy defeat on the caliph's troops, of whom 12,000 were killed in battle in addition to those drowned in the flood. Of the survivors some few, with the davāt-dār at their head, made their way back to Baghdad, whilst others fled as far as Ḥilla and Kūfa.

Following up this victory Baiju's troops had by 22 January reached the western suburbs of Baghdad. In the meantime, Ket-Buqa, coming up from the south, had passed through Ṣarṣar and penetrated the market district of Karkh; and Hülegü himself, leaving his heavy baggage at

[1] Transl. Arends, p. 41.

Khānaqīn, had reached the eastern walls of Baghdad simultaneously with Baiju's approach to the western side. In accordance with their practice in siege operations the Mongols ringed the whole circumference of the town with a kind of palisade called *sibē*; inside this fence they sunk a moat and set up their mangonels. The assault began on 29 January. On 4 February a breach in the Burj al-'Ajamī ("Persian Tower"), the great bastion to the south-east of the Halba Gate, gave the Mongols access to the fortifications. Swarming in through this gap they drove the defenders to right and left along the wall tops and by evening were in control of the whole of the battlements. The situation was now desperate, and the davāt-dār made a vain attempt to escape by boat down the Tigris, while the caliph initiated a series of parleys which led to nothing and were finally broken off by Hülegü in annoyance at the wounding of one of his officers. The caliph's commander-in-chief, Sulaimān-Shāh, the Ive Türkmen, and the davāt-dār had been handed over to the Mongols during the parleying: they were now both of them executed. Left with no adviser except his unsympathetic and probably disloyal vizier Musta'ṣim decided upon surrender. On 10 February he came out of the town accompanied by his three sons and presented himself before Hülegü. The Īl-Khān addressed him with apparent kindness and affability and then asked him to order the inhabitants to lay down their arms and come out of the town. The caliph had a proclamation made to this effect, and the people poured through the gates only to be slaughtered as they issued into the open. Musta'ṣim himself and his sons were lodged, in the custody of Mongol guards, at the Kalwādhā Gate, the present-day Southern Gate, near Ket-Buqa's encampment.

The sack of Baghdad began on 13 February, and the killing, looting and burning continued for seven days, only the houses of Christians being spared. On the 15th Hülegü went on a tour of the caliph's palace and caused the terrified Musta'ṣim to disclose the whereabouts of his treasures. This is the occasion which gave rise to the story, familiar from the pages of Marco Polo and Sir John Mandeville, of the caliph's being starved to death in a tower full of gold and silver. The nucleus of this story is the account of the interview between Hülegü and Musta'ṣim as given by Naṣīr al-Dīn Ṭūsī,[1] who may well have been actually present. The Īl-Khān "set a golden tray before the Caliph and said: 'Eat!' 'It is not edible,' said the Caliph. 'Then why didst thou keep it,' asked

[1] Boyle, "The Death of the Last 'Abbāsid Caliph", p. 159.

the King, 'and not give it to thy soldiers? And why didst thou not make these iron doors into arrow-heads and come to the bank of the river so that I might not have been able to cross it?' 'Such', replied the Caliph, 'was God's will.' 'What will befall thee,' said the King, 'is also God's will.'"

The caliph's death was in fact imminent. On 20 February, having called an end to the pillage and slaughter, Hülegü left Baghdad for the village of Waqaf, which has not been identified but must have lain somewhere along the road to Khānaqīn. It was in this village on that same day that Musta'ṣim met his end. Both Naṣīr al-Dīn and Rashīd al-Dīn in his much fuller account are silent as to the manner of the caliph's death, but the late Muslim authorities are almost certainly right in stating that he was rolled up in a carpet and trampled or kicked to death, to avoid the shedding of his blood, such being the Mongols' method of executing their own princes.

The vizier and the ṣāḥib-dīvān were both confirmed in their offices, a circumstance which throws some doubt on the latter's loyalty also, and were ordered, in collaboration with other officials appointed by Hülegü, "to rebuild Baghdad, remove the slain and dead animals and reopen the bazaars".[1] And dispatching his cousin Buqa-Temür to complete the conquest of southern 'Irāq-i 'Arab and Khūzistān the Īl-Khān withdrew northwards, first to his ordu near Hamadān, and then into Āzarbāījān, where he was to remain for over a year before embarking upon a third campaign, against the Aiyūbid states in Syria. He seems to have passed the earlier part of the summer in Marāgheh, which he was to make his capital city. It was here that Naṣīr al-Dīn Ṭūsī now began, under his patronage, to erect his famous observatory, and it was here, too, on 12 July 1258, that he received his vassal the nonagenarian Badr al-Dīn Lu'lu' of Mosul, to whom he owed the capture of Irbil, vainly besieged by the noyan Urqatu. He appears, however, soon to have moved on to Tabrīz, the capital of his son Abaqa and the later Īl-Khāns; here he was visited by both of the sultans of Rūm and also by the Atabeg Abū Bakr of Fārs, who came to offer his congratulations on a victory on which his *protégé* the poet Sa'dī had composed a famous *marthiya* or *qaṣīda* of mourning. The spoils of this and Hülegü's earlier victory over the Ismā'īlīs had already been transported to Āzarbāījān, where they had been stored in a castle on the island of Shāhī in Lake Reżā'īyeh (Urmīyeh). From these treasures a selection had been made as

[1] Boyle. *op. cit.* p. 160.

presents to the Great Khan to whom Hülegü had dispatched a report on his conquests in Persia and Iraq and on his contemplated campaign against Syria.

The motives underlying the invasion of Syria are somewhat obscure. The hostility between Hülegü and the Ayyūbid Nāṣir Yūsuf, "personnage médiocre et sans courage", as Grousset[1] calls him, is too insubstantial of itself to account for so vast an operation. Christian influences may well have been in play, and it is perhaps only a simplification of the actual circumstances when the Armenian Haithon[2] represents his kinsman and namesake Het'um I of Little Armenia as holding counsel with Hülegü on the conquest of Palestine and as saying to the Īl-Khān: "Sire, the Sultan of Aleppo holds the lordship of the kingdom of Syria; and since you wish to recover the Holy Land, it seems to me best that you first of all lay siege to the city of Aleppo. For if thou canst take that city the others will soon be occupied." Aleppo was certainly Hülegü's first and main objective. He set out from Āzarbāījān on 12 September 1259, having sent on Ket-Buqa ahead with the advanced forces. As before, he commanded the centre in person, entrusting the right wing to Shiktür and Baiju and the left to Suqunchaq and his other commanders. The armies passed through the mountain pastures of Ala-Tagh to the east of Lake Vān: Hülegü was pleased with this region, afterwards a favourite summer resort of the Īl-Khāns, and gave it a Mongol name. The route continued through Akhlāṭ and the Hakkārī mountains, where there was great slaughter of the Kurdish inhabitants, into Diyārbakr. Here Hülegü set about the systematic subjugation of Upper Mesopotamia. Dispatching his son Yoshmut to Mayyāfāriqīn, which surrendered only after a long and desperate siege, and Malik Ṣāliḥ, the son of Badr al-Dīn Lu'lu', to Āmid, he himself captured Edessa, Dunaisir, Nasībīn and Ḥarrān. Then crossing the Euphrates, the Mongols appeared suddenly and unexpectedly before Aleppo, where they were joined by allies unmentioned by the Muslim sources, King Het'um and his son-in-law, Bohemond VI of Antioch. The siege of the town lasted less than a week, from 18 to 24 January 1260; the citadel held out till 25 February. There was the usual methodical massacre lasting six full days; and King Het'um had the satisfaction of setting fire to the great mosque. The fate of Aleppo led to the bloodless surrender of Ḥamā; and when the news reached Damascus Nāṣir Yūsuf fled towards Egypt while a deputation of

[1] *L'Empire des steppes*, p. 434.

[2] P. 302.

notables offered Hülegü the keys of the town. Ket-Buqa made a triumphal entry on 1 March accompanied by King Het'um and Bohemond; and the administration of Damascus was entrusted to a Mongol shaḥna with three Persian deputies.

By the early summer of 1260 the Īl-Khān's troops had penetrated as far as Gaza, and it seemed that the conquest of Syria would be followed by the invasion of Egypt. It was at this juncture that Hülegü received the news of the Great Khan's death (which had in fact occurred nearly a year ago, on 11 August 1259); and he at once returned to Persia, leaving Ket-Buqa in command of an army considerably reduced in numbers, only 20,000 men, according to Kirakos,[1] 10,000, according to Haithon[2] and Barhebraeus.[3] The motive for Hülegü's withdrawal can hardly have been, as Rashīd al-Dīn[4] implies, simply sorrow for the loss of his brother; he may have already felt some apprehension of a threat to his northern flank by Berke of the Golden Horde; but Haithon[5] is possibly right in suggesting that he saw himself as a candidate for the vacant throne. Rashīd al-Dīn[6] mentions only one point in his eastward journey: Akhlāṭ, which he reached on 7 June. According to Haithon,[7] he left his son Abaqa in command at Tabrīz and continued for several days in an easterly direction. Then, receiving news of the election of Qubilai as Great Khan, he returned to Tabrīz. It was probably here that he learnt, not, as stated by Haithon,[8] of encroachments by Berke in the Caucasus area, but of a disastrous defeat in Syria.

Before leaving Syria Hülegü had sent an embassy to Qutuz, the Mamlūk ruler of Egypt. His ambassadors, who offered the usual alternative of submission or war, had, on the advice of Baibars, Qutuz's commander-in-chief and successor (1260–77), been summarily executed, and the Egyptians had invaded Syria to gain a decisive victory over the Mongols. Crushing the forward post at Gaza they were able, thanks to the benevolent neutrality of the Franks of Acre, who had fallen foul of Ket-Buqa, to push forward along the coastline still held by the Crusaders. At Acre, revictualled by these temporary allies, they turned eastwards through Galilee towards the Jordan. The armies collided on 3 September at 'Ain Jālūt near Zarīn, and the Mongols were overwhelmed by the superior numbers of their opponents. The heroism of Ket-Buqa is described by Rashīd al-Dīn[9] in language reminiscent of the

[1] P. 388. [2] P. 303. [3] P. 436.
[4] Transl. Arends, p. 50. [5] P. 303. [6] *Loc. cit.*
[7] *Loc. cit.* [8] P. 304. [9] Transl. Arends, pp. 52–3.

native saga, the *Secret History of the Mongols*. The greater part of his forces turned in flight; he refused to follow their example. In a last message to his master he declares: "Let not the Khan be distressed with the loss of a single Mongol army. Let him imagine that during one year the wives of his soldiers did not conceive and the mares in their herds did not foal." Deserted by his men he fights on until his horse stumbles and he is taken prisoner. The exchange of taunts with his captor is in true Homeric style; and in his last words, before his head is struck off, he contrasts his own faithful service of his khan with the Mamlūk's rise to power by treachery and regicide.

The news of Ket-Buqa's defeat and death reached Hülegü in all probability at Tabrīz; it must have been shortly followed by reports of the Mongols' expulsion from the whole of Syria and their withdrawal across the Euphrates. It so happened that on the previous day Hülegü had received Nāṣir Yūsuf of Aleppo, on whom, in recognition of his renewed homage, he had conferred the governorship of Damascus. Doubts being now cast upon the Ayyūbid's loyalty, a detachment of horsemen were dispatched to intercept him on the journey back to Syria: they overtook and massacred the whole of the party, only the astronomer Muḥyī al-Dīn Maghribī being spared because of his profession. The re-conquest of Syria was attempted by a large force commanded either by Ilge, the ancestor of the Jalayirids, or by Köke-Ilge of the Uriyangqat, a kinsman of the great Sübedei. The Mongols advanced as far as Ḥimṣ, where, on 10 December, they were defeated in battle by the Egyptians and, for the second time, driven back across the Euphrates. So ended the first phase in the struggle between the Mongols and Mamlūks for the possession of Syria, a struggle in which the Īl-Khāns enjoyed the support of Armenian Cilicia and sought in vain the co-operation of Christian Europe: Öljeitü, the great grandson of Hülegü and the penultimate ruler (1304–16) of the dynasty, still hoped for some such united action against the common foe.

Hülegü's attention was now diverted to his northern frontier. The causes of the war with Berke, the ruler of the Golden Horde (1257–66), are variously given. Berke is represented by some authorities as the defender of Islam and as reproaching Hülegü for his devastation of so many Muslim countries and particularly for the execution of the caliph. It is more likely that the heirs of Jochi felt their rights endangered by the establishment of a Mongol kingdom in Persia. Arrān and Āzarbāījān, which had been incorporated in that kingdom, had already been trodden by "the hoof of Tartar horse"[1] in the reign of Chingiz-Khān and were therefore, according to the Conqueror's directions, part of the *yurt* or appanage of Jochi. The *casus belli* seems to have been the death, in apparently suspicious circumstances, of the three Jochid princes, Balaghai, Tutar and Quli, who had accompanied Hülegü to Persia.

Balaghai, according to Rashīd al-Dīn, in one place,[2] Tutar in another,[3] had been accused and convicted of sorcery, a capital offence with the Mongols, and had been sent to Berke as the head of his *ulus*. The latter, satisfied as to his guilt, had sent him back to Hülegü, who had carried out the sentence. The crime, as attributed to Balaghai, had taken place as early as 1256 or 1257, the execution (of Tutar) on 2 February 1260. The other two princes, Tutar (or Balaghai) and Quli, were alleged to have been poisoned. After the death of the princes their troops fled, some by way of Darband to the territory of the Golden Horde, others by way of Khurāsān to the Ghazna region, led by a general called Nīgūdar (Nigüder), whence the name of Nīgūdarīs by which they were afterwards to be known. The flight of these troops was apparently consequent upon a battle fought at some time in Shawwal 660/August–September 1262. It was at about the same time, on 2 Shawwal/ 20 August, that Hülegü set out from Ala-Tagh to meet Berke's army, which, led by the famous general Noqai (a kinsman, as Rashīd al-Dīn[4] is careful to point out, of the dead Tutar), had advanced southwards through Darband and encamped in the region of Shīrvān to the south of the south-eastern spur of the Caucasian range. Hülegü's advanced forces made contact with the army at Shamākhī in Dhu'l-Ḥijja/October–November and suffered some kind of defeat. Berke's men must nevertheless have retreated, for on 29 Dhu'l-Ḥijja/14 November they were in contact once again with these forward troops near Shābarān in the region of the present-day Kuba, well to the north of the mountains. This time victory went to the Persian Mongols, and Noqai himself was put to flight. On 20 November Hülegü advanced from Shamākhī at the head of the main army; Darband was taken by storm on 8 December and Noqai's forces routed for the second time on the 15th. Hülegü's triumph was, however, short-lived. A force under the nominal command of Hülegü's son and successor Abaqa was sent in pursuit of the fleeing army. Crossing the Terek they came upon their deserted but well-stocked encampment, where they feasted and caroused for three

[1] Juvainī, transl. Boyle, vol. I, p. 42.
[2] Transl. Verkhovsky, p. 81.
[3] Transl. Arends, p. 54.
[4] *Ibid.*

days before being attacked by Berke in person at the head of a great army. The battle raged all day (13 January 1263), and when the Persian Mongols, overwhelmed by their opponents' superior numbers, were withdrawing across the frozen Terek the ice gave way under their weight and many were drowned. Abaqa got back in safety to Shābarān, and the victorious Berke, after chasing his defeated enemies to the south of Darband, returned into his own territory, leaving Hülegü to retire in discomfiture to Tabrīz, where he arrived on 23 March. He began elaborate preparations for the renewal of the campaign against the Golden Horde, but in the event it was his son and successor Abaqa who liquidated the war with Berke.

Hülegü had also in these last years of his reign to cope with rebellious vassals. The faithful Badr al-Dīn Lu'lu' of Mosul had died in 1261 at an age of 96 lunar years, and his son Ṣāliḥ had entered into relations with the Mamlūk ruler Baibars. The Īl-Khān was warned of these activities by Ṣāliḥ's own wife, a daughter of Sulṭān Jalāl al-Dīn brought up by the Mongols, and an army was dispatched against Mosul. During a siege which seems to have lasted a full year an attempt was made by Baibars to relieve the town with Syrian troops: it fell in July or August 1262, the inhabitants being massacred and Ṣāliḥ himself, at Hülegü's express orders, subjected to a lingering death by a particularly loathsome form of torture. With the execution of Ṣāliḥ's infant son every memory of the dynasty founded in 1127 by 'Imād al-Dīn Zangī, the great champion of Islam against the Crusaders, was finally extinguished. In Fārs, meanwhile, another old vassal, the Atabeg Abū Bakr (1226–60) had died, and the behaviour of his third successor, Saljuq-Shāh (1262–4), led to the intervention of a Mongol army. Saljuq-Shāh fled to Kāzarūn, where he was captured and killed, and Hülegü bestowed the throne upon Princess Abish, a grand-daughter of Abū Bakr, whom he gave in marriage to his eleventh son, Mengü-Temür (1256–82): she was the last of the Salghurids.

Hülegü died on 8 February 1265 in his winter quarters on the Jaghatu (the present-day Zarīneh Rūd), one of the four rivers which discharge into Lake Reẓā'īyeh from the south: he was in his 49th year. He was laid to rest in the castle on the island of Shāhī where his treasures were stored, his grave being the traditional Royal Tomb of the Northern peoples: this is the last occasion on which human victims are recorded as having been buried with a Chingizid prince. His death was shortly followed (17 June 1265) by that of his chief wife, Doquz

Khatun, the niece of the Kereit ruler Ong-Khān, to whose influence is to be largely attributed his benevolent attitude towards the Christians.

The achievements of Hülegü as a conqueror and empire-builder have not perhaps been fully appreciated. In either capacity he will bear comparison with his cousin Batu or his brother Qubilai, the founders respectively of the Golden Horde and the Yüan dynasty. Having destroyed both the 'Abbāsid Caliphate and its Ismā'īlī opponents he extended the Mongol conquests to the shores of the Mediterranean and left to his successors dominion (subject, nominally, to the Great Khan) over a territory corresponding to the greater part of what we now call the Middle East. It is, however, not for nothing that we speak of the Īl-Khāns of *Persia*, just as to William Adam Hülegü was *imperator Persidis*.[1] The Mongol was, in fact, *mutatis mutandis* as much Emperor of Iran as the Norman William was King of England. He and his successors created at least the pre-conditions for a national state; Iran ceased to be a mere geographical expression, and its rulers, for the first time since late antiquity, entered into direct diplomatic relations with the West. The dynasty founded by Hülegü may be said to have paved the way, however unwittingly, for the centralizing and nationalistic policies of the Ṣafavids.

ABAQA

Immediately upon Hülegü's death the roads were closed, in accordance with the Mongol custom, and a ban laid on all movement from place to place. Summoned from his winter-quarters in Māzandarān Abaqa, the Īl-Khān's eldest son and heir-apparent and the most obvious candidate for the throne, did not in fact present himself until 9 March. Another candidate, his younger brother Yoshmut, had arrived on the Jaghatu only a week after his father's death but, realizing his lack of support, had returned almost at once to his post on the northern frontier at Darband. Abaqa, upon his arrival, was received with respect and deference and, the mourning ceremonies once completed, was, by the unanimous decision of the assembled princes and amīrs, invited to ascend the throne. In accepting, after the conventional show of hesitance, he stipulated that his election should first have the sanction of the Great Khan. The ceremony of enthronement took place on 19 June, a date selected as auspicious by Naṣīr al-Dīn Ṭūsī, on the shores of the Chaghan Na'ur ("White Lake"), the modern Tualā, in the

[1] See Boyle "The Death of the Last 'Abbāsid Caliph", p. 149 n. 5.

Farāhān district to the north of Sulṭānābād (Arāk). Here the new Īl-Khān proceeded to appoint his commanders and officials: Shams al-Dīn Juvainī, chosen as vizier by his father, was retained in that office, while his brother, the historian, whom Hülegü had made governor of Baghdad, now became lieutenant to the noyan Suqunchaq, the viceroy of 'Irāq-i 'Arab and Fārs. For his capital Abaqa chose Tabrīz in preference to Marāgheh favoured by his father; his summer residences he fixed at Ala-Tagh and Siyāh-Kūh (the range which forms the watershed between the Jaghatu and the Qizil Uzūn) and his winter residences in Baghdad, Arrān and the warm valley of the Jaghatu.

Hostilities with the Golden Horde were resumed at the very commencement of Abaqa's reign. On 19 July 1265 Yoshmut advanced northwards against Noqai, who had invaded the Īl-Khān's territory at the head of a large army. In a fierce battle fought on the Aq-Su, a river descending into Shīrvān from the southern slopes of the Caucasus, Noqai was wounded and put to flight. Abaqa now followed his brother over the Kur to collide with Berke at the head of 300,000 horse; he recrossed the river and for a fortnight the two armies faced each other across the water, exchanging volleys of arrows. In search of a crossing Berke proceeded upstream towards Tiflis; he died *en route*, his body was carried back to Sarai for burial and his leaderless troops dispersed to their homes. As a kind of Hadrian's Wall along his northern frontier Abaqa caused a great *sibē* or palisade to be erected along the left bank of the Kur, a day's journey in length according to Haithon,[1] a deep moat being dug between the sibē and the river. Leaving his brother Mengü-Temür with a mixed force of Mongols and Muslims to defend these fortifications the Īl-Khān set out for Khurāsān, passing the winter of 1266–7 in various encampments in Māzandarān and Gurgān.

It was during this winter, or perhaps a year or two later, that Abaqa was visited by Mas'ūd Beg, the son of the celebrated Muḥammad Yalavach and the governor of the whole agricultural zone of Central Asia from the Uighur country westwards. The object of this visit was ostensibly to collect revenues due to Baraq, the ruler (1266–71) of the Chaghatai Khanate, and to his eastern neighbour Qaidu, of whom Baraq was first a rival and then a satellite; but the real purpose of Mas'ūd Beg's journey was to spy out the land for Baraq, who had been encouraged by Qaidu in his plans for invading the territories of Abaqa.

[1] P. 336. He takes Cyba (Ciba), i.e. *sibē*, to be the name of a place in the vicinity of the wall.

A day after Mas'ūd's departure the news was received of the appearance of a hostile army on the Oxus. The Īl-Khān dispatched a party to apprehend him, but he eluded their pursuit and crossed the Oxus just as they reached the left bank. In the course of another embassy to Abaqa (apparently in the winter of 1267–8, when the Īl-Khān was again in Māzandarān and Gurgān) the emissaries of Baraq presented Prince Tegüder, a grandson of Chaghatai who had led a contingent westward under Hülegü, with a special kind of arrow known as *toghana*, discreetly indicating that there was a message hidden inside it. In the message Baraq apprised his kinsman of his intention and appealed for his co-operation. Returning to his fief in Georgia Tegüder, after consulting with his amīrs, decided to make his way into Baraq's territory by way of Darband. The Īl-Khān's suspicions had by now been aroused, and the noyan Shiremün, the son of Chormaghun, was sent in his pursuit; finding the passage through Darband barred, he returned to Georgia, still pursued by Shiremün, hid for a while in a great forest, was overtaken and defeated in battle and finally, in the autumn of 1269, surrendered to Abaqa. He was imprisoned for a year on an island in Lake Urmīyeh and then released after Baraq's defeat. Until his death, though not perhaps restored to favour, he enjoyed free access to the Īl-Khān's court. The story of his revolt is told with many curious details in the Georgian Chronicle[1] and in the *History of the Nation of the Archers* of the Armenian Grigor.[2] Tegüder's name has often been misread as Nigüder (Nīgūdar) and has in consequence been connected with the Nīgūdarīs, who, as we have seen, were in fact the troops of the Jochid princes Tutar and Quli.

Baraq's first hostile move was to demand that Tübshin, Abaqa's younger brother and commander in Khurāsān and Māzandarān, should evacuate the meadowlands of Bādghīs, which he claimed, along with the territories stretching southwards to the Indus, to be the hereditary property of his own ulus. It was only after an exchange of angry messages with Tübshin and Abaqa himself that he moved his forces towards the Oxus. Qaidu, to whom he had appealed for assistance, had sent, according to Vaṣṣāf,[3] a whole host of princes to swell his army; but Rashīd al-Dīn mentions only two, Qïpchaq and Chabat, a grandson and great grandson respectively of the Great Khan Ögedei. The Chaghatai princes crossed the river in the spring of 1270 and advanced to Marū-

[1] Quoted by Howorth, vol. II, pp. 229–31.

[2] Transl. Blake and Frye, pp. (107)–(109).

[3] Transl. Hammer-Purgstall, p. 134.

chaq, where Tübshin was awaiting them. Qaidu, who saw himself in the role of *tertius gaudens* in this conflict, had instructed his two kinsmen, according to Rashīd al-Dīn,[1] to find some pretext for withdrawing their forces upon the first contact with Tübshin, and this they contrived to do, to Baraq's no small embarrassment. Tübshin, who was accompanied by the veteran Arghun Aqa, seems nevertheless to have been unequal to opposing the invader and retired into Māzandarān to await the approach of his brother at the head of the main army.

Abaqa set out from Mīāneh in Āzarbāījān on 27 April 1270. The crops were beginning to come up and the Īl-Khān, so Rashīd al-Dīn[2] tells us, "out of his perfect justice" forbade his troops to harm even a single ear. In the great plain between Abhar and Zanjān, which the Mongols called Qongqur-Öleng ("Brown Meadow") and where Öljeitü afterwards built his capital Sulṭānīyeh, he was met by an ambassador from the Great Khan, a man called Tekechük, who had been detained by Baraq, had managed to escape and was able to inform Abaqa of the conditions prevailing in the enemy's camp. The Īl-Khān accelerated his pace and, passing through Ray, was welcomed by Tübshin and Arghun Aqa in Qūmis. They proceeded together to the meadows of Rādkān, where Abaqa distributed largesse to the troops and presents to the amīrs, and from thence by way of Bākharz into Bādghīs. Abaqa, whose patrols had already made contact with Baraq's forces, now sent an emissary to offer terms of peace. Baraq was in the Ṭāliqān area, which he had made his headquarters. Despite the defection of Qïpchaq and Chabat he had succeeded in conquering the greater part of Khurāsān. On 19 May 1270 his troops had attacked and pillaged the town of Nīshāpūr, razed to the ground by their forebears nearly fifty years before, but had vacated it the next day. He had also meditated a similar attack on Herāt but had been persuaded of the unwisdom of such an action and had sought instead to win over the allegiance of the ruler of Herāt, the Malik Shams al-Dīn Kart. The latter was rescued from an embarrassing position by the news of the approach of Abaqa at the head of a great army; he withdrew into his castle to wait upon events.

The terms which Abaqa's emissary transmitted to Baraq were generous enough. In return for the cessation of hostilities the Īl-Khān offered to cede the territory stretching from Bādghīs southwards to the Indus. One at least of Baraq's amīrs was in favour of accepting these terms, but he was overruled by the bellicose majority and, despite the

[1] Transl. Arends, p. 74.

[2] *Op. cit.* p. 77.

warning of Baraq's astrologer, it was decided to launch an immediate attack. Doubt had been cast on the actual presence of Abaqa in Khurāsān, and it was suggested that this was a false report put about by Tübshin and Arghun Aqa for their own ends. Accordingly three scouts were sent on ahead to ascertain the facts. They were captured by Abaqa's men on the very spot that had been selected for the battlefield. This was a broad plain at the foot of the mountains with a river, which the Mongols called Qara Su, flowing in front of it. Brought before Abaqa the scouts were soon intimidated into declaring the nature of their mission; and the Īl-Khān conceived the idea of deceiving the enemy by means of their own spies. Leaving his tent for a moment he gave the necessary instructions to one of his men. He then returned to resume the drinking bout with his generals, the three scouts remaining, as heretofore, bound to the tent pole. An hour or two later the officer whom he had so instructed entered in the guise of a courier to declare, with simulated agitation, that Abaqa's territories had been invaded by a great army from the Golden Horde and that all was lost unless the Īl-Khān returned immediately. Affecting to believe this message Abaqa ordered his forces to abandon the camp and baggage and leave for Māzandarān that very night. At the moment of departure he detailed an officer to execute the three scouts but told him *sotto voce* to let one escape. As the army passed Herāt the governor was ordered to close the gates of the town to Baraq; they halted at the place chosen for the battlefield which Rashīd al-Dīn here calls Dasht-i Chīna, perhaps the Plain of the Wolf (Mongol *china* "wolf").

Meanwhile the sole surviving scout had made off post-haste to bear the imagined good tidings to Baraq. Elated with the news the Chaghatai army advanced westwards the next morning in pursuit, as they thought, of a fleeing army. The Herātīs had closed their gates as ordered but Baraq, though angered by their action, was in no mood to turn aside from the chase. Crossing the Harī Rūd the troops beheld the deserted encampment spread out before them and fell gleefully to pillaging it. Finally sated with plunder they halted to the south of Herāt and passed the remainder of the day in feasting and revelry. The next day they continued the advance westwards along the river and had ridden for about two hours when they suddenly emerged on to a broad plain covered from end to end with Abaqa's men. Baraq drew up his forces on the river bank, to meet, as best he could, the Īl-Khān's attack. Despite the advantage of surprise all did not at first go in Abaqa's favour, and his left wing was driven back as far as Pūshang (on the site of the modern Ghurian); but their pursuers were thrown into disarray, and, with the third charge of Abaqa's army, the enemy broke before them. Baraq's horse was killed beneath him and he escaped across the Oxus on the mount of one of his guards; he was accompanied by only 5,000 of his men, whose losses would have been even greater but for rear-guard action on the part of Jalayirtai, the same general who had driven back Abaqa's left wing. The Battle of Herāt (as it may be called) was fought on 22 July 1270: henceforth, apart from the incursions of Esen-Buqa and Yasa'ur in the reign of Öljeitü, the eastern frontiers of Iran were to remain comparatively inviolate until the rise of Tīmūr.

Leaving Tübshin in command of Khurāsān and Māzandarān the Īl-Khān returned to Āzarbāijān, reaching Marāgheh on 18 October and the *ordus* of his wives in the Jaghatu valley on 6 November. Here he received the ambassadors of the Great Khan, the bearers of a yarlīgh conferring upon him the Khanate of Iran; and here, in accordance with that yarlīgh, the ceremony of enthronement was performed for a second time on 26 November. It is now that we hear for the last time of Naṣīr al-Dīn Ṭūsī. During an hunting expedition in the Jaghatu valley the Īl-Khān had been gored by a bison (*gāv-i kūhī*). The primitive first aid of an attendant had stopped the bleeding, but the wound suppurated and an abscess was formed which none of Abaqa's physicians dared to open. Naṣīr al-Dīn gave it as his opinion that the operation could be performed without danger; and the lancing was successfully carried out, under his supervision, by a Muslim surgeon. The great philosopher died four years later in Baghdad and Rashīd al-Dīn[1] records some curious details about the circumstances of his burial. His scientific work has been dealt with elsewhere in this volume. A true disciple of Avicenna, "he held fast"—in the words of Barhebraeus,[2] a Christian collaborator at Marāgheh—"to the opinions of the early philosophers, and he combated vigorously in his writing those who contradicted them".

In the following decade the Īl-Khān himself took little or no part in military operations. In 1271 there was an echo from the past when the Ismā'īlī castle of Gird-Kūh finally surrendered. It had withstood a continuous siege of eighteen years, having been first invested by Ket-Buqa in May 1253. In Transoxiana, which remained without an effective ruler from the death of Baraq (9 August 1270) till the accession of his son Du'a (1282), Abaqa was able to avenge himself for the invasion of

[1] Transl. Verkhovsky, p. 200. [2] P. 452.

Khurāsān. In the course of a campaign (1272–3) suggested and partially led by a renegade Chaghatai officer, Bukhārā was sacked and burnt and as a result of this and subsequent troubles remained depopulated for seven years. Only in Asia Minor was Abaqa called upon to intervene in person.

Of the two sultans of Rūm Kai-Kā'us II was now an exile in the Crimea and Qïlïch-Arslan IV had been put to death by his vizier Mu'īn al-Dīn Sulaimān, better known as the Parvāna (*Ṣāḥib Parvāna*, "Keeper of the Seals"). Though Qïlïch-Arslan's infant son was the titular ruler the administration of the country was and remained in the hands of the Parvāna. That he was in correspondence with the Mamlūks seems indisputable; whether he authorized the deputation of Rūmī notables (including, according to Rashīd al-Dīn, his own son) who in 1276 invited Baibars to attempt the conquest of Rūm is not so clear. The invitation was in any case accepted and, in the spring of 1277, the Mamlūk sultan invaded the territory of the Saljuqs, inflicted a crushing defeat on the Mongol army of occupation at Abulustān (the modern Albustan) on the Upper Jaiḥān (15 April), made a triumphal entry into Qaiṣariyya (Kayseri) a week later and then, with equal rapidity, withdrew into his own territory. News of this disaster was brought to Abaqa at Tabrīz, and he set out forthwith for Asia Minor. At Abulustān he inspected the battlefield, and shed tears over the piles of Mongol dead; then angered with the lukewarmness of his Saljuq allies, he gave orders for the devastation of an area stretching from Qaiṣariyya to Erzerum, calling a halt to the rapine and slaughter only upon the intercession of his vizier the *ṣāḥib-dīvān* Shams al-Dīn Juvainī. It was at first his intention to enter Syria in pursuit of Baibars but, convinced of the difficulties of military operation in the height of summer, he postponed till the following winter a campaign which in the event was not to be launched till the autumn of 1281. He spent the remainder of the summer in Ala-Tagh, whither the Parvāna, who had discreetly withdrawn to Ṭūqāt (Tokat) during the hostilities, was brought for trial. His guilt established, he was put to death on 2 August 1277. There is perhaps some truth in Haithon's[1] story that his body was cut up and eaten in some sort of cannibalistic ritual.

Some weeks after the execution of the Parvāna the ṣāḥib-dīvān was sent to restore peace and order in the Saljuq territories. This task completed we find him in the Darband area pacifying the mountain tribes of what

[1] P. 309

is now Daghestan, "peoples", says Rashīd al-Dīn,[1] "that have never been subdued by anyone in any period". It was at this time, about the year 1277, that the great minister was first exposed to the machinations of rivals seeking to encompass his downfall. Of these the most dangerous and persistent was a certain Majd al-Mulk, a former protégé of Shams al-Dīn. On the basis of some chance remarks by one Majd al-Dīn, a confidant of the ṣāḥib-dīvān's brother 'Alā' al-Dīn, he accused both brothers of being in league with the Mamlūks. The accusation was made in a statement to Yesü-Buqa, a son-in-law of Hülegü, and in due course was brought to the notice of Abaqa, who ordered an inquiry. The unfortunate Majd al-Dīn was put to the question but refused to make any admission of guilt, so that Majd al-Mulk was not able to press the charge. However, three years later in the spring of 1279, he succeeded in gaining access to Prince Arghun, Abaqa's elder son and second successor (1284–91), and convincing him not only that the ṣāḥib-dīvān was in treasonable correspondence with the Egyptians but also that he had embezzled huge sums from the Treasury. Arghun repeated these accusations to his father, who did not, however, take any action until he had himself been approached by Majd al-Mulk in the spring of the following year. It was only through the intercession of one of the royal ladies that Shams al-Dīn was saved from the Īl-Khān's wrath, though Abaqa's suspicions do not seem to have been entirely allayed and the ṣāḥib-dīvān was not fully restored to favour. Against Shams al-Dīn's brother 'Alā' al-Dīn, the historian and governor of Baghdad, the intrigues of Majd al-Mulk were more successful: he was twice arrested and was actually being taken to Hamadān for trial at the time of Abaqa's death.

The Īl-Khān's plans for an attack on Syria, for which, as we shall see, he had long been seeking an alliance with the powers of the Christian West, were interrupted by a threat from an unexpected quarter. In the winter of 1278–9 a force of Nīgūdarīs or Qaraunas (as they called themselves and are called by Marco Polo) invaded Kirmān and Fārs from their base in southern Afghanistan. Rashīd al-Dīn's[2] and Vaṣṣāf's[3] accounts of these operations are difficult to reconcile; the latter authority writes in much greater detail and speaks of a second campaign three years later in which the invaders penetrated to the shores of the Persian Gulf. The present incursion seems to have little more than a large-scale

[1] Transl. Arends, p. 92. [2] *Ibid.* p. 94.
[3] Bombay ed. pp. 199–202.

raid, from which they returned, with their prisoners and booty, to the region of Sīstān. Here in the town of the same name (the earlier Zarang) they were besieged by Prince Arghun in the summer (July–August) of 1279; they offered but slight resistance and, upon the surrender of the town, their leaders, including a grandson of the Chaghatai khan Mubārak-Shāh (1266) were taken to Herāt, where they paid homage to Abaqa (12 August 1279). The ruler or commander of these freebooters was until 698/1298–9 a great-grandson of Chaghatai called 'Abdallāh, a convert (as his name indicates) to Islam. He was then recalled by the Chaghatai khan Du'a (1282–1306) and replaced by the latter's son, Qutlugh-Khwāja, under whom in 1300 the Nīgūdarīs launched yet another attack upon Fārs, an action, says Rashīd al-Dīn,[1] on which they would not have ventured but for the preoccupation of Ghazan's forces in Syria.

To Syria Abaqa was now at last able to give his full attention. He had been in correspondence with the pope since 1267 (and apparently earlier); in 1273 he had written both to the pope and to Edward I of England. In the following year his envoys had repeated the message at the Council of Lyons; in 1276 they were in Italy and in 1277 in England. To these appeals for an alliance against a common enemy Abaqa had received no positive reply, and he decided to act alone. In September 1281 an army of some 40,000 men under the command of the Īl-Khān's brother Mengü-Temür entered Syria by way of 'Ain Ṭāb. As in Hülegü's invasion twenty years earlier, the King of Little Armenia, now Het'um's son Leon III, had contributed his contingent of troops. The clash with the Egyptians occurred near Ḥimṣ on 30 October. The battle is described in the greatest detail by the Egyptian historians; Rashīd al-Dīn, writing for Ghazan and Öljeitü, is naturally disinclined to dwell upon a humiliating defeat of their grandfather's forces. The Mongol right wing, composed of Oirats, Armenians and Georgians, drove back their opponents to the gates of Ḥimṣ, but in the centre, Mengü-Temür, a young and inexperienced commander, was wounded by an Egyptian officer and turning in flight was followed by the greater part of his army. He recrossed the Euphrates with such of his forces as had not drowned in the river or died of thirst in the desert and made for his mother's apanage in Upper Mesopotamia.

News of this *débacle* was brought to Abaqa in the Mosul area. For some unaccountable reason, instead of taking personal charge of the

[1] *Loc. cit.*

campaign, he had chosen to remain to the east of the Euphrates, engaged apparently on a large-scale hunting expedition, first on the Khābūr and then on the Euphrates opposite Raḥbat al-Shām: fighting broke out with the inhabitants, though Rashīd al-Dīn[1] specifically mentions that the Īl-Khān did not cross the river. On 15 October he turned back towards Sinjār and on the 30th rejoined his ordus in the vicinity of Mosul. He was extremely angry with the news, declaring that those responsible would be called to account in a quriltai to be held the next summer and that he would then take the field in person to avenge his brother's defeat. He was to be denied this satisfaction. After passing the greater part of the winter in Baghdad (it was during this period that 'Alā' al-Dīn Juvainī was arrested, released and re-arrested) he set out for Hamadān, where he arrived on 18 March 1282 and where, after a bout of heavy drinking, he died in a state of *delirium tremens* on 1 April. He was laid to rest alongside his father on the island of Shāhī.

"Khulagu and Abaka", says Howorth,[2] "were two important figures in Asiatic history. They conquered and controlled a vast empire with vigour and prudence. Their successors, until we reach the reign of Ghazan, were for the most part weak and decrepit rulers, whose authority was gradually disintegrating. Had it not, in fact, been for the utter desolation and prostration caused by the campaigns of Jingis and Khulagu in Persia, they would undoubtedly have been driven out and displaced; and, as it was, a very little more aggressive vigour on the part of the Egyptian rulers who controlled the various forces of Islam would no doubt have led to the collapse of the empire of the Ilkhans." It is certainly true that not until the accession of Ghazan was the Īl-Khānid state ruled by a prince capable of reviving and continuing the policies of Hülegü and Abaqa.

TEGÜDER (AḤMAD)

After Abaqa's death the royal ladies, the princes of the blood and the great amīrs gathered together in Marāgheh to observe the usual ceremonies of mourning; they then proceeded to the Jaghatu valley to elect his successor. Of the two candidates for the throne Tegüder, Hülegü's seventh and eldest surviving son, was the more strongly supported, and the other candidate, Abaqa's eldest son Arghun, was persuaded to stand down in his favour. He was proclaimed on 6 May

[1] Transl. Arends, p. 98.

[2] Vol. III, p. 393.

1282, apparently still in the winter residence on the Ja<u>gh</u>atu; but the actual enthronement took place in Ala-Ta<u>gh</u> more than a month later, on 21 June. As a convert to Islam (it is not known of how long standing) he assumed the name of Aḥmad and the title of sultan.

It was at Ala-Ta<u>gh</u> that 'Alā' al-Dīn Juvainī was cleared of Majd al-Mulk's charges and reinstated in the governorship of Baghdad, whilst his accuser, condemned in turn, was lynched by the mob before the death sentence could be carried out. His brother, the ṣāḥib-dīvān, was likewise fully restored to favour, and it was at his advice that Tegüder now sought to establish friendly relations with the sultan of Egypt, a step diametrically opposed, as he admits himself in his letter to Qïla'un, to the wishes of his fellow princes, who at the quriltai just concluded had unanimously resolved upon the resumption of hostilities with the Mamlūks. The embassy which set out from Ala-Ta<u>gh</u> on 25 August was coolly received. A mission in the following year fared even worse. The ambassador and his staff were cast into prison, where the former actually died. He could in any case have accomplished nothing for the delivery of his message had been anticipated by the news of Tegüder's dethronement and death.

Relations between the khan and his disappointed rival had rapidly deteriorated. Much of the latter's animus was directed against Tegüder's protégés, the Juvainī brothers, particularly <u>Sh</u>ams al-Dīn, whom he accused—and the charge seems to have been widely believed—of having poisoned his father. The winter of 1282–3 he spent in Baghdad, where he revived the old charge of embezzlement against 'Alā' al-Dīn, whose agents he arrested and put to the torture: he caused the body of one man, who had recently died, to be exhumed and flung upon the highway. News of these activities reached 'Alā' al-Dīn in Arrān and brought on a stroke: he died on 5 March 1283. In the spring Ar<u>gh</u>un returned from Baghdad to <u>Kh</u>urāsān, of which his father had made him viceroy and where he now began to prepare for open rebellion against Tegüder. He had an ally and perhaps a rival in his uncle Prince Qongqurtai, the ninth son of Hülegü and viceroy of Rūm. In Arrān, where he was in attendance on Tegüder, Qongqurtai formed, or was said to have formed, a conspiracy to seize the khan's person during the celebration of the Mongol New Year falling in January 1284. He was arrested by Tegüder's son-in-law, the Georgian general Alinaq, on 17 January and executed on the following day; and with Qongqurtai out of the way the khan at once moved against his fellow conspirator Ar<u>gh</u>un. From an army of 100,000 men now at his disposal he dispatched, on 29 January, an advanced force of 15,000 horse under the command of Alinaq; he himself, at the head of the main army, set out from Pīl-Suvār in Mūghān on 26 April. On the 31st he received news of the approach of Arghun's army and instructed Alinaq to offer battle if his forces were superior in number but otherwise to await his own arrival. There was a clash between the advance parties of either army at Khail-i Buzurg between Qazvīn and Ray, and a pitched battle was fought at Aq-Khwāja (Sumghān) to the south of Qazvīn on 4 May. Though the result seems on the whole to have been a victory for Arghun, he saw fit to withdraw eastwards, and the khan's forces continued to advance. At Aq-Khwāja Tegüder received a deputation bearing a conciliatory message from Arghun. Against the advice of his generals he rejected these overtures and pressed onwards. A second deputation headed by Prince Ghazan, the future Īl-Khān, reached him in the Simnān area on 31 May. His reply was that Arghun should demonstrate his sincerity either by presenting himself in person or by sending his brother Geikhatu. This message he caused to be delivered by a deputation of princes and amīrs, one of whom, Buqa, was secretly in sympathy with Arghun. Despite an undertaking made to Buqa that, as a conciliatory gesture, he would halt at Khurqān, Tegüder advanced to a place called Kālpūsh to the north of Jājarm, where it had been Arghun's intention to make a stand. At Kālpūsh, on 28 June, he was rejoined by his ambassadors bringing with them Prince Geikhatu and two of Arghun's amīrs, one of them the famous Nauruz. Buqa was annoyed to find that Tegüder had not kept his word; he ventured to argue with the khan, who expressed his displeasure by the use of threatening language and by deposing him from his office. As the result of this treatment Buqa became, in Rashīd al-Dīn's[1] words, "still more ardent a partisan of Arghun" with the direst consequences to Tegüder. Meanwhile, at Qūchān, which he reached on 7 July, the Īl-Khān learnt that Arghun, with only a small following, had taken refuge in the famous mountain stronghold of Kalāt (the later Kalāt-i Nādirī). Approached by Alinaq at the head of Tegüder's advanced forces he was persuaded to come down from the castle and surrender to his uncle (11 July 1284). Tegüder, after receiving him with apparent kindness, handed him over to Alinaq to be kept under guard until such time as he could be tried in the presence of the khan's mother, Princess Qutui. Then, conceiving a

[1] Transl. Arends, p. 109.

desire for the company of his most recently married wife, he set out for his *oghruq* or base camp at Kālpūsh, leaving Alinaq in charge of the prisoner and the princes in command of the army. Buqa availed himself of his opportunity. Arghun was released, and Alinaq killed; and, with the co-operation of the princes and commanders favourable to Arghun, all supporters of Tegüder had soon been eliminated. "At night", says Rashīd al-Dīn,[1] "Arghun was a prisoner, and in the morning he was monarch of the face of the earth."

News of this reversal of his fortunes reached Tegüder while still *en route* to Kālpūsh. He halted for a brief space and then, on 10 July, fled westwards along the great Khurāsān road. Within three days he was in Qongqur-Öleng, where he looted Buqa's ordu and was only restrained by the Amīr Suqunchaq from harming his wife and family. On 17 July he reached his own ordus, probably in Soghurluq (in Turkish "the place abounding in marmots"), the Mongols' summer residence at Shīz (Takht-i-Sulaimān), the site of the famous fire-temple.[2] It was his intention to make for Darband and escape into the territory of the Golden Horde; but messengers arriving from Arghun with news of his changed circumstances, he was placed under close arrest by the officers in charge of the ordus. It was at this juncture that a band of Qaraunas, whom Buqa had caused to be dispatched in his pursuit, burst into the camp, which they pillaged with an indiscriminate savagery graphically described by Vaṣṣāf:[3] "nothing was left", says Rashīd al-Dīn,[4] "save the ashes in the fire-places." They took Tegüder into their own custody handing him over to Arghun when, on 26 July, he arrived in the ordus. At a place called Āb-i-Shūr ("Salt Water") near Yüz Aghach (in Turkish "Hundred Trees"), an unidentified summer residence somewhere in the Ūjān region, Tegüder was brought to trial, the main charge being the execution of Qongqurtai. He expressed contrition for his past actions, and Arghun himself was in favour of clemency, but the protests of Qongqurtai's family and the possibility of a rising in Hamadān prevailed upon him to pass the death sentence. It was carried out on 10 August 1284: as in the case of his victim Qongqurtai his back was broken, a form of execution designed, like the use of the bowstring, to avoid the shedding of royal blood.

There is little or no evidence to support Howorth's[5] contention that

[1] *Op. cit.* p. 111.
[2] See Minorsky, *Iranica* p. 101.
[3] See d'Ohsson, vol. III, p. 605; Howorth, vol. III, p. 307.
[4] Transl. Arends, p. 113.
[5] Vol. III, p. 308.

his death "was mainly due to his patronage of Muhammedanism, which set against him the conservative feeling, both political and religious, of the Mongol chieftains". His overtures to the Mamlūks might well have offended national susceptibilities but can hardly have been widely known of during his lifetime. In patronizing the Juvainīs he merely followed the example of his shamanist or Buddhist father and brother. Like them he was, according to Barhebraeus,[1] favourably disposed towards the Christian sects; and Ra<u>sh</u>īd al-Dīn[2] specifically mentions his employment of Georgian and Armenian troops in his campaign against Ar<u>gh</u>un. He does not, in short, despite the contrary testimony of Haithon,[3] give the impression of a bigoted convert to Islam; and his downfall was probably due, not to an active or passive religious policy, but simply, as afterwards in the cases of his nephews Geikhatu and Baidu, to his ineffectiveness as a ruler.

ARGHUN

The enthronement of Ar<u>gh</u>un followed closely upon the execution of his uncle; it took place, according to Ra<u>sh</u>īd al-Dīn,[4] on the next day, i.e. 11 August 1284. Only the royal ladies and the amīrs were present, the princes, Ar<u>gh</u>un's brothers, cousins and uncles, having not yet arrived. Ra<u>sh</u>īd al-Dīn,[5] it is true, speaks of his uncle Hula<u>ch</u>u as playing a leading part in the ceremony; but this is probably an anachronistic reference to the second ceremony, held on 7 April 1286, after Ar<u>gh</u>un's accession had been officially sanctioned by the Great Khan. At the time of the first ceremony Hula<u>ch</u>u still saw himself as a rival candidate for the throne; it was only at the quriltai held in the spring or summer of 1285 that he was reconciled with his nephew and accepted, jointly with Ar<u>gh</u>un's brother Geikhatu, the viceroyalty of Rūm. At the same quriltai Ar<u>gh</u>un's son <u>Gh</u>azan received the provinces of <u>Kh</u>urāsān, Māzandarān, Qūmis and Ray. Buqa's services had been recognized much earlier. Already in the autumn of 1284 Ar<u>gh</u>un had appointed him his vizier and, as a more spectacular demonstration of his gratitude, had caused gold to be poured over him until he was all but buried in the pile. Buqa's predecessor, <u>Sh</u>ams al-Dīn Juvainī, fared very differently. After his master's downfall he had made his way first to Iṣfahān and then to Qum, from whence he had been urged to escape to

[1] P. 467.   [2] Transl. Arends, p. 106.   [3] P. 312.
[4] Transl. Arends p. 115.   [5] *Loc. cit.*

India by way of Hurmuz. However, reassured by the proclamation of a general amnesty, he decided to throw himself on the mercy of the new khan. Arghun was then at Qurban Shire (in Mongol "Three Thrones"), somewhere in the vicinity of Soghurluq. Here Shams al-Dīn arrived on 23 September 1284, and through the good offices of Buqa, with whom he had previously been on friendly terms, he was appointed the latter's deputy. This improvement in his fortunes was of very brief duration; the victim of intriguers, who had once been his *protégés*, he was put to death at the gates of Ahar on 16 October 1284.

Such was the end of the great minister, whose role under the Īl-Khāns may be compared, not unaptly, with that of Niẓām al-Mulk under the Saljuqs. Barhebraeus,[1] an observer certainly not prejudiced in his favour, bears witness that "the whole kingdom of the House of Mâghôgh [i.e. Magog, the Mongols] hung on his finger, for he was very sagacious with an understanding nature; and he was well instructed in the greater number of the sciences and the various kinds of learning". His successor's term of office lasted little more than four years. His arrogance soon raised him enemies; their numbers increased as the result of his activities in Fārs (still nominally ruled by Princess Abish), where he had been sent to restore order after a popular rising against the Mongols; and perceiving that he had lost the khan's favour he became involved in a conspiracy in which several of the princes seem to have been implicated. Betrayed by Arghun's cousin Jüshkeb, who had affected an interest in the plot in order to obtain the names of the conspirators, Buqa was put to death on 16 January 1289. He was succeeded as vizier by a Jewish physician, Sa'd al-Daula of Abhar, "the most influential Jew not only of Azerbaijan but of Persia as a whole, after Mordecai and Esther, and after Ezra and Nehemiah, ever to play a role in the political arena of Persia".[2] Sa'd al-Daula had first won the Īl-Khān's confidence as a financial administrator, when sent to Baghdad to restore the economy after the large-scale peculations of Buqa and his brother Aruq. A man of pleasing address conversant with both the Turkish and the Mongol languages, he so ingratiated himself with Arghun that the latter, in June 1289, bestowed upon him the vizierate of his Empire. The rule of a Jew over a predominantly Muslim community must of itself have caused widespread resentment, and such resentment was naturally aggravated by his practising the usual nepotism of his age and time and distributing the key posts in the

[1] P. 473.

[2] Fischel, "Azerbaijan in Jewish History", p. 8 n. 19

administration amongst his relations and co-religionists. Nevertheless even a hostile witness such as Vaṣṣāf is constrained to admit that Sa'd al-Daula "established the administration on the basis of law and justice; that his reforms led to the disappearance of oppression, robbery and thieving, to security and facilitation of the pilgrimage to Mecca; that the finances of the state were consolidated and that all the inhabitants benefited from his successful efforts".[1] The story, recounted by Vaṣṣāf,[2] that he contemplated founding a new religion with the khan as its prophet is probably pure invention. Despite his unpopularity he retained Arghun's favour to the very end, his adversaries venturing to attack him only when the Īl-Khān was on his death-bed.

Though he had won his throne by the sword Arghun appears only twice to have taken the field during the course of his reign: in the spring of 1288 and again in the spring of 1290, the forces under his command repelled an invasion launched by the ruler of the Golden Horde, Töle-Buqa (1287–91) and led by his successor Toqta (1291–1312). These seem however to have been little more than large-scale raids. Of far greater potential danger to the Īl-Khānid state was the insurrection of Nauruz, the son of Arghun Aqa, who, as military governor of Khurāsān, was the second-in-command to Prince Ghazan. The rebellion lasted for five years (1289–94), continuing into the reign of Geikhatu: at the time of Arghun's death Ghazan was in full retreat before his former lieutenant, who proceeded to rapine and slaughter upon such a scale as Rashīd al-Dīn[3] terms "beyond description". The terror which Nauruz had inspired became proverbial, and the natives of Khurāsān, when their cattle refused to drink, would say it was because they had seen his reflection in the water. Such was the instrument whereby the Īl-Khāns were to be brought into the fold of Islam.

Like his father Arghun wished to resume the war against the Mamlūks, and he too sought a military alliance with the Christian West. Already in 1285 he had sent a letter to Pope Honorius IV, of which the Latin translation has been preserved in the Vatican archives. The correspondence seems to have had the sanction of the Great Khan himself, one of whose officials, a Nestorian Christian called 'Īsā Kelemechi, took part in the embassy.

And now let it be [says the Īl-Khān], because the land of the Saracens is not ours, between us, good father, us who are on this side and you who are on

[1] Fischel, *op. cit.* p. 8.
[2] See below, p. 541.
[3] Transl. Arends, p. 152.

your side; the land of Scami [Shām, i.e. Syria] to wit the land of Egypt between us and you we will crush. We send you the said messengers and [ask] you to send an expedition and army to the land of Egypt, and it shall be now that we from this side and you from your side shall crush it between us with good men; and that you send us by a good man where you wish the aforesaid done. The Saracens from the midst of us we shall lift and the lord Pope and the Cam [i.e. the Great Khan Qubilai] will be lords.[1]

In 1287 a second embassy, led by a Nestorian prelate from China called Rabban Sauma, set out for Europe, returning in the following year with letters from Pope Nicholas IV, Edward I of England and Philippe le Bel of France. The last-named at least seems to have given a favourable reply, for in a letter written in the summer of 1289 Arghun refers to his promise to send troops to his aid in a forthcoming campaign against the Mamlūks. He himself, he continues, would set out at the beginning of January 1291, so as to reach Damascus on 15 February. And he adds: "Now if, fulfilling thy sincere word, thou sendest thy troops at the time agreed upon, and if, blessed with good fortune by Heaven, we conquer these people, we shall give you Jerusalem."[2]

Arghun must soon have abandoned the idea of such an expedition, for we find him in September 1289 at Marāgheh *en route* for Arrān, where he passed the winter of 1289–90 and where, in the following spring, he became involved, as has already been mentioned, in a brief collision with the forces of the Golden Horde. He took a great interest in the sciences, true and false, and Rashīd al-Dīn[3] records an interview with the famous scientist Quṭb al-Dīn al-Shīrāzī in the Vān area, during the late summer of 1290, in which the latter showed him a map of the Mediterranean coast of what is now Turkey and answered the Īl-Khān's questions about it. Arghun had on a former occasion exchanged views with Quṭb al-Dīn on the alchemist's art, upon which and its practitioners he had lavished large sums of money; and at Marāgheh in the previous autumn he had been offered by an Indian yogi the elixir of life, in the form of an electuary compounded mainly of sulphur and mercury.[4] This medicament he continued to take over a period of nearly eight months, at the end of which, having now returned to Tabrīz, he retired into the castle to hold a forty-day fast in the company of Buddhist priests, apart from whom only Sa'd al-Daula and two other

[1] Moule, *Christians in China*, p. 106.

[2] Mostaert and Cleaves, *Les Lettres de 1289 et 1305 des ilkhan Aryun et Olǰeitü à Philippe le Bel*, p. 18.

[3] Transl. Arends, p 128.

[4] See also Yule, *The Book of Ser Marco Polo*, vol. II, pp. 365 and 369 n. 5.

favourites were admitted to his presence. In Arrān, where he passed the winter of 1290–1, he was taken dangerously ill, but in response to treatment by a Muslim or Jewish physician was showing some signs of recovery, when a Buddhist priest or doctor appeared at his bedside and gave him some kind of potion which had the effect of bringing on a relapse. His illness, which now became chronic, was put down by some to the evil eye, for the aversion of which they recommended the giving of alms; the *qams* or shamans, on the other hand, diagnosed witchcraft; and one of his ladies, who confessed under torture to having administered a love-philtre, was thrown into the river (presumably the Kur) along with a number of other women. The khan's life was now despaired of and on 16 February 1291 a group of amīrs hostile to Sa'd al-Daula and Arghun's other favourites formed a conspiracy to overthrow them. They were all of them seized and put to death, Sa'd al-Daula himself being formally tried and executed on 5 March. His death, as was to be expected, became the signal for savage pogroms in Tabrīz and Baghdad. He was survived by his master for less than a week. Arghun died on 10 March 1291 in Bāghcha, one of his residences in Arrān; he was in his early thirties, having been born *c.* 1258. It is a curious thought that but for the measures he took to ensure longevity he might have lived to match the achievements of his father, Abaqa, and his son, Ghazan.

He was the last of the Īl-Khāns to be accorded the traditional secret burial, being laid to rest on a mountain side near Sujās. The place was concealed and the whole area made a *qorugh* or sanctuary, to which entry was prohibited, but the ban was lifted in after years when his daughter Öljei founded a *khānqāh* or convent for dervishes at the site of his tomb.

GEIKHATU AND BAIDU

A week after Arghun's death messengers were sent to summon the three candidates for the throne: his son Ghazan in Khurāsān, his brother Geikhatu in Rūm and his cousin Baidu at Baghdad. Ghazan, retreating before the rebel Nauruz, received the news, which was at first kept from him, at Simnān; it was followed by reports of the manoeuvres by the partisans of the other candidates and then of Geikhatu's election as Īl-Khān; and he halted where he was, in the Simnān–Fīrūzkūh area, to resume, in due course, the struggle against Nauruz and his Transoxianan allies. Certain of the amīrs, and particularly those involved in the death of Sa'd al-Daula, had favoured Baidu, in whom they saw a more lenient and easy-going ruler; but the supporters of Geikhatu, amongst whom we now hear for the first time of the Amīr Choban, had won the day, and he was proclaimed khan at a quriltai held near Akhlāṭ on 23 July 1291, though the actual enthronement ceremony did not take place until a year later.

Immediately after the celebrations an inquiry, over which the Īl-Khān presided in person, was held into the execution of Sa'd al-Daula's Mongol colleagues. On this, as on later occasions, Geikhatu showed remarkable clemency. One alone of the conspirators was put to death, the remainder receiving only light punishment when they were not pardoned outright. The new khan's unwillingness to spill blood was apparently due to the advice of the qams, who attributed the shortness of his predecessor's reign to the quantity of blood he had shed. He was soon to demonstrate this same leniency towards offenders against his own interests. After the trial was concluded he returned to Rūm to put down a rising and, availing themselves of his absence the Amīr Taghachar, the ringleader of the conspirators so recently pardoned, and Ṣadr al-Dīn Zanjānī, a former associate of Juvainī's enemy Majd al-Mulk, plotted together to set up one of his uncles in his stead. Their plot uncovered, Taghachar was sent under escort to the quriltai held at Ala-Tagh in the summer of 1292, at which the ceremony of enthronement was to take place, and Ṣadr al-Dīn was cast into prison at Tabrīz. Not only was their act of treason forgiven them, but we find Ṣadr al-Dīn invested, before the year was out, with the combined office of vizier and ṣāḥib-dīvān, a post for which he had had the effrontery to canvass when just released from prison, while Taghachar was actually chosen as one of the commanders dispatched from Ala-Tagh to the relief of Qa'lat al-Rūm.

This fortress, on the right bank of the Euphrates, had been invested by the Mamlūk Sulṭān Ashraf Ṣalāḥ al-Dīn Khalīl (1290–3), fresh from his victories over the Franks of Acre and Tyre. In June 1292 a force of which Taghachar was apparently second-in-command, was sent to raise the siege, and reinforcements followed a week or so later; but the fortress had fallen to the Egyptians already before the first troops arrived. Ashraf did not follow up this success, contenting himself, in an exchange of letters with Geikhatu, with a threat to invade the latter's territory and re-establish Baghdad as the metropolis of Islam. Meanwhile there was a *détente* in relations with the Golden Horde. Toqta

(1291–1312), who before his accession had led two campaigns across the Caucasus, dispatched, in the spring of 1294, a peace mission which was honourably received by Geikhatu at Dalan Na'ur (in Mongol "Seventy Lakes"), a settlement at the western end of the Great Wall along the Kur. The period of peace thus inaugurated was to last, more or less uninterruptedly, until the reign of Abū Sa'īd.

On the profligacy of Geikhatu's morals the authorities are with one exception unanimous. He was concerned, says the continuator of Barhebraeus,[1]

> with nothing except riotous living, and amusement and debauchery. He had no thought for anything except the things that were necessary for Kings, and which they were bound to have, and how he could get possession of the sons and daughters of the nobles, and have carnal intercourse with them... And very many chaste women among the wives of the nobles fled from him, and others removed their sons and daughters and sent them away to remote districts. But they were unable to save themselves from his hands, or to escape from the shameful acts which he committed with them.

Rashīd al-Dīn's total silence on this subject is due no doubt to a desire not to embarrass his patrons, the nephews of Geikhatu; but even he is constrained to refer to the Īl-Khān's wild extravagance, one of the reasons given for the curious experiment for which his reign is chiefly remembered, the attempt to substitute for metallic currency the paper money of China known as *ch'ao*.

In describing the situation which led up to this experiment Vaṣṣāf[2] alludes not only to the depletion of the treasury by the gross prodigality of the khan and his vizier Ṣadr al-Dīn Zanjānī but also to a disease called by the Turkish name of *yut* which had caused great havoc in the Mongols' herds in the days following on the death of Arghun. This was not in fact an epidemic but simply the consequences of a cold spell following abruptly upon a period of mild weather.[3] It was probably this natural disaster rather than the exhaustion of the exchequer which led to the situation in which, according to the continuator of Barhebraeus,[4] not a single sheep could be killed for the Īl-Khān's food. The possibilities of ch'ao as a means of overcoming their difficulties had

[1] P. 494. [2] Bombay ed. p. 271.

[3] The Kazakh *dzhut*(*jut*). Cf. Wheeler, *The Modern History of Central Asia*, p. 34: "The whole of Kazakh life was regulated by the search for summer grazing grounds with adequate water, and winter pastures sheltered from the wind and cold and particularly from the dreaded *dzhut*—the freezing over of previously thawed snow which made it impossible for cattle to reach fodder."

[4] P. 496.

been discussed by Ṣadr al-Dīn and his colleagues on several occasions. At Pīl-Suvār in the spring of 1294, they broached the subject to Geikhatu, who turned to Bolad Ching-Sang, the representative of the Great Khan at his court, for further information on the nature and working of this type of currency. It was decided, despite some opposition, to proceed with the experiment, which seems to have been put fully into practice only in Tabrīz. Here on 13 August a proclamation was issued imposing the death penalty on all who refused to accept the new currency. Considerable quantities of ch'ao were then prepared and, on 12 September, put into circulation. For a week after their first issue these notes were taken from motives of fear, but soon all trade had come to a standstill and the bazaars were completely deserted. In face of public uproar Ṣadr al-Dīn was forced first to allow the use of gold for the purchase of food and then to suppress the paper currency altogether. The experiment lasted little more than two months and is perhaps most noteworthy as being the first recorded instance of block printing outside of China. It is remarkable that Marco Polo, who with his father and uncle had spent nine months in Tabrīz at about this time, should make no mention of this episode, the more so as he describes at length the use of paper currency in China. One can only assume that the Polos left on their homeward journey before the scheme had been set in motion.

Unbridled licentiousness and reckless extravagance would no doubt of themselves have brought about the Īl-Khān's downfall, which was, however, precipitated by his ill-considered behaviour towards Baidu. Rashīd al-Dīn[1], as one would expect, is extremely reticent about this incident, which took place in Ala-Tagh in the summer of 1294. He says simply that Baidu joined Geikhatu in his summer residence on 12 June, that the latter rebuked him for some unspecified reason and that he was allowed to leave on 11 July having apparently been under some kind of detention. The continuator of Barhebraeus,[2] on the other hand, gives a detailed account of the episode, with which Vaṣṣāf's[3] briefer version is in basic agreement. Insulted by Baidu during a drinking bout Geikhatu caused his cousin to be beaten up by his attendants and then, repenting of his action, sought to make amends. Concealing his resentment Baidu returned to his residence at Daqūqā, where, in the winter of 1294–5, he rose in rebellion. From Tabrīz Geikhatu dispatched the perfidious Taghachar against his advancing enemy; Taghachar deserted to Baidu,

[1] Transl. Arends, p. 136. [2] Pp. 494–5. [3] Bombay ed. p. 275.

and Gei<u>kh</u>atu fled, first to Ahar and then to Pīl-Suvār. Here he was overtaken by pursuers whom he thought to be in prison in Tabrīz. These were the amīrs who, under the leadership of Ta<u>gh</u>a<u>ch</u>ar, had been responsible for the deaths of Sa'd al-Daula and his Mongol colleagues. Warned of their complicity in Baidu's rebellion Gei<u>kh</u>atu had been persuaded by Ta<u>gh</u>a<u>ch</u>ar to imprison rather than to execute them; and they had then, on Ta<u>gh</u>a<u>ch</u>ar's orders, been released. They showed no mercy to the man who had twice spared their lives. Gei<u>kh</u>atu was strangled with the bowstring on 26 March 1295, apparently on the amīrs' own authority without Baidu's sanction or knowledge; he was 24 years of age. Vaṣṣāf concludes his account of the catastrophe with a phrase of which d'Ohsson[1] renders the sense but not the concision and the elegance: "A la fin l'empire montra à Gaïkhatou ce qu'il aimait, c'est-à-dire, *le derrière*."

The brief reign of Baidu is ignored by Ra<u>sh</u>īd al-Dīn, who mentions this prince only in connexion with <u>Gh</u>azan's campaign against him. His enthronement took place, according to Vaṣṣāf,[2] in the neighbourhood of Hamadān in April 1295. On the other hand, the continuator of Barhebraeus[3] speaks of a ceremony at Ūjān, whither he had caused to be transported from Tabrīz the "great throne" on which his predecessors, from Abaqa onwards, had been inaugurated. Ta<u>gh</u>a<u>ch</u>ar now received, as reward for his perfidy, the post of commander-in-chief, Ṣadr al-Dīn Zanjānī was replaced as vizier by Jamāl al-Dīn Dastajirdānī and the executioners of Gei<u>kh</u>atu were each appointed to the governorship of a province.

<u>Gh</u>azan first heard of Baidu's revolt at Qara-Teppe near Sara<u>kh</u>s when returning from a victory gained over the Transoxianan Mongols. He took no notice and proceeded on his way to Rādkān, where, according to Ra<u>sh</u>īd al-Dīn,[4] he received a message from Baidu himself formally inviting him to ascend the throne. Having consulted his amīrs and sent for Nauruz, with whom he was now reconciled, he returned to his headquarters at Sulṭān Duvīn in the plain between the Atrak and the Gurgān river, from whence, after a few days, he set out for Āzarbāijān by way of Māzandarān and 'Irāq-i 'Ajam. At Simnān he was met by emissaries dispatched, before his death, by Gei<u>kh</u>atu with a consignment of ch'ao for use in the provinces under <u>Gh</u>azan's jurisdiction.

---

[1] Vol. IV, p. 113 n. 1. In the original (Bombay ed. p. 279): ...*tā salṭanat u pād<u>sh</u>āhī nīz maḥbūb-i ū ya'nī pu<u>sh</u>t bi-numūd.*

[2] Bombay ed. p. 283.   [3] P. 500.   [4] Transl. Arends, pp. 285–6.

He caused it all to be burnt, remarking that even iron would not stand up to the damp climate of Māzandarān, to say nothing of paper. At Khail-i Buzurg he learnt, as Rashīd al-Dīn[1] puts it, that Baidu had changed his mind and now wanted the Khanate for himself; he probably learnt, in actual fact, that Baidu's enthronement was now a *fait accompli*. He decided to continue his advance despite the smallness of his forces: his unpreparedness for battle is illustrated by Rashīd al-Dīn[2] by the fact that he had left behind his sacred banner (*tuq*) and royal war drum. He dispatched ambassadors to Baidu to announce his coming and to ask for a safe conduct. Baidu's reply, delivered at Aq-Khwāja, though conciliatory in tone, was to the effect that Ghazan should turn back. Disregarding this warning he still pressed on: at Qongqur-Öleng he gathered, from a close questioning of Baidu's envoys, that his reception might well be hostile, and from thence onward the troops proceeded in battle order. On 16 May they crossed the Safīd Rūd, and three days later the two armies came face to face at Qurban Shire.

After a charge by Ghazan's left wing a truce was called for, apparently on Baidu's initiative, and the two princes, each accompanied by a small group of followers, conferred together on rising ground between the armies. Their negotiations that day did not extend beyond general expressions of good intent, which they affirmed, according to the Mongol custom, with the drinking of wine mixed with gold, a ceremony for which the converts to Islam such as Nauruz substituted an oath and handshake. At nightfall each returned to his own quarters. The next day the two armies proceeded side by side to Qurban Shire, where they encamped so close together as to drink from the same spring; but there was mutual distrust and the troops remained under arms throughout the whole of the night. The following day, 23 May, the representatives of the two princes met to continue their discussions, and it was agreed that the ordus of his father Arghun should go to Ghazan and that he should have control of 'Irqā-i 'Ajam, Khurāsān, Qūmis, Māzandarān and one half of Fārs. As the negotiations proceeded Baidu's troops had been strongly reinforced, and Ghazan, fearing treachery, decided to withdraw, leaving Nauruz behind to complete the negotiations. He decamped in the night of 24–5 May, crossed the Safīd Rūd at dawn and by nightfall had reached Zanjān; the next day he continued on his journey to Damāvand, where he was to spend the summer. Baidu's troops set out at once in his pursuit and advanced as

[1] *Op. cit.* p. 287. [2] *Loc. cit.*

far as Qongqur-Öleng before giving up the chase. As for Nauruz, he and his colleagues were arrested and detained, and one at least of Baidu's amīrs demanded his execution. He was, however, not without friends in the Īl-Khān's entourage, and prompted, it is said, by Ṣadr al-Dīn Zanjānī, he undertook upon oath to deliver either Ghazan's head or his person bound hand and foot. Released on the strength of this undertaking he fulfilled the letter of his oath, upon reaching Ghazan at Fīrūzkūh, by sending Baidu a cauldron (in Turkish *qazan* or *ghazan*) tied up in a sack.

In Ghazan's councils Nauruz, himself a Muslim of long standing, now impressed upon his master (as he had done during the parleys at Qurban Shire) the desirability of following his example and adopting Islam. Ghazan, who had been brought up as a Buddhist and had himself erected Buddhist temples in Khurāsān, responded to the suggestion with alacrity, partly no doubt out of genuine conviction, as Rashīd al-Dīn,[1] himself a convert from Judaism, is careful to insist, but partly also for reasons similar to those that weighed with Henry of Navarre. His declaration of faith, an important moment in the history of Persia and of Islam, took place on 19 June 1295 in the mountain pastures of the Lār valley, high up in the Alburz.[2] After performing the ritual ablution he entered a pavilion frequented in former times by his father Arghun and, instructed by Shaikh Ṣadr al-Dīn Ibrāhīm Ḥamawī, repeated several times the *Kalima* or Muslim Creed. His amīrs followed his example in a body, and the month of Ramaḍān coming round shortly afterwards (15 July to 13 August in that year) they observed for the first time the precepts of their new religion in the company of *shaikhs* and *imāms*. The fasting over Ghazan set out, as the Muslim commander of a Muslim army, to overthrow the last non-Muslim ruler of Persia.

His advance westwards was in the nature more of a triumphal procession than of a military campaign. Already before his departure he had learnt from Baidu's own envoy of the support he enjoyed in the latter's camp; and at every stage of the journey he met with fresh evidence of that support. At Fīrūzkūh he received Ṣadr al-Dīn Zanjānī, the promoter of the ch'ao experiment, now the first of Baidu's officials to defect to his rival. Near Ustūnāvand, a castle in that same area, he welcomed the Amīr Choban and Qurumshi, the son of Alinaq, whom, at their own request, he sent on ahead to join Nauruz in the advanced

[1] Transl. Arends, p. 297.

[2] See also below, pp. 541–3.

party. At Aq-Khwāja he learnt that Taghachar had abandoned Baidu, as he had abandoned Geikhatu before him and was now allied with Nauruz in pursuit of his master. To the west of Sujās Ghazan was met by his brother Khar-Banda, the future Īl-Khān Öljeitü; and on the banks of the Safīd Rūd, a group of powerful amīrs came to place their services at his disposal. He halted at Yüz Aghach to await the latest news of Baidu, who had fled before Nauruz's troops towards the Araxes and Nakhchivān. Hearing nothing he went on to Ūjān, where he learnt that the Īl-Khān had been captured and brought back to Tabrīz and that he had requested an interview with Ghazan. Suspecting the motives of this request Ghazan gave orders not to bring the prisoner to his presence but to execute him on the spot. He was put to death in a garden outside Tabrīz on 4 October 1295.

Haithon[1] speaks of Baidu as a "good Christian" and indeed ascribes his downfall to his patronage of the Christians. His pro-Christian attitude was due, according to the continuator of Barhebraeus, to the influence of Abaqa's wife Despoina, the natural daughter of Michael Palaeologus.[2] The same authority goes on to say that he became a Muslim but "was never able to learn the ablutions and the fasts". The probability is that he was one of the minority that still clung to the old shamanistic deism which showed equal respect to all faiths and religions.

GHAZAN

Ghazan arrived at the gates of Tabrīz on 4 October, the very day of his predecessor's execution. Already the first decree of the new Islamic régime was being enforced within the town, viz. that all churches, synagogues and Buddhist temples were to be destroyed here, at Baghdad and throughout the Īl-Khān's domains.

And in those days [says the continuator of Barhebraeus],[3] the foreign peoples stretched out their hands to Tâbrîz, and they destroyed all the churches which were there, and there was great sorrow among the Christians in all the world. The persecutions, and disgrace, and mockings, and ignominy which the Christians suffered at this time, especially in Baghdâd, words cannot describe. Behold, according to what people say, "No Christian dared to appear in the streets (or, market), but the women went out and came in and bought and sold, because they could not be distinguished from the Arab women, and could not be identified as Christians, though those who were recognized as Christians were disgraced, and slapped, and beaten and mocked...

[1] P. 315. [2] P. 505. [3] P. 507.

But it was on the Buddhists that the decree and its consequences weighed heaviest. "And this after the honour to which they had been promoted by the Mongol kings, and which was so great that one half of the money which was gathered together in the treasury of the kingdom had been given to them, and it had been expended (?) on the work of images of gold and silver. And a very large number of the pagan priests, because of the way in which they were persecuted became Muslims."[1] Measures such as these were, it seems, due to the fanaticism of men like Nauruz who had brought Ghazan to power and whose policies, for a time at least, he was obliged to follow. Once established on the throne he reverted, as far as was consistent with his Muḥammadanism, to the religious tolerance of his predecessors, and we are told by Rashīd al-Dīn[2] that when two years later, on 21 July 1298 (significantly a Sunday), the Tabrīz mob proceeded to wreck such churches as were still left standing the Īl-Khān was angry and saw to it that the ringleaders were punished.

On 17 October Ghazan left Tabrīz to spend the winter in Arrān. He halted in the early stages of the journey to go through the Muslim marriage ceremony with a lady who had been the wife of his father Arghun and then (apparently against her will) of his uncle Geikhatu. The custom of a son's marrying his father's widows other than his own mother can be traced back, as Togan[3] has shown, through the whole history of the Altaic peoples: it had been observed by Ghazan's father, grandfather and great grandfather, the Christian wife of Hülegü, the celebrated Doquz Khatun, having been previously married to Tolui. That a Muslim divine should have been willing to solemnize such a marriage seems almost incredible; that an apparently sincere convert to Islam should have formed a union expressly condemned in the Qur'ān[4] shows how strong the old traditions still remained. After the wedding celebrations Ghazan proceeded by way of Ahar into Mūghān, where he halted for a while near Bakrābād and where he was joined by Nauruz. The latter, now appointed the Īl-Khān's lieutenant-general and commander-in-chief, had been left behind in Tabrīz to deal with various administrative matters including the raising of a loan from wealthy Tabrīzīs, the treasury being, as was to be expected, completely exhausted. From Bakrābād they crossed the Araxes into the Qarabāgh Steppe,

[1] *Loc. cit.* [2] Transl. Arends, p. 327.

[3] *Ibn Faḍlān's Reisebericht*, pp. 129–31.

[4] Sūra IV, verse 26: "And marry not women whom your fathers have married: for this is a shame, and hateful, and an evil way—though what is past may be allowed."

where, at a ceremony held on 3 November 1295, Ghazan was enthroned as khan, assuming as a Muslim ruler the name of Maḥmūd and the title of sultan.

Ghazan had many problems to cope with in the first winter of his reign. Prince Süge, an uncle of the Īl-Khān, sent eastwards to repel a Chaghatai invasion, halted on the Karaj to plot rebellion; Nauruz, in command of the advance forces, turned back to engage him in battle; he was defeated, captured and executed. A fellow conspirator, Prince Arslan, a descendant of Chingiz-Khān's brother Jochi-Qasar, continued the rebellion in the Pīl-Suvār area. Engaged by Qutlugh-Shāh, one of the most capable of Ghazan's generals, at Bailaqān he was finally put to flight after a hotly contested battle. With his execution on 29 March 1296 the rebellion came to an end: it had cost the lives of three princes of the blood. Whilst this civil war was still in progress, a horde of Oirat, who had their grazing lands in the Diyārbakr area, migrated *en masse* into Syria and placed themselves under the protection of the Mamlūk sultan, then Ket-Bugha (1294–6). At about the same time Prince Ilder, a grandson of Hülegü, fled for some unspecified reason into Asia Minor, was defeated in battle, hid for a while in the neighbourhood of Erzerum and was finally captured and killed. Taghachar too now met his end. In November 1295 Ghazan had sent him to Rūm on the grounds that he was a man of fickle character (*sarī' al-inqilāb*)[1] and that it was safer to keep him at a distance. Shortly afterwards he caused him to be discreetly put to death. The Īl-Khān had some compunction about this treatment of a man to whom he owed a debt of gratitude and who was only of potential danger; and in justification of his action he recounted to his intimates an analogous episode in the history of China. The removal of Taghachar was not without its consequences. Baltu, the military commander in Asia Minor, who had been involved in his death, now rose in revolt, egged on by Prince Ildei, another of Ghazan's great uncles. The revolt was suppressed by an expedition led by Qutlugh-Shāh in the winter of 1296–7. Ildei, who was tried and executed in the previous autumn, was no less than the fifth prince of the blood to come to a violent end within the first twelve months of Ghazan's reign.

In June 1296 Ghazan held a quriltai in pasture lands with the Mongol name of Sayin ("Good") between Ardabīl and Sarāb. It was here that he received Nauruz, towards whom, for reasons that shall appear, his

[1] Rashīd al-Dīn, ed. Alizade, p. 302.

feelings had begun to cool. Upon Nauruz's approach the Chaghatai army had quickly withdrawn. A brief reconnaissance raid satisfied him as to the fact of their withdrawal and he at once returned to Āzarbāījān to visit his sick wife. His departure and the rumours to which it gave rise led to large-scale desertions so that the defences of Khurāsān were greatly depleted. Hearing of his return Ghazan was angry and ordered him back to his post; and his reply, to the effect that he must first see his wife (a daughter of Abaqa), only increased the Īl-Khān's anger. At Sayin he was accorded every honour, but the amīrs perceived the change in the Īl-Khān's attitude and impressed upon him the inadvisability of sending this arrogant and unscrupulous man back to Khurāsān. Ghazan was inclined to agree with them but his sense of gratitude prevailed over his judgment, and on 3 July Nauruz took his leave for the last time. His downfall and death little more than a year later were due, in the event, not to disloyal ambition but to the machinations of his enemies.

On his journey to Baghdad in the following autumn Ghazan halted for a while in the Hamadān region, where he received the *maliks* of 'Irāq-i 'Ajam, as also Afrāsiyāb I, the atabeg of Greater Luristān (1288–96), who had risen in rebellion at the time of Arghun's death. Afrāsiyāb, despite his record, was treated with favour and had started on the homeward journey, when he was arrested by the general Horqudaq just returning from Fārs and, on the strength of the latter's accusations, put to death. It was at Hamadān, too, that Jamāl al-Dīn Dastajirdānī was appointed ṣāḥib-dīvān in place of Sharaf al-Dīn Simnānī, who in turn had displaced Ṣadr al-Dīn Zanjānī, disgraced after only a brief tenure of office. Jamāl al-Dīn's appointment lasted little more than a month. Brought to trial on charges instigated by Ṣadr al-Dīn he was executed on 27 October 1296 and was succeeded in the office of vizier or ṣāḥib-dīvān (the two posts seem at times to merge into one) by his antagonist.

It was during the trial of Jamāl al-Dīn Dastajirdānī that the full facts of Nauruz's correspondence with the Mamlūk sultan were first brought to light. He had, in the last months of Baidu's reign, appealed to the ruler of Egypt for help in the overthrow of the infidel Īl-Khān. The sultan's reply arrived after Ghazan's triumph, when the situation was altogether changed; and Nauruz judged it prudent to show his master, not the real text, but a substitute version prepared, at his orders, by Jamāl al-Dīn Dastajirdānī. Nauruz's emissary had been a certain 'Alam al-Dīn Qaiṣar, the clerk of a Baghdadi merchant, who in the course of his duties made frequent visits to Egypt. He was arrested at Baghdad on 13 March 1297 and Ṣadr al-Dīn Zanjānī, seizing this opportunity of avenging himself on Nauruz, caused a number of forged letters to be secreted in the prisoner's effects. Qaiṣar was taken before Ghazan at Shahr-Abān to the north-east of Baghdad on the Khurāsān road. Questioned by the Īl-Khān in person he recounted the true facts of the correspondence. His belongings were then searched and the letters, apparently addressed by Nauruz to Egyptian amīrs, discovered. Ṣadr al-Dīn and his associates attested that the writing was that of Nauruz's secretary, and Ghazan, enraged by this seemingly damning evidence, had Qaiṣar executed on the spot and gave orders for the extirpation of the whole of Nauruz's family, three of his brothers (two of them implicated in the spurious correspondence) and a son being seized and put to death within the space of little more than a month.

At Asadābād, as he returned northwards, the Īl-Khān was joined by Qutlugh-Shāh from Mūghān and by the amīrs Choban and Bolad-Qaya from Ray. Bolad-Qaya was at once dispatched to join advance parties under the amīrs Horqudaq and Sönitei in pursuit of Nauruz; and was followed shortly afterwards by Qutlugh-Shāh at the head of the main army. At Dāmghān Qutlugh-Shāh learnt that Nauruz's shaḥnas here and in all towns from Ray eastwards had been put to death by Horqudaq's forces. East of Isfarā'in he was joined by a deserter from Nauruz's army, an officer called Dānishmand Bahadur, whom he sent on ahead with the vanguard. Dānishmand overtook Nauruz somewhere to the east of Nīshāpūr and, despite the smallness of his own force, inflicted a heavy defeat upon him. Nauruz abandoned his baggage and fled in the direction of Herāt, pursued now by Horqudaq and the whole of the advance forces. At Jām, under cover of darkness, he sprang an ambuscade on his pursuers and then continued his flight. Arrived before Herāt he was offered asylum by the Malik Fakhr al-Dīn Kart. His amīrs urged him not to trust himself to the malik; he replied that for three days past he had been unable to perform the *namāz* and that he could neglect his religious duties no longer. He entered the town accompanied only by 400 horse, and was accommodated by Fakhr al-Dīn in the citadel. Meanwhile Qutlugh-Shāh, also a good Muslim, arriving at Mashhad, had visited the shrine of the Imām Riḍā and prayed that his enemy might be delivered into his hands. His prayer was to be granted. Summer was at its height when Qutlugh-Shāh invested Herāt, and because of the great heat and the strength of the fortifications he was advised to abandon the siege and withdraw. He indignantly rejected this advice and soon found means of achieving his purpose. The *shaikh al-Islām* of Jām was made to write a letter to Fakhr al-Dīn urging him to surrender Nauruz if he wished to save the town from destruction. The letter was smuggled into the town and produced its effect. Despite the great debt of gratitude which Fakhr al-Dīn owed to Nauruz (who during his father's lifetime had secured his release from imprisonment by a personal guarantee of his good behaviour) he decided in the end to betray his guest rather than risk Ghazan's wrath. A device was found to separate Nauruz from his followers and he was overpowered and bound. The severed head of his secretary, the same man whose handwriting Ṣadr al-Dīn had affected to recognize in the forged letters, was sent to Qutlugh-Shāh as proof of his master's detention, and in return for a written assurance confirmed by oath, that no harm should come to the town, Nauruz himself was handed over to his pursuers. The jubilant Qutlugh-Shāh attempted to interrogate him. It was for Ghazan, Nauruz said, and not for the likes of him, to question him, and he refused to answer, "knowing that he had committed no crime".[1] Qutlugh-Shāh ordered him to be cut in two, and his head was sent to Baghdad, where for some years it was exposed on one of the city gates. So ended the career of this powerful and turbulent man, probably destined, had his life been spared, to have played the same role of king-maker and mayor of the palace in Persia as had his elder contemporary Prince Noqai in the Golden Horde. The death of the "second Abū Muslim", as Vaṣṣāf[2] aptly calls him, occurred on 13 August 1297.

In Tabrīz, on 2 November, there took place a ceremony that would have gladdened Nauruz's heart. The Īl-Khān and his amīrs in a body formally exchanged their broad-brimmed Mongol hats for the Muslim turban. In our own days we have witnessed, in the very regions over which Ghazan ruled, the reversal of this process by laws which substituted for the fez and the *kulāh* a form of headgear as ill-suited as the Mongol for the performance of the *namāz*.[3] Soon after the ceremony Ghazan left for Arrān, where he spent the winter of 1297–8 and where, in the following spring, the execution of a prince of the blood was

[1] Rashīd al-Dīn, transl. Arends, p. 181. [2] Bombay ed. p. 313.

[3] In Turkey a law was passed in 1925 requiring all men to wear hats and making the wearing of the fez a criminal offence. In Iran the change was made in two stages. In 1928 a peaked cap replaced the *kulāh*, for which in 1935 the normal European headgear was substituted.

shortly followed by that of his vizier, the infamous Ṣadr al-Dīn Zanjānī.

The prince of the blood was Taichu, a son of Mengü-Temür and therefore Ghazan's great uncle. His crime seems to have been little more than lending a credulous ear to a prophecy made by a Muslim divine that within forty days he would succeed to the throne. He was arrested on 13 April 1298 on the banks of the Qara-Küderi (in Mongol "Black Musk Deer"), apparently a canal cut from the Kur, and was put to death on the 15th near Dalan Na'ur. His fate was shared by the prophet and by all who had been present when he made his prophecy. Whether or not Taichu's guilt was such as to justify the death penalty, it is impossible, on the evidence available, to reach an opinion; the punishment of Ṣadr al-Dīn, the *Ṣadr-i Jahān* as his title went, was certainly richly deserved. On 28 March 1298 he was accused before Ghazan of having embezzled state funds. A couple of days later, no doubt with these accusations in mind, Ṣadr al-Dīn taxed Rashīd al-Dīn (who now appears on the scene for the first time, apparently as a subordinate to Ṣadr al-Dīn) with having traduced him behind his back. He was silenced by Ghazan, who took Rashīd al-Dīn's part but seemed otherwise disposed to let matters rest. At this juncture Qutlugh-Shāh, returning from a campaign in Georgia, upbraided Ṣadr al-Dīn for the economic conditions in that country. To avert the blame from himself the vizier told Ghazan that it was in fact Qutlugh-Shāh's officers who had ruined Georgia. Puzzled at the khan's attitude of disapproval Qutlugh-Shāh asked Ṣadr al-Dīn who it was that had spoken ill of him. He said that it was Rashīd al-Dīn. It so happened that Qutlugh-Shāh was on familiar terms with Rashīd al-Dīn and he took the first occasion to reproach him for this unfriendly act; he refused, however, to disclose the name of his informant. Rashīd al-Dīn then approached the Īl-Khān in person, and when Ghazan sent for Qutlugh-Shāh he had no option but to name the vizier. Ghazan's patience was now at an end. Ṣadr al-Dīn was arrested and put on trial; he answered his interrogators with the utmost aplomb and might, given time, have extricated himself even from this situation. However, he was handed over to Qutlugh-Shāh and, on 4 May, met the same end at the hands of the same executioner as his great antagonist the Amīr Nauruz. Soon after these executions Ghazan left Dalan Na'ur for Tabrīz, where on 3 June, the brother and nephew of Ṣadr al-Dīn were likewise put to death.

From Tabrīz, on 11 September, the Īl-Khān set out for his winter-quarters in the Baghdad area, at about the same time appointing Sa'd al-Dīn Sāvajī as Ṣadr al-Dīn's successor with, apparently, Rashīd al-Dīn as his associate or deputy. Travelling by way of Hamadān and Burūjird he arrived on 29 November in the region of Wāsiṭ, where he remained until February 1299 and where he received the news of Sülemish's revolt in Asia Minor. Sülemish had been sent by Qutlugh-Shāh in pursuit of Baltu after the latter's defeat in the winter of 1296–7, and it was presumably he who had brought Baltu to Tabrīz, where he had been executed on 14 September 1297. It was then that Ghazan had appointed Sülemish commander-in-chief in Rūm. He had at the same time deposed the Saljuq ruler Mas'ūd II, the son of Kai-Khusrau II, suspected of complicity in Baltu's rising, and had replaced him by his nephew 'Alā' al-Dīn Kai Qubād II (1297–1300). Mas'ūd, it may be anticipated here, was restored to the throne in 1300 and reigned for four years: he was the last of the Saljuqs of Rūm. In the winter of 1298–9 there were heavy snowfalls in Asia Minor cutting off all communications with the East, and Sülemish took advantage of this situation to spread the rumour that Ghazan had been dethroned. He then rose in revolt, killing the generals whom Ghazan had associated with him in the command, gathering together a force of some 50,000 men and obtaining the promise of support from Syria. To suppress the rebellion an army under the command of Qutlugh-Shāh set out from Wāsiṭ on 15 February 1299. On 27 April a battle was fought near Aq-Shahr between Sīvās and Arzinjān on the high road to Persia. Sülemish was defeated and put to flight; he escaped into Syria and proceeded to Cairo, where he was favourably received by the sultan; but deciding to return to Rūm in search of his family, he was captured by the Armenians upon entering Cilicia and handed over to Ghazan.

Ghazan, meanwhile, whilst journeying from Najaf to Baghdad, had received in audience a group of dissident Mamlūk amīrs led by Saif al-Dīn Qïpchaq, the governor of Damascus. Their quarrel had been with Sulṭān Lachïn (1296–8) and learning at Ra's al-'Ain of his death, they had regretted their decision to defect to the Īl-Khān. It was, however, too late to turn back and, admitted to Ghazan's presence, they assured him, with such conviction as they could muster, of their support in the invasion of Syria and Egypt. Ghazan remained in Baghdad for less than a fortnight (8–20 March 1299) before setting out on the journey back to Āzarbāījān. In Ūjān, where he arrived on 28 May, he held a quriltai shortly followed by the execution of several of Sülemish's officers. Sülemish himself was put to death in Tabrīz on 27 September. Of the form of execution Rashīd al-Dīn says[1] only that it was "horrible" (*shanī'*): his body was burnt and the ashes flung to the wind. Ghazan, at about this time, was affected with ophthalmia; and wild rue was burnt and prayers offered up in order to avert the evil eye.

At Tabrīz Ghazan learnt of a Syrian incursion into Upper Mesopotamia. The invaders had captured Mārdīn and attacked Ra's al-'Ain; they had desecrated the mosques by their scandalous behaviour in them, and this during Ramaḍān (falling that year in June); and they had carried off great numbers of prisoners when they withdrew. Ghazan had no difficulty in obtaining a *fatwā* for a war of retaliation, and on 16 October he set out for Syria. Proceeding by way of Mosul and Nasībīn he crossed the Euphrates on 7 December at Qal'at Ja'bar. On the western bank of the river in the Plain of Ṣiffīn, the scene of the famous battle between 'Alī and Mu'āwiya, he was heartened with news of dissension amongst the enemy, presumably reports of the attempt by the Oirat refugees to overthrow Sulṭān Nāṣir. The Mongol forces arrived before Aleppo on 12 December but did not attempt to invest the town; instead they turned southwards, passing to the east of Ḥamā on the 20th and encamping near Salamiyya on the edge of the Syrian Desert. The enemy, as Ghazan now learnt, had concentrated their forces near Ḥimṣ in the same strategically favourable position from which, eighteen years before, they had inflicted a crushing defeat on Mengü-Temür. He decided not to make a frontal attack but, by turning eastwards into the desert, to outflank the Mamlūks and take them from the rear. On the banks of a stream some ten miles north of Ḥimṣ the troops, in accordance with this change of plan, were ordered to draw three days' supply of water. This was on 22 December. The enemy had intended to attack the next day, but mistaking the purpose of the Mongols' movements and thinking they were about to retreat they decided to give battle at once. As the enemy approached Ghazan drew up such of his forces as were at hand, Qutlugh-Shāh commanding on the right and he himself in the centre. Qutlugh-Shāh caused the great war-drums to be beaten and the Egyptians, imagining this to indicate the presence of the khan, charged in great strength upon the right wing, which broke before them; but the centre, where Ghazan himself, contrary to Mongol usage, took part in the fighting and where he was

[1] Ed. Alizade, p. 332, transl. Arends, p. 185.

joined by Qutlugh-Shāh from the routed right, stood firm until the left wing was able to take up its position. The battle, which lasted from eleven o'clock until nightfall, ended in the total defeat of the Mamlūks. Advancing slowly in the tracks of the retreating enemy Ghazan encamped some three miles from Ḥimṣ. Town and citadel surrendered without a blow, and Ghazan found himself in possession of the Sultan's treasure abandoned by the Mamlūks in their precipitate flight. He distributed the contents amongst his amīrs, keeping for himself, according to Haithon, only a sword and a leather bag containing the title deeds of the kingdom of Egypt and the muster roll of its army. As for his prowess in the battle, says Haithon, himself present in the suite of Het'um II, "it will be talked of amongst the Tartars for all time".[1] A *fatḥ-nāma* or bulletin proclaiming the victory, penned by none other than Vaṣṣāf, was dispatched to Tabrīz and all the chief cities of Ghazan's empire; and the next day, 28 December, the Mongols advanced on Damascus deserted, like Ḥimṣ, by its defenders. On 31 December a deputation of Damascene notables came to sue for quarter, and three days later Ghazan was encamped in the famous meadows of Marj Rāhiṭ to the east of the town, where he received the homage of the populace. On the following Friday, 8 January 1300, the *khuṭba* was read in Damascus in Ghazan's name; on the 23rd he learnt from the officer sent in their pursuit that the Egyptians had been driven out of Syria.

The Mongols evacuated the country as quickly as they had occupied it. Ghazan left Damascus as early as 5 February, possibly because of reports of the Qarauna inroads in Southern Persia; whatever the reason for his departure, it cannot have been, as Rashīd al-Dīn[2] appears to suggest, the approach of the hot season. He crossed the Euphrates, again as before at Qal'at Ja'bar, on a bridge of his own invention consisting of inflated skins lashed together with bark rope. In the Mosul area, which he reached on 8 March, he was joined in early April by Qutlugh-Shāh, whom he had left in command at Damascus. After Ghazan's departure Qutlugh-Shāh had laid siege to the citadel, which had continued to offer resistance after the capitulation of the town, but discouraged by his lack of success had abandoned these operations after a matter of days and followed in his master's wake. According to Rashīd al-Dīn,[3] he brought news of rebellious activities on the part of Qïpchaq, whom the Īl-Khān had reinstated as military governor of

[1] P. 318. [2] Transl. Arends, p. 188. [3] *Op. cit.* p. 190.

Damascus; but this is probably only an anticipation of subsequent events. On leaving Damascus Qutlugh-Shāh had handed over the command to Mulai, the same officer who had pursued the Egyptians to the frontier. Alarmed by rumours put about by Qïpchaq, now in correspondence with Sulṭān Nāṣir, he too withdrew from Syria, catching up with Ghazan on 8 May at or near Darband-i Zangī between Ḥulwān and Shahrazūr. By this time the Egyptians had already reoccupied Damascus; by the end of May they had restored Mamlūk rule throughout the whole of Syria.

Ghazan, however, had no intention of renouncing his conquests; and in the autumn he returned to the attack. The summer he had spent in Āzarbāijān: first in Marāgheh, where he had inspected the observatory and explained to the scientists his plans for another and more elaborate one in Tabrīz; then in Ūjān, where, on 13 July, he had summoned a quriltai; and finally in Tabrīz, where he had remained till the end of September, watching the progress in the building of the Gunbad-i ʿĀlī, his future mausoleum. On 30 September he left for Syria; Qutlugh-Shāh at the head of large forces, had been sent on in advance on the 16th. Ghazan followed the same route as on the previous expedition, crossing the Euphrates on 30 December, again at Qalʿat Jaʿbar. From Jabbūl, which they reached on 3 January 1301, the Mongols approached the outskirts of Aleppo (which, as in the previous campaign, they made no attempt to invest) and then turned southwards, encamping on the 18th in the vicinity of Qinnisrīn. They advanced no further and the forces under Qutlugh-Shāh were ordered to halt at Sarmīn. Ghazan, according to Rashīd al-Dīn,[1] had received no reports of enemy movements and wished to spare a Muslim country from devastation. In point of fact military operations by either side had been rendered impossible by torrential and continuous rains, and the consequent floods and the cold had caused havoc amongst the horses and camels: Rashīd al-Dīn[2] himself speaks of the plight of two Mongol amīrs entrapped with their men and beasts in a sea of mud. Ghazan turned back on 2 February, crossing the Euphrates at Raqqa, where he visited the tombs of the martyrs of Ṣiffīn, and reaching the ordus of his ladies at Chahār Ṭāq near Sinjār on the 25th. On 19 May he crossed the Tigris into the Kurdish country and directed a punitive expedition against the inhabitants. It was from here that he sent an embassy to the Mamlūk sultan. On 2 June he was back in Ūjān.

[1] Transl. Arends, p. 191. [2] *Loc. cit.*

Ghazan passed the whole of the summer in Ūjān, during which time a conspiracy against his minister Sa'd al-Dīn was uncovered and suppressed, three officials of the Dīvān being put to death. The Īl-Khān, remarks Rashīd al-Dīn,[1] *à propos* of these executions, was so tender-hearted that if a fly fell in his food he would lift it out and set it gently down so that its wings might not be broken. "It is more difficult for me," he would say, "to kill an innocent gnat than a guilty human being; for to allow a mischievous man to live only leads to disorders, especially in affairs of state." After a brief stay in Ala-Tagh Ghazan left, on 23 November, for his winter-quarters in Arrān. It was here, in the Qarabāgh country on 19 December, that he received his ambassadors on their return from Egypt with the Sultan's reply to his message. Versions of both documents have been preserved by the Egyptian historians.[2] Nāṣir's letter, though mainly concerned with a rebuttal of Ghazan's charges, ended on a conciliatory note with an offer of peace and an alliance. From Qarabāgh Ghazan now went on a hunting expedition into the mountains of Shīrvān and Lakzistān, i.e. the south-eastern spur of the Caucasian range; from thence he proceeded to the plain called Gāvbārī in the Mūghān Steppe, where he passed some time hunting and fishing before moving into the area to which he had given the Turkish name of Qush-Qapugh ("Bird Gate"). This was the narrow coastal strip stretching northwards from the Gulf of Kirov (as it is now known) to the present-day Divichi (formerly Barmakī). Rashīd al-Dīn speaks of cranes and waterfowl flying overhead on their way back from their winter to their summer range; and in fact the shores of the gulf are to this day a resting place for migrating birds, which in 1929 was established as a nature reserve. It was from Qush-Qapugh, on 12 April 1302, that Ghazan wrote a letter to the pope (then Boniface VIII), of which the Mongol original was discovered in the Vatican archives in 1921. After referring to a message from the pope delivered by the Genoese Buscarel the Īl-Khān speaks of a yarlīgh transmitted in reply by a mission composed of the same Buscarel and two Mongols. This yarlīgh was apparently, as suggested by Mostaert and Cleaves,[3] a detailed plan of campaign for the invasion of Syria proposed by Ghazan to Boniface and the Christian princes. "As for now," he goes on, "we are making our preparations exactly in the manner [laid down in our yarlīgh]. You too should prepare your troops, send word to the

[1] Transl. Arends, p. 192.
[2] See d'Ohsson, vol. IV, pp. 288–93 and 295–309.
[3] "Trois documents mongols des Archives secrètes vaticanes", p. 469.

rulers of the various nations and not fail to keep the rendezvous. Heaven willing we [i.e. Ghazan] shall make the great work [i.e. the war against the Mamlūks] our sole aim."[1]

On the preparations to which Ghazan referred in this letter there is no precise information in the Muslim sources; but the dispatch of Qutlugh-Shāh to Diyārbakr at the end of September 1301, and his recall a month later had presumably some connexion with the proposed campaign. Ghazan himself seems not to have returned to Tabrīz until the early summer of 1302. From the coastal strip he had gone back into the mountains to receive the submission of the Lakz, the modern Lezghians, the same tribesmen subdued twenty-five years earlier by Shams al-Dīn Juvainī. Then, returning southwards, he had entered the jungles of Tālish, where he had held a great *battue*, constructing for this purpose a kind of vast stockade, consisting of two wooden fences a day's journey apart at the one end and converging to a width of less than fifty yards. Rashīd al-Dīn enumerates the various species of animals entrapped in this enclosure but, curiously enough, does not mention the tiger, still in modern times a native of that region. From Tālish Ghazan made his way, by easy stages, to Tabrīz and from thence, at the end of July, to Ūjān, where he was lodged in a huge tent of gold cloth, which it had taken three years to construct and a whole month to erect. Three days of religious devotion and reading from the Qur'ān were followed by feasting and revelry, and the festivities concluded with a quriltai at which dispositions were made for the contemplated campaign in Syria. Ghazan's brother Khar-Banda, the future Öljeitü, was placed, as heretofore, in command of the eastern frontiers; Qutlugh-Shāh was sent into Georgia to recruit a Georgian contingent to join the Mongol forces in Diyārbakr; and Ghazan himself set out on 26 August 1302, by a circuitous route which took him southwards to Ḥilla by way of Kirmānshāh and then north-westwards along the right bank of the Euphrates to Raḥbat al-Shām.

From Hamadān he even made an easterly détour to the pasture lands on the Chaghan-Na'ur in Farāhān before turning back and striking the Khurāsān trunk road near Bīsitūn. As he passed by Kirmānshāh he recalled how in that region, five years previously, he had slept with his followers under a great rock with a solitary tree casting its shade over them. It was during the supposed revolt of Nauruz and his party; Nauruz's brother Lakzī had not yet been captured; Nauruz himself was

[1] *Op. cit.* p. 471.

still all-powerful in distant Khurāsān; and Ghazan had passed an uneasy night, filled with anxiety for the future. He revisited the spot with all his amīrs and ladies and was moved to tears at the contrast between his circumstances then and now. After he had offered up prayers of thanksgiving his amīrs, reverting to a custom of their pagan forefathers, attached streamers to the branches of the tree and danced around it to the strains of music. Bolad Ching-Sang, the representative of the Great Khan, who was present in Ghazan's suite, related how Qutula, a great uncle of Chingiz-Khān, had performed a similar ceremony to celebrate a victory over the Merkit; and how he and his warriors continued to dance until the pressure of their feet had formed a circular trench around the tree. Ghazan was pleased with the tale and, good Muslim though he was, himself for a while joined in the dancing.

He was apparently still in the mountains of Kurdistān when messengers arrived from Qutlugh-Shāh escorting a party of Syrian amīrs who had come to offer their allegiance: these were apparently distinct from a deputation of three who had joined him at Bīsitūn. At about the same time he received an embassy from the Byzantine Emperor Andronicus II (1282–1328), who offered the hand of a daughter in marriage and sought the Īl-Khān's protection against his Turkish neighbours. Ghazan now descended into the plains of Iraq somewhere to the north of Bandīnjān[1] on the Khūzistān border, where he stayed for three days at the beginning of December before embarking upon a hunting expedition in the Wāsiṭ region. By the end of the month he was in Ḥilla, where he received two embassies: from the Mamlūk sultan and from Toqta, the ruler of the Golden Horde. Of the sultan's message Rashīd al-Dīn[2] says only that it was not to Ghazan's liking: it was, according to Mīrkhwānd,[3] a rejection of a demand by the Īl-Khān for annual tribute and the insertion of his name in the khuṭba and on the sultan's coinage. As for Toqta's embassy Rashīd al-Dīn gives no indication whatsoever of its purpose, which was, again according to Mīrkhwānd,[4] to revive the old claim of the House of Jochi upon Arrān and Āzarbāījān. The ambassadors had an escort of 300 horse—too few, as Ghazan sarcastically remarked, to conquer the country and too many for the delivery of a message. The Mongol New Year occurring at this time the members of both embassies were included in the celebrations,

[1] The modern Mandalī.
[2] Transl. Arends, p. 197.
[3] Vol. v, p. 412.
[4] *Op. cit.* pp. 413–14.

the sultan's envoys being afterwards sent to Tabrīz as prisoners on parole.

On 29 January, Ghazan crossed the Euphrates at Ḥilla on the famous bridge of boats and on 5 February visited the shrine of Ḥusain at Karbalā. He then turned northwards along the western bank of the river. At Ḥadītha the greater part of the womenfolk were sent across to the eastern bank to await the Īl-Khān's return at Sinjār; his favourite wife accompanied him as far as 'Āna ("there is", says Rashīd al-Dīn,[1] "no more delightful place in the whole world"), which he reached on 2 March. His pace along this stretch of the route had been leisurely in the extreme, averaging less than ten miles a day; and the whole of one week had been spent in pursuit of game still apparently as plentiful as in the days of Xenophon,[2] the Arabian ostrich. It was at 'Āna that Vaṣṣāf presented the Īl-Khān with the first three books of his history and was encouraged to continue with his work. The Mongols remained here for a week before advancing on Raḥbat al-Shām, which they reached on 18 March. The inhabitants at first made some show of resistance but after some days of negotiations, in which Rashīd al-Dīn played a leading part, were induced to surrender. On the 26th, as Ghazan continued northwards, he was heartened with news of the defeat and death of Qaidu in a battle with the Great Khan's forces; he learnt at the same time that Qutlugh-Shāh and the Amīr Choban had crossed the Euphrates at Raqqa and approached Aleppo. He halted for three days on the river bank, dispatched his amīrs and troops to join Qutlugh-Shāh, and then recrossed the Euphrates *en route* for Sinjār and Mosul. Why he chose to withdraw from personal participation in the campaign is by no means clear. Rashīd al-Dīn[3] ascribes his retirement, unconvincingly, to the approach of the hot weather and the seasonal floods, while Haithon[4] speaks of an invasion of his eastern frontiers by Qaidu, who in point of fact had been dead for more than a year and a half. Of his itinerary Rashīd al-Dīn,[5] who evidently accompanied him, gives a detailed account. The passage of the Euphrates took place on 2 April; he crossed the Khābūr at Mākīsīn and advanced at a very leisurely pace across the desert, then covered with spring flowers, hunting the game animals as he went; on the 14th he joined his womenfolk at Chahār Ṭāq near Sinjār, on the 19th he was at Tall A'far, where he conferred the Sultanate of Northern Mesopotamia upon Najm al-

[1] Transl. Arends, p. 198.
[2] *Anabasis* I, v.
[3] Transl. Arends, p. 199.
[4] P. 319.
[5] Transl. Arends, pp. 199–200.

Dīn II (1294–1312), the Artuqid ruler of Mārdīn; crossing the Tigris at Mosul he encamped on the plain of Kushāf, apparently to be identified with the town of Ḥadītha above the confluence of the Great Zāb: here he awaited the outcome of the campaign.

Qutlugh-Shāh's army advanced through Syria without meeting serious resistance; they reached the Damascus area on 19 April and on the following day passed on through Kiswa to encounter the sultan's army drawn up on a famous battle-field of early Islam, the meadows of Marj al-Ṣuffar. A charge by the Mongol left wing on the Mamlūk right inflicted heavy casualties on the Egyptians and drove them back in headlong rout. Meanwhile Qutlugh-Shāh, who had gone to their assistance from the centre, was attacked by the Mamlūk centre and left and forced back on to a neighbouring hill, where he was joined by the troops returning from their pursuit of the enemy's right wing. Here the Mongols were compelled to pass the night, the hill completely encircled by Mamlūk troops. In the morning, suffering by now from thirst, they were unable to break through the cordon until the Egyptians deliberately opened their ranks to let them through, the more easily to destroy them in their flight. The Mongols made their way down to the river, apparently the modern Wādī 'Arrām, losing a great number of their horses in the muddy terrain, and the Egyptians then launched their attack, pursuing the fleeing enemy until nightfall: the pursuit was taken up in the morning by a Mamlūk amīr who continued to follow them as far as Qariyatain.

Travelling with what appears to have been indecent haste Qutlugh-Shāh reached Ghazan at Kushāf on 7 May, and was presumably the first to inform him of the Mongols' disastrous defeat. Of the Īl-Khān's reaction to the news and his reception of the messenger Rashīd al-Dīn says not a word. According to Maqrīzī[1] the effect of the report was so violent as to bring on a nasal haemorrhage: his attitude towards Qutlugh-Shāh may be deduced from the Egyptian's account of his subsequent behaviour at the court of inquiry held in June–July at Ūjān. Ghazan left the next day for Irbīl, celebrating the 'īd al-fiṭr (falling that year on 18 May) at Darband-i Zangī in the foothills of Kurdistān and proceeding from thence to Marāgheh. On 4 June, at some point along this route, he was joined by Choban, who, in contrast to his colleague, had remained with the defeated army, attending to the wants of the horseless and the wounded, and leading them slowly back by way of

[1] Transl. Quatremère, vol. II, p. 204.

Baghdad. From Marāgheh Ghazan sent his womenfolk ahead to Ūjān and spent a few days hunting on the slopes of Mount Sahand; he reached Ūjān himself on 26 June and two days later inaugurated the *yarghu* or court of inquiry, which lasted till 18 July. Of the results of this investigation Rashīd al-Dīn[1] mentions only the execution of two obscure officers; it is natural perhaps that he should not refer to the humiliation of Qutlugh-Shāh, with whom he was on terms of friendship. According to Maqrīzī's[2] account, the Īl-Khān was with difficulty restrained from putting his commander to death; and the onlookers are said to have rushed at the prisoner and spat in his face. Maqrīzī adds that Qutlugh-Shāh was banished to Gīlān; in fact, like the other commanders, he seems to have been sentenced to be beaten with the rod; even Choban, whose conduct had earned and received the Īl-Khān's praises, was not excepted from this punishment.

On 8 September 1303 Ghazan arrived in Tabrīz and had begun warlike preparations, presumably for a fourth invasion of Syria, when he was attacked for the second time with some form of ophthalmia. After treatment by his own doctors had failed to cure the disease he finally, on 19 October, had recourse to Chinese physicians (probably in the suite of Bolad Ching-Sang), who cauterized his body in two places, apparently in the abdominal region. He left on 1 November for his winter-quarters in Baghdad; unable to sit a horse on account of the cauterization he was obliged to travel in a litter, averaging little more than three or four miles a day. By 25 November he was on or near the Safīd Rūd and finding the route southwards to Hamadān to be blocked with heavy snowfalls he abandoned his intention of wintering in Baghdad and made instead for a residence at some unidentified spot on the banks of the river to which he had given the Mongol name of Öljeitü-Nuntuq[3] ("Auspicious Encampment"). Here he imposed upon himself the discipline of a *chilla*, i.e. a forty-day period of retirement, fasting and meditation such as was practised by dervishes and seekers after occult powers. His motives may well have been medical rather than spiritual, for it is clear that the Īl-Khān's infirmity—whatever its nature—was no longer a mere inflammation of the eyes.

[1] Transl. Arends, p. 201. [2] Transl. Quatremère, vol. II, pp. 204–5.

[3] The Oeuldjaïtou-yamouc of d'Ohsson (vol. IV, p. 349) and Oldzheitu-Buinuk of Arends (p. 206), the second element of the name being corruptly spelt in the MSS of Rashīd al-Dīn. Howorth, vol. III, p. 484, takes the first element for the name of the Īl-Khān and speaks of "a yurt or camp of the Mongols, which Uljaitu named Boinuk or Yamuk"!

It was during this period of seclusion that the "Mazdakite" conspiracy (to which reference will be made elsewhere in this volume)[1] was uncovered and suppressed. Ala-Fireng, the eldest son of Geikhatu, whom the conspirators sought to place on the throne, is depicted by Rashīd al-Dīn as playing a purely passive role in their machinations; it is significant, however, that one of the first acts of Ghazan's successor was to order his execution. On 10 January 1304 the Īl-Khān emerged from his retreat to take part in the New Year celebrations and to resume the administration of affairs. A few days later Keremün, the youngest of his wives, died suddenly of a stroke; her death produced a deep impression on Ghazan, perhaps already conscious of his own approaching end. At the beginning of April, he set out eastwards travelling light and accompanied only by his immediate entourage: the womenfolk had been left, along with the heavy baggage, at a place called Qal'achuq ("Little Castle") on or near the Safīd Rūd. No reason is given for this journey: it is possible that the Īl-Khān had conceived a desire to revisit his old viceroyalty of Khurāsān. His health was apparently fully restored and he was even able to indulge his passion for hunting whilst passing through the Sulṭān Bulāgh hills *en route* for Sāveh. From Sāveh, where a feast had been prepared by the vizier Sa'd al-Dīn, a native of the town, he continued, after a three days' halt, in the direction of Ray. It was at this stage that he suffered a relapse; he forced himself to ride on in spite of his infirmity, but by the time he had reached the district of Khail-i Buzurg between Ray and Qazvīn he was critically ill. He sent for his chief and favourite wife Princess Bulughan, whom he had married in defiance of the sharī'a in 1294,[2] and returning slowly westwards was reunited with her in the district of Pushkil Darra to the east of Qazvīn at the beginning of May. Assembling his ministers he exhorted each of them individually and confirmed his previous designation of his brother Khar-Banda as his heir. This duty accomplished he passed the greater part of his time in retirement, retaining full possession of his faculties until the end. He died on Sunday, 11 May 1304 in the thirty-third year of his life, and his body, transported amid universal mourning to Tabrīz, was laid to rest in the Gunbad-i-'Ālī, the mausoleum he had himself designed and erected.

Ghazan was without question the greatest of the Īl-Khāns, a remarkably gifted man by the standards of any age of history. What strikes one above all is the catholicity of his interests. He was conversant not only

[1] See below, p. 548.

[2] See above, p. 380.

with arts or sciences such as natural history, medicine, astronomy and chemistry (or more strictly alchemy) but also with several handicrafts. He could, so Rashīd al-Dīn[1] assures us, perform the tasks of a goldsmith, a blacksmith, a carpenter, a painter, a founder or a turner more expertly than the masters of these trades. "No one surpassed him", says Pachymeres,[2] "in making saddles, bridles, spurs, greaves and helmets: he could hammer, stitch and polish, and in such occupations employed the hours of his leisure from war." In addition to his native Mongol he was said to have had some knowledge of the Arabic, Persian, Hindī, Kashmīrī, Tibetan, Chinese and Frankish (i.e. French or perhaps Latin) languages. Despite his conversion to Islam he took a great interest in the history and traditions of his forefathers, on which he was an authority second only to Bolad Ching-Sang, the representative of the Great Khan. It was, in fact, at his suggestion and with his encouragement that Rashīd al-Dīn embarked upon the first part of the *Jāmiʿ al-tawārīkh*, "a vast historical encyclopaedia such as no single people, either in Asia or in Europe, possessed in the Middle Ages".[3] His measures to reform the fiscal system will be examined elsewhere in this volume.[4] In his person he was short and of unprepossessing appearance, in complete contrast to his father Arghun, a tall and handsome man. After describing his gallantry in the Battle of Ḥimṣ the Armenian Haithon, in a passage already referred to above,[5] continues as follows: "And the most remarkable thing of all was that within a frame so small, and ugly almost to monstrosity, there should be assembled nearly all those high qualities which nature is wont to associate with a form of symmetry and beauty. In fact amongst all his host of 200,000 Tartars you should scarcely find one of smaller stature or of uglier and meaner aspect than this Prince."[6]

ÖLJEITÜ

Through his agents in Ghazan's court Khar-Banda had received early intelligence of his brother's death and had at once taken steps to remove a possible rival. This was his cousin Ala-Fireng, recently involved in the "Mazdakite" conspiracy.[7] The unsuspecting prince was struck down

[1] Transl. Arends, p. 213.
[2] Quoted by Yule, *The Book of Ser Marco Polo*, vol. II, p. 478.
[3] Barthold, *Turkestan*, p. 46.
[4] See below, pp. 494–500.
[5] P. 388.
[6] Quoted by Yule, *loc. cit.*
[7] See above, p. 396.

in the course of a private interview by one of Khar-Banda's emissaries (30 May 1304), himself killed shortly afterwards in a collision with the forces of the Amīr Horqudaq. The latter, also apparently regarded as an obstacle in Khar-Banda's path, was captured and summarily executed. Against the deaths of these two men should be set the fact that during the first year of Ghazan's reign no less than ten princes of the blood had met a violent end: it is possible that the new Īl-Khān's prompt if ruthless action may have prevented the recurrence of bloodshed on a similar scale. The way now clear, he set out on the journey from Khurāsān to Āzarbāījān. Progress was slow because of the heavy rainfalls: he reached Ūjān on 9 July, and ten days later the ceremony of enthronement took place still, apparently, with all the traditional rites as observed and described by John de Plano Carpini nearly sixty years before. He assumed the throne name of Öljeitü (in Mongol "Fortunate" or "Auspicious") in addition to that of Khar-Banda (in Persian "Ass-Herd") given him either at birth, in accordance with the Mongol custom of naming a child after the first person or object that caught the mother's eye after the confinement, or at a later stage, in accordance with the custom of altering a child's name to protect him against the evil eye. Partly, at least, for euphemistic reasons the name was afterwards changed to Khudā-Banda ("Slave of God", the Arabic ʿAbdallāh), the Īl-Khān's full title being Ghiyāth al-Dīn Muḥammad Khudā-Banda Öljeitü Sulṭān.

After three days of feasting Öljeitü turned his attention to affairs of state, confirming Saʿd al-Dīn and Rashīd al-Dīn in their offices and appointing Qutlugh-Shāh his commander-in-chief. On 6 August he left Ūjān for Tabrīz where, on the following day, he visited his brother's tomb. It was somewhere near Marāgheh, in the Jaghatu valley according to Vaṣṣāf,[1] that he received the ambassadors of the Great Khan Temür, the grandson and successor (1294–1307) of Qubilai, accompanied by those of Chabar, the son of Qaidu, and Du'a, the son of Baraq: the object of this composite mission was to apprise the Īl-Khān of a pact that had put an end to the longstanding quarrels between these branches of the House of Chingiz-Khān. From Marāgheh, where he installed Aṣīl al-Dīn, the son of Naṣīr al-Dīn Ṭūsī, in the observatory founded by his father, Öljeitü made his way to winter-quarters in Mūghān, halting *en route* at Tabrīz to pay a second visit to the Gunbad-i ʿĀlī. In Mūghān, on 9 December, he received the ambassadors of

[1] Bombay ed. p. 475.

Toqta, the ruler of the Golden Horde, who presumably made some allusion to the reconciliation of the princes of Central and Eastern Asia, of which Toqta also had been informed. To this development, apparently betokening the restoration of the Mongol world empire as it had existed under Möngke, Öljeitü refers in a letter addressed to Philippe le Bel, which has been preserved in the French national archives. He begins this letter, written at Alīvān (Barzand) in Mūghān on 5 April 1305, by affirming this desire to maintain the traditional ties of friendship between the Īl-Khāns and the "sultans of the Frankish people". He then proceeds: "...we, Temür Qa'an, Toqta, Chabar, Du'a and others, the descendants of Chingiz-Khān, after recriminating one another for forty-five years down to these recent times, have now, protected by Heaven, all of us, elder and younger brothers, reached a mutual agreement, and from the land of the Chinese, where the sun rises, to the sea of Talu [the Caspian, or perhaps the Mediterranean], our states joining with one another [i.e. re-establishing communications], we have caused our post stations to be linked together." The letter concludes with a veiled hint at possible concerted action against the Mamlūks: "Now, as for those who shall not agree, either with us, or with you, let Heaven decide on the manner in which, by the strength of Heaven, leaguing against them all of us together, we shall take our stand."[1] The Īl-Khān's meaning, as appears from the contemporary Italian version of the letter, was intended to be amplified by word of mouth.

Öljeitü, in fact, as the Persian authorities explicitly state, had every intention of continuing the anti-Mamlūk policy of his predecessors. In December 1305, the Egyptian ambassadors detained by Ghazan were allowed to depart; they were accompanied by Öljeitü's own ambassadors bearing a message to the sultan. That this was not a conciliatory move is clear from the tone of the message as reproduced by Vaṣṣāf:[2] the Īl-Khān wished no doubt to gain time whilst making his own preparations and awaiting the response to his appeal to the princes of Christendom. In the meantime he set his hand to the task for which he is chiefly remembered: the building or rather the completion (for the work had been begun by his father Arghun) of a new town on the plain of Qongqur-Öleng to which he (or perhaps already Arghun) had given the name of Sulṭānīyeh and which, though "neither geographically nor

[1] Mostaert and Cleaves, *Les Lettres de* 1289 *et* 1305 *des ilkhan Aryun et Öljeitü à Philippe le Bel*, pp. 56–7.

[2] Bombay ed. p. 472.

historically suited for such a high destiny",[1] he now made his capital. Here was erected his mausoleum, still to this day "one of the most celebrated buildings in the whole of Persia".[2]

It was from Sulṭānīyeh that he set out, in May 1307, upon a campaign against, not the Egyptians, but an enemy much nearer home, the people of the Caspian province of Gīlān. That this territory, contiguous to the Mongols' summer and winter quarters in Arrān and Āzarbāījān, should still have remained unsubjugated after fifty years of Īl-Khānid rule is readily accounted for by the inaccessibility of the country with its dense forests and impenetrable jungles and, above all, humid, unhealthy climate. Stung, it is said, by the jeers of the Chaghatai Mongols Öljeitü resolved upon an elaborate military operation against Gīlān. Four armies entered the country at four different points: Choban advancing from Ardabīl, Qutlugh-Shāh from Khalkhāl and Toghan and Mu'min from Qazvīn, whilst Öljeitü himself, passing through Ṭārum halted for three days on the slopes of Mount Dulfak, before pushing forward in the direction of Lāhījān. He was joined *en route* by Choban, to whom the rulers of Āstārā and Gaskar had surrendered without a fight. Toghan and Mu'min were equally successful in Southern Gīlān, and Öljeitü, who had occupied Lāhījān and received the submission of its ruler, was in the region of Kūhdum on the return journey when he learnt the news of Qutlugh-Shāh's defeat and death in battle. Advised at Khalkhāl to proceed with caution in this difficult terrain the commander-in-chief, ignoring counsel so little in keeping with his character, sent on ahead Bolad-Qaya in command of a force which defeated the Gīlakīs in three bloody battles. The latter then sued for peace, and Qutlugh-Shāh was in favour of accepting their submission but was dissuaded by his son Siba'uchi, who seems to have inherited all of his father's impetuosity. Displacing Bolad-Qaya at the head of the advanced forces Siba'uchi carried fire and sword through the land until confronted by a great host of Gīlakīs on a battle-field of their own choosing between Rasht and Tūlim. The Mongols were defeated with great slaughter, their horses sinking in the mud as they turned in flight. Qutlugh-Shāh's own troops withdrew in panic when they heard the news, and he was left with only a handful of men to meet the oncoming enemy: he was killed by an arrow shot, and the triumphant Gīlakīs possessed themselves of the whole of the immense booty which the Mongols had captured in their territory. Such was the end of this

[1] Minorsky, *Iranica*, p. 47. [2] *Ibid.*

powerful and headstrong man, the Cotolossa of Haithon: he was a descendant of Jedei Noyan of the Manqut tribe, a general of Chingiz-Khān. His death carried incalculable consequences for the future of the Īl-Khānate; had he survived, the Amīr Choban, who now succeeded him as commander-in-chief, might well not have achieved the all-powerful position which he occupied in the following reign. A detachment sent to avenge this disaster almost met with the same fate; the dispatch of reinforcements caused the Gīlakīs to disperse into their forests, and, on 29 June Öljeitü struck camp to leave Gīlān, having gained what seems to have been at most a Pyrrhic victory over its inhabitants.

In the previous year the Īl-Khān had dispatched an army against Fakhr al-Dīn Kart, the malik of Herāt, with whom he had clashed during his viceroyalty of Khurāsān because of his support for the Nīgūdarīs. Fakhr al-Dīn closed the gates of the town upon the approach of the Mongol commander, Dānishmand Bahadur, but after a few days' siege entered into negotiations, as the result of which he surrendered the town to Dānishmand, leaving one of his officers, Jamāl al-Dīn Muḥammad Sām, in command of the citadel; he himself withdrew to the neighbouring castle of Amān-Kūh. Whilst visiting the citadel with a small following Dānishmand was attacked and killed; the Mongols inside the town were slaughtered and the army outside the walls then withdrew. Reinforcements were sent under the command of Dānishmand's son Bujai to avenge his father's death; they invested the town on 5 February 1307. The siege, which lasted till 24 June, is described in considerable detail by Ḥāfiẓ-i Abrū[1] and Mīrkhwānd,[2] as one would expect of historians writing of their Tīmūrid patrons' capital. Here it is sufficient to say that Fakhr al-Dīn Kart, who was certainly in collusion with Sām, died in the early days of siege; that a plot to kill Sām and so save the town was betrayed and the conspirators executed; and that Bujai finally negotiated terms of surrender with his father's murderer in order to deny another general the credit of capturing the town.

Öljeitü, baptized in infancy with the Christian name of Nicholas, had become in turn a Buddhist and a Sunnī (Ḥanafī) Muslim. Reference will be made elsewhere[3] to a curious disputation which took place in his presence, apparently in Arrān in the winter of 1307–8, between representatives of the Ḥanafī and Shāfi'ī schools, "who, in the heat of controversy, brought against each other such abominable accusations that Úljáytú was greatly annoyed with both, and even the Mongol

[1] Pp. 18–39. [2] Pp. 443–68. [3] See below, p. 544.

nobles who were by no means squeamish, professed disgust, and began to ask whether it was for this that they had abandoned the faith of their ancestors, to which they now called on Úljáytú to return".[1] Shortly afterwards, during a violent thunderstorm, several of the Īl-Khān's companions were killed by lightning. It was put to him by some of his amīrs that he should purify himself according to the ancient Mongol (and indeed Altaic) custom, by passing between two fires;[2] and *bakhshis*, who must have been, not Buddhist priests but qams or shamans, were produced to supervise the ceremony. They attributed the disaster to Öljeitü's conversion to Islam, which they called upon him to abjure. A return to shamanism was of course altogether out of the question, but his anti-Sunnī feelings persisted and he was gradually persuaded to become a Shī'ite, making the final decision after a visit to Najaf in the winter of 1309–10.

The vizier Sa'd al-Dīn Sāvajī, who had always enjoyed Ghazan's confidence and favour, fell from grace under his successor. The basic cause of his downfall seems to have been an arrogance bred from long years of power; he made enemies, one of whom was his colleague Rashīd al-Dīn; and it was the latter's report to Öljeitü on the peculations of his subordinates that led to his arrest and execution (19 February 1312). He was succeeded in his office by Tāj al-Dīn 'Alī-Shāh, a dealer in jewels and precious stuffs who had insinuated himself into the Īl-Khān's good graces; with no previous knowledge of public finance (*'ilm-i daftar u siyāqat*)[3] and in no way more honest than his predecessor, he achieved, in the following reign, the distinction of being the first Īl-Khānid vizier to die in his bed.

Öljeitü must by now have long abandoned the hope of a European alliance against the Mamlūks. There is no record of Philippe le Bel's having answered (or even received) the Īl-Khān's letter; but a similar letter addressed to Edward I of England was acknowledged in a letter from his son Edward II dated at Northampton, 16 October 1307, and in a second letter[4] dated 30 November and written at Langley the English king replies to what must have been an oral message conveyed by the Īl-Khān's ambassadors. He wishes Öljeitü well in his enterprise, which he takes quite naturally, and without necessarily being misled by the envoys, to be the extirpation of the "abominable sect of Mahomet",

[1] E. G. Browne, *A Literary History of Persia*, vol. III, p. 50.
[2] See Rockhill, *The Journey of William of Rubruck*, pp. 240–1 n. 2.
[3] Ḥāfiẓ-i Abrū, p. 46.
[4] Quoted by Howorth, vol. III, p. 576.

but regrets that the distance and other difficulties prevent his co-operating in this "laudable design". Pope Clement V, in a letter[1] dated at Poitiers, 1 March 1308, disclosed some of the details of the proposed alliance: "We have noticed with pleasure, from these letters and communications, that appealing to our solicitude on behalf of the Holy Land, you have offered us 200,000 horses and 200,000 loads of corn, which will be in Armenia when the army of the Christians arrives there, and in addition to march in person with 100,000 horsemen to support the efforts of the Christians to expel the Saracens from that Holy Land." He expresses his appreciation of the offer, which, he says, "has strengthened us like spiritual food", but makes only a vague reference to future collaboration. He and his brethren, he assures the Īl-Khān, "will execute as far as we can what God had inspired us to do, and when a favourable season for crossing the sea shall come we will advise you by letters and messengers so that you may accomplish what your magnificence has promised".

It was encouragement from another quarter that prompted Öljeitü's one and only invasion of Mamlūk territory. At Sulṭānīyeh, in August 1312, he welcomed the arrival of a group of dissident Syrian amīrs headed by Qara-Sonqur, the governor of Damascus, and Aq-Qush al-Afram, the governor of Tripoli. On Qara-Sonqur, whose Turkish name ("Black Gerfalcon") he changed, on account of his years, to Aq-Sonqur ("White Gerfalcon"), he bestowed the governorship of Marāgheh and on al-Afram that of Hamadān; both men accompanied him on a campaign for which they must have convinced him the time was now propitious. Setting out from his capital at the beginning of October he proceeded by way of Mosul, crossed the Euphrates at Qirqīsiyā and, on 23 December, sat down before Raḥbat al-Shām. He had been encouraged by Qara-Sonqur and al-Afram to think that the governor, a protégé of the former amīr, could be induced to surrender the town. In this he was disappointed: the townsfolk offered fierce resistance, and because of their heavy casualties and lack of provisions the Mongols, on 26 January 1313, raised the siege and withdrew across the Euphrates, never to return.

So ended, after a lapse of fifty years, the Mongol–Mamlūk struggle for the possession of Syria. That the outcome would have been different had the princes of Europe accepted the proffered alliance cannot seriously be doubted. Nor need we question the sincerity of the Mongols'

[1] Quoted by Howorth, vol. III, pp. 576–7.

promises with respect to Palestine; the restoration of the Kingdom of Jerusalem would have been as much in their interest as was the preservation of Little Armenia. The views of the Armenian Haithon, dictated in Avignon in 1307 when the question of such collaboration was still under earnest consideration, deserve more attention than has perhaps been accorded them.[1] Having captured the district of Tripoli the Christian expeditionary force should, according to the strategy laid out in his work, rebuild the city, make it their base of operations "and thus be ready when the Tartars had completed their conquest of the Holy Land to take over from them the towns there, which he was confident they would make over to the Christians for custody, because they could not endure the heat of the summer in those parts; nor did they fight with the Sultan to conquer more lands, for they were masters of all Asia, but because the Sultan was very unfriendly to them and always doing them some injury, especially when they were at war with the neighbouring Tartars (i.e. those of Kipchak and Jagatai)".[2] There were, of course, disadvantages to an alliance with the Mongols.

> If Karbanda, or some one sent by him, should invade Egypt with a very large army, it would be well to avoid him, for the Lord of the Tartars would deem it derogatory to follow the counsel of the Christians, and would insist on their following his commands. Besides which, the Tartars were all mounted and marched rapidly, and a Christian army, much of which marched on foot, could not keep up with them. The Tartars, again, when in small numbers and humble were obsequious, but when in large numbers were overbearing and arrogant, insulting to their allies who were weaker than themselves, and would be found unbearable by the Christians.[3]

In the event of a large-scale campaign of this sort Haithon recommends that while the Mongols follow their normal route to Damascus the Christian army should advance along a parallel route to Jerusalem. "And in this way, because of the distance between them, peace and friendship would be preserved between the Christians and the Tartars..."[4] Some kind of collaboration must in fact have been possible, and it is interesting to speculate what might have happened if, for example, the Crusade of Edward I and Abaqa's invasion of Syria in 1281 had, by accident or design, exactly coincided, instead of occurring nearly ten years apart.

In the last years of his reign the Īl-Khān's attention was directed

[1] The *Flos Historiarum Terrae Orientis* is dismissed by Spuler, p. 231, as "nur ein Tendenzwerk".
[2] Quoted by Howorth, vol. III, p. 578. [3] *Ibid.* p. 579. [4] P. 361.

eastwards. His annexation, in 1313, of the Nīgūdarī territories in Southern Afghanistan provoked an invasion of Khurāsān by a Chaghatai army led by Kebek, the brother of the khan (Esen-Buqa), Dā'ūd Khwāja, the ousted Nīgūdarī ruler, and Prince Yasa'ur, a grandson of Baidar, Chaghatai's sixth son. Crossing the Oxus in the middle of January 1314, they inflicted a heavy defeat on the army of Khurāsān near the banks of the Murghāb, pursuing their fugitive opponents to the gates of Herāt. Upon receiving news of this disaster Öljeitü at once set out from Sulṭānīyeh (18 February 1314), and the enemy withdrew as he approached, recalled, apparently, by Esen-Buqa, who was being hard pressed by the troops of the Great Khan. It was about this time that Öljeitü appointed his son Abū Sa'īd to the viceroyalty of Khurāsān, a post traditionally held by the heir-apparent, the actual duties being carried out by Abū Sa'īd's atabeg, the Amīr Sevinch, for the prince was only an eight-year old child. The situation in the East was somewhat eased by the defection of Prince Yasa'ur, accused by Kebek of collusion with the Persian Mongols during the invasion of Khurāsān. Öljeitü's troops crossed the Oxus to intervene in a battle between Yasa'ur and the Chaghatai forces and to swing the balance in the former's favour: he accompanied them back into Khurāsān, where Öljeitü allowed him to occupy the pasture lands of Bādghīs and where, as we shall see, he rose in rebellion against Öljeitü's successor.

It was the expenses of the army of Khurāsān that occasioned the first rift between Rashīd al-Dīn and 'Alī-Shāh. Abū Sa'īd's requests for funds were passed on by Öljeitü to the two viziers. Rashīd al-Dīn disclaimed all responsibility, saying that he had never had the management of the finances nor affixed his seal to assignations made upon the revenue.

"I only possess the robe that covers me, and have not a single coin, and, inasmuch as we govern the empire together," replied Ali-Shah, "why should we separate from one another when it is a question of paying?" "Because you have undertaken that responsibility yourself", said Rashid. "You are the guardian of the Great Seal, and are charged with the carrying out of the Sultan's orders." "Why then not affix your seal after mine?" was the reply. "I do not want to join myself with you who profess poverty when asked for money, while each of your employés has made a hundred tumans and become a Carun..."[1]

After listening to this dispute Öljeitü ordered the division of his empire into two administrative spheres, Rashīd al-Dīn becoming responsible

[1] Howorth, vol. IV, pp. 570–1. His ultimate source is Kāshānī: the passage is quoted by Bayānī in his edition of Ḥāfiẓ-i Abrū, pp. 65 ff., n. 1.

for Central and Southern Persia to the confines of Khurāsān whilst 'Alī-Shāh was placed in charge of North-western Persia, Mesopotamia and Asia Minor. But even this segregation of their fields of operation failed to restore harmony, and 'Alī-Shāh, having survived an investigation into his accounts, continued a vendetta which resulted, in the following reign, in his colleague's disgrace and execution.

Öljeitü died in Sulṭānīyeh on 17 December 1316; he was in his thirty-sixth year. The cause of his death seems to have been some kind of digestive disorder brought on by the intemperate habits common to all the Mongol princes (with the exception, if we may believe Rashīd al-Dīn,[1] of Ghazan) and aggravated by the excessive administration of astringent medicines. Without his brother's energy and strength of character Öljeitü was an even greater patron of the arts. It was at his suggestion that Rashīd al-Dīn, having completed the first volume of his work, the *Ta'rīkh-i Ghāzānī*, dealing with the history of the Mongols from the beginnings down to the death of Ghazan, embarked in a second volume upon "the first attempt to record the history of all the great nations of the continent of Eurasia",[2] an enterprise which "has not as yet been accorded the recognition it deserves as a unique achievement...".[3] We think of Öljeitü, however, first and foremost as a builder. In addition to Sulṭānīyeh he constructed, at the foot of Mount Bīsitūn, a second capital called Sulṭānābād Chamchimāl or simply Chamchimāl (Mongol *chabchimal* "hewn"), of which the ruins still exist and which has given its name to the Chamchamāl plain. Mustaufī[4] speaks of his interest in the surveying of his dominions: roads were measured and milestones set up and in 1311, presumably when the foundations of Chamchimāl were being laid, Mustaufī himself, on the instructions of the Īl-Khān and with the assistance of engineers, made a calculation to ascertain the height of Bīsitūn.

ABŪ SA'ĪD

The heir-apparent, still only in his twelfth year, was in Māzandarān at the time of his father's last illness. It was not until the spring of the following year that he arrived in Sulṭānīyeh, the enthronement ceremoney following in the middle of April or, according to the *Mujmal-i Faṣīḥī*,[5] not until 4 July. The delay in his arrival appears to have been

[1] Transl. Arends, pp. 215–16.
[2] Jahn, *Rashīd al-Dīn's History of India*, pp. ix–x.
[3] *Op. cit.* p. x.
[4] Pp. 160–1 and 183.
[5] Vol. II, p. 26.

due to the ambition of his atabeg the Amīr Sevinch, who for a while had aspired to the post of amīr of the ulus or commander-in-chief before conceding the superior claims of the Amīr Choban, who had occupied this office ever since the death of Qutlugh-Shāh and to whose charge Öljeitü, upon his deathbed, had specifically committed his son.

The new Īl-Khān retained the services not only of Choban but also of Rashīd al-Dīn and 'Alī-Shāh. The two viziers were still at loggerheads, and 'Alī-Shāh, jealous of the credit his colleague enjoyed with the now all-powerful amīr of the ulus, renewed his former intrigues to such purpose that, at the beginning of October 1317, Rashīd al-Dīn was dismissed from office. The Amīr Sevinch wished to secure his reinstatement, but died near Baghdad, where Abū Sa'īd was passing the winter of 1317–18, before he could achieve his object. In the spring, when the Court moved northwards, the Amīr Choban summoned Rashīd al-Dīn from Tabrīz, where he was living in retirement and persuaded him, against his better judgment, to re-enter the Īl-Khān's service: he was, Choban said, as necessary to the state as salt to food. 'Alī-Shāh and his henchmen now redoubled their efforts to discredit him; they accused him of having poisoned the Īl-Khān's father; the accusation was believed and Choban, far from defending his protégé, seems actually to have assumed the role of prosecutor. Rashīd al-Dīn was put to death on 17 July 1318, having first been made to witness the execution of his son, a lad of sixteen, who, as the cupbearer, was alleged to have actually administered the poison. His death was the signal for the looting of Rub'-i Rashīdī, the suburb of Tabrīz which he had founded and given his name, and all his lands and property were confiscated by the Dīvān, even his pious foundations (*vaqfs*) being robbed of their endowments. His severed head, according to Nuwairī,[1] was taken to Tabrīz and carried about the town for several days with cries of: "This is the head of the Jew who abused the name of God; may God's curse be upon him!" Such was the ignominious end of the celebrated statesman and historian, "the greatest vizier of the Il-Khan dynasty, and one of the greatest men the East has produced";[2] he was a little over seventy years of age. His Jewish origin, denied by some scholars and queried by others, has been fully established by the researches of Fischel[3] and Spuler.[4]

[1] Quoted by d'Ohsson, vol. IV, p. 611.

[2] Howorth, vol. III, p. 589.

[3] See "Azarbaijan in Jewish History", pp. 15–18.

[4] See *Die Mongolen in Iran*, pp. 247–9.

Yasa'ur, the Chaghatai prince established in Bādghīs, had at first professed towards the young Īl-Ḵhān a loyalty with which his activities in Ḵhurāsān were difficult to reconcile, but early in 1319 he rose in open revolt, and news of his invasion of Māzandarān was received simultaneously with a report that Öz-Beg, the ruler (1313–41) of the Golden Horde, was approaching Darband at the head of a great army. It was decided that the Amīr Ḥusain—the father of Ḥasan-i Buzurg or Ḥasan the Great, the founder (1336–56) of the Jalayir dynasty—should be sent against Yasa'ur, whilst the Īl-Ḵhān marched in person against Öz-Beg. Choban, reviewing his troops near Bailaqān,[1] learnt that Abū Sa'īd was facing the enemy across the Kur with a force of no more than a thousand men at arms and the like number of grooms, muleteers and camel-men, his advanced forces having retired in disorder upon the mere report of Öz-Beg's approach. It had been Choban's intention to proceed to Ḵhurāsān, being alarmed by exaggerated accounts of Yasa'ur's strength; he now hurried to his sovereign's assistance, crossed the Kur at the head of 20,000 men and inflicted heavy losses upon an enemy already in full retreat. The fighting over, disciplinary action was taken against the officers who had deserted their posts: the most culpable were beaten with the rod, a display of severity which was not without its consequences. In 1325 Choban repulsed a second invasion by Öz-Beg and even carried the war into the enemy's own territory. Thirty years later Öz-Beg's son and successor Janï-Beg (1340–57) succeeded where his father had failed and for a brief space of time Āzarbāïjān was incorporated in the territories of the Golden Horde.

Yasa'ur's revolt was soon suppressed. He withdrew from Māzandarān as Ḥusain's forces advanced against him; from Ṭūs he sent an army to invest Herāt, where the Malik Ghiyāth al-Dīn had rallied to Choban and the Īl-Ḵhān; in April he sat down in person before the town but raised the siege upon the approach of the Īl-Ḵhān's army and withdrew into Southern Afghanistan. In the following year he was defeated and killed, not by the Persian Mongols, but by the troops of his Chaghatai kinsman Kebek, who had now succeeded to the Khanate. A rebellion nearer home was of far greater danger. The officers subjected to corporal punishment after the battle with Öz-Beg sought to take their vengeance on Choban; they waylaid him near Lake Sevan in Armenia; he escaped, made his way to Tabrīz, and thence to Sulṭānīyeh. The malcontents, meanwhile, had been joined by the Amīr Irenjin, whom Choban had

---

[1] Near Shusha in the present-day Soviet Āzarbāïjān.

dismissed from the governorship of Diyārbakr; they collected an army at Nakhchivān and advanced on the capital. A fierce battle was fought near Mīāneh (June 1319); the Īl-Khān's men were on the point of giving way, when they were rallied by Abū Saʿīd's personal intervention and, returning to the charge, completely routed the enemy. Many of the rebel amīrs were killed in the fighting; Irenjin, captured in the village of Kāghadh-Kunān, was taken with two of the other ringleaders to Sulṭānīyeh, where they were suspended from hooks and fires kindled beneath them. Because of the bravery he had displayed in this battle the young Īl-Khān received the title of Bahādur[1] ("Hero") and in subsequent firmans and the like his name appeared as al-Sulṭān al-ʿĀdil ("the just Sultan") Abū Saʿīd Bahādur Khān. The fatḥ-nāma announcing this victory was issued from Qarabāgh, whither Abū Saʿīd had betaken himself to pass the winter of 1319–20. For the part he had played in the battle Choban was rewarded with the hand of the Īl-Khān's sister, the Princess Sati Beg.

The mayor of the palace—for such Choban had by now to all intents and purposes become—had soon to cope with the rebellion of his own son. In 1322 Temür-Tash, appointed viceroy of Rūm at the beginning of the reign, proclaimed himself the independent ruler of that province, causing coin to be struck and the khuṭba to be recited in his name; he gave himself out to be the Mahdī or Messiah whom the Muslims expect at the end of the world and sought the alliance of the Egyptians in the conquest of Persia. With the Īl-Khān's permission Choban intervened in person. Though suffering from gout he advanced through the snows of an Anatolian winter to secure his son's surrender; and Temür-Tash was for his father's sake not only pardoned but actually reinstated in his post, in which, attacking now the Turks and now the Greeks, he extended the Mongol conquests to the very shores of the Mediterranean.

Early in 1324 occurred the death of the vizier ʿAlī-Shāh, the first and only holder of his office under the Īl-Khāns to die of natural causes. He was succeeded in due course by Rukn al-Dīn Ṣā'in (Mongol *sayin* "good"), a protégé of Choban, who, however, soon began to intrigue against his benefactor. The latter's power was now at its zenith, and Abū Saʿīd was "only king in name",[2] the whole of his dominions being parcelled out amongst Choban and his sons, one of whom, Dimashq

[1] On this ancient Altaic title see Doerfer, vol. II, pp. 366–77 (no. 817).
[2] *The History of Shaikh Uwais*, transl. van Loon, p. 54.

Khwāja ("Master Damascus"),[1] the viceroy of Āzarbāījān and the two 'Irāqs, also exercised the authority nominally vested in Rukn al-Dīn. A natural impatience with such tutelage was aggravated by the whisperings of the new vizier, the arrogant and dissolute behaviour of Dimashq Khwāja and, above all, a violent passion which the Īl-Khān, now in his 21st year, had conceived for Baghdād Khatun, the latter's sister and the wife of Shaikh Ḥasan. In accordance with the Yasa[2] of Chingiz-Khān the sovereign could exercise a kind of *droit de seigneur* with respect to any married woman who took his fancy. In Ūjān in the late summer of 1325 Abū Sa'īd approached the Amīr Choban through an intermediary with a view to claiming this right. Without making a direct reply Choban extricated himself from an embarrassing situation by persuading the Īl-Khān to pass the following winter in Baghdad and then, after the departure of the Court, dispatching his son-in-law and daughter to Qarabāgh. Absence did not, however, have the effect that Choban had expected and Abū Sa'īd's feelings for Baghdād Khatun remained unchanged. Early in 1326 the fear of an invasion of Khurāsān caused Choban to lead an army to the eastern frontiers, where in the autumn of that year the Chaghatai khan Tarmashirin (1326–34) crossed the Oxus to be defeated by Choban's son the Amīr Ḥasan in a battle near Ghazna. The vizier Rukn al-Dīn Ṣā'in had accompanied Choban on this campaign, leaving Dimashq Khwāja in complete and untrammelled control of the administration. Disgusted with his excesses and ashamed of his own complete destitution of authority, the Īl-Khān was seeking some opportunity for ridding himself of Dimashq when the pretext was provided by the discovery of an intrigue with a former concubine of Öljeitü; and Dimashq, trapped in the citadel of Sulṭānīyeh, was killed whilst trying to escape on 25 August 1327.

The Īl-Khān was now resolved to extirpate the whole race of Choban. The amīrs in Khurāsān, notified of his intention, at first affected to take the part of their commander-in-chief, who set out westwards to avenge his son. At Simnān he persuaded Shaikh 'Alā' al-Daula, the local religious leader, to intercede with Abū Sa'īd, then encamped near Qazvīn. The shaikh's arguments producing no effect Choban continued his march, his troops pillaging and burning as though in enemy

[1] Cf. the name of his sister Baghdād Khatun ("Lady Baghdad"). Dimashq might well have been born in Damascus during the Syrian campaign of 1299–1300.

[2] Ḥāfiẓ-i Abrū, p. 117, seems to be our only authority for the existence of such a law, which Togan, p. 220, believes to have obtained amongst the ancient Turks.

territory, until he reached the village of Qūha to the south-east of Ray, only a day's journey distant from the Īl-Khān's camp. Here, under cover of darkness, the greater part of his amīrs with a force of 30,000 men went over to Abū Saʿīd, and in the morning he found himself with no alternative but a rapid withdrawal. He made off in the direction of Sāveh, from whence he sent his royal wife, Princess Sati Beg, back to her brother, and then struck eastwards across the desert to Ṭabas. It had at first been his intention to seek refuge in Transoxiana, but upon reaching the Murghāb he changed his mind and made for Herāt, where history was to repeat itself almost exactly. Like Nauruz before him, he trusted his life to the Kart ruler and like Nauruz he too was betrayed. Ordered by Abū Saʿīd to execute the refugee, Ghiyāth al-Dīn, though bound by ties of friendship to Choban (as his brother Fakhr al-Dīn had been to Nauruz), had no choice but to obey. At his own request Choban was not beheaded but suffered an honourable death by strangulation, a finger of his hand being sent to the Īl-Khān as proof of his execution. His last wish that his body should be buried in Medina was carried out under the supervision of his daughter Baghdād Khatun, whom Abū Saʿīd had now at last married, having compelled her husband Shaikh Ḥasan to divorce her. Choban, according to Ibn Baṭṭūṭa, was laid to rest, not in the mausoleum he had caused to be built for himself near the Mosque of the Prophet, but in the famous cemetery of Baqīʿ. "It was al-Jubān", Ibn Baṭṭūṭa[1] adds, "who had the water brought to Mecca", referring to his restoration of the conduit of Zubaida "with the result that good water became abundant and cheap in Mecca during the Pilgrimage, and plentiful enough to grow vegetables in the city".[2] The pious Muslim did not forget his Mongol origins: his son by Princess Sati Beg was called Sorghan Shira after his ancestor the Süldüs tribesman who had helped the youthful Chingiz-Khān to escape from capitivity amongst the Taichi'ut.[3]

Temür-Tash learnt of his father's death at Qaisariyya; he fled by way of Lāranda (now Karaman) into the territories of the Mamlūk sultan, who had offered him asylum. At Cairo he was received at first with every honour but was afterwards imprisoned and put to death (22 August 1328). Nāṣir, desirous of keeping on good terms with Abū Saʿīd, found it expedient to execute his guest rather than accede to the Īl-Khān's request for his extradition. Had Temür-Tash survived he might, after

[1] Transl. Gibb, pp. 339–40.
[2] *Ibid.* p. 340, n. 227.
[3] See Waley, *The Secret History of the Mongols*, pp. 230–1.

the collapse of the Īl-Khānid dynasty, have founded a successor state in Anatolia and so hampered and perhaps prevented the rise of the Ottoman empire. "His death", says Grousset,[1] "followed seven years later by that of Abū Sa'īd, left Anatolia without a master and liberated the local Turkish amīrs, the Qaraman in the South-East and the Ottoman in the North-West. Thus the rise of the Ottoman Empire was an indirect consequence of events at the Īl-Khānid court in the crucial years 1327–1335."

The duties of vizier were confided, after the death of Dimashq Khwāja, to Ghiyāth al-Dīn, the son of Rashīd al-Dīn, a minister, according to the contemporary historian Mustaufī,[2] of such "angelic temperament" that "instead of punishing those who had wrought towards his noble family ill deeds whereof the recapitulation would disgust the hearts of my hearers, he drew the pen of forgiveness through the record of their crimes, recompensed their evil actions with good, and made each one of them an exemplar of the prosperity of this empire, raising them to the highest ranks, and entrusting to them the most important functions..." Such indeed was the vizier's complaisance or simplicity that we find him interceding with the Īl-Khān on behalf of the rebellious viceroy of Khurāsān, Narin-Taghai, who was plotting his downfall. The execution of Narin-Taghai and his fellow conspirator the Amīr Tash-Temür in September 1329 ended the last serious threat to Abū Sa'īd's authority. Three years later Shaikh Ḥasan-i Buzurg, accused of conspiring with his former wife, Baghdād Khatun, to assassinate her husband, was banished to the castle of Kamākh (the modern Kemah) on the Western Euphrates. He was cleared of the accusation and in 1333 returned to Rūm as viceroy, a post which he still occupied when called to intervene in the struggles that followed Abū Sa'īd's death. In the summer of 1335 there were rumours that Öz-Beg was again preparing an invasion of the Īl-Khān's dominions. The armies of Baghdad and Diyārbakr were dispatched to Arrān and stationed along the Aq-Su. Abū Sa'īd followed in person; he died in the Qarabāgh area on 30 November 1335, his death being apparently due to poisoning though he had previously been attacked by some epidemic disease. The poison according to Ibn Baṭṭūṭa,[3] was administered by Baghdād Khatun, jealous of a younger rival, Dil-Shād Khatun, the daughter of her brother Dimashq Khwāja and afterwards the wife

[1] *L'Empire des steppes*, p. 464.
[2] Quoted by Browne, vol. III, pp. 56–7.
[3] Transl. Gibb, p. 340.

of Shaikh Ḥasan-i Buzurg and the mother of his son and successor (1356–74) Shaikh Uvais.

The last of his line, Abū Saʿīd was in no way degenerate or effete. He is described by Ibn Taghrībirdī[1] as "a brave and brilliant prince of majestic appearance, generous and witty". He wrote an excellent hand in both the Mongol and the Arabic scripts, was a good musician and composed poetry in Persian, of which two specimens are preserved in the *Ta'rīkh-i Shaikh Uvais*.[2] Ibn Taghrībirdī also praises him for demolishing churches, though in fact in matters of religion he seems to have continued the tolerant policy of his predecessors. It was during his reign that Pope John XII, by a bull dated 1 May 1318, had founded the archbishopric of Sulṭānīyeh, of which the first incumbent was Francis of Perugia, succeeded in 1323 by William Adam. And if he ignored the pope's exhortation to embrace Christianity he at least paid some attention to his appeal to protect the Christian Armenians against their Muslim neighbours.

THE COLLAPSE OF THE ĪL-KHĀNID STATE

With the death of Abū Saʿīd the House of Hülegü had become virtually extinct. A prince of another line, Arpa Ke'ün,[3] a great grandson of Tolui's youngest son Arïgh Böke, was raised to the throne as his successor. A Mongol of the old school he showed himself during his brief reign a strong and energetic ruler in complete contrast to the puppets that were to follow him. One of his first acts was to order the execution of Baghdād Khatun, accused of correspondence with the Golden Horde and at least suspected of having poisoned her husband. In the depths of winter he confronted Öz-Beg across the Kur and, by an outflanking movement, put his forces to flight. Returning from this victory he consolidated his position by marrying Princess Sati Beg, the sister of Abū Saʿīd and the widow of Choban; at the same time he put to death several Chingizid princes whom he saw as possible rivals. He had reckoned, however, without ʿAlī Pādshāh, the Oirat governor of Baghdad, who proclaimed a new khan, Mūsā, a grandson of Baidu, and took up arms against Arpa. A battle was fought on the Jaghatu on 29 April 1336; Arpa fled, defeated, was captured in Sulṭānīyeh and

[1] Quoted by d'Ohsson, vol. IV, p. 717.
[2] Persian text, pp. 155–6.
[3] I.e. *Prince* Arpa, the Mongol *ke'ün* "son", like its Turkish equivalent *oghul*, being used as the title of princes of the blood.

brought to Ūjān, where, on 15 May, he met his end at the hands of the son of one of his own victims. His vizier Ghiyāth al-Dīn, the son of Rashīd al-Dīn, was already dead, having been executed by the amīrs against 'Alī Pādshāh's wishes.

It was now that Shaikh Ḥasan-i Buzurg intervened in the struggle for power, setting up as his own claimant a great grandson of Mengü-Temür, a young child called Muḥammad. A battle between the rival khans in the Ala-Tagh area (24 July) resulted, through an act of treachery on the part of Shaikh Ḥasan, in the defeat of Mūsā and the death of 'Alī Pādshāh. After pursuing Mūsā in the direction of Baghdad and inflicting heavy losses on his followers Ḥasan accompanied Muḥammad to Tabrīz, where he fixed his residence and where he married Princess Dil-Shād, the favourite wife of Abū Sa'īd, who had recently borne him a posthumous child—a daughter. Meanwhile the amīrs in Khurāsān, hostile to Shaikh Ḥasan, had elected their own khan, Togha-Temür, a descendant in the sixth generation of Chingiz-Khān's brother Jochi-Qasar. Under his leadership they undertook the conquest of Āzarbāījān and 'Irāq-i 'Ajam, arriving in March 1337, before Sulṭānīyeh. Shaikh Ḥasan judged it prudent to withdraw from Tabrīz into Arrān, and the Khurāsānīs proceeded to overrun the greater part of 'Irāq, clashing with Mūsā's men and finally making common cause with them against Shaikh Ḥasan. The two princes encountered their opponent in the Marāgheh area, at Soghurluq, according to the *Ta'rikh-i Shaikh Uvais*,[1] on 15 June. For some unexplained reason Togha-Temür at once retired from the battlefield and did not draw rein until he had reached Bisṭām. Mūsā for his part stood firm and gave a good account of himself, but was none the less defeated, captured in flight and taken to Shaikh Ḥasan, by whom, on 10 July, he was put to death. Despite his apparently pusillanimous conduct Togha-Temür maintained control over Khurāsān and Māzandarān, while Shaikh Ḥasan's authority in Āzarbāījān and 'Irāq was challenged from an altogether unexpected quarter.

His new antagonist was another Shaikh Ḥasan, the son of Temür-Tash and the grandson of Choban, called Shaikh Ḥasan-i Kūchak or Shaikh Ḥasan the Little to distinguish him from his namesake. To advance his cause Ḥasan-i Kūchak conceived the idea of passing off a Turkish slave as his father Temür-Tash who, he claimed, had escaped from prison in Egypt and had wandered for several years in distant

[1] Transl. van Loon, p. 64.

lands. By this pretence he attracted to his party both the supporters of the Choban family and also the Oirat tribesman who had fought under Mūsā. Advancing under the banners of his spurious father he engaged Ḥasan-i Buzurg at a place called Naushahr ("New Town") in the Ala-Tagh area on 16 July 1338. The latter, deceived by a ruse of Ḥasan-i Kūchak, withdrew on Tabrīz leaving in the lurch his protégé, the young khan Muḥammad, who was captured and killed.

The pseudo-Temür-Tash now thought to exploit this victory to his own advantage. He attempted to assassinate Ḥasan-i Kūchak, who, however, escaped and made his way to Georgia; he then advanced on Tabrīz, hoping to occupy the town before his secret became known. He was defeated by Ḥasan-i Buzurg and, joining the Oirat whom the latter had expelled from Sulṭānīyeh, accompanied them to their encampment in the Baghdad region. Meanwhile Ḥasan-i Kūchak, who had joined Princess Sati Beg in Arrān, proclaimed that lady, the sister of Abū Sa'īd and the widow of his grandfather, as khan and advanced against his rival. The latter fell back on Qazvīn, and Ḥasan-i Kūchak's forces occupied Āzarbāījān; Ḥasan-i Buzurg then launched a counter attack, but before they actually came to blows an uneasy peace had been patched up between them. The advantage now being with his opponent Shaikh Ḥasan-i Buzurg tried another tack: he offered the throne of Abū Sa'īd to Togha-Temür, who arrived in 'Irāq-i 'Ajam with his following in January or February 1339. By a Machiavellian ruse Ḥasan-i Kūchak succeeded in so discrediting this prince that he withdrew into Khurāsān in the early summer. Ḥasan-i Buzurg then set up yet another khan, Jahān-Temür, the son of Ala-Fireng and grandson of Geikhatu. Ḥasan-i Kūchak, not to be outdone, deposed Princess Sati Beg and replaced her by Sulaimān, a great grandson of Hülegü's third son Yoshmut, whom he forced her to marry. The two Ḥasans with their rival khans met in battle on the Jaghatu at the end of June 1340: Ḥasan-i Buzurg was defeated and fled to Baghdad, where he deposed Jahān-Temür and himself assumed sovereignty as the founder of the Jalayir dynasty.[1]

The deposition of Jahān-Temür may be regarded as the final dissolution of the Īl-Khānid state. His rival, it is true, retained his nominal power a year or two longer, surviving the death[2] of his protector, but

[1] Called also the Īlkānī dynasty after Ḥasan's great grandfather, Ilge (Īlkā) Noyan, one of Hülegü's generals. See van Loon, p. 6.

[2] He was murdered by his wife in a manner described by Salmān of Sāveh in verses which, as Browne, who reproduces them (*A Literary History of Persia*, vol. III, p. 60), says, "hardly bear translation".

then he too was deposed by Ḥasan-i Kūchak's brother and, like Jahān-Temür, vanishes into obscurity. So insignificant had these figureheads become that we are not even informed as to the time and manner of their death. The same applies to another puppet, Anushīrvān, of Persian, Turkish or Īl-Khānid origins, who replaced Sulaimān in 1344 and in whose name his Chobanid masters continued to strike coin until 1353. In the latter year Togha-Temür, the last of the Persian Chingizids, was killed by the first of the Sarbadārs of Sabzavār, who, along with the Jalayirs in Baghdad and Tabrīz, the Muẓaffarids in Fārs and the Karts in Herāt, were to fill the vacuum left by the Īl-Khāns until the advent, towards the end of the century, of another Mongol or semi-Mongol conqueror, Tīmūr,[1] born, by a curious coincidence, in the same year in which Abū Sa'īd died.

The Īl-Khāns, and before them the viceroys of the Great Khan, had dominated Western Asia for a period of more than 100 years. The economic decline of that region, induced by the havoc of the invasion, aggravated by the taxation policy of the earlier rulers and only partially arrested by the reforms of Ghazan will be examined elsewhere[2] in this volume. Here is perhaps the place to consider the more positive consequences of Mongol rule. Unlike the Saljuqs, who entered the Iranian world already converted to Islam and with their backs turned upon their Oghuz past, the Mongols, whilst gradually abandoning their shamanist, Christian or Buddhist beliefs, never forgot their historical origins or severed their ties with their kinsmen in Eastern, Central and Northern Asia. The persistence of national feeling amongst their conquerors may well have strengthened the Persians' own sense of nationalism, reinforcing the effect of what Minorsky has called the "Iranian intermezzo", i.e. the period between the withdrawal of the Arabs and the arrival of the Ghaznavids and Saljuqs, an "interval of Iranian domination" but for which "the national tradition would have become blunted and the Ṣafavids would have found it infinitely more difficult to restore the particular moral and cultural character which distinguishes Persia from her Muslim neighbours".[3] Certainly this process of differentiation must have been greatly facilitated by the existence, for almost a century, of a centralized state occupying approximately the same area as the Sassanian

[1] Strictly speaking *Temür* (in Turkish "Iron"), the Taimūr/Teimūr usual in Middle Eastern countries and even the conventional European Tamerlane representing the original pronunciation more closely than the Orientalist's *Tīmūr*.

[2] See below, chapter 6.

[3] *Studies in Caucasian History*, p. 110 n. 1.

empire and entering, for the first time since the Sassanians, into direct relations with the Christian West. The fact that Persian, under Īl-Khānid patronage, now finally displaced Arabic as the vehicle of historical writing must also have encouraged nationalistic tendencies. But perhaps the greatest, if the least tangible, benefit of Mongol rule was the widening of Persia's horizons. Situated on the communication routes between East and West, Īl-Khānid Iran was exposed to the influence of both China and Europe. The first Chinese to reach Persia seem to have been artillery men—mangonel experts—in the armies of Chingiz-Khān and Hülegü. Among the "numerous company of wise men from various countries"[1] that were gathered around Naṣīr al-Dīn Ṭūsī in his Marāgheh observatory was one Fu Meng-chi who explained to him the principles of Chinese astronomy. There were, as we have seen, Chinese physicians at the Court of Ghazan. Chinese artists, operating for the most part, we must presume, in the Buddhist temples, were to leave an indelible impression upon Persian miniature painting. European contacts were mainly in the fields of commerce and diplomacy. Since the reign of Hülegü Italian merchants had been established in Tabrīz, where they remained and prospered until after the death of Abū Sa'īd; it was from their numbers that the Īl-Khāns recruited their ambassadors and interpreters for the various missions to Europe; the most famous of them, the Polos, escorted from China to Persia a Mongol princess destined to be the bride of Ghazan. There is some evidence of the employment of European artisans: in the correspondence of Rashīd al-Dīn[2] there is a letter addressed to his son, then governor on the Byzantine frontier, asking for the dispatch of twenty weavers, apparently to be purchased as slaves from a Cypriot slave-dealer. Of intellectual relations the only concrete evidence is Rashīd al-Dīn's *History of the Franks*, which is based on a Latin work translated for him by some unknown scholar, perhaps a monk or friar resident in Tabrīz. The collapse of the Īl-Khānid state followed by the rise of the Ming in Eastern and the Ottomans in Western Asia brought an end to all such intercourse. Had Ghazan lived longer or had he shed less royal blood at the commencement of his reign, relations with Europe would have been continued and perhaps intensified with incalculable consequences for the future. What is certain is that the Middle East would today bear an altogether different aspect if the House of Hülegü had retained its full vigour for a decade or two longer.

[1] Barhebraeus, p. 51. [2] Quoted by Minorsky, "La Perse au Moyen Age", p. 421.

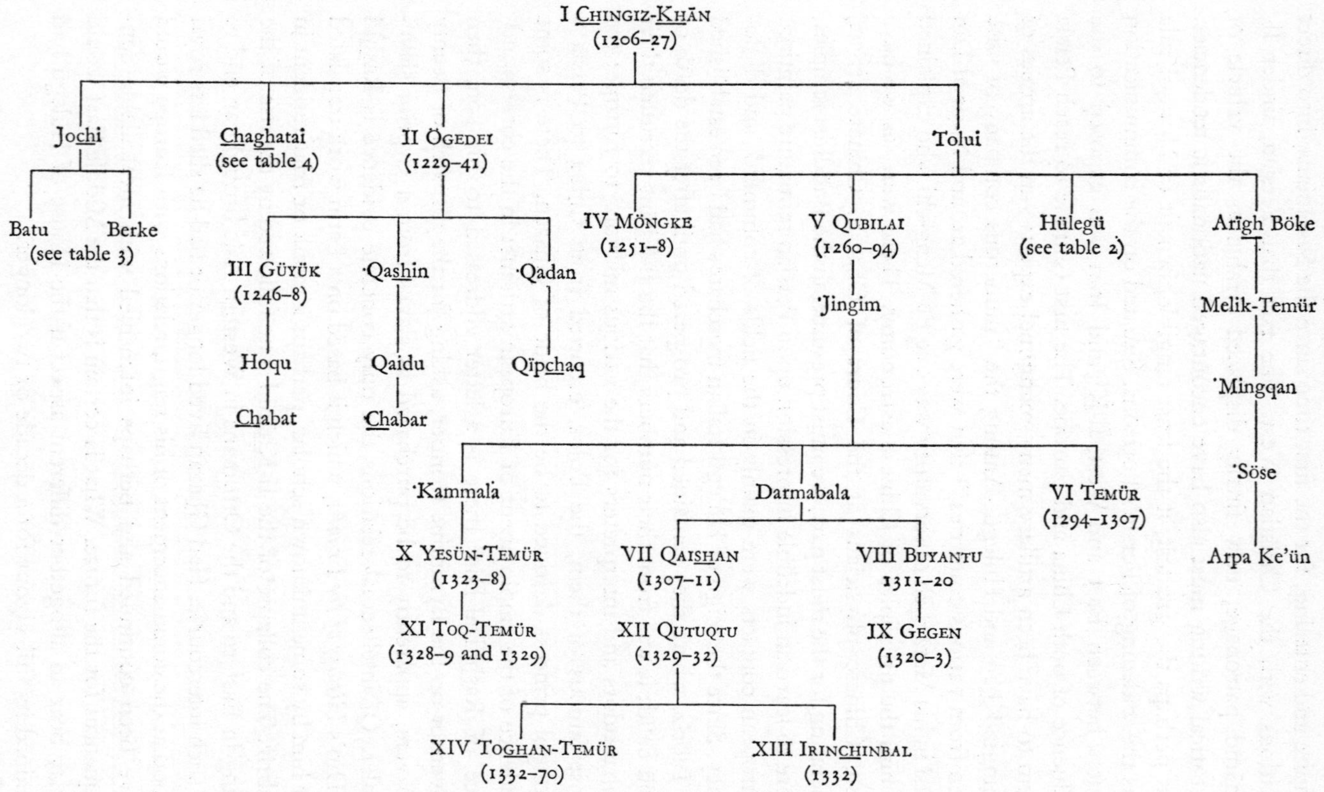

Table 1. The Great Khans and the Yüan Dynasty of China.

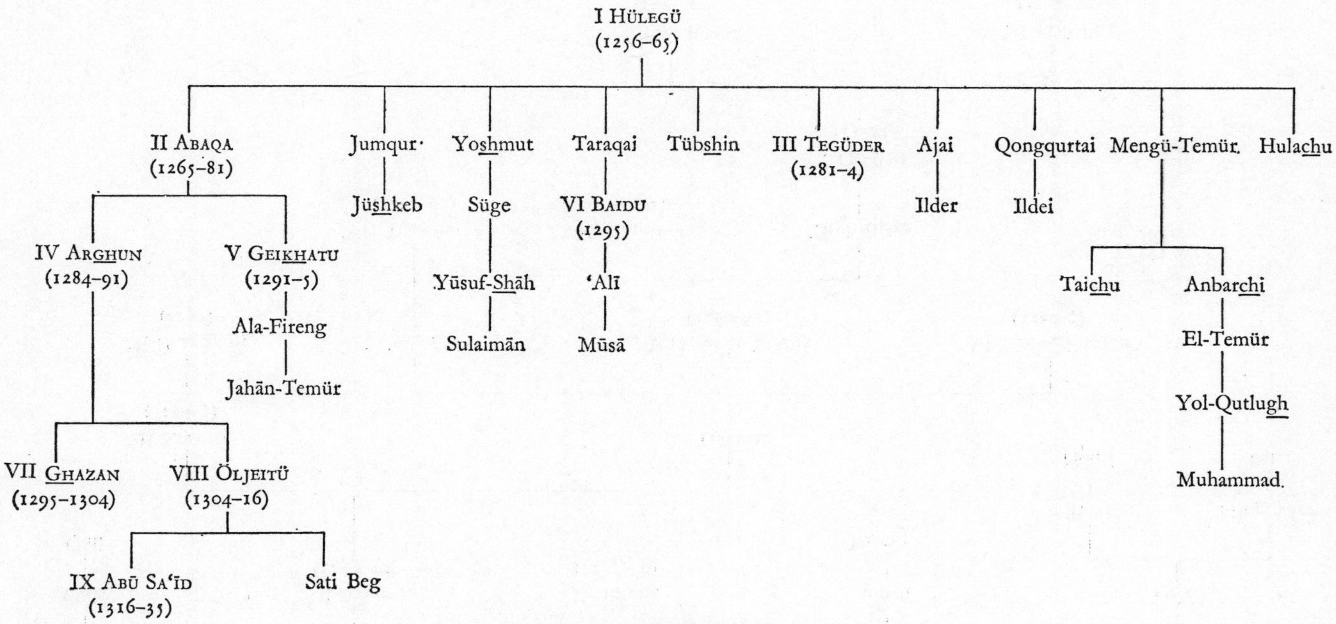

Table 2. The Īl-Khāns of Persia.

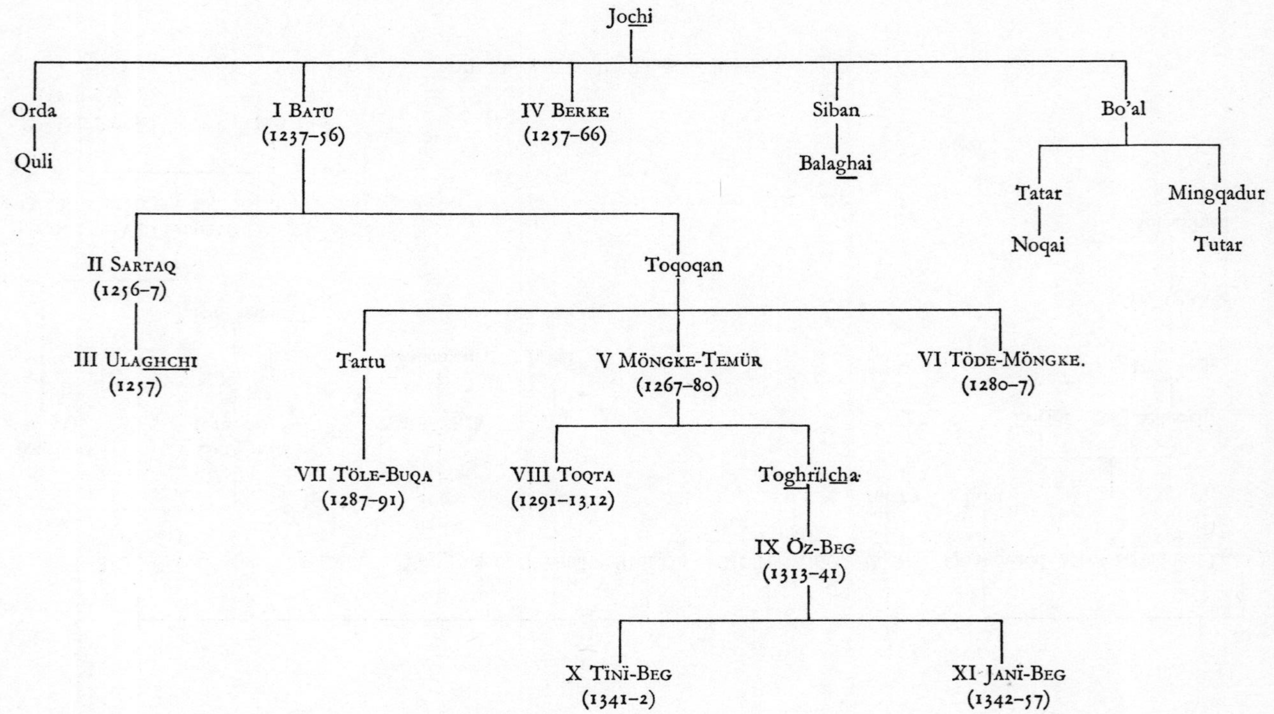

Table 3. The Khans of the Golden Horde, 1237–1357.

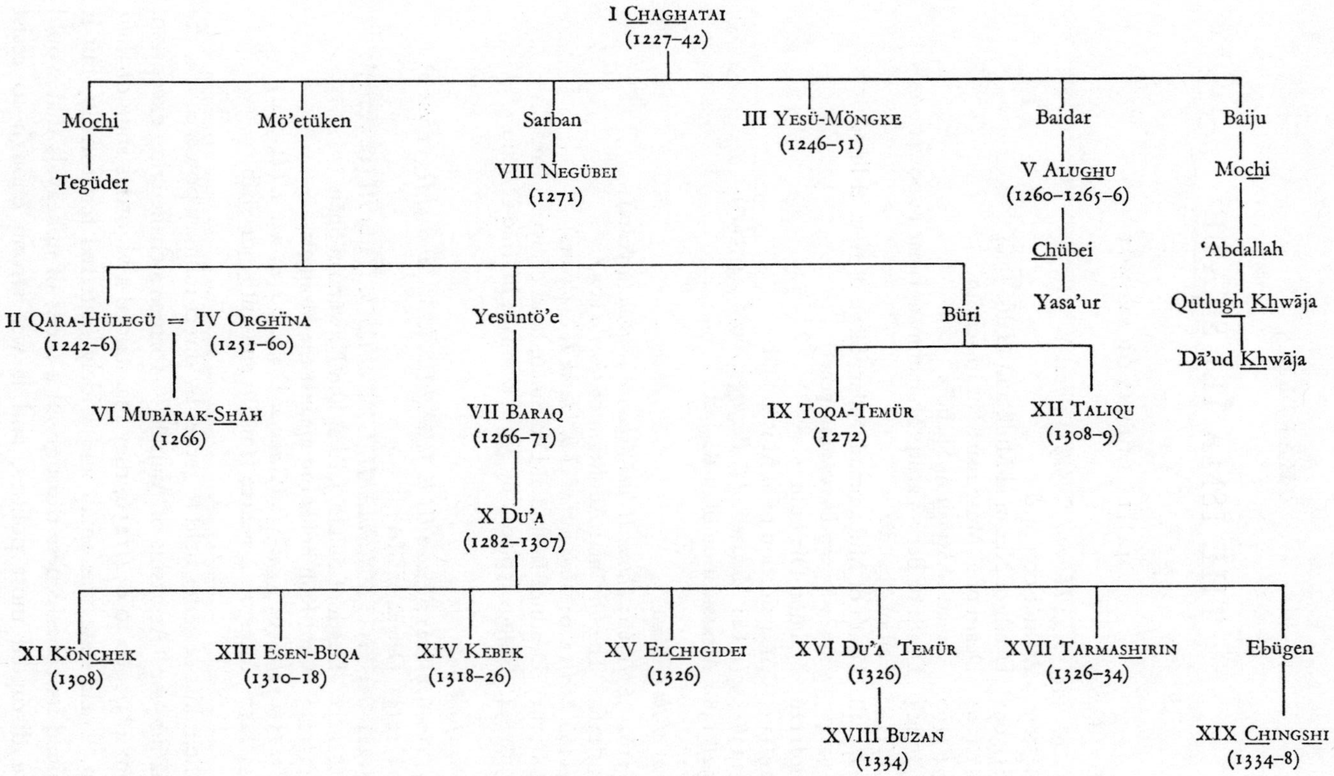
I Chaghatai (1227–42)
Mochi
Tegüder
Mö'etüken
Sarban
VIII Negübei (1271)
III Yesü-Möngke (1246–51)
Baidar
V Alughu (1260–1265–6)
Chübei
Yasa'ur
Baiju
Mochi
'Abdallah
Qutlugh Khwāja
Dā'ud Khwāja
II Qara-Hülegü (1242–6) = IV Orghïna (1251–60)
VI Mubārak-Shāh (1266)
Yesüntö'e
VII Baraq (1266–71)
X Du'a (1282–1307)
Büri
IX Toqa-Temür (1272)
XII Taliqu (1308–9)
XI Könchek (1308)
XIII Esen-Buqa (1310–18)
XIV Kebek (1318–26)
XV Elchigidei (1326)
XVI Du'a Temür (1326)
XVIII Buzan (1334)
XVII Tarmashirin (1326–34)
Ebügen
XIX Chingshi (1334–8)

Table 4. The Chaghatai Khanate, 1227–1338.

CHAPTER 5

THE ISMĀʿĪLĪ STATE

ISMĀʿĪLĪ RULERS OF ALAMŪT

Dāʿīs of Dailam

483/1090–518/1124: *Ḥasan-i Ṣabbāḥ* (34 years)
- 483/1090 Alamūt occupied
- 485/1092 Death of Niẓām al-Mulk and Malik-Shāh
- 487/1094 Death of al-Mustanṣir; Nizārī schism
- 494/1100 Aḥmad-i ʿAṭṭāsh in Shāhdīz
- 498/1104 Death of Berk-Yaruq; Muḥammad Tapar in power
- 500/1107 Fall of Shāhdīz
- 511/1118 Death of Muḥammad Tapar; Siege of Alamūt lifted

518/1124–532/1138: *Buzurg-Ummīd* (14 years)
- 520/1126 Maimūn-Diz built
- 529/1135 Assassination of al-Mustarshid

532/1138–557/1162: *Muḥammad b. Buzurg-Ummīd* (24 years)
- 532/1138 Assassination of al-Rāshid

Imāms of the Qiyāma

557/1162–561/1166: *Ḥasan II ʿalā-dhikrihi ʾl-salām* (4 years)
- 559/1164 The Qiyāma: Abolition of *sharīʿa* law

561/1166–607/1210: *Muḥammad II b. Ḥasan II* (44 years)
- 588/1193 Death of Rāshid al-Dīn Sinān, head of Syrian Ismāʿīlīs
- 590/1194 Saljuqs replaced by Khwārazmians in ʿIrāq-i ʿAjam

Imāms of the Satr

607/1210–618/1221: *Ḥasan III b. Jalāl al-Dīn b. Muḥammad II* (11 years)
- 612/1215 Defeat of Mengli

618/1221–653/1255: *Muḥammad III ʿAlāʾ al-Dīn b. Ḥasan III* (34 years)
- 628/1231 Death of Sulṭān Jalāl al-Dīn Khwārazm-Shāh
- 651/1253 Gird-Kūh holds out against the Mongols

653/1255–654/1256: *Khur-Shāh Rukn al-Dīn b. Muḥammad III* (1 year)
- 655/1257 Mongols massacre Ismāʿīlīs and kill Khur-Shāh

In the midst of states held together by direct military power alone, the Ismāʿīlīs—or "Assassins of Alamūt"—formed a challenging exception. From 483/1090 to 654/1256, they maintained a vigorous state of their own. Their state was small and widely scattered territorially, but it retained its cohesiveness throughout a series of upheavals that would have disrupted most polities, and it was strong enough to resist successfully the relentless enmity of the rest of Muslim society. In the cultural life of the time, moreover, the Ismāʿīlī state played a perceptible role—even to the point of acting as host to prominent non-Ismāʿīlī intellectuals. We cannot yet trace all the sources of its vitality, but we can make out some of them.

The student of Ismāʿīlī history is faced with problems that do not arise in the study of most dynasties. No Ismāʿīlī chronicles have survived intact. We must depend on the Sunnī chroniclers, who were most of them blindly hostile to, and ignorant of, Ismāʿīlī internal developments. The most important exception is Rashīd al-Dīn Faḍl Allāh, who was not only fair-minded but excerpted extensively the Ismāʿīlī chronicles surviving in his time.[1] But the hostility of the chroniclers is a less serious obstacle than our ignorance of the institutions and intellectual assumptions of the Ismāʿīlīs. To understand the conditions prevailing among Sunnī Muslims, we have access to a large body of literature which has been preserved in the Sunnī tradition. The Ismāʿīlī tradition has preserved very little from that period—only a few doctrinal works. Often we are at a loss to understand what a given event meant in its Ismāʿīlī context, even when we are tolerably sure of the date of the event and some of its more visible features. Yet we understand better now than we used to.

Earlier Western scholarship, basing itself on the impressions of the Crusaders as well as on the Sunnī tradition, was inclined to see in the Ismāʿīlīs a romantically diabolic "order of assassins", not quite human in their fanatical subservience to an enigmatic but self-seeking and all-powerful master, the "Old Man of the Mountain". This picture can no longer be taken seriously. As we use such Ismāʿīlī materials as are available and learn to sift the chronicles more cautiously, it proves to be chiefly legendary. But the reality that is emerging turns out to be almost as extraordinary as the legend. That this handful of villagers and small townsmen, hopelessly outnumbered, should again and again reaffirm their passionate sense of grand destiny, reformulating it in every new historical circumstance with unfailing imaginative power and persistent courage—that they should be able so to keep alive not

[1] Rashīd al-Dīn's section on the Ismāʿīlīs has now been edited by M. J. Dānesh-Pajuh and M. Modarresy (Tehrān, 1960). See also Juvainī, vol. III, tr. J. A. Boyle, vol. II. Other chronicles, notably that of Ibn al-Athīr, are cited in the relevant notes of Marshall G. S. Hodgson, *The Order of Assassins: the Struggle of the Early Nizari Isma'ilis against the Islamic World* (The Hague, 1955). See also pp. 25–6 of that work; and for the relationship between Rashīd al-Dīn and Juvaini, see *ibid.* p. 73 n.

only their own hopes but the answering fears and covert dreams of all the Islamic world for a century and a half—this in itself is an astonishing achievement. To comprehend it at all, we must understand the vital religious convictions out of which it grew.[1]

THE ISMĀ'ĪLĪ MOVEMENT UNDER THE GREAT SALJUQS

Shī'īs had never been satisfied with the compromises of official Muslim life, which Sunnīs had accepted as more or less inevitable up to a point. Shī'īs held fast to the hope that, if only Muslims would accept divinely approved leadership, then the high Islamic ideals of equality and godliness among the faithful and an equitable order throughout mankind could be realized in practice. Loyalty to the house of 'Alī had early become identified with such hopes: the true *imāms* (leaders of the Muslim community) were specially designated descendants of 'Alī. Those who maintained loyalty to these imāms considered themselves a Muslim élite (*khāṣṣ*): they alone were true to the real principles of Islam, while the common mass was led astray by temporary appearances of power on the side of other claimants to authority, whom God had not authorized.

For many Shī'īs it readily followed that the true imāms were not merely the proper rulers of the world. The imāms, even if unrecognized, represented God's will in the world at all times. Whether in power or not, they were divinely guided to the proper interpretation of religious truths; their interpretation of Qur'ān and of the law was alone binding on Muslims. Indeed, without the insight which originated with the imām, who in turn had inherited it from the Prophet, the text of the Qur'ān could be quite misunderstood by the ordinary unthinking Muslim; for behind the literal reference of its words lay a deeper meaning, more or less symbolical, which only the imām could

[1] The main steps in the development of Nizārī studies by modern Westerners are traced in Hodgson's *Order of Assassins* (hereafter cited as *OA*), pp. 22–32. W. Ivanow has done especially important work; but his translations and interpretations are often very arbitrary and misleading, and warnings on their use are to be found in *OA*, pp. 31–2, 329, 232 n., 233 n. and 235 n. *The Order of Assassins* (unfortunately mistitled) seems to remain the standard work and will be referred to throughout this chapter. It suffers from some immaturity of scholarship: references are sometimes too imprecise and translations from the Persian too clumsy; above all, too slight an acquaintance with the general political life of the time occasioned some vagueness of focus. Several of its interpretations have been sharpened in this chapter (and some details made more precise). Nevertheless, the argument of the book seems to remain sound, so far as it goes; both political and theological history need to be further explored, however.

elucidate with authority. But only the élite, wholly devoted to Islam, could recognize the special role of the imāms or appreciate the spiritual insight which resulted from their teaching. Exposure of these sacred matters before the common Sunnīs would not enlighten them but might rather lead to profanation and persecution of the imām's cause. Until the time was ripe for all mankind to see the truth, Shīʿīs were invited to exercise *taqiyya* (pious dissimulation), disguising their true convictions under a seeming conformity to the standards of the world. Only at the end of the age, with God's aid, would the imām appear, in triumph, to vindicate his true adherents, and set the world to rights.

Among the several Shīʿī movements, that of the Ismāʿīlīs was distinguished by being organized hierarchically and secretly. Ismāʿīlīs recognized Ismāʿīl son of Jaʿfar al-Ṣādiq, and Ismāʿīl's son, as the authorized imāms. But for many years the imāms were held to be in hiding and inactive. Meanwhile, the organization seems to have been self-perpetuating. Adherents were ranked in several grades, in principle according to the degree to which they had advanced in the esoteric teachings ascribed to the imām. An adherent of an upper rank was set over adherents of a lower rank in his own area. Set over all adherents in a given province was the *dāʿī*, or head of religious teaching.

The whole organization was kept secret on the principle of taqiyya. Among Ismāʿīlīs this taqiyya was more far-reaching than among most Shīʿīs: the adherent was initiated in a special ceremony and forbidden under oath to reveal anything about the teachings or membership of the community. The doctrine presented as the inner meaning, the *bāṭin*, of the Qur'ān was correspondingly more elaborate. Whereas for some Shīʿīs it went little beyond the identification of various Qur'ānic phrases as symbolic references to the imām and to the Shīʿīs' loyalty to him, for Ismāʿīlīs a whole spiritual cosmos was to be traced in the Qur'ān by those who held the clue—not only in the immediate symbolism of its words but in an extensive set of numerical correspondences. To be an Ismāʿīlī was to share in the secrets of the universe. The historical origin of the hierarchism and secrecy of the Ismāʿīlīs is not clear, but in any case they made possible two things as disquieting to Sunnīs as they were heartening to many Shīʿīs: a proliferation of cosmological and historical speculation, often rather sophisticated, without regard to its intelligibility to the masses; and at the same time an extensive preparation of disciplined cadres to support any political move which the leadership should find desirable.[1]

After the triumph of Ismā'īlī power in Egypt in 257/969, when the Fāṭimid dynasty of caliphs was established, Ismā'īlī hopes everywhere were high. Some Ismā'īlīs may once have doubted the claims to the imāmate put forward by the leader of that section of the Ismā'īlī movement which now seemed to be blessed with success. But soon almost all Ismā'īlīs rallied to the Fāṭimid line. Throughout Iran they recognized the Egyptian Fāṭimids as the true 'Alid imāms, descendants of Ismā'īl and entitled, as custodians of the spiritual inheritance of the Prophet, to exclusive obedience among all Muslims. The imām had at last appeared in power. As Fāṭimid arms were attended with victory in Syria and the Ḥijāz, and as Fāṭimid prestige and naval power ensured the new caliph's recognition from Sicily to Sind, Ismā'īlīs could hope that the promised days were at hand, when the imām was to reunite the Muslims, overwhelm the infidels, and "fill the earth with justice as it is now filled with injustice", the long-standing dream of all Shī'īs.

Now the whole movement was focused in Cairo at the Fāṭimid court, under the direction of the chief dā'ī there. Dā'īs in the Iranian highlands seem to have been responsible to the chief dā'ī in points of doctrine and in planning overall strategy for the victory of the Ismā'īlī cause in their area—a victory identified with submission to the Egyptian caliphate. Efforts were made to convert local rulers, many of whom were in any case Shī'ī in the tenth and early eleventh centuries, or to find support for military coups on behalf of the imām. As the result of one such coup, Baghdad itself was held briefly in the name of the Fāṭimid caliph. When an Ismā'īlī propagandist was ready to retire from such activities, or to withdraw from them for a time, he went to Cairo, where a number of Iranian Ismā'īlī philosophers, commonly persecuted at home, ended their lives as respected officials. Indeed, the intellectual leadership of Cairo was largely of Iranian origin.

But after the rise of Saljuq power, confidence in Egypt could not but be undermined. In Iran, the several localized dynasties established in

[1] In addition to the references appearing in *OA* (especially pp. 13–14, 17), see three articles by S. M. Stern: "Ismā'īlīs and Qarmaṭians", *L'Elaboration de l'Islam* (Paris, 1961–2), pp. 99–108; "Heterodox Ismā'īlism at the time of al-Mu'izz", *B.S.O.A.S.* (1955), pp. 10–33; and "Abu'l-Qāsim al-Bustī and his refutation of Ismā'īlism", *J.R.A.S.* (1961), pp. 14–35. Likewise Wilferd Madelung, "Fatimiden und Baḥrainqarmaṭen", *Der Islam* (1959), pp. 34–88, with corrections in the same volume; and Madelung, "Das Imamat in der frühen ismailitischen Lehre", *Der Islam* (1961), pp. 43–135.

Būyid times were replaced by a single strong power, ardently Sunnī. The Egyptian government itself was manifestly weakening; under al-Mustanṣir in the 1060s it went through a period of internal chaos which paralysed its foreign policy. After this crisis, from 468/1074 on, the government was directed by a military man, Badr al-Jamālī, who kept the imām under his control. His foreign policy was defensive, and it was clear that he did not expect the Egyptian government to recover the lead it had once had. Its power remained visibly inferior to that of the Saljuqs during the rest of the eleventh century. The promised days of victory and justice seemed indefinitely postponed.

But the Ismā'īlī movement in Saljuq lands, and especially in the Iranian highlands, continued as strong as and perhaps stronger than it was before the Egyptian Fāṭimids appeared and stirred the temporary hope of victory by way of their armies. Ismā'īlīs seem to have been numerous in towns in all parts of Iran, but in this period we have evidence of them in the countryside only in a few areas. Many are reported to have been craftsmen and some appear as merchants; they were often led by men of the liberal professions. They made many converts among common soldiers and occasionally among lesser officers. It is easier to tell what they opposed than whether they had any very concrete positive plans. We have a few details which suggest dislike of the Turks, not surprising among Iranian and Arab populations whom military rule must have irked. (Ḥasan-i Ṣabbāḥ is reported as saying the Turks were *jinn*, not men.) Certainly, at least in a generalized way, they stood against the social injustice of a stratified society, which the occupation by Turkish troops seemed to aggravate; there is a story that the Ismā'īlīs boasted of assassinating a vizier (Niẓām al-Mulk) in revenge for his treatment of a carpenter—who was thus drastically asserted to be his equal. Finally, and perhaps most important, it is clear from the nature of their propaganda that they despised and resented the pettiness and aridity of the personal outlook sometimes encouraged by that *sharī'a*-minded Islam which was taught in the multiplying Sunnī madrasas. The Ismā'īlīs were resisting the Sunnī intellectual and moral synthesis that is often regarded as the glory of the age—an age then being introduced by the Sunnīs after the victory of Sunnī power over the various Shī'ī dynasties.

Iranian Ismā'īlīs, in their struggle with the spirit of the age, did not have to look so far as Egypt to find the means of some sort of co-ordination of their activities. The Ismā'īlīs of the upper Oxus valleys, beyond the Saljuq presence, had, at least at one time, a local dāʿī independently responsible to Cairo; at any rate they do not seem to have been involved, at least at first, in the movements which took place among the Ismāʿīlīs in the Saljuq lands. But many, if not most, of the Ismāʿīlīs under Saljuq rule seem to have owned the authority of a single superior dāʿī, whose headquarters were at Iṣfahān, the chief Saljuq capital. We know that ʿAbd al-Malik-i ʿAṭṭāsh, dāʿī at Iṣfahān in the 1070s, was head of the movement throughout the west Iranian highlands, from Kirmān to Āzarbāījān, if not beyond. We do not know whether any dāʿīs for Khurāsān and Kūhistān or for Iraq or the Jazīreh were subordinated to him. It does appear that the Syrian Ismāʿīlīs, even though their province was being occupied by the Saljuqs, were not placed under Iṣfahān. But ʿAbd al-Malik-i ʿAṭṭāsh was respected for his scholarship even in Sunnī circles, and seems to have been a focus of widespread renewed Ismāʿīlī activity in the Saljuq dominions.[1]

During the 1080s the Ismāʿīlīs of the Saljuq lands were preparing active insurrection on an unprecedented pattern. Before any overt moves were made, the Ismāʿīlīs at Sāveh in ʿIrāq-i ʿAjam were accused of murdering a muezzin lest he betray their secrets. More than one dedicated young man was sent to Egypt and came back ready to seize a fortress in revolt. By 483/1090, revolt broke out simultaneously in Dailam and Kūhistān, and in the next few years in many other areas as well. This time the Ismāʿīlī hopes were not concentrated on a great army to sweep over all the Muslim lands from a single centre, on the model of the rise of the Egyptian Fāṭimids. Now they were looking to a multiplicity of risings everywhere at once, to overwhelm the established social structure from within.

I. REVOLT

The Ismāʿīlīs of the Iranian highlands and the Fertile Crescent were not destined to overthrow the Saljuqs but rather to found a society apart, which was set over against Muslim society as a whole. We shall trace the fate of this society in four phases, each representing a new departure in their relations with the outside world. After the failure of the initial revolt came the second period, that of stalemate, in which the Ismāʿīlīs were regrouped on a more permanent basis. From this basis they went

[1] On the organization of those Ismāʿīlīs who were to become Nizārīs, see *OA*, pp. 45, 64, and 69.

on, in a third period, to attempt a spiritual defiance, consummating their apocalyptic vision among themselves on the level of the inward life. Later yet, as history impinged even on their inwardness, they dreamed of world leadership in a quest which sent their envoys far beyond the old Saljuq territories, and which was terminated only by a special effort of the all-conquering Mongols. But the first and decisive moment was that of their great revolt.

Ḥasan-i Ṣabbāḥ at Alamūt

The role of any one man in great historical events is hard to isolate and is limited at best. In the case of Ḥasan-i Ṣabbāḥ, the most famous figure in the revolt, we have even less basis than usual for judging the role he played. Yet the accounts present him as more than just an ordinary leader, and his personality may well have offered the other Ismā'īlīs a crucial rallying-point of unyielding strength. In any case, our story must revolve about him if only because he is the only figure about whom we have even moderately detailed evidence.

Ḥasan-i Ṣabbāḥ tells us, in an autobiographical passage, that he was brought up as a Shī'ī, but that he had supposed Ismā'īlism was just heretical philosophy till a friend whom he respected for his uprightness convinced him—without at first revealing himself as an Ismā'īlī—that the Ismā'īlī imām was the true one. Even so, Ḥasan hesitated to commit himself in the face of the popular opprobrium which the Ismā'īlīs suffered. Only after an illness that had seemed fatal, when he thought he would die without having acknowledged the true imām, did he seek out an Ismā'īlī propagandist and become initiated.[1]

He came to the attention of 'Abd al-Malik-i 'Aṭṭāsh in due time, and was appointed to a post in the Ismā'īlī organization and sent to Egypt, arriving there in 471/1078. On the way, he had to make a detour in southern Syria because of Turkish military operations at the very doorstep of the imām. What we have about his experiences in Egypt, then under the rule of Badr al-Jamālī, seems to be mostly legendary, but he did not see the imām himself and he cannot have been much encouraged to rely on Egyptian power to achieve anything for the Iranians in their own confrontation with Turkish military power. When he came back to Iran after two years, he set out on extensive travels throughout the west Iranian highlands, presumably

[1] On the biography of Ḥasan-i Ṣabbāḥ, see *OA*, pp. 43–51.

propagandizing and getting acquainted with local circumstances. In the later 1080s he is represented as seeking an appropriate base for carrying out his part in the Ismāʿīlī revolt that was to come. We do not know whether this work was still under the direction of ʿAbd al-Malik-i ʿAṭṭāsh, but this is likely, for his repute in the Sunnī chronicles suggests he was still chief dāʿī in that period.

Eventually Ḥasan was appointed dāʿī of Dailam, potentially an important post since that was one of the few regions where the bulk of the population were already Shīʿī. He chose the fortress of Alamūt in Rūdbār (the valley of the Shāhrūd) in the Alburz [Elburz] mountains north of Qazvīn as his base (see the map of Rūdbār and vicinity, p. 431). He won over the garrison to his views by way of secret emissaries, infiltrated the place with converts from elsewhere, and finally arrived himself under a pseudonym. The commandant, realizing the danger, had feigned conversion so as to ferret out the Ismāʿīlī leaders and get rid of them, but he had shown his hand too soon and now found himself impotent. Forced to come to terms with Ḥasan, he accepted a check in payment for the fortress and left. The date was 483/1090. Both Ismāʿīlīs and Sunnīs regarded this as the first great blow in the revolt.

At about the same time, and at least partly inspired from Alamūt, the Ismāʿīlīs of several small towns in Kūhistān, the arid lands south of Khurāsān, declared their independence from the Saljuqs. Taking advantage of insults made by a Saljuq amīr to the locally respected Sīmjūrid family, they identified their cause with local self-respect, and seem to have won solid support in the population. When it became apparent that the local amīrs could not cope with the Ismāʿīlīs either at Alamūt or in Kūhistān, larger Saljuq forces were sent in 485/1092 against them in both places. At Alamūt the Ismāʿīlīs were few in number at the moment, but some 300 Ismāʿīlīs were brought in from around Kazvin and Ray for the emergency, and the reinforced garrison, supported by Ismāʿīlīs from other parts of Rūdbār, was able to make a sally against the Saljuq forces. The Saljuqs were defeated and withdrew. Before they could make a new effort, first the vizier Niẓām al-Mulk was assassinated and then Malik-Shāh himself died. The Saljuq force in Kūhistān concentrated on one small town, Dareh, but failed to take it before Malik-Shāh's death led to the break up of the expedition. The Ismāʿīlīs had established permanent footholds.[1]

Alamūt was physically a large towering rock, with steep slopes hardly

[1] On the early revolt, see *ibid.* pp. 72–5.

Map 5. Rūdbār and vicinity.

negotiable on most sides, but with a considerable expanse at its top where extensive building could be done. Situated in mountainous terrain, its approaches could be guarded with relative ease. Yet it was strategically placed, commanding the shortest passage between Qazvīn and the Caspian coast, while control of Rūdbār as a whole could permit harassment of the main route between all 'Irāq-i 'Ajam and the Caspian. The Dailamī inhabitants of the area had been long noted for their military capabilities as well as for their Shī'ī inclinations. It was not the first time Alamūt had served as a rebel's stronghold.[1]

In the years following 485/1092, while intestine Saljuq quarrels gave the Ismā'īlīs a respite, Ḥasan-i Ṣabbāḥ made Alamūt as impregnable as possible. He strengthened the fortifications and built up a great store of provisions. It is said he caused vast storerooms to be hollowed out in the rock, in which large amounts of food could be kept in good condition for a long time—presumably largely cut off from air and especially from warmth. He also took care to arrange irrigation for the fields immediately around Alamūt. Physically, Alamūt became as nearly self-sufficient as might be, ready to resist an indefinite siege. Likewise the mood of Alamūt became martial. Personally, Ḥasan set an austere example. Once he had taken up residence there, he is said to have left the four walls of his house only twice, and twice to have gone up on the roof; he spent his time writing and directing operations.

[1] On Alamūt as a site, see Freya Stark, *The Valleys of the Assassins* (London, 1934), pp. 197–251.

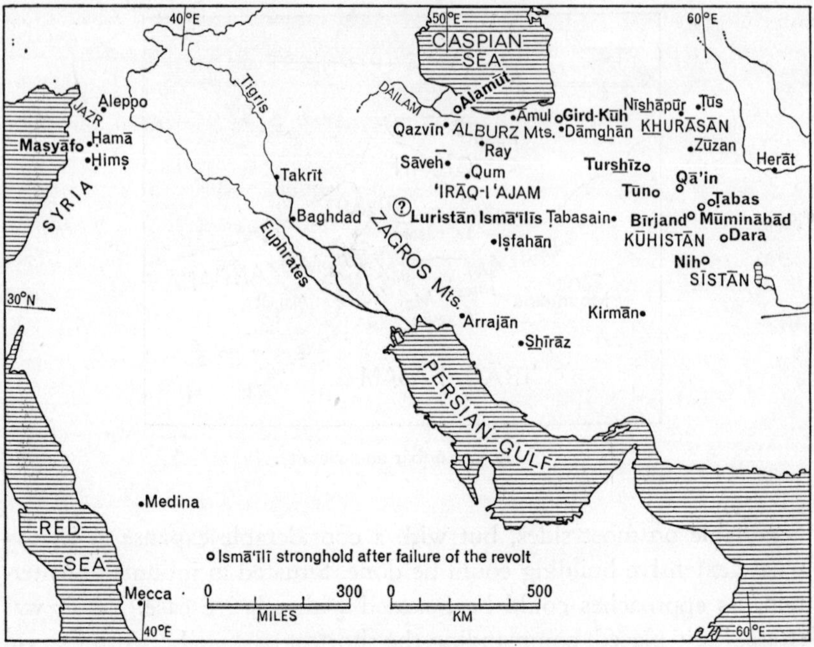

Map 6. The Ismāʿīlī State, with important centres in the revolt.

He had his two sons executed, one on the charge of murder (which later proved false) and the other on that of wine-drinking; he sent away his wife and daughters to spin along with other women in a distant fortress at a time of difficulty, and never brought them back. It is said that Ismāʿīlī chiefs followed his precedent and never had their women with them while they were executing military command, in contrast to usual Muslim practice. Though Alamūt was probably not the official centre of the movement at first, it was in a position to offer leadership at need.

Once Alamūt was secured and much of Kūhistān independent, the rising proceeded rapidly. A year before Malik-Shāh's death, another fortress had been seized (in 484/1091): Sanamkūh near Abhar, in the mountains westward from Qazvīn. On Malik-Shāh's death (485/1092), the quarrels between Berk-Yaruq and Tutush and then Muḥammad Tapar called troops away from any efforts they might have made against the Ismāʿīlīs; moreover, they created just the conditions of uncertainty and disorder in which the Ismāʿīlīs found numerous opportunities for action and also, perhaps, a more sympathetic hearing for their message of resistance against the Turkish rulers.

Within a few years the Ismāʿīlīs held strongholds in a number of mountainous zones in the Iranian highlands. (See the map of the Ismāʿīlī state.) Along with Alamūt and some neighbouring places at the western end of the Alburz, they seized at least two other places of defence at the eastern end of that range. In Kūhistān—not a mighty mountain range yet mountainous enough and relatively inaccessible in central Iran just east of the deserts—they controlled a group of towns extending north and south over 200 miles. In the Zagros range, especially in the south around Arrajān, they seized several forts at key spots. In 488/1095, a captain said to be an Ismāʿīlī was entrusted with the town of Takrīt on the Tigris, north of Baghdad; but this town does not seem to have become Ismāʿīlī in sentiment. Less decisive Ismāʿīlī activity is reported from many towns throughout the area of Saljuq rule—even where fortresses were not seized, the Ismāʿīlīs became an active faction in the cities, even, as in Kirmān and Aleppo, winning the support of Turkish amīrs themselves, at least for a time.[1]

The new doctrine

The official Ismāʿīlī doctrine at Cairo had developed into a complex and sophisticated cosmological system, in which one might think the only role of the dāʿīs and other ranks in the organization was to learn and teach a proliferating stock of esoteric lore. All this learning was certainly not rejected by those Ismāʿīlīs who were launching the rebellion. But observers got the impression that there was a "new teaching" associated with the movement which could be contrasted with the old; and this would not be surprising. If there was, however, it was not a wholly new system but a new emphasis and development of a doctrine of long standing among Ismāʿīlīs and indeed among Shīʿīs generally: the doctrine of *taʿlīm*, authoritative teaching. Those Sunnīs who were most closely acquainted with the Ismāʿīlī movement at the time concentrated on this doctrine as the main Ismāʿīlī thesis, and later Ismāʿīlī writings refer to the doctrine in contexts which likewise associate it with the time of the revolt. In its fully developed form, the doctrine is ascribed in particular to Ḥasan-i Ṣabbāḥ, who expounded it in a Persian essay. But we cannot assume that he is the one who developed it; ʿAbd al-Malik-i ʿAṭṭāsh, for instance, was intellectually

[1] Cf. ʿIzz al-Dīn Ibn al-Athīr, *al-Kāmil fiʾl-taʾrīkh*, *A.H. 492, 494, 500*; and *OA*, pp. 75–8, which the present account makes more precise.

active and was more prominent than Ḥasan at the time when the doctrine was first taken notice of; but we have no writings of his to go by.[1]

The Shīʿīs had always condemned the Sunnīs for presuming to choose for themselves in religious questions—starting with the choice of Abū Bakr as first caliph, admittedly not designated by Muḥammad as his successor, whereas the Shīʿīs were sure that ʿAlī had been divinely indicated as the successor. Then the Sunnīs had continued, in the Shīʿī view, to interpret religious truth and in particular the sharīʿa law arbitrarily, according to their own sense of propriety: they even called the founders of their great schools of law imāms, though these founders could claim no special status except that which resulted from the respect accorded them by their own followers. The Shīʿīs, in contrast, claimed to base their understanding of religious truth and law on the teaching of true imāms, designated not by human choice but (like the Prophet himself) by divine election. If Islam could be founded only by divine authority, surely it must be interpreted also by divine authority. Men were no more in a position to decide on ultimate truth in subsequent times than in the time of Muḥammad himself. Accordingly, over against the Sunnī systems of determining law the Shīʿīs set their own doctrine, that one must seek the only authoritative teaching, taʿlīm, that of the authoritatively designated ʿAlid imāms.

As to how Muslims were to know who was the true imām, Shīʿīs were not at a loss to adduce evidentiary miracles; but every sophisticated person knew how limited the evidentiary strength of any wonder is; hence on a sophisticated level the Shīʿī case was really made to rest on history. If one were once convinced, by the logic of the situation, that a true imām *must* have been designated (for God would not be so inconsistent as to appoint a prophet and then leave mankind in the dark as to the imāms to come after him), then one looked for any relevant indications; and it was not hard to find anecdotes about the Prophet which could be construed as designating ʿAlī to succeed him. ʿAlī in turn, and each of the other imāms, could be assumed to have designated his own successor.

But such a proof of the imām's identity is by no means rigorous. Moreover it presupposes that one has already accepted Muḥammad as Prophet. In Ḥasan's book, mentioned by several writers and sum-

[1] On the authorship and role of the new doctrine, see *OA*, p. 52; also pp. 131–2.

marized for us by Shahrastānī, this argument was transformed into an incisive and self-contained instrument for validating the Ismā'īlī position regardless of one's prior commitment. Ḥasan's work established four propositions. First, either one needs a teacher to know ultimate truth—truth about God—or one does not; but if not, one has no grounds for preferring one's own speculations to those of another, since this is implicitly to teach the other, or at least to accept one's own authority in preference to his. With this proposition, the position of Muslims generally was asserted against philosophers who denied the need for any authority at all. The second proposition was that either the required teacher must be authoritative, or any teacher will do; but if any teacher will do, we are in as bad a situation as if we had no teacher at all, for we have no ground for preferring one teacher to another. With this proposition, the Shī'īs' insistence on authoritative teaching, ta'līm, was asserted against the Sunnīs, who, in any given generation, must depend on a host of learned men none of whom is inherently more authoritative than the others. But Ḥasan's third proposition brought out the weakness of the ordinary Shī'īs themselves. Either the authority of the authoritative teacher must be proved or any teacher may be accepted as authoritative, which would leave us where we were before; but how can his authority be proved except on the basis of some further authority?—which authority would have to be proved in turn.

With the fourth proposition, Ḥasan showed how the authority of the final teacher could be known not through something beyond itself but by way of the structure of knowledge itself. All true knowledge requires a contrast of two opposites, which can be known only through each other; thus we can conceive the (Aristotelian) "necessary" only by contrast to what is merely possible—and the "possible" only by contrast to what is inherently necessary. Neither can be conceived without the other. Again, in the phrase "no god but God", the unique God can be conceived properly only by contrast to the many godlings; while we see the inanity of these godlings only by contrast to God Himself. The phrase "no god but God", in turn, cannot stand without its complement, "Muḥammad is God's Prophet": God's unity can be properly known only by way of the Prophet's revelation, while the very notion of prophethood presupposes the idea of God. A like conjunction of opposites determines the very source of ultimate knowlege itself—the relation between the individual person who wishes to know and the authoritative teacher whom he must discover. The reasoning of the individual, if he pursues it rigorously, leads him to the dilemma presented in the third proposition: not only can the reason not discover ultimate truth for itself, it cannot even determine what authority to turn to. On the other hand, the claimant to ultimate authority, the imām, cannot substantiate his claims by recourse to any proof beyond himself, or he ceases to claim ultimate authority. But put the individual's reasoning and the authoritative teacher, the imām, together, and each solves the other's dilemma. What the individual's reasoning does is show him, not the imām, but his need for the imām and for his teaching, his taʿlīm. It is only when reasoning has reached this point that the imām can present himself as fulfilling this very need. That imām, then, is true who does not allege extraneous proofs for his imāmate but only his own existence as fulfilling the need which, and only which, reasoning can demonstrate. This imām, said Ḥasan, is the imām of the Ismāʿīlīs.[1]

Such an argument presupposes that there is a truth which is absolute and ultimate and yet unconditionally rational—a common enough assumption, in pre-modern times at least, which only Ṣūfīs were successfully challenging in Ḥasan's day. Given this intellectual atmosphere, the argument was hard to refute directly. Moreover, as compared with the general S͟hīʿī notion of taʿlīm, the more refined doctrine of taʿlīm which Ḥasan presented was not only more rigorous logically but more self-sufficient. It did not deduce the position of the imām from the position of the Prophet, but rather deduced the prophethood of Muḥammad from the office of the imām, whose authoritative teaching provided the only ultimate demonstration of the validity of prophethood. Thus the Ismāʿīlī doctrine was supported on its own terms independently of any doctrine accepted by the Sunnī community at large.

The rigor and self-sufficiency of the doctrine were appropriate to the new sternness required of a movement in active and universal revolt. In effect, it laid its emphasis upon the movement itself, rather than on any ulterior reality or purpose to which the movement was the means. The imām was self-sufficient and the movement to establish his authority was self-contained, not to be justified by any given practical consequences. The critics complained that, in effect, this authoritative teacher taught nothing but his own authority. For men in the stress

[1] S͟hahrastānī's summary of Ḥasan's book is translated in the appendix to *OA* and analysed there on pp. 52–61.

of an all-encompasing rebellion, it was precisely loyalt ment—expressed as loyalty to the imām as its head— once they were committed to the revolt, there was no l sider questions which might divide or at least confuse t ably, indeed, older and less urgent Ismā'īlī doctrines con taught, but Ḥasan's doctrine of ta'līm could well help t discipline the movement in its immediate urgency.

The schism

In the midst of the risings, the Ismā'īlī movement suffered an internal schism which tested the vitality of its doctrine. In 487/1094 died al-Mustanṣir of Egypt. The Fāṭimid state was now in the hands of al-Afḍal, son of Badr al-Jamālī, as vizier. Badr had married al-Afḍal's sister to a younger son of al-Mustanṣir, whom al-Afḍal now raised to the caliphate as al-Musta'lī. But it was an older son, Nizār, who had been known to have been designated by al-Mustanṣir as future imām. Nizār revolted with the support of an anti-Afḍal military faction and of the Ismā'īlī *qāḍī* of Alexandria, and was put down only the next year. Within Egypt and in the Yemen, the majority of Ismā'īlīs went along with al-Afḍal and accepted al-Musta'lī as the true imām; but in Syria the Ismā'īlīs were sharply divided, and in the rest of the Saljuq-ruled lands they insisted on the rights of Nizār, which they continued to recognize even when he was finally executed. The Iranian Ismā'īlīs did not, however, attempt then to interfere actively in Egypt, nor did they even identify any one of the descendants of Nizār as claimant to power in Egypt.

For the Egyptian state it was an advantage to retain power in the vizierial family by recognizing their creature, al-Musta'lī. Al-Afḍal continued the cautious and firm policies of his father. But what was advantageous to the conservative Egyptian state would have been at most an encumbrance to the rebels against the Saljuqs, to whom the state gave no effective support. For the Iranians, it may well have been with relief that they found themselves no longer tied to the Fāṭimid power, free to pursue their own policies without the danger of inappropriate intervention from Cairo.

The justification of the schism, however, was quite legitimately doctrinal. The basis on which the Ismā'īlīs, at least retrospectively, had justified their adherence to Ismā'īlī and his son (as against Mūsā, whom the Twelvers followed) was that Ja'far al-Ṣādiq had explicitly designated Ismā'īl as the next imām, and that a subsequent designation of another son—supposing it had occurred—could not validly supersede the first designation. Al-Afḍal claimed that al-Mustanṣir had designated al-Musta'lī on his deathbed, but it was understandable that pious Ismā'īlīs should hold by the earlier designation of Nizār. Nevertheless, on Nizār's death a difficulty arose. Nizār seems to have designated no one of his sons as his successor; at any rate, no Nizārid rose to claim the imāmate. Who then was the imām of the rebel Ismā'īlīs (who now called themselves Nizārīs)?[1]

Before long, many outsiders and probably some Nizārī Ismā'īlīs believed that a son or grandson of Nizār had been smuggled out of Egypt and was kept secretly at Alamūt. But we have no evidence that this was done, and some evidence that it was not: later, the Egyptian government could claim to know that all the male descendants of Nizār were quiescent; the notion of a descendant of Nizār being at Alamūt had to take the form of his having been a posthumous son by a slave girl, and hence unknown in Cairo. At any rate, at Alamūt no account seems to have been taken of the presence of any Nizārid. If we may judge by bits and shreds of evidence in later Ismā'īlī works, no imām at all was named, after Nizār. It was known that one of the Nizārids must be he, but not which one. Eventually, it seems, Ḥasan-i Ṣabbāḥ, as the most important of the dā'īs, was recognized as *ḥujja*, "proof", of the imām. The term *ḥujja* had already been used, at least informally, of a figure in the ideal spiritual hierarchy ranking next after the imām; now its use seems to have become more precise: Ḥasan was custodian of the Ismā'īlī mission until the imām should reappear, at which time he would point out the imām to the faithful.

When this interpretation was adopted we cannot tell, but there is nothing against its having been adopted already in Ḥasan's lifetime; perhaps it was accepted at the same time as his leadership of the whole movement. We have still less way of knowing how Ḥasan himself felt about the doctrine, which presumably had not been taught him by any actual imām though it concerned the most ultimate truths, which should come by ta'līm. Yet the imām had been inaccessible to the faithful before, in the days before the rise of the Fāṭimids, and Ḥasan might

[1] The Nizārīs are properly to be distinguished, not from "Musta'lians", but from the Ṭayyibīs on the one hand and the Ḥāfiẓīs on the other. For a discussion of the schism see *OA*, pp. 62–9.

well feel himself divinely singled out, with his logical gifts, for bearing a burden now which someone had borne before. For the faithful generally, the expectation of the near-coming of a promised imām, whose mere humanity meanwhile was veiled by absence, might be more inspiring than a present and all-too-human ruler who in fact contributed nothing positive to the cause anyway. In Ḥasan's doctrine, the role of the imām had become so abstract as to amount to little more than a guarantee of the validity of the Ismā'īlī movement as such. In the atmosphere of total dedication and imminent expectations which must have surrounded the Ismā'īlī risings, such a role could be played perhaps as well by an abstract postulate as by a distant and irrelevant monarch.

Methods of struggle

The revolt was unprecedented in form. The very leadership of the risings in their first years seems to have been as decentralized as the sites of their activity. After 'Abd al-Malik-i 'Aṭṭāsh's death, there is no assurance that the dā'ī of Iṣfahān had even a nominal precedence over an important dā'ī like that of Dailam. But the dā'īs did co-operate, and the revolt soon showed a characteristic overall pattern precisely in its co-ordinated decentralization.

Many movements which aimed at reforming Muslim society had taken as their model Muḥammad's emigration to Medina, accordingly, they set up a *dār al-hijra*, a place of emigration, as headquarters for their campaign, from which to return victoriously into Muslim society at large as Muḥammad had returned to Mecca. For the early Khārijīs this had been a military camp to which all the truly faithful ought to move, and which commonly was shifted freely about the countryside as a base for something like guerilla warfare. For the Shī'is it had usually been a fixed base, where a strong army could be recruited and from which the other provinces could be conquered in regular military operations, as had happened in the rise of the 'Abbāsids and of the Fāṭimids. For the rebel Ismā'īlīs now there were many dār al-hijras, as many as there were local groups who could seize a stronghold for themselves and hold out against the established rulers. But all these dār al-hijras formed one community, and if one of them was lost, its people could find refuge in another.

At almost every town there was an Ismā'īlī cell. Such cells seem to have become the nucleus for armed bands, which—like some other armed bands formed in the artisan population—could even be accepted as allies in the fighting by one Saljuq faction against another. It was such armed bands that seized key fortresses as defensible headquarters—or occasionally were granted them by an amīr who was glad to use their support. Such fortresses were garrisoned in a fairly conventional way: in each case, the troops were likely to owe allegiance first to their immediate commander, and only through him to the Saljuq regime or some faction in it. Hence it was not always immediately clear whether a given fortress was in Ismā'īlī hands or merely in the hands of a commander willing to use Ismā'īlī manpower. When necessary, an Ismā'īlī garrison could maintain its position by offering submission to some Saljuq amīr—which merely meant that it would send him part of any taxes raised on the surrounding lands and send forces to join in his battles. In the towns themselves, naturally, the ambiguity was even greater. Since the Ismā'īlīs kept their allegiance secret, only the fulltime leaders were likely to be identified with any certainty by public rumour. As the Sunnī public came to recognize the revolt as a serious threat, the Ismā'īlīs still in the towns began to look like a secret fifth column within the gates.

The decentralized pattern of the revolt was appropriate to the times. There was no longer, after Malik-Shāh's death, a single all-powerful Saljuq ruler to be replaced. But even before his death, with the decay of a centralized bureaucracy, the Islamic lands had come to be increasingly parcelled out in the hands of individual commanders of garrisons; to subdue the Saljuq domains meant subduing them all piecemeal. Even on the civilian side, the social structure put power in the hands of individuals of local standing, qāḍīs or prominent '*ulamā*—individuals whose power often resulted less from any special office dependent on a central authority than from relatively informal ties of local prestige and private patronage. There scarcely existed any single target for a military conquest by a regularly organized army, conquest which would have resulted in the submission of an obedient realm as had happened in Egypt. If the Ismā'īlīs were to win, it was reasonable to expect that, at least at first, it would be locality by locality, fort by fort.

The same atomization of power suggested the use of an important auxiliary technique for achieving military and political aims: assassination. Where local authority was relatively personal, so that an official furnished with basically the same means of power as another official did not automatically succeed him, the elimination of a key individual could disrupt any social undertaking. Thus the death of Malik-Shāh automatically terminated the expedition against Kūhistān; it was thought of, not as a project of the state, but as the personal command of Malik-Shāh himself, and the new ruler would have to launch it all over again it he cared to. In these circumstances, assassination was quite commonly resorted to by all factions.

At first, doubtless, the Ismāʿīlīs resorted to it as an occasional convenience, as did anyone else. But before long they made a relatively systematic use of it. It is clear that they did not rely solely on assassination or the threat of it, nor did they always bring it into play even in the case of notorious enemies. But they used it sufficiently often so that almost any assassination was likely to be ascribed to them, and many prominent Sunnī figures took precautions against it—even to wearing armour beneath their regular clothes. The Ismāʿīlīs seem to have thought of it as a specially meritorious service in the war for the holy cause; those ready to accomplish missions of assassination were called *fidāʾīs*, devotees, and received special honour. (And if they were killed in action they would be rewarded as martyrs in Paradise, of course, according to the general Muslim doctrine.) Perhaps it was felt that it was better to kill one great man who caused trouble than to slaughter many ordinary men on a battlefield—a viewpoint presumably more acceptable to the Ismāʿīlīs, who looked on the Sunnī leaders as traitors to Islam, than to the Sunnīs, who thought that the death of a great man, on whom the social order depended, was more disastrous than the death of many peasants. Certainly the risky action of killing a great man, who was normally surrounded by armed servants, was glorified as heroic. The Ismāʿīlīs preferred to do it in as public a setting as possible, since part of the purpose was to intimidate any others who took too strong a position against them. Many of the murders were consequently highly dramatic; and the assassins did not often escape with their lives.

The Ismāʿīlīs' readiness to use assassination went so far, it seems, that already in the days of the revolt they were willing to use it not only for their own immediate purposes but also in aid of non-Ismāʿīlī political allies. Much later the Ismāʿīlī chiefs were willing to hire out assassins to relatively friendly rulers for pay, but in the time of the revolt, even if an assassination were on behalf of a friend, it was clearly undertaken with an eye to the strategic advantage to the Ismāʿīlīs of that friend's career; no clear line could be drawn between the several purposes for which assassination might be used. It is doubtful if the assassinations were specially ritualized at that period, or that the assassins formed a special corps, as later they probably did; all Ismāʿīlīs called one another "comrades", and presumably all were in principle ready to perform any needful act in the common struggle. But doubtless some men held themselves in special readiness and were likely to be called on. It seems that at some point the practice arose of sending Ismāʿīlīs to insinuate themselves into the households of various great men as servants, who would be in a position to kill such men if they made themselves troublesome. A dramatic warning could be given—a knife by the sleeping man's cushion, with a note attached—so that the man would realize his peril without being able to identify the responsible member of the household, and be persuaded, by way of precaution, to curb his hostility to the Ismāʿīlīs.[1] It is not clear how often such means were used, but one or two cases would be sufficient to stimulate a general fear of such secret Ismāʿīlī agents; no one knew whether he was one of those selected for secret surveillance. That fear would be quite as effective in many cases as the actual presence of an Ismāʿīlī in a given household. Nevertheless, normally assassination was carried out not by members of the household but by men specially sent to perform it, who stalked their victim till an appropriate occasion offered—as at a mosque or in a bath.

The assassinations were balanced almost from the beginning by massacres. The assassination of a popular leader or preacher who had initiated or incited action against the Ismāʿīlīs could rouse the Sunnī population of a town to round up all those in town who were suspected of being Ismāʿīlīs and then kill them summarily. Those who took the lead in such a massacre became themselves, in turn, the targets of assassination attempts. Massacres and assassinations appear together, frequent in some periods and areas, infrequent in others; rarely was one phenomenon unaccompanied by the other. The massacres were spurred by tales of Ismāʿīlī atrocities—Ismāʿīlīs were accused of bearing an indiscriminate hostility against mankind, or at least against all Muslims, and no sadistic practice seemed too improbable to be ascribed to them. About 486/1093 Iṣfahān was outraged by the report that a certain couple had been luring passing young men into an obscure alley (a blind man would ask a young man to guide him home there) and

[1] Such a ruse was employed, according to Juvainī (transl. Boyle, pp. 681–2), by Ḥasan-i Ṣabbāḥ himself in order to intimidate Sulṭān Sanjar.

putting them to death in their house in exquisite and gradual tortures; the couple were identified as Ismā'īlī, and they and all others accused of the same allegiance were dragged to a large bonfire and burned alive. As in all such cases of mass fright, many besides Ismā'īlīs fell victim to the massacres: anyone could get rid of an enemy by making a plausible accusation.[1]

Between assassinations and massacres, popular feeling hardened against the Ismā'īlīs. They were called by many names, notably *Bāṭiniyya* (men of the *bāṭin*, the inner meaning of texts); *Malāḥida* (heretics *par excellence*); and in Syria *Ḥashīshiyya* (smokers of *ḥashīsh*, narcotic hemp). The latter name was sufficiently current locally to be picked up by the Crusaders, under the form "Assassin" (from *Ḥashāshīn*); it became the normal Occidental designation of the Nizārī Ismā'īlīs and was ultimately used, as a common noun, for anyone who committed what readers of Crusading history associated most with them: public murders. The name also became the basis for several modern misunderstandings. It has been supposed, for instance, that the fida'īs sent on assassination missions were drugged with ḥashīsh—which would have been singularly inappropriate to the patient waiting and perfect timing which the assassinations required. It has also been supposed, on the basis of a modern reinterpretation of Muslim legends, that ḥashīsh was used to give the fidā'īs dreams of Paradise, convincing them to kill the more readily so as to go to Paradise as their reward; but for this there is no more real evidence than for the other. The name seems to have been used simply as an ugly sobriquet, perhaps on the basis of some now-forgotten local incident. In any case, it represented the popular feeling, which combined contempt and hatred with a bewildered astonishment at the Ismā'īlīs' mad courage.[2]

The Saljuq counteroffensive

At the start of the revolt is was still possible to evaluate the Ismā'īlīs in differing ways. It seems that several, but not all, captains on Berk-Yaruq's side looked on the Ismā'īlī bands as little more than another faction among the subject population, to be co-operated with when convenient, as would be done with local bands of Sunnīs. Berk-Yaruq's

[1] On the methods used in the struggle and in its repression, see *OA*, pp. 77–84, 87–9, 110–15; on assassination, see especially pp. 82–4, 110–15.

[2] On the name "Assassin", see *OA*, pp. 135–7, and references there.

brothers and enemies, Muḥammad and Sanjar, gained prestige among the more consciously Sunnī by refusing any dealing with the Ismāʿīlīs. But whatever the amīrs' attitude, none of them on either side had leisure to campaign against the Ismāʿīlīs, except sporadically as the occasion arose in the course of other activities. From the time of the schism with Egypt till the death of Berk-Yaruq (498/1104), the Ismāʿīlī fortunes seemed to be steadily on the rise.

About 492/1099 the *ra'īs* Muẓaffar, a secret Ismāʿīlī well connected among the Saljuq officers at Iṣfahān, persuaded one of Berk-Yaruq's amīrs to acquire Gird-Kūh, a strong fortress in the Alburz near Dāmghān in Qūmis, and to install him there as his lieutenant. Gird-Kūh was along the main route between western Iran and Khurāsān—part of the famous route between the Fertile Crescent and the Mediterranean to the west and the Tarim Basin and China to the east. As Ḥasan had done at Alamūt, the ra'īs Muẓaffar strengthened and stocked up the fortress as for an indefinite siege. A troop of Ismāʿīlīs from Kūhistān intervened on Berk-Yaruq's side shortly after, in 493/1100, in a battle near there between the ra'īs's patron and Sanjar, but they were unable to save the day for Berk-Yaruq; and the ra'īs's patron was killed in the fighting. The ra'īs nevertheless carried his patron's treasure to Gird-Kūh and held that stronghold, some time afterward openly declaring himself an Ismāʿīlī.

But even closer to the middle of things, at least politically, was the seizure of the fortress Shāhdīz not far from Iṣfahān. Aḥmad-i ʿAṭṭāsh, the son of ʿAbd al-Malik, set up as schoolmaster at the garrison, which was composed of presumably Shīʿī Dailamīs, and won them over; by about 494/1100 he was master of the place, and soon the Ismāʿīlīs were able to collect taxes in the nearby lands to the detriment of the Saljuq treasury. The Ismāʿīlīs seized a second fortress in the vicinity, Khālinjān, about the same time. Aḥmad's father is said to have retired to Alamūt under Ḥasan's protection at about this time, as a result of rising hostility in Iṣfahān; but the report seems questionable. In any case, he was no longer active by now. Aḥmad had the reputation of being a learned man, though not so much so as his father; the Sunnī reports speak of him as if he were his father's successor as dāʿī at Iṣfahān and probably as head of the whole Nizārī movement.

By this time, the association of some of Berk-Yaruq's captains with the Ismāʿīlīs was proving disastrous. While the opposing Saljuq forces accused all Berk-Yaruq's men of Ismāʿīlism, and Berk-Yaruq was held responsible for Ismā'īlī attacks on amīrs who opposed him, he was himself attempted by assassins when he appointed a vizier who was strongly anti-Ismā'īlī. In 494/1101, Berk-Yaruq in western Iran and Sanjar in Khurāsān came to an agreement to regard the Ismā'īlīs no longer as local bands but as a general threat to Saljuq power, and to act against them. The chief fruit of Berk-Yaruq's resolve was a grand massacre of suspected Ismā'īlīs at Iṣfahān, Baghdad, and elsewhere. Army officers were especially affected and several of them fled. Sanjar, with fewer friends of the Ismā'īlīs to purge within his own ranks, sent instead an expedition against Ṭabas in Kūhistān, which was said to have been bought off after causing much devastation; and three years later he sent another which wrecked Ṭabas and destroyed as much else as possible. The second expedition, as a *jihād* (holy war), was joined by many Sunnī volunteers in addition to the regular troops, and the Ismā'īlī captives, as apostates, were enslaved. Yet the next year Ismā'īlīs from Turshīz in Kūhistān were in a position to raid a Sunnī caravan as far west as Ray; and in Berk-Yaruq's lands no Ismā'īlī fortresses seem to have been overthrown at all.

Meanwhile, the Ismā'īlī position was being consolidated in Rūdbār, where several other fortresses were aligned with Alamūt, apparently in many cases by agreement with the local leaders, who received aid from the Ismā'īlīs against domination from Ray and Qazvīn. The most important addition was Lanbasar, considerably west of Alamūt in the Shāhrūd valley. After its garrison went back on their first agreement with the Ismā'īlīs, it was re-subjugated by Ḥasan's lieutenant Buzurg-Ummīd and built into a major stronghold. In Syria in this period the Ismā'īlīs controlled as yet no fortresses, but they were strong in Aleppo and in the nearby towns of the Jazr region, and they enjoyed the patronage of Riḍwān, Saljuq amīr of Aleppo.

With the advent to power of Muḥammad Tapar, however, the more important dynastic disputes ended and the Saljuq forces made greater headway against the Ismā'īlī revolt. Even in Syria, Riḍwān turned gradually against the Ismā'īlīs, who had become embarrassing, and he allowed more than one massacre of them; on his death in 507/1113, they were scattered from their headquarters in Aleppo and for some time sought vainly a citadel which they could hold for their own. Most of the Ismā'īlī strongholds in the Zagros mountains seem to have fallen during Muḥammad's reign. In 500/1107 Muḥammad sent an expedition against Takrīt; to avoid letting it fall into his hands, its master turned it over to an Arab chief, Ṣadaqa, who was a Shīʿī but no Ismāʿīlī.

The most important project, led by Muḥammad in person, was to rid the neighbourhood of Iṣfahān of its Ismāʿīlīs. Aḥmad-i ʿAṭṭāsh negotiated long and, for a time, successfully to maintain himself in Shāhdīz, arguing that he was a Muslim and should be accepted as a legitimate garrison chief so long as he submitted to Muḥammad's overall direction—that is, above all, paid him tribute and served in his wars. There were those in Iṣfahān who were willing to let him serve if in future he would indeed be obedient to the Saljuq ruler. But the more zealous Sunnī ʿulamā turned the day by arguing that the Ismāʿīlīs were not in fact true Muslims; that by exalting the bāṭin, the supposed inner meaning of the law, they had abandoned Islam even though they still observed the law, as they did. In this case no accommodation could be made with them. Finally a capitulation was agreed to in 500/1107 in which many of the Ismāʿīlīs were allowed safe-conduct to more distant Ismāʿīlī fortresses while the nucleus of the garrison was to surrender outright when the others had got away. In the end the nucleus resisted nonetheless, fighting even for the last turrets. Aḥmad was finally captured, paraded ignominiously through the town, and skinned alive.

Sanjar was encouraged to send a further expedition against the Ismāʿīlīs of Kūhistān. But we hear more of the expedition against Alamūt. After the fall of Shāhdīz and the death of the dāʿī of Iṣfahān, if not even earlier (as some reports seem to suggest, at least in some Ismāʿīlī circles), Ḥasan-i Ṣabbāḥ presumably was acknowledged as head of the whole Nizārī Ismāʿīlī movement, and Alamūt as its headquarters. After a futile expedition by the vizier himself, a son of Niẓām al-Mulk, the reduction of Alamūt was entrusted to Shīrgīr, the amīr of Sāveh. He tried attrition, taking some places fairly near Qazvīn, but above all Rūdbār in a yearly expedition for seven years. At length, in 511/1118, he was ready for a full-scale siege. Other amīrs were sent to help him. But as the surrender of Alamūt seemed to draw near, the news of Malik-Shāh's death arrived and the army broke up despite Shīrgīr's pleas. Alamūt was saved.[1]

[1] On the Saljuq counteroffensive, see *OA*, pp. 76–8, 84–9, 95–8.

II. STALEMATE

Though Alamūt was safe, the revolt as such was over. In the almost thirty years since Alamūt had been seized, the Ismā'īlīs had done their best to establish themselves throughout the Saljuq domains; they had posed a serious threat to Saljuq rule for a time, with considerable strength in and around Iṣfahān itself. But their partisans in the cities had been massacred or disorganized, and many of their strongholds had been destroyed. What remained could not seriously serve as a base for general revolt, at least not till their party had been widely rebuilt and a new effort prepared. The imām had never appeared in power to save the situation, and the times did not seem propitious for him to do so now. To be sure, the rebellion had been successful on a local basis in Rūdbār and Kūhistān, where whole districts had asserted and maintained their independence of the Saljuqs. But with the failure of the overall effort, one might have expected the surviving Ismā'īlīs to break up into local groupings and to be assimilated into the evolving Sunnī social and political structure on a local *ad hoc* basis. Yet the Ismā'īlīs held together from Kūhistān to Syria. The sons of the rebels were still dedicated. A further generation with essentially the same puritan and power-oriented outlook had to pass before a new beginning would be attempted. Meanwhile the Ismā'īlīs carried on the old struggle as best they could.

Definition of the territorial position

Though there was no major succession dispute on Muḥammad Tapar's death, his successor at Iṣfahān, Maḥmūd, and Sanjar, as general head of the Saljuqs, were sufficiently occupied with other troubles not to press much further against the Ismā'īlīs. Sanjar is said to have made a truce with the Ismā'īlīs, persuaded by a dagger which Ḥasan contrived to have thrust into the floor next to Sanjar's pillow. The historian Juvainī found conciliatory letters from Sanjar in the Ismā'īlī archives. The Ismā'īlīs at Alamūt reoccupied fortresses which they had given up to S͟hīrgīr. During the rest of his life (to 518/1124) Ḥasan-i Ṣabbāḥ, while remaining dā'ī of Dailam, seems to have been regarded as head of the community. He presumably devoted himself to consolidating its position in the territories it had won, and perhaps also to reaffirming, in some degree, a central authority over them.

These territories consisted primarily of two main districts: Rūdbār and a large part of Qūhistān. Rūdbār was felt to be the core portion of Dailam and inherited the militant and particularist temper of the Dailamī mountaineers. There were dozens of fortresses in its mountains, not only in the Alburz proper north of the Shāhrūd but in the lower mountains between that valley and Qazvīn; the Ismā'īlīs sometimes held a fortress or so sufficiently near Qazvīn to serve as a special irritant to the Qazvīnīs. The chief of the Rūdbār Ismā'īlīs, who was also head of the whole community, commonly resided at Alamūt, but by no means always. The most immediate neighbours and enemies of Rūdbār were Qazvīn to the south and Rūyān to the north (between the Alburz and the sea); accordingly, the rulers of 'Irāq-i 'Ajam at Iṣfahān and of Māzandarān at Āmul, the respective suzerains of those two neighbours, intermittently felt it their duty to destroy the Ismā'īlī power, which lay between their territories. The Ismā'īlī territory in Kūhistān was distinctly more extensive, including several towns more substantial than any in Rūdbār. In the north, Turshīz was readily involved in hostilities with the authorities in Khurāsān, while Nih in the south was commonly at odds with Sīstān. The Kūhistānī Ismā'īlīs owned the authority of a single chief, appointed at Alamūt, who resided usually, but not always, in either Tūn or Qā'in or in the fortress of Mu'minābād.

In addition to the two main territories, the Ismā'īlī state included three other scattered tracts. The other fortresses in the eastern Alburz seem to have been lost, but Gird-Kūh at Dāmghān was held and stood isolated but firm as an Ismā'īlī outpost. Though the fortresses in the southern Zagros had been lost, farther north in the Zagros, in Luristān, some fortresses were retained or else soon after acquired, with the support of some local Jewish clans. Lastly, after Ḥasan's death, the Ismā'īlīs in Syria finally acquired their long-sought independent base in the mountains west of Ḥamā and Ḥimṣ, where they acquired a small group of fortified towns; here they were ruled by an appointee of Alamūt, who sometimes resided at Maṣyāf.

For a time, even after Ḥasan's death, the Ismā'īlī community included not only those in the independent territories but a substantial number in at least some Iranian cities. Correspondingly, not everyone in Rūdbār or (probably) in Ismā'īlī Kūhistān was an Ismā'īlī. But gradually we cease to hear of Ismā'īlīs outside of their own territories, except in the Jazr district of Syria, east of Aleppo, and possibly in parts of Kūhistān and Sīstān that were not ruled by Ismā'īlīs. Doubtless some such Ismāʿīlīs persisted, though without playing a large role in the Ismāʿīlī state, or presumably, in the fortunes of the religious community. At some time, but we do not know whether in the Alamūt period, the numerous Ismāʿīlīs of the upper Oxus basin were won over to the Nizārī position. But in large measure the state formed henceforth an independent Ismāʿīlī society with little stake in the wider Sunnī society except so far as its often active trade and, indeed, its continuing intellectual interests, enforced interaction.[1]

The continuing struggle

On Ḥasan-i Ṣabbāḥ's death in 518/1124, his position as dāʿī of Dailam and as head of the community fell to his lieutenant at Lanbasar, Buzurg-Ummīd. This man was well connected, at least by marriage, with ruling families in the Caspian region, but clearly he was chosen also for his personal qualities. He moved to Alamūt and carried on the rigorous policies of his predecessor, aided by a council of three advisers who had also been appointed by Ḥasan. One gets the impression that the Ismāʿīlīs' enemies hoped he would prove a lesser man than Ḥasan; within two years of his accession, the Saljuqs were attacking both Rūdbār and Kūhistān. At Āmid there was a massacre of suspected Ismāʿīlīs. But the attacks seem to have had no success. On the contrary, in the first years of Buzurg-Ummīd's rule, the Ismāʿīlī position in Rūdbār was strengthened. The fortress of Ṭāliqān was taken, then or earlier—this was presumably the strongest place in the Ṭāliqān mountains; and a new fortress, Maimūn-Diz, was built at the border of the Ismāʿīlī territory downstream from Alamūt.[2]

Meanwhile, the Ismāʿīlīs were becoming embroiled on a more local basis. The Bāvandid rulers of Māzandarān, who had refused to join Muḥammad Tapar against Alamūt, had become their active enemy by the time of Maḥmūd's campaign. Then the Ismāʿīlīs' envoy to Maḥmūd at Iṣfahān had been lynched, and they avenged themselves, not on the Iṣfahānīs, but on the more accessible Qazvīnīs, thus exacerbating an enmity with that city which persisted even when the ruler of ʿIrāq-i ʿAjam was inactive. At least some of the Kūhistānī Ismāʿīlīs were at war with the amīrs of Sīstān with little regard to what arrangements

[1] On the Ismāʿīlī territorial pattern, cf. *OA*, pp. 115–16, pp. 244–5. The maps given here supplement the vaguer data there.

[2] The site of Maimūn-Diz has now been identified. See Peter Willey, *The Castles of the Assassins* (London, 1963), pp. 158–92.

Sanjar might make. The greatest triumph of Buzurg-Ummīd's reign seems to have been the defeat and execution by fire of a Zaidī imām, Abū Hāshim, who had arisen to power in the non-Ismāʿīlī districts of Dailam.[1]

When Buzurg-Ummīd died in 532/1138, his son Muḥammad became dāʿī, and, like him, held the allegiance of all the several Ismāʿīlī territories. In the earlier part of his reign, at least, he increased the area under the control of Alamūt, seizing some fortresses in the direction of Gīlān. But the quarrels with the Ismāʿīlīs' neighbours sometimes seemed little more exalted than personal feuds. An amīr of Ray campaigned against them in Rūdbār after his master's assassination, perhaps even despite Sanjar's orders; he built a tower of Ismāʿīlī heads. The ruler of Turshīz tried at one point to restore Sunnism there, was expelled, and failed to regain his position even with an army from Sanjar. For at least six years after 545/1150, one of Sanjar's amīrs, Ibn Anaz, carried on an almost personal series of raids in Kūhistān. Perhaps the most disastrous such vendetta for the Ismāʿīlīs was the hostility of Shāh Ghāzī of Māzandarān, who built several towers of Ismāʿīlī heads gathered from his Rūdbār campaigns, though even he does not seem to have made permanent conquests of land. The raids and counter-raids exchanged with Qazvīn persisted throughout; the Ismāʿīlīs' chronicler has recorded the number of sheep taken on each raid.[2]

Though the Nizārīs had made no serious attempt to support the Nizārid cause in Egypt after the schism, bitterness yet remained between the two parties, especially in Syria. Under al-Mustaʿlī's son al-Āmir (personal rule, 515/1121–524/1130), beginning with what was held to be a Nizārī assassination of the vizier al-Afḍal, the Nizārī cause seems to have been especially active even in Egypt. The succeeding vizier took extensive measures to guard against a new assassination, allegedly even trying to keep track of any who might be setting out from Alamūt, and at any rate blaming directly on Alamūt the activity of Nizārī agents uncovered. A public defence of al-Āmir's rights as imām, as against those of his uncle Nizār, was deemed necessary. But in 524/1130 al-Āmir was assassinated (again, but more clearly, by Nizārīs); thereupon the Egyptian Ismāʿīlīs themselves split. He seems to have had a son in that last year, al-Ṭayyib; but whether because the infant died or because he otherwise disappeared, on al-Āmir's

[1] On Buzurg-Ummīd's reign, see *OA*, pp. 99–104.
[2] On Muḥammad b. Buzurg-Ummīd's reign, see *OA*, pp. 143–6.

death there seemed to be no male heir. After a time of confusion, al-Āmir's cousin (by another uncle) took power as al-Ḥāfiẓ and claimed the imāmate. The main body of Egyptian Ismā'īlīs accepted him, being called Ḥāfiẓiyya; the Ismā'īlīs of the Yemen, the chief body of non-Nizārī Ismā'īlīs outside Egypt, rejected him in the name of al-Ṭayyib, and they became the Ṭayyibīs. Henceforth, though the Nizārīs and Ḥāfiẓīs seem to have had occasional hostile and even friendly relations, the Nizārīs seem to have taken no further account of the Fāṭimid caliphate.[1]

After a spate of assassinations and massacres at the beginning of Muḥammad's reign—these were now limited pretty much to the relatively northerly lands from Kūhistān to Syria, without the involvement of such cities as Baghdad—traces of Ismā'īlī activity in cities away from the Ismā'īlī-ruled territories become few. It is said that under Jahān-Sūz Ghūrī (d. 556/1161) Ismā'īlī propagandists were invited into Ghūr, where his successor had to kill them along with their converts. But even if this is not a case of maliciously mistaken identity, it is not typical of the Ismā'īlī activity of the time. Nevertheless, the Ismā'īlīs continued to maintain a large sense of their mission. The chroniclers of Buzurg-Ummīd and his son stressed their acts of generosity—as in the case of a militant enemy amīr whose fortunes at home had changed and who sought refuge with the Ismā'īlīs and was not yielded up to his enemies despite their reminder that previously he had acted treacherously against the Ismā'īlīs. The Ismā'īlīs gloried especially in two acts that seemed to take them on to the world stage again for a moment: the assassinations of the 'Abbāsid caliphs al-Mustarshid and then of his son, al-Rāshid. Neither caliph was master any longer of a caliphal empire: indeed, both were out of favour with their Saljuq masters, and were either in prison or in exile. Yet the Ismā'īlīs gave their assassins the accolade of *al-'Abbāsī*, victors over the house of 'Abbās, and they even interpreted the necessary exile of al-Rāshid as an expedition by the lord of all Sunnīs against the Ismā'īlīs to avenge his father.

Reactions among the Sunnīs

By the end of Muḥammad b. Buzurg-Ummīd's reign, the picture of a great life-and-death struggle with the 'Abbāsid caliphate was as inappropriate to the Ismā'īlī state as it was to the 'Abbāsid. Yet the

[1] On the later relations with the Fāṭimid Ismā'īlīs, see *OA*, pp. 107–10.

Ismāʿīlī sense of their own grandeur was answered by the Sunnīs' corresponding feeling that they still constituted a major threat to Sunnī Muslim society. The impact of the Ismāʿīlī revolt had been far-reaching and was only then losing its immediacy. Zealous Sunnīs were still inclined to see the Ismāʿīlīs as the arch-enemies of Islam.

The first results of the revolt had been, of course, highly disruptive—not only by way of direct Ismāʿīlī action but also by way of the Sunnīs' panic in response to it, which launched indiscriminate massacres. But apart from immediate political and social consequences, the movement had significant intellectual and imaginative consequences among the Sunnīs which were more enduring. The first question that was raised was what limits should be put to the Sunnī doctrine that membership of the Muslim community should be determined by external acts—notably by acknowledgement of Muḥammad and performance of the *ṣalāt* in the direction of Mecca—while hearts could be judged by God alone. At Iṣfahān those who insisted that the privileges of being a Muslim should be less freely granted had their way when the Ismāʿīlīs were excluded despite their external conformity; many later Muslims followed this precedent. This problem as presented in the Ismāʿīlīs was also a major one for Ghazālī, who wrote an incisive treatise to resolve it; he then cited that treatise in many other connexions, as fundamental to deciding what sort of intellectual position was and was not compatible with Islam.

But Ghazālī was touched by the Ismāʿīlī position, and especially by Ḥasan's doctrine of taʿlīm, more deeply than this. He wrote many works designed to refute the Ismāʿīlīs, some of which seem equally designed to settle his own conscience with regard to their challenge. In the *Munqidh min al-ḍallāl* he came to terms with four categories of seekers of the truth, as representative of all the intellectual positions worthy of serious consideration: the philosophers of the Greek tradition; the *mutakallimūn*, taken *en bloc* as those who argue on behalf of historical revelation; the Ṣūfīs with their immediate mystical consciousness—and the Ismāʿīlīs with their doctrine of taʿlīm. To each of the first three groups he allowed a carefully defined role in his total vision of truth-seeking; and though he condemned the Ismāʿīlīs roundly, it can be argued that, if not to them, at least to their position he likewise allowed a certain role. He claimed that Muḥammad himself was the true authoritative teacher whose existence, as the Ismāʿīlīs showed, reason posited and might verify, but whose teaching it could not reach by itself. In doing so he not only undercut the Ismāʿīlī doctrine but introduced a new approach into the Sunnī doctrine itself: the historical revelation was to be kept central yet was to be tested and interpreted by the inner need of the human being—at its highest, of course, in Ṣūfī experience. The Ismāʿīlī logic helped make possible this integration of history with personal inwardness.

No other Sunnī was so intimately influenced by the Nizārī Ismāʿīlī doctrine as was Ghazālī; but few other Sunnī writers were so influential. Other Sunnīs of the time wrestled with the questions raised, but less perceptively. Probably the last to whom the questions were intellectually actual was Shahrastānī (d. 548/1153), who debated with Ismāʿīlīs and was more irritated than challenged by them (though he may have used their writings incidentally in his history of doctrine). For later writers, the doctrine of taʿlīm was something out of the past —Fakhr al-Dīn Rāzī used it to make a debating point against Ghazālī, for instance.

The stimulus to the Muslim imagination was more lasting and has carried over into the Occident. At the time of the revolt itself, the popular reaction came to be an unthinking enraged terror, which created as its objects diabolically clever and ruthless leaders manipulating gullibly stupid followers. The people of Rūdbār were so stupid, it was said, that one of them would saw off the branch he sat on; while Ḥasan-i Ṣabbāḥ was felt to have almost superhuman powers of insight, by which he could win the blind devotion of many skilled individuals and direct them successfully in the most widely ramified and delicate undertakings. The old explanation of Ismāʿīlism—that it was invented by a Persian Zoroastrian who resented the Arab victory and wanted to subvert Islam and replace it with dualism, to which doctrine Ismāʿīlism would lead—no longer sufficed; it was not dropped, but rather than Islamic doctrine, the Ismāʿīlīs' target was now said to be the Muslims themselves: their whole purpose, some believed (as during the panic at Iṣfahān), was to kill as many Muslims as cruelly as possible.

Soon this temper was crystallized into romantic legends. The idea that Ḥasan used drugs to make his human tools more manipulable appeared early in a crude form (walnuts, coriander, and honey to expand the brain). By the time of Marco Polo, the tale was current in Iran that Ḥasan had had a garden made to resemble Paradise, with beautiful maidens at the disposal of the young man who (drugged asleep so as to be transported there unawares) was told (when he awoke a second time and the garden had vanished) that Ḥasan could send him to that Paradise at will, and would send him there permanently if he died in his service. In Arabic, too, the story turned up in a historical novel set in al-Ḥākim's time, in which the master of the garden was one Ismāʿīl at Maṣyāf, a subsequent headquarters of the Syrian Nizārīs. It was a Western scholar, Silvestre de Sacy, who later put together the nickname *Ḥashīshiyya* and the notion of the drug, and surmised that the drug was no mere sleeping powder but a vision-engendering narcotic, and that no real garden was necessary. But the garden was too fascinating a theme to be dispensed with, and modern popular lore has retained both the ḥashīsh and the garden.

Other tales were told: at a nightly orgy, males and females would gather and mingle sexually at will with no regard to status or relationship; then the next day, at a word from their master, Ismāʿīlī fidā'is would leap from a turret to their death, for the edification of a visitor. For ordinary Muslims—and for medieval Westerners, whose imaginations proved quite as lurid—the Ismāʿīlīs became a dreamworld embodying whatever fascinating horror the sober actuality ruled out from their prosaic lives. But some of the tales seem to have originated with the Ismāʿīlīs themselves, notably the tale of the three schoolfellows, which FitzGerald retold in his introduction to the *Rubaiyyat*. As the Ismāʿīlīs told it, Ḥasan-i Ṣabbāḥ was the hero. Since the three students had agreed to share among themselves the good fortune that any of them should achieve, Ḥasan came, as did ʿUmar Khayyām, to Niẓām al-Mulk when he became vizier, expecting his favour. But when Ḥasan, duly established at court, proved much more capable than Niẓām al-Mulk, the latter's condescension to his old friend gave way to jealousy, and he plotted to cover the unsuspecting Ḥasan with ignominy and have him disgraced. It was thus the vizier who began the hostility which Ḥasan brought to a conclusion by launching the revolt and getting the vizier assassinated in revenge. The efforts of Sunnī versions to whitewash the vizier were only partly successful, but the story was so appealing that it continued to circulate nonetheless. In the realm of the imagination, the Ismāʿīlī inspiration, direct or indirect, ruled unchallenged even after their political power disappeared.[1]

[1] On the imaginative and intellectual repercussions among the Sunnīs, see *OA*, pp. 121–39.

The continuing vitality of the Ismāʿīlīs

Indeed, the Ismāʿīlī imaginative power may have contributed to the unwonted vitality which the Ismāʿīlī state continued to show even in its reduced form. That vitality is already exhibited in its very survival. In the Islamic society of that age, when so much in the political sphere depended on direct military power, the authority of a government did not normally extend beyond the range of its armies. The five parcels that went to make up the Ismāʿīlī state could obviously not be controlled militarily from any one centre; its unity could in no way be enforced. Nor were the Ismāʿīlīs of one area able to send much material assistance to another area; there was no immediate profit to be gained from the unity. Yet the state remained one; the governors of Kūhistān and of Syria were regularly appointed by the authority at Alamūt until Alamūt itself fell, despite drastic changes of policy which some of the rulers of Alamūt were to institute. Surely it was a common vision as much as mutual service that kept those widely dispersed territories together for five generations.

The vitality of the state is also attested by the stability of its dynasty. There seem to have been no succession disputes, either at first when it was a dāʿī who ruled, or later when the imāmate was at stake. Twenty years is a relatively long reign in a Muslim dynasty where the effective power is vested in the ruler; but of the seven reigns at Alamūt (the eighth was cut short by the Mongols), four are longer than that: twenty-four, thirty-four, thirty-four, and even forty-four years. Two rulers were murdered (and just possibly a third); one of them after a peculiarly drastic change of policy, the other after his personality showed signs of deterioration—he was the only ruler of the seven who was not fully competent personally (and even he may have been blackened posthumously). The rulers were supported by a vigorous and independent community life in each of the Ismāʿīlī districts, and though they could initiate extreme changes of policy they were not allowed to grow soft.[1]

Considering the small extent and limited economy of the state, it retained a disproportionate power: repeatedly the Ismāʿīlīs were able to expand beyond their holdings, and their diplomacy often ranged far and effectively—at more than one period they were respectfully listened to as far away as in the courts of Western Europe. To the

[1] On the stability of the state, see *OA*, pp. 115–20, 244–6.

Sunnīs, their power seemed greater than it really was: the continuing intense hatred for the Ismā'īlīs, which finally led Sunnīs to call the Mongols down on them when no Muslim power seemed capable of defeating them, bears witness to the Ismā'īlī reputation. It has been suggested that this power was based on the weapon of assassination. Doubtless that played a role; but the Ismā'īlīs were by no means the only ones who resorted to assassination, nor could such a weapon have been systematically effective over many generations unless it were backed up by strong institutions.

The Ismā'īlī society was not a typical mountaineer and small-town society, despite the counting of sheep after raids. Each community maintained its own sense of initiative in the framework of the wider cause, and probably a sense of larger strategy was never completely absent: the immediate consequence everywhere of changes in their overall external policy suggest this. But what was most distinctive was the high level of intellectual life. The prominent early Ismā'īlīs were commonly known as scholars, often as astronomers, and at least some later Ismā'īlīs continued the tradition. In Alamūt, in Kūhistān, and in Syria, at the main centres at least, were libraries which included Qur'āns and religious literature of all sorts, but also scientific books and equipment; visitors were impressed with the libraries, which were well known among Sunnī scholars. To the end the Ismā'īlīs prized sophisticated interpretations of their own doctrines, and were also interested in every kind of knowledge which the age could offer.

The vitality of their community was reinforced by the continuing arrival of a certain number of outsiders into the Ismā'īlī centres. We hear of few Ismā'īlīs coming in from outside; after the time of Buzurg-Ummīd the Ismā'īlīs of the diaspora would not have been sufficiently numerous to help much, either in supporting Ismā'īlī external policies or in revitalizing the isolated communities. Yet the Ismā'īlīs did challenge the imagination and were able to attract individuals of high calibre. Some of these were political refugees—amīrs who had lost out in quarrels within the Sunnī world and who knew the Ismā'īlīs would never give them up to their enemies. Some were adventurous youths who adopted Ismā'īlism, such as Rāshid al-Dīn Sinān, who later became head of the Syrian Ismā'īlīs; he seems to have been brought up in a Nuṣairī community in Iraq, and to have gone to Alamūt when he wanted to get away from home. Finally, in the later period, there were a number of outside scholars attracted to the Ismā'īlī libraries and to their generous patronage of learning; most of them seem to have remained frankly non-Ismāʿīlī, but they helped maintain the high intellectual tone of the community. The greatest of them, Naṣīr al-Dīn Ṭūsī, even wrote major Ismāʿīlī treatises.

Accordingly, we must attribute the Ismāʿīlī strength only in part to their military methods or to the political genius of their early leaders, and to the irrationally persistent reputation which the later generations retained. In large part it resulted from the solidarity they could maintain among themselves under outside pressure; from their ability to renew a social and religious tradition which encouraged their continued independence; and from the special appeal they made, in the contemporary Muslim society, to the exceptional individual.

III. RESURRECTION

Theological doctrines usually serve as a criticism and discipline of religious practice, warning of pitfalls to be avoided in terms of a given tradition. But sometimes they can form a positive charter for spiritual renewal, as was now to be the case. Doctrines cannot really describe such a renewal, but the nature of its spiritual life can be deduced from them. By the shifts they make in terminology and emphasis, and in particular by the points which prove crucial at moments of polemic with other viewpoints, they indicate what sorts of mood, insight, aspiration, and commitment are to be legitimized and given social encouragement. We know the next stage of the Ismāʿīlī community life almost exclusively through its theological production; from this we must try to deduce the life of the time. But such a procedure is not entirely inappropriate. Theological doctrines are especially important in a community like that of the Nizārī Ismāʿīlīs, which depended so much on a continual revitalizing of their distinctive group orientation.

Ḥasan II: sublimation of expectations

In the later years of Muḥammad b. Buzurg-Ummīd, there was a movement among the younger Ismāʿīlīs to revive what had always been a popular doctrine in Ismāʿīlī circles, though it had been suppressed by the Ismāʿīlī leadership: the doctrine that the sharīʿa ritual law no longer applied to those who understood the bāṭin, the inner meaning of it, for the sharīʿa was simply a set of symbols intended to incite to more understanding beyond itself, and when it had fulfilled its function it was no longer binding. Those who believed this had seen the imposition of shariʿa on enlightened and devoted Ismāʿīlīs as a kind of taqiyya, or dissimulation designed only to help keep the ignorant, wilful Sunnīs in place—lest they follow the free Ismāʿīlīs' example prematurely and, without even the symbols of truth to restrain them, give rein to their evil natures and cast aside all law and order altogether. In any case, at the end of the age, when the imām established full justice in the world—an eschatological time which many Ismāʿīlīs identified with the Last Judgment and the coming of Paradise—the sharīʿa would be abolished, for it would no longer be relevant when the imperfect conditions of the present life were past. But many Ismāʿīlīs were restive, at least in their private lives, at waiting for the grand consummation. During the active revolt the Ismāʿīlī puritanism had been accentuated as all energies were focused on the immediate goal of material victory. But now it would seem that in their own districts, set apart from the Sunnī world, the Ismāʿīlīs no longer had any responsibility to set a cautious example to the Sunnīs. Why shouldn't the Ismāʿīlīs assume their rightful freedom from the petty restrictions of the sharīʿa and live in full recognition of the spiritual truths of their faith, which preoccupation with the sharīʿa ritual tended to obscure?

When Muḥammad found that among the young men who inclined to this viewpoint was his own son Ḥasan, who was expected to succeed him as dāʿī, he took drastic action. It is said that Ḥasan drank wine in secret to show that he was above the law, and that some of the Ismāʿīlīs took this to be a sign that he was the true imām. Muḥammad had 250 men killed and exiled 250 more, and Ḥasan denied publicly that he was the imām; apparently from that time till Muḥammad's death Ḥasan curbed his tongue. But Ḥasan had read widely not only in the older books of the Ismāʿīlīs but also in philosophic and Sūfī writings. He seems to have learned to interpret the old Ismāʿīlī hopes in the light of Ṣūfī psychological insights. He is said to have been very affable and popular in Rūdbār, where he was regarded as more learned than his father; on his father's death (557/1162) he succeeded without dispute and proceeded to prepare the way, cautiously, for a reform. After two years he was ready.[1]

On 17 Ramaḍān 559/1164 he gathered together at Alamūt representatives from the various dispersed Ismāʿīlī groups, at least those in

[1] On Ḥasan II's youth, see *OA*, pp. 146–8.

Iran (the Syrians are not mentioned, and the new dispensation may not have been fully introduced to them till later). He read them a message supposed to be from the imām, naming Ḥasan as the imām's special representative with plenary authority, entitling him not only dāʿī but also ḥujja, proof of the imām (like Ḥasan-i Ṣabbāḥ), and finally caliph, representative of the imām, presumably a higher rank yet. At last the imām was emerging. But he announced yet more: the long-foretold Last Day had arrived—*qiyāma*, the Resurrection—when all mankind would be judged and committed forever to either Hell or Paradise; henceforth those who refused to accept the imām were cast into Hell, which was spiritual non-existence, while those who accepted him were in Paradise. Finally, as was fitting in Paradise, taqiyya was no longer necessary and the sharīʿa was at an end. Accordingly, the fast of Ramaḍān (which in the bāṭin had been held to stand for taqiyya) was broken with a feast then and there. Toward the time of the *ḥajj* pilgrimage, a similar ceremony was held at the fortress Mu'minābād in Kūhistān, where Ḥasan's position as caliph was explicitly identified with that of the Fāṭimid caliph al-Mustanṣir—who had in fact been imām.[1]

The great resurrection, the end of the world, was thus understood (in a typically Ismāʿīlī manner) in a symbolic sense. It was the end of a religious era, and the beginning of a spiritual dispensation of moral, not physical, perfection. The end of earthly life, of the external level of reality, at least as possessing religious significance, and also the end of the sharīʿa law, was the moment when the inward meaning of reality became evident and what mattered henceforth would be a purely spiritual life of inward states of the soul. The event may be compared with the advent of the dispensation of grace and the end of the dispensation of the law as Paul presented them. More properly, it must be interpreted in Ṣūfī terms: the inner life of moral and mystical experience was the sole reality henceforth to be attended to. Those who could respond were, spiritually, already in eternal life, and those who could not were spiritually lifeless. This was the long-awaited culmination; the faithful Ismāʿīlīs who understood were to leave behind all material compromise and rise to the spiritual level which was the only true victory; that is, they were to become spiritually perfect; while the Sunnīs were defeated in the most final sense possible, in that all their

[1] On the declaration of qiyāma, see *OA*, pp. 148–58. The chief sources are Rashīd al-Dīn, Juvainī, and *Haft Bāb-i Abī Isḥāq*. The latter is to be found in *Kalām-i Pīr*, ed. W. Ivanow (Bombay, 1935), as indicated by Ivanow in an appendix.

further efforts were rendered spiritually meaningless. Thus was established the doctrine of the qiyāma, the Resurrection, as the new basis of Ismāʿīlī life.

From one point of view, Ḥasan's proclamation was the natural fulfilment of Ismaʿīlī hopes. But it raised serious difficulties, covered over for the time being by the enthusiasm of the reform and the personal popularity of Ḥasan himself. The dominant moral tone of Nizārī Ismāʿīlism had been a rigorous moral purism founded on the sharīʿa as such; the doctrine of the qiyāma made a radical reversal in this. The reversal was not merely permissive: Ḥasan seems to have insisted that the Ismāʿīlīs must all live according to the new dispensation, in inward spiritual alertness and without the law, just as previously they all had to live according to the old legalistic dispensation. Some persons are said to have emigrated rather than comply. Then the doctrine of the qiyāma itself presented difficulties: though Ismāʿīlīs might be willing to find that the new heaven and the new earth were not geophysically new but only spiritually new, yet it had been supposed that the eschatological event would still produce a drastic transformation at least of all human society. The first moment was doubtless exhilarating; perfection often does seem within reach at the moment of revolution. But the Ismāʿīlīs had yet to learn to live with the implications of the new doctrine.

Muḥammad II: formulation of the doctrine

Ḥasan did not live to solve the problems. A year and a half after the declaration of the Resurrection, he was murdered by a brother-in-law, a partisan of the sharīʿa. However, his nineteen-year-old son Muḥammad succeeded to his position, reaffirmed Ḥasan's policies, and devoted his life to elaborating the doctrine of the qiyāma in numerous treatises.

The doctrine of the qiyāma effectively replaced the doctrine of taʿlīm as central in the theory of the Nizārī Ismāʿīlīs. Each of these doctrines carried one aspect of older Ismāʿīlī teaching to its extreme: as the doctrine of taʿlīm exalted the lone authority of the imām, so that of the qiyāma exalted the lone validity of the bāṭin. The doctrine of the qiyāma was even more extreme than that of taʿlīm and presented a contrasting temper, substituting high personal consciousness for group rigorism. It was surely facilitated by the legacy of radical Ismāʿīlī ideas which had always been present among Ismāʿīlīs (sometimes transformed into folklore), and which might be expected to come to the fore in out-of-the-way areas when the discipline of city-bred scholars was relaxed. In the case of the Syrian Ismāʿīlīs, at least, we have good evidence that such radical ideas, taking popular form, did prevail. Notions of reincarnation and even of transmigration, rejected by most official Ismāʿīlī teachers, had long been associated with extreme emphasis on the bāṭin, and now reappeared. But the Ismāʿīlīs remained sufficiently sophisticated to require a scholarly defence even of popularly appealing ideas.

The first theoretical problem lay in the person of the imām. At the qiyāma, the great Resurrection, the imām must be present in person: it was precisely the role of culminating imām (called the *qā'im*) to usher in the qiyāma, for which all his followers were waiting and to which the other imāms were but as links in a chain. Indeed, if taqiyya was lifted, if the bāṭin became evident and the inner secrets were revealed, the first of those was precisely the identity of the imām and his true position. Where then was the imām? It would seem that before the end of his life Ḥasan II had hinted that he was himself not merely the caliph, representative of the imām, but the imām himself. But the imām ought to be a direct descendant of ʿAlī and in particular of Nizār, which Buzurg-Ummīd, Ḥasan's grandfather, certainly had not been. Probably Ḥasan maintained that he was imām in the bāṭin, to which the external descent in the flesh would be indifferent. Muḥammad II took the step of announcing that Ḥasan had been imām according to physical descent also; and thus Muḥammad II likewise, being his son, was imām. The story which he seems to have sponsored was that Ḥasan was not the son of Muḥammad b. Buzurg-Ummīd but of a descendant of Nizār who had in fact been hidden in Alamūt just as the outside tales had had it. Either the babies had been interchanged or the imām (not bound to the law) had actually slept with the dāʿī's wife. In any case, the Nizārid line of imāms had appeared and was acting on its own authority in Alamūt. If one believed that the qiyāma was valid to begin with, some such conclusion followed almost necessarily in the ingrown community and the particular way chosen to show how it could have happened was perhaps of secondary consequence.

The second theoretical problem lay in the qiyāma itself. The great Resurrection, even if merely regarded as a turning-point in human history and not as a geophysical epoch, was still expected to be a time of evident wonders in which the faithful would triumph and their opponents disappear. The dead were to be raised, nature was to be purified, no labour was henceforth to be needed, no sin could be committed, all was to be well. Indeed, personal spiritual perfection was sufficiently wondrous already, that the wonders and the transformations of the world at large could readily enough be rendered at such a moment into symbolic terms; thus the "world" of the Ismā'īlī religious organization came to an end with the ending of the old system of rankings and their hierarchy (which must have been inappropriate to the isolated communities anyway); at the Resurrection all the faithful were equal in the realm of religion. But the imām's appearance had led, still less than in the early Fāṭimid period, to a visible triumph over the Sunnī world. The Resurrection was the moment when Hell and Paradise were no longer distant possibilities but immediate actualities. To justify the high claims, it could be said that the Sunnīs had been resurrected in that they had been offered the opportunity—which Ismā'īlism had not offered before—not merely of a high promise and meanwhile a deeper insight, but of the immediate, perfected living of the life of the spirit unencumbered by sharī'a; and in the Sunnīs' refusal they had *ipso facto* been judged and condemned to a spiritual non-existence that was all the more absolute the more complete was the spiritual reality offered them. But the doctrine of the qiyāma introduced a further element which distinguished the Ismā'īlīs from the Sunnīs more graphically: the figure of the imām-qā'im.

Turning back to various religious traditions of the Islamic region, Muḥammad II pointed to a darkly known figure, the eternally living man Elijah, who had been swept up to heaven, and Enoch, and, in a more strictly Islamic context, Khiḍr, the Qur'ānic figure whose literary ancestry went back not only to Elijah but to Utnapishtim in the Gilgamesh epic and to Alexander's cook, who had drunk of the water of life and would live forever. Khiḍr had been adopted by the Ṣūfīs as an eternally wandering mystic, ready to bring material and spiritual sustenance to lonely dedicated Ṣūfīs in their hour of extremest need. Among some Christians Melchizedec, the priest forever whom Abraham honoured and who was a type of Christ, had likewise captured the imagination. This ever-living, recurrently reappearing figure of unlimited wisdom and irresistible authority had always been at best marginal to the Sunnī world, mysterious and inaccessible. Muḥammad II now identified with that figure the imām-qā'im, the special imām who was master of the qiyāma.

Some Ismāʿīlīs (and not only Ismāʿīlīs among the Shīʿīs) had always been inclined to exalt ʿAlī over Muḥammad, the imām over the prophet, on the ground that the inward meaning of external symbols (the meaning that ʿAlī was charged with teaching) was of higher status than the external symbols themselves (which Muḥammad had brought). Until now, however, such a doctrine was not admitted officially among the Ismāʿīlīs, perhaps lest it undermine the status of the sharīʿa. Muḥammad II now adopted it, and, by identifying ʿAlī as a figure with Melchizedec and Khiḍr-Elijah, he endowed the newly exalted imām with all the potency of their tradition. What had happened in the qiyāma, then, was much more than any mere conquest of the Sunnī world might have been, an event already foreshadowed in the time of the Fāṭimids. Into a different world, the elusive world of Khiḍr-Elijah, which the Sunnīs only glimpsed in fragments of legend or occasional momentary experiences of Ṣūfīs, the Ismāʿīlīs had been admitted in full and permanently. It was as if Dailam and Kūhistān had been wrapt, like Elijah himself, and carried out of sight of the Sunnīs, and their inhabitants were privileged to walk, as on everyday ground, the sacred soil upon which Moses removed his shoes to tread, when, in the incident of the burning bush, God spoke to him through Melchizedec, the imām-qā'im of his time.[1]

Ismāʿīlism and Ṣūfism

It is not easy to estimate what all this could mean, substantively and psychologically. For some, transcendence of ordinary life by way of symbolism was probably quite enough. At the very least, the qiyāma meant the declaration of the Ismāʿīlīs' psychological independence from the world outside, an independence in some ways quite real once the wider revolt was abandoned; and this abandonment was likewise symbolized in the qiyāma, in that it declared the Sunnī world irrelevant. For others, the qiyāma could mean a personal transformation. This was summed up in the doctrine that the perfected faithful should no longer see anything but the imām, and God in the imām.

The great boon of Paradise, according to Muslim tradition, was

[1] On the doctrine of the qiyāma under Muḥammad II, see *OA*, pp. 160–80. The chief sources are: the *Haft Bāb-i Abī Isḥāq*, just cited; the *Haft Bāb-i Bābā Sayyidnā*, in W. Ivanow, *Two Early Ismaili Treatises*, Islamic Research Association Series II (Bombay, 1933); and Nāṣir al-Dīn Ṭūsī's *Rawḍat al-taslīm*, ed. W. Ivanow: *Taṣawwurāt*, Ismaili Society Series B, vol. VII (Leiden, 1952).

that there one could see God face to face. In the Paradise of the qiyāma, the locus of divinity was the imām, now reinterpreted as the Elijah–Khiḍr–Melchizedec figure. The imām was God made visible. To see the imām was to see God—and it was in this seeing that Paradise essentially consisted, not in being in Rūdbār or in Kūhistān. But to see the imām was a matter of viewpoint. To see just the body of the imām (which might, moreover, appear to have its imperfections) was useless: one had to see him in his spiritual reality. If one saw the imām, i.e. understood and concentrated on him in his spiritual reality, then all else that one saw and did would follow from that—one would see the whole world from his viewpoint and no longer from one's own personal vantage-point at all: one would see the imām only and not oneself, as they put it. Thus one would live the totally enlightened and spiritual life which was the afterlife the Ismāʿīlīs had expected—and it would make no difference whether this was in the body or not. Accordingly, in the qiyāma the faithful were summoned not to the worship of God, which was their own imperfect activity, but to God Himself, now present in the imām, in Whom their own selves no longer mattered.

The imām, then, was to serve for the Ismāʿīlīs as a Ṣūfī *pīr* sometimes did for his disciples. They were to cultivate their own divine awareness by focusing their attention on him, seeing the divine presence hidden within him, and forgetting their separate selves. But the imām was more than a Ṣūfī pīr. Muḥammad II is reported to have written his discourses in the language of the philosophers, and certainly he made use also of the Ismāʿīlī tradition. The doctrine of the qiyāma and its discipline formed a new synthesis among traditions. The imām was not simply one experienced Ṣūfī teacher among many, who might be the object of a transference process in those disciples who chose to explore their inward selves under his guidance. Beyond that, he was felt to be a unique, single cosmic individual who summed up in his position the whole reality of existence; the perfect microcosm, for whom no lesser pīr could be substituted. In him the faithful found not only a guide to personal awareness but also the embodiment of a whole symbolic system in terms of which he could place himself in the whole cosmos.

This new sense of the cosmos into which the deepening sense of self-awareness fitted was described in Ismāʿīlī terms as a third level of being, in effect a bāṭin behind the bāṭin. This third level, that of ultimate reality, went beyond the old Ismāʿīlī interpretations of the sharīʿa as these had gone beyond the shariʿa itself. On that level all things were one in the imām. Only personal relations counted, for only persons had an inward, spiritual life; and even persons, when perfect, were merged into their idealized roles as expressions of cosmic harmony. Every imām, when seen rightly, was seen to be ʿAlī; every disciple was again Salmān, the faithful disciple of Muḥammad and adherent of ʿAlī. The accidents of space and time did not matter. On this level not only the arbitrary rules of the sharīʿa were pointless, but even the hierarchically organized discipline of the Ismāʿīlī organization in the time of taqiyya. The qiyāma was a declaration of spiritual adulthood, in which all rules and discipline were outgrown and the individual acted directly from his inmost self—which was at one with all the rest of existence in the present and revealed imām.

Even this cosmic aspect of the qiyāma doctrine contained much that was analogous to the doctrines of cosmic unity professed by the Ṣūfīs of that time and especially later. The cosmic position of the imām was very like that of the Perfect Man, who is the microcosm, i.e. the final end of creation in that God brings the world to full consciousness of Himself through that saint. But such general and abstract teachings about an invisible Perfect Man, or *quṭb* among the Ṣūfīs, could not offer a full equivalent of the sense of joint spiritual experience which the Ismāʿīlīs seem to have shared in the presence of their quite visible and present one true imām, who was at once pīr and quṭb.

On the whole, the doctrine of the qiyāma seems to have had far less impact on the Sunnī world than did Ḥasan-i Ṣabbāḥ's doctrine of taʿlīm. Until the time of Juvainī, writing after the fall of Alamūt, the Sunnī chroniclers and theologians seem scarcely to have been aware of it. To be sure, if it had any effect it would have been among the Ṣūfīs, to whose ideas the doctrine was most congenial, and who travelled widely and were commonly receptive to new ideas; and movements of thought among the Ṣūfīs were little chronicled by the standard authors unless they caused special scandal. The Sunnī Ṣūfī doctrines of cosmic unity and of the Perfect Man, in fact, were brought to full flower only by Ibn ʿArabī, who was eighteen years the junior of Muḥammad II. But such ideas were already developing in Ṣūfī circles. Ibn ʿArabī, indeed, made use of Ismāʿīlī concepts and terms, but presumably not of the doctrine of the qiyāma. Rather, it was the earlier forms of such doctrines among the Ṣūfīs which will have served as suggestions to Ḥasan II and Muḥammad II.

What is more likely is that the doctrine of the qiyāma may have influenced later Shī'ī thinking. If there is one person in Twelver Shī'ī history who answers to Ghazālī among the Sunnīs as legitimizer of philosophy and mysticism, it is Naṣīr al-Dīn Ṭūsī, the leading figure in Shī'ism at the time of its revival in the thirteenth century. He was one of the earliest within the Twelver community of a synthesis of the Ṣūfī experience developed among Sunnīs with a strongly Shī'ī attitude on the imāmate—a synthesis which was later made yet more explicit, with the imām in the role of Perfect Man, and became a primary basis for Shī'ī thought under the Ṣafavids. But Ṭūsī himself in his earlier years lived among the Ismā'īlīs and wrote works of theology for them, expounding the doctrine of the qiyāma in a slightly later form, when the imām was again technically hidden (as he was to the Twelvers). It seems likely that later Twelvers did not need the Ismā'īlī example to suggest to them the possibility of such a synthesis, but in fact that example was present in the most intimate way to one of the Twelver Shī'īs' first and greatest expounders of Ṣūfism.[1]

In any case, the qiyāma laid the foundation for the ultimate identification of Nizārī Ismā'īlism as a Ṣūfī *ṭarīqa*, which was the guise it appeared in after the fall of Alamūt. In the time of the qiyāma, the Ismā'īlīs remained consciously opposed to Ṣūfism as such, yet already they found it convenient to borrow Ṣūfī terminology. Later, when a new taqiyya was necessary after their state could no longer protect them from Sunnī wrath, the protean forms of Ṣūfism were easily available to them with almost no alteration in their own ways.

The Resurrection within history

Among the Ismā'īlīs the qiyāma meant, along with independence from the Sunnī world and its opinion, an admission of their failure in the attempt to transform that world. The attempt to rival Sunnism within that world came to an end with the revolt itself. From the viewpoint of both Sunnīs and Twelver Shī'īs, however, what mattered was not the end of the revolt as such, which might have made for easier relations, for in any case hostilities continued on both sides. For them the great

[1] Henry Corbin has studied closely the relations among Shī'ism, Ismā'īlism, and Ṣūfism. In his *Histoire de la philosophie islamique*, vol. I (Paris, 1964), see especially pp. 47–50; but all of Parts I and II are highly relevant. He discusses the doctrine of the qiyāma quite soundly and perceptively (pp. 137–51), though with almost no regard to its historical conditions and development.

fact was that the sharīʿa was abolished. In the time of Aḥmad-i ʿAṭṭāsh (494/1100) it could be debated whether the Ismāʿīlīs were Muslims, entitled to the privileges and immunities of membership in the Muslim community. At that time the Ismāʿīlīs' chief plea was that they kept the Muslim sharīʿa law and differed from other Muslims only on the question of the imāmate. But now, for those who chose to notice at all the changes within the Ismāʿīlī society, the worst suspicions of the Ismāʿīlīs' opponents were confirmed. Rejecting the sharīʿa, the Ismāʿīlīs put themselves beyond the pale of Islam by any obvious standard: variations in the sharīʿa could be tolerated, but now the Ismāʿīlīs were no longer even "people of the Qibla", who performed worship (as prescribed by the sharīʿa) in the direction of Mecca. Thus they failed the minimal test of adherence to Muḥammad's mission.

Technically, Paradise was not in history. On the level of ultimate reality, in the doctrine of the qiyāma, only the type, i.e. the role that persons played in the eternal drama with the imām, was real; not the dated and placed individual event. As the faithful was always Salmān, so he who rejected the summons was forever ʿUmar, banished from Paradise and so in reality non-existent. Yet already in the time of Ḥasan II warfare with the outsiders seems to have flared up more intensely than it had for some years—warfare waged on a lower level than that of ultimate reality, but necessary in its own way. Ibn Anaz continued his raids in Kūhistān. More significantly, the Rūdbārīs intensified their quarrel with Qazvīn after a lapse of years without much raiding; building a fortress just outside the city, we are told, they harassed it almost to the point of siege (560/1165).

In the first half of the reign of Muḥammad II, however, the Ismāʿīlīs were relatively at peace with their neighbours; or at least we hear little of warfare in either Sunnī or Ismāʿīlī chronicles. A ruler of Rūyān, at odds with the local gentry and with his superior, the ruler of Māzandarān, fled to the Ismāʿīlīs for refuge and with their help carried out some raids—in which he was worsted. But for the most part little of headline note happened among the Iranian Ismāʿīlīs. In Syria it was the time of the Muslim struggle to oust the Crusaders, of Nūr al-Dīn and Saladin. There the Ismāʿīlīs were under the leadership of Rāshid al-Dīn Sinān, a companion of Ḥasan II who seems to have been sent there to introduce the doctrine of the qiyāma. He was occupied in consolidating the independence of the Ismāʿīlī fortresses, which straddled the line between Muslims and Franks, and also in establishing their relations with their several neighbours. He seems to have interpreted the qiyāma in his own way, perhaps with relatively little reference to Muḥammad II, and to have managed a quite personal foreign policy in his very limited territory. There was a rumour that Alamūt would have liked to be rid of him. Nonetheless, at his death there was no question of the succession: Alamūt appointed the chief in Syria as elsewhere.

In the last sixteen years or so of Muḥammad II's reign—after Sinān's death (588/1193), that is—we hear increasingly of petty warfare in which the Ismāʿīlīs were often on the defensive. The Kūhistānīs had trouble with the rulers of Sīstān to the south and then with the rulers of Ghūr (the great Ghūrid dynasty that overwhelmed the Ghaznavids), who delighted in destroying any Ismāʿīlīs whom they might chance to discover in their path. The Ismāʿīlīs were reduced to making humble terms with the Ghūrid Ghiyāth al-Dīn, when he was setting about conquering Khurāsān; and when his brother began attacking them all over again, they had to beg Ghiyāth al-Dīn to intervene with him in their favour. Rūdbār had trouble again with Māzandarān, supporting a rebel ruler of Rūyān—evidently with such success that the Ismāʿīlīs were granted some villages as a reward. Then the Khwārazmians established themselves as the partisans of Qazvīn against the Ismāʿīlīs, taking the place of the Saljuqs; but their activities were relatively minor and at least partly defensive. Though the Ismāʿīlīs of Rūdbār could still undertake daring ventures, one gets the impression that many Ismāʿīlīs had grown used to peace and did not care for interruptions of their commercial activity. Occasionally assassination was still used, but in one case, the assassination of the Ghūrid Shihāb al-Dīn, the Ismāʿīlīs laid claim to an act which may well not have been their own—and did so as a pretext for winning favour with the rising Khwārazmian power, enemy of the Ghūrids. Even the vigour of Rūdbār could be turned to winning tributary villages in alliance with a Sunnī ruler. Politically the Ismāʿīlī situation carried little glamour.[1]

IV. ACCOMMODATION

The great revolt, after it was contained, was followed by a period in which the Ismāʿīlīs, even while retaining the doctrines and viewpoints of the revolt itself, in fact were defending a limited territorial state

[1] On Ḥasan II's reign, see *OA*, pp. 157–9; on Muḥammad II's reign, pp. 182–4, 210–14; on Sinān, pp. 185–209.

against its neighbours. Such ideals were at odds with such a practice. The high sense of mission the Ismāʿīlīs retained had led finally to the proclamation of the spiritual Resurrection and to the whole inward-turning discipline of the qiyāma, in which they tried to raise their own little society to the highest conceivable level of human realization and relegated the rest of the world to insignificance. But again the bold effort was checked, though again not fully defeated. The outer world refused to remain insignificant; but what was more important, for an effort aimed at inner perfection rather than outer empire, the effort faltered internally. It failed in the person of the imām himself; but not only in him.

In the fourth and last phase of the Ismāʿīlī state, the Ismāʿīlīs retained the ideal of perfection but restricted it to a limited spiritual sphere and in fact were working out an accommodation, both inward and external, with its human and historical limitations. The rising generation wanted peace and normalcy. After some hesitation they did not wholly reject (as did their imām for himself) the ideal of the qiyāma; but they adapted it to a more limited estimate of the human condition. Then they supplemented its crippled inward grandeur with revived political ambition: ambition both within the Sunnī world and even beyond it, not hesitating to dream of material world domination. Thus the sense of mission persisted, if anything growing more comprehensive as the Ismāʿīlī state itself grew weaker.

Ḥasan III: recognition of Sunnism

The shift of phase was more unmistakably marked at the end of the time of the qiyāma than it had been at the end of the active revolt. That the death of Muḥammad Tapar and the abandonment of Shīrgīr's siege of Alamūt would be the end of generalized military involvement became evident only in the years that followed. The end of the effort for perfection in the qiyāma was announced as abruptly as had been the qiyāma itself.

Muḥammad II's son Ḥasan did not like the Ismāʿīlī isolation and rejected the doctrine of the qiyāma. Relations between father and son were strained during Muḥammad's last years, and it is said they each went in mortal fear of the other; but there is no reason to suppose, as some later claimed, that Muḥammad was murdered when he died at a ripe age (607/1210). In any case, Ḥasan III's accession was well prepared. From an Ismā'īlī point of view he was undeniably the imām: he had received the irrevocable designation by the preceding imām and whatever he ordered was to be received in faith. At the same time, Ḥasan had written to a number of Sunnī rulers assuring them that he abjured Ismā'īlism and intended to lead his flock into the fold of Sunnī Islam. Accordingly, his accession was accepted by the Ismā'īlīs and acclaimed by the Sunnīs too. Many Sunnī rulers were glad to receive by conversion the dread enemy whom they had never been able to overcome by conquest. Ḥasan's rights to the territory which the Ismā'īlīs happened to hold were acknowledged, and he was accepted as a Sunnī amīr among other amīrs.

This did not happen without effort, however. Ḥasan's mother, said to have been a Sunnī from the first, went on pilgrimage to Mecca under the patronage of the Caliph al-Nāṣir and received an honoured place in the Baghdad caravan. At Mecca the pilgrims from Syria challenged the honour paid to her, and so to the ex-Ismā'īlīs, and a fracas ensued. But Ḥasan did his best to convince everyone that the community was really reformed and had readopted the shari'a—this time, the Sunnī shari'a, not the Shī'ī shari'a which Ḥasan's grandfather had done away with. He had every village build a proper mosque and also a bath, to prove its status as a full-fledged centre of normal Muslim life; we know that this was done at least in some places in Syria. He imported Sunnī scholars (of the Shāfi'ī school) and insisted that all his people obey them. The Qazvīnīs naturally remained sceptical, recalling the Ismā'īlī propensity to taqiyya, or dissimulation of their true religious position; he allowed their religion scholars to come up into Alamūt and burn whatever they disliked of the books in the famous library—a procedure which, like many men of religion, they found much to their taste and which seems to have won them over. Thus from chief of an execrated and increasingly marginal sect, Ḥasan made himself into a celebrated hero, whose actions reverberated throughout the Islamic lands. What remained unchanged was that his repute and the role he could play still waxed far out of proportion to the material resources of his little state.

All the Ismā'īlī territories seem to have obeyed Ḥasan's orders without any question. Whether he laid claim to the dignity publicly or not, he was still the imām: indeed, he never renounced the power which was based on that position, even though he denounced the position that had brought him the power. Ḥasan himself was almost certainly sincere in his adoption of Sunnism. His people, however, almost certainly regarded his action as a reimposition of taqiyya; and, given the extensive meaning that had been assigned to taqiyya by implication when its lifting was decreed at the qiyāma, this could imply any sort of accommodation with the world, even to the concealment, doctrinally, of the person of the imām. In fact, the adoption of the Sunnī sharī'a brought immediate tactical advantages in both Kūhistān and Syria, though Rūdbār had been less threatened and now benefited less politically. In Kūhistān, the Ghūrid attacks were effectively ended. In Syria the Ismā'īlīs had just got into serious trouble with the Franks and now received opportune assistance from Aleppo. The Ismā'īlīs found occasion to reciprocate the Sunnī friendliness. Toward the end of Ḥasan's reign the Mongol terror swept over much of the Islamic lands, including Khurāsān. Many refugees, and in particular Sunnī scholars, found asylum in the Ismā'īlī towns of Kūhistān (these were relatively less attractive, or less accessible, to the Mongols), and they were given lavish hospitality by the head of the Ismā'īlīs there, himself a scholar.

Ḥasan III's reform was accepted sufficiently by his own people to allow him not only to impose it without recorded disruption in all their territories, but even to leave Rūdbār, accompanied by an Ismā'īlī army, for a couple of years of foreign adventure without losing control at home. When Ḥasan first acceded to power, he had the khuṭba recited in the name of the Khwārazm-Shāh, the most potent monarch in Iran at the time and successor to the Saljuqs. However, fairly soon he shifted to the alliance of the Caliph al-Nāṣir, the great opponent of the Khwārazmians. The caliph was in a position to show Ḥasan much honour—as in the pilgrimage of his mother; then Ḥasan wanted to marry into the noble Sunnī houses of Gīlān, and the caliph's letters persuaded those nobles to allow their daughters to go to Alamūt. Perhaps even more important, the shift brought with it an alignment with Öz-Beg of Āzarbāījān, an important member of the caliph's alliance. Ḥasan seems to have struck up a real friendship with that other ruler; when they decided to make a joint campaign, Ḥasan went to his court for a long stay to make preparations.

The campaign was a major one. 'Irāq-i 'Ajam was a primary point of contention between the Khwārazm-Shāh and the caliphal alliance. The Āzarbāījānī forces had succeeded in gaining control of the greater part of it, but then Mengli, Öz-Beg's lieutenant there, made himself independent and threatened seriously to weaken the alliance. The caliph persuaded troops to come from as far away as Syria to help Öz-Beg, but Ḥasan's help seems to have been reckoned of considerable importance. Öz-Beg subsidized Ḥasan substantially, and after the victory (which was not a very brilliant one, though immediately effective enough), Ḥasan was given Abhar and Zanjān. Thus the Ismāʿīlī state was expanding more decisively than in its whole history since the revolt—not through either settlement or conversion, but simply by annexing tribute-paying dependent territory. Ḥasan seems to have lost that territory later, presumably to the Khwārazmians.

After the campaign, Ḥasan retired to Rūdbār and stayed there. When Öz-Beg's next lieutenant in ʿIrāq-i ʿAjam also broke with him and went over to the Khwārazm-Shāh, there was no great campaign; rather, at the caliph's bidding, Ḥasan sent Ismāʿīlī fidāʾīs, who assassinated him. Ḥasan seems not to have been very venturesome by nature, despite his one fling, and he looked well to the constellation of forces around him: he was the first Iranian ruler to submit to the Mongols after they crossed the Oxus. After an otherwise undistinguished reign of eleven years, he died of dysentery while still a fairly young man (618/1221). His Sunnī wives were (most implausibly) accused by his vizier of having poisoned him, and they were done away with; but in principle his Sunnī policies were maintained under the nominal headship of his little son Muḥammad III.[1]

Adjustment of the doctrine

Under Muḥammad III (618/1221–653/1255) the ṣalāt worship prescribed by the sharīʿa was carried on, at least in the main centres, till the end; the community remained officially Sunnī. But gradually the sharīʿa came to be little enforced, and the ideas and practices associated with the qiyāma revived. In any case, the community regarded itself as specifically Ismāʿīlī. Muḥammad III himself seems to have been brought up as an Ismāʿīlī imām. He clearly accepted that role and probably also felt himself to be dispensed from the sharīʿa law and perhaps from many other human limitations. However, he was no scholar and probably contributed little personally

[1] On Ḥasan III, see *OA*, pp. 215–22. There has been some question of Ḥasan's sincerity and as to whether, if converted, he was in fact Sunnī or Twelver Shīʿī; on this cf. *ibid.* pp. 222–5.

to Ismā'īlī thinking; indeed, he seems to have looked to a Ṣūfī pīr in Qazvīn for his personal spiritual guidance, or at least for some sort of blessing; he sent gifts to the pīr as an admirer. If it was not the Sunnī teachers of the sharī'a, neither was it the imām in person who guided the community spiritually. Rather, it was others, thrown up by the community itself.

Ḥasan III and his Sunnism were not repudiated: they were explained. In the course of this explanation the doctrine of the qiyāma was reinterpreted to allow for ordinary human and historical processes without repudiating the work of Ḥasan II either. In the process "popular" and folkloric ideas gained a still larger place over against the older learned tradition. The result was a doctrinal system in which the Ismā'īlīs were prepared to maintain their spiritual independence under almost any circumstances. Their potential affinity to a Ṣūfī ṭarīqa was increased, and the way was further prepared—as it turned out—for the community to survive intact even though the Ismā'īlī state itself fell.

It was explained that the qiyāma, the resurrection, was not simply a final event but a condition of life which could, in principle, be withheld or granted by the imām-qā'im to mankind, or to the élite among mankind, at any time. The tacit identification between sharī'a law and taqiyya, implied in the teaching of Ḥasan II, was confirmed, and with it the identification of *ḥaqīqa* (spiritual reality) with qiyāma. Human life, then, alternated between times when reality was manifest and spiritual perfection could be sought directly; and times when reality was veiled and, instead of perfection, even the élite, for the most part, were directed to an outer symbolic acting-out of the tokens of reality, as laid down in the sharī'a. Ḥasan II had introduced a brief period when reality was manifest; Ḥasan III had closed that period again.

This could be because any imām was potentially imām-qā'im, immediate representative of God on earth, and hence could decree whether there should be a time of qiyāma or not. It was still expected, as earlier among Ismā'īlīs, that full qiyama would come only at the end of the sixth millennial period after Adam: that is, at the end of the millennial period introduced by the sixth great prophet, Muḥammad, which would also be the end of the present cycle (roughly seven thousand years) of history. But within the millennial period of Muḥammad, and in special honour of his greatness, there could be anticipatory periods of qiyāma, each one a foretaste of the final period of qiyāma: such was the qiyāma of Ḥasan II. Correspondingly, the rest of the time, when taqiyya and the sharī'a prevailed, was a time of *satr*, or "concealment".

The term *satr* had originally referred to those periods when the whereabouts of the imām was unknown to the world at large, or even, at times, to the faithful, as had been the case among Ismā'īlīs before the rise of the Fāṭimids and again after the death of Nizār. But now it came to mean not merely concealment of the person of the imām but any concealment of his ultimate reality, of his true religious role as the point where God became visible. In particular, Ḥasan III was known in his outward person as a wordly ruler, but he chose not to be recognized in his inner reality as imām; hence, despite his physical availability, his reign was a time of satr. Moreover, it was pointed out retrospectively that even the period when the imāms ruled in splendour in Egypt and the Ismā'īlī bāṭin was officially taught in Cairo had been a time of satr. In comparison with the qiyāma, all lesser degrees of the imām's manifestation were equally concealment; hence the concealment ordered by Ḥasan III differed only in degree from what had happened often before. If reality was to be hidden, it might as well be by imposition of the Sunnī sharī'a as by that of the Shī'ī; and the imām might as well deny his own special relation to Muḥammad along with his status as visible locus of the divine.

Satr, the period of concealment, carrying with it sharī'a and taqiyya, was the more normal lot of mankind because of human weakness.[1] Even within the period of satr, spiritual reality was not entirely suppressed and could be known on a certain level. A small élite within the community of the faithful could even then look on the reality of the imām and so live the life of spiritual perfection. But, in theory the members of this élite, like the imām himself, were born to their status. In the time of Ḥasan III and perhaps even, in principle, in that of Muḥammad III, this élite may have been reduced to a single figure, the ḥujja, the "proof" of the imām—a position that had been filled by Ḥasan-i Ṣabbāḥ and now again rose to prominence, though we cannot identify the actual individuals who filled it in this last period of the Ismā'īlī state. It sufficed for most persons to remain on the second level, the level of the bāṭin, understanding what lay behind the sharī'a and seeing the secret status of the imām, without going beyond that to the full personal realization in which they beheld nothing but the imām's ultimate reality.

[1] On the doctrines of the satr, see *OA*, pp. 225–37.

For most Ismā'īlīs, what was primarily retained from the qiyāma times was not so much the hope for spiritual perfection as the imaginative richness which found its fullest embodiment in the Khiḍr–Elijah–Melchizedec imām-qā'im figure. If the élite still existed, even in the person of a single man, then at least such secrets could still be expounded, even though they were not fully lived out by most of the faithful; their exposition was what most mattered. Under Muḥammad III, however, a way was left open for the practice of qiyāma perfection by the more spiritually minded even of ordinary persons. The faithful were divided into "strong" and "weak", and the "strong" could hope to achieve what seems to have amounted to a status of secondary or derived élite alongside the few élite who were born to their roles. Thus those who were devoted not merely to the imaginative splendour of the qiyāma but also to its moral and spiritual practice could devote themselves to this, freely transcending the sharī'a as did the imām and his ḥujja themselves.

With such a distinction, the Ismā'īlīs moved even closer to the practice of a Ṣūfī ṭarīqa, which allowed both for close disciples dedicated wholly to the pīr, and for a wider circle of adepts who looked to the pīr's wise teachings and especially to his blessing but did not attempt to enter into the pīr's spiritual life themselves. The qiyāma was losing even such social dimensions as it had still had under Muḥammad II, when it was the foundation for the life of the whole state, and was becoming, like the Ṣūfī mystical life, a special vocation for an individually selected few. Even so, the Ismā'īlī imām retained his unique cosmic position, to which a flesh-and-blood Ṣūfī pīr, himself no quṭb or Perfect Man, could not pretend.

The only religious writings which we can certainly date to the time of Muḥammad III are those ascribed to Naṣīr al-Dīn Ṭūsī, who figures as the most important Ismā'īlī writer of the whole period of the satr following Ḥasan III. Legal work of his—presumably Shī'ī rather than Shāfi'ī—expounded the sharī'a for later Iranian Ismā'īlīs; his theological works expounded the spiritual situation under conditions of satr. In them he answered with sophistication the numerous problems of detailed adjustment which arose when the doctrines of the satr and of the qiyāma, and also of Fāṭimid Ismā'īlism were mutually confronted; and he dealt with the more strictly philosophical problems that arose in the new doctrine taken for itself. (He was also very careful to give as little leeway as possible to those who might wish to fancy themselves among the "strong"—who must have been rather too numerous in fact.) We have from him a work of technical precision on Ismāʿīlī theology, and a briefer work clearly designed for the ordinary Ismāʿīlī, yet written with a wonderfully succinct clarity. Moreover his famous work on ethics was originally dedicated to an Ismāʿīlī chief in Kūhistān and furnished with an Ismāʿīlī preface.[1]

Ṭūsī may not have been, even then, an Ismāʿīlī; later he was certainly a Twelver. But it was not entirely by chance that the Ismāʿīlīs were able to make use of the services of so able a writer. From the time of Ḥasan III, at least, though especially after the Mongol holocaust, they attracted to their libraries and to their learned patronage a large number of scholars like him, if not quite so eminent, from the outer world. Such scholars were free to maintain their prior religious convictions, and though Ṭūsī and some of the other non-Ismāʿīlī scholars who were in Rūdbār at the time of the Mongol invasion claimed that they were being kept there by force, it seems unlikely that such force long antedated the Mongol invasion itself, when special measures must have been unavoidable. At any rate, they were on terms of mutual confidence with the Ismāʿīlī leadership. The Ismāʿīlīs of the satr had worked out a religious system which allowed the most extreme spiritual daring of their heritage to coexist with a folkloric Shīʿī imaginativeness and even with the religious scholarship of the wider Muslim world. In such an atmosphere, their out-of-the-way fortresses were becoming centres of an intellectual life no longer limited to their own particular tradition; perhaps more important, the Nizārī Ismāʿīlī tradition itself was ceasing to be necessarily dependent upon the Ismāʿīlī state as such.

Persisting ambitions

As in religion, so in political action the Ismāʿīlīs developed a flexible policy, one which allowed for co-operation with the Sunnī powers without abandonment of Ismāʿīlī solidarity or even of Ismāʿīlī ambitions. In this sphere also Muḥammad III was not the central figure, though he played his role. In his first years he was a minor, having become imām at the age of nine, and the chiefs of the community acted with little reference to him—and without leaving much trace of quarreling among themselves. When he grew up he seems to have been moody and capable of violent fits of anger; he could be drunk for

[1] On Ṭūsī's Ismāʿīlī work, see *OA*, pp. 239–43.

days at a time. The chroniclers have accused him of being mentally deranged, and say that his courtiers were afraid to bring unpleasant news to him; but in fact he seems to have kept pretty well in touch with events and was probably less brutal and unpredictable than many another tyrant born to absolute power. Nevertheless, though he maintained his authority effectively enough, most of the initiative in practical decisions probably came from others.[1]

Muḥammad III's reign began (618/1221) just after the first wave of the Mongol conquest had destroyed the Khwārazmian power. The scholarly refugees came to the Ismā'īlī towns at this time, not simply because they were out of the way and so ignored by the Mongols, but because at that point the Ismā'īlī state was proving stronger than most. The prudently early submission to the Mongols, which gave it an initial immunity, did not preclude an independent policy. In Kūhistān the Ismā'īlīs maintained an island of prosperity and stability from which all benefited when in so many other places even what the Mongols had spared was being disrupted by the lesser warrings they left in their wake. The scholarly gentleman Shihāb al-Dīn, a ruler whom even bigoted Sunnīs spoke highly of, aroused complaints that his policy of wholesale hospitality was lavishing too freely the resources of the community upon non-Ismā'īlī strangers, and he was eventually replaced. But Shams al-Dīn, the replacement, sent from Alamūt, also compelled respect among the Sunnīs. After an attempt on his life by a Sunnī foreigner, he was able to prevent a spontaneous lynching of all the resident Sunnīs, taking soldierly command of a mob situation and drastically enforcing order. The Kūhistānīs were able to take a forward policy in Sīstān, but by and large they limited their objectives to defence. Sunnīs whose style of life had been interrupted by the Mongols could go to Kūhistān to renew their wardrobes, and the main burden of negotiations between the Ismā'īlīs and their neighbours seems to have been the reopening of trade.

In Rūdbār the Ismā'īlī policy was more aggressive, though in one sense it likewise was on the side of order, being favourable to the caliph and opposed to Khwārazmian disruption. In the first six years after the fall of the Khwārazmian empire, the Ismā'īlīs annexed a number of places, including Dāmghān near Gird-Kūh. At some point, perhaps earlier but most probably in this period, they seized other places in Qūmis, presumably in the Zagros mountains, and in the Ṭārum

[1] On the personality of Muḥammad III, see *OA*, pp. 256–8.

mountains of western Dailam where once they had had little foothold. The arrival of the Khwārazmian adventurer Jalāl al-Dīn put an end to this expansion. The old Ismā'īlī quarrel with the Khwārazmians was renewed with him. A Khwārazmian chief who had raided Ismā'īlī Kūhistān was assassinated, and Jalāl al-Dīn's vizier was secretly surrounded by Ismā'īlīs in his service, ready to cut him down at a word from the imām (these latter were burned alive when their presence was revealed—and Alamūt was duly compensated financially for their deaths). Before long the Ismā'īlīs agreed to pay Jalāl al-Din tribute for Dāmghān; but they continued to co-operate with both the caliph and the Mongols in opposition to him. The heirs to power in both Āzarbāijān and 'Irāq-i 'Ajam whom he had dispossessed took refuge in Rūdbār and received Ismā'īlī help.

After the death of Jalāl al-Dīn in 628/1231, the Ismā'īlī began to shift their hostilities once more: from the Saljuqs they had shifted their enmity to the Khwārazmians, who were the Saljuqs' most powerful successors; from the Khwārazmians they shifted it now to the Mongols. The Mongols took Dāmghān from them, the only major (and Sunnī) city that they then had a garrison in. The breach with the Mongols became decisive only after more than a decade, when the Mongols refused to recognize the Ismā'īlī envoys in Mongolia. The breach may have been exacerbated by the attitude of Muḥammad III, who eventually, at least, proved much more insistent than most Ismā'īlī leaders in resisting the Mongols. But it was made inevitable by an outlook which was popular with the Ismā'īlīs quite independently of the imām's attitude. The Ismā'īlīs continued, as before, to be involved in neighbouring quarrels: again supporting a chief of Rūyān against his overlord in Māzandarān, for instance. But in the open political situation that the first Mongol operations had left behind, they were envisaging a field of action wider than had been possible since the time of Ḥasan-i Ṣabbāḥ.

Soon after the death of Ḥasan III, Ismā'īlī agitators were already at work in Ray, evidently looking toward winning a new popular following and perhaps arousing a new general revolt. Syrian Ismā'īlīs, on a rumour of Jalāl al-Dīn's death, boasted to the ruler of Anatolia that the Ismā'īlīs of Rūdbār would now take over all 'Irāq-i 'Ajam, whose previous Khwārazmian ruler was a refugee among them. Prophecies of how the imām was going to conquer the world had long appeared in Ismā'īlī works, but we find an unusually detailed prophecy in one of

Ṭūsī's works of this period. After occupying Dailam, the imām would conquer the several other districts south of the Caspian—Māzandarān, Gīlān, and Mūghān—and would then carry the holy war to India, China, and Europe—that is, to all the main civilized regions, beyond the Islamic lands in the eastern hemisphere. At this juncture, all this need not have seemed too fantastic. The nearest we know of Ismā'īlīs getting to China is by way of embassies in Mongolia. But Indian tradition places the first Nizārī Ismā'īlī missionary activity, which produced the Khoja sect there, at just this time. And the Ismā'īlīs are reported to have sent envoys in 1238 to the courts of France and England in Western Europe to try to arrange for joint action by Christians and Muslims against the Mongols: a project which would presuppose the Ismā'īlīs still having some common understanding with the caliph, even that late in Muḥammad III's reign. Popular fantasy—presumably not discouraged by the Ismā'īlīs—represented many of the rulers of the earth as sending regular ransom payments to the Ismā'īlīs, at least to those in Syria, to avoid being assassinated; kings were named as distant as the Yemen and Germany and Spain. But pretensions to any sort of world domination could only conflict irreconcilably with the overriding ambitions of the Mongols, who regarded themselves as the only masters of the world.[1]

The collapse

The Ismā'īlīs were playing a larger role in the outer world after the first Mongol conquests than they had played since the original revolt, and their political structure, like their intellectual life, seems to have been vigorous and sound. Nevertheless, they had not ceased to be a marginal power in territory and manpower. Though the Būyid family had once dominated all western Iran on the basis of the loyalty of Dailam and of its peasant soldiery, the times called for more than the stop-gap regime which the Būyids had been able to supply. To be successful, the Ismā'īlīs would have to depend on the Shī'īs of the Islamic lands; but the Shī'a was still at a low ebb then, and most Shī'īs had rejected the Ismā'īlī imāms anyway; nor was Alamūt in a position to come to an arrangement with Twelver Shī'ism such as Shāh Ismā'īl could later make to found the Ṣafavid state on. In any case, many of the Ismā'īlīs were more concerned to avoid hindrances to

[1] On politics under Muḥammad III, see *OA*, pp. 244–8, 250–6.

commerce than to conquer the world. The Mongols, on the contrary, were fully serious about their intention to rule everywhere and to suppress every possible rival.

With time, the Mongols consolidated their position in Iran, and the Ismāʿīlīs—who, apart from the caliph himself, were almost alone in remaining hostile—became isolated. The welcome accorded Ḥasan III as a convert had long since been dissipated, and most Sunnīs were again eager to see the old enemies of orthodoxy suppressed. At last Möngke, urged on by Muslims at his court, decided in 650/1252 to send a major expedition against the two powers that still held out in the central Muslim lands: the Ismāʿīlīs and the ʿAbbāsid caliphate. Hülegü took his time in making the long trip from Mongolia with the main Mongol force, but his advance armies joined with the Mongol garrisons already in Iran to attack as many Ismāʿīlī fortresses as possible. In Dailam they did little more than raid. They failed to take Gird-Kūh; it seemed impregnable until disease decimated the garrison, and in that emergency men from Rūdbār were successfully thrown in to bring the garrison up to strength: on which the Mongols gave up. They managed to take Tūn and some other places in Kūhistān, on which they then concentrated; but later the Ismāʿīlīs regained what had been lost even there. When Hülegü finally arrived, however, the Mongols more successfully overran a great part of Kūhistān, destroying Tūn and deporting its artisans according to their custom. Then Hülegü moved toward Rūdbār.

This situation seems to have aggravated a tension between Muḥammad III and his chief officers, who wanted to come to an agreement with the Mongols. It was said, perhaps for political reasons later, that after the Mongol armies approached, Muḥammad's mental aberration became more marked, so that the leading Ismāʿīlīs feared for their lives. Muḥammad's son and designated successor as imām, Kh̲ur-Sh̲āh, had long been on bad terms with his father (it is said the Ismāʿīlīs, holding to their principles, would not let Muḥammad designate any other son, though he wished to). Now Kh̲ur-Sh̲āh likewise began to be frightened. He came to an agreement with the Ismāʿīlī chief men that Muḥammad was to be set aside without suffering any harm to his person, and Kh̲ur-Sh̲āh, as effective regent, was then to negotiate with the Mongols. But before the plan could be put into operation, Kh̲ur-Sh̲āh fell ill and was confined to his bed. At this point (653/1255), a favourite of Muḥammad's, whom Muḥammad had injured, murdered him.

Kh̲ur-Sh̲āh and his advisers set about a change of policy with due caution. First they completed a campaign in western Dailam, where the Ismā'īlīs seized a fortress they had been besieging. Then Khur-Shāh sent letters to the neighbouring rulers announcing his father's death and his own accession. At the same time he ordered all the Ismā'īlīs to follow the sharī'a more closely than they had generally been doing, clearly hoping to conciliate the Sunnī powers again. Then he sent to the Mongols, offering his submission.

Unfortunately, the Mongols were not ready to be satisfied with anything less than total surrender. They required Khur-Shāh's personal attendance on Hülegü and the demolition of the Ismā'īlī fortresses, including Alamūt. Khur-Shāh asked for a delay of a year in his own appearance and for exemption of Alamūt and Lanbasar from the demolition order. Meanwhile the chiefs in Gird-Kūh and in Kūhistān submitted personally, but the fortress nonetheless held out. Khur-Shāh was finally permitted to send his son in his place, but the seven-year-old lad was sent back as being too young. By this time, Hülegü himself was near Ray and speeding his pace as he moved nearer Rūdbār; he demanded that Khur-Shāh demolish immediately at least Maimūn-Diz, the fortress where he was staying, and then come himself to Rūdbār. Khur-Shāh still lingered, and suddenly found himself besieged in Maimūn-Diz by the full Mongol force.

There is some evidence that, given the spirit of an earlier time, the key Ismā'īlī fortress might have been held at least long enough to persuade Hülegü that some accommodation, leaving the Ismā'īlī power humbled but still essentially intact, would be expeditious. The Mongols themselves were doubtful whether they should press the siege of Maimūn-Diz at that time; subsequently, when they found how massively constructed and well-provisioned were such fortresses as Alamūt, they congratulated themselves on their good fortune in persuading their master to surrender them. Muḥammad III may have been correct in his calculation that the Ismā'īlīs could resist the Mongols as well as they had the Saljuqs or the Khwārazmians. Indeed, the Ismā'īlī spirit was not wholly gone. No traitors are recorded, and at least Gird-Kūh, which later elected to resist despite Khur-Shāh's final surrender, held out alone for a long time. But Khur-Shāh seems to have listened to the foreign scholars at the court, such as Naṣīr al-Dīn Ṭūsī, who were eager to see the Ismā'īlī state at an end, and to be free to taste of the yet larger munificence of the Mongols (which they did); nor did his Ismā'īlī advisers strongly counteract that influence, though the lesser fidā'īs threatened to kill him if he tried to surrender. Before long, Khur-Shāh came down to Hülegü's camp, and the greater number of the Ismāʿīlīs followed his lead (654/1256). A devoted band which yet attacked the Mongols as they entered Maimūn-Diz was exterminated, and with some trouble most of the fortresses were persuaded by Khur-Shāh, now a puppet of the Mongols, to surrender. The Mongols, who could not expect to hold them themselves in a hostile Dailam, undertook the major labour of dismantling them stone by stone.

Gird-Kūh and Lanbasar still held out for a time, but isolated they could no longer hope for such succour as had come earlier to Gird-Kūh from Rūdbār; after some years they too had to surrender.[1] Meanwhile, the Sunnī Muslims persuaded the Mongols to destroy the whole Ismāʿīlī people so far as they could. The library of Alamūt was burned as a matter of course (though Juvainī, a Sunnī scholar, was first allowed to take out copies of the Qur'ān and other "safe" items). Rather less expected was a general massacre of all the Ismāʿīlīs who, exiled from their fortresses, were relatively accessible to the Mongol sword. The men of Kūhistān were summoned to great gatherings—presumably on the pretext of consultation—and slaughtered. The slave markets of Khurāsān were glutted with Ismāʿīlī women and children, denied the privileges of Muslims. Khur-Shāh was sent to Mongolia but was rejected by Möngke and killed on the way back;[2] however, the remnant of the Ismāʿīlīs claimed to have saved and hidden away his son to father a continuing line of imāms.[3]

In the next decades there were attempts in both Rūdbār and Kūhistān to restore the Ismāʿīlī state, but without success. The Syrian Ismāʿīlīs, situated at the farthest limit of the Mongol tide, barely managed to survive it, only to become dependent on the Mamlūk state, whose ruler they were bound to furnish with assassins on demand. In Iran, the surviving Ismāʿīlīs at last took refuge in obscurity, cloaked by the forms of a Ṣūfī ṭarīqa whose pīr was the imām.

[1] Gird-Kūh did not in fact surrender until 29 Rabīʿ II 669/15 December 1270. See Rashīd al-Dīn, ed. Alizade, p. 140, also above, p. 360.

[2] Apparently in the Khangai mountains. See Juvainī, tr. Boyle, p. 724 n. 8, also above, p. 345.

[3] On the Mongol operations, see *OA*, pp. 258–71. The basic references are Juvainī and Rashīd al-Dīn; each of these must be consulted at two points: when he describes the expedition of Hülegü, and then also when he describes the history of the Ismāʿīlīs, under the reign of Khur-Shāh.

CHAPTER 6

THE SOCIO-ECONOMIC CONDITION OF IRAN UNDER THE ĪL-KHĀNS

We can distinguish the following periods in the socio-economic history of Iran during the Mongol dominion.

The first period—from the twenties to the nineties of the thirteenth century—is marked by the colossal economic decline of Iran, caused both by the devastation wrought during the Mongol conquest, and still more by the administrative practices, in particular the taxation policy, of the first conquerors (the viceroys of the Great Khan, and then from 1256 the Īl-Khāns). Typical phenomena of the time are a reduction in population and cultivated land, the decline of agriculture, the migration of fresh multitudes of Mongol and Turkish nomads, and the expansion of migrational cattle-breeding, a decline in urban life, the growth of tendencies of natural economy, an increase in state taxes and feudal rent, the attachment of peasants to the soil, and the growth of a peasant insurrectionary movement.

The second period—from the nineties of the thirteenth century to the middle thirties of the fourteenth century (to the death of Īl-Khān Abū Sa'īd in November 1335) is characterized by something of an economic upsurge, especially in agriculture, as a result of the reforms of Ghazan. During this and the following periods conditional private ownership of land and large-scale unconditional landownership expanded at the expense of state and small-scale peasant landowning. The economy of the country did not however attain its pre-1220 level.

The third period extends from the mid-thirties to the eighties of the fourteenth century (to the beginning of Timur's conquest). This period is marked by feudal dismemberment, the struggle for power of feudal groups, and the political disintegration of the Īl-Khānid state as a result. This disintegration began in 1336 and was completed in 1353 on the occasion of the killing of the last Īl-Khān, Ṭogha-Temür, and the destruction of his headquarters—*ordu*—in Gurgān by rebel Sarbadārs. The restoration of pre-Ghazan methods of peasant exploitation provoked violent rebellions among the peasantry (the Sarbadārs of Khurāsān in 1337–81, analogous movements in Māzandarān and Gīlān from the fifties to the seventies of the fourteenth century, and others), which were supported by minor Iranian landowners as well as urban artisans.

THE CONSEQUENCES OF THE MONGOL INVASION

In the Middle Ages invasions by conquering nomads of cultivated settled areas were normally devastative. The Saljuq conquest of Iran in particular was accompanied by pillage and destruction.[1] The destructive nature of the invasion of Khurāsān by the Oghuz of Balkh in the fifties of the twelfth century is notorious.[2] But the Mongol conquest brought to Iran as it did to other lands destruction and decline on an incomparably greater scale. This was because the conquests of Chingiz-Khān, uniting under his rule most of the Mongol, Turkish, and other nomads of Central Asia, were accompanied not by spontaneous cruelty, but by the systematic extermination of the civilian population in a series of towns (Balkh, Marv, Nīshāpūr, Herāt, Ṭūs, Ray, Qazvīn, Hamadān, Marāgheh, Ardabīl, etc.) and the laying waste of whole regions. This mass-killing was a complete system, put into practice on initiative from above, and had as its goal the planned destruction of those elements of the population that were capable of resistance, the intimidation of the remainder, and sometimes the providing of pasture for the nomads.

Ibn al-Athīr spoke of the Mongol invasion as of an enormous universal catastrophe.[3] Even the pro-Mongol historian Juvainī, speaking of the massacres perpetrated by the generals of Chingiz-Khān, concludes with this assertion: "... where there had been a hundred thousand people there remained ... not a hundred souls alive."[4] More than a century after the invasion, in 740–1339/40, the historian and geographer Ḥamd Allāh Qazvīnī refers to the "ruin (in the present day) as a result of the irruption of the Mongols and the general massacre of the people which took place in their days" and adds: "Further there can be no doubt that even if for a thousand years to come no evil befalls the country, yet will it not be possible completely to repair the damage, and bring back the land to the state in which it

[1] See, for example, Gurgānī, *Vīs u Rāmīn*, pp. 23–4 (preface of the author concerning the destruction of the villages of the Iṣfahān oasis); Ibn al-Balkhī, *Fārs-Nāma*, pp. 132, 134 (about the devastation of Shīrāz).

[2] Ibn al-Athīr, vol. XI, pp. 117; Rāvandī, *Rāḥat al-ṣudūr*, pp. 180 ff.

[3] Ibn al-Athīr, ed. Tornberg, vol. XII, pp. 233–5.

[4] *Ta'rīkh-i Jahān-Gushā*, vol. I, p. 17; transl. J. A. Boyle, vol. I, p. 25.

was formerly."[1] Such is the testimony of the contemporaries of the Mongol invasion.

Thus the economic and cultural decline of Iran after the conquest, as also of neighbouring lands, cannot be doubted. But we can only conceive the scale of the decline clearly if we collect and correlate the separate and varying pieces of information given by historians and geographers of the thirteenth and fourteenth centuries, and compare them with information from the pre-Mongol period.

The primary result of the Mongol conquest was a fall in population, mostly among the working people in town and country, due to massacre and abduction into slavery and captivity, the flight of the remaining population, and the desertion of areas that had been thickly populated at an earlier date. Arab and Persian sources, speaking of the universal slaughter in a series of towns and districts, give figures which stun the imagination. Thus at the taking of Nīshāpūr, in 1220, 1,747,000 men alone are said to have been massacred.[2] At the capture of Marv, according to Ibn al-Athīr, about 700,000 people were killed,[3] according to Juvainī, 1,300,000.[4] At the second Mongol capture of Herāt, at the end of 1222, 1,600,000 people were said to have been killed.[5] The number killed at the capture of Baghdad by Hülegü is fixed by Ḥamd Allāh Qazvīnī at 800,000.[6] Describing massacres in the lesser towns, the sources give smaller figures: in Nasā 70,000 were killed;[7] in the district of Baihaq (of which the chief town was Sabzavār) 70,000 dead were counted;[8] 12,000 were killed in Tūn (Kūhistān),[9] and so on.

Of course we cannot accept these figures as entirely reliable. Such sizeable numbers are difficult to accept for a population living in a feudal economy, even in the case of such major cities as Nīshāpūr and others like it, and even assuming that the figures refer to the country

[1] *Nuzhat al-qulūb*, p. 27, transl. le Strange, p. 34.

[2] Saifī, *Ta'rīkh-Nāma-yi Harāt*, p. 63. This figure is of course improbable.

[3] Ibn al-Athīr, vol. XII, p. 257.

[4] Juvainī, vol. I, p. 128. This figure is arrived at in an arbitrary manner by the author, who considers that the total ought to be 1,300,000, as the counting of the dead lasted thirteen days, and 100,000 corpses could be counted in a day and a night. See the English translation by J. A. Boyle, vol. I, p. 164.

[5] Saifī, p. 60; similar figures are given by other sources. Ḥamd Allāh Qazvīnī informs us that there were 440,000 households in Herāt under the Ghūrids, that is 2,000,000 people, since household signifies family (*Nuzhat al-qulūb*, p. 152). According to Saifī (p. 67), 190,000 men took to arms in Herāt and district; if men fit for military service were 10 per cent of the population, we arrive at a figure of 1,900,000 souls for Herāt and district.

[6] *Ta'rīkh-i Guzīda*, p. 580.

[7] Nasawī, p. 52.

[8] Juvainī, vol. I, p. 138; translation of J. A. Boyle, vol. I, p. 175.

[9] *Nuzhat al-qulūb*, pp. 54–5; Clavijo, edition of I. Sreznevsky, p. 187.

districts surrounding the towns. But admitting exaggeration, we cannot however dismiss these figures as pure products of fantasy: the very fact that such numbers could be given, and in different sources, both pro- and anti-Mongol in orientation, implies a grandiose scale of mass-extermination, astounding the imagination of contemporaries. So does the fact that such towns as Ray were never rebuilt and remained uninhabited and in ruins for centuries. We should take into consideration also that many people were led away into slavery and captivity, or died of epidemics or hunger—the normal concomitants of foreign invasion.[1] Taking all this into account, we cannot doubt that between 1220 and 1258 the population of Iran declined several times over, the northern and eastern areas suffering most of all. Regrettably, the sources do not contain any overall figures for the population of Iran before and after the Mongol conquest.

Khurāsān suffered most of all. Yāqūt in the second decade of the thirteenth century speaks of the prosperity of the districts of Khurāsān.[2] According to Nasawī, all the towns and castles had been ruined and the major part of the population both in the towns and the rural areas either killed or carried off into slavery during the first Mongol invasion of Khurāsān in 1220–23, whilst the young men had been taken away for employment in siege operations; the conquerors left nobody in peace.[3] Juvainī says that in a couple of months, Tolui so ravaged many regions of Khurāsān that he made them like the "palm of the hand".[4] Writing about the year 720/1321 Saifī cites the stories of old men, based on the memories of eye-witnesses, to show that at the time of the invasion there were in Khurāsān "neither people, nor corn, nor food, nor clothing",[5] and that "from the frontiers of Balkh as far as Dāmghān people ate only human flesh, dogs and cats for a whole year,[6] because the warriors of Chingiz-Khān had burnt down all the granaries".[7]

What life was like in the Herāt region of Khurāsān, one can judge from the stories of Saifī: after the slaughter of 1220 only sixteen

[1] According to a writer continuing the *Ta'rīkh-i Sīstān* (p. 396), about 100,000 died of famine and a disease of the legs, mouth and teeth (scurvy?) at the Mongol siege of Sīstān (Zarang) in 632/1234–5.

[2] *Mu'jam al-buldān*, *passim* under the names of the towns and districts of Khurāsān; among other things are given the numbers of villages in districts. In the region of Ṭūs alone there were about 1,000 villages (*ibid.* vol. III, p. 560).

[3] Nasawī, p. 52–4.

[4] Juvainī, vol. I, p. 119; translation of J. A. Boyle, vol. I, p. 152.

[5] Saifī, p. 83.

[6] 618 = 1220–21.

[7] Saifī, p. 87.

people survived in the city of Herāt, and only forty, if we include fugitives from other places,[1] whilst not more than a hundred survivors remained in the surrounding countryside.[2] Saifī relates a vivid tale drawn from the memories of old men about the life of the forty chance survivors in their ruined and devastated city: first they fed upon the corpses of animals and men, then for a period of four years this handful of people were only able to get food by attacking passing caravans; and this too at distances of from 150 to 800 kilometres from Herāt.[3] When in 1236 the Great Khan Ögedei gave assent to the rebuilding of Herāt and brought back some of the weavers (*jāma-bāfān*) who had been carried off into captivity, these latter had first of all to restore one of the canals that had been destroyed and then to harness themselves to the plough and sow corn, because there were neither peasants nor cattle in the countryside around the town.[4]

The Balkh region, according to Yāqūt,[5] at the beginning of the thirteenth century before the Mongol conquest abounded in riches, producing silk and such a quantity of corn that it was the granary of the whole of Khurāsān and Khwārazm. From the life of the great Persian poet and mystic Jalāl al-Dīn Rūmī we learn that Balkh had about 200,000 inhabitants in the twelfth and at the beginning of the thirteenth centuries.[6] The Mongols sacked it, massacring the whole population.[7] Travellers who passed through Balkh, the Chinese Taoist Ch'ang-ch'un (1223),[8] Marco Polo (the second half of the thirteenth century),[9] and Ibn Baṭṭūṭa (the thirties of the fourteenth century),[10] inform us that it and its environs were derelict and deserted.

After the Marv oasis had been destroyed three times by the Mongols (1221–3), its agriculture and the dam on the river Murghāb were ruined, cattle had been driven away, and corn had been taken. Massacre followed massacre until "in the town and the villages there were not a hundred souls alive and not enough food even for these enfeebled few".[11] In Ṭūs only fifty houses remained occupied.[12] Nīshāpūr was

[1] Saifī, p. 83.
[2] *Ibid.* pp. 182–3.
[3] *Ibid.* pp. 89–90. For more detail see: I. Petrushevsky, *Zemledelie i agrarnïe otnosheniya v Irane XIII–XIV vv.*, pp. 67–69.
[4] Saifī, pp. 110–11.
[5] *Mu'jam al-buldān*, vol. I, p. 713.
[6] Aflākī, vol. I, p. 15 (Huart's translation).
[7] Juvainī, vol. I, pp. 103–5; transl. Boyle, vol. I, pp. 130–3.
[8] Ch'ang-ch'un, p. 111.
[9] Marco Polo, trans. Yule, vol. I, p. 158.
[10] Ibn Baṭṭūṭa, vol. III, p. 58.
[11] Juvainī, vol. I, pp. 125–32; transl. Boyle, vol. I, pp. 159–68.
[12] *Ibid.* vol. II, p. 238; transl. Boyle, vol. II, p. 501.

completely empty and ruined after the wholesale slaughter;[1] in the town there was not a wall still standing and the rural area was also devastated.[2]

According to the poet Nizārī, many villages were still deserted in Kūhistān in the seventies, the town of Qā'in being still without water;[3] 12,000 people had been killed in Tūn; all the Ismā'īlīs in Kūhistān had been slaughtered in accordance with the decree of Hülegü.[4]

The Mongol conquest took an equally heavy toll in Ṭabaristān (Māzandarān). In the words of the historian of the region Ibn Isfandiyār (beginning of the thirteenth century) "all land was cultivated from the mountains to the shores of the sea, and villages adjoined one another, so that there was not one span of waste land that did not bear the fruits of the earth";[5] here "the whole countryside was garden or orchard, so that the eye saw nothing but green".[6] Harvests were such that there were many fresh vegetables at each season of the year and a great quantity of corn, rice, millet, and every kind of meat and fowl;[7] in the area "there had never been poverty, such as there was in other places".[8] The same historian states that the region was desolate after the Mongol conquest and that throughout the whole of Khurāsān there were crowds of slave-captives from Ṭabaristān.[9] The local historian Ẓahīr al-Dīn Mar'ashī, writing about 1470, speaks of the terrible devastation of Māzandarān by the Mongols and says that the ruins and heaps of ashes were still there in his time.[10] Yāqūt wrote of neighbouring Gurgān at the beginning of the thirteenth century as of a rich district, abundant in *garmsīr* (i.e. subtropical) crops and silk. As an example of the wealth of the region Yāqūt cites the case of an estate which cost 1,000,000 dirhams and was leased for 500,000.[11] But Hamd Allāh Qazvīnī speaks of the destruction of Gurgān by the Mongols, and says that in his time (1340) there were few people living there.[12] The decay of the irrigation network is referred to by Ghazan in his decree concerning the cultivation of desolate land.

[1] *Ibid.* vol. I, pp. 133–40; transl. Boyle, vol. I, pp. 169–78.

[2] *Mu'jam al-buldān*, vol. III, p. 230; vol. IV, p. 859.

[3] Nizārī, *Kulliyyāt*, manuscript in the Institute of Language and Literature of the Academy of Sciences of the Tajik S.S.R. no. 100 (manuscript) of 972/1564–5), 1.292*a*.

[4] Juvainī, vol. III, p. 277; transl. Boyle, vol. II, p. 724.

[5] *Ta'rīkh-i Tabaristān*, ed. of Persian text of 'Abbās Iqbāl, vol. I, p. 74.

[6] *Ibid.* vol. I, p. 76. [7] *Ibid.* [8] *Ibid.* vol. I, p. 81.

[9] Ibn Isfandiyār, *Ta'rīkh-i Ṭabaristān*, abridged English translation by Browne, GMS, p. 258.

[10] Ẓahīr al-Dīn Mar'ashī, p. 264. [11] *Mu'jam al-buldān*, vol. I, p. 49.

[12] *Nuzhat al-qulūb*, p. 159.

OTHER FACTORS IN THE DECLINE

The dislocation in the life of Iran during the conquest was not however the only cause of the catastrophic decline in the economy of the country. There were other factors aggravating the decline. First of all, the conquest of Iran did not create a stable peace inside the land. The invasions of the armies of the Qïpchaq and Chaghatai rulers, enemies of the Īl-Khāns, were almost as destructive as the first Mongol invasion. We shall quote here only one example: in 1295 the Chaghatai ruler Du'a terribly ravaged and burnt the rural areas of Khurāsān (especially the Herāt oasis), the rural districts of Māzandarān, and the Yazd oasis, driving 200,000 prisoners (women and children) into servitude.[1] Equally devastating were the incursions of the Nīgūdarī Mongols, who led a nomadic existence in Afghanistan and did not recognize the authority of the Īl-Khāns,[2] into Khurāsān, Sīstān, Kīrmān and Fārs,[3] and the punitive expeditions of the Īl-Khāns themselves against their recalcitrant vassals, or in order to put down popular revolt (for example the revolt in Fārs led by the *qāḍī* Sharaf al-Dīn, who proclaimed himself Mahdī in 663/1265).[4] It is sufficient to say that Khurāsān remained desolate;[5] the Herāt oasis and Herāt itself were devastated with the loss of part of the population in 1270, 1288, 1289, 1295, 1306–07 and 1319.[6]

The increase in the number of nomads in the country had a part in the decline of the economy, especially that of agriculture. Contrary to the opinion of V. V. Barthold that "the Mongol invasion was not connected, as was the Germanic invasion of the Roman Empire, with transmigration of people",[7] the sources permit us to speak of a considerable migration of Mongol nomadic tribes into the territory of the Īl-Khāns,[8] not to mention that of Turkish nomads. Some previously agricultural territory became pasture for the nomads, as for example Bādghīs in Khurāsān, where before the Mongol conquest there were

[1] Saifī, pp. 402, 408, 416.

[2] Ancestors of the present-day Hazāra Mongols in Afghanistan.

[3] Vaṣṣāf, pp. 199–202; Saifī, pp. 379–83; for details see Marco Polo, trans. Yule, vol. I, pp. 99–100.

[4] Vaṣṣāf, pp. 191–92.

[5] Saifī, p. 346 (under the year 975 or 1276).

[6] Saifī, pp. 379 ff., 381 ff., 402 ff., 461 ff., 503 ff., 716 ff. For details see: I. Petrushevsky, *Trud Saifī kak istochnik po istorii Vostochnogo Khorasana.*

[7] *Istoria kul'turnoi zhizni Turkestana*, p. 86.

[8] *Nuzhat al-qulūb*, pp. 64, 66, 83, 85; Shabāngāraī, ff. 228*a*, 237*b*; *Mukātibāt-i Rashīdī*, pp. 273–8 (no. 46; Marco Polo, trans. Yule, vol. I, pp. 99–100); Evliya Chelebi, *Siyāḥat-Nāma*, vol. II, pp. 291 ff.

several towns with populations of 20,000–30,000.[1] The influence of the nomads proved unfavourable to Iran in the economic sphere. Nomadic cattle-rearing, without knowledge of fodder-grass cultivation and based upon cattle being at grass the whole year round, was extensive in character and required great uninhabited expanses of summer and winter pasture. The nomads, always armed and strong by reason of their tribal organization, ruined grass and trampled crops underfoot in their migrations, not scrupling to rob unorganized, unarmed, and defenceless peasants.[2] But the political rule of the nomads or, more exactly, of their feudal military aristocracy, who regarded the subjugated Persians as a permanent source of plunder and revenue and no more, also created great difficulties for Iran. Because, although nomad cattle-breeding was known in Iran from ancient times,[3] it had never occupied as important a position in the economy, as it did under the Mongols and later. Neither under the Umayyads, nor even under the Saljuqs did the military nobility of nomad tribes play such a leading role, as it did under the Īl-Khāns and their successors, the Jalayirids, Qara-Qoyunlu, Aq-Qoyunlu, and the first Ṣafavids.

The most important factor hindering the economic renaissance of the country and contributing to further economic decline was the fiscal policy of the viceroys of the Great Khan, and of the Īl-Khāns. This policy was particularly hard on peasant farmers, since the taxes were not precisely established, were levied in an arbitrary manner,[4] were collected several times over,[5] and were often of arbitrary size. We shall speak later in greater detail about the fiscal system of the Īl-Khāns. Let us for the time being note that towards the end of the thirteenth century the peasants had been brought to the verge of poverty and mass-flight. Thus even those regions which had not fallen prey to the invasion of Chingiz-Khān and Hülegü, as for example Fārs, were ruined. Vaṣṣāf gives a typical example of the decline of agricultural productivity in the Fārs region. The district of Kurbāl, considered one of the most fertile, watered by canals from the river Kur, on which were two large dams (the Band-i Amīr and Band-i Qaṣṣār),[6] yielded about

[1] Ḥāfiẓ-i Abrū, geographic works, f. 228*a*.

[2] *Mukātibāt-i Rashīdī*, pp. 177 (no. 33), 277–8 (no. 46); *Dastūr al-kātib*, ff. 34*a*, 224*b*, 233*b*, etc.

[3] Herodotus, *History*, Book I, chapter 125.

[4] See Juvainī, vol. II, pp. 244, 261, 269, 274, 277–8; trans. Boyle, vol. II, pp. 508, 524, 533, 539, 541–3.

[5] *Jāmi' al-tawārīkh*, ed. Alizade, p. 453.

[6] Ibn al-Balkhī, *Fārs-Nāma*, pp. 151–2; *Nuzhat al-qulūb*, p. 124.

700,000 *kharvārs* (ass-loads)[1] of grain in the annual harvest under Būyid 'Aḍud al-Daula (949–83). Under the atabeg Sa'd b. Abī Bakr, a vassal of the Īl-Khāns, the annual harvest there about the year 1260 fell to 300,000 kharvārs, and before the reforms of Ghazan fell even further, and the *kharāj* of Kurbāl consisted of only 42,000 kharvārs of grain.[2] The deliveries of grain from the other districts of Fārs decreased in a like manner.[3]

Rashid al-Dīn gives the following general characterization of the decline of Iran and neighbouring countries before the reforms of Ghazan:

At the time of the Mongol conquest they submitted the inhabitants of great populous cities and broad provinces to such massacres, that hardly anyone was left alive, as was the case in Balkh, Shuburqān, Ṭāliqān, Marv, Sarakhs, Herāt, Turkestan, Ray, Hamadān, Qum, Iṣfahān, Marāgheh, Ardabīl, Barda'a, Ganjah, Baghdad, Irbīl and the greater part of the territories belonging to these cities. In some areas on the frontiers, frequently traversed by armies, the native population was either completely annihilated or had fled, leaving their land waste, as in the case of Uighuristān and other regions that now formed the boundary between the *ulus* of the Qa'an and Qaidu. So also were several districts between Darband and Shīrvān and parts of Abulustān and Diyārbakr, such as Harrān, Ruḥa,[4] Sarūj, Raqqa and the majority of cities on both sides of the Euphrates, which were all devastated and deserted. And one cannot describe the extent of the land laid waste in other regions as a result of the slaughter, such as the despoiled lands of Baghdad and Āzarbāījān or the ruined towns and villages of Turkestan, Iran and Rūm [Asia Minor], which people see with their own eyes. A general comparison shows that not a tenth part of the lands is under cultivation and that all the remainder is still lying waste.[5]

TENDENCIES IN THE SOCIAL POLICY OF THE ĪL-KHĀNS

We can trace two political trends in the upper strata of the Mongol victors and the leading group of Iranian aristocracy allied to them. The supporters of the first trend, admirers of Mongol tradition and the nomadic way of life, were antagonistic to a settled life, to agriculture

[1] Conventional measure of weight; 1 *kharvār* = 100 *mans*, but the *man* varied in different districts; Shīrāz *man* = 3·3 kg, Tabrīz *man* = app. 3 kg.

[2] Vaṣṣāf, p. 445. Taking the *kharāj* to be 20–24 per cent of the crop, the overall crop can be estimated at from 221,000 to 175,000 *kharvārs*. See calculations in: I. Petrushevsky, *Zemledelie* . . ., pp. 81–2; also reference to sources.

[3] Vaṣṣāf, p. 445; see *ibid.* p. 435.

[4] The ancient Edessa, now called Urfa.

[5] *Jāmi' al-tawārīkh*, ed. Alizade, pp. 557–8.

and to towns,[1] and were supporters of unlimited, rapacious exploitation of settled peasants and town-dwellers. These representatives of the military feudal–tribal steppe aristocracy regarded themselves as a military encampment in enemy country, and made no great distinction between unsubjugated and subjugated settled peoples. The conquerors wished to plunder both, albeit in different ways, the former by seizure of the spoils of war, the latter by exacting burdensome taxes. The supporters of this policy did not care if they ended by ruining the peasantry and the townspeople; they were not interested in their preservation. The most self-seeking and avaricious members of the local Iranian bureaucracy supported the adherents of this first trend,[2] as did the tax-farmers, who closely linked their interest to that of the conquerors and joined with them in the plunder of the settled population subject to taxation—the *ra'iyyat*.

As well as being supported by a small group of nomad aristocrats, closely connected by service with the family of the Īl-Khān in his headquarters (*ordu*) and demesne (*injü*), the second trend was mainly supported by the majority in the Iranian bureaucracy, by many of the Muslim clergy,[3] and by the large-scale merchants. This tendency aimed at the creation of a strong central authority in the person of the Īl-Khān, the adoption by the Mongol state of the old Iranian traditions of a centralized feudal form of government, and in connexion with this the curbing of the centrifugal proclivities of the nomad tribal aristocracy. To do this it seemed necessary to reconcile the feudal leaders of Iran to the Īl-Khān, to reconstruct the disrupted economy of the country, particularly of agriculture, and to foster town-life, trade, and the merchants. Some lightening of the fiscal burden, an exact stabilizing of imposts and obligations (there was no stability in these under the first Īl-Khāns) laid upon the ra'iyyat, and protection from such taxes and services as would ruin them completely, were necessary conditions of this.[4] The conflict between these two tendencies is complicated by the

[1] The Yasa of Chingiz-Khān required the Mongols to lead a nomadic existence, not to settle nor to dwell in the towns: see the *Ta'rīkh-i Guzīda*, manuscript in Leningrad State University, no. 153, 472 (not in edition of E. G. Browne); quotation in W. Barthold, *Turkestan*, G.M.S. N.S. (London, 1958), p. 461 n. 5.

[2] Such were the great *bitikchi* Sharaf al-Dīn Juvainī, the *ṣāḥib-dīvān* Shams al-Dīn Muḥammad Juvainī (the brother of the historian), and particularly his son Bahā' al-Dīn Juvainī.

[3] Under the first Īl-Khāns Christians also (mostly of the Nestorian and Monophysite clergy).

[4] For more about these two trends see: I. Petrushevsky, *Zemledelie i agrarnïe otnosheniya v Irane v XII–XIV vv.*, pp. 46–53; there are also references to sources and literature for research.

conflict between the pristine trends of the Iranian Middle Ages, towards feudal disintegration and feudal centralization.

A policy in the spirit of the first tendency predominated under the first six Īl-Khāns. For this reason, although there was no lack of attempts by individual rulers to rebuild cities and irrigation networks, nevertheless these attempts were not successful, because of the policy of unbounded exploitation of the ra'iyyat—both peasant and city-dweller. Since the work of construction was carried out by unpaid forced labour, it only laid an extra burden upon the ra'iyyat, who were ruined previous to this, and in general such work was not completed.[1]

The second trend gained the upper hand in the *ulus* of the Īl-Khāns during the reign of Ghazan, from 1295 to 1304. His vizier, the historian, Shafi'ite theologian and encyclopaedist Rashīd al-Dīn Faḍl Allāh Hamādānī (1247–1318), who carried out the reforms of this Īl-Khān, was the most notable representative and ideologist of this policy. After the publication of the correspondence of Rashīd al-Dīn, we cannot doubt but that his was the initiative in the reforms of Ghazan. In a letter to his son Shihāb al-Dīn, governor of Khūzistān, Rashīd al-Dīn expressed in the following words the idea that it was necessary to keep the well-being of the ra'iyyat up to a certain level, since they were the fundamental payers of taxes:

It is fitting that rulers have three exchequers; firstly of money; secondly of weapons; thirdly of food and clothing. And these exchequers are named the exchequers of expenditure. But the exchequer of income is the *ra'iyyat* themselves, since the treasuries that I have mentioned are filled by their good efforts and their economies. And if they are ruined, the king will have no revenue. After all, if you look into the matter, the basis of administration is justice, for if, as they say, the revenue of the ruler is from the army, and the government (*salṭanat*) has no revenue but that paid by the army,[2] yet an army is created by means of taxation (*māl*), and there is no army without taxation. Now tax is paid by the *ra'iyyat*, there being no tax that is not paid by the *ra'iyyat*. And the *ra'iyyat* are preserved by justice. There are no *ra'iyyat*, if there is no justice.[3]

This same idea is expressed by Ghazan in a speech made to amīrs, i.e. to the Mongol-Turkish military and nomad aristocracy. In this speech he says amongst other things:

[1] *Jāmi' al-tawārīkh*, ed. Alizade, p. 558; cf. Saifī, pp. 440, 444.
[2] That is, out of plunder, one-fifth of which went to the state.
[3] *Mukātibāt-i Rashīdī*, pp. 118–19 (no. 22).

I am not on the side of the Tāzīk[1] *ra'iyyat*. If there is a purpose in pillaging them all, there is no-one with more power to do this than I. Let us rob then together. But if you wish to be certain of collecting grain (*taghār*)[2] and food (*āsh*) for your tables in the future, I must be harsh with you. You must be taught reason. If you insult the *ra'iyyat*, take their oxen and seed, and trample their crops into the ground, what will you do in the future? . . . The obedient *ra'iyyat* must be distinguished from the *ra'iyyat* who are our enemies.[3] How should we not protect the obedient, allowing them to suffer distress and torment at our hands.[4]

GHAZAN'S REFORMS AND THEIR CONSEQUENCES

The most important of Ghazan's reforms aimed at restoring the Iranian economy were: a new method of levying the land tax (*kharāj*) and other taxes payable to the dīvān, fixing a precise sum for each particular area in money or kind to be paid twice yearly, in spring and autumn:[5] the cutting by half of the impost on trades and crafts (*tamgha*)[6] in some towns and its complete abolition in others:[7] this measure was intended to assist the revival of town life. Other reforms important for the Iranian economy were enacted during the reign of Ghazan:[8] the abolition of *barāt*, i.e. the system of payment of state liabilities to soldiers, officials, pensioners, and creditors of the state by means of notes drawn against local exchequers, transferring payment on them to peasants, on whose shoulders was thus laid an additional fiscal burden; abolition of the practice of quartering military and official personnel in the homes of the ra'iyyat, which practice, accompanied always by extortion and maltreatment of the taxable population, was one of the heaviest

[1] I.e. Tajik; this term was then used to describe Iranians in general; see W. Barthold's article, "Tādjīk", *EI*.

[2] I.e. payment in kind of the military personnel of the state out of taxes.

[3] I.e. rebels.

[4] Probably this manifesto of Ghazan to the amīrs was inspired by Rashīd al-Dīn, if not written by him and ascribed by him to his master. The same speech in a somewhat varying form is in the Jalayirid collection of official documents *Dastūr al-kātib* (ff. 34*a*–*b*); we find it in another slightly varied form in the "Introduction" to the Persian tract on agriculture *Irshad al-zirā'a* of the year 915/1509–10; the text and the Russian translation of the latter (from the manuscript of E. M. Peshchereva, Leningrad; in the lithographed edition of 'Abd al-Ghaffār, 1323/1905–6, the "Introduction" is omitted) are to be found in: I. Petrushevsky, *Zemliedelie*..., pp. 57–8.

[5] *Jāmī' al-tawārīkh*, ed. Alizade, p. 478.

[6] *Jāmi' al-tawārīkh*, ed. Alizade, vol. III, pp. 466–77; a copy of a new tax-roll for Kkūzistān is cited in the *Mukātibāt-i Rashīdī*, pp. 122–3 (no. 22).

[7] See the *Mukātibāt-i Rashīdī*, pp. 32–4 (no. 13), 122–3 (no. 22).

[8] Copies or descriptions of Ghazan's decrees are to be found in *Jāmi' al-tawārīkh*.

impositions upon them; limitation of carriage and postal services, which were a heavy burden; the decree permitting the settlement and cultivation of deserted and neglected land belonging to the Dīvān and private owners, together with the creation of fiscal incentives; the restoration of the currency and the establishment of a firm rate for silver coin: 1 silver dīnār, containing 3 mithqāls of silver = 13·6 grammes = 6 dirhams: the establishment of a single system of weights and measures (using the Tabrīz system) for the whole state. It is true that even after these measures taxes were still quite high.[1] But in comparison with the previous system of pure club-law and unrestricted pillage, the new regime was an improvement from the point of view of the ra'iyyat. The decrees of Ghazan, forbidding the use of violence by amīrs, their households, servants of the khan, messengers, officials and nomads against the ra'iyyat also played a part in this development. Ghazan also enacted wide-ranging measures for the restoration of the ruined irrigation network[2] and for the revival of agriculture.[3]

The reforms of Ghazan and the temporary transfer of a leading political role in the State from the nomad Mongol-Turkish aristocracy to the Iranian civil bureaucracy made some economic improvement possible, especially in agriculture. Rashīd al-Dīn evidently exaggerated the importance of Ghazan's reforms: Vaṣṣāf speaks of them in a more modest manner. Ḥamd Allāh Qazvīnī however witnesses to the revival of agriculture in his factual description of the state of agriculture in a series of regions: he speaks of rich harvests, low prices, an abundance of foodstuffs, the export of corn and fruit, and so on.[4] The effect of Ghazan's reforms was still felt during the reign of his brother Öljeitü (1304–16), when control of affairs remained in the hands of Rashīd al-Dīn. The information that we are given concerning the social policy of Abū Sa'īd (1316–35) is contradictory. Vaṣṣāf speaks of fresh fiscal oppression and of the arbitrary abuse of power by financial officials about the year 718/1318.[5] Fifteenth-century writers like Ẓahīr al-Dīn Mar'ashī and Daulatshāh, on the other hand, describe Abū Sa'īd as a most ra'iyyat-loving ruler, under whom the country flourished.[6] These pieces of information probably contradict one another because they

[1] See below for more on this point.

[2] *Jāmi' al-tawārīkh*, ed. Alizade, pp. 411–12; *Mukātibāt-i Rashīdī*, pp. 157–58 (no. 28), 180–1 (no. 33), 245–7 (no. 38, 39); *Nuzhat al-qulūb*, pp. 208–28.

[3] *Jāmi' al-tawārīkh*, ed. Alizade, p. 415.

[4] *Nuzhat al-qulūb*, pp. 49–55, 59, 71–89, 109–12, 147–58; see also the description of Khurāsān in the geographical work of Ḥāfiẓ-i Abrū.

[5] Vaṣṣāf, pp. 630 ff.

[6] Ẓahīr al-Dīn Mara'shī, pp. 101–2; Daulatshāh, pp. 227–8.

refer to different periods—either to the beginning of Abū Sa'īd's reign, when the influence of the nomadic military aristocracy again predominated under the amīr and favourite Choban, or to the end of his reign, when the vizier Ghiyāth al-Dīn Muḥammad Rashīdī, the son of Rashīd al-Dīn, reintroduced his father's policy.

After the death of Abū Sa'īd civil wars between feudal cliques (connected with the development of a system of military feoffs)[1] the political disintegration of Iran and the inclination of certain local dynasties to use pre-Ghazan methods of government put an end to further economic revival. If the earlier Jalayirids (Ḥasan-i Buzurg, 1340–56, and Shaikh Uvais, 1356–74) had attempted to rule in the spirit of Ghazan,[2] the Chobanids, having established themselves in Āzarbāījān and Persian 'Irāq (1336–56) and basing their power exclusively on the Mongol-Turkish nomad aristocracy, resurrected the system of unrestricted and unregulated force and the unrestrained pillage of the ra'iyyat. This distinction between the policies of the two dynasties is made by the author of *Ta'rīkh-i Shaikh Uvais* in a story in which he relates the following: At the gates of Baghdad, before a battle, the amīrs of the Jalayirid army said to the amīrs of the Chobanid forces: "You are tyrants, but when we left you Āzarbāījān it was like Paradise, and we have made Baghdad into a flourishing city"; the Chobanid amīrs answered: "We were in Rūm and wrought havoc; you made Āzarbāījān flourish, we drove you from it, and ravaged the country as we did before; now we have come here and shall drive you out and ruin this region also."[3]

In spite of a certain revival at the end of the thirteenth and beginning of the fourteenth centuries, the economy had far from reached its pre-conquest level. We can deduce this if we compare the numbers of villages in various regions (*vilāyat*) before and after the Mongol conquest.

In the vilāyat of Herāt there were about 400 villages in the tenth century,[4] at the beginning of the fifteenth 167.[5] In the vilāyat of Iṣfahān alone the number had increased.[6]

[1] See below.

[2] *Dastūr al-kātib*, passim, especially ff. 36*b*–37*a*, 47*b*–48*b*, 51*a*–51*b*.

[3] *Tārīkh-i Shaikh Uvais*, ed. J. B. van Loon, facsimile, f. 173; cf. Ḥāfiz-i Abrū, *Dhail-i Jāmi' at-tawārīkh*, ed. Bayānī, pp. 171–85.

[4] Ibn Rusta, *BGA*, vol. VII, p. 173.

[5] Ḥāfiẓ-i Abrū, Geographical Works, manuscript quoted, ff. 225*a*–227*b* (list of villages).

[6] According to Yāqūt (f. 292)—360 villages; according to *Nuzhat al-qulūb* (p. 50)—400 villages, not including hamlets; according to the *Tarjuma-yi Maḥāsin-i Iṣfahān*, p. 47 (in 1329)—800 villages (*dīh*) and hamlets (*mazra'a*).

Vilāyat	Yāqūt (early thirteenth century)[a]	Ḥamd Allāh Qazvīnī (approx. 1340)[b]	Ḥāfiẓ-i Abrū (early fifteenth century)[c]
Hamadān	660 villages	212 villages	—
Rūdhrāvar	93 villages	73 villages	—
Khwāf	200 villages	—	30 villages (*qarya*), excluding hamlets (*mazra'a*)
Isfarā'in	451 villages	50 villages	26 villages, excluding hamlets
Baihaq[d]	321 villages	40 villages	84 villages, excluding hamlets
Juvain	189 villages	—	29 villages, etc.
Turshīz (Busht)	226 villages	—	20 villages, etc.

[a] *Mu'jam al-buldān*, respectively: vol. iv, p. 988; vol. i, p. 246; vol. ii, pp. 911, 486; vol. i, p. 804; vol. ii, p. 165; vol. i, p. 628.

[b] *Nuzhat al-qulūb*, respectively: pp. 72, 73, 149.

[c] Geographical Works, quoted manuscript, ff. 251*a*, 229*b*, 231*a*–233*a*.

[d] According to the *Ta'rīkh-i Baihaq* of Ibn Funduq (approx. 1168), p. 34—395 villages.

Ḥamd Allāh Qazvīnī names more than thirty towns that were still in ruins in his time, among them Ray, Khurramābād, Saimara, Tavvaj, Arrajān, Dārābjird and Marv. According to the same author some cities had become small towns, such as Qum and Sīrāf. A series of former towns had become villages such as Ḥulwān, Mīāneh, Barzand, Kirmānshāh and Kirind.[1]

We can judge the condition of Iran's economy in the Īl-Khānid period from the tax-returns received by the dīvān of the central government. According to Vaṣṣāf, previous to the reign of Ghazan the dīvān received each year 18,000,000 dīnārs,[2] according to Ḥamd Allāh Qazvīnī the sum was 17,000,000, whilst after Ghazan's reforms the figure rose to 21,000,000 dīnārs;[3] but in 1335–40 the sum was 19,203,800.[4] It is interesting to compare these figures with the returns of the Saljuq period (in Īl-Khānid dīnārs) also quoted by Ḥamd Allāh Qazvīnī in his work,[5] as well as with the figures given in the *Risāla-yi Falakiyya*.[6]

[1] *Nuzhat al-qulūb*, *passim* (see index).

[2] Vaṣṣāf, p. 271.

[3] *Nuzhat al-qulūb*, p. 27.

[4] These calculations were made by adding the figures given for separate districts in the *Nuzhat al-qulūb*.

[5] As an important official of the finance department, Ḥamd Allāh Qazvīnī had access to the account-books of this department and had seen the overall roll composed by his grandfather Amīn al-Dīn Nāṣir, former head of the financial administration of the Saljuq sultans of 'Irāq. He also worked out the value of the returns in dīnārs of the Īl-Khānid period.

[6] Composed by 'Abdallāh Māzandarānī about 1364. It is not clear whether the figures given here refer to the time of the Īl-Khān Abū Sa'īd or Sulṭān Uvais. This *risāla* is examined and analysed in: Walter Hinz, "Das Rechnungswesen orientalischer Reichsfinanzämter im Mittelalter", *Der Islam*, vol. 29/1–2 (1949). We quote this article below.

Regions of Īl-Khān state	Dīvān taxes of pre-Mongol period (*Nuzhat al-qulūb*)	Dīvān taxes 1335–40	Dīvan taxes (*Risāla-yi Falakiyya*)
Arabian 'Irāq	Over 30,000,000	3,000,000	2,500,000
Persian 'Irāq ('Irāq-i 'Ajam)	Over 25,000,000	2,333,600	3,500,000
Lur Great	—	90,000 (1,000,000)	320,000
Lur Little	—	90,000 (1,000,000)[a]	280,000
Āzarbāījān	Approx. 20,000,000	2,160,000	—
Arrān and Mūghān	Over 3,000,000	303,000	—
Shīrvān	1,000,000	113,000	820,000
Gushtāsfī (delta of the Kur and the Araxes)	Approx. 1,000,000	118,500	—
Gurjistān and Abkhāz (Georgia)	Approx. 1,000,000	1,202,000	400,000

[a] In both regions of Lur 1,000,000 dīnārs were collected, but the central dīvān received only 90,000, the rest being kept by the dīvāns of the local atabegs.

Regions of the Īl-Khān state	Dīvān taxes of pre-Mongol period (*Nuzhat al-qulūb*)	Dīvān dues in 1335–40	Dīvān taxes (*Risāla-yi Falakiyya*)
Rūm (Asia Minor)	Over 15,000,000	3,300,000	3,000,000
Great Armenia	Approx. 2,000,000	390,000	—
Diyārbakr and Diyār Rabī'a (Upper Mesopotamia)	10,000,000	1,925,000	—
Kurdistān (Eastern, now Iranian)	Approx. 2,000,000	201,500	—
Khuzistān	Over 3,000,000	325,000	1,100,000
Fārs	Approx. 10,500,000[a]	2,871,200	—
Shabānkāra	Over 2,000,000	266,100	4,000,000
Kirmān and Makrān	880,000	676,500	—
Total[b]	100,580,000	19,203,800	15,920,000

[a] In 310 or 922.
[b] In Īl-Khānid dīnārs. Detailed calculations and references to *Nuzhat al-qulūb* in: I. Petrushevsky, *Zemledelie* . . ., pp. 96–100; see for figures from the *Risāla-yi Falakiyya* Walter Hinz, *op. cit.* pp. 133–4.

Thus, according to Ḥamd Allāh Qazvīnī, the seventeen regions forming the Īl-Khānid state paid the central dīvān 19,203,800 dīnars in 1335–40 as against 100,580,000 before the Mongol conquest, both sums being in Īl-Khānid dīnārs. In other words the revenue of the Īl-Khānid dīvān was but 19 per cent of that of the pre-Mongol period, and in some districts even less, 9–13 per cent. Also in the pre-Mongol and Mongol budgets sums which were paid to the dīvāns of vassal landowners and sums derived from the rent or tax on military fiefs—*iqṭā'*, which had fiscal immunity, were not taken into account. Inasmuch as the situation remained the same in this respect,[1] the abrupt fall in tax-receipts can hardly be explained in any other way than by the general economic decline of Iran.

Ḥamd Allāh Qazvīnī does not give figures for eastern and northern Iran, since all taxes in Sīstān, Kūhistān, Khurāsān, Gurgān and Mazandarān were expended on the local budgets, and the central dīvān received nothing at all,[2] whilst it received only a tiny share of the local revenue of Gīlān—a mere 20,000 dīnārs.[3] *The Risāla-yi Falakiyya* gives the returns on the rent-tax of *khāṣṣa* lands, i.e. from the private estates of the Īl-Khān and his family, according to district:

	Dīnārs		Dīnārs
Khurāsān	4,220,000	Armenia	540,000
Māzandarān	2,370,000	Diyārbakr	430,000
Ray	754,220$\frac{5}{6}$[a]	Āzarbāijān	2,600,000
Gīlān	1,220,000		
Kurdistān	300,000	Total from lands of the khāṣṣa[b]	12,434,220$\frac{5}{6}$

[a] According to the *Nuzhat al-qulūb* (p. 55), 151,500 dīnārs were paid by the Ray *vilāyat* to the central dīvān; in pre-Mongol times Ray and its *vilāyat* paid 7,000,000 dīnārs.

[b] W. Hinz, *op. cit.* pp. 133–4.

As is well known, taxes from khāṣṣa lands were not paid to the Great Dīvān (the central dīvān), but were paid to the private dīvān of the khāṣṣa for the upkeep of the Īl-Khan's quarters and those of his wives and the princes. According to the *Risāla-yi Falakiyya*, only 28,354,220$\frac{5}{6}$ dīnārs were paid annually by dīvān and khāṣṣa lands.[4] The divergence in the figures—both the overall figures and those for particular districts quoted in the *Nuzhat al-qulūb* and *Risāla-yi Falakiyya*—makes us think that the budget given in the latter source cannot refer to 1334–5, as Hinz supposes. The *Nuzhat al-qulūb* in fact gives nominal figures for the years 1335–40, years of feudal civil strife and peasant uprisings. According to the *daftars* not a half of the amount collected under Ghazan was collected.[5]

[1] There were no fewer iqṭā' lands under the Saljuqs, in all probability, than there were under Ghazan, judging by the fact that Malik-Shāh (1072–92) granted iqṭā's to 46,000 soldiers (Rāvandī, ed. Iqbāl, pp. 130–1).

[2] *Nuzhat al-qulūb*, p. 147.

[3] *Ibid.* p. 162.

[4] In Hinz's article (pp. 133–4) the incorrect figure 28, 264,220$\frac{5}{6}$ dīnārs is given, as a result of a miscalculation.

[5] *Nuzhat al-qulūb*, p. 27.

Therefore it is possible to assert that the economy of Iran during and especially after Ghazan's reign did not reach its pre-Mongol level. A certain relative improvement was experienced mainly in agriculture. Hamd Allāh Qazvīnī gives reason for thinking that from Ghazan's time the irrigation works of all four types in use from ancient times in Iran—mountain springs, river channels, wells and *kārīz*, i.e. underground galleries (with clay pipelines, timbering and inspection-wells) for bringing underground water to the surface—were to a considerable extent restored. The same author gives almost complete information concerning the kind of irrigation in use in each district or *vilāyat*.[1]

THE CONDITION OF AGRICULTURE AT THE END OF THE ĪL-KHĀNID PERIOD

We can judge the condition of agriculture in Iran after Ghazan's reforms not only from the *Nuzhat al-qulūb* but also from the anonymous Persian agrotechnical tract *Kitāb-i 'ilm-i falāḥat u zirā'at*, the author of which speaks of himself as a contemporary of Ghazan,[2] from regional historico-geographical works, from information given by travellers, and from the letters of Rashīd al-Dīn.

According to these sources wheat and barley were cultivated wherever there were water supplies and wherever agriculture had been preserved. The author of the *Falāḥa* mentions many kinds of wheat and barley; millet was less widely distributed. Ḥamd Allāh Qazvīnī names more than twenty districts (including Ray, Qum, Tabrīz, Iṣfahān, all Khūzistān and some regions of Fārs and Khurāsān) with especially high yields of corn. Bread made from barley or millet, frequently with the admixture of beans, chestnuts, or acorns, was the bread of the poor.[3] Rice was grown in the territory near to the Caspian and in a series of regions in Āzarbāījān, Persian 'Irāq (Zanjān, etc.) and Fārs (Kurbāl, Fīrūzābād, etc.), and also in Khūzistān.[4] The author of

[1] For the table based on this information see *Zemledelie*..., pp. 130–6.

[2] *Kitāb-i 'ilm-i falāḥat u zira' at, ta'līf-i shakhṣ-i 'ālim va 'āmil va siyāḥī dar 'ahd-i Ghāzān Khān.* Lithographed edition of Persian text of Najm ad-Daula 'Abd al-Ghaffar, Tehrān, 1322/1905. Henceforth we shall use the abbreviation *Falāḥa.* See concerning this tract: doctor Taqī Bahrāmī, *Ta'rīkh-i kishāvarzī-yi Irān*; I. Petrushevsky, *Persidski Traktat po agrotekhnike vremeni Ghazan-khāna*, pp. 586-99.

[3] See Sa'dī, *Gulistān*, chapter I, ḥikāyat 7; Farhang Shams-i Fakhrī, pp. 103 (no. 87), 124 (no. 96), 134 (no. 194). Ibn Baṭṭūṭa, vol. II, p. 32; *Nuzhat al-qulūb*, p. 130.

[4] *Nuzhat al-qulūb*, pp. 62, 117, 163; *Mukātibāt-i Rashīdī*, pp. 254–5 (no. 41), 271 (no. 45). Ẓahīr al-Dīn Mar'ashī, p. 413; Yāqūt, vol. II, p. 496; Zakariyyā Qazvīnī, vol. II, p. 102.

the *Falāḥa* informs us of various methods of cultivating rice. In some areas crops were a hundredfold and more, whilst the best rice was considered to be that of Gīlān, the second best being that of Māzandarān. The same author says that under the Ghazan experiments were carried out (in which the author took part) to sow the best kind of Indian rice in Iran, but without result.[1] Evidently the *zurrat*[2] of the author of the *Falāḥa* is wheat-sorghum (*anthropogon sorghum*). Much dhurrat was sown in the vilāyats of Kāshān and Iṣfahān, and the crops are supposed to have been nearly three-hundredfold.[3] Rye and oats were unknown in Iran, as now.

First place amongst fodder-crops was taken by lucerne,[4] used to feed horses. Greek clover was also known.[5] Cotton was the most common of the textile plants, the cultivation of which pushed flax and other textile plants into the background. Ḥamd Allāh Qazvīnī speaks of the cultivation of cotton in a series of regions, some fifty or so, of Persian 'Irāq (among them Ray, Qum, Nihāvand, Yazd); of Fārs—such as Shīrāz, Abarqūh, Kāzarūn, Lār; of Kirmān, Kūhistān, and Khurāsān (Khabūshān, Zāveh); throughout the whole of Khūzistān and Gurgān; and also in Māzandarān, Gīlān, Qūmis, and Āzarbāījān.[6]

According to the author of the *Falāḥa* cotton gave its finest crops in the *garmsīr* regions, but was also cultivated on *sardsīr* land,[7] primarily in sandy clay areas (*rīgbūm*). Fine cotton (*narm*) and coarse cotton (*zibr*) were known, but in general Indian cotton was thought of as better than Iranian.[8] Flax (*kattān*) was less widely grown in the fourteenth century than it had been in the tenth century, mostly in the south-west of Iran (the districts of Kāzarūn, Rīshahr, Sīnīz in Fārs), and not as a textile plant for the most part, but as a source of lamp-oil.[9] Hemp was culti-

[1] *Falāḥa*, pp. 86–8.

[2] زرت for the correct ذره *dhurra* (Arabic).

[3] *Falāḥa*, pp. 88–9.

[4] Strabo mentions the culture of lucerne (μηδιχή) in Media, *Geography*, XI, 13.

[5] Shams-i Fakhrī, p. 33 (no. 32), under the term *Shanbalīd*.

[6] See a table based on the *Nuzhat al-qulūb* in *Zemledelie* . . ., p. 195; also references. The list in the *Nuzhat al-qulūb* is not complete. Other cotton-producing regions are given in other sources, in particular the Herāt region (Saifī, p. 111).

[7] As is well-known, medieval geographers in Moslem countries distinguished land according to its height, between "cold" (Arabic *ṣurūd*, Persian *sardsīr*, more than 1,000–1,200 m above sea-level) and "hot" (Arabic *jurūm*, Persian *garmsīr*, less than 1,000–1,200 m above sea-level) districts. The coasts of the Caspian Sea and of the Persian Gulf belonged to the garmsīr, as did the province of Khūzistān. Sardsīr were the Iranian uplands, excepting the various depressions (Sīstān, the Balkh oasis, etc.). In conformity with this idea cultivated plants were divided into *garmsīr* = subtropical, and *sardsīr* = all the rest.

[8] *Falāḥa*, pp. 93–4.

[9] *Nuzhat al-qulūb*, pp. 126, 130–1.

vated not so much as a textile, but rather for the production of a well-known narcotic (Arabic *ḥashīsh*, Persian *bang*); evidently the distribution of hemp was not widespread, judging by the fact that Ḥamd Allāh Qazvīnī and Ḥāfiẓ-i Abrū do not mention it in their geographical works. The same can be said of the castor-oil plant (*ricinus communis*) and of safflower (*carthamus tinctorius*). Saffron was made from the plant called in Arabic *zaʿfarān* which yielded a yellow-orange dye (Burūjird, Rūdhrāvar, Qum, Hamadān, Kūhistān).[1] Other dye-yielding plants were madder, which gave a red dye (Khwāf in Khurāsān,[2] and other regions), henna, which gave an orange dye and was used for cosmetic and medicinal purposes,[3] and indigo, which yielded a blue dye and had been cultivated in Persia from the sixth century but was only commonly met with in Kirmān.[4] Ḥamd Allāh Qazvīnī does not mention it in the fourteenth century, but the author of the *Falāḥa* says that the cultivation of indigo had ceased in Iran, and that it was imported from India, despite the fact that Ghazan had attempted to revive its cultivation.[5] Cultivation of the opium poppy, known in Iran from the end of the eleventh or twelfth centuries, was insignificant, to judge from the rarity of references to it in the sources. Sesame occupied the leading position amongst the oil-plants, and sesame oil had practically replaced olive oil.

The melon was grown everywhere in Iran, in the words of the author of *Falāḥa*, "in every garden",[6] and there were many varieties of it. In the garden of one "refuge of a *naqībat* (*naqābat panāh*)", i.e. of an elder (*naqīb*) of the Sayyids, a religious fief-holder, the Herāt soil grew fifty kinds of melon.[7] Ḥamd Allāh Qazvīnī names ten regions (amongst others, Iṣfahān, Tabrīz and Marv) producing the best melons which were exported.[8] The pumpkin was also grown throughout Iran,[9] as were cucumbers (particularly in Gīlān, Māzandarān, Shīrāz, Iṣfahān).[10] The water-melon is however rarely spoken of; Ḥamd Allāh Qazvīnī only mentions it as growing in Qazvīn.[11]

Vegetable-growing was less developed in the period under consideration than fruit-growing; vegetables were to be found for the most

[1] *Ibid.* pp. 70, 73, 144, 146; *Falāḥa*, p. 112.
[2] *Nuzhat al-qulūb*, p. 154. The author of the *Falāḥa* also mentions the regions of Yazd and Nā'īn (p. 94).
[3] Continuation of the *Ta'rīkh-i Sīstān*, p. 396.
[4] *Ḥudūd al-ʿālam*, Persian text, f. 26*b*, English translation, pp. 123–4.
[5] *Falāḥa*, pp. 92–3.
[6] *Ibid.* pp. 94–5.
[7] *Irshād az-zirāʿa*, manuscript of Peshchereva, f. 87 (types of melon named).
[8] *Nuzhat al-qulūb*, pp. 49, 58, 67, 77, 144, 152, 153, 155, 157.
[9] *Falāḥa*, p. 105.
[10] *Ibid.* p. 100.
[11] *Nuzhat al-qulūb*, p. 58.

part near to the large commercial cities, such as Iṣfahān.[1] The *Falāḥa* describes in detail the vegetables and spices which were cultivated in Iran at the beginning of the fourteenth century; the most common of them were cabbages, carrots, onions, garlic, rue, mangel-wurzels and also leguminous plants.

As at an earlier date, fruit-growing occupied an outstanding position in the economy of Iran under the Mongols. Ḥamd Allāh Qazvīnī enumerates more than eighty regions of Iran where fruit-growing was widespread and produced abundant crops. Among them was for example Sīstān where horticulture has almost disappeared nowadays. The fig-palm occupied the foremost position amongst the *garmsīr* plants, and was cultivated in Gurgān and Māzandarān, as well as Khuzistān, Fārs, Kirmān and Sīstān. The citrus fruits—the lemon, orange, and bitter orange—were grown in the southern and Caspian regions. The coconut-palm only grew in the regions of Hurmuz and Wāsiṭ,[2] whilst the olive grew only in Khūzistān and near to the Caspian in small quantities. The sugar-cane was cultivated in Khūzistān, Kirmān and Balkh, and its export and cultivation had greatly declined in comparison with the previous centuries. According to the author of the *Falāḥa* the sugar produced in his time was poor in quality and reddish in colour, and Iranian craftsmen were unable to make refined sugar (*qand*).[3] The peach, apricot, plum, pear, apple (of which there were more than nowadays), pomegranate, mulberry tree, walnut, almond, pistachio (wild in eastern districts only) were the commonest sardsīr plants. The fig was also widely distributed, both the garmsīr and the sardsīr varieties.[4] The remaining sardsīr fruits were less widespread. In particular it was not the custom to grow the black and red cherry, the filbert and chestnut, in the garden; but the hazel-nut and the other fruits and nuts just mentioned were plentiful in the wild.[5] Viticulture was also highly developed.

Ḥamd Allāh Qazvīnī and other authors name about seventy regions in which the best vines were cultivated. There were many varieties. In one district alone, Pūshang (Khurāsān) a hundred kinds of vine were being grown.[6] In the horticultural enterprise of the naqīb near Herāt, which we mentioned, exactly a hundred varieties of vine were under cultivation.[7] Apparently after Ghazan's reforms viticulture did not

[1] See, for example, *Tarjuma-yi Maḥāsin-i Iṣfahān*, pp. 46, 64.
[2] *Falāha*, p. 46. [3] *Ibid.* p. 102. [4] *Ibid.* pp. 7.
[5] *Ibid.* pp. 15, 21, 29. [6] *Nuzhat al-qulūb*, p. 153.
[7] *Irshād al-zirā'ā*, cited manuscript, f. 80.

achieve the level it had attained around the beginning of the thirteenth century. Thus Ibn Funduq, writing about 1168, informs us of the abundance of vines in the regions of Baihaq and Nīshāpūr, but Ḥamd Allāh Qazvīnī says nothing of Nīshāpūr grapes, and states that few grapes were grown in Baihaq.[1] Dried fruit and grapes were exported from a number of regions (Iṣfahān, etc.) to such distant countries as Asia Minor (Rūm), India and China (via Baṣra).[2] Wine-making and the drinking of wine were very widespread, despite the Islamic prohibition. Date-palm brandy and other alcoholic drinks were produced and consumed.[3] The cultivation of flowers and scented plants (*mashmūmāt*) had also been preserved in Iran—in Fārs and Māzandarān[4]—and they were used in the production of perfumes, cosmetics, medicaments, aromatic essences (flower-waters), and flower-oils, especially the renowned rose-oil, etc.[5]

Unlike other branches of agriculture silk-growing (i.e. the culture of the silk-worm) not only showed no sign of decline in the second half of the thirteenth and the fourteenth century, but showed progress. If in the tenth century the main areas of silk-production were the Marv oasis, Gurgān, Māzandarān, and the Barda'a valley in Arrān and Shīrvān, and the silk-weavers of, say, Khūzistān worked the raw imported silk of Barda'a, in the period under consideration silk-weaving existed also in the Yazd oasis, in Fārs (in the region of Bishāpūr), Kūhistān (Turshīz, Gunābād), Khurāsān (Khwāf and Zāveh) and Gīlān,[6] as well as the areas previously mentioned. At the beginning of the thirteenth century Gīlān silk was still considered to be of poor quality,[7] but by the end of the thirteenth century its quality had so improved that merchants came from Genoa to buy it.[8] Italian sources of the thirteenth–fourteenth centuries—the commercial records of the Florentines Pegolotti and Uzziano, the statutes of Pisa, etc., utilized by W. Heyd in his book—know of the following sorts of raw silk imported from Iran for manufacture in the towns of Italy: *seta ghella*—Gīlān silk;

[1] *Ta'rīkh-i Baihaq*, p. 273; cf. *Nuzhat al-qulūb*, pp. 147, 150.

[2] *Nuzhat al-qulūb*, pp. 37, 49.

[3] For details see the article of I. Petrushevsky, "Vinogradarstvo i vinodelie v Irane v XIII–XV vv.", *Vizantiyskiy Vremennik*, vol. XI (1956).

[4] *Nuzhat al-qulūb*, pp. 118, 160; Ibn al-Balkhī repeats other details in this source in the *Fārs-Nāma*, pp. 134, 142, 143, 147, 148.

[5] See *Falāḥa*, pp. 40–3 (the method of making rose-oil is also described here); *Mukātibāt-i Rashīdī*, pp. 54 (no. 18), 93 (no. 21), 272 (no. 45).

[6] *Nuzhat al-qulūb*, pp. 74, 126 (compare Ibn al-Balkhī, p. 142), 143–5, 154, 159–60, 163.

[7] Yāqūt, vol. IV, p. 344.

[8] Marco Polo, trans. Yule, vol. I, p. 54. Compare V. V. Barthold, *Istoriko-geograficheskii obzor Irana*, p. 157.

seta masandroni—Amul silk from Māzandarān; *seta stravatina* or *seta stravai*—Astrabad silk from Gurgān; *seta talani*—Dailam (?) silk; *seta mardacascia*—silk from Marv-i Shāhijān, etc.[1]

According to the author of the *Falāḥa* a special kind of mulberry tree (white mulberry) was used for the culture of the silkworm. It did not have much fruit, but many leaves, "for one *diram* of *pupae* (*tukhm-i kirm*) eats 500 *mans* of leaves and gives one *man* of silk".[2] The organization of silk-production was best managed in the Yazd oasis. There one mulberry tree yielded 500 *mans* of leaves and one *man* of raw silk, as much as was yielded in other regions by 4–5 dirams of silkworm.[3] The culture of cochineal still had some importance—although incomparably less than that of silk—and was used in the manufacture of red dye which was then exported to a number of countries. Cochineal was collected near Mārand in Āzarbāījān,[4] and to the south of Ararat.[5]

In general an impression is created that irrigation (in particular the construction of *karīzes* and channels, and the building of dams)[6] and agricultural engineering were kept up in Iran after the Mongol conquest. But there was no noticeable progress in the application of the tools of labour. This is most readily explained by the dominant form of feudal exploitation of the peasantry (the quit-rent system) and the high rates of feudal rent, as a consequence of which the introduction of improvements in tools (the same that have survived into the twentieth century) was advantageous neither to the peasant nor to the landowner.

THE TOWN IN THE FOURTEENTH CENTURY

From what has been said previously, it is evident to what extent the towns had suffered after the Mongol conquest—in particular the large cities such as Marv, Balkh, Herāt, Nīshāpūr, Ray, Qazvīn and so on. Some of the shattered and ravaged cities were restored, as was Herāt in 1236, but they were now much smaller. In 639 or 1241/2 there were 6,900 people in Herāt.[7] But Herāt was again sacked several times, as we have already seen, and only became a large city again under the

[1] W. Heyd, *Geschichte des Levanthandels*, pp. 650–3.

[2] *Falāḥa*, p. 23;1 *diram* is here equivalent to 3 grammes (*diram* = *dirham*) approx.; 1 *man* (here Tabrīz) equals about 3 kilogrammes.

[3] *Falāḥa*, pp. 21–5.

[4] *Nuzhat al-qulūb*, p. 88.

[5] Clavijo, p. 156.

[6] The Ṣāhib-Dīvān Shams al-Dīn Muḥammad Juvainī (executed in 1284) built a great dam on the river Gāvmāsā near Sāveh (*Nuzhat al-qulūb*, p. 221); Rashīd al-Dīn spent 700,000 dīnārs on the reconstruction of the dam on the river Kārūn (*Mukātibāt-i Rashīdī*, p. 180, no. 33).

[7] Saifī, p. 238.

Tīmūrids. According to the well-informed Rashīd al-Dīn, on the eve of Ghazan's reforms five out of every ten houses in the sacked cities of Iran were uninhabited.[1] In Nakhchivān as late as the reign of Sulṭān Uvais five out of six houses were empty, the occupants having gone to live elsewhere.[2] The heavy tax on crafts and trade, which had not existed under the pre-Mongol rulers,[3] hampered the rivival of town-life. If we take into consideration the remarks of Ḥamd Allāh Qazvīnī that many towns were still ruined and that others had become villages we can make the deduction that in general urban life had suffered a decline in Iran during the Mongol period.

But this decline did not affect all towns. Some towns and cities revived after the reforms of Ghazan and made considerable economic progress. This depended not only on the fact that there were towns which had not been destroyed during the conquest (Tabrīz for example avoided destruction by paying the conquerors), but also on the economic nature of the town. In medieval Iran towns could be divided into several economic types. First of all there were many small and medium-sized towns occupied in commerce and craft-industry serving a limited local market. Other towns of a moderate size were centres of craft-industry producing exports for the international market such as Kāzarūn—the centre of flax-spinning, Yazd—weaving silk—and Kāshān—the centre of the ceramics industry—which also weaved silk and made carpets.

There were city-emporiums lying on international caravan and shipping routes, which were storing places, points for trans-shipping, and exchanges for the export and transit trades, such as Tabrīz, Marāgheh, Hamadān, Qazvīn, Iṣfahān, Shīrāz, Nīshāpūr, etc. Hurmuz, transferred from the coast to a bare little island in the Persian Gulf, flourished entirely thanks to the transit of Iranian, Arabic, Western European, Indian and Chinese goods. Frequently such towns were also centres of craft-industry serving the international market, as Iṣfahān (cotton and silk-weaving) and Shīrāz (iron goods, wool-weaving, the production of rose and other flower oils and aromatic essences).[4] There is no

[1] *Jāmiʿ al-tawārīkh*, ed. Alizade, pp. 558–9. [2] *Dastūr al-kātib*, p. 167*a*.

[3] *Nāṣir ad-dīn Ṭūsī*, p. 761. *Tamgha* was collected on each business transaction, even in the case of prostitution and the sale of wine. The exact size of the *tamgha* is not known, but from one of the letters of Rashid al-Dīn (no. 13, see below) it is possible to conclude that until the time of Ghazan it was paid at the rate of 10 per cent of the value of each deal. The *tamgha* was retained in Iran, but at a reduced rate, until the reign of Ṭahmāsp I.

[4] Rose water and other aromatic liquids were even exported to China from Fārs in the twelfth–thirteenth centuries; see Chau Ju-Kua, p. 134.

doubt that the great city-emporiums by far surpassed the greatest cities of Western Europe of the late medieval period, such as Venice, Milan, Florence or Paris, in the scale of their economic activities and their populations (at least before the Mongol invasion). Thus we should pay a certain respect to the figures given in the sources for the populations of the giant cities of the pre-Mongol period.[1] In general we do not possess reliable statistical information for the Mongol period as regards population, but we do have some figures for the fifteenth century. Clavijo fixes the population of Tabrīz in 1403 at 200,000 households.[2] An anonymous historian of S͟hāh Ismā'īl, more modestly, and probably more correctly, gives the figure as from 200,000 to 300,000 people. The Mongols are supposed to have slaughtered about 800,000 people in Baghdad in 1258, whilst Tīmūr is said to have killed 90,000 in 1401. Josapha Barbaro gives the population of Iṣfahān[3] as a mere 50,000 in the second half of the fifteenth century. That of Kās͟hān he gives as 20,000 households (= families, i.e. approx. 90,000 people), and that of S͟hīrāz as 200,000 households (about 900,000 people), which is probably a great exaggeration.[4] Such towns were able to recover quickly after the Mongol conquest and even to prosper because of income from exports and the transit trade, despite high rates of taxation (*tamg͟ha*). This prosperity however came to a rapid end and such towns were deserted when the trade routes altered, as happened in the case of the south Iranian port of Sīrāf, the importance of which passed to Hurmuz. Towns living off the transit trade had comparatively little influence on the economic development of Iran as a whole, although of course they influenced the economies of the suburban regions. It is in part possible to assess the development of such towns, as well as the market character of their suburban agriculture, from their tax-returns. Regrettably Ḥamd Allāh Qazvīnī rarely gave figures for tax (*tamg͟ha*) paid by cities separately from that paid by the cities and their surrounding districts (see p. 508).

The residences of the Īl-K͟hāns represented a peculiar type of town or city. Such were Marāg͟heh, Tabrīz, Ūjān, and the bazaar-cities that had arisen around the Īl-K͟hānid headquarters (*ordu*)—the summer camps

[1] See above, pp. 485–6.

[2] That is "families". Persian *k͟hāna*, lit. house, signified "family" ordinarily. Assuming that the average family consisted of 4·5 persons, we obtain 900,000 inhabitants of Tabrīz. This is an evident exaggeration.

[3] Iṣfahān was sacked twice after the Mongols had pillaged it (1237), by Tīmūr and during the reign of Jahān-S͟hāh.

[4] Barbaro, pp. 72–4.

(Ala-Tagh, Sulṭānīyeh) and the winter ones (Maḥmūdābād). According to Ḥamd Allāh Qazvīnī the tamgha paid in Sulṭānīyeh rose from 200,000 to 300,000 dīnārs when the khan had his residence (*ordu*) there. The satisfaction of the requirements of the Court and trade with the nearby summer camps (*yailaq*) of the Mongols gave both wages and income to the motley population of craftsmen and traders gathered in Sulṭānīyeh.[1] Ibn Baṭṭūṭa calls Marāgheh a little Damascus.[2]

Vilāyat	Tax (*tamgha*) from cities in dīnārs	Tax (*kharāj*) from the country district in dīnārs
Tabrīz	875,000	275,000
Baghdad	800,000	—
Shīrāz	450,000	—
Wāsiṭ	448,000	—
Iṣfahān	350,000	500,000
Hamadān	105,000	136,000
Marāgheh	70,000	185,000
Qazvīn	55,000	55,000[a]

[a] *Nuzhat al-qulūb*, pp. 78, 36, 116, 47, 50, 71–2, 87, 59 respectively.

It is worthy of note that, whereas the Arab geographers of the ninth and tenth centuries and an anonymous Persian at the end of the tenth century give detailed information concerning articles produced by craftsmen and their export from the towns of Iran, Ḥamd Allāh Qazvīnī and Ḥāfiẓ-i Abrū say almost nothing about the economic life of the towns, although they dwell upon the agricultural production of various regions in some detail. In this it is impossible not to see reflected the decline of the towns. Essentially we know very little about the economy of the towns and life in them during the thirteenth and fourteenth centuries. Nevertheless *objets d'art* in museums and various collections witness to the fact that Iranian craftsmanship remained at a high level.[3] In the correspondence of Rashīd al-Dīn the following articles of export from various towns are mentioned: Tabrīz—monochrome woven silks (*kīmkhā*), cloth of camel-hair, variously coloured velvets (*qaṭīfa-yi alvān*), shagreen and leather footwear, fur and fur goods; Shīrāz—cotton cloths (*karbās*) and printed cotton goods, linen (*qadaq* of Kāzarūn), leather footwear; Iṣfahān—cotton cloths *valad*, *ābyārī*, *shamsiyya*, etc.; Kāzarūn—cotton cloths; Kāshān—woven silks; Herāt—*kimkhā* and other silken cloths.[4]

[1] *Ibid.* pp. 55–6.

[2] Ibn Baṭṭūṭa, vol. I, p. 171.

[3] For more detail see: Zakī Muḥammad Ḥasan, *Ṣanāyi'-i Irān ba'd Islām*, tarjuma-yi Fārsī-yi Muḥammad 'Ali Khalkhālī.

[4] *Mukātibāt-i Rashīdī*, pp. 183 ff. (n. 34).

The towns of the pre-Mongol period and after had no overall self-government such as that given by statute to the city communes of the eleventh–sixteenth centuries and the German imperial cities in western Europe. There was however self-administration within the limits of the quarter (*maḥalla*; the householders of the quarter, gathering in the mosque, elected their mayor, discussed their business) and the guild or corporation—either merchant, craft, or religious. The corporations of the Sayyids and their elders—*naqīb*—in particular were very influential; there were about 1,400 Sayyids in the Shīrāz corporation.[1] The influence of the Ṣūfī-dervish shaikhs was also enormous. At the beginning of the thirties of the thirteenth century the majority of the population in Balkh were *murīds* of Shaikh Bahā' al-Dīn Valad, the father of Jalāl al-Dīn Rūmī.[2] A century later the inhabitants of Ardabīl were thought to be mostly murīds of Shaikh Ṣafī al-Dīn Isḥāq, the ancestor of the Ṣafavid dynasty.[3] In the towns the power of the local feudal landowner, known generally under the title of *malik*, was interwoven with the power of the khan's vicegerent (Mongol *basqaq*, Persian *shaḥna*) who controlled the activities of the malik, collected taxes and was endowed with military might.[4]

The town nobility as previously had great influence in the towns forming a kind of patriciate. These were landowners or feudalists of the surrounding area who before the Saljuq conquest had lived in their castles, but who now lived more often in the towns than upon their estates. The characteristic peculiarity of this nobility was its close connexion with the great commercial companies and with big wholesale and transit trade. They invested a part of their income in the companies of the great wholesale merchants, called usually *urtaq* (Turkish *ortaq*—"partner in a share", investor), "the Emperor's own merchants" (*tujjār-i khāṣṣ*), or "trustworthy merchants" (*tujjār-i amīn*), who returned the feudal lords their share of the profit in goods, mostly textiles. Thus the above-mentioned vizier, the historian Rashīd al-Dīn, himself a great feudal landowner,[5] invested a major part of his fortune, 32,500,000 dīnārs out of 35,000,000, in a large wholesale undertaking; "the greater part of the money I gave to trustworthy merchants (*tujjār-i amīn*)", writes Rashīd al-Dīn in his will, "and they conduct their trade with this money, and I have written down their names in my

[1] Ibn Baṭṭūṭa, vol. II, p. 78.

[2] *Aflākī*, trans. Huart, pp. 7–9, 15.

[3] *Nuzhat al-qulūb*, p. 81.

[4] For more on the inner structure of the towns and corporations see A. K. S. Lambton, *Islamic Society in Persia*.

[5] See below, pp. 521–2.

account book".[1] In his letters Rashīd al-Dīn gives huge lists of goods, mostly textiles, and partly leather and fur goods, etc., which he had received from the merchants.[2] Such a rapprochement of some groups of feudalists with the large-scale merchants is a phenomenon typical of medieval Iran, as also of other lands of the Near and Middle East. Thus in contrast to Western Europe from the eleventh to the fifteenth centuries the merchants did not oppose the great feudal landowners, but made common cause with them against the craftsmen, the lower classes of the towns and the local peasantry.[3]

The town authorities—*ra'īs* (mayor), *qāḍī* (the religious judge and head of the religious estate in the area), *khaṭīb* (the imam of the mosque meeting), *muḥtasib* (the censor of morals supervising bazaars, social life, and morals of the citizens), and others—came from the local patriciate. Often they inherited their positions. As did the family of the Qāḍīyān in Shīrāz, the Mustaufīyān in Qazvīn[4] and the Juvainīyān in Khurāsān.[5] The writer of these lines analysed the information given by Ḥamd Allāh Qazvīnī concerning the aristocratic families of his native town of Qazvīn in order to give an idea of the nature of the urban nobility of his time.[6] It appears that despite the fact that on 7 Sha'bān 717/7 October 1220 the Mongols had carried out a "wholesale massacre",[7] many of the local noble families survived or were spared. Of the 28 families mentioned by the author 25 had settled in Qazvīn long before the Mongol conquest,[8] and only three (one of Mongol, one of Turkish, and one of Persian origin) again distinguished themselves in the service of the Mongol Īl-Khāns. These families possessed estates in the district of Qazvīn and carried out state and religious duties.[9]

[1] *Mukātibāt-i Rashīdī*, p. 238 (no. 36). [2] *Ibid.* pp. 183–93 (no. 34), 282–9 (no. 47).

[3] See Barthold, *K istorii krestyanskikh dvizheniy v Persii*, pp. 61–2.

[4] The hereditary heads of the financial administration of the district. From this family came the historian and geographer Ḥamd Allāh Mustaufī Qazvīnī (approx. 1280–1350).

[5] From these came the ṣāḥib-dīvān Shams al-Dīn Muḥammad Juvainī and his brother 'Alā' al-Dīn 'Aṭā-Malik Juvainī.

[6] *Ta'rīkh-i guzīda*, Persian text, pp. 842–9; abridged English translation, pp. 233–6. More detail in I. Petrushevsky, *Gorodskaya znat' v gosudarstve Hulaguidov*, pp. 88–96.

[7] Dramatically described by Ḥamd Allāh Qazvīnī in his *Ẓafar-nāma*; see text in E. G. Browne, *LHP*, vol. III, pp. 96–8.

[8] Amongst this ancient aristocracy outstanding were the Zākānīyān, from whom stemmed the poet 'Ubaid-i Zākānī (died 1371) and the Ghaffārīyān, from whom sprang the Shāfi'ite theologian Najm al-Dīn 'Abd al-Ghaffār (died 1267), and the theologian of the sixteenth-century, Aḥmad Ghaffārī.

[9] Ṣadr al-Dīn Khālidī was the grand vizier under Geikhatu; for more than sixty years, from 651 = 1253/4, the maliks of Qazvin were by inheritance of the Iftikhārīyān family.

Noble families owned large estates with servants and slaves, suburban gardens, and sometimes whole quarters, in the towns. The enormous quarter or rather suburb rebuilt by Rashīd al-Dīn in Tabrīz, belonging to him by right of unconditional ownership (*mulk*), is described not without boasting in his letter to his son Sa'd al-Dīn, the governor of Qinnisrīn and 'Awāṣim.[1] In this quarter (Rub'-i Rashīdī) he claims that there were 30,000 homes (= families),[2] 24 caravansarais, 1,500 shops, bath-houses, gardens, mills, workshops for weaving (*sha'r-bāfī*) and papermaking (*kāghadh-sāzī*), a dye-works (*rangraz-khāna*), a mint (*dār al-ḍarb*), etc. Rashīd al-Dīn brought tradesmen (*ṣanā'ī va muḥtarafa*) from a variety of towns to his suburb, and asked his son to send 50 wool-weavers (*ṣūf-bāfān*) from Antioch and Cilicia, and 20 from Cyprus. Four-hundred theologians and lawyers were settled here in the "quarter of the learned" (*kūcha-yi 'ulamā'*), and there were 1,000 students (*ṭālib-i 'ilm*).[3] Fifty of the best doctors of Syria, Egypt, India, and China (oculists, surgeons, bonesetters) worked in the hospital (*dār al-shifā*), and so on. In Hamadān Rashīd al-Dīn had his own quarter with 1,500 houses. Nobles, mosques, theological academies or madrasas, and religious bodies owned by right of mulk or vaqf caravansarais, bazaars, and shops, which they leased for rent and from which they derived income.

In medieval Iran there were four fundamental centres of social life in a town: the *shahristān* and the quarters of the patriciate; the madrasas, the *khānqāhs* of the dervishes, and other religious institutions together with religious corporations and dervish brotherhoods; the bazaar centre (Persian *chārsū*, Arabic *murabba'a*), together with the caravansarais, big merchants, and wholesale trade; and the quarters of the craftsmen, and their corporations (Arabic *ṣinf*, plural *aṣnāf*), the lesser bazaars with their petty retail trade. Wares were sold by craftsmen in the workshops, the latter also serving as shops (*dukkān* in Arabic). Most often but not always craftsmen of one and the same trade lived in the same quarter; in every town there were quarters occupied by silk-weavers, cotton-carders, shoemakers, saddlemakers, dyers, potters, etc.

The sources are meagre concerning the craftsmens' corporations.[4] Ibn Baṭṭūṭa mentions them, saying that the Iṣfahān craftsmen elected

[1] *Mukātibāt-i Rashīdī*, pp. 315–27 (no. 51).

[2] *Ibid.* p. 318: سی هزار خانه; سی "thirty" is perhaps a mistake for سه "three".

[3] *Ibid.* pp. 318–20; apart from the 1,000 students mentioned there were another 6,000 supported by Rashīd al-Dīn who studied in Tabrīz itself.

[4] Concerning the corporations see A. K. S. Lambton, *Islamic Society in Persia*, pp. 17 ff.

elders from amongst themselves (*al-kulū*, Persian *kulū*, *kulūi*).[1] He also mentions guilds of craftsmen in Shīrāz. In the sources rank is mentioned: *ustād* "master", *khalīfa* "apprentice",[2] and *shāgird* "pupil", apprentice. The craft guilds in the towns of Iran were much weaker than the guilds of western Europe. They could not obtain a corporative monopoly nor could they fix the price of their products to their greatest satisfaction, as was the case in western Europe. A connexion is traceable between the craft guilds and the dervish brotherhoods.[3] In literature there is more than one mention of the connexion between the corporations and the movement of the *futuwwa*—the unions of the ākhīs.[4] The ākhīs are also mentioned in the towns of the fourteenth century,[5] but there is no information concerning a connexion between them and the guilds. There were also corporations of declassé indigent elements (*'ayyārān*)[6] and guilds of beggars (*sāsānīyān* or *sāsiyān*).[7]

Corporate craftsmen were freemen although they had to give part of their produce to the treasury or to the local landowner, and take part without recompense in the construction of public buildings and in the decoration of the city for festivals organized by the authorities. But there were also unfree craftsmen working in the towns of Iran and Central Asia under the Mongols. At the time of the Mongol invasion many craftsmen were turned into slaves; some of them (for example

[1] Ibn Baṭṭūṭa, vol. II, p. 45.

[2] Ethnological investigation of Central Asian craft guilds show that there were thought to be two ranks in the corporations—apprentice (*shāgird*) and master (*ustād*); *khalīfa* was the title of a person who had qualified as a master but who did not have the means to start his own *dukkān* and who worked for another craftsman. When a *khalīfa* was able to start his own workshop he required no new initiation. The initiation of a master necessitated a threefold act: the reading of the first *sura* of the Qur'ān, the tying on of a belt (*kamarbandī*), and a ritual feast, called *arvāḥ-i pīr*. See, for example, E. M. Peshchereva, *Goncharnoe proizvodstvo v Srednei Azii* (Moscow, 1959), pp. 313–72. The Persian guilds are first mentioned in the Georgian hagiographic source of the sixth century —*The Life of St Eustaphius of Mtskheta*.

[3] Aflākī, translated by Huart, p. 117, says that during the lifetime of Jalāl al-Dīn Rūmī the greater part of the dervishes of the Maulavī order consisted of craftsmen and poor people; the life of Ṣafī al-Dīn also mentions many murīd craftsmen of the Shaikh Ṣafī al-Dīn (*Ṣafvat al-ṣafā*, *passim*).

[4] Ibn Baṭṭūṭa, vol. II, pp. 260–5.

[5] *Ṣafvat al-ṣafā*, ff. 54*b*, 142*b*, 155*b*, 163*b*, 332*b*, 353*b*, 484*b*, 497*b*, 497*a*, etc.

[6] A. K. S. Lambton, *op. cit.* pp. 117 f., and for the *Akhavi* and the *Futuwwa* Vl. Gordlevsky, *Gosudarstvo Sel'dzhukov Maloi Azii*, pp. 103–106; see also the bibliography of the subject in the latter work.

[7] Legend connected the creation of a guild of beggars with the descendants of the Sassanids (see the *Burhān-i Qāṭi'* under ساسان Sāsān). Regarding the Sāsīyān and their secret language or argot see the *qaṣida* of Abū Dulaf (tenth century; Tha'ālibī, *Yatīmat al-Dahr*, Damascus, 1304, vol. III, pp. 179–94) and the manuscript of the fourteenth century in the *Kitāb-i Sāsīyān*.

the silkweavers of Herāt) were taken to Mongolia, some remained in Iran and worked in special large workshops (*kār-khāna*) belonging to the treasury, or the Īl-Khānid family, and so on. Rashid al-Dīn mentions kār-khānas in Khabūshān, Nīshāpūr, Ṭūs, Isfarā'in, Tabrīz;[1] Vaṣṣāf speaks of kār-khānas and craftsmen belonging to individual Chingizids in Bukhārā and Samarqand;[2] whilst Saifī mentions a kār-khāna in Herāt.[3] It is evident from a decree of Ghazan that craftsmen working in such large workshops—saddlers, tanners, armourers, etc.—were slaves (*asīrān*), and received no wages in money. Payment was in kind, but most of this payment was stolen by officials running the workshops. The whole product of the enslaved craftsmen went to the Dīvān. Since such labour was not very productive, Ghazan put the craftsmen on a fixed tax, after paying which the slaves could work for themselves.[4]

A general phenomenon of the Iranian economy during the Īl-Khān period was the decline of commodity economy (which remained in the areas near the main caravan routes and the large towns) and the growth of natural economy. Taxes from agricultural districts were mostly paid in kind—primarily in grain.[5] And although the geographical work of Ḥamd Allāh Qazvīnī shows taxes in money, it is evident from a list of taxes from Khūzistān quoted by Rashīd al-Dīn in a letter to his son Shihāb al-Dīn, ruler of Khūzistān, that the basic tax—the land tax—was paid in kind, in the form of grain and as a share of the crop.[6] The wages (*mavājib*) and pensions (*marsūmāt*) of the military caste, theologians, shaikhs and others were mostly paid in kind—in the form of wheat, barley, rice, cattle, etc.[7] In one of his letters Rashīd al-Dīn gives a list of fruits which his estates were to supply him with for the winter. The estates, lying in different parts of the country, had to send 50,000 *mans* of grapes, 62,000 *mans* of pomegranates, 37,000 *mans* of apples, 5,900 *mans* of raisins, 4,500 *mans* of fine raisins (*kishmish*), 9,000 *mans* of pears, 7,000 *mans* of quince, 100,000 *mans* of dates, 200,000 oranges, 20,000 lemons and other fruits and fruit-juices.[8] The fact that Rashīd al-Dīn did not buy this mass of fruit on the spot at his

[1] *Jāmiʿ al-tawārīkh*, ed. Alizade, pp. 30, 179, 414.

[2] Vaṣṣāf, pp. 67, 68; see *ibid.* p. 51, concerning the dependants (craftsmen?) of the Chingizids in Bukhara; analysis of text in I. Petrushevsky, *Iz istorii Bukharï v XIII v.*, pp. 114–17.

[3] Saifī, p. 285.

[4] *Jāmiʿ al-tawārīkh*, ed. Alizade, pp. 542–5.

[5] *Jāmiʿ al-tawārīkh*, ed. Alizade, pp. 474–5; *Mukātibāt-i Rashīdī*, pp. 122–3 (no. 22); cf. *ibid.* p. 121: "with the stipulation that they be paid in kind."

[6] *Ibid.*

[7] *Ibid.* pp. 252–6 (no. 41), 265–72 (no. 45).

[8] *Ibid.* pp. 198–206 (no. 34).

winter residence in Tabrīz, but brought it from distant regions, shows that the historian-minister extracted feudal rent from his estates primarily in kind.

FEUDAL RELATIONSHIPS. THE CATEGORIES OF LANDOWNERSHIP

The Mongol conquest had a great and in general evil influence on the economic development of Iran; it had much less influence on the social structure of the country. The most typical features of specifically Iranian feudalism antedating the conquest survived it also. Such were the outstanding importance of irrigation; the coexistence of settled agriculture and nomadic and semi-nomadic cattle-breeding; the absence of demesne and *corvée* in the villages; the combination of large-scale feudal landownership with small-scale peasant tenants; the predominance of product rent (money and labour rent had only secondary importance); the growth of the military fief system; the close connexion between the big merchants and the caravan trade and a group of feudal lords, and even their coalescence; the absence of self-governing towns, so typical of western Europe in the Middle Ages; and the widespread use of slave labour in the crafts and agriculture (irrigation and market gardening) alongside the exploitation of the labour of dependent peasants. Rashīd al-Dīn employed 1,000 (500 men and 500 women) and 200 (100 men and 100 women) enslaved prisoners (*asīrān va ghulāmān*) respectively in the great gardens Fatḥābād and Rashīdābād near Tabrīz—Georgians, negroes, Abyssinians, Greeks and Kurds (?), who "showed zeal in the planting of the vine and of fruit trees, in the digging of channels underground (*qanavāt*) and on the surface (*anhār*), in the watering and gathering of fruit".[1]

The governing class of feudal lords consisted of four main groups: (1) the military aristocracy of the nomad tribes—Mongol, Turkish, Kurd, etc.; (2) the settled local provincial nobility, not connected by service with the central government; (3) the civil service; (4) the Muslim religious caste, more exactly the theologians. The last three groups were primarily composed of Iranians. These feudal groups, who struggled with one another to control the State, expressed two parallel political tendencies in Iranian society—that of feudal disintegration together with a system of military fiefs, and that of a centralized feudal state

[1] *Mukātibāt-i Rashīdī*, p. 53 (no. 17); cf. *ibid.* pp. 194–5 (no. 34), 236 (no. 36).

together with a ramifying bureaucratic apparatus. Opposed to this class of exploiters was the principal exploited class—the settled peasantry. The nomads were also exploited by their nomad feudal lords, but on a much smaller scale. The nomad feudalists exploited not only the nomads subject to them, but also the settled peasants who dwelt on their fiefs. Along with the class division there existed that of estates:[1] "people of the sword" (*ahl-i shamshīr*—the first two groups mentioned), "people of the pen" (*ahl-i qalam*—the last two groups of feudalists mentioned), and the taxable estate or the *ra'iyyat* (Arabic *ra'āyā*, plural of *ra'iyyat*, literally "herd" or "flock")—the peasants and townspeople. This latter division of the population, not reflected in Muslim law, was evidently a survival from the Sassanian period, when society was divided into soldiers, priests, clerks, and the taxable people, composed of peasants, craftsmen and merchants.

The old categories of feudal landownership long recognized by Muslim law (to be more explicit, conditional and unconditional ownership of land and water, i.e. irrigation works) continued to exist under the Īl-Khāns: (1) State lands (Arabo-Persian *arāḍī-yi dīvānī*); (2) the private demesne of the Īl-Khān and the members of his family (Arabic *khāṣṣa*, Mong. synonym *injü*); (3) the lands of the religious and charitable institutions (*arāḍī-yi vaqfī*); (4) the lands of private persons belonging to them by unconditional right, Arabic *mulk*, *milk*, Arabo-Persian *arāḍī-yi mālikī*, *arbābī*), corresponding to the western European allodium.

A peculiarity of State ownership of land was that the State itself exploited its tenants—the village communes (*jamā'at-i dīh*)—by means of finance officials (*'ummāl*). In this case the notions of rent and tax coincided, and the rents or taxes (the land-tax, etc.), paid in cash and kind to the State by the tenants, were then distributed amongst the military caste as wages, pensions, subsidies, gifts, etc. The abundance of state-owned lands was a characteristic of Asiatic feudalism. In the time of the caliphate such land was absolutely predominant in Arab 'Irāq, in Egypt, and possibly in certain areas of Iran, but by no means in all. In Fārs for example privately-owned lands (*mulk*) prevailed until the tenth century.[2] After the Mongol conquest the area of the Dīvān lands greatly increased at first as a result of confiscations or the exter-

[1] By class is understood union on the basis of attitude towards production and by estate union on a legal basis.

[2] Ibn al-Balkhī, *Fārs-Nāma*, pp. 171–2; cf. Istakhri, p. 158.

mination of the previous owners. But afterwards under the Īl-Khāns the greater part of these lands were converted into private property, unconditionally (*mulk*) or conditionally (*iqṭā'*),[1] by means of payment, sale,[2] or seizure.

If the income of the Dīvān lands was spent on the upkeep of the State apparatus and the army, the income from khāṣṣa properties (*injü*) was spent on the upkeep of the Īl-Khān, of his legal wives (*khatun*), of his sons, and of their residences (*ordu*). These lands were under the control of a special ministry—the *dīvān-i īnjū*. Often injü and state-owned lands were leased.[3] Lands belonging to the ruling house (*injü*) were distinguished from lands belonging to the Īl-Khān himself (*īnjū-yi khāṣṣ*, *mulk-i pādshāh*).[4] Rent coincided with tax in these lands also. By the term *injü* was understood not only the land, but also the people living on the land, both peasants and landowners, who were personally dependent on the Īl-Khān, his wives or sons, on the basis of commendation (Arabic *iltijā*) and patronage (Arabic *iljā*, *ḥimāyat*).[5]

The injü land fund was composed of lands confiscated from the Iranian nobility after the Mongol conquest and of lands granted to members of the Īl-Khānid family by the previous owners.[6] This fund was extremely large. The lands of Ghazan himself amounted to 20,000 *faddāns* (plough-strips),[7] that is to 120,000–140,000 hectares of irrigated land. The injü land of Fārs district was leased for four years in 682/1292–3 for the sum of 10,000,000 dīnārs, i.e. for 2,500,000 dīnārs a year. If we consider that State taxes from Fārs (from dīvān and mulk land) were 2,871,200 dīnārs,[8] we can conclude that the injü lands of Fārs gave a slightly smaller income than all the remaining lands. According to the *Risāla-yi Falakiyya*, the overall income from the lands of the khāṣṣa (injü) amounted to 12,434,220$\frac{5}{6}$ dīnārs per annum.[9]

A certain kind of land mentioned in the sources was called *khāliṣāt* ("clean lands", i.e. those free of taxes payable to the dīvān). Nowadays in Iran the term signifies precisely lands belonging to the Dīvān or the State. But in the period under consideration, as is obvious from the

[1] See for more about this A. A. Alizade, *Zemel'naya Politika Ilkhānov*, pp. 5–23.

[2] Thus under Arghun, the governor of Rūm, Fakhr al-Dīn Aḥmad Arkūshī sold State land (*amlāk-i dīvānī*) to men of standing (*arbāb-i manāṣib*), and most of the land in Rūm became thereby *mulk* (*Ta'rīkh-i Guzīda*, p. 485).

[3] Vaṣṣāf, pp. 231, 268, 317, 336, 404, etc.

[4] See A. A. Alizade *K voprosu ob institute inju*, p. 98.

[5] See Quatremère, *Histoire des Mongols de la Perse*, pp. 130–2, n. 12; Alizade, *op. cit.* pp. 95–108.

[6] *Jāmi' al-tawārīkh*, ed. Alizade, p. 479.

[7] Vaṣṣāf, p. 349.

[8] *Ibid.* p. 268.

[9] See above, p. 499.

explanations of Vaṣṣāf and Rashīd al-Dīn,[1] this name was given to ruined and deserted land (*kharāb u bā'īr*) which was leased to landowner tenants (*tānī* pl. *tunnā'* in both authors) under a decree of Ghazan,[2] on condition that it was restored and occupied again, and that part of the kharāj was paid in the form of a share of the crop (*muqāsama*). Conditions of ownership were favourable to the tenants. These lands formed a separate part of the ruler's lands (*khāṣṣa-yi pādshāhī*) under the administration of a special *dīvān-i khāliṣāt* which made contracts with landowner tenants.

The character of the *vaqf* as an institution, and therefore of vaqf landowning also, suffered no change under the Īl-Khāns. Inasmuch as the expenditure of vaqf income was limited by conditions laid down by legators, vaqf land may be regarded as a conditional form of feudal landowning. The income of owners of vaqf land did not only come from the exploitation of land and peasants, but also from canals, bazaars, shops, bathhouses, mills and other items of income which were leased for a money rent (Arabic *ijāra*). Owners of vaqf land paid nothing to the Dīvān, since they had tax immunity. The vaqf constituted the main source of income for dervish shaikhs and theologians. A whole body of religious persons and their servants lived on the income of each large vaqf, receiving from its curator (*mutavallī*) pensions (*marsūmāt*) partly in money but mainly in kind (bread or grain, rice, meat, soap, cloths, etc.), as is shown by the list of expenditure of the vaqf set up by Ghazan in Baghdad.[3] After the Mongol conquest many vaqf estates were seized by the "despoilers" (Arabic *mutaghalliba*)—the Mongols. But under the Muslim Īl-Khāns vaqf landownership expanded and formed a large part of the land fund.

By *mulk*, *milk*, or *arbābī* is meant a feudal institution completely analogous to the western European allodium: the full ownership by the landowner (*malik*) of land and water (channel or *kārīz*), unconditional and without obligation of service to the State, free to be sold and bequeathed. *Mulk* or *milk* denoted small-scale peasant landownership as well, providing the land did not belong to the commune. Mulk land as a rule paid land tax to the dīvān but mostly paid a tenth (Arabic *'ushr*, Persian *dah-yak*) and not the kharāj. It is evident from the correspondence of Rashīd al-Dīn that the arbābī regions of Iṣfahān and

[1] Vaṣṣaf, pp. 349, 389, 445; *Jāmi' al-tawārikh*, ed. Alizade, pp. 556–9.
[2] *Ibid.* pp. 559–63.
[3] *Mukātibāt-i Rashīdī*, pp. 34–40 (no. 14).

Khūzistān were obliged to pay a tenth part of the harvest (*'ushr*) in kind (*bi-jins*).[1] But there were also "free" mulks (*mulk-i ḥurrī*) with fiscal immunity.[2]

Military fiefs were formally accounted a part of the State lands—iqṭā'. But in fact they were a form of conditional private property, equivalent to the Western fiefs, with fiscal immunity and the transfer to the fief-holder (Arabic *muqṭa'*, Arabo-Persian *iqṭā'-dār*) of the right to collect the taxes for himself. Thus tax was the same as rent on these lands and the land tax and other taxes benefited the iqṭā'-dār. The feudal institution of the iqṭā' had evolved from the tenth century, from the time of the Umayyads, up to the time of the Saljuqs. It changed from a peculiar kind of free benefice (a grant by the State to a member of the military caste of the right to collect for himself the kharāj, the 'ushr, the *jizya* from a certain fixed territory great or small for the period of service or for life; in which case the taxes became rent) into a military fief or grant of land with the people on it, which was already usually hereditary in the tenth century.[3] Under the Saljuqs the hereditary iqṭā' had become the general rule, but this practice apparently only became established in law under Ghazan. From the time of the Saljuqs the iqṭā' became the specific form of domination by the Turkish, and, from the thirteenth century, by the Mongol-Turkish nomad military aristocracy, of the Iranian farmers settled on the iqṭā' lands.[4]

Under the Saljuqs iqṭā' land was very common in Iran.[5] Under the first six Īl-Khāns also iqṭā' land was granted to the military,[6] but not to all soldiers, the grants being mainly to the higher ranks. The mass of ranker soldiers, mostly nomads, received only wages in kind (grain), and some money under the name of *jāmagī*. Under Ghazan iqṭā' fiefs were given to all Mongols who were warriors of the general levy, and according to Rashīd al-Dīn whole regions became iqṭā' "in every *vilāyat*". Ḥamd Allāh Qazvīnī locates iqṭā' land in Āzarbāījān, Arrān,

[1] *Mukātibāt-i Rashīdī*, pp. 33 (no. 13), 121–3 (no. 22).

[2] Nāṣir al-Dīn Ṭūsī, pp. 760–1.

[3] See Cl. Cahen, *Evolution de l'iqta' du IX au XIII siècle.*

[4] Concerning the *iqṭā'* and other categories of landownership in Iran under the Īl-Khāns see: B. Spuler, *Die Mongolen in Iran*, 2nd ed. (Berlin, 1955), pp. 327–32; A. M. Belenitsky, "K voprosu o sotsial'nïkh otnosheniyakh v Irane v Hulaguidskuyu epokhu", *Sovetskoe Vostokovedenie*, vol. v (1948), pp. 112–15; A. K. S. Lambton, *Landlord and Peasant in Persia* (London, 1953), pp. 53–104; A. A. Alizade, *Sotsialno-ekonomicheskaya istoria Azerbaijana v XIII–XIV vv.* (Baku, 1956), pp. 135–92; I. P. Petrushevsky, *Zemledelie i agrarnïe otnosheniya v Irane XIII–XIV vv.* (1960), pp. 233–83.

[5] Rāvandī, pp. 130–1.

[6] Juvainī, vol. 1, p. 23; transl. Boyle, vol. 1, p. 32.

Shīrvān and Khurāsān,[1] which is completely explained by the fact that the main summer (*yailaq*) and winter (*qïshlaq*) camps of the Mongol and Turkish tribes forming the backbone of the Īl-Khānid army were there. Cultivated land with settled peasants near to nomad camps was given as iqṭāʿ.

Ghazan's decree of the year 703/1303, dealing with the apportionning of iqṭāʿ land amongst the Mongol levy, was formally an act of beneficence on the part of the Īl-Khān, but was in fact made necessary by the pressing importunity of the army, about which Rashīd al-Dīn speaks. This explains the publication of this decree, which was in contradiction to the general centralizing policy of Ghazan and stimulated thereafter the growth of feudal distintegration. According to the decree, a certain fixed area was granted in fief to the amīr of a thousand, i.e. to the leader of a branch of the Mongol tribe who provided the army with a thousand horsemen. The amīr of a thousand divided this amongst the amīrs of hundreds by sortition (casting lots with a whip). In the same way amīrs of hundreds divided land amongst amīrs of tens, and these did likewise amongst the rankers. All of the soldiers received a large portion by right of iqṭāʿ—a village or part of a village—and the amīrs received correspondingly more. The ownership of iqṭāʿ was conditional upon doing military service; the iqṭāʿ could be taken back upon execution of poor service. In accordance with the decree iqṭāʿ lands were to be inherited, but not necessarily by the son, but by whomsoever of the family could best carry out military service. The sense of the decree indicates that taxes which were previously paid to the dīvān could now be collected as a right by the landowner himself (apart from a small tax of 50 mans of grain). Thus the possessor of iqṭāʿ land had fiscal immunity but not administrative immunity. The inspector of the dīvān of the army—*bītīkchī-yi ʿāriḍ*—was required every year to carry out an inspection of iqṭāʿ lands and to take back the fiefs of those who had failed to do their military service or did not care to cultivate their land.[2] The decree gives the rights of fief-holder in respect of peasants living on the iqṭāʿ lands.[3] This decree firmly established the caste-hierarchical system of military fiefs.

Jalayirid charters (of Sulṭān Uvais) granting iqṭāʿ to an amīr of a *tümen*,[4] an amīr of a thousand, and a lower rank, possibly an amīr of a

[1] *Nuzhat al-qulūb*, pp. 82, 92, 93, 147.

[2] *Jāmiʿ al-tawārīkh*, ed. Alizade, pp. 508–17.

[3] See below, pp. 522ff.

[4] Military-administrative district capable of providing approximately 10,000 men.

hundred,[1] have come down to us. In these decrees there is also talk of the granting of a whole district to the complete control (*taṣarruf*) of a grantee. The terms *jāmagī* and *iqṭā'* are here used as synonyms. Along with a clearly expressed fiscal immunity the iqṭā'-dār also received the right of administrative immunity, with a prohibition against officials of the Dīvān entering upon immune territory, set apart (*mafrūz*) from the vilāyat and not subordinate to local authority.[2] Thus we have here a further evolution of the iqṭā'.

Apart from the fiefs of the military nobility (*iqṭā'*) there existed conditional grants of land and rent to members of the bureaucracy and the religious bodies. The grant for life of rent in kind (corn, barley, rice) or money was called *ma'īshat* (Arabic literally "livelihood") and when granted into heredity (*maurūth*) or when it was "eternal" (*abadī*) it was called *idrār* (literally "pension"). Often such a grant was replaced by the grant of a village of the Dīvān, the income (= amount of taxes) from which equalled the sum of the ma'īshat or the *idrār*. This kind of grant was called the *muqāṣṣa* and was either for life (*muqāṣṣa-yi ma'-'īshat*) or for eternity (*muqāṣṣa-yi idrār*).[3] It is clearly evident from the charters of Sulṭān Uvais that the owner of muqāṣṣa lands not only had fiscal immunity but also administrative immunity. The latter is expressed in the formula (which is met with in the charters of the fifteenth and sixteenth centuries): "Let them [the officials of the Dīvān] make brief and remove quills and feet"[4] (that is, let them not carry on correspondence nor trespass on immune land).

Further development of the iqṭā' led to the *soyurghal* (Mong. literally "grant")—a military fief which appeared under the Jalayirids, was hereditary, and had fiscal and administrative immunity.[5] After the middle of the fourteenth century the term *soyurghal* had replaced *iqṭā'*. The latter term is encountered thereafter from time to time in narrative sources as an archaic and bookish expression ordinarily signifying soyurghal. The sources do not bear out the opinion expressed earlier that the soyurghal was introduced into Iran by Tīmūr.

Pasture lands can be distinguished as a special category of land. The nomads—Mongol, Turkish, Lur and Arab—utilized it for their summer

[1] *Dastūr al-kātib*, ff. 182*b*–183*b*. [2] *Ibid.*

[3] *Ibid.* ff. 221*b*–223*b*; for more about the *idrār* see also Nāṣir al-Dīn Ṭūsī, p. 760; Juvainī, vol. II, p. 277; Vaṣṣāf, p. 453; *Mukātibāt-i Rashīdī*, pp. 255–6 (no. 41).

[4] *Dastūr al-kātib*, f. 22*b*.

[5] See: V. Minorsky, *A Soyūrghāl of Qāsim Āq-Qāyūnlū*; A. M. Belenitsky, *K istorii feodalnogo zemlevladeniya . . .*; I. P. Petrushevsky, "K istorii instituta soyurgāla", *Sovetskoe Vostokovedenie*, vol. VI (1949), pp. 227–46.

camps in high mountainous regions and for their winter camps in the plains, with great distances between. Such pasture was normally designated by the terms *yurt* (Turkish) or *'alaf-khwār* (Arabo-Persian, literally "pasture").[1]

The iqṭā', soyurghal, or yurt could encompass territory great or small and could include the land of landowners lower in rank (e.g. the iqṭā' land of an amīr of a thousand contained the lands of ranks subordinate to him). Both this system and the confusion of the concepts of state-owned land and the feudal estate which we find in the sources were in general typical of feudal societies with their hierarchic disintegrated form of property.

As we have said, private ownership, both conditional (*iqṭā'*) and unconditional (*mulk*), greatly expanded at the expense of state-ownership under the last Īl-Khāns.[2] A general feature of this process was the concentration of land in the hands of great landowners. There were various ways in which this occurred: the granting of land by the Īl-Khāns, law-suits (in respect of land the title-deeds of which had been lost),[3] purchase (*mulk*-land), and often straightforward seizure by the strong. The term *mutaghallib*, meaning "seizer of land", is often met with in the documents of the period. Already under the first two Īl-Khāns the powerful Shams al-Dīn Muḥammad Juvainī, taking advantage of his position, bought land (*mulk*) worth 40,000,000 dīnārs. The greater part of the estates of Rashīd al-Dīn consisted of mulks which he bought in small pieces scattered about various regions. One supposes that this land was bought in separate lots from small landowners driven by ruin to sell their lands. The historian-minister also possessed deserted and neglected land (*zamīnhā-yi kharāb u bā'ir*), which he had taken on the basis of Ghazan's decree granting all such lands to those who would cultivate them.[4] Lastly he derived income from vaqf lands of which he was the trustee (*mutavallī*).

From Rashīd al-Dīn's will it is evident that, beside those lands which he had given to his sons earlier, he intended to leave his sons and daughters, friends and trusted servants, 12,770 faddāns (plough-strips) of mulk ploughland, i.e. approx. 75–85,000 hectares of irrigated ploughland, and 39,000 date-palms in Arab 'Irāq and the southern

[1] See Quatremère, *Histoire des Mongols de la Perse*, p. 137 n. 12: "The sulṭān ordered every tribe to be given an *iqṭā'* and a *'alaf-khwār*."

[2] See Alizade, *Zemel'naya politika Il'khanov*; see reference to sources there as well.

[3] *Jāmi' al-tawārīkh*, ed. Alizade, pp. 446–50.

[4] *Mukātibāt-i Rashīdī*, pp. 14 (no. 6), 21 (no. 9), 22–3 (no. 10), 180–1 (no. 33).

regions of Iran. As well as this he bequeathed to them an enormous number of gardens (1,200 men and women were slaves in but two of them near Tabrīz), vineyards, 30,000 horses, 250,000 rams, 10,000 camels, and so on. Rashīd al-Dīn had elders of nomad tribes (*aḥsham*) pasture his cattle and used to give his poultry and geese to dependent peasants (*dahāqīn*) to be fed.[1] The Īl-Khān Abū Sa'īd presented the Shīrāzī qaḍī Majd al-Dīn Fālī with 100 settlements in the Fārs valley of Jamkān.[2]

THE PEASANTS UNDER THE ĪL-KHĀNS

As is well known, Moslem law did not recognize serfdom and a special category of serfs. It knew only of free Muslims, *dhimmis* (*ahl al-dhimma*); the heterodox, Christians, Jews, Zoroastrians—who were personally free but had limited civil rights; and finally the slave,[3] in principal a heterodox prisoner or the descendant of a heterodox prisoner. The taxable estate (*ra'āyā*)—peasants and townspeople—were formally regarded as personally free. *De facto* feudal dependence existed as a result of bondage to the soil, in virtue of which the State transferred populated land conditionally (*iqṭā'*, *vaqf*) or unconditionally (*mulk*) to the military caste and to the *faqīh*, together with the right to receive either wholly or in part the kharāj and other taxes, in which case tax became rent. Thus the relationship between the landowner and the peasant had the character not of personal but of territorial dependence. Niẓām al-Mulk said that the muqṭa' had no rights over the person (*tan*) of the peasant, nor over the members of his family, nor over his plot of land, nor over his household; he had only the right to collect the rent.[4] Such was the formal legal position of the peasant. Things were of course different in practice. As early as the twelfth century the owners of iqṭā' land exercised legal and police powers over their peasants. The confusion of administrative and State functions with the rights of the landowner was a feature typical of both Western and Eastern feudalism.

[1] *Mukātibāt-i Rashīdī*, pp. 224–40 (no. 36), 194–5 (no. 34), 53 (no. 17). See for more detail I. Petrushevsky, *Feodalnoe khozyaystvo Rashīd ad-dīna*.

[2] Ibn Baṭṭūṭa, vol. II, p. 61.

[3] In the period under consideration the words for slave were usually *ghulām*, *asīr* and *barda*. The terms '*abd* (Arabic) and *banda* (Persian) on the other hand were most often used in a different sense—"slave of God", or "humble servant". In the sources slaves are never confused with feudal bondsmen—the *ra'iyyat*.

[4] *Siyāsat-Nāma*, ed. Schefer, p. 28; ed. Khalkhāli, p. 22.

The self-government practised from ancient times by the village communes in Iran limited to an extent the arbitrary powers of the landowners and the financial officials in State lands. However, this communal self-government had begun to decay long before the Mongol conquest as a result of the inner stratification of the village commune already noticeable under the last Sassanians—the small landowners, the *diqhāns*, were then distinguished from the commune—and also as a result of the arbitrary practices of the financial officials and, after the Saljuq period, of the possessors of military fiefs. The village commune is rarely mentioned in the sources of the Mongol period and is usually called *jamā'at-i dīh*, *jamā'at-i qurā*, or *jamā'at-i ahālī-yi dīhhā*.[1] However we did not chance upon any material descriptive of life in the commune in the sources, although we are told here and there of conflicts and lawsuits between commune and landowner. We completely failed to find any mention of the periodic redistribution of land or about communal crop-rotation; it is evident that both had disappeared about the beginning of this period. The impression is created that the village commune was in a state of decline under the Mongols.

Before the thirteenth century we have no information that the feudal dependence of the peasants had taken the form of serfdom, with prohibition of travel. The binding of the peasants to the soil occurs apparently only after the Mongol conquest.[2] It was provoked primarily by the general economic decline of the country and by the catastrophic curtailment in the number of its inhabitants with the concomitant lack of workers and taxpayers on the land. There was now too much uncultivated and empty land and too few hands. In addition the fiscal policy of the conquerors and unbridled lawlessness on their part drove the peasants to mass flight.[3] For these reasons the State and the feudal classes had a stake in prohibiting the right of movement of peasants and their forced return if they should flee. On the other hand the "Great Yasa" of Chingiz-Khān looked upon the dependence of the low-ranking Mongol warrior from his lord as a personal dependence. The Mongol warrior (*qarachu*) was considered a serf and was attached, but of course not to the soil, for this would not make sense amongst nomads, but to

[1] See *Ṣafwat al-ṣafā*, ff. 184*b*, 192*a*–192*b*, 196*a*, 325*a*, 469*a*, 474*b*; *Mukātibāt-i Rashīdī*, p. 236 (no. 36); *Dastūr al-kātib*, f. 51*a*.

[2] For more detail see I. Petrushevsky, *Zemledelie . . .*, pp. 324–39; references to sources and also literature on the question.

[3] See *Jāmi' al-tawārīkh*, ed. Alizade, pp. 458–9, 514; *Mukātibat-i Rashīdī*, pp. 12 (no. 5), 146 (no. 27); Saifī, p. 464; Ḥāfiẓ-i Abrū, *Dhail-i Jāmi' al-tawārīkh*, p. 20; *Dastūr al-kātib*, ff. 119*b* 120*a*, 167*a*–167*b*, 177*b*, 183*a*, 198*a*–198*b*, 200*a*, 229*a*.

the person of his hereditary lord, the nomad aristocrat. The Mongol conquerors attempted to extend this notion to include the Iranian raʿiyyat. The Yasa prohibited movement to another place under pain of death to "any man from a thousand, hundred, or ten", and forbade the concealing of fugitives.[1] And although this law only applied to soldiers of the Mongol levy at first, it produced the feudal attachment of the raʿiyyat, in so far as the Yasa was extended to them[2] and in so far as the basis of the Yasa was the principle of universal attachment to the service of the State. The Armenian historian Grigor of Akner relates how tax-payers who had run away from the place of their registration were captured, bound and whipped without mercy.[3] The Mongol view of the peasants as the personal property of the lord is recorded in a decree of Ghazan, in which it is clear that the fief-holders are speaking of their peasants: "They are given to us in the iqṭāʿ, they are our slaves."[4] This is a confusion of slaves with the raʿiyyat, previously impossible and inadmissible in Muslim law.

The decree of Ghazan concerning the military fiefs or iqṭāʿ confirms the previously existing attachment of peasants to the soil. Peasants who had fled from inhabited and deserted villages granted as iqṭāʿ were ordered to return to their former habitations, unless thirty years had elapsed from the time of their flight, or unless they were included in the tax lists (*qānūn*) of other vilāyats. All were forbidden to shelter fugitive raʿiyyat.[5] Another decree of Ghazan prohibited the further movement of peasants settled upon land.[6] Thus attachment to the soil had spread to all peasants.

At the same time the decrees of Ghazan of the period after his conversion to Islam must be regarded as an attempt at judicial compromise between the Yasa of Chingiz-Khān and Muslim law. The right of movement of peasants was denied, but they were treated as free in law. It was emphasized that landowners should not move the peasants from village to village arbitrarily and they were forbidden to call them slaves. The peasants were not attached to the landowner but to the place of registration, to the tax list of a given area. This tendency to compromise between the Mongol Yasa and Muslim law is characteristic of the whole of Ghazan's domestic policy. Of course the formal freedom of peasants was pure fiction in their actual situation without rights.

[1] Juvainī, vol. I, p. 24; trans. Boyle, vol. I, p. 32. [2] *Ibid.* p. 25.
[3] Grigor of Akner, ed. Blake and Frye, pp. 324–5.
[4] *Jāmiʿ al-tawārīkh*, ed. Alizade, p. 514.
[5] *Ibid.* [6] *Ibid.* ed. Alizade, vol. III, p. 562.

The attachment of peasants to the soil was also in existence under the Jalayirid sultans. Frequent orders for the search for peasants and their return to their former homes can be found in the documents collected in the *Dastūr al-kātib*.[1] One document mentions the return of fugitive ra'iyyat of the Hamadān vilāyat.[2] The reasons for flight given in these documents were the heaviness of the taxes, the arbitrary and illegal exactions of the local authorities, and sometimes the devastation of an area.

Quit-rent (*muzāra'a*) was the basic form of exploitation of the peasants in Iran both before and after the Mongol invasion. Peasants regarded as free in law depended on the landlord as tenants or subtenants, and in most cases hereditary tenants. The rent they paid was mostly feudal rent, a share of the crop, or in regions near to towns and there only, rent half in kind and half in money. The predominance of quit-rent was due to the fact that the landowners' own demesne was by and large absent from the economy. It is at least true that landlords did not possess, as a rule, their own grain-producing properties. Thus the peasants did not do the *corvée*. In so far as landowners still worked their own estates (gardens and virgin land—*bāqī*), they employed slave prisoners and not peasants.[3]

The five part division of the harvest between the landlord and the farmer (one part for the land, irrigation, draught animals, seed, and workmen) which exists at the present day is not mentioned in the medieval sources. Then also the share of the landowner (in other words, the feudal rent) varied according to local conditions and depended for its size on whether the tenant received from his landlord land only, or oxen, seed, and the benefits of his irrigation as well. The share of the landlord was designated by the term *ḥiṣṣa-yi māliki*, *bahra-yi mālikāna*.[4]

In general there was not a clear distinction between this rent and taxes. Both were either paid wholly to the State, as was the case on the land of the Dīvān where tax and rent were one; or to the Īl-Khān and his family, if the land was injü land; or wholly to the landlord on vaqfī, iqṭā', muqāṣṣa, and *mulk-i ḥurr* territory; or lastly income from

[1] See above p. 523, n. 2; see especially *Dastūr al-kātib*, f. 229*a* (three documents).

[2] *Ibid.* the first document.

[3] *Mukātibāt-i Rashīdī*, pp. 53 (no. 17), 236 (no. 36); *Jāmi' al-tawārīkh*, ed. Alizade, p. 513: "Let virgin land be worked by their slaves oxen, teams of draught animals, and with their seed."

[4] Vaṣṣāf, p. 630; *Dastūr al-kātib*, f. 151*b*.

land would be divided between the State as tax and the landlord as rent in fixed proportion on mulk and *khāliṣāt* land. What was this proportion? We have but little information on this point. We see from the tax regulations of Khūzistān that the Dīvān took 60 per cent of the harvest on state-owned land and 10 per cent from arbābī or mulk land in kind.[1] Assuming that the same amount was paid by the tenant on the latter land as on the former, we may conjecture that the landowner derived 50 per cent after the State's 10 per cent (*dah-yak*) had been paid to the dīvān, and that the peasant kept 40 per cent of his crop. We can suppose that the same applies to the Iṣfahān vilāyat where the dīvān took 10 per cent.[2] On khāliṣāt land in Arab Iraq however the tenant (*tānī*) had one-third of the crop, one-third was paid to the dīvān, and the subtenant farmer (*barzgar*) kept one-third for himself.[3]

Money rent existed in suburban regions near to large towns (money rent on land—*ijāra*); auxiliary forms of rent were the labour rent and rent in kind. Labour rent signified the forced labour of the ra'iyyat on behalf of the State or their landlords and consisted of irrigation work such as the digging of channels and kārīz and their periodic cleansing,[4] building work such as the construction of houses, palaces, fortress walls, etc.,[5] and the clearing of woodland for the plough in the lands near the Caspian.[6] The words used for this labour rent were *bīgār*, *shīgār*, and *ḥashar*.

The terms *akkār*, *muzāri'*, and *barzgar* meaning "farmer, sower", as the sources show, took on the sense of quit-rent tenant. The economic unit was *juft-i gāv*, literally a "team of oxen" (synonyms were *faddān*, *zauj*, and *pāgāv*). This term had a twofold technical sense: (1) a team of oxen together with light or heavy plough and ploughmen, the team often consisting of several pairs of beasts and sometimes as many as twelve; (2) a strip of land for ploughing which could be worked by one team in one season. The size of the *juft* or faddān varied in different

[1] *Mukātibāt-i Rashīdī*, pp. 121–3 (no. 22).

[2] *Ibid.* pp. 33–4 (no. 13).

[3] *Nuzhat al-qulūb*, p. 31; instead of بانی and بزرگ as in the edition of le Strange, should be تانی and برزگر.

[4] *Mukātibāt-i Rashīdī*, pp. 244–45 (no. 38; Rashīdī gathered together 20,000 *ra'iyat* from Jazīreh, Rūm, and Armenia in order to dig a canal), 246–7 (no. 39); compare *Rashaḥāt 'ayn al-ḥayāt*, p. 227 (3,000 peasants from the estates of Khwāja Aḥrār sent to clean channels).

[5] *Jāmi' al-tawārīkh*, ed. Alizade, p. 558; Kirakos transl. Brosset, p. 193; Saifī, pp. 440, 444, 739–472; cf. Juvainī, vol. 1, p. 20.

[6] Ẓahīr al-Dīn Mar'ashī, p. 413.

regions but an average would possibly be 6–7 hectares.[1] The juft normally included several peasant farms and served as the unit of taxation of the peasants.[2] It was a unit for fixing the returns—the injü estates of Ghazan in Fārs were leased at 61 dīnārs and 4 dāngs per annum from each faddān[3] and also as the unit for the distribution of compulsory labour amongst the peasants.[4]

The official acts rarely touch upon the condition of the peasants on privately owned estates and give meagre information. This is understandable since the State regarded the relationship between the peasant and his malik as the private affair of the latter; narrative sources rarely mention this subject. On the other hand we possess much information from the most varied sources concerning the condition of the peasants on injü and Dīvān land, and they all paint a dark picture. Ḥamd Allāh Qazvīnī gives us to understand that the position of the peasant was better on the estates of the private landowners (*arbāb*), and that they took care to preserve their own property. Managers of Dīvān and vaqf land, in which there was a rapid turnover, were in a hurry to get rich, and did not worry about the prosperity of their estates, with the result that they ruined them.[5] The poet Nīzārī in the seventies of the thirteenth century saw an estate (privately owned) in Kūhistān which had been deserted because of the oppression of a tyrant landlord.[6] The same poet gives the following description of the practice of collecting tax in kind (wine) in the same province. The tax collector (*muḥaṣṣil*) arrived at the village of Baidan and presented the elder (*mihtar-i dīh*) with an assignation (*barāt*) on 100 mans of wine. The elder announced that his village was ruined and that he did not have a single man of wine. He was given 200 blows with a stick, which only ceased when the hidden jars of wine were discovered.[7] Rashīd al-Dīn, speaking about the mass flight of peasants from their villages, continues: "When the tax collectors went around the locality, they found some villain or other who knew the houses, and at his direction discovered the people in corners, cellars, gardens, and ruins. If they could not find the men, they seized their wives. Driving them before them like a flock of sheep,

[1] See for calculations I. Petrushevsky, *Feodalnoe khozyaystvo Rashīd ad-dīna*, pp. 90–3; references and literature on the question.

[2] *Dastūr al-kātib*, f. 151*b*.

[3] Vaṣṣāf, p. 349.

[4] Rashaḥāt *'ayn al-ḥayāt*, pp. 227–8; *Silsilat an-nasab-i Safavīya*, pp. 113–14.

[5] *Tārīkh-i Guzīda*, pp. 485–6.

[6] *Dastūr-Nāma*, ed. Bertel's, pp. 65–6, *Vostochnï sbornik*, vol. 1 (1918).

[7] *Dastūr-Nāma*, pp. 67–8.

they brought them to the tax officials who had them hung up on ropes so that the wails and plaints of the women rose up to the heavens."[1] The same author relates that one of the landowners (*mallāk*) arrived at his village in Fīrūzābād in the region of Yazd to collect the rent and could find neither elder nor peasant: they had all fled. On the other hand he saw seventeen tax collectors, come with barāts to be met from the taxes of the village. They had managed to capture three ra'iyyat who had hidden in the steppe. They brought them back to the village and hung them on ropes to force them to tell where the other peasants were hidden, but they discovered nothing.[2] Rashīd al-Dīn wrote to his son Maḥmūd, governor of Kirmān, about the poverty-stricken condition of the peasants of the province of Bam, ruined and in flight because of the extortion and violence practised by the military.[3] Rent and taxes not only devoured a great part of the peasant's crops, but were often more than the peasant could pay, so that arrears (*baqāyā*)[4] mounted from year to year, and the peasant remained an eternal debtor. Tax-farming did more than a little to ruin the peasants, and this practice, called *muqāṭa'a* or *ḍamān*, remained in existence after the reign of Ghazan.[5] Tax-farmers were mainly nomad aristocrats,[6] local landlords, officials or moneylenders attempting to get as much out of the ra'iyyat as possible, and not caring if they drove them to total ruin. Rashīd al-Dīn and Vaṣṣāf give us much information concerning the malpractices and exactions of the tax-farmers.[7] The fiscal system established by the Mongols and tax-farming were primary reasons for the calamitous situation of the ra'iyyat, particularly the settled peasants, almost the majority of whom were on the verge of penury previous to Ghazan's reforms. The lawlessness and violence of the feudal lords, first and foremost, of the Mongol-Turkish nomad nobility and the military caste down to its lowest ranks, were causes no less important.[8] These are typified by the remarks of Ghazan, that "in the eyes of the governors and others even clods of earth call forth esteem, but the ra'iyyat do not" that "the rubbish on the roads was not trodden underfoot as were the ra'iyyat", and that the Iranian ra'iyyat were so demeaned and terrorized,

[1] *Jāmi' al-tawārīkh*, ed. Alizade, p. 458. [2] *Ibid.* p. 460.

[3] *Mukātibāt-i Rashīdī*, pp. 10–11 (no. 5).

[4] Juvainī, vol. II, pp. 223, 244, etc.; transl. Boyle, vol. II, pp. 487, 507–8.

[5] *Mukātibāt-i Rashīdī*, p. 269 (no. 45).

[6] *Jāmi' al-tawārīkh*, ed. Alizade, pp. 453, 468.

[7] *Jāmi' al-tawārīkh*, ed. Alizade, pp. 448–53, 468 476; Vaṣṣāf, pp. 231, 268 298–9, 302–3, 404, 436–9.

[8] *Jāmi' al-tawārīkh*, ed. Alizade, pp. 478–9, 567–9.

that were a fly to steal their bread, they would not dare oppose it.[1] These words show clearly the contrast between the fiction of freedom in law (in accordance with Moslem law) and the actual unprivileged and depressed position of the ra'iyyat.

THE FISCAL SYSTEM UNDER THE ĪL-KHĀNS

The fiscal system, like the whole Mongol system of government, was a monstrous and self-contradictory combination of methods introduced by the nomad conquerors (partly influenced by China—taxation per head of the population) and ancient Iranian traditions kept up by the 'Abbāsid caliphate. The Mongol fiscal system has attracted the attention of a number of investigators.[2] Nevertheless the meaning of certain terms used in taxation and the nature of the taxes they designated are still very often unclear and have not been determined. This is explained by the insufficiency and in some cases the vagueness of the sources, and also by the fact that one and the same term had a different meaning at different times and in different regions. The latter circumstance is evidently to be explained by the fact that the different areas had dissimilar fiscal regulations and traditions, whilst the tendency of Moslem lawyers to consider the tax system as a unified whole inclined them to use a common terminology for taxes that differed at times in various districts.

The sources mention about 45 terms for taxes and obligations of the Īl-Khān period that survived in part into the following period. Some of these terms are however synonyms. The majority of them were known before the Mongols, under the Saljuqs or even earlier. The tax system of the Mongols nonetheless weighed much more heavily upon the population of Iran than the fiscal systems of earlier epochs. This was because of the high, inexactly ascertained rates of tax and the arbitrary methods of collection practised by the authorities, and not because of the imposition of new taxes. (Rashīd al-Dīn and Vaṣṣāf note the practice of exacting one and the same tax several times in one year or exacting it several years in advance.) A final reason for this was the fact that a

[1] *Jāmi' al-tawārīkh*, ed. Alizade, pp. 469, 477.

[2] Besides the well-known work of d'Ohsson and the notes of Quatremère on his *Histoire des Mongols de la Perse*, see V. V. Barthold, *Persidskaya nadpis' na stene aniiskoi mecheti Manuche*; V. Minorsky, *A Soyūrghāl . . .*; V. Minorsky, *Fārs in 881 = 476*; B. Spuler, *Die Mongolen in Iran*, pp. 306–35; 'Abbās Iqbāl, *Ta'rīkh-i mufaṣṣal-i Irān*, vol. 1, pp. 285–307; A. K. S. Lambton, *Landlord and peasant in Persia*, pp. 102–4; A. A. Alizade, *Sotsialno-ekonomicheskaya i politicheskaya istoriya Azerbaidzhana XIII–XIV vv.*, pp. 198–253; I. P. Petrushevsky, *Zemledelie i agrarnïe otnosheniya v Irane XIII–XIV vv.*, pp. 340–402 (ch. VIII).

ruined country could not bear such a tax burden. The burden was made more heavy by tax-farming and by covering State expenditure with assignations (*barāt*, *ḥavāla*), payment of which was imposed on the ra'iyyat. Whilst it is true that both practices existed under previous rulers, they greatly expanded under the Mongols, and Ghazan's fiscal policy was only a palliative. The whole weight of the tax burden fell of course on the peasant ra'iyyat, and the lower and middle ranks of the town dwellers; the upper classes—"the people of the sword" and the "people of the pen" were either free from taxes or passed them on to the quit-rent peasants of their estates.

The main tax before the Mongol conquest was, as is known, the *kharāj*—the land tax. A new tax came into existence alongside it in the Mongol period, and in some cases replaced the kharāj. This was the *qubchur*. As Quatremère has shown,[1] the qubchur was at first only a tax on pasture land. *Qubchur* kept its original technical meaning of one out of every 100 head of cattle or 1 per cent amongst the Mongols under the Īl-Khāns,[2] from which it is evident that taxes paid by the nomads remained insignificant. But shortly after the Mongol conquest the Mongol authorities began to use the word *qubchur*, a term familiar to them, to designate the basic direct tax paid by town and country dwellers. Thus the qubchur meant two basically distinct taxes: the 1 per cent paid by the nomads; and the tax on the settled population, which, as can be seen from Juvainī and Rashīd al-Dīn, was paid in money even after Ghazan's reforms, and must have been very difficult for the peasants to pay, since they had to sell their grain to raise the money. The nature of the qubchur remains far from clear. The opinion has been expressed that the qubchur paid by the settled population corresponds to the kharāj, but this has not been proved, as is shown by Minorsky.[3] It has also been shown that in some areas only one of the taxes was collected—the qubchur in one, the kharāj in another.[4] Indeed Rashid al-Dīn mentions "qubchur regions" (*vilāyāt-i qubchūrī*);[5] in other vilāyats, for example Khūzistān, only the kharāj was exacted.[6] But there were regions like Fārs where both the qubchur and the kharāj were paid.[7] It is not known what the basis of the distinction was.

[1] See Quatremère, *op. cit.* p. 256 n. 83; compare B. Vladimirtsov, *Obshchestvennii stroi mongolov*, p. 112.

[2] Naṣīr al-Dīn Ṭūsī, p. 761; *Dastūr al-kātib*, ff. 201*b*, 226*a*.

[3] *A Soyūrghāl of Qasim Aq-Qoyunlu*, p. 955 n. 2.

[4] A. A. Alizade, *op. cit.* p. 204.

[5] *Jāmi' al-tawārīkh*, ed. Alizade, p. 461.

[6] *Mukātibāt-i Rashīdī*, pp. 122–3 (no. 22).

[7] Vaṣṣāf, p. 347.

From information given by Naṣīr al-Dīn Ṭūsī,[1] we can see that the qubchur was a poll tax under Hülegü (and evidently later) and that it was imposed on all subjects first of all by the Mongols contrary to Muslim law, which exempted the Mohammedans. The qubchur was graded according to the property of the tax-payer, and its rate changed often.[2] Rashīd al-Dīn relates that the qubchur was usually farmed out, and that there were governors who took 10 times, and even 20 or 30 times the qubchur from the ra'iyyat of their vilāyats (the latter being evidently an exaggeration).[3] Qubchur returns under Ghazan are not known. One can deduce from the decree of Ghazan only that the overall sum from each district was ascertained on the basis of fixed estimated expenditure (*ikhrājāt-i muqarrarī*) and was then divided amongst the ra'iyyat on the basis of previous tax lists.[4] The term *qubchur* disappears from documents under the Jalayirids, but the tax itself—poll tax, paid by Muslims as well—was still in existence later under the name of *sar-shumāra* or *sarāna*.

As we have already said, the kharāj was mostly collected in kind as part of the crop (the ancient *muqāsama*) in the Īl-Khānid period, but it was paid in cash[5] on a measured area (the ancient *misāha*) in the country-side near to such towns as Baghdad and Shīrāz. The rate of the tax was not the same in each vilāyat. In one of Ghazan's decrees the part of the crop given by the peasant to the Dīvān (kharāj) was fixed at 1/3 to 1/4.[6] But in Khūzistān, as we have said, the kharāj from state-owned land was fixed during the reign of Ghazan at 6/10 of the crop. In one Jalayirid document the rate of the kharāj is stipulated as 2/10 of the harvest in kind (*bahra*), "according to the custom of the vilāyat".[7] Apart from the basic kharāj (*aṣl-i kharāj* or simply *aṣl*) there was also an additional sum—*far'*.[8] The far' was supposed to be 1/10 of the basic kharāj, according to Vaṣṣāf, and from 1/10 to 2/10, according to Naṣīr al-Dīn Ṭūsī.[9] The terms *aṣl-i kharāj* and *far'* were known long before the Mongol conquest.[10]

The tithe (*'ushr* or *dahyak*), in other words the lands tax at the

[1] Nāṣir al-Dīn Ṭūsī p. 763.
[2] Juvainī, vol. II, pp. 254, 256, 261; trans. Boyle, vol. II, pp. 517, 517, 524.
[3] *Jāmi' al-tawārīkh*, ed. Alizade, p. 453.
[4] *Ibid.* p. 462. [5] *Ibid.* pp. 472–3. [6] *Ibid.* p. 551.
[7] *Dastūr al-kātib*, f. 199*b*.
[8] Vaṣṣāf, pp. 438, 439.
[9] *Ibid.* p. 435; Naṣīr al-Dīn Ṭūsī, p. 762.
[10] Firdausī, *Shāh-Nāma*, ed. Mohl, vol. VII, p. 502 (chapter 50, verse 899); cf. Rāvandī, p. 32.

alleviated rate of 1/10 of the crop in kind,[1] was exacted from privately owned lands (*mulk*, *arbābī*)[2] under the Īl-Khāns. Apparently this was a special privilege of the landowners. It did not apply to peasants paying quit-rent, who had to pay rent to landlords (*bahra-yi mālikāna*), as well as 'ushr to the dīvān.

The sources give conflicting information on the *qalan*, which is evidently explained by the fact that it signified different taxes and duties at different times and in different places. Grigor of Akner and Rashīd al-Dīn speak of the qalan as a kind of military service. But the table of taxes of Khūzistān show it to be the upkeep of the military aristocracy (amīrs) during their tours and military expedition,[3] whilst the amount raised by the qalan was a meagre 1,200 dīnārs from the whole of Khūzistān, compared with the total tax from the region of 325,000 dīnārs.[4] But the thirteenth-century Persian poet Pūr-i Bahā, in a *qaṣīda* in honour of the historian and administrator 'Alā' al-Dīn Juvainī speaks of the qalan and the qubchur as the two main taxes that bore heavily and with ruinous effect upon the population.[5] We conclude from this that the term *qalan* was here used in place of *kharāj*.

Earlier we mentioned the tax that the Mongols introduced for the first time, the *tamgha*, which was paid on all forms of trade and urban crafts, even prostitution,[6] and which replaced the Moslem *zakāt* at the rate of 2·5 per cent. (There is no mention of zakāt in documents of the thirteenth century and after.) The rate of the tamgha is not known exactly. But from the letter of Rashīd al-Dīn to his spiritual counsellor Ṣadr al-Dīn Turkā'ī[7] we can conclude that the rate was 10 per cent of the value of each commercial transaction originally, and that Ghazan cut it by half in some towns and in other towns abrogated it for a period (for example, in the towns of Khūzistān).

The term *'avāriḍ* meant a special tax to cover extraordinary expenses, but was in fact regularly imposed and was extremely ruinous.[8] We can

[1] Concerning the origin and original character of the *'ushr* see A. N. Poliak, *Classification of Lands . . .*, pp. 40–62; F. Lokkegaard, *Islamic Taxation*, pp. 72–91.

[2] At least from all private estates in Khūzistān and the Iṣfahān *vilāyat*; see the *Mukātibāt-i Rashīdī*, pp. 33–4 (no. 13), 121–3 (no. 22); cf. *Rashaḥāt 'ayn al-ḥayāt*, p. 227.

[3] *Mukātibāt-i Rashīdī*, pp. 122–3.

[4] *Ibid.*

[5] See V. Minorsky, *Pūr-i Bahā and his poems*, pp. 194–7 (Persian text), 198–200 (English translation), especially verse two:

> "The whole world has become scattered and homeless
> Because of the immense *qalan* and endless *qopčur*."

[6] *Dastūr al-kātib*, f. 227*a*.

[7] *Mukātibāt-i Rashīdī*, p. 34 (no. 13).

[8] See Vaṣṣāf, p. 197; *Mukātibāt-i Rashīdī*, p. 28 (no. 11).

judge its character from a tale of Saifī. In 716/1317 the governor of Khurāsān, the Amīr Yasa'ul, desiring to organize a celebration in honour of his daughter on the occasion of her marriage with the son of Prince Yasa'ur, imposed 'avāriḍ of 300,000 dīnārs on the ra'iyyat of Khurāsān, 50,000 of which were to be paid by Herāt. Two *nā'ibs* with fifty horsemen, arriving in Herāt on the day of the Festival of the Sacrifice (*'īd-i qurbān*), drove the inhabitants out of the mosque with sticks, and laid 100 to 200 dīnārs tax on all whom they caught and bound. They extorted it on the spot, beating and torturing, wounding and making invalids of about 200 citizens. By sunset they had collected 50,000 dīnārs.[1] 'Avāriḍ was already resorted to under Maḥmūd of Ghazna.[2]

The words *'alafa* and *'ulūfa* (lit. fodder, forage) signified a collection in kind to provide food and fodder for the military caste and the army in a given district. According to the sources, this exaction consisted of grain, straw, oxen, sheep, poultry, wine, and sometimes money. In 707/1307 the general Muḥammad Sām demanded 500 kharvārs of grain, 500 rams, 50 horses, 30 slaves (*barda*) and 10,000 dīnārs for his army from the vassals of the lord of Herāt.[3] The *taghār* was the same tax, but in a narrower sense, being only paid in grain, at the rate of 100 mans (= 1 kharvār, or ass load).

The general poll-tax (*sar-shumāra*, *sarāna* = *qubchur*) introduced by the Mongols, which we have already mentioned, must not be confused with the ancient poll-tax based on Moslem law, exacted from the non-Moslems—the *jizya*. After the Mongol conquest the jizya ceased to exist. Ghazan restored the jizya paid by the heterodox (October 1295) after his conversion to Islam, but quickly abolished it (1296)[4] because of the intercession of the Nestorian patriarch Mar Yabalaha III, an Uighur by birth (1281–1317). But in 1306 the jizya was restored again by Öljeitü, and this time for good.[5] Under Sulṭān Uvais the jizya paid by Christians and Jews (men only) was 8 dīnārs from the rich, 6 from those of middle condition, and 4 from the poorer people.[6] It is not clear whether the jizya was paid by the heterodox instead of the sar-shumāra, or together with it. In some districts *khāna-shumāra*[7] (i.e. tax paid by household or family) was exacted in place of sar-shumāra.

Tax on gardens was paid in fruit—*bāgh-shumāra*[8]—and was evidently

[1] Saifī, p. 649.
[2] Nizāmī-y 'Arūḍī Samarqandī, p. 18.
[3] Saifī, p. 522.
[4] Mar Yabalaha, pp. 115–16.
[5] *Ibid.* p. 149.
[6] *Dastūr al-kātib*, f. 220*a*.
[7] *Ibid.* ff. 225*a*–225*b*.
[8] *Ibid.*

identical with the *thamārāt* (fruit).[1] This tax derives from the time of Khusrau I Anushīrvān, who laid a tax on fruit trees.[2]

Increases in the kharāj and other taxes were reflected in the terms *tafāvut* (difference), *taufīr* (increase),[3] *zavā'id* (excess), and *nemeri* (Mongol: addition).[4] Details and rates of these taxes are not specified more exactly.

The term *ikhrājāt* (lit. expenditure), frequently encountered in the sources, evidently referred to the whole group of circumstantial and permanent taxes paid by the ra'iyyat to cover the cost of officials touring the latters' districts (*ikhrājāt-i ṣādir u vārid*).[5] Expenditure covered by estimates (*muqarrarī*) was distinguished from expenses beyond the estimates (*khārijīyat*). The following taxes evidently belonged to the group: *ḥaqq al-taqrīr* (synonym—*rasm al-vizāra*)—as we see from the correspondence of Rashīd al-Dīn;[6] a tax in kind (grain, sugar, etc.) for the support of the Grand Vazīr: *rasm al-ṣadāra* (*ḥaqq al-tauliyya*)—a tax collected from the ra'iyyat of vaqf lands for the Grand Ṣadr at the rate of 10 per cent:[7] *rusūm-i shaḥnagī* or *dārūghakī*—a tax for the governor of a province (*shaḥna*, *darugha*, *basqaq*); *rusūm-i 'immāl* (*rasm-i khazāna*, Arabic-Persian)—a tax for the upkeep of officials of the Exchequer (*khazīna*, *bait al-māl*), fixed at 2 out of every 100 dīnārs tax from the time of Ghazan;[8] *ḥaqq at-taḥsīl* ("share of the tax")—for the tax collector (*muḥaṣṣil*, *taḥṣīldār*);[9] and *ḥarz*—a tax at the preliminary estimate of a crop, and similar taxes.

The term *ṭarḥ* signified the compulsory sale of products by the ra'iyyat to the Exchequer or local ruler at prices much below market value, and the compulsory purchase by the ra'iyyat of goods lying in government stores at prices far beyond that value. The meaning of the term is explained by A. A. Alizade.[10]

[1] Vaṣṣāf, p. 439, مال وخراج ثمره; *Mukātibāt-i Rashīdī*, pp. 121 ff., ثمرات is the reading of Professor Muhammad Shafi'; the manuscript had نمارات

[2] Ṭabarī, ser. 1, pp. 960–2; Th. Noeldeke, *Geschichte der Perser und Araber* . . ., pp. 244–5 n.

[3] This term was already known in the eleventh century, see the *Siyāsat-Nāma*, p. 209.

[4] Vaṣṣāf, p. 326; also mentioned in the Ani inscription.

[5] Juvainī, vol. 1, p. 23; Vaṣṣāf, p. 339; *Dastūr al-kātib*, ff. 112*a*, 201*a*–201*b*, 221*b*, 225*a*–229*a*. (All the documents granting immunity shown here speak of liberation from the *ikhrājāt* as well as other taxes.)

[6] *Mukātibāt-i Rashīdī*, pp. 236–7 (no. 36), 243 (no. 37).

[7] *Dastūr al-kātib*, f. 213*a*.

[8] *Jāmi' al-tawārīkh*, ed. Alizade, vol. III, pp. 540–41.

[9] *Dastūr al-kātib*, f. 206*b*.

[10] A. A. Alizade, *Termin ṭarḥ*, pp. 109–13; there also references to sources; in particular there is the story from Vaṣṣāf (p. 363) about how, at a time of famine in Fārs, the ra'iyyat were ordered to provide the Exchequer with a *ṭarḥ* of corn at 6 dīnārs per *kharvār*, when the market price was 30 dīnārs per *kharvār*.

"Presents" from the ra'iyyat to the Īl-Khān, to members of his family, to dignitaries, and to the local feudalists (Persian *pīshkash*, Mongol *sa'uri*, Turkish *tuzghu*) were obligatory upon their arrival in a district, or upon the occasion of some festivity, and their proportions were established. Thus one of Ghazan's decrees states that a wine-skin of fruit-juice should contain 50 Tabrīz mans in payment of *sa'uri* to the residence of Īl-Khān, whilst a wine-skin of fruit-juice given on the occasion of a festivity should hold 40 mans.[1]

The gathering of ra'iyyat for forced labour has already been mentioned. It was one of their heaviest duties. No less heavy for them was the obligation to billet (Arabic *nuzūl*, Turkish *qonalgha*)—the duty of taking into their houses the innumerable messengers, amīrs, military persons, and officials, together with their staffs, and then to feed and entertain them. According to Rashīd al-Dīn, every *basqaq* who toured a region with his staff occupied at least a hundred houses at one time. "In every neighbourhood", he says, "where a messenger decided to stay, the inhabitants were immediately subjected to constraint, since his slaves and military servants lowered themselves into neighbouring courtyards from the flat roofs, and stole whatever their eyes fell on. They shot their arrows at pigeons and chickens, and often hit children. Whatever they found that was eatable or drinkable or could be fed to their cattle, no matter to whom it belonged, they stole for themselves."[2] Since the messengers were arriving all the time, when one left a house, another would be billeted in it the very same day. "Every year", relates Rashīd al-Dīn, "under various pretexts messengers took away several thousand cows, bedding, cauldrons, pots and utensils belonging to the inhabitants. They stabled saddle animals and beasts of burden in the gardens, and in one day would ruin a garden which was the product of ten years' work and a thousand difficulties overcome."[3] Ghazan abolished the right to billet in the houses of the ra'iyyat and ordered the construction of special government hostelries. But already by the time of the Īl-Khān Abū Sa'īd the obligation to billet had appeared yet again. We can ascertain this from the fact that the reason for the uprising of the Sarbadārs in Khurāsān (737/1337) was the unbridled licence of a Mongol messenger who stopped for lodging at the village of Bāshtīn and demanded wine and a woman. Under Sulṭān Uvais decrees were again issued to forbid billeting in the houses

[1] *Jāmi' al-tawārīkh*, ed. Alizade, p. 499.
[2] *Ibid.* p. 564.
[3] *Ibid.* p. 460.

of the ra'iyyat.[1] Of course the obligation to billet existed in Iran before the Mongol conquest,[2] but never before did it assume such proportions of national disaster as it did under the Mongols, according to Rashīd al-Dīn, when many of the ra'iyyat deliberately kept their houses in a delapidated condition, which however did not always help.

The carriage duty (Turkish *ulagh*)—the obligation of the ra'iyyat to provide animals for riding and carrying on the postal service (*barīd*, Turkish *yam*)—was already in existence at the time of the caliphate. But only in the Mongol period do the sources describe it as a national calamity.

"It is impossible to calculate", says Rashīd al-Dīn, "how many asses the *ulagh* took each year from the *ra'iyyat*, the merchants, and others, and how many thousands of *ra'iyyat* had their heads, arms, and legs broken by the messengers. The *ra'iyyat* were all the time wandering about in search of their animals, taken from them for government transport, and did not know what to do. Some of their animals had been driven away for good, and were not returned. Others were left by the roadside to die; and the *ra'iyyat* neglected the farms and their work."[3]

Such were in general the system of taxes and obligations and its terminology under the Īl-Khāns. We shall not dwell here upon a number of fiscal terms which are insufficiently clear. Taxes and obligations not based on Moslem law (that is, apart from the kharāj, 'ushr, jizya, and zakāt) were covered by the term *takālīf*, *taklīfāt-i dīvānī*.[4] But beside these there were taxes arbitrarily fixed by local authorities, denoted in the sources by the terms *shiltāqāt* (Arabicized plural of the Mongol *shiltaq*, pretext (for extortion) and *shanāqiṣ* (plural of Arabic *shanqaṣa*—synonym of *istiqṣā'*—"draining to the uttermost, exhausting utterly").[5]

The system of taxes and services of the Īl-Khān state was without a doubt based on the merciless exploitations of the settled working population by both the state and the feudal leadership connected with it. The scale of feudal rent and taxation was completely out of proportion with the economic development of the country. Attempts to

[1] *Dastūr al-kātib*, ff. 50*b*, 166*b*–168*b*.

[2] Ibn al-Athīr, vol. XI, p. 180; Rāvandī, pp. 33, 513 (note of the editor on the term *nuzūla*).

[3] *Jāmi' al-tawārīkh*, ed. Alizade, p. 556; cf. *ibid.* pp. 479–83.

[4] See Khwāndamīr, *Ḥabīb al-siyar*, vol. III, pt. 4, p. 21, where there is an abridgement of the decree of Sulṭān Aḥmad Aq-Qoyunlu (902/1497) abolishing the taxes *takālīf-i dīvānī* and *ikhrājāt-i shiltāqāt*, by reason of their not being based on Moslem law.

[5] See Rāvandī, p. 507 (editor's note on the word *shanqaṣa*).

reform this system and make it less hard on the peasants and town dwellers—under Ghazan and the early Jalayirids—gave but temporary and relative periods of economic revival. In sum, this system, together with the general ruin of the period of the Mongol conquest, was the main factor in the inability of Iran to regain the level that it had reached by the beginning of the thirteenth century. High rates of feudal rent and tax were the chief causes of the popular uprisings in Iran.

CHAPTER 7

RELIGION UNDER THE MONGOLS

As we have already seen, at the time of the Mongol conquest most of Iran was Sunnī; indeed, says Molé, this was "one of the most Islamized countries in the Middle and Near East".[1] Small Zoroastrian minorities existed in one or two centres, but played only a secondary role in the country's religious life. There were also Jews and Christians, but the latter were far less numerous than in the Arabic-speaking countries of Syria, Egypt, and Iraq. A summary of the distribution of the various Muslim schools and sects in Iranian territory has been given above, pp. 283–302.

The Mongol invasion of Persia, which began in 1220, together with the subsequent fall of the Baghdad caliphate (1258) and the killing of the last ʿAbbāsid caliph, al-Mustaʿṣim billāh, brought the entire Muslim world and especially Persia face to face with unexpected and formidable problems. For the first time in the history of Islam a great part of the Muslim world found itself under the rule of a non-Muslim power—and not only non-Muslim, but one which, to begin with, was in general *anti*-Muslim. At the same time, however, when the Mongols destroyed the external and political power of the reformed Ismāʿīlism of Alamūt, they thus saved orthodox Islam from the continual menace which it represented. And their destruction of the Sunnī caliphate in Baghdad meant that for the first time Sunnism was deprived of every semblance of political authority, and this could only be an advantage for S͟hīʿism. The presence of a S͟hīʿī theologian, and one of the greatest of the time, among Hülegü's advisers was, to say the least, significant.

There has been a tendency to exaggerate the unimportance of the decadent Sunnī caliphate under the last ʿAbbāsids. In reality, it was precisely the decline of the caliphs' political power that led them to accentuate certain more specifically "religious" aspects (in the Western sense) of this institution. For example, when they were trying to dissuade Hülegü from attacking the capital, the caliph's ambassadors said to him: "If the caliph is killed, the whole world will be disorganized, the Sun will hide his face, the rain will cease to fall and the plants

[1] "Les Kubrawiya entre sunnisme et Shiʿisme . . .", *Revue des Etudes Islamiques*, p. 65.

will no longer grow."[1] This is the typical notion of the "sacred monarch" to be found in many Asiatic traditions, and it is significant that the Mongols themselves, who in some respects had similar ideas concerning the sanctity of sovereignty, seem to have believed the ambassadors up to a certain point. In fact, when Musta'ṣim was taken prisoner by Hülegü's hordes, some of the Sunnīs who were with the Mongols said that "if Hülegü spills the blood of the caliph on the ground, he and his infidel Mongols will be swallowed up by the earth. He must not be killed.... The accursed Hülegü feared that if he let the caliph live, the Muslims would rise in revolt, and that if he slew him with a sword and his blood was spilled on the ground, there would be an earthquake." He therefore had him killed by the well-known method, without any shedding of blood.[2] Contemporary sources are full of interesting references to this sacral aspect of the caliph; even Hülegü's court astrologer, Ḥusām al-Dīn, had predicted six disasters if Baghdad were to be attacked. Fortunately for Hülegü his Shī'ī adviser Naṣīr al-Dīn Ṭūsī was able to show that Ḥusām al-Dīn's astrological deductions were wrong.[3] That the Shī'īs were not very grieved by the fall of the 'Abbāsid caliphate is evident in practically all the sources, even if one disregards the "treachery" of the last 'Abbāsid's Shī'ī minister, Ibn al-'Alqamī (d. 656/1258), and the presence in Hülegü's retinue of Naṣīr al-Dīn Ṭūsī. Certain *ḥadīths* had been circulating for some time, which might well have persuaded the Shī'īs to collaborate with Hülegü: according to one, for example, the "Turks" would help the *Mahdī* or the *Qā'im* to achieve victory;[4] and there were other similar stories. It is known that while Hülegü was preparing to lay siege to Baghdad, several Shī'ī communities surrendered to him, and a rumour also spread that, under the influence of Naṣīr al-Dīn Ṭūsī, he had become a Muslim.

On the other hand, the fall of the caliphate had a disastrous effect on the Sunnīs, and all the Sunnī historians speak of it as if it were a cosmic catastrophe, while poets wrote elegies on the death of al-Musta'ṣim, on that occasion Sa'dī, the great Persian poet, composed two *qaṣīdas*, one in Arabic and the other in Persian. But while the psychological effects on the Sunnīs are evident, the theological consequences

[1] Ibn al-Ṭiqṭaqa, *Al-Fakhrī*, transl. Amar, p. 225; cf. Rashīd al-Dīn, transl. Arends, p. 38.

[2] Jūzjānī, *Ṭabaqāt-i Nāṣirī*, ed. Ḥabībī, vol. II, pp. 197–8. See also Boyle, "The Death of the Last 'Abbāsid Caliph", p. 150 and note 5.

[3] See above, p. 346.

[4] Qazvīnī, *Kitāb al-naqḍ*, pp. 510–11.

are less clear. The true caliphate, which combined the spiritual with the temporal power, had long since ceased to exist. Despite the fact that princes even in distant lands like India had theoretically to be invested by the Caliph of Baghdad, it is no exaggeration to say that his effective authority during the decadence of the ʿAbbāsid dynasty was spiritual rather than temporal. The comparison between the pope and the caliph is not a recent European invention, but can be found for the first time in the diary of the Shāfiʿī *qāḍī* Jamāl al-Dīn Muḥammad b. Sālim of Ḥamā, in Syria, who in 1260, that is shortly after the fall of Baghdad, visited Italy and went to the court of King Manfred, son of Frederick II, as envoy of the Mamlūk Sulṭān Baibars. Here he speaks of the pope, as "the Caliph of the Franks". This is interesting, because it was Baibars who in 1261 with great pomp installed an uncle of the dead al-Mustaʿṣim as "Caliph", conferring upon him functions which were somewhat "spiritual" and nominal. Ignoring the realities of the situation, Sunnī writers of treatises continued to repeat the old notion of a caliphate pure and simple, even at a time when it had become a fairy tale or had disappeared altogether. The more intelligent among them, such as Ibn Khaldūn in the fourteenth century, admitted that after the disappearance of Arab dominion nothing was left of the caliphate but the name;[1] while al-Nasafī (d. 537/1142) and Ibrāhīm Ḥalabī (d. 1549) maintained that the real caliphate had lasted only thirty years, until the death of ʿAlī. It is therefore not surprising that the theological effects of the fall of the Baghdad caliphate were very slight.

The Mongol invasion, then, strengthened the non-Muslim communities in Persia. Chingiz-Khān and Ögedei were shamanists who had no desire to be converted to any other religion, though Chingiz-Khān was interested in other creeds and made inquiries, both directly and indirectly, about the usages and customs of foreign religious communities. Güyük had strong leanings towards Christianity, even if he actually remained a shamanist. Möngke seems to have been somewhat indifferent to religious matters, but as soon as Qubilai embraced the Buddhist faith and his brother Hülegü also showed leanings towards that religion (in fact it is almost certain that the latter became a Buddhist), shamanism lost all its official significance. This did not happen, however, with the traditional religious customs of the Mongols. Sorcerers were still numerous and respected, and Abaqa greeted with joy a magician (*sāḥir*) named Baraq, who visited him in 1278.[2] The

[1] *Muqaddima*, transl. Rosenthal, vol. 1, pp. 402–78.

[2] Rashīd al-Dīn, vol. 1, p. 267.

figure of the shaman in the religious world of the Mongols in Iran disappeared more or less definitely during the reign of Arghun (1284–91), when Buddhism was being practised more thoroughly and conscientiously. But the real nature of Buddhism in Īl-Khānid Iran and its influence on the Muslims of that country is an unsolved, and perhaps insoluble, problem, chiefly because of the lack of reliable sources. (In contrast, we know that the Mongols had a considerable influence on the Persian language.) Iran must have been full of Buddhist temples —we hear of them only when they were destroyed in 1295–6—and in these temples there must have been numerous priests. Buddhism was particularly strong under Arghun, who even caused Buddhist priests to be brought from India, and is said to have died as a result of treatment prescribed for him by an unidentified "Indian yogi". (For contacts between Ṣūfīs and Buddhist priests, see below, pp. 545–6.) Nestorian Christianity was also widespread, especially among the women of the Īl-Khāns' family; Möngke's mother, several of his wives, and Hülegü's wife were all Christians, as were many other women (including, of course, Abaqa's wife Maria, known as Despoina Khatun, who was an illegitimate daughter of the Byzantine Emperor Michael VIII). These women often had their children baptized, and at least two Īl-Khāns, Aḥmad Tegüder and Öljeitü, were Christians in their childhood. As regards the Jews, their position was considerably strengthened by the success of individual Jews in obtaining court appointments, a notable case being the physician and minister of Arghun, Sa'd al-Daula, who was a mortal enemy of the Muslims and favoured his fellow-Jews in every possible way by using his influence over the sovereign. But even royal favour was not enough to save him from popular fury, and he was executed in 1291. According to Vaṣṣāf (d. first half of fourteenth century), Sa'd al-Daula tried to gain the favour of the Īl-Khān by declaring that Chingiz-Khān was a prophet, that the gift of prophecy was hereditary, and that Arghun should follow in the footsteps of the prophet Muḥammad and found a new *umma* (religious nation), which would be universal and would turn the Ka'ba into a pagoda! Another important figure of the Īl-Khānid period is also said to have been a Jew, at all events by origin. This was Rashīd al-Dīn, a physician and a famous historian of the Ghazan period; he too was killed, in 1318, but his death did not completely put an end to the influence of Jews at the Īl-Khānid court.

The 16th of June 1295 (1 Sha'bān 694) was a very important day in the history of religion in Īl-Khānid Persia, for on that day, a few months before his accession to the throne, Prince Ghazan was converted to Islam and assumed the Muslim name of Maḥmūd, at Fīrūzkūh in the presence of Shaikh Ṣadr al-Dīn Ibrāhīm al-Ḥamawī. It is true that the Īl-Khān Tegüder (d. 1284) had previously been converted to Islam and had taken the name of Aḥmad, but this was purely a personal matter and had no sequel. Ghazan, on the other hand, made the whole of his court and large numbers of the Mongols in Iran become Muslims. Thus, after a lapse of some seventy years, Islam again became the official religion of Iran; moreover Ghazan started a veritable persecution of Buddhists and other believers. Of particular interest is the following passage from the *Jāmiʿ al-tawārīkh*:

When the Lord of Islam, Ghazan, became a Muslim, he commanded that all the idols should be broken and all the pagodas (*but-khāna*) and (*ātash-kada*) destroyed, together with all the other temples the presence of which in Muslim countries is forbidden by the *sharīʿa*, and that all the community (*jamāʿat*) of the idolatrous *bakhshi* [a Turkish word derived from the Chinese *po-shih* "teacher"] should be converted [forcibly] to Islam. But since the Most High God did not aid them, they had no true faith, but were Muslims only outwardly and by necessity, and in their district (*nāḥiya*) there were signs of unbelief (*kufr*) and of aberration (*ḍalālat*). After a certain time the King of Islam perceived their hypocrisy and said to them: "Let those among you who wish it return to India, to Kashmīr, to Tibet, and to the countries whence they came; and let those who remain here cease to be hypocrites, and let them believe in that which they have in their hearts and cease from defiling with their hypocrisy the true religion of Islam. And if it should come to my ears that they are building fire-temples or pagodas, I will without hesitation put them to the sword." But some persevered in their hypocrisy, while others again returned to their wicked beliefs. And Ghazan said: "My father was an idolater and died an idolater and built for himself a temple which he made *vaqf* for that community [of the *bakhshi*]. That temple I have destroyed; go ye there and live on alms [among those ruins]."[1]

It would seem that this "temple of Arghun", like other temples, contained portraits of the deceased sovereign, which the women of his family tried in vain to save from the iconoclastic zeal of the neophyte Ghazan.

Besides destroying the temples of the idolaters, Ghazan also embarked on an active cultural policy in support of Islam. According to the sources he was a frequent visitor of the mosques, arranged for public readings of the Qur'ān, had a particular reverence for the Shīʿī

[1] Ed. Alizade, pp. 396–7.

holy places in Mesopotamia, built mosques in every village, and founded numerous religious institutions for the poor in the larger towns and also in Mecca. He seems to have devoted particular care to the building of *dār al-siyādas*, which were kinds of hostels in which the descendants of the Prophet (*sayyids*) were accommodated free of charge. Among the holy foundations he created, Rashīd al-Dīn even mentions a kind of shed in which birds could find shelter and food during the winter months, and in this Ghazan may have been influenced by similar Hindu and Buddhist practices.

In his definite leaning towards Shīʿism Ghazan visited the Shīʿī sanctuaries in Mesopotamia, and it would seem that he even had coins struck bearing inscriptions of the Shīʿī type. His brother and successor Öljeitü went still further. Originally a Christian, he subsequently became a Buddhist and eventually a Muslim. But even after embracing the Muslim religion he still seemed uncertain, since he was first a Ḥanafī, then a Shāfiʿ, until, disgusted with the sectarian squabbles among the various Sunnī schools, and influenced by Tāj al-Dīn Āvajī of Mashhad and by Jamāl al-Dīn Muṭahhir, Öljeitü finally went over to Shīʿism, despite the efforts to win him back to Buddhism made by the *bakhshis*[1] who had remained in Iran. His son and successor Abū Saʿīd, however, was a Sunnī. This in itself is sufficient to show that these conversions must be ascribed mainly to the activities of preachers and propagandists of the various sects in court circles. For example, it is not clear whether Öljeitü's Shīʿī tendencies brought about any spread of Shīʿism among his Persian subjects, and some of the sources even tell us that before he died he was converted once again to Sunnism.

Most Persian Muslims, even during the Mongol and Īl-Khānid eras, remained Sunnites. In addition to Baghdad, Iṣfahān and Shīrāz were the citadels of Sunnism in Iran, and during the reign of Öljeitü, according to Ibn Baṭṭūṭa (fourteenth century), it was in these centres that the population and the scholars offered the most vigorous resistance to the unsuccessful attempts to convert them forcibly to Shīʿism. Despite such sporadic attempts, however, it may be said that the traditional hostility between the two great branches of Islam became less acute after the end of the Sunnī caliphate in Baghdad and when the Īl-Khānid government—unlike that of the Saljuqs—began to show more sympathy for Shīʿism, i.e. Twelver Shīʿism (we shall deal later with the

[1] [*Ed.:* Some at least of these *bakhshis* must have been Mongol shamans. See above, p. 402.]

extremist sects). An example of this rapprochement is the *Aurād al-aḥbāb wa fuṣūṣ al-ādāb*, a mystical book of devotions written in 723/1323 by the Sūfī Sunnite Abū'l-Mafākhir Yaḥya Bākharzī, which contains prayers handed down by Shī'ī imams whose names are each followed by the formula *raḍiya 'llāhu 'anhu*, "May God be pleased with him". On the Shī'ī side, too, a more conciliatory attitude became perceptible. The great theologian and mystic Ṣadr al-Dīn Ibrāhīm (644/1246–722/1322), who influenced Ghazan to become a Muslim, was, like his father, a Sunnī, but nevertheless he studied under Naṣīr al-Dīn Ṭūsī and other learned Shī'īs, and there are many pro-Shī'ī features in his work, *Farā'id al-simṭain fī manāqib al-rasūl wa 'l-batūl wa 'l-murtaḍā wa 'l-sibṭain*. A proof of the interest Ghazan himself took in the "family of the Prophet" are the numerous hostels he founded, these being rather like *vaqfs* endowed with funds in order to help the *sayyids* in the various districts. In some cases people sought refuge in Shī'ism because they were disgusted with the squabble among the different Sunnī schools, and especially, as regards Iran, between Shafi'ites and the Ḥanafites. Typical of these was the quarrel at Öljeitü's court between some Ḥanafite scholars and the Shāfi'ī qāḍī Niẓām al-Dīn 'Abd al-Malik of Marāgheh, which became so violent that "the Mongol amīr Qutlugh-Shāh turned to the other amīr and said: 'Why have we abandoned the *Yasa* of Chingiz-Khān and the religion of our forefathers and accepted this religion of the Arabs, which is divided into so many sects?'"[1] It would seem that this episode was one of the reasons why Öljeitü embraced Shī'ism.

But it was during the Mongol and Īl-Khānid period that Twelver Shī'ī theology became stabilized in forms which were to become canonical, and, though subjected to modifications, were never supplanted. The two leading representatives of Shī'ī thinking at this time were Naṣīr al-Dīn Ṭūsī (d. 672/1274) and his disciple 'Allāma Ḥillī (d. 726/1326). Of the former, who was an astronomer, philosopher, jurist, and a theologian of encyclopaedic knowledge, it is difficult to give a concise description, and here we will only add that he was one of the founders of Imamite theology and that his innumerable works have been the subject of many commentaries. The second man, like his uncle Muḥaqqiq Ḥillī (d. 676/1277), was a theologian and jurist rather than a philosopher, and his treatises form the basis of all subsequent Shī'ī canonical law.

[1] Ḥāfiẓ-i Abrū, pp. 50–1 n.

The trend towards Shī'ism in many circles was due above all to mysticism, which at this time revealed many interesting Shī'ī features.

At the time of the Mongol invasion two *ṭarīqas* had a predominant influence in Iran: the Kubrāviyya in the East and the Suhravardiyya in the West. A characteristic of the Ṣūfism of this period is its deeper study of the philosophical and theoretical aspect of doctrine, this being partly due to the influence of Ibn 'Arabī, whose disciples in the East included Ṣadr al-Dīn Muḥammad b. Isḥāq Qonavī (d. 673/1274), author of *Fukūk*, *Miftāḥ al-ghaib*, and *Nafaḥāt-i Ilāhiyya*, and Qonavī's disciple the well-known Persian poet 'Irāqī (d. 688/1289), who wrote the famous *Lama'āt* annotated by Jāmī. Ecstatic Ṣūfism was gradually being transformed into *'irfān* (gnosis) and penetrating more and more into Persian lyric poetry, nearly all of which at this time was strongly influenced by Ṣūfism. But parallel with this esoteric level ran the "practical" form of Ṣūfism, whose leading exponents were Farīd al-Dīn 'Aṭṭār (who is said to have been killed by the Mongols in 618/1221 at a very advanced age) and later Jalāl al-Dīn of Balkh (d. at Qonya in 672/1273), founder of the famous ṭarīqa called the *maulaviyya*, in which particular importance was attached to mystic dancing. The *Mathnavī-i Ma'navī* and the *Dīvān-i Shams-i Tabrīz* by Maulānā Jalāl al-Dīn are two of the best works produced by Persian religious genius.

In the progressive penetration of Shī'ism into Persian Ṣūfism, the *kubrāviyya* school was particularly important. Kubrā himself was the great Ṣūfī master of the Khwārazm, and he was killed about 618/1221 at the time of the Mongol invasion. Although a Shāfi'ī Sunnite, he is said to have had leanings towards Shī'ism, but his eulogies of 'Alī and of the *ahl al-bait* are common to all Ṣūfis, and they do not prove that Kubrā favoured Shī'ism more than other writers. His first-generation disciples appear to have been all Sunnīs, and uncommon trends are to be found only in the works of Sa'd al-Dīn Ḥamūya, who is said to have taught that the *auliyā'* of the Muslim community are twelve in number, and that the twelfth is the *ṣāḥib al-zamān*, who will return to bring justice to all the world: an interesting adaptation of the Ṣūfī doctrine of the twelve imāms. Later, in the person of the Kubrāvī Shaikh 'Alā' al-Daula Samnānī (d. 756/1335), we meet a writer of unusual originality. Of particular interest for our study are the relations with the religious leaders at the court of Arghun, in whose service he spent some time during the Mongol period. He had a great admiration for the ascetic achievements of the bakhshis, one of whom helped him to solve certain problems in his spiritual life, but he distrusted the monistic tendencies in the Indian religions. Nevertheless, Indian influences may perhaps have inspired his theory of the "inner" or subtle "senses" (*laṭīfa*). In the interesting "confessions", which form part of his *Ṣafwat al-ʿurwa*, Samnānī clearly showed his partiality for Sunnism, but he was scandalized by the quarrels among the various juridical schools and did not adhere to any single school. Finally his soul found rest in Sunnism, but in admitting that ʿAlī alone of all the caliphs achieved perfection in all *three* aspects of the imamate—*khilāfa*, *varātha*, and *valāya*—he came in many respects closer to Shīʿism than to Sunnism. We may thus conclude with Molé that "his conception of Ṣūfism and its role enabled him to construct something resembling a Sunnite Shīʿism, which, although opposed to the *ravāfiḍ*, exalts the role of the *ahl al-bait*, and especially that of ʿAlī". The remaining links in this chain of Kubrāvī Ṣūfism tinged with Shīʿism would take us beyond the Mongol and Īl-Khānid era. After Kubrā's Sunnī Ṣūfism, in which he acknowledged ʿAlī, and after the frank and tolerant Sunnism of Samnānī, we have in the works of ʿAlī Hamadānī (d. 786/1584) a vigorous Sunnism in *sharīʿa* side by side with extreme Shīʿī ideas in ṭarīqa, followed by the openly professed Shīʿism of Nūrbakhsh (d. 869/1464). The imperceptible transition from Sunnism to Shīʿism, which first appears in the Kubrāviyya ṭarīqa, exercised a great influence on Islam in Iran, and is the explanation for the acceptance of confessional Shīʿism in the Ṣafavid era.

The Shīʿī tendencies in the kubrāviyya, however, were not the only instances of the curious Shīʿī Ṣūfism which began in Iran at this time. Another is the Shaikhiyya-Jūriyya *silsila* in Khurāsān, which had considerable political importance since it was linked with the Sarbadārid movement. The Shaikhiyya of Khurāsān were followers of Shaikh Khalīfa (killed in 736/1335), who was a Māzandarānī by origin and —an interesting point—a disciple of ʿAlāʾ al-Daula Samnānī, with whom, however, he seems to have had certain disagreements. At Sabzavār in Khurāsān Khalīfa founded a school of mysticism, which many of the inhabitants of the city joined. Sabzavār had long been a centre of Shīʿism, but we know very little about the teachings of Shaikh Khalīfa. At all events they were considered heretical by the Sunnī *faqīh* of the city who in vain implored the Īl-Khān Abū Saʿīd to get rid of Khalīfa. Eventually he was secretly murdered by local Sunnites and was succeeded by one of his disciples, Ḥasan Jūrī, who gave the movement a character which was more markedly Shīʿī and at the same time more military than it had been. The names of all the adherents were recorded in writing and they were advised "to keep themselves hidden until the day of the rising".[1] The movement, unlike the other ṭarīqas, which were far more peaceful in their attitude towards the ruling powers, had all the characteristics of a social revolt (it would appear that Ḥasan Jūrī himself was of peasant origin). After the death of the founder, Ḥasan Jūrī found a large number of new supporters in Nīshāpūr, in Ṭūs, Khabūshān, Abīvard, and so on, who joined forces with the Sarbadārids and helped to create the curious "Shī'ī republic" of Sabzavār. The military and political vicissitudes of the Sarbadārids, however, are outside the scope of our argument, since they continued into the post-Īl-Khānid period. Ḥasan Jūrī was arrested about the year 739/1338 and died shortly afterwards.

The mixture of militarism, social reform, and Shī'ism characteristic of the Shaikhiyya-Jūriyya ṭarīqa is also found in the movement of the followers of Mīr Qivām al-Dīn Mar'ashī, in Māzandarān, which the sources definitely describe as a branch of the Shaikhiyya-Jūriyya ṭarīqa, and in fact it was Ḥasan Jūrī who granted the title of *Shaikh* to Qivām al-Dīn's father, 'Izz al-Dīn Sūgandī. The latter died while returning from Sabzavār to Māzandarān, and his son succeeded him as head of the Māzandarānī branch of the ṭarīqa. At Āmul, about the middle of the century, Qivām al-Dīn became the head of a mass movement and founded a miniature Shī'ī state. His confraternity, like the Shaikhiyya-Jūriyya, was definitely Shī'ī, and the Mar'ashī were a family of sayyid descended from 'Alī Zain al-'Ābidīn.

Another group of Ṣūfīs who first sympathized with Shī'ism and then embraced it completely were the Ṣafavids, who were destined to be the founders of the Ṣafavid dynasty two centuries later, under which the whole of Persia was converted to Shī'ism. The founder of this confraternity, Shaikh Ṣafī al-Dīn Isḥāq of Ardabīl (d. 735/1335), was a disciple of Shaikh Zāhid Gīlānī (d. 700/1301), who in turn was a disciple of Jamāl al-Dīn Jīlī (d. 651/1253), himself a follower of Najm al-Dīn Kubrā. Nevertheless Shaikh Ṣafī was undoubtedly a Sunnī, and the "military" and Shī'ī trends in his brotherhood did not make their appearance until after the Mongol period.

In any case, Ṣūfism with a Shī'ī tinge remains the most important religious feature in Iran at this time, especially in view of later developments.

[1] *Ḥāfiẓ-i Abrū*, p. 474.

No description of the religious movements in Iran during the Mongol and Īl-K͟hānid eras would be complete without some mention of the extremist movements, some of which, rightly or wrongly, were accused of "Mazdakism"; in our discussion we shall exclude the Ismā'īlīs, who are dealt with elsewhere in this volume. One such movement began during the ninth year of the reign of Ögedei (1229–41), when a "maker of sieves" named Maḥmūd appeared in the village of Tārāb, near Buk͟hārā, who claimed to have remarkable magical powers, in particular that of curing the sick and receiving messages from spirits concerning occult matters. These powers were rumoured to have been taught to him by his sister, for, as Juvainī says, "in Transoxiana and in Turkestān many persons, especially women, claim to have magical powers, and when anyone has a pain or falls ill, they visit him, summon the exorcist, and perform dances and similar nonsense, and in this manner convince the ignorant and the vulgar".[1] Maḥmūd Tārābī even managed to occupy Buk͟hārā with the help of the peasants and artisans, who were living in dire poverty; but according to the hostile chronicler Juvainī, his adherents also included nobles and learned Muslims. The Mongols had to despatch what was practically an expeditionary force to quell this rebellion, which, apart from its economic and social significance, throws an interesting light on popular beliefs in Iran at this time, and especially on the presence of messianic and thaumaturgical elements among the oppressed lower orders.

Somewhat sketchy and incomplete are the references found in sources such as the *Jāmi' al-tawārīk͟h* and the *Nuzhat al-qulūb*, to real or pretended "Mazdakite" movements in Īl-K͟hānid Iran. These played an important role in the conspiracy of Prince Ala-Fireng, the elder son of Geik͟hatu (Jumādā I 703/December 1303), who was persuaded by a "Mazdakite" sect to take over the reins of government. According to Ras͟hīd al-Dīn,[2] the promoters of this conspiracy "passed themselves off as *s͟haik͟hs* [mystics]", but in reality they had subversive social ideas. The heads of the sect were the *pir* Ya'qūb Bāg͟hbānī, a *s͟haik͟h* named Ḥabīb, who had once been *k͟halīfa* (deputy) to S͟haik͟h Ras͟hīd Bulg͟hārī, a sayyid named Kamāl al-Dīn, and various others. Under a veil of mysticism, coupled with stories of miracles, and of the apparitions of angels, prophets, and saints, there lay concealed, says Ras͟hīd al Dīn, the ancient "way of thinking of Mazdak". Ideas of this kind were

[1] Transl. Boyle, p. 109.
[2] Transl. Arends, p. 203.

widespread among the populace, though many influential personages were also said to be members of the sect, some of them from the entourage of the notorious finance minister Ṣadr al-Dīn, who was responsible for the introduction of paper money into Persia. The minister himself was said to have been a disciple of Shaikh Rashīd Bulghārī, mentioned above. In any case the conspiracy was discovered and its religious leaders were executed. But these followers of Ya'qūb Bāghbānī were not the only "Mazdakites" in Iran during those days. In his *Nuzhat al-qulūb*, a geographical treatise written in 1340, Mustaufī Qazvīnī gives a description of the province of Rūdbār in Māzandarān, not far from the Ismā'īlī fortress of Alamūt, and after telling us that the inhabitants were *Bāṭinīs* (Ismā'īlīs), he adds that there also existed a group of people calling themselves *Marāghiyyān*, who were believed to be "Mazdakites". If Schwarz's unconvincing hypothesis is correct, the word *Marāghiyyān* means "men of Marāgheh", and thus they would be the last remnants of the descendants of the followers of Pāpak, who had fled from Āzarbāījān after the collapse of the Khurramite movement. A more probable explanation is that, by calling them "Mazdakites", the sources wished to stress certain extremist social tendencies, real or imaginary, in the ideas professed by these interesting sects, about whose real religious theories we know very little.

In the history of religion in Iran, the Mongol period is important for a number of reasons. First, it saw a strengthening of Shī'ism as a consequence of the fall of the 'Abbāsid caliphate, and this was accompanied by a proportionate mitigation of the Shī'ī–Sunnī dispute, the appearance within Ṣūfism of trends towards Shī'ism, and a leaning towards a certain *tashayyu' ḥasan* ("moderate" Shī'ism) in Sunnī circles. In addition, certain Ṣūfī and Shī'ī movements of a military kind were formed, which were the forerunners of the Ṣafavid movement, while pseudo-Mazdakite eschatological and social movements occurred sporadically. And finally, Ṣūfism made particularly noteworthy progress, especially in its doctrinal tendencies.

CHAPTER 8

POETS AND PROSE WRITERS OF THE LATE SALJUQ AND MONGOL PERIODS

This chapter touches on the era of the "Great Saljuqs" only in its last phase, that is, towards the end of the reign of Sulṭān Sanjar (d. 552/1158), a monarch who was then decadent though he was later idealized. The Saljuqs are a remarkable phenomenon, and we should therefore cast at least a cursory glance back to the period of their real greatness; for this wholly Turkish dynasty, holding sway over an immense area, played a very considerable part in the expansion of the Persian literary language and of Persian culture in general. That the principal Saljuq rulers themselves showed a lack of culture was no obstacle to this, mainly because their internal policy was in the hands of Iranian counsellors and trusted advisers, without whose help these barbarian warriors could scarcely have held their own in such a highly cultivated milieu. Moreover the example set by the policy of Sulṭān Maḥmūd of Ghazna had a lasting effect: the Saljuq court teemed with Iranian scholars and Iranian writers. The official language was Persian, and in it was conducted the official correspondence of the court, in contrast to the practice under Maḥmūd. This is one side of the picture. On the other, the waves of Turkish expansion were hastening the influence of that language in certain areas, with Turkish idioms even beginning to approach the position of the literary language.

Whereas the expansion of the Saljuqs was to the west, embracing Syria, Asia Minor, and the Caucasus, the ousted Ghaznavids strove to establish a firm footing in Multān, the Punjab, and Sind, at the same time extending the sway of the Persian language and Persian literature in the upper social strata of their remaining Indian possessions. Similarly the courts of the Khwārazm-Shāhs (1077–1231) and the Ghūrids (1100–1206) were unable to dispense with Persian culture, though its vitality—measured by the number and importance of their poets and other writers at this time—was certainly not comparable to that in neighbouring territories to the west. The same is true of the Qara-Khitai.

Thus from the cultural point of view the Saljuq era does represent one of the high-water marks of Iranian history and civilization. This cultural expansion is reflected in the development of the towns, in the founding of remarkable schools (*Niẕāmiyyas*), not only in Baghdad but also in other important centres; in the transference of the administrative machine from the hands of the old aristocratic families to those of a new middle-class intelligentsia; and also, as Bausani suggests, in the imponderable, if not always noticeable, influence of Ismā'īlism. What novel and unprecedented developments might have taken place, had not the disastrous Mongol cataclysm occurred![1]

Poetry also flourished during the period of the decline and fall of Saljuq rule, but the forms perfected by the old masters were already dying out and poetry was developing in an entirely new direction. Sanā'ī had pointed to such new ways during the first half of the sixth/twelfth century. The panegyric ode (*qaṣīda*) reached its greatest heights in the works of Anvarī and Khāqānī, because both these outstanding poets realized that the old paths could no longer be trodden and that the crisis would have to be resolved. Searching for fresh ideas and imagery, they saw a way out in the combination of poetic experience with erudition and refined rhetoric, in which—and this cannot be overemphasized—genuine poetry did not in any way suffer. This was the case with the great poets at least; with the lesser, however, virtuosity of technique tended to take the place of ideas. Their verses are more suited to private reading, for in public recitation their deeper significance and refinement would vanish without a trace, as would all likelihood of any brilliant effect. The tradition of recitation was already dying out by the end of the Saljuq period. All this, together with increasing Arabicization, led in poetry to the "'Irāqī" style and in prose to artificiality.

From the social point of view the poets no longer stood on so high a pedestal as they had done previously. They faced each new day with fear, for the vast Saljuq empire was gradually disintegrating into states of varying sizes. Jealous of one another and easily bought for money, the poets were not treated with any great tenderness by the rulers, and thus it is common to find them languishing in prison or wandering from one court to another. They were compelled by the search for daily bread and their own prodigality to hunt for material rewards, and this in turn made begging, which even the most famous amongst them condoned, the most effective means of support for their poetic activity. Their distress was heightened by the universal sense of insecurity and the con-

[1] *I Persiani*, p. 139.

stant threat of invasion. Lamentations and vindictive or scornful verses provide a good barometer for measuring prevalent social conditions.

This alone was enough to cause the qaṣīda to lose its formerly privileged position. Additional factors were a growth in the power of the towns, guilds, and bazaars, and an increasing antagonism to feudal overlords on the part of their tenants. This development found its expression in the increasing popularity of both the *ghazal* and the quatrain from the second half of the sixth/twelfth century on, with the ghazal gradually taking pride of place. The chaste language of these and other similar forms, compared with the exaggerated bombast of the qaṣīdas, was a natural outcome of this change. The origin of the ghazal is sometimes traced back to the old independent song, and sometimes to the detachment of the purely lyrical exordia in the qaṣīdas and their division into smaller units, singing being an essential feature in both cases. The poets took refuge in these forms when eulogistic verse could no longer provide sure hope of success. Ṣūfism, particularly widespread in the non-feudal layers of society, adopted the ghazal and the quatrain for its own ends. The strength of this movement grew in proportion to the economic and social distress of the empire, but was not confined only to certain well-defined social strata. Although it embraced more or less all poetry, it would be mistaken to assume that only with Ṣūfism did poetry exist at all. Nevertheless Shiblī Nu'mānī is convinced that a ghazal untouched by Ṣūfism is a rose without a scent.[1] It is interesting to note that a definite *nom de plume* in the last line of a ghazal occurs a hundred years earlier in Ṣūfī writings than in non-Ṣūfī ghazals (sixth/twelfth century). Bertel's thinks that the earliest Ṣūfī poets imitated the artisans with whom they were closely connected, whose practice it was to mark their products with their names, while Bausani and with him Ateş see in the *nom de plume* the poet's own emotional self-exhortation.[2] The artisans and their circles formed a secret society, the *Futuwwa* or "young men's association", closely linked to Ṣūfism. A link between the *Futuwwa* and the *Akhis*, a secret brotherhood existing in Asia Minor and Transcaucasia, is very probable.[3]

There is another poetic form that came strongly to the fore in the late Saljuq period. This was not the heroic epic, whose inappropriate subject matter and antiquated language did not permit it to continue into this period; it was the romantic epic. After 'Unṣurī (and countless other

[1] *Shi'r*, vol. v, p. 30. [2] Cf. *Dějiny perské a tádžické literatury*, p. 84.

[3] Franz Taeschner in a letter: "As far as I can make out, the *Futuwwa* and the Akhī brotherhood are indistinguishable."

mathnavī writers), this form was to reach such perfection in the hands of Niẓāmī (d. 605/1209) that he in turn became the model for all Iranian poets in subsequent centuries. The romantic tale, indeed even an early type of romantic epic, is known to have already existed in Middle Persian literature. It should not surprise us that something so profoundly characteristic of Persia reappeared quite naturally in Islamic–Iranian culture, a fact which is confirmed by the *Vīs u Rāmīn* (an Iranian counterpart of the medieval European Tristan and Isolde epics), which existed in Pahlavī, probably in a Pāzand or Pārsī version, at least as a tale and, in the earliest New Persian period, as an epic. Rūdakī (d. 329/940) also helped to keep the romantic tradition alive. A closer examination of this development reveals moreover that very many lines in mathnavīs must have been taken from romantic epics.[1] We know the titles of two such epics by 'Unṣurī (d. 431/1039), and a considerable portion of a third (*Vāmiq u 'Adhrā*) has recently been discovered in India by Muḥammad Shafi'. Three survive in their entirety: 'Ayyūqi's *Varqa u Gulshāh* (early fifth/eleventh century), the *Vīs u Rāmīn* of Fakhr al-Dīn Gurgānī (d. after 448/1039), and the *Yūsuf u Zalīkhā* of Amānī, written after 476/1083. The production of romantic epics cannot have ceased all of a sudden, although no titles, let alone actual texts, survive. The fact that so many echoes of *Vīs u Rāmīn* are discernible in Niẓāmī suggests that he was indebted to the works of his predecessors, and these must therefore still have been extant. The preference for the didactic, ethical or Ṣūfi epic undoubtedly sprang from the immorality and depression of the period; Sanā'ī was to become one of its greatest exponents.

The weakening of Saljuq power led to the disintegration of the empire. Amongst the principalities which arose during the second half of the sixth/twelfth century, that of the Khwārazm-Shāhs became increasingly powerful, since, apart from the personal energy of these rulers, the territory possessed numerous geographical and political advantages. The Khwārazm-Shāhs were well on the way to restoring the Saljuq empire to the size it had enjoyed at its zenith, but there was to be a reversal whose effects on the whole Iranian world were truly tragic. The catastrophe came from the East.

The fact that a clash occurred between the Khwārazm-Shāh and

[1] It is the merit of Maḥjūb in his *Mathnavī-Sarā'ī* to have clarified our ideas about the early history of the *mathnavī* in New Persian down to the fifth/eleventh century. On a manuscript of the *Humāi-Nāma* prior to A.D. 1200 see A. J. Arberry, "An early Persian epic", *Mélanges Massé* (Tehran, 1963), pp. 11–16.

Chingiz-Khān is insufficiently explained by the arrogant behaviour of the sultan: that would be too superficial a reason to account for events which were of the greatest historical importance. The clash became inevitable once Chingiz-Khān had unified Mongolia and consolidated its fighting power; indeed, since he depended on a feudalized nomadic aristocracy, he had to subordinate his policies to its requirements. The power of the Khwārazm-Shāhs, on the other hand, as the spies of Chingiz-Khān soon found out, was by no means as solid as its expansion implied. The outcome of the struggle was thus already decided in advance. The Mongol invasion took place in two waves, beginning in 1219 under Chingiz-Khān himself, and continuing under the leadership of the first Īl-Khān Hülegü, who in 1256 broke the power of the Assassins and in 1258 destroyed Baghdad and the caliphate.[1] Neither phase of the invasion touched the southern half of Iran; but the northern districts, including Khwārazm and Transoxiana, were struck with indescribable brutality. The invasion of course embraced a much vaster area, but here we are concerned only with the Mongol conquests in Iran and her neighbouring territories. The eastern Islamic areas in particular suffered greatly from this terror. The ruthless invaders massacred wholesale, destroying everything so as to instil fear and prevent counter-attack from behind. Indeed this catastrophe is one of the causes of Iran's subsequent backwardness. Not only the political but also the cultural development of the country was brought almost to a halt for many years to come, even though it cannot be denied that the concentration of such immense areas in the hands of the conquerors brought with it certain economic advantages.

Under Hülegü (654–63/1256–65), the bounds of the Īl-Khānid empire had been more or less definitely established. It was to become "an essentially Iranian state which for the first time for many years incorporated the greater part of the Iranian people. The importance this had for the development of Persian civilization and for the continuation of Iranian culture is not to be under-estimated."[2] Although the Īl-Khāns (654–736/1256–1336) strove to make good the brutality of the conquerors, they were nevertheless foreigners in Iran. A shattered economic system—these nomadic shepherds finding themselves in countries where feudalism was flourishing—was to remain with them until the end of the seventh/thirteenth century, when Ghazan

[1] See Boyle, "The Death of the Last 'Abbāsid Caliph".
[2] Spuler, *Die Mongolen*, p. 59

(694–703/1295–1304) attempted to carry out reforms: much too late, however, to preserve the power of the dynasty from its imminent dissolution. Nor could the conversion to Islam of the last rulers and the Mongol regiments help to avert this.

To the handfuls of survivors in the smouldering ruins, art could be of little consequence. Writers and scholars fled to take refuge in places less sorely smitten. That part of their cultural heritage which they could not take with them was doomed to destruction. Only the archives of the Assassins reached the hands of the historians after the destruction of the stronghold at Alamūt. The culture of the north-eastern provinces shifted to those of the south-east and elsewhere. This is why Jalāl al-Dīn Rūmī was to appear in Saljuq Qonya, Sa'dī in Shīrāz, Amīr Khusrau and 'Irāqī in India. When, under Hülegü, Tabrīz was raised to the position of capital city, political and intellectual life moved away to this particular region, and Āzarbāījān remained the heart of the empire for eighty years. The 'Irāqī style becomes predominant at this time, and the first signs of the Indian style begin to appear. If the old qaṣīda lost its former eminence, this was for the reasons usually given, namely, that there were no great Iranians left, and that, to begin with, the Mongols could not understand Persian. At all events the Īl-Khāns themselves produced not a single poet or prose writer,[1] and their courts displayed not the slightest interest in poetry. Moreover under the Mongols there was a new growth of towns, for which the panegyric ode had no appeal. The ghazal and the mathnavī were the forms in which their interests could be expressed.

The distress of the towns was by no means slight; disturbances and oppressions continued, encouraging the retreat into Ṣūfism. This suffering expressed itself in the mystical and didactic qaṣīda[2] (as opposed to the purely panegyric ode), and even more in the short ghazal, which reached its greatest perfection in the hands first of Sa'dī and later of Ḥāfiẓ. The long mystical poem reached its culmination in these years ('Attār, Maulavī); versified teachings of the Ṣūfī system now made their appearance; and the influence of Ṣūfism became altogether more evident. These phenomena clearly demonstrate an attempt to escape from a horrible reality. The Īl-Khāns showed interest in

[1] [Ed. With the possible exception of Abū Sa'īd. See above, p. 413.]

[2] Pūr-i Bahā's "combination of encomium with blame" admirably fits the times. On the introduction of Turco-Mongol expressions into the qaṣīda, cf. Minorsky, "Pūr-i Bahā's 'Mongol' Ode" and Kubīčková, "La qasīda à l'honneur de Wağihuddīn Zangī".

learning only in so far as they were able to appreciate it. Hülegü founded an observatory, entrusting it to his favourite and counsellor Naṣīr al-Dīn Ṭūsī (597–672/1200–74). Since the reason for its erection lay not in any interest in science but solely in astrological superstition, the fact that the Persian scholars used it for genuine astronomical research deserves all the more credit. Another subject which flourished during this period, reaching unprecedented heights, was historiography, for Chingiz-Khan and the Īl-Khāns were intent on immortalizing their deeds and the fame of the Mongols.

The Mongols slaughtered far too much of the population of Persia and destroyed too much of its economic structure and cultural heritage, for the catastrophe they had caused not to leave permanent scars. In this account the poets, the real essence of New Persian literature, take up the first and by far the largest portion of our interest, while the second, much smaller portion deals with the prose writers. The poets themselves will be examined in chronological order, less as individuals than as members of groups which emerge quite naturally. The importance of mysticism will make it necessary to devote a special section to its main representatives. Since panegyric poetry had been all-important until the Mongol period (its chief mode being the qaṣīda), it forms a magnificent gateway through which to enter upon a detailed study of New Persian literature. Nevertheless, special circumstances require that an exception be made at the start.

SANĀ'Ī

Sanā'ī is a poet on whom little research has been done.[1] Only the last phase of his life and work comes within the scope of this study, and both are unfortunately hidden in great obscurity. The dates variously given for his death are as much as seventy years apart (520–90/1126–94), and the discrepancy between the dates for his last poem is eleven years (524–35/1129–41). More important is the question: can he be regarded as an adherent of *taṣavvuf* or not? In their appreciation of him, West and East diverge greatly. Nonetheless the significance and lasting influence of Sanā'ī as a poet were so great that it would be impossible to omit him from this survey.

Ḥakīm ("the scholar") Abu'l-Majd Majdūd b. Ādam Sanā'ī was born

[1] Y. E. Bertel's, *Istoriya*, pp. 402–55, is the only authority to have based his account on a thorough examination of the poet's work.

about 473/1080–81 in Ghazna, where he spent his youth. He had already begun to write poetry during the rule of the Ghaznavid Abū Sa'īd Mas'ūd (492–508/1099–1115), but was not to remain a writer of panegyrics for long. A profound psychological upheaval made him turn to the opposite extreme. Legend attributes this to a quarrel picked with him by a madman, who accused him of the rankest heresy for his praise of rulers. This horrible experience—which was probably what led him later to undertake a pilgrimage to the holy places of Islam—occurred around 1105 during his sojourn at Balkh, where he wrote the satirical poem, *Kār-Nāma-i Balkh*, "The Book of the Deeds of Balkh". His life after his return to Balkh was interrupted by journeys to Khurāsān and Khwārazm, until he reappeared at his birthplace around 518/1124–25. But not even the entreaties of Bahrām-Shāh (510–52/1117–57) could induce him to return to the court. Nevertheless it was to Bahrām-Shāh that he dedicated his last and most celebrated work, the mathnavī *Ḥadīqat al-ḥaqīqa* ("The Garden of Truth"), and because of this he was accused of an heretical desire for innovation and had to beg for an edict of purification from Baghdad. He was then already seriously ill, and died immediately after the completion of the poem.

The complications do not end here, however. Whereas Persian scholars are at pains to present Shī'ism as the poet's creed, Sanā'ī's qaṣīda on Abū Ḥanīfa points instead to Sunnism, even though the tenor of his utterances regarding the family of the Prophet is clearly sympathetic. Tradition insists that he was a disciple of Shaikh Yūsuf Hamadānī, and European orientalists, too, accept his taṣavvuf, and even see him as one of the most typical of the mystic poets. This is contrary to the most recent view, that of Y. E. Bertel's, who concedes at most a small degree of mysticism, while emphasizing all the more Sanā'ī's critical, didactic, and ascetic (though not Ṣūfī) tendencies.

Even when items of doubtful authorship are excluded, Sanā'ī's works consist of a whole series of mathnavīs and an extensive dīvān. The shorter mathnavīs are generally grouped among the so-called "Six of Sanā'ī", the best-known being the *Sair al-'ibād ila 'l-ma'ād* ("The Pilgrimage of the Servants of God to the Place of the Return"), a poem the theme of which is in some ways reminiscent of Dante's *Divine Comedy*, especially the *Inferno*. Moreover this theme had already occurred in the Middle Persian *Artāk Virāz Nāmak* ("The Book of Artak Viraz"), and in Avicenna's, that is Ibn Tufail's, *Ḥayy ibn Yaqẓan*.

"The Garden of Truth" (sometimes also called the *Ilāhī-Nāma*, "The Divine Book") overshadows all Sanā'ī's ma<u>th</u>navīs—both in length (according to its author it has 10,000 lines, but 12,000 would be more correct); and also in importance, not only for its own sake, but for the further development of this type of ma<u>th</u>navī, as it is the first to be so long and to contain parables. Sanā'ī began his *magnum opus* in 524/1129–30 and finished it eleven years later at the age of 60, immediately before his death. The *Ḥadīqa* consists of ten chapters, each with a different title, arranged in different orders in different manuscripts; the content of the chapters is heterogeneous.

Most orientalists regard the *Ḥadīqa* as an "encyclopaedia of Ṣūfism", whereas Bertel's prefers the description "encyclopaedia of all Sanā'ī's accumulated knowledge". He reminds us that the poet frequently speaks of asceticism but never of spiritual discipline (*ṭarīqat*), and that he never mentions the "way of the Ṣūfīs" by name. Bertel's concedes some mysticism only in the chapter on love. In so doing he comes into conflict with Western opinion, but this is less important than the fact that Oriental scholars are unanimous about the Ṣūfī character of Sanā'ī's poetry. Moreover, with the exception of Bertel's, European orientalists do not recognize in Sanā'ī such exceptional qualities as do the Persian scholars, who show marked enthusiasm for him. Niẓāmī's *Ma<u>kh</u>zan al-asrār* ("The Treasure-chamber of Secrets") and <u>Kh</u>aqānī's *Tuḥfat al-'Irāqain* ("The Gift from the two Iraqs") follow most closely in time on the great master's example. The description of night in Niẓāmī's poem was obviously influenced by the *Ḥadīqa*. Yet Sanā'ī's language distinguishes itself from that of others, and, unlike the older, simpler language, his delights in learned allusions. Another difficulty for a reader lies in his use of brachylogy. Thus it is comprehensible that the Ṣūfīs encountered difficulties when trying to gain instruction from the *Ḥadīqa*; at the request of his pupils, Jalāl al-Dīn Rūmī ("Maulavī") is said to have decided to write his own ma<u>th</u>navī, whose revelation of truths was more accessible to them than the *Ḥadīqa*. Although the *Ḥadīqa* was one of Maulavī's models, the techniques of the two authors differ: the *Ḥadīqa* does not delight in anecdotes, whereas they are interwoven everywhere in Maulavī's work.

Sanā'ī was also one of the first to make the <u>gh</u>azal a medium for mystical ruminations; and in doing so, he provided an example for succeeding generations. Many of his <u>gh</u>azals cannot fail to move the reader. The anacreontic manner is present, and there are outspoken attacks on poetry written for mercenary motives, as well as severe judgments on contemporary life in all its aspects (and on the Turks too); the poet refrains neither from invective nor from obscenity. But his real significance lies in his effective, far-reaching introduction of an ascetic and mystic attitude as an ingredient of the didactic mathnavī of varying length (Nāṣir-i Khusrau, d. 465–10/1072–77, had already introduced philosophic ideas into poetry). Sanā'ī led poetry away from simple and mundane things to spheres more elevated and intellectually more ambitious; in doing so he became a great innovator. Particularly notable is his social message that all Moslems are equal.

THE PANEGYRIC POETS

(i) *In Transoxiana*

Shihāb al-Dīn 'Am'aq of Bukhārā served the Qarakhānids in Samarqand, and, being an outstanding poet, was honoured with the title "Prince of Poetry". 'Am'aq enjoyed the highest esteem and favour at court, acquired great wealth, and insisted that other poets should revere him. He was a man of culture and had a thorough command of all the devices of rhetoric; in one of his qaṣīdas he worked the words *mūi u mūr* "the hair and the ant" into every half-line, a unique feat indeed! But he was too good a poet to be guilty of the barrenness of mere artificiality. His similes are tender and heartfelt, whether founded on fancy, reason or reality. Only one line seems to have survived from his epic *Yūsuf and Zalīkhā*, and this is no less intricate since it can be scanned in two metres—the reason, no doubt, for the loss of the epic.[1] He died in 542–43/1147–49 at the age, it is said, of 100, and in the loneliness which elderly court poets, superseded by younger rivals, knew only too well.

'Abd al-Vāsi' Jabalī of Gharchistān, born about 555/1160, sang the praises of various contemporary dynasties. He is noteworthy as the precursor of a stylistic change that was to dominate the sixth/twelfth century: this consisted of a more frequent use of the colloquial language by cultured people, together with an increased number of Arabic expressions. He had a predilection for rhetorical ornaments, in particular for the figure *laff u nashr* (chiasmus). His dīvān of animal names is a real treasury of information.

More important as a prose writer than as a poet is Rashīd al-Dīn

[1] On this epic and its forerunners and imitations see Khayyām-Pūr (1338), p. 242.

Muḥammad ʿUmarī (meaning "a descendant of Caliph Uʿmar"), usually called Rashīd-i Vaṭvāṭ ("the Bat"), because he was a small, unprepossessing man with a bald head.[1] He was born at Balkh in 508–09/1114–16,[2] and died either in 578/1182–83 or, more probably, five years earlier. After acquiring an excellent education in his home town and in Khwārazm, he became the most outstanding stylist in Persian and Arabic in the court of the Khwārazm-Shāh Atsïz and his successors. Although he was often out of favour, Rashīd was constantly in the shah's entourage. His poetic sphere was naturally that of Persian and Arabic court poetry. Rhetorical ornaments came easily to a man who wrote an excellent guide to poetry; in handling these ornaments he was a master. In his works there is therefore little place for feelings, although, as the impressive qaṣīda on the visit of his beloved old mother shows, he was capable of capturing the right tone when occasion demanded. Elsewhere all the fireworks of rhetorical figures and tropes, all the ingenuity of language and form, are unable to conceal the coldness of feeling in his poems. The poet had to devote much attention to the description of martial events which he witnessed, and many of these descriptions are certainly very good. Rashīd's rhetorical talent was greatly, if not unanimously, admired: a master such as Khāqānī placed it below that of Adīb Ṣābir.

Rashīd cultivated lively relations with the literary world, and in this he was helped considerably by his high position as a court dignitary, since it made those more or less close to him seek his favour unless political antagonisms forced them to do otherwise. This was the case, for instance, in his relations with Adīb Ṣābir, a poet at the hostile court of Sanjar. Political hostility does not account for every such breach, however. Rashīd was a self-satisfied and arrogant man, full of personal sympathies and antipathies, fond of criticizing others. Those poets who listened to his advice and gave way to his suggested alterations to their poems, enjoyed his favour even to the extent of being invited to live with him. In such cases Rashīd could be generous in material ways also. His relationship to Khāqānī is interesting: it began with expressions of mutual praise, short-lived however, since Khāqānī suspected Rashīd of obstructing his access to the court of the Khwārazm-Shāh. Rashīd possessed a large library, collected manuscripts and compared variants. A strict Sunnī, he condemned all philosophers.

[1] The name means "sand martin" according to Safā, *Ta'rīkh*, vol. II, p. 628.

[2] Vil'chevsky in a letter.

Rashīd's prose is particularly valuable. Pride of place goes to his "Art of Rhetoric", the *Ḥada'iq al-siḥr fī daqā'iq al-shi'r*, or "Magic Gardens of the Niceties of Poetry", written because Muḥammad b. 'Umar Rādūyānī's *Tarjumān al-Balāgha*, "Guide to Eloquence" (composed between 481/1088 and 507/1114) had become out of date. In Rashīd's book almost thirty Persian poets are represented by examples, 'Unsurī in particular; amongst the Arab poets, Mutanabbī is most often cited. Sanā'ī and Firdausī are, in Rashīd's eyes, non-existent, and he never mentions his own contemporaries.[1] Nevertheless this is a valuable book, though its artificiality was probably an unfortunate influence on the development of Persian poetry. It was followed by a host of imitations.

Apart from his Persian works, there is also a collection of Rashīd's Arabic writings. Outstanding examples of his prose are the collections of his Persian and Arabic letters, both official and private: it is in these and in his poetics that his real significance can be seen.

A particularly arresting and indeed welcome exception in the grey monotony of more or less well-known panegyric poets is the satirist Ḥakīm ("The wise") Shams al-Dīn Muḥammad b. 'Alī (or possibly Mas'ūd), of Samarqand or its vicinity, who according to his own claim was a scion of the family of Salmān, the Persian companion of the Prophet. He was generally known as Sūzanī, the "needlemaker", a *nom de plume* said to have arisen because of his violent passion for a needlemaker's apprentice under whose influence he supposedly took up the twin crafts of needlemaking and poetry; this seems, however, a clumsy explanation when the relevance of "nomen omen" is so obvious. Details of his life (he died in 562/1166) are lacking, apart from what we can gather from his works. Obviously he was a very cultured writer: he took a knowledge of Arabic for granted. Countless allusions of his, and what seem to us now his extremely interesting quotations, lead to the conclusion that he was remarkably well read, and that his knowledge of Christianity and Manichaeism was exceptional, while his frequent use of Turkish words shows how widely known that language was. When he alludes to situations in everyday life, his level of meaning is often obscure—a problem which arises often enough with literary figures. In order, apparently, to make his livelihood, he addressed eulogistic verses to greater and lesser rulers, though he himself probably never left

[1] Firdausī afforded no material on account of the simplicity of his style. But cf. my article, "Ritoricheskiye priyemī Firdausi", *Sbornik Orbeil* (Moscow–Leningrad, 1960), pp. 427–32.

Samarqand. Despite all their rhetorical erudition, however, these panegyrics show a general poverty of language. His qaṣīdas are hardly likely to have aroused much admiration for him, in contrast with the *fontaines lumineuses* of the court poets, even if those to whom they were addressed could scarcely understand them. But their delight in Sūzanī's broad and non-literary humour must have been all the more spontaneous and unfeigned. He never hesitated to include lewd and insulting remarks, travesties and parodies, in his satire, for which he had many a down-to-earth metaphor and turn of phrase. He possessed unmistakable poetic talent, but too often lacked all sense of good taste. Nevertheless Sūzanī was a genuinely realistic poet, worthy of the most thorough study.

(ii) *Ghaznavid*

A somewhat later poet, hitherto less well known, is Sayyid Ashraf al-Dīn Abū Muḥammad Ḥasan b. Muḥammad Ḥusainī Ghaznavī, called Ashraf for short. His poetic career began towards the end of the fifth/eleventh century under the Ghaznavids. He was active for a long time at the court of Bahrām-Shāh, where he enjoyed the favour and esteem both of the ruler and the viziers. After 543/1148 his life became less peaceful; harassed, he made his way through Khurāsān and 'Irāq to Baghdad and Mecca, singing the praises of minor Saljuq princes and of the great Sulṭān Sanjar. He died suddenly in 556/1160–61 on the way from Hamadān to Khurāsān, in Āzādvār, where his grave can still be seen. His dīvān, which contains *inter alia* eighty-three ghazals, is particularly significant for the development of this form. Occasionally signed with the pseudonym "Ḥasan", and essentially lyric in manner, his ghazals frequently contain eulogies of Bahrām-Shāh, often just in the final lines. In his qaṣīdas the panegyric manner alternates with the didactic. Although not impervious to the influence of his predecessors and contemporaries, he possessed a voice original and strong enough to influence poets of the latter half of the sixth/twelfth century. Simplicity and lucidity are not the least of his merits.

(iii) *Saljuq*

It is well known that poets of the Saljuq period went from court to court in search of better conditions; there is nothing surprising in this. But at the same time they could also have other motives for so doing.

A case in point is a man who was made to suffer for a mode of conduct that happened not to be spontaneous but was enjoined on him.

Shihāb al-Dīn Adīb Ṣābir b. Ismā'īl Tirmidhī, a panegyric poet at the court of Sulṭān Sanjar, was a fluent writer of conventional "love and wine" poetry; his sensitive verses are marked by the usual mannerisms, and by a predilection for certain rhetorical figures. But at heart he was a pessimist and probably for that reason a night-reveller. He imitated masters old and new and was in contact with the leading poets of his day; even Anvarī regarded himself as insignificant in comparison with Tirmidhī. His exceptional knowledge of Arabic proves how highly educated he was; not only was he conversant with Arabic literature, he even translated Persian verse into Arabic. At the beginning of the hostilities between Sanjar and the Khwārazm-Shāh Atsïz, he was despatched to the latter, ostensibly as an ambassador—as proof of the high regard in which he was held—but in reality as a spy. When he discovered Atsïz's plans to assassinate Sanjar, he was cruelly punished, being drowned in the Oxus (538/1143 or 542/1148).

The qaṣīda, flourishing generally throughout the twelfth century, reached its culmination in the works of two poets who were contemporaries of each other: Anvarī of Khurāsān and Khāqānī of Caucasia, masters of a poetic genre particularly neglected and underestimated by Western scholars. Both were poets who outshone their predecessors, and whom their own followers could not surpass. Both were men not only of intellectual and poetic genius, of profound thought and wisdom, but of genuine feeling too. Erudition is the hallmark of their poetry, as is virulent invective. They wrote both qaṣīdas and ghazals, and other slighter types of verse. But whereas Khāqānī's works include an extensive mathnavī, tradition ascribes some didactic prose writings to Anvarī. Since they both enjoyed considerable fame in their own lifetimes, it is all the more surprising that details concerning them are so deficient and distorted, in the case of Anvarī perhaps even more than with Khāqānī. Traditional biographies are full of attractive but unfortunately fictitious anecdotes which contain only grains of truth at most. Factual pictures of their lives could not be pieced together as long as reliable editions of their works were lacking. It is indeed fortunate that there has recently been an improvement in this respect. Anvarī and Khāqānī are amongst the most difficult poets to understand; to do so requires the greatest philological, historical, and cultural penetration. (For further discussion on Khāqānī, see below, pp. 569 ff.)

Anvarī's name and genealogy can be established with relative ease and accuracy: they are Auḥad al-Din 'Ali b. Vahīd al-Din Muḥammad b. Isḥāq Abīvardī. He was born in the village of Badana, not far from the small town of Abīvard (or Bāvard), between Nasā and Sarakhs. Badana was situated in Dasht-i Khāvarān, and therefore the poet is said to have signed his earliest poems with the name Khāvarī before assuming his well-known *nom de plume* of Anvarī.[1] As is often the case in the biographies of early poets, the precise year of his birth is not known, but there is good reason for supposing it was 510/1116–17, since his first known qaṣīda dates from 530/1135–36. His father left him a modest fortune, which he soon squandered in riotous living. A tendency to drink, already apparent in his youth, was later to find expression in notorious passages in his qaṣīdas where he begs for wine. He parried the reproaches of his friends in a probably unfinished mathnavī, the surviving torso of which shows that the author's propensity for invective was present in him from the start. He studied the customary sciences, in particular philosophy, mathematics, medicine, and astrology, and his works are permeated with a deep knowledge of them. Yet it was not to science and learning that he was to devote his life. A delightful anecdote tells us why he gave his preference to poetry; no doubt it is apocryphal, yet it has a core of truth: the prodigality of the court poets must have appeared attractive to a man of such unbridled inclinations. He did in fact make his way to the court of Sulṭān Sanjar, to whom he was undoubtedly akin in temperament, and there he became one of the ruler's intimates. He probably resided in the sultan's palace at Marv until the catastrophic Ghuzz invasion (548/1153–54). He then lived in Nīshāpūr and above all in Balkh. It was in Balkh that he underwent a disagreeable experience, when some verses lampooning the city appeared. The inhabitants, deeply offended, threatened Anvarī, supposing him to be the author. Even a long qaṣīda, full of praises of Balkh, might not have been enough to placate them had he not been protected by respected worthies of the town who were also his friends. It was finally discovered that the lampoon had been foisted on him by Athīr al-Dīn Futūḥī. Between 560 and 565 (1164–70) he visited Baghdad and Mosul. It cannot yet be established how long he spent there, but it is certain that after 568/1172–73 he was back in Balkh, where he presumably lived until his death.

[1] Nafīsī, *Divān-i Anvarī*, p. 37, assumes that Khāvarī is a mistake due to the incorrect explanation of Anvarī-yi Khāvarī as "Anvarī of Khāvar".

One of the hardest problems in his biography is to establish the date of his death. If circulating rumours are sifted, we are left with a range of dates from 540 to 597 (1145–1201), a period of almost sixty years. The foremost Iranian scholars are working on the solution of this problem. One clue is offered by the conjunction of the seven planets, with Saturn in Libra, a celestial occurrence which was regarded by astrologers and especially by Anvarī as the portent of a cataclysm of the first order. The terrified population of Balkh abandoned their homes and fled to the woods and mountains in the hope of finding some refuge there from the hurricane that was supposedly threatening, while on the critical day, 29 Jumādā II 582 (15 August 1186), the flame of the little lamp on the minaret did not even flicker. Events justified those who disagreed with Anvarī, e.g. the poet Ẓahīr Fāryābī, and the resulting scorn must inevitably have injured Anvarī's reputation. Embittered, he retired to complete solitude, writing nothing more, and died either in 583/1187–88, or, more probably, in 585/1189–90.

Lyric poetry was completely reformed by this poet of genius. It might be added that he practised poetry in all its forms, though as a court poet he favoured the qaṣīda. Though appreciating the masters of this style, he was well aware that it was static and inflexible in both form and expression, and he set about taking it apart and reshaping it. He did not regard its traditional sequence as sacrosanct, and was fond of beginning with praise of the person to be eulogized and then passing on to another subject. The customary types of exordium vanish, their lyrical qualities being allowed to appear wherever they like. He does not attach any particular value to romantic feelings, not even in a dialogue between a lover and his beloved; amorousness is obviously not identical with passion, it conceals something else: it is directed at the person eulogized. To create lyrical episodes he had recourse either to descriptions of nature, in which he was most successful, or to philosophical reflexions. He was a master of description, be it of personal experiences (his crossing of the Oxus) or of public happenings (the catastrophe brought about by the Ghuzz, 548/1153).

His language, too, departed from tradition. He could not help making use of the ornaments provided by poetics, and his command of the whole range of rhetoric was perfect; but here too he was in search of something new. He was no lover of trifling play with words and letters; instead he delighted in tropes, metaphors, similes, and allusions. He seldom, however, sacrificed a thought to a rhetorical embellishment.

Extreme elegance of first and last lines, of transitions, and of the invocation is characteristic of him. His use of hyperbole, in which his thoughts and their effect are expressed to maximum advantage, is striking. So sovereign was his command of language—indeed he could improvise at a moment's notice—that he could express any idea with ease, though this does not mean that his ideas are immediately accessible to one and all. The stiff and antiquated language of his predecessors did not suit Anvarī, and he used contemporary colloquial language, in particular the cultivated speech of the educated. This, together with his unusually comprehensive knowledge, drove him to replace the customary and hackneyed images with fresh ones drawn from the most varied fields of knowledge, as familiar to him as was poetry itself. This ushered in a wave of Arabicization such as had not hitherto occurred, though this does not mean that Anvarī added an unnatural or inappropriate element to poetry.

An essential ingredient of Anvarī's dīvān is the g͟hazal, which in his unique way he brought to a high degree of perfection—the highest perhaps until Sa'dī. Nor could a man of his intellectual brilliance ignore the quatrain. But there was another genre which was particularly congenial to his easily excitable temperament, namely the "fragment" (*qiṭ'a*).[1] This form gave poets the opportunity of treating their subject matter as freely as they wished; like other poetic forms, fragments allowed invocations and tokens of gratitude, but they also permitted attacks, and this was grist to Anvarī's mill. While his qaṣīdas and g͟hazals gleam with immaculate purity, his fragments were the ideal vehicle through which to work off his vanity, his sarcasm, his sense of injustice, and his petty jealousy of other poets. In them he incorporated his satires, or rather lampoons, for which he did not hesitate to use the coarsest, most scandalous expressions, whether his irritation was justified or not; for his sharp tongue spared no one, and indeed he sometimes hoped to incur his masters' favours by these means. He raised his voice against the stupidities prevalent at all levels of society, against sycophancy, against anomalies in administration; he satirized women, blind fate, and so on. Lampoons cannot fail to be personal, and paradoxically their very subjectivity sheds a most informative light on society. Anvarī's most likeable facet is his humour, found especially in his petitionary verse.

Anvarī's originality as a writer lies in his dīvān taken as a whole.

[1] Occasional poems of the most diverse content with the rhyme scheme, ba, ca, da....

Yet he was not only a great poet but a great scholar too, as is proved by the multitude of allusions in the dīvān. It is also known that he was an admirer of Avicenna's philosophy and that he knew G͟hazālī's *Destructio Philosophiae*. When in Mosul he wrote a learned petition in honour of Quṭb al-Dīn Maudūd and promised to write more. There are also reports of a commentary on astronomical tables and of an astrological work of his called *Mufīd*, "The Useful One"; but these writings have been lost, and only incomplete references to them survive.

Anvarī himself seems to have been a man fond of good living, merry to the point of licentiousness, and a great drinker of wine (indeed he once fell off a roof when intoxicated). In his petitionary verse he could be quite shamelessly importunate, though elsewhere he condemned begging as unworthy of poetry and the poet. Poetry itself he called unnecessary and worthless, though here he was obviously thinking of panegyric poetry. His inconsiderate delight in abusing others shows that he was irascible and easily hurt; on the other hand the discrepancy between the volume of his praise and the worth of its object was obvious enough to so perspicacious a man. Nevertheless he remained loyal to Sanjar and to the Saljuqs in general, even though the uncertainty of the times forced him to bestow praise on all kinds of people. His fluctuating attitude to various problems must be seen as a result both of the upheavals and dangers of the period, and of his exuberant talent and explosive, violent temperament.

Eastern scholars are trying to discover which sect Anvarī belonged to. Whereas in the past they would have liked to regard him as a S͟hīʿī, it is now openly admitted by Iranian scholars that he was a Sunnī.

Anvarī was not uninfluenced by his predecessors, in particular by Abu'l-Faraj Rūnī, who probably died after 492/1098–99. Anvarī was acquainted with the poetry of K͟hāqānī, and in his turn exerted a considerable influence on contemporary and subsequent poets. Ẓahīr Fāryābī (d. 598/1201–02) adopted Anvarī's manner to such an extent that later generations could not decide which poet to prefer. But the initiated opted, and quite rightly, for Anvarī. Now regarded as one of the greatest figures in Persian literature, he has been prevented from becoming universally known only because panegyric poetry is foreign to the West.

THE ĀZARBĀĪJĀN SCHOOL

Transcaucasia and its neighbour Āzarbāījān provide a good example of an area which produced a homogeneous group of poets, each of whom nevertheless had his own characteristics. There are of course other examples (see, e.g., pp. 584–6); but literary history has not yet studied this aspect of Persian literature in sufficient detail. Although the great Saljuq rulers strove to bring this territory under the strong and centralized administration of their empire, they were unable to subdue the local feudal organization for long and to prevent its disintegration into independent principalities. The feudal conditions of Transcaucasia were very much closer to those of Europe than to those elsewhere in Iran.

Its poetry is proof of its high degree of culture. Not only were there innumerable Caucasian and Āzarbāījānī writers and scholars, but they were especially original. Their modes of expression, their vocabulary, and their syntax contain certain features found seldom or not at all in the poets of eastern Iran. This does not mean that there were no connexions between this school and the poets of the other parts of Iran. All these developments in poetry had sprung from the same roots, but had afterwards been subjected to local influences, in this case to the propinquity of non-Iranian and non-Muslim territories, whose languages were foreign or, at most, merely related to Persian. With the exception of Niẓāmī's works, the entire poetic output of the region was confined to lyric poetry, to the qaṣīda in particular. Moreover all these poets were employed by royal courts. Here, too, although there was no specifically Ṣūfī literature, the Ṣūfī mask allowed poets to express opinions which would have been unthinkable in normal circumstances. Under the influence of Ṣūfism, of the urban classes that is, the g͟hazal became very popular; and under the growing influence of the towns, themes were occasionally chosen from outside the courtly sphere. One of the striking features of the Transcaucasian school is its complicated technique. In their language the poets desisted from archaism, but drew all the more extensively from Arabic vocabularly. There are even traces of local folklore.

The school, which began with Qaṭrān (d. 465/1072), formed a well-defined group of teachers and pupils of whom two, K͟hāqānī and Niẓāmī, were to exert a lasting influence on the entire development of their respective genres: K͟hāqānī being the greatest exponent of the qaṣīda and Niẓāmī the most brilliant writer of romantic epics. Apart from the latter poet, all the others were attached to courts, even though Persian was not the language of the princes whose praises they sang. But these patrons should not be over-idealized; their moods, often arbitrary and hostile, and the possibility of their disfavour and of ensuing imprisonment were common perils for the poets. One result was that the court poets could not display a definite moral attitude. The first such poet was the courtier Niẓām al-Dīn Abu'l-'Alā Ganjavī (d. 554/1159), the first notable figure of the school of Shīrvān, a critic and teacher highly regarded by the generations after him. Little of his writing has survived.

An attempted comparison has already been made above (p. 563), and now it can be taken further. Khāqānī and Anvarī were undoubtedly great poets, and only their almost exclusive concentration on the panegyric seems to me to have prevented them from becoming known outside the bounds of Iranian culture. Khāqānī's biography abounds with problems, though Anvarī more than rivals him in this respect. The infusion of learning into poetry, a characteristic they shared with their times, contributed towards their greatness. Anvarī was well acquainted with philosophy and acknowledged its place in his writings; Khāqānī was no lover of it. They were well aware of the shady side of panegyric writing and often even expressed a disgust for poetry. Both, however, were excellent lyric poets, and the genuine feeling in their ghazals clearly points the way to Sa'dī and Ḥāfiẓ. Neither of them was pampered by life. The choleric Anvarī inclined to laughter, while Khāqānī surveyed the world with a sombre gaze. Their sharp tongues gave them such a reputation that they almost came to grief, for each had certain invective poems falsely attributed to him; in spite of this, they each had to make atonement and beg for pardon. And in the end, both of them retired into solitude.

Of all the poets in this period, Afḍal al-Dīn Badīl (Ibrahīm) b. 'Al Khāqānī of Shīrvān (b. 515/1121–22) was most closely bound to his native country, Āzarbāījān, and therefore his poetry cannot be understood without a thorough knowledge of the political and cultural life of eastern Transcaucasia, a central meeting-point of Muslim and Christian religious influences. Khāqānī remembers his father, the cabinet maker 'Alī, but his deepest affection was for his mother, who had once been a Nestorian slave, and who, although she had embraced Islam, must certainly have taught her son the elements of the Christian faith and its rites. Khāqānī, unlike the majority of Islamic Persian writers, was remarkably well informed on the subject of Christianity; he did not of course owe this knowledge solely to his mother, for the interest in religion prevailing amongst those around him had much to do with it. His dīvān abounds in images and symbols which are sometimes Christian, sometimes Muslim, both blended together; at times he also quotes from Christian prayers and sacred texts. A dīvān of this kind could not have been composed anywhere except in Transcaucasia.

His youth was spent in poverty and distress, and nothing would have come of him, the child of an ordinary artisan family, had not his talent and quite exceptional sagacity attracted the attention of his uncle, the doctor Mīrzā Kāfī al-Dīn ʿUmar b. ʿUthmān,[1] a cultured man who himself taught the boy the rudiments of Arabic (Khāqānī was also to write Arabic qaṣīdas). Then followed a thorough education in every branch of science, which left its mark on Khāqānī and his work. Ghazals and eulogies of the Prophet (*naʿt*), written under the mystical *nom de plume* of Ḥaqāʾiqī, "the searcher after truth", soon gave the young student the reputation amongst his companions of being a reasonably good poet; but the naʿts of his maturity were to earn him the name of Ḥassān al-ʿAjam, "the Persian Ḥassān". When the court poet Abu'l-ʿAlā Ganjavī (p. 569 above) took him as a disciple, he was so well pleased with him that he gave him his daughter's hand in marriage, and even presented him to the Shīrvān-Shāh, who at that time was Abu'l-Muẓaffar Khāqān-i Akbar Manūchihr b. Farīdūn. It seemed that Khāqānī (who had been led by these favourable auspices to request this pseudonym) had indeed succeeded. But his father-in-law soon became jealous, and this put an end to all the young poet's hopes: there could be no question of a career for him when ʿAlī the cabinet-maker had sold his possessions to support his son and the latter's family.

This was the actual background to the impassioned quarrel which broke out between the two poets, and which continued until Khāqānī accused Abu'l-ʿAlā of sympathizing with the ideology of Ḥasan-i Ṣabbāḥ, the founder of the Assassins: an accusation of considerable gravity in the eyes of the Sunnī prince. Khāqānī then tried to establish himself elsewhere, especially at the court of the famous Khwārazm-Shāh ʿAlāʾ al-Dīn Atsïz, but this the poet Rashīd Vaṭvāṭ (pp. 559 ff.) would not allow. To Rashīd's friendly approach, Khāqānī replied with

[1] On Khāqānī's alleged relationship to him cf. Vil'chevsky's (and K. G. Zaleman's) opinion in O. L. Vil'chevsky, "Khakani", pp. 74–5.

an angry satire, and though he soon regretted his act, he did not improve his relations with Rashīd. When 'Umar the doctor, his "uncle" and teacher, died in 545/1150, Khāqānī was filled with anchoretic yearnings, a mood that was to reappear later though he was able to indulge it at the end of his life. His attempt to reach the court of Sulṭān Sanjar failed; he had got only as far as Ray when the destruction of the Saljuq empire reduced all his hopes to naught. In 551–52/1156–57 he undertook his first pilgrimage to the holy places of Islam, a concession accorded him probably at the request of the Georgian king Dmitri I. One fruit of this pilgrimage was the *Tuḥfat al-'Irāqain* ("The Gift from the Two Iraqs"), the first book of travels in mathnavī form to be written in Persian. He met with a most unfriendly reception in Iṣfahān on his return journey: the city rose in indignation against him on account of an offensive and scandalous satire which had been foisted on him by Mujīr Bailaqānī. Khāqānī was driven to appease the city with a long qaṣīda meant to clear up the deceit. Shortly afterwards he was thrown into prison (554/1159), his laments finding utterance in the so-called "prison qaṣīdas". The cause of this must be sought in the upheavals that followed the death of the Shīrvān-Shāh Manūchihr (554–57/1159–62), since Khāqānī probably refused to support the shah's widow Tamara in her conception of the succession.

In Vil'chevsky's biography a definite clue to this event is furnished by a qaṣīda written in 564/1168 and addressed to the Byzantine Emperor Manuel Comnenus (1143–80) rather than to the latter's nephew and rival Andronicus Comnenus.[1] This qaṣīda proves that Khāqānī visited the court of the Emperor at Constantinople: in it he speaks of the religious controversy which was at that time engrossing Constantinople and Orthodox Christianity, namely, the interpretation of the words: "I go unto the Father: for the Father is greater than I" (John xiv. 28). Khāqānī's interpretation concurred with the opinion of the Church Council, which had been influenced by Manuel to oppose Andronicus. Later, however, Khāqānī showed a different attitude to Andronicus, when the latter, an exile, wandering from place to place with his consort Theodora, eventually arrived in Transcaucasia at the court of the Georgian king Giorgi III (1156–84). There Andronicus was greeted with all due pomp and took part in the allied campaign of Georgia and Shīrvān to ward off the Russian attack on Transcaucasia in 569/1173. In one of his qaṣīdas the poet offers Andronicus his services, describing

[1] Vil'chevsky, *op. cit.* p. 67; but cf. Minorsky, "Khāqānī".

him as the only man capable of defeating the Russian armies, and going so far as to call him the worthiest claimant to the Imperial throne, which in fact Andronicus never ceased to strive for. This complete reversal in Khāqānī's attitude was caused not so much by Andronicus's hostility to Russia, as by the poet's own dissatisfaction with the court of Akhsitān and with Shīrvān in general; this unhappiness was the reason for his never-ending attempts to break away. He was able to disguise his service to Andronicus by another pilgrimage (which was probably again brought about by the intercession of a member of the Byzantine Imperial family). Thus in 570/1175, entrusted with a political mission on behalf of Andronicus, he set out for Iraq; and he remained in Baghdad for some time, where, despite invitations, he refused to enter the service of the Caliph. Soon after his return to Shīrvān he suffered the cruel blow of the death of his son Rashīd al-Dīn (571/1176), and probably other misfortunes besides. His struggles to escape from his surroundings at Shīrvān became increasingly desperate; yet each time his hopes were dashed. Although Akhsitān was by no means fond of him, he was reluctant to lose him. Finally Khāqānī began to long for Khurāsān, by then already under the dominion of the Khwārazm-Shāh; he would willingly have established himself there, now that Rashīd Vaṭvāṭ was dead (573/1177–78). In 580/1184 he either went or fled to Tabrīz, but never got any farther; from there he visited Baghdad and various other places, but Tabrīz remained his principal place of residence. Many of the poems in his dīvān date from this period, but his activities, apart from writing poetry, remain obscure. While he was at Tabrīz his wife died, in Shīrvān, and he poured out his grief in eight elegies. After living in what seems to have been solitude, he died at Tabrīz in 595/1199.

A comparison between Vil'chevsky's biography of the poet and of the traditional native ones will reveal many discrepancies. In order to establish the truth, it is wiser to follow the example of various Iranian and Soviet scholars and rely on the evidence of Khāqānī's dīvān itself, since it contains a host of autobiographical details. Conversely, we can appreciate the poetry fully only by continually bearing in mind the history and culture of the Muslim and Christian Caucasus, and by remembering Khāqānī's ties with Constantinople. The poet provides some help in this, with allusions and frequent, although well hidden, chronograms. A speciality of Khāqānī's (as of other poets of the Āzarbāījān school, no doubt) is the double chronogram calculated according to both the Hijrī and the Julian calendars, though its presence is not immediately obvious. A good example occurs in the famous qaṣīda on the ruins of Madā'in (Ctesiphon), a poem erroneously attributed to the poet's second pilgrimage. That it was written instead in 561/1166 is clearly indicated by a double chronogram within it.[1] Thus Khāqānī did not write the qaṣīda while bewailing the actual ruins of the celebrated metropolis; he wrote it six years after his return from the pilgrimage and even used a similar qaṣīda by the Arabic poet Buḥturī (d. 284/897) as his model. There can be no question of any patriotic feelings or of any echoes of Iranian national ideals in Khāqānī's qaṣīda; rather, it is a beautiful variation of the usual lament on the transitoriness of worldly things.

Within his dīvān, every description of Khāqānī's life shows the unrest in which he lived. The poet was continually complaining and lamenting. This was not the fault of his milieu only; its moral standards were by no means high, but he too was to blame for his sufferings. Nor can it be maintained that he never accepted any gifts or emoluments from the Shīrvān-Shāhs. Nevertheless he was always convinced that he was being treated unjustly, and because of this he was continually fleeing from place to place in search of something better. He was a poet of genius, but a man of boundless conceit and always apt to take offence. This is the key to the correct understanding of his inconsistent behaviour.

Khāqānī was a panegyric poet, though not quite in the usual sense; he was not just a poetic craftsman, but a genuine poet of an exceptional and brilliant kind. Outwardly his writing is beset with innumerable difficulties, so that it yields its treasures to few, and then only with the help of the numerous commentaries which this peculiarity has rendered necessary. A man of outstanding learning, he made use of every detail that contemporary knowledge could offer, displaying them all with the fireworks of his rhetorical virtuosity. In both science and poetry he was in his element; but as he was first and foremost a poet, science had to be the servant of his poetry. The nature of the difficulties which encompass it is a result of this; they stem not from any desire to dazzle and impress nor from any superficial delight in artificiality, but from his intellectual richness: Khāqānī presupposes like-minded readers. These difficulties are present in his panegyric verse and in his more heartfelt passages—in his powerful and moving laments and elegies on the deaths of his

[1] Letters of O. L. Vil'chevsky dated 22 July and 26 September 1959.

son and wife, for instance, and on the murder of a scholar during the Ghuzz incursion; they are present when he meditates on the transience of the things of this world in the qaṣīda on the ruins of Ctesiphon, when he is suffering from jealousy, lack of friends, betrayal, and imprisonment. Particularly magnificent are his descriptions of landscapes and of nature, of morning and sunrise in particular; here, as in other passages, we sense the beauty of his Caucasian homeland. Nor is love entirely absent, though its presence is rare. The manifestation of Allah as the Beloved is a concept quite foreign to him. In his panegyric verse, which often rises to tones of the most exaggerated adulation, his purpose is not just empty praise, for he also imparts instruction and advice. At the same time, his ability to attack and to slander is equally remarkable. His enthusiasm is for religious and especially Ṣūfī wisdom, rather than for anything philosophical. In his originality he reveals affinities with the poets of Āzarbāījān and ʿIrāq, but his qaṣīdas, as he himself admitted, reflect the direct influence of Sanāʾī. He knew, admired, and imitated the great poets of Khurāsān, such as Manūchihrī, and he strove to surpass ʿUnṣurī in ornamentation. He used the ghazal both for the expression of its customary themes and for its laments.

A master of language, a poet of sense and sensibility, constantly inclining towards introspection, and a man of unique personality; with such qualities Khāqānī is assured of a place in the front ranks of Persian literature. (This being so, the praise he consciously and not infrequently bestows upon himself does not sound hollow.) He reveals the heights to which the qaṣīda can aspire in the hands of a genius. Unfortunately the art of the qaṣīda is in all respects esoteric. Khāqānī exerted an incalculable influence on the entire subsequent development of panegyric poetry. His qaṣīda on Ctesiphon even influenced the "Ode on the Kremlin" by the modern poet Lahūtī (d. 1957). It is also likely that Maulavī adopted the form of Khāqānī's exordia and ghazals for many of his own ghazals; on the other hand the picaresque tone of some of his poems is reminiscent of Ḥāfiẓ two hundred years later.

This picture of Khāqānī would not be complete without further mention of his *Ṭuḥfat al-ʿIrāqain*, "The Gift from the Two Iraqs" (i.e. from Persian and Arabian Iraq), the author's poetic description of his first pilgrimage to Mecca and Medina. The title was not his original one, since he himself calls the work *Tuḥfat al-khawāṭir va zubdat al-ḍamāʾir*, "The Gift made up of Memories and a Selection of Thoughts". The work is immediately remarkable because it has nothing in common with any other existing mat͟hnavī; nor can it be described as a continuous travel narrative, because the author constantly interrupts it with digressions. In fact, it is an Oriental counterpart to Byron's *Childe Harold's Pilgrimage*. At the very beginning K͟hāqānī apostrophizes the sun, and during the course of the poem he repeatedly alludes to it on all manner of occasions and in its most diverse aspects. In six cantos of varying length, he treats of places and important people, of nature, events, traditions, and customs, and of his own life and family. His style varies from description to direct address and dialogues, of which one of the most striking is a long conversation with the prophet K͟hiḍr. The poet praises and laments, but he also inveighs against people (not sparing his own father-in-law).

Yet even this does not complete the picture of K͟hāqānī, for the man's real thoughts and feelings are not to be found in his eulogies any more than in his invectives. Rather, it is in many lesser-known qaṣīdas—either messages to, or laments for, relatives and friends, for artisans, stallkeepers, poets, and other simple folk in S͟hīrvān: works written not for hope of reward but out of sincerity of heart, and thus permeated with deep feeling for their respective heroes—it is in these qaṣīdas, together with his intimate, essentially lyrical g͟hazals and quatrains, and finally in his "Fragments", where he often expresses the purest and most lofty humanism, that K͟hāqānī translated into superlative poetry the thoughts and ideals of an oriental town in the Middle Ages, thus preserving them for posterity.

K͟hāqānī's disciple and his rival in courtship was Abu'l-Niẓām Muḥammad Falakī S͟hīrvānī, a native of S͟hamāk͟hī (b. 501/1107, d. 549–51/1154–57). Calligrapher, Arabic scholar, and mathematician, he was also well versed in astronomy and therefore surnamed Falakī, meaning both "heavenly" and "ill-starred"; indeed he is said to have written a book on astronomy. It is strange that Falakī does not seem to have thought any contemporary poet worthy of mention; instead he regarded himself as the equal of Abū Tammām (d. 230/846) and of Abū Nuwās (d. 198/810). He spent his whole life at the court of the famous S͟hīrvān-S͟hāh Manūc͟hihr II b. Farīdūn, and, unlike the other poets, praised only his master in his finely wrought qaṣīdas. Yet he too, like K͟hāqānī, Mujīr, and probably Abu'l-'Alā, was thrown into prison as a result of the calumny of rivals, an experience which had a deep effect on him. Of his poetic works some 1,512 scattered lines have survived, and they are relatively simple, even when they touch on science. He generally includes essentially lyrical passages, on wine and the beloved, at the end of a qaṣīda. He admires neither bigotry nor boastfulness. From prison he spoke as a true poet; but originality was never his most salient feature. Nevertheless ʿIṣmat Bukhārāʾī (d. 829/1425–26) imitated him, as did Salmān Sāvajī (see p. 613), though the latter did not acknowledge his model.

Another of Khāqānī's pupils was Abu'l-Makārim Mujīr al-Dīn of Bailaqān (part of Shīrvān), an excellent though pugnacious poet: in fact after his apprenticeship he became an enemy who attacked the master in a lampoon. Virtually nothing is known of his life except that he came of a family in no way distinguished and that his mother was an Abyssinian. In his qaṣīdas he extolled amongst others the atabegs of Āzarbāījān (Eldigüzids) and the Saljuq sultan Arslan b. Toghril. His relations with these, alternating between favour and disgrace, between fame in the eyes of the envious and public ignominy, indeed imprisonment, cannot be described here. Mujīr's dīvān is impressive because of its good taste, the harmony of its language, and its lucidity, simplicity, and forceful impact (indeed Amīr Khusrau Dihlavī preferred it to Khāqānī's); he is at his best when imitating old masters, rather than his own teacher. He was not inclined to display his knowledge, either literary or scientific, in his verse, and had no great understanding of philosophy; his mysticism was nothing more than superficial asceticism and pessimism. His lampoon on Iṣfahān (written because of allegedly inadequate hospitality) caused much suffering for Khāqānī, who was taken to be the author. It was in Iṣfahān that Mujīr died in about 594/1197–98, though whether by natural causes is not known.

To the same group as Khāqānī and the Āzarbāījān poets connected with him belongs Athīr al-Dīn Abu'l-Faḍl Muḥammad b. Ṭāhir (d. 577/1181 or 579/1183–84), a native of the distant town of Akhsikat, in Farghāna; his pseudonym was Athir or Athir-i Akhsikat. His earliest works date from before the time he left his home for the west, following the brutal Ghuzz incursion. In Āzarbāījān he entered the service of the Eldigüzids and acquired a brilliant literary reputation. His panegyric qaṣīdas are very much in the manner of Khāqānī, with whom, as with Mujīr, he maintained relations. He could not, however, restrain himself from attacking them both. An egotist, he loved himself most, while regarding Khāqānī as his equal and honouring Mujīr with the epithet "Robber of the caravans of poetry". His ghazals and quatrains are worthy of attention, and certainly his ingenuity of content and form cannot be denied; but this is counterbalanced by the frequent obscurity resulting from his erudite manner.

Born about 551/1156 in Fāryāb (to the south-west of Balkh), Ẓahīr al-Din Ṭāhir b. Muḥammad, who wrote under the name Ẓahīr, came of a learned family. That he was probably of Turkish origin, or brought up in Turkish surroundings, would account for the large proportion of Turkish words in his divan. When Anvarī and his supporters made their prophecy, that a catastrophic hurricane would occur in 582/1186, Ẓahīr was amongst those who disputed its accuracy, and in doing so he aroused the enmity of Toghan-Shāh b. Mu'ayyad. He then betook himself to Iṣfahān and from there to Māzandarān and Āzarbāījān, praising a whole series of patrons on the way. He dedicated the majority of his panegyric qaṣīdas to Nuṣrat al-Din Abū Bakr Eldigüz, the atabeg of Āzarbāījān and 'Irāq (587–607/1191–1211), though at this court he was not immune from the animosities created by intrigues. He finally came to prefer seclusion in Tabrīz, where he died at the age of forty-seven.

Ẓahīr was unashamedly a writer of panegyrics, a follower of Khāqānī and Anvarī, both of whom he surpassed in exaggerated adulation, though he lacked their emotional depth, not to mention their genius. He was an obsequious man whose begging was in the worst taste; but cupidity was a feature of the period. He despatched poems of praise far and near, in Arabic as well as Persian. In his conceit he criticized Anvarī, Niẓāmī, and others, because he regarded no one as his equal, though he himself did not write any satires. But he did undoubtedly possess certain poetic gifts, which must have enabled him to exert a considerable influence, since later generations were undecided whether to give preference to him or to Anvarī, whom he in fact imitated. Their indecision was sadly misplaced, it is true, for Ẓahīr was far from being a great poet; in the eyes of his contemporaries his chief merit lay in the relative comprehensibility of his verse. The reading of his dīvān presupposes a good knowledge of the troubled age in which he lived. The praise which Ḥāfiẓ bestows on him is for a line falsely attributed to him. However, Sa'dī himself imitated Ẓahīr's lyrical preambles.

The romanticism of Niẓāmī may be identified with a conception of humanity of the most sublime kind. What a difference there is between this conception and the sober utilitarianism of Sa'dī! Niẓāmī comes first not only as a socially conscious philosopher but also as a psychologist, a story-teller, a verbal artist, and a rhetorical virtuoso.

As the scene of the greatest flowering of the panegyrical qaṣīda, southern Caucasia occupies a prominent place in New Persian literary history. But this region also gave to the world Persia's finest creator of romantic epics. Ḥakīm Jamāl al-Dīn Abū Muḥammad Ilyās b. Yūsuf b. Zakī b. Mu'ayyad Niẓāmī, a native of Ganja in Āzarbāījān, is an unrivalled master of thoughts and words, a poet whose freshness and vigour all the succeeding centuries have been unable to dull. Little is known of his life, the only source being his own works, which in many cases provide no reliable information. We can only deduce that he was born between 535 and 540 (1140–46) and that his background was urban. Modern Āzarbāījān is exceedingly proud of its world-famous son and insists that he was not just a native of the region, but that he came of its own Turkish stock. At all events his mother was of Iranian origin, the poet himself calling her Ra'īsa and describing her as Kurdish. The only fact known about his youth is that he was orphaned early. It can be assumed that his family was relatively wealthy, for otherwise he could scarcely have enjoyed that excellent education in all the known branches of science and learning which his works so incontestably reveal. His native Ganja seems to have cast a spell on him: he left its walls only once, in 581 or 582 (1185–87), and then against his will: when the ruler of Āzarbāījān, Qïzïl-Arslan, who was on a progress some thirty *farsakhs* (117 miles) away, expressly requested to meet him. Did Niẓāmī make his living from poetry alone? Was poetry his only source of livelihood? An answer of a kind is to be found in *Lailī u Majnūn*, an epic of over 4,000 lines which Niẓāmī conjured up in less than four months; there he says that he might have been able to complete it in a fortnight had it not been for another occupation.[1] If he visited royal courts in his early years, he soon abandoned the practice; he was no court sycophant, indeed his whole way of thinking was against it. He did dedicate his great epics as well as occasional ghazals to princes; but it was then customary to do so in the hope of some reward or, rather, fee. Bahrām-Shāh, in return for the dedication of the epic *Makhzan al-asrār*, sent him 5,000 dīnārs and five nimble mules. Niẓāmī's reward for *Khusrau u Shīrīn* (he was given the village of Ḥamdūniyān) seems to have been less satisfactory, for it was made fun of by one of his rivals. It may therefore be justifiably deduced that he did not enjoy an excess of worldly goods. Tradition

[1] *Lailā u Majnūn*, ed. Dastgirdī, p. 29, ll. 10–11.

associates him with certain of the *Akhīs*, a kind of masonic society of the period, which recruited its supporters not from high-ranking circles but rather from the artisan classes. He was not an adherent of Ṣūfism. 599/1203 has generally been taken to be the year of his death, but the chronology of the persons he praised points to a later date, the most credible being that inscribed on an old gravestone, namely 605/1209, though the inscription itself contains a mistake and is therefore not entirely trustworthy. People have for centuries made pilgrimages to Niẓāmī's mausoleum as though to the burial-place of a saint; it has now been lovingly restored.

Niẓāmī's epics consist of five independent poems, each with its own metre which were only later grouped together in a collection known as the *Khamsa* or "Quintet". In the first poem, *Makhzan al-asrār*, "The Treasure-Chamber of Secrets", the topical allusions are dated, but a difficult and still unsolved problem arises. The earliest manuscripts of the epic give three different dates for its completion. These are apparently approximate only, and unfortunately happen to be metrically interchangeable. However, on the basis of various other allusions, the year 570/1174–75, when Niẓāmī was approximately thirty-five, appears the most likely one for its completion. Unlike all his other epics, this poem has an ethical and philosophical content, though Ṣūfī symbolism is apparent only in the introductory passage concerning the heart. He does not avoid criticism of the rulers and of their system, he defends the rights of the ordinary man, and holds up truth as a categorical imperative. As regards its content, Niẓāmī's work has a precursor in Sanā'ī's *Ḥadīqa*, but both in metre and in the clear-cut organization of the poem, he went his own way: his desire was, as he proudly announced, to stand on his own feet. The introduction is made up of eulogies of God and of the Prophet; a description of the latter's ascent into heaven in the space of a second; a eulogy of Bahrām-Shāh; a description of the poem's genesis, and a passage in praise of words and poetry: in other words, a series of passages of the kind which later occur regularly in every conceivable epic. Each of the poem's twenty chapters has a theoretical introduction and an illustration in the form of a parable, which often refers only to the last idea in the introduction, while at the same time forming a transition to the next chapter. The mastery with which the poet handles the theoretical reflexions and then devises appropriate parables must be particularly emphasized. The subject matter itself is not easily digestible; but the perfect way in which such intractable material is adapted proves the greatness of Niẓāmī. There is no trace of the diffuseness characteristic of Sanā'ī; the poetry is drawn from the living language, yet this remains Niẓāmī's most difficult work.

The repercussions of the poem on Persian literature were extremely far-reaching and made themselves felt on the literature of neighbouring countries also. Indeed the fame which Niẓāmī acquired with *Makhzan al-asrār* spread so far that the ruler of Darband, though the poem was not dedicated to him, expressed his admiration with the gift of a Qïpchaq slave girl called Afaq (i.e. "Blanca"), whose beauty obviously must have captivated the poet, since he married her in 569/1173–74. Their happy union was blessed with a son to whom Niẓāmī repeatedly refers in his works, but unfortunately in 1180 her death put an end to their happiness.[1] When the 'Irāqī Saljuq Toghril II requested a love epic from the poet without specifying the subject further, Niẓāmī picked on the story of the lovers Khusrau and Shīrīn, a theme set in his own region and based at least partly on historical fact, though an aura of legend already surrounded it. Niẓāmī completed the work in feverish activity after Afaq's death (*c.* 576/1181), with Shīrīn and Afaq, two figures of the utmost purity, blending into one in his imagination. The poem is really a romance of the love and suffering of a princess as a girl and then as a wife, and is unequalled for its pure beauty in the whole of Persian literature. Some of the events narrated in it were obviously suggested by the unworthiness of the ruling classes; the shāh's vacillation, for example, leads to an uprising of his vassals and the downfall of all the main characters. Niẓāmī's motivation is psychological; his portrayal of character is brilliant. We have the constant Shīrīn and the vacillating Khusrau; her love shines with purity, his feelings spring from egotism. The episode of Farhād stands out as an example of love sacrificing itself. The animal passion of the shāh's son Shīrūye is of the basest kind: in him the loose morality of a feudal lord is depicted in even worse light than it is in Khusrau. How much more noble, by comparison, is the labourer Farhād!

The subject of the third epic, written in 584/1188, is not taken from Persian history but is borrowed from the Arabian world: not that of the Bedouins, but one closer to the Persian conception of Arabia. *Lailī u Majnūn* was composed at the request of the Shīrvān-Shāh Akhsitan, and Niẓāmī undertook its composition unwillingly, fearing

[1] He lost his second wife after completing his *Lailī u Majnūn*; he married for the third time whilst writing the *Sharaf-Nāma*. The third wife also died before him.

that the subject would prove too slight; for this reason he chose the shortest metre. The subject is in fact similar to that of *Romeo and Juliet.* It is an epic full of feeling and passion, and quite unlike the colourless Arabic sources on which Niẓāmī drew. The drama of the story culminates in the casting off of the iron fetters, symbolic of a deliberate break with human society. Majnūn ("Fool") lives only for the spiritual bond uniting him with Lailī; this is why the external appearances seem not to change after the death of the husband she had been compelled to marry. The whole conception is entirely psychological without any trace of Ṣūfism. Majnūn has to suffer as a poet too, but grief enhances the passion of his songs. Bertel's has pointed out the didactic element concealed in the epic. On the one hand we have the exceptional mildness of Majnūn's father, on the other the unnatural tyranny of Lailī's; and a third concept of fatherhood is apparent in the relationship of Niẓāmī to his son, which is expressed in the preamble to the poem. When in a special chapter the poet addresses the son of the ruler, it seems that he really has in mind the ruler himself, who, being a father, might be able to perceive the lesson of the tragic story which he had himself suggested for the epic.

It has been maintained that *Lailī u Majnūn* is inferior to the previous epic, but I do not share this opinion.[1] In the development of plot and in emotional depth, not to mention language and rhetoric, it is certainly quite the other's equal. Moreover the exceptional number of imitations of it attest to its popularity, and although this has naturally decreased with the decline of feudalism, the theme of the epic still recurs today in Turkish and Persian novels.

The fourth of Niẓāmī's epics in terms of chronology, but the first in merit, is the *Haft Paikar*, "Seven Pictures" (completed in 593/1197), whose elegant, graceful metre corresponds to the lighter nature of the poem. It is dedicated to the Aqsunqurid 'Alā' al-Dīn Körp-Arslan, the Prince of Marāgheh, who had commissioned it without specifying a theme. Its subject is the life of the Sassanian Emperor Bahrām V Gūr (420–38), a monarch less celebrated in history than in legend; in other words, it is taken once again from Iranian history. Bahrām is the central figure, but his story does not occupy the entire poem, more than half of it being made up of the seven delightful tales of the seven princesses whom Bahrām married, and these, taken together, amount to a second plot.

[1] Bausani. *Istoria*, p. 665.

In the *Haft Paikar* the shāh does not appear in the same light as the heroes of the *Shāh-Nāma* or those portrayed by the followers of Firdausī. Bahrām is made to correspond to the new conditions, as can be clearly seen if Firdausī's version is compared with Niẓāmī's. The attitude of the poet is obvious: he upholds the people against the misrule of the princes and potentates, and offers the latter a lesson cast in the most exquisite poetic form. In the tales of the seven princesses, Niẓāmī's narrative art reaches the highest degree of perfection he ever attained. The most varied aspects of love are brilliantly conveyed, always with a profound moral basis. In his description of passion, Niẓāmī commands the whole range from the utmost delicacy to the most extreme violence. He avoids the make-believe of the fairy tale, transposing it into illusion and thus into subjective reality. His language is not antiquated; rather, it corresponds exactly to the times and provides an admirable vehicle for describing events and emotions.

Niẓāmī's last epic is the *Iskandar-Nāma*, "The Lay of Alexander", or more properly *Sharaf-Nāma*, "Book of Honour" and *Iqbāl-Nāma*, "Book of Fortune", which, if taken together, form his most extensive work. Its dating, however approximate, provides insuperable difficulties, chiefly because the dates of Niẓāmī's death and of the accession of 'Izz al-Dīn Mas'ūd, the ruler of Mosul (1211–19) clash. The *Sharāf-Nāma* can with some hesitation be ascribed to the years between 1196 and 1200, and the *Iqbāl-Nāma* to the years between 1200 and the poet's death (600/1203–605/1209?). Dārāb solves the problem by regarding the dedication to 'Izz al-Dīn Mas'ūd as a later interpolation.[1] These dates, however, are all extremely doubtful. A peculiarity of the epic is the apostrophization of the "cup-bearer" in the first part and of the "singer" in the second, as a prelude to each.

Niẓāmī took the material for the entire poem from Arabic and Persian chronicles, but certainly not from monographic sources. Desire for war and conquest is quite foreign to his Iskandar; he fights and conquers only when obliged to do so or when helping others. He appears first as a warrior, in the *Sharāf-Nāma*, then as a philosopher, and finally as a prophet in the *Iqbāl-Nāma*. For this reason Niẓāmī attaches no importance to Iskandar's origin. In the later sections especially, the poet's indebtedness to Greek wisdom can frequently be detected, though anachronisms are numerous. However, the sublimity of his thoughts could allow him at times to dispense with historical accuracy.

[1] *The Treasury of Mysteries*, p. 64.

All his life he was preoccupied with the problems of social order and the struggle against its disturbers and enemies—indeed from this point of view, his works can be seen as a gradual crescendo culminating in the *Iskandar-Nāma*. His last epic can be called a product of his old age only in the sense that here his humanism found its profoundest expression. The sumptuous style of his earlier poems would here have been out of place; the *Iskandar-Nāma* is less colourfully written than the others, its allegories and symbolism standing out all the more for this reason. While *Khusrau u Shīrīn* is rich in imagery, all the later epics become increasingly simple in form, reaching their artistic culmination in the *Haft Paikar*.

Niẓāmī's great virtues are his wealth of ideas, his powerful imagination and infinite religious depth, command of *le mot juste*, perfect poetic technique, ability to choose and order his material, philosophic profundity, and understanding of social questions; indeed he often voices the attitude of the towns. He did much to further the introduction of vernacular current language into epic poetry, giving it the same vocabulary which had already penetrated court poetry; in doing so, he dealt a decisive blow to the ancient epic tradition, since the latter, through its reluctance to accept the influence of Arabic, was becoming increasingly difficult to understand; indeed, Gurgānī in his romantic epic *Vīs u Rāmīn* (1040–54) had not been entirely able to avoid the influence of Arabic. The heroic epic was becoming less and less important, not only because of social changes and a diminishing interest in its old style, but because it had proved incapable of casting off the studied purity of language which was its characteristic. Moreover the influence of the language of lyric poetry tended to emphasize certain aspects of epic poetry that had hitherto been overlooked, namely, the lyrical approach and psychological motivation. As the ideals of chivalry died out, the personal element came to the fore and the tragedy of the individual acquired increasing scope, all of which coincided with the rise of an urban middle class which eclipsed the other social strata. In the metrical field, on the other hand, Niẓāmī was in no way an innovator, since all the metres he uses can be found in earlier epics. Ṣafā is undoubtedly right when he claims that in the disputes between Khusrau and Shīrīn, Niẓāmī imitated the corresponding passages in Gurgānī's *Vīs u Rāmīn*;[1] he may elsewhere have borrowed from other mathnavī writers also. But even if he did, he impressed the unique stamp of his genius on all his borrowings.

[1] *Ḥamāsa*, p. 321.

His lyrical dīvān is said to have amounted to almost 20,000 couplets, but apart from a number of ghazals and a handful of qaṣīdas, is entirely lost. It would appear that tradition has greatly exaggerated the original number of lines, though what little remains is enough to show that Niẓāmī was a great master of the ghazal. His lyric poetry is permeated with passionate emotion, and its unusual dichotomy between the poet and the person addressed generates a sense of perpetual tension. He must certainly have been writing lyric poetry throughout his life.

The number of imitators of Niẓāmī's *Khamsa* was exceptionally great both in Iran and in areas within the sphere of Persian culture, i.e. Turkey, Central Asia, and India.[1] These writers mirrored its form and its subject-matter, and chose analagous and sometimes identical themes, often reproducing them in similar groups of five. The first and foremost imitator was Amīr Khusrau (see below, pp. 606–9), who in turn influenced others after him. From the point of view of poetic quality, the magnificent epic *Lailī u Majnūn* (895/1489–90) by Maktabī of Shīrāz comes closest to Niẓāmī's own poem, though Maktabī achieves new effects by the inclusion of ghazals, a practice for which there is evidence already at the beginning of the eleventh century. Maktabī's poem was in due course to have a counterpart in Fuḍūlī's treatment of the same subject in the language of Āzarbāījān, in whose literature Fuḍūlī's poem occupies a high place. The intense admiration which was felt for Niẓāmī is also reflected in arts such as miniature-painting, many of whose subjects are taken from the *Khamsa*.

THE IṢFAHĀN SCHOOL

The poet Jamāl al-Dīn Muḥammad b. 'Abd al-Razzāq Iṣfahānī is less well known than Niẓāmī, but he merits attention because of his plebeian origins and especially because he represents the Iṣfahān School in the literature of Persian 'Irāq. Born in Iṣfahān of a local family who appear to have been artisans, he worked as a goldsmith and miniature-painter. His education and knowledge were of the usual kind. From early youth he began writing poetry, and although he produced much panegyric verse, he was not attached to any court. He suffered from an impediment of speech, and was left by smallpox with faulty eyesight. He attempted

[1] On the familiarity of Shota Rustaveli, the greatest poet of medieval Georgia, with Niẓāmī's work, cf. D. I. Kobidze, *Iz gruzino-persidskikh literaturnïkh svazei. Literaturniye razïskaniya*, vol. III (1946), pp. 203–23. (In Georgian with a résumé in Russian.)

to establish himself both in Āzarbāījān (visiting Ganja, where he must certainly have met Niẓāmī) and in Māzandarān, no doubt in the hope of obtaining a better livelihood from the local rulers; but he appears to have met with no success since he eventually returned to his home town, where he spent the rest of his life. He was well aware of Iṣfahān's shortcomings and censured them, but he was too patriotic to restrain his indignation when Mujīr ridiculed the city.

He practised all the less ambitious forms of lyric verse, though chiefly the qaṣīda and ghazal. His qaṣīdas sing the praises of numerous distant and nearby princely personages—especially the Iṣfahānī families Sa'īd and Khujand (the former of the Shāfi'ite and the latter of the Hanafite persuasion)—as well as of members of learned circles. He was influenced by the great panegyric poets who were his contemporaries: Khāqānī, Anvarī, and Rashīd Vaṭvāṭ, actually quoting from them on occasion (though they never quote him); but in contrast to their displays of erudition, he never abandons his simplicity. He had dealings of a friendly or polemical nature with many writers. In his own writings he delighted in proffering advice to all and sundry, in admonishing and criticizing, and in imitating Sanā'ī, though unsuccessfully. His qaṣīdas dispense with the exordium and plunge at once *in medias res* with the eulogy itself; descriptions of nature are infrequent throughout. He occupies an important position in the development of the ghazal, which he did much to perfect; its possibilities must have been particularly congenial to him, since he comes near to striking the tender notes of the ghazal in his qaṣīdas also. Vaḥīd praises Jamāl's choice of metaphors.[1] The subjects of his poems attracted attention, as is shown by the echoes found in later masters of the ghazal, including Sa'dī. The ideas expressed in his works are idiosyncratic: he is constantly longing for renunciation but never practises it. His reflexions are based on traditional and formal theology rather than on philosophy or mysticism.[2] "The qaṣīda known as *āshūb-i rūzgār* [confusion of the times] sums up all the bitterness of human life."[3] He died in 588/1192.

His son Kamāl al-Dīn Ismā'īl of Iṣfahān (b. 568/1172–73) was one of the great poets of Iṣfahān and one of the very last important panegyric poets. Although he was prevented from completing his education by the financial difficulties which beset his family after his father's death, the technical expressions recurrent in his writings show that he was

[1] *Armaghān*, vol. XVIII, p. 86. [2] Badī' al-Zamān, *Sukhan*, vol. II, pt. I, pp. 215 ff.
[3] Abdullah, *The Value*, p. 5.

soundly versed in all the customary branches of knowledge. Besides Persian he wrote Arabic poetry; but this has perished along with his prose writings. Like his father he was a Sunnite of the Shāfi'ite persuasion, though he was also a member of the Ṣūfī order. But asceticism was by no means the keynote of his life; he was an excellent backgammon player and a lover of wine, which he used to request from those whose praises he sang. He began to write verses when a boy, and at the age of twenty composed the famous elegy on the death of his father, a work of high perfection. The influence of a member of the Sa'īd family secured him a public position, but he lost it as a result of envious calumny and even suffered a fine. Although he was pardoned, he gave up the idea of an official career and thenceforth devoted himself solely to poetry. The influential persons to whom he addressed his eulogies ensured him a quiet life, and a considerable income too, which enabled him to support others less fortunate than himself. Besides praising the two distinguished Iṣfahānī families (Sa'īd and Khujand), he wrote eulogies of the Khwārazm-Shāhs, the atabegs of Fārs and the princes of Ṭabaristān. His love for his home town was even greater than his father's. For all his Ṣūfism, he was fond of luxury, ostentation, and the society of the great; and he lacked neither presumption nor desire for fame. On the other hand, he never harmed others. At the approach of the Mongol invaders he fled into the outskirts of the city disguised as a dervish, but this did not save him; he died in 635/1237 at the hands of the Mongols, when it was discovered quite by chance that he had hidden people's valuables in a well. His tomb has been preserved.

Kāmal was most at home in panegyric poetry. In contrast to his father's, his verse contains less depth of feeling, though it is more polished and exceptionally rich in new and striking ideas. Because of this he was called *Khallāq al-ma'ānī*, "Creator of subtle thoughts". The lack of lyrical exordia in his qaṣīdas is compensated by the frequent interjection of didactic advice, mystical reflexions, laments on life, sickness, transitoriness, and the all-pervading decay of civilization. His descriptions have always attracted unanimous praise. Kamāl was the creator of the standard 'Irāqī type of qaṣīda, which was later—like his father's ghazal—brought to its fullest perfection by Sa'dī. He also practised the shorter forms of lyric poetry, but did not reach very great heights in the ghazal because he often chose inappropriate modes of expression. Ritter has recorded the existence of a mathnavī by Kamāl on the subject of mystic love.[1]

[1] "Philologika VII", p. 105, no. 20.

THE GREAT MYSTICS

There is probably no author in the whole of Persian literature whose biography and works present so many riddles as do those of ʻAṭṭār. Virtually nothing is known about him because the works themselves, in so far as they are reliable and authentic, betray virtually nothing. The story that Abū Ḥamīd Muḥammad b. Abū Bakr Ibrāhīm, generally known as Farīd al-Dīn ʻAṭṭār, lived the same number of years as there are *suras* in the Qur'ān (114) must be firmly rejected. Since the date of his death can be ascertained with relative accuracy, the date of his birth can best be placed in 537/1142–43 or three years later. He was born in Nīshāpūr or in a neighbouring suburb or town. In his poems he calls himself ʻAṭṭār, which means both "apothecary", which in fact he was, and also "doctor". In the pharmacy in Nīshāpūr, which he had inherited from his father, about five hundred people had their pulses taken daily; yet in spite of this he was soon able to complete the epics *Muṣībat-Nāma* and *Ilāhī-Nāma*, which he had begun in his shop. There were advantages as well as drawbacks to his noisy surroundings, as he met people from all walks of life and was able to learn much from them. Amongst them were adherents to Ṣūfism, who introduced him to the miraculous world of the saints, and he certainly had links with Ṣūfī circles. It is nowadays considered possible that he came into contact in 616–17/1219–21 with Maulavī, who was at that time a boy, for it was to Maulavī, when on his wanderings, that the aged ʻAṭṭār dedicated his epic *Asrār-Nāma*, while to Maulavī's father he prophesied that Maulavī would scorch with fire those whom the world had scorched. ʻAṭṭār himself writes that he visited the doctor Majd al-Dīn Khwārazmī (drowned in 606/1209–10 or in 616/1219–20), who was a follower of Shaikh Najm al-Dīn Kubrā (d. 618/1221); but he himself was never Najm al-Dīn's disciple. A venerable old man, he was killed during a massacre in 618/1221, when, according to ʻAṭā Malik Juvainī, his native town was taken by the Mongols. Thus he reached the age of eighty-one. His grave can still be seen in Shādyākh, a suburb of Nīshāpūr, not far from the mausoleum of the saint Muḥammad Maḥrūq and the tomb of ʻUmar Khayyām.

ʻAṭṭār regarded himself as a prolific writer, but it is extremely difficult to ascertain exactly what he wrote. Once again we are confronted with numbers that cannot be trusted: a total of sixty-six works is reached if genuine, dubious, and spurious works are all included. But even if we confine ourselves to extant and definitely genuine mathnavīs (*Khusrau-*

Nāma, *Asrār-Nāma*, *Manṭiq al-ṭair*, *Muṣībat-Nāma*, *Ilāhī-Nāma*), together with a dīvān of lyric poetry, a collection of quatrains entitled *Mukhtār-Nāma*, and the insignificant *Pand-Nāma*, we are still faced with an impressive total of approximately 45,000 lines.

'Aṭṭār's best-known epic, and crowning achievement in the art of the mathnavī, is the *Manṭiq al-ṭair*, "The Language of the Birds" (an expression taken from the Qur'ān, S. xxvii, 16), which is often called *Maqāmāt-i Ṭuyūr*, or "The Stations of the Birds". He was not the first to pick such a theme: Abū 'Alī Sīnā had already written the symbolical *Risālat al-ṭair*, "Treatise on Birds", in Arabic, and a poem of the same title, also in Arabic, is ascribed to Muḥammad Ghazālī (d. 505/1111). 'Aṭṭār's immediate sources or models were Ghazālī's work, the allegorical dialogues about birds in the famous Ismā'īlī-slanted encyclopaedia of the tenth-century *Ikhwān al-Ṣafā* ("Brothers of Purity"), and Sanā'ī's *Sair al-'ibād* (see above, p. 557). 'Aṭṭār blended his models, changed the object of the quest from the mythological bird 'Anqā and the mythological bird Sīmurgh, and made brilliant use of the double meaning of the name Sīmurgh. In his version all kinds of birds assemble and decide to go and search for a king to rule over them. Hudhud, the hoopoe, assumes the leadership of the expedition because he knows where the Sīmurgh, the rightful king of the birds, lives; but he cannot set out alone. The birds are deterred by the difficulties ahead of them, and talk each other into pursuing aims which, though not despicable, are earthly and of little value for their quest; but the hoopoe always dissuades them from these aims. The journey is long and arduous, since the pilgrims have to pass through seven perilous valleys. Many of the birds fall by the wayside, but the survivors journey on for many years; the majority perish, until only thirty birds remain (*sī murgh*). Finally they reach the court of the Sīmurgh. There the sun of his presence shines, and in their own reflexions they recognize themselves, the thirty birds, *sī murgh*, the Sīmurgh. When they gaze on the Sīmurgh they behold themselves, and when they gaze on themselves they behold the Sīmurgh: and if they look on both at once, they see only one Sīmurgh. After many ages have passed, the birds are restored to their own identity and enter the state of "continuing to exist after having ceased to be".

The *Ilāhī-Nāma* or "Book of God" also takes the form of a story within a story, its principal theme being *zuhd*, i.e. renunciation of worldly desires and wishes, whose place should be taken by the higher ideals of mystic ethics and piety. The king asks his six sons what it is that they most desire. The first asks for the daughter of the king of the Peris, the second for knowledge of the magic arts, the third for Jamshīd's magic goblet, the fourth for the elixir of life, the fifth for Solomon's magic ring, and the sixth for the philosophers' stone. The king convinces each in turn of the thoughtlessness of his wishes and guides them towards higher goals.

While dialogue and persuasive speeches are the structural basis of the *Ilāhī-Nāma*, dialogue plays a noticeably less important role in the epic *Muṣībat-Nāma*.[1] The subject of the story within the narrative framework is the soul's journey during the meditation of mystical seclusion. It is possible that the accounts of spiritual journeys by the famous mystic Bāyazīd Bisṭāmī (d. 261/874), which 'Aṭṭār himself recorded in the *Tadhkirat al-Auliyā*, specifically suggested this poem to him, or at least influenced his writing of it. In the *Muṣībat-Nāma* the thought of the soul in meditation wanders through the mythical and physical cosmos, personified as a traveller who is the disciple of a *pīr* (master of a mystic order). The traveller passes through forty stations corresponding to the forty days of his meditative seclusion, and after each of his visionary dialogues with one of the mythical, cosmic, and physical beings, or personified virtues of the soul, he receives instruction from the *pīr* concerning his interlocutor; thus here too the sequence of speech, reply, and concluding lesson is preserved. The attitude of the traveller is one of spiritual distress, perplexity, irresolution, and despair. From the beings he visits he is seeking help, guidance, and deliverance from his tormenting condition. Each time he begins his speech with a *captatio benevolentiae*, by enumerating the being's claims to fame, but all his requests receive negative answers, which always derive from the difficulties of each being's own position. The prophets direct him to Muḥammad, who at last shows him the right way, the way into his own soul.

Quite different in structure is the relatively less extensive *Asrār-Nāma*, constructed in the manner of Sanā'ī's *Ḥadīqa*, the later *Mathnavī* of Maulavī. In this small work many of the themes whose variations dominate the great epics are briefly sounded, the passages of theoretical instruction and the exhortations taking up more space than in the other works. The *Khusrau-Nāma* or *Khusrau u Gul* is the complete antithesis of all four works so far mentioned. Logical and compact in structure,[2]

[1] Ritter, *Das Meer*, pp. 18–30. Ritter is my authority in all this section.
[2] Detailed contents in Ritter, "Philologika X", pp. 160–73.

it is a romantic story about two lovers, a piece of fiction of the usual adventure type without any trace of mysticism; it was probably an early work composed shortly after the death of the poet's mother. The real heroine of the epic is a most enchanting woman whose great beauty involves her in sufferings of all kinds, but who at the end victoriously maintains her feminine purity.[1]

It must be emphasized that all 'Aṭṭār's epics except for the last-named contain a much greater amount of abstract thought than their basic plots would suggest, since these are mainly taken up with the individual stories illustrating the underlying theme.

'Aṭṭār's dīvān contains about 10,000 lines of lyric poetry in the form of qaṣīdas and g͟hazals. It is almost devoid of descriptions of nature, and is completely lacking in panegyric verse (which 'Aṭṭār eschewed completely, being quite indifferent to all holders of power); but his poetry is marked by transports of ecstatic fervour (and often *rindī*).[2] In this he exerted a certain influence on Sa'dī and Ḥāfiz. He constantly uses word-repetition and regular refrains, no doubt to bring about a heightening of emotion. In comparison with Sanā'ī's g͟hazals, those of 'Aṭṭār are distinguished by a great emphasis on mystical symbolism and by infectious enthusiasm. The *Muk͟htār-Nāma*, "Book of Selections", forms an independent collection of 2,010 quatrains which 'Aṭṭār himself selected as the best in his entire works and arranged in fifty chapters according to their content.

Exceptionally important is the *Tad͟hkirat al-auliyā*, which consists of ninety-seven biographies of early mystics and is an excellent example of old, straightforward Persian prose. Twenty-three of the items, however, must be ascribed to Aḥmad al-Ṭūsī (twelfth century) and four to a later author.

'Aṭṭār deepens the pantheistic *taṣavvuf* by making the quest for the absolute more thorough—a quest whose central idea is the deification of the self. To set free the divine substance in himself completely and become God, a human being must take the way of *fanā*, or cessation of being. The only force which can make this possible is that love which is prepared to make the utmost sacrifices.[3] Passionate tones accompany this mystical speculation. Jalāl al-Dīn Rūmī expresses his admiration for

[1] *En miniature*: *Ilāhī-Nāma*, ed. Ritter, pp. 31 ff., transl. Rouhani, pp. 71 ff.

[2] When there is kindness of heart, the religious law is valid only within certain limits.

[3] Cf. Ritter, "Das Proömium", p. 179.

Sanā'ī, but regards himself as nothing better than a slave in comparison to 'Aṭṭār.

As in other cases, modern research has shown how the biography of Maulānā Jalāl al-Dīn Rūmī (whom the Persians generally call Maulavī) has in the course of time been distorted and endowed with legendary features, though it must be admitted that the romantic vicissitudes of his life provided good grounds for this. Born in 604/1207, he came of an old and learned family in Balkh, where his father, Bahā' al-Dīn Muḥammad Valad, was a well-known preacher by no means averse to mystical speculation. He compiled a collection of memorable fragments from his sermons under the title *Ma'ārif*, "Gnoses", echoes of which can be heard even in Maulavī's dīvān and mathnavī. Fear of the Mongols, together with the pressures of various controversies, impelled Bahā' al-Dīn to leave Balkh in about 616/1219–20, first for the holy places and then via Damascus to Qonya (*c.* 618/1221–22). After Bahā's death (628/1230–31) Maulavī came under the influence of the mystic Burhān al-Dīn Muḥaqqiq of Tirmidh, a disciple of his father.[1] Following no doubt the suggestion of this spiritual guide, he set out for Aleppo and Damascus to further his education. It may have been in Damascus that he first met the wandering dervish Shams al-Dīn Muḥammad Tabrīzī, for whom he conceived a passionate attachment after the death of Burhān al-Dīn in 638/1240–41. When Shams al-Dīn appeared in Qonya in 642/1244, he was at that time allegedly sixty years old. Nevertheless his physical beauty and his novel mystical-narcissistic theories concerning the higher world of the beloved (*ma'shūq*) completely captivated Maulavī. When this passionate affair had aroused the antipathy of his disciples, Shams departed for Damascus in high dudgeon, but he allowed his pupil's fervent supplications to weaken his resolve, and finally consented to return to Qonya, only to arouse another immediate outbreak of hostility (645/1247), which once again compelled him to leave the place. After this he vanished into thin air, but not without leaving some traces, because his sayings were later collected under the title *Maqālāt-i Shams-i Tabrīz*. Although these are difficult to understand, the ideas they have in common with Maulavī's writings indicate the influence of Shams al-Dīn on the latter.

In vain the pupil searched for his master. It is thought that the dance

[1] Gölpınarlı in his article "Mawlānā" comes to the conclusion that Maulavī at the time of his meeting with Shams al-Dīn was already 62 years old. He bases his argument on a *ghazal* of the poet. This hypothesis strikes me as very doubtful.

which members of the Maulavī order still perform to the languid sound of a reed flute and the gentle beating of a miniature double-drum represents the vain and desperate search for this mysteriously lost friend. This whirling dance is the centre-piece of all the rites of the Maulavī dervishes and was instituted by Maulavī himself. His longing and his anxiety made him a truly great poet; he identified himself with the vanished *ma'shūq*, and in so doing found him again spiritually. His poems are not sung by himself, they are sung by his teacher reimbodied in him. He even wrote under the name of *Shams-i Tabrīz*, "Sun of Tabrīz", though occasionally he uses the name *Khāmūsh*, i.e. "Silent One", which Gölpınarli thinks he had adopted as a pseudonym before his meeting with Shams al-Dīn. The playing of music and the singing of passionate hymns and dances were well able to rouse his turbulent emotions; they were roused too by his new mystical and emotional attachment to an illiterate "goldsmith", Ṣalāḥ al-Dīn Farīdūn Zarkūb, with whom he became so infatuated that the jealousy and animosity of his other disciples were once again aroused, leading to a grave crisis in the order. After Ṣalāḥ's death (662/1263–64) the master turned his affections to Ḥusām al-Dīn Ḥasan, who was the actual inspiration of his principal work. Jalāl al-Dīn's mortal pilgrimage came to an end on Sunday, 5 Jumādā II, 672/7 December 1273; his bier was accompanied to the grave by the entire population of Qonya, not only the Muslims but the Christians and Jews also, all of whom remembered the master's boundless tolerance.

The lyrical *Kulliyyāt-i Shams*, "The Complete [lesser] Poems of Shams", amount to a total of 36,349 lines in the excellent critical edition by Professor Badī' al-Zamān Furūzānfar. From first to last these poems are permeated with the mystical idea of the identification of subject with object, which leads on the one hand to pantheism and on the other to self-deification, "in which the narcissistic theme of the identification of the self with the loved object, of its fusion with it, is very prominent". In the impassioned ecstasy with which ideas and visions well up in them, these lyrics far exceed all Persian poetry previously written; indeed they were dictated in what amounts to a trance and, by contrast with the works of other poets, are in fact relatively simple in style. Despite this, the grandiose scale of the underlying ideas has a tiring effect because it is expressed with a monotonous seriousness to which all the lyrical variations, however, colourful and fiery, are unable to impart sufficient variety and interest. Diversity, it must be emphasized, has never been one of the virtues of Persian poetry; on the other hand, the remarkable subtlety with which spiritual processes are described—in Maulavī's work too—must be counted to its credit.

Jalāl al-Dīn's principal work, an encyclopaedia or rather bible of Ṣūfism and theosophy, is the *Mat̲h̲navī-i Ma'navī*, "The Mat̲h̲navī concerned with the Inner Meaning of all Things".[1] It is in six books, amounting to a total of 27,000 lines, the sixth book being unfinished and the seventh spurious. It is less passionate than the g̲h̲azals, but possesses great poetical beauty and other artistic qualities, quite apart from its importance for Ṣūfī philosophy and ethics. The poem lacks the customary opening cantos and begins with the lament of the reed flute, which was suggested by (Pseudo?-)'Aṭṭār.[2] The sustained feat of imagination is astonishing when one considers that the work was dictated, to the one who inspired it, over a period of more than ten years which included several intervals; but this is partially offset by a certain lack of harmony in its contents (in this respect Maulavī resembles Sanā'ī) and by some slight formal aberrations. Reflexions alternate with parables and stories of the most varied kinds, the one often interrupting the other; emotions alternate with thoughts, erudition and rhetoric with simplicity, yet the language is so flexible that it always suits the content exactly. There can be no doubt that the technique of the narrative episodes in his *Mat̲h̲navī* is carried to even greater perfection than in the works of 'Aṭṭār. A difficulty of a special kind lies in "the sequence of ideas, which is loosely associative and reminiscent almost of a train of thought. Another peculiarity is the relation of each story to the teachings attached to it. Often the story is not an allegory or moralizing parable; its purpose is simply to arouse the listener's interest in what is to follow, the latter being only loosely connected. One would expect the moral to be based on the actual point of the story. This is, however, by no means always the case."[3] Here too the influence of 'Aṭṭār can be detected. Thanks to Nicholson's critical edition, which provides both a translation and a commentary by the same scholar, it has at last become possible to penetrate into

[1] It should not pass unnoticed that, according to Gölpınarlı the Maulavī dervishes did not regard themselves as Ṣūfīs and stood aloof from the Ṣūfī orders. Cf. Ritter, *Oriens*, vols. XIII–XIV, p. 346. Was this perhaps only the case in the early days of the order?

[2] Ritter, "Das Proömium", pp. 169 ff.

[3] Ritter, "Zum Meṯnewī-Text", *OLZ* (1928), p. 8. But cf. Ritter, *Persiens Mystiker Dschelāl Eddīn Rūmī*.

Maulavī's theological system and to trace its connexions with Sanā'ī and particularly with 'Aṭṭār. Ritter fears that the results of such an inquiry, though likely to be considerable, might be less rewarding than could be expected, and he therefore suggests that Maulavī's philosophy should be studied above all with the help of other authentic sources. These, says Ritter, are his letters and sermons, the sayings contained in his *Fīhī mā fīhī*, i.e. "Miscellanies", the works of his father, the surviving tradition of his teacher Shams-i Tabrīzī, the memoirs of Aḥmad Aflakī (d. 761/1360), and lastly the works of Maulavī's son Sulṭān Valad (d. 712/1312), who was also a Ṣūfī poet and with whom the history of the Maulavī order really begins. The establishment and growth of the order and the initiation of its first rituals were all the work of Valad. He also applied the concept of theophany to saints and shaikhs and made three hitherto unknown favourites of his father famous. He wrote a mathnavī in three parts, which provides authentic information about his father and his doctrines; the second part, usually known as the *Rabāb-Nāma*, "Book of the Rebec", consists of two sections which are very important philologically, for one is in Saljuq Turkish and the other in Greek.

SA'DĪ

We think of the most popular moralist in Persian literature, indeed one of the most famous of all Persian poets, not as a stern mentor but as a jovial, laughing person, with perhaps a glimmer of good-humoured roguishness. That is at any rate the kind of person who emerges from his works. The biographical facts that have been handed down contribute little towards his portrait. And even Sa'dī's own words cannot altogether be trusted; they cannot be taken literally and this makes it extremely hazardous to base a reconstruction of his life on the many stories which he tells, presumably only to entertain and instruct.[1] There is no contemporary information about him; uncertainties abound at every point. As to the dating of his life prior to 655/1257 and after 680/1281–82, there is nothing definite to go on and we must be content with hypotheses.[2]

The oldest records give us these names: Muṣliḥ al-Dīn Abū Muḥammad 'Abdallāh b. Musharraf b. Muṣliḥ b. Musharraf, known

[1] No one will, for example, believe the story of the dervish who crossed a river on his cloak.

[2] Iqbāl, *Sa'dī-Nāma*, p. 632.

as Sa'dī Shīrāzī,[1] but there are numerous variants. Both his own works and tradition confirm that he was born in Shīrāz, a town to which he remained most movingly loyal throughout his life and for which, no doubt, he longed passionately when travelling abroad. The date of his birth is based entirely on hypothesis, the most plausible suggestion being that of 'Abbās Iqbal: 610–15/1213–19. Even then Sa'dī would have reached a great age, though not the legendary one of 120. Thanks largely to the considerable culture of his father, Sa'dī received a careful education from an early age; he often recalls his father's love and wise guidance. His mother continued the same routine after his father died, when Sa'dī was only about twelve. Shīrāz was by no means short of schools, and Sa'dī began his studies there; these were cut short by his move to Baghdad, made through fear of the "Turks" (or so at least he says in the *Gulistān*). Tradition maintains that he was sent to Baghdad where he was supported by the Salghurid atabeg of Shīrāz; but he certainly cannot have gone there as early as 592/1196, since it is said that he studied at the famous Shāfi'ite university, the Niẓāmiyya. Moreover it is scarcely credible that the atabeg would have accorded such a favour to a boy of humble albeit educated background. Attempts have been made to derive specific dates from the names, which he himself gives, of his teachers in Baghdad: yet here, too, difficulties arise. Nor can anything be learnt from the passages in which Sa'dī apparently addresses himself as a man aged fifty or sixty. We only know that after completing his studies he set off on travels which took him to Iraq, Syria, and the Ḥijāz. On the other hand it is hard to believe that he travelled in eastern Iran, Transoxiana, and India. The many impossible ingredients in the story of how he destroyed the infamous idol in the temple of Somnat exclude the likelihood that he visited India. Equally untenable is the description of his meeting with a boy in Kāshghar, which, if true, would suggest that even before the completion of the *Gulistān* his fame as a poet had spread to such remote areas; this is quite unlikely even if the date of the peace treaty between the Khwārazm-Shāh and the Qara-Khitai (probably 1210) is arbitrarily moved forward. This objection is corroborated by the fact that the best Persian *Ars Poetica*, *al-Mu'jam* (630/1232–3) by Shams-i-Qais, contains no quotations from Sa'dī, though there are a great many from other poets of that period.

The *Gulistān* mentions a visit to Tabrīz, where Sa'dī is said to have

[1] Nafisī, *Ta'rīkh-i durust*, p. 65.

met the Ṣāḥib-Dīvān Shams al-Dīn Muḥammad Juvainī, his brother ʿAlāʾ al-Dīn ʿAṭā-Malik Juvainī (see below, pp. 622–3), and the Īl-Khān Abaqa himself, to all of whom he gave advice at their request—advice, however, which is much too naïve for the episode to be credible. That Saʿdī was famous at that time can be accepted without difficulty (Abaqa ruled from 663 to 680/1265–82), but it is very doubtful that he would have set out alone from Shīrāz to Tabrīz since he declined other journeys at that time, though he did sing the praises of Ṣāḥib-Dīvān Juvainī. Other meetings with famous people provide the material for favourite anecdotes, not a word of which can be true. For example, in Shīrāz he is supposed to have met Shaikh Ṣafī al-Dīn, the earliest ancestor of the Ṣafavid dynasty, whom he represents as holding strong Shīʿī beliefs; the fact that both men were Sunnīs was readily overlooked for the purposes of the anecdote. Saʿdī's return to Shīrāz after many years of travel brings us to the first reliable dates. Soon afterwards he completed his didactic epic *Būstān*, "The Orchard" (655/1257), and a year later he finished his *Gulistān*, "Rose-Garden", which is written in both prose and verse, the former poem being dedicated to the ruling atabeg Muẓaffar al-Dīn Abū Bakr b. Saʿd Zangī, the latter to his son Saʿd b. Abū Bakr b. Saʿd Zangī, from whom Saʿdī took his *nom de plume*. Its derivation from the name of a prince has no significance, for there are other instances, the best-known being Qāʾānī in the nineteenth century. Saʿdī had certainly begun writing before this time, but he had not yet acquired fame. He left Shīrāz unknown, and returned there equally unknown. Fame—and it was quite phenomenal—came only with the *Būstān* and then especially with the *Gulistān*, two works from which he has been universally quoted ever since.

Saʿdī's assertion that he composed the *Būstān* immediately after his return to Shīrāz and the *Gulistān* only a year later must be understood in the sense that he completed sketches brought back from his travels, because such short periods of composition would scarcely be possible for works so replete with details and original perceptions, not to mention their formal elegance and indeed perfection. Saʿdī settled permanently in his beloved Shīrāz, where in monk-like seclusion he devoted himself to meditation and poetry; from the abundant experience which he had gained in his own life he imparted advice to rulers and subjects, disciples and admirers, and in turn delighted in their benevolence, their gifts and the subsistence they provided. This period probably saw the composition of most of his lyric poetry, comprising both the ghazals and didactic panegyrical qaṣīdas, in which he admonishes the great and comments on current events.[1] It is curious that he nowhere alludes to the death of the two brothers Juvainī; did he fear to do so, or had he already ceased writing? Nafīsi has established the correct date of Sa'dī's death, from among a great many put forward, as 27 Dhu'l-Hijja 691/9 December 1292.[2]

It cannot be disputed that Sa'dī was an adherent of Ṣūfism. The ambiguity of his ghazals may be overlooked, because this was customary. The most convincing proof of his Ṣūfī outlook is the chapter on love in the *Būstān*. His tendency, however, was not towards speculation but at most towards asceticism, and his motives were dictated more by utilitarianism than by philosophical ethics. This is why, as a moralist, he shows little regard for consistent adherence to ethical doctrines which he himself has propounded elsewhere, but prefers to countenance exceptions which are quite their reverse when he feels there is no alternative. Truth is holy, certainly, but there can be occasions when prudence ordains a lie. This Sa'dī illustrates in the very first anecdote in the first chapter of the *Gulistān*, where infringement of the principle of truth is dictated by common humanity, since otherwise the caprice or stupidity of the king and the ruthlessness of his advisers would undoubtedly have led to bloodshed. A whole series of similar antinomies could be cited. In his own life, too, Sa'dī did not always act in accordance with strict ethical principles. If he belonged to those rare figures in Persian literature who valued freedom of literary expression, who disliked the obsequiousness of panegyric verse and preferred to express admonition in their qaṣīdas, thus virtually committing themselves to controversies with the rulers, why then did he sing the praises of Hülegü, the very man who had removed the Salghurid Saljuq-Shāh, destroyed Baghdad, and put the last 'Abbasid Caliph al-Musta'ṣim to a most ignominious death? Why again did he lament this very caliph in a heart-rending elegy—quite out of line with the policy of his lord and master in Shīrāz, Abū Bakr b. Sa'd, who, while professing to accept the Sunna, led his army in support of the Mongol campaign to destroy the centre of Sunnī Islam? Shiblī supposes that Sa'dī, although usually included amongst the greatest Ṣūfīs, was really no Ṣūfī by nature, but had to make an intense effort to accept Ṣūfism, being

[1] We also have verses composed in the dialect of his native town.

[2] *Ta'rīkh-i durust.*

naturally more inclined to externals in the manner of the mullas;[1] indeed, he tells how his father castigated him when a small boy for his egotism and his critical eye for the faults of others. Sa'dī also criticizes pederasty, though he is not immune to similar tendencies himself.

This literary output embraces every kind of lyric poetry, as well as the didactic epic and elegant prose. The heroic epic did not suit his pacific nature (the prelude to a battle scene in the *Būstān* is a display of bravura written to prove he could do it if he wished). A brilliant story-teller, he lacked the patience to allow himself to be tied to a single theme, which is necessary in romantic epics often thousands of lines in length, but not in didactic epics with their varied contents. Though he brought the ghazal to the highest degree of perfection in the period, he won most esteem for the prose of his world-famous *Gulistān*. He was thus a master of both prose and verse.

Sa'dī's principal didactic works are the *Būstān* and the *Gulistān*. Moralizing verse had long been in existence, it is true, but the great poet of Shīrāz was the first to raise it to the level of true poetry. The *Būstān*, or perhaps more correctly *Sa'dī-Nāma*, is an epic in the *mutaqārib* metre (three bacchic and one iambic foot), which was erroneously regarded as a prerogative of the heroic epic. The poem is almost 4,500 lines long and, apart from the opening (Sunnī) doxology, is divided into ten chapters which deal in turn with various virtues. The poet begins each chapter with the outline of a theoretical problem and then illustrates it either from his own experience or from legends, history, and so on, in the manner usual in all didactic mathnavīs. These parables, which are almost always brief, occur more frequently than in other comparable works.

The *Gulistān* follows the same ideological pattern. Its form may not have been beneficial to the development of Persian prose, for the work was written in rhyming and rhythmic prose interspersed with verses (which take up about a third of the book) in the manner of the *Munājāt* ("Prayers"), by Anṣārī (d. 481/1088), who seems to have been Sa'dī's model. In contrast with the *Būstān*, where the parables are linked to ethical problems, the anecdotes form the body of the *Gulistān*, one or two lines of pithy wisdom being deduced from each: in fact this is a kind of miniature *maqāma* (see below, p. 618). The book consists of an introduction and eight chapters in which the anecdotal material is arranged under particular headings. Sometimes the title does not fit

[1] *Shi'r*, vol. II, p. 34.

the anecdote, at other times the deduction has no recognizable connexion with it. Sa'dī's style is characterized by a sovereign command of language, refined simplicity (lacking only in the somewhat over-ornamental introduction), and by a terseness at that time rare. If the *Būstān* cannot be said to contain any deep philosophy (except perhaps in the Ṣūfī third chapter concerning love), this is even more true in the thoroughly practical and sociologically more down-to-earth *Gulistān*, where the deductions are usually no more than the most obvious commonplaces, clothed admittedly in matchless poetry. An attempted translation will, to one's surprise, produce shapeless banality, because nothing can replace the magic of Sa'dī's own simplicity. He can strike a spark of poetry from the most insignificant everyday occurrence, and the occurrence does not necessarily have to contain a lesson. The tone of the work is kaleidoscopic, the serious alternating with the comic, the sublime with the frivolous. There are also certain difficult passages; a good example is Sa'dī's dispute with a dervish about rich people, who are criticized for their indifference to the poor and to those in distress. At first sight it appears that Sa'dī is trying to defend the rich; but a deeper insight into his polished but bitter irony shows on whose side he was really.

Sa'dī's two main works have produced a host of imitations (the *Gulistān* understandably even more than the *Būstān*). The best-known are Jāmī's *Baharistān* ("Spring Garden") written in 892/1487, and Qā'ānī's *Kitāb-i Parīshān* ("Pell-Mell"), written in 1152/1836.

Although popular at courts, Sa'dī was certainly no court poet; despite this he could not entirely resist the attraction of panegyric verse, for all his condemnation of it. In the traditional order the catalogue of his lyric poetry contains four collections of qaṣīdas and one extensive strophic poem. But there is one great difference between him and his precursors. He came into contact with a great many courts, but he never renounced his belief in freedom of thought and freedom of the pen; nor did he ever beg. His eulogies are restrained; he rightly accuses Ẓahīr Fāryābī of exaggeration, and all the more eager to fill his own qaṣīdas with good advice and wise remarks addressed to the shāhs, in which he urges generosity and goodness, appeals to their better selves, and emphasizes the transitoriness of the world. To do this he had to choose his mode of expression judiciously, otherwise his audacity might have brought risks; he was, however, protected by his personal authority. In these lyric poems the didactic element is most prominent, the lyric least. Not all the qaṣīdas can be said to be valuable, for many are marred by diffuseness and monotony.

As regards content and scope, the main part of Sa'dī's output lies in the books of ghazals, together with a collection of aphorisms and maxims called *Ṣāḥibiyya*, and finally his "Fragments", i.e. quatrains and single lines. The century-long development of the ghazal before Ḥāfiẓ culminates in Sa'dī. What is his particular merit? Above all, he does not merely play with words in his praises of the beloved, but allows himself to be moved by feelings of genuinely experienced love, whether we regard it as realistic or transcendental. According to Bahār, many of the poems come near to declaring their political themes under the guise of wine and the beloved. Certainly Sa'dī the moralist is true to himself when he opposes hypocrisy in all its forms. He also creates many subjects which are new and gives new colours to old ones. Not the least of his characteristics are the simplicity of the language, the appropriateness of his metres, the lightness of his refrains, and the direct way in which each story makes its single point.

Critical studies of Sa'dī's literary remains have recently been undertaken by Furūghī and Aliyev. Six treatises written in ornate prose (that is, prose alternating with verse, as in the *Gulistān*) have survived under Sa'dī's name, though at least one of them cannot be deemed authentic. To these can be added a seventh, which is a shallow parody of the mystical and religious homily in the second treatise, and is also probably spurious. Sa'dī himself, however, is undoubtedly the author of some short tales in the fifth chapter of the *Gulistān* which are far removed from the fragrance of the rose-garden. Indeed their existence helps to prove the authenticity of the extremely scabrous (*Muṭāyabāt* "Jokes", also known as *Khabīthāt* or *Hazlīyyāt*, "Facetiae"), a collection of somewhat monotonous poems quite lacking in artistic taste, which Sa'dī claims, in an apology in his preface, that he was ordered to write. In this aspect of the work of Sa'dī, and of all similar writers, Bausani sees the only example of realism in traditional Persian literature: an extremely barren one at that. The authorship of the *Pand-Nāma* "Book of Maxims" is disputed; it was at one time a favourite text for study in the West, and contains many sound principles without ever aspiring to great artistic heights.

Sa'dī is one of the most lively and colourful figures in Persian and indeed world literature. Yet it is quite impossible to co-ordinate his ideas into an integral system. Too impulsive and too much of a poet to be without inconsistencies, he is nevertheless always convincing, and his great attraction possibly lies in the very contrariety of his paradoxical ideas. These are for the most part truisms, but they are so superbly expressed that they are comprehensible even to the simplest person. Many have become proverbs, if they were not proverbs originally. Echoes of Firdausī, Asadī, Sanā'ī, Anvarī, Ẓahīr Fāryābī, and even the Arabic poet Mutanabbī (d. 354/965) show Sa'dī's wide reading and good taste, while an inimitable lightness of touch pervades all his work. One of his most sublime ideals was the brotherhood of man, and his Ṣūfism served the common people by encouraging activity and a balanced life; and in like manner he attacked intolerance, injustice, exploitation, and hypocritical or extravagant piety. But Sa'dī's unique and lasting success lies above all in his universally accessible and accommodating moral philosophy. The Persian, as indeed any human being, can see himself in Sa'dī.

SA'DĪ'S CONTEMPORARIES

(*a*) *Panegyric writers*

The Mongol invasion wrought such havoc in Khurāsān, Āzarbāījān, and finally in central Iran, that poetry took a long time to recover in those areas. The great poets of the seventh/thirteenth century lived in unscathed peripheral lands, i.e. the south-west (Sa'dī), Asia Minor (Maulavī), and India (Amīr Khusrau). In Iran proper, literary life was concentrated at Shīrāz, which had been left more or less untouched by the Mongols. The central figure here was undoubtedly Sa'dī; the rest were merely imitators of earlier writers or of Sa'dī himself. One writer deserving mention is Raḍī al-Dīn Abū 'Abdallah Muḥammad b. Abū Bakr Imāmī of Herāt (d. 676/1277–79), who wrote panegyrics of the amīrs and viziers of Kirmān. His qaṣīdas and ghazals are simple in style and reflect the spirit of taṣavvuf. Imāmī's work has received obviously exaggerated praise from his better-known contemporary Majd al-Dīn Hamgar (b. 607/1210–11, d. 686/1287), who was at first a functionary and a panegyric writer at the court of the Salghurid atabegs of Shīrāz. After their downfall, he was active at Iṣfahān and Baghdad, travelled through Khurāsān, and finally returned to his native city. As a poet he shows a command of delicate ideas, and his quatrains, varied in theme and expression and personal rather than speculative in tone, are extremely beautiful.

(*b*) *Mystics*

Fakhr al-Dīn Ibrāhīm b. Shahryār 'Irāqī was a contemporary of Sa'dī and, like him, had been a pilgrim in the eastern half of Islam; but in contrast to Sa'dī, he was a profound theosophist. A serene thirst for knowledge and a capacity for love were the dominant traits in his character, and they shaped his whole life. Born at Hamadān in 610/1213, he astonished those around him by his unusual talent and erudition. At the age of seventeen, he joined a band of wandering dervishes, amongst whom was a beautiful youth for whom he conceived a passionate admiration (an occurrence which was to repeat itself later). He abandoned everything, and wandered with them about Persia and India, where for twenty-five years he lived with Bahā' al-Dīn Zakariyyā of Multān, a disciple of Shihāb al-Dīn Suhravardi. But at last the jealousy of his colleagues in the order forced him to leave secretly for Mecca. After completing the pilgrimage he visited Qonya, where he was enthralled by the lectures of Shaikh Ṣadr al-Dīn Qonavī on the speculations of the famous mystic philosopher Muḥyī al-Dīn ibn 'Arabī (d. 638/1240). Under the impact of these lectures 'Irāqī wrote his *Lama'āt* ("Lightning Flashes"), which are ecstatic meditations on Ibn 'Arabī's *Fuṣūṣ al-Ḥikam* ("Ring-Stones of Wisdom"). Circumstances led him to travel to Cairo and thence to Damascus, a place sanctified by the presence of Ibn 'Arabī's and other tombs. In both cities he was received with unprecedented pomp. He ended his days in Damascus in 688/1289 and was buried next to the grave of the man who in his eyes represented the most sublime theosophy.

The *Lama'āt*, 'Irāqī's principal work, is not large in size but is profound and truly poetic. It is written in prose interspersed with Persian and Arabic verse. With this work a new influence began to affect the theory of love, namely that of Ibn 'Arabī's theosophy, whose monotonous outpourings were soon to inundate the last remaining islands of independent mystic thought within Islam.[1] Of the various commentaries on the book, that of Jāmī, entitled *Ashi''a-yi Lama'āt* ("Flashes of Lightning", 886/1481), became the most famous. 'Irāqī's dīvān and his delightful *'Ushshāq-Nāma* "Book of Lovers", also known as *Dah Fasl*, "Ten Chapters"), a short mathnavī incorporating ghazals, move along the same erotic–mystic lines, reaching their peak of

[1] Ritter, "Philologika VII", p. 96.

ecstasy in the ghazals of the dīvān.[1] Compared with Maulavī's poems, 'Irāqī's are more polished in form. 'Irāqī's theoretical statements on mystical love are all the more important because, thanks to an extant detailed biography of him, much is known about his personal experiences of mystical love, which is rarely the case with Persian poets.

Afḍal al-Dīn Muḥammad Kāshī, generally called Bābā Afḍal, was born around 582/1186–87 or 592/1195–96 in Maraq near Kāshān, and died after 654/1256 or 664/1265–66; according to Minovi, however, he lived considerably earlier, at the beginning of the seventh/thirteenth century; he is buried in Maraq. There is scant information about his life, and it has little importance. His thought was influenced by the Bāṭiniyya and by Avicenna, whom he also resembles in his attempts to substitute Persian technical terms for Arabic ones. His writings are chiefly in Persian, but sometimes also in Arabic. His prose works are concerned with philosophy, theosophy, metaphysics, ethics, and logic; they are partly original, partly editions or translations of the writings of others, are distinguished by a simple, intelligible, and lucid style. Bahār regards Afḍal's translation of Aristotle's *Kitāb al-nafs* (*De Anima*) as exemplary. Bābā Afḍal's quatrains are extremely attractive, and their occasional notes of revolt were remarked on long ago by Whinfield.[2] It is no wonder that several of them have gained currency as purported works of Khayyām. Bābā Afḍal must also be included amongst the principal theorists of Ṣūfism.

A figure of much more questionable importance is Shaikh Maḥmud Shabistarī (d. *c.* 720/1320–21), whose *Gulshan-i Rāz* ("Rose-Garden of Secrets") written in 710/1311 has received some notice in the East and undue admiration in the West. It is a relatively brief compendium of symbolic "Ṣūfī" terminology, and was in fact a series of versified replies to versified questions by Mir Husainī Sādāt (d. 718/1318). The fact that the then Aga Khan interested himself in a Bombay (1280/1863) edition of this work suggests that the author (if indeed he was Shabistarī) may have had Ismā'ilī leanings.[3] Whoever he was, he was no outstanding poet.

Rukn al-Din Auḥadī Iṣfahānī (b. in Marāgheh about 670/1271–72, d. 738/1338) has been much admired and imitated in the West for

[1] 'Ubaid-i Zākānī's mathnavī of the same name written in 75/1350 was probably inspired by this work but is concerned with worldly love.

[2] Browne, *A Literary History of Persia*, vol. II, pp. 109–10.

[3] See Arberry, *Classical Persian Literature*, p. 304.

his artistic expression of Ṣūfī ideas. This is particularly true of his principal work, the mathnavī *Jām-i Jam* ("The Cup of Jamshīd", i.e. the mirror of the whole universe), written in 733/1332–33 in the manner of Sanā'ī's *Ḥadīqa*, though not in blind imitation, since Auḥadī adapted his work to the requirements of his own age. For us today his importance lies not so much in his mysticism as in his social and pedagogic interests, such as social intercourse, the rebuilding of cities, the education of children, criticism of magistrates, and so on, to which he gives greater attention than do most Persian poets. His poem "is thus in some sort an amalgam of the *Qābūs-nāma* with the *Ḥadīqat al-ḥaqīqa*".[1] Some of Auḥadī's ghazals were even incorporated in the dīvān of Ḥāfiẓ. A poet and critic as sensitive as Muḥammad Bahār has observed that a ghazal by Auḥadī can be fully the equal of one by Ḥāfiẓ himself.[2] Auḥadī seems to have owed his *nom de plume* to the head of his order, Shaikh Abū Ḥamīd Auḥad al-Dīn of Kirmān (d. 697/1298), who was the author of a mathnavī entitled *Miṣbāḥ al-arwāḥ* ("Light of Souls").[3] This is an allegorical pilgrimage through imaginary cities, displaying basic ideas which are strikingly similar to those of Dante's *Divine Comedy*. Auḥad of Kirmān was suspected of heresy, which is not surprising since he was a disciple of Muḥyī al-Dīn ibn 'Arabī: he advanced the doctrine of man deified and "belongs together with Aḥmad Ghazālī and 'Irāqī to that group of Ṣūfīs who revered heavenly in earthly beauty".[4]

NIZĀRĪ

Ḥakīm Sa'd al-Dīn b. Shams al-Dīn b. Muḥammad Nizārī Kuhistānī (b. 645/1247–48 at Birjand, d. there in 720/1320–21) stands out among Persian poets for his individuality. He came of an old but impoverished family of the landed aristocracy, and lost what little wealth he had inherited during the Mongol invasion, so that he was reduced to a life of hardship. He acquainted himself with Persian and Arabic literature, and 'Umar Khayyām had a particularly strong and lasting influence on him. Although some of his teachers were Sunnī, he held fast to the religious beliefs of his father. Nizārī was ostensibly a Shī'ī of the traditional kind, but he undoubtedly had leanings towards Ismā'īlism,

[1] Arberry, *Classical Persian Literature*, p. 307. [2] *Baḥth*, p. 184.

[3] According to Eghbal, *MDAT*, vol. II, pt. 3, p. 8, it is the work of Muḥammad b. El-Toghan Bardāsīrī and is only ascribed to Auḥad al-Dīn Kirmānī.

[4] Ritter, "Philologika IX", p. 60.

particularly in his interpretation of the Qur'ān and of external observances (for instance with regard to wine-drinking), and also in his refusal to believe in the existence of Hell. From his youth on he served at the court and in the chancellery of the Kart rulers of Herāt, and he had perforce to sing their praises in qaṣīdas. As if in loyalty to the Ismā'īlī tradition, he longed for detailed knowledge of other lands and peoples, and of their opinions; and both in his official capacity and on his own initiative he undertook many journeys. The fruit of his two years of pilgrimage (678–79/1280–81) was the *Safar-Nāma* ("Travel Book" about 1,200 lines long), in which, far from recording trivialities, he describes the life of the cities and regions he saw, his meetings with people, and other experiences. After returning to Herāt he re-entered the service of the court, but was so slandered that he lost his position. A self-defence written in verse, the *Munāẓara-i Shab u Rūz* ("Dispute between Night and Day") resulted in his pardon, though only for a time. He then withdrew into solitude, and poetry itself is said to have become repugnant to him; eventually he set himself up as a farmer, a way of life which he, like Ibn Yamīn, valued highly.

His dīvān contains about fifteen sections, amongst them the long mathnavī (about 10,000 lines) called *Aẓhar u Maẓhar*, concerning the fidelity of two lovers; it was written in 700/1300. Nizārī's ghazals go beyond the traditional literary models, and in so doing mirror all the more clearly the social discontent which resulted from the Mongol oppression and exploitation. Another work that bears the stamp of originality is the *Dastūr-Nāma* (in 576 lines), a kind of parody of the popular "books of maxims", which in its language and poetic form is extremely polished; it was written for the poet's sons, but in fact "gives to those who lead a dissipated life and are partial to a goblet of wine rules of conduct which are in direct opposition to those laid down in the Qur'ān". Daulatshāh says that the work was much appreciated by connoisseurs and men of the world, but he does not conceal the attitude of the clergy towards the poet—to them he was a heretic indeed.[1]

Nizārī is little known and certainly underrated. The reasons for this lie in his convictions, his opinions, and the attitude of his poetry. Bertel's regards him as an outspoken free-thinker and blasphemous underminer of the very foundations of orthodoxy.[2]

[1] "Destūr-nāme Nizārī", p. 42.

[2] Leiden ed., p. 231, l. 24; p. 233, l. 7; Bertel's, *op. cit.* p. 44.

INDO-PERSIAN LITERATURE

The earlier phase of Islamic contact with India goes back to the eighth century; but it was little more than a prelude. In fact Islam began to take root only with Maḥmūd of Ghazna (early eleventh century), whose Indian policy was continued by his successors and, later, by members of other dynasties; though all were Turkish, they brought the Persian language and customs of India with their courts, because they themselves had come under the sway of Persia's highly developed culture. The influence of the courts, and the presence of Indians at them, caused Persian to spread throughout the conquered territories, where anyone wishing to enter the civil service had to master that language. The upper classes were naturally the ones affected, and it was from their ranks that the Indo-Persian poets were drawn, in so far as these were not Iranian immigrants. As foreigners, they showed many peculiarities in their writings—writings which Persians proper regard as un-Persian. Nevertheless there were several Indo-Persian men of letters—a surprisingly large number in all—who exerted an influence in Iran itself and in Central Asia. The greatest of them was Yamīn al-Dīn Abu'l- Ḥasan Amīr Khusrau Dihlavī, who was born in 651/1253 at Patyali and died at Delhi seventy-five years later.

Amīr Khusrau was an Indian only on his mother's side; his father, an illiterate Turk from Central Asia, was a man of some importance, who had moved to India with his tribe, the Hazāra-yi Lachin, during the Mongol invasions, either from Transoxiana or from Balkh. Although he belonged to the Chishtī order of Ṣūfīs and was completely devoted to its shaikh, the saint and scholar Niẓām al-Dīn Auliyā (d. 725/1324), Amīr Khusrau worked as a court poet in the service of various rulers and dynasties in Delhi and Multān. This did not in the least disturb the mystical bent of his lyric poetry. The poetic works of this *Ṭūṭī-yi Hindī* ("The Indian Parrot") were formerly estimated to run to 400,000 lines, but this total is quite fanciful and cannot stand up to critical examination, even though Khusrau was undeniably an extremely prolific poet and also a prose writer. He collected his best lyrics in five dīvāns which contain eulogistic qaṣīdas and also examples of all the other lyric genres, especially the ghazal. In qaṣīdas Amīr Khusrau followed the example of Khāqānī, though without the latter's incomprehensibility, while also imitating Sanā'ī and later his own contemporary Kamāl al-Dīn Iṣfahānī; in the ghazal, however, Sa'dī was his model. Muḥammad Waḥīd Mīrzā, while not wishing to underrate the poet's other works, regards the ghazals as the most important part of his output and emphasizes their simplicity, internal coherence, wealth of feeling, and *joie de vivre*, their melodious sound (whence their popularity amongst Ṣūfīs), and finally their intellectual sublety, a quality which he claims is lacking in the Persian poets of Iran, apart from Jāmī (d. 898/1492) and Naẓīrī (d. 1021/1612–13).[1]

Amīr Khusrau's work culminates in his epic poetry, which is an essential link in the development of the Persian mathnavī. It consists of historical poems and of parallels to Niẓāmī's *Khamsa*, each group, like the *Khamsa*, being divided into five parts, as is Khusrau's lyric poetry too. The themes for the first group of epics are taken entirely from contemporary local history; thus Khusrau inaugurated a new development by rejecting the romanticism of the fairy tale and the myth in a daring attempt at historical and local realism. This branch of his epic poetry, which occupied him from 688/1289 until his death, includes: *Qirān al-sa'dain* ("The Conjunction of the Two Lucky Stars"), written in 688/1289, which describes the struggle for the throne and reconciliation between Kai-Qubād, the son, with Bughra-Khān, the father; *Miftāḥ al-futūḥ* ("The Key to Victories"), written in 690/1291, which describes the four victories won by Jalāl al-Dīn Fīrūz-Shāh Khaljī in the single year 689/1290; and the *Tughlaq-Nāma*, which deals with the events during the short life of Ghiyath al-Din Tughlaq-Shāh, and was composed towards the end of Khusrau's life.

The first of these poems was written at the behest of Kai-Qubād himself. Though the theme was not exactly attractive, the command did enable Amīr Khusrau to realize his long-held ambition of trying his hand at an epic of some length, possibly in emulation of the masterly Niẓāmī. He succeeded in avoiding the obvious pitfall of monotony and produced a work of outstanding merit, which is recognized by critics as his finest mathnavī, but to do so he had to call upon all his powers of narrative and lyric invention, interspersing a whole series of ghazals and poetic descriptions among the sections of narrative, a feature which recurs in the other poems in this group. Each chapter has a title in the form of *abyāt-i silsila*, i.e. uniformly versified titles for each canto, and this practice is repeated in several of his other epics and dīvāns. In the *Miftāḥ al-futūḥ* historical accuracy is emphasized; and as in the previous work, the panegyrical origin of the poem is transparent. The *Tughlaq-*

[1] *The Life and Works of Amir Khusrau*, pp. 205 ff.

Nāma was likewise written at a royal behest. "The mathnavi does not offer many attractions to a student of literature. It is on the whole a plain narrative but with a few of those lively and imaginative passages that characterize Khusrau's other poetical works."[1]

Unique features are discernible in *Nuh Sipihr* ("Nine Heavens"), written in 718/1318, an epic of heterogeneous content. Epic descriptions alternate with passages praising India and more or less directly extolling Mubārak-Shāh Khaljī (716–20/1316–20). "The poem, in fact, is replete with things of immense historical and sociological interest and may safely be claimed to be a composition unique, in style and spirit, in the whole range of mathnavi literature—a poem which would amply repay a careful study and would be appreciated much better after a thorough perusal."[2] In contrast with Khusrau's other versified narratives, *'Ashīqa* or *'Ishqiyya* (715/1316) is built around "the central theme of the romantic love and the tragic fate of Khizr Khan and the beautiful princess Devaldi".[3] This epic undoubtedly influenced Salmān Sāvajī, who was one of the first to follow the lead of the great Indian poet.

Amīr Khusrau was the first poet who wrote on the model of Niẓāmī's "Quintet", and he did so in a way that was to have a decisive effect on later imitations. The Indian poet took the same subjects as in the *Khamsa*, altering the various episodes, the motivation, and the language to a greater or lesser extent, and displaying an erudition which, though considerable, by no means equals Niẓāmī's. The clear-cut outlines of Niẓāmī's poetry here give way to a certain nebulous quality, and its philosophical profundity and social preoccupation vanish. But it was precisely this undisputed lowering of levels and euphuization of style which accorded with the taste of the times. There have been occasions, though only in periods of literary decadence, when critics have given preference to Khusrau's *Khamsa*. The great Niẓāmī, despite his verve and creative ebullience, spent half a lifetime on the composition of his *Khamsa*, whereas Amīr Khusrau completed his task in just under three years (698–701/1298–1301). His *Khamsa* does not amount to much more than half Niẓāmī's in length. Notwithstanding all his talent and wealth of imagination, the speed of composition alone would prevent his being the equal of the master of Ganja. Vahīd Dastgirdī does not attribute any very great poetic value to Khusrau's *Khamsa*.[4]

[1] Waḥīd Mīrzā, *op. cit.* p. 252. [2] *Ibid.* p. 189. [3] *Ibid.* p. 178.
[4] *Ibid.* p. 192, for various views on the subject.

Some of Khusrau's quatrains are reminiscent of Khayyām, and there are several others in praise of apprentices, the latter reputedly drawn from a collection of amorous epigrams entitled *Shahr-Āshūb*, "Disturbers of the City". (Humorous poems of this kind appeared both before and after Khusrau.) The question of Khusrau's Hindī poetry remains unsolved. Though the poet must certainly have known his own vernacular (after all, his mother was of Indian origin), the authenticity of the poems ascribed to him in this idiom is extremely doubtful. He did, however, make use of Hindī words in his Persian poetry.

What is of interest is his prose, even if the titles of the numerous works traditionally ascribed to him must be reduced to no more than three. The principal one of these is his *I'jāz-i Khusravī* ("Khusrau's Inimitability") or *Rasā'il al-I'jaz* ("Treatises on Inimitability"), an extensive work dating from between the years 682/1283–84 and 719/1319–20, which consists of six treatises on various stylistic and rhetorical questions together with examples of letters, etc. "It introduces a healthy change by his innovations inasmuch as he attached more importance to ideas and intellectual figures of speech than to senseless alliterations, quips and puns."[1] His *Ta'rīkh-i 'Alā'i* ("History of 'Alā'"), or *Khazā'in al-futūḥ* ("Treasure-Chambers of Victories"), written in 711/1311–12, describes events during the years 695–711/1296–1312, when 'Alā' al-Dīn was reigning. The style is extremely bombastic and precious, though the work remains an important historical source. Khusrau's *Afḍal al-fawā'id* ("The Most Excellent Moral Precepts") is a compendium of the sayings of Niẓām al-Dīn Auliyā, his Ṣūfī guide.

Information has survived of the poet's musical abilities and it is probable that he did much to bring about the fusion of Persian and Indian music in India though unfortunately there are no works on music by him.

Amīr Khusrau is the greatest representative of Indo-Persian classicism. His style, which Bertel's[2] calls "powdered", may be seen as a prelude to the "Indian style" proper, which was to arise almost three hundred years later. Although he liked to follow precedents, there is no denying that he made considerable efforts to be independent; his epics, in so far as they are based on his own experience and observations, are certainly original. Emotional depth and a sense of humour are outstanding qualities of his writing.

[1] *Ibid.* p. 220.

[2] *Ocherk*, p. 41; *idem*, "Navoi i Nizami", p. 81.

One of Amīr K̲h̲usrau's close friends was Amīr Najm al-Dīn Ḥasan Sijzī, surnamed Ḥasan Dihlavī (b. 651/1253, d. 729/1328), a court poet, though perhaps reluctantly, since it is likely that under the influence of his spiritual mentor Niẓām al-Dīn Auliyā he regarded panegyrics as unworthy of a poet. His eight hundred or so g̲h̲azals, which are much admired both in and outside India, are distinguished by simplicity of language and poetic technique and by an emotional force even greater than in K̲h̲usrau's, though Ḥasan knew how to be mordant as well as delicate. Marek also refers to romantic and didactic epics and prose works by Ḥasan.[1] Although his poetry seems at first sight simple, it is in fact written with great skill. It is not surprising that he influenced even Persian and Central Asian poets such as Kamāl K̲h̲ujandī (d. 803/1400–01) and Ḍamīr Iṣfahānī (d. after 985/1578); Kamāl was even called "Hasan's Plagiarist". Like K̲h̲usrau, Ḥasan took Saʿdī as a model. Compared with those of many other poets, his g̲h̲azals have a remarkable internal coherence.

PANEGYRIC POETS AT MINOR COURTS

A poet whose fame was great even in his own lifetime is Kamāl al-Dīn Abuʾl-ʿAṭā Maḥmūd b. ʿAlī, whose poetic pseudonym K̲h̲wāju ("The Little Lord") was probably a childhood nickname. Born in 689/1290 or 679/1281 at Kirmān, he was very much a court poet, as his qaṣīdas, dedications, and epics prove. His patron was the last Īl-K̲h̲ān Abū Saʿīd; he then served the Muẓaffarids and the Jalayirids, finally settling at the court of Abū Isḥāq Īnjū in S̲h̲īrāz, where he died in 753/1352 or 762/1361. Much of his life was spent wandering from place to place, and in so doing he became acquainted with many people and joined a Ṣūfī order, which was to make its mark on his writing. He was twenty-seven when one of his qaṣīdas was immortalized in plaster on the walls of the bath-house at Yazd. Even if later generations have somewhat modified the hasty judgments of their merit, his writings are numerous and remarkable, especially his dīvān entitled Ṣanāyiʿ al-kamāl, "Arts of Perfection" (alluding to his name Kamāl al-Dīn). Because he was a court poet, the panegyric element is very much to the fore, though he praised not only temporal rulers but also the imāms, especially ʿAlī. Much of his poetry springs from religious—mostly Ṣūfī—and ethical considerations. His qaṣīdas were obviously

---

[1] *Dějiny perské a tadžické literatury*, p. 524.

written under the influence of the 'Irāqī school, while Sa'dī influenced his ghazals, even though he himself maintained that he wrote in the manner of Ḥāfiẓ. While it is not true that Ḥāfiẓ actually praises him in so many words, the number of identical subjects in the dīvāns of both poets suggests that they shared sympathies; a likelihood confirmed by the fact that their ghazals have been confused by later generations. Their common sphere of activity, together with the fact that they probably knew each other personally, makes it easy to believe that they influenced each other, and Khwājū is more likely to have influenced the young Ḥāfiẓ than *vice versa*. Köprülü sees in Khwājū's ghazals a connecting link between Sa'dī and Ḥāfiẓ,[1] Shiblī Nu'mānī perceives a lack of mysticism in his poetry and in consequence regards him as nothing more than a colourful flower without a scent.[2] Khwājū even wrote riddles and logogriphs, both decadent literary genres but widely popular for this very reason; on the other hand he was adept at choosing the *mot juste*, and was versed in intricacies of poetic technique and stylistic art to the point of artificiality.

In writing a "Quintet" Khwājū modelled his work on Niẓāmī's, but also introduced alterations which were to be perfected one and a half generations later by Jāmī. Khwājū's mathnavīs belong to his maturity, perhaps even to his old age. Two of them are love stories, the other three being devoted to religious themes, either ethical, Ṣūfī, or inspired by the poet's membership of his order. The love stories concern the adventures of two couples, *Humāi u Humāyūn* (732/1331–32) and *Gul u Naurūz* ("Rose and New Year", 742/1341–42), the latter being the better mathnavī, though its subject matter is not original. Both are almost like fairy tales from the Arabian Nights, with a tendency to veer into mysticism.[3] The next phase in Khwājū's epic-writing is represented by his *Rauḍat al-Anwār* ("Garden of Lights", 743/1342), an imitation of Niẓāmī's *Makhzan al-asrār* (see above, pp. 579–80); then follow two Ṣūfī ethical mathnavīs, the *Kamāl-Nāma* ("Book of Perfection", 744/1343–44) and the *Gauhar-Nāma* ("Book of the Pearl", ? 746/1345–46).

As to the *Sām-Nāma*—an epic, more in the form of a courtly novel, about the ancient Iranian hero Sām—Safa favours Khwājū's authorship for a variety of reasons, although the old sources make no mention

[1] *IA*, vol. v, p. 40*a*.
[2] *Shi'r*, vol. v, p. 30, where he makes the same reservation with regard to Salmān Sāvajī.
[3] Bausani, *Istoria*, p. 752.

of the work;[1] Köprülü, on the other hand, doubts its authenticity and regards it as a feeble effort. Several prose treatises are also ascribed to Khwājū; they are all written in an artificial prose style in the manner of the *Maqāmas*.

In spite of his reputation, Khwājū is a poet without personality; it is truer to say that he was a successful imitator of greater poets both in his lyric poetry and in the romantic and reflective mathnavī. Indeed he was so skilful at imitation that his contemporary Ḥaidār of Shīrāz accused him of plagiarism in a versified lampoon, doubtless prompted by nothing more than spiteful envy of the reputation that Khwājū was already enjoying.

A remarkable exception to the general monotony of Persian poetry in this period is presented by Amīr Maḥmūd b. Amīr Yamīn al-Dīn Ṭughrā'ī of Faryūmad (this was not his actual birthplace), named Ibn Yamīn for short, born in 685/1286 or 687/1288. After the death of his father, who was also a poet, he succeeded to the latter's office as a director of finance to the vizier of Khurāsān in 722/1322, but this gave him no satisfaction as he was denounced by his colleagues and finally dismissed. In the unusually uncertain circumstances prevailing after the death in 736/1336 of the last ruling Īl-Khān, namely Abū Sa'īd, Ibn Yamīn shuttled between the courts of various rival petty princes. At the Battle of Zāveh, fought between the poet's patrons, the Sarbadārs of Sabzavār, and the Karts of Herāt (743/1342), he lost the only manuscript of the dīvān he had composed during the first half of his life, and probably all his wealth as well. He was taken prisoner by the victorious Karts and remained in captivity for several years. He was not badly treated, but he had to sing his captors' praises until he managed to return from Herāt to the Sarbadārs at Sabzavār. He died in 769/1368 at Faryūmad, where he was living a withdrawn life as a farmer.

The loss of the dīvān was a bitter blow; but it was not lost entirely beyond recall, because Ibn Yamīn pieced it together again as far as possible from his own memory and that of his friends. In Leningrad an old manuscript is preserved in which there are also poems dating from the first half of his poetic career. Since this manuscript certainly does not contain all his poetry, it can be assumed that Ibn Yamīn's total output was more than has actually survived; nevertheless 16,000 lines are a substantial amount, double the 8,000 lines in the printed

[1] *Ḥamāsa*, p. 335.

edition. He eulogized approximately sixty-five rulers, some of whom were mutual enemies, but his qaṣīdas are all thoroughly average, often repeating themselves and full of plagiarisms. His ghazals are equally mediocre; it is in *vers d'occasion* (*qiṭ'a*) that he excels, rivalling Anvarī as an exponent of this form. These short poems are the products of the inspiration of the moment, and as a result contain inconsistencies and even contraditions. In them Ṣūfism alternates with rationalism, encouragement to activity with a desire for isolation from the world; they are, in other words, true products of their times. Ibn Yamīn was in many ways a forward-looking poet, not without a touch of materialism. In these poems he attacks the feudal overlords whom he praises in his qaṣīdas, confesses reverence for women, shows pity for the suffering, and extols the virtues of husbandry—but without ceasing to be the loyal servant of the sultans. He accepted the Shī'ī convictions of the Sarbadārs as his creed and was amongst the earliest poets to praise the imāms and Karbalā. All this, together with his knowledge of rural life, renders his "fragments" important for the understanding of social and peasant life in the period, while the document itself is almost unique amongst the Persian classics. Ibn Yamīn captivates the reader not with the excellence of his style but with his down-to-earth ideas and his realism.

A country nobleman, Khwāja, Jamāl al-Dīn Salmān Sāvajī, i.e. of Sāveh (b. *c.* 709/1309, d. 778/1376), was the last notable pre-Ṣafavid panegyric writer. He eulogized the Jalayirids, though he did not hesitate to praise their temporary conquerors. Because he was a "prince of poets" and in the ruler's confidence, his favour was courted by many, and he soon acquired fame and esteem through the preciosity of his "over-artificial qaṣīdas" written in the manner of the panegyric poet Sayyid Dhu'l-Fiqār Shīrvānī (d. 689/1290). This type of poetry had been in vogue before and was often to be cultivated with greater perfection afterwards, particularly by poets in the ninth/fifteenth century who put Salmān in the shade. As a compensation for their lack of ideas, the writers of panegyrics pursued a line of "art for art's sake" all the more vigorously. Salmān was especially skilful in his use of the *double entendre*. But writing of this type was chiefly a way of attracting notice at the outset of his career. He wrote works of greater literary merit when he began to think up new subjects and new metaphors. Despite this, his qaṣīdas still contain echoes of Kamāl al-Dīn Ismā'īl, of Ẓahīr Faryābī, and Anvarī, and even of the early panegyrist

Manūchihrī (died *c.* 432/1040–41), while the great mystic poets can be recognized as the models of his ghazals. Salmān wrote hymns glorifying God, the Prophet, and the imāms, in particular 'Alī, who until then had not been praised very much in Iran; on the other hand, it cannot be maintained that Salmān was an out-and-out Shī'ī. Apart from these poems and other traditional forms of lyric verse, he wrote a *Sāqī-Nāma* ("Book of the Cup-Bearer"), which probably antedates Ḥāfiẓ and was therefore one of the earliest lyric poems; a romantic epic called *Jamshīd u Khurshīd* (763/1361–62), an adaptation of *Khusrau u Shīrīn* under another name; and a romantic tale *Firāq-Nāma* ("The Book of Separation"), written to console Sulṭān Uvais on the loss of his favourite; the separation was temporary at first, but after the reconciliation it was to become permanent, since his beloved died. Since the poem was based on an actual occurrence—and here Salmān was following the example of Amīr Khusrau—his *Firāq-Nāma* was to become a model for many later poets. In general Salmān's works display accomplishment rather than genuine poetic fire. The praise he was given in the dīvān of Ḥafiẓ was based on spurious poems, though Ḥāfiẓ certainly knew his works, as Salmān knew those of Ḥāfiẓ; and in fact their styles are so similar that some of Salmān's ghazals have passed into the other's dīvān. His frivolous verses ("Jokes") recall those of Sa'dī. 'Ubaid-i Zākānī reproached him for writing in the language of women, saying he must have written his poems for his wife; nevertheless the two men became friends.

Judaeo-Persian literature lies somewhat outside the scope of this study. Towards the end of the Mongol period, Maulānā Shāhīn of Shīrāz, taking as his subjects biblical material and Judaeo-Persian traditions, became a kind of Firdausī or Niẓāmī of the Iranian Jews. Before his time translations of the Pentateuch had already been made. The Judaeo-Persian writers all used the Hebrew script exclusively.

At this point the Mongol period comes more or less to an end, and poetry moves into the age of Tīmūr with the outstanding figure of Ḥāfiẓ.

PROSE

This section does not touch on strictly scientific prose, but is confined in the first place to *belles-lettres*; then to prose lying on the border between literature and science: didactic prose with literary pretensions; and finally, historiography.

Though New Persian prose has not acquired the fame of New

Persian poetry, and with a few exceptions has not received the same notice or critical scrutiny as the poetry, it must on no account be underrated, as regards either quantity or quality. Immeasurable riches still lie hidden in manuscripts. A peculiarity of Persian literary prose, and often of scientific prose too, during this period is a tendency—to an even greater extent than in earlier periods—to approximate to poetry as the true voice of Persia. To this end literary prose favoured a florid style and the inclusion of verse, accompanied by an increasing use of Arabic. In didactic and scientific prose the same means were used, especially in prefaces and historical works, and sometimes even to the point of including verse in the text itself. Furthermore, in literary prose rhythm and rhyme were brought into the structure of the sentence, particularly in the short story in dialogue form known as *maqāma*; indeed the whole gamut of rhetorical ornamentation and excessive Arabic borrowing were the essential features of this curious genre, and became much more important than the story itself. Tendencies of this kind had already been discernible during the Saljuq era, and Mongol rule only sharpened the taste for this ornamentation and preciosity in both literary and didactic prose. This trend, however, was not wholly uniform. Although it is indisputable that artificiality increased and that prose became highly elaborate and tended towards poetry, still there were always certain writers who cultivated simple or at least relatively chaste modes of expression. Two currents were thus at work in the same period. While historians delighted in styles of every kind, including the most pretentious, Ṣūfī writers in general preferred a simpler tone. History apart, bombast tended to occur most frequently in biography and literary history, essays, and epistolary writings. In these genres may be found a style which is flowery, high-flown, often excessively verbose, and lacking in content sometimes to the point of utter vacuity; a style, moreover, which swelled the proportion of Arabic vocabulary in Persian to such extreme limits that only professional aesthetes were capable of understanding it. The requirements of reality were simply lost from sight.

I. *Literary prose*

The oldest Persian novel, *Samak-i ʿAyyār* ("Samak the Magnanimous") was written down, according to the oral tradition of Ṣadaqa b. Abu'l-Qāsim Shīrāzi, by Farāmurz Khudādād b. ʿAbdallāh Kātib al-Arrajānī in 585/1189. It records the fabulous adventures of the various knights who courted the Emperor of China's daughter. Another novelist, Abū Ṭāhir Muḥammad Ṭarsūsī, whose dates are quite uncertain, imitated Firdausī in the sphere of historical romance, and became famous for various prose novels based on Persian legends; his *Dārāb-Nāma* has been published.[1] There is also a novel by Ḥamīd al-Dīn Jauharī Zargar dating from the sixth/twelfth century and telling about the poetess Mahsitī; only a small number of the quatrains quoted in it, however, can be accepted as genuinely hers.

Collections of anecdotes, arranged under various unifying titles, have also come down. The most important is *Jawāmi' al-ḥikāyāt va lawāmi' al-riwāyāt* ("Necklaces of Anecdotes and Lightning-Flashes of Tales"), comprising 2,113 stories gathered by Sadīd al-Dīn Muḥammad 'Aufī. A descendant of 'Abd al-Raḥmān 'Auf, one of the Prophet's companions, 'Aufī came of a cultured Transoxianian family who engaged in literary pursuits; he was born between 567 and 572 (1171–77). He travelled widely, and worked at royal courts in Transoxiana, Sind, and finally Delhi; he seems to have had no moral scruples about changing masters. There is no further record of him after 630/1232–33. The collection of stories dates from the author's later years and is distinguished by its simplicity, which contrasts with the pomposity of the *Lubāb al-albāb* ("Quintessence of Hearts"), written in 618/1221–22. The latter, besides being more characteristic of his style, is the oldest work of its kind in Persian literature. It is a sort of history of literature or rather a collection of biographies of poets, written in a flowery style, in place of which one would prefer more facts. 'Aufī was not an outstanding master of style and the importance of both works lies in their usefulness. The *Jawāmi' al-ḥikāyāt*, a veritable fountain of anecdotes drawn from a great many sources, was in turn a source for the parables of the didactic writers and is important for this reason alone, quite apart from its occasionally valuable historical comments. In 620/1203 'Aufī made a Persian translation of *Al-Faraj ba'd al-shidda* ("Joy after Sorrow"), from the Arabic of the Qāḍī Abū 'Alī al-Muḥsin al-Tanukhī (d. 384/994); but it has not survived. The original was again translated between 651/1253–54 and 656–73/1258–75 by Ḥusain Dihistānī Vazīrī, but it is not certain whether this was in fact a new translation or simply

[1] See the Bibliography *s.v.* Bīghamī. To judge from the manuscript, Bīghamī must have written the text in the eighth/fourteenth or ninth/fifteenth century. The narrator, however, must have died a little earlier.

an adaptation of the older one; even now all the uncertainties about this so-called second translation and its author are far from having been removed.

Among the collections of moralizing fables or tales incorporated in a framework, first and foremost stands *Kalīla u Dimna*, for countless ages one of the most treasured books of the peoples of East and West; it is also known by the name "Bidpai's Fables". For present purposes, its origin lies in the excellent Arabic translation by the Persian 'Abd-allāh b. al-Muqaffa' (executed *c.* 142/759), whose text was taken from the Middle Persian adaptation by Burzoe of various Indian models. Several Persian versions were based on the translation by Ibn al-Muqaffa', but they were all superseded by that of Abu'l-Ma'ālī Naṣr Allāh, probably a native of Shīrāz, who at the command of the Ghaz-navid Bahrām-Shāh (511–52/1118–52) undertook a new adaptation. Khusrau Malik (555–82/1160–86) rewarded his ministerial services by having his executed. The versified version by Rūdakī has been lost. And even Naṣr Allāh's work (written between 515 and 537/1131–53), which, in spite of much rhetorical ornamentation adapted to the exigencies of contemporary taste, is still a masterpiece of Persian prose by virtue of its elegance and comparative simplicity, was not to remain unscathed. The ornamentation which he gave it seemed insufficient to later writers, who outdid each other in their customary stylistic con-tortions and bombast, though it is not surprising that so popular and highly valued a work should have been subject to such influences. The elegance of Naṣr Allāh's style became obscured and his text underwent such brutal distortion that it is virtually impossible to form any clear idea of its original state without the aid of a critical reconstruction. In or about 658/1260 Bahā' al-Dīn Aḥmad Qāni'ī of Ṭūs cast Naṣr Allāh's version into the form of a mathnavī in the *mutaqārib* metre for 'Izz al-Dīn Kai-Kā'ūs, the Saljuq ruler of Rūm. The version by Ḥusain Vā'iẓ Kāshifī entitled *Anvār-i Suhailī* ("The Lights of the Canopus") is far more blatantly rhetorical than that of Naṣr Allāh; but this belongs to the end of the ninth/fifteenth century.

The *Marzubān-Nāma*, written in the Tabari dialect by Ispahbud ("Prince") Marzban b. Rustam b. Shahryār b. Sharvin around the turn of the tenth to eleventh century, provides a valuable parallel to *Kalīla u Dimna*. Only two mutually independent New Persian verions have survived, both written in an over-elaborate style. These are the *Marzubān-Nāma* by Sa'd-i Varāvīnī of Āzarbāījān, written between

607/1210 and 622/1225 and the *Rauḍat al-ʿuqūl* ("The Garden of Sensible Minds"), written at the end of the twelfth century, by a vizier of the Saljuqs of Rūm, Muḥammad b. Ghāzī of Malatiya. Three works resembling the Arabian Nights, viz. the *Sindbād-Nāma* ("The Book of the Seven Viziers"), the related *Bakhtiyār-Nāma* ("The Book of the Ten Viziers"), and the *Ṭūṭī-Nāma* ("The Parrot-Book"), date from this period and were at one time extremely popular. They are collections of tales arranged within the framework of a definite "moralizing" idea (mainly that same objectionable disparagement of and disrespect for women which underlies the Arabian Nights). One collection without any underlying idea is the *Qiṣṣa-yi Chahār Darvīsh* ("The Tale of the Four Dervishes"), a fantastic work strongly impregnated with the romantic spirit. The origins of these collections lie for the most part in India and Sassanian Iran, though their texts have of course undergone the most varied and colourful developments. Sooner or later they were all clothed in a more elevated prose style. The original version of *Sindbād-Nāma*, written in a primitive style by Khwāja Amīr al-Dīn Abu'l-Fawāris Qanārizī in 339/950–51, has disappeared, together with a poetic replica by Azraqī (d. before 465/1072); the latter was recast in a more elevated style by Muḥammad al-Ẓahīrī al-Kātib of Samarqand in 556–57/1160–61. The oldest version of the *Bakhtiyār-Nāma*, dating from the beginning of the seventh/thirteenth century, is by a certain Muḥammad Daqā'iqī of Marv, to whom a version of the *Sindbād-Nāma* is also attributed; it exists in several different versions, and was versified by an otherwise unknown poetaster named Panāhī at the Qara-Qoyunlu court in 851/1447. The *Ṭūṭī-Nāma*, the anonymous original version of which has disappeared, is preserved in an "extremely tasteful new version" (Ethé) of 730/1330 by Ḍiyā al-Dīn Nakhshabī, as well as in shortened versions by Muḥammad Khudāvand Qadīrī (ninth/tenth century) and Abu'l-Faḍl b. Mubārak (d. 1011/1602–03), and in a metrical version by Ḥamīd of Lahore.

A nobler type of rhetorical art is represented by the *maqāma*, a true expression of art for art's sake, in the form of tales in prose interspersed with verse about the adventures of witty vagrants, an attenuated offshoot of the classical mime. The principal examples are in Arabic, although the creator of the genre, which was later to be brought to perfection by Ḥarīrī (d. 516/1122), is generally considered the Persian Badīʿ al-Zamān of Hamadān (d. 398/1007), unless chronological precedence is given to his rival Abū Bakr al-Khawārizmī (d. 383/993 or 393/1002). The Arabic works of two principal exponents of the *maqāma* were then imitated in Persian by the qāḍī Ḥamīd al-Dīn (d. 559/1163–64), who employed fewer unfamiliar and *recherché* expressions than Ḥarīrī, and whose style was closer to that of his fellow-countryman Badī' al-Zamān. After an interval came Sa'dī's *Gulistān*, which had its first imitation in the *Nigaristān* ("Picture Gallery") by Mu'in al-Dīn Juvainī (735/1335).

II. *Literary prose bordering on the scientific or didactic*

A work of Ṣūfī character, *Asrār al-tauhid fī Maqāmāt al-Shaikh Abū Sa'īd* ("The Secrets of God's Oneness on the Spiritual Stations of Shaikh Abū Sa'īd"), provides valuable information about the life of the celebrated mystic who died *c.* 570–80/1174–85. According to this biography, written by his great-great-grandson Muḥammad b. al-Munavvar, Shaikh Abū Sa'īd did not himself write poetry; the poems generally attributed to him must therefore be by others. The work also possesses great literary merit, and except in its introduction avoids the artificialities fashionable in the sixth/twelfth century.

Shihāb al-Dīn Suhravardī blended taṣavvuf with Zoroastrian and Neo-Platonist ideas in his Arabic and Persian works, and put forward the heretical philosophy of Monism; for so doing he was executed in Aleppo in 587/1191, and he is therefore called *al-Maqtūl*, "the executed one", to distinguish him from other writers of the same name. His treatises in Persian are consciously artistic in style (H. Corbin calls them visionary) and are amongst the earliest allegories ever written in that language. Written in relatively simple language, these tales are remarkably effective. Other prose of this kind includes 'Aṭṭār's hagiographic *Tadhkirāt al-auliyā*, and the *Mirṣād al-'ibād* ("Observatory of God's Servants") of Najm al-Dīn of Ray. In the latter work, besides important and varied themes drawn from Ṣūfism, there are valuable quotations from the poets, including the earliest reference to 'Umar Khayyām's quatrains.[1] It was written at the request of the author's disciples in 618–20/1221–23 in Qaiṣariyya and Sīvās, where he had taken refuge from the Mongol hordes. For 'Irāqī's *Lama'āt* ("Lightning Flashes") see above p. 602; three minor prose works are ascribed to Shabistarī (p. 603 above); and the Arabic and Persian writings of Bābā Afḍal should also be mentioned (p. 603 above).

[1] Arberry, *op. cit.* p. 252, stresses "the detailed account of the mystical commemoration (*dhikr*), and the curious discussion of the kinds of 'light' seen in ecstasy".

To the category of didactic prose belongs the *Akhlāq-i Nāṣirī* ("Ethics of Nāṣir"), so called in honour of the Ismā'īlī Nāṣir al-Dīn 'Abd al-Raḥīm of Kūhistān, which was written in 633/1235–36 and is the first of three famous treatises on ethics. The author, Khwāja Naṣīr al-Dīn Ṭūsī (597–672/1200–73), was one of Hülegü's most influential advisers, an outstanding polymath who composed innumerable scientific works in Arabic and Persian. He was at the same time a moralist of a very strange kind—"Professor Levy remarks that the verdict of history is a most unfavourable one"[1]—who was able to be of service both to the Assassins and to their Mongol enemies, and to contribute to the downfall of the last 'Abbāsid, an action allegedly prompted by his Shī'ī convictions. It is known that the *Akhlāq-i Nāṣirī*, and in particular its introduction, was originally composed in the spirit of his then masters, the rulers of Alamūt, but was later submitted to a thorough revision under Hülegü, who had put an end to the rule of the Assassins. Naṣīr al-Dīn exonerated himself by claiming that he had written the earlier version under duress as a captive of the Assassins; in the changed circumstances, he was quite naturally at pains to conceal his past as far as possible. His writings deal with mathematics, astronomy (a short introduction to the subject in verse is ascribed to him), cosmology, mineralogy, geography, history, the science of calendars, law, medicine, education and morals, geomancy, logic, theology, poetry, and letter-writing. When the seven hundredth anniversary of the death of Khwāja Ṭūsī was celebrated at Tehrān in 1956, the city justly honoured one of Iran's greatest geniuses. He converted his ruthless utilitarianism into an active policy and ended by making a great contribution to the relief of Persia after the Mongol catastrophe, just as Shams al-Dīn Juvainī did somewhat later, though the latter's motives were undoubtedly more idealistic.

A second non-fictional prose includes works concerned with literary history. The *Chahār Maqāla* ("Four Treatises"), written in 550–51/1155–57 by Aḥmad b. 'Umar b. 'Ali of Samarqand, generally known by the name Niẓāmī-yi 'Arūḍi, is a work of fundamental importance for the study of contemporary and earlier movements in literature. The reader must bear in mind, however, that it was written in the atmosphere of the Ghūrid dynasty, and consequently supports their attitudes and opposes those of their enemies, especially the Ghaznavids. On Rashīd Vaṭvāṭ's *Ḥadā'iq al-siḥr* ("Magic Gardens"), see above, p. 561;

[1] *Ibid.* p. 253.

and on 'Aufī's *Lubab al-albāb* ("Quintessence of Hearts"), see p. 616. A work on the subject of Persian prosody, versification and poetics, attributed to Naṣīr al-Dīn Ṭūsī, is said to be no great masterpiece. This subject received its finest treatment in *al-Mu'jam fī ma'āyīr ash'ār al-'Ajam* ("An Explanation of the Criteria of the Poems of the Persians"), written between 614/1217 and 630/1232–33 by Shams al-Dīn Muḥammad b. Qais of Ray, first in Arabic and subsequently in Persian at the request of the scholars of Shīrāz. Its value lies in the exactitude of the rules which it sets down and to an equal degree in many reliable quotations which it contains, often from poets whose dīvāns have since been lost.

III. HISTORIOGRAPHY

Amongst the historical works dating from the close of the Saljuq period, the following are important for their content and style. The *Tarīkh-i Baihaq* ("The History of Baihaq") by Abu'l-Ḥasan 'Alī b. Zaid al-Baihaqī, called Ibn Funduq (d. 565/1169–70), must be clearly distinguished from the much earlier *Ta'rīkh-i Baihaqī* ("The History of Baihaqī") or *Ta'rīkh-i Mas'ūdī*, a history of Sulṭān Mas'ūd of Ghazna by Abu'l-Faḍl Muḥammad Baihāqī (d. 470/1077–79). Of historical importance is the *Kitāb al-tawassul ila al-tarassul* ("An Exploration of the Approaches to Letter-Writing"), an epistolary collection by Bahā' al-Dīn Muḥammad Mu'ayyad al-Baghdādī (d. not before 588/1192), which was completed in 578–79/1182–84. The *Ta'rīkh-i Ṭabaristān* ("History of Ṭabaristān"), was written in 613/1216 by Muḥammad b. Isfandiyār. Finally the *Rāḥat al-ṣudūr wa āyāt al-surūr* ("Repose of Hearts and Signs of Joy", 599/1203), a history of the Saljuqs by Najm al-Dīn Abū Bakr Muḥammad Rāvandī, is "certainement un plagiat de *Saljuq-nama-i Zahiri* [Nishapuri] puisqu'il n'y a pas un mot de plus et s'arrête absolument à la même date. Ravendi a tout simplement changé le style de Zahiri sans rien y ajouter".[1]

Although the Mongol invasion inevitably had a most catastrophic effect on the development of Persian culture (except in those marginal areas which remained unscathed or were in any case not Iranian), Persian historiography reached its apogee precisely during this unfortunate period; indeed the principal historical works of the Mongol period are amongst the finest ever produced by any of the Islamic

[1] Nafīsī in a letter dated 12 October 1963.

peoples. The Īl-Khāns were eager to have their conquests and actions immortalized and they soon found subjects who were willing to undertake this task. As these writers had access to the relevant documents, especially those concerning the history of the Mongols and Turks, and as they had witnessed at first hand the events they described, they were able to provide penetrating and accurate accounts; even though they were court officials, they did not necessarily indulge in eulogies. The consolidation of the Mongol empire was the main factor in the remarkable development of Persian historiography during the thirteenth and fourteenth centuries;[1] other factors were the Crusades and the increase of caravan and sea trade in Asia and the Mediterranean, both of which served to tighten the political, economic, and cultural fabric of Iran and to broaden the horizon of Persian historians.

The complex sentence structure and wealth of vocabulary which characterize the styles of these historians can best be seen as a legacy of the Saljuq period in its decline. Two works in which this kind of writing is particularly evident are Nūr al-Dīn Muḥammad Nasawī's *Nafthat al-maṣdūr* ("Expectorations of the Consumptive") 632–37/1234–40, and Ḥasan Niẓāmī Nīshāpūrī's *Tāj al-ma'āshir* ("Crown of Glorious Deeds"), which is a bombastic and superficial history of India covering the years 587–614 (1191–1217). To this group also belongs the *Tarjama-yi Yamīnī* ("Translation of Yamini's Book") of Abu'l-Sharaf Naṣīḥ Jarbadhaqānī (early seventh/thirteenth century), which owes its rhetorical style to its Arabic original of 1021. These works are the historical counterparts of the purely literary *belles lettres* of the period, both reflecting a stylistic development that continued throughout the Mongol period and eventually reached the most distasteful extremes, destined in their turn to have a harmful influence on later Persian historical prose. Because of their ornamentation—a feature which undoubtedly had an aesthetic appeal to contemporary taste—factual works of this kind enter the sphere of literature.

'Alā' al-Dīn 'Aṭā Malik Juvainī (623–81/1226–83) is a typical representative of this style, although he had already begun writing during the early part of the Īl-Khānid period. He came of a family which had transferred its services from the Khwārazm-Shāhs to the Mongols. While his brother Shams al-Dīn Muḥammad occupied the position of a *ṣāḥib-dīvān* or finance minister to the Mongol khans, 'Aṭā Malik was

[1] For a good synopsis see M. Murtaḍavī, "Jāmi' al-Tawārīkh", *NDAT*, vol. XIII, pt. 1, pp. 37–57. Cf. K. Jahn, "Study".

the governor of Baghdad and indeed a very benevolent one. The Juvainīs were the leaders of a group who furthered the Mongol regime, but none of the family earned any thanks for their services; they were removed at the instigation of the Mongol nobility, who were hostile to them, and their immense wealth was confiscated. ʿAṭā Malik has been immortalized by his *Ta'rīkh-i Jahān-Gushā* ("History of the World-Conqueror"), completed in 658/1260, which in three volumes deals in turn with: (*a*) the history of Chingiz-Khān, his ancestors and descendants, from the first campaign to the death of the Great Khan Güyük Khān (647/1248); (*b*) the history of the Khwārazm-Shāhs and of the Mongol viceroys in Iran until 656/1258; and (*c*) the entry of Hülegü into Iran in 1256–58 and the history of the Ismāʿīlis or Assassins (1090–1258). The author visited Mongolia and was present at the destruction of the Assassin stronghold at Alamūt, from whose valuable library he tried to save what he could. On the basis of the (no longer extant) *Sar-Gudhasht-i Sayyidnā* ("Incidents in the Life of our Lord", i.e. Ḥasan-i Ṣabbāḥ, the founder of Ismāʿīlī rule in Alamūt), he wrote a description of the fortunes of this curious sect. Juvainī was a supporter of his masters, he neither concealed nor tried to exonerate them from their misdeeds. In his inquiry into the reasons for the fall of Iran he anticipated Ibn Khaldūn. Juvainī's style alternates between a greater and lesser degree of ornamental rhetoric.

Rashīd al-Dīn Faḍl Allāh of Hamadān (645–817/1247–1318) is regarded as Persia's greatest historian. An exceptionally cultivated man, he was originally a physician and later became vizier, a position he continued to hold until the reign of Abū Saʿīd, when he was accused of poisoning the latter's father, Öljeitü, and executed. Not even the insults heaped upon his corpse could satisfy the hatred felt for him; in 1399 his remains were exhumed and reburied in a Jewish cemetery. His enormous fortune was confiscated and his library of 60,000 volumes dispersed. His letters[1] provide a useful historical source, but his principal work is the *Jāmiʿ al-tawārīkh* ("Compendium of Histories"), written at the behest of Ghazan. The first part, called *Ta'rīkh-i Ghāzānī* in honour of its sponsor, was devoted to the history of the Mongol empire and the Īl-Khāns up to the death of Ghazan in 703/1304; the second part was dedicated to Öljeitü (703–16/1304–16) and is devoted

[1] He also composed *qaṣīdas* in the Mongol, Arabic, Persian and Turkish languages, cf. Spuler, *Die Mongolen*², p. 457, n. 2. [Ed.: It is in fact highly doubtful whether Rashīd al-Dīn had more than a smattering of Mongol. See Doerfer, *Türkische und mongolische Elemente im Neupersischen*, vol. 1, pp. 44–8.]

to general world history; and the third, a geography of the "seven climes", probably either was never written or was lost at the dissolution of the author's library. The entire work, written in a comparatively simple style, is noteworthy for several reasons. The first part, which contains more detailed and comprehensive information than any comparable works, including those in Chinese and Mongolian, is particularly valuable. The general history is not confined to the Islamic countries but looks farther east and west. In his task Rashīd al-Dīn had the collaboration of specialists on the language or nation in question; indeed for Mongolia his authority was Ghazan himself. Their contributions may well have been considerable, and it has even been doubted whether Rashīd al-Dīn can really be called the author of *Jāmi' al-tawārīkh*; however, these doubts have been convincingly dispelled by Murtaḍavī.[1] Rashīd al-Dīn always takes social and economic factors into consideration. Himself a bureaucrat from the middle class and a supporter of the centralizing policies of the Īl-Khāns, he opposed the particularist tendencies of feudalism, and therefore the Mongolian nomadic aristocracy.

A work in which bizarre and distorted writing reaches its climax, but which is nevertheless a mine of information, is the *Tajziyat al-amṣār wa tazjiyat al-a'ṣār* ("The Partition of Territories and the Lapse of Ages") by Sharaf al-Dīn 'Abdallāh of Shīrāz, generally called Vaṣṣāf-i Ḥaḍrat, i.e. "Court Panegyrist" (663–735/1264–1334). It continues the work of Juvainī, embracing the years 656–723 (1258–1323). Being a court official, Vaṣṣāf had access to the archives and therefore provides a great deal of factual detail, though unfortunately in a most intimidating manner. He himself admits that he was concerned primarily with literary effect, historical events serving merely as a basis. The work is thus an exercise in style on a lavish scale. To judge by their lasting effect, Vaṣṣāf's extreme fondness for Arabic words and his excessively bombastic, florid, and precious style were amongst the most harmful influences on Persian prose. On social and economic matters, however, Vaṣṣāf must be regarded as an excellent authority. In his political opinions he followed Rashīd al-Dīn, eulogizing the Mongols but never hesitating to reveal their inhumane and unjust acts.

Alongside the supporters of the Īl-Khāns there were other historians who were outspokenly opposed to them. Apart from the Arab Ibn al-Athīr (d. 630/1234), particular mention should be made of Muḥam-

[1] *Loc. cit.*

mad Nasawī (see above, p. 622) and Minhāj al-Dīn 'Uthmān Jūzjānī (b. *c.* 589/1193, d. after 664/1265); and there were others of lesser significance.

Views similar to Rashīd al-Dīn's were held by another historian, Ḥamd Allāh Mustaufī Qazvīnī, an advocate of centralization. His *Ta'rīkh-i Guzīda* ("Selected History") begins with the creation of the world and runs to 730/1329. In about 735/1355 he completed his immense *Ẓafar-Nāma*[1] ("Book of Victories"), an imitation of Firdausī's *Shāh-Nāma* containing about 75,000 lines of verse. His third work was a cosmography and geography entitled *Nuzhat al-qulūb* ("Restoration of Hearts") written in 740/1339–40, which is outstanding for the accuracy of its dates and other facts.

Works on the history of India include Ḍiyā' al-Dīn Bārānī's *Ta'rīkh-i Fīrūz-Shāhī*, dealing with events during the years 1265 to 1357; the *Ta'rīkh-i 'Alā'i* of Amīr Khusrau (see above, p. 609), a *Ta'rīkh-i Vaṣṣāf* in miniature; and Jūzjānī's general history entitled *Ṭabaqāt-i Nāṣirī* (657–58/1259–60).

In conclusion, it must be stressed that this survey covers only a very small proportion of the vast quantity of prose writing produced during the period. In selecting works to be discussed, I have given thought to their stylistic and other aesthetic aspects. Works confined to science, mathematics and so on, have been omitted entirely.[2]

[1] Two further historical epics of the Mongol period are listed by Murtaḍavī, *Taḥqiq*, p. 149 (they are completely worthless); he also, *ibid.* p. 323, quotes a doublet of Rashīd al-Dīn by Shams al-Dīn Kāshānī.

[2] For a general survey of such works see Felix Tauer, "Persian Learned Literature from its Beginnings up to the end of the 18th Century" in Rypka, *History of Iranian Literature* (Dordrecht, 1968). [Ed.: Professor Rypka's chapter was completed on 9 November 1963.]

CHAPTER 9

THE VISUAL ARTS, 1050–1350

The period of Iranian history covered in this discussion began with the rise of the Turkish dynasties of the Ghaznavids and of the Great Saljuqs and ended with the small Iranian or Mongol dynasties which followed and contributed to the fall of the Īl-Khānid empire. The specific dates quoted above are only approximations since stylistic and thematic changes do not necessarily coincide with major historical events, but the period as a whole is one in which all provinces of Islamic Iran and all media of artistic creation underwent considerable changes and in fact established architectural, formal, iconographic, and aesthetic standards which were to remain for many centuries thereafter those of Islamic Iranian art in general. This statement is valid in the sense that the arts of the following centuries can almost always be shown to be in a definable kind of relationship to forms, ideas, and techniques created or developed between the eleventh and the fourteenth centuries. Yet, if these filiations with later centuries can indeed be established, it is far more difficult to define the relationship of this art to that of previous centuries. In fact our documentation on and conceptual framework for the arts of the first four centuries of Islamic Iranian art are so limited and so much tied to the interpretation of a few texts or to purely accidental finds, that, with a few exceptions to be mentioned in due course, we will consider the art of Iran during the centuries under consideration as a new creation. If it is perhaps too adventurous to call it a renaissance in the sense that it does not seem to be in continuous but in revolutionary relationship to what preceded, it is not too far-fetched to talk of an artistic explosion, for, regardless of its complexity in details, the period which produced the mosque of Iṣfahān, the minaret of Jām, the mausoleum of Sanjar in Marv, that of Öljeitü in Sulṭānīyeh, Kāshān and Ray ceramics, the "Bobrinski" kettle, the Wade cup, the "Demotte" *Shāh-Nāma*, and the manuscripts of the Rashīdiyya can by any account be considered as one of the most productive and most brilliant periods of Iranian art.

The period is not an easy one to define properly. First, the disastrous lack of proper monographic studies—except in the case of a very few objects and buildings[1]—makes any generalization somewhat hazardous. Secondly, the periodization of the different artistic entities which can be defined is impossible in anything but the most general terms. To give but a few examples, one may point out that the period of the Great Saljuqs (roughly from 1050 to 1150) is almost totally *terra incognita* in all but architecture, while the century which followed the death of Sanjar is tremendously rich in properly dated objects but exhibits an original architecture only in a few small monuments from areas peripheral to the Iranian world, primarily Āzarbāījān, and a few cities of Central Asia. Other instances are ceramics, in which some of the most remarkable objects of the so-called "Saljuq" style were demonstrably manufactured after the Mongol conquest; and manuscripts, among which the greatest masterpiece of the fourteenth century, the "Demotte" *Shāh-Nāma*, has never found the artistic and intellectual or social milieu in which it was made. Thus it is, at this stage of our research, still almost impossible to co-ordinate properly the monuments with the events of the time; and often in trying to explain the monuments one misses the human and spiritual context in which they were made and used. Hence, even though one must be cognizant of the classical divisions of styles into a *Saljuq* period (roughly until the third or fourth decade of the thirteenth century) and the Īl-Khānid one (roughly after the last decade of the same century), we shall in this chapter avoid these distinctions on the ground that neither the monuments nor the social and cultural history of Iran have as yet been sufficiently explained to make the time distinctions more than convenient labels for museum identification.

Yet this lamentable historical vacuum is not the only methodological deficiency with which we have to cope. An equally frustrating problem is posed by what may be called the geographical co-ordinate of the arts. It is clear for instance that the third, fourth, and fifth decades of the twelfth century witnessed a remarkable building activity known primarily through large congregational mosques in the area of Iṣfahān, that the last decades of the twelfth century and the thirteenth

[1] Among the few examples are D. S. Rice, *The Wade Cup* (Paris, 1955), to be consulted together with R. Ettinghausen, "The 'Wade' Cup", *Ars Orientalis*, vol. II (1957); R. Ettinghausen, "The Iconography of a Kāshān Luster Plate", *Ars Orientalis*, vol. IV (1961); M. B. Smith, "Material for a Corpus of Early Iranian Islamic Architecture", *Ars Islamica*, vols. II, IV, VI (1935–9).

century saw major constructions of mausoleums in Āzarbāijān, that inlaid metalwork was developed to a particularly remarkable degree in Khurāsān in the second half of the twelfth century, and that Rashīd al-Dīn sponsored a major school of painting in Tabrīz in the first two decades of the fourteenth century. In all four of these instances there is no evidence that any other part of Iran enjoyed the same developments. Should any of them then be considered as regional growths to be explained by some local needs or purposes? Or are they purely accidentally preserved and should a style or an idea formed in Khurāsān in the middle of the twelfth century be construed as valid for the rest of Iran? It is of course clear that each such definable group of monuments will provide different answers to these questions. The Rashīdiyya school of painting *did* have a greater importance in the development of Iranian art after the death of its founder in 1318 than the architectural style of Āzarbāijān in the thirteenth century. Yet almost no attempt has yet been made by archaeologists or historians to separate pan-Iranian trends from local ones or to assess the exact character of any one provincial development,[1] and to the questions raised almost thirty years ago by Professor Minorsky,[2] scholarship has still not provided answers.

These methodological and intellectual difficulties in any attempt to discover the structure—the word is used here in the sense given to it by linguists or ethnographers—around which one can explain the monuments of Iranian art and their development makes our task of discussing them in a few pages particularly arduous. To attempt a chronological description would take us too long and is somewhat meaningless without at least partial solutions to the questions raised in the preceding paragraphs. A discussion of techniques separately from each other would correspond to traditional methods of treating Islamic art, but its underlying assumption of separate developments for each major medium would have to be demonstrated for this particular period and in any event it would not provide a clear summary of the visually perceived world created during these centuries. Our choice, therefore, has been to avoid any attempt at total coverage but rather to select a more limited number of precise topics through which, it is hoped, one may be able to define the major characteristics of the arts of the eleventh to fourteenth centuries and also point to the problems which still need

[1] Preliminary remarks for the fourteenth century by D. Wilber, *The Architecture of Islamic Iran: The Ilkhānid Period* (Princeton, 1955), pp. 88 ff.

[2] V. Minorsky, "Geographical Factors in Persian Art", *B.S.O.S.* vol. IX (1937–9).

to be solved. Three such topics were chosen: the architecture of the mosque, the objects of the twelfth–thirteenth centuries, the painting of the fourteenth century. Each of these, as we will try to show, serves as a focal point around which most of the major monuments and problems can be discussed. Much in the interpretations which will be proposed is still hypothetical, but it is our belief that only through working hypotheses can the actual significance of an insufficiently studied art properly emerge.

THE ARCHITECTURE OF THE MOSQUE AND ITS IMPLICATIONS

The central phenomenon of the architecture of Iran during these centuries is the formation of what may be called the classical Iranian mosque. Almost its most perfect example is found in the now ruined *masjid-i jumʿa* of Varāmīn (fig. 1; pls. 1, 2), near Tehrān. It is a rectangle, 66 by 43 metres, with a remarkably clear plan. A courtyard in the centre was lined with an internal façade; on either side lies an axial *īvān* (definable as a rectangular vaulted hall of which one side opens directly to the outside) framed by two or four smaller arched openings. The īvāns are not of equal size and the centrally planned balance of the court is overshadowed by the strong longitudinal axis of the wider īvān on the *qibla* side (pl. 2) which is followed by a superbly majestic dome rising high above the rest of the building. The area between īvāns is at the same time quite open for circulation and yet definable through a series of long vaults carried on square or rectangular supports. A curious sort of ambiguity remains as to whether these supports are actually piers imagined as separate entities or walls opened up by wide arches. There are three entrances to the building, each of which is a shallow īvān leading into the axial īvāns of the court. The main entrance, on the longitudinal axis, is architectonically articulated through a series of niches and prefigures the composition of the *īvān qiblī*.

The medium of construction is brick throughout. Its fabric varies from place to place and thus serves at the same time as a mode of construction and as decoration. The vaults are usually pointed barrel vaults. The īvāns and the zone of transition to the dome are provided with a characteristic architectonic composition known as the *muqarnas*. It consists of a combination—variable in structure and extent—of complete units of construction, such as half-domes and vaults, or segments thereof, used, at least in appearance, either to give variety to a wall surface or to organize the passage from one form to the other, as from square to octagon or from walls to vault. Throughout the building decoration is at the same time omnipresent and subordinated to architectural lines. Several different techniques are used: imaginative

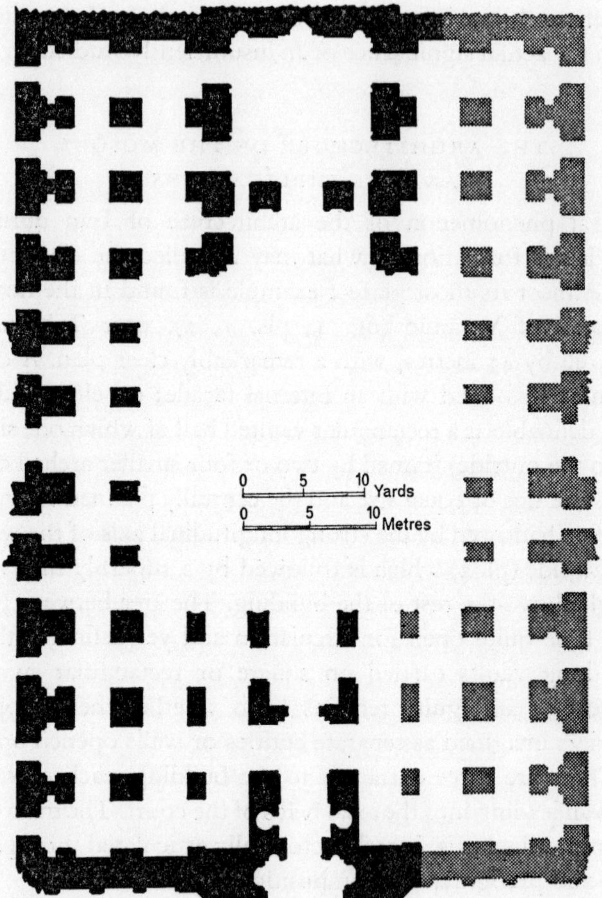

Fig. 1. Plan of mosque at Varāmīn.

variations in the fabric of construction, stucco, terra-cotta, colour faïence. Although vegetal motives do exist, the main designs are either epigraphical or geometric. The former, with their religious or historical subject-matter, serve also to identify the purpose, quality, and time of execution of the building. The latter are used to strengthen the main lines of the building and have been used in a particularly effective fashion.

Such are briefly the major characteristics of the mosque of Varāmīn.[1] Their significance is that almost all of them were created or developed during the two and a half centuries which preceded the building of the mosque. The time of invention, history, or purpose of most of these features are still not well understood and each one deserves a separate monographic treatment. We shall limit ourselves here to a rapid discussion of some of the problems posed by the most striking identifying characteristics of the building.

The first one is the plan of a mosque with four īvāns around a court (pl. 3) and with a large dome on the axis in front of the *miḥrāb*. The establishment of this plan, which remained characteristic of Iranian architecture for many centuries, has been the subject of much controversy and the question of the origins of this plan demands some elaboration. It seems clear that, toward the end of the first half of the twelfth century, a whole group of cities in the western Iranian province of Jibāl either acquired totally new congregational mosques or replaced older, presumably hypostyle buildings with new ones. The reasons for these transformations are not certain. There may have been local reasons in each instance, like the 1121–22 fire which destroyed most, if not all, of the older mosque of Iṣfahān. Or else these mosques simply reflected the growth in wealth and population of the province under the rule of the Great Saljuqs. Whatever the reasons, in Iṣfahān, Ardistān, Gulpāīgān, Barsian and Zavāreh,[2] new mosques were erected, all of which exhibit sufficiently related characteristics of style and plan that they form a clearly identifiable architectural school.

The masterpiece of this school is undoubtedly the mosque at Iṣfahān, but it also has a number of internal peculiarities due to the presence of older remains (to some of which we shall return) and to a particularly complicated later history.[3] As a result it is perhaps less immediately useful to define *typical* features than it is to illustrate the higher technical and aesthetic values of the style. More typical is the

[1] Latest description with bibliography in Wilber, pp. 158–9.

[2] In addition to the studies by M. B. Smith quoted previously (especially in *Ars Islamica*, vol. IV), the most convenient introduction to this group of monuments is by A. Godard, "Les Anciennes mosquées de l'Iran", *Āthār-é Īrān*, vol. I (1936), and "Ardistan et Zavare", *ibid.*

[3] A. Godard, "Historique du Masdjid-é Djum'a d'Isfahan", *Āthār-é Īrān*, vols. I, II, III (1936–8); A. Gabriel, "Le Masdjid-i Djum'a d'Isfahan", *Ars Islamica*, vol. II (1935).

mosque at Zavāreh (fig. 2), built in 1136. It is a simple rectangle with an unobtrusive side entrance, an appended minaret, a courtyard with four īvāns prominently contrasted in plan and elevation from the rest of the building where clearly identified piers support barrel vaults: a large dome appears behind the īvān qiblī. This basic kind of plan was imposed elsewhere on more or less complex older remains and in a more refined way appears at Varāmīn.

But there is a further complicating factor. Whereas in Zavāreh the whole building was conceived as a unit, in a number of other examples,

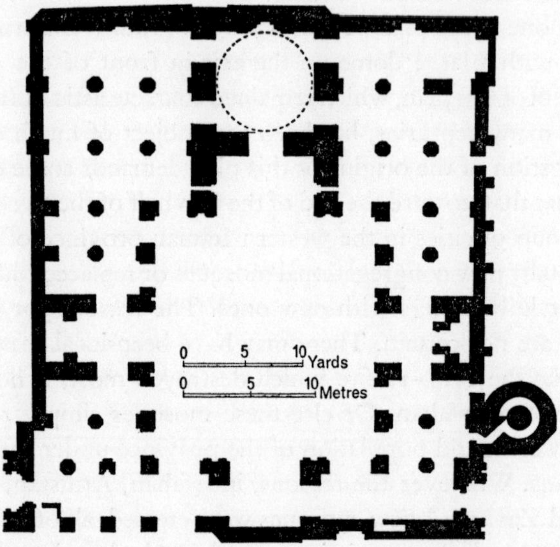

Fig. 2. Plan of mosque at Zavāreh.

the dome appears to have been built separately and often the presently known areas surrounding the domes are considerably later than the dome itself.[1] Hence there is the possibility that the large dome in the back of the traditional Iranian mosque had a history independent of that of the court with four īvāns.

From this observation there has emerged the one consistent theory explaining the growth of the Iranian mosque. A. Godard has introduced the hypothesis of a "kiosk-mosque", which originated in the single domical fire-temple of Sassanian Iran and which consisted in a single domical structure at one end of a large open space. It is only little

[1] A list of such buildings is in A. Godard, *L'Art de l'Iran* (Paris, 1962), p. 343.

by little, argued Godard, that such open areas became entirely built up, and it is a peculiarity of the early decades of the twelfth century that the architects of western Iran introduced a court with four īvāns to surround the dome. The origin of the four īvāns is found in eastern Iran, where it is assumed to be the characteristic plan for the private house. And the reason of this impact of eastern Iran would have been the impact of the one new kind of building known to have been created in the eleventh century, the *madrasa*, an institution created in part for the re-education of the masses in orthodoxy and presumed to have originated in activities carried out first in the private houses of eastern Iran.[1]

Such is, in a slightly simplified form, the presently accepted theory; but there is much in it which is hypothetical and uncertain. First the degree of archaeological and historical precision which is required in such hypotheses does not exist for the monuments of eastern Iran[2] and the little that is known of eleventh- and twelfth-century architecture in Transoxiana and Khurāsān offers no example known to me of mosques with four īvāns.[3] There is much danger in relating relatively well-known monuments, like those of Jibāl, with far less well studied ones and, as was mentioned before, our understanding of the character of the provinces of Iran is far too uneven to allow for generalizations. Secondly, even if it is quite likely that there were instances of fire-temples transformed into Muslim oratories and that single domical sanctuaries were indeed built, it is nonetheless true that the small space thus provided is not very well suited to Muslim cultic practices, especially in larger cities. Furthermore, there is a tradition of a dome in front of the miḥrāb going back to the Umayyad mosque in Medina; in this instance the domed areas also served as a *maqṣūra* (reserved area) for the caliph or his representative. It so happens that, in the case of the mosque of Iṣfahān, the domed room in front of the miḥrāb is provided with a

[1] The clearest statement of the position is in A. Godard, "L'origine de la madrasah", *Ars Islamica*, vols. xv–xvi (1951). An earlier but particularly acute criticism of these and other arguments for the kiosk-mosque appears in J. Sauvaget, "Observations sur quelques mosquées seldjoukides", *Annales Institut d'Etudes Orientales, Université d'Alger*, vol. iv (1938). For the madrasa as an institution, see now G. Makdisi, "Muslim Institutions of learning in eleventh century Baghdad", *B.S.O.A.S.* vol. xxiv (1961).

[2] This is particularly true of the presumably critical madrasa at Khargird; cf. the objections raised by K. A. C. Creswell, *The Muslim Architecture of Egypt*, vol. ii (Oxford, 1959), pp. 132–3.

[3] There is no easily accessible and complete description of Central Asian monuments taken all together; the most convenient introduction is G. A. Pugachenkova, *Puti razvitiia arkhitekturï Yuzhnogo Turkmenistana* (Moscow, 1958); now also *Istoriya iskusstv Uzbekistana* (Moscow, 1966).

formal inscription giving the name of Niẓām al-Mulk and thus dating it between 1070 and 1092. This together with other bits of evidence analysed by Sauvaget[1] suggests that some, if not all, of these large domes had a ceremonial princely significance. Or, alternatively, all of them could have had a primarily religious and symbolic significance in emphasizing the orientation of the building and the direction of prayer.

This latter point may be strengthened by the third difficulty involved in the classical scheme explaining the formation of this type of mosque. It is that the plan of the court with four īvāns itself is not particularly adapted to the ceremony of prayer. It is a centrally arranged plan revolving around a court and it does not in its simple form provide the automatic orientation which is essential in a mosque; hence the widening of one īvān and the large size of the dome could be interpreted as necessary adaptations of a given type of plan to new purposes. Moreover, there is considerable evidence that the plan was a ubiquitous one, i.e. that it was a sort of standard arrangement which could be—and was—used for many purposes. This is shown partly by its impact on regions west of Iran, but also by its occurrence in secular structures, such as the magnificent twelfth-century caravanserai of Ribāṭ S͟haraf[2] or the G͟haznavid palace of Las͟hkarī Bāzār.[3]

Pending further studies and especially excavations of pertinent buildings, it would seem, therefore, preferable to argue that, while the *fact* of the creation of a new type of mosque in the early twelfth century in western Iran is undeniable, the *reasons* for its creation in this particular form are not yet eludicated. Yet, even though the peculiar combinations and uses of īvāns and domes which were thus created appear as new, their immediate adaptation and their continued utilization over several centuries indicate that in some way these elements of plan and elevation struck a particularly meaningful chord in the Iranian vision of its monuments. Was it a revival with modifications of the forms of Sassanian architecture with its domes and īvāns? Then one may indeed suggest that it was a renaissance. Or did these forms continue over the preceding centuries in ways of which we are not aware? Then it would be more appropriate to talk of a blossoming of seeds planted earlier. Or was this new architecture the result of the impact of the new Turkish masters of political power who would have served as catalysts to the

[1] Cf. above note 1, p. 633.
[2] A. Godard, "Khorasan", *Āt͟hār-é Īrān*, vol. IV (1949).
[3] D. Schlumberger, "Le Palais ghaznévide de Lashkari Bazar", *Syria*, vol. XXIX (1952).

formalization of indigenous traditions or brought new ones from the East? Then indeed these monuments may appropriately be called *Saljuq*.

Yet, until new research has brought answers to these questions, it may be preferable to talk more modestly of a western Iranian type of mosque plan created in a clearly defined period and with considerable impact on later centuries. Through its form in Varāmīn in the early fourteenth century, one can imagine the changes brought into it: strengthening of a longitudinal axis through an elaborate gateway (the *pīsh-ṭāq*), simplification and standardization of systems of support, partial decrease in relative size of the court, more elaborate proportions between parts. The ways in which these changes were brought in and their chronology are still matters which have to await investigation.

Although the plan with four īvāns became the standard plan for mosques, it should be noted that it does not define all types of mosque buildings erected during these centuries. Especially in the early fourteenth century there were many instances of repairs and reconstructions in older buildings[1] and a particularly noteworthy feature was that a large building like the mosque of Iṣfahān was subdivided into smaller units, thereby suggesting a change in the religious practices of the time and the apparent uselessness of the large early congregational mosque. More extraordinary is the one significant remaining mosque which clearly identifies the Īl-Khānid imperial style. Built in Tabrīz between 1310 and 1320 by 'Alī-Shāh, a vizier of Öljeitü, it is known today as the "Fortress", the *Arg*. Originally there was a large court with a pool in the centre of the building, but its main unit was an īvān, 48 metres deep, 25 metres high, and 30 metres wide. Its walls were between 8 and 10 metres thick and its vault, which was meant to be larger than that of Ctesiphon, fell shortly after its completion.[2] This astounding construction was clearly megalomaniac and illustrates an odd variant within the traditional plan of the mosque.

Next to the plan, the most significant feature of the Iranian mosque as it appears in Varāmīn is its construction. And here again the main threads lead back to the architecture of the twelfth century in western Iran. Although stone was used consistently in many parts of Āzarbāījān and unbaked brick or rubble in mortar in more prosaic buildings,

[1] There is no list available of these reconstructions but many instances can be found throughout Wilber's book and in several studies by M. Siroux, esp. in "Le masdjid-e djum'a de Yezd", *Bull. Inst. Fr. Arch. Or.* vol. XLIV (1949).

[2] Wilber, pp. 146–9.

the standard medium of construction of most of Iran became baked brick. The significance of this point is twofold. On the one hand, it appeared in the late eleventh century with the domes of Iṣfahān as a comparatively new medium of construction in western Iran, while its sophisticated use can be demonstrated as early as in the ninth and especially tenth centuries in north-eastern Iran.[1] Thus the possibility does indeed exist that the development of brick architecture was part of a possible impact of one region of Iran over the other. On the other hand, as early as the first major datable constructions of the late eleventh century, the masons of Iran used their brickwork ambiguously, in that they transformed it into a medium of decoration. As a result wall surfaces can vary from the superb nakedness of the mosque of 'Alī-Shāh in Tabrīz to the involved complexity of the dome in Varāmīn.

But the most noteworthy constructional characteristic of these centuries occurred in the development of a new and more magnificent type of dome than had been known in Iran until then. It is not only the large miḥrāb domes which made this development possible. In a mosque like Iṣfahān there were several hundred smaller domes covering the areas between īvāns; few of these have been preserved and the identification of those which are of the twelfth century is another unfinished task of archaeological scholarship. Also in Iṣfahān there remains the probable masterpiece of early Iranian domes, the so-called north dome of the mosque (pls. 4, 5), originally probably a ceremonial room for the prince's entrance into the sanctuary. But in addition the eleventh, twelfth, thirteenth, and fourteenth centuries witnessed a remarkable spread of monumental mausoleums, some of which continued to be tower-tombs as before, while others were squares or polygones covered with cupolas.[2] The greatest concentrations of the mausoleums remaining from the twelfth and thirteenth centuries are in Transoxiana and Āzarbāījān, while the fourteenth-century ones are more evenly spread all over Iran.[3] Many of these mausoleums had a primarily religious character and this was the time of the formation of the large sanctuaries

[1] The recent discovery by D. Stronach and T. C. Young, Jr., of two eleventh-century mausoleums with extensive brick designs in western Iran will lead to new hypotheses on this subject, "Three Seljuq Tomb Towers", *Iran*, vol. IV (1966).

[2] For the period up to 1150 see the lists and bibliographies prepared by O. Grabar, "The earliest Islamic commemorative buildings", *Ars Orientalis*, vol. VI (1966); for later periods see D. Wilber, *passim*, and A. U. Pope, ed. *A Survey of Persian Art* (London, 1939), pp. 1016 ff. and 1072 ff.

[3] In addition to the works quoted previously see M. Useinov, L. Bretanitskij, A. Aalamzade, *Istoriya arkhitekturï Azerbaidzhana* (Moscow, 1963), pp. 44 ff.

of Mashhad and Qum, not to mention many smaller ones, like those of Bisṭām,[1] whose exact significance in contemporary piety is more difficult to assess. But the two greatest memorial tombs were primarily secular: the large (27 by 27 metres outside) square mausoleum of Sanjar in Marv and the even more spectacular octagonal (25 metres in interior diameter) mausoleum of Öljeitü, with a particularly complex history.[2]

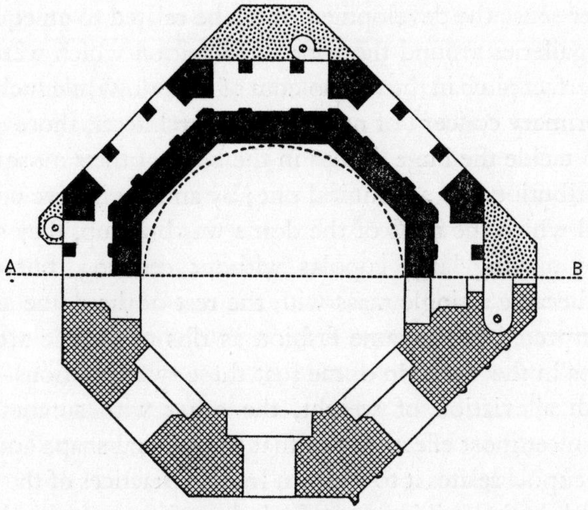

Fig. 3. Plan of mausoleum of Öljeitü at Sulṭānīyeh.

In spite of several pioneering studies,[3] the exact characteristics and development of these Iranian domes are still insufficiently documented and I should like to limit myself to three features which seem to me to be of particular importance. The first one concerns the general appearance of these domes. During these centuries two separate changes were introduced in the construction of cupolas. One is the creation of a double shell, i.e. in effect two domes more or less parallel to each other. The phenomenon is peculiar to northern and north-eastern Iran and its first appearance occurs in monuments which have been variously dated in the eleventh or twelfth centuries.[4] But, while it is obvious that this

[1] *Survey*, pp. 1080 ff.

[2] For the mausoleum of Sanjar see now Pugachenkova, pp. 315 ff.; for the Sulṭānīyeh one of the best studies is by Godard in *Survey*, pp. 1103 ff.

[3] A. Godard, "Voûtes iraniennes", *Āthar-é Īrān*, vol. IV (1949), and remarks by M. B. Smith in *Ars Islamica*, vol. IV.

[4] In addition to Pugachenkova, pp. 275 ff., see A. M. Prubytkova, *Pamyatniki arkhitekturï XI veka v Turkmenii* (Moscow, 1955). It seems still uncertain whether an eleventh-

development will have considerable importance for the changes brought into domes in the fifteenth century, the exact assessment of the reasons for the invention of the double dome is more difficult to make. It should probably be connected with a general interest on the part of north-eastern Iranian architects for the lightening of the mass of the dome, both in the literal sense of making cupolas less heavy and in the aesthetic sense of giving to the upper part of the building an airier look. In this latter sense the development must be related to an equally great interest in galleries around the zone of transition which were brought to a most perfect pitch in the mausoleum of Öljeitü. While such appeared to be the primary concern of north-eastern architects, those of western Iran had to tackle the huge domes in the back of their mosques. Their major contribution was a technical one; by an imaginative use of brick ribs around which the mass of the dome was built up, they solved the problem of making large cupolas without centring, but these ribs eventually became a single mass with the rest of the dome and should not be interpreted in the same fashion as ribs of Gothic architecture. It is perhaps in the Varāmīn dome that these two traditions—one concerned with alleviation of weight, the other with sureness of construction—meet most effectively in that the general shape and massiveness of the cupola relates it to western Iranian practices of the preceding centuries, while the striking use of windows is more typical of north-eastern tendencies.

The second noteworthy feature of these Iranian domes is their zone of transition effecting the passage from the square to the circular base of the cupola. The technique used throughout was based on the squinch creating an octagon. In a number of instances of larger domes, an additional sixteen-sided area was provided above the octagon. However, the most striking feature of the zone of transition during these centuries was the remarkably architectonic use made of the muqarnas by western Iranian architects. The origin and the exact purpose of this combination of architectural units is not known, but it seems likely, within our present evidence, that it developed in eastern Iran in the tenth century as a primarily decorative form.[1] In the eleventh century in western Iran the muqarnas acquired a more meaningful

century date is preferable to a twelfth-century one for many of these monuments. However, the discovery of the Kharraqān buildings clearly proves that the form existed in the eleventh century.

[1] The crucial building for this problem is the Tim mausoleum, whose latest discussion is by G. A. Pugachenkova, *Istoriya Zodchikh Uzbekistana*, vol. II (Tashkent, 1963).

function as a working element in the upward movement of the dome. Logically constructed around a few basic axes of symmetry the muqarnas became the visible means by which masonry was articulated, at least as far as the viewer is concerned, for whether or not the actual thrusts from above were carried down the lines of the muqarnas is still a moot question. That an interest in the logical articulation of walls and masonries existed in Iranian architecture of the eleventh and twelfth centuries is clear from other instances as well, such as the unique structure of the piers in the north-eastern dome in Iṣfahān or the fascinating system of interlocking ribs in the mausoleum of Sanjar.

Yet it would be wrong to consider these interests, some of which were short-lived, or the muqarnas exclusively as actual or imitative constructional devices. They were also decorative ones and, even though during the period with which we are concerned the decorative function did not always overshadow other purposes in the domes as such, it did so in façades, cornices, and other parts of buildings. Thus the fascination with transforming constructional units into decorative ones, or in the better monuments, the creation of an ambiguous balance between decorative and architectonic values clearly appears in the uses of the muqarnas as early as in the eleventh century and is continued over the next two centuries.[1]

On the last significant aspect of Iranian architecture at this time, we may be briefer, because this aspect has been treated with greater thoroughness than the others.[2] A look at the mosques and mausoleums shows the considerable part played by various decorative techniques in the final state of the buildings. Some involved the medium of construction, others were specifically ornamental techniques, such as stucco, terra-cotta, and coloured bricks or tiles. The former two techniques are not new, but the latter appears indeed to have been a creation of these centuries, still used sparingly when compared to what will happen in later times, but portentous of a new and highly original relationship between colour and architecture. On the whole, however, the major characteristic of decoration in the large congregational

[1] Several preliminary studies on the subject by J. Rosintal, *Pendentifs, Trompes et Stalactites* (Paris, 1928), and *Le Réseau* (Paris, 1937).

[2] For a general survey limited in its monuments to Central Asia but with principles valid elsewhere see L. Rempel, *Arkhitekturnï ornament Uzbekistana* (Tashkent, 1962) which has superseded the shorter *Arkhitekturnï ornament Srednei Azii* by B. P. Denike (Moscow, 1939). For the specific problem of colour see D. Wilber, "The Development of Mosaic Faience", *Ars Islamica*, vol. VI (1939). Useful notes in *Survey*, pp. 1279 ff.

mosques is their subordination to architectural values. Rich though it may be in Varāmīn or the two large domes of Iṣfahān, its effectiveness lies in the way in which it emphasizes, strengthens, and accentuates lines and ideas of a preponderantly architectural vision of buildings. Nowhere is this more striking than in the superb masses of the domical exteriors. Yet, while this is generally true of the congregational mosques, it is less so of mausoleums, smaller sanctuaries, or the few known secular buildings. Pīr-i Baqrān, near Iṣfahān, a small sanctuary for a local holy man dated between 1299 and 1312, is a true museum of stucco designs.[1] The mausoleums of Āzarbāījān carry an extensive surface decoration which all but obliterates their actual walls.[2] Ribāṭ Sharaf, a twelfth-century caravanserai, or the eleventh-century palace at Tirmidh had most of their walls covered with decorative designs and, in the former case, included even stucco imitiations of brick walls.[3] And the Jām minaret (pl. 6), like several other such structures perhaps more secular than religious in purpose, also has an almost total covering of decorative designs.[4] It is as though the closer one comes to the little-known secular art of the time or to the more popular cults of saints the more brilliant and overbearing becomes the decoration, whereas the mosques maintain something of an ascetic dignity, more in keeping perhaps with the severity of official Islam.

It is difficult to sum up the characteristics of the architecture of Iran during some three centuries of numerous and varied building activities. Two major points seem to stand out. The first one is the apparent polarization in the twelfth century of major inventions in two areas: the north-east and the west, with a more minor but highly original centre developing late in the century in north-western Iran. While the contacts and influences between those centres are matters for debate, recent evidence seems to suggest that it is western Iran which created, at this time, the most unified architectural school, perhaps because it had been less developed and less creative than Khurāsān in the preceding centuries. The forms and ideas of plans and construction developed then were picked up by the Īl-Khānids in the early decades of the fourteenth

[1] Wilber, pp. 121 ff.

[2] In addition to relevant passages in Useinov and others, *Survey*, and Wilber, see various remarks by Godard in *Āthār-é Īrān*, esp. vol. 1 (1926).

[3] Cf. note 2, p. 639 above and for Tirmidh Denike's general study; on this whole point see also D. Hill and O. Grabar, *Islamic Architecture and its Decoration* (London, 1965).

[4] A. Maricq and G. Wiet, *Le Minaret de Jam* (Paris, 1959). For other minarets see M. B. Smith, "The Manars of Isfahan", *Āthār-é Īrān*, vol. 1 (1936) and J. Sourdel-Thomine, "Deux minarets d'époque Seljoukide", *Syria*, vol. xxx (1953).

1 Varāmīn, mosque, entrance.

2 Varāmīn, mosque: (*a*) *īvān* on the *qibla* side; (*b*) dome from inside.

3 Iṣfahān, mosque: (*a*) court and *īvāns*; (*b*) south dome, zone of transition.

4 Iṣfahān, north dome, elevation.

5 Iṣfahān, north dome, from inside.

6 Jām, minaret.

7 (*a*) Sulṭānīyeh, upper part of mausoleum.
(*b*) Goblet with *S̲h̲āh-Nāma* scenes.

8 (*a*) Bowl with the story of Farīdūn.
(*b*) Bowl signed by ʿAlī b. Yūsuf.

9 (*a*) Dish signed by Shams al-Dīn al Ḥasanī.
(*b*) Dish.

10 (*a*) Kettle, inlaid bronze.
(*b*) Cup, inlaid bronze.

11 Incense burner.

12 (*a*) A scene from the story of Jacob.
(*b*) The tree of the Buddha.

13 (*a*) *S͟hāh-Nāma*, 1341: Rustam lifts the stone over Bīz͟han's pit.
(*b*) *S͟hāh-Nāma*, fourteenth century: Alexander and the talking tree.

14 *Shāh-Nāma*, fourteenth century: the bier of Alexander.

15 Rustam slays Isfandiyār.

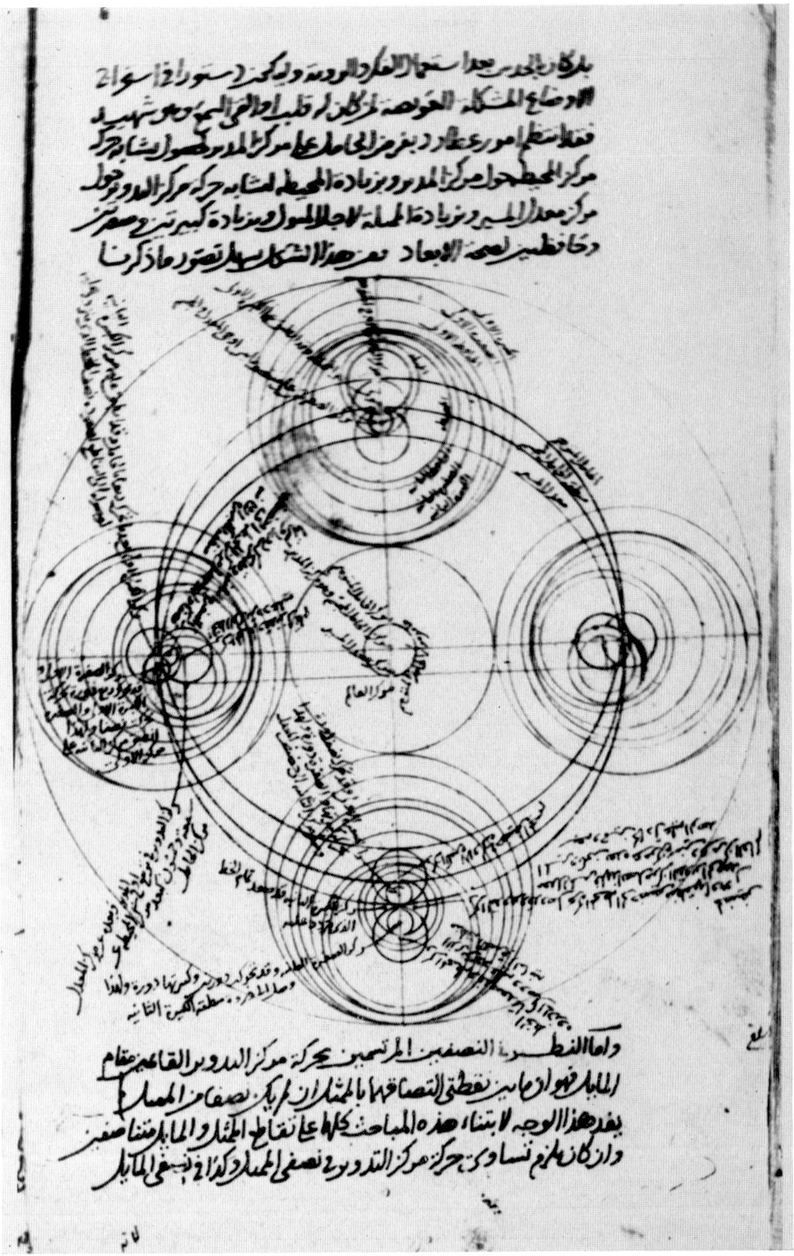

16 Illustration of a planetary model from a copy of Quṭb al-Dīn al-S͟hīrāzī's *al-Tuḥfat al-s͟hāhiya*.

century and, in conjunction with their own monumental ambitions and renewed eastern Iranian traditions, created the monuments of Tabrīz, Sulṭānīyeh (pl. 7*a*), and Varāmīn. But the permanent coagulation of a series of definitive types and techniques seems, for the most part, to have been effected around 1100 in the West.

The second point concerns the character of this architectural typology, for it established the basis of almost all later developments in Iranian art. The building with an internal façade opening a court, the rhythms of fulls and voids based on īvāns, the mighty dome, the varieties of decorative techniques modifying the surface of the wall, and, among features which were not discussed, the tall, cylindrical minarets, and, at this time less developed, the high screen-like portal, these were all to become permanent features of medieval Iranian architecture. Whatever technical or decorative novelties were introduced in subsequent centuries, they were, for the most part, variations —sometimes far superior in actual quality and aesthetic merit—on the vocabulary of forms created in the twelfth century. That this happened altogether is more difficult to explain and, to a degree, the explanation lies in features of Iranian culture other than those of the visual arts alone. One possibility is that these immensely active centuries established the formal and aesthetic system of Iranian architecture in monuments—mosques, mausoleums, caravanserais—which by their very function remained in use for many centuries and thus forced themselves by their presence as permanent models. But whatever the explanation, there is little doubt that the monumental infrastructure created in the twelfth century may truly be called the classical period of Iranian Islamic art, for it consisted of monuments magnificent in their own right and at the same time sufficiently abstract in their formal and technical components to be used for centuries to come.

THE PORTABLE OBJECTS OF THE TWELFTH AND THIRTEENTH CENTURIES

Whereas the architecture created in the twelfth and subsequent centuries was the beginning of a fairly coherent development in which the innovating position of the twelfth century is clearly apparent, things are far less tangible when we turn to the other arts. As far as painting, mural or manuscript, is concerned, it is at the end of the thirteenth century that there begins a definite movement whose steps can be partly traced and explained. To these we shall return later. For the earlier centuries we have a few texts, some more or less understandable fragments, and a few manuscripts which still await proper analysis.[1] A curious revival of monumental sculpture seems to have occurred at this time,[2] but its instances are few, its genuineness not always secure, and in any case its future development limited. There is, however, one area of artistic activity where the reverse is true, i.e. a tremendous development in the twelfth–thirteenth centuries and a partial decadence in the fourteenth. It is the area of the *objet d'art*. Furthermore, whereas both painting and architecture are hardly known in Iran before the latter part of the eleventh century, this is not so with respect to objects. Be it in ceramics or in metalwork, glass, and textiles, as early as in the ninth century major objects were made and definable schools are identified. Thus, at least on the level of the existence of a semi-industrial manufacturing tradition, a certain continuity seems to exist and in Iran, as elsewhere in the Islamic world, there appeared a fascination, unknown since Antiquity, with the transformation of the everyday useful object into a work of aesthetic quality.

Difficulties of interpretation arise, however, primarily from the enormous mass of objects which have been attributed to the twelfth and thirteenth centuries. Almost no museum in the world seems to lack a "Saljuq" ceramic or tile or a bronze stand in the shape of a bird. Furthermore, a rather indiscriminate scholarship abetted by the activities of clandestine commercial diggers in Iran itself, has created a terminology of styles and types based on cities or provinces—such as Ray, Gurgān, Kāshān, Sāveh—which only too often do not correspond to more than the alleged place of origin of the first-known objects of the given type. Finally, the lack of properly dated objects, and especially considerable uncertainty about the actual archaeological index of those objects which are dated have added to the confusion prevailing in the field, although no one can deny the aesthetic qualities and the sheer variety of the things made during these centuries nor the fact that their existence is one of the main features of the arts of this time.

In view of the unsettled state of our knowledge of these objects, our remarks will be limited to three points which seem to be somewhat more

[1] The most significant works involved are the mural paintings found at Lashkarī Bāzār, above, note 3, p. 364, and the Istanbul manuscript of Warqah and Gulshāh, A. Ateş, "Un vieux poème romanesque persan", *Ars Orientalis*, vol. IV (1961).

[2] R. M. Riefstahl, "Persian Islamic Stucco Sculpture", *The Art Bulletin*, vol. XIII (1931); *Survey*, pls. 514 ff.

clearly definable than any attempt at the explanation of styles or at the periodization and localization of types.

The first of these points involves techniques. In ceramics the most astounding variety of techniques were used in Iran: simple *sgraffiato* wares, moulded wares, translucent wares, underglaze painted, overglaze painted, lustre painted, and especially the so-called *mīnā'i* technique which permitted the clear fixation of many different colours on the surface of the object. Combinations of several techniques are not unknown.[1] A further significant development of ceramics was the tile. Sometimes used as a section in a larger frieze of consistent designs, the tile of the thirteenth century in particular was also often conceived as a single object, decoratively and iconographically self-sufficient, and it is with these that we will mostly be concerned. In metalwork, in addition to numerous gold objects, usually jewels, whose study has never been made, and a few silver ones, we encounter mostly bronze which was cast, chased, *repoussé*, or, most characteristically for the time, inlaid with silver.[2] None of these techniques, except mīnā'i, were new in themselves, but there is little doubt that techniques such as mīnā'i and inlaid metal were particularly developed because they allowed a greater refinement of designs on the surfaces of the objects.

The time of these changes in technical emphasis can probably be set in the middle of the twelfth century. For bronze the first-known object to illustrate the change is an 1148 penbox in the Hermitage Museum,[3] although the most celebrated early example is the 1163 bucket (also in the Hermitage), well known by the name of its former owner as the "Bobrinski kettle".[4] For ceramics the earliest dated faïence, a fragment in the British Museum, is from 1179 and we may probably assume that the main development of new ceramic techniques was probably contemporary with that of bronze.[5] For other media our information is fragmentary, but the crucial ones of bronze and ceramics seem to indicate the middle of the twelfth century as the beginning of the main explosion of new types of objects. We are very badly informed on the late eleventh and early twelfth centuries. There are very few securely dated pieces and their position in the history of Iranian art is quite

[1] Best introduction in A. Lane, *Early Islamic Pottery* (New York, 1948).

[2] Best introduction by D. Barrett, *Islamic Metalwork in the British Museum* (London, 1949).

[3] L. T. Giuzalian, "Bronzevoi kalemdan 1148 g.", *Pamyatniki epokhi Rustaveli* (Leningrad, 1938).

[4] R. Ettinghausen, "The Bobrinski 'kettle'", *Gazette des Beaux-Arts*, vol. XXIV (1943).

[5] *Survey*, pp. 1672 ff.

unclear.[1] Tentatively and barring major archaeological discoveries, we may assume then that it is after the fall of the Great Saljuqs that the manufacture of objects developed in particularly striking new ways and that until then older techniques were preserved, but the explanation of these dates is a still unsolved problem of historical scholarship. A fairly clear ending to the series of ceramics developed in the middle of the twelfth century is provided by a study of the dated examples. The bulk of the objects are thirteenth century, without apparent effect from the Mongol invasion, but only lustre-painted tiles continue through the first third of the fourteenth century. After about 1340 there is a sudden lack of dated objects until around 1400. Metalwork, on the other hand, seems to have suffered from the invasion from the East. Practically no dated Iranian pieces are known after about 1225 until the latter part of the century when new objects were made for the new masters of the Near East and eventually a distinguishable school was established in southern Iran. Even though it may be assumed that new Iranian metalwork gave, in the twelfth century, a major impetus to Islamic metalwork in general, it is in the Fertile Crescent and Egypt that its greatest thirteenth-century masterpieces will be made.[2]

There is one last remark to be made about the techniques. They also, like the monuments of architecture, have regional associations. For metalwork it is quite certain that Khurāsān, or, more generally, north-eastern Iran, was the main centre from which new techniques derived and in which they were pursued until the Mongol invasion. A separate school has been suggested for north-western Iran, but its existence above the artisanal level is not secure. Ceramics are more difficult to localize properly, but there it would seem clear that the major impetus was in western Iran. Kāshān, of course, is the best-known centre and there is no doubt that its potters had acquired a particularly high reputation.[3] The exact significance of the prominence of Kāshān for the evaluation of styles and techniques and for the attribution of pieces to specific centres is less easy to determine, for potters from Kāshān may indeed have worked elsewhere. But, in any event and regardless of the fact that ceramics of similar types were produced all over Iran, it seems that the new techniques and the new subjects originated primarily in western Iranian cities.

[1] This is particularly true of the so-called Alp-Arslan dish (*Survey*, pp. 2500 ff.).

[2] E. Kühnel, *Islamische Kleinkunst* (Braunschweig, 1962), pp. 175 ff.

[3] R. Ettinghausen, "Evidence for the Identification of Kashan Pottery", *Ars Islamica*, vol. III (1936).

It is thus primarily with the new ceramics of the late twelfth and thirteenth centuries and the new metalwork which can be dated between *c.* 1150 and *c.* 1220 that I should like to deal in introducing the second general point to be made about these objects. Their most striking feature is their use of human and animal figures. Such representational themes existed before, but clearly in a more limited way; they were either more or less sophisticated reflexions of folk art (especially in ceramics) or a limited princely vocabulary with many Sassanian reminiscences. The peculiarity of the iconography apparent in the twelfth and thirteenth centuries is at the same time its variety and the suggestion of a meaningful visual system of images, even though we are not yet able to translate the language in its entirety. But that we are dealing at this time with a conscious fascination with the animation of the object through figures is made evident by one of the most unusual phenomena of this time, the concomitant animation of inscriptions which occurs on the objects themselves and even on a few monumental inscriptions.[1]

What were these scenes? At one extreme stand very precise iconographic subjects: an episode from the *S̱ẖāh-Nāma* redone in comic-strip fashion (pl. 7 *b*),[2] the story of Bahrām Gūr and Āzāda in many forms,[3] the story of Farīdūn (pl. 8),[4] illustration of a specific (but unidentified) battle with the names of the personages involved in it,[5] and, especially in tiles, a wide variety of subjects which can be described (an animal, a man reading a scroll, the façade of a building) but whose contemporary meaning usually escapes us. At the other extreme is found what may be called a generalized, abstract iconography, i.e. an imagery whose individual elements are easy enough to identify but whose significance on the object or for the viewer is less immediately clear. Three main cycles can be defined. One is the traditional princely cycle, with enthroned personages, male and female attendants, hunting, polo-playing, music and dancing. The cycle is usually shown in an expanded and full form on metal objects (pls. 10, 11), while one or the other of its elements occurs on ceramics, often in a very decorative fashion as frames for other subjects. Oddities and confusions do occur within the cycle, such as the backgammon players on the Hermitage kettle, but on the whole the cycle can easily be recognized and is consistent. The same is true of the second definable cycle, the astronomical one. It includes primarily the

[1] Best discussion published so far in D. S. Rice, *The Wade Cup* (Paris, 1955), pp. 21 ff.

[2] G. D. Guest, "Notes on the Miniatures on a Thirteenth Century Beaker", *Ars Islamica*, vol. x (1943).

[3] *Survey*, pl. 664.

[4] *Ibid.* pl. 692 c.

[5] *Ibid.* pls. 674–5.

signs of the zodiac and symbols of the planets, but a particularly interesting group probably made in Āzarbāījān included also labours of the month.[1] These themes are less common on ceramics but they do occur, usually on objects whose style and composition reflect metalwork.[2] The third cycle is more difficult to describe and it is possible that it may not be more than a variant of the princely cycle. It occurs primarily on ceramics and shows, at its simplest, one or two personages, of either sex, motionlessly sitting next to each other, or playing a musical instrument, at times near a body of water or beside a tree. The facial types are usually distinguishable by their heavy lower jaws, very simplified facial features, and narrow slit eyes.[3] In a few instances, such as celebrated plates in the Freer Gallery and in the Metropolitan Museum (pl. 9), more personages are added and the possibility is suggested that these images belong to our first group of precise stories or events. Yet these objects differ in style from those which do show precisely defined iconographic subjects and all of them are pervaded by a curious sense of immaterial reality. For reasons to be explained below, we may call this a cycle of love or of meditation.

The peculiarity of these themes is that, except for the princely ones, they all seem to belong exclusively to the period between 1150 and around 1300. They almost totally disappear from later pottery, which tends to a far more limited representational vocabulary,[4] and the themes of metalwork in later decades are either consciously imitative of early models or traditional in their use of princely themes. It must be added that any eventual complete survey of iconographic cycles on Iranian objects of this period should also include decorative designs which appear to be purely ornamental but may at times also have more precise meanings[5] and a whole category of objects in the shape of animals, human beings, and even houses[6] whose importance is as considerable as their number and as the paucity of attempts to explain them. But, even though often quite original and aesthetically spectacular, as a type these latter categories of objects are not as original in Iranian art as the ones we have described and the hypothesis we shall formulate presently to explain the latter may apply to them as well.

Our third general point about this whole category of works of art

[1] D. S. Rice, "The Seasons and the Labours of the Months", *Ars Orientalis*, vol. I (1954).
[2] *Survey*, pls. 712–13. [3] *Ibid.* pls. 686, 687, 693, 710, etc.
[4] A. Lane, *Later Islamic Pottery* (London, 1957).
[5] R. Ettinghausen, "The Wade Cup", *Ars Orientalis*, vol. II (1957), esp. pp. 341 ff.
[6] *Survey*, pls. 739 ff.

concerns the meaning which should be attributed to them. Regardless of their quality of execution, they were all useful objects, i.e. symbolically or actually they were meant to fulfil some function, whether it be pouring water or wine or holding flowers or sweets. It is therefore possible that in some fashion the imagery on them reflects either the precise function to which they were destined or some relationship between owner and object, or maker and owner, or giver and owner. In order to suggest the kind of relationship that was involved, a clue is provided by the inscriptions. The most common ones consist of a series of good wishes to an anonymous owner; at other times the owner is known and the object acquires a "personalized" meaning. Then there are inscriptions referring to the function of the object and wishing successful performance of the function. On ceramics are also encountered excerpts from celebrated literary texts or, more often, shorter poems dwelling in more or less successful fashion on various themes of love, separation, happiness, well-being, but especially love.[1] It is very rarely that one can find a direct and immediate correspondence between images on objects and inscriptions. However, it could be argued that the correspondence between them did not necessarily exist on a narrative and illustrative level but on some other level, just as the text and the image of a Christmas card do not necessarily relate to each other, although both reflect a series of more or less concrete sentiments accepted as being appropriate to the occasion. Since the inscriptions so consistently bring out themes of love and well-being, it may be suggested that the images should be interpreted in like fashion. No problem is raised around interpreting in this fashion the astrological images or the zoomorphic shapes of objects, since both of these themes have had a long history of apotropaic meanings.[2] Nor is the princely cycle particularly anomalous, since a semi-magical significance of power and success is traditional with any princely cycle since ancient Egyptian art. Illustrations of romances of references to well-known legendary or actual events can easily also be so interpreted. As to the theme of love or meditation, one could interpret it as a new iconography peculiar to these times and specifically related to the new development during the twelfth and thirteenth centuries of an esoteric poetry which was mystical and

[1] These texts have never been published systematically. For examples see M. Bahrami, *Recherches sur les carreaux de faïence* (Paris, 1937), and *Gurgan Faïences* (Cairo, 1949), and articles by L. T. Giuzalian in *Epigrafika Vostoka*, vols. III, IV, V, VII (1947–53); cf. summary by O. Grabar in *Ars Orientalis*, vol. II (1957), pp. 550–1.

[2] See article quoted in note 1, p. 646.

religious but ambiguously used an erotic vocabulary for its deeper purposes. Such was the hypothesis suggested by R. Ettinghausen in a brilliant study devoted to a plate in the Freer Gallery.[1] Its ultimate significance was that there is a series of levels of meaning at which these Iranian objects can be understood and that, in all probability, a certain ambiguity was consciously maintained in the images, in part because the visual and poetic system of the literature itself was ambiguous but also because these objects were ambiguous in themselves, partly works of art and partly implements for daily living.

There is one last remark of significance to be made about the meaning of these objects. The Hermitage bucket was made for a merchant, as were a number of other known bronze objects from Iran. The excerpts from the *S̲h̲āh-Nāma* on the ceramics followed a popular, spoken version of the text, not the learned manuscript one. The poems are almost always in Persian. Various Ṣūfī groups had already by that time permeated the social organizations of the cities and provided them with an esoteric vocabulary which may or may not have always been understood at all levels of possible meaning. As a result one may draw the conclusion that it is the urban bourgeoisie of Iran which was the primary sponsor and inspirer of the astonishing development given to the beautiful object in the twelfth and thirteenth centuries. Parts of its themes were shared with the aristocratic milieu of princes but it is the city merchant and artisan who may be identified as the prime mover in the explosion of the art of the object. The development in Iran finds parallels in the Arab world with the illustrations of the *Maqāmāt* and its short-lived character can be explained by the decadence of urban life after the Mongols. As to why it was precisely in the second half of the twelfth century that this unique development took place, the question is still difficult to answer. Could it be a primary document for a shift in the power and prestige of the bourgeoisie at the moment when the strong arm of the Great Saljuqs was weakening?

PAINTING IN THE FOURTEENTH CENTURY

It is generally recognized that, whatever its past, Iranian miniature painting began its known development with the Mongol conquest. One manuscript from the end of the thirteenth century, the *Manāfiʿ al-*

[1] R. Ettinghausen, "The Iconography of a Kāshān Luster Plate", *Ars Orientalis*, vol. IV (1961).

ḥayawān in the Morgan Library in New York dated 1291, is usually considered to be the first document identifying a major stylistic change. Then the school established by Rashīd al-Dīn (pl. 12) in the quarter of his creation near Tabrīz is assumed, by the very character of its universal aspirations and the cosmopolitan position of the Īl-Khānid capital, to have been a major catalyst in gathering new styles and ideas from many different sources. Out of it, with two extraordinary masterpieces, the "Demotte" *Shāh-Nāma* divided between many collections all over the world and the *Kalīla and Dimna* in the University Library in Istanbul, a fully Iranian artistic tradition was established, although the exact dates of these two manuscripts is not known and the proposed dates vary from 1330 to the 1370's. These two unique masterpieces are usually felt to be related to a number of manuscripts dated in the 1350's, a *Kalīla and Dimna* in Cairo and a *Garshāsp-Nāma* in Istanbul.[1] Parallel to this "high" development, there is assumed a "lower" or more provincial development, whose roots may go back to pre-Mongol times. It consists mostly of a group of *Shāh-Nāma* manuscripts, usually attributed in part to Shīrāz thanks to one manuscript dated in 1331, but it is agreed that other schools probably existed. In all of these manuscripts except perhaps the Istanbul *Kalīla and Dimna* there always appears something experimental, as though Iranian painters were trying to discover new modes of expression and, fascinating though many of them are, these miniatures give more rarely the sense of self-assured perfection which begins later in the fourteenth century under new and different sponsors and influences. Although no absolutely definite date can be provided for the change, 1370 seems to be as good a date as any, since several fragments of that time in Istanbul clearly show a very different style.[2] That, however, it is under the Īl-Khānids that a new Iranian art of painting began has been fully recognized by the Iranian view of their own painting, since sixteenth-century writers clearly acknowledged that the reign of Abū Sa'īd (1317–36) saw the birth of painting and recognized the names of two artists of the time, Aḥmad Mūsā and Shams al-Dīn.[3]

In its general lines this schematic outline probably corresponds to the reality of historical development of painting in the first two-thirds of the fourteenth century. While there are certainly many obscure moments

[1] R. Ettinghausen, "On some Mongol Miniatures", *Kunst des Orients*, vol. III (1959).
[2] B. Gray, *Persian Painting* (Geneva, 1961), pp. 40 ff.
[3] E. Schroeder, "Aḥmad Mūsā and Shams al-Dīn", *Ars Islamica*, vol. VI (1939).

in this development especially as long as there are many documents which remain both unpublished and unclearly fitted within it,[1] the outline may serve as a sort of backbone which has the merit of identifying two precise strands, an imperial Īl-Khānid one with cosmopolitan overtones, and several local schools, around which various miniatures or manuscripts can be arranged in a sequentially meaningful fashion. It is somewhat more difficult to relate the stylistic scheme to the political and cultural history of the time but these problems should be resolved whenever a clear picture emerges of Iranian history between the decline of the Īl-Khānids around 1330 and the new Tīmūrid order in the last decades of the century.

If, then, we leave for the time being the historical problems as being as adequately stated as evidence permits,[2] what remains is to try to explain what was meant by Dūst Muḥammad in the sixteenth century when he wrote: "It was then (the rule of Abū Sa'īd) that Ustādh Aḥmad Mūsā...withdrew the covering from the face of painting and invented the kind of painting which is current at the present time."[3] Since we are inadequately informed on the intellectual framework within which Dūst Muḥammad made his remark, it is from the manuscripts themselves that we must try to discover in what ways the painting of the fourteenth century appeared revolutionary. Without attempting to be exclusive, it seems that there are two broad areas in which this painting is both new and the first step toward the art of the following period. These are first, subject-matter and the interpretation given to it, and secondly, the more precise problems of the representation of man and of landscape.

The subject-matter of Īl-Khānid painting has a number of very traditional elements. The book on the usefulness of animals known in several manuscripts of the late thirteenth and of the fourteenth centuries is not by itself a new genre and instances of the same sort of illustrated books exist in earlier Islamic art. The book of *Kalīla and Dimna* was illustrated as early as the tenth century, although we do not have any remaining manuscripts before the thirteenth. A more original case is

[1] The unpublished documents include in particular the Istanbul albums and the Berlin one, about which we only know individual pictures which have been discussed. For fourteenth-century examples see R. Ettinghausen, "Persian Ascension Miniatures", *Accademia di Lincei, Rendiconti* (1956).

[2] In addition to B. Gray's recent book, one should consult I. Stockhoukine, *La Peinture iranienne* (Bruges, 1936) and E. Kühnel's chapter in *Survey*, pp. 1829 ff.

[3] L. Binyon, R. Wilkinson and B. Gray, *Persian Miniature Painting* (Oxford, 1931), p. 184.

provided by the *Shāh-Nāma* and in general the epic tradition. Many of the illustrated texts had been written a long time before the Mongols; yet, until the Mongols, there is very little evidence of epic images on manuscripts (the main exception being probably the Freer beaker mentioned before,[1] but even there it may be questioned whether a consecutive narrative of its type is really characteristic of manuscripts) and the little we know is that there were mural paintings with epic scenes,[2] perhaps in the manner of the pre-Islamic Soghdian paintings from Panjikent. If we add to this that there are practically no known manuscript texts of the *Shāh-Nāma* clearly dated before the fourteenth century, it would follow that interest in and development of an epic art illustrating books on the legendary past of Iran appears to be an Īl-Khānid creation, or at the very least, underwent a tremendous increase in the fourteenth century.

Several reasons may be given to explain this phenomenon. One is the importance of aristocratic taste and patronage which would naturally be concerned with legendary heroes. Another may have been the rediscovery through the Mongols of the old Soghdian epic traditions.[3] But the most compelling reason was probably the activities sponsored by the Mongol princes themselves, especially Ghazan Khān, which led to the foundation of Rashīdiyya. For, as Ghazan and Öljeitü wanted to have the past deeds and mores of the Mongols recorded for posterity, they or their Persian executors had this specific aim fitted within a general world history, the *Jāmi' al-tawārīkh*. Manuscripts of this work were copied and illustrated and several examples are preserved of the presumably original group, especially those in the Edinburgh University Library and the Royal Asiatic Society, dated respectively 1306 and 1314, and in Istanbul (pl. 12). A fascination for history and the past was not limited to official sponsors and it has been recognized that the writing of history was a major characteristic of Īl-Khānid times.[4] The *Āthār al-bāqīya*, also in the Edinburgh Library, dated in 1307–08 preserved illustrations of another compendium. It is only natural, under these circumstances, that the *Shāh-Nāma*, the most complete of the historical epics, be brought back into favour and

[1] Above, note 2, p. 645.

[2] *Survey*, p. 1374. Cf. also *Ta'rīkh-i Baihaqi* (Tehran, 1324), p. 501, among several other examples.

[3] O. Grabar, "Notes on the Iconography of the Demotte *Shah-nameh*", *Studies in Honour of B. Gray* (forthcoming).

[4] E. G. Browne, *A Literary History of Persia* (Cambridge, 1961), vol. III, pp. 62 ff.

popularity and thus it is that aside from the uniquely superb "Demotte" manuscript[1] we have preserved several small *S̲h̲āh-Nāmas* (pl. 13) of varying quality whose detailed study still remains to be made.[2] All of them can be understood as the product of an awareness of more ancient times which was in fact an Īl-K̲h̲ānid phenomenon.

There were variations in the ways in which the past, legendary or not, was treated. The *Jāmi' al-tawārīk̲h̲* and the *Āt̲h̲ār al-bāqīya* were primarily narrative books in which precise events were depicted and, especially in the former, long lists of rulers were given. As a result we meet with a re-discovery of portraits, neither likenesses nor fictitious authors' portraits, but set types identifying certain series of kings and emperors. Then we see specific scenes illustrated, and among these a number of images are clearly derived from models from the cultures whose histories or geography were described. Thus the representation of Tibet in the Royal Asiatic Society manuscript shows personages and building of Far Eastern character, while an Annunciation in the Edinburgh *Āt̲h̲ār al-bāqīya* has Christian models. But for the most part new iconographic cycles had to be created, such as a cycle for the life of Muḥammad, the first such cycle in Islamic art. This was made possible by the introduction into Iranian art of new compositional principles and of a small number of units of composition which were sufficiently flexible to be used meaningfully in different contexts and thus illustrate different subjects with a comparatively small number of elements. Among them one may distinguish a clear tripartite composition of each image, the groupings of personages in two's or three's to make a crowd and several variations within these arrangements, a landscape which is at the same time very simple and conscious of spatial values, a superb utilization of gestures of the head and especially of fingers, and a limited use of colour. The small number of these features lends a certain monotony to the scenes from the *Jāmi' al-tawārīk̲h̲*, a monotony which is not always alleviated by the astounding quality of the drawing. But this monotony pertains also to the literary genre that was so illustrated. What seems far more significant is that these manuscripts and the school which produced them created and popularized

[1] D. Brian, "A Reconstruction of the Miniature Cycle in the Demotte *Shāh-nāmeh*", *Ars Islamica*, vol. VI (1939).

[2] The most convenient list will be found in K. Holter, "Die islamischen Miniaturhandschriften vor 1350", *Zentralblatt f. Bibliothekswesen*, vol. LIV (1937), to be supplemented by H. Buchthal, O. Kurz and R. Ettinghausen, "Supplementary Notes", *Ars Islamica*, vol. VII (1940).

a new vocabulary of forms without which later Iranian painting is not quite understandable. As we shall see below, much of this new vocabulary was of Chinese origin, and this is easy enough to understand if we consider the world-wide character of the Mongol empire. What seems far more important is that a court-appointed school of painting succeeded in imposing its new patterns. That it happened must be attributed to the new interest in history and to the systematic distribution all over Iran of Rashīd al-Dīn's historical volumes.

If we turn to the more specifically Iranian *Shāh-Nāmas*, a clear distinction can be established between the small and more provincial manuscripts and the "Demotte" codex. The former are primarily narrative and show only to a limited degree, if at all, influences from the Rashīdiyya. Their origins may well go back to pre-Mongol times and perhaps even to media other than book illustrations.[1] Their quality varies, but in some of the more successful ones a rather effective result has been achieved by the puppet-like, richly coloured personages on a gold background with only limited landscape or architectural props. Only in the aesthetically less rewarding 1341 manuscript do we encounter a somewhat more developed landscape.

The "Demotte" *Shāh-Nāma* (pls. 13–15), on the other hand, is undoubtedly one of the most complex masterpieces of Iranian art. Its fifty-six known miniatures have been the subject of many discussions and controversies about both their dates and technical problems of retouching or altogether later additions to the manuscript.[2] That almost all the miniatures have been tampered with is clearly true and the original style of some of them is irretrievably lost. Yet it may be argued that on two counts essential for our discussion here practically all the miniatures can be used as evidence: the choice of illustrated subject-matter and the basic compositional pattern. In the first instance the miniatures have tended to emphasize certain subjects at the expense of others: legitimacy in large throne scenes and in specific stories dealing with the ways in which Iranian kings were discovered; the miraculous and the fantastic especially in the story of Alexander the Great (pl. 13); battles given monumental proportions either in single combats or in the dusty clash of competing armies; and especially death and mourning which inspired some of the most stunning compositions of the manuscript and which have led to the definition of one of the probable artists as a *maître du*

[1] B. Gray, *Persian Painting*, p. 58.
[2] The basic bibliography will be found in B. Gray's book, p. 173.

pathétique.[1] As far as compositional patterns are concerned, the striking feature of the "Demotte" *Shāh-Nāma*, when seen in relation to the *Jāmi' al-tawārīkh*, is that, while it clearly relied on the latter for many details especially in the grouping of personages, it expanded the image both iconographically by adding more personages and a far more developed landscape and spatially by devising more complex oblique and circular compositions, by multiplying planes of action, and by diffusing excellent draftsmanship with a far more expanded palette. In short, the artist or artists of the "Demotte" manuscript transformed the purely illustrative tradition of the small manuscripts and the technically perfect narrative of the Rashīdiyya ones into an intellectually and emotionally sophisticated interpretation of the Persian epic. In this sense it inaugurates what may be called a *heroic* tradition in Iranian art, just as the *Jāmi' al-tawārīkh* inaugurated a *historical* one.[2]

It is, thus, particularly unfortunate that we are still unable to define the milieu in which the manuscript was produced. Whether it should, in part, be interpreted as reviving a very ancient heroic tradition of painting almost unknown since the eighth century in Iran, whether it should be attributed to Tabrīz because of its quality, of its relations to Chinese, Rashīdiyya, and even western arts and also because of its interest in Iranian legitimacy, a very Mongol concern, or whether it should be related to some Iranian milieu which saw in the tragically represented fate of Alexander the Great a parallel to the Īl-Khānids, these questions we simply cannot answer for the time being and yet they clearly are preliminaries to any proper understanding of the period and of its masterpiece.

In discussing the subject-matter illustrated by the *Jāmi' al-tawārīkh* and by the *Shāh-Nāma*, we have repeatedly mentioned an evolution in the representation and use of landscape, the importance of human groups and expressions, and the existence of a strong Chinese impact on some aspects of miniatures. These three features are actually closely related to each other and had a considerable impact on later Iranian painting. Therefore, they deserve some comment.

The most striking feature of the 1291 manuscript of the *Manāfi' al-ḥayawān* in the Morgan Library is that, next to a group of images which are relatable to thirteenth-century Arab painting with their single plane

[1] E. de Lorey, "L'Ecole de Tabriz", *Revue des Arts Asiatiques*, vol. IX (1935).

[2] This point has come out in a completed dissertation at the University of Michigan on the Istanbul Rashīd al-Dīn manuscript by Dr G. Inal.

indicated by a grassy band and their strong colouristic effects, there occurs a very different style in which ink drawing predominates, several planes are distinguished by a series of parallel or oblique lines, trees are no longer shown in their entirety, their trunks have strongly emphasized knots, some of the animals are even shown in monochrome against a bare sky. All these changes with their linear qualities and spatial concerns are clearly of Chinese origin. An even stronger Far Eastern influence occurs in the Rashīd al-Dīn landscapes with the introduction of Chinese-type mountains and a greater sophistication in the use of planes and of drawing techniques. The groupings of personages also bear the earmark of Far Eastern painting,[1] as do certain types of clothes, certain facial features, and the ubiquitous cloud form. These themes all remain in the "Demotte" *Shāh-Nāma* and the Istanbul *Kalīla and Dimna* in the sense that clouds, mountains, trees, certain flowers, groupings and personages, and certain spatial arrangements based on series of lines continue to be derived from Far Eastern art. And one can agree that Chinese painting—through its accidental impact by the nature of the Mongol empire and through the deliberate recourse to Chinese painters and works of art—created, or, at the very least, considerably enlarged the formal vocabulary available from then on to Iranian painters. It can further be agreed that the Rashīdiyya was one of the primary centres for the assimilation and dissemination of this vocabulary.

The new vocabulary which was thus created was rapidly transformed or, more precisely, it was used for purposes and in ways which have no relation to the place of its origins. Three principal areas can be identified in which Iranian artists so elaborated on their models as to make them not more than characteristic details. First, a great deal of the effectiveness of Chinese spatial and figural representations was lost when themes created in large scroll paintings were translated into the language of the more restricted illustrative miniatures. The frame of the *Jāmiʿ al-tawārīkh* miniatures often seems more like a straight-jacket and the tendency to explode the limits of the traditional miniature frame will remain a constant characteristic of fourteenth-century Iranian painting culminating in the highly original use of the margin and relations between text and image found, for instance, in the Istanbul *Kalīla and Dimna*.[2] A result of this concern with the frame of the

[1] For an analysis of a miniature from the manuscript, see J. Travis, "The battle of Ardavan and Ardashir," *The Art Quarterly*, vol. XXXI (1968).
[2] B. Gray, pp. 34 ff.

individual image, tied with the consistent importance of precise subject-matter, led to a growing tendency to crowd the interior of the miniature with many natural, architectural, or human and animal elements. Each one of these has probably its own story before it became a *type* or a *cliché*[1] but, in many of the "Demotte" miniatures, they filled almost all spaces and replaced the excitement of Chinese empty spaces (still evident in some of the earlier Persian miniatures) with the very Iranian fascination with colour.

The second area of Iranian elaboration concerns more specifically landscape. As one moves from the *Jāmiʿ al-tawārīkh* miniatures to those of the "Demotte" *Shāh-Nāma* or to the Istanbul *Kalīla and Dimna*, the individual elements of the landscape—the ground with its flowers or tufts of grass, the grey mountains in which fabulous monsters live, the trees which talk—become adapted to the needs of the story; they become real actors and not merely supports for action or brilliant symbols of space. As Alexander the Great reaches the end of the world, the ground suddenly changes into a striking deformed conception of the non-world. And nothing illustrates better the tragedy of the battle between Rustam and Isfandiyār than the blossoming setting with its little genre scene in one corner and the almost chiastic arrangement of a blooming and of a dying tree in the centre of the composition (pl. 15). As these elements of the landscape increase in colourfulness and significance, they become more involved and more complex and, in an image like that of the king of the monkeys and the tortoise in the Istanbul *Kalīla and Dimna*,[2] the landscape almost overshadows the incidents of the story and becomes an end in itself, but perhaps its sombre symphony of colours reflects the gruesome and cynical moral of the story. Thus, pending necessary detailed analysis, one might suggest that, as it became involved in the complexities of illustrated events, the Far Eastern vocabulary of landscape forms acquired a very Iranian nationality and also became at the extreme limit almost an end in itself.

The final characteristic feature of this painting is its transformation of man into a hero. As early as in the *Jāmiʿ al-tawārīkh* the tall personages in their long robes and with their slightly bent heads become the principal subjects of the illustrations. The whole conception of the "Demotte" *Shāh-Nāma* further emphasized the point of the importance of man in the story and the human element is quite striking in the Istanbul *Kalīla and Dimna*, although perhaps more conventional in the provincial

[1] R. Ettinghausen, in *Kunst des Orients*, vol. III, for one such *type*.

[2] B. Gray, p. 35.

small *Shāh-Nāma*. But, even if one may agree on the preponderance of man in the fourteenth-century painting, the ways in which it is achieved were not consistently the same. Two main systems of representation may be identified. One may tentatively be called *aristocratic*. Its elongated personages are usually quiet and almost motionless, with perhaps a long finger or a slight movement of the head indicating emotional involvement. Facial features are usually carefully drawn and outlined. At the other extreme occurs a sort of *caricatural* or *pathetic* tradition. Bodies are grotesquely overdrawn, often shown in violent movements. But it is in faces, especially in some of the mourning faces of the "Demotte" *Shāh-Nāmas* or in the figures of executioners that a deformed expression serves both as a masterful vehicle for the representation of pain and horror and at times also for the ridiculous. In origin these two modes of representation may be related in part to certain Far Eastern ways; and the strangely unexplained drawings in an Istanbul album may be a later example of the caricatural style.[1] At the same time both modes hark back to obscure Iranian traditions as early as the eighth-century Soghdian ones continued in part in Central Asian painting.[2]

These remarks cannot be construed as providing a complete account of fourteenth-century Iranian painting. This task is impossible without many more detailed investigations than have been accomplished so far. Our attempt has been rather to focus attention on a few themes which seem to identify the first steps of a new Iranian art of painting: its relation to books and stories, its historical interest, the impact of Chinese painting as a creator of visual forms, the pre-eminence of human elements, the development of the landscape, the key position of the Rashīdiyya school. There is a constant feeling in surveying these paintings of an art in "becoming", i.e. of an art in search of the themes and forms which will best express the needs and aspirations of the culture which sponsored it. But we are still too ill-informed on the character of the culture and especially on what it expected of its painting to give an adequate account of the latter's meaning. That in the process an extraordinary masterpiece like the "Demotte" *Shāh-Nāma* could have been produced is a testimony to the vitality of the aspirations at work and to the fermentation of ideas out of which will emerge the more classically perfect painting of the Tīmūrids.

[1] See the preliminary studies by O. Aslanapa, R. Ettinghausen and M. Loehr in *Ars Orientalis*, vol. 1 (1954).

[2] For a general summary and a bibliography see M. Bussagli, *Central Asian Painting* (Geneva, 1964).

CONCLUSIONS

In attempting to summarize the character of the visually perceived world of Iran between 1050 and 1350, two points may be brought out as being of particular significance. First, this is the time during which Iran acquired its permanent monumental Islamic infrastructure, in the same sense that the contemporary Gothic world accomplished it for the Ile-de-France or for England. Whatever earlier religious architecture of Iran had been, it is after the growth of the monuments of the area of Iṣfahān in the early twelfth century and of monumental tombs everywhere that the more or less permanent forms of most Iranian architecture were established: court with *īvāns*, domes, and decorative techniques. However spectacular, and even at first glance revolutionary, most later developments will almost always appear as variations on themes of the twelfth century.

In painting and the decorative arts, if we except the unique but comparatively short-lived art of objects on a broad social base which developed in the twelfth and thirteenth centuries, the principal novelty of the period consists in the first moments of the known history of Iranian painting. In this realm one cannot argue as well that the miniatures of the fourteenth century formed the permanent taste of Iranian painting. Yet later painting cannot entirely be explained without the experiments of the early fourteenth century and especially without the body of influences at work at that time and the visual vocabulary which slowly emerged out of them. *Mutatis mutandis* and without in any way suggesting a relation of cause and effect between the two traditions, it may be suggested that Iranian painting of the fourteenth century stands toward later painting in the same relationship as Giotto and the International Style stand to the Italian Quattrocentro.

CHAPTER 10

THE EXACT SCIENCES IN IRAN UNDER THE SALJUQS AND MONGOLS

PRE-SALJUQ SCIENCES

In commencing a description of the mathematical sciences as practised and developed in Iran during the three and a half centuries beginning with, say, 430/1038, it is useful to review accomplishments in the field up to that time. Having assessed the accumulated scientific capital available, as it were, to the mathematicians and astronomers of the period, consideration can then be given to the manner in which they maintained, enhanced, or neglected the fund of knowledge they inherited.

One essential tool for any serious work, a place-value number system, had been at hand for three millennia. The calculus of sexagesimals, which had been developed in Mesopotamia, came to the Islamic world via the Greeks. It continued to be fully exploited for numerical operations throughout medieval times. The decimal system (but without fractions) was introduced into the Middle East from India during the ʿAbbāsid period. It did not become a serious competitor to sexagesimals until much later, nor was there any reason why it should.

Following the Pythagorean discovery of irrational ratios, the Greeks constructed a rigorous theory of the continuum, the process entailing a clear formulation of the notion of a limit. This body of doctrine likewise was taken over by the Muslims and subjected to repeated critical examination by numerous scholars. The same goes for geometric algebra, including a systematic treatment of the quadratic equation and a few cubics, euclidean plane and solid geometry, Apollonius' work on conic sections, "analemma" methods (i.e. descriptive geometry), various categories of analogue computers, e.g. the astrolabe based on stereographic mapping, planetary equatoria, and so on.

As for trigonometry, in order to obtain numerical solutions to problems on the celestial sphere, Hellenistic astronomers had worked out a cumbersome discipline involving a single tabulated function, that of chord lengths in terms of the corresponding arcs. The basic configuration was not the triangle, but the complete quadrilateral, relations between the sides being given by Menelaos' theorem. The spherical angle as such played no role. Some time later, we do not know just when, the Indians substituted for the chord, tables of half-chords, thus introducing the sine function, the fundamental periodic function in science and technology. Long before, as a by-product of time-reckoning from the height of the sun, shadow tables had appeared in various places. They were the immediate ancestors of the tangent and cotangent functions.

These disparate elements were assimilated by the astronomers of the ʿAbbāsid empire and developed into a proper trigonometry. The now standard periodic functions of the discipline were defined, and the relationships between them explored. Extensive and precise tables of all were computed by the use of facile and powerful numerical techniques which were then new to mathematics and which were characteristic of Islamic work throughout. Shortly before the advent of the Saljuq dynasty several investigators stated and proved the plane and spherical cases of the sine theorem for oblique triangles. This made possible the abandoning of the Menelaos configuration in favour of relations involving the triangle alone, including functions of its angles as well as its sides.[1]

The above leads naturally to a consideration of astronomy, the only branch of natural science susceptible of both extensive and exact development in ancient and medieval times. For many centuries the most challenging astronomical problem was that of predicting, for any given time, the positions of the planets, celestial objects which in the course of years trace out curiously looped paths in the night sky against the backdrop of the fixed stars. Two solutions to the problem of planetary motion were developed almost simultaneously in the last centuries B.C. One, the Babylonian, based upon sequences of numbers making up periodic relations now known as linear zigzag or step functions, had disappeared completely long before the rise of Islam. The other, of Hellenistic provenience, regarded the planetary paths as resulting from combinations of circular motions. Numerical results were then inferred by trigonometric calculations based on the geometric models. In the second century A.D. this type of approach culminated in

[1] See Paul Luckey, "Zur Entstehung der Kugeldreiecksrechnung", *Deutsche Mathematik* vol. v (1941), pp. 405–46.

Ptolemy's *Almagest*, easily the finest and most original astronomical work of antiquity. Meanwhile, some knowledge of pre-Ptolemaic Greek (and Babylonian) planetary theory had reached the Indian subcontinent. There the basic geometric model was subjected to modifications of considerable originality by individuals whose work gives the impression that they felt far more at home manipulating numerical rather than geometric concepts.[1] Sassanian Iran, thus enveloped on two sides and influenced by techniques emanating both from the eastern Mediterranean and from India, produced astronomical work of its own, of what degree of originality it is as yet difficult to say.[2]

In any event, three distinct and competing sets of astronomical doctrine were cultivated in the flourishing scientific centres of the 'Abbāsid hegemony. There were active partisans respectively of the (Sassanian) Zīj-i Shāh, the Sindhind (from Sanskrit *siddhānta*) and the Almagest. But in the course of time the clear superiority of Ptolemaic theory over the other two was amply demonstrated, and by the beginning of our period they had effectively disappeared from the field.

The quickening of interest in astronomical theory from the ninth century A.D. on, was more than matched by activity in observational astronomy carried on predominantly at Baghdad, but also at Būyid, Ghaznavid, Sāmānid, and many other dynastic capitals[3] stretching from Spain to Central Asia. An incomplete count yields a hundred and four dated observations between 800 and 1050 attested in the manuscript literature. These are mostly of equinoxes and solstices, but they include also planetary conjunctions, positions of individual planets, eclipses, and fixed star observations. For continuity this cannot touch the three-hundred year span of the single Babylonian archive now being studied.[4] But it demonstrates that the active cultivation of astronomy was far more widespread and intensive in the ninth and tenth centuries than at any previous time in history.

The fruits of observation and theory combined were sets of numerical tables (*zījes*) appearing in great profusion during the same period. Their contents run the gamut of requirements for the practising astronomer-astrologer from purely mathematical tables of trigonometric functions

[1] See O. Neugebauer, "The Transmission of Planetary Theories in Ancient and Medieval Astronomy", *Scripta Mathematica*, vol. XXII (1956), pp. 165–92.

[2] See David Pingree, "Astronomy and Astrology in India and Iran", *Isis*, vol. LIV (1963), pp. 229–46.

[3] See Aydin Sayili, *The Observatory in Islam* (Ankara, 1960).

[4] Cf. Bryant Tuckerman, "Planetary, Lunar, and Solar Positions, 601 B.C. to A.D. 1..." *Mem. Am. Phil. Soc.* vol. LVI (1962), p. v.

and tables for calculating planetary positions through co-ordinate tables of fixed stars and famous cities.[1]

Thus, the scientists of Saljuq Iran found their subject in a vigorous and flourishing state. What they did with it is the next consideration.

THE FOUNDATIONS OF MATHEMATICS

Throughout the Middle Ages a succession of Muslim scholars worked along two lines, one of which led them to generalize the concept of a number. The second can be thought of as an examination of the nature of euclidean geometry which, in modern times, culminated in the appearance of the various non-euclidean geometries. Of the latter, only the first faint foreshadowing occurred in Saljuq and Mongol Iran. Both are sketched herewith.

Nowadays the domain of the real numbers is regarded as including various other categories of numbers: the *integers*, or whole numbers; the *rationals*, or common fractions—ratios between pairs of integers, expressible as terminating or repeating decimals; and the *irrationals*, expressible as non-terminating, non-repeating decimals. For the Greeks, however, the term "number" meant only a member of the infinite set 2, 3, 4,..., i.e. a positive integer greater than unity. Frequently this definition sufficed, as in the comparison of geometric entities, say the lengths of a pair of "commensurable" lines. Commensurable magnitudes are those for which a common unit can be found. For a finite set of such magnitudes the use of fractions can be avoided by choice of a unit sufficiently small.

However, it had been discovered as early as the fifth century B.C. that for some pairs of easily constructed magnitudes, the diagonal and side of a square ($\sqrt{2}:1$), for instance, no such common unit can be found. In order to deal with the "irrational" ratios between such magnitudes Eudoxus worked out a definition of proportion (found in Book V of Euclid's *Elements*) which is equivalent to the celebrated definition of real numbers given in the nineteenth century by R. Dedekind. This involves dividing the set of all rational numbers by a "cut". Each cut constitutes a real number, and the set of all such cuts makes up the system of real numbers.[2]

[1] E. S. Kennedy, "A Survey of Islamic Astronomical Tables", *Trans. Am. Phil. Soc.* N.S. vol. XLVI (1956), pt. 2.

[2] See *The Thirteen Books of Euclid's Elements* (Dover reprint, New York, 1956), transl. and ed. by T. L. Heath, vol. II, p. 120.

Eudoxus' version of the doctrine was completely rigorous, but it excluded common fractions and incommensurable ratios from the domain of numbers, and it presented no ready means for the carrying out of operations, say multiplication, between pairs of irrationals.

The early Muslim geometers resurrected and used a second definition of proportion which seems to have been known to the Greeks, but which appears explicitly nowhere in the Greek literature. In effect, it makes use of the procedure for expressing a ratio as a continued fraction. Examples are

$$43:19 = 2+\cfrac{1}{3+\cfrac{1}{1+\frac{1}{4}}} \quad \text{and} \quad \sqrt{2}:1 = 1+\cfrac{1}{2+\cfrac{1}{2+\cfrac{1}{2+\dots}}}$$

If the fraction terminates the ratio is rational; otherwise it is irrational.[1] The continued fraction approach has the advantage that, in the case of an irrational, cutting off the development at any stage yields a finite continued fraction which is a rational approximation to the ratio sought. In the computation of trigonometric tables the Islamic mathematicians were continually confronted with irrational ratios for which they used rational approximations, and already in pre-Saljuq times a tendency was evidenced to think of these ratios as numbers.[2]

The matter was carried much farther by ʿUmar Khayyām (*fl.* 1100) in his treatise on the difficulties of Euclid's Elements.[3] Like his predecessors, he defined two irrational ratios as equal if and only if their continued fraction developments are equal. Still employing continued fractions he went on to give conditions for determining which of two unequal ratios, rational or irrational, is the greater. By showing the equivalence of his and the Eudoxian definition he was enabled to take over all the properties of proportions in the Elements. In this connexion he hypothesizes a magnitude whose ratio to a unit is to be regarded as completely abstract "connected to numbers, (but) not an absolute, genuine number" (*taʿallaqu biʾl-ʿadad, lā ʿadadan muṭlaqan ḥaqīqiyyan*). Later

[1] See E. B. Plooij, *Euclid's Conception of Ratio* (Rotterdam, 1950).

[2] E.g. in al-Bīrūnī's *Al-Qānūn al-Masʿūdī* (Hyderabad-Dn. 1954), vol. 1, p. 303, l. 7. See also A. P. Juschkewitsch and B. A. Rosenfeld, *Die Mathematik der Länder des Ostens in Mittelalter* (Berlin, 1960), p. 132.

[3] *Fī sharḥ mā ashkala min muṣādarāt kitāb Uqlīdus*; text, Russian translation, and commentary are published by B. A. Rozenfel'd and A. P. Yushkevich in *Omar Xaiiām*, Traktatï (Moscow, 1961). See, in particular: transl. p. 145, text p. 61.

in the same passage he says "regarding it (*ta'tabar fīhi*) as a number, as we have mentioned". Thus the irrational has very nearly, but not quite, been admitted to the status of a number.

Later Naṣīr al-Dīn Ṭūsī (*fl.* 1250) in his trigonometrical work on the complete quadrilateral[1] demonstrated the commutative property of multiplication between pairs of ratios (i.e. real numbers). He also asserts that every ratio can be regarded as a number.

The topic involving the foundations of geometry has the same two protagonists just mentioned and can be dealt with more briefly. It concerns the fifth postulate of Euclid, which states that if a transversal cuts two other lines in such manner that the sum of the interior angles on the same side of the transversal is less than a straight angle, the two lines will meet on that side if produced. It had been thought since classical times that this postulate was in fact provable in terms of the assumptions of the Euclidean system, and many geometers essayed such a proof. In the same tract referred to above[2] Khayyām criticizes an atttempt by Ibn al-Haitham (*fl.* 1000) and has a go at the problem himself. He considers a quadrilateral *ABCD*, say, with equal sides *AB* and *DC*, both perpendicular to *BC*. This is the "birectangular quandrilateral" to which much later the name of Saccheri[3] was attached. Khayyām easily shows, without using the fifth postulate, that angles *A* and *D* must be equal. Hence they both must be either (1) acute, or (2) obtuse, or (3) right angles. He then launches into the proof of a series of theorems designed to demonstrate the absurdity of hypotheses (1) and (2). If they can be demolished then (3) is valid, and (3) is equivalent to the fifth postulate. Naṣīr al-Dīn follows a somewhat different course, striving toward the same end.[4] Their attempts were foredoomed to failure, for the fifth postulate is in fact independent of the others. If it is denied, and a different assertion substituted for it, a variety of geometries result which are different from that of Euclid, but no more and no less valid than it. It may turn out, for instance, that from a point outside a given line, two distinct parallels may be drawn to it. If either hypothesis (1) or (3) is substituted for the fifth postulate, one of the two now classical non-Euclidean geometries results. This lay far in the future

[1] *Traité du quadrilatère, attrib. a Nassirud-din el-Toussy* (Istanbul, 1891), ed. and transl. by A. Caratheodory.

[2] Rozenfel'd and Yushkevich, *op. cit.* transl. p. 120, text p. 42.

[3] See D. E. Smith, "Euclid, Omar Khayyam and Saccheri", *Scripta Mathematica*, vol. III (1935), pp. 5–10.

[4] Juschkewitsch and Rosenfeld, *op. cit.* p. 150.

and unsuspected by Khayyām and Naṣīr al-Dīn. Meanwhile they demonstrated properties characteristic of these unborn disciplines. For instance, both realized that acceptance of hypothesis (1) implies that the angle sum of any triangle is less than two right angles. This is a property enjoyed by triangles in the geometry of Lobachevskii.

ALGEBRA—KHAYYĀM AND THE CUBIC EQUATION

The expression

$$x^3 + 200x = 20x^2 + 2000$$

is an example of a cubic equation. To find a solution for it, a root, is somehow to obtain a particular number such that when x is replaced by it the resulting number on the left (the root cubed plus two hundred times the root) equals the resulting number on the right. This equation appears in a recently discovered treatise[1] written by Khayyām. He shows that it is equivalent to the following geometric problem: Find a right triangle having the property that the hypotenuse equals the sum of one leg plus the altitude on the hypotenuse. He demonstrates in turn the equivalence of this with a second question in geometry; he finds a geometric solution of the equation at the intersection between a circle and a hyperbola, and a numerical solution by interpolation in trigonometric tables. This particular equation stimulates Khayyām to review the work done by others with similar problems, to make a classification of types of such equations, and to undertake the systematic solution of all.

His treatise is useful as giving an indication of the methods, motivation, content, and background of the algebra of his time, as well as its interrelations with other branches of mathematics.

In the example cited, the highest power of the unknown quantity is three. Had this highest power been a two the equation would have been a quadratic, if four a quartic, five a quintic, and so on. General procedures for the solution of quadratics had appeared early in the second millennium B.C. Isolated examples of cubics also had turned up centuries before Khayyām's time. Thus Archimedes, in seeking so to place a plane that it splits the volume of a sphere in a given ratio, formulated the problem in terms of a cubic equation. He, like Khayyām after him, solved it by means of intersecting conic sections.

A conic section is any one of the curves (circle, ellipse, hyperbola, or parabola) formed when a circular cone is cut by a plane. The theory of

[1] Translated by A. R. Amir-Moez in *Scripta Mathematica*, vol. XXVI, pp. 323–37.

conics as developed in classical times included manifold metric properties. For instance, if a point moves so that its distances, x and y, from a fixed pair of perpendicular lines always satisfies the relation $xy = 4$, it will trace out an hyperbola. If the relation is $y = x^2$ the point will move along a parabola. At any intersection of the two curves both relations will be satisfied simultaneously. Hence at such a point the x-distance will satisfy the relation $xy = x(x^2) = x^3 = 4$, a cubic equation. And the distance from the point to the line is a root of the equation.

In his major work in algebra Khayyām exploits this variety of technique to work out solutions for all possible types of cubic equations. In his classification, not only the equation

$$x^3 = 20x^2 + 2000,$$

but also

$$x^3 + 20x^2 = 200x + 2000$$

demands an approach different from the example given at the beginning of the section. This is because not only the number of terms but also the inadmissibility of negative terms affects the category of a given equation.

Khayyām's solutions appear as line segments, not numbers; he is usually satisfied with a single root per equation; no negative roots are admitted. All his expressions are written out in words—the symbolism we associate with algebra still lay centuries in the future. Nevertheless Khayyām left the subject of polynomial equations in a state much farther along than that in which he found it.[1]

TRIGONOMETRY AND COMPUTATIONAL MATHEMATICS

Saljuq and Mongol times are to be regarded as a period of consolidation in trigonometry rather than one of innovation. This was natural, since they followed hard after the significant forward steps taken by Abu'l-Wafā' al-Buzjānī, Abū Naṣr Manṣūr, and others.[2] The work of these people is assembled and integrated into much earlier material in the book of Naṣīr al-Dīn referred to above,[3] the *Kitāb shikl al-qiṭā'*, com-

[1] There are several translations of Khayyām's algebra into European languages, the first being F. Woepeke's *L'Algebre d'Omar Alkhayyāmī* (Paris, 1851) which includes the Arabic text. An English version is by D. S. Kasir, *The Algebra of Omar Khayyam* (New York, 1931). The most recent is in the *Traktatī* cited above, which also contains the Arabic text. See also Juschkewitsch and Rosenfeld, *op. cit.* pp. 113–24, and Rozenfel'd and Yushkevich, *op. cit.* pp. 250–9.

[2] Cf. Luckey, *op. cit.*

[3] Caratheodory, *op. cit.*

pleted in 1260. As its name indicates, it has mainly to do with the complete quadrilateral, the basic configuration of Menelaos' spherics. However, the last of the five treatises is written with the avowed purpose of eliminating the quadrilateral from the subject in favour of the simpler triangle. The author lists the six combinations of known sides or angles of a spherical triangle under which the triangle is determinate. He then systematically indicates the solution of each case without recourse to the Menelaos Theorem. In this sense the book is the first treatment of trigonometry (the measurement of the triangle) as such.

It is a landmark also in a second sense. The subject evolved in response to a need on the part of astronomers to transform and apply in various ways the information yielded by observations of celestial bodies. Until the work of Naṣīr al-Dīn, trigonometric techniques were closely associated with problems in spherical astronomy. This did not cease in his time or later, but his book makes no reference to astronomy, and marks the emergence of trigonometry as a branch of pure mathematics.[1]

Numerical analysis also received its impetus from astronomy because of the need for tables of the trigonometric and other functions encountered in solving problems on the celestial sphere. The apogee of Islamic work in computational mathematics did not occur until the Tīmūrid period, but steady progress in the field was maintained during the twelfth and thirteenth centuries. As an illustration we cite the table of the tangent function which appears in the *Zīj-i Īlkhānī* turned out at Naṣīr al-Dīn's Marāgheh observatory. Up to forty-five degrees it proceeds at intervals of one minute of arc. Hence there are

$$45 \times 60 = 270 \text{ entries,}$$

each to three sexagesimal places, which implies precision to the order of one in ten million, say. The function increases ever more rapidly as it approaches ninety degrees, so the interval between values of the argument is increased to ten minutes, up to eighty-nine degrees, and fifty minutes. The last entry in the table has five sexagesimal places. The design and carrying through of a project such as this involves much more than hiring a sufficient number of adept calculators.

[1] A. von Braunmühl, *Vorlesungen über Geschichte der Trigonometrie*, vol. 1 (Leipzig, 1900). See also the outline history of trigonometry in the thirtieth Yearbook of the National Council of Teachers of Mathematics, *Historical Topics for the Mathematics Classroom* (Washington, to be published in 1968).

PLANETARY THEORY—THE MARĀGHEH SCHOOL

The earth and its sister planets of the solar system rotate in nearly circular orbits about the sun, all lying pretty much in a single plane, the ecliptic. Think of each orbit as the rim of a spinning wheel, the poet's *charkh-i gardūn*, of which the line between sun and planet is a spoke. If, which is natural, we regard the earth as fixed, then the turning of the earth–sun spoke constrains the sun itself to move in an orbit about the earth, whilst it remains the hub of the independently rotating sun–planet spoke. Now the planet, riding upon the rim of its own wheel, alternately approaches the earth and recedes from it as the wheel spins. At the same time it alternately moves forward, ahead of the earth–sun spoke, thence receding behind it, and so on.

This figure of wheels upon wheels provides a valid if simplified explanation for the looped paths of the planets as seen from the earth. Moreover, if the larger orbit is called the *deferent* (*al-ḥāmil*), the smaller, rotating upon its periphery, the *epicycle* (*al-tadwīr*), and if for the wheel-spoke the modern technical term *vector* is substituted, the configuration becomes the standard one of ancient and medieval planetary theory. For the superior planets, those whose orbits are larger than the earth's, the deferent cannot be thought of as the orbit of the sun; nevertheless, for these planets also a deferent-epicycle combination is valid.

This general approach antedates Ptolemy, as does the realization that to obtain a closer correspondence to observation it is necessary for each planet that the earth's position be slightly displaced from the deferent centre. Also pre-Ptolemaic is the notion, strongly held until the sixteenth century, that any celestial motion must be uniform and circular, or a combination of such motions. Stated in modern form, this requires that the motion of any celestial body be expressible as that of the end-point of a linkage of constant length vectors, each vector rotating at constant angular velocity, and the initial point of the first vector being at the earth.

Ptolemy's observations led him to the realization that the centre of equal motion for the epicycle centre is neither the earth nor the deferent centre, but a point distinct from both, the *equant* (*muʿaddal al-masīr*). The presence of the equant in the Ptolemaic model makes possible a high degree of precision in predicting planetary positions, but it violates the principle of uniform circularity as stated above.

This alleged flaw in the planetary theory was the object of criticism by many astronomers, but until Īl-Khānid times no one seems to have produced a model capable of competing with Ptolemy's in terms of accuracy, and which would at the same time involve only uniform circular motions. Such a development was, however, inaugurated by Naṣīr al-Dīn Ṭūsī and carried through by associates of his at the Marāgheh observatory. He seems to have been the first to notice that if one circle rolls around inside the circumference of another, the second circle having twice the radius of the first, then any point on the periphery of the first circle describes a diameter of the second. This rolling device can also be regarded as a linkage of two equal and constant length vectors rotating at constant speed (one twice as fast as the other), and hence has been called a *Ṭūsī-couple*. Naṣīr al-Dīn, by properly placing such a couple on the end of a vector emanating from the Ptolemaic equant centre, caused the vector periodically to expand and contract. The period of its expansion being equal to that of the epicycle's rotation about the earth, the end-point of the couple carries the epicycle centre with it and traces out a deferent which fulfils all the conditions imposed upon it by Ptolemy's observations. At the same time, the whole assemblage is a combination of uniform circular motions, hence unobjectionable, and it preserves the equant property, also demanded by the phenomenon itself.

Other astronomers of the Marāgheh group continued work along these lines, although their results have not as yet been fully recovered. In all cases their efforts, usually successful, seem to have been to construct combinations of uniform circular motions satisfying Ptolemaic boundary conditions and preserving the equant.

Among the five planets visible to the naked eye, Mercury is by far the most irregular. Hence the construction of a satisfactory model for predicting its positions offers more difficulty than does that for any other planet. After repeated efforts, made long after he had left Marāgheh, Quṭb al-Dīn Shīrāzī, a younger associate of Naṣīr al-Dīn, produced the equivalent of the configuration illustrated in fig. 4. It satisfies all the conditions demanded by Ptolemy for the orbit of Mercury, and as such probably marks the apex of the techniques developed by the Marāgheh school. Without going into details we note that, exclusive of the epicycle radius (not shown in the figure), it involves some six rotating vectors, of which two pairs ($r_2 r_3$ and $r_4 r_5$) are Ṭūsī-couples with different periods.

In sketching these developments, it has been necessary to omit many aspects of the general problem of planetary motion which were considered by the scientists named. For instance, the planes of all the planetary orbits diverge slightly from the ecliptic, thus giving rise to motions in latitude for which machinery must be provided. Some appreciation of the inevitable complexity of a complete model may be gained by contemplating pl. 16, reproduced from a copy of one of Quṭb al-Dīn's books.

Developments along the lines indicated did not cease with the disappearance of the Marāgheh group. The work of the Damascene astronomer known as Ibn al-Shāṭir (*fl.* 1350) falls outside our domain geographically, though not in time. It is relevant to say, however, that he succeeded where Quṭb al-Dīn failed, producing a lunar model free of the very serious defects in the Ptolemaic one, and in fact identical with the lunar model of Copernicus (*fl.* 1520). Indeed, it has been shown that most of the Copernican planetary models are duplicates of those exhibited either by the Marāgheh scientists or by Ibn al-Shāṭir. All that is left to Copernicus is the philosophically important reintroduction of a heliostatic universe.[1]

OBSERVATIONAL ASTRONOMY

It is safe to say that in Saljuq Iran many astronomers were engaged in making observations, but it is impossible to give a precise description of this activity because the available sources yield incomplete and conflicting information. That Sulṭān Malik-Shāh had a new solar calendar inaugurated is indubitable, its epoch coinciding with the day of the vernal equinox of A.D. 1079, each Nau-Rūz day thereafter to fall on the succeeding vernal equinox. However, one report states that a group of astronomers including Khayyām was commissioned to work out the calendar, and that to do so large sums were spent on an observatory which was in operation about twenty years. A second source claims that the king proposed a programme of observations, at which the astronomers demurred and suggested the calendar as a counter-proposal, the implication being that no observatory was involved. The *Naurūz-*

[1] The subject of planetary motion cannot be discussed adequately without the introduction of technical material. The reader will find an exposition of the Ptolemaic system in O. Neugebauer's *The Exact Sciences in Antiquity* (2nd ed., Providence, R.I., 1957; there is a paperback edition by Harpers), appendix I. Descriptions of the Marāgheh and Ibn al-Shāṭir models are given in the following papers in *Isis*: vol. XLVIII (1957), pp. 428–32; vol. L (1959), pp. 227–35; vol. LV (1962), pp. 492–9; vol. LVII (1966), pp. 208–19, 365–78.

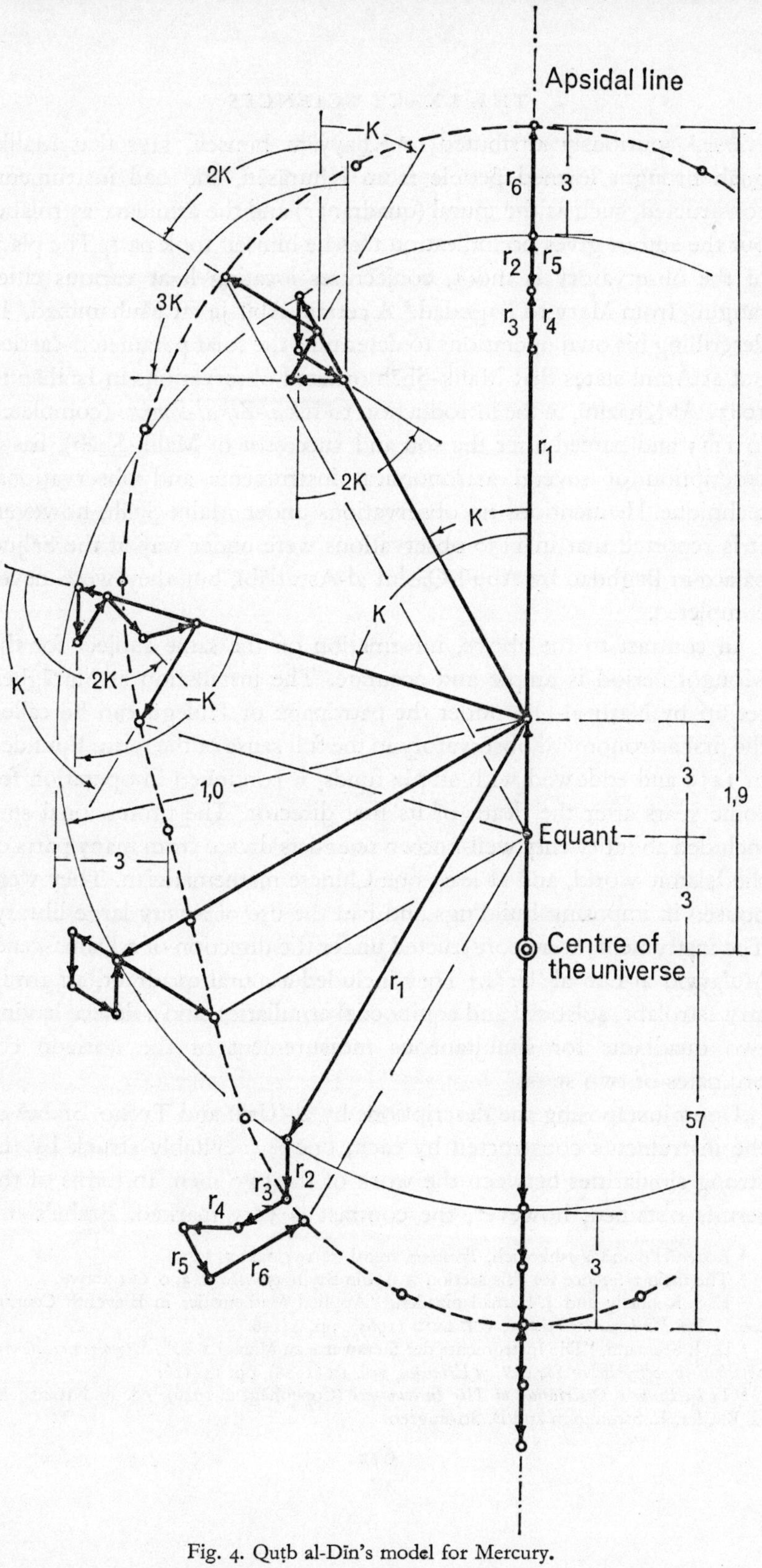

Fig. 4. Quṭb al-Dīn's model for Mercury.

Nāma,[1] spuriously attributed to Khayyām himself, says that Malik-Shāh brought learned people from Khurāsān, and had instruments constructed, such as the mural (quadrant?) and the armillary astrolabe, but the author gives no indication that he himself took part. The place of the observatory is moot, conjectures locating it at various cities ranging from Marv to Baghdad.[2] A certain Abū Ja'far Muḥammad,[3] in describing his own operations to determine the solar parameters carried out at Āmul states that Malik-Shāh ordered observations in Iṣfahān in 1083. Al-Khāzinī, in the introduction to his *al-Zīj al-Sanjarī* (completed in 1115 and named after the son and successor of Malik-Shāh), has a description of several astronomical instruments and observational technique. He mentions no observations under Malik-Shāh, however. It is reported that in 1130 observations were under way at the Saljuq palace in Baghdad by Abu'l-Qāsim al-Asṭurlābī, but they were never completed.

In contrast to the above, information on the same subject for the Mongol period is ample and accurate. The installation at Marāgheh set up by Naṣīr al-Dīn under the patronage of Hülegü can be called the first astronomical observatory in the full sense of the term. Founded in 1259 and endowed with ample funds, it continued in operation for some years after the death of its first director. The professional staff included about twenty well-known scientists drawn from many parts of the Islamic world, and at least one Chinese mathematician. They were housed in imposing buildings and had the use of a very large library. The instruments were constructed under the direction of a Damascene, Mu'ayyid al-Dīn al-'Urḍī.[4] They included a mural quadrant, an armillary astrolabe, solsticial and equinoctial armillaries, and a device having two quadrants for simultaneous measurement of the horizon coordinates of two stars.

Upon juxtaposing the descriptions by al-'Urḍī and Tycho Brahe[5] of the instruments constructed by each, one is inevitably struck by the strong similarities between the work of the two men. In terms of the results obtained, however, the contrast is very marked. Brahe's un-

[1] Rozenfel'd and Yushkevich, *Traktatï*, transl. p. 193, text p. 127.

[2] The main reference for this section is Aydin Sayili, *op. cit.*, n. 3, p. 661 above.

[3] E. S. Kennedy and J. Hamadanizadeh, "Applied Mathematics in Eleventh Century Iran", *The Mathematics Teacher*, vol. LVIII (1965), pp. 441–6.

[4] H. J. Seemann, "Die Instrumente der Sterawarte zu Maragha...", *Sitzungsberichte der physikalischmedizinischen Sozietät zu Erlangen*, vol. LX (1928), pp. 15–126.

[5] *Tycho Brahe's Description of His Instruments* (Copenhagen, 1946), ed. and transl. by H. Raeder, E. Stromgren and B. Stromgren.

precedentedly precise observations enabled Kepler to make fundamental advances in theory, whereas we have seen above that observation played no role in the Marāgheh work in planetary theory. Furthermore, it can be shown (as charged by al-Wābkanwī)[1] that the planetary mean motion parameters in Naṣīr al-Dīn's *Zīj-i Īlkhānī* have been taken over from the earlier work of Ibn al-A'lam, hence they were not based on work at Marāgheh. And these determinations require no elaborate instruments at all.

After the death of Hülegü, later rulers of the same dynasty also sponsored astronomical work. Ghāzān is said to have built a minor observatory at Tabrīz.[2] It was probably from this centre that a Byzantine text[3] relays a lunar eclipse report from Tabrīz in 1295, and a solar eclipse the next year. Working successively under Öljeitü and Abū Sa'īd, al-Wābkanwī reports planetary conjunctions observed in 1286, 1305, and 1306.

MATHEMATICAL GEOGRAPHY

In order to predict the positions of celestial objects as observed from his own station, the astronomer must know the position of his locality with respect to the base co-ordinates and epoch of the tables he is using. In response to this need, most medieval zījes give lists of cities, together with their latitudes and longitudes. A partial collection involving thirty such tables runs to about 2,500 localities in Asia, Africa, and Europe.[4] Only one of these tables dates from the Saljuq period, but about a third of the total seem to have been put together in Īl-Khānid Iran. Localities appearing most frequently in all the sources are concentrated in Iran and Central Asia. On the basis of this it can be inferred that this time was the peak of activity in this particular field, perhaps as a result of the excellent communications maintained by the Mongol bureaucracy. On the other hand, a count was made of localities listed in five or more tables including the *Zīj-i Īlkhānī* but not before. This yielded only twenty-nine place-names, of which only Qara-Qorum, Besh-Balïq, and Farghāna are easily identifiable Central Asiatic centres.

[1] See Aya Sofya MS. 2694, f. 3r. [2] See above, p. 389.

[3] O. Neugebauer, "Studies in Byzantine Astronomical Terminology", *Trans. Am. Phil. Soc.* vol. L (1960), pt. 2, p. 28.

[4] Fuad I. Haddad and E. S. Kennedy, "Place Names of Medieval Islam", *Geographical Review*, vol. LIV (1964), pp. 439–40.

SPECIFIC GRAVITY DETERMINATIONS

Archimedes had discovered that whenever a heavy object is immersed in a liquid its apparent weight is decreased by the weight of whatever amount of the liquid it displaces. This fact was used by him in his celebrated investigation of the purity of Hieron's gold crown.

The same principle is easily applicable to the calculation of the specific gravity of substances heavier than water, the ratio between the weight of any quantity of the substance and the weight of an equal volume of water. A succession of Muslim physicists, from the time of the caliph al-Ma'mūn on, developed varieties of balances for such determinations. The work was continued in Saljuq times by Khayyām, a certain Abū Ḥātim al-Muẓaffar al-Isfazārī, and 'Abd al-Raḥmān al-Khāzinī, the author of *al-Zīj al-Sanjarī*. Al-Khāzinī has left an account of these researches in a work called *Kitāb mīzān al-ḥikma*.[1]

The title of the book is the name of the main instrument it describes, a balance equipped with five pans, two of which were suspended from the same point on one side of the balance arm, the lower pan being immersed in water. Moreover, the other side of the balance arm bore a set of marks, one for each of the varieties of substance to be tested. Two of the remaining pans could be slid along this balance arm so as to be suspended at will from any one of the marks. The fifth pan was suspended at a fixed point on the arm, its distance from the knife-edge fulcrum being equal to that of the double pan on the other side.

Suppose now that a piece of metal were presented, alleged to be of, say, pure gold. One of the movable pans is suspended, empty, at the mark for gold; the sample is placed in the upper (air) pan of the double pan arrangement, and the sample is weighed in the usual manner. The sample is then transferred to the submerged pan, i.e. it is now weighed under water, and the weight which counter-balanced it in the fifth pan is transferred to the pan suspended at the mark for gold. If the instrument still balances, the sample indeed has the specific gravity of gold.

[1] The text was published by the Oriental Publications Bureau, Osmania University Hyderabad-Dn., 1359 A.H. Large portions of the text had previously been published, translated, and commented upon by N. Khanikoff, as "Book of the Balance of Wisdom", *J.A.O.S.* (1860), pp. 1–128. The subject has been extensively studied by Eilhard Wiedemann and his associates. See, e.g. *Sitzungsberichte der physikalischmediziniscben Sozietät zu Erlangen*, vol. XL (1908), pp. 133–59, which lists other papers. A short treatise on the balance by Khayyām is published in the *Traktati*, *op. cit.* note 10.

If a mixture of two substances is presented, say an alloy of gold and silver, its composition is determined as follows. Set one of the two movable pans at the gold mark and the other at the silver mark. Now place the sample in the air balance and weigh it in the usual manner. Then transfer the sample to the water pan, and remove from the fifth pan the weight which counterbalanced the sample in air. Place part of this weight in the pan at the gold mark and the rest in the silver mark pan, in such manner that the instrument balances. The division of this weight is the proportion of gold to silver in the sample.

Implicit in the above is a reasonably precise knowledge of the specific gravity of any material to be assayed, and tables of such specific gravities are given in the texts, most of the constants stemming from al-Bīrūnī. Also implicit is the realization that densities are affected by temperatures. The whole is an elegant application of theory to practise, typical of the Muslim medieval penchant for scientific instruments of many varieties.

RAINBOW THEORY

In antiquity a few individuals, notably Aristotle and Seneca, had attempted explanations of rainbow formation, but with little success. However, considerable progress was made in the study of more general optical problems, notably the phenomena of reflexion and refraction.

In the late thirteenth and early fourteenth centuries this knowledge was applied independently in Western Europe and in Iran by investigators who made strikingly similar advances in rainbow theory. This involved a realization that (1) the effect is produced by the behaviour of rays of sunlight falling upon spherical droplets of water, and (2) that this behaviour is a combination of refractions and reflexions after the ray has entered the drop.

Kamāl al-Dīn al-Fārisī (d. *c.* 1320) studied at Marāgheh under Quṭb al-Dīn Shīrāzī, the latter previously mentioned in connexion with planetary theory. Quṭb al-Dīn himself does not seem to have written extensively on optics, but his leading ideas were seized upon by Kamāl al-Dīn and developed in detail in a very extensive reworking of the optics (*Kitāb al-manāẓir*) of Ibn al-Haitham (*fl.* 1000). In so doing, Kamāl al-Dīn simulated experimentally the behaviour of sunlight falling upon raindrops by the use of a spherical glass container filled with water. This he suspended in a dark room, and he then proceeded to study the directions taken by an isolated ray of sunlight admitted through a hole in such manner as to impinge upon the sphere. Thus he showed that the primary rainbow is the result of two refractions and one reflexion within the drop, while the secondary bow arises from two refractions and two reflexions.

The same conclusions were reached at almost the same time by Theodoric of Freiberg, whose work also was based on that of Ibn al-Haitham. Because of a lack of a measure of refraction equivalent to Snell's law, the results obtained both in Europe and in the Orient were qualitative rather than quantitative. Both Kamāl al-Dīn and Theodoric sought to explain the colours of the rainbow, both unsatisfactorily.[1]

THE STATE OF THE SUBJECT—THE SOURCES

Any broad survey such as this is ultimately dependent upon scientific writings produced during the period under review. Many such works, known to have been written, are no longer extant. Their absence would be felt more, however, if those sources which have survived had been completely exploited. On the contrary, most of the available Arabic and Persian scientific manuscripts have not been read in modern times, much less studied, and those texts which have been published are to a great extent the results of chance encounters. The current general picture may be altered significantly with the study of any additional text. For instance, the existence of the non-Ptolemaic planetary models discussed above was uncovered in the course of a few hours casual browsing in the Bodleian in order to kill time after a particular group of other manuscripts had been examined.

A number of topics are known to have been cultivated during the eleventh and twelfth centuries, but it is not presently possible to say whether they originated at this time or whether they had been passed on from earlier times or other regions. An example is furnished by the *Dastūr al-munajjimīn*,[2] an astronomical and chronological anthology put together by some member of the Ismāʿīlī sect, and perhaps part of the

[1] See Carl B. Boyer's *The Rainbow from Myth to Mathematics* (New York and London, 1959), chap. v. This in turn is based upon the work of Eilhard Wiedemann, e.g. "Über die Brechung des Lichtes in Kugeln...", *Sitzungsberichte der physikalisch-medizinische Sozietät zu Erlangen*, vol. XLII (1910), pp. 15–58. Also "Zur Optik von Kamāl al-Dīn", *Archiv für die Gesch. der Naturwissenschaften...*, vol. III (1910–12), pp. 161–77. The text of Kamāl al-Dīns' work has been published as *Kitāb tanqīḥ al-Manāẓir...*, 2 vols. (Hyderabad-Dn., 1347–8 A.H.). In the preparation of this and other sections the counsel of Professor Seyyed Hossein Nasr is gratefully acknowledged.

[2] Paris B.N. MS. Ar. 5968, ff. 75–8.

library found by Hülegü at the taking of Alamūt. This describes several interpolation schemes employing second-order difference sequences to fill in values for an arbitrary function between given tabular values. Another such method[1] is described in the *Zīj-i Ashrafī*, written in Shīrāz early in the fourteenth century.

An anonymous manuscript, probably written after the time of Khayyām, gives a solution for a particular quartic equation,[2] and the presumption is that additional work was done in this field.

An anonymous and undated manuscript probably composed in Iran or Central Asia during the latter part of the eleventh century employs a certain period relation between days and anomalistic months to give auxiliary tables for determining solar and lunar true positions. The period relation used is also found in Seleucid cuneiform tablets, Greek papyri, and Indian texts dating from the fourth century A.D. Hence its appearance in an Arabic text gives one of the few instances where the ancient "arithmetic methods" (as contrasted with the employment of functions of continuous variables) were taken over by Muslim scientists. At the same time, the unknown author combined with his application of the period relation a highly intelligent exploitation of the Ptolemaic lunar model and the facile computational technique characteristic of his time.[3]

Because the Muslim calendar is a strictly lunar one, the methods for predicting the evening of first new moon visibility were of interest to Islamic astronomers. Some twenty-two different solutions to this problem have thus far been encountered in the literature, ranging from simple applications of a linear zigzag function to others (like that of al-Khāzinī in the *al-Zīj al-Sanjarī*) employing a high degree of mathematical sophistication. Many of these are of unknown provenience, but many stem from Saljuq and Mongol times.

[1] See Javad Hamadanizadeh, "A Medieval Interpolation Scheme for Oblique Ascensions", *Centaurus*, vol. IX (1963), pp. 257–65.

[2] A. P. Yushkevich, *Istoriya Matematika v Srednie Veka* (Moscow, 1961), p. 258. A translation of this is A. P. Juschkewitsch, *Geschichte der Mathematik im Mittelalter* (Leipzig, 1964).

[3] E. S. Kennedy, "A Set of Medieval Tables for Quick Calculation of Solar and Lunar Ephemerides", *Oriens* (to appear).

AN ASSESSMENT

If a frequency plot is made against time of the output of medieval astronomical tables arranged by geographical place of origin[1] it will be seen that, beginning already with the tenth century, the path of the centroid commences veering east from the region of Baghdad. By A.D. 1100 the distribution is clustered on the Iranian plateau, where it remains for the next four centuries. The tables plotted represent only one genre of scientific writing. Nevertheless, in them are embodied the results of observation and theory, of astronomy and mathematics. The plot conveys about as true an impression of scientific activity during our period as can presently be expected.

From its position of strength Iran exported science to the regions adjoining it. A certain Orthodox bishop, resident in Tabrīz in 1295 translated *al-Zīj al-Sanjarī* and *al-Zīj al-ʿAlāʾī* into Greek upon his return to Constantinople.[2] His work was basic in the revival of astronomy then taking place in the Byzantine Empire. It is known that Chinese astronomers assisted Naṣīr al-Dīn at the Marāgheh observatory, and that their presence facilitated intensive study of the Chinese and Uighur calendars[3] on the part of Islamic scholars. But it is also known from Chinese records, that, at the request of the Great Khan Qubilai, a Muslim astronomer, a certain Jamāl al-Dīn, was sent to Pekin with drawings or models of instruments of the Marāgheh type to be used at the imperial observatory there.[4] The *Zīj-i Īlkhānī* of Naṣīr al-Dīn was translated from its original Persian into Arabic for use in the Arab world. The process going on in Byzantium, China, and the Arab regions was also taking place in India. In the fourteenth century the Tughluq sultan of Delhi maintained a translation service. Among the works he had put into Sanskrit was a Muslim treatise on the astrolabe, and doubtless other scientific books were translated. In Western Europe, particularly Spain, the twelfth century was the time of translations from Arabic into Latin, although many of the translations (such as the *zīj* of al-Khuwārizmī) were based on theories by then long obsolete in the Middle East. Even in the

[1] See, e.g. Kennedy, "Survey", p. 168.

[2] David Pingree, "Gregory Chioniades and Palaeologan Astronomy", *Dumbarton Oaks Papers*, vol. XVIII (1965), p. 152–82. The material on India is also from Professor Pingree.

[3] E. S. Kennedy, "The Chinese-Uighur Calendar as described in the Islamic Sources", *Isis*, vol. LV (1964), pp. 435–43.

[4] W. Hartner, "The Astronomical Instruments of Cha-ma-lu-ting", *Isis*, vol. XLI (1956), pp. 184–94. See also Joseph Needham, *Science and Civilization in China* (Cambridge, 1959), vol. III, p. 373.

following century, only one European, Leonardo of Pisa, is known to have done original work in mathematics, and he travelled and studied in the Orient.

In contrast, we have noted significant advances in the foundations of mathematics, algebra, optics, and planetary theory. That these achievements were of a lesser order than those of Archimedes, and that their consequences were incomparably less significant than the scientific breakthrough which followed the work of Newton and Leibniz is perhaps irrelevant. The scientists of Saljuq and Mongol Iran were the best of their age.

BIBLIOGRAPHY

Volume Editor's Note

The bibliographies printed below are selective and incomplete. Their purpose is not to list all publications that bear directly or indirectly on the subject, but to enable readers to carry further the study of selected topics. A later volume in this series (vol. 8) will present at much greater length a systematic bibliography. As a rule, books and articles superseded by later publications have not been included, and references to general treatises not directly relevant to the subject-matter of individual chapters have been reduced to a minimum.

Within the limits set by these principles, contributors were free to compile bibliographies as they thought best. The "layout" of the lists, therefore, varies from chapter to chapter. The editor did not even find it desirable to produce a uniform method of abbreviating references to learned periodicals. Form of presentation is, therefore, the decision of the individual author.

BIBLIOGRAPHY

CHAPTER I

1. *Primary sources*

Abū Ḥāmid Muḥammad b. Ibrāhīm. *Dhail-i Saljūq-Nāma.* Tehrān, 1332/1954.

Anushīrvān b. Khālid. *See under* Bundārī.

Baihaqī, Abu'l-Faḍl. *Ta'rīkh-i Mas'ūdī.* (1) Ed. Q. Ghanī and 'A. A. Fayyāḍ. Tehrān, 1324/1945. (2) Ed. Sa'īd Nafīsī. 3 vols. Tehrān, 1319–32/1940–53. (3) Russian tr. A. K. Arends. *Istoriya Mas'uda 1030–1041.* Tashkent, 1962.

Barhebraeus. *Chronography.* Tr. E. A. Wallis Budge. Oxford, 1932.

Bīrūnī. *al-Āthār al-bāqiya 'an al-qurūn al-khāliya.* Tr. E. Sachau: *The Chronology of Ancient Nations.* London, 1879.

Bundārī. *Zubdat al-nuṣra wa-nukhbat al-'uṣra.* Ed. M. T. Houtsma in *Recueil de Textes Relatifs à l'Histoire des Seljoucides*, II. Leiden, 1889.

Fakhr-i Mudabbir Mubārak-shāh. *Adab al-mulūk wa-kifāyat al-mamlūk.* India Office Persian MS. no. 647.

Fāriqī, Ibn al-Azraq. *Ta'rīkh Mayyāfāriqīn.* Extracts in Ibn al-Qalānīsī. *See below.*

Gardīzī. *Zain al-Akhbār.* Ed. M. Nazim. Berlin, 1928.

Ḥamd Allāh Mustaufī. *Nuzhat al-qulūb.* Ed. and tr. G. Le Strange. Gibb Memorial Series, XXIII, nos. i–ii. London, 1916–19.

—— *Ta'rīkh-i Guzīda.* Facsimile text and abridged tr., E. G. Browne. G.M.S., XIV, nos. i–ii. London, 1910–13.

Anon. *Ḥudūd al-'ālam.* Tr. V. Minorsky. G.M.S., n.s. XI. London, 1937.

Ḥusainī, Ḥusain b. Muḥammad. *Tarjuma-yi Maḥāsin-i Iṣfahān.* Ed. 'Abbās Iqbāl. Tehrān, 1328/1949.

Ḥusainī, Ṣadr al-Dīn 'Alī. *Akhbār al-daula al-Saljūqiyya.* Ed. Muḥammad Iqbāl. Lahore, 1933.

Ibn al-Athīr. *al-Kāmil fi-'l-ta'rīkh.* Ed. C. J. Tornberg. 13 vols. Leiden, 1851–76.

Ibn al-Balkhī. *Fārs-Nāma.* Ed. G. Le Strange and R. A. Nicholson. G.M.S., n.s. I. London, 1921.

Ibn Faḍlān. *Risāla.* Ed. and tr. A. Z. V. Togan. *Ibn Faḍlāns Reisebericht. Abhandlungen für die Kunde des Morgenlandes*, vol. XXIV, no. 3. 1939. Leipzig, 1939.

Ibn Funduq and 'Alī b. Zaid. *Ta'rīkh-i Baihaq.* Ed. A. Bahmanyār. Tehrān, 1317/1938.

Ibn Ḥauqal. *Kitāb ṣūrat al-arḍ.* Ed. J. H. Kramers. 2 vols. 2nd ed. Leiden, 1938–9.

Ibn Isfandiyār. *Ta'rīkh-i Ṭabaristān.* Abridged tr. E. G. Browne. G.M.S., II. Leiden, 1905.

Ibn al-Jauzī. *al-Muntaẓam fī ta'rīkh al-mulūk wal-umam*. 7 vols. Hyderabad, 1357–9/1938–41.

Ibn Khallikān. *Wafayāt al-a'yān*. Tr. Baron M. G. de Slane: *Ibn Khallikan's Biographical Dictionary*. 4 vols. Paris, 1843–70.

Ibn al-Qalānisī. *Dhail ta'rīkh Dimashq*. Ed. H. F. Amedroz. Leiden, 1908.

Ibn al-Ṭiqṭaqā. *Kitāb al-Fakhrī*. Cairo, 1317/1899. Tr. C. E. J. Whitting: *Al Fakhri*. London, 1947.

'Imād al-Dīn. *See under* Bundārī.

Iṣṭakhrī. *Kitāb masālik al-mamālik*. Ed. M. J. de Goeje, in Bibliotheca Geographorum Arabicorum, I. 2nd ed. Leiden, 1927.

Juvainī, 'Alā' al-Dīn 'Aṭā'-Malik. *Ta'rīkh-i Jahān-Gushā*. Tr. J. A. Boyle: *The History of the World-Conqueror*. 2 vols. Manchester, 1958.

Juvainī, Muntajab al-Dīn. *'Atabat al-kataba*. Ed. 'Abbās Iqbāl. Tehrān, 1329/1950.

Jūzjānī. *Ṭabaqat-i Nāṣirī*. Ed. 'Abd al-Ḥayy Ḥabībī. 2 vols. Kabul, 1342–3/1963–4. Tr. H. G. Raverty: *The Ṭabakāt-i Nāṣirī*. 2 vols. London, 1881–99.

Kai-Kā'ūs b. Iskandar. *Qābūs-Nāma*. Ed. R. Levy. G.M.S., n.s. XVIII. London. 1951. Tr. Levy: *A Mirror for Princes*. London, 1951.

Kāshgharī, Maḥmūd. *Dīwān Lughāt al-Turk*. Facsimile text and Turkish tr., Besim Atalay: *Divanü lûğat-it Türk*. 5 vols. Ankara, 1939–41.

al-Khwārazmī, Abū 'Abdallāh Muḥammad. *Mafātīḥ al-'Ulūm*. Ed. G. van Vloten. Leiden, 1895.

Māfarrūkhī. *See under* Ḥusain b. Muḥammad Ḥusainī.

Maqdisī. *Aḥsan al-taqāsīm fī ma'rifat al-aqālīm*. Ed. M. J. de Geoje. Bibliotheca Geographorum Arabicorum, III. 2nd ed. Leiden, 1906.

Mīrkhwānd. *Rauḍat al-ṣafā'*. Ed. Riḍā Qulī Khān. 6 vols. Tehrān, 1270–4/1853–6.

Muḥammad b. Ibrāhīm. *Ta'rīkh-i Saljūqiyān-i Kirmān*. Ed. M. T. Houtsma in *Recueil de Textes*, I. Leiden, 1886.

Anon. *Mujmal al-tawārīkh wa'l-qiṣaṣ*. Ed. Malik al-Shu'arā' Bahār. Tehrān, 1318/1939.

Narshakhī. *Ta'rīkh-i Bukhārā*. Ed. Mudarris Riḍawī. Tehrān, ?1939. Tr. R. N. Frye: *The History of Bukhara*. Cambridge, Mass., 1954.

Nasawī. *Histoire du Sultan Djelal ed-Din Mankobirti*. Ed. and tr. O. Houdas. Publications de l'École des Langues Vivantes Orientales, III. vols. IX–X. Paris, 1891–5.

Nāṣir-i Khusrau. *Safar-Nāma*. Ed. Muḥammad Dabīr Siyāqī. Tehrān, 1335/1956.

Niẓām al-Mulk. *Siyāsat-Nāma*. Ed. M. Qazvīnī and M. M. Chahārdihī. Tehrān, 1334/1956. Tr. H. Darke: *The Book of Government, or Rules for Kings*. London, 1960.

Niẓāmī 'Arūḍī Samarqandī. *Chahār Maqāla*. Ed. M. Qazvīnī and M. Mu'īn. Tehrān, 1333/1954. Revised tr., E. G. Browne in G.M.S., XI, no. ii. London, 1921.

Rāvandī. *Rāḥat al-ṣudūr wa-āyat al-surūr*. Ed. Muḥammad Iqbāl. G.M.S., n.s. II. London, 1921.

Sibṭ b. al-Jauzī. *Mir'āt al-zamān fī ta'rīkh al-a'yān.* 2 vols. Hyderabad, 1370–1/1951–2.

Subkī, Tāj al-Dīn. *Ṭabaqāt al-Shāfi'iyya al-kubrā.* 6 vols. Cairo, 1323–4/1905–6.

Anon. *Ta'rīkh-i Sīstān.* Ed. Malik al-Shu'arā' Bahār. Tehrān, 1314/1935.

Tha'ālibī. *Laṭā'if al-Ma'ārif.* Ed. P. de Jong. Leiden, 1867. Tr. C. E. Bosworth: *The Book of Curious and Entertaining Information.* Edinburgh, 1968.

'Utbī. *al-Ta'rīkh al-Yamīnī.* With commentary of Shaikh Manīnī. Cairo, 1286/1869.

Yāqūt. *Mu'jam al-buldān.* Beirut, 1374–6/1955–7.

Ẓahīr al-Dīn Mar'ashī. *Ta'rīkh-i Ṭabaristān u Rūyān u Māzandarān.* Ed. A. Shāyāl. Tehrān, 1333/1954.

Ẓahīr al-Dīn Nīshāpūrī. *Saljūq-Nāma.* Tehrān, 1332/1954.

2. *Selected secondary sources*

Allen, W. E. D. *A History of the Georgian People.* London, 1932.

Amedroz, H. F. "The Marwānid dynasty at Mayyāfāriqīn in the tenth and eleventh centuries A.D." *Journal of the Royal Asiatic Society.* 1903.

—— "The assumption of the title Shâhanshâh by Buwayhid rulers". *Numismatic Chronicle*, ser. 4, vol. v, 1905.

Arberry, A. J. *Classical Persian literature.* London, 1958.

Aubin, J. "La Ruine de Sîrâf et les Routes due Golfe Persique aux XIe et XIIe Siècles." *Cahiers de Civilisation Médiévale*, vol. II, no. 3. 1959.

Barthold, V. V. *Turkestan down to the Mongol invasion.* Gibb Memorial Series, n.s. v. 2nd ed. London, 1928.

—— *Histoire des Turcs d'Asie Centrale.* Paris, 1945.

—— "A Short history of Turkestan" in *Four Studies on the History of Central Asia*, I. Leiden, 1956.

—— "History of the Semirechye" in *Four Studies*, I.

—— "A history of the Turkman people" in *Four Studies*, III. Leiden, 1962.

—— "Shirwānshāh" and "Takash". *Encyclopaedia of Islam.* 1st ed. Leiden, London, 1913–42.

Bosworth, C. E. "Ghaznevid military organisation." *Der Islam*, vol. XXXVI. 1960.

—— "The early Islamic history of Ghūr". *Central Asiatic Journal*, vol. VI. 1961.

—— "The imperial policy of the early Ghaznawids." *Islamic Studies, Journal of the Central Institute of Islamic Research*, vol. I, no. 3. 1962.

—— "The titulature of the early Ghaznavids." *Oriens*, vol. XV. 1962.

—— "Early sources for the history of the first four Ghaznavid sultans (977–1041)." *Islamic Quarterly*, vol. VII. 1963.

—— *The Ghaznavids: their Empire in Afghanistan and Eastern Iran 994–1040.* Edinburgh, 1963.

—— "On the chronology of the Ziyārids in Gurgān and Ṭabaristān." *Der Islam*, vol. XL. 1964.

—— "Ghazna" and "Ghūrids". *Encyclopaedia of Islam.* 2nd ed. Leiden, London, 1960– .

Bosworth, C. E. *The Islamic Dynasties, a Chronological and Genealogical Survey.* Edinburgh, 1967.

Bowen, H. "The last Buwayhids." *J.R.A.S.* 1929.

—— "The *sar-gudhasht-i sayyidnā*, the 'Tale of the Three Schoolfellows' and the *wasaya* of the Nizām al-Mulk." *J.R.A.S.* 1931.

—— "Notes on some early Seljuqid Viziers." *Bulletin of the School of Oriental and African Studies*, vol. xx, 1957.

—— "Niẓām al-Mulk." *Encyclopaedia of Islam.* 1st ed.

Browne, E. G. *A Literary History of Persia*, 4 vols. London, Cambridge, 1902–24.

—— "Account of a rare manuscript history of Iṣfahán." *Journal of the Royal Asiatic Society*, 1901.

—— "Account of a rare, if not unique, manuscript history of the Seljúqs..." *J.R.A.S.* 1902.

Cahen, C. "La Campagne de Mantzikert d'après les sources musulmanes." *Byzantion*, vol. IX. 1934.

—— "La Premiere Pénétration Turque en Asie-Mineure." *Byzantion*, vol. XVIII. 1948.

—— "Les Tribus Turques d'Asie Occidentale pendant la période Seljukide." *Wiener Zeitschrift für die Kunde des Morgenlandes*, vol. LI. 1948–52.

—— "Le Malik-Nameh et l'histoire des origines Seljukides." *Oriens*, vol. II. 1949.

—— "L'évolution de l'Iqtaʿ du IXe au XIIIe siècle. Contribution à une histoire comparée des sociétés médiévales." *Annales: Économies, Sociétés, Civilisations*, vol. VIII. 1953.

—— "The Turkish invasions: the Selchükids." *A History of the Crusades.* Vol. I: *The First Hundred Years.* Ed. K. M. Setton and M. W. Baldwin. Philadelphia, 1955.

—— *Mouvements populaires et Autonomisme Urbain dans l'Asie Musulmane du Moyen Âge.* Leiden, 1959. (Originally in *Arabica*, vol. v. 1958; vol. VI. 1959.)

—— "The historiography of the Seljuqid period." *Historians of the Middle East.* Ed. B. Lewis and P. M. Holt. London, 1962.

—— "The Turks in Iran and Anatolia before the Mongol invasions." *A History of the Crusades.* Vol. II: *The Later Crusades, 1189–1311.* Ed. R. L. Wolf and H. W. Hazard. Philadelphia, 1962.

—— "L'Iran du Nord-Ouest face à l'expansion seljukide, d'après une source inédite." *Mélanges d'Orientalisme offerts à Henri Massé.* Tehrān, 1963.

—— "Qutlumush et Ses Fils avant l'Asie Mineure." *Der Islam*, vol. XXXIX. 1964.

—— "Alp Arslan", "Atabak", "Barkyāruḳ", and "Buwayhids'. *Encyc. of Islam.* 2nd. ed.

Frye, R. N. "The Samanids: a little-known dynasty". *Muslim World*, vol. XXXIV. 1944.

—— "Remarks on Baluchi history". *Central Asiatic Journal*, vol. VI. 1961.

Frye, R. N. and A. M. Sayïlï. "Turks in the Middle East before the Saljuqs." *Journal of the American Oriental Society*, vol. LXIII. 1943.
Grousset, R. *Histoire de l'Arménie des origines à 1071*. Paris, 1947.
—— *L'Empire des steppes*. 4th ed. Paris, 1952.
Haig, Sir T. W. "Maḥmūd of Ghazna" and "Salghurids". *Encyc. of Islam*. 1st ed.
Hodgson, M. G. *The Order of Assassins; the Struggle of the Early Nizârî Ismâ'îlîs against the Islamic World*. The Hague, 1955.
Honigmann, E. *Die Ostgrenze des Byzantinischen Reichs von 363 bis 1071 nach griechischen, arabischen, syrischen und armenischen Quellen* (= A. A. Vasiliev. *Byzance et les Arabes*, vol. III). Brussels, 1935.
Houtsma, M. T. "Zur Geschichte der Selǵuqen von Kermân". *Zeitschrift der Deutschen Morgenländischen Gesellschaft*, vol. XXXIX. 1885.
—— "Die Ghuzzenstämme." *W.Z.K.M.*, vol. II. 1888.
—— "The death of the Niẓām al-Mulk and its consequences". *Journal of Indian History*, ser. 3, vol. II. 1924.
—— "Some remarks on the history of the Saljuks." *Acta Orientalia*, vol. III. 1924.
—— "Ildegiz", "Malikshāh", "Muḥammad b. Malikshāh", "Maḥmūd b. Muḥammad b. Malikshāh", "Ṭughril II b. Arslan", and "Ṭughril b. Muḥammad". *Encyc. of Islam*. 1st ed.
Huart, C. "Les Ziyârides.' *Mémoires de l'Academie des Inscriptions et Belles-Lettres*, vol. XLII. 1922.
—— "Les Mosâfirides de l'Adherbaïdjân." *Essays to E. G. Browne*. Cambridge, 1922.
—— "Kākōyids." *Encyc. of Islam*. 1st ed.
Kabir, M. *The Buwayhid Dynasty of Baghdad*. Calcutta, 1964.
Kafesoğlu, I. "Doğu Anadoluya ilk Selçuklu akïnï (1015–21) ve tarihî ehemmiyeti." *Köprülü Armağanï*. Istanbul, 1953.
—— *Sultan Melikşah devrinde Büyük Selçuklu imparatorluğu*. Istanbul, 1953.
—— "Selçuklu tarihinin meseleleri." *Belleten*, vol. XIX. 1955.
—— "Büyük Selçuklu Veziri Nizâmü'l-Mülk'ün eseri Siyâsetnâme ve türkçe tercümesi." *Türkiyat Mecmuasï*, vol. XII. 1955.
—— *Harezmşahlar devleti tarihi (485–617/1092–1229)*. Ankara, 1956.
Kasravī, Aḥmad. *Shahriyārān-i gum-nām*. 3 vols. Tehran, 1928–30.
Khan, Gulam Mustafa. "A history of Bahram Shah of Ghaznin." *Islamic Culture*, vol. XXIII. 1949.
Köprülü, M. F. "Afshār". *Encyc. of Islam*. 2nd ed.
Köymen, M. A. "Büyük Selçuklular Imparatorluğunda Oğuz Isyanı", and "Büyük Selçuklu Imparatorluğu Tarihinde Oğuz istilâsı." *Ankara Üniversitesi Dil ve Tarih-Coğrafya Fakültesi Dergisi*, vol. V. 1947.
—— *Büyük Selçuklu Imparatorluğu tarihi*. Vol. II: *Ikinci Imparatorluk Devri*. Ankara, 1954.
Krenkow, F. "al-Ṭughrā'ī." *Encyc. of Islam*. 1st ed.
Lambton, A. K. S. *Landlord and Peasant in Persia*. London, 1953.
—— "The Administration of Sanjar's Empire as illustrated in the *'Atabat al-Kataba*." *Bulletin of the School of Oriental and African Studies*, vol. XX. 1957.

Laurent, J. *Byzance et les Turcs Seldjoucides dans l'Asie Occidentale jusqu'en 1081.* Nancy, 1913.
—— "Des Grecs aux Croisés; Étude sur l'Histoire d'Edesse entre 1071 et 1098." *Byzantion*, vol. I. 1924.
Le Strange, G. *The Lands of the Eastern Caliphate.* Cambridge, 1905.
—— *Description of the Province of Fars in Persia at the Beginning of the Fourteenth Century A.D.* London, 1912.
Makdisi, G. "Notes on Hilla and the Mazyadids in Mediaeval Islam." *Journal of the American Oriental Society*, vol. LXXIV. 1954.
—— "Muslim institutions of learning in eleventh-century Baghdad." *Bulletin of the School of Oriental and African Studies*, vol. XXIV. 1961.
Maricq, A. and G. Wiet. "Le Minaret de Djam, la Découverte de la Capitale des Sultans Ghorides (XIIe–XIIIe siècles)." *Méms. de la Délégation Archéologique Française en Afghanistan*, XVI. Paris, 1959.
Marquart, J. "Ērānšahr nach der Geographie des Ps. Moses Khorenacʿi." *Abh. der Königl. Gesell. der Wissenschaften zu Göttingen*, Phil.-Hist. Kl., N.F. vol. III, no. 2. 1901.
Miles, G. C. "The coinage of the Kākwayhid dynasty." *Iraq*, vol. V. 1938.
Minorsky, V. *La Domination des Daïlamites.* Paris, 1932.
—— *Studies in Caucasian History.* London, 1953.
—— *A History of Sharvān and Darband in the 10th–11th Centuries.* Cambridge, 1958.
—— "Kurds", "Marāgha", "Musāfirids", "Tabrīz", and "Tiflis", *Encyc. of Islam.* 1st ed.; "Aḥmadīlīs" and "Daylam", *Encyc. of Islam.* 2nd ed.
—— and C. Cahen. "Le recueil transcaucasien de Masʿūd b. Nāmdār (début du VIe/XIIe siècle." *J.A.*, vol. CCXXXVII. 1949.
Nāẓim, M. *The Life and Times of Sulṭān Maḥmūd of Ghazna.* Cambridge, 1931.
—— "The Pand-Nāmah of Subuktigīn." *J.R.A.S.*, 1933.
Nöldeke, T. *Das Iranische Nationalepos.* 2nd ed. Berlin, Leipzig, 1921.
Pritsak, O. "Karachanidische Streitfragen 1–4." *Oriens*, vol. III. 1950.
—— "Von den Karluk zu den Karachaniden." *Zeitschrift der Deutschen Morgenländischen Gesellschaft*, vol. CI. 1951.
—— "Āl-i Burhān." *Der Islam*, vol. XXX. 1952.
—— "Der Untergang des Reiches des Oğuzischen Yabğu." *Köprülü Armağanї.* Istanbul, 1953.
—— "Karahanlïlar." *Islam Ansiklopedisi.* Istanbul, 1941–? German version: "Die Karachaniden." *Der Islam*, vol. XXXI. 1953–4.
Qazvīnī, Mīrzā Muḥammad. "Masʿud-i Saʿd-i Salman." *J.R.A.S.*, 1905, 1906.
Rabino di Borgomale, H. L. "Les Dynasties du Māzandarān de l'an 50 avant l'Hégire à l'an 1006 de l'Hégire (572 à 1597–8) d'après les Chroniques Locales." *J.A.*, vol. CCXXVIII. 1936.
—— "L'Histoire du Mâzandarân." *J.A.*, vol. CCXXXIV. 1943–5.
—— "Les dynasties locales du Gîlân et du Daylam." *J.A.*, vol. CCXXXVII. 1949.
Rippe, K. "Über den Sturz Nizām-ul-Mulks." *Köprülü Armağanї.* Istanbul, 1953.

Ross, Sir E. D. "On three Muhammadan dynasties in northern Persia in the tenth and eleventh centuries." *Asia Major*, vol. II. 1925.
—— "Shaddādids." *Encyc. of Islam*. 1st ed.
Sachau, E. "Zur Geschichte und Chronologie von Khwârazm." *Sitzungs-Berichte der Wiener Akademie der Wissenschaften*, Phil.-Hist. C., vol. LXXXIII, 1873; vol. LXXIV, 1873.
Sanaullah, M. F. *The Decline of the Saljūqid Empire*. Calcutta, 1938.
Shafi, I. M. "Fresh Light on the Ghaznavîds." *Islamic Culture*, vol. XII. 1938.
Sourdel, D. *Inventaire des Monnaies Musulmanes Anciennes du Musée de Caboul*. Damascus, 1953.
Spuler, B. *Iran in früh-islamischer Zeit*. Wiesbaden, 1952.
—— "Ghaznavids." *Encyc. of Islam*. 2nd ed.
Taeschner, F. "Das Futuwwa-Rittertum des Islamischen Mittelalters." *Beiträge zur Arabistik, Semitistik und Islamwissenschaft*. Leipzig, 1944.
—— "al-Nāṣir." *Encyc. of Islam*. 1st ed.
Tibawi, A. L. "Origin and character of *al-Madrasah*." *B.S.O.A.S.*, vol. XXV. 1961.
Togan, A. Z. V. *Umumî Türk Tarihine Giriş*. Istanbul, 1946.
—— *The Khorezmians and their Civilization*. Preface to Fasc. Ed. of the Glossary to Zamakhsharī's *Muqaddimāt al-Adab*. Istanbul, 1951.
—— and W. Henning. "Über die Sprache und Kultur der alten Chwarezmier." *Z.D.M.G.*, vol. XC. 1936.
Tolstov, S. P. *Auf den Spuren der altchoresmischen Kultur*. Berlin, 1953.
Wittek, P. "Deux chapîtres de l'histoire des Turcs de Roum." *Byzantion*, vol. XI. 1936.
Yïnanç, Mükrimin Halil. *Anadolu'nun Fethi*. Istanbul, 1944.
Zettersteen, K. V. "Ḳïzïl Arslan", "Pehlewān Muḥammad b. Ildegiz", "Sandjar", "Sulaimān b. Ḳutulmush", and "Zengī 'Ilmād al-Dīn". *Encyc. of Islam*. 1st ed. Leiden, London, 1913–42.

CHAPTER 2

Amedroz, H. F. "The mazalim jurisdiction in the *Ahkam sultaniyya* of Mawardi." *J.R.A.S.*, 1911.
Binder, L. "Al-Ghazali's theory of Islamic government." *Muslim World*, vol. XLV. 1955.
Bowen, H. C. "Niẓām al-Mulk." *Encyclopaedia of Islam*, 1st ed.
Cahen, C. "L'évolution de l'iqta' due ixe au xiiie siècle." *Annales E.S.C.*, vol. VIII. 1953.
Ghazālī. *Ghazali's Book of Counsel for Kings* (*Naṣīḥat al-Mulūk*), transl. F. R. C. Bagley. Oxford, 1964.
Gibb, Sir H. A. R. "An interpretation of Islamic history", in *Studies on the Civilization of Islam*, ed. Stanford J. Shaw and William R. Polk. London, 1962.
—— "Al-Mawardi's theory of the Caliphate." *Ibid.*

Horst, H. *Die Staatsverwaltung der Grosselǧuqen und Ḫorazmšahs (1038–1231)*. Wiesbaden, 1964.
Houtsma, M. T. "The death of Nizam al-Mulk and its consequences." *Journal of Indian History*, vol. 3. 1924.
Ibn Khallikān. *Wafayāt al-aʿyān*, transl. de Slane, 4 vols. Paris and London, 1842–71.
Iqbāl, ʿAbbās. *Vizārat dar ʿahd-i salāṭīn-i buzurg-i Saljūqī*. Tehran, 1959/60.
Kai Kā'ūs b. Iskandar. *A Mirror for Princes (the Qābūs Nāmeh)*, transl. R. Levy. London, 1951.
Lambton, A. K. S. "Quis Custodiet Custodes: Some Reflections on the Persian Ṭheory of Government." *Studia Islamica*, fascs. v and vi.
—— "Justice in the medieval Persian theory of kingship." *Studia Islamica*, fasc. xvii.
—— "Reflections on the *iqṭāʿ*", in *Arabic and Islamic studies in honor of Hamilton A. R. Gibb*, ed. George Makdisi. Leiden, 1965.
—— "The administration of Sanjar's Empire as illustrated in the *ʿAṭabat al-Kataba*." *B.S.O.A.S.*, vol. xx. 1957.
—— "The theory of kingship in the *Naṣīḥat ul-Mulūk* of Ghazālī." *The Islamic Quarterly*, vol. I, 1954.
Makdisi, G. "Muslim institutions of learning in eleventh century Baghdad." *B.S.O.A.S.*, vol. XXIV. 1961.
Margoliouth, D. S. "The Devil's delusion, by Ibn al-Jauzī." *Islamic Culture*, vols. IX, X, XI, XII, XIX, XX, XXI and XXII (1935–48).
Massignon, L. "Les Medresehs de Baghdad." *B.I.F.A.O.*, vol. VII. 1909.
Nāṣir-i Khusrau. *Sefer Nameh, Relation du Voyage de Nasseri Khosrau*, transl. C. Schefer. Paris, 1881.
Niẓām al-Mulk. *Siasset Nameh, Traité de Gouvernement*, transl. C. Schefer. Paris, 1893.
Ribera y Tarragó, J. "Origen del Colegio Nidamí de Baghdad." *Disertaciones y opúsculos*, vol. I. 1928.
Sanaullah, M. F. *The decline of the Saljuqid Empire*. Calcutta, 1938.
Siddiqi, Amir Husain. "Caliphate and kingship in medieval Islam", in *Islamic Culture*, vols. X/3 and XI/1.
Talas, Asad. *La madrasa Nizamiyya et son histoire*. Paris, 1939.

For original sources in Arabic and Persian see footnotes to the text.

CHAPTER 3

In the preparation of this chapter I have drawn amply from various sections of the valuable work by Dhabīḥu'llāh Ṣafā, *Ta'rīkh-i Adabīyāt dar Irān*, vol. II. Tehrān, 1336/1957.

Important sources for the religious history of Saljuq Iran are:

Niẓām al-Mulk. *Siyāsat-Nāma*. Tr. Schefer. Paris, 1891, 1897. New ed.: Mudarrisī. Tehrān, 1335/1956. Russian tr.: B. N. Zakhoder. Moskow–Leningrad, 1949; English tr.: H. Darke. London, 1960.

Naṣīr al-Dīn Abu'l-Rashīd 'Abd al-Jalīl b. Abi'l-Ḥusain al-Qazvīnī al-Rāzī. *Kitāb al-naqḍ*, ed. Muḥaddith. Tehrān, 1331/1952.

Sayyid Murtaḍā Rāzī. *Tabṣirat al-'awāmm fī ma'rifa maqālāt al-anām*. Ed. A. Iqbāl. Tehrān, 1313/1934.

Rāvandi. *Rāḥat al-ṣudūr*. Ed. M. Iqbāl. Leiden, 1921.

Ibn al-Jauzī. *Talbīs Iblīs*. Cairo, 1928.

Shihābu, a'l-Dīn Suhravardī. *Opera Metaphysica et Mystica*. Ed. Henry Corbin. Vol. I. Istanbul, 1945: vol. II, Tehrān, 1952.

Further references are given in the body of this chapter. There is an important bibliography, though devoted chiefly to the period immediately preceding the Saljuqs, in: B. Spuler. *Iran in früh-islamischer Zeit*. Wiesbaden, 1952. (See especially pp. 133–224 and the map of religions at the end of the volume.)

CHAPTER 4

ABBREVIATIONS

B.S.O.A.S.	*Bulletin of the School of Oriental and African Studies.*
C.A.J.	*Central Asiatic Journal.*
H.J.A.S.	*Harvard Journal of Asiatic Studies.*
J. A.	*Journal Asiatique.*
J.R.A.S.	*Journal of the Royal Asiatic Society.*
J.S.S.	*Journal of Semitic Studies.*

Abū Bakr al-Quṭbī al-Ahrī. *Ta'rīkh-i Shaikh Uwais*. Ed. and tr. J. B. van Loon. The Hague, 1954.

Abu'l-Fidā. *Ta'rīkh Ismā'īl Abi'l-Fidā*. 4 vols. Constantinople, 1869–70.

Admiralty, Naval Intelligence Division. *Persia*. 1945.

Alizade, A. A. *See* Rashīd al-Dīn.

Arends, A. K. *See* Rashīd al-Dīn.

Atalay, B. *See* Kāshgharī.

Barhebraeus. *The Chronography of Gregory Abû'l Faraj*. 2 vols. Tr. and ed. E. A. W. Budge. London, 1932.

Barthold, W. *Four Studies on the History of Central Asia*. Tr. V. and T. Minorsky. Vol. I. Leiden, 1956.

—— *Turkestan down to the Mongol Invasion*. London, 1928.

Blake, R. P. *See* Grigor of Akner.

Blochet, E. *See* Rashīd al-Dīn.

Borghezio, G. "Un episodio delle relazioni tra la Santa Sede e i Mongoli (1274)." *Roma*, vol. XIV, no. 11. 1936.

Boyle, J. A. "The death of the last 'Abbāsid Caliph: a contemporary Muslim account." *J.S.S.* vol. VI, no. 2. 1961.

—— "A form of horse sacrifice amongst the 13th- and 14th-century Mongols." *C.A.J.*, vol. X, nos. 3–4. 1965.

—— "*Iru* and *Maru* in the *Secret History of the Mongols*." *H.J.A.S.*, vol. XVII, nos. 3 and 4. 1954.

Boyle, J. A. "The journey of Het'um I, King of Little Armenia, to the court of the Great Khan Möngke." *C.A.J.*, vol. IX, no. 3. 1964.

—— "Kirakos of Ganjak on the Mongols." *C.A.J.*, vol. VIII, no. 3. 1963.

—— "The longer introduction to the *Zīj-i-Īlkhānī* of Naṣīr-ad-Dīn Ṭūsī." *J.S.S.*, vol. VIII, no. 2. 1963.

—— "The Mongol commanders in Afghanistan and India according to the *Ṭabaqāt-i-Nāṣirī* of Jūzjānī." *Islamic Studies*, vol. II, no. 2. 1963.

—— "On the titles given in Juvainī to certain Mongolian princes." *H.J.A.S.*, vol. XIX, nos. 3 and 4. 1956.

—— *See also* Juvainī.

Bretschneider, E. *Medieval Researches from Eastern Asiatic Sources.* 2 vols. London, 1888.

Browne, E. G. *A Literary History of Persia.* Vol. III. Cambridge, 1928.

Budge, E. A. W. *See* Barhebraeus.

Carpini. *Histoire des Mongols.* Tr. and ed. Dom J. Becquet and L. Hambis Paris, 1965.

—— *The Tartar Relation.* Tr. G. D. Painter in *The Vinland Map and the Tartar Relation* by R. A. Skelton, etc. New Haven and London, 1965.

Cattenoz, H. G. *Tables de concordance des ères chrétienne et hégirienne.* 2nd ed. Rabat, 1954.

Ch'ang-ch'un. *The Travels of an Alchemist.* Tr. A. Waley. London, 1931.

Doerfer, G. *Türkische und mongolische Elemente im Neupersischen.* Vols. I–III. Wiesbaden, 1963, 1965 and 1967.

Eghbal, Abbas. *Ta'rīkh-i mufaṣṣal-i Īrān.* Vol. I, 2nd ed. Tehrān, 1341/1962.

Faṣīḥ, Aḥmad. *Mujmal-i Faṣīḥī.* Ed. Maḥmūd Farrukh. 3 vols. Mashhad, 1960–2.

Fischel, W. J. "Azarbaijan in Jewish history." *Proceedings of the American Academy for Jewish Research*, vol. XXII. 1953.

—— "On the Iranian paper currency الچاو of the Mongol period." *J.R.A.S.*, 1939.

—— "Über Raschid ad-Daulas jüdischen Ursprung." *Montaschrift für Geschichte und Wissenschaft des Judentums*, vol. LXXX. 1937.

Frye, R. N. *See* Grigor of Akner.

Gibb, H. A. R. *See* Ibn Baṭṭūṭa.

Gottschalk, H. L. *Al-Malik al-Kāmil von Egypten und seine Zeit.* Wiesbaden, 1958.

Grigor of Akner. *History of the Nation of the Archers.* Ed. and tr. R. P. Blake and R. N. Frye. Cambridge, Mass., 1954.

Grousset, R. *Le Conquérant du monde.* Paris, 1944.

—— *L'Empire des steppes.* Paris, 1939.

Haenisch, E. *See Secret History of the Mongols.*

Ḥāfiẓ-i Abrū. *Dhail-i Jāmi' al-Tawārīkh.* Ed. Khān-Bābā Bayānī. Tehrān, 1939.

Haithon. *Flos Historiarum Terre Orientes* in *Recueil des Historiens des Croisades, Documents arméniens.* Paris, 1906.

Hambis, L. *See Yüan shih* and *Sheng-wu ch'in-cheng lu.*

Hammer-Purgstall, J. von. *See* Vaṣṣāf.

Harva, U. *Die religiösen Vorstellungen der altaischen Völker*. Helsinki, 1938.

Howorth, H. H. *History of the Mongols*. 4 vols. London, 1876–1927.

Ibn al-Athīr. *Chronicon, quod perfectissimum inscribitur*. Ed. K. J. Tornberg. Vol. XII. Leiden, 1853.

Ibn Baṭṭūṭa. *The Travels of Ibn Baṭṭūṭa*. Tr. H. A. R. Gibb, vol. II. Cambridge, 1962.

Ibn Bībī. *Die Seltschukengeschichte des Ibn Bībī*. Tr. Herbert W. Duda. Copenhagen, 1959.

Ibn Faḍlān. *Ibn Faḍlāns Reisebericht*. Ed. and tr. A. Zeki Validi Togan. Leipzig, 1939.

Jahn, K. "Das iranische Papiergeld." *Archiv Orientální*, vol. x. 1938.

—— *Rashīd al Dīn's History of India*. The Hague, 1965.

—— *See* Rashīd al-Dīn.

Jūzjānī. *Ṭabaḳāt-i-Nāṣirī*. Tr. H. G. Raverty. 2 vols. London, 1881.

—— *Ṭabaqāt-i-Naṣirī*. Ed. H. Ḥabībī. Vol. II. Kabul, 1964.

Kāshgharī. *Divanü Luğat-it-Türk*. Tr. B. Atalay. 3 vols. Ankara, 1939–41.

Kirakos Gandzakets'i. *Patmut'yun Hayots'*. Ed. K. A. Melik'-Ohanjanyan. Erevan, 1961.

Lane-Poole, Stanley. *The Mohammadan Dynasties*. London, 1894.

Lessing, F. D. (ed.). *Mongolian-English Dictionary*. Berkeley and Los Angeles, 1960.

Le Strange, G. *The Lands of the Eastern Caliphate*. Cambridge, 1930.

—— *Palestine under the Moslems*. London, 1890.

—— *See also* Mustaufī.

Loon, J. B. van. *See* Abū Bakr al-Quṭbī al-Ahrī.

Maqrīzī. *Histoire des sultans mamlouks de l'Egypte*. Tr. M. E. Quatremère. 2 vols. Paris, 1837–45.

Minorsky, V. *A History of Sharvan and Darband in the 10th–11th Century*. Cambridge, 1958.

—— "Geographical factors in Persian Art." *B.S.O.S.*, vol. IX, no. 3. 1938.

—— *Iranica*. Tehrān, 1964.

—— "A Mongol decree of 720/1320 to the family of Shaikh Zāhid." *B.S.O.A.S.*, vol. XVI, no. 3. 1954.

—— "Mongol place-names in Mukri Kurdistan." *B.S.O.A.S.*, vol. XIX, no. 1. 1957.

—— "Roman and Byzantine Campaigns in Atropatene." *B.S.O.A.S.*, vol. XI, no. 2. 1944.

—— "La Perse au Moyen Age." In *Proceedings* of XII Convegno "Volta", Accademia Nazionale dei Lincei. Rome, 1957.

—— *Studies in Caucasian History*. London, 1953.

Mīrkhwānd. *Rauḍat al-ṣafā*. Vol. v. Tehrān, 1960.

Mostaert, A. and Cleaves, F. W. *Les Lettres de 1289 et 1305 des ilkhan Aryun et Öljeitü*. Cambridge, Mass., 1962.

—— "Trois documents mongols des Archives secrètes vaticanes." *H.J.A.S.*, vol. XV, nos. 3 and 4. 1952.

Moule, A. C. *Christians in China before the Year 1550*. London, 1930.
Mustaufī. *The Geographical Part of the Nuzhat-al-Qulūb*. Tr. G. le Strange. Leiden and London, 1919.
Nasawī. *Histoire du Sultan Djelal ed-Dīn Mankobirti*. Ed. and tr. O. Houdas. 2 vols. Paris, 1891–5.
d'Ohsson, C. *Histoire des Mongols*. 4 vols. The Hague and Amsterdam, 1834–5.
Pelliot, P. *Notes on Marco Polo*. 2 vols. Paris, 1959 and 1963.
—— *Notes sur l'histoire de la Horde d'Or*. Paris, 1950.
—— See *Secret History of the Mongols*.
Petech, L. "Les Marchands italiens dans l'empire mongol." *J.A.*, vol. CCL. 1962.
Polo, Marco. *The Book of Ser Marco Polo*. Tr. and ed. Sir Henry Yule. 3rd ed. by Henri Cordier. 2 vols. London, 1903.
Poppe, Nicholas. *Grammar of Written Mongolian*. Wiesbaden, 1954.
Rashīd al-Dīn. *Djami el-Tévarikh*. Vol. II. Ed. E. Blochet. Leiden and London, 1911.
—— *Dzami-ät-Tävarikh*. Vol. III. Ed. A. A. Alizade, tr. A. K. Arends. Baku, 1957.
—— *Histoire des Francs*. Ed. and tr. K. Jahn. Leiden, 1951.
—— *Geschichte Ġāzān-Ḫāns*. Ed. K. Jahn. Leiden, 1940.
—— *Sbornik letopisei*. Vol. I, part 2. Tr. O. I. Smirnova. Moscow–Leningrad, 1952. Vol. II. Tr. Y. P. Verkhovsky. Moscow–Leningrad, 1960.
—— *Ta'rīḫ-i mubārak-i Ġāzānī* (History of the Īl-Khāns Abaqa to Geikhatu). Ed. K. Jahn, Prague, 1941.
Richard, J. "Le Début des relations entre la Papauté et les Mongols en Perse." *J.A.*, vol. CCXXXVII. 1949.
Rubruck. *The Journey of William of Rubruck to the Eastern Parts of the World*. Tr. W. W. Rockhill. London, 1900.
Ṣaifī. *Ta'rīkh-Nāma-yi Harāt*. Ed. M. Z. Siddiqi. Calcutta, 1944.
Secret History of the Mongols. Die Geheime Geschichte der Mongolen. Tr. E. Haenisch. 2nd ed. Leipzig, 1948.
—— *L'Histoire secrète des Mongols*. Tr. P. Pelliot. Paris, 1949.
—— *See also* Waley, A.
Sheng-wu ch'in-cheng lu. Histoire des campagnes de Gengis-Khan. Tr. and ed. P. Pelliot and L. Hambis. Vol. I. Leiden, 1951.
Smirnova, O. I. *See* Rashīd al-Dīn.
Spuler, B. *Die Goldene Horde*. 2nd ed. Wiesbaden, 1965.
—— *Die Mongolen in Iran*. 2nd ed. Berlin, 1955.
Togan, A. Z. V. *See* Ibn Faḍlān.
Vaṣṣāf. *Geschichte Wassaf's*. Ed. and tr. J. von Hammer-Purgstall. Vol. I. Vienna, 1856.
—— *Kitāb-i mustaṭāb-i Vaṣṣāf*. Lithograph ed. Bombay, 1852–3.
Verkhovsky, Y. P. *See* Rashīd al-Dīn.
Waley, A. *The Secret History of the Mongols and Other Pieces*. London, 1963.
Wheeler, G. *The Modern History of the Soviet Central Asia*. London, 1964.
Willey, P. R. E. *The Castles of the Assassins*. London, 1963.
Yüan shih. Le chapitre CVII du Yuan che. Ed. and tr. L. Hambis. Leiden, 1945.

CHAPTER 5

Bibliographical information is given throughout the notes to this chapter. Marshall G. S. Hodgson, *Order of Assassins* (discussed in note 1 on p. 423), has been translated into Persian by Farīdūn Badra'ī as *Firqa-yi Ismā'īliyya* (Tabrīz, 1964). The translator had trouble finding the exact equivalent of the English wording, and some of his *hijrī* dates are merely from a date-table and so incorrect, but he worked conscientiously and has made precisions in some details. See now also Bernard Lewis, *The Assassins* (London, 1967).

CHAPTER 6

ABBREVIATIONS

B.G.A.	*Bibliotheca geographorum Arabicorum.*
B.S.O.A.S.	*Bulletin of the School of Oriental and African Studies.*
G.M.S.	Gibb Memorial Series.
E.I.	*Encyclopaedia of Islam.*
H.S.	Works issued by the Hakluyt Society.
Z.D.M.G.	*Zeitschrift der Deutschen Morgenländischen Gesellschaft.*
S.S.I.A.	Sbornik statei po istorii Azerbaijana, Baku.
L.	Leningrad.
M.	Moscow.
SPb	St Petersburg.

Primary sources

Abū Bakr al-Quṭbī al-Ahrī. *Ta'rīkh-i Shaikh Uwais.* Ed. and tr. J. B. van Loon. The Hague, 1954.

Aflākī, Afḍāl ad-Dīn. *Aflaki, Manaqib al-arifin. Cl. Huart, Les saints des derviches tourneurs*, vol. I, 1918 (Fr. transl.).

Barbaro, Josafa. *Travels to Tana and Persia.* Ed. Lord Stanley of Alderley... Hakluyt series, vol. 49, part I. London, 1873.

Burhān-i Qāṭi'. *Kitāb-i Burhān-e Qāṭi' ta'līf-i Moḥammad Ḥusain.* Calcutta, 1233/1818 (Pers.).

Ch'ang-ch'un. *Si Yu-tsy, puteshestvie na Zapad. Perevod s primechaniyami arkhimandrita Palladia Kafarova. Trudy chlenov Russkoi dukhovnoi missii v Pekine*, vol. IV. SPb, 1866.

Chao Ju-kua, His Work of the Chinese Trade in the XII and XIII Centuries... Tr. E. Hirth and W. W. Rockhill. SPb, 1912.

Clavijo, R. G. *Dnevnik puteshestvya ko dvoru Timura* ("Diary of a visit to the court of Timur"). Ed. I. I. Sreznevsky. SPb, 1881. (Spanish text and Russian tr.)

Dastūr al-kātib. See Muḥammad b. Hindūshāh-i Nakhchivānī.

Daulatshāh. *The Tadhkirat al-shu 'ará of Dawlatsháh.* Ed. E. G. Browne. London–Leiden, 1901.

Fāḍil Haravī. *Irshād al-zirā'a*. Ed. 'Abd al-Ghaffār Najm al-Daula. Tehrān, 1323/1905 (Pers. text).

Falāḥa. *Kitāb-i 'ilm-i falāhat u zirā'at, ta'līf-i shakhṣ-i 'ālim va 'āmil va siyāhī dar 'ahd-i Ghāzān Khān*. Ed. 'Abd al-Ghaffār Najm al-Daula. Tehrān, 1323/1905 (Pers. text, lithogr.).

Firdausī. *Shāh-Nāma. J. Mohl, Chah-nama, édition complète*, vol. I–VII. Paris, 1830–78 (texte pers.).

Grigor of Akner. *History of the Nation of the Archers (Mongols)*... The Armenian text ed. with an English tr. and notes by Robert P. Blake and Richard N. Frye. Cambridge, Mass., 1954.

Gurgānī, Fakhr al-Dīn. *Vīs u Rāmīn*. Ed. M. Minovi. Tehrān, 1314/1935 (Pers. text).

Ḥāfiẓ-i Abrū. Geographical work without title, manuscript of the Oriental Institute of the Academy of Sciences of the Uzbek, No. 5361 (Tashkent).

—— *Dhail-i Jāmi' al-tawārīkh*. Ed. Khānbābā Bayānī. Tehrān, 1317/1938.

Ḥudūd al-'ālam. Manuscript of Tumansky (phototype of the Persian text), with tr. by V. V. Barthold. L., 1930.

—— V. Minorsky, *Ḥudūd al-'ālam*... London, 1937. G.M.S., n.s. XI (English tr. and commentary).

Ḥusain Āvī. *Tarjuma-yi Maḥāsin-i Iṣfahān*. Ed. 'Abbās Iqbāl. Tehrān, 1328/1949 (Pers. text).

Ibn al-Athīr. *Ibn el-Athiri Chronicon*... Ed. C. J. Tornberg, vol. XII. Leiden–Upsala, 1853–64 (Arab. text).

Ibn al-Balkhī. *The Fārs-nāma*... Ed. by le Strange and R. Nicholson. London, 1921. G.M.S. n.s. I (Pers. text).

Ibn Baṭṭūṭa. *Voyages d'Ibn Batoutah*... Par C. Defrémery et le Dr. B. R. Sanquinetti, vol. I–IV. Paris. 1854–9 (texte arabe et traduction française).

Ibn Funduq, Abū-l-Ḥasan Baihaqī. *Ta'rīkh-i Baihaq*. Ed. Aḥmad Bahmanyār. Tehrān, 1317/1938 (Pers. text).

Ibn Isfandiyār. *Ta'rīkh-i Ṭabaristān*. Ed. 'Abbās Iqbāl, vol. I. Tehrān, 1320/1941 (Pers. text).

—— *An abridged translation of the History of Tabaristan...by E. G. Browne*. Leiden–London, 1905. G.M.S., II.

Ibn Rusta. *Kitāb al-a'lāq an-nafīsa*... Ed. M. I. de Goeje. *B.G.A.*, vol. VII. Leiden, 1892 (Arab. text).

Irshād az-zirā'a. See Fāḍil Haravī.

Jūzjānī, Minhāj ad-Dīn. *Tabaqāt-i Nāṣirī*. Ed. W. Nassau-Lees. Calcutta, 1863–4 (Pers. text).

Juvainī, 'Alā' al-Dīn 'Aṭā Malik. *The Ta'ríkh-i-Jahán-Gushá*... Ed. by Mīrzā Muḥammad ibn 'Abd al-Wahhāb-i Qazvīnī, parts I–III. London–Leiden, 1912–37. G.M.D., XVI, 1–3 (Pers. text).

Juvainī (tr. by J. A. Boyle). *The History of the World-Conqueror*, vols. I–II. Manchester, 1958.

Kāshifī, Fakhr al-Dīn 'Ali ibn Ḥusayn-i Vā'iẓ. *Rashaḥāt 'ain al-ḥayāt*. Tashkent 1329/1911 (Pers. text, lithogr.).

Khwandamīr. *Ḥabīb al-siyar*. Bombay, 1253/1857 (Pers. text, lithogr.).
Kirakos Gandzaketsi. M. Brosset, *Deux historiens arméniens...Kirakos de Gandzak...* SPb, 1871 (trad. franç.).
Kitāb-i ʻilm-i falāḥat u zirāʻat. See *Falāḥa*.
Marʻashī, Ẓahīr al-Dīn. *Sehir ed-din's Geschichte von Tabaristan*. Ed. B. Dorn. SPb, 1850 (Pers. text).
Mar Yabalaha. *Histoire de Mar Yabalaha III, patriarche des Nestoriens...*, Traduite du syriaque par J. B. Chabot. Paris, 1895 (trad. franç.).
Muḥammad b. Hindūshāh-i Nakhchivānī. *Dastūr al-kātib fī-taʻyīn al marātib*. Manuscript of the Institute of the Nations of Asia of the Soviet Academy of Sciences, unnumbered. Copy of V. G. Tischenhausen from the Vienna manuscript F-185 (Leningrad: Pers.).
Saifī, Saif, ibn Muḥammad al-Haravī. Saifī, *Ta'rīkh-Nāma-yi Harāt*. Ed. Prof. Muḥammad Zubair al-Ṣiddīqī. Calcutta, 1944 (Pers. text).
Shabāngāraī, Muḥammad. *Majmaʻ al-ansāb*. Manuscript of the Institute of the Nations of Asia, no. 372 (Leningrad: Pers.).
Shams-i Fakhrī. *Shams-i Fachrii Ispahanensis Lexicon Persicum*. Ed. C. Salemann. Kazan, 1887 (Pers. text and indices).
Ṭabarī, Muḥammad ibn Jarīr. *Annales*. Ed. M. J. de Goeje, Ser. I. Leiden, 1879 (Arab. text).
—— Th. Noeldeke, *Geschichte der Perser und Araber zur Zeit der Sasaniden*. Leiden, 1879.
Ta'rīkh-i Baihaq. *See* Ibn Funduq.
Ta'rīkh-i Sīstān. Ed. Malik al-Shuʻarā Bahār. Tehrān, 1314/1935 (Pers. text).
Vaṣṣāf. *Kitāb-i tajziyat al-amṣār wa tazjiyat al-aʻṣār*. Bombay, 1269/1852–3 (Pers. text, lithogr.).
Yāqūt ar-Rūmī al-Hamawī. *Jacut's geographisches Woerterbuch*. Ed. F. Wuestenfeld, Bd. I–IV. Leipzig, 1866–70.

Secondary sources

Alizade, A. A. *K istorii feodal'nīkh otnoshenii v Azerbaidzhane XIII–XIV vv.— terminī "ṭarḥ" i "qopchūr"*. S.S.I.A., vīp. I. Baku, 1949.
—— *K voprosu ob institute ikṭāʻ v Azerbaidzhane, sbornik statei po istorii Azerbaidzhana* (S.S.A.), vīp. I. Baku, 1949.
—— *K voprosu ob institute īndzhū v Azerbaidzhane*. S.S.I.A., vīp. I. Baku. 1949.
—— *K voprosu o polozhenii krstyan v Azerbaidzhane v X–XIV vv*. Trudī Instituta istorii Akad. Nauk Azerb. SSR, vol. III. Baku, 1949.
—— *Sotsial'no-ekonomicheskaya i politicheskaya istorya Azerbaidzhana XIII–XIV vv*. Baku, 1956.
—— *Zemel'naya politika il'khanov v Azerbaidzhane*. Trudī Instituta istorii Akademii Nauk Azerb. SSR, vol. I. Baku, 1947.
Barthold, V. V. "Ḥāfiẓ-i Abrū i ego sochineniya." *Sbornik "al-Muzaffariya" v chest' V. R. Rozena*. SPb, 1897.
—— *Istoriko-geografichesky obzor Irana*. SPb, 1903.
—— *Istoria kulturnoi zhizni Turkestana*. L., 1927.

Barthold, V. V. "K istorii krestyanskikh dvizhenii v Persii." *Sbornik "Iz dalekogo i blizkogo proshlogo v chest' N. I. Kareeva"*. SPb, 1923.

—— "K voprosu o feodalizme v Irane." *Novy Vostok*, no. 28. M., 1930.

—— *Mesto prikaspiyskikh oblastei v istorii musulmanskogo mira*. Baku, 1926.

—— *Persidskaya nadpis' na stene aniyskoi mecheti Manuche*. SPb, 1911.

—— "Tadjik." *E.I.*, vol. IV.

—— *Turkestan down to the Mongol Invasion*. London, 1958; G.M.S., n.s. v.

—— *Turkestan v epokhu Mongol'skogo nashestvia* (Works, vol. I). M., 1963 (2nd Russian edn).

Becker, C. H. "Steuerpacht und Lehnwesen in den moslemischen Staaten." *Der Islam*, vol. v, I. 1914.

Belenitsky, A. M. "K voprosu sotsialnïkh otnosheniyakh v Hulaguidskuyu epokhu." *Sovetskoe vostokovedenie*, vol. v. M.-L., 1948.

Browne, E. G. *A Literary History of Persia*. vol. III. Cambridge, 1951.

Cahen, Claude. "L'évolution de l'iqṭā' du IX au XIII siècle." *Annales (Economies, Sociales, Civilisation)*, vol. 8, N. I. Paris, 1953.

Gordlevsky, V. A. *Gosudarstvo Sel'jukidov Maloi Azii*. M., 1941.

Heyd, W. *Geschichte des Levantehandels im Mittelalter*, Bd. I–II. Stuttgart, 1879.

Hinz, Walter. "Das Rechnungswesen orientalischer Reichsfinanzämter im Mittelalter." *Der Islam*, Bd. 29/1–2. Berlin, 1949.

Iqbāl (Eghbāl), 'Abbās. *Ta'rīkh-i mufaṣṣal-i Īrān az istilā-yi Mughūl tā i'lān-i mashrūṭiyyat, jild-i I. Az Chingīz tā Tīmūr*. Tehrān, 1312/1933.

Lambton, A. K. S. *Islamic Society in Persia*. London, 1954.

—— *Landlord and Peasant in Persia*. London, 1953.

Le Strange, G. *The Lands of the Eastern Caliphate*. Cambridge, 1905.

Minorsky, V. "A civil and military review in Fars in 881/1476." *B.S.O.A.S.*, vol. x, part I. 1959.

—— "A Mongol decree of 720/1320 to the family of Shaykh Zahid." *B.S.O.A.S.*, vol. XVI, part 3. 1954.

—— "A Soyurghal of Qasim B. Jahangir Aq-Qoyunlu 903/1498." *B.S.O.A.S.*, vol. IX, part 4. 1939.

—— "Pūr-i Bahā and his Poems." *Charisteria* (J. Rypka). Prague, 1956.

Petrushevsky, I. P. "Feodalnoe khozyaystvo Rashid ad-dina." *Voprosï istorii*, no. 4. 1951.

—— "Gorodskaya znat' v gosudarstve Hulaguidov." *Sovetskoe vostokovedenie*, vol. v. M.-L., 1948.

—— "Iz istorii Bukharï v XIII v..." *Uchenye zapiski Leningradskogo gosud. universiteta*, no. 179 (Seria vostokovedcheskikh nauk, vïpusk I). L., 1949.

—— "Persidskii traktat po agrotekhnike vremeni Gazan-khana." *Materialï pervoi vsesoyuznoi nauchnoi konferentsii vostokovedov 1957g*. Tashkent, 1958.

—— "Trud Seifi kak istochnik po istorii Vostochnogo Horasana." *Materiali Yuzhno-Turkmenskoi arkheologicheskoi kompleksnoi ekspeditsii*, vol. v. Ashkabad, 1955.

—— *Zemledelie i agrarnïe otnosheniya v Irane XIII–XIV vv*. M.-L., 1960.

Poliak, A. N. "Classification of lands in the Islamic law." *Amer. Journ. Semitic Lang. Literatures*. 1940.

Poliak, A. N. "La féodalité islamique." *La Revue des Etudes Islamiques*, vol. x. Paris, 1936.
Schwarz, P. *Iran im Mittelalter nach den arabischen Geographen*, vols. I–IX. Leipzig, 1896–1936.
Spuler, B. *Die Mongolen in Iran*, 2nd ed. Berlin, 1955.
—— "Quellenkritik der Mongolengeschichte Irans." *Z.D.M.G.* vol. 92 (17), 1939.

CHAPTER 7

A bibliography of the sources used here and of much other material may be found in the following three works:
B. Spuler. *Die Mongolen in Iran*. Berlin, 1955 (see especially pp. 167–249).
Z. Safa. *Ta'rīkh-i adabiyyāt dar Irān*. Vol. II, part I. Tehrān, 1341/1962 (pp. 103–98).
I. P. Petrushevsky. *Zemledelie i agrarnïe otnošeniya v Irane XIII–XIV vekov*. Moscow, Leningrad, 1960 (especially pp. 403–71).
On "Shī'ite" Sūfism, see especially:
M. Molé. "Les Kubrawiya entre sunnisme et shiisme aux huitième et neuvième siècles de l'hégire." *Revue des Etudes Islamiques*. 1961. Pp. 61–142.
On Shī'ism, see also:
R. Strothmann. *Die Zwölfer-Schī'a, Zwei religionsgeschichtliche Charakterbilder aus der Mongolenzeit*. Leipzig, 1926.

CHAPTER 8

ABBREVIATIONS

B.S.O.A.S.	*Bulletin of the School of Oriental and African Studies.*
J.A.	*Journal Asiatique.*
J.R.A.S.	*Journal of the Royal Asiatic Society.*
J.S.S.	*Journal of Semitic Studies.*
N.D.A.T.	*Nashriyya-yi Dānishkada-yi Adabiyyāt-i Tabrīz* (Journal of the Tabriz Faculty of Arts).
N.D.A.Te.	*Nashriyya-yi Dānishkada-yi Adabiyyāt-i Tihrān* (Journal of the Tehrān Faculty of Arts).
ZDMG	*Zeitschrift der deutschen morgenländischen Gesellschaft.*

Further details in J. Rypka, *History of Iranian Literature*.
'Abd al-Vāsi' Jabalī. *Dīvān*, ed. Dh. Ṣafā. I. (*Qaṣīdas*). Tehrān, 1339/1960–1.
Abdullah, S. M. "The Value of Persian Poetry", in *Islamic Research Association Miscellany*, vol. I. Oxford, 1949.
Adīb Ṣābir. *Dīvān*, ed. 'Alī Qavīm. 1334/1955–6.
'Am'aq. *Dīvān*, ed. S. Nafīsī. Tehrān, 1339/1960–1.
Anṣārī. "Munājāt", transl. A. J. Arberry. *Islamic Culture*, 1936, pp. h 369–80.
Anvarī. *Dīvān*, ed. S. Nafīsī. Tehrān, 1337/1958–9; 2 vols., ed. Muh. T. Mudarris Rażavī. Tehrān, 1337/1958–9, 1340/1961–2./V. A. Zhukovskiy, *Ali Aukhadeddin Enveri. Materialī dlya ego biografii i kharakteristiki*. St Petersburg, 1883.

Arberry, A. J. *An Introduction to the History of Ṣūfism*. London, n.d./*Sufism. An Account of the Mystics of Islam*, London, 1950./*British contributions to Persian Studies*. London, 1942./"Persian Literature", in *The Legacy of Persia*. Oxford, 1953, pp. 199–229./*Classical Persian Literature*. London, 1958./*Immortal Rose. An Anthology of Persian Lyrics*. London, 1948.

Athīr al-Dīn Akhsīkatī. *Dīvān*, ed. Rukn al-Dīn Humāyūn-Farrukh. 1337/1958–9.

'Aṭṭār. *Kullīyāt*. Lucknow, 1872./*Dīvān-i qaṣā'id va ghazalīyāt*..., ed. S. Nafīsī. Tehrān, 1319/1940–1; ed. Taqī Tafaḍḍulī. Tehrān, 1341/1962–3./*Mantiq al-Ṭair*, ed. Muḥ. Javād Mashkūr. Tehrān, 1337/1958–9, 1341/1962–3./*Mantic Uttaïr; ou Le langage* des *oiseaux, poème de philosophie religieuse*, ed. M. Garcin de Tassy. Paris, 1857; transl. Garcin de Tassy, 1863./*The Conference of the Birds*, transl. C. S. Nott from Garcin de Tassy's version. London, 1954./Garcin de Tassy, *La poésie philosophique et religieuse d'après le Mantic Uttaïr de Fariduddin Attar*. 4th ed. Paris, 1864./*Ilahi-name. Die Gespräche des Königs mit seinen sechs Söhnen. Eine mystische Dichtung*, ed. H. Ritter. Istanbul, 1940; ed. F. Rouhani. Tehrān, 1340/1961–2; *Le Livre Divin*, transl. F. Rouhani. Paris, 1961./*Muṣībat-Nāma*, ed. Nūrānī Visāl. Tehrān, 1338/1959–60./*Asrār-Nāma*, ed. Ṣādiq Gauharīn. Tehrān, 1338/1959–60./*Khusrau-Nāma*, ed. Aḥmad Suhailī Khwānsārī. Tehrān, 1340/1961–2./*Ushtur-Nāma*, ed. Mahdī, Muḥacciq. Tehrān, 1340/1961–2./*Pand-namèh, ou Le Livre des Conseils*, transl. and ed. Silvestre de Sacy. Paris, 1819./*Tadhkiratu'l-Awliyā* ("Memoirs of the Saints"), ed. R. A. Nicholson. 2 vols. London–Leiden, 1905–7; abridged and transl. into English by B. Behari. Lahore, 1961./S. Nafīsī, *Justujū dar aḥvāl va āthār-i Farīd al-Dīn 'Aṭṭār-i Nīshābūrī*. Tehrān, 1320/1941–2./H. Ritter, *Das Meer der Seele. Mensch, Welt und Gott in den Geschichten des Farīduddīn 'Aṭṭār*. Leiden, 1955./Badī' al-zamān Furūzānfar, *Sharḥ-i aḥvāl va naqd u taḥlīl-i āthār-i Shaikh Farīd al-Dīn Aṭṭār*. Tehrān, 1340/1961–2./W. Lentz, "'Attār als Allegoriker. Bemerkungen zu Ritters 'Meer der Seele'." *Der Islam*, vol. 35 (1960), pp. 52–96./H. Ritter, "'Aṭṭār. Philologika x. (I.) Zur Vita." *Der Islam*, vol. 25 (1939), pp. 134–73; XIV. (II.) *Oriens*, vol. 11 (1958), pp. 1–76; XV. (III.) "Der Dīwān." *Ibid.* vol. 12 (1959), pp. 1–88; XVI. "*Muxtarnāme*." *Ibid.* vols. 13–14 (1961), pp. 195–239.

Aufī. *Jawāmi' al-ḥikāyāt wa lawāmi' al-riwāyāt*, ed. Muḥāmmad T. Bahār, vol. 1. Tehrān, 1324/1945–6; ed. Muḥāmmad Mu'īn, vol. 1. Tehrān, 1335/1956–7; 1340/1961–2./Muḥāmmad Nizāmuddīn, *Introduction to the Jawámi' u 'l-Hikáyát*... London, 1929./*The Lubábu 'l-albáb*, ed. E. G. Browne and Muḥāmmad Qazvīnī. 2 vols. London, 1903, 1906; ed. S. Nafīsī. Tehrān, 1333–5./R. A. Nicholson, *Studies in Islamic Poetry*. Cambridge, 1921.

Auhadī. *Jām-i Jam*, ed. Vaḥīd Dastgirdī. Tehrān, 1307/1928–9./*Kulliyyāt*, ed. S. Nafīsī. Tehrān, 1340/1961–2./*Dīvān*, ed. Sayyid Yūsha. Madras, 1951; ed. Ḥamīd Sa'ādat. Tehrān, 1340/1961–2.

Bābā Afḍal. *Muṣannafāt*, ed. M. Minovi and Yahyā Mahdavī. 2 vols. Tehrān, 1330/1951–2, 1337/1956–7./*Rubā'ilyāt*, ed. S. Nafīsī. Tehrān, 1311/1932–3.

Bahā' al-Dīn Muḥāmmad al-Baghdādī. *Al-Tavassul ilā al-tarassul*, ed. Aḥmad Bahmanyār. Tehrān, 1315/1936–7.

Bahā' al-Dīn Muḥāmmad Ḥusain Khaṭībī Balkhī ("Bahā' Valad"). *Ma'ārif*, ed. Badī' al-Zamān Furūzānfar. Tehrān, vols. I. 1333/1954–5, II. 1339/1960–1.

Bahār, Malik al-shu'arā Muḥāmmad Taqī. *Sabk-shināsī yā taṭavvur-i nathr-i fārsī*. 2 vols. Tehrān, 1321/1942–3; 2nd ed. 1337–8/1958–1960.

Baihaqī, Abu'l-Faḍl Muḥāmmad. *Ta'rīkh-i Baihaqī*, ed. Ghanī and Faiyāż. Tehrān, 1324/1945–6./*Ta'rīkh-i Mas'ūdī ma'rūf bi-Ta'rīkh-i Baihaqī*, ed. S. Nafīsī. 3 vols. Tehrān, 1319/1940–1, 1326/1947–8, 1332/1953–4./ *Istoriya Mas'uda (1030–1041)*, transl. A. K. Arends. Tashkent, 1962.

Baihaqī i. Funduq. *Ta'rīkh-i Baihaq*, ed. Aḥmad Bahmanyār. Tehrān, 1317/ 1938–9./Kalimullah Husayni, "Life and Works of Zahiru'd-din al-Bayhaqi", *Islamic Culture*, vol. 28/1 (1954), pp. 297–318; cf. *ibid.* vols. 33 (1959), pp. 188–202; 34 (1960), pp. 49–59 and 77–89.

Bakhtiyār-Nāma, ed. Vaḥīd Dastgirdī (1310), ed. Y. E. Bertel's (with Glossary). Leningrad, 1926./*Idem*, "Novaya Versiya", *Izvestiya Akad. Nauk, otdeleniye gumantarnikh nauk* (1929), pp. 249–76./Transl. W. Ouseley. London, 1801; Larkhall, 1883; French, M. Lescallier. Paris, 1805; Azesbaijani, Fedai, ed. G. Mammeddi. Baku, 1957./Th. Nöldeke, "Über die Texte des Buches von den zehn Veziren [Bakht-yār-nāma], besonders über eine alte persische Rezension desselben." *Z.D.M.G.*, vol. 45 (1891), pp. 97–143.

Baranī (Barnī). *Tā'rīkh-i Fīrūzshāhī*, ed. Saiyid Ahmad Khan. Calcutta, 1862.

Bausani, A. *I Persiani*. Florence, 1962.

Bertel's, Y. E. *Ocherk istorii persidskoi literaturī*. Leningrad, 1928./*Istoriya persidsko-tadshikskoi literaturī*. Moscow, 1960.

Bīghamī, Maulānā Shaikh Ḥājjī Muḥāmmad. *Dārāb-Nāma*, ed. Dh. Ṣafā. 2 vols. Tehrān, 1339, 1342.

Boyle, J. A. "The Death of the Last 'Abbāsid Caliph: a Contemporary Muslim Account." *J.S.S.*, vol. VI, no. 2 (1961).

Browne, E. G. *A Literary History of Persia*, vol. II. London, 1906.

Dhahīr al-Dīn Fāryābī. *Dīvān*, ed. by Taqī Bīnish. Mashhad, 1337/1958–9; ed. Hāshim Raḍī. Tehrān, 1338/1959–60.

Ethé, Hermann. *Neupersische Literatur*. (Grundriss der iranischen Philologie, ed. W. Geiger and E. Kuhn. Vol. II.) Stuttgart, 1896–1904, pp. 212–368.

Falakī, Hadi Hasan, vol. I. *Falakī-i Shirvānī. His time, life and works*; vol. II. *Dīwān*. London, 1929. See also *Islamic Culture*, 1950, April, pp. 77–107 and July, pp. 145–186; *Researches in Persian literature*. Hyderabad, 1958.

Gabrieli, Francesco. "Letteratura Persiana", in *Le Civilta dell'Oriente*, vol. II, pp. 345–94. Rome, 1957.

Ḥamd Allāh Mustaufī. *Ta'rīkh-i-guzīda*, facsimile, ed. E. G. Browne. Leiden and London, 1910; abridged in English by E. G. Browne. Indices by R. A. Nicholson. Leiden and London, 1913./*Târîkhè Gozîdè*, ed. and transl. J. Gantin, vol. I. Paris, 1903./*Nuzhat al-qulūb*, ed. Muḥāmmad Dabīr Siyāqī. Tehrān, 1336/1957–8; *The Geographical Part*, ed. and transl. G. le Strange. Leiden and London, 1915 and 1919; *The Zoological Section*, ed. and transl. J. Stephenson. London, 1928.

Hamgar. S. Nafīsī, *Majd al-Dīn Hamgar-i S̲h̲īrāzī*, reprinted from *Mihr*. 1314.

Ḥamīdī. *Maqāmāt*, ed. Sayid ʻAlī Akbar Abarqūʼī. Iṣfahān, 1339/1960–1.

Ḥasan Dihlavī. *Dīvān*. Hyderabad, 1933./M. I. Borah, "The life and Work of Amir Hasan Dihlavi", *Journal and Proceedings of the As. Soc. of Bengal*, 1941/3, vol 7, pp. 1–59./Salim, Muḥāmmad, "Amir Najmuddin Hasan Sijzi", *Or. Coll. Mag.* vol. 34, pts. II–III (1958), pp. 11–39.

Ḥasan G̲h̲aznavī. *Dīvān*, ed. T. Mudarris Raẓavī. Tehrān, 1328/1949–50.

Hekmat, Ali Asg̲h̲ar. *Glimpses of Persian literature*. Calcutta, 1956.

Humay-Nama, transl. A. J. Arberry. London, 1963.

Ibn al-Arabī. *La sagesse des prophètes (Fuṣūṣ al-ḥikam)*, transl. T. Burckhardt. Paris, 1955.

Ibn al-Muqaffaʻ, D. Sourdel, "La biographie d'Ibn al-Muqaffaʻ d'après les sources anciennes". *Arabica*, vol. 1/3 (1954), pp. 307–23.

Ibn-i Yamīn. *Dīvān*, ed. R. Yāsimī. Tehrān, 1317/1938–9; ed. S. Nafīsī. Tehrān, 1318/1939–40./*100 short poems*. The Persian Text with paraphrase by E. H. Rodwell. London, 1933./*Bruchstücke*, transl. Ott. M. von Schlechta-Wssehrd. Vienna, 1952.

ʻIraqi. *Kulliyyāt*, ed. S. Nafīsī. Tehrān, 3rd ed. 1339/1960–1./*ʻUs̲h̲s̲h̲āq-Nāma*, ed. and transl. A. J. Arberry. London, 1939./Y. D. Ahuja, "Early years of Shaykh ʻIraqi's Life", *Islamic Culture*, vol. 30 (1956), pp. 95–105;/*Idem*, "ʻIraqi in India", *ibid.* vol. 32 (1958), pp. 57–70./*Idem*, "Shaykh ʻIraqi's travels and his stay in Rum", *ibid.* vol. 33 (1959), pp. 260–77.

Jalāl al-Dīn Rūmī (Maulavī). *The Mathnavī*, ed. R. A. Nicholson. 8 vols. London, 1925–40./*Kulliyyāt-i mas̲navī-i maʻnavī*, ed. M. Darvīs̲h̲. Tehrān, 1341./*Tales of mystic meaning*, transl. R. A. Nicholson. London, 1931./A. J. Arberry, *Tales from the Masnavi*. London, 1961./R. A. Nicholson, *Selections* (from the *Mas̲navī*, *Dīvān* and *Fīhi mā fīh*), ed. A. J. Arberry. London, 1950./H. Ritter, "Das Proömium des Matnawī-i Maulawī", *Z.D.M.G.*, vol. 93 (1939), pp. 169–96./*Kulliyyāt-i S̲h̲ams yā Dīvān-i Kabīr*, ed. Badīʻ al-Zamān Furūzānfar, 6 vols. Tehrān, 1336–40./ *Selected Poems from the Dīvāni Shamsi Tabrīz*, ed. and transl. R. A. Nicholson. Cambridge, 1898, 1952./*The Rubāʻiyāt*. Select translations into English verse by A. J. Arberry. London, 1949./*Maktūbāt*, ed. Yūsuf Jams̲h̲īdīpūr and Gh.-Ḥ. Amīn, 1337/1958–9./"Fīhi mā fīhi. The Table-tale of Jalālu'd-Dīn Rūmī", *J.R.A.S.*, 1929; ed. Badiʻ al-Zamān Furūzānfar. Tehrān, 1330/1951–2; ed. "Shirkat-i sihāmī", Tehrān, 1339/1960–1./*Discourses of Rumi*, tr. A. J. Arberry. London, 1961./ R. A. Nicholson, *Rūmī, Poet and Mystic*. London, 1950./Afzal Iqbal, *The Life and Thought of Rumi*. Lahore, 1956./A. Gölpınarlı, *Mevlânâ Celâleddîn*. 3rd ed. Istanbul, 1959./*Idem*. "Mawlānā Sams-i Tabrīzī ile altmış iki yaşinad bulundu", *Türkiyat Mecmuasi*, vol. 3 (1959), pp. 156–61./G. Richter, *Persiens Mystiker Dschelâl-Eddîn Rūmī, eine Stildeutung*. Breslau, 1933./ H. Ritter, "Philologika XI. Maulānā Dschalāladdīn Rūmī und sein Kreis", *Der Islam*, vol. 26 (1942), pp. 116–58, 221–49./*Idem*,"Neue Literatur", *Oriens*, vols. 13–14 (1960), pp. 342 ff./*Idem*, "Die Mewlānâfeier in

Kouya, vol. 11.–17 December 1960./*Oriens*, vol. 15 (1962), pp. 248–76./ *Idem*, "Der Reigen der Tanzen-den Derwische", *Zeitschrift f. vergleich. Musikwissenschaft*, vol. 1 (1933), pp. 28–40 and 5–23./A.-M. Schimmel, *Die Bildersprache Dschelâladdîn Rûmîs*. Walldorf Hessen, 1949./*Yād-nāma-yi Maulavī*, ed. 'Alī Akbar Mushīr Salīmī. Kumīsyūn-i millī-i Yūneskō. Tehrān, 1337/1958–9.

Jamāl al-Dīn Iṣfahānī. *Dīvān*, ed. Vaḥīd Dastgirdī. Tehrān, 1320/1941–2.

Jarbādhqānī Abu'l-Sharaf, Nāṣiḥ. *Tarjuma-i ta'rīkh-i Yamīnī*. Lith. Tehrān, 1272/1856./*The Kitab-i Yamini, historical memoirs of the Amīr Sabaktagīn, and Sultān Mahmūd of Ghazna*, transl. from the Persian version of the contemporary Arabic chronicle of Al Utbi by the Rev. J. Reynolds. London, 1858.

Juvainī. *Ta'rīkh-i Jahān-Gushāi*, ed. Mīrzā Muḥāmmad Qazvīnī. 3 vols. London, 1912, 1916, 1937;/*The History of the World-Conqueror*, transl. J. A. Boyle. 2 vols. Manchester, 1958.

Kamāl al-Dīn Ismā'īl. *Kullīyāt*. Bombay, 1307/1889, etc./*The Hundred Love Songs*, transl. L. H. Gray and done into English verse by Ethel W. Mumford. London, 1903.

Khāqānī. *Dīvān-i Ḥassān al-'Ajam*, ed. 'Alī 'Abd al-Rasūlī. Tehrān, 1316/ 1937–8; *Dīvān-i Khaqānī-i Shirvānī*, ed. "Amīr Kabīr", Tehrān, 1336; ed. Żiyā' al-Dīn Sajjādī. Tehrān, 1338./*Tuḥfat al 'Irāqain*, ed. Yaḥyā Qarīb. Tehrān, 1333, with commentary by Ismail Khan Abjadi, Madras Univ., 1940./N. Khanikoff, "Mémoire sur Khâcâni, poète Persan du XII siècle", *J.A.*, 1864–5/4, pp. 137–200; vol. 5, pp. 296–367./V. Minorsky, "Khāqānī and Andronicus Comnenus", *B.S.O.A.S.*, vol. 11 (1945), pp. 550–78./O. L. Vil'chevskiy, "Khakani. Nekotoriye chertī tvorchestva i mirovozreniya poeta", *Sovetskoye vostokovedeniye*, (1957/4), pp. 62–76./*Idem*, "Khronogrami Khakani", *Epigrafika vostoka*, vol. 13 (1960), pp. 59–68./'Alī Dashtī, *Shā'irī dīr-āshnā*. Tehrān, 1341./J. Rypka, "Khākānī-i Shirvānī", *N.D.A.T.* vol. 15/1 (1342/1962–3), pp. 101–11.

Khusrau Dihlavī. *Kulliyyāt-i 'Anāṣir-i Davāvīn*. (4 dīvāns.) Cawnpore, 1871, 1334/1916;/(Odes 1–60). The text with an introduction, literal translation and notes. By A. O. Koreishi. Bombay, 1316/1901./*The Nuh Sipihr. An Historical Mathnavī on the Reign of Mubārak-Shāh*, ed. Muḥāmmad Waḥīd Mīrzā. Oxford–Calcutta, 1949./*Qirān al-Sa'dain*, ed. by S. Ḥasan Barnī. 'Alīgarh, 1918./"Miftāḥ al-Futūḥ", ed. Yāsīn Niyāzī. *Orient. Coll. Mag.* vols. XII–XIII, 1936–7./*Duwal-Rānī va Khiżr Khān* (= 'Ashīqa, 'Ishqīya), ed. Rashīd Aḥmad. 'Alīgarh, 1336/1917./*Tughlaq-nāma*, ed. S. Hāshimī Farīdābādī. Awrangabad, 1352/1933./Maṭla'. *al-Anvār*. With commentary by Muḥāmmad Akram Multānī. Delhi, 1293/1876./*Shīrīn u Khusrau*, ed. Yur. Aliyev. Moscow, 1961./*Majnūn Laylī*, ed. Muḥāmmad Ḥabīb al-Raḥmān-Khān. 'Alīgarh, 1335/1917./*Hasht Bihisht*, ed. by Muḥāmmad Sulaimān Ashraf. 'Alīgarh, 1336/1918./*I'jāz* (parts 1–2 only). Lucknow, 1876; Cawnpore, 1877./*Khazā'in al-Futūḥ*, ed. Muḥāmmad Waḥīd Mīrzā. Calcutta, 1950./Moḥāmmad Wahid Mirza, *The life and works of Amir Khusrau*. Calcutta, 1935.

K͟hwājū Kirmānī. *Dīvān*, ed. Aḥm. Suhailī K͟hwānsārī. Tehrān, 1336/1955–6./*Rauḍat al-Anwār*, ed. Kūhī Kirmānī. Tehrān, 1308/1929–30./*Sām-Nāma*, ed. S. Nafīsī. 2 vols. Bombay, 1319–20/1940–2./S. Nafīsī, *Aḥvāl va Muntak͟hab-i As͟h'ār-i K͟hwājū-yi Kirmānī*. Tehrān, 1307/1928–9.

Levy, R. *Persian Literature. An Introduction*. London, 1923.

Maḥjūb, Muḥāmmad Ja'far. "Mat͟hnavī-sarā'ī dar zabān-i Fārsī tā pāyān-i qarn-i panjum-i hijrī." 1 .*N.D.A.T.* vol. 15 (1342/1962–3), pp. 183–213, 261–85.

Maḥmūd S͟habistarī. *Gulshan i Raz: the Mystic Rose Garden*, ed. and transl. E. H. Whinfield. London, 1880./*Mir'at al-Muḥaqqiqin*. S͟hīrāz, 1317.

Massé, H. *Anthologie persane*. (XIe-XIXe siècles.) Paris, 1950.

Meier, Fritz. *Die schöne Mahsatī. Ein Beitrag zur Geschichte des persischen Vierzeilers*, vol. I. Wiesbaden, 1963.

Minhāj Jūzjānī. *Ṭabaqāt-i Nāṣirī*, vol. XI. XVII–XXIII, ed. Captain W. N. Lees, K͟hadim Hosain and 'Abd al-Hai. Calcutta, 1864; ed. 'Abd al-Ḥai Ḥabībī Qandahārī. 1949./*A general history of the Muhammadan Dynasties*, transl. Major H. G. Raverty. London–Calcutta, 1881, 1897.

Muḥāmmad b. al-Munavvar. *Asrār al-Tauhīd fī Maqāmāt al-Shaikh Abī Sa'īd*, ed. Z̲ānīḥ Allāh Ṣafā. Tehrān, 1332/1953–4.

Murtaḍazvī, M. "Muqallidīn-i S͟hāh-Nāma dar Daura-yi Mughūl va Tīmūrī va Ta'rīk͟h-i Manẓūm-ī S͟hams al-Dīn Kās͟hānī". *N.D.A.T.* vol. 14/2–3 (1341/1962–3), pp. 141–75, 323–52./*Taḥqīq dar bāre-i Īlk͟hānān-i Īrān*. Tabriz, 1341/1962–3.

Najm al-Dīn Dāya. *Mirṣād al-'ibād*, ed. Ḥusain al-Ḥusainī al-Ni'mat-allāhi. Tehrān, 1312/1933.

Nak͟hs͟habī (Qādirī). *The Tooti Namah, or Tales of a Parrot*, ed. and transl. [F. Gladwin]. London, 1801./*Das persische Papageienbuch*, transl. C. J. L. Iken. Berlin, 1905./*Touti-Nameh ou les Contes du Perroquet*, transl. Henri Muller. Paris, 1934.

Naṣīr al-Ṭūsī. *Ak͟hlāq-i Nāṣirī*, ed. Jalāl Humā'ī. Tehrān, 1320/1941–2; = *Akhlāq-i Muḥtas͟hamī*, ed. Muḥammad Taqī Dānis͟hpuz͟hūh. Tehrān, 1960./*Muqaddima*, ed. Jalāl Humā'ī. Tehrān, 1320/1941–2./*The Nasirean Ethics*, transl. G. M. Wickens. London, 1964./*Auṣāf al-as͟hrāf*, ed. Naṣr Allāh Taqavī. Tehrān, 1306/1927–8./*Maṭlūbu al-mu'minīn*, ed. W. Ivanow. Bombay, 1933./*The Rauḍatu't-taslīm* (*Taṣawurat*), ed. and transl. W. Ivanow. Leiden, 1950./*Zīj-i Īlk͟hānī*, ed. J. Greaves. London, 1650./M. Minovi and V. Minorsky, "Naṣīr al-Dīn Ṭūsī on Finance". *B.S.O.A.S.* vol. 10/3 (1941),pp.755–89./"The Longer Introduction to the *Zīj-i-Īlkhānī* of Naṣīr-al-Dīn Tūsī", by J. A. Boyle. *J.S.S.* vol. VIII, no. 2 (1963)./*Biographie. Congrès commémoratif (1335/1956) du 7ème centenaire de la mort*. Tehrān (n.d.). (On this occasion the University of Tehrān published a number of his writings.)

Naṣr Allāh. *Kitāb-i Kalīla u Dimna*, ed. 'Abd Allāh Qarīb. 4th ed. Tehrān, 1319/1940; ed. Ḥasanzāda Āmulī. Tehrān, 1341/1961–2./Ed. M. Minovī. Tehran, 1343/1964./Ḥusain Vā'iẓ Kās͟hifī. *Anvār-i Suhailī*.

Niẓāmī. *Kulliyyāt-i Khamsa*. Tehrān, 1341/1962–3./*Makhzan al-asrār*, ed. Vaḥīd Dastgirdī. Tehrān, 1313/1936–7; ed. A. A. Alizade. Baku, 1960./ *The Treasury of Mysteries*, transl. with introd. essay on the life and times of Nezāmī by G. H. Dārāb. London, 1945./*Khusrau u Shīrīn*, ed. Vaḥīd Dastgirdī. Tehrān, 1313/1934–5; ed. L. A. Khetagurov. Baku, 1960./ H. W. Duda, *Farhād und Schīrīn*. Prague, 1933./*Lailī u Majnūn*, ed. Vaḥīd Dastgirdī. Tehrān, 1313./*Leila und Madschnun*, transl. R. Gelpke. Zürich, 1963./*Haft Paikar*, ed. Vaḥīd Dastgirdī. Tehrān, 1315/1936–7./*Heft Peiker*, ed. H. Ritter and J. Rypka. Prague, 1934./*The Haft Paikar* (*The Seven Beauties*), transl. C. E. Wilson. 2 vols. London, 1924./*Die sieben Geschichten der sieben Prinzessinnen*, trans. R. Gelpke. Zürich, 1959./*Sharaf-Nāma*, ed. Vaḥīd Dastgirdī. Tehrān, 1316/1937–8; ed. A. A. Alizade. Baku, 1947./*The Sikandar Nāmae, Barā*, transl. H. Wilberforce Clarke. London, 1881./*Iskanders Warägerfeldzug*..., transl. Jacob. Glückstadt, 1934./*Iqbāl-Nāma*, ed. by Vaḥīd Dastgirdī. Tehrān, 1317/1938–9; ed. F. Babayev. Baku, 1947./*Dīvān*, ed. M. Ṭabāṭabā'ī. 1333/1954–5./*Dīvān-i Qaṣā'id va Ghazaliyyāt*, ed. S. Nafīsī. Tehrān, 1338/1959–60./*Lirika*, ed. Y. E. Bertel's and K. A. Lipskerov. Moscow, 1947./*Idem*, "Navoji i Nizami". *Sbornik Alisher Navoi*. Moscow–Leningrad, 1946, pp. 68–91./H. Ritter, *Über die Bildersprache Nizamis*. Berlin–Leipzig, 1927.

Niẓāmī 'Arūḍī. *Chahár Maqála*, ed. Muḥāmmad Qazvīnī. London, 1910; rev. ed. by Muḥāmmad Mu'īn. Tehrān, 1341/1962–3; rev. transl. E. G. Browne. London, 1921.

Nizārī. "Dastūr-Nāme", ed. and transl. Y. E. Bertel's. *Vostochnïi sbornik*, vol. 1, pp. 37–104.

Nūr al-Dīn Muḥāmmad Khurandīzī Nasavī. *Nafthat al-maṣdūr*, ed. Riḍā-Qulī-Khān Hidāyat. Lith., 1308/1890.

Pagliaro, A. and Bausani, A. *Storia della letteratura persiana*. Milan, 1960.

Pizzi, I. *Storia della poesia persiana*. 2 vols. Turin, 1894.

Qaṭrān. *Dīvān*, ed. Muḥammad Nakhjavānī. 2nd ed. Tabriz, 1335.

Rashīd al-Dīn Faḍl Allāh. *Jāmi' al-tawārīkh*, ed. et trad. E. Quatremère. Vol. 1 (Hülegü). Paris, 1836; Tome II. ed. E. Blochet. London, 1911./ *Geschichte Ġāzān-Ḫāns aus dem Ta'rīḫ-i mubārak-i Ġāzānī*, ed. Karl Jahn. London, 1940./*Ta'rīḫ-i mubārak-i-Ġāzānī* (Abāġā-Gaiḫātū), ed. Karl Jahn. Prague, 1941./*Qismat-i Ismā'īliyyān u Fāṭimiyyān u Nizāriyyān u Dā'iyān u Rafīqān*, ed. Muḥāmmad Taqī-Dānish-puzhūh and Muḥāmmad Mudarrisī Zanjānī. Tehrān, 1338/1959–60./*Sbornik letopisei*, vol. 1/1, by L. A. Khetegurov. Leningrad–Moscow, 1952; 1/2, by O. I. Smirnova: *ibid*. 1952; II. *ibid*. 1960; III. by A. K. Arends. 1946./III. *Jami-ät-tävarikh*, ed. A. A. Alizade, transl. A. K. Arends (= Leningrad, 1946). Baku, 1957./ *Histoire Universelle I. Histoire des Francs*, ed. and transl. K. Jahn. Leiden, 1951./*Mukātabāt-i Rashīdī*, ed. Muḥāmmad Shafi'. Lahore, 1947./E. Blochet, *Introduction à l'histoire des Mongols par Fadl Allah Rachid al-Din*. London, 1910./M. Murtaḍavī, "Jāmi' al-tavārīkh va mu'allif-i vāqi'ī-i ān". *N.D.A.T.* vol. 13 (1340), pp. 31–9, 311–50, 516–26.

Rashīd al-Dīn Vaṭvāṭ. *Dīvān*, ed. S. Nafīsī. Tehrān, 1339/1960–1./*Ḥadā'iq al-shi'r*, ed. 'Abbās Iqbāl. Tehrān, 1308/1929–30, ed. S. Nafīsī. Tehrān, 1339/1960–1./*Alis hundert Sprüche*, ed. and transl. H. L. Fleischer. Leipzig, 1837./*Nāmahā*, ed. Qāsim Tūisarkānī. Tehrān, 1339/1960–1.

Rāvandī, Najm al-Dīn Muḥāmmad. *Ráḥat as-Ṣudúr va Áyat as-Surúr*, ed. Muḥāmmad Iqbāl. London, 1921; rev. ed. by M. Minovi. Tehrān, 1333/1954–5.

Ritter, H. "Philologika VII, IX–XI *Der Islam*, XIV–XVI", *Oriens*, vols. 21/1933, 24/1937, 25/1939 and 26/1942.

Rypka, Jan. *Iranische Literaturgeschichte*. Unter Mitarbeit v. Ot. Klíma, V. Kubíčkovā, J. Bečka, J. Cejpek, I. Hrbek. Leipzig, 1959./*History of Iranian literature*. Written in collaboration with O. Klíma, V. Kubíčková, F. Tauer, J. Becka, J. Cejpek, J. Marek, I. Hrbek and J. T. P. de Bruyn. Under the supervision of K. Jahn. Dordrecht, 1968.

Sa'd al-Dīn Varāvīnī. *The Marzubān-nāma*, ed. by Mīrzā Muḥāmmad of Qazvīn. London, 1909./*The Tales of Marzuban*, transl. R. Levy. London, 1959./Gabrieli Francesco, "Il settimo capitolo del Marzbān-Nāmeh", *Rivista degli studi orient.* vol. 19 (1940), pp. 125–60.

Ṣadaqa (Farāmurz Khudādād). *Kitāb-i Samak-i 'Ayyār*, ed. P. N. Khanlari. Tehrān. Vol. I. 1339/1960–1, vol. II, 1345/1966–7.

Sa'dī. *Kulliyyāt*, ed. Muḥāmmad-'Alī Furūghī. Tehrān, 1337, 1338, 1340./*Matn-i Kāmil-i Dīvān u Būstān u Gulistān* (based on Furūghī), ed. M. Muṣaffā. Tehrān, 1340/1961–2./*Būstān*, ed. Furūghī. Tehrān, 1316/1937–8./*Gulistān*, ed. Abd al-Aẓīm [Qarīb] Garakānī. Tehrān, 1310; ed. Furūghī. Tehrān, 1316/1937–8; ed. and transl. R. M. Aliyev. Moscow, 1959; ed. S. Nafīsī. Tehrān, 1341/1962–3; ed. M. J. Mashkūr. Tehrān, 1342/1963–4./*Stories from the Bustān, together with selections from Francis Gladwin's translation of Gulistān...*, by R. Levy. London, 1928./*Kings and Beggars. The first two chapters of Sa'di's Gulistan*, transl. A. J. Arberry. London, 1945./*Ṭaiyibāt*, ed. L. W. King. Calcutta, 1919–21; transl. L. W. King. London, 1926./*Badā'i'*, ed. and transl. L. W. King. Berlin, 1304/1925./*Pand-Nāma: Sadi's Scroll of Wisdom*. Persian and English text, transl. A. N. Wollaston. London, 1906./H. Massé, *Essai sur le poète Saadi, suivi d'une bibliographie*. Paris, 1919./S. Nafīsī, "Ta'rīkh-i durust-i Dargudhasht-i Sa'dī", *M.D.A.Te*, vol. 6/1 (1337), pp. 64–82.

Ṣafā, Dhabīh Allāh. *Ta'rīkh-i adabiyyāt dar Īrān*. II (middle 5th/11th–beginning 7th/12th century). Tehrān, 1336./*Ḥamāsa-sarā'i dar Īrān*. Tehrān, 1324; pt. 2. 1336./*Ganj-i sukhan*. 3 vols. Tehrān, 1339–40.

Salmān Sāvajī. *Kulliyyāt-i Ash'ār*, ed. R. Yāsimī. Tehrān, 1337/1958–9./*Dīvān*, ed. Manṣūr Mushfiq. Tehrān, 1337/1958–9./R. Yasimi, *Salmān-i Sāvajī*. Tehrān, n.d.

Sanā'ī. *ḥadīqat al-ḥaqīqa*, ed. Mudarris Raḍavī. Tehrān, 1329./*The first book of the "Hadīqat al-Haqīqa"; or, The enclosed Garden of the Truth*, ed. and transl. J. Stephenson. Calcutta, 1911./*Sair al-'Ibād ilā al-Ma'ād*, ed. S. Nafīsī. Tehrān, 1316./*Dīvān*, ed. Muḥammad Taqī Mudarris Raḍavī. Tehrān, 1320/1941–2, 1341/1962–3; ed. by Maẓāhir Muṣaffā, Tehrān,

1336/1957–8./R. A. Nicholson, *A Persian forerunner of Dante*. Towyn-on-Sea, 1944./H. Ritter, "Philol. VIII. Anṣārī Herewī-Senā'i Ġaznewī", *Der Islam*, vol. 22 (1935), pp. 89–105./H. Ritter, "Philog. XV. 'Aṭṭār III, 7. Der Diwan", *Oriens*, vol. 12/1–2 (1959), pp. 1–88.

Shams al-Dīn Qais. *Al-Mu'jam fī Ma'āyir Ash'ār al-'Ajam*, ed. Mīrzā Muḥāmmad of Qazwīn. London, 1908.

Shiblī Nu'mānī. *Shi'r al-'Ajam*. In Urdu: Lahore, vols. I–V, 1924. In Persian: Tehrān, vols. I, 1316, 1335; II, 1327; III, 1335; IV, 1314; V, 1318.

Storey, C. A. *Persian Literature. A bio-bibliographical survey*. In progress. London, 1927– .

Suhravardī Maqtūl. *Mu'nis al-'Ushshāq. The Lovers' Friend*, ed. O. Spies. Stuttgart, 1934; transl. O. Spies and S. K. Khatak. *Muslim Univ. Journal*, 'Alīgarh, vol. 3/1 (1936)./*Three Treatises on Mysticism*, ed. and transl. O. Spies and S. K. Khatak. Stuttgart, 1935./"Le bruissement de l'aile de Gabriel", ed. and transl. H. Corbin and P. Kraus. *J.A.*, vol. 227 (1935), pp. 1–82./*Opera metaphysica et mystics*, ed. H. Corbin; I. Istanbul, 1945, II. Tehrān–Paris, 1952./H. Corbin, *Suhrawardî, fondateur de la doctrine illuminative (ishrâqî)*. Paris, 1938./*Idem*, *Les motifs zoroastriens dans la philosophie de Sohrawardi*. Tehrān, 1946.

Sulṭān Valad. *Valad-Nāma*, ed. Jalāl Humā'ī. Tehrān, 1315–16/1936–8./*Dīvān*, ed. Kilisli R. Bilge. İstanbul, 1941; ed. Asghar Rabbānī. Tehrān, 1338/1959–60.

Sūzanī. *Dīvān*, ed. Nāṣir al-Dīn-Shāh Ḥusainī. Tehrān, 1338/1959–60.

Tanūkhī. *Faraj ba'd al-shidda*, ed. M. Mudīr. Tehrān, 1333/1954–5./Alfred Wiener: "Die Farağ ba'd aš-Šidda-Literatur von Madā'inī (gest. 225 H.) bis Tanūḫī (gest. 384 H.)", *Der Islam*, vol. 4 (1913), pp. 270–98, 387–430./Fr. Gabrieli, "Il valore letterario e storico del Farağ ba'da š-šidda di Tanūḫī", *Rivista degli studi orientali*, vol. 19 (1940), pp. 17–44.

Vaṣṣāf. *Tajziyat al-amṣār va tazjiyat al-a'ṣār*, in various lithographs./*Geschichte Wassaf's*, vol. I (all published) ed. and transl. J. von Hammer-Purgstall. Vienna, 1856.

Ẓahīr al-Dīn Fāryābī. *See* Dhahīr al-Dīn Fāryābī.

Ẓahīr al-Dīn Nīshāpūrī (d. *c*. 582/1186). *Saljūq-nāma*, ed. Ismā'īl Afshār. Tehrān, 1332/1953–4.

Ẓahīrī. *Sindbād-Nāma*, ed. A. Ateş. İstanbul, 1949; ed. 'Alī Qavīm. Tehrān, 1333/1954–5./*The Book of Sindibâd*... from the Persian and Arabic, by W. H. Clouston. [Glasgow] 1884./Transl. M.-N. Osmanov. Moscow, 1960./B. E. Perry, "The origin of the Book of Sindbad", *Fabula*. Berlin, 1960.

CHAPTER 9

General

Beside general, and usually unsatisfactory, works on Islamic art, the only truly usable introduction to the art of Iran is to be found in A. U. Pope, ed., *A Survey of Persian Art*, 6 vols. (Oxford, 1939), partly out of date. Familiarity with the contents of three periodicals is also essential: *Ars Islamica*, 16 vols. (1934–51); *Ars Orientalis*, 6 vols. to date (1953–66); *Âthâr-é Iran*, 4 vols. (1936–49). For recent literature it is possible to keep up to date through the *Abstracta Islamica* published every year by the *Revue des Etudes Islamiques*.

Architecture

Photographs and brief introductions can be found in A. U. Pope, *Persian Architecture* (New York, 1965) and D. Hill and O. Grabar, *Islamic Architecture and its Decoration*, 2nd ed. (London, 1967). Most important articles or special studies will be found quoted there or in the notes to the pertinent chapter in this volume. Special mention should be made of recent efforts in Iran to provide systematic surveys, city by city, of the major monuments of the country. An excellent example is that of Lutfallah Hunarfar, *Ganjīna-yi āthār-i ta'rīkh-i Iṣfahān* (Iṣfahān, 1964).

Painting

The most convenient introduction to the subject is provided by B. Gray, *Persian Painting* (Geneva, 1961), with an excellent bibliography. Among more recent publications two merit special attention: E. J. Grube, *Muslim Miniature Paintings* (Venice, 1962) and B. W. Robinson, *Persian Miniature Painting* (London, 1967). Both are exhibition catalogues which do not claim completeness but which are provided with important commentaries on exhibited paintings.

Decorative Arts

There is at present no convenient introduction to the ceramics, metalwork, glass, or textiles of the centuries under consideration in this volume and one would have to begin with the specific studies quoted in our notes. Some important preliminary remarks may be found in Charles K. Wilkinson, *Iranian Ceramics* (New York, 1963) and D. Barrett, *Islamic Metalwork in the British Museum* (London, 1949).

CHAPTER 10

al-Bīrūnī. *Al-Qānūn al-Mas'ūdī*. Hyderabad-Dn., 1954.

Amir-Moez, A. R. *Scripta Mathematica*, vol. XXVI, pp. 323–37.

Boyer, Carl B. *The Rainbow from Myth to Mathematics*. New York and London, 1959.

Braunmühl, A. von. *Vorlesungen über Geschichte der Trigonometrie*, vol. I. Leipzig, 1900.

Caratheodory, A. (ed.). *Traité du quadrilatère, attrib. à Nassirud-din el-Toussy*. Istanbul, 1891.

Haddad, Fuad I. and E. S. Kennedy. "Geographical tables of Medieval Islam."

Hamadanizadeh, Javad. "A medieval interpolation scheme for oblique ascensions." *Centaurus*, vol. IX (1963), pp. 257–65.

Hartner, W. "The astronomical instruments of Cha-ma-lu-ting." *Isis*, vol. XLI (1956), pp. 184–94.

Juschkewitsch, A. P. and B. A. Rosenfeld. *Die Mathematik der Länder des Ostens in Mitterlalter*. Berlin, 1960.

Kamāl al-Dīn. *Kitāb tanqīḥ al-Manāẓīr...*, 2 vols. Hyderabad-Dn., 1347, 8 A.H.

Kasir, D. S. *The Algebra of Omar Khayyam*. New York, 1931.

Kennedy, E. S. "A survey of Islamic astronomical tables." *Trans. Am. Phil. Soc.* n.s. vol. XLVI (1956), pt. 2.

—— "The Chinese–Uighur calendar as described in the Islamic sources." *Isis*, vol. LV (1964), pp. 435–43.

—— and J. Hamadanizadeh, "Applied mathematics in eleventh-century Iran." *The Mathematics Teacher*.

Khanikoff, N. "Book of the Balance of Wisdom." *J.A.O.S.* (1860), pp. 1–128.

Luckey, Paul. "Zur Entstehung der Kugeldreieckspechnung." *Deutsch Mathematik*, vol. V (1941), pp. 405–46.

Needham, Joseph. *Science and Civilization in China*, vol. III. Cambridge, 1959.

Neugebauer, O. "The transmission of Planetary Theories in Ancient and Medieval Astronomy." *Scripta Mathematica*, vol. XXII (1956), pp. 165–92.

—— *The Exact Sciences in Antiquity*, 2nd ed. Providence, R.I., 1957.

—— "Studies in Byzantine Astronomical Terminology." *Trans. Am. Phil. Soc.* vol. L (1960), pt. 2, p. 28.

Pingree, D. "Astronomy and astrology in India and Iran." *Isis*, vol. LIV (1963), pp. 229–46.

—— "Gregory Chioniades and Palaeologan astronomy." *Dumbarton Oaks Papers*, pp. 152–82.

Plooij, E. B. *Euclid's Conception of Ratio*. Rotterdam, 1950.

Raeder, H., Stromgren, E. and B. Stromgren (ed.). *Tycho Brahe's Description of His Instruments*. Copenhagen, 1946.

Rosenfeld, B. A. and A. P. Yushkevich. *Omar Xaiiām, Traktatï*. Moscow, 1961.

Sayili, Aydin. *The Observatory in Islam*. Ankara, 1960.

Seemann, H. J. "Die Instrumente der Sterawarte zu Maragha..." *Sitzungsberichte der physikalisch-medizinischen Sozietät zu Erlangen*, vol. LX (1928), pp. 15–126.

Smith, D. E. "Euclid, Omar Khayyam and Saccheri." *Scripta Mathematica* (1935).

Wiedemann, Eilhard. "Uber die Brechung des Lichtes in Kugeln..." *Sitzungsberichte der physikalisch-medizinische Sozietät zu Erlangen*, vol. XLII (1910), pp. 15–58.

—— "Zur Optik von Kamäl al-Din." *Archiv für die Gesch. der Naturwissenschaften...*, vol. III (1910–12), pp. 161–77.

—— *et al. Sitzungsberichte der physikalisch-medizinischen Sozietät zu Erlangen*, vol. XL (1908), pp. 133–59.

Woepeke, F. *L'Algebre d'Omar Alkhayyāmi*. Paris, 1851.

INDEX

Figures in italics indicate a main entry.

Ḥasan III of Alamūt
and his father Muḥammad II, 469
adoption of Sunnism, 469–71, 473–4
his mother's pilgrimage, 470, 471
alliance with the Caliph al-Nāṣir, 471–2
Ḥasan or Ḥasanūya, brother of Faḍlūya, 60
Haṣan b. 'Alī, ruler of Samarqand, 139, 140
Ḥasan b. 'Alī al-Ṭughrā'ī, vizier to Mas'ūd, 121
Haṣan b. al-Mubāriz of Fasā, Kurdish tribal chief, 117
Ḥasan Dihlavī, poet, 610
Ḥasan-i Buzurg, 408, 412, 413–16
deposes Jahān-Temür, 415
founder of Jalayir dynasty, 415
Ḥasan-i Kūchak, Ḥasan the Little, son of Temür-Tash, 414–15
Ḥasan-i Ṣabbāḥ, 101–2, *429–49*, 453–4
conquers mountain regions of Ṭabaristān, 27
early career, 429–30
established at Alamūt, 430–2
and doctrine of ta'līm, 433–7
recognized as *ḥujja*, of the imām, 438–9
as head of Nizārī Ismā'īlī movement, 446
Sar-Gudhasht-i Sayyidnā, 623
Ḥasan Jūrī, 546–7
Ḥasan Qaṭṭān, physician, 288
Ḥasan, Sayyid, poet, 159
Ḥasan, Shaikh, son of Choban, 410–11
Ḥasanūya, 60
Ḥasanūyids, 24
ḥashar, 526
ḥashīsh, 443, 454, 501–2
Ḥashīshiyya, 443, 454
hats, 384
ḥavāla, 530
Hazārasp, fortress in Khwārazm, 144, 145
Hazārasp b. Bānkīr, Tāj al-Mulūk, Kurd, 61, 245 and n. 1
Hazāra-yi Lachin, 606
Helmand, 51
hemp, 501–2
Herāt, 49, 50, 65, 90, 149, 154, 160, 161, 254, 297, 341, 363, 405, 416, 533, 601
surrenders to Saljuqs, 20–1
returns to Ghaznavids, 52
Niẓāmiyya, 72
under Ghūrids, 163–6, 185
capture by Khwārazm-Shāh, 166, 192
and Ai-Aba, 185–7
Saifī's History, 315
capture by Mongols, *315–16*, 321, 485 and n. 5, 491
and Baraq, Battle of Herāt, *358–60*
and Nauruz, 383–4
survivors of massacre, 486–7
rebuilding of town, 487, 505–6
besieged by Dānishmand and Bujai, 401
besieged by Yasa'ur, 408
betrayal of Choban, 411
devastation by Du'a, 489
numbers of villages, 496
horticulture, 502, 503
products, 508, 513
tax-collectors, 533
Nizārī the poet, 605
heresy, 118, 619
viziers and, 248
Hermitage Museum, Leningrad
penbox, 643
Bobrinski kettle, 643, 645, 648
Het'um I of Little Armenia, 350–1
Het'um II, 388
Ḥijāz, 85, 98–9, 595
Ḥilla, 24, 108 n. 1, 115, 122, 132, 133, 175, 241, 347, 391–3
Ḥillī, 'Alāma, theologian, 544
al-Ḥillī, Ibn Idrīs, 295
Ḥillī, Muḥaqqiq, 544
Ḥimṣ, 448
capture by Zangī, 127
Mongol defeat by Mamlūks (1260), 352
battle of Ḥimṣ (1281), 363–4
Ghazan's victory over Mamlūks (1299), 387–8
Hindi, 609
Hindū Khān, grandson of Tekish, 164, 192
Hindu Kush mountains, 9
Hindū-Shāh, author of *Tajārib al-salaf*, 263
Ḥiṣn Kaifā, 24
Ḥiṣn Manṣūr, 97
ḥiṣṣa-yi māliki, 525
historiography, Persian, 33, 621–5, 651–2
History of the Franks, of Rashīd al-Dīn, 417
History of the Nation of Archers, 357
Hīt, 108
Honorius IV, Pope, 370
Horqudaq, 382, 383, 397–8
horses, 5, 226, 228–30, 245, 252, 254, 325–6, 389, 403, 522
hospices, see *ribāṭs*
hospitals, 217, 229, 511
hostels, 543, 544
Ḥudūd al-'Ālam, Persian geographical treatise, 6
ḥujja, "proof", 438, 459
Hujvīrī, 297
Hulachu, 368
Hülegü, 339–40, *340–55*, 531, 554–6
campaign against the Ismā'īlīs, *340–5*, *480–2*; in Kūhistān, 488

Ibn Jahīr, Za'īm al-Ru'asā', 99
Ibn al-Jauzī, 44, 99
on Niẓām al-Mulk's alleged support of Shāfi'ism and Ash'arism, 73
on Ṣadaqa, 115
on Dubais, 121
on Toghrïl Beg's projected marriage, 212
on Toghrïl Beg's wife, 224
on taxes in Baghdad, 250 n. 2
on the 'ayyār and futuwwa, 273–4
on story-tellers, 277
Ibn al-Jauzī, theologian, author of *Talbīs Iblīs*, 287
on Ṣūfīs, 299–300
Ibn Kākūya ('Alā' al-Daula Muḥammad), Kākūyid ruler of Iṣfahān, 37 and n. 2, 38
in conflict with Ghaznavids, 38
relations with "Irāqī" Türkmen, 38
fortifies Iṣfahān, 40
forced to evacuate Ray, 41
Ibn Khafīf, 297
Ibn Khaldūn, 540
Ibn Khallikān
on Alp-Arslan and Niẓām al-Mulk, 239
on grants to viziers, 261
Ibn al-Muqaffa', 214, 617
Ibn al-Muslima, vizier to caliph al-Qā'im, 46, 47, 60
Ibn al-Muṭṭalib (Hibat Allāh Muḥammad b. 'Alī), 292
Ibn Muyassar, 63
Ibn Qaṣṣāb, Mu'ayyid al-Dīn, vizier to the Caliph al-Nāṣir, 172, 182
Ibn Rushd (Averroes), 288
Ibn Shādān, 'amīd of Balkh, 264
Ibn al-Shāṭir, 670
Ibn Sīna, *see* Avicenna
Ibn Taghrībirdī on Abū Sa'īd, 413
Ibn al-Ṭiqṭaqā on Ṣadaqa, 115
Ibn Tufail, 557
Ibn Yamīn, 605, *612–13*
Ibn Zur'a, 90
Ibrāhīm, chief of Dārābjird, 117
Ibrāhīm b. Marzbān, Musāfirid, 31–2
Ibrāhīm b. Mas'ūd, 65
on loss of Khurāsān, 50
makes peace treaty with Chaghrī, 53
prosperity of Ghaznavid empire under, 53, 93–4
relations with Malik-Shāh, 93–4
Ibrāhīm b. Naṣr, Tamghach-Khān, 64–5
Ibrāhīm b. Quraish, 'Uqailid, of Mosul, 106
Ibrāhīm Ḥalabī, 540
Ibrāhīm Ïnal, leader of the Ināliyān, 19, 22, 38, 44, 49, 58–9
established at Ray and Hamadān, 41
in Kurdistān, 42
arrested by Toghrïl, later released, 42
raids Byzantine territories, 43
revolt and death, 44
reliance on Türkmen, 197
Iconium, *see* Konya
idrār, 520
Iftikhārīyān family, 510 n. 9
īghār, 232
Ïghlamïsh, Saif al-Dīn, 183–4
Ïghraq, Saif al-Dīn, 318–19
ijāra, money rent, 517, 526
ikhrājāt, 534, 536 n. 4
Ikhtiyār al-Dīn Muḥammad Khaljī, commander under Mu'izz al-Dīn, 162
Ikhwān al-Ṣafā, 588
Īlāq, 3, 12, 91
al-Īlāqī, 288
Il-Arslan, Tāj al-Dunyā wa'l-Dīn, son of Atsïz, Khwārazm-Shāh, 145–6, 178, 185
Il-Begi, 110
Ildei revolts against Ghazan, 381
Ilder, grandson of Hülegü, 381
Ilge (Īlkā) Noyan, 352, 415 n. 1
Il-Ghāzī b. Artuq, 108, 111, 116, 121, 123, 241
shaḥna of Baghdad, 246
Ilig, title held by Qarluq chiefs, 5
Īlkānī dynasty, 415 n. 1
Īl-Khāns
the name, 345 n. 4
survey of their rule, 416–17
Ilyās, made governor of Chaghāniyān by Alp-Arslan, 66, 235
'Imād al-Dīn, historian of the Saljuqs
on Toghrïl's rule in Nīshāpūr, 23
on Toghrïl's meeting with the caliph, 47
on Ḥanafī's favoured treatment, 73
on the Qarluq, 149
on Muḥammad b. Maḥmūd, 169
on Arslan b. Toghrïl, 175, 180
'Imād al-Dīn Kiyā Harāsī, pupil of Juvainī, 287
'Imād al-Dīn Muḥammad b. Aḥmad, diploma for office of *qāḍī* of Nīshāpūr, 209
Imām al-Ḥaramain (Juvainī), 266, 287
Imāmī, panegyric writer of Herāt, 601
Imāmites (Twelvers), 290–1, 302
Ïnal b. Anūsh-Tegin, 109, 112
Ïnalchuq, 305
Ināliyān, section of Türkmen, 19, 22
Ïnal-Tegin, brother of Atsïz, 146
Ïnanch Bilge Ulugh Jāndār, 152
shaḥna of the Türkmen in Gurgān, 246
Ïnanch Khatun, wife of Pahlavān, 180–1
execution, 181

Ïnanch Sonqur, governor of Ray, 177–8, 180
Ïnanch Yabghu (?Bighu), governor of Ṭabaristān, 66, 235
India, 13, 93–4, 157–8, 297, 511, 541, 550, 555, 584, 595
Ghūrids in, 161, 162, 166
Jalāl al-Dīn in, 322–3
Mongol invasion, 341
trade with, 502, 504
literature, 600, 606–10
the poet 'Irāqī, 602
historical works; *Tāj al-Ma'āthir*, 622; other works, 625
mathematics, decimal system, 659
astronomy, 678
indigo, 502
Indus, 322–3
battle of the Indus, 320–1
initiation
Ṣūfī ritual, 296
in craft guilds, 512 n. 2
injü, demesne, 492, 515, 516, 525–6, 527
Ioanne, brother of queen Tamara of Georgia, 179
iqṭā'āt al-istighlāl (assignments of revenue for living-allowances), 82
iqṭā's, *81–4*, 112, 198–9, 222, 224, 227, 230, *231–9*, 244, 245, 261, 499 n. 1 (ii), *518–21*
allotted to caliph, 99, 100, 234
held by women, 224, 234
early history, 231–3
iqṭā' al-tamlīk, 232; iqṭā' al-istighlāl, 82–3, 232
variety of practice and terminology, 233–4
grants of administrative iqṭā's to Saljuq maliks, 235–6; to amīrs and local rulers, 236–7
financial control over, 237–8
hereditary tenure of, 238
court offices and, 238
Niẓām al-Mulk and, 81–3, 199, 230–1, 234–5
fiscal immunity, 498–9
under the Īl-Khāns, *518–21*; Ghazan's decree, 518–19; annual inspection, 519; administrative immunity, 520
muqāṣṣa lands, 520
soyurghal, 520–1
rent from, 525–6
iqṭā'-dār, see *muqṭa'*
Iram, 294
Īrān-Shāh, Bahā' al-Daula, 90
'Irāq, 'Irāq-i 'Ajam, 59, 118, 255, 283, 291, 306, 309, 311, 323, 337, 338, 382, 414, 415, 562, 584
Oghuz in, 41
revenue, 255
Ismā'īlīs, 448, 478
Ḥasan III's campaign, 471–2
tax-returns, 498
rice-growing, 500; cotton, 501
Iraq, 'Irāq-i 'Arab, 24–5, 36, 39, 41, 43–8, 57, 61, 67, 99–101, 102–34 *passim*, 167–84 *passim*, 200–1, 214, 222, 291, 324–5, 349, 572, 595
'Irāqī, the poet, 545, 555, *602–3*, 604
Lama'āt, 545, 602, 619
life, 602
'Ushshāq-Nāma, 602–3
"'Irāqī" Türkmen
entry into Khurāsān, 19
migrations, 27, 32, 33
as mercenaries, 38
attack Ray and Hamadān, 38, 40
in Iraq and al-Jazīreh, 41
and Toghrïl, 41
Irbīl, 240, 325, 335, 349, 394, 491
Irenjin, 408–9
Irgiz river, 306
irrigation and water supplies, 85–6, 342, 514, 517, 526 and n. 4
in Fārs, restored by Chavlï, 117
in Khwārazm, 142
qanāts, 253, 342, 514
destruction by Mongols, 487, 488
reconstruction, 493, 495, 500, 505 and n. 6
kārīz, 500, 505, 517
Irtish, river, 305, 307, 322
'Īsā Böri, Türkmen beg, 95
'Īsā Kelemechi, 370
Iṣfahān, 40, 79, 88, 90, 103, 106, 112, 125, 131, 132–3, 137, 170, 172, 175, 176, 181, 240, 252, 335
Toghrïl's capital, 38, 222
madrasas, 72, 216
under Malik-Shāh, 85, 223
besieged by Berk-Yaruq, 109, 110–11, 255, 261
and Ismā'īlīs, 101–2, 446, 449, 453; dā'ī of Ismā'īlīs in, 428, 444, 446; massacres of Ismā'īlīs, 442–3, 445
and Muḥammad of Kirmān, 134
under Alp-Arslan, 223
shaḥna, 244
Nāṣir-i Khusrau on, 22, 274, 277
Jews, 275
commerce, 277
Sunnism, 283, 285, 543
battle with Mongols, 330–2
and Mongol conquest, 491
numbers of villages, 496 and n. 6

'Izz al-Dīn Murtaḍā, 295
'Izz al-Dīn Nassāba, 314
'Izz al-Dīn Sa'd, ruler of Fārs, 172–3
'Izz al-Dīn Saltuq of Erzerum, 178
'Izz al-Dīn Satmaz, 177
'Izz al-Dīn Sūgandī, 547
'Izz al-Mulk Ḥusain, 105
'Izz al-Mulk Ṭāhir b. Muḥammad Burūjirdī, vizier to Qara-Sonqur, 256, 260, 268

Jabbūl, 389
Jabriyya, 284
Ja'far, Banū, of Tiflis, 123
Ja'far, Abu'l-Faḍl, son of caliph al-Muqtadī and Malik-Shāh's daughter, 100–1, 213, 220
Ja'farak, court jester, 75
Jaghatu river, 354, 356, 360, 398, 413, 415
Jahān-Sūz ("world-Incendiary"), *see* 'Alā' al-Dīn Ḥusain
Jahān-Temür, 415
Jahrūm, 238
Jalāl al-Daula Abū Ṭāhir Shīrzil, Būyid ruler in Baghdad, 39, 41
Jalāl al-Dīn, son of 'Alā' al-Dīn Muḥammad, Khwārazm-Shāh, 166, 168, 182, 184, 306–7, *322–35*, 354
victory over Mongols at Parvān, 317–19
battle of the Indus, 320
in India, 321–3
and Baraq Ḥājib, 323, 329
feud with the caliph, 324–6
and Öz-Beg, 325–7
war against the Georgians, 327–30, 332–3
and Akhlāt, 328–9, 332–4
encounters with Mongols, 330–2; battle of Iṣfahān, 330–2
campaign against Kai-Qubād and Ashraf, 333–4
Mongol invasion under Chormaghun, 334–5
his death, 335
personal characteristics, 325–6, 335
and Ismā'īlīs, 478
Jalāl al-Dīn Fīrūz-Shāh Khaljī, 607
Jalāl al-Dīn Ḥasan III b. Muḥammad, Grand Master of Alamūt, 168–9, 183
Jalāl al-Dīn Muḥammad, son of Maḥmūd Khān, 186
Jalāl al-Dīn Rūmī (Maulavī), 298, 487, 545, 555, 558, 574, *591–4*
Kulliyyāt-i Shams (*Dīvān-i Shams*), 545, 592–3
Mathnavī-i Ma'navī, 545, 593–4
Jalāl al-Dīn Rūmī, 555
and 'Aṭṭār, 587, 589, 590–1
his life, 591–2
Fīhī mā fīhī, 594
Jalāl al-Dīn 'Ubaidallāh b. Yūnus, vizier to Caliph al-Nāṣir, 180
Jalāliyya Khatun, *see* Terken Khatun
Jalayir dynasty, 408, 415 and n. 1, 416, 496
Jalayirtai, 360
Jām, 383
minaret, 640 and pl. 6
jāmagī, 518, 520
jāma-khāna, royal wardrobe, 238
Jamāl al-Dīn Dastajirdānī, 376, 382
Jamāl al-Dīn Iqbāl, 216
Jamāl al-Dīn Jīlī, 298, 547
Jamāl al-Dīn Muḥammad b. 'Abd al-Razzāq Iṣfahānī, poet, 584–6
Jamāl al-Dīn Muḥammad b. Sālim, of Ḥamā, Shāfi'ī qaḍi, 540
Jamāl al-Dīn Muṭahhir, 543
Jamāl al-Dīn Rāzī, 295
Jamāl al-Mulk Manṣūr, son of Niẓām al-Mulk
governor of Balkh, 69
poisoned on Malik-Shāh's orders, 75
Jambul, *see* Talas
Jāmī, 545, 599, 607
Bahāristān, 599
Ashi''a-yi Lama'āt, 602
Jāmi' al-tawārīkh of Rashīd al-Dīn, 397, 548, 623–4
on Ghazan, 542
manuscripts of, 651 and pl. 12, 652–7
Jand, 16, 143–4, 189, 191, 305
Saljuq in, 18
visit of Alp-Arslan, 65, 140
occupied by Atsïz, 145–6
jāndār, chief executioner, 226
Janī-Beg, 408
Jarbadhaqānī, Abu'l-Sharaf Naṣīḥ, *Tarjama-yi Yamīnī*, 622
Jarīriyya (Sulaimāniyya), 290–1
Jārūdiyya (Sarḥūbiyya), 290–1
Jauhar, daughter of Sulṭān Mas'ūd, 133
Jauhar, Fāṭimid general, 71
Jauhar, governor of Ray under Sanjar, 131, 236, 244
Jauhar Khatun, daughter of Malik-Shāh, 94
Jazīrat ibn 'Umar, 97–8, 109, 216
al-Jazīreh, 24, 41, 92, 97, 101, 109–11, 121, 183, 242
under Muḥammad, 115–16
career of Zangī, 126–7
Saladin and, 171
Jazr, 445, 448
Jebe, 305, 307–11

Jedei Noyan, 401
Jerusalem, 103, 371, 404
jewellery, 158, 255, 257, 643
  pearls, 257, 312
Jews, 274–5, 289, 369–70, 522, 538, 592
  Sa'd al-Daula, 369–70, 372, 541
  Rashīd al-Dīn, 407, 541, 623
  Ibn 'Allān, 74, 245 and n. 2
  and Ismā'ilīs, 448
  jizya, 533
  literature, 614
  Maulānā Shāhīn, 614
Jibāl, 41, 42, 105, 111, 116, 120, 124–6, 133, 170, 175–6
  Khwārazm-Shāh Tekish and, 182–3
  massacre of Khwārazmians, 183
  construction of new mosques, 631
Jīruft, 56, 59, 134, 173
jizya, poll-tax, 213, 249–50, 518, 533
Jocelyn II of Edessa, 127, 241
Jochi, eldest son of Chingiz-Khān, 305, 307, 319
  appanage, 352–3
John XII, Pope, 413
John of Plano Carpini, 141, 318, 398
Josapha Barbaro, 507
al-Jubān, *see* Choban
juft-i gāv, 526–7
Jürchet, 148
Jūrī, Ḥasan, 546–7
Jüshkeb, 369
Justān b. Ibrāhīm, 31
Justānids, Dailamī dynasty, 30
justice
  the sultan and, 86, 209–11, 227–8
  courts of, see *maẓālim* and *qāḍī*
Juvain
  office of shaḥna, 244 n. 3
  numbers of villages, 497
Juvainī, Abu'l-Ma'ālī, scholar, 46
Juvainī, 'Alā' al-Dīn 'Aṭā-Malik, the historian, 192, 193, 338, 339, 510 and n. 5, 532, 587, *622–3*
  his restoration of Khabūshān, 342
  as Hülegü's secretary, 344
  accused of embezzlement, 362, 365
  governor of Baghdad, 362, 365
  and library of Alamūt, 447, 482, 623
  and Ismā'ilīs, 623
  and Sa'dī, 595–6, 597
  Ta'rīkh-i Jahān-Gushā, 623
  on Atsïz, 143
  on Qara-Khitai, 145
  on Kamāl al-Dīn, 145
  on Sanjar's captivity, 154
  on Mu'izz al-Dīn, 164
  on the Mongols, 304–45 *passim*
  on public order under the Mongols, 337
  on death of Rukn al-Dīn, 345
  on Mongol massacres, 484, 485 and n. 4
  on devastation of Khurāsān, 486
  on Maḥmūd Tārābī, 548
Juvainī, Bahā' al-Dīn, father of the historian, 336–7, 338
Juvainī, Bahā' al-Dīn, son of Shams al-Dīn, 492 n. 2
Juvainī, Imām al-Ḥaramain, theologian, 266, 287
Juvainī, Mu'īn al-Dīn, *Nigaristān*, 619
Juvainī, Shams al-Dīn, ṣāḥib-dīvān, 391, 492 n. 2, 505 n. 6, 510 n. 5
  vizier to Abaqa, 356, 361–2
  intrigues of Majd al-Mulk, 362, 365
  execution, 368–9
  Barhebraeus on, 369
  purchases of land, 521
  and Sa'dī, 595–6, 597
Juvainī, Sharaf al-Dīn, 492 n. 2
Juvainīyān, 510 and n. 5
Jūzjānī, Minhāj al-Dīn, historian, 158, 159, 160, 161, 303–4, 319, 624–5
  on enmity between Ghaznavids and Ghūrids, 160
  on Ghiyāth al-Dīn, 163
  on Tekish, 192–3
  on siege of Herāt, 315–16
  Ṭabaqāt-i Nāṣirī, 159, 625

Kabul, 3, 157
Kāghadh-Kunān, 409
Kai-Kā'ūs b. Hazārasp, 29
Kai-Kā'ūs b. Iskandar, 'Unṣur al-Ma'ālī, 26–7, 51
  Qābūs-Nāma, 26
  on the futuwwa, 273
Kai-Kā'us II of Rūm, 361, 617
Kai-Khusrau b. Qïlïj-Arslan, Ghiyāth al-Dīn, Saljuq sultan of Rūm, 15
Kai-Qubād, sultan of Rūm, campaign against Jalāl al-Dīn, 333–4
Kai-Qubād II, 'Alā' al-Dīn, of Rūm, 386
Kākā Balīmān, 90
Kākūyids, dynasty of Dailamī origin, based on Iṣfahān, 9, 37–8, 117–18
  become Saljuq vassals, 38
  operations against, 42
Kālābāgh, 320
Kalāt-i Nādirī, 306, 366
Kalila u Dimna, 159, 617, 650
  Istanbul manuscript, 649, 655–7
  Cairo manuscript, 649

Malatya, 44, 63, 97
Malāzgird (Manzikert), 24, 43, 44, 129, 179, 334
battle of, 61, 96, *63–4*, 230
malik, title of Saljuq princes, 218 and n. 1
duties, 235–6
Malik Dīnār, Ghuzz leader, 173–4, 189
ruler of Kirmān, 174, 190 n. 1
Malik al-Kāmil, of Egypt, 333–4
Mālikī, 284
Malik-Nāma, 17, 18
al-Malik al-Raḥīm, eldest son of Abū Kālījār, 38, 45, 46
Malik-Shāh b. Berk-Yaruq, 111, 221
Malik-Shāh b. Maḥmūd, sultan, 126, 129, 169, 175, 176
Boz-Aba's revolt, 126, 131–2
further revolts, 133
his reign, 175
death, 176–7
Malik-Shāh, b. Muḥammad, 172, 176
Malik-Shāh b. Tekish, governor of Nīshāpūr, 190
Malik-Shāh b. Toghrīl, 181–2
Malik-Shāh, Jalāl al-Daula Mu'izz al-Dīn Abu'l-Fatḥ, sultan, *66–102*, 195–202 *passim*, 203–82 *passim*
nominated as heir, 57, 61, 66, 87, 220, 229, 235
with Alp-Arslan on Armenian campaign, 62
his reign as zenith of Great Saljuqs, 66–7, 84–7
campaigns and visits to Georgia and Caucasus, 67, 95
campaign against Marwānids, 67, 97–8
reaches the Mediterranean, 67, 98
and the Qarakhānids, 66–7, 91–3; recovers Samarqand, 92–3
and Ibrāhīm of Ghazna, 66, 93–4
served by Niẓām al-Mulk as vizier, 68–102 *passim*, 260–7; his relations with, 68, 74–7, 102, 262, 266
dismissal of Armenian mercenaries, 74–5, 81, 90, 229–30
choice of successor, 77, 78, 220
his empire: composite character, 78; strength of Turkish traditions, 79, 220; Türkmen claims, 79
and the army, 80–1
his revenues, 85
his buildings and fortifications, 85, 223
his reputation for justice, 86, 227; and Khumar-Tegin, 238
economic conditions under, 86
accession, 87
revolt of Qavurt, 88–9
revolts of Tekish, 90–1
Samarqand, 92–3
his policy in Āzarbāījān and Arrān, 94–5
and Anatolia, relations with sons of Qutlumush, 96
relations with caliph, 99–102; his daughter married by caliph, 100–1, 213, 265
his first visit to Baghdad, 100, 248
later visits, 101
plans to depose caliph, 101, 102, 213
and Ismā'īlīs, 102, 446
opposition from Saljuq family, 220
his alms-giving, 254
and taxes, 250; tribute, 253
inaugurates new solar calendar, 670
and astronomy, 670, 672
Mamlūks of Egypt, 351, 354, 361, 382–3, 540
Ma'mūn b. Ma'mūn, Abu'l-'Abbās, 8
Ma'mūnids, rulers of Khwārazm, 8
man, measure of weight, 491 n. 1
Manāfi' al-ḥayawān, manuscript of, 648–9, 654–5
manāqib-khwāns, singers, 293
Manbij, 63
Mandalī, *see* Bandīnjān
Mandeville, Sir John, 348
Manfred, 540
Mangüjekids, 43
Manichaeism, 561
Manqīshlaq, 66, 140, 143–4, 151, 317
Mansūr, son of Qutlumush
raids on Byzantine territory, 67
relations with Malik-Shāh, 67, 96
death, 96
Manṣūriyya, Saljuq palace at Ṭūs, 338, 342
Manūchihr, son of Abu'l-Asvār, Shaddādid, ruler of Ani, 35, 95
Manūchihr II b. Farīdūn, 123, 570, 575
Manūchihr b. Qābūs, Falak al Ma'ālī, Ziyārid, 12–13, 25–6
Manūchihrī Dāmghānī, Ghaznavid poet, 25, 574, 613–14
Manuel Comnenus, Byzantine Emperor, 571
Manzikert, *see* Malāzgird
maps, 371
maqāma, 598, 612, 615, 618–19, 648
Maqdisī, geographer, reference to Türkmen, 17
Maqrīzī, 394–5
maqṣūra, 633
Maqtūl, *see* Suhravardi Maqtūl
Marāgheh, 32–4, 128, 129, 131, 176, 280, 326, 360, 371, 394, 403, 549, 581
assassination of Caliph al-Mustarshid, 127–8

painting, 584, 626–9, 641–2, *648–58*, pls. 12–15
Rashīd al-Dīn's school in Tabrīz, 628, 649, 651, 653–5, 657
mural, 642 n. 1
Chinese influence, 652–7
Pamir mountains, 9
Panāhī, 618
Panjāb, 162, 165, 306
Panj Dih, suburb of Marv, 85, 223
Panjikent, 651
Panjshīr, river, 318
Pāpak, 549
paper, 147, 511
paper money, 374–5, 376–7
parasol, 326
Parvān, 320, 321
battle, 317, 318–19
Parvāna, the, Mu'īn al-Dīn Sulaimān, 361
Pashto, 198 and n. 1
pearls, 312
peasants, 234, 259, 499, 505, 514, *522–9*
and Mongol invasion, 489–91
attachment to the soil, 523–5
quit-rent, 525–7; money rent, 526
forced labour, 526 and n. 4, 527; other obligations, 535–6
condition of life on injü and Dīvān land, 527–9
taxes and exactions, 529–37
Pechenegs, 141
Pegolotti, 504
Peking, 303–4
pensions, 513, 517
perfume, 256
Philaretos, 97, 98
Philippe le Bel of France, 371, 399, 402
physicians, *see* medicine
Pīl-Suvār, 375–6, 381
Pīr-i Baqrān, 640
pīshkash, 535
Pishkil-Dara, 344
pīsh-ṭāq, 635
poetry, *550–614*
in the Saljuq period, 551
insecurity of poets, 551–2
the qaṣida, 551–2, 555 and n. 2, 556
the ghazal, 552, 555; Ṣūfism and, 568
the romantic epic, 552–3
the mathnavī, 553, 555
under the Mongols, 555–6
polo, 332, 645
population, effects of Mongol invasion on, 484–8
Prester John, 147
printing, paper money, 374–5
Prophet, the
his cloak and sceptre, 150
na't, eulogies, 570
prose, *614–25*
historiography, 33, 621–5, 651–2
novels, 615–16
collections of anecdotes, 616–17
fables and stories, 617–18
didactic prose, 619–20
literary history, 621–2
see also *maqāma*
prostitution, 506 n. 3, 532
pseudo-Temür-Tash, 414–15
Ptolemy
Almagest, 660–1
planetary theory, 668–9, 670 n. 1
Pūr-i Bahā, 532, 555 n. 2
Pūshang, 49, 81, 186, 359–60, 503
Pushkil Darra, 396

Qā'ānī, *Kitāb-i Parīshān*, 599
qabāla, tax farm, 231
Qābūs b. Vushmagīr, Shams al-Ma'ālī, 25, 28
Qābūs-Nāma, of Kai-Kā'ūs b. Iskandar, 26
on futuwwa, 273
qāḍī, 244, 248, 259, 510
qāḍī's court, 269
functions and position in the administration, 269–72
qāḍī al-quḍāt, 270–1
qāḍī-i jumla-i mamālik, 271–2
qāḍī-i lashkar, 272
Qadīr Khān Jibrā'il b. 'Umar, 139
Qadīr Khān Yūsuf of Kāshghar and Khotan, 18–19, 65, 91
Qadīrī, Muḥammad Khudāvand, 618
Qādiriyya, branch of Ṣūfīs, 296–7
Qāḍīyān, 510
Qaghan (Arabic Khāqān), title of head of the Qarluq, 5
Qaidu, 356–8, 393
al-Qā'im, 'Abbāsid caliph, 44–9 *passim*, 212
Sunnī revival under, 36–7
marriage to daughter of Chaghrī Beg Dā'ud, 48, 212
Toghrīl marries daughter of, 48–9, 55, 212
and Alp-Arslan's accession, 55
and vizier Ibn Jahīr, 60–1
Qaimaz, 140
Qā'in, 58, 448, 488
Qais, island off coast of Fārs, 87, 174
Qaiṣar, 133
Qaiṣar, 'Alam al-Dīn, emissary of Nauruz, 382–3
Qaiṣariyya, 63, 97, 361, 411, 619

Qutlugh-Shāh, one of Ghazan's generals, 381, 383–4, 386–9, 391, 544
battle of Ḥimṣ, 387–8
Syrian campaign, defeat at Marj al-Suffar, 393–5
commander-in-chief to Öljeitü, 398
in Gīlān, 400
death, 400–1
Qutlugh-Tegin, Rukn al-Daula, 107
appointed amīr of Fārs by Malik-Shāh, 89
atabeg, 240
Qutlumush b. Arslan Isrā'īl, 22, 49
attacks Ganja, 34
raids Armenia, 44
prepares to seize power on Toghrïl's death, 54
revolts against Alp-Arslan, 58, 219
reliance on Türkmen, 197
Qutui, 366
Qutula, 392
Qutuz, 351

Rabāb-Nāma, of Sulṭān Valad, 594
Rabban Sauma, 371
Rādkān, 10, 310, 338, 340, 342, 358, 376
Rādūyānī, Muḥammad b. 'Umar, 561
Rāfiḍīs (extremist Shī'īs), 73
Rāgh-i Zar, 163
Rāghib, Abu'l-Qāsim Ḥusain b. Muḥammad, 295
Raḥbat al-Shām (Raḥba), 241, 242, 364, 391, 393, 403
Rahhāṣiyya, order, 168
ra'īs, local official, 236, 251, 252, 276, *279–81*
Ra'īsa, mother of Niẓāmī, 578
ra'iyyat, settled population subject to taxation, 492–6, 515, 522–37 *passim*
personal freedom, 522 and n. 3, 524
forced labour, 526 and n. 4, 527
oppression of, 527–9, 536–7
billeting, 535–6
carriage duty, 536
Rāmjird, 117
Rang, 319
Raqqa, 389, 393, 491
Ra's al-'Ain, 386, 387
al-Rāshid, caliph
in alliance with Zangī, 127
hostilities with Mas'ūd, boss of Baghdad, 128
deposed, 127, 128–9
further resistance, 129
murdered, 129, 451
Rashīdābād, near Tabrīz, 514
Rashīd Bulghārī, Shaikh, 548–9
Rashīd al-Dīn, son of Khāqānī, 572
Rashīd al-Dīn, Faḍl Allāh Hamādānī, historian, 393, 505 n. 6, 517–18, *623–4*
on murder of Niẓām al-Mulk, 102
on the Mongols, 311, 317, 341–397 *passim*
on death of Rukn al-Dīn, 345
on Hülegü and Caliph Musta'ṣim, 346
on Ket-Buqa, 351–2
on destruction of churches, 380
made deputy to Ghazan's vizier, 385–6
on Ghazan, 390, 406
on hunting, 391
Jāmi' al-tawārīkh, 397, 542, 548, 623–4; manuscripts, 651–7 and pl. 12
Ta'rīkh-i Ghāzānī, 406, 623–4
and Ghazan, 397, 493–5
office retained under Öljeitü, 398
and Öljeitü, 406
fall of vizier Sa'd al-Dīn Sāvajī, 402
division of authority with vizier 'Alī-Shāh, 405–6
dismissal and execution, 407
Jewish origin, 407
rebuilds suburb of Tabrīz, 407, 511
History of the Franks, 417
request for weavers, 417, 511
and Ismā'īlī chronicles, 423
on Mongol devastation, 491, 506
his letter to Shihāb al-Dīn, 493
and agriculture, 500, 513–14
and products for export, 508
investments in trading enterprises, 509–10
his estates, 513–14; slave labour on, 514
on workshops, 513
on khāliṣāt land, 516–17
on iqṭā's, 518
purchases of land, 521
his will, 521–2
on oppressive tax-collectors, 527–8; on tax-farmers, 528
on taxes, 530, 532
on billeting, 535–6
on carriage duty (ulagh), 536
on Mazdakites, 548
his qaṣīdas, 623 n. 1
his geography, 624
his school of painting in Tabrīz, 628, 649, 651, 653–5, 657, pl. 12
Rāshid al-Dīn Sinān, head of Syrian Ismā'īlīs, 456, 467–8
Rashīd al-Dīn Vaṭvāṭ, the poet, 139, 145, *559–61*, 585
and Khāqānī, 560, 570–1, 572
Ḥadā'iq al-siḥr..., 561
Rasht, 400
rasm-i khazāna, 534
rasm al-ṣadāra, 534